WILEY CIA EXAM REVIEW

VOLUME 3

Business Analysis and Information Technology

THIRD EDITION

S. RAO VALLABHANENI

JOHN WILEY & SONS, INC.

This book is printed on acid-free paper. ♾

Published by John Wiley & Sons, Inc., Hoboken, New Jersey.
Published simultaneously in Canada.

For general information on our other products and services, or technical support, please contact our Customer Care Department within the United States at 800-762-2974, outside the United States at 317-572-3993 or fax 317-572-4002.

Wiley also publishes its books in a variety of electronic formats. Some content that appears in print may not be available in electronic books. For more information about Wiley products, visit our Web site at www.wiley.com.

ISBN 10: 0-471-71881-5 (Volume 3)

ISBN 0-471-71883-1 (Set)

ISBN 13: 978-0-471-71881-9

Printed in the United States of America

10 9 8 7 6 5 4 3 2 1

CONTENTS

CIA EXAM CONTENT SPECIFICATIONS

The CIA exam tests a candidate's knowledge of current internal auditing practices and understanding of internal audit issues, risks, and controls. The exam is offered in four parts, each part consisting of 125 multiple-choice questions. The following is a breakdown of Part III:

Part III: Business Analysis and Information Technology

A. Business Processes (15-25%)

1. Quality management (e.g., TQM)
2. The International Organization for Standardization (ISO) framework
3. Forecasting
4. Project management techniques
5. Business process analysis (e.g., workflow analysis and bottleneck management, theory of constraints)
6. Inventory management techniques and concepts
7. Marketing—pricing objectives and policies
8. Marketing—supply chain management
9. Human Resources (Individual performance management and measurement; supervision; environmental factors that affect performance; facilitation techniques; personnel sourcing/staffing; training and development; safety)
10. Balanced scorecard

B. Financial Accounting and Finance (15-25%)

1. Basic concepts and underlying principles of financial accounting (e.g., statements, terminology, relationships)
2. Intermediate concepts of financial accounting (e.g., bonds, leases, pensions, intangible assets, R&D)
3. Advanced concepts of financial accounting (e.g., consolidation, partnerships, foreign currency transactions)
4. Financial statement analysis
5. Cost of capital evaluation
6. Types of debt and equity
7. Financial instruments (e.g., derivatives)
8. Cash management (treasury functions)
9. Valuation models
   a. Inventory valuation
   b. Business valuation
10. Business development life cycles

C. Managerial Accounting (10-20%)

1. Cost concepts (e.g., absorption, variable, fixed)
2. Capital budgeting
3. Operating budget
4. Transfer pricing
5. Cost-volume-profit analysis
6. Relevant cost
7. Costing systems (e.g., activity-based, standard)
8. Responsibility accounting

D. Regulatory, Legal, and Economics (5-15%)

1. Impact of government legislation and regulation on business
2. Trade legislation and regulations
3. Taxation schemes
4. Contracts
5. Nature and rules of legal evidence
6. Key economic indicators

E. Information Technology—IT (30-40%)

1. Control frameworks (e.g., eSAC, COBIT)
2. Data and network communications/connections (e.g., LAN, VAN, and WAN)

3. Electronic funds transfer (EFT)
4. e-commerce
5. Electronic data interchange (EDI)
6. Functional areas of IT operations (e.g., data center operations)
7. Encryption
8. Information protection (e.g. viruses, privacy)
9. Evaluate investment in IT (cost of ownership)
10. Enterprise-wide resource planning (ERP) software (e.g., SAP R/3)
11. Operating systems
12. Application development
13. Voice communications
14. Contingency planning
15. Systems security (e.g. firewalls, access control)
16. Databases
17. Software licensing
18. Web infrastructure

1 BUSINESS PROCESSES (15–25%)

THEORY

1.1 Quality Management

Total Quality Management (TQM) is a strategic, integrated management system for achieving customer satisfaction.[1] It involves all managers and employees and uses quantitative methods to improve continuously an organization's processes. It is not an efficiency (cost-cutting) program, a morale-boosting scheme, or a project that can be delegated to operational managers or staff specialists. Paying lip service to quality improvement by merely using quality slogans to exhort workers is equally disastrous.

KEY CONCEPTS TO REMEMBER: LESSONS LEARNED FROM TQM

- Learn quality concepts first and tailor them to fit your organization.
- The commitment to change must come from the top management.
- Begin TQM with managers and supervisors who are models and trend setters.
- Data is crucial. You should not guess at what the symptoms or problems are, but go out and look at the facts and let that guide the improvement process.
- Recognition of the team members creates enthusiasm.
- TQM is a management system, hence, cannot be delegated to a quality control department.
- Quality is profit, not cost.
- TQM will reduce costs and risks, increase productivity, and enhance customer satisfaction.

In TQM context, the standard for determining quality is meeting customer requirements and expectations the first time and every time. There are many potential requirements and expectations that customers have, depending upon the particular product or service and needs of the customer. Rather than the organization attempting to specify what it views as quality, a TQM approach to quality systematically inquiries of its customers what they want, and strives to meet, and even exceed, those requirements. Such an approach helps to identify the elements of quality that are of paramount importance to customers. It also recognizes that customers' expectations may change over time. TQM can be applied equally to manufacturing and service organizations.

(a) **Elements of TQM.** The three essential requirements or principles of TQM are: (1) the pursuit of complete customer satisfaction by (2) continuously improving products and services, through (3) the full and active involvement of the entire workforce.

These three principles are met by integrating seven key operating practices.

1. Demonstrating personal leadership of TQM by senior management
2. Strategically planning the short- and long-term implementation of TQM throughout the organization
3. Assuring that everyone focuses on customers' needs and expectations
4. Developing clearly defined measures for tracking progress and identifying improvement opportunities
5. Providing adequate resources for training and recognition to enable workers to carry the mission forward and reinforce positive behavior
6. Empowering workers to make decisions and fostering teamwork
7. Developing systems to assure that quality is built in at the beginning and throughout operations.

(b) **What Is Different about TQM?** Although the adoption and integration of the seven operating practices are essential, leaders beginning a TQM effort should bear in mind that to realize the full potential of

[1] ***Introduction to Total Quality Management,*** *U.S. Office of Personnel Management, Washington, D.C. 1991.*

TQM requires a fundamental cultural change. When this transformation has occurred, everyone in the organization is continuously and systematically working to improve the quality of goods and services, and the processes for delivering them, in order to maximize customer satisfaction. TQM has become a way of managing that is embedded in the culture and environment of the organization, not simply a set of specific management techniques and tools. TQM emphasizes doing each job right the first time.

Components of TQM

- Process management
- Quality teams
- Quality councils
- Ongoing training

It follows that a successful approach to quality improvement requires a long-term commitment and recognition that the effort is an unending journey. Although some early successes can be achieved, a cultural transformation to full use of the TQM approach will occur only gradually.

(c) **Common Areas of Agreement on Quality.** Although each of the quality experts (i.e., Deming, Juran, and Crosby) has developed his individual approach to quality improvement, the following are some significant common areas of agreement:

- Producing a quality product costs less because there is less waste.
- Preventing quality problems is better than detecting and correcting them.
- Statistical data should be used to measure quality.
- Managers need to take a leadership role in improving quality.
- Managers and employees need training in quality improvement.
- Companies need to develop a Quality Management System.

A TQM approach to management represents a unique blending of: the objective, practical, and quantitative aspects of management, for example, focus on processes and reliance on quantitative data and statistical analysis for decision making; and the "soft" aspects of management, for example, providing a visionary leadership role, promoting a spirit of cooperation and teamwork, and practicing participative management. Many organizations, when deciding to undertake a TQM effort, focus on one or the other of these general approaches. A fully successful effort requires balanced attention to both.

The following areas need to be improved:

- Many managers encourage employee involvement and empowerment, but few organizations adopt the specific practices that bring them about, such as reliance on teams of employees to identify and resolve specific operating problems. Where teams are used, few have been delegated sufficient authority to make changes or have been trained to use the full array of TQM tools.

KEY CONCEPTS TO REMEMBER: PITFALLS TO AVOID WHEN IMPLEMENTING TQM

- Overemphasizing the technical tools at the expense of leadership and management issues
- Applying the tools before the needs are determined
- Tendency to rush the quality improvement process
- Viewing TQM as a budget-cutting tool or employee productivity program
- Conducting mass training before support systems for TQM have been set up

- Although many organizations recognize the importance of measurement and analysis to decision making, many measure the wrong things. Also, few organizations focus on internal processes across functions in order to assure that quality is built into the production and service system on a continuing basis.
- Many organizations have in place a system they call "Quality Assurance," but these systems are often designed to check for adherence to quality standards at the end of the production process. TQM creates procedures for assuring quality throughout the production and service process.

- Many organizations claim to serve the customer first, but few systematically and rigorously identify the needs of customers, both internal and external, and monitor the extent to which those needs are being met.

(d) **Characteristics of a Quality Organization.** When organizations adopt TQM principles and practices, the results have been startling. Workers at all levels focus on their customers' needs and become committed and involved in the quest for quality. Management and workers form a team in seeking continuous improvement. The cumulative result of these changes frequently is a profound change in the overall culture and atmosphere of the organization. Organizations become more streamlined, a larger percentage of workers are involved in line operations, and there is a greater spirit of cooperation and working toward common goals. Perhaps most significantly, a spirit of energy and excitement, even fun, permeates the organization.

Some specific contrasting characteristics that frequently result between the traditional approach and the TQM approach to managing are summarized in Exhibit 1.1.

<u>Traditional approach to managing</u>

- The organization structure is hierarchical and has rigid lines of authority and responsibility.
- Focus is on maintaining the status quo (don't fix it if it ain't broke).
- Workers perceive supervisors as bosses or cops.
- Supervisor/subordinate relationships are characterized by dependency, fear, and control.
- The focus of employee efforts is on individual effort; workers view themselves as competitors.
- Management perceives labor and training as costs.
- Management determines what quality is and whether it is being provided.
- Primary basis for decisions is on "gut feeling" or instinct.

<u>TQM approach to managing</u>

- The organization structure becomes flatter, more flexible, and less hierarchical.
- Focus shifts to continuous improvement in systems and processes (continue to improve it even if it ain't broke).
- Workers perceive supervisors as coaches and facilitators. The manager is seen as a leader.
- Supervisor/subordinate relationships shift to interdependency, trust, and mutual commitment.
- The focus of employee effort shifts to team effort; workers see themselves as teammates.
- Management perceives labor as an asset and training as an investment.
- The organization asks customers to define quality, and develops measures to determine if customers' requirements are met.
- The primary basis for decisions shifts to facts and systems.

Exhibit 1.1: Comparison of traditional approach to managing with TQM approach to managing

(e) **Quality Assurance, Quality Control, Quality Audit, Quality Circles, and Quality Councils.** In order to meet customer quality requirements, the work processes used to produce their products and services must be designed to prevent problems and errors from occurring in the first place.

Quality assurance focuses on the front end of processes, beginning with inputs, rather than the traditional controlling mode of inspecting and checking products at the end of operations, after errors are made. Processes are designed both to prevent errors and to detect and correct them as they occur throughout the process. As part of the emphasis on prevention and early detection, employees are trained to analyze incoming supplies. Suppliers are asked to assure, assess, and improve their processes and products or services. The organization establishes a partnership with suppliers and customers to assure continuous improvement in the quality of the end products and services.

Quality control is an evaluation to indicate needed corrective action, the act of guiding, or the state of a process in which the variability is attributable to a constant system of chance causes. Quality control includes the operational techniques and activities used to fulfill requirements for quality. Often, quality assurance and quality control are used interchangeably, referring to the actions performed to ensure the quality of a product, service, or process.

QUALITY ASSURANCE VS. QUALITY CONTROL

- Quality assurance focuses on front end of processes
- Quality control focuses on middle and back end of processes
- Quality assurance is a management issue
- Quality control is a technical issue

Quality audit is a systematic, independent examination and review to determine whether quality activities and related results comply with planned arrangements, and whether these arrangements are implemented effectively and are suitable to achieve the objectives.

Quality circles refer to a team of employees (6 to 12) voluntarily getting together periodically to discuss quality-related problems and issues and to devise strategies and plans to take corrective actions. Participative management places a premium on teamwork as the way to solve problems and initiate process improvements, especially issues with cross-functional implications. The focus is on teamwork and processes rather than on individual efforts and tasks. Quality circles should be introduced in an evolutionary manner so that employees feel that they can tap their creative potential.

Establishment of a **quality council** is a prerequisite of implementing a total quality management program in the organization. The quality council is similar to an executive steering committee. By establishing a quality council, senior management provides an identity, structure, and legitimacy to the quality improvement effort. It is the first concrete indication that senior management has recognized the need to improve and has begun to change the way the organization conducts its business. The direction that this change will take becomes clear when the Quality Council publishes its vision, guiding principles, and mission statement. Management needs to support and promote the total quality management program, not just sponsor it.

(f) **Concurrent Engineering.** Long lead times for introducing new products have been a major problem for many manufacturers. This slowness in introducing new products is clearing the way for competitive products entering the market.

The focus of concurrent engineering is to reduce the overall product cycle time, which is measured as the elapsed time between research, development, and marketing of a new product. This is called time to market a new product, which is aimed at increasing performance and productivity.

Concurrent engineering is defined as a systematic approach to the integrated and overlapping design of products and their related processes, including design, manufacturing, and support. It requires that, from the beginning, all elements of product life cycle be evaluated across all design factors to include user requirements, quality cost, and schedule.

The foundation of concurrent engineering is that some 80 to 85% of a product's cost is determined at concept development. Additionally, the integration of support processes early on cuts manufacturing costs while raising quality and reducing development time.

The significant benefits to be obtained from concurrent engineering include

- Improved quality of design, leading to a reduction in change orders
- Reduction in product cycle time as a result of using concurrent design, rather than sequential design
- Reduction in manufacturing costs as a result of using multifunction teams to integrate product and process
- Reduction in scrap and rework as a result of product and process design optimization

Involving suppliers in product design is also a strategic move for a successful concurrent engineering practice. Concurrent design, a part of concurrent engineering, makes the design relatively fixed, requiring limited engineering change orders, so that little line disruption results. This enables new versions of popular products to be introduced with great speed and ease.

(g) **Cost of Quality.** The Cost of Quality (COQ) measurement identifies areas for process improvement. The focus of this measurement is to express quality in terms of quantitative and financial language, that is, costs, return on investment, cost of poor quality, cost of rework, and so on.

The COQ definition includes the following three items:

1. COQ is the cost of making a product conform to quality standards (i.e., quality goods).
2. COQ is the cost of not conforming to quality standards (i.e., waste, loss).
3. COQ is a combination of item 1 and 2.

COQ = The cost of conformance (A) + The cost of nonconformance (B)

where (A) includes cost to prevent and detect a failure and (B) includes cost to correct a failure.

Costs related to quality are usually separated into at least three areas: prevention costs, appraisal costs, and failure costs (see Exhibit 1.2).

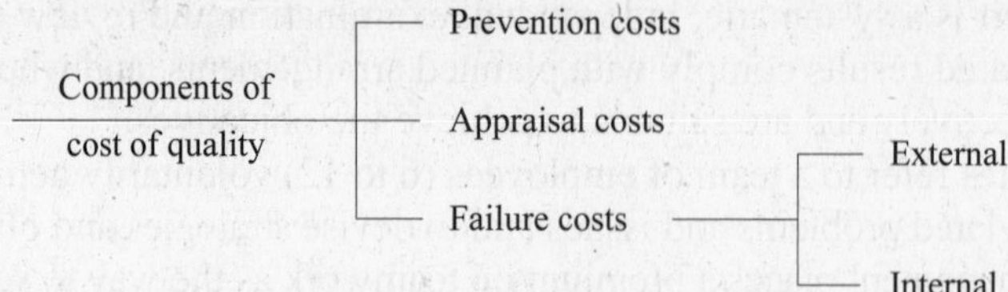

Exhibit 1.2: Components of cost of quality

(i) **Prevention costs.** These costs are associated with all the activities that focus on preventing defects. It is the cost of conformance to quality standards. Some major cost categories included in this cost classification are: operator inspection costs, supplier ratings, supplier reviews, purchase-order technical data reviews, training, supplier certification, design reviews, pilot projects, prototype test, vendor surveys, quality design, and quality department review costs.

KEY CONCEPTS TO REMEMBER: BASIC INTERRELATIONSHIPS AMONG QUALITY COSTS

The basic relationships among the three types of quality costs are that money invested in prevention and appraisal can substantially reduce failure costs. In addition to reducing expenses, the reduction in external failure costs results in fewer customer complaints. A dollar invested in a prevention program saves money many times in failure costs.

(ii) **Appraisal costs.** These costs are associated with measuring, evaluating, or auditing products to assure conformance with quality standards and performance requirements. Some major cost categories included in this cost classification are purchasing appraisal costs, qualifications of supplier product, equipment calibration, receiving and shipping inspection costs, tests, and product quality audits.

(iii) **Failure costs.** These costs are associated with evaluating and either correcting or replacing defective products, components, or materials that do not meet quality standards. Failure costs can be either internal failure costs that occur prior to the completion or shipment of a product or the rendering of a service, or external failure costs that occur after a product is shipped or a service is rendered. Examples of internal failure costs include repair, redesign, reinspection, rework, retesting, sorting, and scrap. Examples of external failure costs include product warranty charges, returns, and recalls; liability suits; and field service staff training costs.

Quality metrics can be developed for the cost of quality measurement to help managers monitor quality. These metrics include

- The total cost of quality as percentage of revenue by year
- The cost of conformance as percentage of total cost of quality
- The cost of nonconformance as percentage of total cost of quality

(h) **Quality Tools.** Either an auditor or an auditee can use quality tools. These tools can be used to analyze processes, prioritize problems, report the results, and to evaluate the results of a corrective action plan. The seven quality control tools include check sheets, histograms, scatter diagrams, Pareto diagrams, flowcharts, cause-and-effect diagrams, and control charts. Later, seven other tools came into effect, called the seven quality management tools. These management tools include affinity diagram (also called KJ method), tree diagram, process decision program chart, matrix diagram, interrelationship digraph, prioritization matrices, and activity network diagram. The seven quality management tools are modern while the seven quality control tools are traditional.

QUALITY CONTROL TOOLS VS. QUALITY MANAGEMENT TOOLS

- The old seven quality control tools are used for quantitative data analysis.
- The new seven quality management tools are used for qualitative data analysis.

(i) **Old seven quality control tools.**

(A) ***Check sheets.*** Check sheets are used for collecting data in a logical and systematic manner. The data collected can be used in constructing a quality control chart, Pareto diagram, or histogram. The most important use of the check sheet is that it enables the user to gather and organize data in a format that permits efficient and easy analysis of data.

Process improvement is facilitated by the determination of what data or information is needed to reduce the difference between customer needs and process performance. Some examples of data that can be collected include: process variables including size, length, weight, and diameter; number of defects generated by each cause; product characteristics; costs; vendors; inspection procedures; customer profiles; employees attitudes; and defect location. The idea is that once this data is collected and analyzed, the cause can be found and a plan to eliminate the problem can be implemented.

(B) ***Histograms.*** A histogram is a frequency distribution diagram in which the frequencies of occurrences of the different variables being plotted are represented by bars. The purpose is to determine the shape of the graph relative to the normal distribution (or other distributions). It is often confused with a bar graph, in which the frequency of a variable is indicated by the height of the bars. In a histogram, the frequency is indicated by the area of the bar. Histograms can only be used with variable data, which require measurements on a continuous scale. Only 1 characteristic can be shown per histogram, and at least 30 observations representing homogeneous conditions are needed.

Old Quality Control Tools

The old seven quality control tools include check sheets, histograms, scatter diagrams, Pareto diagrams, flowcharts, cause and effect diagrams, and control charts.

A histogram is a frequency distribution, in which the area of each bar is always proportional to the actual percentage of the total falling in a given range. If the bars are of equal length, then the histogram is equivalent to a bar graph, in which the relative size of the bars depends only on their heights. A histogram can be compared to the normal distribution (or other distribution). For example, if the graph is off-center or skewed, this may indicate that a process requires adjustment. Histograms are essentially used for the same applications as bar graphs, except that the horizontal scale in a histogram must be numerical, usually representing a continuous random variable.

A bar graph is a frequency distribution diagram in which each bar represents a characteristic or attribute, and the height of the bar represents the frequency of that characteristic. The horizontal axis may represent a continuous numerical scale (e.g., hours), or a discrete nonnumerical scale (e.g., phases of a project). Generally, numerical-scale bar graphs in which the bars have equal widths are more useful for comparison purposes; numerical-scale bar charts with unequal intervals can be misleading because the characteristics with the largest bars (in terms of area) do not necessarily have the highest frequency. Bar graphs are used to compare the frequencies of different attributes (e.g., number or percentage of problem reports by phase).

(C) ***Scatter diagrams.*** A scatter diagram is a plot of the values of one variable against those of another variable to determine the relationship between them. These diagrams are used during analysis to understand the cause and effect relationship between two variables. Scatter diagrams are also called correlation diagrams.

If the data points fall approximately in a straight line, this indicates that there is a linear relationship, which is positive or negative, depending on whether the slope of the line is positive or negative. Further analysis using the method of least squares can be performed. If the data points form a curve, then there is a nonlinear relationship. If there is no apparent pattern, this may indicate no relationship. However, another sample should be taken before making such a conclusion.

Method of least squares can be used in conjunction with scatter diagrams to obtain a more precise relationship between variables. It is used to determine the equation of the regression line (i.e., the line that "best fits" the data point). With this equation, one can approximate values of one variable when given values of the other.

(D) ***Pareto diagram.*** A Pareto diagram is a special use of the bar graph in which the bars are arranged in descending order of magnitude. The purpose of Pareto analysis, using Pareto diagrams, is to identify the major problems in a product or process, or more generally, to identify the most significant causes for a given effect. This allows a developer to prioritize problems and decide which problem area to work on first.

Pareto analysis is based on the 20/80 rule, which states that approximately 20% of the causes (the "vital few") account for 80% of the effects (problems). The "vital few" can be determined by drawing a cumulative percent line and noting which bars are to the left of the point marking 80% of the total count. The vital few are usually indicated by significantly higher bars and/or a relatively steep slope of the cumulative percent line.

Pareto diagrams (charts) can be helpful in determining whether efforts towards process improvement are producing results. These diagrams are useful when the process is stable; it will not be effective if used on a chaotic process because the process is not ready for improvement. The process must first be stabilized through the use of control charts. *Root cause analysis is performed using the Pareto diagrams.*

Pareto diagrams can be drawn showing before and after improvements, demonstrating the effect of the improvements through the use of Pareto diagrams. This is a powerful tool when used in this way because it can mobilize support for further process improvement and reinforce the continuation of current efforts. Pareto diagrams are based on 80/20 rule indicating that 20% of things account for 80% of problems, and are usually drawn as pie charts, histograms, or vertical bar charts. Pareto diagrams focus on "vital few" instead of "trivial many." When arranged from greatest to least, the Pareto chart graphically indicates which problems should be handled first.

(E) ***Flowcharts.*** A flowcharting tool can be used to document every phase of a company's operation, for example, from order taking to shipping in a manufacturing company. It will become an effective way to break down a process or pinpoint a problem. Flowcharting can be done at both the summary level and the detailed level serving different user needs.

Flowcharting is a first step towards the documentation of a process required for ISO 9000 and other quality awards. In this way, problems can be traced quickly to the right source and corrected properly. Also, the flowcharts can be used as a training tool or a reference document on the job.

A process map is similar to a flowchart. Mapping is the activity of developing a detailed flowchart of a work process showing its inputs, tasks, and activities in sequence. A process map provides a broader perspective than typical flowcharts.

(F) ***Cause-and-effect diagrams.*** One form of a cause-and-effect (C&E) diagram is used for process analysis. It is used when a series of events or steps in a process creates a problem and it is not clear which event or step is the major cause of the problems. Each process or subprocess is examined for possible causes; after the causes from each step in the process are discovered, significant root causes of the problem are selected, verified, and corrected. The C&E diagrams are also called fishbone or Ishikawa (the inventor) diagrams.

The C&E diagrams should be used as a framework for collecting efforts. If a process is stable, it will help organize efforts to improve the process. If a process is chaotic, the C&E diagram will help uncover areas that can help stabilize the process.

(G) ***Control chart.*** A control chart assesses a process variation. The control chart displays sequential process measurements relative to the overall process average and control limits. The upper and lower control limits establish the boundaries of normal variation for the process being measured. Variation within control limits is attributable to random or chance causes, while variation beyond control limits indicates a process change due to causes other than chance—a condition that may require investigation. The upper control limit and lower control limit give the boundaries within which observed fluctuations are typical and acceptable. They are usually set, respectively, at three standard deviations above and below the mean of all observations.

There are many different types of control charts (e.g., np, p, c, u, X, XB, R, XM, and MR). "np" is number of nonconforming units, "p" is fraction of nonconforming units, "c" is number of nonconformities, "u" is number of nonconformities per unit, "X" is a single observed value, "XB" is X-Bar, "R" is a range, "XM" is a median, and "MR" is a moving range.

A run chart is a simplified control chart, in which the upper and lower control limits are omitted. The purpose of the run chart is more to determine trends in a process, rather than its variation. Run charts can be used effectively to monitor a process, for example, to detect sudden changes and to assess the effects of corrective actions. Run charts provide the input for establishing control charts after a process has matured or stabilized in time. Limitations of this technique are that it analyzes only one characteristic over time, and it does not indicate if a single data point is an outlier.

Dr. Genichi Taguchi, a Japanese statistician and Deming Prize winner, developed what is called Taguchi method, the off-line quality control method, which includes product and process design. This is contrasted to on-line quality control in which quality control activities are focused on control charts and process control methods. Taguchi's methods provide a system to develop specifications, design those specifications into a product and/or process, and produce products that continuously surpass said specifications. *There are seven aspects to off-line quality control.*

1. The quality of a manufactured product is measured by the total loss to society created by that product.
2. Continuous quality improvement and cost reduction are necessary for an organization's health in a competitive economy.
3. Quality improvement requires the never-ending reduction of variation in product and/or process performance around nominal values.
4. Society's loss due to performance variation is frequently proportional to the square of the deviation of the performance characteristic from its nominal value.
5. Product and process design can have a significant impact on a product's quality and cost.
6. Performance variation can be reduced by exploiting the nonlinear effects between a product's and-or process's parameters and the product's desired performance characteristics.
7. Product and/or process parameter settings that reduce performance variation can be identified with statistically designed experiments.

(ii) **New seven quality management tools.** The original quality tools were adequate for data collection and analysis, but the seven new tools allow better identification, planning, and coordination in quality problem solving. These new tools include affinity diagram (also called KJ method), tree diagram, process decision program chart, matrix diagram, interrelationship digraph, prioritization matrices, and activity network diagram. Each tool is discussed briefly.

(A) ***Affinity diagram.*** The affinity diagram is a data reduction tool in that it organizes a large number of qualitative inputs into a smaller number of major categories. These diagrams are useful in analyzing defect data and other quality problems, and used in conjunction with cause-and-effect diagrams or interrelationship digraphs.

(B) ***Tree diagram.*** A tree diagram can be used to show the relationships of a production process by breaking it down from few larger steps into many smaller steps. The greater the detail of steps, the better simplified they are. Quality improvement actions can start from the right-most of the tree to the left-most.

(C) ***Process decision program chart.*** The process decision program chart (PDPC) is a preventive control tool in that it prevents problems from occurring in the first place and mitigates the impact of the problems if they do occur. From this aspect, it is a contingency planning tool. The objective of the tool is to determine the impact of the "failures" or problems on project schedule.

(D) ***Matrix diagram.*** A matrix diagram is developed to analyze the correlations between two groups of ideas with the use of a decision table. This diagram allows one to systematically analyze correlations. Quality Function Deployment (QFD) is an extension of the matrix diagram. The American Supplier Institute defines QFD as: "A system for translating consumer/customer requirements into appropriate company requirements at each stage, from research and product development, to engineering and manufacturing, to marketing/sales and distribution."

The QFD is a structured method and uses a series of charts called "quality tables" to provide the discipline and communication required to focus on answering three action-oriented questions: what? how? and how much? QFD can be used both for products and services.

(E) ***Interrelationship digraph.*** The interrelationship digraph is used to organize disparate ideas. Arrows are drawn between related ideas. An idea that has arrows leaving it but none entering is a "root idea." More attention is then given to the root ideas for system improvement. The digraph is often used in conjunction with affinity diagrams.

(F) ***Prioritization matrices.*** Prioritization matrices are used to help decision makers determine the order of importance of the activities being considered in a decision. Key issues and choices are identified for further improvement. These matrices combine the use of a tree diagram and a matrix diagram.

New Quality Management Tools

The new seven quality management tools include affinity diagram (also called KJ method), tree diagram, process decision program chart, matrix diagram, interrelationship digraph, prioritization matrices, and activity network diagram.

(G) ***Activity network diagram.*** Activity network diagrams are project management tools to determine which activities must be performed, when they must be performed, and in what sequence. These diagrams are similar to PERT and CPM, the popular tools in project management. Unlike PERT and CPM, activity network diagrams are simple to construct and require less training to use.

(iii) **Plan-do-check-act (PDCA) cycle.** The PDCA cycle was first known as the Shewhart cycle and later known as the Deming cycle. It is a core management tool for problem solving and quality improvement. The PDCA cycle can be used for planning and implementing quality improvements. The "plan" calls for developing an implementation plan for initial effort followed by organization-wide effort.

The "do" part carries out the plan on a small scale using a pilot organization, and later on a large scale. The "check" phase evaluates lessons learned by pilot organization. The "act" phase uses lessons learned to improve the implementation. It supports both old and new quality tools.

(iv) **Stratification.** Stratification is a procedure used to describe the systematic subdivision of population or process data to obtain a detailed understanding of the structure of the population or process. It is not to be confused with a stratified sampling method. Stratification can be used to break down a problem to discover its root causes and can establish appropriate corrective actions, called countermeasures.

Stratification is important to the proper functioning of the Deming PDCA cycle. *Failure to perform meaningful stratification can result in the establishment of inappropriate countermeasures, which can then result in process or product deterioration in quality.*

STRATIFICATION VS. PARETO DIAGRAM VS. C & E DIAGRAM

- Stratification can be used when performing root cause analysis with Pareto diagrams. A problem can be broken down into subcomponents, and each subcomponent can be further broken down into its subcomponents, and so on. Then, attention should be paid to one or more of the root causes of a process or product problem, from which countermeasures can be established to resolve the problem.
- Stratification can also be used when performing root cause analysis with C&E diagrams. A C&E diagram can be used to stratify one bar from a Pareto diagram at a time to get an in-depth understanding of the corresponding cause (bar) before any other cause (bar) is studied.

(i) **Quality Models and Awards.** A system should be put in place to allow the organization to determine systematically the degree to which product and services please customers, and focus on internal process improvement. Data should be collected on features of customer satisfaction such as responsiveness, reliability, accuracy, and ease of access. The measurement systems should also focus on internal processes, especially on processes that generate variation in quality and cycle time. *Cycle time is the time required from conception to completion of an idea or a process.* When customer data indicates a problem, or when the organization wants to raise the level of customer satisfaction, the organization should focus on improving the processes that deliver the product or service.

In order to assure that processes are continuously improved, data should be collected and analyzed on a continuing basis, with particular attention to variation in processes. The causes of variation are examined to determine whether they result from special circumstances (special causes) or from recurring ("common") causes. Different strategies should be adopted to correct each occurrence. The immediate objectives of the analysis and measurement effort are to reduce rework, waste, and cycle-time and to improve cost-effectiveness and accuracy. The ultimate objectives are to assure that the organization understands the extent to which customer satisfaction is being realized, where there are deficiencies, and why, and to isolate causes that can be attacked systematically.

(i) **Three quality preachers.** We will discuss quality models from three quality preachers' viewpoints: (1) Deming, (2) Juran, and (3) Crosby.

(A) ***Deming quality model.*** According to Deming, good quality does not necessarily mean high quality. It is, rather, "a predictable degree of uniformity and dependability, at low cost, and suited to the market." He recognizes that the quality of any product or service has many scales, and may get a high mark on one scale and a low mark on another. In other words, quality is whatever the customer needs and wants. And since the customer's requirements and tastes are always changing, the solution to defining quality in terms of the customer is to constantly conduct customer research.

Deming said people are eager to do a good job and are disturbed when they are unable to because of limitations imposed by management. Deming's basic philosophy on quality is that productivity improves as variability decreases. Since all things vary, he says, that is why the statistical method of quality control is needed. "Statistical control does not imply absence of defective items. It is a state of random variation, in which the limits of variation are predictable," he explains.

There are two types of variation: chance and assignable, and says Deming, "The difference between these is one of most difficult things to comprehend." It is a waste of time and money to look for the cause of the chance variation, yet, he says, this is exactly what many companies do when they attempt to solve quality problems without using statistical methods. He advocates the use of statistics to measure performance in all areas, not just conformance to product specifications. Furthermore, he says it is not enough to meet specifications; one has to keep working to reduce the variation as well.

Inspection, whether of incoming or outgoing goods, is, according to Deming, too late, ineffective, and costly. "Inspection does not improve quality, nor guarantee it," he says. Moreover, inspection is usually designed to allow a certain number of defects to enter the system. For example, a company that buys items with an acceptable quality level of three percent is, in effect, telling the vendor that it can send three bad items out of every 100. "The vendor will be pleased to meet these requirements," says Deming.

Deming says that judging quality requires knowledge of the "statistical evidence of quality," and that companies dealing with vendors under statistical control can eliminate inspection. "You will note from the control charts that came along with the product, far better than any inspection can tell you, what the distribution of quality is, and what it will be tomorrow." In this way, quality is predictable, and one can also safely predict that the vendor's quality will improve over time. "One of the first steps for managers of purchasing to take is to learn enough about the statistical control of quality to be able to assess the qualifications of a supplier, to be able to talk to him in statistical language," says Deming.

Deming also points out that simply checking the specifications of incoming materials may not be enough if the material encounters problems in production. "Specifications cannot tell you the whole story. The supplier must know what the material is to be used for," he says. He is critical of most producers for qualifying vendors on quality because once qualified, the vendor, "has discharged his responsibility, and the purchaser accepts whatever he gets." The only effective way to qualify vendors is to see if their management abides by his 14 points, uses statistical process control, and is willing to cooperate on the tests and use of instruments and gauges.

The best recognition one can give a quality vendor, according to Deming, is to give that vendor more business. He points out that requiring statistical evidence of process control in selecting vendors would mean, in most companies, a drastic reduction in the number of vendors they deal with simply because not that many vendors would qualify. Nevertheless, he says, this is the only way to choose vendors, even if that means relying on a single source for critical items.

In fact, Deming advocates single sourcing. "A second source, for protection, for every item purchased is a costly practice," he says. The advantages of single sourcing include better vendor commitment, eliminating small differences between products from two suppliers, and simplifying accounting and paperwork. A disadvantage is the risk of depending on one supplier without any backup alternatives.

As to the fact that relying on a single source can often mean paying a higher price, Deming says, "The policy of forever trying to drive down the price of anything purchased, with no regard to quality and service, can drive good vendors and good service out of business. The ways of doing business with vendors and customers that were good enough in the past must now be revised to meet new requirements of quality and productivity."

DEMING'S FOURTEEN POINTS FOR MANAGEMENT

1. Create constancy of purpose toward improvement of products and services.
2. Adopt the new philosophy. We can no longer live with commonly accepted levels of delays, mistakes, defective materials, and defective workmanship.
3. Cease dependence on mass inspection. Require, instead, statistical evidence that quality is built in.
4. End the practice of awarding business on the basis of price tag.
5. Find problems. It is management's job to work continually on the system.
6. Institute modern methods of training on the job.
7. Institute modern methods of supervision of production workers. The responsibility of foremen must be changed from quantity to quality.
8. Drive out fear, so that everyone may work effectively for the company.
9. Break down barriers between departments.
10. Eliminate numerical goals, posters, and slogans for the work force, asking for new levels of productivity without providing methods.
11. Eliminate work standards that prescribe numerical quotas.
12. Remove barriers that stand between the hourly worker and his right to pride of workmanship.
13. Institute a vigorous program of education and retraining.
14. Create a structure in top management that will push every day on the above thirteen points.

(B) ***Juran quality model.*** According to Jospeh M. Juran, there are two kinds of quality: "fitness for use" and "conformance to specifications." To illustrate the difference, he says a dangerous product could meet all specifications, but not be fit for use. He pointed out that the technical aspects of quality control had been well covered, but that firms did not know how to manage for quality. He identified some of the problems as organizational, communication, and coordination of functions—in other words, the human element.

Juran talks about three basic steps to progress: (1) structured annual improvements combined with devotion and a sense of urgency, (2) massive training programs, and (3) upper management leadership. In his view, less than 20% of quality problems are due to workers; the remainder is caused by management.

JURAN'S TEN STEPS TO QUALITY IMPROVEMENT

1. Build awareness of the need and opportunity for improvement.
2. Set goals for improvement.
3. Organize to reach the goals (establish a quality council, identify problems, select projects, appoint teams, designate facilitator).
4. Provide training.
5. Carry out projects to solve problems.
6. Report progress.
7. Give recognition.
8. Communicate results.
9. Keep score.
10. Maintain momentum by making annual improvement part of the regular systems and processes of the company.

(C) ***Crosby quality model.*** According to Philip B. Crosby's definition, quality is conformance to requirements, and it can only be measured by the cost of nonconformance. "Don't talk about poor quality or high quality. Talk about conformance and nonconformance," he says. This approach means that the only standard of performance is zero defects. Crosby encourages "prevention (perfection)" as opposed to "inspection," "testing," and "checking."

CROSBY'S FOURTEEN STEPS TO QUALITY IMPROVEMENT

1. Make it clear that management is committed to quality.
2. Form quality improvement teams with representatives from each department.
3. Determine where current and potential quality problems lie.
4. Evaluate the cost of quality and explain its use as a management tool.
5. Raise the quality awareness and personal concern of all employees.
6. Take actions to correct problems identified through previous steps.
7. Establish a committee for the zero defects program.
8. Train supervisors to actively carry out their part of the quality improvement program.
9. Hold a "zero defects day" to let all employees realize that there has been a change.
10. Encourage individuals to establish improvement goals for themselves and their groups.
11. Encourage employees to communicate to management the obstacles they face in attaining their improvement goals.
12. Recognize and appreciate those who participate.
13. Establish quality councils to communicate on a regular basis.
14. Do it all over again to emphasize that the quality improvement program never ends.

(ii) **Malcolm Baldrige National Quality Award.** The Malcolm Baldrige National Quality Award (NQA) is an annual award to recognize US companies that excel in quality management and quality achievement. The award promotes

- Awareness of quality as an increasingly important element of competitiveness
- Understanding of the requirements for quality excellence
- Sharing of information on successful quality strategies and the benefits derived from implementation of these strategies

Award criteria goals include delivery of ever-improving value to customers and improvement of overall company operational performance. The Award criteria are built on a set of core values and concepts. Together, these values and concepts represent the underlying basis for integrating the overall customer and company operational performance requirements. These core values and concepts include customer-driven quality, leadership, continuous improvement, employee participation and development, fast response, design quality and prevention, long-range outlook, management by fact, partnership development, and corporate responsibility and citizenship.

The core values and concepts are embodied in seven categories, including leadership, information and analysis, strategic quality planning, human resource development and management, management of process quality, quality and operational results, and customer focus and satisfaction.

(iii) **European Quality Award.** The European Quality Management Association has set up a European equivalent to the US Baldrige program, the European Quality Award (EQA). **Quality measures** for EQA include: leadership, information and analysis, strategic quality planning, human resource development and management, management of process quality, quality and operational results, customer focus and satisfaction, financial results, and environmental concerns.

(j) **Six-Sigma.** Six-sigma is an approach to measuring and improving product and service quality. In six-sigma terminology, a defect (nonconformance) is any mistake or error that is passed on to the customer. It redefines quality performance as defects per million opportunities (dpmo), as follows:

dpmo = (Defects per unit) × 1,000,000/opportunities for error where defects per unit = Number of defects discovered/Number of units produced

Six-sigma represents a quality level of at most 3.4 defects per million opportunities. Its goal is to find and eliminate causes of errors or defects in processes by focusing on characteristics that are critical to customers.

(i) **Six-sigma metrics.** The recognized benchmark for six-sigma implementation is General Electric (GE). GE's six-sigma problem solving approach (DMAIC) employs five phases: (1) define, (2) measure, (3) analyze, (4) improve, and (5) control.

The define (D) phase focuses on identifying customers and their priorities, identifying a project suitable for six-sigma efforts based on business objectives as well as customer needs and feedback, and identifying critical-to-quality characteristics (CTQs) that the customer considers to have the most impact on quality. Specific tools useful in the define phase include cause-and-effect diagram, brainstorming, and process mapping ("as is").

The measure (M) phase focuses on determining how to measure the process and how it is performing and identifying the key internal processes that influence CTQs and measure the defects currently generated relative to those processes. Specific tools useful in the measure phase include systems analysis, cause-and-effect diagram, process mapping, and common cause and special cause identification.

The analyze (A) phase focuses on determining the most likely causes of defects and understanding why defects are generated by identifying the key variables that are most likely to create process variation. Specific tools useful in the analyze phase include statistical process control (SPC) and process mapping.

The improve (I) phase focuses on identifying means to remove the causes of the defects, confirming the key variables and quantifying their effects on the CTQs, identifying the maximum acceptable ranges of the key variables and a system for measuring deviations of the variables, and modifying the process to stay within the acceptable range. Specific tools useful in the improve phase include brainstorming (idea gathering), process mapping ("should be"), and quality function deployment (house of quality and voice of the customer).

The control (C) phase focuses on determining how to maintain the improvements and putting the tools in place to ensure that the key variables remain within the maximum acceptable ranges under the modified process. Specific tools useful in the control phase include mistake proofing and institutionalization.

The concept behind the six-sigma is similar to TQM, which is the integration of human and process elements of improvement. Human elements include management leadership, a sense of urgency, focus on results and customers, team processes, and culture change. Process elements include the use of process management techniques, analysis of variation and statistical methods, a disciplined problem-solving approach, and management by fact.

According to American Society for Quality (ASQ), several key principles are necessary for effective implementation of six-sigma.

- Committed leadership from top management
- Integration with existing initiatives, business strategy, and performance measurement

- Process thinking
- Disciplined customer and market intelligence gathering
- A bottom-line orientation
- Leadership in the trenches. It includes technical and nontechnical employees and managers. It also includes: champions, who are fully trained business leaders who promote and lead the deployment of six-sigma in a significant area of the business; master black belts, who are fully trained quality leaders responsible for six-sigma strategy, training, mentoring, deployment, and results; black belts, who are fully trained six-sigma experts who lead improvement teams, work projects across the business, and mentor green belts; green belts, who are full-time teachers with quantitative skills as well as teaching and leadership ability; they are fully trained quality leaders responsible for six-sigma strategy, training, mentoring, deployment, and results; and team members, who are individuals who support specific projects in their area.
- Training
- Continuous reinforcement and rewards

(ii) **Six-sigma tools.** Six-sigma tools can be categorized into eight general groups, which will integrate the tools and the methodology into management systems across the organization.

1. Elementary statistical tools include basic statistics, statistical thinking, hypothesis testing, correlation, and simple regression.
2. Advanced statistical tools include design of experiments, analysis of variance, and multiple regression.
3. Product design and reliability tools include quality function deployment (QFD) and failure mode and effects analysis (FMEA).
4. Measurement tools include process capability and measurement systems analysis.
5. Process improvement tools include process improvement planning, process mapping, and mistake-proofing (Poka-Yoke).
6. Implementation tools focus on organizational effectiveness and facilitation of meetings and communication.
7. Teamwork tools focus on team development and team assessment.
8. Process control tools include quality control plans and statistical process control (SPC).

1.2 International Organization for Standardization Framework

ISO 9000 consists of a series of generic standards with appropriate guidelines published by the International Organization for Standardization (called ISO) for vendor certification programs. ISO 9000 addresses quality system processes not product performance specifications. In other words, the ISO 9000 covers how products are made, but not necessarily how they work. ISO 9000 focuses on processes, not on products or people. It is based on the concept that one will fix the product by fixing the process. The ISO 9000 is a standard to judge the quality of suppliers. It assumes that suppliers have a sound quality system in place and it is being followed. ISO 9000 can be used as a baseline quality system to achieve Total Quality Management objectives.

The standards are becoming an acceptable worldwide approach to vendor certification and international trade. The real push is from companies throughout the world who are requesting that their suppliers become certified. The ISO 9000 standards are equally applicable to manufacturing and service industries, and remove the nontariff barriers that arise from differences and inadequacies among national, local, or company standards. Major categories of nontariff barriers include quantitative import restrictions such as quotas, voluntary export restraints, and price controls.

There are two kinds of standards: (1) product standards dealing with technical specifications and (2) quality standards dealing with management systems. Quality measures for ISO 9000 include: leadership, human resource development and management, management of process quality, and customer focus and satisfaction.

(a) **ISO Certification Process.** To earn ISO 9000 certification, a company must set up and document all procedures that relate to the process to be certified. These procedures can include everything from procuring and storing raw materials, to designing products, to issuing change orders on designs, to controlling inventory, to answering customer phone calls. Flowcharts can be used to document the procedures in place.

Documentation of these procedures ensures that they are followed throughout the organization. The idea is that by rethinking and documenting every step of the corporate process, companies can identify and eliminate trouble spots—and thus improve overall quality. *The probability of producing a high-quality product increases because the risk that leads to poor quality decline as the processes are documented and followed. ISO 9000 forces discipline into the system.*

After an application for certification is filed, registrars or auditors accredited by a national quality board will conduct on-site audits. During the audit, registrars ask questions about company procedures and policies.

(b) **Benefits of ISO 9000.** The painstaking certification process yields several benefits for customers of certified manufacturers and service providers. These benefits include

- Products from ISO 9000-certified suppliers are likely to be more reliable.
- When every step of a manufacturing process is documented, it is easier to spot problems and trace them back to an exact point in the manufacturing line. Problem tracking is facilitated.
- Its document-it-all approach makes it easier for users to evaluate products and services and to anticipate potential problems.
- Costs will be lower for both the manufacturer and the customer due to efficient operations. Lower design costs translate to lower product costs, which should mean lower prices for users.
- Buying products from ISO-certified suppliers can save customers the time and expense of conducting on-site visits of manufacturing facilities.
- It saves time and money by not having to test incoming parts from ISO-certified suppliers because its suppliers' procedures include testing.

(c) **Types of ISO 9000 Standards.** There are several types of ISO 9000 family of standards, including the 9000 and 10000 series.

- **ISO 8402.** It presents vocabulary for quality management and quality assurance.
- **ISO 9000.** It presents quality management and quality assurance standards. It serves as an introduction to the other standards in the series. Part 1 provides guidelines for selection and use. Part 2 provides generic guidelines for the application of ISO 9001, 9002, 9003. Part 3 provides guidelines for the application of ISO 9001 to the development, supply, and maintenance of software. The key process is the design phase. Part 4 deals with application for dependability management. It focuses on the reliability, maintainability, and availability characteristics of products such as transportation, electricity, telecommunications, and information services.
- **ISO 9001.** It addresses quality systems. It is the most comprehensive model for quality assurance in design, development, production, installation, and servicing.
- **ISO 9002.** It addresses quality systems and it is a model for quality assurance in production, installation, and servicing.
- **ISO 9003.** It addresses quality systems and it is a model for quality assurance in final test and inspection.
- **ISO 9004.** It deals with quality management and quality system elements. There are four parts in this standard.
  - **Part 1** provides general guidelines for most of the quality system elements contained in ISO 9001, 9002, and 9003 in greater detail. It addresses various areas such as organizational goals (consider costs, benefits, and risks); management responsibility (establish quality policy); quality system elements (configuration management, quality plans, quality records, audits and reviews, quality improvement); financial considerations of quality systems (quality-costing approach, process-cost approach, quality-loss approach); quality in marketing (defining product requirements, obtaining customer feedback); quality in specification and design (translating customer needs into technical specifications); quality in purchasing (agreement on quality assurance, selection of contractors and suppliers); quality of processes (process capability, product handling); control of processes (material control, traceability, process control and change control); product verification (verifying incoming materials, in-process, and finished product); control of inspection, measuring and test equipment (corrective action, outside testing); control of nonconforming product (segregation, disposition, action and avoidance); corrective action (analyzing the problem, investigation and elimination of causes); post production activities (storage and service, postmarketing surveillance); quality records (inspection

reports, test data, drawings, specifications, procedures); personnel (qualifications, motivation); product safety (standards, tests, product recall methods, emergency plan for contingencies); and use of statistical methods (graphical methods, regression analysis, control charts, analysis of variance methods, design of experiments, statistical sampling).

- **Part 2** provides guidelines for services. It applies to organizations that provide services or whose products include a service component.
- **Part 3** provides guidelines for processed materials. It applies to organizations whose products consists of processed materials such as solids, liquids, or gases that are delivered in pipelines, drums, tanks, or cans. It includes guidelines on process control, process capability, equipment control, maintenance, and documentation. It points out the importance of statistical sampling.
- **Part 4** provides guidelines for quality improvement. This standard states "the motivation for quality improvement comes from the need to provide increased value and satisfaction to customers." An important concept is that companies should "seek opportunities for improvement, rather than waiting for a problem to reveal opportunities. It also talks about performing processes more efficiently and effectively with less waste and resource consumption.

- **ISO 10005.** It deals with quality management providing guidelines for quality plans.
- **ISO 10007.** It provides guidelines for configuration management. It describes the technical organizational activities of configuration identification, control, status accounting, and audit. It is applied over the life cycle of a product to provide visibility and control of functional and physical characteristics.
- **ISO 10011.** It provides guidelines for auditing quality systems. Part 1 deals with auditing and includes first-, second-, and third-party audits. Part 2 covers qualification criteria (education, training, and experience) for quality systems auditors. Part 3 addresses management of an audit from initial planning to the closing meeting.
- **ISO 10012.** It deals with quality assurance requirements for measuring equipment. It assumes that quality depends upon accurate measurements.
- **ISO 10013.** It deals with guidelines for developing quality manuals. It describes the development and control of quality manuals, tailored to the specific user needs.
- **QS-9000.** This guideline makes it easier for suppliers to do business with auto manufacturers and other original equipment manufacturers. This guideline applies to all internal and external suppliers that provide production materials, production or service parts, or heat treating and other finishing services. QS-9000 was developed because ISO 9001 was not current for the automotive industry; the QS-9000 interpretations updated the ISO 9001 requirements.

WHICH ISO STANDARD IS WHICH?

- ISO 9001, 9002, and 9003 are called conformance standards and quality assurance models. They are used for external quality assurance to provide confidence to the customer that the company's quality system is capable of providing a satisfactory product or service. They are not levels of quality and are used in contractual situations. They are prescriptive documents.
- ISO 9000-1 and 9004-1 are guidance standards. They are used for internal quality assurance activities aimed at providing confidence to the management of an organization that the intended quality is being achieved. They are used in noncontractual situations. They are descriptive documents.
- ISO 10005, 10011, and 10013 deal with quality plans, auditing, and quality manuals respectively.
- QS-9000 is not a standard, but it contains the ISO 9001 standard; its reqirements are much broader than ISO 9001.
- The ISO 9000 standards provide a baseline or foundation for a Total Quality Management (TQM) program

BALDRIGE VS. ISO 9000 VS. EQA

- Compared with Baldrige and EQA, ISO 9000 offers somewhat thin coverage of specific quality categories.
- ISO 9000 only covers four categories, compared with the seven covered by Baldrige and nine by EQA. For example, ISO 9000 does not address the "information and analysis" category, which defines how to collect corporate data, internally and externally, to measure management quality.
- ISO 9000 does not cover "strategic quality planning," a category used to judge the importance of improving quality as part of the corporate planning process, or "quality and operational results," which deals with the financial soundness of a company.
- EQA actually goes beyond Baldrige to encompass nine specific quality categories, in which categories 8 and 9 are additional items in the EQA.

1.3 Forecasting

The simplest form of forecasting is the projection of past trends called extrapolation. Model building activities are examples of analytical techniques. A model breaks down a major problem into parts or subproblems and solves it sequentially. Some examples of applications of forecasting models in managerial accounting are pricing, costs, revenue, and inventory decisions.

For example, when forecasting purchases of inventory for a firm, factors such as knowledge of the behavior of business cycles, econometrics, and information on the seasonal variations in demand are important.

Models require a set of predetermined procedures. If there are no well-ordered and fully-developed procedures there is no need to model. That is, *no procedure, no model.* For example, a onetime crisis situation cannot be modeled due to lack of a preset procedure.

A key concept in all forecasting models dealing with probabilities is the expected value. The expected value equals the sum of the products of the possible payoffs and their probabilities.

(a) **Time Series Analysis.** Time series analysis is the process by which a set of data measured over time is analyzed. Decision makers need to understand how to analyze the past data if they expect to incorporate past information into future decisions. Although the factors that affect the future are uncertain, often the past offers a good indication of what the future will hold. *The key is to know how to extract the meaningful information from all the available past data.*

All time series contain at least one of four time series components: long-term trend, seasonal, cyclical, and random or irregular components. Time series analysis involves breaking down data measured over time into one or more of these components. Time series analysis is similar to regression analysis in that both techniques help to explain the variability in data as much as possible. The four types of components of time series analysis help explain that variability (see Exhibit 1.3). The purpose of time series analysis is to use these components to explain the total variability in past data. The problem is how to best separate each component from the others so that each can be analyzed clearly.

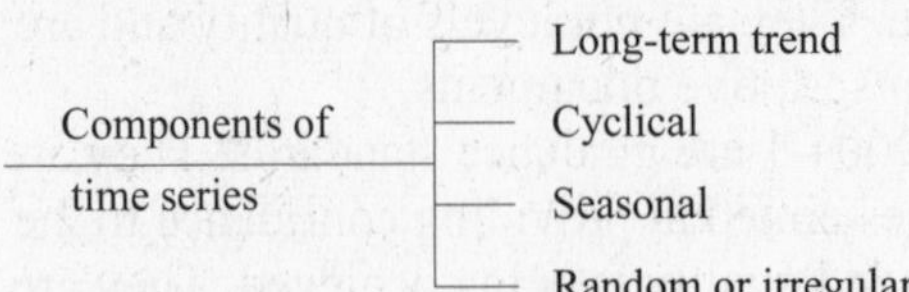

Exhibit 1.3: Components of time series

(i) **Long-term trend.** The trend component is the long-term increase (growth) or decrease (decline) in a variable being measured over time. An example is annual sales over the past 10 to 15 years. Because long-term forecasting is becoming increasingly important due to severe global competition, the trend component in time series analysis is important to all organizations.

Long-term growth patterns have a wide variety of shapes such as the first-degree, exponential, and Gompertz curves. The easiest method to fit trend lines to a series of data is to graph the data and draw the trend line freehand. Another way of fitting a trend line to a set of data is to use the least square regression method. *Two methods are available to fit a trend line to a series of data: (1) draw the trend line freehand, and (2) use the least square regression method.*

(ii) **Seasonal component.** The seasonal component represents those changes in a time series that occur at the same time every year. An example is peak sales occurring once in the spring and once in the fall season.

Some organizations (e.g., toy stores, food processors, lumber mills) are affected not only by long-term trends but also by seasonal variations. The demand for products or services is highly dependent on the time of year. Those organizations facing seasonal variations are interested in knowing how well or poorly they are doing relative to the normal seasonal variation. The question is whether the increase or decrease is more or less than expected, or whether it occurs at more or less than the average rate.

A seasonal index known as the ratio to moving average can be calculated to measure seasonal variation in a time series. A 12-month moving average is used here. *Seasonal variation affects the overall planning process, especially in labor requests, inventory levels, training needs, and periodic maintenance work.*

Some prefer to eliminate irregular components in the data by taking the normalized average of the ratio to moving averages. A requirement prior to separating the irregular components from the data is to make sure that the ratio to moving averages is stable from year to year. Another assumption to be made prior to eliminating irregular components is that the irregular fluctuations are caused by purely random circumstances.

(iii) **Cyclical component.** In addition to the seasonal component, data can contain certain cyclical effects. Cyclical effects in a time series are represented by war-like fluctuations around a long-term trend. These fluctuations are thought to be caused by pulsations in factors such as interest rates, money supply, consumer demand, market conditions, and government policies. Cyclical fluctuations repeat themselves in a general pattern in the long term, but occur with differing frequencies and intensities. Thus, they can be isolated, but not totally predicted. *Firms affected by cyclical fluctuations are those vulnerable to unexpected changes in the economy. The effect is different each time it occurs.*

Cyclical variations in time series data do not repeat themselves in a regular pattern as do seasonal factors, but they cannot be considered random variations in the data either.

The organizations hardest hit by the cyclical component are those connected with items purchased with discretionary income (e.g., big-ticket items such as home appliances and automobiles). Consumers can postpone purchasing these items and consequently these producing organizations are the most affected by a downturn in the economy.

The cyclical component is isolated by first removing the long-term trend and seasonal factors from the time series data. Then statistical normal values are calculated by multiplying the trend value by the seasonal index values. Finally, the cyclical component, which also contains the irregular component, is determined for each time period.

(iv) **Random or irregular component.** The random or irregular component is the one that cannot be attributed to any of the three components already discussed, namely long-term trend, seasonal, and cyclical components (see Exhibit 1.4). Random fluctuations can be caused by many factors, such as economic failures, weather, political events.

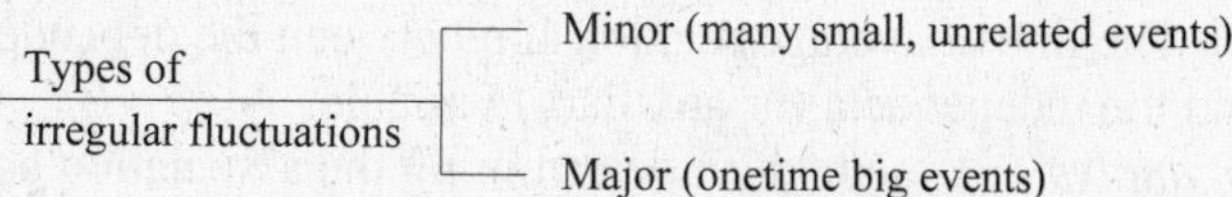

Exhibit 1.4: Types of irregular fluctuations

Minor irregularities show up as sawtooth-like patterns around the long-term trend. Individually, they are not significant, but collectively they can be significant and could cause problems to many organizations.

LARGE VS. SMALL IRREGULAR VARIATIONS

- Large irregular variations cause greater problems.
- Small irregular variations cause lesser problems.

Major irregularities are significant onetime, unpredictable changes in the time series due to such extended and uncontrolled factors as a war, an oil embargo, a summer drought, or a severe winter storm.

Almost all industries and organizations are affected by irregular components. Agriculture, insurance, and mining companies will be more interested in this component. Minor irregularities can be smoothed out by using a moving average method. The goal is to eliminate as much as possible the irregular influences so that the true, seasonal, and cyclical components can be recognized and used. *A random component is unwanted. Buying insurance coverage is one way to mitigate the risks resulting from major irregular fluctuations.*

(b) **Regression Analysis.** Regression analysis is a statistical technique used to measure the extent to which a change in the value of one variable, the independent variable, tends to be accompanied by a change in the value of another variable, the dependent variable.

Most measures of associations are nondirectional, that is, when calculated, it is not necessary to indicate which variable is hypothesized to influence the other. Measures of association show to what degree, on a zero-to-one scale, two variables are linked.

DEFINITION OF KEY TERMS: REGRESSION ANALYSIS

- *Analysis of covariance.* A method of analyzing the differences in the means of two or more groups of cases while taking account of variation in one or more interval-ratio variables.
- *Analysis of variance.* A method for analyzing the differences in the means of two or more groups of cases.
- *Asymmetric measure of association.* A measure of association that makes a distinction between independent and dependent variables.
- *Auxiliary variable.* Another name for independent variable.
- *Correlation.* Correlation is a synonym for association and it is one of several measures of association. Correlation means the interdependence between two sets of numbers or a relation between two quantities, such that when one changes, the other changes. Simultaneous increasing or decreasing of quantities is called "positive correlation"; when one quantity increases while the other decreases, it is called "negative correlation."
- *Dependent variable.* A variable that may, it is believed, be predicted by or caused by one or more other variables called independent variables. It will show the "effect."
- *Discriminant analysis.* A tool for discriminating between effective and ineffective policies or procedures. It is based on subjective assessment (not based on statistics), and discrete values.
- *Explanatory variable.* Another name for independent variable.
- *Independent variable.* A variable that may, it is believed, predict or cause fluctuation in a dependent variable.
- *Primary variable.* Another name for dependent variable.
- *Regression.* The line of average relationship between the dependent (or primary) variable and the independent (or auxiliary) variable.
- *Regression analysis.* A method for determining the association between a dependent variable and one or more independent variables.
- *Regression coefficient.* A measure of change in a primary variable associated with a unit change in the auxiliary variable. An asymmetric measure of association; a statistic computed as part of a regression analysis.
- *Regression estimate.* An estimate of a population parameter for one variable that is obtained by substituting the known total for another variable into a regression equation calculated on the basis of the sample values of the two variables. Note that ratio estimates are special kinds of regression estimates.
- *Symmetric measure of association.* A measure of association that does not make a distinction between independent and dependent variables.

Managers often need to determine the relationships between two or more variables prior to making a decision or for predicting and planning purposes or when analyzing a problem. When two variables are involved, simple linear regression and correlation analysis are the most often applied statistical tools for decision making. They provide a basis for analyzing two variables and their relationship to each other.

When more than two variables are involved, multiple regression analysis will be useful. Where only one independent variable is involved in the analysis, the technique is known as simple regression analysis; where two or more independent variables are involved, the technique is called multiple regression analysis (see Exhibit 1.5).

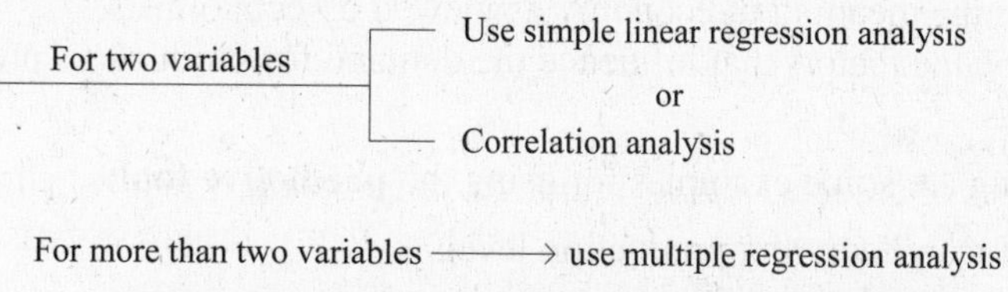

Exhibit 1.5: Simple regression and multiple regression

The basic diagram, or scatter plots, can be used to depict potential relationships between a dependent variable Y (e.g., sales) and an independent variable X (e.g., advertising). The scatter plot provides a visual feel for the relationship between variables (qualitative measurement). A dependent variable is the variable whose variation is of interest. An independent variable is a variable used to explain variation in the dependent variable. The independent variable is also called an explanatory variable. Three possible relationships can emerge from the scatter plots: (1) linear, (2) curvilinear, and (3) no relationship (see Exhibit 1.6).

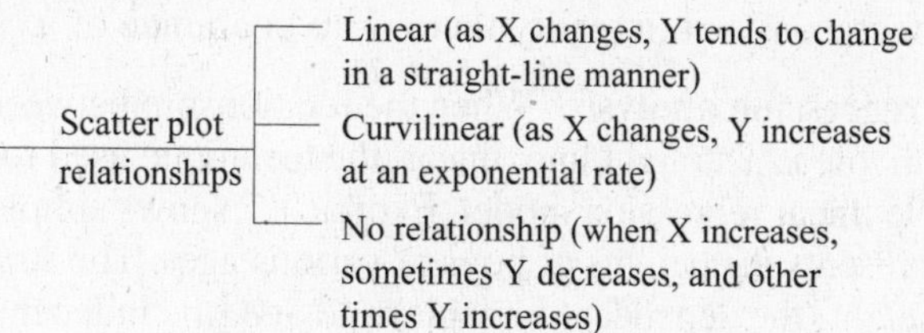

Exhibit 1.6: Scatter plot relationships

- **Linear.** As X changes, Y tends to change in a straight line or near straight-line manner. It can be positive change (Y increases as X increases) or negative change (Y decreases as X increases).
- **Curvilinear.** As X increases, Y increases at an exponential rate (example, as production increases, overtime is increasing at an exponential rate). As X increases, Y increases at a diminishing rate (example, as advertising is allowed to grow too large, diminishing returns will occur for sales).
- **No relationship.** When X increases, sometimes Y decreases, and other times Y increases.

In addition to qualitative measure (i.e., visual feel), quantitative measurement using *correlation coefficient* is needed to measure the strength between two variables. The correlation coefficient can range from a perfect positive correlation (+1.0) to a perfect negative correlation (-1.0). If two variables have no linear relationship, the correlation between them is zero. Consequently, the more the correlation differs from zero, the stronger the linear relationship between the two variables. The sign of the correlation coefficient indicates the direction of the relationship, but does not aid in determining the strength.

Example

Given four values of correlation coefficient, -0.15, -0.75, 0.19, and 0.35, which value indicates the weakest linear association between two variables. The value -0.15 has the weakest linear association because it is farther from -1.0.

USES OF REGRESSION ANALYSIS

Two basic uses of regression analysis are as a descriptive tool and as a predictive tool. The following are some examples for using the **descriptive tool:**

- To describe the relationship between a loan's term (number of months) and its dollar value by a loan officer in a bank. A positive linear relationship might exist between time and amount in which smaller loans would tend to be associated with shorter lending periods whereas larger loans would be for longer periods.
- To explain the meaning of economy as viewed by economists.
- To describe the factors that influence the demand for products as presented by market researchers.

The following are some examples for using the **predictive tool:**

- To predict manufacturing production levels
- To forecast annual tax revenues
- To predict inventory levels

To determine whether the linear relationship between sales and advertising is significant requires us to test whether the sample data support or refute the hypothesis that the population correlation coefficient is zero. A 't' statistic is used to test the hypothesis that the population coefficient is zero.

The correlation does not imply cause and effect, since two seemingly unconnected variables could often be highly correlated. When a correlation exists between two seemingly unrelated variables, the correlation is spurious at best. Even in the case of sales and advertising one might be tempted to say that a cause and effect exist, but in reality there is no guarantee of a cause-and-effect situation.

(i) **Simple linear regression analysis.** When the relationship between the dependent variable and the independent variable is a straight line, linear, the technique used for prediction and estimation is called the simple linear regression model. Exhibit 1.7 shows simple linear regression where the plotted data represents the heights of boys of various ages. The straight line represents the relationship between height (the dependent variable) and age (the independent variable) as disclosed by regression analysis. If the change in the dependent variable associated with a change in the independent variable does not occur at a constant rate, the relationship can be represented by a curved line and is referred to as curvilinear.

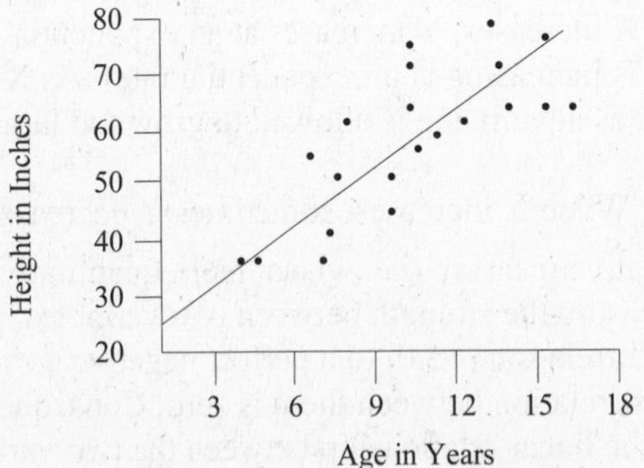

Exhibit 1.7: Simple linear regression

The simple linear regression model is represented by the following equation:

$$Yi = ß0 + ß1\ Xi + ei$$

Where *Yi* is the value of the dependent variable, *Xi* is the value of the independent variable, ß0 is the *Y*-intercept (a regression coefficient defining the true population model), ß1 is the slope of the regression line (a regression coefficient defining the true population model), and *ei* is the error term or residual and is a random component.

The random component is the difference between the actual *Y* value and the value of *Y* predicted by the model, and *i* could be positive or negative, depending on whether a single value of *Y* for a given *X* falls above or below the regression line. These *ei* values will have a mean of zero and a standard deviation called the standard error of the estimate. If this standard error is too large, the regression model may not be very useful for prediction.

Here, the regression model connects the averages of dependent variable *Y* for each level of the independent variable, *X*. The regression line, a straight line, is determined by two values, ß0 and ß1.

Simple Regression Analysis

In simple regression analysis, the correlation coefficient measures the strength of the linear relationship between any two variables (X and Y); the analysis of variance "F" test indicates whether the regression model explains a significant proportion of variation in the dependent variable.

Managers would like to estimate the true linear relationship between dependent and independent variables by determining the regression model using sample data. A scatter plot can be drawn with the sample data to estimate the population regression line. The least squares criterion is used to select the best line since many possible regression lines exist for a sample of data. According to the least squares criterion, the best regression line is the one that minimizes the sum of squared distances between the observed (X,Y) points and the regression line. *Residual is the difference between the true regression line and the actual* Y *value.*

(ii) **Assumptions of the simple linear regression model.** The following list provides assumptions of the simple linear regression model:

- Individual values of the dependent variable, *Y*, are statistically independent of one another.
- For a given *X* value, there can exist many values of *Y*. Further, the distribution of possible *Y* values for any *X* value is normal.
- The distribution of possible *Y* values have equal variances for all values of *X*.
- The means of the dependent variable, *Y*, for all specified values of the independent variable can be connected by a straight line called the population regression model.

The following are some major considerations in using regression analysis as a predictive tool:

- Note that conclusions and inferences made from a regression line apply only over the range of data contained in the sample used to develop the regression line. The applicable range of data is called the" relevant range of data." Any predictions beyond the relevant range of data would lead to "overpredictions." Thus, the range of data in the sample should cover the range of data in the population. Then only a true relationship between the dependent variable and the independent variable will emerge.
- Be aware of the fact that a significant linear relationship existing between two variables does not imply that one variable causes the other. Although there may be a cause-and-effect relationship, managers should not infer the presence of such a relationship based only on regression and/or correlation analysis. Other factors such as judgment, experience, and knowledge of the specific area of interest should also be considered.
- A cause-and-effect relationship between two variables is not necessary for regression analysis to be used for prediction. It is important to make sure that the regression model accurately reflects the relationship between the two variables and that the relationship remains stable.
- A high *coefficient of determination* (R^2) does not guarantee that the regression model will be a good predictor. The R^2 applies only to the sample data—measuring the fit of the regression line to the sample data—not to any other data.

The least squares regression line minimizes the sum of squared residuals. This value is called the sum of squares error (SSE). It represents the amount of variation in the dependent variable that is not explained by the least squares regression line, the amount of variation in the dependent variable that is explained by the regression line is called the sum of squares regression (SSR).

$$SSR = TSS - SSE$$

where TSS is the total sum of squares explaining the amount of total variation in the dependent variable.

The percentage of the total variable in the dependent variable which is explained by the independent variable is called the coefficient of determination (R^2). R^2 can be a value between zero and 1.0. R^2 indicates how well the linear regression line fits the data points (X,Y). *The better the fit, the closer R^2 will be to 1.0.*

INTERPRETATION OF R^2

- R^2 is 1.0 when there is a perfect linear relationship between two variables.
- R^2 will be close to zero when there is a weak linear relationship or no linear relationship at all.

When R^2 is 1.0, it corresponds to a situation in which the least squares regression line would pass through each of the points in the scatter plot. Least square criterion ensures that R^2 will be maximized. R^2 applies only to the sample data used to develop the model.

APPLICATION OF REGRESSION ANALYSIS

Example 1

XYZ Company derived the following cost relationship from a regression analysis of its monthly manufacturing overhead cost.

$$C = \$80,000 + \$12\ M$$

where C is monthly manufacturing overhead cost and M is machine hours. The standard error of estimate of the regression is $6,000. The standard time required to manufacture a case of the company's single product is four machine hours. XYZ applies manufacturing overhead to production on the basis of machine hours, and its normal annual production is 50,000 cases.

Question: What is the estimated variable manufacturing overhead cost for a month in which scheduled production is 5,000 cases?

Answer: In the cost equation C = $80,000 + $12 M, $80,000 is the fixed cost component and $12M is the variable cost component. That is, $12 x 5,000 cases x 4 machine hours per case = $240,000.

Question: What is the predetermined fixed manufacturing overhead rate?

Answer: Since $80,000 is the fixed component per month, we need to multiply this by 12 to obtain one year fixed cost. The predetermined overhead rate per machine hour is ($80,000 x 12)/(50,000 x 4) = $4.80.

Example 2

The linear regression equation, Y=15.8 + 1.1(x), was used to prepare the data table below.

Actual X	Predicted Y	Actual Y	Residual
0	15.8	10	-5.8
1	16.9	18	1.1
2	18.0	27	9.0
3	19.1	21	1.9
4	20.2	14	-6.2

Question: What do you conclude from the above data table?

Answer: The best description of the data is that the relationship is not linear. A linear equation was used with nonlinear relationship. If the relationship was linear, the results of actual Y would have been higher than or equal to 15.8; it is not. Two values (10 and 14) are less than 15.8, indicating a nonlinear relationship.

(iii) **Multiple regression analysis.** Regression analysis is used for prediction and description to determine the relationship between two or more variables. The multiple regression analysis technique analyzes the relationship between three or more variables, and is an extension of the simple regression analysis. *In simple regression analysis, there is only one independent variable. In multiple regression analysis, there is more than one independent variable.* Exhibit 1.8 presents a comparison between simple regression and multiple regression analysis.

<u>*Characteristics of simple regression*</u>

- Sales is a dependent variable and advertising expenditures is an independent variable.
- The model is an equation for a straight line in a two-dimensional space.
- Each regression coefficient represents a slope and involves a matrix algebra.
- Can use graph or calculator to solve the problem. Use of computer is optional.
- The correlation coefficient is calculated.

<u>*Characteristics of multiple regression*</u>

- House price is a dependent variable and square feet of house, age of house, number of bedrooms, and number of bathrooms are examples of independent variables.
- The model forms a hyperplane through multidimensional space.
- Each regression coefficient represents a slope and involves a matrix algebra.
- Must use computer to solve the problem.
- The correlation matrix is calculated.

Exhibit 1.8: A comparison between simple regression and multiple regression

From a theoretical viewpoint, the sample size required to compute a regression model must be at least one greater than the number of independent variables, that is, for a model with four independent variables, the absolute minimum number of case samples required is five. Otherwise, the model will produce meaningless values. From a practical standpoint, the sample size should be at least four times the number of independent variables.

SIMPLE REGRESSION VS. MULTIPLE REGRESSION

- When there are two variables (one dependent and one independent), we call it a bivariate or simple regression.
- When thee are more than two variables (one dependent and more than one independent), we call it a multivariate or multiple regression.
- The multivariate model offers a better fit than the bivariate model.

(iv) **Assumptions of the multiple regression model.** The following list provides assumptions about the multiple regression model:

- The errors are normally distributed.
- The mean of the error terms is zero.
- The error terms have a constant variance for all combined values of the independent variables.

In multiple regression analysis, additional independent variables are added to the regression model to explain some of the yet-unexplained variation in the dependent variable. Adding appropriate additional variables would reduce the standard error of the estimate where the value of the latter is too large for the regression model to be useful for prediction.

The *correlation matrix* is useful for determining which independent variables are likely to help explain variation in the dependent variable. A value of ± 1.0 indicates that changes in the independent variable are linearly related to changes in the dependent variable.

Similar to simple regression, multiple regression uses R^2, the multiple coefficient determination, and is determined as follows:

$$R^2 = \frac{\text{Sum of squares regression}}{\text{Total sum of square}} = \frac{SSR}{TSS}$$

Example

If R^2 is 0.75, then 75% of the variation in the dependent variable can be explained by all independent variables in the multiple regression model.

When highly correlated independent variables are included in the regression model, a condition of overlapping called **multicollinearity** can exist. Specifically, when two independent variables are correlated with each other, adding redundant information to the model, multicollinearity does exist in practice. The best practical advise is to drop the independent variable(s) that is the main cause of the multicollinearity problems from the model.

Multicollinearity influences the regression model negatively—the regression coefficient sign is the opposite of the expected sign. The independent variable causing multicollinearity is not necessary to the functioning of the model and hence can be removed without any loss. It is highly correlated with other independent variables and has low correlation with the dependent variable.

(v) **Symptoms of multicollinearity in regression.** The following list provides symptoms of multicollinearity in regression analysis:

- Incorrect signs on the coefficients
- A change in the values of the previous coefficients when a new variable is added to the model
- The change to insignificant of a previously significant variable when a new variable is added to the model
- An increase in the standard error of the estimate when a variable is added to the model

Not all independent variables contribute to the explanation of the variation in a dependent variable. Some variables are significant, but not all. *The significance of each independent variable can be tested using a "t" test. It is calculated by dividing the regression coefficient by the standard deviation of the regression coefficients.*

"F" TEST VS. "t" TEST

- The "F" test is used to explain the significance of just one independent variable.
- The "t" test is used to explain the significance of each independent variable. Multicollinearity affects the "t" test.

The regression model used for prediction should contain significant independent variables only. If insignificant variables exist, they should be removed and the regression model rerun before it is used for prediction purposes. *Any coefficient with an unexpected sign indicates a problem condition. Unexpected sign implies unreasonable relationships between variables.*

Developing a multiple regression model is an art and requires judgment when selecting the best set of independent variables for the model that are less in conflict and contributing to best predictor.

(vi) **Dummy variables in regression models.** When an independent variable in a regression model is a nominal or ordinal variable, it is called a qualitative variable. For example, in a model for predicting individual income, each manager may assign different values for a potential qualitative variable, for example, sex (male or female), affecting the regression analysis.

In order to assign unique numerical values for these qualitative variables, dummy variables are added to the regression model. Rules for dummy variables include: if the qualitative variable has two possible categories (e.g., male or female), one dummy variable is added, and for more than two possible categories, one less than the number of possible categories is added (i.e., for five categories, only four dummy variables). Not following these rules would introduce the unwanted multicollinearity and the fact that least squares regression estimates cannot be obtained if the number of dummy variables equals the number of possible categories. Dummy variables take on values of zero and one, and they represent the qualitative variables in the regression analysis.

(vii) **Regression methods.** Basically, there are two methods for developing a regression model: (1) ordinary regression and (2) stepwise regression (see Exhibit 1.9).

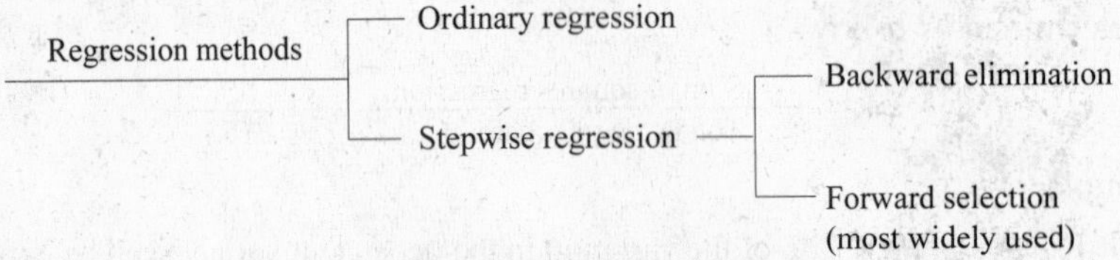

Exhibit 1.9: Regression methods

In the **ordinary regression method,** all independent variables are brought into the model at one step. The **stepwise regression method** develops the least squares regression equation in steps, either through backward elimination or through forward selection.

(A) ***Backward elimination.*** The backward elimination stepwise method begins by developing an ordinary regression model using all independent variables. All insignificant independent variables are eliminated in a stepwise fashion. The only independent variables left are the ones that have coefficients that are significantly different from zero. The advantage is that the manager has the opportunity to look at all the independent variables in the model before removing the variables that are not significant.

(B) ***Forward selection.*** The forward selection procedure works in the opposite direction of the backward elimination procedure. It begins by selecting a single independent variable that is highly significant—the one highly correlated with the dependent variable. In the next step, a second independent variable is selected based on its ability to explain the remaining unexplained variation in the dependent variable.

The forward selection procedure prevents multicollinearity from occurring. It does this by dropping an insignificant variable that is causing the overlap from the model. The forward selection procedure is widely used in decision-making applications and is generally recognized as a useful regression method. Because the selection process is automatic by the computer, the manager needs to use his judgment to make sure the regression model is usable and meaningful.

(viii) **Econometrics.** The application of statistical methods to economic data is called econometrics. It analyzes the relationships between economic variables. Econometrics uses multiple regression analysis.

Example

Recent events caused the time-series used by an electric utility company to become too unpredictable for practical use. An econometric model is developed to predict the demand for electricity based on factors such as (1) class of service, (2) population growth, and (3) unemployment in the area of service. Since there are three independent variables, multiple regression is used.

(c) **Sensitivity Analysis.** Sensitivity analysis is an evaluation of how certain changes in inputs results in what changes in outputs of a model or system (see Exhibit 1.10).

Changes in inputs —Lead to→ Changes in outputs

Exhibit 1.10: Scope of sensitivity analysis

The primary reason that sensitivity analysis is important to managers is that real-world problems exist in a dynamic environment. Change is inevitable. Prices of raw materials change as demand fluctuates, changes in the labor market cause changes in production costs. Sensitivity analysis provides the manager the information needed to respond to such changes without rebuilding the model. For example, bank management can use sensitivity analysis technique to determine the effects of policy changes on the optimal mix for its portfolio of earning assets.

Computer simulation techniques can be used to perform sensitivity analysis. The capability to ask "what if" questions is one of the biggest advantages of computer simulation. Next, sensitivity analysis is presented for manufacturing applications, linear programming applications, financial applications, network applications, and inventory applications.

(i) **Manufacturing applications.** The linking of production process improvement to financial results is critical to a successful computer-integrated manufacturing implementation. Management has established priorities: to decrease process variability, to shorten feedback time, and to reduce support functions. A process model was developed with the following parameters: facilities and equipment cost, theoretical materials consumption, actual materials consumption, and supplies cost. Sensitivity analysis was used to study the behavior of those parameters.

Sensitivity analysis was applied to the process model to compare the cash flows associated with various plan alternatives. Testing the model for changes in several parameters indicated that the model is sensitive to process inefficiency, product yields, volume variation, and price variations. Conversely, the model is relatively insensitive to change in labor costs.

The relationships between increased labor efficiency and gross profit can be studied using sensitivity analysis in a manufacturing plant environment.

(ii) **Linear programming applications.** Sensitivity analysis is the study of how changes in the coefficient of a linear program affect the optimal solution. The optimal solution is a feasible solution that maximizes or minimizes the value of the objective function. The objective function is used to measure the profit or cost of a particular solution.

Sensitivity analysis associated with the optimal solution provides valuable supplementary information for the decision maker. In the linear programming case, sensitivity analysis can be used to answer questions such as

- How will a change in a coefficient of the objective function affect the optimal solution?
- How will a change in the right-hand side value for a constraint affect the optimal solution?

However, there is one prerequisite prior to making the above changes, that is, optimal solution to the original linear programming problem needs to be in place. The changes are applied to the optimal solution. For this reason sensitivity analysis is often called postoptimality analysis. For example, in a production environment, sensitivity analysis can help determine how much each additional labor hour is worth and how many hours can be added before diminishing returns set in.

(iii) **Financial applications.** Integer linear programming techniques have been successfully used to solve capital budgeting problems. Only the integer variables are permitted to assure the values of zero or one. They could be of either the all-integer or the mixed-integer type. Fractional values of the decision variable are not allowed. The firm's goal is to select the most profitable projects and budgets for the capital expenditures. The outcome is usually whether the project is accepted (a value of 1) or rejected (a value of zero).

Another advantage of using an integer linear programming technique in a capital budgeting is its ability to handle multiple-choice constraints such as multiple projects under consideration and only one project can be selected in the end.

Sensitivity analysis is more critical for integer linear programming problems than that for linear-programming problems because a small change in one of the coefficients in the constraints can cause a large change in the value of the optimal solution. An example would be that one additional dollar in the budget can lead to a $20 increase in the return.

(iv) **Network applications.** Sensitivity analysis can be performed on the network. It provides the ability for checking the feasibility of current schedules and for permitting management to "experiment" with or evaluate the effects of proposed changes.

(v) **Inventory applications.** It is good to know how much the recommended order quantity would change if the estimated ordering and holding costs had been different. Depending on whether the total annual cost increased, decreased, or remained the same, we can tell whether the economic order quantity (EOQ) model is sensitive or insensitive to variations in the cost estimates.

(d) **Simulation Models.** The primary objective of simulation models is to describe the behavior of a real system. A model is designed and developed and a study is conducted to understand the behavior of the simulation model. The characteristics that are learned from the model are then used to make inferences about the real system. Later, the model is modified (asking "what if" questions) to improve the system's performance. The behavior of the model in response to the "what if" questions is studied to determine how well the real system will respond to the proposed modifications. Thus, the simulation model will help the decision maker by predicting what can be expected in practice. A key requisite is that the logic of the model should be as close to the actual operations as possible. In most cases, a computer is used for simulation models.

Computer simulation should not be viewed as an optimization technique, but as a way to improve the behavior or performance of the system. Model parameters are adjusted to improve the performance of the system. When good parameter settings have been found for the model, these settings can be used to improve the performance of the real system.

The steps involved in a computer simulation model include

- A computer simulation model that "behaves like" or simulates the real world system is developed.
- A series of computer runs or experiments is performed to learn about the behavior of the simulation model.
- The design of the model is changed to determine if the modifications improve the system performance. "What if" questions are asked of the model in this step. Thus, the simulation model helps the manager in predicting the future.

Usually, a computer simulator is used to conduct a simulation exercise on a computer. The simulator run by computer programs would perform mathematical calculations and keep track of the simulation results. Examples of calculations in a retail store environment include

- Number of customers serviced at a retail store during the twenty hours of simulated operations
- The average profit per hour per store
- Number of lost customers at a store per hour
- Average dollar loss per hour per store due to lost customers

Generic computer programming languages such as BASIC, FORTRAN, and PASCAL can be used to develop computer simulators. More specific simulation languages such as SIMSCRIPT, GPSS are favored due to their powerful and few programming statements required compared to many statements needed for generic languages.

(i) **Simulation applications in forecasting.** The following list describes simulation applications in forecasting:

- To perform a role play in order to reflect reality in a person being trained
- To study the performance of a waiting line system
- To simulate traffic flow through a busy street intersection to determine the number of traffic signals required for improving the traffic
- To simulate airplane flight conditions for training pilots
- To simulate the behavior of an inventory system in order to determine the best order quantity and reorder point
- To undergo a "dry run" evacuation in an office due to fire in a high-risk building
- To create mock disasters to provide experience in dealing with crisis situations such as product tampering, power outages, and flood
- To train auditors by providing financial statements and operating data to conduct a financial audit or an operational audit, respectively

(ii) **Simulation procedures and approaches.** Computer simulation is performed using the two basic procedures: (1) heuristic and (2) probabilistic, as shown in Exhibit 1.11.

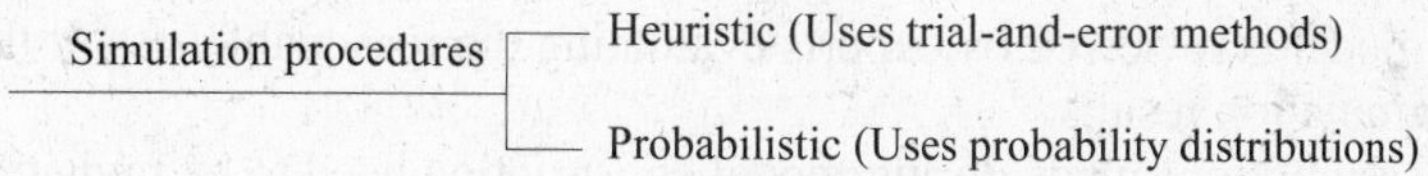

Exhibit 1.11: Simulation procedures

Heuristic procedures do not require probabilistic components. A variety of deterministic values are generated for the decision variables, and the best of the feasible solutions is selected.

When **probabilistic distributions** are involved, it is called the Monte Carlo simulation. Model inputs such as the number of customer arrivals in a service center are generated from probability distributions. These models are based on probabilities and time intervals of outcomes. When probabilities are involved, it is called a stochastic model.

Two approaches exist to the logic and recordkeeping of a simulation model: fixed time period and next event. In the fixed time period approach, each time period is of equal length, and the state of the system is updated at either the beginning or the end of each time period. The time between system updates is fixed.

In the next event approach, the time between arrivals and the time to complete service is randomly generated for a customer. The state of the system would be updated each time there was either a customer arriving or a customer completing service. The time between system updates is variable. Exhibit 1.12 presents advantages and disadvantages of simulation models.

ANALYTICAL PROCEDURES VS. COMPUTER SIMULATION

- Analytical procedures are best used to solve simple problems.
- Computer simulation is best used to solve complex problems.

Advantages of simulation models	Disadvantages of simulation models
• Solves complex problems where analytical procedures cannot be used. • Provides a convenient experimental laboratory. "What if" questions can be asked of the model. • Then danger of obtaining bad solutions to a problem is slight and the consequences have no effect on the organization. • The model can be run long enough to reach a steady state that will enable the manager to identify the apparent best decisions. • Learning is active for participants. • Mistakes are made in a risk-free environment. • Time spans can be compressed for key problems • Provides immediate feedback concerning proper and improper actions or decisions. Corrective action is timely	• There is a high cost of model development for design and programming. • The model does not guarantee an optimal solution to a problem. Decision variables are selected that have a good chance of being near the optimal solution. Also, not all values of the decision variables are tried in the model because it is costly to do so. • Simulation may not be able to replicate all situations or complexities that may arise in a real-world case. • Participants may tend to generalize from the model. It can create a "false sense of confidence" concerning their ability to cope with reality.

Exhibit 1.12: Advantages and disadvantages of simulation models

The sequence of model activities is

Model validation → Model implementation

Model validation is a step in the simulation procedure.

(iii) **Simulation model validation.** Validation involves verifying that the simulation model accurately describes the real-world system it is designed to simulate. The purpose of model validation is to make sure that it is a reasonable reflection of the real world. *The following methods will help to validate the model:*

- The simulation results can be compared with the current and past behavior of the real system. The model is run with an actual set of past observations and the output is compared directly with the behavior of the actual system.
- The model is reviewed by experts evaluating the reasonableness of the simulation model and the simulation results.
- The assumptions made during model construction need to be revisited, clarified, expanded, and adjusted as needed.
- The model is peer reviewed or desk-checked by programming staff to detect errors. *Improper programming of the model can lead to inaccurate results.*
- The simulated distributions for the probabilistic components can be compared with the corresponding probability distributions in the real system.
- It is good to collect the data on the system after it has reached a stable, or steady-state condition. Management is interested in what happens during "normal" business hours of operation. The steady-state condition of the model is synonymous with the "normal" hours of operation.

(iv) **Simulation model implementation.** Model implementation includes steps such as searching for errors, searching for exceptions, searching for gaps between actual and expected, searching for overlaps or duplications between procedures, and searching for root causes of poor implementation.

1.4 Project Management Techniques

In order for projects to be successfully implemented, they must be well managed. Many organizations apply a variety of project management techniques to optimize project success and enhance the likelihood of meeting project-specific as well as organization-wide goals. These techniques include monitoring project performance, establishing incentives to meet project goals, and developing a project management team with the right people and the right skills. This can help avert cost overruns, schedule delays, and performance problems common to many organizations.

It is important to develop **performance measures** and link project outcomes to business unit and strategic goals and objectives. The key is monitoring project performance and establishing incentives for accountability, and using cross-functional teams to involve those with the technical and operational expertise necessary to plan and manage the project.

Typically, a **project plan** is used to manage and control project implementation and includes performance measurement baselines for schedule and cost, major milestones, and target dates and risks associated with the project. By tracking cost, schedule, and technical performance, a project team is aware of potential problem areas and is able to determine any impact of the deviation and decide if corrective action is needed. Regular review of the status of cost, schedule, and technical performance goals by individuals outside the project team allows for an independent assessment of the project and verification that the project is meeting stated goals.

Major projects should include **multidisciplinary teams,** consisting of individuals from different functional areas and led by a project manager, to plan and manage projects. Typically, a core project team is established early in the life cycle of a project and additional individuals with particular technical or operational expertise are added during appropriate phases of the project. The team must not only possess technical and operational expertise, but it must also be composed of the "right" people. The selection of the team members is critical—they must be knowledgeable, willing to trade off leadership roles, and able to plan work and set goals in a team setting. The successful team will have a high spirit, trust, and enthusiasm. A sense of ownership and the drive of the team committed to a project are key factors in the successful completion of a project. This integrated and comprehensive approach improves communication between upper management and project managers and among the various stakeholders in the project. It also increases the likelihood that potential problems will be identified and resolved quickly, thus increasing the chances that the project will remain on schedule and within budget.

(a) **Why Project Management?** Management needs to know what parts of the project or program are most likely to cause serious delays. This knowledge will lead to management actions that will achieve the project or program objectives and deadlines.

When is project management preferred? The project management approach is the preferred method for dealing with projects defined onetime. The task is very complex and involves interdependence between a number of departments. The task has great significance to the organization. Onetime tasks can be accomplished with a minimum interruption of routine business. Exhibit 1.13 shows factors responsible for a successful performance of a project as well as symptoms of project management failures.

Managers need to coordinate diverse activities toward a common goal. Management must devise plans, which will tell with reasonable accuracy how the efforts of the people representing these functions should be directed toward the project's completion. In order to devise such plans and implement them, management must be able to collect pertinent information to accomplish the following tasks:

- To form a basis for prediction and planning
- To evaluate alternative plans for accomplishing the objective
- To check progress against current plans and objectives
- To form a basis for obtaining the facts so that decisions can be made and the job can be done

A single master plan for a project should include planning, scheduling, and controlling functions. The plan should point directly to the difficult and significant activities—the problem of achieving the objective. For example, the plan should form the basis of a system for management by exception. It should indicate the exceptions (red flags). Under such a system, management need act only when deviations from the plan occur.

A reporting system should be designed for middle to senior management to use. The monthly progress report calls for specific reestimate only for those events on critical paths and subcritical events. It should accomplish the following tasks:

- Preparing a master schedule for a project
- Revising schedules to meet changing conditions in the most economical way
- Keeping senior management and the operating department management advised of project progress and changes

Plans should be separated from scheduling. Planning is the act of stating what activities must occur in a project and in what order these activities must take place. Scheduling follows planning and is defined as the act of producing project timetables in consideration of the plan and costs. Controlling is ensuring that plans are accomplished. The correct sequence is

Planning → Scheduling → Controlling

Project structure is a characteristic of all projects that provides for all work being performed in some well-defined order. For example: In research and development and product planning, specifications must be determined before drawings can be made. In advertising, artwork must be made before layouts can be done.

Factors responsible for successful performance of a project	Symptoms of project management failures
• The organization of the project	• High costs
• The authority of the project manager	• Schedule overruns
• Scheduling and planning techniques used	• Poor-quality product
• The project manager's good relationship with senior management	• Failure to meet project objectives
• The use of resources, including slack time	• Customer or user dissatisfaction with the end result

Exhibit 1.13: Successful factors and symptoms of project management

(b) **Project Management's Basic Guidelines.** The following list provides basic guidelines for project management:

1. **Define the objective(s) of the project.** This includes defining management's intent in undertaking the project, outlining the scope of the project, and describing the end results of the project including its effects on the organization.
2. **Establish a project organization.** This includes appointment of one experienced manager to run the project full-time, organization of the project management function in terms of responsibilities, assignment of manpower to the project team, and maintenance of a balance of power between the functional department managers and the project manager.
3. **Install project controls.** This includes controls over time, cost, and quality.

(c) **Project Controls.** In any project, there will be at least three types of controls applied: (1) time control, (2) cost control, and (3) quality control.

(i) **Time control.** Project network scheduling begins with the construction of a diagram that reflects the interdependencies and time requirements of the individual tasks that make up a project. It calls for work plans prepared in advance of the project. Once the overall schedule is established, weekly or biweekly review meetings should be held to check progress against schedule. Control must be rigorous, especially at the start, so that missed commitments call for immediate corrective action.

(ii) **Cost control.** Periodic reports showing the budget, the actual cost, and variances is a good start for cost controls. It is necessary to break the comprehensive cost summary reports into work packages or major tasks and focus on major problems and opportunities. The cost reports should be distributed to technical as well as functional managers alike.

(iii) **Quality control.** Quality control comprises three elements: defining performance criteria, expressing the project objective in terms of quality standards, and monitoring progress toward these standards. Examples of performance criteria include market penetration of a product line, processing time for customer inquiries, and the like. Both quantitative and qualitative measures need to be defined.

(d) **Project Organization.** Project organization is where the reporting relationships and the work location rest predominantly with the project manager. Three common types of project organization include traditional structure, matrix organization, and hybrid form (see Exhibit 1.14).

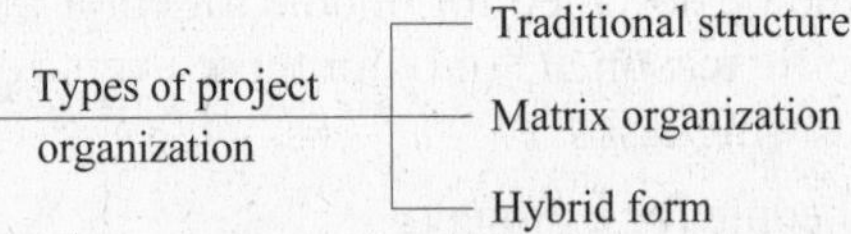

Exhibit 1.14: Types of project organization

In **traditional structure,** the basic interrelationship was with the functional manager. A hierarchy of reporting relationships is followed. In **matrix organization,** most of the personnel were directly responsible to the project manager for work assignments but remained physically located with their functional manager. Other forms include combining a large project team with several small functional teams or basic functional teams with a small project task force.

The matrix team members must learn new ways of relating and working together to solve cross-functional problems and to attain synergy. According to Dr. Jack Baugh[2] of Hughes Aircraft Company, the matrix management structure must be used when there is (1) a rapid technological advancement, a need for timely decisions, (2) a vast quantity of data to be analyzed, (3) an increased volume of new

[2] ***WINGS: Project Leaders Guide,*** *Volumes 1 and 2, AGS Management Systems, King of Prussia, PA, 1986. Original citation by Dr. Jack Baugh of Hughes Aircraft Company.*

products and services to be introduced, (4) a need for simultaneous dual decision making, and (5) a strong constraint on financial and/or human resources.

He also cited reasons for using a matrix management structure as (1) providing a flexible adaptive system, (2) providing timely, balanced decision making, (3) permitting rapid management response to a changing market and technology, (4) training managers for ambiguity, complexity, and executive positions, and (5) helping in synergizing and motivating human resources.

Hybrid form is the best possible option since it can achieve technical excellence, and, at the same time, meet cost and schedule deadlines.

Project authority is a measure of the degree of control the project manager has over all the activities necessary to complete the project successfully. Delays can be reduced if the project manager can make decisions without having to wait for the approval of someone "higher up." This type of delay is often the cause of schedule and cost overruns.

The authority of the project manager is seldom spelled out in formal directives or policies. The traditional forms of management—one man, one boss—is simply not adequate for completing projects.

The conflict is between the project manager and the functional manager. It is the influence rather than authority that matters. What counts is the priority assigned to the project, and the experience and personal characteristics of the project manager. *There may not be any relation between the formal authority of the project manager and the actual success of the project.*

KEY CONCEPTS TO REMEMBER: MOST COMMON REASONS FOR PROJECT MANAGEMENT FAILURES

- The basis for a project is not sound.
- The wrong person is appointed as the project manager.
- Company management fails to provide enough support.
- Task definitions are inadequate.
- Management monitoring techniques are not appropriate.
- Project termination is not planned properly (that is, to reduce adverse effect on the employee's progress in the company after the project is completed).
- Redefinitions of the project's scope are unclear.
- Large-scale design changes are occurring.
- The need for additional funding is not approved.

(e) **Problems in Project Management.** Project managers face unusual problems in trying to direct and harmonize the diverse forces at work in the project situation. Their main difficulties arise from three sources: (1) organizational uncertainties, (2) unusual decision pressure, and (3) inadequate senior management support (see Exhibit 1.15).

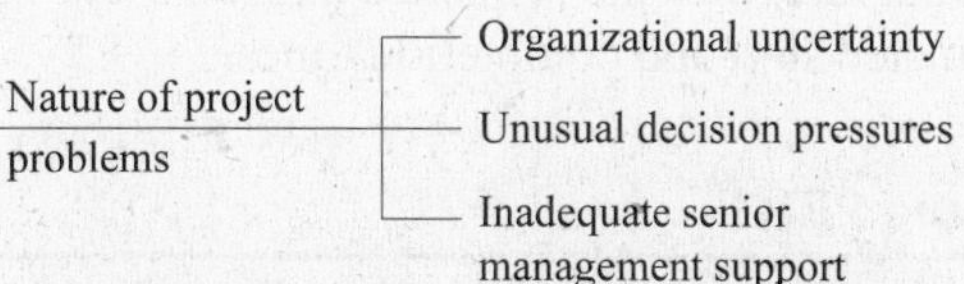

Exhibit 1.15: Nature of project problems

(i) **Organizational uncertainty.** The working relationships between the project manager and the functional department managers have not been clearly defined by senior management. Uncertainties arise with respect to handling delays, cost overruns, work assignments, and design changes. Unless the project manager is skillful in handling these situations, senior management may resolve them in the interest of functional departments, at the expense of the project as a whole.

(ii) **Unusual decision pressures.** When uncertainties are added to the situation, the project manager has to make his decisions based on limited data and with little or no analysis. He must move fast, even if it means an intuitive decision that might expose him to senior managements' criticism. *Decisions to sacrifice time for cost, cost for quality, or quality for time, are common in most projects.* There is a clear indication that the project manager needs support from senior management due to these tradeoffs.

(iii) **Inadequate senior management support.** Senior management can seldom give the project manager as much guidance and support as his line counterpart gets. Delays in initial approval of the project by senior management, inability to resolve conflicts between the project manager and the functional department managers, and delays in allocating resources are the most common issues on which the project manager needs more attention from senior management. Otherwise, project performance can be hampered.

(f) **Project Scheduling Techniques.** Six project scheduling techniques are discussed in this section, including program evaluation and review techniques, critical path methods, line-of-balance method, graphical evaluation and review techniques, work breakdown structure, and Gantt chart (see Exhibit 1.16).

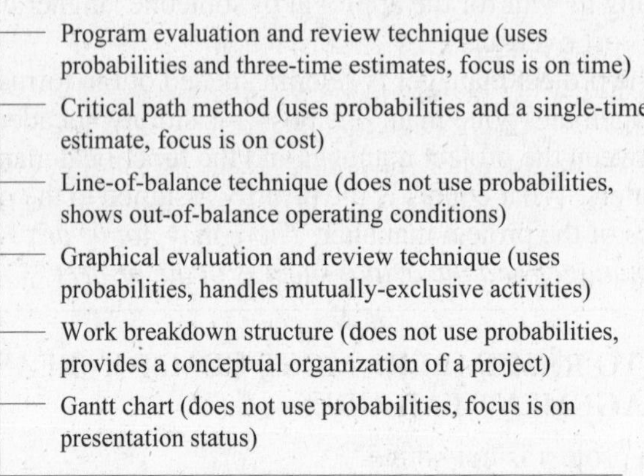

Program evaluation and review technique (uses probabilities and three-time estimates, focus is on time)
Critical path method (uses probabilities and a single-time estimate, focus is on cost)
Line-of-balance technique (does not use probabilities, shows out-of-balance operating conditions)
Graphical evaluation and review technique (uses probabilities, handles mutually-exclusive activities)
Work breakdown structure (does not use probabilities, provides a conceptual organization of a project)
Gantt chart (does not use probabilities, focus is on presentation status)

Exhibit 1.16: Project scheduling techniques

(i) **Program evaluation and review techniques.** Project management frequently uses network diagrams to plan the project, evaluate alternatives, and control large and complex projects toward completion. Program evaluation and review techniques (PERT) requires extremely careful plans from the very outset of the project. This allows management to allocate resources to critical areas before they become critical. This will alert a manager to trouble areas or bottlenecks before they become a major problem and the source of a project overrun. PERT also helps to allocate resources, but has no influence on the excellence of the end product.

PERT improves communication upward to the manager and the customer (client). PERT lets the supervisor believe that the project manager is doing a superior job, regardless of how well the project manager is actually performing.

(A) ***PERT features.*** The following list provides features of PERT:

- Manages "one-of-a-kind programs, as opposed to repetitive tasks. It develops a network diagram that identifies the sequence of events and their relationships to one another along with estimated start and completion times.

Sensitivity Analysis and PERT

Sensitivity analysis can be performed on the network. It provides the ability for checking the feasibility of current schedules and for permitting management to "experiment" with or evaluate the effects of proposed changes.

- Uncertainties involved in programs can be handled where no standard cost and time data are available.
- It includes a network comprised of events and activities. An event represents a specified program accomplishment at a particular instant in time. An activity represents the time and resources, which are necessary to progress from one event to the next.
- Events and activities must be sequenced on the network under a highly logical set of ground rules, which allow the determination of critical and subcritical paths. These ground rules include: the fact that no successor event can be considered completed until all of its

predecessor events have been completed, and no looping is allowed, that is, no successor event can have an activity dependency which leads back to a predecessor event.

- Time estimates are made for each activity of the network on a three-way basis: optimistic, most likely, and pessimistic. The three time estimates are required as a gauge of the "measure of uncertainty" of the activity, and represent the probabilistic nature of many tasks. The three estimates are reduced to a single expected time and a statistical variance.

(B) ***PERT assumptions.*** Interrelationships of activities are depicted in a network of directed arcs (arcs with arrows, which denote the sequence of the activities they represent). The **nodes,** called events, represent instants in time when certain activities have been completed and others can then be started. All inwardly-directed activities at a node must be completed before any outwardly-directed activity of that node can be started. A **path** is defined as an unbroken chain of activities from the origin node to some other node. The origin node is the beginning of the project. An **event** is said to have occurred when all activities on all paths directed into the node representing that event have been completed.

Another assumption of PERT is that all activities are started as soon as possible. This assumption may not hold true when scarce resources must be allocated to individual activities.

(C) ***PERT applications.*** The development of a critical path network is accomplished by establishing the major milestones that must be reached. Construction of the network diagram requires identification and recording of the project's internal time dependencies—dependencies that might otherwise go unnoticed until a deadline slips by or impacts other activities. A new activity can be added by identifying its successor and predecessor.

An ordered sequence of events to be achieved would constitute a valid model of the program. The network provides a detailed, systematized plan and time schedule before the project begins. As the project progresses, the time estimates can be refined. A top-down approach is taken when developing the network. The total project is fully planned and all components of the plan are included.

Applications of PERT and CPM

- Construction and maintenance of chemical plant facilities, highways, dams, buildings, railroads, and irrigation systems
- Planning of retooling programs for high-volume products in plants such as automotive and appliance plants
- Introduction of a new product
- Installation of a computer system
- Acquisition of a company

Critical path scheduling helps coordinate the timing of activities on paper and helps avert costly emergencies. The network diagram must be developed in detail as much as possible so that discrepancies, omissions, and work coordination problems can be resolved inexpensively, at least to the extent that they can be foreseen.

Project diagrams of large projects can be constructed by sections. Within each section the task is accomplished one arrow at a time by asking and answering the following questions for each job:

- What immediately preceded this job?
- What immediately succeeds (follows) this job?
- What can be concurrent with this job?

If the maximum time available for a job equals its duration, the job is called critical. A delay in a critical job will cause a comparable delay in the project completion time. A project contains at least one contiguous path of critical jobs through the project diagram from beginning to end. Such a path is called a critical path.

Meaning of the Critical Path

Typically only about ten to fifteen percent of the jobs in a large project are critical. The primary purpose of determining the "critical path" is to identify those activities that must be finished as scheduled if the new program or project is to be completed on time. The "critical path" of those activities cannot be delayed without jeopardizing the entire program or project.

If the maximum time available for a job exceeds its duration, the job is called a **floater**. Some floaters can be displaced in time or delayed to a certain extent without interfering with other jobs or the completion of the project. Others, if displaced, will start a chain reaction of displacements downstream in the project.

The technological ordering is impossible if a cycle error exists in the job data (i.e., job "a" preceded "b," "b" precedes "c," and "c" precedes "a"). The time required to traverse each arrow path is the sum of the times associated with all jobs on the path. The critical path (or paths) is the longest path in time from start to finish; it indicates the minimum time necessary to complete the entire project.

In order to accurately portray all predecessor relationships, "dummy jobs" must often be added to the project graph. The critical path is the bottleneck route; only by finding ways to shorten jobs along the critical path can the overall project time be reduced; the time required to perform noncritical jobs is irrelevant from the viewpoint of total project time.

(D) ***PERT approach.*** The status of a project at any time is a function of several variables such as resources, performance, and time. Resources are in the form of dollars, or what "dollars" represent—manpower, materials, energy, and methods of production; and technical performance of systems, subsystems, and components. An optimum schedule is the one that would properly balance resources, performance, and time.

Information concerning the inherent difficulties and variability in the activity being estimated are reflected in the three numbers: the optimistic, pessimistic, and most likely elapsed time estimates should be obtained for each activity. The purpose of the analysis is to estimate, for each network event, the expected times (mean or average) and calendar time of occurrence (TE).

When PERT is used on a project, the three time estimates (optimistic, most likely, and pessimistic) are combined to determine the expected duration and the variance for each activity.

- **Optimistic.** An estimate of the minimum time an activity will take. This is based on everything "going right the first time." It can be obtained under unusual, good luck situations.
- **Most likely.** An estimate of the normal time an activity will take, a result which would occur most often if the activity could be repeated a number of times under similar circumstances.
- **Pessimistic.** An estimate of the maximum time an activity will take, a result that can occur only if unusually bad luck is experienced.

The expected times determine the critical path, and the variances for the activities on this path are summed to obtain the duration variance for the project. A probability distribution for the project completion time can be constructed from this information. However, the variances of activities, which do not lie on the critical path are not considered when developing the project variance, and this fact can lead to serious errors in the estimate of project duration.

An estimate of the length of an activity is an uncertain one. A stochastic model can be used to reflect this uncertainty. This model measures the possible variation in activity duration. This may take the form of a distribution showing the various probabilities that an activity will be completed in its various possible completion times. Alternatively, this may be nondistribution such as range or standard deviation.

$$\text{The expected time} = 1/6\,(a + 4m + b)$$

Where a is optimistic time, m is most likely time, and b is pessimistic time. The expected activity times derived from a three-estimate, PERT-type calculation provides a more accurate estimate and allows the activity time variance to be calculated and included in the estimates of project duration.

APPLICATION OF PERT

Example

A company is planning a multiphase construction project. The time estimates for a particular phase of the project are

Optimistic	2 months
Most likely	4 months
Pessimistic	9 months

Question: Using PERT, what is the expected completion time for this particular phase?

Answer: The expected completion time would be 4.5 months, as shown below.

The expected time = $1/6\ (a + 4m + b) = 1/6\ (2 + 4x4 + 9) = 27/6 = 4.5$.

The latest calendar time at which an event must be accomplished so as not to cause a slippage in meeting a calendar time for accomplishing the objective event is referred to as the "latest time," and denoted as *TL*. The difference between the latest and expected times, *TL–TE*, is defined as **slack**. Slack can be taken as a measure of scheduling flexibility that is present in a workflow plan, and the slack for an event also represents the time interval in which it might reasonably be scheduled. Slack exists in a system as a consequence of multiple path junctures that arise when two or more activities contribute to a third.

What is Slack Time?

Slack time is a free time associated with each activity as it represents unused resources that can be diverted to the critical path. Noncritical paths have slack time while critical paths have no slack time.

A slack is extra time available for all events and activities not on the critical path. A negative slack condition can prevail when a calculated end date does not achieve a program date objective established earlier.

The manager must determine valid means of shortening lead times along the critical path by applying new resources or additional funds, which are obtained from those activities that can "afford" it because of their slack condition. "Safety factor" is another name for "slack." Alternatively, the manager can reevaluate the sequencing of activities along the critical path. If necessary, those activities, which were formerly connected in a series can be organized on a parallel or concurrent basis, with the associated trade-off risks involved. Alternatively, the manager may choose to change the scope of work of a critical path alternative in order to achieve a given schedule objective.

When some events have **zero slack,** it is an indication that the expected and latest times for these events are identical. If the zero-slack events are joined together, they will form a path that will extend from the present to the final event. This path can be looked upon as "the critical path." Should any event on the critical path slip beyond its expected date of accomplishment, then the final event can be expected to slip a similar amount. The paths having the greatest slack can be examined for possible performance or resource trade-offs.

When jobs or operations follow one after another, there is no slack. The criteria for defining a subcritical event is related to the amount of slack involved in the event. Those events having as much as five weeks slack have been deemed subcritical.

The PERT analysis permits a quantitative evaluation of conceivable alternatives. Each job in the project is represented by an arrow, which depicts the existence of the job and the direction of time-flows from the tail to the head of the arrow. The arrows are then connected to show graphically the sequence in which the jobs in the project must be performed. The junctions where arrows meet are called events. These are points in time when certain jobs are completed and others must begin.

The difference between a job's early start and its late start (or between early finish and late finish) is called total slack (TS). Total slack represents the maximum amount of time a job may be delayed beyond its early start without necessarily delaying the project's completion time.

KEY CONCEPTS TO REMEMBER: PERT TIME DIMENSIONS

ES = Earliest start time for a particular activity
EF = Earliest finish time for a particular activity
EF = ES + t, where t is expected activity time for the activity
LS = Latest start time for a particular activity
LF = Latest finish time for a particular activity
LS = LF – t, where t is expected activity time for the activity
Slack = LS – ES = LF –EF

The manager examines the work demand and indicates if sufficient resources are available to accomplish all jobs by their early finish. If resources are insufficient, activities are rescheduled within their late finish, using project priority, and available slack. Later, the manager is asked for additional resources or for a decision to delay an activity beyond its late finish.

Critical jobs are those on the longest path throughout the project. That is, critical jobs directly affect the total project time.

If the target date (T) equals the early finish date for the whole project (F), then all critical jobs will have zero total slack. There will be at least one path going from start to finish that includes critical jobs only, that is, the critical path. There could be two or more critical paths in the network, but only one at a time.

If T is greater (later) than F, then the critical jobs will have total slack equal to T minus F. This is a minimum value; since the critical path includes only critical jobs, it included those with the smallest TS. All noncritical jobs will have greater total slack.

Another kind of slack is **free slack** (FS). It is the amount a job can be delayed without delaying the early start of any other job. A job with positive total slack may or may not also have free slack, but the latter never exceeds the former. For purposes of computation, the free slack of a job is defined as the difference between the job's EF time and the earliest of the ES times of all its immediate successors.

When a job has zero total slack, its scheduled start time is automatically fixed (i.e., ES + LS); and to delay the calculated start time is to delay the whole project. Jobs with positive total slack, however, allow the scheduler some discretion in establishing their start times. This flexibility can usefully be applied to smoothing work schedules.

Peak load may be relieved by shifting jobs on the peak days to their late starts. Slack allows this kind of juggling without affecting project time.

Possible data errors in PERT

- The estimated job time may be in error.
- The predecessor relationship may contain cycle errors (job *a* is a predecessor for *b*, *b* is a predecessor for *c*, and *c* is a predecessor for *a*).
- The list of prerequisites for a job may include more than the immediate prerequisites; (e.g., job *a* is a predecessor of *b*, *b* is a predecessor of *c*, and *a* and *b* both are predecessor of *c*).
- Some predecessor relationships may be overlooked.
- Some predecessor relationships may be listed that are spurious.
- The errors in the PERT calculated project's mean and standard deviation will tend to be large if many noncritical paths each have a duration approximately equal to the duration of the critical path. However, the more slack time there is in each of the noncritical paths, the smaller will be the error.

One way to minimize errors and omissions is to continually back-check the data and challenge the assumptions. Exhibit 1.17 presents advantages and limitations of PERT.

Advantages of PERT	*Limitations of PERT*
• Greatly improved control over complex development work and production programs. • Capacity to distill large amounts of data in brief, orderly fashion. • Requires a great deal of planning to create a valid network. • Represents the advent of the management-by-exception principle. • People in different locations can relate their efforts to the total task requirements of a large program. • "Downstream" savings are achieved by earlier and more positive action on the part of management in the early stages of the project.	• There is little interconnection between the different activities pursued. • Requires constant updating and reanalysis of schedules and activities. • Requires greater amount of detail work. • Does not contain the quantity information; only time information is available.

Exhibit 1.17: Advantages and limitations of PERT

(E) ***PERT implementation issues.*** The following list provides issues that should be considered during PERT implementation:

- The people and organization of a project are more important considerations than the use of a particular planning and control technique.
- Consideration should be given to managerial issues such as project organization, personalities of project members, and operating schemes.
- There is a big difference between the criteria of success for the task to be accomplished and the criteria of success for the management system.
- The project manager is a miniature general manager. He usually lacks the commensurate authority and depends on various management techniques to carry out his job.
- The project management approach is the preferred method to deal with onetime defined projects.
- The qualifications of a person making time estimates must include a thorough understanding of the work to be done.
- Precise knowledge of the task sequencing is required or planned in the performance of activities.

APPLICATIONS OF PERT

Example

The network in Exhibit A describes the interrelationships of several activities necessary to complete a project. The arrows represent the activities. The numbers above the arrows indicate the number of weeks required to complete each activity.

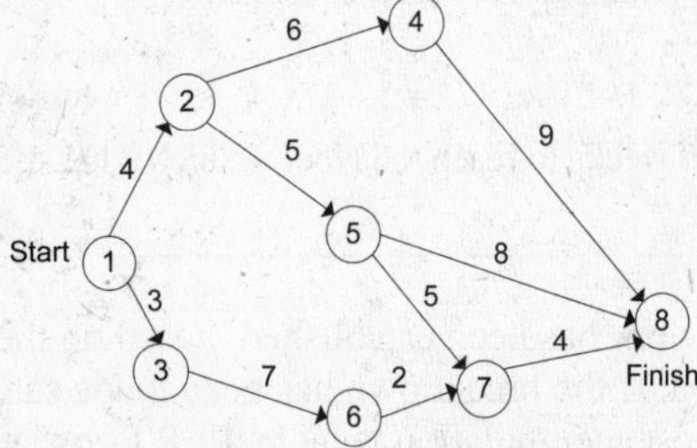

Exhibit A: PERT network

Question: What is the shortest time to complete the project?

Answer: The longest path from node (1) to node (8) is path 1-2-4-8. Since all other paths are shorter in duration than path 1-2-4-8, the activities along those paths can be completed before the activities along path 1-2-4-8. Therefore, the amount of time to complete the activities along path 1-2-4-8, which is 19 weeks (4+6+9), is the shortest time to complete the project.

Question: What is the critical path for the project?

Answer: The critical path is the sequence of activities that constrains the total completion time of the project. The entire project cannot be completed until all the activities on the critical path (the longest path) are completed.

Path 1-2-4-8 which takes 19 weeks is the critical path. Activities along each of the other three paths can be completed (each requires less than 19 weeks) before the activities along 1-2-4-8 can. The other three paths are: 1-2-5-8 (requires 4 + 5 + 8 = 17 weeks), 1-2-5-7-8 (requires 4 + 5 + 5 + 4 = 18 weeks), and 1-3-6-7-8 (requires 3 + 7 + 2 + 4 = 16 weeks).

Example

During an operational audit, an internal auditing team discovers the following document, entitled Project Analysis.

Project Analysis

Activity	*Time in weeks*	*Preceding activity*
A	3	--
B	3	A
C	7	A
D	4	A
E	2	B
F	4	B
G	1	C, E
H	5	D

Using the Project Analysis document, the audit supervisor prepares the PERT diagram shown in Exhibit B.

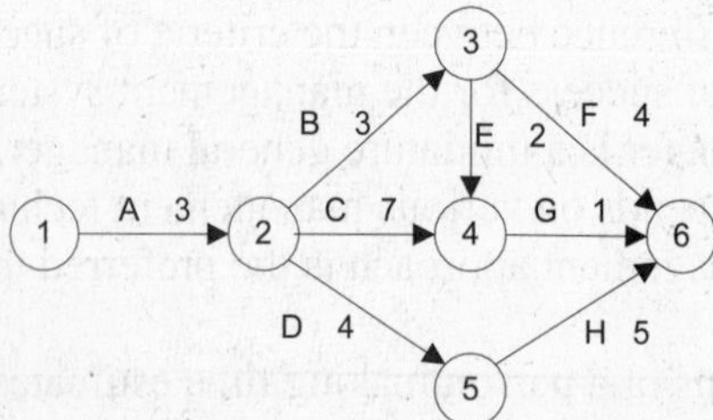

Exhibit B: PERT project analysis

Question: What is the earliest completion time that is indicated by the project analysis?

Answer: There are three paths.

Path 1	A–B–F	=	3 + 3 + 4	=	10 weeks
Path 2	A–C–G	=	3 + 7 + 1	=	11 weeks
Path 3	A–D–H	=	3 + 4 + 5	=	12 weeks

Path 3 has the earliest completion time of 12 weeks since it has the longest time to complete.

Question: What is the earliest time by which Node 4 would be reached?

Answer: There are two paths by which Node 4 can be reached.

Path A	A–C	=	3 + 7	=	10 weeks
Path B	A–B–E	=	3 + 3 + 2	=	8 weeks

Path A has the earliest time of 10 weeks to reach the Node 4 since it has the longest time.

(F) ***PERT cost.*** Once the network has been established, based on the project work breakdown structure, costs can be estimated. If the breakdown has been made satisfactorily, it will serve as both an estimating and actual cost accumulation vehicle. PERT cost adds the consideration of resource costs to the schedule produced by the PERT procedure. *The basic PERT handles the problem of time uncertainty while PERT cost addresses cost uncertainty.* Cost uncertainty as it relates to time can be handled by different cost estimates for three-time differences. The ultimate objective is not only to improve planning and control, but also to assess possibilities for "trading off" time and cost, that is, adding or subtracting from one at the expense of the other.

There is an "optimum" time-cost point for any activity or job as indicated by the "U" shape of the curve drawn between total direct cost (on y-axis) versus time (on x-axis). It is assumed that total costs will increase with any effort to accelerate or delay the job away from this point in the case where resource application varies. *Crashing the project involves shortening the critical path or paths by operating on those activities that have the lowest time-cost slopes.*

At least three approaches are available to develop the cost estimates.

- A singe cost estimate of expected cost
- Three cost estimates
- Optimum time-cost curves

A **single cost estimate** of expected cost is based upon the summation of the individual cost elements. The three-cost estimate approach determines the "expected cost." The advantage of the **three-cost estimate** over the single-cost estimate is that the result is subject to probability analysis. With this expected cost, the manager cannot assume that he has the optimum time-cost mix.

The third approach to estimate is the **optimum time-cost curve concept**. This is differential costing with time as the variability factor. The intention of this approach is to optimize time and costs by using optimum estimated costs. It assumes there is a direct relationship between time and costs on any activity. This relationship can be expressed by a continuous curve. This method is also based upon the concept that activities are subject to time-cost tradeoffs. The optimum time-cost curve method is difficult to put into practice due to the need to develop continuous time-cost curves.

(ii) **Critical path method.** The critical path method (CPM) is a powerful but basically simple technique for analyzing, planning, and scheduling large, complex projects. In essence, the tool provides a means of determining which jobs or activities, of the many that comprise a project, are "critical" in their effect on total project time, and how best to schedule all jobs in the project in order to meet a target date at minimum cost. CPM is an extension of PERT.

Characteristics of project for analysis by CPM are

- The project consists of a well-defined collection of jobs or activities which, when completed, mark the end of the project.
- The jobs may be started and stopped independently of each other, within a given sequence.
- The jobs are ordered in a technological sequence (for example, the foundation of a house must be constructed before the walls are erected).

CPM focuses attention on those jobs that are critical to the project time, it provides an easy way to determine the effects of shortening various jobs in the project, and it enables the project manager to evaluate the costs of a "crash" program.

Normal Time and Crash Time

Time estimates for both normal and crash options are used in the CPM method. Crash time is the time required by the path if maximum effort and resources are diverted to the task along this path. A balance can be obtained when a project manager knows what the normal time and the crash time would be.

As needed, it is a costly practice to "crash" all jobs in a project in order to reduce total project time. If some way is found to shorten one or more of the critical jobs, then not only will the whole project time be shortened but the critical path itself may shift and some previously noncritical jobs may become critical. It is physically possible to shorten the time required by critical jobs by assigning more people to the jobs; working overtime; and using different equipment, materials, and technology.

When CPM is used in a project to develop a crashing strategy, two or more paths through the network may have nearly the same length. If the activity duration is allowed to vary, a decrease in the length of the critical path may not result in an equivalent decrease in the project duration because of the variance inherent in the parallel or alternate paths. These variations of activity times can even allow the alternate path to become a critical path. Thus, simply allowing the activity times to vary slightly from their estimates in order to make the length of the paths different can cause serious errors in a CPM crashing strategy and lead to wasted resources and cost overruns.

(A) ***Characteristics of CPM networks.*** The following list defines characteristics of CPM networks:

- CPM networks attempt to build the entire project "on paper" at a very early stage of the project—even when the scope is not defined, vaguely defined, or incorrectly defined. In a way, CPM is to project management what modeling or simulation is to economic studies, production problems, plant design, and transportation problems.
- CPM provides a graphic view of the entire project with completion dates, support activities, and costs affixed to every stage of the project.

Value of the Critical Path Techniques

The critical path techniques are as valuable on short- and middle-range planning jobs as they are on major and extremely complex projects.

- CPM's single time estimate fails to consider the effects of variability in path completion times on the crashing strategy.
- The CPM chart is an excellent tool for communicating scope as well as details of the job to other persons directly and indirectly concerned with the development and completion of its various phases.
- The CPM chart serves as a permanent record and reminder of the substance of this communication to all management levels.
- The CPM chart shows the timing of management decisions.
- CPM enables the manager to measure progress (or lack of it) against plans and to take appropriate action quickly when needed. And the underlying simplicity of CPM and its ability to focus attention on crucial problem areas of large projects makes it an ideal tool for the senior manager.

(B) ***CPM vs. PERT.*** CPM and PERT methods are essentially similar in general approach and have much in common. However, important differences in implementation details exist. They were independently derived and based on different concepts. Both techniques define the duration of a project and the relationships among the project's component activities. An important feature of the PERT approach was its statistical treatment of the uncertainty in activity time estimates, which involves the collection of three separate time estimates and the calculation of probability estimates of meeting specified schedule dates.

CPM differs from PERT in two areas.

1. The use of only one time estimate for each activity (and thus no statistical treatment of uncertainty)
2. The inclusion, as an integral part of the overall scheme, of a procedure for time/cost trade-off to minimize the sum of direct and indirect project costs

Common features of PERT and CPM.

- They both use a network diagram for project representation, in which diagram circles represent activities with arrows indicating precedence.
- They both calculate early and late start and finish times and slack time.

Exhibit 1.18 provides a comparison between CPM and PERT.

CPM	*PERT*
• CPM uses a single deterministic time estimate to emphasize minimum project costs while downgrading consideration of time restraints. • It is the choice of cost-conscious managers.	• PERT uses three time estimates to define a probabilistic distribution of activity times which emphasizes minimum project duration while downgrading consideration of cost restraints. • It tends to be used by time-conscious managers.

Exhibit 1.18: A comparison between CPM and PERT

While these two techniques are based on different assumptions, they are related to each other because of the obvious relationship between time and cost. *The "ideal" network technique would combine the concepts of CPM's crashing strategy with PERT's probability distribution of activity times to derive the optimum project duration and cost.*

(iii) **Line-of-balance technique.** Line-of-balance (LOB) is a basic tool of project management and was an early forerunner of PERT and CPM. LOB was not as popular as was PERT and CPM. The most successful applications involve methods such as CPM and PERT, which combine simplicity and clarity. These are managerial tools involving planning, scheduling, and control. *CPM and PERT require complicated mathematical models while LOB does not.*

Scope of LOB Technique

- LOB can be performed manually and can be used on large production jobs, maintenance jobs, research and development jobs, and construction jobs.
- LOB requires little training.
- Complex, large-scale LOB problems may require a computer to solve.

LOB is a managerial tool that can show, at a glance, what is wrong with the progress of a project. It can also point to future bottlenecks. The tool is easy to develop and maintain, manually or by computer. It forces the manager to make a plan for the program's completion, and it presents graphical information, which is sometimes unnoticeable in a large volume of data.

LOB is a dynamic tool that tells the manager what is wrong while the project is still going on. It is a simple technique, requiring no equations or models. It does not attempt to optimize operations, but it is a sound basic tool.

The main purpose of the LOB method is to prepare a progress study on critical operations at given times during the actual progress of the job. Each operation is checked against some target; that is, we find where each operation is with respect to where it ought to be. Operations that fall short of target are pointed out for further analysis. LOB uses the principles of "management by exception." *LOB allows the manager to pay special attention only to those activities which are both critical and do not conform to the schedule.*

The LOB technique involves four steps.

1. Developing an objective chart or delivery schedule
2. Preparing a program chart or plan of operation
3. Developing a progress chart including the line of balance
4. Performing analysis

The **objective chart** presents the cumulative delivery schedule of finished goods or services for the entire project in a graphical form. The LOB is graphically derived from the objective chart. It can also be calculated analytically, manually, or by computer.

The **program chart** is best constructed by working backwards, starting with the delivery of the finished product as lead time zero. It will show the schedule of each of the critical operations with completion dates and the source and/or responsibility for each operation.

The **progress chart** is a flow process with all critical operations performed from receipt of raw materials to completion.

The objective chart and the program chart are constructed only once whereas the progress charts must be developed from scratch each time the project is analyzed. The progress chart is therefore good only for a specified date. **Performing analysis** of the progress chart is the core of LOB. The analysis pinpoints "out-of-balance" operations. *It is customary to draw the objective chart, the program chart, and the progress chart on one sheet to get a big, quick picture of the entire project.*

LOB and PERT/CPM are complementary, although each can be used effectively by itself. The distinction between them is that PERT is primarily a planning and evaluation tool for "one-unit type" projects such as research and development with one completion date. PERT's major objective is to identify critical operations, but it can also be used as a control tool by pinpointing deviations from actual performance and rescheduling accordingly.

The line-of-balance monitors a project involving many units to be shipped at certain intervals. LOB can also be used in large projects with one completion date. LOB deals both with operations and components and inventories. PERT deals with only one unit and its critical operations. PERT in general requires a computer while LOB is essentially a graphic, manual tool.

LOB and PERT are related to each other. LOB can complement PERT in the following way: Once the critical path has been identified, it can be used as part of the "program" or the "production plan" of LOB. Other thinking is that these two techniques can be integrated into a single management planning and control system that can be employed from planning stages through production and delivery for a given quantity of items.

Major assumptions of LOB include: that the production method is independent of quantities, that critical operations do not change with time, and that lead time is constant or known with certainty. These assumptions can be related, making the LOB method more complex.

Reasons for low popularity of LOB:

- Lack of awareness of the technique and its potential applicability and advantages
- Management skepticism, which is common to all new managerial techniques
- The lack of a "canned" computer program for LOB
- Lack of a sound delivery forecast which is necessary and which is difficult to obtain considering the difficulty of obtaining market demand and supply forecast
- Requires deterministic lead times (i.e., a single estimate) when in fact, a range is better

PERT VS. CPM VS. LOB

- PERT considers time domain only.
- CPM considers cost information only.
- LOB considers quantity information only.
- PERT is good for production prototype construction, assembly, and test of final production equipment that are still "high on the learning curve."
- PERT can be applied to smaller projects, single projects, large projects, and multi-projects.
- PERT, CPM, and LOB can be integrated to get maximum benefits.

(iv) **Graphical evaluation and review technique.** The Graphical Evaluation and Review Technique (GERT) system permits the modeling of a wide variety of situations not possible with traditional PERT\CPM models. Simulation programs can be used to implement GERT, since it uses "stochastic" networks, that is, networks in which certain arcs (representing activities) have designated probabilities of occurrence. GERT allows the performance of alternative, mutually-exclusive activities, which are not allowed in the PERT/CPM method. In GERT, activity performance times can be expressed as probability distributions. Heuristic sequencing rules are used to give good resource-feasible schedules.

(v) **Work breakdown structure.** The work breakdown structure (WBS) was first intended as the common link between schedules and costs in PERT cost application. Later, it became an important tool for conceptual organization of any project. The WBS provides the necessary logic and formalization of task statements. The WBS prepares the work packages, which usually represent the lowest division of the end items.

(vi) **Gantt chart.** The Gantt chart is a bar chart and is essentially a column chart on its side, and is used for the same purpose. The bar chart is horizontal. The bar chart is a tool that allows a manager to evaluate whether existing resources can handle work demand or whether activities should be postponed. The Gantt chart is used for milestone scheduling where each milestone has a start and completion date. A milestone represents a major activity or task to be accomplished (e.g., a design phase in a computer system development project).

The Gantt chart is a graphical illustration of a scheduling technique. The structure of the chart shows output plotted against units of time. It does not include cost information. It highlights activities over the life of a project and contrasts actual times with projected times using a horizontal (bar) chart. It gives a quick picture of a project's progress in knowing the status of actual time lines and projected time lines. Exhibit 1.19 presents advantages and disadvantages of PERT and Gantt charts.

Advantages

PERT

- A good planning aid.
- Interdependencies between activities can be shown.
- Network diagram is flexible to change.
- Activity times are probabilistic.
- A good scheduling tool for large, nonroutine projects.
- A good tool in predicting resource needs, problem areas, and the impact of delays on project completion.

Gantt chart

- A good planning tool.
- A graphical scheduling technique, simple to develop, use and understand.
- Useful for large projects.
- Shows a sequencing of steps or tasks.
- Actual completion times can be compared with planned times.

Disadvantages

PERT

- Difficult to apply to repetitive assembly-line operations where scheduling is dependent on the pace of machines.
- Large and complex projects are difficult to draw manually.
- Requires computer hardware and software to draw a complex network.
- Requires training to use the computer program.

Gantt chart

- Interrelationships among activities are not shown on the chart.
- Inflexible to change.
- Activity times are deterministic.
- Difficult to show very complex situations.
- Cannot be used as a procedure documenting tool.
- Does not show the critical path in a chain of activities.

Exhibit 1.19: Advantages and disadvantages of PERT and Gantt charts

WHAT ARE SOPHISTICATED TECHNIQUES FOR PROJECT MANAGEMENT?

- PERT, GERT, and CPM techniques are more sophisticated scheduling methods due, in part, to the consideration of probabilities.
- LOB, WBS, Gantt charts, bar charts, and milestones are less sophisticated scheduling methods due, in part, to not considering the probabilities.
- GERT handles alternate, mutually exclusive activities, while PERT/CPM cannot.

There may be a lower probability of a cost/schedule overrun if PERT is used because of its sophistication as a scheduling method compared to less sophisticated scheduling methods such as Gantt charts, milestone scheduling, line of balance, and bar charts. If there is a slack time, there is no need to use sophisticated and tight scheduling methods such as PERT.

1.5 Business Process Analysis

In a manufacturing company, the scope of process analysis starts from raw materials and ends up with finished goods shipping to customers. It includes all the transformation (processing) stages, inspection steps, and transportation stages. Similarly, in a service company the scope of process analysis starts, for example, with claims application and ends up with making payment to the claimant. The goal of process analysis is to facilitate change for improvement. This requires looking at not only the individual processes where problems exist but also the upstream and downstream processes that are related to the process in question. Process improvements can be made by rearranging equipment layout, plant layout, inspection points, and testing stages with the help of motion study, material study, time study, and material handling studies. In this effort, both product processes and service processes should be examined for waste, delays, and improvement.

(a) **Workflow Analysis.** Workflow analysis looks at the overall flow of work to find ways of improving this flow. It can reveal value-added and non-value-added activities (e.g., waste and delays) and identify interdependence among departments. The outcome would be eliminating the non-value-added activities and waste and improving efficiency and effectiveness. Assembling tasks, whether subassembly or final assembly, and process time are value-added activities of a manufactured product, while other activities are non-value-added activities. Examples of non-value-added activities from a customer's viewpoint include inspection time, move time, reporting time, governmental compliance time, storage time, wait time, and queue time.

Workflow systems would make organizations undergo huge managerial and cultural changes, help employees apply business rules, enable process reengineering, provide parallel processing of documents, eliminate information float or overload, and ensure that established policies and procedures are followed.

Workflow software allows business processes to be redesigned and streamlined and automatically routes work from employee to employee.

Interdependence means the extent to which departments depend on each other for resources or materials to accomplish their tasks. Low interdependence means that departments can do their work independent of each of other and have little need for interaction, consultation, or exchange of materials. High interdependence means departments must constantly exchange resources and materials.

There are three types of interdependence that influence organization structure: (1) pooled, (2) sequential, and (3) reciprocal. Pooled interdependence is the lowest form of interdependence among departments. Work does not flow between units. Each department is part of the organization and contributes to the common good of the organization, but works independently. When interdependence is of serial form, with parts or documents produced in one department becoming inputs to another department, then it is called sequential interdependence. Here departments exchange resources and depend upon others to perform well. The management requirements for sequential interdependence are more demanding than for pooled interdependence. These requirements include coordination, communication, integrators, and task forces. The highest level of interdependence is reciprocal interdependence. This exists when the output of operation A is the input to operation B, and the output of operation B is the input back again to operation A. The outputs of departments influence those departments in reciprocal fashion. Management requirements for the complex reciprocal interdependence include greater planning, coordination, communication, permanent teams, and frequent adjustments in the work and its associated plans.

(b) **Bottleneck Management.** Bottleneck is a constraint in a facility, function, department, or resource whose capacity is less than the demand placed upon it. For example, a bottleneck machine or work center exists where jobs are processed at a slower rate than they are demanded. Another example is where the demand for a company's product exceeds the ability to produce the product.

Bottleneck influences both product profitability and product price. The contribution margin per bottleneck hour or the value of each bottleneck hour should be analyzed. This measure is better than the normal contribution margin per unit. The contribution margin per hour of bottleneck can be used to adjust the product price to better reflect the value of the product's use of a bottleneck. Products that use a large number of bottleneck hour per unit require more contribution margin than products that use few bottleneck hours per unit.

(c) **Theory of Constraints.** Theory of constraints (TOC) is a manufacturing strategy that attempts to remove the influence of bottlenecks on a process. According to Dr. Eliyahu M. Goldratt, TOC consists of three separate but interrelated areas: (1) logistics, (2) performance measurement, and (3) logical thinking. Logistics include drum-buffer-rope scheduling, buffer management, and VAT analysis. Performance measurement includes throughput, inventory and operating expense, and the five focusing steps. Logical thinking process tools are important in identifying the root problems (current reality tree), identifying and expanding win-win solutions (evaporating cloud and future reality tree), and developing implementation plans (prerequisite tree and transition tree).

Drum-buffer-rope scheduling is the generalized process used to manage resources to maximize throughput. The drum is the rate or pace of production set by the system's constraint. The buffers establish the protection against uncertainty so that the system can maximize throughput. The rope is a communication process from the constraint to the gating operation that checks or limits material released into the system to support the constraint.

Buffer management is a process in which all expediting in a factory shop is driven by what is scheduled to be in the buffers (constraint, shipping, and assembly buffers). By expediting this material into the buffers, the system helps avoid idleness at the constraint and missed customer due dates. In addition, the causes of items missing from the buffer are identified, and the frequency of occurrence is used to prioritize improvement activities.

VAT analysis is a procedure for determining the general flow of parts and products from raw materials to finished products (the logical product structure). A "V" logical product structure starts with one or few raw materials, and the product expands into a number of different products as it flows through divergent points in its routings. The shape of an "A" logical product structure is dominated by converging points. Many raw materials are fabricated and assembled into a few finished products. A "T" logical product structure consists of numerous similar finished products assembled from common assemblies, subassemblies, and parts. Once the general parts flow is determined, the system control points (gating operations, convergent points, divergent points, constraints, and shipping points) can be identified and managed.

The five focusing steps is a process to continuously improve organizational profit by evaluating the production system and the marketing mix to determine how to make the most profit using the system constraint. The steps consist of (1) identifying the constraint to the system, (2) deciding how to exploit the constraint to the system, (3) subordinating all nonconstraints to the system, (4) elevating the constraint to the system, and (5) returning to step 1 if the constraint is broken in any previous step, while not allowing inertia to set in.

1.6 Inventory Management Techniques and Concepts

From inventory management viewpoint, demand is of two types: independent demand and dependent demand. Independent demand inventory systems are based on the premise that the demand or usage of a particular item is independent of the demand or usage of other items. Examples include finished goods; spare parts; material, repair, and operating (MRO) supplies; and resale inventories.

(a) **Independent Demand Inventory Systems.** Independent demand inventory systems are "pull" systems in that materials are pulled from the previous operation as they are needed to replace materials that have been used. An example: finished goods are replaced as they are sold. These types of inventory systems answer the question of when to place the replenishment order and how much to order at one time. Reorder point models and fixed/variable order quantity models (e.g., Economic order quantity, or EOQ) are examples of independent demand inventory systems as they do review inventory either continuously or periodically. Four possibilities exist, including

- Continuous review and fixed order quantity
- Periodic review and fixed order quantity
- Continuous review and variable order quantity
- Periodic review and variable order quantity

(b) **Dependent Demand Inventory Systems.** Dependent demand inventory systems are based on the premise that the demand or usage of a particular item is dependent on the demand or usage of other items. Examples include raw materials, work-in-process inventories, and component parts.

(c) **Inventory Levels and Investment Levels.** A company manages its inventory by using various methods and approaches (e.g., EOQ). Inventory consists of raw materials, work in process, and finished goods. Efficient inventory management is needed to support sales, which is necessary for profits. Benefits such as high turnover rate, low write-offs, and low lost sales can be attributed to efficient inventory management. These benefits, in turn, contribute to a high profit margin, a higher total asset turnover, a higher rate of return on investment, and a strong stock price. Inventory management is a major concern for product-based organizations (e.g., manufacturing, retail), since 20 to 40% of their total assets is inventory and as such, poor inventory control will hurt the profitability of the organization.

KEY CONCEPTS TO REMEMBER: INVENTORY MANAGEMENT

- The larger the amount of inventories held, the longer the inventory conversion period, hence the longer the cash conversion cycle.
- The smaller the amount of inventories held, the shorter the inventory conversion period, hence the shorter the cash conversion cycle.
- A shorter cash conversion cycle is preferred over a longer cash conversion cycle.
- Errors in establishing inventory levels can lead to lost sales, lost profits, or increased costs.
- A lower investment in inventories will increase the rate of return on investment, and the value of the firm's stock increases.
- Too much of reduced investment in inventories could lead to lost sales due to stockouts or to costly production slowdowns.

Inventory levels and account receivables levels directly depend upon sales levels. Receivables arise after sales have been made while inventory must be acquired or produced ahead of sales. Inventory managers have the responsibility to maintain inventories at levels which balance the benefits of reducing the level of investment against the costs associated with lowering inventories. A company's inventory is related to the amount of expected sales. The company's financial forecasting of inventory in the following year would be most accurate when applying simple linear regression method.

(d) **Efficient Inventory Management.** Efficient inventory management focuses on three areas: (1) investment in inventory, (2) optimal order quantity, and (3) reorder point (see Exhibit 1.20).

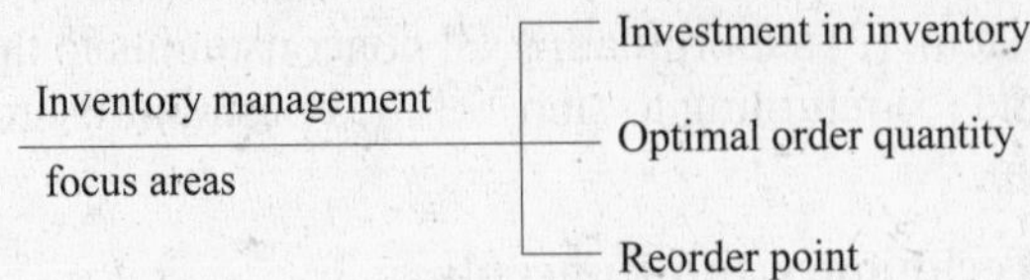

Exhibit 1.20: Inventory management focus areas

(e) **Investment in Inventory.** Investment in inventory depends on the actual level of inventory carried. The relevant question is how many units of each inventory item the firm should hold in its stock. Two types of stock concepts must be understood: (1) working stock and (2) safety stock. The actual level of inventories carried will equal the sum of the working stocks and safety stocks.

Working stock. A working stock is needed to meet normal, expected production and sales demand levels. Producing more goods than are currently needed increases the firm's carrying costs and exposes it to the risk of obsolescence if demand should fall. Remember that demand for sales is uncertain. Economic order quantity (EOQ) establishes the working stock amount. EOQ is discussed later in this section.

Safety stock. A safety stock is needed to guard against changes in sales rates or delays in production and shipping activities. Safety stock is additional stock beyond the working stock and satisfies when demand is greater than expected. The additional costs of holding the safety stock must be balanced against the costs of sales lost due to inventory shortages. Safety stock will not affect the reorder quantities.

KEY CONCEPTS TO REMEMBER: SAFETY STOCK

- The optimum safety stock increases with the uncertainty of sales forecasts, lost sales resulting from inventory shortages, and probability of delays in receiving shipment.
- The optimum safety stock decreases as the cost of carrying it increases.

Effective management requires close coordination and communication among the various functional departments of the organization such as the marketing, sales, production, purchasing, and finance departments. Sales plans need to be converted into purchasing and production plans producing finished goods and for acquiring raw materials; financing plans are needed to support the inventory build-up.

Since inventories need to be available prior to sales, an increase in production to meet increased sales requires an increase in notes payable (a liability account). Since assets (inventories) are increasing, liability (notes payable) must also increase.

Investment in inventory is not complete without discussing the various costs associated with inventories due to their direct relationships. The cost structure affects the amount and type of investment needed. Three types of inventory-related costs are: (1) carrying costs, (2) ordering costs, and (3) stock-out costs, as shown in Exhibit 1.21.

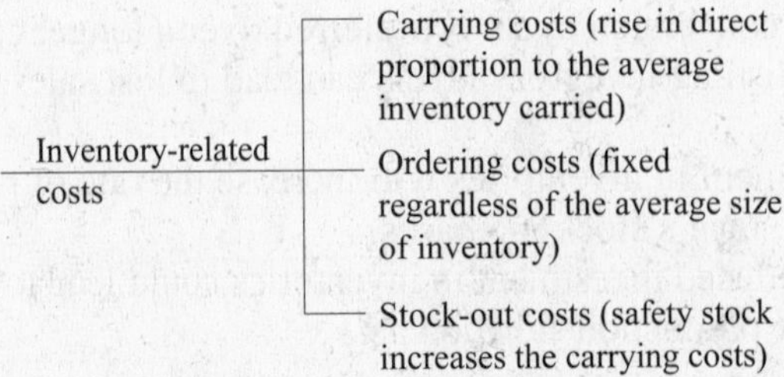

Exhibit 1.21: Inventory-related costs

(i) **Carrying costs.** The costs associated with carrying inventories, including storage, capital, and depreciation costs are known as carrying costs. Carrying costs rise in direct proportion to the average amount of inventory carried which, in turn, depends on the frequency with which orders are placed. That is, an increase in the frequency of inventory ordering will reduce total carrying costs.

$$\text{Annual total carrying costs} = (C)(P)(A)$$

Where C = Percentage cost of carrying inventory, that is, capital cost + storage cost + insurance + depreciation and obsolescence cost + property taxes divided by average inventory value. P = Percentage price per unit. A = Average number of units, i.e., (annual sales\number of orders) divided by 2. (P). (A) = Average inventory value.

(ii) **Ordering costs.** The cost of placing and receiving an order is known as the ordering costs, which is fixed regardless of the average size of inventories.

$$\text{Total ordering costs} = (F)(N) = (F)(S \backslash Q)$$

Where F = Fixed costs associated with ordering inventories, N = Number of orders per year, S = Sales in units, and Q = Quantity ordered in units.

$$\text{Total inventory cost} = \text{Total carrying cost} + \text{Total ordering cost}$$

(iii) **Stock-out costs.** Safety stock reduces stock-out costs. The safety stock is useful in protecting against delays in receiving orders. However, safety stock has a cost. The increase in average inventory resulting from the safety stock causes an increase in inventory carrying costs.

CARRYING COSTS VS. ORDERING COSTS VS. STOCK-OUT COSTS

- The components of **carrying costs,** which increase in proportion to the average amount of inventory held, include the costs of capital tied up in inventory, storage, and handling costs, insurance premiums, property taxes, depreciation, and obsolescence cost.
- The components of **ordering costs,** which are fixed regardless of the average size of inventories, include the cost of placing orders including production setup and shipping and handling costs.
- The components of **stock-out costs,** which are costs of running short, include the loss of sales, the loss of customer goodwill, and problems or delays in production schedules.

(f) **Optimal Order Quantity.** How many units should be ordered or produced at a given time is a major question faced by the inventory manager. Either too much or too little inventory is not good. An optimum inventory level is designed and is found through the use of the economic order quantity (EOQ) model. EOQ provides the optimal, or least-cost, quantity of inventory that should be ordered.

If a company's cost of ordering per order increases while carrying costs per order remain the same, the optimal order size as specified by the EOQ model would increase.

EOQ cost characteristics.

- The point at which the total cost curve is minimized represents the EOQ, and this, in turn, determines the optimal average inventory level. Here, total cost is the sum of ordering and carrying costs.
- Some costs rise with larger inventories whereas other costs decline.
- The average investment in inventories depends on how frequently orders are placed.
- Ordering costs decline with larger orders and inventories due to reduced order frequency.

If Q is the order quantity, then the how-much-to-order decision involves finding the value of Q that will minimize the sum of holding and ordering costs.

$$Q = EOQ = \sqrt{\frac{2D\,Co}{Ch}}$$

Where D is annual sales demand in units, Co is cost of placing one order, Ch is cost of holding (or carrying) one unit in inventory for the year.

Note that the data needed to calculate EOQ includes: the volume of product sales, the purchase price of the products, the fixed cost of ordering products, and carrying costs. It does not include: the volume of products in inventory, inventory delivery times, delays in transportation, or quality of materials.

Due to the square root sign, a given increase in sales will result in a less than proportionate increase in inventories, and the inventory turnover ratio will thus increase as sales grow.

(g) **Reorder Point.** Another major problem facing the inventory manager is at what point should inventory be ordered or produced. The point at which stock on hand must be replenished is called "reorder point." It is also the inventory level at which an order should be placed. The formula is

Reorder point = Lead time × Usage rate

Where lead time is the time lag required for production and shipping of inventory. Usage rate is the usage quantity per unit of time (note: the time period should be the same in both lead time and usage rate (i.e., days, weeks, or months).

A complication in the calculation of the reorder point arises when we introduce a concept of "goods-in-transit." This situation occurs when a new order must be placed before the previous order is received. The formula for a reorder point when goods-in-transit is considered is

Reorder point = (Lead time × Usage rate) – (Goods-in-transit)

KEY CONCEPTS TO REMEMBER: REORDER POINT

- Goods-in-transit are goods that have been ordered but have not been received.
- A goods-in-transit situation exists if the normal delivery lead time is longer than the time between orders.

(h) **Inventory Decisions.** Inventory managers face two decision rules in the management of inventories: "how-much-to-order" and "when-to-order" that will result in the lowest possible total inventory cost. The how-much-to-order decision rule can be satisfied with the use of an economic order quantity (EOQ). This decision rule involves selecting an order quantity that draws a compromise between (1) keeping smaller inventories and ordering frequently (results in high ordering costs), and (2) keeping large inventories and ordering infrequently (results in high holding costs). The when-to-order decision rule can be satisfied with the use of a reorder point.

ORDERING COST VS. HOLDING COST

- Ordering costs are the costs associated with placing an order and include salaries of the purchasers, paper, postage, telephone, transportation, and receiving costs.
- Holding costs are the costs associated with carrying a given level of inventory; these costs are dependent on the size of the inventory. They include interest cost for the capital tied up in inventory, opportunity cost associated with not being able to use the money for investment, insurance fees, taxes, pilferage, and damage, as well as other warehouse overhead costs.

(i) **Calculating How Much to Order.** The focus of EOQ method is on the quantity of goods to order that will minimize the total cost of ordering and holding (storing) goods. EOQ is a decision model that focuses on the trade-off between carrying costs and ordering costs. It calculates the order quantity that minimizes total inventory costs. Calculus is used in determining the EOQ.

EOQ is appropriate for managing the finished goods inventories, which have independent demands from customers or from forecasts. The holding cost, the ordering cost, and the demand information are the three data items that must be prepared prior to the use of the EOQ model. If Q is the order quantity, then the how-much-to-order decision involves finding the value of Q that will minimize the sum of holding and ordering costs.

$$Q = EOQ = \sqrt{\frac{2D\,Co}{Ch}}$$

Where *D* is annual demand, *Co* is cost of placing one order, *Ch* is cost of holding one unit in inventory for the year.

Annual inventory holding cost is directly related to the amount of inventory carried. The EOQ will rise following an increase in the fixed costs of placing and receiving an order.

Exhibit 1.22 describes costs for inventory. Line A represents annual total cost, Line B represents total annual inventory holding costs, Line C represents the minimum-total-cost order quantity, and Line D represents total annual ordering cost.

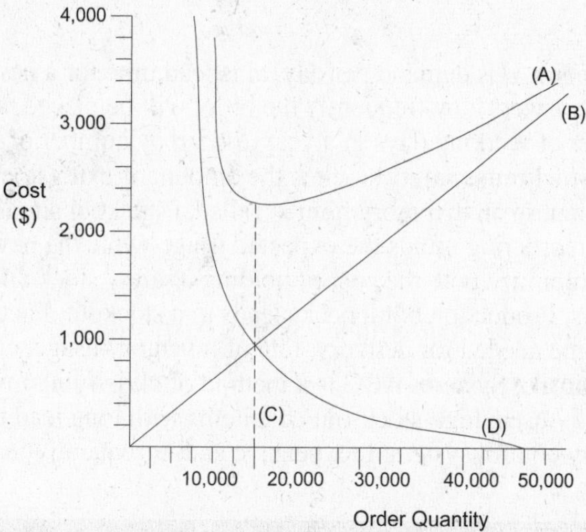

Exhibit 1.22: Cost for inventory

CALCULATION OF OPTIMUM ORDER SIZE

Example

A firm expects to sell 1,000 units of product X during the coming year. Ordering costs are $100 per order and carrying costs (holding costs) are $2 per unit per year.

Question: Using the EOQ model, what is the optimum order size?

Answer: The optimum order size is 217, as shown below.

The answer is to find the square root of (2 × $100 × 1,000)/$2. This is the square root of 100,000, or 317.

(j) **EOQ Assumptions.** Two major assumptions of EOQ include the following: (1) The demand for an item is constant. Since the constant demand assumption is not realistic, managers would have to be satisfied with the near-minimum-cost order quantity instead of a minimum-total-cost order quantity. (2) The entire quantity ordered arrives at one point in time. Again, this may not be realistic because some vendors will deliver partial shipments. Managers usually add a judgmental value-based order quantity to the EOQ suggested order quantity to accommodate unrealistic assumptions of constant demand rate by the EOQ model.

Specific assumptions of the EOQ model include

- Sales can be forecasted perfectly. This is unreal.
- Sales are evenly distributed throughout the year. This is not real. What about seasonal or cyclical demands?
- Orders are received without delay. This is also unreal.
- Fixed costs, carrying costs, and purchase prices are all fixed and independent of the ordering procedures. This is not possible either.

Controls in Material Requirement Cycle

EOQ models, ABC inventory analysis, JIT, and Kanban systems are commonly used controls in material requirements cycle.

(k) **Sensitivity Analysis and EOQ.** It is good to know how much the recommended order quantity would change if the estimated ordering and holding costs had been different. Depending on whether the total annual cost increased, decreased, or remains the same, we can tell whether the EOQ model is sensitive or insensitive to variations in the cost estimates.

(l) **Calculating When to Order.** The when-to-order decision rule is expressed in terms of a reorder point as follows:

$$r = d\,m,$$

Where r is reorder point, d is demand per day, m is lead time for a new order in days.

The cycle time answers how frequently the order will be placed, and it can be calculated as follows: cycle time is number of working days in a year *divided by* number of orders that will be placed in a year.

(m) **Safety Stock and Stockouts.** Safety stock is the amount of extra stock that is kept to protect against stockouts. Running out of an inventory item is called a stockout situation. Safety stock is the inventory level at the time of reordering minus the expected usage while the new goods are in transit.

The goal is to minimize both the cost of holding a safety stock and the cost of stockouts. EOQ is not relevant to stockouts. Production bottlenecks leads to a stockout. Factors to be considered in controlling stockouts include time needed for delivery, rate of inventory usage, and safety stock.

(n) **ABC Inventory Control System.** ABC is a method of classifying inventory based on usage and value. Expensive, frequently used, high stock-out cost items with long lead times are most frequently reviewed in an ABC inventory control system. Inexpensive and infrequently used items are reviewed less frequently.

APPLICATION OF ABC INVENTORY SYSTEM

Example

A firm uses an ABC inventory control system. About 10% of inventory items are classified into group A. Another 20% are in group B. The remainder are in group C. Which classification is most likely to hold the greatest number of days of supply?

a. Group C
b. Group B
c. Group A
d. All groups are likely to have an equal number of days of supply

Answer **(a)** is the correct answer. Group C items are low-dollar-value items and receive less management attention. Extensive use of models and records is not cost effective. It is cheaper to order large quantities infrequently. Group A items are high-dollar value and management would try to keep investment in such items low. Therefore, by definition, choices b, c, and d are incorrect.

(o) **Effects of Inflation on Inventory Management.** There is no evidence that inflation either raises or lowers the optimal level of inventory of firms in the aggregate level. It should be considered since it will raise the individual firm's optimal inventory holdings if the rate of inflation is above average, and vice versa.

Decision rules and consequences of inflation are

- For a moderate inflation, it is safe to ignore inflation and the benefit is not worth the effort.
- For a relatively constant inflation, subtract the expected annual rate of inflation from the carrying cost percentage (C) in the EOQ model and recalculate the EOQ. Since the carrying cost will be smaller, the recalculated EOQ and the average inventory will increase.
- For higher inflation, the higher the rate of inflation, the higher the interest rates will be, and this will cause carrying cost to increase and thus lower the EOQ and average inventories.

(p) **Just-in-Time Systems.**

(i) **JIT strategy.** Just-in-time (JIT) is a production strategy to continuously improve productivity and quality. It is based on the belief that small could be better, not "more" is better. An effective JIT strategy encompasses the entire product life cycle from the acquisition of raw materials to delivery of the end product to the final customer. *The scope includes topics such as JIT purchasing, processing, inventory, and transportation.* Each topic is discussed next.

JIT is based on management principles such as eliminate waste; produce to demand and one-at-a-time; think long-term; develop, motivate, trust, and respect people; and achieve continuous improvement. This is made possible when the focus is "quality at the source" and the tools used are statistical process control methods, fail-safe methods, and problem-solving methods. Quality at the source means producing perfect parts every time and all the time. The major benefits of JIT strategy are improved productivity, quality, service, and flexibility and reduced costs, inventory investment, lead times, lot sizes, and physical space.

(ii) **JIT purchasing.** JIT purchasing requires a partnership between a supplier and a customer, which is a major departure from the traditional purchasing. JIT supplier relations call for long-term partnerships with single source suppliers who provide certified quality materials while continuously reducing costs. The JIT supplier's manufacturing processes must be under statistical process control and their capability should be certified by the customer. The statistical process control charts serve as the documentation to assure that the process stayed in control during the time the parts were made.

Just-in-Time (JIT) Purchasing

Under JIT purchasing, competitive bidding may not occur prior to selecting a supplier because of sole sourcing, single sourcing, or dual sourcing approaches taken. The supplier is selected based on quality, commitment to excellence, and performance, not cost.

A JIT supplier is expected to support the production flow with frequent, small lot shipments, which can be used immediately by the customer. Usually, no inspection is required at the receiving side of the materials.

A JIT supplier will have to become a JIT producer with the idea of pushing costs out of the supply chain, not to pass costs down to the next supplier. Since the JIT supplier is considered as a partner, the customer must notify plant disruptions, temporary shutdowns, or anticipated engineering changes so that the supplier can make adjustments to his production schedules and inventory plans. This requires sharing of information and open communications.

TRADITIONAL PURCHASING PRACTICES VS. JIT PURCHASING PRACTICES

- Traditional purchasing practices call for infrequent, large-lot shipments.
- JIT purchasing practices call for frequent, small-lot shipments.
- Traditional purchasing practices call for inspection, since they focus on continuous checking by the customer. These practices are reactive due to their focus on "after the fact."
- JIT purchasing practices call for no inspection, since they focus on continuous improvement by the supplier. JIT is proactive due to its focus on "before the fact."

(iii) **JIT production processing.** JIT production processing requires setup reduction, focused factory, group technology, uniform scheduling and mixed model scheduling, and the pull system. The objective here is to produce many varieties of products in small quantities on short notice. Manufacturing flexibility is the hallmark of the JIT production processing strategy.

(A) ***Setup reduction.*** Traditional production systems require large lot sizes due to excessive setup or changeover time. JIT suggests reduced setup time so that lot sizes are reduced or evolve to lot size of one with first piece made good every time. The goal is to accomplish any setup in single minutes (i.e., at less than ten minutes). Setup reduction requires eliminating equipment downtime and machine adjustments as much as possible combined with good housekeeping in the manufacturing plant.

With reduction in setup time comes many other benefits such as increased quality due to closer tie-in between the machine operator and the setup, increased productivity and profitability due to elimination of many non-value-added activities associated with moving, storing, inspecting, and reworking, reduced manufacturing lead time resulting in lower inventories and associated physical space requirements, and reduced scrap, lowering unit costs.

(B) ***Focused factory.*** Focused factory is a concept where the plant layout is dedicated to a single product family that maximizes overall productivity and quality while minimizing space and resource requirements. It is intended to physically link all the involved manufacturing operations together to minimize the distance between them, minimize the complexity, maximize the integration of tasks, and enhance the interaction between the workers. This approach eliminates waste and increases communications.

(C) ***Group technology.*** While focused factory is a macro approach, group technology is a micro approach where equipment is laid out to produce a family of parts, one at a time, by physically linking all possible operations in the process. It can be viewed as self-contained, integrated parts factories within the focused factory.

Group technology uses a "cell" concept where the shape of the cell is a "U" or "C" so the starting and ending points are near each other to save walking time. The idea is that a single worker performs every operation, in the proper sequence, to make one finished unit at a time. All operations are close together as much as possible with little or no staging space between workstations. A worker in a group technology cell not only performs every operation in the process but also sees how they relate to one another. This improves productivity and quality.

GROUP TECHNOLOGY VS. TRADITIONAL TECHNOLOGY

- Group technology is a low-volume, high-mix work center for an entire family of similar parts.
- Traditional technology is a high-volume, single-part work center.

(D) ***Uniform and mixed model scheduling.*** Uniform scheduling calls for smaller lot sizes, eventually making every part every day. It is a variable flow management concept instead of trying to coordinate "lumps" of production. It provides level loading for manufacturing operations, building the same product mix every day during a given month. Levels may change from month to month, and hence the term "variable" flow. Under uniform scheduling the interval between like units is called cycle time. The shorter the cycle time, the faster the parts will be made.

Mixed model scheduling is employed to produce parts every hour the same. Yet, production levels will change from month to month to meet customer demand.

(E) ***Pull system.*** Conventional scheduling systems pushes orders through the production shop, making it difficult to synchronize the diverse activities required to produce the end products. This results either in excess inventory or insufficient inventory.

Like uniform scheduling, the pull system is based on the variable flow manufacturing principle to make parts repetitively in a low-volume production. The pull system links every process in the plant using simple signaling cards to synchronize production with changing customer demands. It uses a production signal to authorize the machine center to produce parts that have been taken from the storage area next to it. It uses a withdrawal signal as a permission to consume.

THE PUSH SYSTEM VS. THE PULL SYSTEM

- The push system is based on a fixed flow manufacturing principle.
- The pull system is based on a variable flow manufacturing principle.
- The traditional (push) production system has a "contingency" (i.e., safety stock) mentality.
- The JIT (pull) production system has "no contingencies" (i.e., no safety stock) mentality.

The pull system uses standard lot sizes and employs standard size containers to enhance visual control on the factory floor. This sets the stage for a "precision" mentality. The pull system ensures that right parts will be in the right place at the right time with a minimal investment in inventory. The pull system provides better production control for less cost.

(iv) **JIT inventory.** A misconception about JIT is that it is just a program to reduce inventory. Fortunately, JIT does more than that. JIT purchasing is called "stockless inventory" since the customer has no inventory to stock as it is used up in the production right after it was received. The major goal is to reduce or eliminate work in process inventory so that all raw materials are consumed in the production process.

(v) **JIT transportation.** While JIT purchasing is the starting point of a JIT cycle, the JIT transportation is the execution part of the JIT cycle. JIT transportation is the physical linkage between the inside and the outside processes. It is a process that starts at a supplier location and ends at a customer location. It requires the analysis of all transport events and eliminating the non-value-added events. The basic value-added events include: move load to dock at a supplier location, load carrier, move load to customer location, return empty trailer to terminal, unload by the customer, and move load to assigned customer location.

Similar to JIT supplier–customer partnership, JIT transportation requires that all three parties—the supplier, the carrier, and the customer—work together more closely than ever before. With frequent, small quantities moved each time, the traffic at both the supplier and the customer plants will increase, creating a demand for rapid load and unload capabilities.

To support JIT flow of production, frequent, time-of-day deliveries will be required. This means receiving parts at a specific customer location on specific days at specific times during those days.

Reusable containers and small delivery windows are new approaches. Reusable containers save money when compared with expendable containers. Small delivery windows means rapid loading and unloading which can be enhanced by using point-of-use doors, driver self-unloading, and innovative equipment such as portable ramps and end-loading trailers.

(q) **Materials Requirements Planning.** Materials requirements planning (MRP) is suitable for managing raw materials, components, and subassemblies, which have dependent demands that may be calculated from the forecasts and scheduled production of finished goods. In other words, the order for component inventory is placed based on the demand and production needs of other items that use these components.

Benefits of MRP include reduced investment in inventory, improved workflow, reduced shortage of raw materials and components, and reliable delivery schedules.

DETERMINISTIC INVENTORY VS. PROBABILISTIC INVENTORY

- Deterministic inventory models assume that the rate of demand for the item is constant (e.g., EOQ).
- Probabilistic inventory models assume that the rate of demand for the item is fluctuating and can be described only on probability terms.

In addition to considering dependent demand in the determination of net requirements for components, an MRP system also determines when the net requirements are needed by using the time-phasing concept. This concept works by starting with the time that the finished product must be completed and working backward to determine when an order for each component must be placed based on lead times.

The approach to determining net requirements whenever a dependent demand situation exists is: Net component requirement = Gross component requirement – Scheduled receipts – Number of components in inventory, where the gross component requirement is the quantity of the component needed to support production at the next higher level of assembly.

EOQ VS. MRP

- The EOQ model is focusing on finished goods inventories, which have an independent demand from customers or from forecasts.
- The demand for raw materials and components in the MRP model is directly dependent on the demand for the finished goods in the inventory system.

OVERVIEW OF MASTER PRODUCTION SCHEDULE AND MATERIAL REQUIREMENTS PLANNING

MRP systems are used to project inventory stock levels because they depend on the amount and timing of finished goods to be produced and then determine the requirements for raw materials, parts, components, and subassemblies at each of the prior stages of finished goods production. Working backward, each end product is sequentially exploded or separated into its necessary components and raw materials (i.e., to project inventory stock levels needed). MRP can also be used to do resource planning (capacity planning and labor scheduling) and materials planning. The relationship between MRP system, Master Production Schedule (MPS) system, and Bill of Materials (BOM) is shown in Exhibit 1.23.

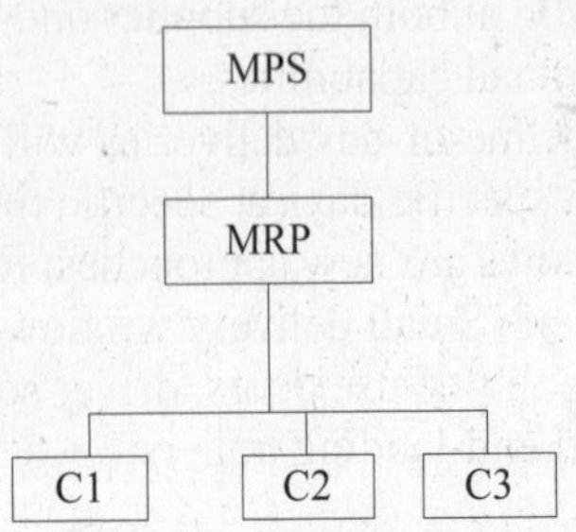

- MPS indicates units of finished goods to be produced each time period.
- BOM defines the components required by each finished product. RMRP uses the BOM to determine the number of components (C1, C2, C3...Cn) required.
- Shows forecasted quantity for each component with dates.

Exhibit 1.23: Relationship between MRP, MPS, and BOM

The inputs to MPS are forecast orders and actual orders. The inputs to MRP are MPS data, BOM data, and the current inventory file. The outputs from the MRP system are the requirements for each item in the BOM along with the dates each item is needed, which, in turn, is used to plan order releases for production and purchasing.

BOM is a structured parts (components) list showing the hierarchical relationship between the finished product and its various components. BOM indicates exactly how many components are needed to produce the quantity of finished goods recommended by the MPS system.

MRP is a computer-based application system and an example of the dependent demand inventory system. It is a system to determine quantity and timing requirements of materials used in a manufacturing operation. Materials can be purchased externally or produced in-house. MRP utilizes a master production schedule, a product bill of materials, and current inventory data to determine current new requirements and timing of materials.

The **objectives** of the MRP system are to determine what, how much, and when to order and also when to schedule deliveries and to keep priorities current for inventory planning, capacity requirements planning, and shop floor control.

The **benefits** of an MRP system come from doing a better job of managing the planning process. Specifically, benefits include lower inventories, better scheduling, early warning system about capacity and supply problems, and long-range plans in terms of equipment and labor needs.

The **prerequisites** for a successful implementation of an MRP system include a feasible master production schedule, accurate inventory records, accurate bill of materials, known lead times, and unique part numbers.

Feasible master production schedule means that the resulting production schedule is practical in terms of material availability, labor capacity, and machine capacity. The planning horizon for the master production schedule should be at least equal to the longest cumulative procurement and manufacturing lead time for an end item. The master production schedule is based upon confirmed customer orders, interplant orders, forecast sales, and current inventory levels. The result is a plan of end items production that translates into the needs for all subassemblies, component parts, and raw materials.

Accurate inventory records are necessary to determine the appropriate quantity and timing of each item to order or manufacture. Cycle counting is generally used to maintain the required inventory accuracy.

Accurate bill of materials (BOM) tells the MRP system what items are used to produce the finished product or subassembly and in what quantity. A variety of display formats exists for BOM, including the single-level BOM, indented BOM, modular (planning) BOM, transient BOM, matrix BOM, and costed BOM. The BOM may also be called the formula, recipe, or ingredient list in certain process industries.

The MRP system requires a lead-time estimate for every part number in the system. This is called *known lead-times.* Incorrect lead-time information leads to incorrect purchasing decisions. It is essential that lead times be updated promptly for all internally produced or externally supplied parts and raw materials.

The MRP system requires that each part be identified with a *unique part number* no matter where it is used in the company. Duplicate part numbers and incorrect part numbers are common problems.

(r) **Distribution Systems.** Inventory in a distribution system can be managed through the use of independent demand models such as continuous and periodic review models. Examples of these models include single order point, double order point, periodic review system, and sales replacement system, which are described below.

The primary **advantage** of the distribution models is that they allow the various levels in the distribution chain to manage their inventories autonomously. The primary **disadvantage** of these models is that they ignore the other stages in the supply chain leading to stockouts and back orders. Excess shipping costs can be incurred since no one is coordinating the movement of materials within the system. Also the demand for replenishment occurs without any regard for what is currently being produced or being planned to be produced. Under these situations, the need for an item incurs extra setup costs, lost productivity, and excess transportation costs.

(i) **Single order point system.** The single order point system basically ignores the fact that the order takes place in a chain and assumes that each element in the distribution system is independent of all other components. This independent behavior can cause large swings caused by a phenomenon called "lumpy demand" at the next level down in the distribution chain. The lumpy demand comes from the lack of communication and coordination between the factory, warehouse(s), distributors, and retailers.

(ii) **Double order point system.** The double order point system considers two levels down in the distribution system, hence the name "double." For example, if a distributor is quoted a lead time from the factory warehouse of two weeks and it takes the factory warehouse three weeks to have stock replenished, the reorder point is set based on the demand for a five-week period. It does not produce lumpy demand, as does the single order point system. An advantage is that it reduces the risk of stockouts. Increasing the safety stock is its disadvantage.

(iii) **Periodic review system.** In a periodic review system, orders are placed on a predetermined time schedule. The advantage is that the order times can be staggered throughout the chain to smooth the demand at each point in the distribution chain. This reduces peaks and valleys caused by several customers ordering at the same time.

(iv) **Sales replacement system.** In the sales replacement system, the supplier ships only what the customer used or sold during the period. The objective is to maintain a stable inventory level in the system. This does require having enough inventory to cover the potential demand during the replenishment cycle. In essence, the sales replacement system is a periodic review model with variable order quantities.

(v) **Distribution requirements planning.** Distribution requirements planning (DRP) is an application of the time-phasing logic of MRP applied to the distribution system. The purpose of DRP is to forecast the demand by distribution center to determine the master production scheduling needs. It uses forecasts and known order patterns from customers in the distribution chain to develop the demand on the master schedule.

DISTRIBUTION REQUIREMENT PLANNING VS. ORDER POINT-BASED DISTRIBUTION SYSTEM

- The DRP anticipates the future needs throughout the distribution chain and plans deliveries accordingly.
- The order point-based distribution system does not anticipate future needs. It simply reacts to the current needs.

(vi) **Inventory distribution methods.** The functions of warehouse distribution, production, and purchasing are closely interrelated and constantly interacting with each other in a manufacturing firm. The decision problems considered during inventory distribution strategy are when, what, and how much of it to ship to a warehouse; when, what, and how much of it to produce at the factory, with what size work force; and when, what, and how much of it to purchase as inputs to the factory warehouse system.

(vii) **Warehouse inventory control.** Warehouses usually stand in a distribution system between a factory and final customers or other warehouses, as shown in Exhibit 1.24.

Exhibit 1.24: Warehouse inventory control

On the sales side, the warehouses face a demand from customers that usually is subject to random demand fluctuations, and usually requires fast service. On the supply side, the warehouse usually faces a significant and sometimes erratic lead-time for receiving shipments of products from factories.

The payments to carriers for making shipments to the warehouse are frequently of major importance in designing the warehouse ordering and distribution system. Economies can usually be achieved by increasing the size of shipment up to some upper limit such as a full truckload or carload. Efforts to economize on shipping costs by increasing the size of shipments have the result of increasing the time between shipments and hence decrease the speed of service.

(viii) **Types of warehouse shipments.** Warehouses usually stock a very large number of products—the larger the shipment size, the more products are involved, and the greater are the problems of controlling the inventories of different products jointly. These are some of the considerations involved in decisions to order shipment to warehouses. Two basic types of shipments can take place: (1) periodic shipments and (2) trigger shipments (see Exhibit 1.25).

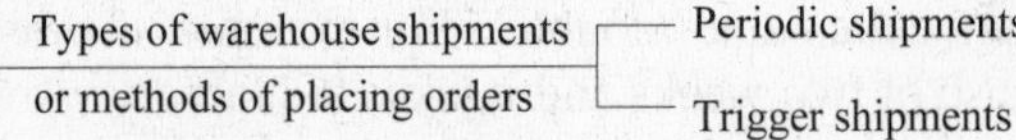

Exhibit 1.25: Types of warehouse shipments

(A) ***Periodic shipments.*** The periodic system of placing orders has the virtue of automatically synchronizing the decisions on many products. Under this system of operation, warehouse shipping decisions can be handled in two steps. First, the product can be considered in the aggregate, and next the shipping costs for different sizes of shipping lot can be weighed against the cost of holding inventory that is associated with each size lot. On this basis, the optimum shipping lot can be determined. By using the forecasted aggregate shipping rate the decision period can be determined.

The shipment received at the beginning of a period is associated with the period because that shipment must carry the warehouse through the period. However, because the lead time *Tl* is required to obtain the shipment, the order for the *t*'th period must be initiated a length of time *Tl* before the beginning of the *t*'th period. When the time arrives for placing an order the inventory records for the products involved are brought up to date. The position of inventories on hand and on order is then known. The orders can then be placed for the amount of each product to be included in the shipment on the basis of the expected product sales, initial inventory position at the time of ordering, and the expected final inventory position at the end of the period.

In calculating the distribution of forecast errors, the forecast span is $(Tl + Td)$ where *Td* is the length of the decision period, which is equal to the interval between the receipt of shipments. It should be noted that with a decision made in advance on the timing of a shipment, any random fluctuations in aggregate sales tend to cause the size of the shipment to vary randomly. This may be quite satisfactory in situations where less than truckload or carload shipments are being made and variations in the size of the shipment can be accommodated readily. If the fluctuations in the size of the shipment exceed the available capacity, a supplementary shipment may be required or alternatively the aggregate inventory buffer changed.

(B) ***Trigger shipments.*** A warehouse may aggregate its products and decide on the optimal size of shipment, but allow timing to be triggered by sales. Because the timing of shipments is irregular, orders for individual products cannot depend on a simple constant lead-time. Instead, *the lead-time for any single product is a random variable, which depends partly upon the orders that are placed for other products.* When the total orders for all products have reached the total desired for a shipping lot, the orders will be placed for a shipment. Under this system the lead-time for any one product is a random variable that depends upon the random sales of other products. The outcome for an individual product depends upon the correlation between its sales and the aggregate sales.

(C) ***Advantages and disadvantages.*** This trigger system is more responsive to fluctuations in sales than the corresponding periodic system. It has the further advantage that the shipment size is predetermined rather than random; hence problems of overburdening carrier capacity are minimized. However, the costs of administering the continuous review of inventory position for a trigger system are usually somewhat higher than under the periodic system.

(ix) **Other warehouse considerations.** In estimating the cost of alternative shipping carriers, the cost of having valuable inventory tied up while the vehicle is in transit should be considered. While this cost will usually not be large, taking it into account will systematically lower the costs of using faster rather than slower carriers. Another economy associated with fast shipments that may be overlooked is the fact that time in transit is one component of the lead-time. *Shortening the lead-time allows a reduction in the inventory buffers, and hence a decrease in inventory holding costs.*

A warehouse may be put under a financial constraint in response to the working-capital needs of the company; the warehouse also may be constrained by the production-smoothing requirements of the factory, and the warehouse itself may have certain constraints on its capacity to receive shipment or its storage space. Some of these may be equality constraints on the exact amount of inventory that should be held, and some constraints may be inequality restraints that establish upper or lower limits. Briefly stated, if an inequality restraint is not violated when the corresponding variable is set to zero, then the constraint can be ignored. If it is violated, then the solution is carried through as if an exact constraint applied.

In estimating the costs of stockouts at the warehouse the least costly alternative should be used. If the warehouse is out of stock on a product it may disappoint a customer, or it may initiate a rush order from another warehouse or from the factory. In the latter cases the cost of depletion may well be the cost of making a special rush shipment, taking into account the communication and expediting costs. Although few warehouses keep adequate records on stockouts and failures to render customer service, this data could be useful in estimating depletion costs as well as costs associated with customer service.

When estimating the cost of holding inventory, the cost of obsolescence should be considered. The indirect costs of having very large inventories in a warehouse may be increased because of product damage resulting from high stacking. Also, increased handling costs from crowded aisles and poor housekeeping and access may show up as overtime payments.

A single warehouse may utilize several different decision systems on different types of products, or products from different suppliers according to particular needs. For example, fast-moving products might be segregated from slow-moving products, and a different decision system used for each.

(s) **Production Scheduling and Control Systems.** Four types of production scheduling and control systems will be discussed in this section. These include: (1) just-in-time systems, (2) traditional systems, (3) Kanban systems, and (4) bar coding systems (see Exhibit 1.26).

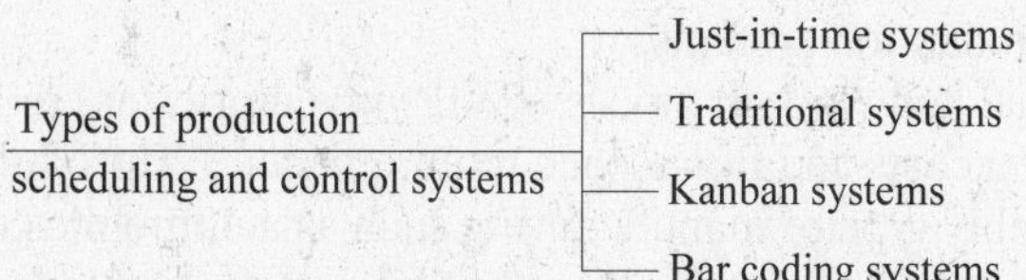

Exhibit 1.26: Types of production scheduling and control systems

(i) **Just-in-time production systems.** Just-in-time (JIT) represents a management philosophy whose objective is to eliminate all sources of waste including unnecessary inventory. The basic principle of JIT is to produce the right products in the right quantity at the right time in the right place. JIT's primary goal is to minimize production inventory levels while providing needed raw materials, parts, and components just before they are used. To facilitate this goal, JIT purchasing places the orders such that delivery immediately precedes usage.

With JIT, products are manufactured or assembled only when they are needed. This means the number of parts produced or purchased at any one time should be just enough to produce one unit of the finished product. Therefore, inventories are better managed to the extent that they are not needed, or at least are minimized.

JIT and Risk

JIT requires a fundamental change in traditional production systems. These changes encompass production layout, material flows, setup times, employee attitudes, and work culture. A risk of JIT is the critical dependency on a few vendors.

JIT requires a commitment to continuously improve activities and the quality of products while eliminating all non-value-added activities and work-in-process inventory. Lead times, waiting time for materials or other, and inspection are grouped as non-value-added activities.

Production flow in a JIT system is "demand-pulled" through the plant by the downstream workstations ordering subassemblies and parts from upstream workstations. These pull-orders are controlled by a Kanban system, which is a system of cards and empty bins. Kanban is explained later in the section.

JIT can be viewed as an intermediate step toward more advanced manufacturing technologies such as computer-integrated manufacturing (CIM). Producing one unit of a finished product at a time allows the implementation of strict quality control standards. The worker under JIT is fully responsible for ensuring that the subassemblies that are received or produced are error-free. If errors are detected, production stops and errors are immediately corrected. *Therefore, the JIT system relies on employee involvement in production operations, quality control, and productivity improvements.*

KEY CONCEPTS TO REMEMBER: BENEFITS OF JIT

- Increased inventory turnover measured as sales divided by inventory. Increased inventory turnover is an indication of increased productivity.
- Increased production rates due to little or no waiting time and increased productivity
- Lower storage space due to lower inventory levels required
- Lower spoilage costs due to high-quality products
- Lower material handling costs since the materials are delivered directly to the assembly floor
- Reduced production lead times due to shorter setup times and better coordination with suppliers
- Reduced indirect labor since most or all non-value-added activities are removed
- Reduced warranty claim costs due to better quality products

The total quality control system developed by D. Deming is an integral part of the JIT philosophy. Frederick Taylor's principles of scientific management influenced the development of the JIT system. Reduction of waste, zero inventories, quality circles, and the use of computer robotics are seen as management tools to increase efficiency and output—a theme familiar to scientific management and JIT production systems.

Raw material and work in process (WIP) inventories are reduced significantly, thereby decreasing carrying costs and floor space requirements. JIT production systems are most appropriate in repetitive assembly type of manufacturing such as automobiles or appliances.

The JIT system requires the setting of daily production targets, so that feedback on worker performance is timely. Workers are given more responsibility for building perfect quality into the product and to produce the desired quantity. The detailed variance reports are no longer needed in the JIT system because defects are becoming fewer and fewer.

JIT promotes work simplification procedures and relies on few suppliers to deliver raw materials and parts on time. Competitive bids are not common. Close ties tend to develop between two parties (customers and suppliers) as they work closely together to improve quality and to implement the JIT philosophy. JIT requires mutual trust between the vendor and the customer. A greater reliance is placed on the vendor to perform and deliver as expected by the customer.

(ii) **Traditional production systems.** Traditional production systems practice a "push" production system concept where each worker produces a subassembly at his own pace and passes the output to the next worker until the final product is completed. A WIP inventory is commonly maintained at each workstation. Plant workers are controlled by work standards and motivated by piece-rate incentive system. This approach leads to producing quantity rather than quality products. Workers have little or no incentive to correct errors or problems.

Workers are encouraged to make good-quality products, not punished for the production of poor-quality work. Under a traditional production system, quality control is the responsibility of a quality control inspector, not the production worker. This quality control inspection is not done quickly enough to trace production problems. Inspection is not done continuously; it is often done for the finished goods only.

Work standards or standards of performance are established by using either imposition or via participation techniques, where the latter approach is more motivating for the worker than is the former. A performance report is issued periodically. A variance investigation occurs when significant discrepancies exist between the standard and the actual output. Investigation could reveal that either the worker is inefficient or the standard is not set properly. Exhibit 1.27 shows a comparison between traditional production systems and JIT production systems.

Characteristics of traditional production systems	*Characteristics of JIT production systems*
• Quality is seen as a hit-or-miss event, and there is no explicit commitment to continuous improvement and production of quality products. • The system is evolutionary. • More WIP is maintained. • No reliance on employee involvement and participation in decision making. • Quality control inspector is responsible for the quality of the product. • The push system begins with the first worker on the assembly line dictating the flow of work. • Workers are compensated based on a piece-rate incentive system. • Inventory investment is increased. • Need for detailed variance reports is great due to many defects. Reports will prove more useful as problem detectors. • Long production runs and long setup times are typical.	• Quality is a planned event, and there is an explicit commitment to continuous improvement and production of quality products. • The system is revolutionary since long-held beliefs are discarded. • Little or no WIP is maintained. • Relies on high employee involvement and participation in decision making. • Production worker is responsible for ensuring the quality of the product. • The pull system begins with the last worker on the assembly line dictating the flow of work. • Workers are compensated based on a group incentive system. • Inventory investment is decreased. • Little or no need for detailed variance reports due to fewer defects. Reports will prove less useful as problem detectors. • Short production runs and short setup times are common.

Exhibit 1.27: Characteristics of traditional production systems and JIT production systems

(iii) **Kanban production and inventory system.** Working under a "pull" system, production procedures and work instructions are communicated by a system of signals sent among workers through the use of a series of cards called *Kanbans*. The JIT production system and Kanban inventory system work together. In Kanban, the last workstation is informed of the day's production needs; all other workstations respond to the Kanban cards and containers, that is, all other workstations are pulled in.

KEY CONCEPTS TO REMEMBER: BENEFITS OF KANBAN INVENTORY SYSTEM

- Paperwork-free system
- Product is made to order
- Diminished need to take physical inventory for income determination purposes
- Lower finished goods inventory amounts

- Simple procedures for taking physical inventory, when needed
- Lower work in process inventory amounts
- Zero or fewer defective products

After the Kanban system informs the final assembly production needs, each workstation then "orders" products or parts from the preceding workstation. This chain moves back to the point of purchasing raw materials. A condition is that a workstation cannot produce unless an order has been placed.

Two kinds of Kanban cards are used for posting and tracking inventory activity and to communicate among workers at the workstation: (1) move card and (2) production card (see Exhibit 1.28).

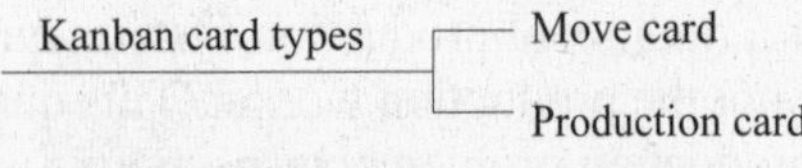

Exhibit 1.28: Kanban card types

The **move card** allows the worker to take one standard container of a specific part from one work center to another. The **production card** tells another production work center to produce the number of parts that will fit a standardized container. There is only one card with each container at any point in time.

Material requirements planning (MRP) is a widely used computerized system that operates under the "push" principle, while Kanban represents the "pull" system. The newer version of MRP is MRP II, which takes the bill of materials for the products to be produced, calculates all subassembly and raw materials needed by time and quantity. Then the workstations are informed as to the number of units to be produced. This method is equated to the "push" system where the work is pushed through the plant.

TRADITIONAL PRODUCTION SYSTEMS VS. MRP VS. JIT VS. KANBAN SYSTEMS

- Traditional manufacturing system practices a "push" production system.
- Materials requirements planning system operate under "push" production system.
- JIT manufacturing system practices a "pull" production system.
- Kanban manufacturing system practices a "pull" production system since it responds to the JIT production plan.

(iv) **Bar coding systems.** Sadhwani and Tyson[3] found that more and more managers are focusing on solutions that collect data in real time, at the point of origin, in a way that ensures the captured data are right the first time. One such solution is the use of automatic identification technologies, such as bar coding, optical character recognition (OCR), voice recognition (VR), and radio frequency (RF) identification. Of these methods, bar coding is the most popular and cost-effective. Bar codes can be used in manufacturing environments such as shop floor and receiving as well as in office environments such as purchasing, inventory, billing, accounts payable, and payroll time-clocking.

Bar codes are symbols that can be processed electronically to identify numbers, letters, or special characters on a receiving report, invoice, time card, or part. They are used to improve data accuracy and increase speed of updating the supporting data in all interfacing systems.

Removing the human element from the data collection process greatly improves data accuracy and updating speed.

Bar code technology supports the JIT production philosophy and continuous improvement program. This is because bar code technology is paperless, which is one of the goals of JIT. Bar codes support continuous improvement due to increased accuracy of data available in the system and establishment of production standards based on such data. This also improves quality of decision making. Exhibit 1.29 presents advantages and disadvantages of bar code technology.

[3] *"Bar Coding Technology, A Research Report," Sadhwani and Tyson, Institute of Management Accountants, Montvale, NJ, 1990.*

Advantages of bar coding technology

- Improved employee productivity
- Timeliness of data collection
- Accuracy of data collection
- Ability to trace labor and material costs directly to specific departments and jobs

Disadvantages of bar coding technology

- High cost of equipment
- Long implementation times
- Continual support in education and training
- Resistance to change by current employees

Exhibit 1.29: Advantages and disadvantages of bar coding technology

For example, the use of bar codes on raw materials will reduce the amount of paperwork that is required to track inventories. Movement of raw materials, subassemblies, and finished products are monitored electronically using bar codes. In addition to speed, accuracy is increased since there is little or no human involvement in reading and interpreting the bar code data. Key entry of data is eliminated.

1.7 Marketing—Pricing Objectives and Policies

Pricing decisions that integrate the firm's costs with its marketing strategy, business conditions, competition, consumer demand, product variables, channels of distribution, and general resources can determine the success or failure of a business. Pricing of products or services is the cornerstone of the marketing function. *If the price is too high, buyers may purchase competitive brands leading to a loss of sales and profits. If the price is too low, profitability may suffer despite increases in sales.*

Effective pricing should consider the following factors: demand influences, supply influences, and environmental influences (see Exhibit 1.30).

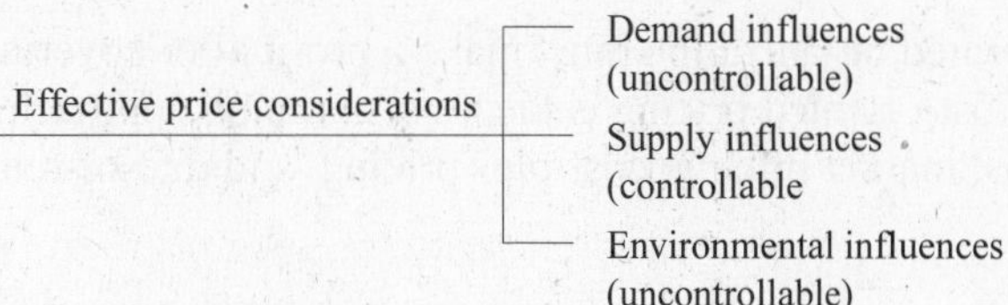

Exhibit 1.30: Effective price considerations

(a) **Demand Influences.** From a demand perspective, three primary considerations are: (1) demographic factors, (2) psychological factors, and (3) price elasticity. **Demographic factors** include: number, location, and economic strength of potential buyers, type of consumer (i.e., resellers or final), and expected quantity of purchases by type of consumer. These demographic factors help determine market potential and are useful for estimating expected sales at various price levels.

The heart of **psychological factors** focuses on how consumers perceive various prices or price changes. It is difficult to predict: how much will potential buyers be willing to pay for the product? and whether potential buyers use price as an indicator of product quality. The best way to find out answers to these questions is to conduct marketing research. Although not conclusive, many research studies have found that persons who choose high-priced product categories and see the consequences of a poor choice as being undesirable. They believe that quality is related to price and see themselves as good judges of product quality. In general, the reverse is true for persons who select low-priced items in the same product categories.

Both demographic and psychological factors affect **price elasticity**. Price elasticity is a measure of consumers' price sensitivity, which is estimated by dividing relative changes in the quantity sold by the relative changes in price. This is expressed as

$$e = (\Delta Q/Q) \text{ divided by } (\Delta P/P) = \text{Change in quantity}/Q \text{ divided by (Change in price}/P)$$

Price elasticity can be estimated from historical data or from price/quantity data across different sales districts and by sampling a group of consumers from the target market and surveying them concerning various price/quantity relationships. However, bear in mind that surveying the consumers can be expensive and time consuming.

(b) **Supply Influences.** Supply influences can be understood in terms of pricing objectives, costs, and nature of the product. To be effective, pricing objectives need to be derived from corporate objectives via marketing objectives as shown in Exhibit 1.31.

Corporate objectives ⟶ Marketing objectives ⟶ Pricing objectives

Exhibit 1.31: Pricing objectives

Marketing research has found that the most common pricing objectives are pricing to achieve a target return on investment, stabilization of price and margin, pricing to achieve a target market share, and pricing to meet or prevent competition.

Additional Pricing Objectives

- Target return on investment and market share
- Maximum short-run and long-run profits
- Growth and stabilization of market
- Desensitize customers to price
- Maintain price-leadership arrangement
- Discourage new entrants with low prices
- Speed exit of marginal firms

The marketing manager focuses on multiple objectives when making pricing decisions. This becomes even more important considering that the manager does not have perfect information about cost, revenue, and market.

Every profit-oriented organization must make a profit after covering production, marketing, and administrative costs. Cost-oriented pricing is the most common approach in practice, and there are at least three basis variations: market pricing, cost-plus pricing, and rate-of-return pricing. This is shown in Exhibit 1.32.

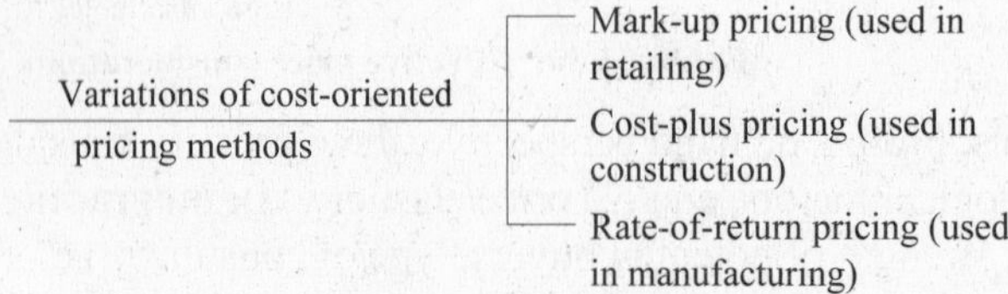

Exhibit 1.32: Variations of cost-oriented pricing methods

Markup pricing is used in the retail industry, where a percentage is added to the retailer's invoice price to determine the final selling price. In **cost-plus pricing,** the costs of producing a product or completing a project are totaled and profit amount or percentage is added on. It is used in job-oriented and nonroutine and difficult to "cost" in advance situations such as military installations. In the **rate-of-return or target pricing**, price is determined by adding a desired rate of return on investment to total costs. Generally, a breakeven analysis is performed for expected production and sales levels and a rate of return is added on.

Advantages of cost-oriented approach

- Simple to calculate
- Simple to understand
- Simple to explain
- Simple to trace
- Provides objective evidence
- Yields a good pricing decision

Disadvantages of cost-oriented approach

- Cost approaches give little or no consideration to demand factors
- Price determined by a markup or cost-plus method has no necessary relationship to what people will be willing to pay for the product
- Little emphasis placed on estimating sales volume in the rate-of-return pricing
- Cost approaches fail to reflect competition adequately considering the fact that costs and markups are different to each producer

Exhibit 1.33: Advantages and disadvantages of cost-oriented approach to pricing

Three important product characteristics that can affect pricing are (1) perishability, (2) distinctiveness, and (3) stage in the product life cycle. Goods that are very perishable in a physical sense (e.g., food, flowers) must be priced to promote sales without costly delays. Perishable items also include high-fashion and seasonal products since their demand is based on time. One of the primary marketing objectives of any firm is to make its product distinctive in the minds of buyers and charge higher prices. Homogeneous goods such as bulk wheat and whole milk are perfect substitutes for each other while most consumer goods are heterogeneous goods.

The price of a product often depends on the stage of the life cycle that a product is in and explained in terms of price skimming and price penetration (see Exhibit 1.34).

Pricing policies	Skimming policy
	Penetration policy

Exhibit 1.34: Pricing policies

A **skimming policy** is one in which the seller charges a relatively high price on a new product. The price may be lowered later as the competition moves in. This pricing strategy is good for monopoly companies and where the demand for the product is price inelastic.

A **penetration policy** is one in which the seller charges a relatively low price on a new product to discourage competition. This pricing strategy is good where competitors can move in rapidly and where demand for the product is price elastic. Regardless of what pricing strategy is used when a new product is introduced, the price may have to be altered later to accommodate changes in the market forces.

(c) **Environmental Influences.** Competitive and government regulations are two uncontrollable variables that have environmental influence on pricing. Many factors help determine whether the firm's selling price should be at, below, or above competition. **Competitive factors** include: number, size, location, and cost structure of competitors, conditions of entry into the industry, degree of vertical integration of competition, number of products sold by competitors, and historical reaction of competitors to price changes.

KEY CONCEPTS TO REMEMBER: COMPETITION AND PRICING

- **Pricing a product** at **competition.** It is called "going-rate pricing," which is the average price charged by the industry and is widely used for homogeneous products.
- **Pricing a product** below **competition.** It can be found in "sealed-bid pricing" where the firm is bidding directly against competitors for project contracts. It is an intentional move to obtain the job contract.
- **Pricing a product** above **competition.** This pricing strategy is used when firm has a superior product or because the firm is the price leader in the industry.

Governmental regulation includes both state and federal government. The scope of state regulation includes pricing by public utility companies while the scope of federal regulation covers price fixing, deceptive pricing, price discrimination, and promotional pricing.

(d) **General Pricing Decision Model.** As mentioned earlier, pricing decisions require the consideration of many factors. Peter and Donnelly[4] suggests a nine-step pricing decision model even though it is difficult to generalize an exact sequence of when each factor is to be considered. *These nine steps include* (1) define target markets, (2) estimate market potential, (3) develop product positioning, (4) design the marketing mix, (5) estimate price elasticity of demand, (6) estimate all relevant costs, (7) analyze environmental factors, (8) set pricing objectives, and (9) develop the price structure.

The *advantages* of this model are that it breaks the pricing decision into nine measurable steps, it recognizes that pricing decisions need to be integrated into overall marketing strategy, and it considers both qualitative and quantitative factors in pricing decisions.

The fact that all pricing decisions will not fit the framework suggested above is its major limitation and *disadvantage.*

1.8 Marketing—Supply Chain Management

(a) **Managing the Supply Chain.** The supply chain is seen as equivalent to an input-transformation-output system. In this context, both customer and supplier goodwill are to be viewed as a key asset to an organization. The supply chain becomes a value chain when all of the transforming activities performed upon an input provide value to a customer. The real challenge is to ensure that value is added at every step of

[4] ***Marketing Management: Knowledge and Skills,*** *J. Paul Peter and James H. Donnelly, Jr. Third Edition, Richard D. Irwin, Homewood, IL, 1992.*

the chain to achieve customer satisfaction. Both purchasing and the supplier play a large role in the value chain.

Managing the supply base includes integration of suppliers, involvement of suppliers, supplier reduction strategies, supplier performance, and supplier certification. The purpose of managing the supply base is to manage quality, quantity, delivery, price, and service.

Integrating suppliers means reducing or balancing the number of suppliers available so that they become part of the buyer operation to lower inventories, to increase response time and quality, and to decrease total cost.

Early *involvement of suppliers* in the product design process reduces cost, improves quality, and shortens product development cycle time. This is achieved through review of product specifications and production standards by the supplier.

Characteristics of Supply Chain Management

Honesty, fairness, and trust have to be the driving values for effective supply management.

Supplier reduction strategies include deciding who will be single sourcing or second sourcing. Approaches to improving *supplier performance* include improved communication, early supplier involvement in the buyer product design, and measuring supplier performance indicators. Improved communication is achieved through designating one or two individuals for all communication that takes place between the buying and supplying firms and conducting supplier conferences and workshops to share information common to both parties (cost, design specifications, and profit).

The supplier performance is measured in terms of quality, delivery, service, and cost/price. **Quality measures** may include incoming defect rate, product variability; number of customer complaints, use of statistical process control, documented process capabilities, and supplier's quality philosophy. **Delivery measures** include on-time delivery, percentage and availability of product within quoted lead time, and quantity accuracy. **Service measures** include invoice accuracy and length of time required to settle claims, availability of a supply plan, and availability of engineering support. **Cost/price measures** include product cost, price reductions, transportation cost, willingness to participate in price reviews, and minimum buy requirements.

Paradigm Shift for Auditors

Internal auditors may not be comfortable with reducing or eliminating incoming inspection of goods, and this requires a paradigm shift on the part of auditors.

Supplier certification is a certification process conducted by the purchasing organization in that their major suppliers are certified so that shipments go directly into use, inventories, or production. The goal of certification is to reduce or eliminate incoming inspection of goods coming from a supplier by a purchaser.

Certification involves evaluating the supplier's quality systems, approving the supplier's processes, and monitoring incoming product quality. The advantages of supplier certification are increased product quality, reduced inspection costs, and reduced process variation.

(b) **Alternative Market Channels.** It takes a considerable amount of time, money, and effort to set up channels of distribution. Because of this heavy commitment of resources, once decisions are made about the channel of distribution they are not easy to retract. Yet these decisions are very critical to the success of the firm. Decisions based on inaccurate or incomplete information can be very costly to the firm. Whether it is a consumer good or industrial good, channels of distribution provide the ultimate consumer or industrial user with time, place, and possession value (utility). *Thus, an efficient channel is one that delivers the product when and where it is wanted at a minimum total cost. Marketing intermediaries exist to bring about product exchanges between buyers and sellers in a reasonably efficient manner.*

(i) **Marketing intermediaries.** The primary role of intermediaries is to bring supply and demand together in an efficient and orderly manner (see Exhibit 1.35).

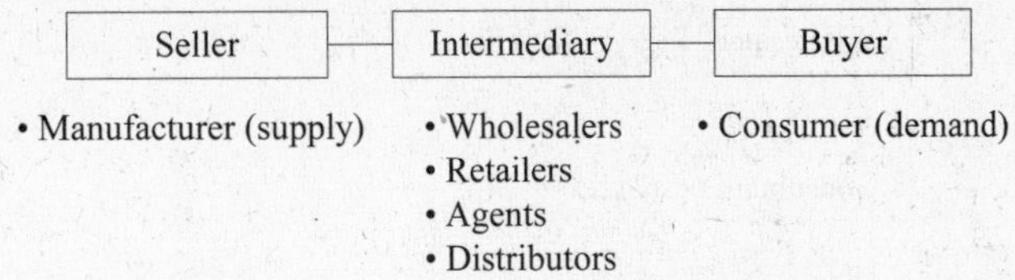

Exhibit 1.35: Primary role of intermediaries

Since it would be very difficult for each consumer to deal with each manufacturer directly for products, the need for intermediaries becomes apparent considering the distance between the seller and the buyer and the product complexity. Therefore, marketing intermediaries can perform product exchange functions more cheaply and more efficiently than the manufacturer can. Also, competition among intermediaries will result in lower costs to the consumer. There are many types of marketing intermediaries, many of which are specialized by function and industry.

Major Types of Marketing Intermediaries

Middleman, merchant middleman, agent, wholesaler, retailer, broker, sales agent, distributor, jobber, and facilitating agent are various types of marketing intermediaries.

(ii) **Channels of distribution.** A channel of distribution is the integration of intermediaries through which a seller markets his products to users or consumers. Agents, wholesalers, and retailers are called intermediaries. These intermediaries are also called middlemen. Channels with one or more intermediaries are referred to indirect channels. The risks assumed and the functions performed by these parties vary as shown in the list that follows.

MARKETING FUNCTIONS PERFORMED IN CHANNELS OF DISTRIBUTION

- **Buying.** Purchasing products from sellers for use or for resale.
- **Selling.** Promoting the sale of products to ultimate consumers or industrial buyers.
- **Sorting.** Function performed by intermediaries in order to bridge the discrepancy between the assortment of goods and services generated by the producer and the assortment demanded by the consumer. This function includes four distinct processes: sorting out, accumulation, allocation, and assorting.
- **Accumulation.** A sorting process that brings similar stocks from a number of sources together into a larger homogeneous supply.
- **Allocation.** A sorting process that consist of building an assortment of products for use in association with each other.
- **Assorting.** A sorting process that consist of building an assortment of products for use in association with each other.
- **Concentration.** The process of bringing goods from various places together in one place.
- **Financing.** Providing credit or funds to facilitate a transaction.
- **Storage.** Maintaining inventories and protecting products to provide better customer service.
- **Grading.** Classifying products into different categories on the basis of quality.
- **Transportation.** Physically moving products from where they are made to where they are purchased and used.
- **Risk-taking.** Taking on business risks involved in transporting and owning products.
- **Marketing.** Collecting information concerning such things as market conditions, research expected sales, consumer trends, and competitive forces.

SOURCE: Dictionary of Marketing Terms, American Marketing Association, Chicago, IL, 1988.

For convenience, the channels of distribution are classified into consumer goods and industrial goods (see Exhibits 1. 36 and 1.37).

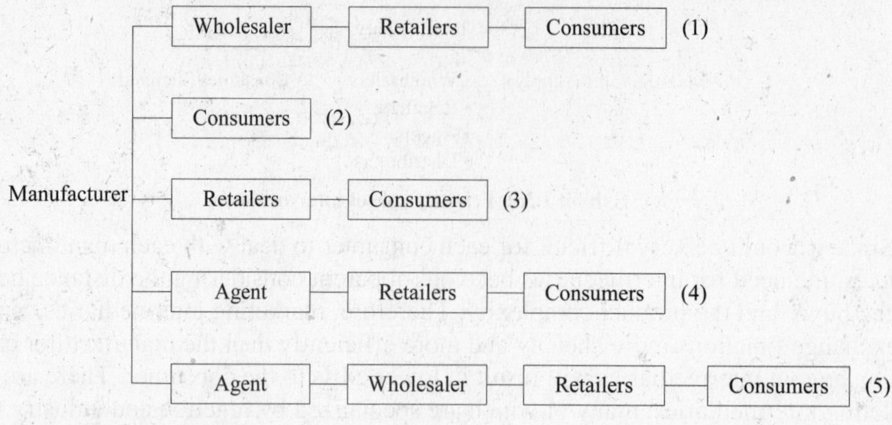

Legend

1. Selling a product through wholesalers to retailers to consumers is the most common channel in the consumer market.
2. Some products are sold directly to consumers.
3. Some private brands are sold to consumers through retailers.
4. Some products are sold to agents to retailers to consumers.
5. Some products are sold to agents to wholesalers to retailers to consumers when intermediaries are few in number.

Exhibit 1.36: Channels of distribution for consumer goods

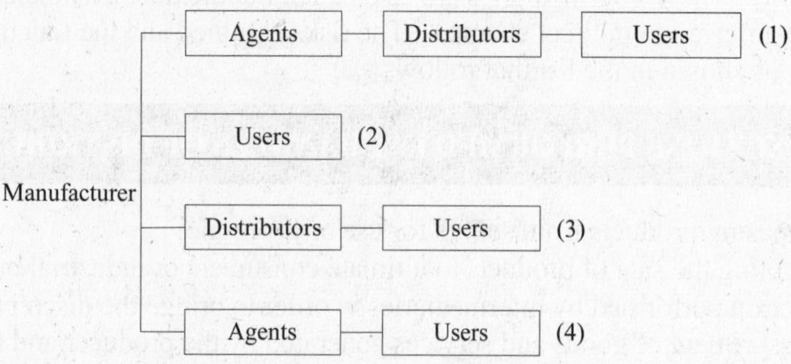

Legend

1. Used by a small manufacturer or when the market consists of many small customers. The manufacturer cannot afford to have a direct sales staff.
2. Used by most manufacturers to market the product to few but large customers. The products require presale and postsale service.
3. Used by manufacturer when the number of buyers is large and the size of the buying firm is small.
4. Used by small manufacturers who do not wish to have their own sales staff contract with agents. Suitable for users who are geographically dispersed.

Exhibit 1.37: Channels of distribution for industrial goods

Selecting the right channels of distribution is not an easy task when considering the geography of consumers and willingness of the intermediary to accept the seller's products. For most products, the intermediaries were well established doing business for many years. Exhibit 1.38 presents six basic considerations in the initial development of channel strategy.

1. **Customer characteristics** include number, geographical dispersion, purchasing patterns, and susceptibilities to different selling methods.
2. **Product characteristics** include perishability, bulkiness, degree of standardization, installation and maintenance services required, and unit value.
3. **Intermediary characteristics** include availability, willingness to accept product or product line, strengths, and weaknesses.
4. **Competitive characteristics** include geographic proximity and proximity in outlet.
5. **Company characteristics** include financial strength, product mix, past channel experience, and present company marketing policies.

6. **Environmental characteristics** include economic conditions and legal regulations and restrictions.

Exhibit 1.38: Considerations in channel planning

In addition, the choice of channels can be improved by considering distribution coverage required, degree of control desired, total distribution cost, and channel flexibility. These are explained next.

(A) ***Distribution coverage required.*** Since the needs and expectations of the potential buyer vary, distribution coverage can be viewed as a range from intensive to selective to exclusive distribution (see Exhibit 1.39).

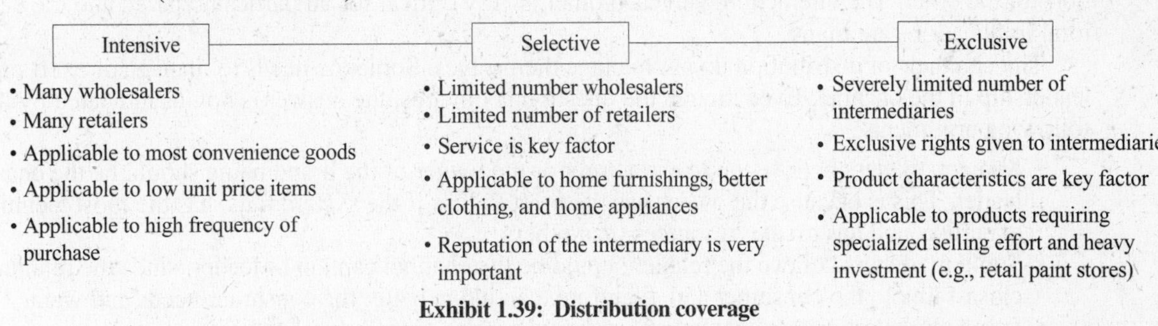
Intensive
Selective
Exclusive
• Many wholesalers
• Many retailers
• Applicable to most convenience goods
• Applicable to low unit price items
• Applicable to high frequency of purchase
• Limited number wholesalers
• Limited number of retailers
• Service is key factor
• Applicable to home furnishings, better clothing, and home appliances
• Reputation of the intermediary is very important
• Severely limited number of intermediaries
• Exclusive rights given to intermediaries
• Product characteristics are key factor
• Applicable to products requiring specialized selling effort and heavy investment (e.g., retail paint stores)

Exhibit 1.39: Distribution coverage

(B) ***Degree of control desired.*** The degree of control desired by the seller is proportional to the directness of the channel. When the market is concentrated in a limited geographic area, with many small buyers, the seller selling directly can influence the buyer significantly with his own policies and procedures. The control by the seller is somewhat diluted when indirect channels are used and the control is more indirect rather than direct. The indirect control can be exercised through sharing promotional expenditures, providing sales training, and sharing the computer-based application system for quick response.

(C) ***Total distribution cost.*** A total cost concept is suggested for the channels of distribution to avoid suboptimization. The concept states that a channel of distribution should be viewed as a total system composed of interdependent subsystems, with the objective to optimize total system performance. Cost minimization is a part of total system performance. The following is a list of major distribution cost factors to be minimized:

- Order processing and transportation costs
- Cost of lost business (an "opportunity" cost due to inability to meet customer demand)
- Inventory carrying cost including storage-space charges, cost of capital invested, taxes, insurance, obsolescence, and deterioration
- Packaging and materials handling costs

Other factors that must be considered include level of customer service desired, sales volume, profit levels, and the marketing mix desired.

(D) ***Channel flexibility.*** This involves forecasting and/or adapting the channels of distribution in relation to changing buyer habits and population moves such as inner cities to suburbs or north to south relocation. Change from individual stores to shopping centers and malls is also a consideration. Under these changing conditions, establishing a new channel of distribution is not that easy and takes time, money, and effort.

(c) **Selecting Intermediaries.** *The two basic methods of selecting intermediaries (middlemen) are* ***pushing*** *and* ***pulling***. Pushing a product through the channel means using normal promotional effort—personal skills and advertising—to help sell the whole marketing mix to possible channel members. This is a common approach with the producer working through a team to get the product to the user. By contrast, pulling means getting consumers to ask intermediaries for the product. This involves distributing samples and coupons to final consumers. If the promotion works, the intermediaries are forced to carry the product to satisfy their customer needs.

Push vs. Pull

- Pushing a product through the channel means using normal promotional effort—personal skills and advertising.
- Pulling a product means getting consumers to ask intermediaries for the product.

(d) **Managing Channels of Distribution.** From a management point of view, entire channels of distribution should be treated as a social system since each party plays a defined role and each has certain expectations of the other. The interaction with each other is very critical for all parties involved and the behavioral implications are many.

The channels of distribution do not manage themselves. Someone needs to manage or exert primary leadership in the channel. Even though the question is obvious, the answer is not, as indicated by the following arguments:

- Some marketers believe the manufacturer or the owner of the brand name should be the channel leader. This is because the owner has the most to lose if the system fails, has the most technical expertise, and has greater resources than others.
- Some marketers believe the retailer should be the channel captain or leader, since the retailer is the closest link to the consumer and, therefore, can judge better the consumer needs and wants.
- Some marketers argue the wholesaler should seek to gain channel control.
- Some marketers suggest that the locus of control should be at the level where competition is greatest.
- Some marketers believe that the powerful member whether it is a manufacturer, wholesaler, or retailer, should assume channel leadership.

Although there are exceptions, the tendency appears to lean toward channels controlled by the manufacturer.

1.9 Human Resources Management

A policy is a statement of how an organization intends to handle an issue or a situation.[5] A policy statement can be brief or expanded. A key element of a policy is that it is a predetermined guideline providing a specified course of action for dealing with prescribed circumstances. Some organizations operate without written policies because they want to handle issues on a case-by-case basis. Employees may see this as a way to show favoritism or discrimination. Unwritten practices tend to become informal policies causing confusion and chaos.

Two choices are available for companies who want to develop written policies: (1) develop policies on a department level or (2) an organization level. Policies developed at the individual department level could create conflicting practices for common items such as attendance, promotions, vacations, sick leave, and employee discipline, leading to low productivity and high morale problems.

Policies developed on an organization level would provide: consistency in handling similar issues, improved communication of policy issues, control over personnel costs, prevention or response to administrative claims and litigations, compliance with government laws and regulations, and delegation of routine personnel decisions to supervisors and managers. Exhibit 1.40 presents various types of organizational policies.

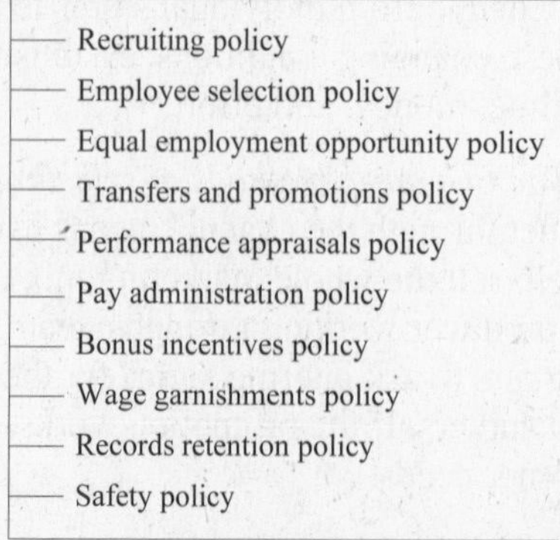

Recruiting policy
Employee selection policy
Equal employment opportunity policy
Transfers and promotions policy
Performance appraisals policy
Pay administration policy
Bonus incentives policy
Wage garnishments policy
Records retention policy
Safety policy

Exhibit 1.40: Types of organizational policies

[5] ***Personnel Policy Handbook,*** *William S. Hubbartt, McGraw-Hill, New York, 1993.*

(a) **Recruiting Policy.**

(i) **Policy guidance.** A human resource policy on recruiting will guide managers to hire the right person for the job. The primary purpose of the recruiting policy is to attract qualified candidates at a minimum cost and time. A recruiting policy also will enable the organization to contact a diverse variety of recruiting resources, which helps to avoid charges of bias in recruiting practices.

In the absence of a defined recruiting policy, hiring managers will do whatever method works best for attracting candidates. Some will ask employees for referrals, some will talk to employment agencies, while others place an advertisement in the local paper. These efforts will produce varying results. Some recruiting methods will be more costly than others. A recruiting policy will help managers to achieve the best results.

(ii) **Ways to minimize potential risks and exposures.** There are various ways to minimize potential risks and exposures. They include

- Although hiring of applicants referred by current employees is a low-cost and effective means for recruiting employees, excessive reliance on this method can be counterproductive and even result in legal problems for the employer. Employee cliques would result in excessive turnover because newly hired workers would feel like outsiders.
- Failure to attract a diverse applicant pool could result in charges of employment discrimination by the Equal Employment Opportunity Commission (EEOC) as discriminating between minority and nonminority applicants. It is a good practice to communicate job opening information to all employees and to all outside communities through various media available.
- Conflict between recruiting policy and promotion-from-within policy could slow down and complicate the hiring process. For example, promotion policies complicate the hiring process by delaying the filling of the job or requiring the promotion of a marginally qualified worker when a fully qualified applicant from outside the company is available.

(b) **Employee Selection Policy.**

(i) **Policy guidance.** Careful employee selection is an important activity because capable, hardworking employees affect the productivity and profitability of the organization. This involves employee screening, testing, physical exam, and orientation. Costs are incurred during selection, termination, and rehiring.

The objective of a policy on employee selection and testing is to provide guidelines on selection procedures that will help managers in selecting a qualified employee while avoiding legal liabilities. Policy guidance facilitates a uniform and thorough approach to employee selection. With selection guidelines, there is a great likelihood that supervisors will make better selection decisions.

In the absence of guidelines, managers will try different employee selection techniques. Some managers conduct detailed interviews. Others may ask only a few questions about job skills or personal interests and then make a hiring decision based on applicant personality. Some managers devise tests for applicants or ask applicants to demonstrate their skill at running a machine used on the job. At best, these techniques will have varying degrees of success and, at worst, such practices have been shown to be improper and discriminatory selection devices. EEOC provides guidelines about employment tests, interviewer rating scales, and the regulation requirements that the test be a valid measure of required performance on the job.

Job Descriptions

A job description is useful in employee recruiting, screening, training, compensating, and evaluating performance. A written job description is needed to effectively analyze the job to determine its exempt or nonexempt status. Management is responsible for developing, using, and maintaining the job description. They should not include gender-based terms (e.g., salesperson), or arbitrary requirements (e.g., high school or college degree), which could be viewed as discriminatory and in violation of antibias laws. Job descriptions should include a disclaimer which asserts management's right to change job duties.

(ii) **Ways to minimize potential risks and exposures.** There are various ways to minimize potential risks and exposures. They include

- Be aware that polygraph testing for preemployment screening of applicants by nongovernmental employees is now a prohibited employment practice under the Polygraph Protection Act of 1990.
- Be aware of the Americans with Disabilities Act (ADA) of 1990 which states that in the event that an applicant with a disability is unable to complete a test due to his disability, the employer is responsible for making a reasonable accommodation by identifying an alternative means to permit the applicant to demonstrate the skill or knowledge that the test purports to measure.
- Avoid inquiries about physical or mental handicaps, age, sex, national origin, or other protected categories on the employment application.
- Avoid misunderstandings by confirming job offers in a letter, which specifies job, start date, and pay rate.
- Use objective, job-related criteria throughout the selection process. Job descriptions are a useful tool in the selection process.
- Be consistent in the use of selection techniques. If a selection procedure, such as reference checks, physical exam, or drug screen, is used on one candidate, it should be used on all candidates for the same job or similar class of jobs. Sporadic use of a selection procedure could be viewed as a discriminatory hiring practice.
- Check employment classifications (e.g., exempt or nonexempt employee) to ensure that they do not create a category that groups employees by race, age, sex, or other protected class defined by antibias laws. Employment classifications help to sort out issues such as eligibility for benefits, payments of salaries, and entitlement to overtime pay.
- Be aware that the preemployment physical exam is now prohibited by ADA. A postoffer physical exam is allowed as long as it is not used to screen out qualified disabled applicants. However, Occupational Safety and Health Administration (OSHA) requires preemployment physical exams on certain jobs such as employees working in a noisy environment. These applicants require a hearing test and periodic retesting.
- Avoid placing a new employee on a new job without complete orientation and training.
- Avoid telling a new employee that he will receive a salary adjustment after 30 or 60 days. Use the term performance appraisal instead of a salary adjustment, where the latter term would imply an automatic increase in the salary.

KEY CONCEPTS TO REMEMBER: JOB ANALYSIS, JOB DESCRIPTIONS, AND JOB SPECIFICATIONS

- A **job analysis** is used to develop job descriptions and job specifications. The **development** function is the place where job analyses are done. The scope of a job analysis includes: (1) analyzing workflows and tasks, (2) observing employees work, (3) studying the methods used to attain work-unit objectives, and (4) interviewing employees about how they accomplish their tasks. The administration of a fair and equitable compensation program should be based on a current job analysis.

  Job analysis → Job descriptions → Job specifications

- A **job/position description** is developed based on a job analysis. A job description includes a listing of job title, job duties, job requirements, and reporting relationships. It summarizes the duties that the employee will be held accountable for performing. Compensation rates are not included in job descriptions although they are developed simultaneously.
- A **job specification** document will contain the job requirements in detail (which becomes a "core" of the job) and the minimum qualifications (e.g., education, experience, other skills) necessary to perform the job satisfactorily.

(c) **Equal Employment Opportunity Policy.**

(i) **Policy guidance.** A policy statement asserting equal employment opportunity, by itself, is not enough to prevent discriminatory practices. Since equal employment laws cover all employment decisions, specific guidelines are needed to guide managers in effectively implementing this policy.

A policy on equal employment opportunity must accomplish a variety of purposes. It must identify protected class employees, specify covered employment decisions, outline guidelines for managers, provide a mechanism for individuals to present claims, and define procedures for resolution of those claims.

(ii) **Ways to minimize potential risks and exposures.** There are various ways to minimize potential risk and exposures. Some of them are

- Avoid using "boilerplate" equal employment policy and expect to be in full compliance with the law. For employees, management actions will speak much louder than words.
- Address nondiscrimination issues when writing personnel policies for recruiting, selection, training, promotions, pay administration, discipline, appraisals, discharges, and other policy areas.
- Implement all policies consistently for all employees. For example, excessive attention to or documentation of the discharge of a minority when other cases are not similarly documented could be viewed as a discriminatory practice. Likewise, a company's failure to document the performance problems of a minority female because of fear of a discrimination claim, and then subsequently terminating that individual, was judged to be a discriminatory employment practice.
- Issue separate policies on preventing sexual harassment or complying with disabilities act provisions in order to get special attention instead of combining with other policies of the organization.

Courts have held that a hostile or offensive working environment constitutes unlawful sexual harassment even if the employee bringing the suit suffers no economic or job benefit losses as a result of such harassment. The EEOC holds the employer accountable for controlling sexual harassment occurring between employees, supervisors, and subordinates, or customers if the employer knows or should have known of the conduct. The EEOC recommends that companies should take proactive measures to prevent sexual harassment by developing a policy and communicating information to employees.

AFFIRMATIVE ACTION VERSUS EQUAL EMPLOYMENT OPPORTUNITY

- Firms having a specified dollar volume of contracts with the federal government or some other government jurisdictions are subject to affirmative action requirements. These require a race–sex breakout of the workforce, compared to a race–sex breakout of the area labor force.
- Equal employment opportunity policies specify nondiscriminatory and nonpreferential treatment for all candidates and employees.

(d) **Transfers and Promotions Policy.**

(i) **Policy guidance on transfers.** Employee transfers can occur between jobs, work locations, operating shifts, or departments. Transfers may be initiated by the organization to move an employee to another assignment in response to staffing requirements. Employees may also request transfers. Transfers may be temporary or permanent.

A personnel policy on transfers helps to sort out these various issues and guide the reassignment of employees to other jobs. The process of transferring employees raises questions about pay rates, shift differential pay, reporting relationships, and duration of assignments. Transfers can also result in relocation for employees and their families. If these issues are not resolved properly, the employee will not be fully effective and productive on the new job assignment, thus costing more than its benefits.

(ii) **Ways to minimize potential risks and exposures.** There are various ways to minimize potential risks and exposures. Some of these are

- Do not give up the flexibility to make temporary transfers when needed to respond to unique business conditions. Protect the management prerogative to assign employees to special tasks.
- Make sure that employee availability for transfer is a condition of employment.
- Avoid hardships to employees by allowing employees to accept or reject the transfer.
- Customize the transfer policies to be responsive to employee needs as well as business requirements.

(iii) **Policy guidance on promotions.** For many employees, career advancements and the opportunity for greater earnings is a significant motivator, which can contribute to organizational loyalty. Promotion policies are generally seen as good for morale. Often, employees seek employment at a particular firm because of career advancement potential. For these reasons, many organizations have a philosophy of trying to promote from within whenever possible (see Exhibit 1.41).

Advantages and disadvantages of promoting from within	*Advantages and disadvantages of hiring an outsider*
• Advantages include increased motivation among employees, less expensive than hiring an outsider, and not difficult to identify proven performers • Disadvantages include possibility of social inbreeding	• Advantages include bringing a new perspective to or fresh look at the problem, and current experience, training, skill, and education • Disadvantages include more expensive than promoting from within and difficult to identify proven performers

Exhibit 1.41: Advantages and disadvantages of promoting from within and hiring an outsider

While advantages of promoting from within are low cost and timeliness, some disadvantages include promotion dilemma (i.e., when two equally qualified subordinates were under consideration for the job), low employee morale, and low productivity if the company disregards qualified employees to hire an outsider.

(iv) **Ways to minimize potential risks and exposures.** There are various ways to minimize potential risks and exposures. Some of them are

- Use job bidding promotion procedures so that only interested employees will come forward to apply.
- Post all jobs covered by the policy on the bulletin board. Failure to post jobs would lead to charges of favoritism. Posting the job and interviewing all candidates allows management to evaluate candidates and counsel those who are not selected.

(e) **Performance Appraisals Policy.**

(i) **Policy guidance.** A performance appraisal is a structured discussion between employee and supervisor. It provides an opportunity for the supervisor to recognize an employee's achievements, offer suggestions for improvement when needed, discuss job responsibilities, define job objectives, counsel on career advancements, and justify a pay adjustment.

A policy on performance appraisals provides guidelines for managers to conduct effective performance appraisal. The policy can identify when performance appraisals should be scheduled, who is responsible for preparation of the appraisal, how the appraisal influences pay adjustments, and how to prepare for and conduct performance appraisals.

(ii) **Ways to minimize potential risks and exposures.** There are various ways to minimize potential risks and exposures. Some of them are

- Use the objective data of performance results rather than subjective opinions. Recognition of good performance can be a motivation for employees. Likewise, when the employee performs poorly, the manager should rate the employee accordingly. If the manager fails to identify poor performance, the employee is likely to assume that performance is satisfactory, unless told otherwise.
- Consider separating performance appraisals and pay discussion. Otherwise, there is a great likelihood that the employee may think that the both of them are the same.
- Avoid low rating from "hard" managers compared to high ratings from "easy" managers. One way to reduce this kind of inconsistency is to include performance-level definitions in the per-

formance appraisal policy guidelines. Another approach is to have the appraisal form reviewed by the human resource specialist.

- Conduct the performance appraisals on time to reduce employee anxiety and tension. This can be achieved by having the human resource specialist remind the functional manager about due dates and monitor appraisal for on-time completion.

(f) **Pay Administration Policy.**

(i) **Policy guidance.** A pay administration policy provides instructions to aid supervisors in understanding the organization's compensation philosophy, formulating pay offers, and having salary adjustments. Further, it can define guidelines which allow supervisors to make pay decisions within prescribed limits. Exceptions to pay policy can be referred to human resources management for approval.

Sequence of Activities in Pay Administration

- Perform job analysis
- Develop job description
- Conduct job evaluation
- Determine salary ranges or pay levels
- Conduct performance appraisal

An organization's compensation philosophy sets the direction for its pay policy. The pay philosophy determines whether the firm is going to be a pay leader or follower, or match competitive norms. Many large firms tend to have defined compensation programs with formalized job evaluation systems and salary ranges. A plan of job classification is the basic element of compensation analysis and job evaluation.

A carefully defined pay administration policy also helps an organization comply with the Equal Pay Act of 1963. This Act prohibits unequal wages for women and men who work in the same company performing substantially equal work with respect to skill, effort, and responsibility under similar working conditions.

(ii) **Ways to minimize potential risks and exposures**. There are various ways to minimize potential risks and exposures. Some of them are

- Minimize the likelihood of inequity in pay rates by having a human resource or compensation specialist review all pay offers and pay adjustments. The specialist should advise the supervisor if pay rates or pay ranges are unusually high or low.
- Improve control and consistency by defining a pay structure. The process for preparing a pay structure includes job evaluation, comparison of pay to an area salary survey, and creation of pay ranges. This process provides an objective basis to define job levels.

KEY CONCEPTS TO REMEMBER: PAY PLANS

Four different pay plans exist: all-salary, skill-based evaluation, lump-sum salary increases, and cafeteria benefits. Advantages, disadvantages, and possible outcomes for each pay plan are presented below.

- **All-salary.** Advantages include: promotes a climate of trust and produces increased satisfaction and job attraction. Disadvantages include: possible higher costs of administration and possible greater absenteeism. Possible favorable outcomes include: supervisors will deal with absenteeism, will produce participative climate, will create a responsible workforce, and jobs will be well designed.
- **Skill-based evaluation.** Advantages include: promotes a more flexible and skilled workforce, promotes increased satisfaction, and promotes a climate of growth. Disadvantages include: higher costs of training and higher salaries. Possible favorable outcomes include: employees will want to develop themselves, and pay would be related to performance.

- **Lump-sum salary increases.** Advantages include: provides increased pay satisfaction and provides greater visibility of pay increases. Disadvantages include: higher cost of administration and short-term salary inequities. Possible favorable outcomes include: provides fair pay rates and pay would be related to performance.
- **Cafeteria benefits.** Advantages include: provides increased pay satisfaction and provides greater job attraction. Disadvantages include: higher cost of administration and possible lack of employee knowledge on various options. Possible favorable outcomes include: will provide a well-educated, heterogeneous work force and provides good data processing.

SOURCE: CIA Exam, Questions and Suggested Solutions, May 1989, Part III, Question 51. The Institute of Internal Auditors, Altamonte Springs, Florida.

(g) **Bonus Incentives Policy.**

(i) **Policy guidance.** Many organizations have considered bonus or incentive pay plans as a way to stimulate desired improvements in productivity and quality levels. The goal of a bonus incentive plan is to reward employees for achievement of specified performance results. It is a win-win situation—the employees benefit from higher compensation based upon their attainment of plan objectives. The employer benefits because increased productivity (or lower costs) promotes higher profits. A good bonus plan should pay for itself.

Varieties of incentive pay plans follow. Premium pay is used by some firms to provide an incentive for certain kinds of work. Premium pay is added to the employee's base pay when certain specified conditions are met. Piece rate is often used in manufacturing firms where employee productivity is measured by the number of pieces produced. Many sales people are compensated on a commission basis. The commission is a designated percent of the selling price or profits on the items sold. Bonus incentives can be an informal payout to employees after a profitable year based on management discretion.

(ii) **Ways to minimize potential risks and exposures.** There are various ways to minimize potential risks and exposures. Some of them are

- A poorly designed bonus plan or unattainable incentive goals will be demotivating.
- Recognize that a bonus incentive plan can cause employees to focus activities solely toward the specified bonus incentive factor, at the expense of other job activities. To balance this conflict situation, both quality and quantity goals should be emphasized.
- Consider implementing two types of bonus incentive plans: one on an individual basis and the other based on group. An individual incentive coupled with a group incentive plan helps promote teamwork throughout the organization and achieve a balance between individual and group goals.

(h) **Wage Garnishments Policy.**

(i) **Policy guidance.** Wage garnishments are a court-ordered process for an employer to withhold a portion of an employee's earnings for payment of a debt. Therefore, the garnishments impose a legal obligation upon the employer. An employer's failure to withhold monies as directed could create financial obligations on the company. Further, failure to properly handle deductions can create legal liabilities for the firm. For these reasons, it is important to define a policy to guide the handling of wage deduction orders.

There are a variety of wage deduction orders: tax liabilities (back taxes) to tax authorities, spouse or dependent (child) support payments, and creditors based on wage assignment agreement when granting credit.

The Consumer Credit Protection Act is one law that defines employer obligations relating to wage garnishments. The Act prohibits employers from discharging an employee whose earnings have been subjected to any one indebtedness. Further the law limits the amount of an employee's wages that can be subject to garnishments.

Until the Hatch Act was amended in February 1994, the federal government agencies were exempted to collect wages from federal government employees for debts incurred outside their employment. The new Act requires federal agencies to honor court orders for withholding amounts of money from an employee's wages, and to make payment of that withholding to another person or organization for the specific purpose of satisfying a legal debt of the employee. The total debt can include recovery of attorney's fees, interest, or court costs.

(ii) **Ways to minimize potential risks and exposures.** There are various ways to minimize potential risks and exposures. Some of them are

- The employer will incur extra costs for handling the wage garnishment orders. As a result, employers may be upset with the employee or with the system and take inappropriate action creating legal liabilities.
- Do not be tempted to fire the employee when a wage garnishment order is received.
- Be alert for official-looking letters from collections agencies demanding wage deductions to pay off indebtedness.
- Specify a priority sequence for handling multiple garnishments received on the same employee. For example, an IRS tax garnishment takes priority over all others, then support garnishment, and then garnishment for other debts. Garnishment orders should be processed one at a time in the order received. When two or more garnishments are received, notify the creditor that their demand notice will be satisfied upon completion of prior notices.

(i) **Records Retention Policy.**

(i) **Policy guidance.** Federal government labor laws, wage hour laws, and many similar state laws specify certain minimum records that must be maintained by employers. These laws define minimum records retention requirements. Some states have laws that deal with the issues of personnel records privacy and employee access to personnel files.

A policy on human resources records is important for the following reasons: to maintain accurate records, to retain records required by law, and to protect records' confidentiality. For example, with accurate personnel records that reflect the individual's education, experience, job history, and performance levels, management can make more informed personnel decisions. Other advantages of accurate personnel records include: helping a company to prevail in unemployment compensation hearings, and providing a basis for defending against discrimination charges or wrongful discharge lawsuits.

(ii) **Ways to minimize potential risks and exposures.** There are various ways to minimize potential risks and exposures. Some of them are

- Protect the confidentiality of personnel records by keeping files in locked drawers or file cabinets and requiring access codes to access computer-based records, and by changing these access codes periodically.
- Avoid the tendency to allow supervisors unrestricted latitude in responding to reference check inquiries by other area employers. A former employee can file a lawsuit because of poor handling of employment references. An untrained supervisor carelessly giving a bad reference about a former employee could create a liability for a libel or defamation lawsuit. The best preventative action is to send reference inquiries to the personnel records specialist. Release references only in response to written inquiries. Limit the reference check to verifying dates of employment and job title(s) and confirming salary if the other employer provided data given by the employee. Avoid detailed subjective evaluation of unverifiable performance information.
- Avoid unnecessary restrictions on employees viewing their own files. When permitting the employee to view the file, the viewing should take place in the presence of a supervisor, manager, or human resource specialist. This prevents unauthorized removal of documents from or insertion of documents into the employee file.

(j) **Safety Policy.** Firms that have successful safety programs typically share three common characteristics: a management commitment to safety, active employee participation in safety activities, and thorough investigation of accidents. Successful safety programs reduce accidents. Fewer accidents mean less work interruptions, fewer worker's compensation claims, and lower insurance costs.

The US Occupational Safety and Health Administration (OSHA) is the federal government agency responsible for defining and enforcing job standards. The OSHA law covers all employers engaged in a business affecting commerce, but excludes self-employed individuals, family firms, and workplaces covered by other federal safety laws. Employers covered by OSHA have a general duty to maintain a safe and healthful workplace. The general duty requirements mean that the employer must become familiar with safety standards that affect the workplace, educate employees on safety, and promote safe practices in the daily operation of the business.

Manufacturing Operations Audit

In a manufacturing operations audit, the audit objective was to determine whether all legal and regulatory requirements concerning employee safety are being properly implemented. The audit procedure would be examining documentation concerning the design and operation of the relevant systems and observing operations for compliance.

(i) **Safety responsibility.** A safety responsibility policy serves as the framework for additional policy guidelines that direct safety activities. Typical safety activities include safety orientation, safety training, safety committee, workplace inspections, and accident investigations. Also effective in promoting safe work practices are safe operating procedures, job safety analysis, and publishing of safety rules. In order to implement this policy, a safety manager should be designated to coordinate day-to-day safety activities, and should be supported by higher-level management for having ultimate responsibility for directing workplace safety.

Safety policy guidelines provide a basis for promoting employee participation in safety activities. Active participation in safety is one important way to keep safety in everyone's mind. A safety mindset helps to prevent accidents.

Some risks that could result from noncompliance, or pitfalls to avoid, include: not holding supervisors and managers accountable for safety in their respective work areas, and not including safety results on a supervisor's performance evaluation, and tendency to publish a few safety rules and then let things slide. Under the law, an employer will be held liable for failing to enforce safety rules. If a company publishes a safety rule, but neglects to require employees to comply with the rule, the firm may be subject to a citation.

(ii) **Accident investigation.** The purpose of accident investigation is to identify the accident's cause so that future accidents can be avoided. In addition to prevention of accidents, accident investigations serve several other important functions such as: eliminating unsafe conditions, identifying training needs, redesigning jobs, preventing or combating fraud related to unethical worker's compensation claims, analyzing accident data, and reporting to government.

1.10 Balanced Scorecard System

Objectives. Most businesses have traditionally relied on organizational performance based almost solely on financial or accounting-based data (e.g., return on investment [ROI] and earnings per share) and manufacturing data (e.g., factory productivity, direct labor efficiency, and machine utilization). Unfortunately, many of these indicators are inaccurate and stress quantity over quality. They reward the wrong behavior; lack predictive power; do not capture key business changes until it is too late; reflect functions, not cross-functional processes; and give inadequate consideration to difficult-to-quantify resources such as intellectual capital. Most measures are focused on cost, not so much on quality.

Kaplan and Norton[6] of Harvard Business School coined the term "balanced scorecard" in response to the limitations of traditional financial and accounting measures. They recommend that key performance measures should be aligned with strategies and action plans of the organization. They suggest translating the strategy into measures that uniquely communicate the vision of the organization. Setting targets for each measure provides the basis for strategy deployment, feedback, and review.

The balanced scorecard system is a comprehensive management control system that balances traditional financial measures with nonfinancial measures (e.g., customer service, internal business processes, and the organization's capacity for innovation and learning). This system helps managers focus on key performance measures and communicate them clearly throughout the organization.

Kaplan and Norton divided the strategy-balanced scorecard into four perspectives or categories as follows:

[6] ***The Strategy-Focused Organization,*** *Robert Kaplan and David Norton, Harvard Business School Press, Boston, MA, 2001.*

1. **Financial perspective.** The financial strategy focuses on matters from the perspective of the shareholder. It measures the ultimate results that the business provides to its shareholders, including profitability, revenue growth (net income), return on investment, economic-value-added, residual income, costs, risks, and shareholder value. Financial measures are lagging measures (lag indicators); they report on outcomes, the consequences of past actions. They tell what has happened. The financial perspective is looking back.
2. **Internal business process perspective.** The internal business process focuses on strategic priorities for various business processes, which create customer and shareholder satisfaction. It focuses attention on the performance of the key internal processes that drive the business, including such measures as quality levels, efficiency, productivity, cycle time, production and operating statistics such as order fulfillment or cost per order. Internal process measures are leading measures (lead indicators); they predict what will happen. The internal process theme reflects the organization value chain. The internal process (operations) perspective is looking from the inside out.
3. **Customer perspective.** The customer strategy is aimed at creating value and differentiation from the perspective of the customer. It focuses on customer needs and satisfaction as well as market share, including service levels, satisfaction ratings, loyalty, perception, and repeat business. The customer perspective is looking from the outside in.
4. **Innovation and learning perspective.** The innovation and learning strategy sets priorities to create a climate that supports organizational change, innovation, and growth. It directs attention to the basis of a future success—the organization's people and infrastructure. Key measures might include intellectual assets, employee satisfaction and retention, market innovation (new product introductions), employee training and skills development, research and development (R&D) investment, R&D pipeline, and time to market a product or service. Innovation and learning perspective is looking ahead.

Measures should include both financial and nonfinancial. Financial measures include ROI, residual income, earnings per share, profit, cost, and sales. Nonfinancial measures include customer measures, internal business process measures, innovation and learning measures, and manufacturing measures. Customer measures include satisfaction, perception, and loyalty. Internal business process measures include efficiency, quality, and time. Innovation and learning measures include research and development (R&D) investment, R&D pipeline, skills and training for employees, and time to market a product or service. Manufacturing measures include factory productivity, direct labor efficiency, and machine utilization.

A good balanced scorecard system contains both leading and lagging indicators, and both financial and nonfinancial measures. For example, customer survey (performance drivers) about recent transactions might be a leading indicator for customer retention (a lagging indicator); employee satisfaction might be a leading indicator for employee turnover (a lagging indicator), and so on. These measures and indicators should also establish cause-and-effect relationships across the four perspectives. The cause-and-effect linkages describe the path by which improvements in the capabilities of intangible assets (people) get translated into tangible customer satisfaction and financial outcomes.

The balanced scorecard provides graphical representation on strategy maps and provides a logical and comprehensive way to describe strategy. They communicate clearly the organization's desired outcomes and describe how these outcomes can be achieved. Both business units and their employees will understand the strategy and identify how they can contribute by becoming aligned to the strategy.

WHICH SCORECARD PERSPECTIVE IS WHICH?

- The financial perspective is looking back.
- The internal process perspective is looking from inside out.
- The customer perspective is looking from outside in.
- The innovation and learning perspective is looking ahead.

MULTIPLE-CHOICE QUESTIONS (1-430)

Quality Management

1. Customers consistently rank which of the following service-quality dimensions as the most important?
   a. Reliability.
   b. Assurance.
   c. Tangibles.
   d. Responsiveness.

2. Which of the following is at the core of the definition of total quality management (TQM)?
   a. Customer surveys.
   b. Continuous improvement.
   c. Employee satisfaction.
   d. Supplier inspections.

3. The total quality management (TQM) program needs to be anchored to an organization's
   a. Policy.
   b. Procedure.
   c. Culture.
   d. Standards.

4. Which of the following service-quality dimensions deals with the employees' knowledge, courtesy, and ability to convey trust and confidence?
   a. Empathy.
   b. Assurance.
   c. Tangibles.
   d. Responsiveness.

5. Which of the following is **not** one of the principles of total quality management (TQM)?
   a. Do it right the first time.
   b. Strive for zero defects.
   c. Be customer-centered.
   d. Build teamwork and empowerment.

6. In the context of total quality management (TQM), a cause-and-effect analysis can be carried out with
   a. Kaizen.
   b. A flow chart.
   c. A fishbone diagram.
   d. Interrelationship digraph.

7. In the context of total quality management (TQM), "vital few and trivial many" analysis can be carried out with a
   a. Pareto diagram.
   b. Run chart.
   c. Fishbone diagram.
   d. Control chart.

8. In the context of total quality management (TQM), the correlation between two product characteristics is carried out with a
   a. Run chart.
   b. Histogram.
   c. Scatter diagram.
   d. Control chart.

9. In the context of total quality management (TQM), the best way to view Kaizen is that it is a
   a. Program.
   b. Procedure.
   c. Destination.
   d. Journey.

10. In the context of total quality management (TQM), the best way to identify and eliminate unnecessary work steps in a process is carried out with a
    a. Flowchart.
    b. Control chart.
    c. Run chart.
    d. Pareto chart.

11. Total quality management (TQM) should be viewed as
    a. Customer centered and employee driven.
    b. Management centered and technology driven.
    c. Policy centered and procedure driven.
    d. Goal centered and standard driven.

12. When a product conforms to its design specifications, it is called
    a. Product-based quality.
    b. Value-based quality.
    c. Transcendent quality.
    d. Manufacturing-based quality.

13. Which of the following TQM process improvement tools tracks the frequency or amount of a given variable over time?
    a. A run chart.
    b. A histogram.
    c. A scatter diagram.
    d. A control chart.

14. Which of the following TQM process improvement tools monitors the actual versus desired quality measurements during repetitive operations?
    a. A run chart.
    b. A histogram.
    c. A scatter diagram.
    d. A control chart.

15. Which of the following TQM process improvement tools indicates deviations from a standard bell-shaped curve?
    a. A run chart.
    b. A histogram.
    c. A scatter diagram.
    d. A control chart.

16. The costs of providing training and technical support to the supplier in order to increase the quality of purchased materials are examples of
    a. Prevention costs.
    b. Appraisal costs.
    c. Internal failure costs.
    d. External failure costs.

17. The costs of repairs made under warranty or product recalls are examples of
    a. Prevention costs.
    b. Appraisal costs.
    c. Internal failure costs.
    d. External failure costs.

18. The costs of inspecting raw materials, testing goods throughout the manufacturing process, and testing the final product are examples of
    a. Prevention costs.
    b. Appraisal costs.
    c. Internal failure costs.
    d. External failure costs.

19. The costs of the material, labor, and other manufacturing costs incurred in reworking defective products and the costs of scrap and spoilage are examples of

a. Prevention costs.
b. Appraisal costs.
c. Internal failure costs.
d. External failure costs.

20. Services can be characterized by all of the following characteristics **except** for:

a. Intangibility.
b. Homogeneity.
c. Perishability.
d. Inseparability.

21. There are four unique characteristics that distinguish goods from services. The one that is the primary source of the other three characteristics is

a. Intangibility.
b. Heterogeneity.
c. Perishability.
d. Inseparability.

22. Customers have a difficult time objectively evaluating services due to which of the following?

a. Intangibility.
b. Heterogeneity.
c. Perishability.
d. Inseparability.

23. The service characteristic that reflects the variation in consistency from one service transaction to the next is

a. Intangibility.
b. Heterogeneity.
c. Perishability.
d. Inseparability.

24. The unique service characteristic that deals specifically with the inability to store inventory of services is

a. Intangibility.
b. Heterogeneity.
c. Perishability.
d. Inseparability.

25. In the six-sigma methodology, the "analyze" stage serves as an outcome of which of the following stages?

a. Define.
b. Control.
c. Measure.
d. Improve.

26. In the six-sigma methodology, the mistake-proofing tool is used in which of the following stages?

a. Define.
b. Control.
c. Measure.
d. Improve.

27. In which of the following six-sigma methodology stages do process or product improvements become institutionalized?

a. Define.
b. Control.
c. Measure.
d. Improve.

28. A process-mapping tool is **not** used in which of the following six-sigma methodology stages?

a. Define.
b. Control.
c. Measure.
d. Analyze.

29. The cause-and-effect diagram is used in which of the following six-sigma methodology stages?

a. Define.
b. Analyze.
c. Improve.
d. Control.

30. Brainstorming techniques are used in which of the following six-sigma methodology stages?

a. Define.
b. Analyze.
c. Measure.
d. Control.

31. Which of the following will be useful throughout the process in the six-sigma methodology?

a. "As is" process map.
b. "Should be" process map.
c. "Could be" process map.
d. "May be" process map.

32. An "as is" process map is used in which of the following stages of the six-sigma methodology?

a. Define.
b. Measure.
c. Analyze.
d. Improve.

33. A "should be" process map is used in which of the following stages of the six-sigma methodology?

a. Define.
b. Measure.
c. Analyze.
d. Improve.

34. Both common causes and special causes are identified in which of the following stages of the six-sigma methodology?

a. Define.
b. Measure.
c. Analyze.
d. Improve.

35. In the six-sigma training environment, which of the following roles is primarily dependent on others to acquire data?

a. Green belts.
b. Black belts.
c. Master black belts.
d. Sponsors.

36. In the six-sigma training environment, which of the following roles is based on the principle of contributing independently and applying the tools and techniques?

a. Green belts.
b. Black belts.
c. Master black belts.
d. Sponsors.

37. In the six-sigma training environment, which of the following roles is based on motivating others so they may contribute to the success of the organization?

a. Green belts.

b. Black belts.
c. Master black belts.
d. Sponsors.

38. In the six-sigma methodology, the quality function deployment (QFD) technique is used to
a. Improve product design and reliability.
b. Measure process capabilities.
c. Implement statistical process control.
d. Improve organizational processes.

39. In the six-sigma methodology, process-mapping techniques are used to
a. Improve product design and reliability.
b. Measure process capabilities.
c. Implement statistical process control.
d. Improve organizational processes.

40. In the six-sigma methodology, mistake-proofing techniques are used to
a. Improve product design and reliability.
b. Measure process capabilities.
c. Implement statistical process control.
d. Improve organizational processes.

41. All of the following are effective ways to prevent service mistakes from occurring **except:**
a. Source inspections.
b. Self-inspections.
c. Sequence checks.
d. Mass inspections.

Items 42 through 44 are based on the following:

After experiencing decreases in performance levels, a company implemented several changes in its management and production methods to improve product quality and productivity. As its first change, management organized quality circles. These groups of employees, including supervisors, met weekly to identify and discuss problems, investigate causes, and recommend and implement corrective actions.

All of the company's products involve high technology, specialized raw materials, and skilled labor. In the past, manufacturing was organized around highly trained, specialized employees. In an effort to further improve production, the company became less specialized by expanding production horizontally. This change meant that both the variety and number of tasks an individual performed increased. As a result, the average number of products for each employee to produce was reduced from seven to four.

42. The implementation of quality circles as described above is an application of which of the following motivational concepts?
a. Participative management.
b. Management by objectives.
c. Offering extrinsic rewards.
d. Motivation-hygiene theory.

43. Grouping production activities by having employees perform more than one task in the horizontal expansion of jobs is an example of job
a. Rotation.
b. Sharing.
c. Enlargement.
d. Enrichment.

44. When making these changes, management told employees that if the company was to stay in business, productivity and product quality needed vast improvement. Management tried to convince employees that by learning additional skills and working within quality circles, both production and quality would be increased. They assured employees that additional training and hard work would enable them to perform new skills and achieve success in quality circles. Management's explanation and arguments are an application of which of the following?
a. Reinforcing positive behavior.
b. Letting employees know what is expected of them.
c. Using identified employee needs to motivate employees.
d. Assuming that employees will work as hard as needed in order to be treated fairly.

45. In an organization with empowered work teams, organizational policies
a. Should define the limits or constraints within which the work teams must act if they are to remain self-directing.
b. Become more important than ever. Without clear rules to follow, empowered work teams are almost certain to make mistakes.
c. Should be few or none. The work teams should have the freedom to make their own decisions.
d. Should be set by the teams themselves in periodic joint meetings.

46. Empowerment is a process that increases an employee's motivation to perform well. Empowerment is **not** facilitated if management
a. Uses participative decision-making.
b. Uses standard (downward) performance appraisals.
c. Decreases the degree of formalization.
d. Educates and trains its employees.

47. Which of the following is a key to successful total quality management?
a. Training quality inspectors.
b. Intense focus on the customer.
c. Creating appropriate hierarchies to increase efficiency.
d. Establishing a well defined quality standard, then focusing on meeting it.

48. One of the main reasons that implementation of a total quality management program works better through the use of teams is
a. Teams are more efficient and help an organization reduce its staffing.
b. Employee motivation is always higher for team members than for individual contributors.
c. Teams are a natural vehicle for sharing ideas, which leads to process improvement.
d. The use of teams eliminates the need for supervision thereby allowing a company to reduce staffing.

49. One of the main reasons total quality management (TQM) can be used as a strategic weapon is that
a. The cumulative improvement from a company's TQM efforts cannot readily be copied by competitors.
b. Introducing new products can lure customers away from competitors.

c. Reduced costs associated with better quality can support higher stockholder dividends.
d. TQM provides a comprehensive planning process for a business.

50. A manager is putting together a new team. What is the most productive action this manager could take to help the team become a long-term high-performing group?

a. Assign a strong team leader from the beginning to help the group determine its goals and to divide up tasks so that the team does not waste time.
b. Select members who have similar backgrounds so that they get along well.
c. Stay out of the team's way and let them develop their own goals.
d. Provide the team with clear goals and give the team time to mature.

51. Which of the following situations would result in the **lowest** productivity for a group of workers?

a. High group cohesion with low alignment with organizational goals.
b. Low group cohesion with moderate alignment with organizational goals.
c. High amount of diversity within the team along with moderate conflict.
d. Weak leadership and strong commitment to organizational goals.

52. Focusing on customers, promoting innovation, learning new philosophies, driving out fear, and providing extensive training are all elements of a major change in organizations. These elements are aimed primarily at

a. Copying leading organizations to better compete with them.
b. Focusing on the total quality of products and services.
c. Being efficient and effective at the same time, in order to indirectly affect profits.
d. Better management of costs of products and services, in order to become the low-cost provider.

53. Total quality management in a manufacturing environment is best exemplified by

a. Identifying and reworking production defects before sale.
b. Designing the product to minimize defects.
c. Performing inspections to isolate defects as early as possible.
d. Making machine adjustments periodically to reduce defects.

54. Which statement best describes the emphasis of total quality management (TQM)?

a. Reducing the cost of inspection.
b. Implementing better statistical quality control techniques.
c. Doing each job right the first time.
d. Encouraging cross-functional teamwork.

55. Which of the following is a characteristic of total quality management (TQM)?

a. Management-by-objectives.
b. On-the-job training by other workers.
c. Quality by final inspection.
d. Education and self-improvement.

56. In which of the following organizational structures does total quality management (TQM) work best?

a. Hierarchical organizational structure.
b. Teams of people from the same specialty.
c. Teams of people from different specialties.
d. Specialists working individually.

57. If a company is customer-centered, its customers are defined as

a. Only people external to the company who have purchased something from the company.
b. Only people internal to the company who directly use its product.
c. Anyone external to the company and those internal who rely on its product to get their job done.
d. Everybody external to the company who is currently doing, or may in the future do, business with the company.

58. The basic underlying principle of the quality-of-work-life view of motivation suggests that an organization should unlock the creative potential of its people by

a. Involving them in decisions affecting their lives and providing them with more control over their work.
b. Providing fair and equitable reward systems that are clearly linked to the employees' effort and performance.
c. Focusing on employees' higher-level needs.
d. Using job enrichment techniques that increase skill variety, task identity and significance, autonomy, and feedback.

59. In a quality cost report, the category of internal failure costs is for costs incurred to correct defects and problems within the production, distribution, and marketing systems. Which one of the following costs is **not** relevant to internal failure?

a. Rework.
b. Union grievance arbitration fees.
c. Freight on returned goods.
d. Scrap.

Items 60 and 61 are based on the following:

Listed below are costs of quality that a manufacturing company has incurred throughout its operations. The company plans to prepare a report that classifies these costs into the following four categories: preventive costs, appraisal costs, internal-failure costs, and external-failure costs.

Cost items	*$ Amount*
Design reviews	275,000
Finished goods returned due to failure	55,000
Freight on replacement finished goods	27,000
Labor inspection during manufacturing	75,000
Labor inspection of raw materials	32,000
Manufacturing product-testing labor	63,000
Manufacturing rework labor and overhead	150,000
Materials used in warranty repairs	68,000
Process engineering	180,000
Product-liability claims	145,000
Product-testing equipment	35,000
Repairs to equipment due to breakdown	22,000
Scheduled equipment maintenance	90,000
Scrap material	125,000
Training of manufacturing workers	156,000

60. The costs of quality that are incurred in detecting units of product that do not conform to product specifications are referred to as

a. Preventive costs.
b. Appraisal costs.
c. Internal-failure costs.
d. External-failure costs.

61. The dollar amount of the costs of quality classified as preventive costs for the manufacturing firm would be

a. $643,000
b. $701,000
c. $736,000
d. $768,000

62. The most important component of quality control is

a. Ensuring goods and services conform to the design specifications.
b. Satisfying upper management.
c. Conforming with ISO-9000 specifications.
d. Determining the appropriate timing of inspections.

63. Under a total quality management (TQM) approach

a. Measurement occurs throughout the process, and errors are caught and corrected at the source.
b. Quality control is performed by highly trained inspectors at the end of the production process.
c. Upper management assumes the primary responsibility for the quality of the products and services.
d. A large number of suppliers are used in order to obtain the lowest possible prices.

64. Quality control circles are now used all over the world. They typically consist of a group of five to ten employees who meet regularly. The primary goal of these circles is

a. To improve the quality of leadership in the organization.
b. To tap the creative problem-solving potential of every employee.
c. To improve communications between employees and managers by providing a formal communication channel.
d. To allow for the emergence of team leaders who can be targeted for further leadership development.

65. A traditional quality control process in manufacturing consists of mass inspection of goods only at the end of a production process. A major deficiency of the traditional control process is that

a. It is expensive to do the inspections at the end of the process.
b. It is not possible to rework defective items.
c. It is not 100% effective.
d. It does not focus on improving the entire production process.

66. Quality control programs employ many tools for problem definition and analysis. A scatter diagram is one of these tools. The objective of a scatter diagram is to

a. Display a population of items for analysis.
b. Show frequency distribution in graphic form.
c. Divide a universe of data into homogeneous groups.
d. Show the vital trend and separate trivial items.

Items 67 and 68 are based on the following:

The management and employees of a large household goods moving company decided to adopt total quality management (TQM) and continuous improvement (CI). They believed that if their company became nationally known as adhering to TQM and CI, one result would be an increase in the company's profits and market share.

67. The primary reason for adopting TQM was to achieve

a. Greater customer satisfaction.
b. Reduced delivery time.
c. Reduced delivery charges.
d. Greater employee participation.

68. Quality is achieved more economically if the company focuses on

a. Appraisal costs.
b. Prevention costs.
c. Internal failure costs.
d. External failure costs.

Items 69 and 70 are based on the following:

An organization has collected data on the complaints made by personal computer users and has categorized the complaints.

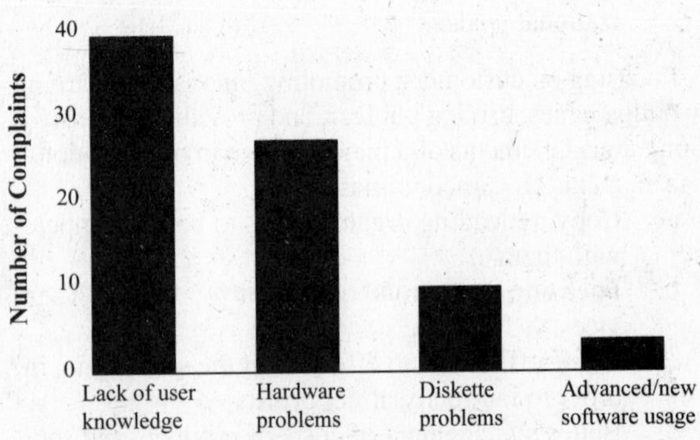

69. Using the information collected, the organization should focus on

a. The total number of personal computer complaints that occurred.
b. The number of computer complaints associated with diskette problems and new software usage.
c. The number of computer complaints associated with the lack of user knowledge and hardware problems.
d. The cost to alleviate all computer complaints.

70. The chart displays

a. The arithmetic mean of each computer complaint.
b. The relative frequency of each computer complaint.
c. The median of each computer complaint.
d. The absolute frequency of each computer complaint.

71. Quality cost indices are often used to measure and analyze the cost of maintaining a given level of quality. One example of a quality cost index, which uses a direct labor base, is computed as

Quality cost index = (Total quality costs)/(Direct labor costs) x 100.

The following quality cost data were collected for May and June:

	May	*June*
Prevention costs	$4,000	$5,000
Appraisal costs	6,000	5,000
Internal failure costs	12,000	15,000
External failure costs	14,000	11,000
Direct labor costs	90,000	100,000

Based upon these cost data, the quality cost index

a. Decreased 4 points from May to June.
b. Was unchanged from May to June.
c. Increased 10 points from May to June.
d. Decreased 10 points from May to June.

72. Which one of the following statements about quality circles is **false**?

a. A quality circle is typically comprised of a group of eight to 10 subordinates and supervisors.
b. Part of the quality circle concept includes teaching participants communication skills, quality strategies, and problem analysis techniques.
c. Quality circles meet on the company premises and on company time.
d. The quality circle has the final control over implementation of recommended solutions.

73. A company is experiencing a high level of customer returns for a particular product because it does not meet the rigid dimensions required. Each return is reworked on a milling machine and sent back through all of the subsequent finishing steps. This is a costly process. Identify the best method for reducing the quality failure costs.

a. Customer surveys.
b. Increased finished goods inspections.
c. Defect prevention.
d. Increased work-in process inspections.

74. Which statement best describes Total Quality Management (TQM)?

a. TQM emphasizes reducing the cost of inspection.
b. TQM emphasizes better statistical quality control techniques.
c. TQM emphasizes doing each job right the first time.
d. TQM emphasizes encouraging cross-functional teamwork.

Items 75 through 77 are based on the following:

The costs of quality can be categorized as follows:

a. **Prevention costs.** This involves eliminating the production of products which do not conform to quality requirements. Costs include product and process design and testing, supplier evaluation and training, employee training, and preventative maintenance.
b. **Appraisal costs.** This involves detecting products which do not conform to quality requirements. Costs include inspection, testing, and statistical quality control.
c. **Internal failure costs.** This involves correcting or scrapping nonconforming products before they are shipped. Costs include rework, scrap, retesting, and changes in the design of the product or process.
d. **External failure costs.** This involves customers detecting nonconforming products after shipment. Costs include allowances, customer complaints, service, warranty, product liability, lost customer goodwill, and returned products.

75. Management of a company is attempting to build a reputation as a world-class manufacturer of quality products. On which of the four costs should it spend the majority of its funds?

a. Prevention costs.
b. Appraisal costs.
c. Internal failure costs.
d. External failure costs.

76. Management of a company is attempting to build a reputation as a world-class manufacturer of quality products. Which of the four costs would be the **most** damaging to its ability to build a reputation as a world-class manufacturer?

a. Prevention costs.
b. Appraisal costs.
c. Internal failure costs.
d. External failure costs.

77. Management of a company is attempting to build a reputation as a world-class manufacturer of quality products. Which of the following measures would **not** be used by the firm to measure quality?

a. The percentage of shipments returned by customers because of poor quality.
b. The number of parts shipped per day.
c. The number of defective parts per million.
d. The percentage of products passing quality tests the first time.

78. Which of the following is **least** related to product or service quality?

a. ISO 9000.
b. Continual Improvement.
c. Economic Order Quantity.
d. Quality Circles.

79. Manufacturing operations which use just-in-time (JIT) inventory delivery must develop a system of total quality control (TQC) over parts and material. The objective of TQC is to

a. Provide an early warning system that detects and eliminates defective items.
b. Statistically estimate the potential number of defective items.
c. Detect and eliminate maintenance and processing problems, which cause bottlenecks.
d. Ensure that the "pull" exerted by each assembly stage includes correct quantities and specifications.

80. Statistical quality control is often used to distinguish between random variation and other sources of variation in an operating process. A control chart that shows the fraction defective of a sample is a(n)

a. R chart.
b. X-bar chart.
c. P-chart.
d. Cusum chart.

81. Because of the difficulty and high cost of measuring the dimensions of the product produced in a certain manufacturing process, statistical quality control is done by classifying sampled products into two categories, acceptable and unacceptable. The appropriate control chart for controlling the proportion of unacceptable units in this process is the

a. P-chart.
b. X-bar chart.
c. R chart.
d. SQC chart.

82. The costs of quality that are incurred in detecting units of product that do not conform to product specifications are referred to as

a. Prevention costs.
b. Appraisal costs.
c. Rework costs.
d. Failure costs.

83. Which of the following would minimize defects in finished goods caused by poor-quality raw materials?

a. Documented procedures for the proper handling of work-in-process inventory.
b. Required material specifications for all purchases.
c. Timely follow-up on all unfavorable usage variances.
d. Determination of the amount of spoilage at the end of the manufacturing process.

84. The use of teams in total quality management is important because

a. Well-managed teams can be highly creative and are able to address complex problems better than individuals can.
b. Teams are quicker to make decisions, thereby helping to reduce cycle time.
c. Employee motivation is higher for team members than for individual contributors.
d. The use of teams eliminates the need for supervision, thereby allowing a company to become leaner and more profitable.

International Organization for Standardization (ISO) Framework

85. Which of the following is **not** a basic requirement of the ISO 9001 quality standard?

a. Establishing and maintaining procedures for controlling documentation.
b. Procedures to verify, store, and maintain purchased items.
c. Reviewing contracts to assess whether requirements are adequately defined.
d. Simultaneous application for the Malcolm Baldrige National Quality award.

86. Which of the following is **not** a reason that firms seek ISO 9000 certification?

a. To met contractual obligations.
b. To market goods in Europe.
c. To remove tariffs.
d. To gain competitive advantage.

87. The ISO 9000 registration process includes all of the following **except:**

a. Rectification.
b. Document review.
c. Preassessment.
d. Assessment.

88. Which of the following is **not** true regarding the ISO 9000 quality standard?

a. ISO 9000 does not guarantee a quality product.
b. Its objective is to ensure conformance to documented procedures and standards.
c. Third-party auditors cannot be used.
d. Recertification is required every three years.

89. Which of the following is true about the ISO 9000 quality standards?

a. The scope of the standards aligns more closely with the US Malcolm Baldrige criteria.
b. Emphasis has shifted toward evaluating product quality.
c. The previous focus on customer expectations has been reduced.
d. The requirements for quality system documentation have increased.

90. Which of the following was specifically designed for automotive suppliers?

a. QS-9000
b. ISO 9001:2000
c. TL 9000
d. AS 9000

91. Which of the following best describes the ISO 9000 standards?

a. They are product quality standards.
b. They are quality system standards.
c. They are environmental quality standards.
d. They are people quality standards.

92. The ISO 9000 standards for quality program focuses most on which of the following areas?

a. Customer satisfaction.
b. Business results.
c. Internal processes.
d. Productivity improvements.

93. Which of the following is designed for environmental standards?

a. ISO 10012
b. ISO 10011
c. ISO 14000
d. ISO 10013

Forecasting

94. Which of the following forecasting techniques refers to the preparation and study of written descriptions of alternative but equally likely future conditions?

a. Informed judgment.
b. Scenario analysis.
c. Surveys.
d. Trend analysis.

95. Which of the following is **not** a type of forecasts?

a. Event input forecasts.
b. Event outcome forecasts.
c. Event timing forecasts.
d. Time series forecasts.

96. "Timing questions" in the event timing forecast can be answered by identifying which of the following?

a. Lagging indicators.
b. Leading indicators.
c. Coincident indicators.
d. Composite indicators.

97. Extrinsic forecasts are based on which of the following?
a. Lagging indicators.
b. Leading indicators.
c. Coincident indicators.
d. Composite indicators.

98. Which of the following is based on the assumption that the future will be an extension of present and past results?
a. Scenario analysis.
b. Survey analysis.
c. Trend analysis.
d. Market analysis.

99. Judgmental forecasts are
a. Fast and expensive.
b. Slow and inexpensive.
c. Fast and inexpensive.
d. Reliable and accurate.

100. Gradual shifting of a time series over a long period of time is called
a. Periodicity.
b. Cycle.
c. Regression.
d. Trend.

101. Seasonal components
a. Cannot be predicted.
b. Are regular repeated patterns.
c. Are long runs of observations above or below the trend line.
d. Reflect a shift in the series over time.

102. Short-term, unanticipated, and nonrecurring factors in a time series provide the random variability known as the
a. Irregular component.
b. Residual.
c. Forecast error.
d. Mean squared error.

103. Causal forecasting models
a. Should avoid the use of multiple regression analysis.
b. Attempt to explain a time series' behavior.
c. Do not use time series data.
d. Should avoid the use of linear regression analysis.

104. Which of the following seasonal indices shows a positive effect?
a. Above one.
b. Exactly one.
c. Less than one.
d. Exactly zero.

105. A deseasonalized time series is calculated by
a. Dividing each original time series observation by the corresponding seasonal index.
b. Subtracting each original time series observation from the corresponding seasonal index.
c. Multiplying each original time series observation with the corresponding seasonal index.
d. Adding each original time series observation to the corresponding seasonal index.

106. Which of the following is **not** an appropriate time series forecasting technique?
a. Least squares.
b. Exponential smoothing.
c. The Delphi technique.
d. Moving averages.

107. To remove the effect of seasonal variation from a time series, original data should be
a. Increased by the seasonal factor.
b. Reduced by the seasonal factor.
c. Multiplied by the seasonal factor.
d. Divided by the seasonal factor.

108. All of the following are useful for forecasting the needed level of inventory **except:**
a. Knowledge of the behavior of business cycles.
b. Internal accounting allocations of costs to various segments of the company.
c. Information about seasonal variations in demand.
d. Econometric modeling.

109. Solution strategies such as "what if" are used with
a. Statistical sampling.
b. Econometric forecasting.
c. Queuing theory.
d. Simulation.

110. A cost-volume-profit model developed in a dynamic environment determined that the estimated parameters used may vary between limits. Subsequent testing of the model with respect to all possible values of the estimated parameters is termed
a. A sensitivity analysis.
b. Statistical estimation.
c. Statistical hypothesis testing.
d. A time-series study.

111. A company is deciding whether to purchase an automated machine to manufacture one of its products. Expected net cash flows from this decision depend on several factors, interactions among those factors, and the probabilities associated with different levels of those factors. The method that the company should use to evaluate the distribution of net cash flows from this decision, and changes in net cash flows resulting from changes in levels of various factors is
a. Simulation and sensitivity analysis.
b. Linear programming.
c. Correlation analysis.
d. Differential analysis.

112. Which of the following is **not** true about simulation models?
a. They are deterministic in nature.
b. They may involve sampling.
c. They mathematically estimate what actual performance would be.
d. They emulate stochastic systems.

113. A large fishing operation has information on the interval, time, and probabilities of shrimp schools staying beneath their fishing boats. In order to use this information to predict when and where to send their boats, which of the following techniques should be used?
a. Simulation.
b. Least squares.
c. Queuing theory.
d. Exponential smoothing.

114. Because of the large number of factors that could affect the demand for its new product, interactions among these factors, and the probabilities associated with different values of these factors, the marketing department would like to develop a computerized model for projecting demand for this product. By using a random-number procedure to generate values for the different factors, it will be able to estimate the distribution of demand for this new product. This method of estimating the distribution of demand for the new product is called

a. Monte Carlo simulation.
b. Linear programming.
c. Correlation analysis.
d. Differential analysis.

115. As part of a risk analysis, an internal auditor wishes to forecast the percentage growth in next month's sales for a particular plant using the past thirty months' sales results. Significant changes in the organization affecting sales volumes were made within the last nine months. The **most** effective analysis technique to use would be

a. Unweighted moving average.
b. Exponential smoothing.
c. Queuing theory.
d. Linear regression analysis.

116. To facilitate planning and budgeting, management of a travel service company wants to develop forecasts of monthly sales for the next twenty-four months. Based on past data, management has observed an upward trend in the level of sales. There are also seasonal variations with high sales in June, July, and August, and low sales in January, February, and March. An appropriate technique for forecasting the company's sales is

a. Time series analysis.
b. Queuing theory.
c. Linear programming.
d. Sensitivity analysis.

117. Recent events caused the time series used by an electric utility to become too unpredictable for practical use. As a result, the utility developed a model to predict the demand for electricity based on factors such as class of service, population growth, and unemployment in the area of service. The discipline that deals with such models is called

a. Linear programming.
b. Network analysis.
c. Operations research.
d. Econometrics.

118. A forecast of time-series data one period ahead using weights, which minimize the error between the actual data and the forecast made of the actual data is termed

a. Time series analysis.
b. Dynamic programming.
c. Exponential smoothing.
d. Econometrics.

119. The statistical analysis of relationships between economic variables is referred to as

a. Macroeconomics.
b. Econometrics.
c. Microeconomics.
d. Socioeconomic.

120. If a firm has a goal of developing a predictive model for sales based on linear, multiple regression analysis and the inherent assumptions embodied within, the science involved is

a. Goal programming.
b. Business statistics.
c. Linear programming.
d. Econometrics.

121. The manager of the assembly department of a company would like to estimate the fixed and variable components of the department's cost. To do so, the manager has collected information on total cost and output for the past twenty-four months. To estimate the fixed and variable components of total cost, the manager should use

a. Regression analysis.
b. Game theory.
c. Sensitivity analysis.
d. Queuing theory.

122. The internal auditor of a bank has developed a multiple regression model, which has been used for a number of years to estimate the amount of interest income from commercial loans. During the current year, the auditor applies the model and discovers that the R^2 value has decreased dramatically, but the model otherwise seemed be working okay. Which of the following conclusions are justified by the change?

a. Changing to a cross-sectional regression analysis should cause the R^2 to increase.
b. Regression analysis is no longer an appropriate technique to estimate interest income.
c. Some new factors, not included in the model, are causing interest income to change.
d. A linear regression analysis would increase the model's reliability.

123. In regression analysis, which of the following correlation coefficients represents the strongest relationships between the independent and dependent variables?

a. 1.03
b. -0.02
c. -0.89
d. 0.75

124. An auditor asks accounting personnel how they determine the value of the organization's real estate holdings. They say that valuations are based on a regression model that uses 17 different characteristics of the properties (square footage, proximity to downtown, age, etc.) to predict value. The coefficients of this model were estimated using a random sample of 20 company properties, for which the model produced an R^2 value of 0.92. Based on this information, which one of the following should the auditor conclude?

a. The model's high R^2 is probably due in large part to random chance.
b. 92% of the variables that determine value are in the model.
c. The model is very reliable.
d. This sample of properties is probably representative of the overall population of company holdings.

125. An internal auditor for a large automotive parts retailer wishes to perform a risk analysis and wants to use an appropriate statistical tool to help identify stores that would be out of line compared to the majority of stores. The most appropriate statistical tool to use would be

a. Linear time series analysis.
b. Cross-sectional regression analysis.
c. Cross tabulations with chi-square analysis of significance.
d. Time series multiple regression analysis to identify changes in individual stores over time.

126. A division uses a regression in which monthly advertising expenditures are used to predict monthly product sales (both in millions of dollars). The results show a regression coefficient for the independent variable equal to 0.8. This coefficient value indicates that

a. The average monthly advertising expenditure in the sample is $800,000.
b. When monthly advertising is at its average level, product sales will be $800,000.
c. On average, for every additional dollar in advertising you get $0.80 in additional sales.
d. Advertising is not a good predictor of sales because the coefficient is so small.

127. An audit manager has just returned from an executive training program and has suggested that the audit department develop a mathematical model to help identify factors that may be causing changes in the cost of production. According to the manager, the model should recognize that the company currently has three separate production (cost) centers. Which of the following approaches would best provide the analysis suggested by the audit manager?

a. Develop a classical variables-sampling estimate of cost of production per department, with the sample stratified by the dollar value of each product produced.
b. Develop a three-year ratio analysis of cost of production compared to cost of raw inventory, across the three departments.
c. Develop a multiple regression analysis of production costs including such variables as raw material inventory costs, number of employees in the department, and overtime pay.
d. Develop a linear regression analysis relating cost of production to cost of goods sold.

128. A chain retailer has outlets in forty nonoverlapping though similar local markets. Recently, the retailer conducted its largest promotional campaign ever. Each outlet was unrestricted in allocating its promotional budget between local print, radio, or television advertising or in underspending the budget. The internal auditor wishes to evaluate the effectiveness of these tactics. In this case

a. Time series analysis should be used since the promotion occurred over time.
b. Multiple regression analysis may be an effective tool for modeling the relationship between sales and promotional tactics.
c. Discriminant analysis would be the best tool for discriminating between effective and ineffective promotional tactics.
d. Since the relationships between promotional expenditures and sales are probably nonlinear, regression analysis should not be used.

129. The management of an airline is interested in the relationship between maintenance costs and the level of operations of its aircraft. Using regression analysis on cost and activity data collected over the past twelve months, the relationship depicted below was estimated.

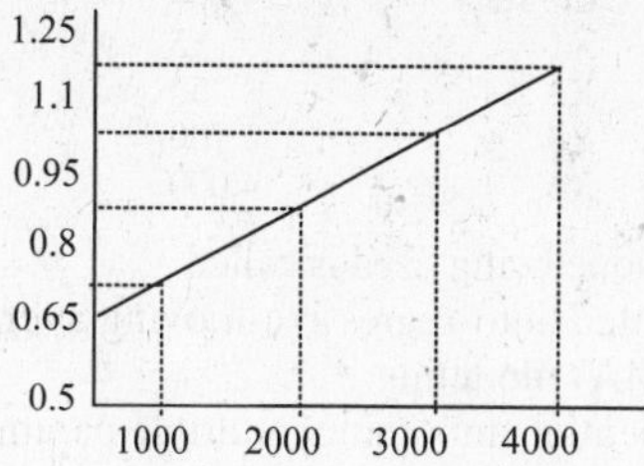

The estimated increase in the monthly maintenance cost for each additional hour of operation is

a. $150 per hour.
b. $300 per hour.
c. $450 per hour.
d. $750 per hour.

130. What coefficient of correlation would result from the following data?

X	Y
1	10
2	8
3	6
4	4
5	2

a. 0
b. -1
c. +1
d. Cannot be determined from the data given.

131. The manager of the shipping department of a company believes that estimation of the fixed and variable components of the department's costs will facilitate forecasting these costs for planning and budgeting purposes. An appropriate technique for estimating fixed and variable cost components is

a. Regression (least squares) analysis.
b. Game theory.
c. Sensitivity analysis.
d. Queuing analysis.

132. A university admissions committee believes that standardized test scores, high school grade point average, and the rigor of high school courses are the most important variables in predicting undergraduate grade point average (GPA). The technique appropriate for modeling expected undergraduate GPA would be

a. Multiple regression analysis.
b. Exponential smoothing.
c. Bivariate regression analysis.
d. Auto-regressive model.

Items 133 through 137 are based on the following:

Many firms have site location models to predict future sales (Y) at locations yet to be developed. Some explanatory variables that could be used are: population density within a specific radius (X1), traffic flow (X2), the number of competitors (X3), and the ease of entry into and out of the proposed site (X4). An abbreviated computer printout of a linear analysis yields:

Dependent variable: Y N: 12
R: .986 R squared: .972
Standard error: 3800

Variable	*Coefficient*
Constant	124,000
X1	5
X2	350
X3	-1,700
X4	4,000

133. The technique being used is called
a. Integrated auto-regressive-moving average (ARIMA) modeling.
b. Exponential smoothing, multiple parameters.
c. Multiple regression analysis.
d. Linear programming.

134. The relationships existing between the dependent variable and the independent variables can best be described as
a. Three direct relationships and one inverse relationship.
b. Three indirect relationships and one direct relationship.
c. Two direct and two indirect relationships.
d. Four direct relationships.

135. One of the variables (X4) is very unusual because either there is a problem with entry into the site or there is not. We may then assign a "0" for no entry problems and a "1" for having entry problems. Such a variable is called a(n)
a. Multicollinear variable.
b. Dummy variable.
c. Omitted variable.
d. Outlier.

136. According to the computer printout, if traffic flow increased by one more unit, sales would
a. Decrease by 1,700.
b. Increase by 350.
c. Increase by 5.
d. Increase by 4,000.

137. If, for a site being considered, X1=10,000, X2=300, X3=9, and X4=1, the predicted sales would equal
a. 124,000
b. 126,655
c. 143,700
d. 267,700

138. The following data on variables x and y was collected from June to October:

	June	*July*	*August*	*September*	*October*
x	24	31	19	15	22
y	104	76	124	140	112

The correlation coefficient between variables x and y is nearest to
a. 1.00
b. -1.00
c. 0.50
d. 0.00

139. The linear regression equation, Y=15.8 + 1.1(x), was used to prepare the table below.

Actual X	*Predicted Y*	*Actual Y*	*Residual*
0	15.8	10	-5.8
1	16.9	18	1.1
2	18.0	27	9.0
3	19.1	21	1.9
4	20.2	14	-6.2

The best description of the existing problem is that
a. Autocorrelation is exhibited.
b. The relationship is not linear.
c. The data is simply not related.
d. The data is inversely related.

140. A company wishes to forecast from time series data covering 20 periods. Which of the following is not an appropriate forecasting technique?
a. Weighted least squares
b. Exponential smoothing
c. The Delphi technique
d. The moving average process

141. A firm plans to develop a sales forecasting model. The requirements are that the model be able to forecast accurately and relate sales to a set of predictor variables, such as, the product's price, advertising expenditures, consumer income per capita, and the price of a competing product. Based on the information given, which of the following quantitative techniques would be most appropriate?
a. Linear programming.
b. Exponential smoothing.
c. Trend extrapolation.
d. Multiple regression.

Project Management Techniques

142. A project is defined as a
a. Temporary endeavor.
b. Continuous endeavor.
c. Expensive endeavor.
d. Endless endeavor.

143. The most important skill for setting priorities and managing time is
a. Learning to say no.
b. Establishing ABC priority system.
c. Following the 80/20 principle.
d. Performing the Pareto analysis.

144. Which of the following is the first stage of the project life cycle?
a. Termination.
b. Conceptualization.
c. Planning.
d. Execution.

145. Budget demands are the highest in which of the following stage of the project life cycle?
a. Termination.
b. Conceptualization.
c. Planning.
d. Execution.

146. Project-based organizations are becoming common today due to
a. Lack of middle management layer.
b. Need for quick response to customers.
c. Vertical organization structure.
d. Profitability goals.

147. Eliminating wasted activities, tasks, and steps is called
a. Job elimination.
b. Work simplification.
c. Job specification.
d. Work measurement.

148. Which of the following is the least desirable skill of a project manager?

a. Leadership skill.
b. Technical skill.
c. Conflict resolution skill.
d. Negotiation skill.

149. Establishing project priorities remains a(n)
a. Subjective process.
b. Objective process.
c. Centralized process.
d. Decentralized process.

150. In the ABC priority system used in project time management, the 'B' system deals with which of the following?
a. "Must do" objectives.
b. "Should do" objectives.
c. "Nice to do" objectives.
d. "Could do" objectives.

151. In which of the following project organizational structures does each group or component concentrate on performing its own activities in support of the company's business mission?
a. Matrix.
b. Functional.
c. Progressive.
d. Project.

152. In which of the following project organizational structures does the project manager **not** have complete authority over the project team?
a. Matrix.
b. Functional.
c. Functional and matrix.
d. Project.

153. In which of the following project organizational structures is the project manager responsible for the project results while functional managers are responsible for providing the resources needed to achieve the results?
a. Matrix.
b. Functional.
c. Mixed-mode.
d. Project.

154. All of the work that must be done in order to satisfy the customer that the deliverables meet the requirements or acceptable criteria agreed upon at the onset of the project is called
a. Scope.
b. Plan.
c. Schedule.
d. Objective.

155. Ultimately, the responsibility of the project manager is to
a. Finish the project as quickly as possible.
b. Finish the project as cheaply as possible.
c. Make sure the customer is satisfied.
d. Make independent decisions.

156. Which of the following describes a hierarchical tree of network elements or end items that will be accomplished or produced by the project team during the project?
a. Workload structure.
b. Project breakdown diagram.
c. Work breakdown structure.
d. Project task distribution list.

157. Which of the following measures actual progress of a project and compares it to planned progress on a timely and regular basis and taking corrective action immediately?
a. Project planning.
b. Work breakdown.
c. Project control.
d. Quality control.

158. The project control process starts with establishing which of the following?
a. A baseline plan.
b. A work order form.
c. A schedule assignment.
d. A time-cost tradeoff.

159. When modifying a project schedule, which of the following activities usually presents the opportunity for larger time reductions?
a. Shorter duration.
b. Longer duration.
c. Near term.
d. Future.

160. Which of the following tradeoffs is used to incrementally reduce the project duration with the smallest increase in cost?
a. Schedule-quality.
b. Cost-production time.
c. Time-quality.
d. Time-cost.

161. In project management, the two basic types of contracts include which of the following?
a. Flat price and cost analysis.
b. Fixed price and incremental cost.
c. Flat price and cost reimbursement.
d. Fixed price and cost reimbursement.

162. Which of the following contracts is most appropriate for projects that involve risk?
a. Fixed price.
b. Flat price.
c. Time and profit.
d. Cost reimbursement.

163. For a project, the objective is usually defined in terms of scope, cost, and which of the following?
a. Plan.
b. Schedule.
c. Controls.
d. Tasks.

164. In project management, each activity has two pairs of duration called
a. Normal and crash time.
b. Normal and budget time.
c. Actual and crash time.
d. Quantity and quality time.

165. In project management, which of the following measures the cost efficiency with which the project is being performed?
a. Cost efficiency index.
b. Cost quality index.
c. Cost production index.
d. Cost performance index.

166. In project management, which of the following computes the difference between the cumulative earned value of the work performed and the cumulative actual cost?
a. Cost performance index.
b. Cost variance.
c. Budgeted costs.
d. Cost quality index.

167. In project management, the cost performance analysis should include identifying those work packages that have a negative cost variance or a cost performance index of less than which of the following?
a. 1.0
b. 1.5
c. 2.0
d. 2.5

168. Which of the following determines a project's duration based on technological and resource contention constraints?
a. Critical parameters.
b. Critical chain.
c. Critical ratio.
d. Critical success factors.

169. In project management, which of the following includes the total value, including overhead, of approved estimates for completed activities?
a. Earned value.
b. Critical value.
c. Planned value.
d. Noncritical value.

170. Which of the following is heavily weighted in calculating a Program Evaluation and Review Technique's (PERT's) expected time?
a. Optimistic time.
b. Most likely.
c. Pessimistic time.
d. Actual time.

171. Which of the following shows the appropriate sequence and interrelationship of activities to accomplish the overall project work scope?
a. Bubble diagram.
b. Network ladder.
c. Network diagram.
d. Responsibility chart.

172. The Gantt chart used in project management combines which of the following functions?
a. Planning and leveling
b. Scheduling and evaluating
c. Planning and scheduling
d. Scheduling and controlling

173. Which of the following techniques used in project management separate the planning and scheduling functions?
a. Gantt chart.
b. Work breakdown structure.
c. Network diagram.
d. Responsibility matrix.

174. In project management, activities are linked in which of the following order?
a. Linear order.
b. Parallel order.
c. Precedential order.
d. Regressive order.

175. Which of the following is used for projects that have a set of activities that are repeated several times?
a. Truncation.
b. Looping.
c. Laddering.
d. Transitions.

176. In project management, which of the following times are determined by calculating forward through the network?
a. Earliest start time and earliest finish time.
b. Latest start time and latest finish time.
c. Earliest start time and latest start time.
d. Earliest finish time and latest finish time.

177. Which of the following describes the latest time by which a particular activity must be finished in order for the entire project to be completed by its required completion time?
a. Earliest start time.
b. Earliest finish time.
c. Latest start time.
d. Latest finish time.

178. Which of the following equations can calculate total slack in a project?
a. Latest finish time minus earliest finish time.
b. Latest finish time minus latest start time.
c. Earliest finish time minus earliest start time.
d. Latest finish time minus earliest start time.

179. In project management, which of the following uses only one time estimate for an activity?
a. Deterministic model.
b. Stochastic model.
c. Probabilistic model.
d. Steady-state model.

180. Which of the following measures planned and completed work for each stage of a project by time elapsed?
a. Time and work chart.
b. Gantt chart.
c. Time and motion chart.
d. Production and delivery chart.

181. One of the drawbacks to the traditional Gantt chart used in project management is that it does not graphically display which of the following?
a. Order of activities.
b. Timeframe of activities.
c. Interrelationships of activities.
d. Structure of activities.

182. The critical path in a program evaluation and review technique (PERT) network is the most
a. Efficient path.
b. Time-consuming path.
c. Labor-intensive path.
d. Expensive path.

183. Program evaluation and review technique (PERT) is most appropriate for
a. Small, routine projects.
b. Small, unique projects.
c. Large, nonroutine projects.
d. Large, repetitive projects.

184. Which of the following Gantt chart features is an improvement over the flowchart?
a. Dollar amounts.
b. Time elements.
c. Task descriptions.
d. Resource requirements.

185. Working from the last node to the start node through the network logic of a project in order to determine late start dates and late finish dates is called
a. Forward pass.
b. Backward pass.
c. Backward integration.
d. Vertical integration.

186. Which of the following would be a long-range rather than a short-range planning topic?
a. Production scheduling.
b. Inventory policy.
c. Product quality.
d. Advertising budget.

187. The process of adding resources to shorten selected activity times on the critical path in project scheduling is called
a. Crashing.
b. The Delphi technique.
c. ABC analysis.
d. A branch-and-bound solution.

188. The following information applies to a project:

Activity	*Time (days)*	*Immediate predecessor*
A	5	None
B	3	None
C	4	A
D	2	B
E	6	C, D

The earliest completion time for the project is
a. 11 days.
b. 14 days.
c. 15 days.
d. 20 days.

189. A bank is designing an on-the-job training program for its branch managers. The bank would like to design the program so that participants can complete it as quickly as possible. The training program requires that certain activities be completed before others. For example, a participant cannot make credit loan decisions without first having obtained experience in the loan department. An appropriate scheduling technique for this training program is
a. PERT/CPM.
b. Linear programming.
c. Queuing theory.
d. Sensitivity analysis.

190. Which of the following terms is **not** used in project management?
a. Dummy activity.
b. Latest finish.
c. Optimistic time.
d. Lumpy demand.

191. Various tools are employed to control large-scale projects. They include all of the following **except:**
a. PERT.
b. CPM.
c. Statistical process control.
d. Gantt charts.

192. Activity scheduling information for the installation of a new computer system is given below.

Activity	*Immediate predecessor*	*Duration (days)*
A	--	4
B	--	3
C	A	9
D	A	6
E	B, D	5

For this project, the critical path is
a. A-C
b. B-E
c. A-D-E
d. B-D-C

193. In a critical path analysis, if slack time in an activity exists, it refers to the fact that the activity
a. Is not essential to the overall project.
b. Is a backup activity to replace a main activity should it fail.
c. Could be delayed without delaying the overall project.
d. Involves essentially no time to complete.

194. A Gantt chart is a graphical scheduling technique typically applied to production applications. The structure of the chart shows
a. Cost in dollars plotted against units of output.
b. The sequencing and relationship of steps in a production process.
c. Output plotted against units of time.
d. The "critical path" in a chain of activities.

195. A corporation uses CPM/PERT to plan the development of a new cordless food processor. The primary purpose of determining the "critical path" related to this project is to identify
a. Those activities that must be completed exactly as scheduled if the development of the new cordless food processor is to be completed on time.
b. The maximum amount of time an activity on the critical path may be delayed without delaying the scheduled development of the new food processor.
c. The optimal size of the new food processor.
d. What features should be incorporated in the new food processor.

Business Process Analysis

196. Which of the following is **not** one of the areas of the theory of constraints?
a. Bottleneck management.
b. Logistics.
c. Performance measurement.
d. Logical thinking.

197. Which of the following is **not** part of the logistics area of the theory of constraints?
a. Drum-buffer-rope scheduling.
b. Problem solving.
c. Buffer management.
d. VAT analysis.

198. Which of the following is **not** part of the performance measurement area of the theory of constraints?
a. Throughput.

b. Inventory.
c. Current reality tree.
d. Operating expense.

199. Which of the following starts with one or a few raw materials in the theory of constraints?
a. A "V" logical structure.
b. An "A" logical structure.
c. A "T" logical structure.
d. A general structure.

200. Which of the following is appropriate for discovering delays or possibilities for mistakes in conveying information in the way office and administrative tasks are carried out?
a. Clerical process analysis.
b. Joint process analysis.
c. Operator process analysis.
d. Product process analysis.

201. A process delivers value through all of the following items **except:**
a. Selling.
b. Quality.
c. Cost reduction.
d. Flexibility.

202. Which of the following structures yields greater efficiency and production and is achieved by reengineering or process redesign?
a. Functional organization.
b. Hierarchical organization.
c. Horizontal organization.
d. Vertical organization.

203. An organization should **not** have which of the following business process orientations?
a. Functional view.
b. Process jobs.
c. Process management and measures.
d. Process structure.

204. Which of the following dimensions of business process orientations is the most important one?
a. Process view.
b. Process jobs.
c. Process management and measures.
d. Process structure.

205. A radical redesign of the entire business cycle is called
a. Business process reengineering.
b. Benchmarking.
c. Best practices.
d. Business process improvement.

206. Which of the following involves identifying, studying, and building upon the best practices of other organizations?
a. Kaizen.
b. Benchmarking.
c. Plan, do, check, and act cycle.
d. Total quality management.

207. Cycle time can be either reduced or speeded up with
a. Business process reengineering.
b. Benchmarking.
c. Best practices.
d. Business process improvement.

208. "The time between when an order is placed and when it is received by the customer" is known as
a. Arrival time.
b. Order cycle time.
c. Shipping time.
d. Order time.

209. "The time it takes to deliver a product or service after an order is placed" is called
a. Order cycle time.
b. Customer response time.
c. Order process time.
d. Inspection time.

210. "The time between when an order is placed and when the order is ready for setup" is called
a. Order receipt time.
b. Order wait time.
c. Order process time.
d. Efficiency time.

211. "The time between when an order is ready for setup and the setup is complete" is called
a. Order receipt time.
b. Order wait time.
c. Order process time.
d. Efficiency time.

212. Which of the following refers to eliminating unnecessary procedures and activities in a business process?
a. Work standardization.
b. Work simplification.
c. Work customization.
d. Work measurement.

213. A company faces a constraint when
a. Its operating fixed costs are excessive.
b. The capacity to manufacture a product is limited.
c. Its capital costs are excessive.
d. It is highly leveraged.

214. If a company is faced with a limited resource, which of the following is **not** a feasible choice for alleviating the constraint?
a. Increase the capacity of the limited resource.
b. Ignore the constraint.
c. Reduce the use of the limited resource in production.
d. Focus on products that require less of the limited resource.

215. The theory of constraints
a. Is best associated with horizontal integration.
b. Is best associated with vertical integration.
c. Identifies bottlenecks in the production process.
d. Identifies throughput in the production process.

216. Which of the following statements is **not** true about bottlenecks?
a. Bottlenecks limit throughput.
b. Bottlenecks should be ignored during crisis situations.
c. Bottlenecks are managed using the theory of constraints.
d. Bottlenecks should be relieved to increase production efficiency.

Items 217 to 219 are based on the following:

A manufacturing company has the following estimates for a specific customer order to produce 50 toy sets.

Wait time	10 hours
Inspection time	1 hour
Processing time	36 hours
Move time	1.5 hours

217. Using these time estimates, what is the value-added time?

a. 36 hours.
b. 37 hours.
c. 38.5 hours.
d. 48.5 hours.

218. Using these time estimates, what is the non-value-added time?

a. 2.5 hours.
b. 10.0 hours.
c. 11.0 hours.
d. 12.5 hours.

219. Using these time estimates, what is the manufacturing cycle time?

a. 36.00 hours.
b. 46.00 hours.
c. 47.00 hours.
d. 48.50 hours.

220. Regarding the theory of constraints, which of the following bonds cause-and-effect relationships and connects all the existing major undesirable effects?

a. The current reality tree.
b. The future reality tree.
c. The prerequisite tree.
d. The transition tree.

221. Regarding the theory of constraints, which of the following is **not** an example of an undesirable effect?

a. Too much production.
b. Too much inventory.
c. Too many orders that are not shipped as scheduled.
d. Too much expediting of orders.

222. Regarding the theory of constraints, each entry to the current reality tree does **not** identify which of the following?

a. A root cause.
b. Most desirable effects.
c. A core problem.
d. Most undesirable effects.

223. Which of the following actions does **not** help in reducing the cycle time?

a. Changing from parallel flow to linear flow in a process.
b. Using alternate flow paths in a process.
c. Changing the layout of a process.
d. Using technology to improve process flow.

224. In reducing cycle time, speed flows from which of the following?

a. Complexity.
b. Simplicity.
c. Homogenity.
d. Heterogeneity.

225. Which of the following is **not** generally associated with reducing cycle time?

a. Expanding work steps.
b. Eliminating work steps.
c. Minimizing work steps.
d. Combining work steps.

226. Which of the following is caused by exceeding the capacity limitation of key resources?

a. Fault points.
b. Check points.
c. Critical points.
d. Choke points.

227. Which of the following actions does **not** help in reducing the cycle time?

a. Eliminating process waste.
b. Creating continuous workflow.
c. Using self-managed teams.
d. Providing the right resources.

228. Which of the following accounting systems aggressively exploits the constraint(s) to make more money for a firm?

I. Constraint accounting.
II. Activity-based accounting.
III. Direct cost accounting.
IV. Throughput accounting.

a. I and II.
b. II and III.
c. I and IV.
d. III and IV.

229. In the theory of constraints, the drum-buffer-rope scheduling system maximizes

a. Inventory.
b. Throughput.
c. Nonconstraints.
d. Constraints.

230. All of the following are effective ways to shorten the cycle time **except:**

a. Small lot sizes.
b. Synchronized production plans.
c. Just-in-time manufacturing.
d. "Push" production method.

231. All of the following are effective methods to alleviate bottleneck production cells in a synchronized production plan **except:**

a. Moving the production to other cells.
b. Increasing the capacity by overtime.
c. Increasing the capacity by overloading the cell.
d. Decreasing the production cell utilization significantly.

232. Input material that does not become part of the finished product and has relatively minor economic value is classified as

a. Scrap.
b. Spoilage.
c. Defective product.
d. Waste.

233. A company has excess capacity in production-related fixed assets. If in a given year these fixed assets were being used to only 80% of capacity and the sales level in that year was $2,000,000, the full capacity sales level is

a. $ 1,600,000

b. $ 2,000,000
c. $ 2,500,000
d. $10,000,000

234. Which of the following is true of benchmarking?
a. It is typically accomplished by comparing an organization's performance with the performance of its closest competitors.
b. It can be performed using either qualitative or quantitative comparisons.
c. It is normally limited to manufacturing operations and production processes.
d. It is accomplished by comparing an organization's performance to that of the best-performing organizations.

235. A means of limiting production delays caused by equipment breakdown and repair is to
a. Schedule production based on capacity planning.
b. Plan maintenance activity based on an analysis of equipment repair work orders.
c. Pre-authorize equipment maintenance and overtime pay.
d. Establish a preventive maintenance program for all production equipment.

236. An internal auditor's involvement in reengineering should include all of the following **except:**
a. Determining whether the process has senior management's support.
b. Recommending areas for consideration.
c. Developing audit plans for the new system.
d. Directing the implementation of the redesigned process.

237. Which of the following will allow a manufacturer with limited resources to maximize profits?
a. The Delphi technique.
b. Exponential smoothing.
c. Regression analysis.
d. Linear programming.

238. Reengineering is the thorough analysis, fundamental rethinking, and complete redesign of essential business processes. The intended result is a dramatic improvement in service, quality, speed, and cost. An internal auditor's involvement in reengineering should include all of the following **except:**
a. Determining whether the process has senior management's support.
b. Recommending areas for consideration.
c. Developing audit plans for the new system.
d. Directing the implementation of the redesigned process.

239. An example of an internal nonfinancial benchmark is
a. The labor rate of comparably skilled employees at a major competitor's plant.
b. The average actual cost per pound of a specific product at the company's most efficient plant becomes the benchmark for the company's other plants.
c. The company setting a benchmark of $50,000 for employee training programs at each of the company's plants.
d. The percent of customer orders delivered on time at the company's most efficient plant becomes the benchmark for the company's other plants.

240. Auditors are operating in organizations in which management is in the process of "reengineering" operations with strong emphasis on total quality management techniques. In their quest to gain efficiency in processing, many of the traditional control procedures are being deleted from the organization's control structure. As part of this change, management is
a. Placing more emphasis on monitoring control activities.
b. Making different assumptions about human performance and the nature of human motivation than was done under traditional control techniques.
c. Placing more emphasis on self-correcting control activities and process automation.
d. All of the above.

241. A company, which has many branch stores, has decided to benchmark one of its stores for the purpose of analyzing the accuracy and reliability of branch store financial reporting. Which one of the following is the most likely measure to be included in a financial benchmark?
a. High turnover of employees.
b. High level of employee participation in setting budgets.
c. High amount of bad debt write-offs.
d. High number of suppliers.

242. An organization has decided to reengineer several major processes. Of the following reasons for employees to resist this change, which is **least** likely?
a. Threat of loss of jobs.
b. Required attendance at training classes.
c. Breakup of existing work groups.
d. Imposition of new processes by top management without prior discussion.

Inventory Management Techniques and Concepts

243. A company's attempt to hold the lowest level of inventory that will still enable it to meet customer demand is known as
a. Order cycle time.
b. Just-in-time management.
c. Supply-chain management.
d. Inventory control.

244. Inventory carrying costs include which of the following?
a. Storage costs.
b. Advertising costs.
c. Packaging costs.
d. Sales promotion costs.

245. Which of the following is defined as the point where inventory carrying costs and ordering costs are at their lowest?
a. Breakeven point.
b. Order cycle time.
c. Economic order quantity.
d. Marginal price.

246. Effective inventory management is key to improving all of the following **except:**
a. Purchasing.
b. Customer service.

c. Cash flow.
d. Profitability.

247. Which of the following shows the dichotomies of inventory control?
a. Customer service.
b. Inventory costs.
c. Stock levels.
d. Operating costs.

248. The primary reason for maintaining safety stock is due to
a. Failure on the supply side.
b. Inability to predict demand.
c. Technical and mechanical breakdowns.
d. Information and communication failures.

249. A company's inventory stockholding practices depend on which of the following?
a. Customer service levels.
b. Inexpensive purchases.
c. Objectives and policies.
d. Volume discount purchases.

250. Which of the following elements of inventory demand management affects customer service?
a. Order receipts.
b. Order processing.
c. Product delivery.
d. Customer feedback.

251. All of the following are effective ways of managing the inventory **except:**
a. Pareto analysis.
b. ABC analysis.
c. JIT approach.
d. Safety stock.

252. In the ABC analysis, class "C" inventory consists of which of the following?
a. Many items and low turnover rate.
b. Few items and high turnover rate.
c. Many items and medium turnover rate.
d. Few items and medium turnover rate.

253. In the ABC analysis, class "B" inventory consists of which of the following?
a. Managed with tight control.
b. Managed by JIT approach.
c. Managed by exception.
d. Managed with minimum supervision.

254. In the ABC analysis, class "A" inventory uses a(n)

I. Sophisticated forecasting system.
II. Simple tracking system.
III. Infrequent ordering rules.
IV. Service level policy.

a. I and II.
b. II and III.
c. I and IV.
d. III and IV.

255. Which of the following buries defects in the manufacturing process?
a. Raw materials.
b. Parts and components.
c. Work-in-process.
d. Finished goods.

256. Which of the following does **not** help in meeting customer expectations and reducing inventories?
a. Reducing cycle time.
b. Reducing inventory levels.
c. Eliminating waste in all processes.
d. Lowering interest rates.

257. Which of the following inventory recordkeeping method reduces the inventory of components before issue at the time a scheduled receipt for their parents or assemblies is created via a bill-of-material explosion?
a. Prededuct inventory transaction processing.
b. Backflush inventory method.
c. Explode-to-deduct inventory method.
d. Postdeduct inventory transaction processing.

258. Which of the following uses more than one level of bill-of-material and extending back to the previous points where production was counted?

I. Count point method.
II. Count point backflush method.
III. Key point backflush method.
IV. Pay point method.

a. I and II.
b. II and III.
c. I and IV.
d. III and IV.

259. In an economic order quantity (EOQ) model, both the costs per order and the holding costs are estimates. If those estimates are varied to determine how much the changes affect the optimal EOQ, such analysis would be called a
a. Forecasting model.
b. Sensitivity analysis.
c. Critical path method analysis.
d. Decision analysis.

260. An appropriate technique for planning and controlling manufacturing inventories, such as raw materials, components, and subassemblies, whose demand depends on the level of production, is
a. Materials requirements planning.
b. Regression analysis.
c. Capital budgeting.
d. Linear programming.

261. If a just-in-time (JIT) purchase policy is successful in reducing the total inventory costs of a manufacturing company, which of the following combinations of cost changes would be most likely to occur?
a. An increase in purchasing costs and a decrease in stockout costs.
b. An increase in purchasing costs and a decrease in quality costs.
c. An increase in quality costs and a decrease in ordering costs.
d. An increase in stockout costs and a decrease in carrying costs.

262. A company sells 1,500 units of a particular item each year and orders the items in equal quantities of 500 units at a price of $5 per unit. No safety stocks are held. If the company has a cost of capital of 12%, its annual cost of carrying inventory is

a. $150
b. $180
c. $300
d. $900

263. The internal auditor of a retailing company is auditing the purchasing area. To evaluate the efficiency of purchase transactions, the auditor decides to calculate the economic order quantity for a sample of the company's products. To calculate the economic order quantity, the internal auditor would need data for all of the following **except:**

a. The volume of product sales.
b. The purchase prices of the products.
c. The fixed cost of ordering products.
d. The volume of products in inventory.

264. A company has a specified inventory that it maintains even if no sales occur. It also maintains additional inventory that is positively related to the amount of expected sales. The company's financial forecasting of inventory in the following year would be most accurate when applying

a. Last year's inventory items as the forecast.
b. Last year's inventory as a percentage of total assets to derive the forecast.
c. The percentage of sales method.
d. Simple linear regression.

265. Which of the following is **not** considered a cost of carrying inventory?

a. Shipping and handling.
b. Property tax.
c. Insurance.
d. Depreciation and obsolescence.

266. The economic order quantity (EOQ) for inventory is higher for an organization that has

a. Lower annual unit sales.
b. Higher fixed inventory ordering costs.
c. Higher annual carrying costs as a percentage of inventory value.
d. A higher purchase price per unit of inventory.

267. An organization has an inventory order quantity of 10,000 units and a safety stock of 2,000 units. The cost per unit of inventory is $5 and the carrying cost is 10% of the average value of inventory. The annual inventory carrying cost for the organization is

a. $3,000
b. $3,500
c. $5,000
d. $6,000

268. As a company increases its inventory order size, the total (List A) cost of inventory (List B)

	List A	*List B*
a.	Carrying	Decreases
b.	Carrying	Is unchanged
c.	Ordering	Decreases
d.	Ordering	Is unchanged

269. When the economic order quantity (EOQ) decision model is employed, the (List A) are being offset or balanced by the (List B).

	List A	*List B*
a.	Ordering costs	Carrying costs
b.	Purchase costs	Carrying costs
c.	Purchase costs	Quality costs
d.	Ordering costs	Stockout costs

270. One of the elements included in the economic order quantity (EOQ) formula is

a. Safety stock.
b. Yearly demand.
c. Selling price of item.
d. Lead time for delivery.

Items 271 and 272 are based on the following:

Using an EOQ analysis (assuming a constant demand) it is determined that the optimal order quantity is 2,500. The company desires a safety stock of 500 units. A five-day lead time is needed for delivery. Annual inventory holding costs equal 25% of the average inventory level. It costs the company $4 per unit to buy the product which it sells for $8. It costs the company $150 to place a detailed order and the monthly demand for the product is 4,000 units.

271. Annual inventory holding costs equal

a. $ 850
b. $1,250
c. $1,750
d. $2,250

272. Total inventory ordering costs per year equal

a. $1,250
b. $1,800
c. $2,880
d. $4,130

273. In forecasting purchases of inventory for a firm, all of the following are useful **except:**

a. Knowledge of the behavior of business cycles.
b. Internal allocations of costs to different segments of the firm.
c. Information on the seasonal variations in demand.
d. Econometric modeling.

274. An organization sells a product for which demand is uncertain. Management would like to ensure that there is sufficient inventory on hand during periods of high demand so that it does not lose sales (and customers). To do so, the organization should

a. Keep a safety stock.
b. Use a just-in-time inventory system.
c. Employ a materials requirement planning system.
d. Keep a master production schedule.

275. The economic order quantity (EOQ) is the size of the order that minimizes total inventory costs, which include ordering and holding costs. It can be calculated using the formula

$$Q = \sqrt{\frac{2Dp}{s}}$$

where Q = order size in units, D = annual demand in units, p = cost per purchase order, s = carrying cost per year for one unit of inventory. If the annual demand decreases by 36% the optimal order size will

a. Decrease by 20%.
b. Increase by 20%.

c. Increase by 6%.
d. Decrease by 6%.

276. The purpose of the economic order quantity model is to
a. Minimize the safety stock.
b. Minimize the sum of the order costs and the holding costs.
c. Minimize the inventory quantities.
d. Minimize the sum of the demand costs and the backlog costs.

277. To be even more effective, the company was considering investing in automated equipment to decrease setup times. The payback period was not considered quick enough to justify the investment. The company could refine the analysis of the investment by considering
a. No other factors since the only benefit from the equipment is to decrease setup times.
b. Reductions in inventory permitted by reducing average batch sizes.
c. Efficiencies gained by getting suppliers to deliver better-quality raw materials.
d. Economies achieved by bar coding batches of raw materials before production.

278. Which of the following inventory items would be the **most** frequently reviewed in an ABC inventory control system?
a. Expensive, frequently used, high stock-out cost items with short lead times.
b. Expensive, frequently used, low stock-out cost items with long lead times.
c. Inexpensive, frequently used, high stockout cost items with long lead times.
d. Expensive, frequently used, high stock-out cost items with long lead times.

279. If a company's cost of ordering (per order) increases while carrying costs per order remain the same, the optimal order size as specified by the economic order quantity model would
a. Be unaffected.
b. Increase.
c. Decrease.
d. Be affected, but the direction of change cannot be determined without additional information.

280. A local charitable organization orders and sells Christmas trees to raise funds. They want to know the optimum quantity to order. Any merchandise not sold will be discarded without scrap value. This is an example of a single-period inventory model, which is solved using
a. Economic order quantity.
b. Payoff tables.
c. Material requirements planning.
d. Game theory.

281. Which of the following inventory control techniques divides items into subclassifications and uses different control systems for each classification?
a. ABC method.
b. Economic order quantity model.
c. Just-in-time system.
d. Material requirements planning system.

282. What are the three factors a manager should consider in controlling stockouts?
a. Holding costs, quality costs, and physical inventories.
b. Economic order quantity, annual demand, and quality costs.
c. Time needed for delivery, rate of inventory usage, and safety stock.
d. Economic order quantity, production bottlenecks, and safety stock.

283. Reordering of specific items from vendors should be based on
a. Computations on the basis of economic order quantities.
b. Demand forecasting based on early orders for the items.
c. Market demographics.
d. Vendor quantity discounts and warehouse space.

284. A company has the following requirement for a part during production of a finished product:

Daily requirement for part	*Probability*
50	0.2
60	0.5
70	0.2
80	0.1
	1.0

To ensure a 90% probability of sufficient stockage the daily beginning balance of the part should be
a. 50
b. 60
c. 70
d. 80

285. A manufacturer is considering using bar-code identification for recording information on parts used by the manufacturer. A reason to use bar codes rather than other means of identification is to ensure that
a. The movement of all parts is recorded.
b. The movement of parts is easily and quickly recorded.
c. Vendors use the same part numbers.
d. Vendors use the same identification methods.

286. A manufacturing company is attempting to implement a just-in-time (JIT) purchase policy system by negotiating with its primary suppliers to accept long-term purchase orders which result in more frequent deliveries of smaller quantities of raw materials. If the JIT purchase policy is successful in reducing the total inventory costs of the manufacturing company, which of the following combinations of cost changes would be most likely to occur?

	Cost category to increase	*Cost category to decrease*
a.	Purchasing costs	Stockout costs
b.	Purchasing costs	Quality costs
c.	Quality costs	Ordering costs
d.	Stockout costs	Carrying costs

287. A risk associated with just-in-time (JIT) production is the
a. Increased potential for early obsolescence of inventories of finished goods.
b. High cost of material handling equipment.
c. Potential for significant costs associated with reworking defective components.
d. Critical dependency on a few vendors.

288. An inventory planning method that minimizes inventories by arranging to have raw materials and subcomponents arrive immediately preceding their use is called

a. A safety stock planning system.
b. An economic order quantity model.
c. A just-in-time inventory system.
d. A master budgeting system.

289. The owner of a large automobile repair facility wants to implement a just-in-time (JIT) system of inventory control for the spare parts inventory. That system would be **inappropriate** because

a. It would be too difficult to identify the items that have to be most closely controlled.
b. An auto parts inventory is too diverse to use JIT inventory control techniques.
c. Both sales rates and order lead times must be known for certain.
d. Delivery of raw material or components has to be coordinated to a schedule.

290. Just-in-time (JIT) inventory systems have been adopted by large manufacturers to minimize the carrying costs of inventories. Identify the primary vulnerability of JIT systems

a. Computer resources.
b. Materials supply contracts.
c. Work stoppages.
d. Implementation time.

291. A manufacturing cell's partial productivity can be measured using data on

a. Inventory shrinkage.
b. Inventory turnover.
c. Direct material usage.
d. Scrap.

292. Increased competition, technological innovation, and a shift from mass production of standardized products to custom-produced products in many industries have increased the need for productivity improvement and flexibility of production systems. In response to these demands, organizations have increased their reliance on automation and the use of advanced technologies in their operations. Which of the following is an example of the use of automation and advanced technologies?

a. Flexible manufacturing system.
b. Just-in-time system.
c. Master budgeting system.
d. Economic order quantity.

293. A major justification for investments in computer integrated manufacturing (CIM) projects is

a. Reduction in the costs of spoilage, reworked units, and scrap.
b. Lower book value and depreciation expense for factory equipment.
c. Increased working capital.
d. Stabilization of market share.

294. Which of the following is an advantage of adopting a just-in-time (JIT) inventory system?

a. A formal receiving department may be eliminated.
b. A bill of materials outlines when all materials will be needed on a week-by-week basis.
c. There will be greater emphasis on reducing per unit purchase costs.
d. Late deliveries of materials are less of a problem.

295. Which of the following is **not** involved with facility layout and design issues?

a. Cellular manufacturing.
b. Operations sequence analysis.
c. Program Evaluation and Review Technique (PERT).
d. Line balancing.

Items 296 and 297 are based on the following:

The following types of electronic advancements might be used by financial service organizations, manufacturing firms, and/or service organizations. In answering these two questions you will be asked to identify which of the following items are used in each type of organization.

I. Flexible manufacturing systems.
II. Automated teller machines.
III. Automated storage and retrieval systems.
IV. Computer-aided design.
V. Computer-integrated manufacturing.
VI. CAT scanners.
VII. Bar code systems.
VIII. Electronic funds transfer.
IX. Autopilot systems.
X. Magnetic-ink character recognition codes.
XI. Automated reservations systems.
XII. Document imaging systems.

296. Which of the above examples of automated systems are used in financial services firms?

a. II, III, IV, and VII.
b. II, VIII, X, and XII.
c. II, III, IV and X.
d. VIII, X, XI, and XII.

297. Which of the above automated systems are used in manufacturing firms and which are used in service firms?

	Manufacturing	*Service*
a.	I, II, III, and IV.	VII, VIII, IX, and X.
b.	II, IV, V, and XII.	VI, IX, X, and XII.
c.	III, IV, V, and VII.	I, VI, VII, and VIII.
d.	I, III, IV, and VII.	VII, X, XI, and XII.

298. A materials requirements planning (MRP) system would be most difficult to apply for a manufacturer which

a. Uses relatively few direct materials.
b. Has long set-up times for its manufacturing equipment.
c. Is in a highly volatile industry.
d. Faces high downtime costs.

299. An appropriate technique for planning and controlling manufacturing inventories such as raw materials, components, and subassemblies whose demand depends on the amounts of finished goods scheduled to be produced is

a. Material requirements planning.
b. Regression analysis.
c. Capital budgeting.
d. Linear programming.

300. The company uses a planning system that focuses first on the amount and timing of finished goods demanded and then determines the derived demand for raw material, components, and subassemblies at each of the prior stages of production. This system is referred to as

a. Economic order quantity.
b. Material requirements planning.

c. Linear programming.
d. Just-in-time purchasing.

301. A company has produced two product lines as though they are separate businesses. The accounting and finance functions were common to both products. A change was made to integrate inventory, purchasing, and production planning and control. Such a change would come under the title of

a. Inventory control.
b. Material requirements planning.
c. A Monte Carlo analysis.
d. Linear programming.

302. Which of the following is a characteristic of just-in-time (JIT) inventory management systems?

a. JIT users determine the optimal level of safety stocks.
b. JIT is applicable only to large companies.
c. JIT does not really increase overall economic efficiency because it merely shifts inventory levels further up the supply chain.
d. JIT relies heavily on good-quality materials.

303. A company stocks, maintains, and distributes inventory. The company decides to add to the safety stock and expedite delivery for several product lines on a trial basis. For the selected product lines the company will experience a(n)

a. Increase in some costs but no change in the service level.
b. Change in the service level.
c. Increase in ordering, carrying, and delivery costs.
d. Decrease in ordering, carrying, and delivery costs.

304. The economic order quantity (EOQ) model calculates the cost minimizing quantity of a product to order, based on a constant annual demand, carrying costs per unit per annum, and costs per order. For example, the EOQ is approximately 447 units if the annual demand is 10,000 units, carrying costs are $1 per unit per annum, and the cost of placing an order is $10. What will the EOQ be if the demand falls to 5,000 units per annum and the carrying and ordering costs remain at $1 and $10 respectively?

a. 316
b. 447
c. 483
d. 500

305. A firm expects to sell 1,000 units of product X during the coming year. Ordering costs are $100 per order and carrying costs are $2 per unit per year. Using the EOQ model, what is the optimum order size?

a. 217
b. 224
c. 317
d. 448

306. A firm uses an ABC inventory control system. About 10% of inventory items are classified into group A. Another 20% are in group B. The remainder are in group C. Which classification is most likely to hold the greatest number of days of supply?

a. Group C.
b. Group B.
c. Group A.
d. All groups are likely to have an equal number of days of supply.

307. With regard to inventory management, an increase in the frequency of ordering will normally

a. Reduce the total ordering costs.
b. Have no impact on total ordering costs.
c. Reduce total carrying costs.
d. Have no impact of total carrying costs.

308. The company uses a planning system that focuses first on the amount and timing of finished goods demanded and then determines the derived demand for raw material, components, and subassemblies at each of the prior stages of production. This system is referred to as

a. Economic order quantity.
b. Material requirements planning.
c. Linear programming.
d. Just-in-time purchasing.

309. A company manufactures banana hooks for retail sale. The bill of material for this item and the parts inventory for each material required are as follows:

Bill of materials		*Parts on hand*
Raw material	*Quantity required*	
Wooden neck	1	0
Wooden base	1	0
Swag hook	1	300
Wood screws	2	400
Foot pads	4	1,000

An incoming order calls for delivery of 2,000 banana hooks in two weeks. The company has 200 finished banana hooks in current inventory. If no safety stocks are required for inventory, what are the company's net requirements for swag hooks and screws needed to fill this order?

	Swag hooks	*Wood screws*
a.	1,500	1,400
b.	1,500	3,200
c.	1,700	3,600
d.	1,800	3,600

Marketing—Pricing Objectives and Policies

310. The most fundamental flaw of cost-plus pricing is that it

a. Fails to account for competition.
b. Ignores demand.
c. Ignores industry-wide standard markup policies.
d. Places too much emphasis on competition.

311. "Selling price = Unit cost + Desired profit" represents which of the following pricing approaches?

a. Profit-maximization.
b. Demand-based pricing.
c. Target return pricing.
d. Standard markup.

312. Assume that the unit cost of making a product is $1.32. For every unit sold, the firm wants 20% to represent profit. Applying the standard markup approach, what should the selling price be?

a. $1.65
b. $1.58
c. $2.38
d. $2.90

313. A retail store sells CDs for $15.00. If the cost per CD is $11.00, what is the store's markup on selling price?

a. 22%
b. 27%

c. 66%
d. 73%

314. A retail store sells CDs for $15.00. What is the cost per CD if the markup on selling price is 25%?
a. $10.50
b. $10.75
c. $11.00
d. $11.25

315. A 50% markup on cost is equivalent to a markup on price of
a. 25%
b. 33%
c. 50%
d. 100%

316. A 50% markup on price is equivalent to a markup on cost of
a. 25%
b. 33%
c. 50%
d. 100%

317. If a firm charges a price of $6 for a product with a cost of $4, the markup on cost equals
a. 33%
b. 50%
c. 67%
d. 150%

318. If a firm charges a price of $5 for a product with a cost of $2, the markup on price equals
a. 40%
b. 60%
c. 150%
d. 250%

319. In the classic economic model, the best price is the
a. Breakeven price.
b. Marginal profit price.
c. Profit-maximizing price.
d. Elastic price.

320. By examining how revenues and costs change for a series of prices, a manager can determine the
a. Breakeven price.
b. Marginal profit price.
c. Profit-maximizing price.
d. Elastic price.

321. Which of the following strategic factors will pay a role in setting a base price?

I. Company objectives.
II. Positioning strategy.
III. New product pricing strategies.
IV. Price-quality differences.

a. I and II.
b. II and III.
c. III and IV.
d. I, II, III, and IV.

322. When there is no patent protection on a product, firms pursue a pricing strategy aimed at
a. Stabilizing of price and margin.
b. Achieving a target ROI.
c. A market share target.
d. Profit maximization.

323. Which of the following objectives requires the most substantial cost and demand information?
a. Stabilization of price and margin.
b. Pricing to achieve a target ROI.
c. Market share target.
d. Profit maximization.

324. The two classic pricing strategies for new products are known as skimming and
a. Penetration.
b. Pricing to achieve a target ROI.
c. Profit maximization.
d. Market share maximization.

325. A consumer relying on price to suggest quality is
a. Price promoting.
b. Quality discounting.
c. Making a price-quality judgment.
d. Making an informed judgment.

326. When introducing an easily copied new product, a marketer would be likely to use a(n)
a. Price penetration strategy.
b. Odd-even pricing strategy.
c. Price skimming strategy.
d. High pricing strategy.

327. A skimming pricing policy works best when demand is
a. Inelastic.
b. Declining.
c. Elastic.
d. Growing.

328. Which of the following pricing strategies is used when a company has developed a clearly differentiated product?
a. Price penetration.
b. Odd-even pricing.
c. Price skimming.
d. High/low pricing.

329. Competitors cannot quickly enter with similar products at lower prices with which of the following strategy?
a. Price penetration.
b. Odd-even pricing.
c. Price skimming.
d. High/low pricing.

330. Which of the following pricing strategy is pursued in the introduction phase of the product life cycle?
a. Elastic price.
b. Odd-even pricing.
c. Price skimming.
d. High/low pricing.

331. A choice between skimming and penetration pricing strategies is most likely to be made in which of the following stages of the product life cycle?
a. Mature.
b. Introductory.
c. Growth.
d. Decline.

332. Stable, competitive prices and price wars are both common in which of the following stages of the product life cycle?
a. Mature.
b. Introductory.
c. Growth.
d. Decline.

333. Prices are kept as high as possible before harvesting in which of the following stages of the product life cycle?
a. Mature.
b. Introductory.
c. Growth.
d. Decline.

334. A company introducing a new product should use a price penetration strategy if
a. Investment costs are low.
b. There is little threat of copycat competition.
c. The price elasticity of demand is inelastic.
d. More volume means lower production costs.

335. A company can effectively set its prices higher than its competitors when the
a. Company's costs are higher.
b. Competitors' costs are higher.
c. Competitors' products are perceived as low-priced alternatives.
d. Company's product is perceived as superior quality.

336. Which of the following is **not** a common reason for a company to change a product's price?
a. Competitive price moves.
b. Sales tax rates change.
c. Price promotion.
d. Unique pricing for different customers.

337. A salesperson who reduces the price during negotiations is
a. Price shading.
b. Geographic pricing.
c. Cash discounting.
d. Volume discounting.

338. When a company reduces the price for customers paying promptly it is called
a. Price shading.
b. Geographic pricing.
c. Cash discounting.
d. Volume discounting.

339. Pricing which leaves the cost and responsibility of transportation to the customer is called
a. Zone pricing.
b. Cargo pricing.
c. Free-on-board pricing.
d. Forward pricing.

340. Discounts given to retailers for putting a manufacturer's goods on sale to consumers for a particular period of time are called
a. Cash discounts.
b. Volume discounts.
c. Price shaded discounts.
d. Sales promotion allowances.

341. Which of the following is **not** a form of price flexing to consumers?
a. Reduction bonuses.
b. Couponing.
c. Segmented pricing.
d. Price promotion.

342. As price promotions increase over time, consumers
a. Switch brands for consistency.
b. Grow more sensitive to advertising.
c. Become more sensitive to price.
d. Find alternatives with lower value.

343. Which of the following is **not** a popular way marketers commonly divide price segments?
a. Political segments.
b. Geographic segments.
c. Usage segments.
d. Demographic segments.

344. Sellers charging different prices to different buyers is called
a. Price differentiation.
b. Price discrimination.
c. Price flexing.
d. Price haggling.

345. A company experiencing financial trouble may seek to just produce an acceptable cash flow to cover marginal costs. This pricing objective is known as
a. Survival.
b. Stabilization of prices and margins.
c. Market share target.
d. Pricing to achieve a target ROI.

346. Which of the following is a negative consequence of price-quality judgments?
a. They can lead to reduced profit for businesses.
b. Low price can harm a high-quality brand name.
c. They make advertising ineffective.
d. A high price can harm a low-quality brand name.

347. Price discrimination exists when
a. Costs vary among customers.
b. Markups vary among customers.
c. Markups are constant among customers.
d. Prices vary among customers.

348. Successful price discrimination require
a. The ability to prevent transfers among customers in different submarkets.
b. Inelastic demand in each submarket.
c. Constant marginal costs.
d. Identical price elasticities among submarkets.

349. With price discrimination, lower prices are charged when the
a. Price elasticity of demand is high.
b. Price elasticity of demand is low.
c. Cross-price elasticity of demand is high.
d. Cross-price elasticity of demand is low.

350. Change in the quantity demanded is caused by a change in
a. Advertising.
b. Wage rates.
c. Price.
d. Raw material costs.

351. Change in the quantity supplied is caused by a change in

a. Income.
b. Weather.
c. Energy costs.
d. Price.

352. With elastic demand, a price increase will

a. Lower marginal revenue.
b. Lower total revenue.
c. Increase total revenue.
d. Lower marginal and total revenue.

353. With inelastic demand, a price increase produces

a. Less than a proportionate decline in quantity demanded.
b. Lower total revenue.
c. Lower marginal revenue.
d. Lower marginal and total revenue.

354. Which of the following is true about pricing during peak periods?

a. Incremental costs are relevant for pricing purposes.
b. Fully allocated costs are relevant for pricing purposes.
c. Facilities are underutilized.
d. Expansion is not required to further increase production.

355. The most prevalent pricing practice employed by business firms is setting price equal to

a. Average revenue.
b. Average cost.
c. Average variable cost plus a charge for overhead and profit margin.
d. Marginal revenue.

356. For which type of product is it appropriate for the seller to accept any price that exceeds the storage and delivery costs for the product?

a. By-product
b. Optional product
c. Captive product
d. Product bundle

Marketing—Supply-Chain Management

357. The process of linking a manufacturer's operations with those of its suppliers and customers is called

a. Just-in-time system.
b. Relationship marketing.
c. Supply-chain management.
d. Vendor marketing.

358. Which of the following describes the logistical system, which emphasizes close cooperation and comprehensive interorganizational management to integrate the logistical operations of the different firms in the marketing channel?

a. Marketing channel power.
b. Supply-chain management.
c. Marketing channel design.
d. Horizontal integration.

359. Each organization in a supply-chain is typically involved in

I. The creation of a product.
II. Marketing processes.
III. Delivery of a product.
IV. Postsale service.

a. I and II.
b. II and III.
c. III and IV.
d. I, II, III, and IV.

360. Buyers involved in a supply-chain management strategy

a. Sometimes reach several tiers back in the supply-chain link to assist second-tier suppliers in meeting their goals.
b. Will work with vendors to find suitable additional sales outlets for their products.
c. Will strive to assist their customers to find alternative sources for competitive products.
d. Sometimes find that short-term relationships are more rewarding.

361. The primary goal of supply-chain management is to

a. Lower all costs of marketing, sales, and logistics.
b. Provide the most effective information to all firms in the supply chain.
c. Reduce the dependence on any single supplier.
d. Improve speed, accuracy, and efficiency in manufacturing and delivery.

362. The reward of becoming a valued partner in a customer's supply-chain is

a. Having fewer demands placed on the marketing staff.
b. Being viewed as an extension of the customer's company.
c. Sharing joint advertising costs with all the firms in the supply chain.
d. Enhancing the ability of the supply chain to use technology.

363. To achieve the reward of being viewed as an extension of a company's customers, a business marketer must be able to

a. Sell their products at lower costs than competitors.
b. Meet quality, delivery, service, and informational requirements.
c. Respond to requests for lower prices.
d. Compromise on the time spent with the customer's top management.

364. Companies that adopt the just-in-time approach to purchasing will typically

a. Decrease the number of suppliers with which they deal.
b. Rely on short-term contracts with their suppliers.
c. Increase the number of inspectors checking incoming materials.
d. Have a streamlined accounts payable system.

365. The essence of the just-in-time concept is to

a. Reduce expenditures on materials and parts.
b. Deliver defect-free parts and materials to the production process just at the moment they are needed.
c. Increase the responsiveness to supplier's needs.
d. Eliminate unnecessary suppliers.

366. The goals of just-in-time concepts are generally focused on

a. Quality, inventory cost, and customer service.

b. Costs, service, price, and quality.
c. Customer service, inventory costs, and production efficiency.
d. Quality, customer service, inventory costs, and production efficiency.

367. The value offerings developed by business marketers must be based on
a. The offerings to close competitors.
b. The value proposition specified by the buyer's purchasing agents.
c. The skills and resources that provide value as perceived by the customer.
d. How the marketing department defines the customer's needs.

368. The purchasing method that involves weighing the comparative value of materials, parts, components, and manufacturing processes from the standpoint of their purpose, relative merit, and cost is called
a. Value analysis.
b. Material analysis.
c. Cost analysis.
d. Vendor analysis.

369. Which of the following is **not** true about value analysis?
a. It looks at ways to improve products.
b. It is an approach for lowering costs.
c. It evaluates the most cost-efficient way of accomplishing a function.
d. It points the way to elimination and reengineering.

370. One of the results of value analysis is that
a. Suppliers may be charged for lost or damaged merchandise.
b. The purchasing department may find materials at competing suppliers at a lower cost.
c. Product design alternatives will produce significant cost savings.
d. Ideas from suppliers are integrated into the firm's marketing strategy.

371. The value of a function is determined by
a. Supply and demand factors.
b. What sellers are asking for it.
c. How it is organized and implemented.
d. The most cost-efficient way of fully accomplishing the function.

372. The evaluation of supplier performance is used
a. As a tool for attracting more suppliers.
b. As a negotiation tool to gain leverage in buyer-seller relationships.
c. To leverage the firm's buying power with other suppliers.
d. To penalize suppliers who are delinquent with deliveries.

373. From the supplier's evaluation perspective, the weighted-point plan is useful in that it
a. Provides evidence of the nature and importance of the evaluative criteria used by the buyer.
b. Can be used as a marketing tool if the scores are high enough.
c. Shows how important a good evaluation forecasting system is.
d. Measures whether the buyer is interested in a long-term relationship.

374. Customers in business markets are interested in a supplier's
a. Ability to reduce prices.
b. Relationship with competitors.
c. Capabilities and contributions.
d. Financial position and capital.

375. Which of the following is concerned with the holding of products until they are ready to be sold?
a. Transportation.
b. Materials handling.
c. Warehousing.
d. Packaging.

376. What is the most important factor to consider when deciding whether to single source or multiple source a critical component?
a. Available supplier capacity.
b. Desire to maintain competition for the business.
c. Cost of tooling and setup.
d. Number of suppliers in the marketplace.

377. Which of the following will be useful in competitive analysis when evaluating the worthiness of a potential supplier?
a. Financial stability.
b. Other customers of the suppliers.
c. Management integrity.
d. Available supplier capacity.

378. What other factors should be considered in addition to supplier rating score prior to making the final selection of a supplier?

I. Management integrity.
II. Financial stability.
III. Design flexibility.
IV. Production standards.

a. I and II.
b. II and III.
c. I, II, and III.
d. I, II, III, and IV.

379. Vendor analysis should be conducted

I. On a periodic basis.
II. When significant changes occur to scoring factors.
III. When frequent changes occur in vendor location.
IV. On a vendor-requested basis.

a. I only.
b. II only.
c. I and II.
d. III and IV.

380. Which of the following would **not** usually be a main factor in selecting a vendor?
a. Price.
b. Quality.
c. Inventory usage.
d. Service.

381. Choosing vendors solely based on which of the following factors is detrimental to the long-term success of a buying firm?
a. Quality.

b. Service.
c. Price.
d. Delivery.

382. Supplier audits are an important first step in
a. Supplier certification.
b. Supplier relationships.
c. Supplier partnerships.
d. Strategic partnerships.

383. Supplier audits usually do **not** focus on which of the following?
a. Supplier capabilities.
b. Quality programs.
c. Delivery programs.
d. Human resource programs.

384. Supplier audits usually do **not** cover which of the following?
a. Management style.
b. Industrial engineering.
c. Quality assurance.
d. Materials management.

385. Certified suppliers mean
a. Less risk.
b. Buyer can eliminate all inspections.
c. Buyer can eliminate all tests.
d. More audits.

386. Supplier certification does **not** mean
a. All vendors are ISO 9000 certified.
b. Some vendors are referred to as world-class suppliers.
c. Some suppliers meet the needs of a buyer.
d. Some suppliers exceed the needs of a buyer.

387. Examination of functions and costs of a finished product, part, or component in an effort to reduce costs and/or to improve performance is called
a. Value analysis.
b. Vendor analysis.
c. Materials analysis.
d. Cost analysis.

388. Value analysis has the greatest potential for cost savings for parts, raw materials, and components that have

I. Low unit cost.
II. High unit cost.
III. Low annual usage.
IV. High annual usage.

a. II only.
b. IV only.
c. I and III.
d. II and IV.

389. Which of the following parties should **not** drive the implementation of value analysis program in a company?
a. Product design engineering.
b. Manufacturing operations.
c. Purchasing or supply chain.
d. Sales and marketing.

390. Which of the following are involved in the bullwhip effect in the supply chain process?

I. Nonvalue stream.
II. Value stream.
III. Upstream.
IV. Downstream.

a. I only.
b. II only.
c. III and IV.
d. II and III.

391. The bullwhip effect in the supply chain can be eliminated by
a. Replenishing the supply chain.
b. Synchronizing the supply chain.
c. Resizing the supply chain.
d. Mixing the supply chain.

392. The inventory situation during the bullwhip effect in the supply chain is at a(n)
a. Excess level.
b. Backordered level.
c. Moderate level.
d. Low level.

393. When suppliers are involved in the design, development, and manufacturing of a new product, component, part, or system, it is called
a. Presourcing.
b. Insourcing.
c. Outsourcing.
d. Cosourcing.

394. Which of the following refers to when manufacturing companies do not own equity of their largest suppliers?
a. Japanese keiretsu.
b. American keiretsu.
c. Kanban.
d. Kaizen.

395. What technique would a company use to determine which advertising mix of radio, television, and newspaper offers the optimal increase in sales and improved public image?
a. Pareto analysis.
b. Value analysis.
c. Linear regression.
d. The Markov process.

Human Resources Management

396. The major shortcoming of the traditional employee's performance measurement process is that it
a. Rarely includes broader organizational criteria.
b. Is usually static in nature.
c. Focuses on reaching agreement on the results of the evaluation.
d. Determines actions that need to be taken.

397. Organizations are moving from an employee's performance measurement process to a performance management process in order to
a. Meet competitive challenges.
b. Refine the job analysis.
c. Increase the employee's performance ratings.
d. Rebut the appraiser's assessment.

398. The major difference between employee's performance measurement system and performance management system is the emphasis on
a. Management.
b. Report card.

c. Evaluation tool.
d. Measurement.

399. Which of the following is **not** an element of an employee's performance management system?
a. Promoting shared responsibility.
b. Molding employee's performance.
c. Establishing effective reward and recognition programs.
d. Measurement is seen as an end in itself.

400. Which of the following is **not** a major part of the human resource management process?
a. Employee selection and recruiting.
b. Employee communication.
c. Employee performance appraisal.
d. Employee training and development.

401. Which of the following is the most frequently used but least successful job-searching method?
a. Internal job posting.
b. Employment agencies.
c. Corporate Web sites.
d. Job fairs.

402. Which of the following is the best way to find a job?
a. Internal job posting.
b. Employment agencies.
c. Newspaper advertisements.
d. Job referrals.

403. Which of the following identifies basic task and skill requirements through observation?
a. Job analysis.
b. Job description.
c. Job specifications.
d. Job matrix.

404. Which of the following should be done before job descriptions are developed?
a. Job analyses.
b. Job rotation.
c. Job specifications.
d. Job matrix.

405. Which of the following outlines the role expectations and skill requirements for a specific job?
a. Job analysis.
b. Job rotation.
c. Job specifications.
d. Job descriptions.

406. Which of the following is the most common tool used for employee selection?
a. Background checks.
b. Interviews.
c. Drug testing.
d. Personality tests.

407. Which of the following is defined as a set of job-related questions with standardized answers?
a. Preinterview.
b. Postinterview.
c. Structured interview.
d. Unstructured interview.

408. Which of the following defines the process of evaluating an individual's contribution as a basis for making objective personnel decisions?
a. Performance appraisal.
b. Environmental factors.
c. Facilitation skills.
d. Training and development.

409. Which of the following is **not** a criterion for legally defensible performance appraisals in the United States?
a. Results reviewed with rates.
b. Performance based on job analysis.
c. Results linked with compensation decisions.
d. Written instructions given to evaluators.

410. In which of the following performance appraisal techniques do managers describe the performance of employees in narrative form?
a. Graphic rating scales.
b. Written essays.
c. Ranking and comparison.
d. Goal setting.

411. In which of the following performance appraisal techniques do managers write down specific examples of employees' good and bad performance as they occur and later use them during performance appraisal?
a. Graphic rating scales.
b. Critical incidents.
c. Multirater appraisals.
d. Weighted checklist.

412. Both graphic rating scales and behaviorally anchored rating scales (BARS) are effective for appraising an employee's job performance when they focus on
a. Traits.
b. Skills.
c. Behavior.
d. Scales.

413. Which of the following employees' performance appraisal techniques take input from multiple raters such as one's supervisor, peers, and subordinates?
a. Ranking and comparisons.
b. A top-down review.
c. A bottom-up review.
d. A 360-degree review.

414. Supervisors and managers need more training in which of the following areas?
a. Workplace substance abuse.
b. Referral and rehabilitation approaches.
c. Employee performance appraisals.
d. Sexual harassment problems..

415. Which of the following is the most preferred instructional and training method?
a. Role playing.
b. Case studies.
c. Computer-based training.
d. Live classroom lectures.

Balanced Scorecard System

416. The balanced scorecard system is a(n)
a. Internal control system.
b. Tactical control system.

c. Management control system.
d. Operational control system.

417. Which of the following is the heart of a balanced scorecard system?
a. Strategic management system.
b. Tactical management system.
c. Functional management system.
d. Operational management system.

418. The balanced scorecard system is a reflection of

I. Lag indicators.
II. Lead indicators.
III. Financial indicators.
IV. Nonfinancial indicators.

a. I and II.
b. II and III.
c. III and IV.
d. I, II, III, and IV.

419. Which of the following is **not** a perspective of the balanced scorecard approach?
a. Timeliness.
b. Productivity.
c. Efficiency.
d. Quantity.

420. The balanced scorecard approach does **not** require looking at performance from which of the following perspectives?
a. Financial.
b. Competitor.
c. Customer.
d. Internal business processes.

421. All of the following are critical success factors under the customer perspective of the balanced scorecard approach **except:**
a. Increasing customer service.
b. Reducing prices.
c. Increasing quality.
d. Reducing delivery time.

422. Which of the following perspectives of the balanced scorecard deal with objectives across a company's entire value chain?
a. Financial.
b. Customer.
c. Internal business processes.
d. Learning and growth.

423. Which of the following perspectives of the balanced scorecard deal with objectives of increasing market share and penetrating new markets?
a. Financial.
b. Customer.
c. Internal business processes.
d. Learning and growth.

424. Which of the following perspectives of the balanced scorecard deal with objectives of product improvement?
a. Financial.
b. Customer.
c. Internal business processes.
d. Learning and growth.

425. Which of the following items represent nonfinancial measures under the balanced scorecard approach?

I. Costs.
II. Sales margins.
III. Quality.
IV. Customer service.

a. III only.
b. IV only.
c. I and II.
d. III and IV.

426. Which of the following statements is **not** true about non-financial measures of performance under the balanced scorecard approach?
a. At times quality may be more important than cost.
b. At times timeliness may be more important than meeting budget.
c. At times customer service may be more important than financial returns.
d. At times traditional measures may be more important than nontraditional measures.

427. Which of the following perspectives of the balanced scorecard deal with the objective of shortening the time to market a new product?
a. Financial.
b. Customer.
c. Internal business processes.
d. Learning and growth.

428. All of the following are examples of customer-performance scorecard measures **except:**
a. Lost customers.
b. Dissatisfied customers.
c. Product or service quality.
d. Machine downtime.

429. Which of the following balanced scorecard measure is difficult to identify and implement?
a. Market-based performance scorecard.
b. Production-based performance scorecard.
c. Stakeholder-based performance scorecard.
d. Human resource-based performance scorecard.

430. A good balanced scorecard system contains

I. Lag measures.
II. Lead measures.
III. Interlinking.
IV. Interrelationship digraph.

a. I and II.
b. III and IV.
c. I, II, and III.
d. I, II, III, and IV.

MULTIPLE-CHOICE ANSWERS AND EXPLANATIONS

1. a	63. a	125. b	187. a	249. c	311. c
2. b	64. b	126. c	188. c	250. c	312. a
3. c	65. d	127. c	189. a	251. d	313. b
4. b	66. a	128. b	190. d	252. a	314. d
5. b	67. a	129. a	191. c	253. c	315. b
6. c	68. b	130. b	192. c	254. c	316. d
7. a	69. c	131. a	193. c	255. c	317. b
8. c	70. d	132. a	194. c	256. d	318. b
9. d	71. a	133. c	195. a	257. a	319. c
10. a	72. d	134. a	196. a	258. b	320. c
11. a	73. c	135. b	197. b	259. b	321. d
12. d	74. c	136. b	198. c	260. a	322. c
13. a	75. a	137. d	199. a	261. d	323. d
14. d	76. d	138. b	200. a	262. a	324. a
15. b	77. b	139. b	201. a	263. d	325. c
16. a	78. c	140. c	202. c	264. d	326. a
17. d	79. a	141. d	203. a	265. a	327. a
18. b	80. c	142. a	204. c	266. b	328. c
19. c	81. a	143. a	205. a	267. b	329. c
20. b	82. b	144. b	206. b	268. c	330. c
21. a	83. b	145. d	207. a	269. a	331. b
22. a	84. a	146. b	208. b	270. b	332. a
23. d	85. d	147. b	209. b	271. c	333. d
24. c	86. c	148. b	210. a	272. c	334. d
25. c	87. a	149. a	211. b	273. b	335. d
26. b	88. c	150. b	212. b	274. a	336. b
27. b	89. a	151. b	213. b	275. a	337. a
28. b	90. a	152. c	214. b	276. b	338. c
29. a	91. b	153. a	215. c	277. b	339. c
30. a	92. c	154. a	216. b	278. d	340. d
31. a	93. c	155. c	217. a	279. b	341. a
32. a	94. b	156. c	218. d	280. b	342. c
33. d	95. a	157. c	219. d	281. a	343. a
34. b	96. b	158. a	220. a	282. c	344. b
35. a	97. b	159. b	221. a	283. b	345. a
36. b	98. c	160. d	222. b	284. c	346. b
37. c	99. c	161. d	223. a	285. b	347. b
38. a	100. d	162. d	224. b	286. d	348. a
39. d	101. b	163. b	225. a	287. d	349. a
40. d	102. a	164. a	226. d	288. c	350. c
41. d	103. b	165. d	227. c	289. d	351. d
42. a	104. a	166. b	228. c	290. c	352. b
43. c	105. a	167. a	229. b	291. c	353. a
44. b	106. c	168. b	230. d	292. a	354. b
45. a	107. d	169. a	231. d	293. a	355. c
46. b	108. b	170. b	232. a	294. a	356. a
47. b	109. d	171. c	233. c	295. c	357. c
48. c	110. a	172. c	234. d	296. b	358. b
49. a	111. a	173. c	235. d	297. d	359. d
50. d	112. a	174. c	236. d	298. c	360. a
51. a	113. a	175. c	237. d	299. a	361. d
52. b	114. a	176. a	238. d	300. b	362. b
53. b	115. b	177. d	239. d	301. b	363. b
54. c	116. a	178. a	240. d	302. d	364. a
55. d	117. d	179. a	241. c	303. b	365. b
56. c	118. c	180. b	242. b	304. a	366. d
57. c	119. b	181. c	243. d	305. c	367. c
58. a	120. d	182. b	244. a	306. a	368. a
59. c	121. a	183. c	245. c	307. c	369. d
60. b	122. c	184. b	246. a	308. b	370. c
61. b	123. c	185. b	247. c	309. b	371. d
62. a	124. a	186. c	248. b	310. b	372. b

373. a __ __	383. d __ __	393. a __ __	403. a __ __	413. d __ __	423. b __ __
374. c __ __	384. b __ __	394. b __ __	404. a __ __	414. c __ __	424. d __ __
375. c __ __	385. a __ __	395. b __ __	405. d __ __	415. d __ __	425. d __ __
376. d __ __	386. a __ __	396. a __ __	406. b __ __	416. c __ __	426. d __ __
377. b __ __	387. a __ __	397. a __ __	407. c __ __	417. a __ __	427. d __ __
378. c __ __	388. d __ __	398. a __ __	408. a __ __	418. d __ __	428. d __ __
379. c __ __	389. c __ __	399. d __ __	409. c __ __	419. d __ __	429. c __ __
380. c __ __	390. c __ __	400. b __ __	410. b __ __	420. b __ __	430. c __ __
381. c __ __	391. b __ __	401. c __ __	411. b __ __	421. b __ __	1st: __/430 =__%
382. a __ __	392. a __ __	402. d __ __	412. c __ __	422. c __ __	2nd: __/430 =__%

Quality Management

1. **(a)** Service quality can be measured in terms of five factors (RATER): reliability (R), assurance (A), tangibles (T), empathy (E), and responsiveness (R). Customers consistently ranked reliability as the most important factor. Reliability is the ability to perform the desired service dependably, accurately, and consistently.

Subject Area: Business processes—quality management. Source: Author.

2. **(b)** Continuous improvement is at the core of the definition of TQM and its principles.

Subject Area: Business processes—quality management. Source: Author.

3. **(c)** TQM involves creating an organizational culture committed to continuous improvement of products or services.

Subject Area: Business processes—quality management. Source: Author.

4. **(b)** Assurance is employees' knowledge, courtesy, and ability to convey trust and confidence.

Subject Area: Business processes—quality management. Source: Author.

5. **(b)** Striving for zero defects is the goal of manufacturing management achieved through statistical process control and six-sigma methodologies, which are subsets of TQM. Striving for zero defects is not one of the principles of TQM.

Subject Area: Business processes—quality management. Source: Author.

6. **(c)** The fishbone diagram helps TQM teams visualize important cause-and-effect relationships.

Subject Area: Business processes—quality management. Source: Author.

7. **(a)** The Pareto diagram helps TQM teams to analyze vital few and trivial many (80/20 pattern or rule). It is most efficient to focus on the few things that make the biggest difference.

Subject Area: Business processes—quality management. Source: Author.

8. **(c)** A scatter diagram is used to plot the correlation between two variables.

Subject Area: Business processes—quality management. Source: Author.

9. **(d)** Kaizen practitioners view quality as an endless journey, not a final destination.

Subject Area: Business processes—quality management. Source: Author.

10. **(a)** A flowchart is a graphic representation of a sequence of activities and decisions. The flowchart identifies unnecessary work steps so that they can either be combined or eliminated.

Subject Area: Business processes—quality management. Source: Author.

11. **(a)** Customers can be internal and external to an organization. Building teamwork and empowerment are employee driven. TQM empowers employees at all levels in order to tap their full potential of creativity, motivation, and commitment.

Subject Area: Business processes—quality management. Source: Author.

12. **(d)** Manufacturing-based quality deals with conformance to requirements such as design specifications, customer requirements, or blueprints.

Subject Area: Business processes—quality management. Source: Author.

13. **(a)** A run chart is also called a time series or trend chart, which tracks the frequency or amount of a given variable over time. Significant deviations from the standard signal the need for corrective action.

Subject Area: Business processes—quality management. Source: Author.

14. **(d)** A control chart helps operations maintain key quality measurements within an acceptable range of upper control limit and lower control limit. It monitors the actual versus desired quality measurements during repetitive operations.

Subject Area: Business processes—quality management. Source: Author.

15. **(b)** A histogram is a bar chart showing whether repeated measurements in an operation conform to a standard bell-shaped curve (normal curve).

Subject Area: Business processes—quality management. Source: Author.

16. **(a)** Prevention costs are costs incurred to prevent defects from occurring during the design and delivery of products or services. Prevention costs can keep both appraisal and failure costs to a minimum.

Subject Area: Business processes—quality management. Source: Author.

17. **(d)** External failure costs are associated with defects found during or after delivery of the product or service to the customer.

Subject Area: Business processes—quality management. Source: Author.

18. **(b)** Appraisal costs are costs to detect, measure, evaluate, and audit products and processes to ensure that they conform to customer requirements and performance standards.

Subject Area: Business processes—quality management. Source: Author.

19. **(c)** Internal failure costs are the costs associated with defects that are discovered before the product is shipped or before the service is delivered to the customer.

Subject Area: Business processes—quality management. Source: Author.

20. **(b)** Services are characterized by their intangibility, inseparability, heterogeneity, and perishability.

Subject Area: Business processes—quality management. Source: CBM, Volume two.

21. **(a)** Of the four unique characteristics that distinguish goods from services, intangibility is the primary source from which the other three characteristics emerge.

Subject Area: Business processes—quality management. Source: CBM, Volume two.

22. **(a)** Because of the service's intangibility, the customer's evaluation of a service will extend beyond what was experienced, the behavior of other customers, and the way the service was delivered.

Subject Area: Business processes—quality management. Source: CBM, Volume two.

23. **(d)** One of the most frequently stressed differences between goods and services is the lack of ability to control service quality before it reaches the consumer. Heterogeneity, almost by definition, makes it impossible for a service operation to achieve 100% perfect quality on an ongoing basis.

Subject Area: Business processes—quality management. Source: CBM, Volume two.

24. **(c)** Perishability distinguishes goods and services. It refers to the fact that services cannot be inventoried in the traditional sense.

Subject Area: Business processes—quality management. Source: CBM, Volume two.

25. **(c)** The five stages of six-sigma include define, measure, analyze, improve, and control. The third stage "analyze" serves an outcome of the "measure" stage. These five stages are a modified adoption of the Deming plan-do-study-act (PDSA) approach.

Subject Area: Business processes—quality management. Source: Author.

26. **(b)** A mistake-proofing tool removes the opportunity for error before it happens. It is a way to detect and correct an error where is occurs and avoid passing the error to the next worker or the next operation. This tool prevents an error from becoming a defect in the process.

Subject Area: Business processes—quality management. Source: Author.

27. **(b)** The control stage monitors the ongoing performance of a process. This stage is a transition from improvement to controlling the process. It ensures that new improvements are implemented.

Subject Area: Business processes—quality management. Source: Author.

28. **(b)** Process mapping is a very useful tool in the "define, measure, analyze, and improve" stages but not in the control stage because the process is already in control. In the control stage, systems and structures are in place to institutionalize the improvements. Process mapping is a high-level visual representation of the current process step looking beyond the functional activities and rediscovering core processes. The objective of the process mapping is to understand the process.

Subject Area: Business processes—quality management. Source: Author.

29. **(a)** The cause-and-effect diagram is a tool for analyzing process variables. The diagram shows the main cause and subcauses leading to an effect (symptom). This tool is used in both the "define and measure" stages.

Subject Area: Business processes—quality management. Source: Author.

30. **(a)** Brainstorming techniques are used to define the problem and to make improvements. It is a way to identify bottlenecks, process/machine breakdowns, and non-value-added work steps.

Subject Area: Business processes—quality management. Source: Author.

31. **(a)** An "as is" process map identifies process inputs and outputs and acts as a benchmark against future improvements. This map is being referred throughout the process, including implementation. The "may be" process map does not exist since it signals uncertainty.

Subject Area: Business processes—quality management. Source: Author.

32. **(a)** The "as is" process map is developed in the define stage of the six-sigma methodology.

Subject Area: Business processes—quality management. Source: Author.

33. **(d)** The "as is" process map is changed to "should be" process map in the "improve" stage to reflect new improvements.

Subject Area: Business processes—quality management. Source: Author.

34. **(b)** Common causes affect everyone working in a process and affect all of the outcomes of a process. They are always present and thus are generally predictable. Special causes are not always present in a process, do not affect everyone working in the process, and do not affect all the outcomes of the process. Special causes are not predictable. The stage "measure" collects data about current performance that pinpoints opportunities and provides a structure for making improvements.

Subject Area: Business processes—quality management. Source: Author.

35. **(a)** Six-sigma green belts work directly with black belts and the cross-functional project leaders to carry out identified improvement projects. They implement six-sigma improvement tools by being competent at detailed and routine tasks and by collecting the required data.

Subject Area: Business processes—quality management. Source: Author.

36. (**b**) The role of six-sigma black belts is based on the principle of contributing independently and applying the appropriate tools and techniques in the process of resolving quality problems and issues in the organization. They assume responsibility for definable projects and posses technical competence and ability.

Subject Area: Business processes—quality management. Source: Author.

37. (**c**) Master black belts will ensure that they contribute through others based on their leadership skills. They are involved as a manager, mentor, or idea leader in developing others. They have the technical breadth, can build a strong network of people, and can resolve conflicts. Sponsors are the champions having project management skills, understand the risk management techniques, and have leadership skills. They have the vision and knowledge of their organization's culture.

Subject Area: Business processes—quality management. Source: Author.

38. (**a**) The quality function deployment (QFD) is a structured method in which customer requirements are translated into appropriate technical requirements for each stage of product development and production. QFD improves product design and reliability. The QFD process is often referred to as listening to the voice of the customer, and it is also called house of quality.

Subject Area: Business processes—quality management. Source: Author.

39. (**d**) Process-mapping techniques are used to improve organizational processes.

Subject Area: Business processes—quality management. Source: Author.

40. (**d**) Mistake-proofing techniques are used to improve organizational processes. Typical mistakes in production are omitted processing, processing errors, setup errors, missing parts, wrong parts, and machine adjustment errors. Poka-yoke is an approach for mistake-proofing processes using automatic devices or methods to avoid simple human or machine errors.

Subject Area: Business processes—quality management. Source: Author.

41. (**d**) Mistake-proofing a service requires identifying when and where failures occur. Once a failure is identified, the source must be found. The final step is to prevent the mistake occurring through source inspections, self-inspections, or sequence checks. Mass or final inspections are expensive, time-consuming, and ineffective as it is too late in the game.

Subject Area: Business processes—quality management. Source: Author.

42. (**a**) Participative management includes subordinates in the decision-making process. A quality circle is an example of participative management. Choice (b) is incorrect because management by objectives (MBO) is a process of goal setting, not decision making and problem solving. Choice (c) is incorrect because quality circles are not rewards; they are workgroups. Choice (d) is incorrect because this theory differentiates between motivator and hygiene factors: those, which satisfy and those, which lead to dissatisfaction.

Subject Area: Business processes—quality management. Source: CIA 597, II-25.

43. (**c**) Job enlargement is a horizontal expansion of the job. It requires an individual to perform multiple jobs, not just one task. Choice (a) is incorrect because job rotation involves shifting a worker from task to task (at the same job level), during different periods of time. Choice (b) is incorrect because job sharing requires two or more people to split the same job, and is an alternative work schedule. Choice (d) is incorrect because job enrichment is a vertical expansion of the job. It involves task combining, establishing client relationships, and opening feedback channels.

Subject Area: Business processes—quality management. Source: CIA 597, II-26.

44. (**b**) The theory behind this response is expectancy theory which is a function of three beliefs: (1) the outcome is attractive (the company stays in business), (2) a particular level of performance will lead to the outcome (new skills and quality circles will lead to productivity and quality increases), and (3) a level of effort will lead to the performance level (training and hard work will lead to skills and success of quality circles). Choice (a) is incorrect because the theory behind this response suggests that reinforcement conditions behavior. Reinforcement theorists argue that behavior is environmentally caused. Choice (c) is incorrect because the theory behind this response suggests that a person's needs motivate the individual to work for success. Choice (d) is incorrect because the theory behind this response holds that employees act in such a way as to bring "equity" to the job, that is, an individual's inputs and outputs are "fair" when compared to others at the same level.

Subject Area: Business processes—quality management. Source: CIA 597, II-27.

45. (**a**) Work teams are not "empowered" to do anything they please. The organization has certain expectations for what is to be accomplished and how the teams are to go about accomplishing these things. Once the organization defines the objectives (what is to be accomplished) and sets appropriate policies (how it is to be done), the work teams can be free to make and implement decisions within those boundaries. Policies in this context are usually quite broad (e.g., relating to ethical business conduct) but nevertheless important. Choice (b) is incorrect because they are important but not "more important than ever." Policies in this context should not be "rules" and the distrust implicit in "is almost certain to make mistakes" is inconsistent with empowerment. Choices (c) and (d) are incorrect because work teams are not "empowered" to do anything they please.

Subject Area: Business processes—quality management. Source: CIA 1196, III-17.

46. (**b**) Downward performance appraisals are more structured and formal than upward performance appraisals. They also decrease the meaningfulness of the task when the reviewer is more interested in measuring performance than the employee is. Choice (a) is incorrect because this is an action management would take to empower employees because it allows employees some self-determination in performing their tasks. Choice (c) is incorrect because this is an action management would take to empower employees because it increases the meaningfulness of the task. Choice (d) is incorrect. Again, this is an action management would take to empower employees because it increases the competency of the employees which, in turn, empowers them to perform the task at hand.

Subject Area: Business processes—quality management. Source: CIA 597, III-16.

47. **(b)** Customer focus, both internal and external, is one of the keys of TQM. Choice (a) is incorrect because TQM deemphasizes specialized quality inspectors. Choice (c) is incorrect because centralization often needs to be reduced to successfully implement a TQM process. Choice (d) is incorrect because TQM involves continuous improvement; once a standard is reached, continuous improvement requires its constant reevaluation.

Subject Area: Business processes—quality management. Source: CIA 597, III-23.

48. **(c)** Teams are an excellent vehicle for encouraging the sharing of ideas and removing process improvement obstacles. Choice (a) is incorrect because teams are often inefficient and costly. Choice (b) is incorrect because although employee motivation may be high for some teams members, such potential high motivation does not directly affect the process improvement which is key to quality improvement. Choice (d) is incorrect because the use of teams in total quality management is not aimed at less supervision and reduced staffing although that may be a by-product.

Subject Area: Business processes—quality management. Source: CIA 597, III-24.

49. **(a)** The cumulative effect of TQM's continuous improvement process can attract and hold customers and cannot be duplicated by competitors. Choice (b) is incorrect because new products can be quickly copied by competitors and therefore do not provide a sustained competitive advantage. Choice (c) is incorrect because TQM does not focus on cost reduction. Choice (d) is incorrect because TQM is only one tool of strategic management; other tools have to be used for proper strategic management.

Subject Area: Business processes—quality management. Source: CIA 597, III-20.

50. **(d)** Clear goals and time to go through the early necessary, but not task-focused, stages of development are key to the long-term productivity of a team. Choice (a) is incorrect because assignment of a strong leader and individual tasks are likely to undermine the benefits of participation that are expected from a team. Choice (b) is incorrect. Although similarity may help ease initial conflict, it can be a strong detriment to long-term productivity, which requires diversity of opinion, background, and skills. Choice (c) is incorrect because clear goals provided by a manager are key to a team's success.

Subject Area: Business processes—quality management. Source: CIA 597, III-30.

51. **(a)** In this situation the group is likely to pursue its own agenda at the expense of the organizational goals. Choice (b) is incorrect because although not ideal, this situation will still lead to moderate productivity. Choice (c) is incorrect because high diversity and moderate conflict are both likely to lead to high productivity. Choice (d) is incorrect because this situation is likely to lead to moderate productivity due to commitment to organizational goals.

Subject Area: Business processes—quality management. Source: CIA 597, III-31.

52. **(b)** All the elements presented in the questions are part of the total quality movement in both the manufacturing and service sectors. Choice (a) is incorrect because competition with leading organizations is not the only goal of the total quality movement. Choice (c) is incorrect because the goal is quality first and foremost. A total quality movement may reduce some costs in the long run. Choice (d) is incorrect because the focus of the elements presented is not cost management.

Subject Area: Business processes—quality management. Source: CIA 597, III-3.

53. **(b)** This response describes the "design-it-in" approach, which promotes keeping quality in mind right from the start. Choice (a) is incorrect because this response describes the "fix-it-in" approach. It was the first approach to develop. Inspectors identify defects and have them reworked. Choice (c) is incorrect because this response describes the "inspect-it-in" approach, which applies the "fix-it-in" approach to in-process work. Choice (d) is incorrect because this response describes the "adjust-it-in" approach, which is the same as the "inspect-it-in" approach.

Subject Area: Business processes—quality management. Source: CIA 597, III-4.

54. **(c)** Superior product quality is not attained just through more inspection, better statistical quality control, and cross-functional team work. Manufacturers must make fundamental changes in the way they produce products and do each job right the first time. Choices (a), (b), and (d) are incorrect because each is only a part of the TQM emphasis.

Subject Area: Business processes—quality management. Source: CIA 596, III-23.

55. **(d)** Education and self-improvement should be the number-one career objective for everyone in the organization. Choice (a) is incorrect because management-by-objectives (MBO) causes aggressive pursuance of numerical quotas. Choice (b) is incorrect because on the job training serves to entrench bad work habits. Choice (c) is incorrect because quality by final inspection is unnecessary if quality is built in from the start.

Subject Area: Business processes—quality management. Source: CIA 596, III-29.

56. **(c)** Small teams of people from different specialties empowered to make decision are highly effective. Choice (a) is incorrect because hierarchical organizational structure actually stifles TQM. Choice (b) is incorrect because TQM works best with teams of people from different specialties. Choice (d) is incorrect because teamwork is essential for TQM.

Subject Area: Business processes—quality management. Source: CIA 596, III-30.

57. **(c)** All employees who deal with outsiders must be customer oriented; in addition customers internal to the organization who depend on you to get their job done are considered internal customers. Choice (a) is incorrect because this is an incomplete response. It doesn't include those within the company who depend on it to get jobs done. Choice (b) is incorrect because influence and reliance can be indirect. Choice (d) is incorrect because internal customers are also included

Subject Area: Business processes—quality management. Source: CIA 596, III-32.

58. **(a)** Involving them in decisions affecting their lives. The quality-of-work-life movement is based on the principle of involving employees in the decision and actions that are likely to affect their lives. The methods used include flexible work schedules, participative management, and workplace democracy, all of which aim at increasing the employees' sense of control. Choice (b) is incorrect because providing fair and equitable reward systems that are clearly linked to the employees' effort and performance is one of the keys to motivation. However, it is much narrower than the overall quality-of-work-life concept and is not the key defining characteristic of the movement. Choice (c) is incorrect because focusing on employees' higher-level needs is also one aspect of motivation according to Maslow. Once again, it is a narrow view of motivation and does not fit within the quality-of-work-life concept. Choice (d) is incorrect because using job enrichment techniques that increase skill variety, task identity and significance, autonomy and feedback can address motivation if there is a need to enrich the job in order to match employees' desire and need for growth. Even when effective, such an approach does not aim at reshaping the workplace and does not constitute a basic principle of the quality-of-work-life movement.

Subject Area: Business processes—quality management. Source: CIA 596, III-34.

59. **(c)** This is incurred as a result of customer dissatisfaction. Choice (a) is incorrect because rework corrects defects caused during manufacture. Choice (b) is incorrect because these arise from internal labor disputes. Choice (d) is incorrect because this results from production processes operating out of specification limits.

Subject Area: Business processes—quality management. Source: CIA 596, III-81.

60. **(b)** Appraisal costs are those costs incurred to detect which products do not conform to specifications. Choice (a) is incorrect because preventive costs are incurred to prevent the production of products that do not conform to specifications. Choice (c) is incorrect because internal-failure costs are incurred when a nonconforming product is detected before it is shipped to a customer. Choice (d) is incorrect because external-failure costs are incurred when a nonconforming product is detected after it is shipped to a customer.

Subject Area: Business processes—quality management. Source: CIA 597, III-96.

61. **(b)** This response identifies the appropriate four costs, which are preventive quality costs. See table and supporting calculations below. Choice (a) is incorrect because this response omits scheduled equipment maintenance from the preventive costs and includes labor inspection of raw materials (appraisal cost) as a preventive cost; the other three costs included are appropriate. See table and supporting calculations below. Choice (c) is incorrect because this response includes product-testing equipment as a preventive cost in addition to the four appropriate preventive costs; product-testing equipment is an appraisal cost. See table and supporting calculations below. Choice (d) is incorrect because this response includes both product-testing equipment and labor inspection of raw materials as preventive costs in addition to the four appropriate preventive costs; both of these costs are appraisal costs. See table and supporting calculations below.

Supporting calculations

Cost items	Choice a	Choice b	Choice c	Choice d
Design engineering	$275,000	$275,000	$275,000	$275,000
Labor inspection of raw materials	32,000			32,000
Process engineering	180,000	180,000	180,000	180,000
Product-testing equipment			35,000	35,000
Scheduled equipment maintenance		90,000	90,000	90,000
Training of manufacturing workers	156,000	156,000	156,000	156,000
Total preventive costs	$643,000	$701,000	$736,000	$768,000

Table showing correct classification of costs of quality (COQ)

Cost items	Amount	COQ type
Design reviews	$275,000	Preventive
Finished goods returned due to failure	55,000	External
Freight on replacement finished goods	27,000	External
Labor inspection during manufacturing	75,000	Appraisal
Labor inspection of raw materials	32,000	Appraisal
Manufacturing product-testing labor	63,000	Appraisal
Manufacturing rework labor and overhead	150,000	Internal
Materials used in warranty repairs	68,000	External
Process engineering	180,000	Preventive
Product-liability claims	145,000	External
Product-testing equipment	35,000	Appraisal
Repairs to equipment due to breakdowns	22,000	Internal
Scheduled equipment maintenance	90,000	Preventive
Scrap material	125,000	Internal
Training of manufacturing workers	156,000	Preventive

Subject Area: Business processes—quality management. Source: CIA 597, III-97.

62. **(a)** The major component of quality is to minimize defects and stay true to design. Choice (b) is incorrect because management satisfaction is not the way organizations measure quality. Choice (c) is incorrect because this is compliance audit, not a component of quality control. Choice (d) is incorrect because in many cases, quality is achieved without any formal quality control inspectors and without formal inspection points, but rather through employee control of their own work on a continuous basis.

Subject Area: Business processes—quality management. Source: CIA 1196, III-23.

63. **(a)** The question addresses one of the key components of TQM which is continuous improvement and control for quality by people who produce the goods and services. Under a TQM approach, all employees, not only managers, are responsible for quality. Choice (b) is incorrect because quality control is performed throughout the process by all concerned. Choice (c) is incorrect because this statement is too broad and applies to anything, not just TQM. Choice (d) is incorrect because TQM philosophy recommends limiting the number of suppliers and considering quality and service in addition to price as criteria for selection of suppliers.

Subject Area: Business processes—quality management. Source: CIA 1196, III-24.

64. **(b)** Although choices (a), (c), and (d) may all be byproducts of quality circles, they are not the primary goal of quality circles. Quality circles are aimed primarily at creative problem solving and benefiting from employee creativity and knowledge.

Subject Area: Business processes—quality management. Source: CIA 1196, III-27.

65. **(d)** The process that is used to produce the manufactured goods is not thoroughly reviewed and evaluated for efficiency and effectiveness. Choice (a) is incorrect because the process is expensive, but other quality control processes can also be expensive. Choice (b) is incorrect because it may be possible, although costly, to rework defective items. Choice (c) is incorrect because no quality control system will be 100% effective.

Subject Area: Business processes—quality management. Source: CIA 1195, III-28.

66. **(a)** This defines the objective of a scatter diagram. Choice (b) is incorrect because this defines a histogram. Choice (c) is incorrect because this defines stratification. Choice (d) is incorrect because this defines a Pareto chart.

Subject Area: Business processes—quality management. Source: CIA 1195, III-11.

67. **(a)** TQM is an integrated system that anticipates, meets, and exceeds customers' needs, wants, and expectations. Choice (b) is incorrect because this is too specific. Delivery time is one of many potential activities that needs improvement. Choice (c) is incorrect because this is too specific. Delivery charge is one of many potential activities that needs improvement. Choice (d) is incorrect because increased employee participation is necessary to achieve TQM, but it is not the primary purpose for establishing the program.

Subject Area: Business processes—quality management. Source: CIA 1195, III-12.

68. **(b)** Prevention costs prohibit poor-quality services from being performed in the first place. Choice (a) is incorrect because appraisal costs are a corrective action that is costly. Choice (c) is incorrect because internal failure costs are a corrective action that is costly. Choice (d) is incorrect because external failure costs are a corrective action that is costly.

Subject Area: Business processes—quality management. Source: CIA 1195, III-13.

69. **(c)** These are the most frequent problems. Choice (a) is incorrect because more detailed information is not available. The chart does not focus on the total quantity of computer complaints. Choice (b) is incorrect because the organization should first focus on the more frequent complaints. Choice (d) is incorrect because this information is not provided.

Subject Area: Business processes—quality management. Source: CIA 1195, III-15.

70. **(d)** The chart does display the absolute frequency of each computer complaint. Choice (a) is incorrect because the chart does not display the arithmetic mean. Choice (b) is incorrect because the chart does not display the relative frequency. Choice (c) is incorrect because the chart does not display the median.

Subject Area: Business processes—quality management. Source: CIA 1195, III-16.

71. **(a)** Quality cost index percentage for June = (5,000 + 5,000 + 15,000 + 11,000)/100,000 = 36,000/100,000 = 0.36 × 100 = 36%. Quality cost index percentage for May = (4,000 + 6,000 + 12,000 + 14,000)/90,000 = 36,000/90,000 = 0.40 × 100 = 40%. Decrease in index from May to June = 40% – 36% = 4%. Therefore, by definition, choices (b), (c), and (d) are incorrect.

Subject Area: Business processes—quality management. Source: CIA 1195, III-98.

72. **(d)** Management retains the right to make the final decisions. Choice (a) is incorrect because a quality circle is a small group of subordinates and supervisors—usually eight to ten people. Choice (b) is incorrect because each member is responsible for the success of the circle, and success depends on members having these skills. Choice (c) is incorrect because quality circles are the way work is accomplished in companies that use them. Participation is part of each worker's job.

Subject Area: Business processes—quality management. Source: CIA 1195, II-33.

73. **(c)** Prevention of a defect is felt in reduced costs throughout the entire manufacturing and quality inspection cycle. Choices (a), (b), and (d) are incorrect because they are examples of feedback controls and are not as effective as a feedforward (preventive) control.

Subject Area: Business processes—quality management. Source: CIA 1190, III-14.

74. **(c)** Superior product quality is not attained just through more inspection, better statistical quality control, and cross-functional teamwork. Manufacturers must make fundamental changes in the way they produce products and do each job right the first time. Choice (a) is incorrect because this is only a part of the TQM emphasis. Choice (b) is incorrect because this is only a part of the TQM emphasis. Choice (d) is incorrect because this is only a part of the TQM emphasis.

Subject Area: Business processes—quality management. Source: CIA 594, III-53.

75. **(a)** The firm would do well to spend the bulk of their funds on prevention through better product and process design and testing, supplier evaluation and training, employee training, and preventative maintenance. That is, prevent quality breakdowns before the product is produced. Choices (b), (c), and (d) are incorrect. While spending funds in these areas will improve quality, the funds are better spent on prevention than on appraisal, internal failure, or external failure.

Subject Area: Business processes—quality management. Source: CIA 594, III-54.

76. **(d)** The firm must avoid external failures. If low-quality products are discovered by a firm's customers, it will not be able to build a reputation as a world-class manufacturer. The firm should spend their funds on prevention, appraisal, and internal failure, in that order. That is, prevent quality breakdowns before the product is produced and shipped so that the customer never receives poor-quality products. Choices (a), (b), and (c) are incorrect because detecting poor-quality products at these earlier stages prevents the customer from ever receiving the poor-quality products.

Subject Area: Business processes—quality management. Source: CIA 594, III-55.

77. **(b)** The number of parts is not a measure of quality. Choices (a), (c), and (d) are incorrect because each one is a measure of the quality of the product.

Subject Area: Business processes—quality management. Source: CIA 594, III-56.

78. **(c)** The economic order quantity model is related to what quantity (not quality) of a product should be purchased to minimize ordering and holding costs. Choice (a) is incorrect because ISO 9000 is an international standard of quality which any firm's products need to meet. Choice (b) is incorrect because TQM is the process of changing organization structure and climate and redirecting product quality programs towards becoming a global quality leader. Choice (d) is incorrect because a quality circle is a small group of workers who volunteer to meet regularly to undertake work-related projects designed to advance the company, improve working conditions, and spur mutual self development through using quality concepts.

Subject Area: Business processes—quality management. Source: CIA 594, III-64.

79. **(a)** This is the purpose of a TQC system. Choice (b) is incorrect because it represents a means to achieve the objective of choice (a). Choice (c) is incorrect because this does not relate to parts and material. Choice (d) is incorrect because this is the purpose of another control in a JIT system.

Subject Area: Business processes—quality management. Source: CIA 1191, I-11.

80. **(c)** P-charts are appropriate when the inspection process classifies products into just two categories. In such processes, the distribution of items in each category follows a binomial distribution. The P-chart is based on the binomial distribution. Choices (a) and (b) are incorrect because X-bar and R charts rely on sampling from the normal distribution. Therefore, they are inappropriate for controlling the proportion of unacceptable items. Choice (d) is incorrect because Cusum charts require that dimensions of the product that are of interest can be measured easily.

Subject Area: Business processes—quality management. Source: CIA 592, III-66.

81. **(a)** P-Charts are appropriate when the inspection process classifies products into just two categories. In such processes, the distribution of items in each category follows a binomial distribution. The p-chart is based on the binomial distribution. Choice (b) is incorrect because X-bar and R charts rely on sampling from the normal distribution. Therefore, they are inappropriate for controlling the proportion of unacceptable items. Choice (c) is incorrect because it is the same as choice (b). Choice (d) is incorrect because SQC charts include X-bar and p-charts.

Subject Area: Business processes—quality management. Source: CIA 591, III-45.

82. **(b)** Appraisal costs are those costs (such as test equipment maintenance and destructive testing) incurred to detect which products do not conform to specifications. Choice (a) is incorrect. Prevention costs are incurred to prevent the production of products that do not conform to specifications. Choice (c) is incorrect. Rework costs, a type of failure cost, are incurred when a nonconforming product is detected and corrections are made. Choice (d) is incorrect. Failure costs are incurred in the repair of nonconforming products.

Subject Area: Business processes—quality management. Source: CIA Model Exam 1998, III-1.

83. **(b)** Specifications for materials purchased provide an objective means of determining that the materials meet the minimum quality level required for production. Choice (a) is incorrect. This would not ensure that raw materials are of sufficient quality. Choice (c) is incorrect. This would only help ensure that raw materials are used in the proper quantities. Choice (d) is incorrect. This would only permit proper determination of spoilage after raw materials have been used in production.

Subject Area: Business processes—quality management. Source: CIA Model Exam 2002, III-25.

84. **(a)** Teams can use the diverse knowledge and skills of all team members. Choice (b) is incorrect because teams are often inefficient and costly. Choice (c) is incorrect. Although employee motivation may be high in teams, the high motivation does not always translate directly to quality improvement. Choice (d) is incorrect. Although need for supervision may be reduced, it is not eliminated.

Subject Area: Business processes—quality management. Source: CIA Model Exam 2002, III-3.

International Organization for Standardization (ISO) Framework

85. **(d)** The work involved in implementing the ISO 9001 quality standards is completely different and separate from applying for the US Malcolm Baldrige National Quality award. There is no connection between these two programs in terms of filing applications.

Subject Area: Business processes—ISO framework. Source: CBM, Volume two.

86. **(c)** Removing tariffs between countries is handled by each country's economic and political system, not by the ISO certification process. The other three are valid reasons.

Subject Area: Business processes—ISO framework. Source: CBM, Volume two.

87. **(a)** After an application for certification is filed, registrars will conduct on-site audits. They review documents and conduct interviews. Prior to that, each applicant will do his own preassessment work. The final step is assessment by the registrars. There is no step of rectification.

Subject Area: Business processes—ISO framework. Source: CBM, Volume two.

88. **(c)** Third-party auditors or registrars are used in the certification process. A national quality board will accredit the auditors.

Subject Area: Business processes—ISO framework. Source: CBM, Volume two.

89. **(a)** The ISO 9000 has four quality measures including (1) leadership, (2) human resource developments and management, (3) management of process quality, and (4) customer focus and satisfaction. The US Malcolm Baldrige has seven categories including (1) leadership, (2) strategic planning, (3) customer and market focus,(4) information and analysis, (5) human resources focus, (6) process management, and (7) business results. Both of them are aligned very closely with each other.

Subject Area: Business processes—ISO framework. Source: CBM, Volume two.

90. **(a)** The QS-9000 standard was developed to make it easier for suppliers to do business with auto manufacturers and other original equipment manufacturers.

Subject Area: Business processes—ISO framework. Source: CBM, Volume two.

91. **(b)** ISO 9000 addresses quality system standards focusing on processes, not on products or people.

Subject Area: Business processes—ISO framework. Source: CBM, Volume two.

92. **(c)** The goal of the ISO 9000 standards is to eliminate non-value-added functions by focusing on improving internal processes such as manufacturing, sales, and technical services. Customer satisfaction and business results are the focus of the Malcolm Baldrige National Quality Award program. Productivity improvement is the focus of the Shingo Prize in quality.

Subject Area: Business processes—ISO framework. Source: CBM, Volume two.

93. **(c)** The ISO-14000 is the international standard for environmental management. The other three are examples of product quality standards.

Subject Area: Business processes—ISO framework. Source: CBM, Volume two.

Forecasting

94. **(b)** Scenario analysis is the preparation and study of written descriptions of alternative but equally likely future conditions. Scenarios are visions of what "could be" and are of two types: longitudinal (describes how the present is expected to evolve into the future) and cross-sectional (describes possible future situations at a given point in time).

Subject Area: Business processes—forecasting. Source: Author.

95. **(a)** There are three types of forecasts: (1) event outcome forecasts, (2) event timing forecasts, and (3) time series forecasts. Event outcome forecasts are used to predict the outcome of highly probable future events. Event timing forecasts predict when given events will occur. Time series forecasts seek to estimate future values in a sequence of periodically recorded data such as sales and inventory levels.

Subject Area: Business processes—forecasting. Source: Author.

96. **(b)** "Timing questions" in the event timing forecast can be answered by identifying leading indicators that historically have preceded the events in question. For example, a declining inflation rate (a leading indicator) prompts banks to lower their prime interest rates.

Subject Area: Business processes—forecasting. Source: Author.

97. **(b)** Extrinsic forecasts are based on correlated leading indicators, such as estimating furniture sales based on housing starts. These forecasts are more useful for large aggregations such as total company sales than for individual product line sales. The intrinsic forecast method is a forecast based on internal factors such as an average of past sales.

Subject Area: Business processes—forecasting. Source: Author.

98. **(c)** Trend analysis is the hypothetical extension of a past pattern of events or time series into the future. An underlying assumption of trend analysis is that past and present tendencies will continue into the future.

Subject Area: Business processes—forecasting. Source: Author.

99. **(c)** Judgmental forecasts are both fast and inexpensive but their accuracy depends on how informed the manager is.

Subject Area: Business processes—forecasting. Source: Author.

100. **(d)** Trend is the long-run shift or movement in the time series observable over several periods of data.

Subject Area: Business processes—forecasting. Source: Author.

101. **(b)** A seasonal component is the component of the time series model that shows a periodic pattern over one year or less. Seasonal components are regular repeated patterns. A cyclical component is the component of the time series model that results in periodic above-trend and below-trend behavior of the time series lasting more than one year (choice c.).

Subject Area: Business processes—forecasting. Source: Author.

102. **(a)** The irregular component is the component of the time series model that reflects the random variation of the actual time series values beyond what can be explained by the trend, cyclical, and seasonal components. The irregular component is short-term, unanticipated, and nonrecurring factors in a time series that provide the random variability. Smoothing methods are used to smooth the irregular component. The residual is the difference between the actual value of the dependent variable and the value predicted by the regression equation. The forecast error is the difference between actual and forecasted values. The mean squared error is an approach to measuring the accuracy of a forecasting mode. This measure is the average of the sum of the squared differences between the actual time series values and the forecasted values.

Subject Area: Business processes—forecasting. Source: Author.

103. **(b)** The causal forecasting model is a forecasting method that relates a time series to other variables that are believed to explain or cause its behavior. A simple linear regression is a method for analyzing the relation between one independent variable and one dependent variable. In multiple regression, there can be several independent variables and one dependent variable.

Subject Area: Business processes—forecasting. Source: Author.

104. **(a)** A seasonal index is a measure of the seasonal effect on a time series. A seasonal index above one indicates a positive effect; exactly one indicates no seasonal effect; and less than one indicates a negative effect.

Subject Area: Business processes—forecasting. Source: Author.

105. **(a)** A deseasonalized time series is a time series that has had the effect of season removed by dividing each original time series observation by the corresponding seasonal index.

Subject Area: Business processes—forecasting. Source: Author.

106. **(c)** The Delphi technique is a qualitative technique, not a quantitative technique. Choice (a) is incorrect. The least squares technique is used in regression models to produce a line that best fits the data. Choice (b) is incorrect. The exponential smoothing technique (single parameter) is appropriate for such a database. Choice (d) is incorrect. The moving average process is used to decompose the time series components

Subject Area: Business processes—forecasting. Source: CIA Model Exam 1998, III-36.

107. **(d)** If the original data (with the four trends) is divided by the seasonal norm, the seasonal component is factored out of the data.

Subject Area: Business processes—forecasting. Source: CIA Model Exam 1998, III-38.

108. **(b)** Internal accounting allocations of costs to different segments of the company are arbitrary assignments of already incurred costs which do not have anything to do with forecasting demand. Choices (a), (c), and (d) are incorrect because knowing the behavior of business cycles, understanding seasonal variations in demand for the product, and using econometric models can be valuable when forecasting the required purchases of inventory.

Subject Area: Business processes—forecasting. Source: CIA Model Exam 1998, III-39.

109. **(d)** Solution strategies of the "what if" class are the essence of simulation. Choice (a) is incorrect because statistical sampling does not involve solution strategies. Choice (b) is incorrect because econometric forecasting uses economics to predict the behavior of selected data. Choice (c) is incorrect because queuing theory is used to solve waiting-line problems.

Subject Area: Business processes—forecasting. Source: CIA Model Exam 1998, III-40.

110. **(a)** Sensitivity analysis reveals the impact of changes in one or more input variables on the output or results. Choice (b) is incorrect because statistical estimation involves the estimation of parameters. Choice (c) is incorrect because statistical hypothesis testing involves testing of hypotheses concerning estimated parameters. Choice (d) is incorrect because a time series study involves forecasting data over time.

Subject Area: Business processes—forecasting. Source: CIA 593, III-66.

111. **(a)** Simulation is a technique used to describe the behavior of a real-world system over time. Most often this technique employs a computer program to perform the simulation computations. Sensitivity analysis examines how outcomes change as the model parameters change. Choice (b) is incorrect because linear programming is a mathematical technique for maximizing or minimizing a given objective subject to certain constraints. Choice (c) is incorrect because correlation analysis is a statistical procedure for studying the relation between variables. Choice (d) is incorrect because differential analysis is a method used for decision making that compares differences in costs (and revenues) under two or more alternatives.

Subject Area: Business processes—forecasting. Source: CIA 1194, III-61.

112. **(a)** Simulation models are probabilistic not deterministic. Choice (b) is incorrect because simulation models may involve sampling. Choice (c) is incorrect because simulation models mathematically estimate what performance would be under various conditions. Choice (d) is incorrect because simulation models are stochastic or probabilistic models.

Subject Area: Business processes—forecasting. Source: CIA 594, III-60.

113. **(a)** A model is designed to understand the behavior of the simulation model. The characteristics that are learned from the model are then used to make inferences about the real system. Choice (b) is incorrect because least squares is a prediction and estimation technique utilizing a single dependent and single or multiple independent variables. Choice (c) is incorrect because a waiting-line technique is used to balance desirable service levels against the cost of providing more service. Choice (d) is incorrect because it is a forecasting technique utilizing arbitrary weights.

Subject Area: Business processes—forecasting. Source: CIA 593, III-65.

114. **(a)** Simulation is a technique in which a probabilistic process is first modeled. The inputs to the model are then varied a large number of times to estimate the distribution of possible outcomes from the model of the variable of interest. Simulations that use a random-number procedure to generate values for the inputs are referred to as Monte Carlo simulations. Choice (b) is incorrect because linear programming is a mathematical technique for maximizing or minimizing a given objective subject to certain constraints. Choice (c) is incorrect because correlation analysis is a statistical procedure for studying the relation between variables. Choice (d) is incorrect because differential analysis is a method used for decision making that compares differences in costs (and revenues) under two or more alternatives.

Subject Area: Business processes—forecasting. Source: CIA 592, III-64.

115. **(b)** Exponential smoothing puts most weight on recent sales data. Choice (a) is incorrect because an unweighted average will not give more importance to more recent data. Choice (c) is incorrect because queuing theory is used to determine waiting time. Choice (d) is incorrect because linear regression analysis is a cross-sectional tool, which does not give more importance to more recent data.

Subject Area: Business processes—forecasting. Source: CIA 594, II-38.

116. **(a)** Time series analysis is a statistical forecasting technique that uses patterns observed in historical data to predict future values. Choice (b) is incorrect because queuing theory is used to minimize the cost of waiting in line plus the cost of servicing waiting lines when items arrive randomly at a service point and are serviced sequentially. Choice (c) is incorrect because linear programming is a mathematical technique for maximizing or minimizing a given objective subject to certain constraints. Choice (d) is incorrect because sensitivity analysis is a method for studying the effects of changes in one or more variables on the results of a decision model.

Subject Area: Business processes—forecasting. Source: CIA 1193, III-68.

117. (d) Econometrics is a forecasting model that uses a number of economic and demographic time series. Choice (a) is incorrect because linear programming is a problem-solving approach developed for situations involving maximizing or minimizing a linear function based on certain linear constraints. Choice (b) is incorrect because network analysis is used to solve management problems in areas such as system design and project scheduling. Choice (c) is incorrect because operations research is a term used interchangeably with management science, an approach to managerial decision making based upon scientific methods and extensive use of quantitative analysis.

Subject Area: Business processes—forecasting. Source: CIA 593, III-71.

118. (c) There are many situations where each observation should not be given equal input in establishing the trend line. In such cases, exponential smoothing technique is good to use since it incorporates the more recent observations. Choice (a) is incorrect because time series analysis uses trend projections. Choice (b) is incorrect because dynamic programming involves linear programming. Choice (d) is incorrect because econometrics is an analysis involving two or more variables.

Subject Area: Business processes—forecasting. Source: CIA 593, III-72.

119. (b) Econometrics deals with statistical inferences about relationships between economic data. Choice (a) is incorrect because macroeconomic and microeconomics do not deal with statistical analysis. They refer to classifications of economic theory. Macroeconomics deals with the behavior of economic aggregates like GNP and the level of employment. Choice (c) is incorrect because microeconomics deals with economic behavior of individual units like consumers and firms. Choice (d) is incorrect because socioeconomics combines social and economic factors.

Subject Area: Business processes—forecasting. Source: CIA 1191, III-99.

120. (d) Econometrics is the application of statistical methods to economic or business data. It analyzes the relationships between variables and uses multiple regression analysis. Choice (a) is incorrect because it does not involve regression analysis. Choice (b) is incorrect because it does not involve model assumptions. Choice (c) is incorrect because it does not involve regression analysis.

Subject Area: Business processes—forecasting. Source: CIA 1193, III-74.

121. (a) Regression analysis is a statistical technique for measuring the relationship between variables. It estimates the component of the dependent variable that varies with changes in the independent variable and component that does not vary (fixed) with changes in the independent variable. Choice (b) is incorrect because game theory is a mathematical approach to decision making in which each decision maker takes into account the courses of action of competitors. Choice (c) is incorrect because sensitivity analysis is a method for studying how changes in one or more variables affect the optimal solution in a linear programming model. Choice (d) is incorrect because queuing theory consists of waiting line models, which can be used to determine the operating characteristics for a waiting line.

Subject Area: Business processes—forecasting. Source: CIA 1194, III-59.

122. (c) The R^2 explains the amount of variation in the dependent variable (interest income) that is explained by the independent variables. In this case, less of the change in interest income is explained by the model, thus, some other factor must be causing the interest income variable to change. This would merit audit investigation. Choice (a) is incorrect. Cross sectional regression analysis would not be appropriate because the auditor is trying to estimate changes in a single account balance over time. Choice (b) is incorrect. Regression analysis may still be the most appropriate methodology to estimate interest income, but the auditor should first understand the factors that may be causing R^2 to be decreasing. It may be caused because there is a systematic error in the account balance. Choice (d) is incorrect. Linear regression models are simpler models. The problem is that the auditor should be looking for either a systematic error in the account balance or to a more complex model.

Subject Area: Business processes—forecasting. Source: CIA 595, II-46.

123. (c) This answer is only 0.11 from the maximum value of -1.0. The negative sign indicates the direction relationship (e.g., inverse) between the independent and dependent variables. Choice (a) is incorrect. The range for the correlation coefficient is between -1.0 and +1.0, inclusive. Thus, this answer is not possible even though it is the largest value among the four alternative answers. Choice (b) is incorrect. This is the weakest correlation coefficient among the four alternative answers. This answer is so close to 0.00 that no relationship exists between the independent and dependent variables. Choice (d) is incorrect. This answer is only 0.25 from the maximum value of +1.0 but answer (c) is closer and therefore, stronger.

Subject Area: Business processes—forecasting. Source: CIA 1194, II-46.

124. (a) Mathematically, R^2 always approaches 1.0 as the number of variables in the regression approaches the number of observations in the sample (even if the predictors are unrelated to the dependent variable). This model has a very large number of predictors for the small sample size. If the R^2 is adjusted for the number of variables, it drops to only 0.24. Choice (b) is incorrect. We do not know what the "true" model is and therefore cannot make this inference. Choice (c) is incorrect. The model has too many predictors for the small sample size. Choice (d) is incorrect. You can have a high R^2 in a bad sample with a bad model just as easily as in a good sample with a good model.

Subject Area: Business processes—forecasting. Source: CIA 1195, II-50.

125. (b) The most appropriate statistical tool is cross section regression analysis because it compares attributes of all store's operating statistics at one point in time. Choice (a) is incorrect. Linear time series analysis would not be applicable because it is a simple model, which compares individual stores over time. Choice (c) is incorrect. Cross tabulations have to be built on a model of expectations. Unless the model is built, the analysis is not useful. Choice (d) is incorrect. The stated objective is to compare stores at one point in time. Multiple regression time series analysis compares the performance of an individual store over a period of time.

Subject Area: Business processes—forecasting. Source: CIA 595, II-47.

126. (c) A regression coefficient represents the change in the dependent variable for a unit change in the independent variable. Choice (a) is incorrect because a regression coefficient tells you nothing about the means of the variables. Choice (b) is incorrect because to predict a specific value of sales, you must multiply the independent variable value by the coefficient and add the intercept value. Choice (d) is incorrect because the absolute size of the coefficient bears no necessary relationship to the importance of the variable.

Subject Area: Business processes—forecasting. Source: CIA 1195, II-30.

127. (c) A multiple regression analysis would help the auditor identify which factors appear to be driving the changes in the company's cost structure. Choice (a) is incorrect because this procedure does not help quantify the reasons for changes in production costs. It only helps estimate production costs and that data should already be readily available in the client's records. Choice (b) is incorrect because this method only identifies one possible cause. Choice (d) is incorrect because the linear regression only addresses one factor and would not be as useful as multiple regression.

Subject Area: Business processes—forecasting. Source: CIA 1196, I-29.

128. (b) Multiple regression is the most effective because we are trying to determine the relative effect of four different variables. Choice (a) is incorrect because the data are cross-sectional. Choice (c) is incorrect because the dependent variable, sales, is continuous. Choice (d) is incorrect because the linearity of the relationships cannot be assessed before the data is analyzed.

Subject Area: Business processes—forecasting. Source: CIA 594, II-39.

129. (a) The change in monthly maintenance cost per hour of operation is the slope of the cost function.

$$\text{Slope} = \frac{1{,}200{,}000 - 900{,}000}{4{,}000 - 2{,}000} \quad \text{or} \quad \frac{1{,}200{,}000 - 750{,}000}{4{,}000 - 1{,}000}$$

Or

$$\frac{900{,}000 - 750{,}000}{2{,}000 - 1{,}000} = \$150 \text{ per hour}$$

Therefore, by definition, choices (b), (c), and (d) would be incorrect.

Subject Area: Business processes—forecasting. Source: CIA 1193, III-65.

130. (b) We note that as X increases (inverse relationship) Y decreases, forcing the coefficient of correlation to be negative. As X increases by 1, Y consistently decreases by 2, hence a perfect association between the data r must equal to –1. Choice (a) is incorrect. No correlation is incorrect; there is a perfect negative correlation. Choice (c) is incorrect. Correlation is perfect, but an inverse not a direct relationship exists. Choice (d) is incorrect. We are able to determine that r = –1.

Subject Area: Business processes—forecasting. Source: CIA 593, III-64.

131. (a) Regression analysis is a statistical technique for measuring the relationship between variables. It estimates the component of the dependent variable that varies with changes in the independent variable and component that does not vary (fixed) with changes in the independent variable. Choice (b) is incorrect because game theory is a mathematical approach to decision making in which each decision maker takes into account the courses of action of competitors. Choice (c) is incorrect because sensitivity analysis is a method for studying the effects of changes in one or more variables on the results of a decision model. Choice (d) is incorrect because queuing theory is a mathematical technique for minimizing the total cost of waiting in line plus the cost of servicing lines when items arrive randomly at a service point and are serviced sequentially.

Subject Area: Business processes—forecasting. Source: CIA 1192, III-43.

132. (a) Multiple regression analysis allows you to consider the three variables. Choice (b) is incorrect because exponential smoothing is a time series technique utilizing arbitrary weights. Choice (c) is incorrect. In bivariate regression analysis there is but one independent variable. We have three. Choice (d) is incorrect. Auto regressive models involve bivariate regression analysis where the independent variable is a lagged value for the dependent variable.

Subject Area: Business processes—forecasting. Source: CIA 592, III-75.

133. (c) When there are four independent variables such as X1 through X4, multiple regression analysis is the best technique to use. When only one independent variable is involved, it is called simple regression analysis. Choice (a) is incorrect because integrated auto-regressive-moving average (ARIMA) modeling is a time series technique. Choice (b) is incorrect because exponential smoothing is also a time series model. Choice (d) is incorrect because linear programming optimizes outputs given scarce resources.

Subject Area: Business processes—forecasting. Source: CIA 592, III-55.

134. (a) Since one slope is negative, X3 is inversely related to Y. Since three slopes are positive, X1, X2, and X4 are directly related to Y. Therefore, by definition, choices (b), (c), and (d) will be incorrect.

Subject Area: Business processes—forecasting. Source: CIA 592, III-56.

135. (b) Dummy variables take on values of zero and one, and they represent the qualitative variables (X4) in the regression analysis. When an independent variable (X4) is a nominal or ordinal variable, it is called a qualitative variable. Choice (a) is incorrect because multicollinearity is a dependence between different independent variables. Choice (c) is incorrect because omitted variables impact regression analysis but do not represent a type of variable. Choice (d) is incorrect because an outlier is an extreme data point not a variable.

Subject Area: Business processes—forecasting. Source: CIA 592, III-57.

136. (b) Each of the answers represent the slopes of the four independent variables. The slope asked for was that of independent variable X2. Therefore, by definition, choices (a), (c), and (d) will be incorrect.

Subject Area: Business processes—forecasting. Source: CIA 592, III-57.

137. (d) Predicted Y = 124,000 + 5(10,000) + 350(300) – 1,700(9) + 4,000(1) = 267,700. Therefore, by definition, choices (a), (b), and (c) will be incorrect.

Subject Area: Business processes—forecasting. Source: CIA 592, III-59.

138. (b) A correlation coefficient of –1.00 implies that the observations fall exactly along a straight line **and** that the value of one variable increases (decreases) as the other decreases (increases). In the above example the equation of the straight line is

$$y = 200 - 4x$$

or

$$x = 50 - 1/4y$$

Choices (a) and (c) are incorrect because a positive correlation coefficient implies that one variable increases (decreases) as the other increases (decreases). The data clearly do not indicate this. Choice (d) is incorrect because a correlation coefficient of zero implies that the two variables are unrelated. The data clearly indicate that the two variables move in opposite directions.

Subject Area: Business processes—forecasting. Source: CIA 591, III-44.

139. (b) A linear equation was used with nonlinear relationship. Choice (a) is incorrect. A distractor, autocorrelation is a nonsense response. Choice (c) is incorrect. The data is related, but not linearly. Choice (d) is incorrect. The data is first directly, then inversely related.

Subject Area: Business processes—forecasting. Source: CIA 1190, III-39.

140. (c) The Delphi technique is a qualitative technique, not a quantitative technique. Choice (a) is incorrect because weighted least squares is used only in regression models that have the specification problem heteroscedasticity. Choice (b) is incorrect because the exponential smoothing technique (single parameter) is appropriate for such a database. Choice (d) is incorrect because the moving average process is used to decompose the time series components.

Subject Area: Business processes—forecasting. Source: CIA 1190, III-45.

141. (d) The end-product of multivariate regression analysis is a mathematical equation that estimates the relationship between a dependent variable such as sales and a set of independent or predictor variables, such as price, advertising expenditures, etc. Given the regression equation, sales can be forecast (predicted) based upon knowledge of the independent variables. Choice (a) is incorrect because it is not a forecasting technique. Linear programming is a mathematical procedure suitable for solving a specific type of optimization problem. Specifically it allows one to solve constrained maxima/minima problems in which the objective function and the constraints are linear. Linear programming is **not** a forecasting technique. Choice (b) is incorrect because exponential smoothing is a forecasting technique but the models only utilize information contained in the series to be forecast (i.e., sales). Thus, in this case an application of exponential smoothing only requires data on sales in order to forecast sales. Thus, the requirement that the model relate sales to a set of predictor variables would not be satisfied. A knowledge of the firm's price and the other specified variables is irrelevant in exponential smoothing methods. Choice (c) is incorrect because trend extrapolation (trend analysis) is a forecasting technique often referred to as curve-fitting. In trend extrapolation, the analyst attempts to determine the mathematical equation that "best" reflects the underlying trend in the series and extrapolates this pattern into the future. However, just as was the case with exponential smoothing, trend extrapolation techniques are pure (naive) time series models and only require data on sales in order to forecast sales. Thus, the requirement that the model relate sales to a set of predictor variables would not be satisfied.

Subject Area: Business processes—forecasting. Source: CIA 590, III-43.

Project Management Techniques

142. (a) A project is defined as a temporary endeavor undertaken to achieve a particular objective, aim, or goal. Each project has a beginning date and an end date.

Subject Area: Business processes—project management techniques. Source: Author.

143. (a) Managers have competing demands placed on them. Establishing priorities and managing time are not easy. Managers should develop the skill of learning to say "no" to others who are adding more demands on them.

Subject Area: Business processes—project management techniques. Source: Author.

144. (b) The project life cycle has four stages of conceptualization, planning, execution, and termination. In the conceptualization stage, ideas are presented, discussed, and finalized. Project goals, budgets, and schedules are prepared. The project is just started to proceed.

Subject Area: Business processes—project management techniques. Source: Author.

145. (d) In the execution stage of the project life cycle, budget demands are the highest because the project is being implemented. Pressure is put on the project team to complete the project on time and within the budget.

Subject Area: Business processes—project management techniques. Source: Author.

146. (b) Project organizations are common today due to a need for quick response demanded by the customers. Decisions are made quickly leading to faster implementations. Cross-functional teams of people with different technical skills are brought together on a temporary basis to complete a specific project.

Subject Area: Business processes—project management techniques. Source: Author.

147. (b) Work simplification means reducing complexity, discontinuing unnecessary and burdensome procedures, and eliminating wasted activities, tasks, and work steps. Work measurement uses time and motion studies to estimate the time it takes to complete a task, step, or an activity.

Subject Area: Business processes—project management techniques. Source: Author.

148. (**b**) Project managers should have greater amount of "people management skills," which include leadership, communication, motivation, conflict resolution, and negotiation skills. Technical skills (hard skills such as engineering, science, and technology skills) are least important when compared to interpersonal skills (soft skills such as people management skills).

Subject Area: Business processes—project management techniques. Source: Author.

149. (**a**) Establishing project priorities remains a subjective process affected by organizational politics and value conflicts. The subjective process uses qualitative techniques while the objective process uses quantitative techniques.

Subject Area: Business processes—project management techniques. Source: Author.

150. (**b**) In the ABC priority system used in project time management, the "A" system deals with "must do" objectives, which are critical to successful performance. The "B" system deals with "should do" objectives, which are necessary for improved performance. The "C" system deals with "nice to do" objectives, which are desirable for, improved performance.

Subject Area: Business processes—project management techniques. Source: Author.

151. (**b**) In the functional project organizational structure, groups consist of individuals who perform the same function, such as engineering or manufacturing, or have the same expertise or skills, such as electronic engineering or testing. Each functional group or component concentrates on performing its own activities in support of the company's business mission.

Subject Area: Business processes—project management techniques. Source: CBM, Volume two.

152. (**c**) In a functional project structure, the project manager does not have complete authority over the project team since the team members administratively work for their respective functional managers. In a matrix project structure, the project manager is responsible for achieving the project results while the functional manager is responsible for providing the resources needed to achieve the results. Under the matrix structure, the project manager is the intermediary between the company and the customer.

Subject Area: Business processes—project management techniques. Source: CBM, Volume two.

153. (**a**) In a matrix-type project organizational structure, the project manager is responsible for the project results, while the functional managers are responsible for providing the resources needed to achieve the results.

Subject Area: Business processes—project management techniques. Source: CBM, Volume two.

154. (**a**) The scope of a project—also known as the project scope or the work scope—is all the work that must be done in order to satisfy the customer that the deliverables (the tangible product or items to be provided) meet the requirements or acceptance criteria agreed upon at the onset of the project.

Subject Area: Business processes—project management techniques. Source: CBM, Volume two.

155. (**c**) Ultimately, the responsibility of the project manager is to make sure the customer is satisfied.

Subject Area: Business processes—project management techniques. Source: CBM, Volume two.

156. (**c**) A work breakdown structure is a hierarchical tree of work elements or items accomplished or produced by the project team during the project. The work breakdown structure usually identifies the organization or individual responsible for each work package.

Subject Area: Business processes—project management techniques. Source: CBM, Volume two.

157. (**c**) The key to effective project control is measuring actual progress and comparing it to planned progress on a timely and regular basis and taking corrective action immediately. The project control process involves regularly gathering data on project performance, comparing actual performance to planned performance, and taking corrective actions if actual performance is behind planned performance.

Subject Area: Business processes—project management techniques. Source: CBM, Volume two.

158. (**a**) A baseline plan provides a roadmap showing how the project scope will be accomplished. When changes are agreed upon, a new baseline should be established and used as the benchmark against which actual project performance will be compared.

Subject Area: Business processes—project management techniques. Source: CBM, Volume two.

159. (**b**) Corrective actions that will eliminate the negative slack from the project schedule must be identified. Activities that have longer duration estimates present the biggest opportunity for larger time reductions. In most cases, eliminating negative slack by reducing duration of activities will involve a tradeoff in the form of an increase in costs or a reduction in scope.

Subject Area: Business processes—project management techniques. Source: CBM, Volume two.

160. (**d**) In the time-cost tradeoff methodology, the project time can be reduced with an increase in cost.

Subject Area: Business processes—project management techniques. Source: CBM, Volume two.

161. (**d**) There are basically two types of contracts: fixed-price and cost-reimbursement. The contract must state the terms by which the customer will make payments to the contractor.

Subject Area: Business processes—project management techniques. Source: CBM, Volume two.

162. (**d**) Cost reimbursement contracts are most appropriate for projects that involve risk. The customer agrees to pay the contractor for all actual cost incurred, regardless of the amount, plus some agreed-upon profit. This type of contract is high risk for the customer due to cost uncertainty.

Subject Area: Business processes—project management techniques. Source: CBM, Volume two.

163. (b) For a project, the objective is usually defined in terms of scope, schedule, and cost. Schedule requires completing the work within budget by a certain time.

Subject Area: Business processes—project management techniques. Source: CBM, Volume two.

164. (a) In project management, each activity has two pairs of duration: normal time and crash time. The normal time is the estimated length of time required to perform an activity, according to the plan. The crash time is the shortest estimated length of time in which the activity can be completed.

Subject Area: Business processes—project management techniques. Source: CBM, Volume two.

165. (d) The cost performance index is a measure of the cost efficiency with which the project is being performed. The formula for determining the index is cumulative earned value divided by cumulative actual cost.

Subject Area: Business processes—project management techniques. Source: CBM, Volume two.

166. (b) The cost variance is the difference between the cumulative earned value of the work performed and the cumulative actual cost.

Subject Area: Business processes—project management techniques. Source: CBM, Volume two.

167. (a) A negative cost variance means that the work performed is not keeping with the actual cost. It also means that there is a gap between the value of the work performed and the actual costs incurred. A cost performance index of less than 1.0 means for every dollar actually expended, less than one dollar of earned value was received. When the index goes below 1.0 or gradually gets smaller, corrective action should be taken.

Subject Area: Business processes—project management techniques. Source: CBM, Volume two.

168. (b) In the theory of constraints, critical chain is the longest route through a project network. It considers both technological and resource contention constraints in completing the project. When no resource contention exists the critical chain would be the same as the critical path. The critical ratio is a job dispatching rule that calculate a priority index number by dividing the time to due date remaining by the expected elapsed time to finish the job.

Subject Area: Business processes—project management techniques. Source: Author.

169. (a) Earned value is the total value, including overhead, of approved estimates for completed activities in a project.

Subject Area: Business processes—project management techniques. Source: Author.

170. (b) Program evaluation and review technique (PERT) times are estimated times for the completion of PERT activities. PERT times are weighted averages of the separate time estimates (optimistic, most likely, and pessimistic). The formula for calculating estimated PERT time is (optimistic time plus 4 times most likely time plus pessimistic time)/6. Thus, the most likely time is more heavily weighted than the other time estimates.

Subject Area: Business processes—project management techniques. Source: Author.

171. (c) A network diagram shows the sequential flow and interrelationships of activities. Network planning is a technique that is helpful in planning, scheduling, and controlling projects that consists of many interrelated activities.

Subject Area: Business processes—project management techniques. Source: CBM, Volume two.

172. (c) The Gantt chart combines the two functions of planning and scheduling. Since these functions are performed simultaneously, it is cumbersome to make changes to the plan manually.

Subject Area: Business processes—project management techniques. Source: CBM, Volume two.

173. (c) Network techniques separate the planning and scheduling functions. A network diagram is the result, or output, of the planning function and is not drawn to a time scale. From the network diagram a schedule is developed. Separating the two functions makes it much easier to revise a plan and calculate an updated schedule.

Subject Area: Business processes—project management techniques. Source: CBM, Volume two.

174. (c) Activities have a precedential relationship; that is, they are linked in a precedential order to show which activities must be finished before others can start. Arrows linking the activity boxes show the direction of precedence. An activity cannot start until all of the preceding activities that are linked to it by arrows have been finished.

Subject Area: Business processes—project management techniques. Source: CBM, Volume two.

175. (c) Some projects have a set of activities that are repeated several times. Laddering is a technique used for these types of projects.

Subject Area: Business processes—project management techniques. Source: CBM, Volume two.

176. (a) The earliest start (ES) time and earliest finish (EF) time are determined by calculating forward, that is, by working through the network diagram from the beginning of the project to the end of the project. There is one rule that must be followed in making these forward calculations. The ES time for a particular activity must be the same as or later than the latest of all the EF times of all the activities leading directly into that particular activity.

Subject Area: Business processes—project management techniques. Source: CBM, Volume two.

177. (d) The latest finish time for a particular activity must be the same as or earlier than the earliest of all the latest start times of all the activities emerging directly from that particular activity.

Subject Area: Business processes—project management techniques. Source: CBM, Volume two.

178. (a) Total slack equals latest finish time minus earliest finish time. Total slack for a particular path of activities is common to and shared among all the activities on that path. If total slack is positive, it represents the maximum amount of time that the activities on a particular path can be delayed without jeopardizing completion of the entire project by its required completion time.

Subject Area: Business processes—project management techniques. Source: CBM, Volume two.

179. (a) When all uncontrollable inputs are known and cannot vary, this situation calls for the use of a deterministic model. Only one time estimate is used for an activity. In a stochastic model, one or more uncontrollable inputs are unknown and subject to variation. A range of time estimates is used for an activity.
Subject Area: Business processes—project management techniques. Source: CBM, Volume two.

180. (b) In the Gantt chart, activities are listed down the left-hand side, and a time scale is shown along the bottom. The estimated time for each activity is indicated by a line or bar spanning the period during which the activity is expected to accomplish. The Gantt chart measures the planned and completed work and indicates the status of each activity.
Subject Area: Business processes—project management techniques. Source: CBM, Volume two.

181. (c) One of the major drawbacks to the traditional Gantt chart is that it does not graphically display the interrelationships of activities. Therefore, it is not obvious which activities will be affected when a given activity is delayed.
Subject Area: Business processes—project management techniques. Source: CBM, Volume two.

182. (b) The critical path is the most time-consuming chain of activities and events in a PERT network.
Subject Area: Business processes—project management techniques. Source: Author.

183. (c) PERT is a graphic sequencing, planning, and scheduling tool appropriate for large, complex, and nonroutine projects.
Subject Area: Business processes—project management techniques. Source: Author.

184. (b) A Gantt chart is a graphic planning and scheduling tool. It improves on the flowchart by specifying the time to be spent on each activity. Both the Gantt chart and the flowchart are cumbersome to draw for large and complex projects. Flowcharts do not show time elements. Gantt charts show time elements.
Subject Area: Business processes—project management techniques. Source: Author.

185. (b) The backward pass works from the last node to the start node while the forward pass works from the start node to the last node. Both the forward pass and the backward pass are used in the critical path method of project planning and management. Forward pass calculates early start dates and early finish dates.
Subject Area: Business processes—project management techniques. Source: Author.

186. (c) This would be a long-range planning topic because it affects market positioning. Choice (a) is incorrect. This would seldom be a long-range topic. Choice (b) is incorrect. This would rarely be a long-range concern. Choice (d) is incorrect. This is certainly a concern, but not for long-range planning.
Subject Area: Business processes—project management techniques. Source: CIA Model Exam 2002, III-33.

187. (a) Crashing is the process of adding resources to shorten activity times on the critical path in project scheduling. Choice (b) is incorrect. The Delphi technique is a qualitative forecasting approach. Choice (c) is incorrect. ABC analysis is an inventory model. Choice (d) is incorrect. The branch-and-bound solution is an integer programming solution.
Subject Area: Business processes—project management techniques. Source: CIA Model Exam 1998, III-30.

188. (c) The two paths are 5 + 4 + 6 = 15 days, and 3 + 2 + 6 = 11 days. The longest path, and therefore the earliest completion time, is 15 days. Choice (a) is incorrect. Eleven days is the shortest, not the longest, time to completion. Choice (b) is incorrect. Fourteen days sums 5 + 3 + 6, but is not a path to completion. Choice (d) is incorrect. Twenty days is the sum of all of the activity times.
Subject Area: Business processes—project management techniques. Source: CIA 597, III-100.

189. (a) PERT/CPM (Program Evaluation and Review Techniques/Critical Path Method) is a technique for scheduling interrelated time series activities and identifying any critical paths in the series of activities. Choice (b) is incorrect because linear programming is a mathematical technique for maximizing or minimizing a given objective subject to certain constraints. Choice (c) is incorrect because queuing theory is used to minimize the cost of waiting in line plus the cost of servicing waiting lines when items arrive randomly at a service point and are serviced sequentially. Choice (d) is incorrect because sensitivity analysis is a method for studying the effects of changes in one or more variables on the results of a decision model.
Subject Area: Business processes—project management techniques. Source: CIA 1195, III-100.

190. (d) Project management deals with managing project teams to deal with special projects. Lumpy demand refers to periodic demand for a product or service from the output of a finished project. Choice (a) is incorrect because a dummy activity is one which consumes no time but shows precedence among activities. Choice (b) is incorrect because the latest finish is the latest that an activity can finish, from the beginning of the project, without causing delay in the completion of the project. Choice (c) is incorrect because optimistic time is the time for completing an activity if all goes well.
Subject Area: Business processes—project management techniques. Source: CIA 594, III-61.

191. (c) This is used for quality control. Choices (a), (b), and (d) are incorrect because each one is used to control large-scale projects.
Subject Area: Business processes—project management techniques. Source: CIA 594, II-40.

192. (c) The critical path is A-D-E which takes 4 + 6 + 5 = 15 days. This is the longest path. Choice (a) is incorrect. The A-C path length is 13 days (i.e., 4 + 9 =13). Choice (b) is incorrect. The B-E path length is 8 days (i.e., 3 + 5 = 8). Choice (d) is incorrect. The B-D-C is not a valid path due to cycle error, in that path D cannot go back to path C.
Subject Area: Business processes—project management techniques. Source: CIA 592, III-69.

193. **(c)** Slack is the free time associated with each activity. Choice (a) is incorrect because an activity involving slack is essential to the overall project. Choice (b) is incorrect because it is not a backup activity. Choice (d) is incorrect because time is involved in a slack activity.

Subject Area: Business processes—project management techniques. Source: CIA 1191, III-37.

194. **(c)** A Gantt chart shows output (steps in an activity) on one axis and units of time on the other. Choice (a) is incorrect because a Gantt chart does not include cost information. Choice (b) is incorrect. Some information regarding sequencing may be assumed from a Gantt chart but the relationship among steps is not shown. Choice (d) is incorrect. The term "critical path" is related to a PERT network, which is a more sophisticated scheduling technique.

Subject Area: Business processes—project management techniques. Source: CIA 1191, III-6.

195. **(a)** The critical path is the sequence of activities that constrains the total completion time for the project. Any delay in completing the activities along the critical path will delay scheduled completion of the project. Choice (b) is incorrect because only activities not on the critical path may be delayed without delaying scheduled completion of the project. Choices (c) and (d) are incorrect because CPM/PERT is not used for determining the size or features to be included in the new product.

Subject Area: Business processes—project management techniques. Source: CIA 590, III-47.

Business Process Analysis

196. **(a)** Dr. Goldratt developed a management philosophy entitled theory of constraints, which can be viewed as three separate but interrelated areas. These areas include logistics, performance measurement, and logical thinking. Bottleneck management deals with identifying and managing resources (facility or department) whose capacity is less than the demand placed upon it.

Subject Area: Business processes—business process analysis. Source: Author.

197. **(b)** Logistics include drum-buffer-rope scheduling, buffer management, and VAT analysis. Problem solving is a part of logical thinking.

Subject Area: Business processes—business process analysis. Source: Author.

198. **(c)** Performance measurement includes throughput, inventory, and operating expense. Identifying problems and root causes and developing implementation plans are part of the logical thinking of the theory of constraints. The current reality tree, future reality tree, prerequisite tree, and transition tree are used in the logical thinking.

Subject Area: Business processes—business process analysis. Source: Author.

199. **(a)** VAT analysis deals with determining the general flow of parts and products from raw materials to finished goods (logical product structure). VAT analysis is a part of the theory of constraints. A 'V' logical structure starts with one or a few raw materials and the product expands into a number of different products as it flows through divergent points in its routings. The shape of an 'A' logical structure is dominated by converging points. Many raw materials are fabricated and assembled into a few finished products. A 'T' logical structure consists of numerous similar finished products assembled from common assemblies, subassemblies, and parts.

Subject Area: Business processes—business process analysis. Source: Author.

200. **(a)** Clerical process analysis centers on studying and improving the way office and administrative tasks are carried out. Joint process analyses deal with operator-machine analysis which centers on studying and improving the combination of operator work and machine work in a factory or office. Operator process analysis centers on studying and improving the movements of the operator in a factory or office. Product process analysis centers on the flow of products, and the way a product is made as it passes through various processes in a manufacturing plant.

Subject Area: Business processes—business process analysis. Source: Author.

201. **(a)** Selling is not the only one that can deliver value. Others such as production, supply chain, and logistics can deliver value equally. The other three items are essential in delivering value.

Subject Area: Business processes—business process analysis. Source: Author.

202. **(c)** The horizontal organization is described as eliminating both hierarchy and functional boundaries and is operated with multidisciplinary teams. Few layers of management are practiced between the top and the bottom of the hierarchy. There are many layers of management in the vertical organization.

Subject Area: Business processes—business process analysis. Source: Author.

203. **(a)** A process view, not the functional view, of the business is required. All the other three items are required for a proper business process orientation.

Subject Area: Business processes—business process analysis. Source: Author.

204. **(c)** Process-oriented measures are, by definition, cross-functional, which contributes to a common cause. It might also be said that what gets measured and rewarded gets done.

Subject Area: Business processes—business process analysis. Source: Author.

205. **(a)** Business process reengineering requires a radical rethinking and redesigning of a process.

Subject Area: Business processes—business process analysis. Source: Author.

206. **(b)** Benchmarking is identifying, studying, and building upon the best practices of other organizations. Benchmarking establishes standards, which provide feed forward control by warning people when they deviate from standards. Kaizen is continuous improvement. Plan, do, check and act (PDCA) is called Shewhart cycle in quality and later was modified by Deming to plan, do, study, and act (PDSA) cycle.

Subject Area: Business processes—business process analysis. Source: Author.

207. (a) Business process reengineering can be used to reduce the cycle time or speed it up.
Subject Area: Business processes—business process analysis. Source: Author.

208. (b) The time between when an order is placed and when the customer receives it is known as order cycle time.
Subject Area: Business processes—business process analysis. Source: Author.

209. (b) The time it takes to deliver a product or service after an order is placed is called customer response time.
Subject Area: Business processes—business process analysis. Source: Author.

210. (a) The time between when an order is placed and when the order is ready for setup is called order receipt time.
Subject Area: Business processes—business process analysis. Source: Author.

211. (b) The time between when an order is ready for setup and when the setup is complete is called order wait time.
Subject Area: Business processes—business process analysis. Source: Author.

212. (b) Work simplification refers to eliminating unnecessary procedures and activities in a business process. Work measurement uses industrial engineering techniques to estimate labor time and material standards.
Subject Area: Business processes—business process analysis. Source: Author.

213. (b) A company faces a constraint when the capacity to manufacture a product is limited.
Subject Area: Business processes—business process analysis. Source: Author.

214. (b) If a company is faced with limited resources, management has the following choices: (1) increase the capacity of the limited resource, (2) reduce the use of the limited resource in production, or (3) focus on products that require less of the limited resource. Constraints cannot be ignored since they can lead to loss of sales and profits.
Subject Area: Business processes—business process analysis. Source: Author.

215. (c) The theory of constraints identifies bottlenecks in the production process. A bottleneck is a facility, function, department, machine or work center whose capacity is less than the demand placed upon it.
Subject Area: Business processes—business process analysis. Source: Author.

216. (b) Bottlenecks (1) limit throughput, (2) are managed using the theory of constraints, and (3) should be relieved to increase production efficiency. Bottlenecks should not be ignored during crisis situations.
Subject Area: Business processes—business process analysis. Source: Author.

217. (a) Processing time (36 hours) is the only task that adds value to a specific customer.
Subject Area: Business processes—business process analysis. Source: Author.

218. (d) Wait time (10 hours), inspection time (1 hour), and move time (1.5 hours) are examples of non-value-added time (12.5 hours) from a customer's viewpoint.
Subject Area: Business processes—business process analysis. Source: Author.

219. (d) The manufacturing cycle time (48.5 hours) is the combination of value-added time (36 hours) and non-value-added time (12.5 hours).
Subject Area: Business processes—business process analysis. Source: Author.

220. (a) The current reality tree is a diagram, which presents a logical picture of the subject matter. It bonds cause-and-effect relationships and connects all the existing major undesirable effects. The future reality tree is a logic-based diagram for constructing and testing potential solutions before implementation. Obstacles are identified in the prerequisite tree. The transition tree will show how changes will be evolved from the current tree to the future tree.
Subject Area: Business processes—business process analysis. Source: Author.

221. (a) One cannot say that too much production is an undesirable effect without knowing the sales forecast and the production policy. The other choices are examples of undesirable effects.
Subject Area: Business processes—business process analysis. Source: Author.

222. (b) Each entry to the current reality tree is a root cause and a core problem. At least one entry leads to the existence of most of the undesirable effects. Also, conflicts will be revealed in the current reality tree.
Subject Area: Business processes—business process analysis. Source: Author.

223. (a) Cycle time can be reduced by (1) reducing process complexity through work or process simplification, (2) changing from linear process flow to parallel flow, (3) using alternate process flow paths, (4) changing the sequence or layout of a process, (5) using technology to improve process flow, and (6) letting customer or suppliers share some of the process work.
Subject Area: Business processes—business process analysis. Source: Author.

224. (b) Speed flows from simplicity of tasks, activities, and operations. On the other hand, complexity reduces speed.
Subject Area: Business processes—business process analysis. Source: Author.

225. (a) The goal of reducing the cycle time is to eliminate, minimize, combine or improve the work steps or time. Expanding the work steps usually increases the cycle time.
Subject Area: Business processes—business process analysis. Source: Author.

226. (d) Choke points in a process are caused by exceeding the capacity limitation of key resources. Here capacity is defined as the potential output over a time period. Choke points cause major delays in the cycle time.
Subject Area: Business processes—business process analysis. Source: Author.

227. (**c**) Cross-functional teams, not self-managed teams, focus on completing a specific work activity to reduce the cycle time. Cross-functional work teams are multidisciplined and are an attempt to organize employees around work itself. Self-managed teams are high-performance teams that assume traditional managerial duties such as planning and staffing. Managers should act as facilitators although they can be at times a barrier to self-managed teams. Members in the self-managed team come from one department whereas members in the cross-functional teams come from multiple departments or functions.

Subject Area: Business processes—business process analysis. Source: Author.

228. (**c**) Constraint accounting is synonymous with throughput accounting and is based on the theory of constraints principles. Throughout accounting is concerned with optimizing the flow of materials through a manufacturing plant. It assists managers in deciding on product profitability and production mix by taking account not only of the contribution a product makes but also of the total flow of production through the plant based upon a selected product mix and volume. Direct costing accounting system takes account only of costs that can be directly identified with the manufacture of a product; overhead costs are not included in the product costs. Activity-based accounting is concerned about the cost of indirect activities and costs within a plant and their relationship to the manufacture of specific products.

Subject Area: Business processes—business process analysis. Source: Author.

229. (**b**) The drum-buffer-rope scheduling system is the generalized process used to manage resources to maximize throughput. The drum is the rate of production, the buffer establishes the protection against uncertainty, and the rope is a communication process to support the constraint. The constraint is viewed as a drum and nonconstraints are viewed as soldiers who march to the drumbeat.

Subject Area: Business processes—business process analysis. Source: Author.

230. (**d**) When products are made in large lot sizes, the cycle times must be long because it is necessary to complete a large quantity each step of the process. Synchronized production plans use just-in-time (JIT) manufacturing to organize the shop floor so that each work cell produces components, subassemblies, and final assemblies in the right quantities and at the right time. The use of Kanban cards can help to synchronize production through the "pull" production methods. In the "push" production methods, products are made before they are needed whereas in the "pull" method products are not made until they are needed.

Subject Area: Business processes—business process analysis. Source: Author.

231. (**d**) Bottleneck production cells are those cells that are loaded above their capacity. The problem can be solved by moving the production to other cells or increasing the capacity by overtime or extra crew. It is important to ensure that no cell is overloaded and that no cell is significantly underutilized.

Subject Area: Business processes—business process analysis. Source: Author.

232. (**a**) Scrap is material residue from a manufacturing process that has measurable but relatively minor recovery value. Choice (b) is incorrect. Spoilage is unacceptable units of production that are discarded or sold for disposal value. Choice (c) is incorrect. Defective units are defined as production that does not meet dimensional or quality standards and that is subsequently reworked and sold through regular channels as firsts or seconds. Choice (d) is incorrect. Waste is material that is lost, evaporates, or shrinks in a manufacturing process, or is residue that has no measurable recovery value.

Subject Area: Business processes—business process analysis. Source: CIA Model Exam 2002, IV-54.

233. (**c**) Full capacity sales can be calculated as follows:

Actual sales/ Percent of capacity at which fixed assets were operated = $2,000,000/ .80 = $2,500,000.

Choice (a) is incorrect. This is 80% of the actual sales, calculated as .80 ($2,000,000) = $1,600,000. Choice (b) is incorrect. This is the actual sales. Choice (d) is incorrect. This is actual sales divided by the proportion of unused, rather than used, capacity, or $2,000,000/.2 = $10,000,000.

Subject Area: Business processes—business process analysis. Source: CIA Model Exam 2002, IV-55.

234. (**d**) Benchmarking is accomplished by comparing an organization's performance to that of the best-performing organizations. Choice (a) is incorrect because benchmarking involves a comparison against industry leaders or "world-class" operations. Benchmarking either uses industry-wide figures (to protect the confidentiality of information provided by participating organizations) or figures from cooperating organizations. Choice (b) is incorrect because benchmarking requires measurements, which involve quantitative comparisons. Choice (c) is incorrect because benchmarking can be applied to all the functional areas in a company. In fact, because manufacturing often tends to be industry-specific whereas things like processing an order or paying an invoice are not, there is a greater opportunity to improve by learning from global leaders.

Subject Area: Business processes—business process analysis. Source: CIA Model Exam 2002, III-15.

235. (**d**) A preventive maintenance program will reduce equipment breakdowns and repairs. Choice (a) is incorrect because scheduling production based on capacity utilization ignores other important factors such as demands. Choice (b) is incorrect because budgeting maintenance department activities based on previous work orders will not prevent equipment breakdowns and repairs. Choice (c) is incorrect because standing authorizations of work orders and overtime will not address the problem posed.

Subject Area: Business processes—business process analysis. Source: CIA Model Exam 2002, III-14.

236. (**d**) Internal auditors should not become directly involved in the implementation of the redesigned process. This would impair their independence and objectivity. Choices (a), (b), and (c) are incorrect because internal auditors should perform these functions.

Subject Area: Business processes—business process analysis. Source: CIA Model Exam 1998, III-8.

237. (d) Linear programming is a mathematical technique for maximizing or minimizing a given objective subject to certain constraints. It is the correct technique to optimize the problem of limited resources. Choice (a) is incorrect because the Delphi technique is a qualitative forecasting method that obtains forecasts through group consensus. Choice (b) is incorrect because exponential smoothing is a forecasting technique that uses past time series values to arrive at forecasted values. Choice (c) is incorrect because regression analysis is a statistical technique used to develop forecasts based on the relationship between two or more variables.

Subject Area: Business processes—business process analysis. Source: CIA Model Exam 1998, III-35.

238. (d) Internal auditors should not become directly involved in the implementation of the redesign process. This would impair their independence and objectivity. Choices (a), (b), and (c) are incorrect because internal auditors should perform these functions.

Subject Area: Business processes—business process analysis. Source: CIA 597, III-32.

239. (d) This is an example of an internal nonfinancial benchmark. Choice (a) is incorrect because this is an example of an external financial benchmark. Choice (b) is incorrect because this is an example of an internal financial benchmark. Choice (c) is incorrect because this is an example of an internal financial benchmark.

Subject Area: Business processes—business process analysis. Source: CIA 595, III-22.

240. (d) See responses given for choices (a), (b), and (c). Choice (a) is incorrect because all of the statements are reflective of the differences in approaches to controls in reengineered organizations. Rengineering places more emphasis on monitoring controls to let management know when an operation may be out of control and signals the need for corrective action. Choice (b) is incorrect because most of the reengineering and total quality management techniques assume that humans will be motivated to actively work in improving the process when they are involved from the beginning. Choice (c) is incorrect because there is an increasing emphasis on self-correcting and automated controls.

Subject Area: Business processes—business process analysis. Source: CIA 1195, I-68.

241. (c) A high level of bad debt write-offs could indicate fraud and the compromising of the accuracy and reliability of financial reports. Choice (a) is incorrect because high turnover of employees may indicate a morale problem but not necessarily a problem with the accuracy and reliability of financial reports. Choice (b) is incorrect because a high level of employee participation in budget setting is an example of decentralization and would not necessarily impact the accuracy and reliability of financial reports. Choice (d) is incorrect because a high number of suppliers would not necessarily indicate a problem with the accuracy and reliability of financial reports.

Subject Area: Business processes—business process analysis. Source: CIA 596, II-1.

242. (b) Employee training programs facilitate doing jobs in a new or different way. Choice (a) is incorrect because real or imagined loss of job(s) is a common reason for employees to resist any change. Choice (c) is incorrect because members of work groups often exert peer pressure on one another to resist change, especially if social relationships are changed. Choice (d) is incorrect because lack of communication and discussion of the need for switching to new processes threatens the status quo.

Subject Area: Business processes—business process analysis. Source: CIA 596, III-18.

Inventory Management Techniques and Concepts

243. (d) Inventory control is a company's attempt to hold the lowest level of inventory that will still enable it to meet customer demand.

Subject Area: Business processes—inventory management techniques and concepts. Source: Author.

244. (a) Storage costs are part of inventory carrying costs while advertising, packaging and sales promotion costs are part of sales and marketing costs.

Subject Area: Business processes—inventory management techniques and concepts. Source: Author.

245. (c) Economic order quantity (EOQ) is defined as the point where inventory carrying costs and ordering costs are at their lowest.

Subject Area: Business processes—inventory management techniques and concepts. Source: Author.

246. (a) Purchasing policies and practices can improve inventory management but not the other way around.

Subject Area: Business processes—inventory management techniques and concepts. Source: Author.

247. (c) One of the dichotomies of inventory control is that at an item level, the more stock the better the availability. However, it has been shown that higher stocks are often associated with poor availability. Stockouts result from holding too little stock due to inadequate forecasts, monitoring, or controls. High stock levels arise because too much stock has been purchased through bad forecasting, monitoring, or controls. High stock and poor availability are caused simultaneously as a result of poor control.

Subject Area: Business processes—inventory management techniques and concepts. Source: Author.

248. (b) The primary reason for maintaining the safety (buffer) stock is due to the inability to predict demand. The other choices are secondary reasons for maintaining the safety stock.

Subject Area: Business processes—inventory management techniques and concepts. Source: Author.

249. (c) A company's policies and objectives define the service level provided to customers, the investment to make in the inventory stock, and the flow of order information. Policy guides the inventory operation.

Subject Area: Business processes—inventory management techniques and concepts. Source: Author.

250. (c) Estimating product delivery times and delivering the product on time causes a high level of customer confidence to be gained or lost. Product delivery due dates must reflect the stock availability and replenishment rules. This, in turn, will decide whether customer service is poor or not.

Subject Area: Business processes—inventory management techniques and concepts. Source: Author.

251. (d) The safety stock is a policy matter to meet unexpected product demand. As such it is not an effective tool to manage inventory although it does benefit a company to some extent. The Pareto analysis (80/20 rule) states that 80% of stock value is caused by 20% of stock items. The ABC analysis shows the relative importance of the stock items. The JIT approach focuses on delivering the inventory on time to where it is needed.

Subject Area: Business processes—inventory management techniques and concepts. Source: Author.

252. (a) Class "C" items consist of many items and low inventory rate, with slow movements or low value items. Class "A" represents few items and high turnover rate (choice b.).

Subject Area: Business processes—inventory management techniques and concepts. Source: Author.

253. (c) Only items requiring management attention are managed in the class "B" inventory items. Class "A" items are managed with tight control and with a JIT approach since they are more valuable and more frequently used. Class "C" items are managed with minimum supervision since they are less valuable and infrequently used.

Subject Area: Business processes—inventory management techniques and concepts. Source: Author.

254. (c) Since class "A" items are few with high turnover rate, they should be managed with sophisticated forecasting systems and with a service level policy to meet customer needs.

Subject Area: Business processes—inventory management techniques and concepts. Source: Author.

255. (c) The plant operator's only concern is whether a defective part or component can be reworked or has to be scrapped. As long as there is work in process (WIP), the manufacturing process exerts no pressure to produce quality parts the first time. The cost of rework of a defective part is hidden in the WIP, which acts as a buffer.

Subject Area: Business processes—inventory management techniques and concepts. Source: Author.

256. (d) Usually, high interest rates in the economy force management to pay attention to inventory reduction. The cycle time management principles can integrate all the other three choices to meet customer expectations and to reduce inventories.

Subject Area: Business processes—inventory management techniques and concepts. Source: Author.

257. (a) In the pre-deduct inventory transaction processing system, the book inventory balance of components is reduced before issue. Choices (b), (c), and (d) are the same. In the case of backflush inventory method, the computer automatically reduces the book inventory of components after completion of activity based on what should have been used as specified on the bill-of-material. All four approaches have the same disadvantage of a built-in differential between the book record and what is physically in the stock.

Subject Area: Business processes—inventory management techniques and concepts. Source: Author.

258. (b) Count point backflush method and the key point backflush method are the same. They use more than one level of the bill-of-materials and extending back to the previous points where production was counted. Count point and pay point are the same. They are specific points in a flow of material or sequence of operations at which parts, subassemblies, or assemblies are counted as being complete. They are also designated as the points at which material transfers from one department to another.

Subject Area: Business processes—inventory management techniques and concepts. Source: Author.

259. (b) An EOQ sensitivity analysis involves varying the holding costs per unit and/or the order costs to determine how much the changes affect the optimal EOQ. Choice (a) is incorrect. Forecasting models involve projecting data over time or developing regression models when time series data are not available. Choice (c) is incorrect. Critical path method involves project scheduling. Choice (d) is incorrect. Decision analysis involves selecting the best option from alternatives.

Subject Area: Business processes—inventory management techniques and concepts. Source: CIA Model Exam 2002, III-37.

260. (a) Materials requirements planning (MRP) is a planning and controlling technique for managing dependent-demand manufacturing inventories. Choice (b) is incorrect. Regression analysis is a statistical procedure for estimating the relation between variables. Choice (c) is incorrect. Capital budgeting is used for analyzing and evaluating long-term capital investments. Choice (d) is incorrect. Linear programming is a mathematical technique for maximizing or minimizing a given objective subject to certain constraints.

Subject Area: Business processes—inventory management techniques and concepts. Source: CIA Model Exam 1998, III-32.

261. (d) In this situation, the company will be receiving fewer materials at any point in time, increasing the likelihood of stockouts and thereby resulting in an increase in stockout costs. At the same time, the average inventory will be less, resulting in a reduction in carrying costs. Choice (a) is incorrect. The supplier may ask for a concession in its selling price, which would raise the manufacturer's purchasing costs. Also, the manufacturing company will be receiving fewer materials at any point in time, increasing the likelihood of stockouts and thereby resulting in an increase in stockout costs. Choice (b) is incorrect. The supplier may ask for a concession in its selling price, which would raise the manufacturer's purchasing costs. Also, the cost of quality would not necessarily be affected by the just-in-time purchasing system. Choice (c) is incorrect. With fewer purchase orders being processed by the manufacturer, the ordering costs are likely to decrease. However, the cost of quality would not necessarily be affected by the just-in-time purchasing system.

Subject Area: Business processes—inventory management techniques and concepts. Source: CIA Model Exam 1998, III-34.

262. (a) The annual cost of carrying inventory is the average inventory level times the cost per unit of inventory times the cost of capital. It is calculated as follows: (average inventory level) × (unit cost) × (cost of capital) = (order size/2) × ($5) × (.12) = (500/2) × ($5) × (.12) = $150. Choice (b) is incorrect because this answer is obtained by using the total annual quantity rather than the average inventory level and by neglecting to multiply by the unit price; = (annual quantity) × (.12) = (1500) × (.12) = 180. Choice (c) is incorrect because this answer is obtained by using the order size rather than the average inventory level; = (order size) × ($5) × (.12) = (500) × ($5) × (.12) = $300. Choice (d) is incorrect because this answer is obtained by using the total annual quantity rather than the average inventory level; = (1500) × ($5) × (.12) = $900

Subject Area: Business processes—inventory management techniques and concepts. Source: CIA 594, IV-37.

263. (d) Economic order quantity (EOQ) formula is related to sales not to inventory. Choices (a), (b), and (c) are incorrect because each choice is a required component of the EOQ formula. In addition, data on carrying costs is needed.

Subject Area: Business processes—inventory management techniques and concepts. Source: CIA 594, IV-38.

264. (d) Simple linear regression can be used to estimate inventories as a constant plus a function of sales: INV = a + b SALES, Where "a" is a constant and "b" is a coefficient estimated by the regression model. Choice (a) is incorrect because this method ignores changes in sales. Choice (b) is incorrect because this method ignores the relationship between sales and inventory. Choice (c) is incorrect because this method ignores the constant dollar amount of inventory.

Subject Area: Business processes—inventory management techniques and concepts. Source: CIA 1193, IV-49.

265. (a) Inventory shipping and handling costs are classified as ordering costs, not as carrying costs. Choices (b), (c), and (d) are incorrect because property tax, insurance and depreciation/obsolescence are classified as inventory carrying costs.

Subject Area: Business processes—inventory management techniques and concepts. Source: CIA 1196, IV-43.

266. (b) The higher the fixed ordering costs, the greater the economic order quantity. Higher quantity orders are made less frequently, resulting in lower fixed ordering costs for the period. Choice (a) is incorrect because the economic order quantity (EOQ) is higher for a company that has higher, not lower, annual unit sales. Everything else equal, greater sales volume means more inventory is needed. Choice (c) is incorrect because higher carrying costs will result in a lowering of order quantities so that average inventory is reduced. Choice (d) is incorrect because higher unit purchase prices will increase inventory costs and reduce the economic order size.

Subject Area: Business processes—inventory management techniques and concepts. Source: CIA 1195, IV-37.

267. (b) The annual inventory carrying cost is calculated as follows:

= Average inventory × Percentage carrying cost
= (Order quantity/2 + Safety stock) (Unit cost) (Percentage carrying cost)
= (10,000/2 + 2,000) ($5) (.10) = 35,000 (.10) = $3,500

Choice (a) is incorrect because this solution is obtained by omitting safety stocks from the calculation of annual inventory carrying cost (see b. for correct solution).

= Average inventory × Percentage carrying cost
= (Order quantity + Safety stock/2) (Unit cost) (Percentage carrying cost)
= (12,000/2) ($5) (.10) = $3,000

Choice (c) is incorrect because this solution is obtained by omitting safety stocks from the calculation and by failing to divide the order quantity by two to calculate average inventory.

Annual carrying cost of inventory = Order quantity (.10) (Unit cost)
= 10,000 (.10) ($5) = $5,000

Choice (d) is incorrect because this solution for the annual carrying cost of inventory is obtained if the order quantity is not divided by two when calculating average inventory.

(Average inventory) (Percentage carrying cost)
= (Order quantity + Safety stock) (Unit cost) (Percentage carrying cost)
= (10,000 + 2,000) ($5) (.10) = $6,000

Subject Area: Business processes—inventory management techniques and concepts. Source: CIA 1195, III-42.

268. (c) As order size increases, the number of orders falls. Total ordering cost of inventory is the fixed costs per order multiplied by the number of orders placed per year. Total ordering cost therefore decreases with an increase in the order size. Choices (a) and (b) are incorrect because average inventory is the order size in units divided by two. As order size increases, the average inventory level rises. Total carrying costs of inventory are calculated as the annual percentage carrying costs multiplied by the average inventory in units. Total carrying costs of inventory will therefore increase with an increase in the average inventory level, rather than decrease or remain unchanged. Choice (d) is incorrect because the total ordering cost of inventory decreases with an increase in the order size.

Subject Area: Business processes—inventory management techniques and concepts. Source: CIA 595, IV-49.

269. (a) The EOQ (economic order quantity) decision model calculates the optimum quantity of inventory to order by incorporating only the ordering costs and carrying costs into the model. These costs behave in the opposite direction of each other. Choice (b) is incorrect because this response is incorrect because only carrying costs are correct; the purchase costs are not directly incorporated into the EOQ model. Choice (c) is incorrect because this response is incorrect because neither the purchase costs nor the quality costs are incorporated into the EOQ model. Choice (d) is incorrect because this response is incorrect because only ordering costs are correct; stockout costs are not directly incorporated into the EOQ model.

Subject Area: Business processes—inventory management techniques and concepts. Source: CIA 597, III-91.

270. (b) Of the four variables mentioned, only yearly demand is required.

Subject Area: Business processes—inventory management techniques and concepts. Source: CIA 595, III-98.

271. (c) Holding costs = Q/2 (holding costs per unit) + Safety Stock. Holding costs = 2,500/2 ($4)(.25) + 500 ($4)(.25) = 1,250 + 500 = $1,750.

Subject Area: Business processes—inventory management techniques and concepts. Source: CIA 595, III-99.

272. (c) Inventory ordering costs = D/Q (order costs). Inventory ordering costs = 48,000/2500 (150) = $2,880.

Subject Area: Business processes—inventory management techniques and concepts. Source: CIA 595, III-100.

273. (b) Internal accounting allocations of costs to different segments of the firm are arbitrary assignments of already incurred costs which do not have anything to do with forecasting demand. Choices (a), (c), and (d) are incorrect because knowing the behavior of business cycles, understanding seasonal variations in demand for the product, and the use of econometric models can be valuable when forecasting the required purchases of inventory.

Subject Area: Business processes—inventory management techniques and concepts. Source: CIA 1196, III-8.

274. (a) Safety stock is inventory maintained in order to reduce the number of stockouts resulting from higher-than-expected demand during lead-time. Choice (b) is incorrect because a just-in-time (JIT) inventory system involves the purchase of materials and production of components immediately preceding their use. Choice (c) is incorrect because materials requirement planning (MRP) is a system for scheduling production and controlling the level of inventory for components with dependent demand. Choice (d) is incorrect because a master production schedule (MPS) is a statement of the timing and amounts of individual items to be produced.

Subject Area: Business processes—inventory management techniques and concepts. Source: CIA 1195, III-66.

275. (a) If D decreases by 36%, the Economic Order Quantity (EOQ) will be 0.8Q, or a decrease by 20%.

$$Q = \sqrt{\frac{2 * 0.64D * p}{s}} = \sqrt{0.64\left(\frac{2Dp}{s}\right)} = 0.8Q$$

Therefore, by definition, choices (b), (c), and (d) are incorrect.

Subject Area: Business processes—inventory management techniques and concepts. Source: CIA 1195, III-97.

276. (b) The purpose of the EOQ model is to minimize the sum of the order costs and the holding costs. Choice (a) is incorrect because although safety stock is important in some versions of the model, one does not want to minimize it (otherwise it would be zero, and the firm may incur substantial stockout costs). Choice (c) is incorrect because in the EOQ model, costs not quantities are the focus of the minimization. Choice (d) is incorrect because quantity demanded is a variable in the model, but order costs not demand costs are relevant to the model. Backlogs are customer orders, which cannot be filled immediately because of stockouts. Backlog costs are not quantified in the model.

Subject Area: Business processes—inventory management techniques and concepts. Source: CIA 594, III-66.

277. (b) Shortening setup times permit smaller average batch sizes which permits reductions in inventory leading to decreased inventory holding costs. Choice (a) is incorrect because there are other factors and not considering them is shortsighted. Choice (c) is incorrect because getting suppliers to deliver better quality raw materials is independent of an investment to decrease setup times. Choice (d) is incorrect because coding batches of raw materials is independent of an investment to decrease setup times.

Subject Area: Business processes—inventory management techniques and concepts. Source: CIA 1193, III-52.

278. (d) All of these items prompt a more frequent review in an ABC inventory control system. Choice (a) is incorrect because long, not short, lead times prompt a more frequent review in the ABC inventory control system. Choice (b) is incorrect because high, not low, stockout costs prompt a more frequent review in an ABC inventory control system. Choice (c) is incorrect because expensive, not inexpensive, items prompt a more frequent review in an ABC inventory control system.

Subject Area: Business processes—inventory management techniques and concepts. Source: CIA 1193, IV-26.

279. (b) The optimal order size is increased, because economic order quantity (EOQ) shows how average ordering costs is inversely related to the order size, but carrying costs are directly related to the order size. If ordering costs increase, it is better to increase the order size so as to reduce the number of orders per year. Choices (a), (c), and (d) are incorrect because the optimal order size is increased. Total costs are minimized where holding costs and ordering costs equate. Fixed costs have no impact on EOQ. Annual inventory holding costs are a linear function of the amount of inventory carried. Annual ordering costs are inversely related to the order quantity and continually decline.

Subject Area: Business processes—inventory management techniques and concepts. Source: CIA 1193, IV-51.

280. (b) Payoff table analysis is appropriate for single-period inventory. Choice (a) is incorrect because economic order quantity (EOQ) models deal with a nearly constant demand. Choice (c) is incorrect because material requirements planning (MRP) is a technique for dependent-demand inventories. Choice (d) is incorrect because game theory is a mathematical approach to decision-making in which each decision-maker takes into account the courses of action of competitors.

Subject Area: Business processes—inventory management techniques and concepts. Source: CIA 1192, III-46.

281. (a) This is a description of the ABC method. A-class items are controlled more tightly than C-class items due to their relative values. Choice (b) is incorrect because the economic order quantity (EOQ) model is used to determine the order quantity that minimizes total inventory costs. Choice (c) is incorrect because a just-in-time (JIT) inventory system involves the purchase of materials and production of components immediately preceding their use. Choice (d) is incorrect because material requirements planning (MRP) system is a planning and controlling technique for managing dependent-demand manufacturing inventories.

Subject Area: Business processes—inventory management techniques and concepts. Source: CIA 592, IV-23.

282. (c) Delivery time, usage rate, and level of safety stock are all considerations in controlling stockouts. Choice (a) is incorrect because these are inventory-related terms but none will controls stockouts. Choice (b) is incorrect because the order quantity and annual demand are not factors in the stockout problem. Choice (d) is incorrect because production bottlenecks are the results of a stockout; they are not a method of control. Also, EOQ is irrelevant to stockouts.

Subject Area: Business processes—inventory management techniques and concepts. Source: CIA 1191, IV-25.

283. (b) A stated requirement is demand forecasting based on early orders for items, which means that company personnel have learned that the best predictor of subsequent sales of a specific item is sales in the first few days after it has been made available. Choice (a) is incorrect. Computations on the basis of economic order quantities (EOQ) will minimize the EOQ objective, but EOQ assumes stationary demand, which is not the case here. Choice (c) is incorrect because this is not the critical ordering factor for a specific item. Choice (d) is incorrect because vendor quantity discounts and warehouse space are valid considerations only if the company would order the item in those quantities anyway.

Subject Area: Business processes—inventory management techniques and concepts. Source: CIA 591, III-92.

284. (c) Availability of 70 units ensures 90% of possible daily needs (.2 + .5 + .2 = .9). Choice (a) is incorrect. Availability of 50 units ensures only 20% of possible daily needs (.2). Choice (b) is incorrect. Availability of 60 units ensures only 70% of possible daily needs (.2 + .5 = .7). Choice (d) is incorrect. Availability of 80 units ensures 100% of possible daily needs (.1 + .5 + .2 + .1 = 1).

Subject Area: Business processes—inventory management techniques and concepts. Source: CIA 591, IV-28.

285. (b) A reason to use bar codes rather than other means of identification is to record the movement of parts with minimal labor costs. Choice (a) is incorrect because the movement of parts can escape being recorded with any identification method. Choice (c) is incorrect because each vendor has its own part-numbering scheme, which is unlikely to correspond to the buyer's scheme. Choice (d) is incorrect because each vendor has its own identification method, although vendors in the same industry often cooperate to minimize the number of bar code systems they use.

Subject Area: Business processes—inventory management techniques and concepts. Source: CIA 597, III-75.

286. (d) In this situation, the company will be receiving fewer materials at any point in time, increasing the likelihood of a stockout; at the same time, the average inventory will be less, resulting in a reduction in the carrying costs. Choice (a) is incorrect. While the supplier may ask for a concession in its selling price which would raise the manufacturer's purchasing costs, the manufacturing company will be receiving fewer materials at any point in time increasing the likelihood of a stockout, thereby resulting in an increase in stockout costs. Choice (b) is incorrect. While the supplier may ask for a concession in its selling price which would raise the manufacturer's purchasing costs, the cost of quality would not necessarily be affected by the JIT purchasing system. Choice (c) is incorrect. With fewer purchase orders being processed by the manufacturer, the ordering costs are likely to decrease. However, the cost of quality would not necessarily be affected by the JIT purchasing system.

Subject Area: Business processes—inventory management techniques and concepts. Source: CIA 597, III-94.

287. (d) Because materials are delivered as needed, it is imperative to establish and maintain good relations with those critical suppliers. Choice (a) is incorrect. To the contrary, finished goods inventories are virtually eliminated. Choice (b) is incorrect. JIT does not necessarily require high-cost material handling equipment. Choice (c) is incorrect. If a defect is discovered, production is stopped.

Subject Area: Business processes—inventory management techniques and concepts. Source: CIA 593, II-16.

288. (c) A JIT inventory system involves the purchase of materials and production of components immediately preceding their use. Choice (a) is incorrect because safety stock is the inventory maintained in order to reduce the number of stockouts resulting from higher-than-expected demand during lead time. Choice (b) is incorrect because economic order quantity is the order quantity that minimizes total inventory costs. Choice (d) is incorrect because the master budget is the detailed financial plan for the next period.

Subject Area: Business processes—inventory management techniques and concepts. Source: CIA 592, III-62.

289. (d) Parts needed for repair could not be predicted in advance. Choice (a) is incorrect because identifying items for close control is an element of the ABC method. Choice (b) is incorrect because diversity of needs is not the issue, it's knowing when they are needed. JIT works well with auto manufacturing. Choice (c) is incorrect because sales rates and order lead times are used to determine safety stock, not an issue with JIT.

Subject Area: Business processes—inventory management techniques and concepts. Source: CIA 592, IV-51.

290. (c) Work stoppages at suppliers or transportation disruptions due to poor weather can cause almost immediate work stoppages at the manufacturer because of the lean inventories. Choice (a) is incorrect because JIT systems can require significant computer resources, but they can also be maintained manually. Choice (b) is incorrect because contracts may have to be renegotiated with strict delivery and quality specifications, but this is usually performed over extended periods of time. Choice (d) is incorrect because JIT can be implemented over an extended period of time or a shorter time frame depending on the manufacturer's immediate needs.

Subject Area: Business processes—inventory management techniques and concepts. Source: CIA 595, III-32.

291. (c) This measures inputs consumed for output produced. Choice (a) is incorrect because this measures effectiveness of internal control. Choice (b) is incorrect because this measures efficiency. Choice (d) is incorrect because this measures economy.

Subject Area: Business processes—inventory management techniques and concepts. Source: CIA 596, III-90.

292. (a) A flexible manufacturing system (FMS) consists of two or more computer-controlled machines linked by automated handling devices such as robots and transport systems. Choice (b) is incorrect because just-in-time (JIT) involves the purchase of materials and production of components immediately preceding their use. Choice (c) is incorrect because a master budget is the detailed financial plan for the next period. Choice (d) is incorrect because economic order quantity (EOQ) model is the order quantity that minimizes total costs.

Subject Area: Business processes—inventory management techniques and concepts. Source: CIA 1195, III-99.

293. (a) This is a major emphasis for computer integrated manufacturing (CIM) as well as for the total quality management (TQM) programs which usually proceed it. Choice (b) is incorrect because these may be either higher or lower with CIM. Choice (c) is incorrect because the normal expectation is that working capital will be reduced as investments shift from current to fixed assets. Choice (d) is incorrect because actual or potential market share changes may trigger investments in CIM.

Subject Area: Business processes—inventory management techniques and concepts. Source: CIA 596, III-35.

294. (**a**) With a JIT system, a formal receiving department may be eliminated because materials are delivered by the vendor directly to the final user on the factory floor. Choice (b) is incorrect because a bill of materials is important in an MRP system, not JIT. Choice (c) is incorrect because more emphasis is placed on quality and timeliness of raw materials purchases than on price in a JIT system. Choice (d) is incorrect because late deliveries can be a major problem because there is no inventory cushion to rely on.

Subject Area: Business processes—inventory management techniques and concepts. Source: CIA 1191, IV-24.

295. (**c**) PERT is a project management technique; it is not related to facility layout and design (The other three techniques are related). Choice (a) is incorrect. In cellular manufacturing all of the machines are grouped into cells to allow the product to flow easily through this "island" within the larger job shop or process layout. Choice (b) is incorrect. Operations sequencing analysis develops a good scheme for the arrangement of departments by graphically analyzing the layout problem. Choice (d) is incorrect. Line balancing is the analysis of production lines which nearly equally divide the work to be done among work stations so that the number of work stations required on the production line is minimized.

Subject Area: Business processes—inventory management techniques and concepts. Source: CIA 594, III-62.

296. (**b**) Items II, VIII, X, and XII are related to financial services. Choices (a) and (c) are incorrect because Item III requires the firm to have substantial inventories. Item IV is only used in manufacturing firms not service firms. Choice (d) is incorrect because Item XI is used in the airline industry.

Subject Area: Business processes—inventory management techniques and concepts. Source: CIA 594, III-58.

297. (**d**) Items I, III, and IV are related to manufacturing firms, items X, XI, and XII are related to service firms, and item VII and XII are related to both manufacturing and services firms. Choices (a) and (b) are incorrect because Item II is only used in the service industry. Choice (c) is incorrect because Item I is only used in the manufacturing industry.

Subject Area: Business processes—inventory management techniques and concepts. Source: CIA 594, III-59.

298. (**c**) Companies in a highly volatile industry probably experience unstable demand for their finished product. An MRP system starts with the master production schedule for finished goods and works backward to derive direct materials inventory requirements. This requires accurate estimation of the amount of finished goods to be produced, which would be practically impossible if demand (and hence production) is constantly fluctuating. Choice (a) is incorrect because few direct materials would facilitate preparing inventory reports, which are needed for an MRP system. Many direct materials can complicate preparing the information, which is needed for an MRP system. Choice (b) is incorrect because an MRP system would be useful to ensure that there is an adequate amount of direct materials on hand. This would minimize the probability of stockouts. If the inventory of a direct material were depleted, the assembly line might have to be shut down, and the long set-up time would have to be incurred to restart operations. Choice (d) is incorrect. Since an MRP system minimizes direct materials stockouts, there is less chance of having to shut down the assembly line.

Subject Area: Business processes—inventory management techniques and concepts. Source: CIA 1192, IV-25.

299. (**a**) Material requirements planning (MRP) is a planning and controlling technique for managing dependent-demand manufacturing inventories, Choice (b) is incorrect because regression analysis is a statistical procedure for estimating the relation between variables. Choice (c) is incorrect because capital budgeting is used for analyzing and evaluating long-term capital investments. Choice (d) is incorrect because linear programming is a mathematical technique for maximizing or minimizing a given objective subject to certain constraints.

Subject Area: Business processes—inventory management techniques and concepts. Source: CIA 592, III-61.

300. (**b**) Material requirements planning (MRP) is the system described in the stem. Choice (a) is incorrect because economic order quantity (EOQ) is a decision model that focuses on the trade-off between carrying and ordering costs. Choice (c) is incorrect because linear programming is a decision model concerned with allocating scarce resources to maximize profit or minimize costs. Choice (d) is incorrect because just-in-time (JIT) purchasing involves the purchase of goods such that delivery immediately precedes demand or use.

Subject Area: Business processes—inventory management techniques and concepts. Source: CIA 1193, IV-25.

301. (**b**) MRP is a technique that can be used to manage dependent-demand manufacturing inventories. Choice (a) is incorrect because inventory control specifically deals with inventory. Choice (c) is incorrect because Monte Carlo analysis deals with computer simulations. Choice (d) is incorrect because linear programming is a maximizing or minimizing model.

Subject Area: Business processes—inventory management techniques and concepts. Source: CIA 1191, III-35.

302. (**d**) Poor-quality materials cause major problems to JIT because it retains no safety stock to use to replace defective materials. Substandard materials cause major production disruptions in JIT systems and defeat its whole purpose of lowering cost and lead time while increasing product quality. Choice (a) is incorrect because safety stocks are not held in JIT systems, whose goal is to minimize inventory by insuring that materials arrive at the plant just-in-time for production. Safety stocks raise inventory levels and increase the risk of defective materials through obsolescence and potential damage during storage. Choice (b) is incorrect because many smaller firms are adopting JIT with favorable results. In fact, smaller companies may have an easier time implementing JIT because it can be easier to redefine job functions and retrain workers. Choice (c) is incorrect because the close coordination required between suppliers and customers usually leads to overall inventory reductions throughout the production-distribution chain.

Subject Area: Business processes—inventory management techniques and concepts. Source: CIA 597, IV-39.

303. **(b)** Since the service level is the average number of stockouts, it must change. Choice (a) is incorrect. Since the service level is the average number of stockouts, it must change. Choice (c) is incorrect. There should be no change in orderings costs as the same number of orders will be made each year. It may increase in the initial year as an additional order may be required to increase the safety stock. Choice (d) is incorrect. Since we will be stocking more inventory, carrying costs will increase as will delivery costs.

Subject Area: Business processes—inventory management techniques and concepts. Source: CIA 1190, III-42.

304. **(a)** The EOQ is the square root of 2 times the rate of demand times the order cost divided by the carrying cost. In this case, the percent of change will be equal to the square root of 1/2, or 0.707. 447 units × 0.707= 316. Therefore, choices (b), (c), (d) will be incorrect.

Subject Area: Business processes—inventory management techniques and concepts. Source: CIA 590, III-45.

305. **(c)** The answer is to find the square roof of: (2 × $100 × 1,000)/$2. This is the square root of 100,000, or 317. Choice (a) is incorrect because order costs and carrying costs are reversed. Choice (b) is incorrect because it failed to multiply by the constant (2). Choice (d) is incorrect because it failed to divide by carrying costs.

Subject Area: Business processes—inventory management techniques and concepts. Source: CIA 590, IV-22.

306. **(a)** Group C items are low-dollar-value items and receive less management attention. Extensive use of models and records is not cost effective. It is cheaper to order large quantities infrequently. Group A items are high-dollar value and management would try to keep investment in such items low. Therefore, by definition, choices (b), (c), and (d) will be incorrect.

Subject Area: Business processes—inventory management techniques and concepts. Source: CIA 590, IV-23.

307. **(c)** As the frequency of ordering increases, total carrying costs are reduced by the average that inventory level is reduced. Choice (a) is incorrect because total ordering costs would increase. Choice (b) is incorrect because total ordering costs would increase. Choice (d) is incorrect because total carrying costs are reduced.

Subject Area: Business processes—inventory management techniques and concepts. Source: CIA 590, III-51.

308. **(b)** Material requirements planning (MRP) is the system described in the question. Choice (a) is incorrect because economic order quantity (EOQ) is a decision model that focuses on the trade-off between carrying and ordering costs. Choice (c) is incorrect because linear programming is a decision model concerned with allocating scarce resources to maximize profit or minimize costs. Choice (d) is incorrect because just-in-time (JIT) purchasing involves the purchase of goods such that delivery immediately precedes demand or use.

Subject Area: Business processes—inventory management techniques and concepts. Source: CIA 1190, IV-26.

309. **(b)**

(2,000 – 200) – 300 =1,500
(2,000 – 200)(2) – 400 = 3,200

Choice (a) is incorrect.

(2,000 – 200) – 300 = 1,500
(2,000 – 200) – 400 = 1,400

Choice (c) is incorrect.

(2,000 – 0) – 300 = 1,700
(2,000 – 0)(2) – 400 = 3,600

Choice (d) is incorrect.

(2,000 – 200) = 1,800
(2,000 – 200)(2) = 3,600

Subject Area: Business processes—inventory management techniques and concepts. Source: CIA 596, III-98.

Marketing—Pricing Objectives and Policies

310. **(b)** Price reflects some unit of value given up by one party in return for something from another party. The setting price based on costs has become a common practice. Two approaches include standard markup pricing and target return pricing. Cost-plus pricing method ignores demand since costs are generated internally and since the demand is created externally to an organization.

Subject Area: Business processes—marketing/pricing objectives and policies. Source: Author.

311. **(c)** Two pricing approaches based on cost include standard markup pricing and target return pricing. Target return pricing adds both cost per unit and desired profit and is calculated as selling price per unit = Unit cost per unit + Desired profit per unit. A standard markup percentage based on management profit goal is added to the cost in the standard markup pricing approach.

Subject Area: Business processes—marketing/pricing objectives and policies. Source: Author.

312. **(a)** With the standard markup approach, the Selling price = Unit cost/(1 – Markup percentage). Selling price = $1.32/(1.00 – 0.20) = $1.32/0.80 = $1.65.

Subject Area: Business processes—marketing/pricing objectives and policies. CBM, Volume two.

313. **(b)** Markup on selling price = (Price – Cost)/Price = ($15 – $11)/$15 = 4/15 = 0.266 = 27%.

Subject Area: Business processes—marketing/pricing objectives and policies. Source: Author.

314. **(d)** Markup on selling price = (Price – Cost)/Price = 25% = ($15 – Cost)/$15 = $3.75 = $15 – Cost. Cost = $15 – $3.75 = $11.25.

Subject Area: Business processes—marketing/pricing objectives and policies. Source: Author.

315. **(b)** Markup on cost is the profit margin for an individual product or product line expressed as a percentage of unit cost. Markup on price is the profit margin for an individual product expressed as a percentage of price. Markup on price = (Markup on cost)/(1+ Markup on cost) = 50%/150% = 33%.

Subject Area: Business processes—marketing/pricing objectives and policies. Source: CBM, Volume two.

316. **(d)** Markup on cost = (Markup on price)/(1 – Markup on price) = 50%/50% = 100%.

Subject Area: Business processes—marketing/pricing objectives and policies. Source: CBM, Volume two.

317. (b) Markup on cost = (Price – Cost)/Cost = ($6 – $4)/$4 = $2/$4 = 50%.
Subject Area: Business processes—marketing/pricing objectives and policies. Source: CBM, Volume two.

318. (b) Markup on price = (Price – Cost)/Price = ($5-$2)/$5 = $3/$5 = 60%.
Subject Area: Business processes—marketing/pricing objectives and policies. Source: CBM, Volume two.

319. (c) Given the information contained in a demand curve (quantity and price), a firm can determine the profit-maximizing price by simply calculating the profit at each point and determining which price produces the highest profit.
Subject Area: Business processes—marketing/pricing objectives and policies. Source: Author.

320. (c) Profit-maximizing price is established by examining how revenues and costs change for a series of prices.
Subject Area: Business processes—marketing/pricing objectives and policies. Source: Author.

321. (d) The following strategic factors play a role in setting a base price: (1) company objectives, (2) positioning strategy, (3) new product pricing strategies, and (4) price-quality differences.
Subject Area: Business processes—marketing/pricing objectives and policies. Source: Author.

322. (c) Companies pursue a pricing strategy aimed at a market share target when there is no patent protection on a specific product.
Subject Area: Business processes—marketing/pricing objectives and policies. Source: Author.

323. (d) Profit maximization objectives require the most substantial cost and demand information.
Subject Area: Business processes—marketing/pricing objectives and policies. Source: Author.

324. (a) Two classic pricing strategies for new products are skimming and penetration. Skimming strategy is setting the price at a relatively high level in the beginning and then gradually reducing it over time. The penetration strategy is setting the price at a relatively low level in the beginning where the goal is to obtain market share and expand demand.
Subject Area: Business processes—marketing/pricing objectives and policies. Source: Author.

325. (c) Price is set at a low level in the penetration strategy. One of the downsides of the penetration pricing is that customers may infer low quality from low price, meaning making a price-quality judgment.
Subject Area: Business processes—marketing/pricing objectives and policies. Source: Author.

326. (a) When introducing an easily copied new product, a marketer would be likely to use a price penetration strategy hoping to lure customers quickly. Also, research and development costs are little to none.
Subject Area: Business processes—marketing/pricing objectives and policies. Source: Author.

327. (a) A skimming pricing policy works best when demand is inelastic, meaning a price increase produces a less than proportionate decline in the quantity demanded so that total revenues rise. Many customers are willing to pay the high price for the unique value that a product provides.
Subject Area: Business processes—marketing/pricing objectives and policies. Source: Author.

328. (c) A firm pursuing a clear differentiation strategy is more likely to follow a price skimming policy by charging a higher price to reflect the product's differentiating features.
Subject Area: Business processes—marketing/pricing objectives and policies. Source: CBM, Volume two.

329. (c) A price skimming strategy is setting the price at a relatively high level in the beginning and then gradually reducing it over time. Competitors have no incentive to enter the market with similar products at lower prices.
Subject Area: Business processes—marketing/pricing objectives and policies. Source: Author.

330. (c) Major phases of a product life cycle include introduction, growth, maturity, and decline (commodity). In the introductory phase, paying attention to costs is important, and the firm may choose to pursue a skimming or penetration price strategy. In the growth phase, the firm is faced with the opposing forces of growing demand, yet increasing competition. This necessitates aggressive pricing if the firm cannot hold on to a unique product advantage. Maturity is likely to bring either stable, competitive prices or price wars if some rival firms attempt to get aggressive. The firm should do its best to maintain stable prices and not rock the boat in the maturity phase. Alternatively, some firms will attempt to innovate to break out of the commodity trap. In the decline phase, the firm should try to keep prices up if the decision has been made to harvest the brand. Predicting when and how much to cut prices is an important task.
Subject Area: Business processes—marketing/pricing objectives and policies. Source: Author.

331. (b) In the introductory stage, paying attention to costs is important, and the firm may choose to pursue a skimming or penetration pricing strategy.
Subject Area: Business processes—marketing/pricing objectives and policies. Source: Author.

332. (a) During the mature stage, stable, competitive prices and price wars are common.
Subject Area: Business processes—marketing/pricing objectives and policies. Source: Author.

333. (d) In the decline stage, the firm should try to keep prices up if the decision has been made to harvest the brand.
Subject Area: Business processes—marketing/pricing objectives and policies. Source: Author.

334. (d) A price penetration strategy makes sense when competitive imitation will occur quickly, costs are likely to drop a good deal with increases in volume, and target consumers are relatively price sensitive. Penetration pricing is the standard strategy followed by low-cost leaders.
Subject Area: Business processes—marketing/pricing objectives and policies. Source: Author.

335. (**d**) A company can effectively set its prices higher than its competitors when the company's product is perceived as superior quality.

Subject Area: Business processes—marketing/pricing objectives and policies. Source: Author.

336. (**b**) Competitive price moves, price promotion, and unique pricing for different customers are the common reasons for a company to change a product's price.

Subject Area: Business processes—marketing/pricing objectives and policies. Source: Author.

337. (**a**) A salesperson who reduces the price during negotiations is practicing price shading, which is most common when the customer is a very valuable client.

Subject Area: Business processes—marketing/pricing objectives and policies. Source: Author.

338. (**c**) Cash discounting is offered to differentiate between fast- and slow-paying customers.

Subject Area: Business processes—marketing/pricing objectives and policies. Source: Author.

339. (**c**) Free-on-board (FOB) pricing leaves the cost and responsibility of transportation of goods to the customer.

Subject Area: Business processes—marketing/pricing objectives and policies. Source: Author.

340. (**d**) Discounts given to retailers for putting a manufacturer's goods on sale to consumers for a particular period of time are called sales promotion allowances.

Subject Area: Business processes—marketing/pricing objectives and policies. Source: Author.

341. (**a**) Price flexing takes place in the form of a wide variety of discounts and allowances. Price flexing approaches to consumers include couponing, segmented pricing, and price promotion. Price flexing with business market is an increasing trend toward customization.

Subject Area: Business processes—marketing/pricing objectives and policies. Source: Author.

342. (**c**) The objective of price promotion is to encourage trial by a customer and to allow the seller to maintain a higher list price. As consumers grow accustomed to low-price specials, any firm that does not price promote is likely to lose sales. As price promotions tend to increase over time, consumers become more sensitive to price.

Subject Area: Business processes—marketing/pricing objectives and policies. Source: Author.

343. (**a**) Marketers often have different marketing programs for different consumer segments such as geographic, usage, demographic, and time segments.

Subject Area: Business processes—marketing/pricing objectives and policies. Source: Author.

344. (**b**) Sellers charging different prices to different buyers is called price discrimination.

Subject Area: Business processes—marketing/pricing objectives and policies. Source: Author.

345. (**a**) Pricing for survival occurs when a company experiencing financial trouble may seek to produce an acceptable cash flow, to cover marginal costs, and simply survive. This may result when competition is especially intense, when consumer needs are changing, and/or when substantial excess capacity exists.

Subject Area: Business processes—marketing/pricing objectives and policies. Source: Author.

346. (**b**) One of the downsides of penetration pricing is that customers may infer low quality from low price.

Subject Area: Business processes—marketing/pricing objectives and policies. Source: Author.

347. (**b**) Price discrimination occurs whenever different classes of customers are charged different markups for the same product. It occurs when different customers are charged the same price despite underlying cost differences and when price differentials fail to reflect cost discrepancies.

Subject Area: Business processes—marketing/pricing objectives and policies. Source: CBM, Volume two.

348. (**a**) For price discrimination to be successful and profitable, different price elasticities of demand must exist in the various submarkets. Also, the firm must be able to efficiently identify relevant submarkets and prevent transfers among affected customers.

Subject Area: Business processes—marketing/pricing objectives and policies. Source: CBM, Volume two.

349. (**a**) If there is a high price elasticity of demand, then the customer is price sensitive. As a result, prices must be kept relatively low.

Subject Area: Business processes—marketing/pricing objectives and policies. Source: CBM, Volume two.

350. (**c**) A change in the quantity demanded is caused by a change in price.

Subject Area: Business processes—marketing/pricing objectives and policies. Source: Author.

351. (**d**) A change in the quantity supplied is caused by a change in price.

Subject Area: Business processes—marketing/pricing objectives and policies. Source: CBM, Volume two.

352. (**b**) If demand is elastic, a price increase lowers total revenue, and a decrease in price raises total revenue.

Subject Area: Business processes—marketing/pricing objectives and policies. Source: Author.

353. (**a**) With inelastic demand, a price increase produces less than a proportionate decline in quantity demanded, so total revenue rises.

Subject Area: Business processes—marketing/pricing objectives and policies. Source: CBM, Volume two.

354. (**b**) Fully allocated costs can be appropriate when a firm is operating at full capacity. During peak periods, when facilities are fully utilized, expansion is required to increase production. Under such conditions, an increase in production requires an increase in all plant, equipment, labor, materials, and other expenditures.

Subject Area: Business processes—marketing/pricing objectives and policies. Source: Author.

355. (**c**) Markup pricing is the most commonly employed pricing method. Markup pricing method is average variable cost plus a charge for overhead and profit margin.

Subject Area: Business processes—marketing/pricing objectives and policies. Source: Author.

356. (a) Any amount received above the storage and delivery costs for a by-product allows the seller to reduce the main product's price to make it more competitive. Choice (b) is incorrect. Optional products are those offered for sale along with the main product. They are unlikely to have a zero production cost so the seller must receive a price above the storage and delivery costs for such products. Choice (c) is incorrect. Captive products are those that must be used along with the main product, such as film for use with a camera. Sellers often make their money on the captive products, rather than on the main product which is sold at a low price. The captive products therefore will be priced well above the storage and delivery costs. Choice (d) is incorrect. Product bundles are combinations of products sold together at a reduced price, such as season tickets for a theater. Products are bundled in order to promote the sale of certain items that consumers might not otherwise purchase. The combined price of the bundle must be low enough to encourage consumers to buy the bundle, but must recover production costs and provide some profit for the seller, so the price must exceed storage and delivery costs.

Subject Area: Business processes—marketing/pricing objectives and policies. Source: CIA Model Exam 2002, IV-63.

Marketing—Supply-Chain Management

357. (c) The process of linking a manufacturer's operations with those of its suppliers and customers is called supply-chain management.

Subject Area: Business processes—marketing/supply-chain management. Source: Author.

358. (b) Supply-chain management describes the logistical system, which emphasizes close cooperation and comprehensive interorganizational management to integrate the logistical operations of the different firms in the marketing channel.

Subject Area: Business processes—marketing/supply-chain management. Source: Author.

359. (d) Each organization in a supply chain is typically involved in developing a product, marketing processes, delivery of a product, and postsale service.

Subject Area: Business processes—marketing/supply-chain management. Source: Author.

360. (a) Buyers involved in a supply-chain management strategy sometimes reach several tiers back in the supply-chain link to assist second-tier suppliers in meeting their goals.

Subject Area: Business processes—marketing/supply-chain management. Source: Author.

361. (d) The primary goal of supply-chain management is to improve speed, accuracy, and efficiency in manufacturing and delivery.

Subject Area: Business processes—marketing/supply-chain management. Source: Author.

362. (b) The reward of becoming a valued partner in a customer's supply chain is being viewed as an extension of the customer's company.

Subject Area: Business processes—marketing/supply-chain management. Source: Author.

363. (b) To achieve the reward of being viewed as an extension of a company's customers, a business marketer must be able to meet quality, delivery, service, and informational requirements.

Subject Area: Business processes—marketing/supply-chain management. Source: Author.

364. (a) Companies that adopt the just-in-time approach to purchasing will typically decrease the number of suppliers with which they deal.

Subject Area: Business processes—marketing/supply-chain management. Source: Author.

365. (b) The essence of the just-in-time concept is to deliver defect-free parts and materials to the production process just at the moment they are needed.

Subject Area: Business processes—marketing/supply-chain management. Source: Author.

366. (d) The goals of just-in-time concepts are generally focused on quality, customer service, inventory costs, and production efficiency.

Subject Area: Business processes—marketing/supply-chain management. Source: Author.

367. (c) The value offerings developed by business marketers must be based on the skills and resources that provide value as perceived by the customer.

Subject Area: Business processes—marketing/supply-chain management. Source: Author.

368. (a) The purchasing method that involves weighing the comparative value of materials, parts, components, and manufacturing processes from the standpoint of their purpose, relative merit, and cost is called value analysis.

Subject Area: Business processes—marketing/supply-chain management. Source: Author.

369. (d) Value engineering, not value analysis, points the way to elimination and reengineering.

Subject Area: Business processes—marketing/supply-chain management. Source: Author.

370. (c) One of the results of value analysis is that product design alternatives will produce significant cost savings.

Subject Area: Business processes—marketing/supply-chain management. Source: Author.

371. (d) The value of a function is determined by the most cost-efficient way of fully accomplishing the function.

Subject Area: Business processes—marketing/supply-chain management. Source: Author.

372. (b) The evaluation of supplier performance is used as a negotiation tool to gain leverage in buyer-seller relationships.

Subject Area: Business processes—marketing/supply-chain management. Source: Author.

373. (a) The buying organization weighs each performance factor according to its relative importance to the organization. The results are used by both the seller and the buyer to meet their specific needs and goals.

Subject Area: Business processes—marketing/supply-chain management. Source: Author.

374. (c) Customers in business markets are interested in a supplier's total capabilities and how they contribute to the customers' success in the market.

Subject Area: Business processes—marketing/supply-chain management. Source: Author.

375. (c) Warehousing is concerned with the holding of products until they are ready to be sold.

Subject Area: Business processes—marketing/supply-chain management. Source: Author.

376. (d) The number of suppliers in the marketplace is the most important factor between a single source and multiple sources. If there is only one supplier available for a component, the decision is obvious.

Subject Area: Business processes—marketing/supply-chain management. Source: CBM, Volume two.

377. (b) Understanding "who the other customers of the supplier are" can help in assessing competitive strengths and weaknesses of a potential supplier.

Subject Area: Business processes—marketing/supply-chain management. Source: CBM, Volume two.

378. (c) Factors such as management integrity, financial stability, and design flexibility should be considered in addition to supplier rating score. Production standards are already considered as part of the "Function" and "Quality" ratings.

Subject Area: Business processes—marketing/supply-chain management. Source: CBM, Volume two.

379. (c) Vendor analysis should be conducted on a periodic basis (item I) or whenever there is a significant change in the weights assigned to the scoring factors (item II).

Subject Area: Business processes—marketing/supply-chain management. Source: CBM, Volume two.

380. (c) Price, quality, and service are major factors used in selecting a vendor. Inventory usage should not be a concern at the time of selecting a vendor. It may be useful after selecting the vendor.

Subject Area: Business processes—marketing/supply-chain management. Source: CBM, Volume two.

381. (c) Suppliers should be viewed as outside partners who can contribute to the long-term success of a buying firm. If suppliers are selected on price only, they will be switched continuously, which will destabilize the purchasing process.

Subject Area: Business processes—marketing/supply-chain management. Source: CBM, Volume two.

382. (a) Supplier audits are an important first step in the supplier certification program.

Subject Area: Business processes—marketing/supply-chain management. Source: CBM, Volume two.

383. (d) Usually, supplier audits focus on supplier's production or service capabilities as well as quality and delivery programs.

Subject Area: Business processes—marketing/supply-chain management. Source: CBM, Volume two.

384. (b) Usually, supplier audits cover management style, quality assurance, materials management, product and process design methods, product and process improvement opportunities, and management policies and procedures for problem identification and corrective action. Industrial engineering is useful in setting material and labor time standards.

Subject Area: Business processes—marketing/supply-chain management. Source: CBM, Volume two.

385. (a) Generally speaking, there is less risk with certified suppliers than with noncertified suppliers due to their increased capabilities.

Subject Area: Business processes—marketing/supply-chain management. Source: CBM, Volume two.

386. (a) The certification process verifies that a supplier meets or exceeds the requirements of a buyer. Certified suppliers are referred to as world-class suppliers. Some companies rely on standard industry certification such as ISO 9000. Some companies have their own certification either in addition to or as a substitute for the ISO 9000.

Subject Area: Business processes—marketing/supply-chain management. Source: CBM, Volume two.

387. (a) The scope of value analysis includes examination of functions and costs to determine whether functions can be added, removed, substituted, or improved to reduce costs and to improve overall performance of the finished product. Here, value is related to a product's function and cost.

Subject Area: Business processes—marketing/supply-chain management. Source: CBM, Volume two.

388. (d) Value analysis is most applicable to parts, raw materials, and components that have high unit cost (item II) and high annual usage (item IV). Since the product of high unit cost and high annual usage is significant in dollar amount, it makes sense to analyze these items for cost reduction.

Subject Area: Business processes—marketing/supply-chain management. Source: CBM, Volume two.

389. (c) Although purchasing management is actively involved in the value analysis, it should not drive its implementation due to their limited knowledge in engineering and operations. Usually, purchasing gives more importance to cost reduction at the expense of valuable functions needed for customers.

Subject Area: Business processes—marketing/supply-chain management. Source: CBM, Volume two.

390. (c) The bullwhip effect is an extreme change in the supply position upstream generated by a small change in demand downstream in the supply chain.

Subject Area: Business processes—marketing/supply-chain management. Source: Author.

391. (b) The bullwhip effect can be eliminated by synchronizing the supply chain's downstream and upstream positions.

Subject Area: Business processes—marketing/supply-chain management. Source: Author.

392. (a) The inventory level during a bullwhip effect can quickly move from being backordered to being excess. The effect creates an extreme change.

Subject Area: Business processes—marketing/supply-chain management. Source: Author.

393. (**a**) Presourcing means choosing suppliers in the concept-development stage of a new product, including the design, prototype development, and manufacturing of a component, part, product, or complete system. The rationale for presourcing is that it permits many engineering tasks to be carried out simultaneously (concurrently) rather than sequentially, thereby speeding up the new product development process.

Subject Area: Business processes—marketing/supply-chain management. Source: Author.

394. (**b**) In the Japanese keiretsu (an informal program), Japanese manufacturers own 20 to 50% of the equity of their largest suppliers. In the American keiretsu (a formal program), American companies could not take similar stakes due to legal restrictions. Kanban is a color-coded production material control system used in the factory floor to signal the demand for and the need for the movement of materials between the upstream and the downstream workstations. Kaizen is a concept of continuous improvement in quality.

Subject Area: Business processes—marketing/supply-chain management. Source: Author.

395. (**b**) Value analysis is primarily designed to optimize performance of a function at a minimum cost. Choice (a) is incorrect because Pareto analysis is a technique for classifying problem areas according to degree of importance, and focusing on the most important. Choice (c) is incorrect because linear regression is used to predict one variable if a correlated variable is known. Choice (d) is incorrect because the Markov process is used in applications such as describing the probability that a machine that is working in one period will work in another.

Subject Area: Business processes—marketing/supply-chain management. Source: CIA Model Exam 1998, III-33.

Human Resources Management

396. (**a**) The traditional employee's performance measurement process is based on a job analysis and rarely includes broader organizational criteria. The process is static in nature in that it captures a summary of an entire year of work at one point in time. The focus of employee feedback is on reaching agreement on the results of the evaluation and determining actions that need to be taken to improve performance.

Subject Area: Business processes—human resources. Source: Author.

397. (**a**) Increased competition leads to innovation in the workplace in an effort to reduce costs and improve product and service quality. Employees are the key to improve business results by producing more at higher levels of quality with fewer resources. Choices (b), (c), and (d) are the elements of the traditional performance measurement system.

Subject Area: Business processes—human resources. Source: Author.

398. (**a**) The major difference between employee's performance measurement and performance management is the emphasis on management rather than measurement. Management includes changing the process from a report card or evaluation tool to an opportunity for a full and fair discussion between manager and subordinates. This discussion includes establishing goals and objectives, noting innovations and efficiencies, reinforcing positive behavior and valuable work efforts, and guiding behavior toward higher achievement.

Subject Area: Business processes—human resources. Source: Author.

399. (**d**) In the employee's performance management system, measurement is continuous, and it is seen as a means to an end rather than an end in itself. It molds employee's performance through employee active participation and continuous feedback. Coupled with effective reward and recognition programs, performance management systems can shape work behavior to reap the benefits desired in the competitive marketplace.

Subject Area: Business processes—human resources. Source: Author.

400. (**b**) The human resource management process includes employee selection and recruiting, employee performance appraisal, and employee training and development. Employee communication is not a major part of the human resource management process because every department or function needs employee communication.

Subject Area: Business processes—human resources. Source: Author.

401. (**c**) A corporate Web site is the most frequently used but least successful job-searching method.

Subject Area: Business processes—human resources. Source: Author.

402. (**d**) Job referrals through friends and colleagues are the best way to find a job because of familiarity of the potential employee.

Subject Area: Business processes—human resources. Source: Author.

403. (**a**) Job analysis identifies basic task and skill requirements through observation.

Subject Area: Business processes—human resources. Source: Author.

404. (**a**) Job analyses should be done before job descriptions are developed.

Subject Area: Business processes—human resources. Source: Author.

405. (**d**) Job descriptions outline the role expectations and skill requirements for a specific job.

Subject Area: Business processes—human resources. Source: Author.

406. (**b**) Interviews are the most common tool used for employee selection because of face-to-face communication.

Subject Area: Business processes—human resources. Source: Author.

407. (**c**) Structured interview is defined as a set of job-related questions with standardized answers.

Subject Area: Business processes—human resources. Source: Author.

408. **(a)** Performance appraisal defines the process of evaluating an individual's contribution as a basis for making objective personnel decisions. Environmental factors include intrinsic and extrinsic rewards. Facilitation skills include diplomacy, negotiating, and communicating skills.
Subject Area: Business processes—human resources. Source: Author.

409. **(c)** The criterion for legally defensible performance appraisals in the United States include (1) results were reviewed with ratees, (2) performance was based on job analysis, and (3) written instructions were given to evaluators.
Subject Area: Business processes—human resources. Source: Author.

410. **(b)** Managers use written essays (narrative form) to describe the performance of an employee.
Subject Area: Business processes—human resources. Source: Author.

411. **(b)** In the critical incident performance appraisal technique, managers write down specific examples of employees' good and bad performance as they occur and later use them during the performance appraisal.
Subject Area: Business processes—human resources. Source: Author.

412. **(c)** Both graphic rating scales and behaviorally anchored rating scales (BARS) are effective for appraising an employee's job performance due to their focus on the employee's behavior.
Subject Area: Business processes—human resources. Source: Author.

413. **(d)** In a 360-degree review technique, a manager takes input from multiple raters such as one's supervisor, peers, and subordinates as part of an employee's performance appraisal.
Subject Area: Business processes—human resources. Source: Author.

414. **(c)** Supervisors and managers need more training in employee performance appraisals since errors can be very costly and risky for both the manager and the employee.
Subject Area: Business processes—human resources. Source: Author.

415. **(d)** Live classroom lectures are the most preferred instructional and training methods due to their face-to-face communication and question and answer session.
Subject Area: Business processes—human resources. Source: Author.

Balanced Scorecard System

416. **(c)** The balanced scorecard system is a comprehensive management control system that balances traditional financial measures with operational (nonfinancial) measures relating to a company's critical success factors.
Subject Area: Business processes—balanced scorecard. Source: CBM, Volume two.

417. **(a)** The balanced scorecard system started as a management control system is now becoming a strategic management system because of its importance to overall progress of a company in terms of long-term value, vision, and strategy.
Subject Area: Business processes—balanced scorecard. Source: Author.

418. **(d)** Financial measures are lag indicators focusing on past actions and promoting short-term behavior. Companies also need lead indicators focusing on value creators or drivers, promoting long-term behavior, and equally emphasizing nonfinancial measures such as quality and service. Examples of financial indicators include return on assets (ROA), net income after taxes, and return on equity (ROE).
Subject Area: Business processes—balanced scorecard. Source: CBM, Volume two.

419. **(d)** The four perspectives of the balanced scorecard approach include measures of quality, productivity, efficiency and timeliness, and marketing success.
Subject Area: Business processes—balanced scorecard. Source: Author.

420. **(b)** The balanced scorecard approach requires looking at performance from four different but related perspectives such as financial, customer, internal business processes, and learning and growth.
Subject Area: Business processes—balanced scorecard. Source: Author.

421. **(b)** Reducing prices has a temporary effect while the other three choices have a permanent effect. The number of product or service warranty claims filed, number of returned products, customer response time, and percentage of on-time deliveries are also critical success factors.
Subject Area: Business processes—balanced scorecard. Source: Author.

422. **(c)** The value chain of a company includes all activities from research and development (R&D) to postsale customer service. The scope of internal business processes also includes improving quality throughout the production process, increasing productivity, increasing efficiency of resources, and timeliness of information.
Subject Area: Business processes—balanced scorecard. Source: Author.

423. **(b)** Customer perspective deals with taking care of interests of customers as well as acquiring and retaining more of them.
Subject Area: Business processes—balanced scorecard. Source: Author.

424. **(d)** Learning and growth perspectives deal with product improvement and innovation, information systems capabilities, efficient and effective use of employees, and overall company growth.
Subject Area: Business processes—balanced scorecard. Source: Author.

425. **(d)** The balanced scorecard approach integrates financial and nonfinancial performance measures of a company. Cost (item I) and sales margins (item II) are financial measures while quality (item III) and customer service (item IV) are nonfinancial measures.
Subject Area: Business processes—balanced scorecard. Source: Author.

426. (**d**) Traditional measures are basically financial and are not adequate to fully assess the performance of companies. Traditional measures mainly deal with historical accounting data and cannot answer questions such as customer satisfaction, quality improvement, productivity, efficient utilization of resources, and employee satisfaction.

Subject Area: Business processes—balanced scorecard. Source: Author.

427. (**d**) Time to market a new product is part of the learning and growth perspective.

Subject Area: Business processes—balanced scorecard. Source: Author.

428. (**d**) Examples of customer-performance scorecard measures include customers (new, dissatisfied, satisfied, or lost); target market awareness or preference; relative product or service quality; and on-time delivery. Machine downtime, rework time, and plant waste are examples of production-performance scorecard measures.

Subject Area: Business processes—balanced scorecard. Source: Author.

429. (**c**) Stakeholder-based performance scorecard measurements are difficult to identify and implement because of (1) various constituents involved (stakeholders, employees, unions, governments, investors and creditors, bankers, distributors, wholesalers and retailers, and suppliers and vendors), (2) difficulty in reaching them on a day-to-day basis, (3) difficulty in communicating with them periodically, (4) difficulty in coordinating them, and (5) difficulty in reaching a conclusion on issues due to their diverging viewpoints and conflicting objectives.

Subject Area: Business processes—balanced scorecard. Source: Author.

430. (**c**) A good balanced scorecard system contains lag measures, lead measures, and interlinking. Financial measures are lag indicators focusing on past actions and promoting short-term behavior. Companies also need lead indicators focusing on value creators or drivers, promoting long-term behavior, and equally emphasizing nonfinancial measures such as quality and service. A good balanced scorecard contains both leading and lagging measures and links them through logical cause-and-effect relationships. Interlinking is the quantitative modeling of cause-and-effect relationships between internal and external performance measures. An interrelationship digraph identifies and explores causal relationships among related concepts or ideas. It shows that every idea can be logically linked with more than one other idea at time, and allows for "lateral thinking" rather than "linear thinking." The graph is used after the affinity diagram has clarified issues and problems.

Subject Area: Business processes—balanced scorecard. Source: Author.

2 FINANCIAL ACCOUNTING AND FINANCE (15–25%)

THEORY

2.1 Basic Concepts and Underlying Principles of Financial Accounting

Financial accounting is the language of business. All business transactions will eventually end up in financial statements. Accounting principles are used to classify, record, post, summarize, and report the business transactions between various parties involved. Accountants apply their professional standards to analyze business transactions, prepare estimations, and report business events. The business transactions data accumulated in the chart of accounts are used to prepare the financial statements of an organization. Topics such as accounting principles and qualities of accounting information, the accounting cycle, different formats of financial statements, and account analysis are discussed in this section.

(a) **Accounting Principles and Qualities of Accounting Information**

(i) **Accounting principles.** If the management of a company could record and report financial data as it saw fit, comparisons among companies would be difficult, if not impossible. Thus, financial accountants follow generally accepted accounting principles (GAAP) in preparing reports. These reports allow investors and other stakeholders to compare one company to another.

Accounting principles and concepts are developed from research, accepted accounting practices, and pronouncements of authoritative bodies. Currently, the Financial Accounting Standards Board (FASB) is the authoritative body having the primary responsibility for developing accounting principles. The FASB publishes *Statements of Financial Accounting Standards* and *Interpretations* to these Standards.

Next, we emphasize accounting principles and concepts. It is through this emphasis on the "why" of accounting as well as the "how" that you will gain an understanding of the full significance of accounting. In the following paragraphs, we discuss the business entity concept, the cost concept, the matching concept, and other accounting concepts.

(A) ***Business entity concept.*** The individual business unit is the business entity for which economic data are needed. This entity could be an automobile dealer, a department store, or a grocery store. The business entity must be identified, so that the accountant can determine which economic data should be analyzed, recorded, and summarized in reports.

The business entity concept is important because it limits the economic data in the accounting system to data related directly to the activities of the business. In other words, the business is viewed as an entity separate from its owners, creditors, or other stakeholders. For example, the accountant for a business with one owner (a proprietorship) would record the activities of the business only, not the personal activities, property, or debts of the owner. The business entity concept can be related to economic entity assumption, which states that economic activity can be identified with a particular unit of accountability; going concern assumption, where the accountant assumes unless there is evidence to the contrary, that the reporting entity will have a life long enough to fulfill its objectives and commitments; and monetary unit assumption, where it provides that all transactions and events can be measured in terms of a common denominator—the dollar.

(B) ***Cost concept.*** The historical cost concept is the basis for entering the *exchange price or cost of an asset* into the accounting records. Using the cost concept involves two other important accounting concepts: (1) objectivity and (2) the unit of measure. The objectivity concept requires that the accounting records and reports be based upon objective evidence. In exchanges between a buyer and a seller, both try to get the best price. Only the final agreed-upon amount is objective enough for accounting purposes. If the amounts at which properties were recorded were constantly being revised upward and downward based on offers, appraisals, and opinions, accounting reports would soon become unstable and unreliable. The unit of measure concept requires that economic data be recorded in dollars. Money is a common unit of measurement for reporting uniform financial data and reports.

(C) ***Matching concept.*** The matching concept, which is based on accrual accounting, refers to the matching of expenses and revenues (hence net income) for an accounting period. Under the accrual basis, revenues are reported in the income statement in which they are earned. Similarly, expenses are reported in the same period as the revenues to which they relate. Under the cash basis of accounting, revenues and expenses are reported in the income statement in the period in which cash is received or paid.

(D) ***Other accounting concepts.*** The materiality concept implies that errors, which could occur during journalizing and posting transactions, should be significant enough to affect the decision-making process. All material errors should be discovered and corrected. The accounting period concept breaks the economic life of a business into time periods, and requires that accounting reports be prepared at periodic intervals. The revenue recognition concept, which is based on accrual accounting, refers to the recognition of revenues in the period in which they are earned.

(ii) **Qualities of accounting information.** The accounting function collects the raw data from business transactions and converts them into information useful to the decision maker. In this regard, the accounting information should contain two qualitative characteristics: (1) primary and (2) secondary qualities.

(A) ***Primary qualities.*** The two primary qualities that distinguish useful accounting information are relevance and reliability. If either of these qualities is missing, accounting information will not be useful. Relevance means the information must have a bearing on a particular decision situation. Relevant accounting information possesses at least two characteristics: timeliness and predictive value or feedback value. Timeliness means accounting information must be provided in time to influence a particular decision. Predictive value means accounting information can be used to predict the future and timing of cash flows. Feedback value means the accounting function must provide decision makers with information that allows them to assess the progress or economic worth of an investment.

To be considered reliable, accounting information must possess three qualities: verifiability, representational faithfulness, and neutrality. Information is considered verifiable if several individuals, working independently, would arrive at similar conclusions using the same data. Representational faithfulness means accounting information must report what actually happened. Neutrality means accounting information must be free of bias or distortion.

(B) ***Secondary qualities.*** "Secondary qualities" does not mean that these characteristics are of lesser importance than the primary qualities. If a secondary characteristic is missing, the accounting information is not necessarily useless. The secondary qualities of useful information are comparability and consistency. Comparability means accounting reports generated for one firm may be easily and usefully compared with the accounting reports generated for other firms. If the two firms use totally different accounting methods, it would be very difficult to make a useful comparison of their data and information. Consistency means that a firm systematically uses the same accounting methods and procedures from one accounting period to the next accounting period.

In addition to the primary and secondary qualities, the accounting information must be understandable to economic decision makers. "Earnings management" strategy can destroy the primary and secondary qualities of accounting information.

(b) **Accounting Cycle.** Financial accounting provides accounting information for use by those outside and inside the organization. This information is used by current investors and potential investors to determine the future benefits they will receive if they hold or acquire ownership in a business. Creditors and lenders use this information to assess the creditworthiness of an organization. Other users of this information include employees, unions, customers, the general public, and governmental units.

Transactions, in accounting, are the result of the exchange of goods and/or services. Two factors allow the recording of a transaction—evidence and measurement. An exchange is an observable event and, therefore, provides evidence of business activity. This exchange takes place at a set price and, thus, provides an objective measure of the economic activity. The accounting cycle is one of four business cycles; the other three being sales, finance, and production.

With the traditional accounting model a double-entry system of recordkeeping is used. The fundamental equation used with this system is

Assets = Liabilities + Owners' Equity

All transactions are analyzed and then recorded based upon their effect on assets, liabilities, and owners' equity. The increases and decreases in these accounts are recorded as debits or credits. In recording these transactions, the total amount of debits must equal the total amount of credits. The requirement that debits and credits must equal gives rise to the double-entry method of recordkeeping. In account form, the rules of debits and credits are

Debits	*Credits*
Increase assets	Decrease assets
Decrease liabilities	Increase liabilities
Decrease owners' equity	Increase owners' equity
Increase owners' drawing	Decrease owners' drawing
Decrease revenues	Increase revenues
Increase expenses	Decrease expenses

(i) **Cash-basis versus accrual-basis.** The two approaches of accounting are **cash-basis** accounting and **accrual-basis** accounting. With the **cash-basis of accounting** revenues are recognized when cash is received, and expenses are recognized when cash is paid out. The primary advantages of cash-basis accounting are the increased reliability due to the fact that transactions are not recorded until complete and the simplicity due to the fact that fewer estimates and judgments are required.

For most businesses the cash-basis of accounting for a period requires recognition and measurement of noncash resources and obligations. Cash-basis accounting is not in accordance with GAAP.

With the **accrual-basis of accounting** revenues are recognized when sales are made or services are performed, and expenses are recognized as incurred. Revenues and expenses are recognized in the period in which they occur rather than when cash is received or paid out.

The attempt to record the financial effect of transactions that have cash consequences in the periods in which those transactions occur rather than in the periods in which cash is received or paid pertains to accrual accounting.

(ii) **Steps in the accounting cycle.** The accounting cycle records the effect of economic transactions upon the assets, liabilities and owners' equity of an organization. The accounting cycle involves eight steps: (1) analysis of transactions, (2) journalizing of transactions, (3) posting to the ledger, (4) trial balance and working papers, (5) adjusting journal entries, (6) closing journal entries, (7) preparing financial statements, and (8) reversing journal entries (see Exhibit 2.1).

1. Analysis of transactions
2. Journalizing of transactions
3. Posting to ledger
4. Trial balance and working papers
5. Adjusting journal entries
6. Closing journal entries
7. Preparing financial statements
8. Reversing journal entries

Exhibit 2.1: Eight steps in the accounting cycle

(A) ***Analysis of transactions.*** Each transaction must be analyzed before being recorded to determine the effect on the assets, liabilities, and owners' equity accounts. Asset, liability, and equity accounts are known as **real** accounts because they are not closed at the end of an accounting period. Revenue and expense accounts, however, are referred to as **nominal** accounts because at the end of an accounting period (usually a year), they are closed and their balances are reduced to zero. Therefore, the real accounts represent the financial position of an organization at any point in time. The nominal accounts represent the results of operations over a given period of time.

(B) ***Journalizing of transactions.*** After analysis to determine the affected accounts, transactions are recorded in the accounting journal, or journalized. Each account affected, the amount of the changes, and the direction of the changes (increases or decreases) are recorded. These transactions are recorded in the general journal or special journals, which serve as a chronological record of all the economic transactions of an organization. Special journals group similar types of transactions to provide more efficient processing of data. These journals systematize the original recording of major recurring types of transactions such as cash receipts, cash disbursements, purchases, and sales.

The general journal is used to make entries that do not fit in the special journals, to make adjusting entries at the end of the accounting period, and to make closing entries at the end of the accounting period.

(C) ***Posting to the ledger.*** The complete collection of all the accounts of an organization is the ledger. Transactions are posted to individual ledger accounts after being journalized. The ledger maintains the current balance of all the accounts.

Most organizations maintain subsidiary ledgers for accounts receivable and accounts payable, because it is difficult to determine amounts due from specific customers and amounts due to specific suppliers using the master Accounts Receivable account in the ledger. When using subsidiary ledgers, entries to the general ledger are totals for a specific period of time, for example, weekly totals, from the special journals. The sums of all subsidiary ledgers should be equal to its master account in the general ledger.

(D) ***Trial balance and working papers.*** Working papers are large columnar sheets of paper for entering and summarizing the information necessary for making adjusting and closing entries and preparing financial statements. Working papers are prepared at the end of an accounting period and are for internal use only.

The first step in the preparation of working papers is the preparation of a trial balance. The trial balance lists all accounts with balances as of the end of the accounting period. Balances of the accounts are entered in the columns and totaled. If postings for the period are arithmetically correct, then debits will equal credits. The trial balance does not provide a means of determining whether transactions have been posted to the correct accounts or journalized and/or posted to the general journal.

(E) ***Adjusting journal entries.*** With the accrual system of accounting, certain adjustments must be made at the end of each accounting period. These adjusting entries convert the amounts actually in the accounts to the amounts that should be in the accounts for proper financial reporting. These adjusting entries allocate the cost of assets used in several accounting periods and revenues earned in several accounting periods, accrue revenues and expenses attributable to the current period that have not been recorded, and make appropriate end of period adjustments in the carrying value of certain assets, that is, marketable securities and inventories.

With accrual accounting the cost of long-term assets must be apportioned to the periods that benefit from their use. The three types of long-term assets are **productive** assets such as buildings and machinery, **wasting** assets such as minerals, and **intangible** assets such as patents and copyrights. These assets are apportioned to periods through depreciation, depletion, and amortization.

Another type of revenue and expense apportionment is to record the portion of unearned revenues earned during the year and the portion of a prepaid expense, which expired during the year. The following steps are necessary to make adjusting entries:

1. Determine the current balance in an account.
2. Determine the appropriate balance for the account.
3. Make the appropriate entry or entries to achieve the desired ending balances.

An adjusting entry may be necessary to reduce an asset to its market value. Some common adjustments are accounts receivable, inventories, and marketable securities. These accounts are adjusted by debiting an expense or loss account and crediting a contra asset account.

(F) ***Closing journal entries.*** After posting adjusting entries, all nominal accounts with existing balances are closed to **real** accounts. These closing entries reduce the nominal account balances to zero to show the effect of these accounts on owners' equity and so that information for the next accounting period may be accumulated. The following steps are required:

1. Close all revenue, gain, expense, and loss accounts to the Expense and Revenue Summary account. This account is used only at the end of an accounting period to summarize revenues and expenses for the period.
2. Close the Expense and Revenue Summary account to Retained Earnings
3. Close the dividend account to Retained Earnings

A postclosing trial balance is prepared after making all necessary closing entries. This provides a check against partial posting of closing entries. The postclosing trial balance reflects the balances to be included in the balance sheet at the end of the period.

(G) ***Preparing financial statements.*** After preparing the adjusting entries and posting them to the working papers, an Income Statement can be prepared using the income statement numbers from the working papers.

After preparing the closing entries and posting them to the working papers, the only accounts with balances should be the asset, liability, and owners' equity accounts. At this time, a Statement of Stockholders' Equity or Statement of Retained Earnings should be prepared. This statement summarizes the transactions affecting the owners' capital account balance or retained earning. Such a statement shows the beginning capital account, plus net income or less net loss, less owners' withdrawals or dividends. The ending capital account is then carried forward to the balance sheet, which helps to relate income statement information to balance sheet information.

Now it is time to prepare the Balance Sheet. The Balance Sheet is divided into assets, liabilities, and owners' equity and reflects the balances in these accounts at the end of the year.

(H) ***Reversing journal entries.*** Reversing entries, the final step in the accounting cycle, are recorded on the first day of the next accounting period. Reversing entries are prepared to reverse the effects of certain adjusting entries to which they relate. These entries reduce the possibility of including a revenue or expense at the time of the adjusting entry and including it again when the economic transaction occurs. The general rule on reversing entries is that all adjusting entries that increase assets or liabilities may be reversed. Therefore, the only adjusting entries that should be reversed are those that accrue revenues or expenses. Reversing entries are optional and are dependent on an organization's bookkeeping system.

Examples of Journal Entries

Next, we will present varied examples of journal entries for better understanding of recording of business transactions with accounting implications.

Example 1. Debiting the Prepaid Insurance account and crediting the Accounts Payable account would correctly record the purchase of a liability insurance policy on account.

Example 2. Debiting the Interest Expense account and crediting the Interest Payable account would correctly record the accrued expense transaction.

Example 3. A company has been sued for $100,000,000 for producing and selling an unsafe product. Attorneys for the company cannot predict the outcome of the litigation. In its financial statements, the company should disclose the existence of the lawsuits in a footnote without making a journal entry. The situation did not meet the criteria for setting up as a contingent liability. Only disclosure is required when a loss contingency is possible. No accrual is required because the loss could not be reasonably estimated.

Example 4. In the December 31, 2003 balance sheet, ending inventory was valued at $140,000. An investigation revealed the true balance should have been $150,000. In the December 31, 2004, balance sheet, ending inventory was shown at $200,000. The correct balance should have been $180,000. All errors were discovered during an investigation in 2005 before the books were closed. Ignoring tax effects, the appropriate journal entry that should be made in 2005 to correct the errors would be debiting the Retained Earnings for $20,000 to correct the decreased income and crediting the Inventory for $20,000 to correct the decreased inventory.

This is an example of counterbalancing error affecting both balance sheet and income statement. An entry to adjust the beginning balance of the retained earnings is necessary as it takes two years for the error to be counterbalanced naturally. Note that the books were not closed for 2005.

Example 5. A retail shoe store purchases a copy machine for its office. The copier is priced at $5,000. The store gives cash of $2,000 and a 10% one-year promissory note in exchange for the copier. The acquisition of the copy machine could be recorded by debiting the Office Equipment account and crediting the Cash account for $2,000 and crediting the Note Payable account for $3,000.

The 10% interest rate seems reasonable and the note can be recorded at its face value since it is only for one year. Otherwise, present value should be used to record the note.

Example 6. A retail company purchases advertising services on account. The appropriate journal entry to record the purchase would be debiting the Advertising Expense account and crediting the Accounts Payable account.

Example 7. A company allows customers to redeem 20 coupons for a toy (cost $3.00). Estimates are that 40% of coupons distributed will result in redemption. Since beginning the promotion this year, 4,000,000 coupons were distributed and 1,000,000 redeemed. The adjusting journal entry to accrue for unredeemed coupons at year-end is debiting Premium Expense account for $90,000 and crediting Estimated Liability for Premiums account for $90,000.

All expenses must be accrued at the end of accounting (fiscal) year. In this case, all unredeemed coupons that are still outstanding at year-end must be accrued. The liability of $90,000 is calculated as follows:

Unredeemed coupons are 4,000,000 × 0.40 – 1,000,000 = 600,000
Equivalent toys are 600,000/20 = 30,000 toys
Liability is 30,000 toys × $3.00 cost per toy = $90,000

Example 8. The debit to supplies and credit to supplies expense is indication of an end-of-period adjusting journal entry. These adjustments may include inventory adjustments and

Example 9. When a perpetual inventory system is used and a difference exists between the perpetual inventory amount balance and the physical inventory count, the following journal entry is needed to adjust the perpetual inventory amount. A debit to inventory over and short account and a credit to inventory. A write-down of inventory has occurred, which is reported as an adjustment of cost of goods sold or as another expense on the income statement.

(c) **Different Formats of Financial Statements.** A full set of four financial statements discussed in this section is based on the concept of financial capital maintenance. For a period, the full set should show

1. Financial position at the end of the period
2. Earnings and comprehensive income for the period
3. Cash flows during the period
4. Investments by and distributions to owners during the period

1. **A statement of financial position** provides information about an entity's assets, liabilities, and equity and their relationships to each other at a moment in time. The statement delineates the entity's resources structure—major classes and amounts of assets—and its financial structure—major classes and amounts of liabilities and equity.

   A statement of financial position does **not** purport to show the value of a business enterprise but, together with other financial statements and other information, should provide information that is useful to those who desire to make their own estimates of the enterprise's value. Those estimates are part of financial analysis, not of financial reporting, but financial accounting aids financial analysis.

2. **Statements of earnings and of comprehensive income** together reflect the extent to which and the ways in which the equity of an entity increased or decreased from all sources other than transactions with owners during a period.

   The concept of earnings in this statement is similar to net income for a period in present practice; however, it excludes certain accounting adjustments of earlier periods that are recognized in the current period—cumulative effects of a change in accounting principle is the principal example from present practice. *Other names given to earnings are: net income, profit, or net loss.*

   The list below provides different meanings of earnings.

   - **Earnings** are a measure of entity performance during a period. It measures the extent to which assets inflows (revenues and gains) associated with cash-to-cash cycles substantially completed during the period exceed asset outflows (expenses and losses) associated, directly or indirectly, with the same cycle.
   - **Comprehensive income** is a broad measure of the effects of transactions and other events on an entity, and comprises all recognized changes in equity (net assets) of the entity during a period from transactions and other events and circumstances except those resulting from investments by owners and distributions to owners. *Other names given to the comprehensive income include total nonowner changes in equity or comprehensive loss.*
   - Earnings and comprehensive income are **not** the same because certain gains and losses are included in comprehensive income but are excluded from earnings. Those items fall into two classes that are illustrated by certain present practices: effects of certain accounting adjustments of earlier periods that are recognized in the current period, and certain other changes in entity assets (principally certain holding gains and losses) that

are recognized in the period but are excluded from earnings, such as some changes in market values of investments in marketable equity securities classified as noncurrent assets, some changes in market values of investments in industries having specialized accounting practices for marketable securities, and foreign currency translation adjustments.

3. **A statement of cash flows** directly or indirectly reflects an entity's cash receipts classified by major sources and its cash payments classified by major uses during a period, including cash flow information about its operating, financing, and investing activities.
4. **A statement of investments by and distributions to owners** reflects an entity's capital transactions during a period—the extent to which and in what ways the equity of the entity increased or decreased from transactions with investors as owners. Each of these four statements is presented in Exhibits 2.2 through 2.5.

Exhibit 2.2: Statement of financial position

The Statement of Financial Position (balance sheet) presents assets, liabilities, and shareholders' equity. The balance sheet provides a basis for assessing the liquidity and financial flexibility of an entity, computing rates of return on investments, and evaluating the capital structure of an entity. It reflects the financial status (health) of an enterprise in conformity with GAAP. The balance sheet reports the aggregate (and cumulative) effect of transactions at a point in time, whereas the Statement of Income, Statement of Retained Earnings, and the Statement of Cash Flows report the effect of transactions over a period of time. The balance sheet is based on historical cost, the exchange price principle, or at the acquisition price.

Assets are classified as "current" if they are reasonably expected to be converted into cash, sold, or consumed either in one year or in the operating cycle, whichever is longer.

Liabilities are classified as "current" if they are expected to be liquidated through the use of current assets or the creation of other current liabilities.

Shareholders' equity arises from the ownership relation and is the source of enterprise distribution to the owners. Equity is increased by owners' investments and comprehensive income and is reduced by distributions to the owners.

The following are limitations of balance sheets:

- It does not reflect current values. Items are recorded at a mixture of historical cost and current values. Historical cost used to record assets and liabilities does not always reflect current value. Monetary assets such as cash, short-term investments, and receivables closely approximate current values. Similarly, current liabilities closely approximate current value, and should be shown on the balance sheet at face value.
- Fixed assets are reported at cost less depreciation, depletion, or amortization. Inventories and marketable equity securities are exceptions to historical cost, where they are allowed to be reported at lower of cost or market. Similarly certain long-term investments, which is another exception, are reported under the equity method. Long-term liabilities are recorded at the discounted value of future payments.
- Judgments and estimates are used to determine the carrying value or book value of many of the assets. Examples include determining the collectibility of receivables, salability of inventory, and useful life of fixed (long-term) assets. Estimations are not necessarily bad except there is no accounting guidance available.
- Appreciation of assets is not recorded except when realized through an arm's-length transaction.
- Internally generated goodwill, customer base, managerial skills and talent, reputation, technical innovation, human resources, and secret processes and formulas are not recorded in the balance sheet. Only assets obtained in a market transaction are recorded.
- It ignores the time value of its elements. Most items are stated at face value regardless of the timing of the cash flows that they will generate. Exceptions are certain long-term receivables and payables, which are discounted.
- It omits off-balance-sheet items (mostly liabilities) such as sales of receivables with recourse, leases, throughput arrangements, and take-or-pay contracts.

1. Classification of assets. In order to properly value an asset on the balance sheet, any related valuation allowance account should be reported contra to the particular asset account. Assets include current assets, noncurrent assets, and other assets.

   Current assets include cash, short-term investments, receivables, inventories, and prepaid expenses. The key criterion to include in current assets is the length of the operating cycle. When the cycle is less than one year, the one-year concept is used. When the cycle is very long, the usefulness of the concept of current assets diminishes. Specific components include

   - *Cash and cash equivalents* include cash on hand consisting of coins, currency, undeposited checks, money orders and drafts, and deposits in banks. Certificates of deposit are not considered as cash because of the time restrictions on withdrawal. Cash that is restricted in use or cash restricted for a noncurrent use would **not** be included in current assets. Cash equivalents include: short-term, highly liquid investments that are readily convertible to known amounts of cash and are near their maturity period, Treasury bills, commercial paper, and money market funds.

- *Short-term investments* are readily marketable securities acquired through the use of temporarily idle cash.
- *Receivables* include accounts receivable and notes receivable, receivables from affiliates, and receivables from officers and employees. Allowances due to uncollectibility and any amounts discounted or pledged should be clearly stated.
- *Inventories* are goods on hand and available for sale. The basis of valuation and the methods of pricing should be disclosed.
- *Prepaid expenses* are assets created by the prepayment of cash or incurrence of a liability. They expire and become expenses with the passage of time, usage, or events. Examples include prepaid rent, insurance, and deferred taxes.

Noncurrent assets include long-term investments; property, plant, and equipment; and intangible assets. Specific components include

- *Long-term investments* include investments that are intended to be held for longer than one operating cycle. Examples are debt and equity securities, tangible assets, investments held in sinking funds, pension funds, amounts held for plant expansion, and cash surrender values of life insurance policies.
- *Property, plant, and equipment* includes machinery and equipment, buildings, furniture and fixtures, natural resources and land. These assets are of a durable nature that are to be used in the production or sale of goods, sale of other assets, or rendering of services.
- *Intangible assets* include goodwill, trademarks, patents, copyrights, and organizational costs. Generally, the amortization of an intangible asset is credited directly to the asset account, although it is acceptable to use an accumulated amortization account.

Other assets include accounts that do not fit in the above asset categories. Examples include long-term prepaid expenses, deferred taxes, bond issue costs, noncurrent receivables, and restricted cash.

2. Classification of liabilities. The liabilities are presented in the balance sheet in the order of payment. It is grouped into three categories: current, noncurrent, and other.

   Current liabilities include: obligations arising from the acquisition of goods and services entering the operating cycle, collections of money in advance for the future delivery of goods or performance of services, and other obligations maturing within the current operating cycle to be met through the use of current assets. **Exceptions** are debt expected to be refinanced through another long-term issue after the balance sheet date but prior to the issuance of the balance sheet, and debt that will be retired through the use of noncurrent assets (bond sinking fund) are treated as noncurrent liabilities. The reason is that liquidation does not require the use of current assets or the creation of other current liabilities. The excess of total current assets over the current liabilities is called "working capital." It provides a margin of safety or liquid buffer available to meet the financial demands of the operating cycle.

   Noncurrent liabilities include: obligations arising through the acquisition of assets, obligations arising out of the normal course of operations, and contingent liabilities involving uncertainty as to possible losses.

   Other liabilities include: deferred charges, noncurrent receivables, intangible assets, deferred income taxes, or deferred investment tax credits.

3. Classification of shareholders' equity. Shareholders' equity is the interest of the stockholders in the assets of an enterprise. It shows the cumulative net results of past transactions. Specific components include

   - *Capital stock* consists of par/stated value of common and preferred stock.
   - *Additional paid-in-capital* includes: paid-in-capital in excess of par/stated value which is the difference between the actual issue price and par/stated value, paid-in-capital stock from other transactions which includes treasury stock, retirements of stock, stock dividends recorded at market, lapse of stock purchase warrants, and conversion of convertible bonds in excess of the par value of the stock.
   - *Donated capital* includes donations of noncash property such as land, securities, buildings, and equipment by either stockholders or outside parties.
   - *Retained earnings* are accumulated earnings not distributed to the shareholders. They are divided into appropriated (certain amount is not available for dividends) and unappropriated (available for dividends).
   - *Treasury stock* representing issued shares reacquired by the issuer. These are stated at their cost of acquisition and as a reduction of shareholders' equity.
   - *Adjustments of equity* include net unrealized losses on noncurrent portfolios of marketable equity securities, the excess of minimum pension liability over unrecognized prior service cost, and unrealized gains or losses on foreign currency transactions.

Exhibit 2.3: Statement of income

The Statement of Income, also known as the Income Statement, Statement of Earnings, or Statement of Operations, summarizes the results of an entity's economic activities or performance for a period of time (i.e., an accounting period). It also measures a firm's profitability over a specific period. Management of the enterprise is concerned with the income statement since it is curious to find out how efficiently or effectively resources are used, and how investors and creditors view the income statement.

<u>Forms of income statement</u>

- Single-step
- Multiple-step
- Condensed

Many accountants prefer **single-step** form of income statement with two groups: revenues and expenses. The single-step income statement is simple to present and all items within expenses and revenues are treated similarly in terms of priorities. Expenses are deducted from revenues to arrive at net income or loss, hence the name single-step. One exception is income taxes, which are reported separately as the last item.

EXAMPLE OF SINGLE-STEP INCOME STATEMENT

Revenues
Net sales
Dividend revenue
Rental revenue
  Total revenues

Expenses
Cost of goods sold
Selling expenses
Administrative expenses
Interest expense
Income tax expense
  Total expenses

Net income
Earnings per common share

However, some accountants prefer a **multiple-step** income statement for more information presentation and for better relationships with many classifications. It separates operating transactions from nonoperating transactions and matches costs and expenses with related revenues. For example, in the multiple-step income statement the item "administrative expenses" in the single-step income statement is further classified into office salaries, officers' salaries, utilities expenses, depreciation of buildings, and so on. Similarly, the item "interest expenses" is broken into interest on bonds, interest on notes, and so forth. Income taxes can be broken into current and deferred.

An unrealized loss resulting from a temporary decline in the market value of short-term investments in marketable equity securities should be reported as another expense or loss item on the multiple-step income statement. The short-term investments in marketable equity securities are carried at the lower of aggregate cost or market. The excess of aggregate cost over market is credited to a valuation account. Any increase in the valuation allowance is reported as a charge to income. These unrealized losses do not meet the criteria for classification as extraordinary and are not to be handled as a prior period adjustment. Unrealized losses on the noncurrent marketable equity securities are to be classified as contra stockholders' equity.

The major distinction between the multiple-step and single-step income statement formats is the separation of operating and nonoperating data.

In addition to revenue, a **condensed income statement** presents only the totals of expense groups, which are supported by supplementary schedules. These schedules can be found in the notes to the income statement.

An example of income statement sections in the order of presentation follows.

Income Statement Sections

1. Operating section
2. Nonoperating section
3. Income from continuing operations before income taxes
4. Income taxes
5. Income from continuing operations
6. Results from discontinued operations (gain/loss)
7. Extraordinary items (gain or loss)
8. Cumulative effect of a change in accounting principle
9. Net income
10. Earnings per share

Irregular transactions such as items 6 through 8 should be reported separately following income from continuing operations for single-step income statement.

The following are limitations of income statements:

- Items that cannot be quantified with any degree of reliability were not included in determining income (i.e., economic income versus accounting income).

- Income numbers are often affected by the accounting methods employed (e.g., depreciation).
- Increases in income may result from a nonoperating or nonrecurring event that is not sustainable over a period of time (e.g., onetime tax forgiveness, exchange of preferred stock).

The following are limitations of accrual-based accounting for earnings:

- Information about the liquidity and potential cash flows of an organization is absent.
- The income statement does not reflect earnings in current dollars.
- Estimates and judgments must be used in preparing the income statement.

Major Components of the Income Statement

The **major components** and items required to be presented in the income statement include: income from continuing operations, results from discontinued operations, extraordinary items, accounting changes, net income, and earnings per share.

1. **Income from continuing operations. Sales or revenues** are charges to customers for the goods and/or services provided during the period. Both gross and net sales/revenues should be presented by showing discounts, allowances, and returns.

   Cost of goods sold is the cost of the inventory items sold during the period for a manufacturing or retail company.

   Operating expenses are primary recurring costs associated with business operations to generate sales or revenues. It does not include cost of goods sold, but includes selling expenses (e.g., salesperson salaries, commissions, advertising) and general and administrative expenses (e.g., salaries, office supplies, telephone, postage, utilities, accounting and legal services). An expense is to be recognized whenever economic benefits have been consumed.

   Gains and losses stem from the peripheral transactions of the enterprise. Examples are write-downs of inventories and receivables, effects of a strike, and foreign currency exchange gains and losses.

CALCULATION OF PURCHASING POWER GAIN OR LOSS ON NET MONETARY ITEMS

EXAMPLE: A corporation has gathered the following data in order to compute the purchasing power gain or loss to be included in its supplementary information for the year ended December 31, 20X1:

	Amount in nominal dollars	
	December 31, 20X0	*December 31, 20X1*
Net monetary assets	$800,000	$943,000

	Index number
Consumer price index at December 31, 20X0	200
Consumer price index at December 31, 20X1	230
Average consumer price index for 20X1	220

Question: What is the purchasing power gain or loss on net monetary items (expressed in average-for-the-year dollars for 20X1) reported at what amount for the year ended December 31, 20X1?

Answer: $121,000 purchasing power loss, as shown below.

The net monetary asset position at the beginning of the period ($800,000) is restated to $880,000 average constant dollars ($800,000 × 220/200 = $880,000). The actual increase in net monetary assets ($943,000 – $800,000 = $143,000) is assumed to have occurred evenly throughout the year so it is already stated in terms of average-for-the-year dollars. The restated beginning balance ($880,000) plus the increase ($143,000) yields a subtotal of $1,023,000. This subtotal is compared with the ending balance restated to an average basis ($943,000 × 220/230 = $902,000) to yield a purchasing power loss of $121,000.

Expenses versus losses. Losses result from peripheral or incidental transactions whereas expenses result from ongoing major or central operations of the entity. Expense accounts are costs related to revenue whereas loss accounts are not related to revenue.

Other revenues and expenses are revenues and expenses not related to the operations of the enterprise. Examples include gains and losses on the disposal of equipment, interest revenues and expenses, and dividend revenues. A material gain on the sale of a fully depreciated asset should be classified on the income statement as part of other revenues and gains. Since the sale of an asset is not an operating item, it should be classified as other revenues and gains.

Income tax expense related to continuing operations.

2. **Results from discontinued operations.** It contains two components. The first component, income (loss) from operations, is disclosed for the current year only if the decision to discontinue operations is made after the beginning of the fiscal year for which the financial statements are being prepared. The second component, gain (loss) on the disposal, contains income (loss) from operations during the phaseout period and gain (loss) from disposal of segment assets. Discontinued operations are presented after income from continuing operations and before extraordinary income on the income statement. The disposal of a line of business is normal and any loss should be treated as an ordinary loss.
3. **Extraordinary items.** Per APB Opinion 30, two criteria must be met to classify an event or transaction as an extraordinary item: unusual nature (high degree of abnormality, clearly unrelated to, or only incidentally related to) and infrequency of occurrence (not reasonably be expected to recur in the foreseeable future). Various SFAS required the following items to be presented as extraordinary even though they do not meet the criteria stated above. Remember that SFAS overrides the APB Opinions. These **exceptional items** include
   - Material gains and losses from the extinguishment of debt except for sinking-fund requirements
   - Profit or loss resulting from the disposal of a significant part of the assets or a separable segment of previously separate companies, provided the profit or loss is material and the disposal is within two years after a pooling of interest
   - Write-off of operating rights of motor carriers
   - The investor's share of an investee's extraordinary item when the investor uses the equity method of accounting for the investee
   - Gains of a debtor related to a troubled debt restructuring

   Extraordinary items should be segregated from the results of ordinary operations and be shown net of taxes in a separate section of the income statement, following "discontinued operations" and preceding "cumulative effect of a change in accounting principle." Extraordinary losses must be both unusual and nonrecurring. Sales price minus net book value is gain or loss. A loss because of an expropriation of assets by a foreign government is classified as an extraordinary item in the income statement.

   APB 28 requires that extraordinary items be disclosed separately and included in the determination of net income for the interim period in which they occur. Extraordinary gain should not be prorated or loss should not be deferred.
4. **Accounting changes.** A change in accounting principles (including methods of applying them) results from adoption of a GAAP different from the one previously used for reporting purposes. The effect on net income of adopting the new accounting principle should be disclosed as a separate item following extraordinary items in the income statement. Changes in accounting estimates (lives of fixed assets, adjustments of the costs) are **not** considered errors or extraordinary items; instead they are considered as prior period adjustments.
5. **Net income.** Obviously, the net income is a derived item by subtracting "results from discontinued operations," "extraordinary items," and "cumulative effect of changes in accounting principles" from "income from continuing operations."
6. **Earnings per share.** Earnings per share (EPS) is a compact indicator of a company's financial performance. It is used to evaluate a firm's stock price, in assessing the firm's future earnings potential, and in determining the ability to pay dividends. *EPS is calculated as net income minus preferred dividends divided by the weighted-average of common shares outstanding*. EPS must be disclosed on the face of the income statement. EPS may be disclosed parenthetically when only a one per share amount is involved.

   EPS is required to be reported for the following items:
   - Income from continuing operations
   - Income before extraordinary items and cumulative effect of changes in accounting principles
   - Cumulative effect of changes in accounting principles
   - Net income
   - Results from (gain/loss on) discontinued operations (optional)
   - Gain or loss on extraordinary items (optional)

Exhibit 2.4: Statement of retained earnings

Statement of retained earnings is a reconciliation of the balance of the retained earnings account from the beginning to the end of the year. This statement tells the reader how much money management is "plowing back" into the business. Prior period adjustments including correction of errors (net of taxes) are charged or credited to the opening balance of retained earnings.

Net income is added and dividends declared are subtracted to arrive at the ending balance of retained earnings. This statement may report two separate amounts: retained earnings free (unrestricted) and retained earnings appropriated (restricted). SFAS 16, *Prior Period Adjustments*, provides additional guidelines.

EXAMPLE OF RETAINED EARNINGS STATEMENT

Retained earnings balance at the beginning of the period
Prior period adjustments, net of taxes (+/–)
Correction of an error, net of taxes (+/–)
Net income (+)
Dividends declared (–)
Retained earnings balance at the end of the period

The Statement of Income and the Statement of Retained Earnings can be shown separately. It is an acceptable practice to combine them into a single statement called the Statement of Income and Retained Earnings for convenience. Net income is computed in the same manner as in a multiple- or single-step income statement. The beginning balance in retained earnings is added to the net income (loss) figure. Any prior period adjustments are included in the retained earnings to obtain adjusted retained earnings. Declared dividends (both for preferred stock and common stock) are deducted to obtain the retained earnings ending balance.

Exhibit 2.5: Statement of cash flows

The Statement of Cash Flows (SCF) replaces the previous Statement of Changes in Financial Position. The primary purpose of the SCF is to provide relevant information about the cash receipts and cash payments of an enterprise during a period. A secondary purpose is to provide information about the investing and financing activities of the enterprise during the same period. The emphasis in the SCF is on gross cash receipts and cash payments. For example, SCF is the most useful financial statement for a banker to evaluate the ability of a commercial loan customer to meet current obligations. Cash flow per share should not be reported in the financial statements. Foreign currency exchange rate effects should be used in the preparation of the consolidated SCF.

Noncash exchange gains and losses recognized on the income statement should be reported as a separate item when reconciling net income and operating activities. SCF includes net income, depreciation, investing activities, financing activities, and operating activities.

Specifically, the SCF should help investors and creditors assess

- Ability to generate future positive cash flows
- Ability to meet obligations and pay dividends
- Reasons for differences between income and cash receipts and cash payments
- Both cash and noncash aspects of entities' investing and financing transactions

Classification

The Statement of Cash Flows requires three classifications: (1) investing activities, (2) financing activities, and (3) operating activities.

Investing activities show the acquisition and disposition of long-term productive assets or securities that are not considered cash equivalents. It also includes the lending of money and collection of loans.

Financing activities include obtaining resources from and returning resources to the owners. It also includes resources obtained from creditors and repaying the amount borrowed.

Operating activities include all transactions that are not investing and financing activities. It includes delivering or producing goods for sale and providing services to customers. It involves cash effects of transactions that enter into the determination of net income for the period.

Although the FASB has expressed a preference for the direct method of presenting net cash from operating activities, the indirect method can also be used. The **direct method** shows the items that affected cash flow. The direct method allows the user to clarify the relationship between the company's net income and its cash flows. It reports only the items that affect cash flow (e.g., real cash inflows and real cash outflows) and ignores items that do not affect cash flow (e.g., depreciation and gains).

Entities using the direct method are required to report the following classes of operating cash receipts and payments:

- Cash collected from customers
- Interest and dividend received
- Cash paid to employees and other suppliers
- Interest and income taxes paid
- Other operating cash receipts and payments

The **indirect method** is most widely used and easy to prepare. It focuses on the difference between net income and cash flows. It emphasizes changes in the components of most current asset and current liability accounts. The amount of interest and income tax paid should be included in the related disclosures. Depreciation expense should be presented as an addition to net income in converting net income to net cash flows from operating activities.

The following tables present examples of the SCF classifications in terms of cash inflows and cash outflows.

Cash Inflows

Operating	*Investing*	*Financing*
Cash receipts exceed cash expenditures	Principal collections from loans	Proceeds from issuing equity securities
Receipts from sale of goods or services	Sale of long-term debt or equity securities	Proceeds from issuing short-term or long-term debt (e.g., bonds, notes)
Returns on loans (interest)	Sale of property, plant, and equipment	
Returns on equity securities (dividends)		

Cash Outflows

Operating	*Investing*	*Financing*
Cash expenditures exceed cash receipts	Loans made to others	Payment of dividends
Payments for inventory	Purchase of long-term debt or equity securities	Repurchase of entity's capital stock (e.g., treasury stock)
Payments to employees	Purchase of property, plant, and equipment	Repayment of debt principal
Payments of taxes		
Payments of interest		
Payments to suppliers		

(d) **Account Analysis.** Account analysis helps the internal auditor to be able to reconstruct balance sheet accounts from account balances and journal entries and understand the account classifications and posting error correction process through journal entries.

The composition of accounts with their balances and the nature of business transactions and their effect on account balances can be analyzed using two approaches (1) worksheet (columnar) approach and (2) T-account approach (see Exhibit 2.6).

Techniques to analyze accounts
- Worksheet approach better organized than the T-account)
- T-account approach (faster than the worksheet)

Exhibit 2.6: Techniques to analyze accounts

Techniques to Analyze Accounts

The **worksheet approach** analyzes the changes that occurred in the balance sheet accounts by considering the income statement items. This approach is better organized than the T-account.

The **T-account approach** analyzes the changes in the noncash accounts and provides details on the cash flows during the period. This approach is faster than the worksheet.

It should be noted that there will always be a cause-and-effect relationship between and among accounts due to interlinking of those accounts. Consideration should be given to the characteristics of accounts such as the number of accounts affected, the time frame involved, and the nature of the effect.

There will be at least two accounts that would be related to each other, and usually more. For example, an income statement classification error has no effect on the balance sheet and no effect on net income.

The time horizons for these cause and effects to materialize would be the past, present, and future accounting periods due to lagging and leading effects of accounts. For example, it takes two accounting periods to correct a counterbalancing error itself while it takes more than two periods to correct a noncounterbalancing error itself.

Two types of effects can be seen: direct or indirect effect. An example of direct effect is overstatement of net income when wage expense is understated. Liability being understated when wage expense is understated is an example of an indirect effect.

It helps the internal auditor to understand account relationships when he is conducting audits, whether financial or operational. This understanding indicates to the auditor what to look for during the account examination and verification process, and how to conduct tracing and vouching work. This, in turn, will assure that all related accounts and their effects are reviewed. Such account analysis will most likely help the auditor in reviewing the completeness, accuracy, and appropriateness of accounting journal entries and not so much who made the entries.

The following is a partial and an independent list of accounts with established interrelationships:

- The balance in inventory accounts will increase prior to sales, while the balance in customer receivable accounts will increase after the sales. The reason is that adequate inventories must be available in advance for sales to take place. Here, sales, inventories, and receivable accounts are being affected.
- The effects of misstating unearned interest as revenue would overstate revenue and receivables for this period and under-state revenue for later periods. Examples of accounts that would be affected include interest, receivables, and income.
- When receivables are collected, the balance in cash accounts rises and the balance in receivable accounts falls. Working capital, which is current assets minus current liabilities, stays the same. Here, the working capital composition has just been rearranged. These transactions have an inverse effect on each other since only asset accounts with opposite change are involved.
- During recession, receivables will likely increase as customers attempt to squeeze their trade credit limits to the maximum. This, in turn, increases funds tied up in working capital. Such an increase in working capital would reduce available cash and increase the need for financing. Cash, receivables, and liabilities accounts are affected here.
- Equal changes in accounts receivables and payables would alter the balance of cash but have no effect on working capital. Here, the change has an offsetting effect since receivables and payables move in the opposite direction of the balance sheet.
- Issuance of common stock will increase cash, thereby increasing working capital. Cash accounts, stock accounts, and liability accounts are involved here.
- The longer the sales cycle is, the more working capital that is required. This is an example of the effect on interrelationships among accounting cycles and accounts within a cycle. Here, both sales cycle and finance cycle are affected.
- An increase in the average length of time to collect receivables from customers would increase bad debts for the same type of customers.
- If credit granting policies become too strict, the company will lose customers. If inventory balances are reduced too much, stockout costs will be increased. Both situations will result in lower profits to the company.
- The just-in-time (JIT) inventory concept minimizes working capital investment because a minimum amount of inventory is maintained by the firm. This is a result of vendors continuously making small deliveries of raw materials and parts that are immediately used on the factory floor.
- Payment of the current portion of the mortgage payable would not affect the net working capital situation.

2.2 Intermediate Concepts of Financial Accounting

(a) Bonds

(i) **Overview.** Bonds result from a single agreement. However, a bond is intended to be broken up into various subunits. Notes and bonds have similar characteristics. These include a written agreement stating the amount of the principal to be paid, the interest rate, when the interest and principal are to be paid, and the restrictive covenants.

The stated interest rate on a note or bond often differs from the market interest rate at the time of issuance. When this occurs, the present value of the interest and principal payments will differ from the maturity, or face value. Possible scenarios include

- When the market rate exceeds the stated rate, the instrument is sold at a **discount** meaning that the cash proceeds are less than the face value.
- When the stated rate exceeds the market rate, the instrument is sold at a **premium** meaning that the cash proceeds are more than the face value.
- When the market and stated rates are the same at the time of issuance, no discount or premium exists and the instrument will be sold at its face value.

The proper valuation is the present value of the future payments using the market rate of interest, either stated or implied in the transaction, at the date the debt was incurred.

EXCEPTIONS TO PRESENT VALUE OR MARKET INTEREST RATES

- Deferred income tax debits should not be discounted.
- Deferred income tax credits should not be discounted.
- Long-term notes should be valued using an imputed interest rate with no stated interest rate.

Nominal rate, stated rate, or coupon rate are all names for the interest rate stated on a bond. The periodic interest payments on a bond are determined by this rate. However, the price at which the bonds are sold determines the actual interest expense incurred on the bond issue. The actual rate of interest incurred is called the effective rate, the yield rate, or the market rate and is determined by the investment market.

When a bond sells at par value or face amount, the effective interest rate and the stated rate are equal. When a bond sells at a **discount** (below par), the effective rate is greater than the stated rate. When a bond sells at a **premium** (above par), the stated rate is greater than the effective rate of the bond; then the bond will sell at a discount. If the prevailing market rate of interest is less than the stated rate, then the bond will sell at a premium.

Long-Term Debt Terminology

Term or serial bonds—Term bonds occur when an entire bond issue matures on a single fixed maturity date. Serial bonds are issues that mature in installments over a period of time.

Income bonds—Income bonds are unsecured debt where interest is paid only to the extent of an organization's current earnings. If interest is not paid due to a lack of earnings, bondholders have no claim against future earnings for the interest not paid in the current period.

Revenue bonds—Generally, revenue bonds are issued by local governmental units, and interest and principal can only be paid from specific revenue sources.

Convertible bonds—Convertible bonds allow the bondholder the option to convert the bonds into a specified number of shares of common stock.

Callable bonds—Callable bonds can be purchased from the bondholder by the issuing corporation at the issuer's option prior to maturity. If interest rates fall or an organization wishes to reduce its outstanding debt, then it may call a bond issue.

When a bond sells at a discount, a contra liability account, Discount on Bonds Payable, is debited for the amount of the discount (excess of face value over cash proceeds). This contra liability account is shown as a deduction from bonds payable on the balance sheet. This discount is then amortized over the life of the bonds by one of two methods.

1. **Straight-line method**—Under this method, the amount to be amortized each period is determined by dividing the discount by the number of periods in the life of the bonds. Therefore, an equal amount of discount is charged to expense each period.
2. **Effective interest method**—This method computes bond interest expense for the period by multiplying the effective interest rate (at the bond issue date) by the bond's carrying value at the beginning of the period.

The difference between interest expense for the period and interest payable for the period is the discount amortized for the period.

The carrying value of the bonds issued at a discount increases as they mature. Therefore, the effective interest expense increases as the bonds mature, since it is based on the carrying value of the bonds.

When a bond sells at a premium, a valuation account, Premium on Bonds Payable, is credited for the amount of the premium (excess of cash proceeds over face amount). This valuation account is shown as an addition to bonds payable on the balance sheet. *One of two methods can be used to amortize the premium over the life of the bonds.*

1. **Straight-line method.** This method is calculated the same as it is for a discount. Premium amortization reduces interest expense for the period. The carrying value of the bonds decreases each period by the amount of bond premium amortization.
2. **Effective interest method.** The periodic bond interest expense for this method is computed in the same manner as for a bond discount. The difference between bond interest payable in cash (stated interest rate times face amount of bonds) and effective bond interest expense (effective interest rate times carrying value of bonds) is the bond premium amortization for the period.

Long-Term Debt Terminology

Secured or unsecured—Secured debt has legal agreements that provide the creditor with liens on certain specified property. The lien allows the creditor to sell the property pledged as security on the loan to obtain money to satisfy any unpaid balance of interest and principal.

Bond indenture—A contract between the corporation issuing the bonds and the bondholders is a bond indenture. The bond indenture includes items such as the amount of bonds authorized, the due date, the interest rate, any dividend or other restrictions, and any property pledged as security.

Trustee—Typically the trustee holds the bond indenture and acts as an independent third party to protect the interests of the bond issuer and the bondholder.

Bond—A bond is a debt instrument that contains a promise to pay a specified principal amount at a determinable future date, together with interest at specified times. Bonds are a good financing arrangement when relatively large sums of money are required for long periods.

Registered or coupon bonds—With registered bonds, interest is paid to the registered owner. With coupon bonds, interest is paid to the individual presenting the periodic interest coupons.

The carrying value of bonds issued at a premium decreases as they mature. Therefore, the effective interest expense decreases as the bonds mature.

Any costs incurred related to the issuance of bonds such as advertising costs, printing costs, and fees paid to underwriters, accountants, and attorneys should be charged to a prepaid expense account. These costs should then be amortized over the life of the bond issue, because revenue results from the use of the proceeds over this period.

The reacquisition of a debt security or instrument before its scheduled maturity (except through conversion by the holder) is early extinguishment of debt. Upon early extinguishment the bond can be formally retired or held as a treasury bond.

The net carrying amount of debt is the amount payable at maturity, adjusted for any unamortized discount, premium, or debt issue costs. The amount paid on early extinguishment, including the call premium and other reacquisition costs, is the reacquisition price of debt. *A gain on early extinguishment occurs when the net carrying amount exceeds the reacquisition price. A loss occurs when the reacquisition price exceeds the net carrying amount. A gain or loss on early extinguishment should be recognized in the period in which extinguishment occurred and reflected as a separate line item on the income statement.*

When serial bonds are sold and each maturity sells at a different yield rate, each maturity should be treated as a separate bond issue. The entire bond issue's discount or premium should be debited or credited to a single account. The amount of discount or premium amortization for each period is determined by performing a separate computation for each maturity. Either amortization method, straight-line or effective interest, may be applied to the discount or premium for each maturity. The amortization amounts for all maturities are then summarized and totaled to determine the periodic amortization.

When a note is issued solely for cash, the present value of the note is the cash proceeds. The present value of the note minus its face amount is the amount of the discount or premium. The interest expense on such a note is the stated or coupon interest plus or minus the amortization of any discount or premium.

When a note is issued in a noncash transaction and no interest rate is stated, the stated interest rate is unreasonable, or the stated face amount of the note is materially different from the current cash sales price for similar items or from the market value of the note at the date of the transaction, then the note issued and the property, goods, or services received should be recorded at the fair value of the property, goods, or services. If the fair value of the noncash item cannot be determined, then the market value of the note should be used.

A discount or premium is recognized when there is a difference between the face amount of the note and its fair value.

Interest Rates on Notes and Bonds

The interest rate is affected by many factors including

- The cost of money
- The business risk factors
- The inflationary expectations associated with the business

This discount or premium should be amortized over the life of the note. If neither the fair value of the noncash item nor the market value of the note is determinable, then the present value of the note should be determined by discounting all future payments on the note using an imputed interest rate.

Short-term obligations that are expected to be refinanced on a long-term basis may be classified as long-term liabilities on the balance sheet. The requirements for classification as long-term are as follows: management intends to refinance the obligations on a long-term basis and demonstrates the ability to obtain the refinancing.

According to APB Opinion 21, *Interest on Receivables and Payables*, **all** contractual rights to receive money or contractual obligations to pay money on fixed or determinable dates are subject to present value techniques including interest imputation.

Suggested Disclosures—Notes & Bonds

- The aggregate amount of debt net of the current portion due within one year and any discount or premium.
- Details of each debt including nature of the liability, maturity dates, interest rates, call provisions, conversion privileges, restrictive covenants, assets pledged as collateral.
- The current portion of the long-term debt is shown as a current liability unless something other than current assets will be used to satisfy the obligation.

Examples include secured and unsecured notes, debentures, bonds, mortgage notes, equipment obligations, and some accounts receivable and payable. However, the following items are **exceptions:**

- Receivable and payables arising from transactions with customers or suppliers in the normal course of business which are due in customary terms not exceeding approximately one year
- Amounts which do not require repayment in the future, but rather will be applied to the purchase price of the property, goods, or service involved (e.g., deposits or progress payments on construction contracts, advance payments for acquisition of resources and raw materials, advances to encourage exploration in the extractive industries)

- Amounts intended to provide security for one party to an agreement (security deposits, retainages on contracts)
- The customary cash lending activities and demand or savings deposit activities of financial institutions whose primary business is lending money
- Transactions where interest rates are affected by the tax attributes or legal restrictions prescribed by a governmental agency (e.g., industrial revenue bonds, tax-exempt obligations, government guaranteed obligations, and income tax settlements)
- Transactions between parent and subsidiary companies and between subsidiaries of a common parent
- Warranty for product performance
- Convertible debt securities

APB Opinion 21 requires the amortization of a bond discount or premium using the **effective interest rate method**. Under this method, the total interest expense is the carrying value (book value) of the bonds at the start of the period multiplied by the effective interest rate. The objective of this method is to arrive at a periodic interest cost that will result in a constant effective rate on the carrying value of the bond at the beginning of each period. By the time the bond matures, the carrying value of the bond will be equal to the face value.

Other methods such as the **straight-line method** can be used if the results are not materially different. Under this method, interest expense is equal to the cash interest paid plus the amortized portion of the discount or minus the amortized portion of the premium. The amortized portion is equal to the total amount of the discount or premium divided by the life of the debt from issuance in months multiplied by the number of months the debt has been outstanding that year.

Bondholders have a prior claim to the earnings and assets of the issuing organization. They rank ahead of preferred and common stockholders. Interest must first be paid to bondholders before dividends can be distributed to stockholders. Bondholders have a prior claim on assets in the case of dissolution or bankruptcy.

The following list shows the hierarchy of bondholders:

High priority	Bondholders	• Prior claim on assets in case of dissolution or bankruptcy • Interest must first be paid before dividends are paid to stockholders
	Preferred stockholders	• Prior claims on assets and dividends are paid during liquidation • Dividends in arrears are paid
Low priority	Common stockholders	• Low priority in case of dissolution or bankruptcy • Receive highest benefit if the organization is successful

(ii) **Extinguishment of debt.** Outstanding debt may be reacquired or retired before its scheduled maturity. Usually, this is caused by changes in interest rates or in cash flows. SFAS 76, *Extinguishment of Debt*, presents accounting treatment for **early** extinguishment of debt. SFAS 76 is applicable to all debt extinguishment other than debt conversions and troubled debt restructuring, where the latter is addressed by SFAS 15. *Debt is now considered extinguished for financial reporting purposes in the following circumstances*:

- The debtor pays the creditor and is relieved of all of its obligations, regardless of whether the securities are cancelled or held as so-called treasury bonds.
- The debtor is legally released from being the primary obligor, either judicially or by the creditor and it is probable that the debtor will not be required to make future payments.
- The debtor irrevocably places cash or other assets in a trust to be used solely for satisfying scheduled payments of both interest and principal of a specific obligation and the possibility that the debtor will be required to make future payments with respect to that debt is remote. In this circumstance, debt is extinguished even though the debtor is not legally released from being the primary obligor under the debt obligation.

The trust shall be restricted to owing only monetary assets that are essentially risk free as to the amount, timing, and collection of interest and principal. A monetary asset is money or a claim to receive a sum of money that is fixed or determinable without reference to future prices of specific goods or services.

Suggested Disclosures—Extinguishment of Debt

- Aggregated gains or losses and unconditionally classified as extraordinary items.
- A description of the transaction and sources of the funds used.
- The income tax effect of the transaction.
- The per share amount of the aggregate gain or loss, net of tax.

The monetary assets shall be denominated in the currency in which the debt is payable. For debt denominated in US dollars, essentially risk-free monetary assets shall be limited to

- Direct obligations of the US government
- Obligations guaranteed by the US government
- Securities that are backed by US government obligations as collateral under an arrangement by which the interest and principal payments on the collateral generally flow immediately through to the holder of the security

According to APB Opinion 26, *Early Extinguishment of Debt*, the difference between the net carrying value and the acquisition price is to be recorded as a gain or loss.

KEY CONCEPTS TO REMEMBER: RULES FOR GAINS AND LOSSES

- If the acquisition price is greater than the carrying value, a loss exists.
- If the acquisition price is less than the carrying value, a gain is generated.
- These gains or losses are to be recognized in the period in which the retirement took place.
- All gains and losses, if material in amount, should be treated as an extraordinary item.
- Any gains or losses resulting from satisfying sinking fund requirements within one year are exempted from extraordinary item treatment.

(b) **Leases.** A lease agreement involves at least two parties (lessor, lessee) and an asset. The lessor, who owns the asset, agrees to allow the lessee to use it for a specified period of time for rent payments. *The key point in leases is the transfer of risk of ownership.* If the transaction effectively transfers ownership to the lessee, then it should be treated as a sale even though the transaction takes the form of a lease. Here, the substance, not the form, dictates the accounting treatment. Two types of leases exist: capital and operating lease.

(i) **Accounting by lessees.** SFAS 13, *Accounting for Leases*, requires lessees to classify every lease as either an operating lease or capital lease. A capital lease, not operating lease, is an installment purchase of the property.

The lessee records a capital lease as an asset and an obligation at an amount equal to the present value at the beginning of the lease term of minimum lease payments during the lease term, excluding that portion of the payments representing executory costs such as insurance, maintenance, and taxes to be paid by the lessor, together with any profit thereon.

However, if the amount so determined exceeds the fair value of the leased property at the inception of the lease, the amount recorded as the asset and obligation shall be the fair value. If the portion of the minimum lease payments representing executory costs, including profit thereon, is not determinable from the provisions of the lease, an estimate of the amount shall be made. At the inception of a capital lease, the guaranteed residual value should be included as part of minimum lease payments at present value.

Suggested Disclosures: Lessee

For capital leases:

- The gross amount of assets recorded
- Future minimum lease payments in the aggregate
- Total of minimum sublease rentals to be received
- Total contingent rentals actually incurred for each period
- Depreciation

For operating leases:

- Future minimum lease payments in the aggregate
- Total of minimum rentals that will be received under noncancelable subleases
- Rental expenses separated into minimum rentals, contingent rentals, and sublease rentals

A lease meeting any one of the following four criteria (criteria 1) should be accounted for as a capital lease by the lessee:

Criteria 1

- The lease transfers ownership of the property to the lessee by the end of the lease term. If the title is transferred, the lease is assumed to be a purchase and the assets should be capitalized.
- The lease contains a bargain purchase option.
- The lease term is equal to 75% or more of the estimated economic life of the leased property. However, if the beginning of the lease term falls within the last 25% of the total estimated economic life of the leased property, including earlier years of use, this criterion shall not be used for purposes of classifying the lease.
- The present value at the beginning of the lease term of the minimum lease payments, excluding that portion of the payments representing executory costs such as insurance, maintenance, and taxes to be paid by the lessor, including any profit thereon, equals or exceeds 90% of the excess of the fair value of the leased property.

Normally, rental on an operating lease shall be charged to expense over the lease term as it becomes payable. If rental payments are not made on a straight-line basis, rental expense nevertheless shall be recognized on a straight-line basis unless another systematic and rational basis is more representative of the time pattern in which use benefit is derived from the leased property, in which case that basis shall be used. *The most significant reason for choosing an operating lease over a capital lease would be to avoid an increase in the debt to equity ratio.*

(ii) **Accounting by lessor.** From the standpoint of the lessor, if at inception a lease meets any one of the preceding four criteria (criteria 1) and in addition meets **both** of the following criteria (criteria 2), it shall be classified as a sales-type lease or a direct financing lease. Otherwise, it shall be classified as an operating lease.

Criteria 2

- Collectibility of the minimum lease payments is reasonably predictable. Estimation of uncollectibility based on experience with groups of similar receivables is not a reason for applying this criteria.
- No important uncertainties surround the amount of un-reimbursable costs yet to be incurred by the lessor under the lease. The necessity of estimating executory costs such as insurance, maintenance, and taxes to be paid by the lessor shall not by itself constitute an important uncertainty.

Suggested Disclosures: Lessor

For sales-type and direct financing leases:

- Components of the net investment in leases including future minimum lease payments, unguaranteed residual values, initial direct costs for direct financing leases, and unearned interest revenue
- Future minimum lease payments
- Total contingent rentals included in income

For operating leases:

- The cost and carrying amount of property leased
- Minimum rentals on noncancelable leases in the aggregate
- Total contingent rentals included in income

A lessor has four types of choices in classifying a lease. These include

1. Sales-type leases
2. Direct financing leases
3. Operating leases
4. Participation by third parties

(A) ***Sales-type leases.*** Sales-type leases should be accounted for by the lessor as follows:

- The minimum lease payments (net of amounts, if any, included therein with respect to executory costs such as maintenance, taxes, and insurance to be paid by the lessor, together with any profit thereon) plus the unguaranteed residual value accruing to the benefit of the lessor shall be recorded as the gross investment in the lease.
- The difference between the gross investment in the lease and the sum of the present values of the two components of the gross investment shall be recorded as unearned income. The interest rate to be used in determining the present values shall be the interest rate implicit in the lease. *The net investment in the lease consists of the gross investment less the unearned income.* The unearned income shall be amortized to income over the lease term so as to produce a constant periodic rate of return on the net investment in the lease. Contingent rentals, including rentals based on variables such as the prime interest rate, shall be credited to income when they become receivable.
- The present value of the minimum lease payments (net of executory costs, including any profit thereon), computed at the interest rate implicit in the lease, shall be recorded as the sales price. The cost or carrying amount, if different, of the leased property plus any initial direct costs, less the present value of the unguaranteed residual value accruing to the benefit of the lessor, computed at the interest rate implicit in the lease, shall be charged against income in the same period.
- The estimated residual value shall be reviewed at least annually. An upward adjustment of the estimated residual value should not be made while permanent reduction in the net investment should be recognized as a loss in the period in which the estimate is changed.

(B) ***Direct financing leases.*** Direct financing leases should be accounted for by the lessor as follows:

- The minimum lease payments (as defined earlier) plus the unguaranteed residual value accruing to the benefit of the lessor should be recorded as the gross investment in the lease.

Initial Direct Cost Definition

Those incremental direct costs incurred by the lessor in negotiating and consummating leasing transaction including commissions and legal fees.

- The difference between the gross investment in the lease and the cost or carrying amount, if different, of the leased property shall be recorded as unearned income. The net investment in the lease should consist of the gross investment less the unearned income.

  Initial direct cost shall be charged against income as incurred, and a portion of the unearned income equal to the initial direct costs shall be recognized as income in the same period. The remaining unearned income shall be amortized to income over the lease term so as to produce a constant periodic rate of return on the net investment in the lease. Contingent rentals, including rentals based on variables such as the prime interest rate, shall be credited to income when they become receivable.
- The estimated residual value shall be reviewed at least annually and, if necessary, adjusted in the manner prescribed in sales-type leases.

(C) ***Operating leases.*** Operating leases should be accounted for by the lessor as follows:

- The leased property shall be included with or near property, plant, and equipment in the balance sheet. The property shall be depreciated following the lessor's normal depreciation policy, and in the balance sheet the accumulated depreciation shall be deducted from the investment in the leased property.
- Rent shall be reported as income over the lease term as it becomes receivable according to the provisions of the lease. However, if the rentals vary from a straight-line basis, the income shall be recognized on a straight-line basis unless another systematic and rational basis is more representative of the time pattern in which use benefit from the leased property is diminished, in which case the straight-line basis shall be used.
- Initial direct costs shall be deferred and allocated over the lease term in proportion to the recognition of rental income. However, initial direct costs may be charged to expense as incurred if the effect is not materially different from that which would have resulted from the use of the method prescribed in the preceding sentence.

(D) ***Participation by third parties.*** Participation by third parties leases should be accounted for by the lessor as follows:

- The sale or assignment of the lease or of property subject to a lease that was accounted for as a sales-type lease or direct financing lease shall not negate the original accounting treatment accorded the lease. Any profit or loss on the sale or assignment shall be recognized at the time of the transaction except that (1) when the sale or assignment is between related parties or (2) when the sale or assignment is with recourse, the profit or loss shall be deferred and recognized over the lease term in a systematic manner (e.g., in proportion to the minimum lease payments).
- The sale of property subject to an operating lease, or of property that is leased by or intended to be leased by the third-party purchaser to another party, shall not be treated as a sale if the seller or any party related to the seller retains substantial risks of ownership in the leased property.

  A seller may be by various arrangements assured recovery of the investment by the third-party purchaser in some operating lease transactions and thus retain substantial risks in connection with the property. For example, in the case of default by the lessee or termination of the lease, the arrangements may involve a formal or informal commitment by the seller to acquire the lease or the property, substitute an existing lease, or secure a replacement lessee or a buyer for the property under a remarketing agreement.
- If a sale to a third party of property subject to an operating lease or of property that is leased by or intended to be leased by the third-party purchaser to another party is not to be recorded as a sale. Instead, the transaction should be accounted for as a borrowing.

(iii) **Lease involving real estate.** Lease involving real estate can be divided into four categories: (1) leases involving land only, (2) leases involving land and buildings, (3) leases involving equipment as well as real estate, and (4) leases involving only part of a building.

(iv) **Sale-leaseback transaction.** Sale-leaseback transactions involve the sale of property by the owner and a lease of the property back to the seller. If the lease meets one of the criteria (criteria

1) for treatment as a capital lease, the seller-lessee shall account for the lease as a capital lease; otherwise, as an operating lease.

Except as noted below, any profit or loss on the sale shall be deferred and amortized in proportion to the amortization of the leased asset, if a capital lease, or in proportion to rental payments over the period of time the asset is expected to be used, if an operating lease. However, when the fair value of the property at the time of the transaction is less than its undepreciated cost, a loss shall be recognized immediately up to the amount of the difference between undepreciated cost and fair value.

If the lease meets criteria 1 and 2, the purchaser-lessor shall record the transaction as a purchase and a direct financing lease; otherwise, he shall record the transaction as a purchase and an operating lease.

(v) **Accounting and reporting for leveraged leases.** From the standpoint of the lessee, leveraged leases shall be classified and accounted for in the same manner as nonleveraged leases. The balance of this section deals with leveraged leases from the standpoint of the lessor.

Leveraged lease is defined as one having all of the following characteristics:

- Direct financing and sales-type leases are not included
- It involves at least three parties: a lessee, a long-term creditor, and a lessor (commonly called the equity participant)

Balance Sheet Presentation

The accounts of subsidiaries (regardless of when organized or acquired) whose principal business activity is leasing property or facilities to the parent or other affiliated companies shall be consolidated. The equity method is not adequate for fair presentation of the subsidiaries because their assets and liabilities are significant to the consolidated financial position of the enterprise.

- The financing provided by the long-term creditor is nonrecourse as to the general credit of the lessor. The amount of the financing is sufficient to provide the lessor with substantial "leverage" in the transaction.
- The lessor's net investment declines during the early years once the investment has been completed and rises during the later years of the lease before its final elimination. Such decrease and increase in the net investment balance may occur more than once.

The lessor shall record this investment in a leveraged lease net of the nonrecourse debt. *The net of the balances of the following accounts shall represent the initial and continuing investment in leveraged leases*:

- Rentals receivables, net of that portion of the rental applicable to principal and interest on the nonrecourse debt
- A receivable for the amount of investment tax credit to be realized on the transaction
- The estimated residual value of the leased asset
- Unearned and deferred income consisting of (1) the estimated pretax lease income (or loss), after deducting initial direct costs, remaining to be allocated to income over the lease term and (2) the investment tax credit remaining to be allocated to income over the lease term

The investment in leveraged leases less deferred taxes arising from difference between pretax accounting income and taxable income shall represent the lessor's net investment in leveraged leases for purposes of computing periodic net income from the lease.

For purposes of presenting the investment in a leveraged lease in the lessor's **balance sheet,** the amount of related deferred taxes shall be presented separately from the remainder of the net investment. In the **income statement** or the notes thereto, separate presentation shall be made of pretax income from the leveraged lease, the tax effect of pretax income, and the amount of investment tax credit recognized as income during the period.

KEY CONCEPTS TO REMEMBER: LEASES

- A major difference between operating and financial leases is that operating leases frequently contain a cancellation clause, while financial leases are not cancelable.
- Lessee corporation has leased manufacturing equipment from lessor corporation in a transaction that is to be accounted for as a capital lease. Lessee has guaranteed lessor a residual value for the equipment. The present value of the residual guarantee should be capitalized as part of the cost of the equipment and be reflected in the financial statements of lessee.
- In accounting for a 20-year operating lease of machinery, lease expense and cash outflow would both be the same in total for the 20-year term of the lease as if the lease were capitalized.
- Rent expense is recognized for operating leases only.
- Prepaid rent is not reported for a capital lease by lessee.
- Depreciation expense is a part of items reported by a lessee for a capital lease.
- Interest expense is a part of items reported by a lessee for a capital lease.

(c) **Pensions.** SFAS 87, *Employers' Accounting for Pensions*, and SFAS 88, *Employers' Accounting for Settlements and Curtailments of Defined Benefit Pension Plans and for Termination Benefits*, are the sources of GAAP in the pension area. The principal focus of SFAS 87 is the present value of the pension obligation, the fair value of plan assets, and the disclosure of the makeup of net pension costs and of the projected benefit obligation. The critical accounting issues are the amount to be expensed on the income statement and the amount to be accrued on the balance sheet.

Application of SFAS 87 and 88

The scope includes unfunded, insured, trust fund, defined contribution, defined benefit plans, and deferred compensation contracts.

The scope does not include (1) independent deferred profit-sharing plans and pension payments to selected employees on a case by case basis, (2) plans providing only life or health insurance benefits or both, (3) postemployment health care benefits, related assets, and obligations.

Employer commitment to employees takes the form of contributions to an independent trustee. The trustee then invests the contributions in various plan assets such as Treasury bills and bonds, certificates of deposit, annuities, marketable securities, corporate bonds and stock. The plan assets generate interest and/or appreciate in asset value. The return on the plan assets provides the trustee the money to pay the benefits to which the employees are entitled. These benefits are defined by the terms of the pension plan using a plan's benefit formula. The formula is used to determine the pension cost for each year. The formula takes into account factors such as employee compensation, service length, age, and other factors to determine pension costs (see Exhibit 2.7).

Pension expense is determined by adding up five components, which affect the pension expense amount as follows:

	Component	Effect
1.	Service cost	Increases
2.	Interest cost	Increases
3.	Actual return on plan assets	Generally decreases
4.	Prior service cost	Generally decreases
5.	Net total of other components (gain or loss)	Increases or decreases
	5 = 1 + 2 + 3 + 4	

Exhibit 2.7: Components of pension expense

- The service cost component is determined by the actuarial present value of benefits attributed by the pension benefit formula to employee service during that period.
- Past service cost is the portion of pension plan expense that relates to years prior to inception of the pension plan.

- The interest cost component is the interest for the period on the projected benefit obligation outstanding during the period.
- The actual return on plan assets is determined based on the fair value of plan assets at the beginning and the end of the period, adjusted for contributions and benefit payments.
- The prior service cost component is the present value of future benefits payable as a result of work done before the start of or change in a pension plan. The cost is amortized over the average remaining service period of the employees expected to receive benefits.
- Gains and losses are changes in the amount of either the projected benefit obligation or plan assets resulting from experience different than that assumed and from changes in assumptions.

(d) **Intangible assets.** Typically intangibles lack physical existence and have a high degree of uncertainty regarding their future benefits. These assets have value because of the business advantages of exclusive rights and privileges they provide. The two sources of intangible assets are

1. Exclusive privileges granted by authority of the government or legal contract, which includes patents, copyrights, trademarks, franchises, and so forth
2. Superior entrepreneurial capacity or management know-how and customer loyalty that is goodwill

Intangible assets are initially recorded at **cost**. Therefore, the costs of intangible assets, except for goodwill, are relatively easy to determine. These assets must be amortized over their expected useful life but not to exceed forty years. An organization must use straight-line amortization, unless it can prove that another method is more appropriate. The amortization of intangible assets over their useful lives is justified by the going concern assumption.

(i) **Copyrights, trademarks, and patents.** Those intangibles that have a separate identity apart from the enterprise as a whole are identifiable as intangible assets. The most common types are

- **Copyrights.** Copyrights protect the owner from illegal reproductions of designs, writings, music, and literary productions. Purchased copyrights are recorded at cost. Research and development costs incurred to produce a copyright internally must be expensed. The only costs that can be capitalized are the legal costs to obtain and defend the copyright. Generally, copyrights are amortized over a period of five years or less.

  A material amount of legal fees and other costs incurred by a holder of a copyright in successfully defending a copyright suit should be capitalized as part of the cost of the copyright and amortized over the remaining estimated useful life of the copyright, not to exceed 40 years. All costs should be charged to the copyright account.

Summary of Amortization Periods

- Copyrights not to exceed 40 years
- Trademarks not to exceed 40 years
- Patents not to exceed 17 years
- Organization costs not to exceed 40 years
- Goodwill not to exceed 40 years

- **Trademarks.** Trademarks are features such as designs, brand names, or symbols which allow easy recognition of a product. The costs to develop or acquire a trademark, except for research and development costs, are capitalized. Trademarks must be amortized over a period not to exceed 40 years.
- **Patents.** Patents are granted by the US government and allow the owner exclusive benefits to a product or process over a 17-year period. Purchased patents are recorded at cost. An internally developed patent includes all costs except research and development. Legal fees incurred to successfully defend the patent should also be capitalized. A patent should be amortized over its useful life or 17 years, whichever is shorter.

Treatment of Research and Development Costs

Research and development costs are normally expensed while organization costs, equipment costs, and goodwill costs are capitalized.

- **Organization costs.** Organization costs are incurred in the process of organizing a business. Legal fees, payments to officers for organization activities, and various state fees may be included in organization costs. A material amount of organization costs should be amortized over five years. The period of their useful life should not exceed 40 years.
- **Franchises.** A franchise grants the right to provide a product or service or use a property. Franchise fees that are paid in advance should be capitalized and amortized over the useful life of the asset.
- **Leases.** A contract between the owner of property (lessor) and another party (lessee) that grants the right to use the property in exchange for payments is a lease. Any portion of the lease payments made in advance are capitalized in the leasehold account, an intangible asset account. Another intangible account, leasehold improvements, is established for any improvements to the leased property by the lessee. Leasehold improvements should be amortized over their useful life or the remaining life of the lease, whichever is shorter, while the leasehold is amortized over the life of the lease.

(ii) **Goodwill.** Some intangible assets, since they cannot be separated from the business as a whole, are not specifically identifiable. Goodwill is a prime example of this type of intangible.

Goodwill arises when an organization's value as a whole exceeds the fair market value of its net assets. This typically occurs when an organization generates more income than other organizations with the same assets and capital structure. Superior management, a superior reputation, or a valuable customer list are factors that may contribute to these excess earnings.

Suggested Disclosures for Intangible Assets

- A description of the nature of the assets
- The amount of amortization expense for the period and the method used
- The amortization period used
- The amount of accumulated amortization

Goodwill is something that develops over time through the generation of these excess earnings. However, since no objective measure of the total value of a business is available until it is sold, goodwill is not recorded unless a business is purchased.

To calculate goodwill, a portion of the total cost of the acquired organization should be allocated to the tangible and intangible assets based on their fair market values. Goodwill is the difference between the cost allocated to these assets and the total cost of the acquisition.

The amortization period for goodwill arising after October 31, 1970, should not exceed 40 years. Goodwill before October 31, 1970, does not have to be amortized until the useful life of the goodwill becomes known.

Negative goodwill is created when the fair market value of the acquired net assets exceeds the cost of the acquired company. This excess is allocated proportionately to reduce noncurrent assets except for long-term investments in marketable securities. If noncurrent assets are reduced to zero, then the excess should be recorded as a deferred credit and amortized over a period not to exceed 40 years.

To estimate the value of goodwill prior to the consummation of a purchase requires estimating future expected excess earnings and calculating their present value. The same result should be achieved by determining the present value of the total expected future earnings of the organization, which is the total value of the firm. The total value of the firm minus the value of the identifiable tangible and intangible net assets is estimated goodwill.

RULES FOR GOODWILL

- If goodwill is internally generated, then expense it.
- If goodwill is purchased, then capitalize it.

(e) **Research and Development**

(i) **Research and development costs.** Statement of Financial Accounting Standards (SFAS) 2, *Accounting for Research and Development (R&D) Costs*, requires R&D costs to be expensed as incurred except for intangible or fixed assets purchased from others having alternative future uses. Thus, the cost of patents and R&D equipment purchased from third parties may be deferred, capitalized, and amortized over the assets' useful life. However, internally developed R&D may not be deferred and therefore should be expensed. R&D done under contract for others is not required to be expensed per SFAS 2. The costs incurred would be matched with revenue using the completed-contract or percentage-of-completion method. The key accounting concept is expense R&D costs as incurred and disclose total R&D expenses per period on face of income statement or notes.

Inclusion of R&D activities in the standard are laboratory research to discover new knowledge, formulation, and design of product alternatives (e.g., testing and modifications); preproduction prototypes and models (e.g., tools, dies, and pilot plants); and engineering activity until product is ready for manufacture.

Exclusion of R&D activities from the standard are (1) engineering during an early phase of commercial production, (2) quality control for commercial production, (3) troubleshooting during commercial production breakdowns, (4) routine, ongoing efforts to improve products, (5) adaptation of existing capability for a specific customer, (6) seasonal design changes to products, (7) routine design of tools and dies, (8) design, construction, and start-up of equipment except that used solely for R&D, and (9) legal work for patents or litigation. Item nine is capitalized while all the other eight items are expensed.

Elements of R&D costs include: materials, equipment, and facilities, salaries, wages, and related costs, intangibles purchased from others are treated as materials, R&D services performed by others, and a reasonable allocation of indirect costs, excluding general and administrative costs not clearly related to R&D.

(ii) **Software developed for sale or lease.** The costs that are incurred internally to create the software should be expensed as R&D costs until technological feasibility is established. Thereafter, all costs should be capitalized and reported at the lower of unamortized cost or net realizable value. Capitalization should cease when the software is available for general release to customers.

The annual amortization of capitalized computer software costs will be the greater of the ratio of current revenues to anticipated total revenues or the straight-line amortization which is based on the estimated economic life. Once the software is available for general release to customers, the inventory costs should include costs for duplicating software and for physically packaging the product. The cost of maintenance and customer support should be charged to expense in the period incurred.

(iii) **Software developed for internal use.** Software must meet two criteria to be accounted for as internally developed software. First, the software's specifications must be designed or modified to meet the reporting entity's internal needs, including costs to customize purchased software. Second, during the period in which the software is being developed, there can be no plan or intent to market the software externally, although development of the software can be jointly funded by several entities that each plan to use the software internally.

In order to justify capitalization of related costs, it is necessary for management to conclude that it is probable that the project will be completed and that the software will be used as intended. Absent that level of expectation, costs must be expensed currently as R&D costs are required to be. Entities which historically were engaged in both research and development of software for internal use and for sale to others would have to carefully identify costs with one or the other activity, since the former would be subject to capitalization, while the latter might be expensed as R&D costs until technological feasibility had been demonstrated.

Under terms of the standard, cost capitalization commences when an entity has completed the conceptual formulation, design, and testing of possible project alternatives, including the process of vendor selection for purchased software, if any. These early-phase costs (i.e., preliminary project stage costs) are similar to R&D costs and must be expensed as incurred.

Costs incurred subsequent to the preliminary project stage, and which meet the criteria under GAAP as long-lived assets, can be capitalized and amortized over the asset's expected economic life. Capitalization of costs will begin when both of two conditions are met. First, management having the relevant authority approves and commits to funding the project and believes that it is probable that it will be completed and that the resulting software will be used as intended. Second, the conceptual formulation, design, and testing of possible software project alternatives (i.e., the preliminary project stage) have been completed.

2.3 Advanced Concepts of Financial Accounting

In this section topics such as business combination, consolidation, partnerships, and foreign currency transactions are discussed.

(a) Business Combination

(i) **Overview.** According to FASB, a business combination occurs when an entity acquires net assets that constitute a business or acquires equity interests of one or more other entities and obtains control over that entity or entities. Business combinations may be friendly or hostile takeovers. Purchase accounting is the only acceptable accounting method for all business combinations; the pooling-of-interest method is not.

FASB Statement 141 identified the following as key components of purchase method of accounting:

- **Initial recognition.** Assets are commonly acquired in exchange transactions that trigger the initial recognition of the assets acquired and any liabilities assumed.
- **Initial measurement.** Like other exchange transactions generally, acquisitions are measured on the basis of the fair values exchanged.
- **Allocating costs.** Acquiring assets in groups requires not only ascertaining the cost of the assets (or net assets) group but also allocating that cost to the individual assets (or individual assets and liabilities) that make up the group.
- **Accounting after acquisition.** The nature of an asset and not the manner of its acquisitions determines an acquiring entity's subsequent accounting for the asset.

According to FASB, the **combinor** is a constituent company entering into a purchase-type business combination whose stockholders as a group retain or receive the largest portion of the voting rights and control over the combined enterprise and thereby can elect a majority of the governing board of directors or other group of the combined enterprise. The **combinee** is a constituent company other than the combinor involved in a business combination.

(ii) **Computation and allocation of cost of a combinee.** The cost of a combinee is the total of the amount of consideration paid by the combinor, the combinor's direct "out-of-pocket" costs of the combination, and any contingent consideration that is determinable on the date of the business combination.

The amount of consideration is the total amount of cash paid, the current fair value of other assets distributed, the present value of debt securities issued, and the current fair value (or market) value of equity securities issued by the combinor.

The direct out-of-pocket costs include some legal fees, some accounting fees, and finder's fees (paid to investment banking firm). Costs of registering with the SEC and issuing debt securities are not part of the direct cost of the combinee. Costs of registering with the SEC and issuing equity securities are not part of direct costs either but can be offset against the proceeds from the issuance of the equity securities.

Contingent consideration is additional cash, other assets, or securities that may be issuable in the future, contingent on future events such as a specified level of earnings or a designated market price for a security that had been issued to complete the business combination. Contingent consideration can be determinable or not determinable for recording as part of the cost of the combination.

The FASB requires that the cost of a combinee must be allocated to assets (other than goodwill) acquired and liabilities assumed based on their estimated fair values on the date of the combination. Any excess of total costs over the amounts thus allocated is assigned to goodwill. Methods for determining fair values include: present values for receivables and most liabilities, net realizable value less a reasonable profit for work in process and finished goods inventories, appraised values for land, natural resources, and nonmarketable securities, and individual fair values for patents, copyrights, franchises, customer lists, and unpatented technology.

(b) **Consolidation.** The purpose of consolidated financial statements is to present for a single accounting entity the combined resources, obligations, and operating results of a group of related corporations such as parent and subsidiaries. Only subsidiaries not actually controlled should be exempted from consolidation. Usually, an investor's direct or indirect ownership of more than 50% of an investee's outstanding common sock has been required to evidence the controlling interest underlying a parent-subsidiary relationship. Actual control is more important than the controlling interest in situations such as liquidation or reorganization (bankruptcy) of a subsidiary or control of a foreign subsidiary by a foreign government. Generally accepted accounting principles require the use of the cost method of accounting for investments in unconsolidated subsidiaries because the subsidiaries generally are neither controlled nor significantly influenced by the parent company.

Assets, liabilities, revenues, and expenses of the parent company and its subsidiaries are totaled; intercompany transactions and balances are eliminated; and the final consolidated amounts are reported in the consolidated balance sheet, income statement, statement of stockholders' equity, statement of retained earnings, and statement of cash flows.

(i) **Consolidation of wholly owned subsidiary using purchase accounting method (on date of purchase combination).** The parent company's investment account and the subsidiary's stockholders' equity accounts do not appear in the consolidated balance sheet because they are intercompany (reciprocal) accounts. Under purchase accounting theory, the parent company assets and liabilities (except intercompany) are reflected at carrying amounts, and the subsidiary assets and liabilities (except intercompany) are reflected at current fair values, in the consolidated balance sheet. Goodwill is recognized to the extent the cost of the parent's investment in 100% (wholly owned) of the subsidiary's outstanding common stock exceeds the current fair value of the subsidiary's identifiable net assets.

(ii) **Consolidation of partially owned subsidiary using purchase accounting method (on date of purchase combination).** The recognition of minority interest is handled differently between the wholly owned subsidiary and the partially owned subsidiary. Minority or noncontrolling interest is the claims of stockholders other than the parent company to the net income or losses and net assets of the subsidiary. The minority interest in the subsidiary's net income or losses is displayed in the consolidated income statement, and the minority interest in the subsidiary's net assets is displayed in the consolidated balance sheet.

Minority interest is accounted for in two ways: the parent company concept, which emphasizes the interests of the parent's shareholders, and the economic unit concept, which emphasizes the legal aspect and the entity theory. The parent company concept treats the minority interest in net assets of a subsidiary as a liability. This liability is increased each accounting period subsequent to the date of a purchase-type business combination by an expense representing the minority's share of the subsidiary's net income or decreased by the minority's share of the subsidiary's net loss. Dividends declared by the subsidiary to minority stockholders decrease the liability to them. Consolidated net income is net of the minority's share of the subsidiary's net income. In the economic unit concept, the minority interest in the subsidiary's net assets is displayed in the stockholders' equity section of the consolidated balance sheet. The consolidated income statement displays the minority interest in the subsidiary's net income as subdivision of total consolidated net income, similar to the distribution of net income of a partnership.

(iii) **Consolidation of wholly owned subsidiary using purchase accounting method (Subsequent to date of purchase combination).** Subsequent to the date of a business combination, the parent company must account for the operating results of the subsidiary: the net income or net loss and dividends declared are paid by the subsidiary. In addition, a number of intercompany transactions and events that occur in a parent-subsidiary relationship must be recorded.

In accounting for the operating results of consolidated purchased subsidiaries, a parent company may choose the equity method or the cost method of accounting. In the equity method, the parent company recognizes its share of the subsidiary's net income or net loss, adjusted for depreciation and amortization of differences between current fair values and carrying amounts of a purchased subsidiary's net assets on the date of the business combination, as well as its share of dividends declared by the subsidiary. In the cost method, the parent company accounts for the operations of a subsidiary only to the extent that dividends are declared by the subsidiary. Dividends declared by the subsidiary from net income subsequent to the business combination are recognized as revenue by the parent company; dividends declared by the subsidiary in excess of post-combination net income constitute a reduction of the carrying amount of the parent company's investment in the subsidiary. Net income or net loss of the subsidiary is not recognized by the parent company when using the cost method.

The equity method is consistent with the accrual basis of accounting, and stresses the economic substance of the parent-subsidiary relationship due to single economic entity concept. The equity method is appropriate for pooled subsidiaries as well as purchased subsidiaries. The cost method recognizes the legal form of the parent-subsidiary relationship. The cost method is compatible with purchase accounting only, and there is no cost to pooled subsidiary. Consolidated financial statement amounts are the same, regardless of whether a parent company uses the equity method or the cost method to account for a subsidiary's operations.

(iv) **Consolidation of partially owned subsidiary using purchase accounting method (subsequent to date of purchase combination).** Accounting for the operating results of a partially owned subsidiary requires the computation of the minority interest in net income or net losses of the subsidiary. Thus, under the parent company concept of consolidated financial statements, the consolidated income statement of a parent company and its partially owned purchased subsidiary includes an expense—minority interest in net income (or loss) of subsidiary. The minority interest in net assets of the subsidiary is displayed among liabilities in the consolidated balance sheet.

(v) **Accounting for intercompany transactions not involving profit (gain) or loss.** Subsequent to the date of a business combination, a parent company and its subsidiaries may enter into a number of transactions with each other. Both the parent and the subsidiary should account for these intercompany transactions in a manner that facilitates the consolidation process. Separate ledger accounts should be established for all intercompany assets, liabilities, revenues, and expenses. These separate accounts clearly identify the intercompany items that must be eliminated in the preparation of consolidated financial statements. After elimination, the consolidated financial statements include only those balances and transactions resulting from outside entities.

(vi) **Accounting for intercompany transactions involving profit (gain) or loss.** Many business transactions between a parent company and its subsidiaries involve a profit (gain) or loss. Among these transactions are intercompany sales of merchandise, intercompany sales of plant assets, intercompany leases of property under capital lease or sales-type lease, and intercompany sales of intangible assets. Until intercompany profits or losses in such transactions are realized through the sales of the asset to an outsider or otherwise, the profits or losses must be eliminated in the preparation of consolidated financial statements.

In addition, a parent or subsidiary company's acquisition of its affiliate's bonds in the open market may result in a realized gain or loss to the consolidated entity. Such a realized gain or loss is not recognized in the separate income statement of either the parent company or the subsidiary, but it must be recognized in the consolidated income statement.

(c) **Partnerships.** A partnership is an association of two or more people to carry on as co-owners of a business for profit. Competent parties agree to place their money, property, or labor in a business and to divide the profits and losses. Each person is personally liable for the debts of the partnership. Express partnership agreements may be oral or written.

Partnerships are not subject to the income tax. The partnership net profit or loss is allocated to each partner according to the partnership's profit-sharing agreement. Each partner reports these items on his own tax return. Several separately reported items (e.g., capital gains, charitable contributions) retain their character when passed through to the partners.

BASIC DEFINITION OF PARTNERSHIP TERMS

- General partner: A partner who is liable for all partnership liabilities plus any unpaid contributions
- Limited partner: A partner who is obligated to the partnership to make any contribution stated in the certificate, even if he is unable to perform because of death, disability, or any other reason
- Silent partner: A partner who does not participate in management
- Secret partner: A partner who may advise management and participate in decisions, but his interest is not known to third parties
- Dormant partner: A partner who is both silent and secret

(i) **Duties, rights, and powers of partners.** The duties, rights, and powers of partners are both expressed (in the agreement) and implied (created by law). The statutory law in most states is the Uniform Partnership Act.

All partners have equal rights in management and conduct of business, even if their capital contributions are not equal. The partners may agree to place management within the control of one or more partners.

Ordinary matters are decided by a majority of the partners. If the partnership consists of two persons who are unable to agree and the partnership agreement makes no provision for arbitration, then dissolution is the only remedy.

The following matters require the unanimous consent of the partners:

- Change the essential nature of the business by altering the original agreement or reducing or increasing the partners' capital.
- Embark on a new business or admit new members.
- Modify a limited partnership agreement.
- Assign partnership property to a trustee for the benefit of creditors.
- Confess a judgment.
- Dispose of the partnership's goodwill.
- Submit a partnership agreement to arbitration.
- Perform an act that would make impossible the conduct of the partnership business.

However, the process of "engaging a new client" does not require unanimous consent of the partners.

Partners are not entitled to payment for services rendered in conducting partnership business, but they may receive a salary. The payment of a salary to a partner requires either an express agreement stating such or may be implied from the partner's conduct.

Capital contributions are not entitled to draw interest; a partner's earnings on his capital investment is his share of the profits. Interest may be paid on advances to the partnership above the amount of original contributed capital. Profits that are not withdrawn but left in the partnership are not entitled to draw interest.

Each partner has the duty to give the person responsible for recordkeeping any information necessary to efficiently and effectively carry on business. Each partner has the right to inspect the records at any time, but he cannot remove the records from the agreed-on location without the other partners' consent. Copies of the records can be made.

Knowledge known to one partner and not revealed to the other partners is considered notice to the partnership. A partner should communicate known facts to the other partners and have them added to the partnership records. *A partner who possesses knowledge and does not reveal it to the other partners has committed an act of fraud.*

Every partner has an equal right to possess partnership property for partnership purposes. Possession of partnership property for other purposes requires the other partners' permission. A partner cannot transfer partnership property or use partnership property in satisfaction of his personal debts.

In the case of a partner's death, his interest in specific partnership property passes to the surviving partners. The surviving partners wind up the affairs of the partnership in accordance with the partnership agreement and the applicable laws.

Partners owe each other the duty of undivided loyalty, since a partnership is a fiduciary relationship. Each partner must exercise good faith and consider the mutual welfare of all the partners in conducting business.

Partners have the following powers:

- **Power to contract.** The general laws of agency apply to partnerships, since a partner is considered an agent for the partnership business. A partner may bind the partnership with contractual liability whenever he is apparently carrying on the partnership business in the usual manner. Otherwise, a partner cannot bind the partnership without the authorization of the other partners.
- *The common implied powers of a partner include:* to compromise, adjust, and settle claims or debts owed by or to the partnership, to sell goods in the regular course of business and make warranties, to buy property within the scope of the business for cash or on credit, to buy insurance, to hire employees, to make admissions against interest, to enter into contracts within the scope of the firm, and to receive notices.
- **Power to impose tort liability.** The law imposes tort liability on a partnership for all wrongful acts or omissions of any partner acting in the ordinary course of the partnership and for its benefit. The partnership has the right of indemnity against the partner at fault.
- **Power over property.** Partners have implied authority to sell to good-faith purchasers personal property that is **held** for resale and to execute the necessary documents to transfer title. To sell the fixtures and equipment used in the business requires the other partners' authorization.
- The right to sell a business' real property is implied only if it is in the real estate business. Other transfers of real property require partnership authorization.
- **Financial transactions.** Partnerships are divided into general classes, trading and nontrading partnerships, to determine the limit of a partner's financial powers. A **trading partnership** engages in the business of buying and selling merchandise. Each partner has an implied power to borrow money and to extend the credit of the firm, in the usual course of business, by signing negotiable paper.

A **nontrading partnership** engages in the production of merchandise or sells services. In these partnerships, a partner's powers are more limited. A partner does not have the implied power to borrow money.

(ii) **Liabilities and authorities of a general partner.** General partners are liable for

- Fraudulent acts of other partners
- Debts attributable to limited partner notes to the partnership
- Debts related to the purchase of real property without each partner's consent

General partners have no authority to

- Do any act in violation of the certificate.
- Do any act that would make it impossible to carry on the ordinary business of the partnership.
- Confess a judgment against the partnership.
- Possess or assign partnership property for other than partnership purposes.
- Admit a person as a general partner.
- Admit a person as a limited partner unless the right to do so is given in the certificate.
- Continue the business with partnership property on the death, retirement, or incapacity of a general partner unless the right to do so is given in the certificate.

(iii) **Partnership accounting.** A partner's share of the partnership assets or profits may be determined in a suit for an accounting. These suits are equitable in nature and must be filed in a court of equity. A partner is entitled to a formal accounting in the following situations:

- The partnership has been dissolved.

- An agreement calls for an accounting at a definite date.
- A partner has withheld profits arising from secret transactions.
- An execution has been levied against the interest of one of the partners.
- One partner does not have access to the books.
- The partnership is approaching insolvency, and all parties are not available.

Partners may make a complete accounting and settle their claims without resort to a court of equity. An accounting is performed on the dissolution of a solvent partnership and winding up of its business. All firm creditors other than partners are entitled to be paid before the partners are entitled to participate in any of the assets.

The assets are distributed among the partners as follows:

- Any partner who has made advances to the firm or has incurred liability for, or on behalf of, the firm is entitled to reimbursement.
- Each partner is entitled to return of his capital contributions.
- Any remaining balance is distributed as profits in accordance with the partnership agreement.

(iv) **Actions against other partners.** Typically a partner cannot maintain an action at law against the other partners, because the indebtedness among the partners is undetermined until there is an accounting and all partnership affairs are settled. *The few exceptions to this rule are if*

- The partnership is formed to carry out a single venture or transaction,
- The action involves a segregated or single unadjusted item or account, or
- The action involves a personal covenant or transaction entirely independent of the partnership affairs.

(v) **Admitting a new partner.** If a partnership admits a new partner, the new partner is liable to the extent of his capital contribution for all obligations incurred before his admission. The new partner is not personally liable for such obligations.

(vi) **Asset distribution of partnership.** If a firm is insolvent and a court of equity is responsible for the distribution of the partnership assets, the assets are distributed in accordance with a rule known as **marshalling of assets**. The firm's creditors may seek payment out of the firm's assets and then the individual partner assets. The firm's creditors must exhaust the firm's assets before recourse to the partners' individual assets. *The descending order of asset distribution of a limited partnership is as follows:*

1. To secured creditors other than partners
2. To unsecured creditors other than partners
3. To limited partners in respect of their profits
4. To limited partners in respect of their capital contributions
5. To general partners in respect of any loans to the partnership
6. To general partners in respect of their profits
7. To general partners in respect of their capital contributions

The **asset distribution hierarchy** of a limited partnership is shown in Exhibit 2.8.

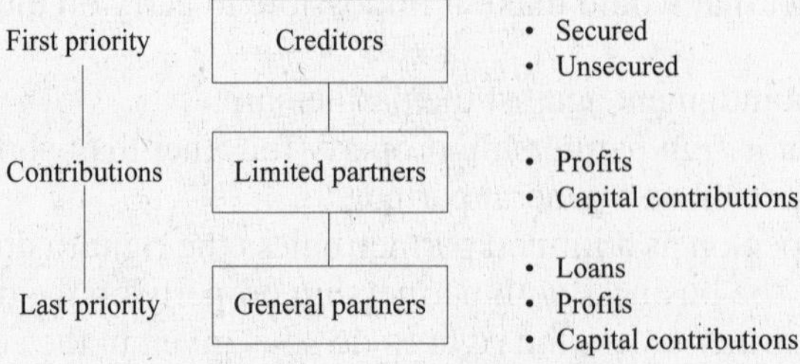

Exhibit 2.8: Asset distribution hierarchy

(d) **Foreign Currency Transactions.** The buying and selling of foreign currencies result in variations in the exchange rate between the currencies of two countries. The selling spot rate is charged by the bank for current sales of the foreign currency. The bank's buying spot rate for the currency is less than the selling spot rate; the spread between the selling and buying spot rates represents gross profit to a trader in foreign currency. Factors influencing fluctuations in exchange rates include a nation's balance of payments surplus or deficit, differing global rates of inflation, money-market variations such as interest rates, capital investment levels, and monetary policies and actions of central banks.

A multinational corporation (MNC) headquartered in the United States engages in sales, purchases, and loans with foreign companies as well as with its own branches, divisions, investees, and subsidiaries in other countries. If the transactions with foreign companies are denominated in terms of the US dollar, no accounting problems arise for the US-based MNC. If the transactions are negotiated and settled in terms of the foreign companies' local currency unit, then the US company must account for the transaction denominated in foreign currency in terms of US dollars. This foreign currency translation is accomplished by applying the appropriate exchange rate between the foreign currency and the US dollar.

In addition to spot rates, forward rates apply to foreign currency transactions to be completed on a future date. Forward rates apply to forward exchange contracts, which are agreements to exchange currencies of different countries on a specified future date at the forward rate in effect when the contract was made. Forward rates may be larger or smaller than spot rates for a foreign currency, depending on the foreign currency dealer's expectations regarding fluctuations in exchange rates for the currency.

Increases in the selling spot rate for a foreign currency required by a US-based MNC to settle a liability denominated in that currency generate transaction losses to the company because more dollars are required to obtain the foreign currency. Conversely, decreases in the selling spot rate produce transaction gains to the company because fewer US dollars are required to obtain the foreign currency. In contrast, increases in the buying spot rate for a foreign currency to be received by a US-based MNC in settlement of a receivable denominated in that currency generate transaction gains to the company; decreases in the buying spot rate produce transaction losses.

(i) **Translation of foreign currency financial statements.** When a US-based MNC prepares consolidated or combined financial statements that include the operating results, financial position (balance sheet), and cash flows of foreign subsidiaries or branches, the US company must translate the amounts in the final statements of the foreign entities from the entities' functional currency to US dollar. Similar treatment must be given to investments in other foreign investees for which the US company uses the equity method of accounting.

Four methods are available to translate foreign currency including current/noncurrent, monetary/nonmonetary, current rate, and temporal method, where the latter method is same as the monetary/nonmonetary method.

(ii) **Current/noncurrent method.** Current assets and current liabilities are translated at the exchange rate in effect on the balance sheet date of the foreign entity (that is, the current rate). All other assets and liabilities, and the components of owners' equity, are translated at the historical rates in effect at the time the assets, liabilities, and equities first were recognized in the foreign entity's accounting records. In the income statement, depreciation expense and amortization expense are translated at historical rates applicable to the related assets, while all other revenue and expenses are translated at an average exchange rate for the accounting period.

This method reflects the liquidity aspects of the foreign entity's financial position by showing the current US dollar equivalents of its working capital components. Inventories are translated at the current rate, which is a departure of the historical rate.

(iii) **Monetary/nonmonetary method.** Monetary assets and liabilities, which are expressed in a fixed amount, are translated at the current exchange rate. All other assets, liabilities, and owners' equity amounts are translated at appropriate historical rates. In the income statement, average exchange rates are applied to all revenue and expenses except depreciation expense, amortization expense, and cost of goods sold, which are translated at appropriate historical rates.

This method emphasizes the retention of the historical-cost principle in the foreign entity's financial statements and parent company aspects of a foreign entity's financial position and operating results. Due to use of the parent company's reporting currency, this method misstates the actual financial position and operating results of the foreign entity.

(iv) **Current rate method.** All balance sheet accounts other than owners' equity are translated at the current exchange rate. Owners' equity amounts are translated at historical rates. To emphasize the functional currency aspects of the foreign entity's operations, all revenue and expenses may be translated at the current rate on the respective transaction dates, if practical. Otherwise, an average exchange rate is used for all revenue and expenses.

(v) **Transaction gains and losses excluded from net income.** Gains and loses from the following foreign currency transactions should be accounted for in the same manner as translation adjustments:

- Foreign currency transactions that are designated as, and are effective as, economic hedge of a net investment in a foreign entity, commencing as of the designation date.
- Intercompany foreign currency transactions that are of a long-term investment nature, when the entities to the transaction are consolidated, combined, or accounted for by the equity method.

(vi) **Functional currency in highly inflationary economies.** The functional currency of a foreign entity in a highly inflationary economy can be identified as the reporting currency (e.g., the US dollar for a US-based MNC). A highly inflationary economy is defined as the one having cumulative inflation of 100% or more over a three-year period. The financial statements of a foreign entity in a country experiencing severe inflation are remeasured in US dollars.

(vii) **Income taxes related to foreign currency translation.** The following are the procedures for the interperiod and intraperiod tax allocation to determine the effects of foreign currency translation.

- Interperiod tax allocation for temporary differences associated with transaction gains and losses that are reported in different accounting periods for financial accounting and income taxes.
- Interperiod tax allocation for temporary differences associated with translation adjustments that do not meet the criteria for nonrecognition of deferred tax liabilities for undistributed earnings of foreign subsidiaries.
- Intraperiod tax allocation for translation adjustments are included in the stockholders' equity section of the balance sheet.

(viii) **Disclosure of foreign currency translation.** Aggregate transaction gains or losses of an accounting period should be disclosed in the income statement or in a note to the financial statements. Changes in cumulative translation adjustments during an accounting period should be disclosed in a separate financial statement, in a note to financial statements, or in a statement of stockholders' equity.

The minimum required disclosures include

- Beginning and ending amounts of cumulative translation adjustments
- Aggregate adjustments during the accounting period for translation adjustments, hedges of net investments, and long-term intercompany transactions
- Income taxes allocated to translation adjustments during an accounting period
- Decreases resulting from sale or liquidation of an investment in a foreign entity

2.4 Financial Statement Analysis

(a) **Overview.** Financial statement analysis requires a comparison of the firm's performance with that of other firms in the same industry, comparison with its own previous performance, and/or both. Three major parties who analyze financial statements from their own perspectives are: (1) managers of the firm to gauge performance, (2) potential investors who want to invest in the firm by purchasing stocks and bonds, and (3) creditors and lenders (e.g., bankers) analyze data in financial statements to assess the financial strength of the firm and the ability to pay interest and principal for the money they lent to the firm. Investors use data in financial statements to form expectations about future earnings and dividends, and about the riskiness of these expected values. *The real value of financial statements is in their predictive power about the firm's future earnings potential and dividends payment strength.*

WHO LOOKS FOR WHAT?

- Investors look for earnings and dividends, and this is reflected in security values. Therefore, cash flows are the major basis for security values.
- Creditors look for asset strength and the ability to pay off the debt.
- Financial statements report accounting profits.
- High accounting profits generally mean high cash flows and the ability to pay high dividends and debt payments.

A company's annual report presents four basic financial statements, including: a Statement of Income (income statement), a Statement of Financial Position (balance sheet), a Statement of Retained Earnings, and a Statement of Cash Flows. Income statement summarizes the firm's revenues and expenses over an accounting period.

An income statement presents the results of operations for a given time period. Net sales are shown at the top; after which various costs, including income taxes, are subtracted to obtain the net income available to common stockholders. A report on earnings and dividends per share is given at the bottom of the statement.

A balance sheet is a statement of the firm's financial position at a specific point in time. The firm's assets are shown on the left-hand side of the balance sheet while liabilities and equity (the claims against these assets) are shown on the right-hand side. *The assets are listed in the order of their liquidity or the length of time it takes to convert assets into cash. The liabilities are listed in the order in which they must be paid.*

A statement of retained earnings shows how much of the firm's earnings were not paid out in dividends. Retained earnings represent a claim against assets, not assets per se. Retained earnings do not represent cash and are not "available" for the payment of dividends or anything else. A positive retained earnings means that the firm has earned an income, but its dividends have been less than its reported income. Due to differences between accrual and cash accounting practices, a firm may earn money, which shows an increase in the retained earnings, but still could be short of cash.

A statement of cash flows reports the impact of a firm's operating, investing, and financing activities on cash flows over an accounting period. This statement shows how the firm's operations have affected its cash flows and presents the relationships among cash flows from operating, investing, and financing activities of the firm.

(b) **Types of Financial Statement Analysis.** Four types of measures that are used to analyze a company's financial statements and its financial position include common size analysis, trend analysis, comparative ratios, and single ratios (see Exhibit 2.9).

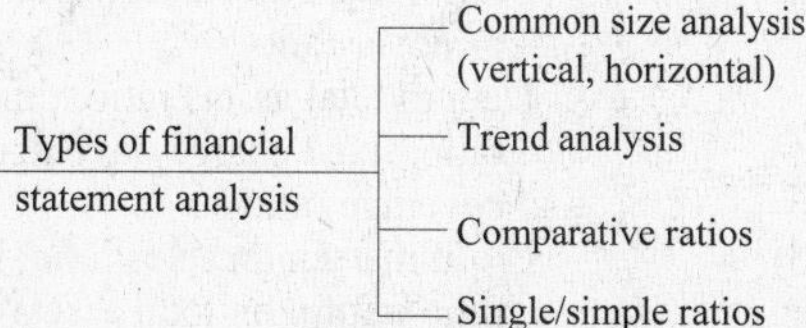

Exhibit 2.9: Types of financial statement analysis

Common size analysis expresses items in percentages, which can be compared with similar items of other firms or with those of the same firm over time. For example, common size balance sheet line items (both assets and liabilities) are expressed as a percentage of total assets (e.g., receivables as X percent of total assets). Similarly, common size income statement line items are expressed as a percentage of total sales (e.g., cost of goods sold as X percent of total sales).

Variations of common size analysis include: vertical analysis and horizontal analysis. **Vertical analysis,** which expresses all items on a financial statement as a percentage of some base figure, such as total assets or total sales. Comparing these relationships between competing organizations helps to isolate strengths and areas of concern.

In **horizontal analysis,** the financial statements for two years are shown together with additional columns showing dollar differences and percentage changes. Thus, the direction, absolute amount, and relative amount of change in account balances can be calculated. Trends that are difficult to isolate through examining the financial statements of individual years or comparing with competitors can be identified.

Trend analysis shows trends in ratios, which gives insight whether the financial situation of a firm is improving, declining, or stable. It shows a graph of ratios over time, which can be compared with a firm's own performance as well as that of its industry.

Comparative ratios show key financial ratios, such as current ratio and net sales to inventory, by industry, such as beverages and bakery products. These ratios represent average financial ratios for all firms within an industry category. Many ratio data-supplying organizations are available and each one designs ratios for its own purpose, such as small firms or large firms. Also, the focus of these ratio is different, too, such as creditor's viewpoint or investor's viewpoint. Another characteristic of the ratio data-supplying organization is that each has its own definitions of the ratios and their components. A caution is required when interpreting these ratios due to these differences.

Another type of comparative analysis is comparing the financial statements for the current year with those of the most recent year. By comparing summaries of financial statements for the last five to ten years, an individual can identity trends in operations, capital structure, and the composition of assets. This comparative analysis provides (1) insight into the normal or expected account balance or ratio, (2) information about the direction of changes in ratios and account balances, and (3) insight into the variability or fluctuation in an organization's assets or operations.

TREND ANALYSIS VERSUS COMPARATIVE RATIO ANALYSIS

- In trend analysis, trends are shown over time between the firm and its industry.
- In comparative ratio analysis, a single point (one-to-one) comparison is shown between the firm and its industry.
- In both analyses, the industry's ratio is an average ratio, while the firm's ratio is not.

Next, our major focus will shift to **single ratios or simple ratios**. Certain accounts or items in an organization's financial statements have logical relationships with each other. If the dollar amounts of these related accounts or items are expressed in fraction form, then they are called ratios. These ratios are grouped into five categories: liquidity ratios, asset management ratios, debt management ratios, profitability ratios, and market value ratios. Exhibit 2.10 presents individual ratios for each ratio category.

Ratio category	*Individual ratios*
Liquidity (1)	Current ratio, quick ratio or acid-test ratio
Asset management (2)	Inventory turnover ratio, days sales outstanding ratio, fixed assets turnover ratio, total assets turnover ratio
Debt management (3)	Debt to total assets ratio, times-interest-earned ratio, fixed charge coverage ratio, cash flow coverage ratio
Profitability (4) = (1) + (2) + (3)	Profit margin on sales ratio, basic earning power ratio, return on total assets ratio, return on common equity ratio, earnings per share ratio, payout ratio
Market value (5) = (1) + (2) + (3) + (4)	Price/earnings ratio, book value per share, market/book ratio

Exhibit 2.10: Individual financial ratios

(c) **Single/Simple Ratios.** Details on liquidity ratios, asset management ratios, debt management ratios, profitability ratios, and market value ratios are presented next.

(i) **Liquidity ratios. Liquidity ratios** measure an organization's debt-paying ability, especially in the short term. These ratios indicate an organization's capacity to meet maturing current liabilities and its ability to generate cash to pay these liabilities.

(A) ***Current ratio (working capital ratio): Current assets divided by current liabilities.*** Current ratio indicates an organization's ability to pay its current liabilities with its current assets and, therefore, shows the strength of its working capital position. A high current ratio indicates a strong liquidity and vice versa. While a high current ratio is good, it could also mean excessive cash, which is not good.

Both short-term and long-term creditors are interested in the current ratio, because a firm unable to meet its short-term obligations may be forced into bankruptcy. Many bond indentures require the borrower to maintain at least a certain minimum current ratio.

(B) ***Acid-test ratio (quick ratio): Quick assets divided by current liabilities.*** Quick assets are cash, marketable securities, and net receivables. This ratio is particularly important to short-term creditors since it relates cash and immediate cash inflows to immediate cash outflows. Purchases of inventory on account would make the quick ratio decrease since it does not include inventory. Current liabilities increase, not current assets. Quick assets are current assets minus inventory.

(ii) **Asset management ratios. Asset management ratios or activity ratios** measure the liquidity of certain assets and relate information on how efficiently assets are being utilized.

(A) ***Inventory turnover ratio: Sales divided by average inventory or cost of goods sold divided by average inventory.*** The inventory turnover indicates how quickly inventory is sold. Typically, a high turnover indicates that an organization is performing well. This ratio can be used in determining whether there is obsolete inventory or if pricing problems exist. The use of different inventory valuation methods (LIFO, FIFO, etc.) can affect the turnover ratio. It is also called inventory utilization ratio. As the obsolete inventory increases, the inventory turnover decreases.

(B) ***Days sales outstanding ratio: Receivables divided by average sales per day.*** Days sales outstanding (DSO) ratio indicates the average length of time that a firm must wait to receive cash after making a sale. It measures the number of days sales are tied up in receivables. If the calculated ratio for a company is 45 days, and its sales terms are 30 days, and the industry average ratio is 35 days, it indicates that customers, on the average, are not paying their bills on time. In the absence of a change in the credit policy about sales terms, the higher the company's actual ratio, the greater the need to speed up the collection efforts. A decrease in the DSO ratio is an indication of effective collection efforts.

Another related ratio is accounts receivable turnover ratio, which is net credit sales divided by average net trade receivables outstanding. The average receivables outstanding can be calculated by using the beginning and ending balance of the trade receivables. This ratio provides information on the quality of an organization's receivables and how successful it is in collecting outstanding receivables. A fast turnover lends credibility to the current ratio and acid-test ratio.

(C) ***Fixed asset turnover ratio: Net sales divided by net fixed assets.*** Fixed asset turnover ratio shows how effectively the firm uses its fixed assets such as plant, equipment, machinery, and buildings. A caution should be noted here that inflation erodes the historical cost base of old assets thus reporting a higher turnover. This inflation problem makes it hard to compare fixed asset turnover between old and new fixed assets. Assets reported on current value basis would eliminate the inflation problem. Fixed asset turnover is also called fixed assets utilization ratio and is similar to the inventory utilization ratio. A high fixed asset turnover ratio may mean either a firm was efficient in using its fixed assets or that the firm is under-capitalized and could not afford to buy enough fixed assets.

(D) ***Total assets turnover ratio: Net sales divided by average total assets.*** The total assets turnover indicates how efficiently an organization utilizes its capital invested in assets. A high turnover ratio indicates that an organization is effectively using its assets to generate sales. This ratio relates the volume of a business (i.e., sales, revenue) to the size of its total asset investment. In order to improve this ratio, management needs to increase sales, dispose of some assets, or a combination of both.

(iii) **Debt management ratios.** Debt management ratios or coverage ratios are used in predicting the long-run solvency of organizations. Bondholders are interested in these ratios, because they provide some indication of the measure of protection available to bondholders. For those interested in investing in an organization's common stock, these ratios indicate some of the risk since the addition of debt increases the uncertainty of the return on common stock.

(A) ***Debt ratio: Total debt divided by total assets.*** Debt ratio impacts an organization's ability to obtain additional financing. It is important to creditors because it indicates an organization's ability to withstand losses without impairing the creditor's interest. A creditor prefers a low ratio since it means there is more "cushion" available to creditors if the organization becomes insolvent. However, the owner(s) prefer high debt ratio to magnify earnings due to leverage or to minimize loss of control if new stock is issued instead of taking on more debt. Total debt includes both current liabilities and long-term debt.

The capitalization of a lease by a lessee will result in an increase in the debt-to-equity ratio. If a firm purchases a new machine by borrowing the required funds from a bank as a short-term loan, the direct impact of this transaction will be to decrease the current ratio and increase the debt ratio.

(B) ***Times-interest-earned ratio: Earnings before interest and taxes divided by interest charges.*** Times-interest-earned ratio provides an indication of whether an organization can meet its required interest payments when they become due, and not go bankrupt. This ratio also provides a rough measure of cash flow from operations and cash outflow as interest on debt. This information is important to creditors, since a low or negative ratio suggests that an organization could default on required interest payments. This ratio measures the extent to which operating income can decline before the firm is unable to meet its annual interest costs. The ability to pay current interest is not affected by taxes since the interest expense is tax deductible. In other words, the interest expense is paid out of income before taxes are calculated.

(C) ***Fixed charge coverage ratio: Earnings before interest and taxes plus lease payments divided by interest charges plus lease payments.*** Fixed charge coverage ratio is similar to times-interest-earned ratio except that the former ratio includes long-term lease obligations. When a company's ratio is less than the industry average, the company may have difficulty in increasing its debt.

(D) ***Cash flow coverage ratio: Earnings before interest and taxes plus lease payments plus depreciation divided by interest charges plus lease payments plus preferred stock dividends (before tax) plus debt repayment (before tax).*** The cash flow coverage ratio shows the margin by which the firm's operating cash flows cover its financial obligations. This ratio considers principal repayment of debt, dividends on preferred stock, lease payments, and interest charges. The reason for putting the dividends on preferred stock and debt repayment amounts on before the tax basis is due to their nontaxdeductibility, meaning that they are paid out of the income before taxes are paid.

(iv) **Profitability ratios. Profitability ratios** are the ultimate test of management's effectiveness. They indicate how well an organization operated during a year. They are a culmination of many policies and decisions made by management during the current year as well as previous years. Typically these ratios are calculated using sales or total assets. Profitability ratios show the combined effect of liquidity, asset management, and debt management performance on operating results.

(A) ***Profit margin on sales ratio: Net income available to common stockholders divided by sales.*** Profit margin on sales ratio indicates the proportion of the sales dollar that remains after deducting expenses. Here, the net income after taxes is divided by sales to give the profit per dollar of sales.

(B) ***Basic earning power ratio: Earnings before interest and taxes divided by total assets.*** Basic earning power ratio shows the raw earning power of the firm's assets, before the influence of taxes and impact of the financial leverage. It indicates the ability of the firm's assets to generate operating income. A low "total asset turnover" and low "profit margin on sales" gives a low "basic earning power ratio." Return on investment (ROI) may be calculated by multiplying total asset turnover by profit margin.

(C) ***Return on total assets ratio: Net income available to common stockholders divided by total assets.*** Return on total assets (ROA) ratio measures the return on total assets after interest and taxes are paid. The net income used in the equation is the net income after taxes. A low ratio indicates a low "basic earning power ratio" and a high use of debt.

Another way of looking at the ROA ratio is by breaking it down into subcomponents as shown below: net income divided by net sales (i.e., profit margin on sales) as one component and net sales divided by total average assets (i.e., total asset turnover) as another component. This breakdown helps in pinpointing problems and opportunities for improvement.

(D) ***Return on common equity ratio: Net income available to common stockholders divided by common equity.*** Return on common equity (ROE) measures the rate of return on common stockholders' investments. The net income used in the equation is the net income after taxes and common equity is the average stockholders' equity. A low ratio compared to the industry indicates high use of debt. This ratio reflects the return earned by an organization on each dollar of owners' equity invested.

(E) ***Earnings per share ratio: Net income minus current year preferred dividends divided by weighted-average number of shares outstanding.*** Earnings per share (EPS) ratio is probably the most widely used ratio for evaluating an organization's operating ability. The complexity of the calculation of EPS is determined by a corporation's capital structure.

An organization with no outstanding convertible securities, warrants, or options has a simple capital structure. An organization has a complex structure if it has such items outstanding. The investor should be careful not to concentrate on this number to the exclusion of the organization as a whole. One danger in concentrating on this number is that EPS can easily be increased by purchasing treasury stock that reduces the outstanding shares.

(F) ***Payout ratio: Cash dividends divided by net income or dividends per share divided by earnings per share.*** Payout ratio indicates the ability to meet dividend obligations from net income earned. There is a relationship between the payout ratio and the need for obtaining external capital. The higher the payout ratio, the smaller the addition to retained earnings, and hence, the greater the requirements for external capital. This says that dividend policy affects external capital requirements. If 'd' is the dividend payout ratio, (1-d) is called the earnings retention rate.

Depending on their tax status certain investors are attracted to the stock of organizations that pay out a large percentage of their earnings, and others are attracted to organizations that retain and reinvest a large percentage of their earnings. Growth organizations typically reinvest a large percentage of their earnings; therefore, they have low payout ratios.

(v) **Market value ratios.** Market value ratios relate the firm's stock price to its earnings and book value per share. It shows the combined effects of liquidity ratios, profitability ratios, asset management ratios, and debt management ratios. The viewpoint is from outside in, that is, from an investors' view about the company's financial performance—past and future.

(A) ***Price/earnings ratio: Price per share divided by earnings per share.*** Price/earnings (P/E) ratio shows how much investors are willing to pay per dollar of reported profits. Financial analysts, stock market analysts, and investors in general use this value to determine whether a stock is overpriced or underpriced. Different analysts have differing views as to the proper P/E ratio for a certain stock or the future earnings prospects of the firm. Several factors such as relative risk, trends in earnings, stability of earnings, and the market's perception of the growth potential of the stock affect the P/E ratio.

P/E RATIOS VERSUS GROWTH VERSUS RISK

- P/E ratios are higher for firms with high growth prospects and low risk.
- P/E ratios are lower for firms with low growth prospects and high risk.

(B) ***Book value per share: Common equity divided by shares outstanding.*** Book value per share ratio is used as an intermediate step in calculating the market/book ratio. Book value per share ratio is used in evaluating an organization's net worth and any changes in it from year to year. If an organization were liquidated based on the amounts reported on the balance sheet, the book value per share indicates the amount that each share of stock would receive. If the asset amounts on the balance sheet do not approximate fair market value, then the ratio loses much of its relevance.

(C) ***Market/book ratio: Market price per share divided by book value per share.*** Market/book ratio reveals how investors think about the company. Market/book ratio is related to ROE ratio in that high ratio of ROE gives high market/book ratio and vice versa. In other words, companies with higher ROE sell their stock at higher multiples of book value. Similarly, companies with high rates of return on their assets can have market values in excess of their book values. A low rate of return on assets gives low market/book value ratio.

CALCULATION OF FINANCIAL RATIOS

Examples 1 through 3 are based on the following selected data that pertain to a company at December 31, 20X4:

Quick assets	$ 208,000
Acid-test ratio	2.6 to 1
Current ratio	3.5 to 1
Net sales for 20X4	$1,800,000
Cost of sales for 20X4	$ 990,000
Average total assets for 20X4	$1,200,000

Example 1: Based on the above, the company's current liabilities at December 31, 20X4, amount to

a. $ 59,429
b. $ 80,000
c. $342,857
d. $187,200

Choice **(b)** is the correct answer. Computations follow.

$$\frac{\text{Quick assets}}{\text{Current liabilities}} = \text{Acid-test ratio}$$

$$\frac{\$208{,}000}{\text{Current liabilities}} = 2.6$$

$$\text{Current liabilities} = \frac{\$208{,}000}{2.6} = \underline{\underline{\$80{,}000}}$$

Choice **(a)** is incorrect. This answer selection incorrectly reflects the computation quick assets ($208,000) divided by the current ratio (3.5). Choice (c) is incorrect. This answer selection reflects the incorrect computation of average total assets ($1,200,000) divided by the current ratio (3.5). Choice (d) is incorrect. This answer selection reflects the incorrect computation of quick assets ($208,000) multiplied by the excess of the current ratio (3.5) over the acid-test ratio (2.6).

Example 2: Based on the above data, the company's inventory balance at December 31, 20X4, is

a. $ 72,000
b. $187,200
c. $231,111
d. $282,857

Choice **(a)** is the correct answer. Computations follow.

$$\frac{\$208{,}000}{\text{Current liabilities}} = 2.6$$

$$\frac{\$208{,}000}{2.6} = \$80{,}000 = \text{Current liabilities}$$

$$\frac{\text{Current assets}}{\text{Current liabilities}} = \text{Current ratio}$$

$$\frac{\text{Current assets}}{\$80{,}000} = 3.5$$

$$\text{Current Assets} = 3.5 \times \$80{,}000 = \$280{,}000$$

Current assets	–	Quick assets	=	Inventory
\$280,000		\$208,000		\$72,000

Choice (**b**) is incorrect. This answer selection reflects the incorrect computation of the current ratio (3.5) minus the acid-test ratio (2.6) multiplied by quick assets (\$208,000). Choice (c) is incorrect. This answer selection reflects the incorrect computation of quick assets (\$208,000) divided by the excess of the current ratio (3.5) over the quick ratio (2.6). Choice (d) is incorrect. This answer selection reflects the incorrect computation of cost of sales (\$990,000) divided by the current ratio (3.5).

Example 3: Based on the above, the company's asset turnover for 20X4 is

a. 0.675
b. 0.825
c. 1.21
d. 1.50

Choice (**d**) is the correct answer. Computations follow.

$$\frac{\text{Net sales}}{\text{Average total assets}} = \frac{\$1{,}800{,}000}{\$1{,}200{,}000} = 1.5$$

Choice (a) is incorrect. This answer reflects the incorrect computation of gross profit (\$1,800,000 – \$990,000) divided by average total assets (\$1,200,000). Choice (b) is incorrect. This answer reflects the incorrect computation of cost of sales (\$990,000) divided by average total assets (\$1,200,000). Choice (c) is incorrect. This answer reflects the incorrect computation of average total assets (\$1,200,000) divided by cost of sales (\$990,000).

(d) **Limitations of Financial Statement Ratios.** Because ratios are simple to compute, convenient, and precise, they are attractive and a high degree of importance is attached to them. Since these ratios are only as good as the data upon which they are based, the following limitations exist:

- The use of ratio analysis could be limiting for large, multidivisional firms due to their size and complexity—two conditions that mask the results. However, they might be useful to small firms.
- Typically, financial statements are not adjusted for price-level changes. Inflation or deflation can have a large effect on the financial data.
- Since transactions are accounted for on a cost basis, unrealized gains and losses on different asset balances are not reflected in the financial statements.
- Income ratios tend to lose credibility in cases where a significant number of estimated items exist, such as amortization and depreciation.
- Seasonal factors affect and distort ratio analysis, which can be minimized by using average figures in calculations.
- Be aware of "window dressing" and "earnings management" techniques used by firms to make them look financially better than what they really are. Management manipulates the financial statements to impress the credit analysts and the stock market investors (i.e., management fraud).
- Certain off-balance-sheet items do not show up on the financial statements. For example, leased assets do not appear on the balance sheet, and the lease liability may not be shown as a debt. Therefore, leasing can improve both the asset turnover and the debt ratios.
- Attaining comparability among organizations in a given industry is an extremely difficult problem, since different organizations apply different accounting procedures. These different accounting procedures require identification of the basic differences in accounting from organization to organization and adjustment of the balances to achieve comparability.

- Do not take the ratios on their face value since a "good" ratio does not mean that the company is a strong one or that a "bad" ratio means that the company is a weak one. This implies that ratios should be evaluated and interpreted with judgment and experience and considering the firm's characteristics and the industry's uniqueness.

2.5 Cost of Capital Evaluation

The rate of return on a security to an investor is the same as the cost of capital to a firm, which is a required return on its investments. Any increase in total assets of a firm's balance sheet must be financed by an increase in one or more of capital components (i.e., debt, preferred stock, retained earnings, common stock). Similar to any other resources, capital has a cost. The cost of capital must reflect the average cost of the various sources of long-term funds used, that is, one or more of capital components used (see Exhibit 2.11). Let us review each component of capital briefly.

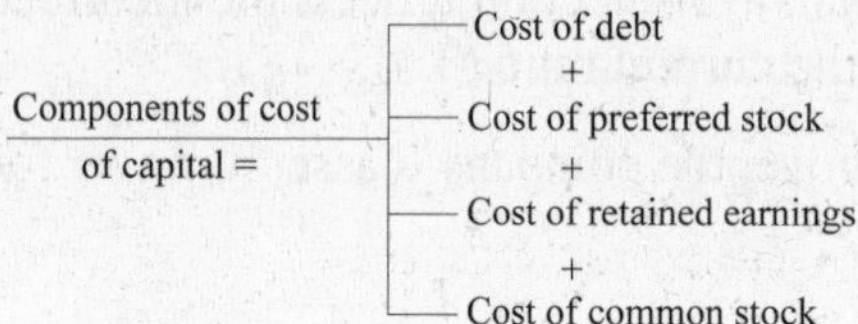

Exhibit 2.11: Components of cost of capital

(a) **Cost of Debt.** The cost of debt is calculated as *Kd* (1-*T*) where *Kd* is the interest rate on debt and *T* is the firm's marginal tax rate. The government pays part of the cost of debt (equal to tax rate) because interest is deductible for tax purposes. The value of the firm's stock depends on after-tax cash flows. Here we are interested in acquiring a new debt (marginal cost of debt) to finance a new asset, and past financing is a sunk cost and is irrelevant for cost of capital calculation purposes.

The key point is to compare the rate of return with after-tax flows. After-tax cost of debt is less than before-tax cost due to tax savings resulting from an interest expense deduction that reduces the net cost of debt.

(b) **Cost of Preferred Stock.** The cost of preferred stock (*Kp*) is the preferred dividend (*Dp*) divided by the net issuing price (*Pn*) or the price the firm receives after deducting flotation costs. This is $Kp = Dp/Pn$. Since preferred dividends are not tax deductible, there are no tax savings unlike interest expense on debt.

(c) **Cost of Retained Earnings.** If management decides to retain earnings there is an opportunity cost involved, that is, stockholders could have received the earnings as dividends and invested this money somewhere else. Because of this opportunity cost, the firm should earn on its retained earnings at least as much as the stockholders themselves could earn in alternative investments of comparable risk.

COST OF DEBT VERSUS COST OF PREFERRED STOCK VERSUS COST OF RETAINED EARNINGS

- The costs of debt are based on the returns investors require on debt.
- The costs of preferred stock are based on the returns investors require on preferred stock.
- The costs of retained earnings are based on the returns stockholders require on equity capital.

When a stock is in equilibrium, its required rate of return (Ks) should be equal to its expected rate of return (*Kes*)

$$Ks = Krf = Rp \text{ or } Kes = (D1/Po) + g$$

where *Krf* is the risk-free rate, *Rp* = Risk premium, *D1/Po* is the stock's dividend yield, *g* is the stock's expected growth rate.

Three methods are commonly used to calculate the cost of retained earnings: (1) the capital asset pricing model (CAPM) approach, (2) the bond-yield-plus-risk-premium approach, and (3) the discounted cash flow (DCF) approach (see Exhibit 2.12).

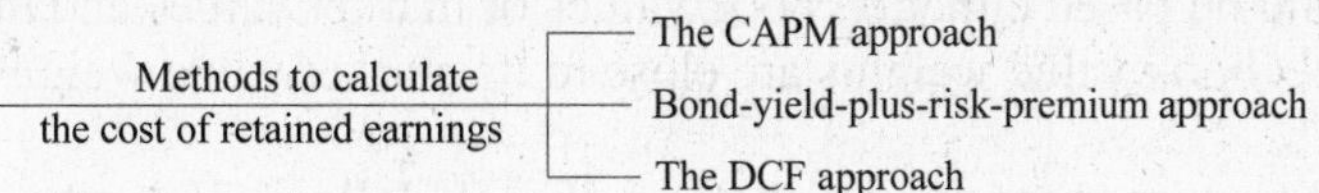

Exhibit 2.12: Methods to calculate the cost of retained earnings

(i) **CAPM approach.** The equation is

$$Ks = Krf + (Km - Krf)\ bi$$

Where *Krf* is the risk-free rate (e.g., US Treasury bond or bill rate), (*Km* – *Krf*) is equal to the risk premium. *Km* is the expected rate of return on the market or on "average" stock. *bi* is the stock's beta coefficient (an index of the stock's risk).

Drawbacks of the CAPM approach include: a stockholder may be concerned with total risk rather than with market risk only. Beta coefficient may not measure the firm's true investment risk. This approach will understate the correct value of the required rate of return on the stock, *Ks*, and it is difficult to obtain correct estimates of the inputs to the model to make it operational. Examples include: deciding whether to use long-term or short-term Treasury bonds for risk-free rate, difficulty in estimating the beta coefficient that investors expect the firm to have in the future, and difficulty in estimating the market risk premium.

(ii) **Bond-yield-plus-risk-premium approach.** This method provides a "ballpark" estimate of the cost of equity, not a precise number, since it uses ad hoc, subjective, and judgmental estimate.

$$Ks = \text{Bond rate} + \text{Risk premium}$$

A firm's cost on common equity is found by adding a risk premium (say 2 to 4%) based on judgment to the interest rate on the firm's own long-term debt.

(iii) **Discounted cash flow approach.** The discounted cash flow (DCF) approach is also called the dividend-yield-plus-growth rate approach, and calculated as

$$Ks = Kes = D1/Po + \text{Expected growth } (g)$$

Investors expected to receive a dividend yield (*D1*/*Po*) plus a capital gain (*g*) for a total expected return of Kes. At equilibrium, this expected return would be equal to the required return (*Ks*). *Ks* = *Kes*.

(d) **Cost of Common Stock.** The cost of common stock (*Ke*) is higher than the cost of retained earnings (*ks*) due to flotation costs involved in selling new common stock. The equation is

$$Ke = \frac{D1}{Po\,(1 - F)} + g$$

Where *D1* is the dividends, *Po is* the stock price, *F* is the percentage flotation cost incurred in selling the new stock, *Po* (1 – *F*) is the net price per share received by the firm.

COST OF COMMON STOCK VERSUS STOCK PRICE

- The firm must earn more than the cost of common stock (*Ke*) due to flotation cost.
- When a firm earns more than *Ke*, the price of the stock will rise.
- When a firm earns exactly *Ke*, earnings per share will not fall, expected dividend can be maintained, and consequently the price per share will not decline.
- When a firm earns less than *Ke*, then earnings, dividends, and growth will fall below expectations, causing the price of the stock to decline.

(e) **Weighted-Average and Marginal Cost of Capital Concepts.** An optimal (target) capital structure is a mix of debt, preferred stock, and common stock that maximizes a firm's stock price. The goal of the finance manager should be then to raise new capital in a manner that will keep the actual capital structure on target over time. The firm's weighted-average cost of capital (WACC) is calculated based on the target proportions of capital and the cost of the capital components.

$$\text{WACC} = WdKd\,(1 - T) + WpKp + WsKs$$

where *Wd*, *Wp*, and *Ws* are the weights used for debt, preferred stock, and common stock, respectively.

The weights could be based either on book values or market values and the latter is preferred over the former. If a firm's book value weights are close to its market value weight, book weights can be used.

As the firm tries to raise more money, the cost of each dollar will at some point rise. The marginal cost concept can be applied here: *The marginal cost of any item is the cost of another unit of that item, whether the item is labor or production. The marginal cost of capital (MCC) is the cost of the last dollar of new capital that the firm raises, and the MCC rises as more and more capital is raised during a given period.* The MCC schedule shows how the weighted-average cost of capital changes as more and more new capital is raised during a given year.

KEY CONCEPTS TO REMEMBER: BREAK POINT, INVESTMENT OPPORTUNITY SCHEDULE, AND COST OF CAPITAL

- A break point (BP) will occur in the marginal cost of capital (MCC) whenever the cost of one or more of the capital components rises. If there are "n" separate breaks, there will be "n+1" different weighted-average cost of capital.
- The investment opportunity schedule (IOS) is a graph of the firm's investment opportunities, with the projects having the highest return plotted first.
- The intersection of the MCC schedule and the IOS schedule is called the corporate cost of capital, which is used to evaluate average risk capital budgeting projects.

The break point is the dollar value of new capital that can be raised before an increase in the firm's weighted-average cost of capital occurs.

The break point (BP) is total amount of lower-cost of capital of a given type divided by fraction of this type of capital in the capital structure

(f) **Issues in Cost of Capital.** There are three major issues in cost of capital: (1) depreciation-generated funds, (2) privately owned and small business firms, and (3) measurement problems.

1. **Depreciation-generated funds.** Depreciation is a source of capital and its cash flows can either be reinvested or returned to investors. The cost of depreciation-generated funds is equal to the weighted-average cost of capital in which capital comes from retained earnings and low-cost debt.
2. **Privately owned and small business firms.** The same principles of cost of capital estimation can be applied to both privately held and publicly owned firms. Input data are difficult to obtain for privately owned firms since its stock is not publicly traded.
3. **Measurement problems.** It is difficult to estimate the cost of equity, obtain input data for the CAPM approach, estimate stock growth rate, and assign different risk-adjusted discount rates to capital budgeting projects of differing degrees of riskiness.

Capital budgeting and cost of capital estimates deal with *ex ante* (estimated) data rather than *ex post* (historical) data. Because of this, we can be wrong about the location of the IOS schedule and the MCC schedule. Consequently, a project that formerly looked good could turn out to be a bad one. Despite these issues, the cost of capital estimates used in this section are reasonably accurate. By solving these issues, refinements can be made.

2.6 Types of Debt and Equity

(a) **Types of Debt.** Debt is of two types: (1) short-term debt and (2) long-term debt. Debt maturities affect both risk and expected returns. For example

- Short-term debt is riskier than long-term debt.
- Short-term debt is less expensive than long-term debt.
- Short-term debt can be obtained faster than long-term debt.
- Short-term debt is more flexible than long-term debt.

(i) **Sources of short-term financing.** By definition, short-term debt (credit) is any liability originally scheduled for payment within one year. The four major sources of short-term credit are: (1) accruals, (2) accounts payable, (3) bank loans, and (4) commercial paper. The order of short-term credit sources is shown below from both cost and importance viewpoints.

In the order of importance	In the order of cost
A. Trade credit (most important)	A. Trade credit (free, no interest paid)
B. Bank loans	B. Accruals
C. Commercial paper	C. Commercial paper
D. Accruals (least important)	D. Bank loans (not free, interest paid)

(A) ***Trade credit.*** Trade credit is granted by the suppliers of goods as a sales promotion device. All firms, regardless of their size, depend on accounts payable or trade credit as a source of short-term financing. Small firms do rely more heavily on trade credit than larger firms due to the former's inability to raise money from other sources. Trade credit, a major part of current liability, is an interfirm debt arising from credit sales and recorded as an accounts receivable by the seller and as an accounts payable by the buyer. Trade credit is a spontaneous source of financing arising from normal course of business operations.

When payment terms are extended, the amount in accounts payable is expanded to provide an additional source of financing. Therefore, lengthening the credit period generates additional financing.

Payment terms vary and usually call for "net 30" meaning that it must pay for goods 30 days after the invoice date. Other terms include "1/10, net 30" which means that a 1% discount is given if payment is made within 10 days of the invoice date, but the full invoice amount is due and payable within 30 days if the discount is not taken. The finance manager has a choice of taking or not taking the discount and he needs to calculate the cost of not taking discounts on purchases. The equation is

$$\text{Percentage cost of not taking discount} = \frac{\text{Discount percent}}{100\% - \text{Discount \%}} \times \frac{360}{A - B}$$

where A = Days credit is outstanding and B = Discount period

COST OF NOT TAKING A DISCOUNT

Example: The approximate cost of not taking a discount when the payment terms are 1/10, net 30, is calculated as follows:

$$\text{Percentage cost of not taking discount} = \frac{1}{100\% - 1\%} \times \frac{360}{30 - 10} = 0.18 = 18\%$$

By paying late (stretching accounts payable), the cost of trade credit is reduced. This is shown below when 30 day bill is paid in 60 days, the approximate cost drops from 18% to 7.2%. That is 1/99 × 360/(60 – 10) = 0.072 = 7.2%.

KEY CONCEPTS TO REMEMBER: COST OF TRADE DISCOUNTS

- The cost of not taking trade discounts can be substantial.
- The cost can be doubled when payment (credit) terms are changed from 1/10, net 30 to 1/10, net 20.
- The cost can be doubled when payment (credit) terms are changed from 1/10, net 30 to 2/10, net 30.
- The cost can be quadrupled, when payment (credit) terms are changed from 1/10, net 30 to 2/10, net 20.
- The cost can be reduced by paying late (i.e., from 2/10, net 30 to 2/10, net 60).

A firm's policy with regard to taking or not taking trade discounts can have a significant effect on its financial statements. A dichotomy exists here in terms of taking discounts or not taking discounts. Careful analysis needs to be performed showing relevant costs and its effects on net income.

Decision Conditions

1. If the company does not take discounts (i.e., uses maximum trade credit), its interest expense will be zero (i.e., no borrowing is necessary), but it will have an expense equivalent to lost discounts.
2. If the company does take discounts (i.e., borrows money from bank), it will incur interest expense on the loan, but it will avoid the cost of discounts lost. The company gives up some of the trade credit and it has to raise money from other sources such as bank credit, common stock, or long-term bonds.

Decision Rules

1. If the discount amount lost exceeds the interest expense, the "take-discounts" policy would result in a higher net income and eventually a higher stock price.
2. If the interest expense exceeds the discount amount lost, the "does not take discount" policy would result in a higher net income and eventually a higher stock price.

(B) ***Bank loans***. Bank loans appear on firms' balance sheets under the notes payable account category. A promissory note is signed by the borrower (customer) specifying the amount borrowed, the percentage interest rate, the repayment schedule, any collateral, and any other terms and conditions. Banks require a compensating balance in the form of a minimum checking account balance equal to a specified percentage (i.e., 10 to 20%) of the face amount of the loan. A compensating balance raises the effective interest rate on the loan.

Examples of Bank Loan Features

- Promissory note
- Compensating balance
- Line of credit
- Revolving credit agreement

Banks also give a line of credit to a borrower and it works like a credit card limit. Line of credit can be based on either formal or informal understanding. It includes the maximum amount of credit the bank will extend to the borrower. A revolving credit agreement, which is similar to a line of credit, is a formal line of credit often used by large firms. The bank has a legal obligation to honor a revolving credit agreement while no legal obligation exists under the line of credit.

The cost of a bank loan (i.e., interest rate) varies depending on economic conditions and Federal Reserve (Fed) money supply policy. Generally, interest rates are higher for riskier borrowers and for smaller loans due to fixed costs of servicing the loan. If a firm is financially strong, it can borrow at the prime rate, which has traditionally been the lowest rates bank charge. If a firm is financially weak, the bank will charge higher than prime rate to compensate for the risk involved.

KEY CONCEPTS TO REMEMBER: LOAN DEMAND AND INTEREST RATES

- When the economy is weak, (i.e., loan demand is weak), the Fed increases the money supply. Consequently, the interest rates on all types of loans decline.
- When the economy is strong, (i.e., loan demand is strong), the Fed decreases the money supply. Consequently, the interest rates on all types of loans increases.

Interest rates on bank loans are quoted in three ways: (1) simple interest, (2) discount interest, and (3) add-on interest. Each method is discussed briefly.

Simple (regular) interest. In a simple interest loan, the borrower receives the face value of the loan and then repays the principal and interest at maturity. Effective rate = Interest/amount received. If a loan period is one year or more, the nominal (stated) rate equals the effective rate. If a loan period is less than one year, the effective rate is higher than nominal (stated) rate.

Discount interest. In a discount interest loan, the borrower receives less than the face value of the loan since the bank deducts the interest in advance. Effective rate = Interest/Amount received. Because of discounting, the effective rate is always higher than a simple interest loan regardless of the loan period. However, the discount interest imposes less of a penalty on a shorter-term than on a longer-term loan because the interest is paid closer to the average date of use of the funds (half the life of the loan).

Add-on interest. Small installment loans employ the add-on interest method. The interest is calculated based on the nominal rate and then added to the amount received to obtain the loan's face value. Effective rate = Interest/0.5 (Amount received). The effective rate can be almost double the stated rate since the average amount actually outstanding is less than the original amount of the loan.

The situation is different when compensating balances are introduced to the simple interest method and discount interest method. In general, compensating balances tend to raise the effective interest rate on a loan because some money is tied up in a checking account (i.e., cannot be used). There are two exceptions: (1) if the firm can use transaction balances as compensating balances, the effective interest rate will be less than otherwise, and (2) if the firm can earn interest on its bank deposits, including the compensating balance, the effective interest rate will be decreased.

(C) ***Commercial paper.*** Commercial paper represents short-term, unsecured promissory notes of large, strong firms and is highly liquid in nature. The interest rate charged on commercial paper is somewhat below the prime rate and its maturity ranges from two to six months. Even though compensating balances are not required for commercial paper, its effective interest rate is higher due to the loan commitment fees involved.

Firms issuing commercial paper are required by commercial paper dealers to have unused revolving credit agreements to back up their outstanding commercial paper. A commitment fee is charged on the unused credit line.

The commercial paper market is impersonal, unlike bank loans. However, the commercial paper market is flexible and provides a wide range of credit sources generally available to financially strong firms with low credit risks.

(D) ***Accruals.*** Accruals are short-term liabilities arising from wages owed to employees and taxes owed to government. These accruals increase automatically as a firm's operations expand and hence little control exist over their levels. No explicit interest is paid on funds raised through accruals.

(ii) **Use of security in short-term financing.** The security agreement of the Uniform Commercial Code (UCC) provides guidelines for establishing loan security. Secured loans are expensive due to recordkeeping costs. Financially weak companies are required to put up some type of collateral to protect the lender, while financially strong companies generally are not even though they are encouraged to do so. Most commonly used collateral for short-term credit is accounts receivable and inventories, which are described in Exhibit 2.13.

Collateral for short-term loans	*Collateral for long-term loans*
Examples of collateral used for short-term loans include accounts receivable, inventories, stocks, and bonds.	Examples of collateral for secured long-term loans include land, building, equipment, stocks, and bonds.

Exhibit 2.13: Collateral for short-term and long-term loans

(A) ***Accounts receivable financing.*** Accounts receivables (A/R) financing involves either the pledging of receivables or the selling of receivables (i.e., factoring) to obtain a short-term loan. Either commercial banks or industrial finance companies are usually involved in pledging and factoring, and a legally binding agent is established between the borrower and the lender (see Exhibit 2.14).

The expensive operation of pledging and factoring functions today will become less expensive tomorrow due to automation and use of debit cards and credit cards. This makes it affordable for small companies to finance their receivables. When a credit card is used to purchase an item, the seller is in effect factoring receivables.

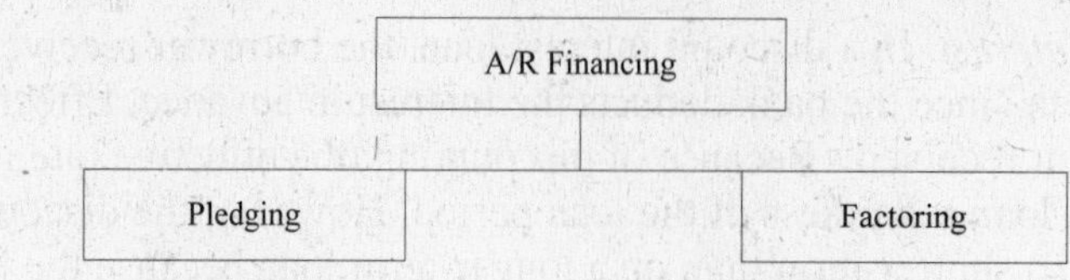

Characteristics of pledging

- Lender has a claim against the receivable
- Lender has recourse against the borrower
- When loan defaults, the borrower must take the loss
- Buyer of the goods (customer) is not notified about pledging
- Loaned amount is less than 100% of the pledged invoices

Characteristics of factoring

- Lender provides money and performs credit checks of the borrower
- Lender has no recourse against the borrower
- When loan defaults, the lender must take the loss
- Buyer of the goods (customer) is notified and asked to make payments directly to the lender
- Performs credit checking, lending, and risk-bearing functions

Exhibit 2.14: Accounts receivable financing methods

(B) ***Advantages and disadvantages of A/R financing.*** Advantages and disadvantages of A/R financing are

Advantages	Flexibility because the financing is tied to the growth of receivables. As sales increase, financing increases. Receivables are put to better use than otherwise. Benefit of an in-house credit department without having one.
Disadvantages	Administrative costs could be higher to handle large volume of invoices with small dollar amounts. Trade creditors may object to selling their goods on credit because receivables (noncash assets) are being pledged or factored. They may have an uneasy feeling about this type of financing arrangement.

(C) ***Inventory financing.*** Inventory financing involves the use of inventory as a security to obtain a short-term loan. Three methods exist: (1) inventory blanket liens, (2) trust receipts, and (3) warehouse receipts (see Exhibit 2.15).

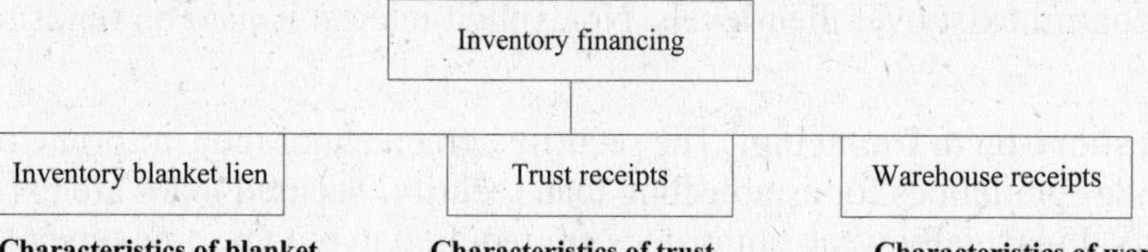

Characteristics of blanket liens

- The lender has a lien against all of the borrower's inventories.
- The borrower has control over the inventory.
- The value of the collateral at any time can be less than the original.

Characteristics of trust receipts

- Trust receipts eliminate drawbacks of blanket liens.
- An instrument exists to acknowledge that the goods are held in trust for the lender.
- The borrower signs and delivers a trust receipt for specific goods.
- The goods can be stored in a public warehouse or be held on the premises of the borrower.
- Proceeds from the sale of the goods are sent to the lender.
- Due to specificity of goods, the borrower could manipulate sales.

Characteristics of warehouse receipts

- Warehousing eliminates all drawbacks of blanket liens and trust receipts.
- Either a public or a field warehouse can be used.
- A public warehouse is an independent third-party operation.
- A field warehouse is established on the borrower's premises.
- Public notice, physical control of the inventory, and supervision by a custodian are required for a field warehouse.
- Lenders insist on having a custodian to control the collateral.

Exhibit 2.15: Inventory financing methods

(D) ***Advantages and disadvantages of field warehouse financing.*** Advantages and disadvantages of field warehouse financing are

Advantages	Flexibility because the financing is tied to the growth of inventories. More sales means more inventory buildup is required and more financing is needed. A convenient method is loan collateral. Better inventory control and warehousing practices, which in turn save handling costs, insurance charges, and theft losses.
Disadvantages	Extensive amount of paperwork is required. Physical separation of goods using fences and signs. High cost of supervision by a custodian of the field warehousing company especially for small firms obtaining the loan.

(iii) **Long-term debt.** Long-term debt is often called funded debt, a term used to define the replacement of short-term debt with securities of longer maturity (e.g., stocks, bonds). Many types of long-term debt instruments are available including term loans, bonds, secured notes, unsecured notes, marketable debt, and nonmarketable debt. Term loans and bonds will be discussed next.

(A) ***Term loans.*** A term loan is a contract under which a borrower agrees to make a series of payments (interest and principal) at specific times to the lender. Most term loans are amortized, which means they are paid off in equal installments over the life of the loan ranging from 3 to 15 years. Amortization protects the lender against inadequate loan provisions made by the borrower.

Since the agreement is between the lender and the borrower, documentation requirements are lower and the speed and future flexibility are greater and the cost is lower compared to a public offering involved in a stock or bond issue. The interest rate on a term loan can either be fixed or variable, and lenders will be reluctant to make long-term, fixed-rate loans.

KEY CONCEPTS TO REMEMBER: TERM LOANS

- If a fixed rate is used, it is set close to the rate on bonds of equivalent maturity and risk.
- If a variable rate is used, it is set at a certain number of percentage points over either the prime rate, the commercial paper rate, the Treasury-bill rate, the Treasury-bond rate, or the London Interbank Offered Rate (LIBOR). When the index rate goes up or down, the rate charged on the outstanding balance will vary accordingly.

(B) ***Bonds.*** A bond is a long-term contract (seven to ten years or more) under which a borrower agrees to make payments (interest and principal) on specific dates to the holder of the bond. The interest rates paid on bonds can be fixed or variable (floating rate bonds) and are generally fixed.

Some debts have specific contractual requirements to meet. The effective cost of the debt is high and many restrictions are placed in the debt contracts, which limits a firm's future flexibility. In order to protect the rights of the bondholders and the issuing firm, a legal document called "indenture" is created and it includes "restrictive covenants." A trustee, usually a bank, is assigned to represent the bondholders and to enforce the terms of the indenture and to ensure compliance with restrictive covenants.

WHAT IS INCLUDED IN RESTRICTIVE COVENANTS?

- Conditions under which the issuer can pay off the bonds prior to maturity
- The level at which the issuer's times-interest-earned ratio must be maintained if the firm is to sell additional bonds
- Restrictions against the payment of dividends when earnings fall below a certain level

Most bonds contain a **call provision** that gives the issuing firm the right to call the bonds before maturity for redemption. The bondholder is paid an amount greater than par value (call premium) for the bond when it is called. The call premium is set equal to one year's interest if the bond is called during the first year, and the premium declines at a constant rate of *I/N* each year thereafter, where *I* equal annual interest and *N* equals original maturity in years.

TERM LOANS VERSUS BONDS

- Bonds and term loans are similar in that both require payments of interest and principal amounts on specific dates.
- Only one lender is involved in a term loan while thousands of investors are involved in a bond issue.
- A bond issue is advertised and sold to many investors whereas a term loan is not advertised and only one borrower is involved.
- A very large term loan can be granted by a syndicate of many financial institutions.
- A bond issue can be sold to one or few lenders (privately placed) for speed, flexibility, and low issuance costs.

Another example of specific debt contract features is **sinking fund** requirements. A sinking fund is a provision that requires annual payment designed to amortize a bond or preferred stock issue. It retires a portion of the bond issue each year. It can also be viewed as buying back a certain percentage of the issue each year. Annual payments are a cash drain on the firm and nonpayment could cause default or force the company into bankruptcy. The firm may deposit money with a trustee who will retire the bonds when they mature.

KEY CONCEPTS TO REMEMBER: CALL PROVISION AND SINKING FUND

- A bond without call provision will protect the bondholder. The investor is not subject to interest rate fluctuations.
- A bond with sinking fund call provision will not protect the bondholder when interest rate falls. The investor loses money on interest.
- Bonds with a sinking fund provision are safer than otherwise. This results in lower coupon rates.

The sinking fund retirement is handled either by calling in for redemption (at par) a certain percentage of the bonds each year or by buying the required amount of bonds on the open market. A sinking fund call requires no call premium while a refunding operation does. A sinking fund requires that a small percentage of the issue is callable in any one year.

The refunding operation works as follows: When a firm sold bonds or preferred stock at high interest rates, and if the issue is callable, the firm could sell a new issue at low interest rates. Then the firm could retire the expensive old issue. This refunding operation reduces interest costs and preferred dividend expenses.

INTEREST RATES VERSUS BOND PRICES

- There is an inverse relationship between bond prices and interest rates.
- If interest rates are increased, the firm will buy bonds in the open market at a discount.
- If interest rates are decreased, the firm will call the bonds.

Various Types of Long-Term Bonds

Mortgage bonds. Under a mortgage bond, the corporation pledges certain fixed assets as security for the bond. Mortgage bonds can be of two types: (1) senior (first) mortgage bonds and (2) junior (second) mortgage bonds. Second mortgage bondholders are paid only after the first mortgage bondholders have been paid off in full. All mortgage bonds are written subject to an indenture. Details regarding the nature of secured assets are contained in the mortgage instrument. From the viewpoint of the investor, mortgage bonds provide lower risk and junk bonds provide greater risk.

Bond Rating Criteria

- Debt ratio
- Times-interest-earned ratio
- Current ratio
- Fixed charge coverage ratio
- Mortgage or other provisions
- Sinking fund requirements

Debentures. A debenture is an unsecured bond. Consequently, it provides no lien against specific property as security for the obligation. Debenture holders come under general creditors. Financially strong companies do not need to put up property as security when they issue debentures. Debentures can be subordinate or not. In the event of liquidation, reorganization, or bankruptcy, subordinate debt has claims on assets only after senior debt has been paid off. Subordinate debentures may be subordinated either to designated notes payable or to all other debt.

Convertible bonds. Convertible bonds are securities that are convertible into shares of common stock, at a fixed price, at the option of the bondholder. Convertible bonds have a lower coupon rate than nonconvertible debt and have a chance for capital gains.

Warrants. Warrants are options, which permit the holder to buy stock for a stated price, thereby providing a capital gain if the price of the stock rises. Bonds that are issued with warrants, like convertible bonds, carry lower coupon rates than straight bonds.

Income bonds. As the name implies, income bonds pay interest only when the interest is earned. These bonds are safer to a company but riskier to an investor than "regular" bonds.

Putable bonds. Putable bonds may be turned in and exchanged for cash at the holder's option. The put option can be exercised only if the issuer is being acquired or is increasing its outstanding debt or other specified action.

Treasury bonds. A treasury bond will have the lowest risk and low opportunity for return to an investor. It has the highest interest rate risk at the date of issue to an issuer (see Exhibit 2.16).

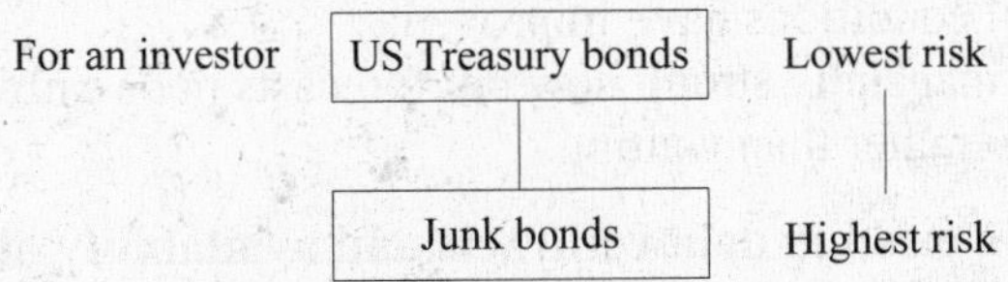

Exhibit 2.16: Bonds and risks

Indexed bonds. Countries faced with high inflation rates issue indexed bonds, also known as purchasing power bonds. The interest paid is based on an inflation index (e.g., consumer price index) so that the interest paid rises automatically when the inflation rate rises. This bond protects the bondholder against inflation.

Floating rate bonds. The interest rate on floating rate bonds fluctuates with shifts in the general level of interest rates. The interest rate on these bonds is adjusted periodically and it benefits the investor and the lender. Corporations also benefit from not having to commit themselves to paying a high rate of interest for the entire life of the loan.

Zero coupon bonds. Capital appreciation is the major attraction in zero coupon bonds rather than interest income. Therefore, zero coupon bonds pay no interest and are offered at a discount below their par values. Both private and public organizations are offering zero coupon bonds to raise money. Zero coupon bonds are also called original issue discount bonds.

Junk bonds. Junk bonds are a high-risk, high-yield bond issued to finance a leveraged buyout, a merger, or a troubled company. In junk bond deals, the debt ratio is high, so the bondholders share as much risk as stockholders would. Since the interest expense on bonds is tax deductible, it increases after-tax cash flows of the bond issuer.

The reason for the availability of so many different types of long-term securities is that different investors have different risk/return tradeoff preferences. Different securities are issued to accommodate different tastes of investors and at different points in time. Short-term US Treasury bills are risk-free and low-return (which act as a reference point), while warrants are high-risk and high-return security.

(iv) **Factors influencing long-term financing decisions.** Long-term financing decisions require a great deal of planning since a firm commits itself for many years to come. The long-term nature combined with uncertainty makes long-term financing risky, requiring careful consideration of all factors involved. Examples of important factors include

- **Target capital structure.** A firm should compare its actual capital structure to its target structure and keep it in balance over a longer period of time. Exact matching of capital structure is not economically feasible on a yearly financing basis due to increased flotation costs involved. It has been shown that small fluctuations about the optimal capital structure have little effect either on a firm's cost of debt and equity or on its overall cost of capital.
- **Maturity matching.** The maturity-matching concept proposes matching the maturity of the liabilities (debt) with the maturity of the assets being financed. This factor has a major influence on the type of debt securities used.
- **Interest rate levels.** Consideration of both absolute and relative interest rate levels is crucial in making long-term financing decisions. The issuance of a long-term debt with a call provision is one example where the interest rate fluctuates. The callability of a bond permits the firm to refund the issue should interest rates drop. Companies base their financing decisions on expectations about future interest rates.
- **The firm's current and forecasted financial conditions.** The firm's financial condition, earnings forecasts, status of research and development programs, and introduction of new products all have a major play in what type of long-term security is issued. For example, the following decision rules apply:
  - If management forecasts higher earnings, the firm could use debt now rather than issuing common stock. After earnings have risen and pushed up the stock price, the firm should issue common stock to restore the capital structure to its target level.
  - If a firm is financially weak, but forecasts better earnings, permanent financing should be delayed until conditions have improved.
  - If a firm is financially strong now but forecasts poor earnings, it should use long-term financing now rather than waiting.
- **Restrictions in existing debt contracts and availability of collateral.** Restrictions on the current ratio, the debt ratio, times-interest-earned ratio and fixed charge coverage ratio can also restrict a firm's ability to use different types of financing at a given time. Also, secured long-term debt will be less costly than unsecured debt. Firms with large amounts of fixed assets (with a ready resale value) are likely to use a relatively large amount of debt.

(b) **Types of Equity.** When management decides to acquire new assets, it has the option of financing these assets either with equity, debt, or a combination. The following is a good financial management policy:

- Long-term assets should be financed with long-term capital.
- Short-term assets should be financed with short-term capital.

The definition of common equity is the sum of the firm's common stock, additional paid-in capital, preferred stock, and retained earnings. The common equity is the common stockholders' total investment in the firm. The sources of long-term capital are shown in Exhibit 2.17.

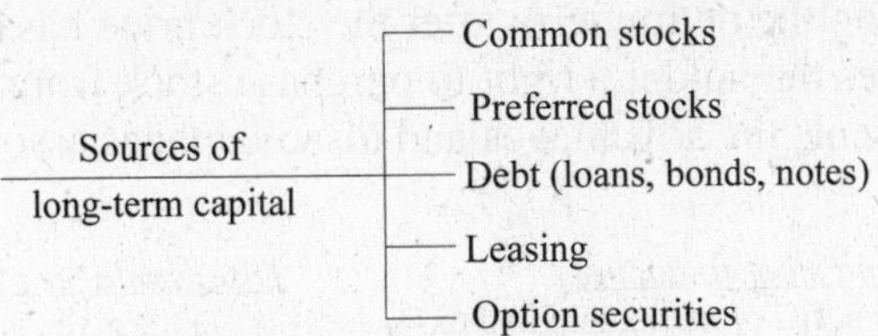

Exhibit 2.17: Sources of long-term capital

Common stocks and preferred stocks will be discussed in this section. Debt was discussed in the previous section. Leasing is presented earlier in this chapter.

(i) **Common stocks.** The common stockholders are the owners of a corporation. Common stock is the amount of stock management has actually issued (sold) at par value. Par value is the nominal or face value of a stock and is the minimum amount for which new shares can be issued. The component "additional paid-in capital" represents the difference between the stock's par value and what new stockholders paid when they bought newly issued shares. Retained earnings are the money that belongs to the stockholders and that they could have received in the form of dividends. Retained earnings are also the money that was plowed back into the firm for reinvestment.

Book value of the firm = Common stock + Paid-in capital + Retained earnings = Common equity
Book value per share = Book value of the firm divided by common shares outstanding

It should be interesting to note that par value, book value, and market value will never be equal due to conflicting relationships.

KEY CONCEPTS TO REMEMBER: RELATIONSHIPS BETWEEN BOOK VALUE, PAR VALUE, AND MARKET VALUE

- If a company had lost money since its inception, it would have had negative retained earnings, the book value would have been below par value, and the market price could have been below the book value.
- When a stock is sold at a price above book value per share, the book value increases.
- When a stock is sold at a price below book value per share, the book value decreases.

Most firms have one type of common stock while others may have multiple types of stock called classified stock. Usually, newer firms issue classified stock to raise funds from outside sources. For example, Class A stock may be sold to the public with a dividend payment but no voting rights. Class B stock may be kept by the founder of the firm to gain control with full voting rights. A restriction might be placed on Class B stock not to pay dividends until the firm reaches a predesignated retained earnings level.

(A) ***Legal rights of common stockholders.*** Since the common stockholders are the owners of a firm, they have the following rights: the right to elect the firm's directors, and the right to remove the management of the firm if they decide a management team is not effective. Stockholders can transfer their right to vote to a second party by means of an instrument known as a proxy. A proxy fight is a situation where outsiders plan to take control of the business by requesting the stockholders transfer their rights to outsiders in order to remove the current management and to bring in a new management team.

Common stock holders have preemptive rights to purchase any additional shares sold by the firm. Preemptive rights protect the power of control of current stockholders and protect stockholders against a dilution of stock value. Selling common stock at a price below the market value would dilute its price. This would transfer wealth from the present stockholders to new stockholders. Preemptive rights prevent such transfer.

(B) ***Put and call options.*** A put option is the right to sell stock at a given price within a certain period. A call option is the right to purchase stock at a given price within a certain period. Selling a put option could force the company to purchase additional stock if the option is exercised. The holder of a put option for a particular common stock would make a profit if the option is exercised during the option term after the stock price has declined below the put price. A warrant option gives the holder a right to purchase stock from the issuer at a given price.

Exhibit 2.18 presents the advantages and disadvantages associated with common stock financing.

Advantages of common stock financing

- It gives the benefits of ownership and expected returns in terms of dividends and capital gains.
- It does not obligate the firm to make dividend payments to stockholders; dividends are optional and dependent upon earnings, investment plans, management practices. This gives flexibility to management.
- It has no fixed maturity date.
- It provides a cushion against losses from the creditors' viewpoint since it increases the creditworthiness of the firm. It lowers the firm's cost of debt due to a good bond rating.
- It provides the investor with a better hedge against unanticipated inflation.
- It provides financing flexibility in that it permits companies (1) to finance with common stock during good times and (2) to finance with debt during bad times. This practice is called "reserve borrowing capacity."

Disadvantages of common stock financing

- It gives voting rights and control to new stockholders when a stock is sold.
- It gives new stockholders the right to share in the income of the firm.
- It increases the cost of underwriting and distributing common stock. Flotation costs are higher than incurred for debt.
- Its average cost of capital will be higher when a firm has more equity than is called for in its optimal capital structure.
- Its dividend payments are not tax deductible for corporations.

Exhibit 2.18: Advantages and disadvantages of common stock financing

(ii) **Preferred stock.** Preferred stock is issued to raise long-term capital for many reasons: when neither common stock nor long-term debt can be issued on reasonable terms, during adverse business conditions, a firm can issue preferred stock with warrants when the common stock is depressed, to bolster the equity component of a firm's capital structure, a firm can issue convertible preferred stock in connection with mergers and acquisitions, and to issue a floating rate preferred stock to stabilize the market price.

Preferred stock is the stock whose dividend rate fluctuates with changes in the general level of interest rates. Thus stock is good for liquidity portfolios (e.g., marketable securities). It is a neat way to obtain new capital at a low cost due to its floating dividend rates, stable market price, and tax exemption for dividends received.

Under US tax laws, if preferred stock with conversion privilege is exchanged for the acquired company's common stock, this constitutes a tax-free exchange of securities (i.e., no gain or loss is recognized for tax purposes). Also, if the buyout were for cash, the acquired stockholders would have to pay capital gain taxes.

Preferred stock is a hybrid stock, meaning that it is similar to bonds in some respects and similar to common stock in others. Therefore, preferred stock can be classified either as bonds or common stock (see Exhibit 2.19).

Preferred stocks as bonds (debt)

- Like bonds, preferred stock has a par value and a call provision.
- Preferred dividends are fixed similar to interest payments on bonds and must be paid before common stock dividends can be paid.
- During financial difficulty, preferred dividends can be omitted without leading the firm to bankruptcy.
- Financial analysts sometimes treat preferred stock as debt.
- Like debt, preferred stocks have coverage requirements for the amount of preferred stock and the level of retained earnings.
- Preferred stock may be redeemed at a given time, at the option of the holder, or at a time not controlled by the issuer—called transient preferreds.

Preferred stocks as common stocks (equity)

- Like most common stock, preferred stock has a par value.
- Like common stock, preferred stocks have no maturity date and are not callable, and hence are perpetuity stocks.
- Unlike common stock, most preferred stock requires dividend payments. This reduces earnings available for common stock shareholders. Preferred stock dividends must be paid before common stock dividends can be paid.
- Like common stock, preferred stock carries a voting right to vote for director.
- Unlike common stock, there is no share in control of the firm.

- Like common stock dividends, preferred dividends can be omitted without bankrupting the firm.
- Financial analysts sometimes treat preferred stock as common stock.

Exhibit 2.19: Characteristics of preferred stock

Preferred stock is usually reported in the equity section of the balance sheet under "preferred stock" or "preferred equity." Accountants and financial analysts treat the preferred stock differently. Accountants treat preferred stock as equity and financial analysts treat it as equity or debt depending on who benefits from the analysis being made. Preferred stock has an advantage in that it has a higher priority claim than common stock (see Exhibit 2.20).

- Has priority over common stock in the assets and earnings
- Can be convertible into common stock
- May be participating
- Cumulative preferred dividends must be paid before common dividends are paid
- Can be treated as a debt due to redeemable feature
- Requires reporting to SEC about redeemable preferred and nonredeemable preferred

Exhibit 2.20: Features of preferred stock

KEY CONCEPTS TO REMEMBER: PREFERRED STOCK, WHOSE VIEWPOINT?

- From the common stockholders' point of view, preferred stock is similar to debt due to fixed dividend payment and reduced earnings for common stock.
- From the debt holder's point of view, preferred stock is similar to common equity due to the high priority of debt holders' claim on assets when the firm is liquidated.
- From management's point of view, preferred stock is safer to use than debt since it will not force them to bankruptcy for lack of dividend payment. Loan defaults would do otherwise.

Exhibit 2.21 shows the relative priorities over assets when the firm is in the liquidation stage.

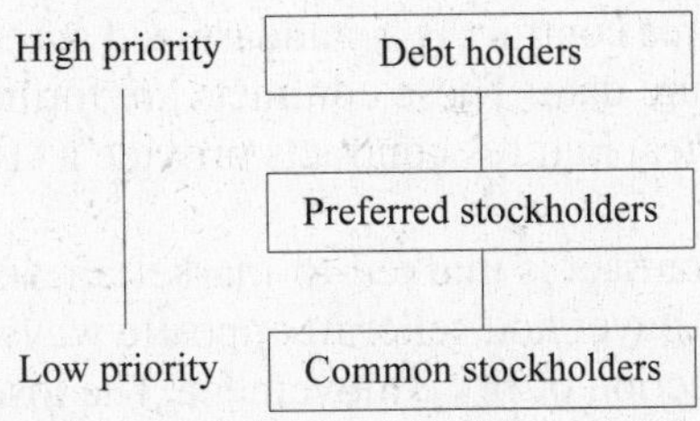

Exhibit 2.21: Relative priorities over assets

(A) ***Major provisions of preferred stocks.*** Major provisions include priority to assets and earnings, par value, cumulative dividends, convertibility into common stock, voting rights, participation in sharing the firm's earnings, sinking fund requirements, maturity date, and call provisions. Some of these provisions are expanded below; others are discussed elsewhere in the chapter.

- **Cumulative dividends.** All preferred dividends in arrears must be paid before common dividends can be paid. This is a protection feature for preferred stock to receive a preferred position and to avoid paying huge common stock dividends at the expense of paying stipulated annual dividend to the preferred stockholders.
- **Sinking fund.** Most newly issued preferred stocks have sinking fund requirements that call for the purchase and retirement of a given percentage (e.g., 2 to 3%) of the preferred stock each year.

- **Call provision.** A call provision gives the issuing corporation the right to call in the preferred stock for redemption. A call premium may be attached where a company has to pay more than par value when it calls the preferred stock.

(B) ***Pros and cons of preferred stock from issuer and investor viewpoints.*** From an issuer's viewpoint, the **advantages** of financing with preferred stock are: fixed financial cost, and no danger of bankruptcy if earnings are too low to meet fixed charges, and avoidance of sharing control of the firm with new investors.

From an issuer's viewpoint, the **disadvantage** of financing with preferred stock is a higher after-tax cost of capital than debt due to nondeductibility of preferred dividends. The lower a company's tax bracket, the more likely it is to issue preferred stock.

From an investor's viewpoint, the **advantages** of financing with preferred stock are: steadier and more assured income than common stock, preference over common stock in the case of liquidation, and tax exemption for preferred dividends received.

From an investor's viewpoint, the **disadvantages** of financing with preferred stock are: no legally enforceable right to dividends, even if a company earns a profit, and for individual investors, after-tax bond yields could be higher than those on preferred stock, even though the preferred stock is riskier.

2.7 Financial Instruments

Financial instruments (currency and credit derivatives) are used by large and small businesses in every industry to hedge against financial risk. One means to hedge currency exposure and risk is through currency market, which includes forward contracts, futures contracts, currency options, and currency swaps.

(a) Currency Derivatives

(i) **Forward contracts.** In the forward exchange market, one buys a forward contract for the exchange of one currency for another at a specific future date and at a specific exchange ratio. This differs from the spot market, where currencies are traded for immediate delivery. A forward contract provides assurance of being able to convert into a desired currency at a price set in advance. A foreign currency sells at a forward discount if its forward price is less than its spot price. If the forward price exceeds the spot price, it is said to sell at a forward premium. Forward contracts provide a "two-sided" hedge against currency movements. Forward contracts are settled only at expiration, and they can be issued at any size.

(ii) **Futures contracts.** A futures contract is a standardized agreement that calls for delivery of a currency at some specified future date. These contracts are formed with the clearinghouse, not directly between the two parties. Futures contracts provide a "two-sided" hedge against currency movements.

Each day, the futures contract is marked-to-market, meaning it is valued at the closing price. Price movements affect the buyer and seller in opposite ways. Every day there is a winner and a loser, depending on the direction of price movement. The loser must come up with more margin (a small deposit), while the winner can draw off excess margin. Future contracts come only in multiples of standard-size contracts.

(iii) **Options.** An option is a contract that gives its holder the right to buy or sell an asset at some predetermined price within a specified period of time. Pure options (financial options) are created by outsiders (investment banking firms) rather than by the firm itself; they are bought and sold by investors or speculators. The leverage involved makes it possible for speculators to make more money with just a few dollars. Also, investors with sizable portfolios can sell options against their stocks and earn the value of the options (minus brokerage commissions) even if the stocks' prices remain constant. Option contracts enable the hedging of "one-sided" risk. Only adverse currency movements are hedged, either with a call option to buy the foreign currency or with a put option to sell it.

Both the value of the underlying stock and the striking price of the option are very important in determining whether an option is in-the-money or out-of-the-money. If an option is out-of-the-money on its expiration date, it is worthless. Therefore, the stock price and the striking price are important for determining the market value of an option. In fact, options are called derivative securities because their values are dependent on, or derived from, the value of the underlying asset and the striking price. In addition to the stock's market price and the striking price, the value of an option also depends on the option's time to maturity, the level of strike price, the risk-free rate, and the variability of the underlying stock's price. The higher the strike price, the lower the call option price. The higher the stock's market price in relation to the strike price, the higher will be the call option price. The longer the option period, the higher the option price and the larger its premium. The exercise value of an option is the maximum of current price of the stock minus the strike price. The price of an option is the cost of stock minus the present value of portfolio. The Black-Scholes model is used to estimate the value of a call option.

Warrants are options issued by a company that give the holder the right to buy a stated number of shares of the company's stock at a specified price. Warrants are distributed along with debt, and they are used to induce investors (a sweetener) to buy a firm's long-term debt at a lower interest rate than otherwise would be required.

Real options are used for investment in real assets and their value is determined as follows:

Project discounted cash flow value = Cash flows divided by 1 plus risk-free cash flow.

(iv) **Swaps.** A swap exchanges a floating-rate obligation for a fixed-rate one, or vice versa. There are two types of swaps: currency swaps and interest-rate swaps. With the currency swaps, two parties exchange interest obligations on debt denominated in different currencies. At maturity the principal amounts are exchanged, usually at a rate of exchange agreed upon in advance. With an interest-rate swap, interest-payment obligations are exchanged between two parties, but they are denominated in the same currency. There is not an actual exchange of principal. If one party defaults, there is no loss of principal per se. However, there is the opportunity costs associated with currency movements after the swap's initiation. These movements affect both interest and principal payments. In this respect, the currency swaps are more risky than interest-rate swaps, where the exposure is only to interest. Currency swaps are combined with interest-rate swaps; there is an exchange of fixed-rate for floating-rate payments where the two payments are in different currencies. Financing hedges provide a means to hedge on a longer-term basis, as do currency swaps.

The swap can be longer term in nature (15 years or more) than either the forward or futures contract (five years). Swaps are like a series of forward contracts corresponding to the future settlement dates at which difference checks are paid. However, a comparable forward market does not exist, nor do lengthy futures or options contracts.

The most common swap is the floating/fixed-rate exchange. The exchange itself is on a net settlement basis. That is, the party that owes more interest than it receives in the swap pays the difference. A basis swap is another popular swap where two floating-rate obligations are exchanged.

Various options exist for swap transactions, which are known as swaptions. One is to enter a swap at a future date. The terms of the swap are set at the time of the option, and they give the holder the right, but not the obligation, to take a swap position.

(b) **Credit Derivatives**

(i) **Total return swaps.** Credit derivatives unbundle default risk from the other features of a loan. The original lender no longer needs to bear the risk; it can be transferred to others for a price. The party who wishes to transfer is known as the protection buyer. The protection seller assumes the credit risk and receives a premium for providing this insurance. The premium is based on the probability and likely severity of default.

The protection buyer is assumed to hold a risky debt instrument and agrees to pay out its total return to the protection seller. This return consists of the stream of interest payments together with the change in the instrument's market value. The protection seller agrees to pay some reference rate and perhaps a negative or positive spread from this rate.

(ii) **Credit swaps.** A credit swap, also known as a default swap, is similar in concept to the total-return swap, but different in the detail. The protection buyer pays a specific premium to the protection seller, insurance against a risky debt instrument deteriorating in quality. The annuity premium is paid each period until the earlier of the maturity of the credit swap agreement or a specific credit event occurring, usually default. If the credit event occurs, the protection seller pays the protection buyer a contingent amount. This often takes the form of physical settlement, where the protection buyer "puts" the defaulted obligation to the protection seller at its face value. The economic cash flow is the difference between the face value of the instrument and its market value. Thus, the protection buyer receives payment only when a specific credit event occurs; otherwise the cash flow from the protection seller is zero. The periodic premium paid is called the credit swap spread. This cost of protection depends on the credit rating of the company, risk mitigation, and likely recovery should default occur.

(iii) **Other credit derivatives. Spread adjusted notes** involve resets based on the spread of a particular grade of security over Treasury securities. An index is specified, and quarterly and semiannual resets occur, where one counterparty must pay the other depending on whether the quality yield spread widens or narrows. Usually the spread is collared with a floor and cap.

Credit options involve puts and calls based on a basket of corporate fixed-income securities. The strike price often is a specified amount over Treasury securities. With **credit-sensitive notes,** the coupon rate changes with the credit rating of the company involved. If the company is downgraded, the investor receives more interest income; if upgraded, less interest income.

GLOSSARY OF CURRENCY AND CREDIT DERIVATIVES

Abandonment options can be structured so that they provide the option to reduce capacity or temporarily suspend operations.

Basis risk is the difference between two risks or prices.

Call option is an option to buy (call) a share of stock at a certain price within a specific period.

A **call swaption** involves paying floating rate and receiving fixed rate in the swap.

A **cap** is a put option on a fixed-income security's value, whereas a **floor** is a call option.

A **collar** is a combination of a cap and a floor, with variation only in the midrange.

Flexibility options permit the firm to alter operations depending on how conditions change during the life of the project.

A **growth option** allows a company to increase its capacity if market conditions are better than expected. Variations of the growth options include: increasing the capacity of an existing product line, expanding into new geographic markets, and adding new products.

In-the-money option occurs when it is beneficial financially for the option holder to exercise the option. A gain will be realized if the option is exercised.

Interest rate risk is the risk that interest rates will change in an unfavorable direction.

Liquidity risk refers to the ability to find a counterparty to enter or terminate a transaction.

Managerial (strategic) options give managers a chance to influence the outcomes of a project. They deal with large and strategic projects.

Market risk is the risk that the value of the agreement will change.

Out-of-the-money option occurs when it is not beneficial financially for the option holder to exercise the option. A loss would be incurred if the option is exercised.

The **protection buyer** pays the protection seller to assume the credit risk.

Put option is the option to sell a specified number of shares of stock at a prespecified price during a particular period.

A **put swaption** involves paying fixed rate and receiving floating rate in the swap.

Striking price or exercise price is the price that must be paid (buying or selling) for a share of common stock when an option is exercised.

(c) **Hidden Financial Reporting Risk**. Off-balance-sheet accounting practices include: hiding debt with the equity method, hiding debt with lease accounting, hiding debt with pension accounting, and hiding debt with special-purpose entities. In all these cases, debt is underreported, which creates a financial reporting risk. Investors and creditors charge a premium for the financial reporting risk. Consequently, the cost of capital goes up and stock prices and bond prices go down.

The equity method hides liabilities because it nets the assets and liabilities of the investee. Since assets are greater than liabilities, this net amount goes on the left-hand side of the balance sheet. This type of accounting practice hides all of the investee's debts.

Use of operating lease accounting "gains" the managers an understatement of their firm's financial structure by 10 to 15 percentage points. Footnotes to financial statements can help investors, creditors, and analysts to unravel the truth.

Huge amounts of money are involved in pension accounting. Pension expenses include the service cost plus the interest on the projected benefit obligation minus the expected return on plan assets plus the amortization of various unrecognized items, such as the unrecognized prior service cost. The only item found on the balance sheet is the prepaid pension asset or the accrual pension cost, which in turn equals the pension assets minus the projected benefit obligation minus various unrecognized items. The netting of the projected benefit obligations and the pension assets is incorrect; consequently, investors, creditors, and analysts must "unnet" them to gain a better understanding of the truth. Another area of concern is the assumptions about interest rates and the need to assess their appropriateness.

Special-purpose entity debt includes securitizations and synthetic leases. Securitizations take a pool of homogeneous assets and turn them into securities. The idea is to borrow money from investors, who in turn are repaid by the cash generated by the asset pool. This process includes mortgages, credit card receivables, transportation equipment, energy contracts, water utilities, and trade accounts receivable. Securitizations are big business and represent a financial risk since these amounts are not shown in the balance sheet. Synthetic leases constitute a technique by which firms can assert that they have capital leases for tax purposes but operating leases for financial reporting purposes. They form a way for companies to decrease income taxes without admitting any debt on their balance sheets.

2.8 Cash Management

(a) **Cash Controls.** The standard medium of exchange is cash, which provides the basis for measuring and accounting for all other items. To be presented as cash on the balance sheet, it must be available to meet current obligations. Cash includes such items as coins, currency, checks, bank drafts, checks from customers, and money orders. Cash in savings accounts and cash in certificates of deposit maturing within one year can be included as current assets preferably under the caption of short-term investments, but not as cash. Petty cash and other imprest cash accounts can be included in other cash accounts.

Current assets are those assets expected to be converted into cash, sold, or consumed within one year or within the operating cycle, whichever is longer. Current assets are properly presented in the balance sheet in the order of their liquidity. Some of the more common current assets are cash, marketable securities, accounts receivable, inventories, and prepaid items.

(i) **Cash items excluded.** The portion of an entity's cash account which is a compensating balance must be segregated and shown as a noncurrent asset if the related borrowings are noncurrent liabilities. If the borrowings are current liabilities, it is acceptable to show the compensating balance as a separately captioned current asset.

RULES FOR COMPENSATED BALANCES

- If related borrowings are noncurrent liabilities, then show the compensated balance as a noncurrent asset.
- If related borrowings are current liabilities, then show the compensated balance as a current asset.

Certain cash items are not presented in the general cash section of the balance sheet. They include compensating balances, other restricted cash, and exclusions from cash.

(A) ***Compensating balances.*** The SEC defines compensating balances as: "that portion of any demand deposit (or any time deposit or certificate of deposit) maintained by a corporation which constitutes support for existing borrowing arrangements of the corporation with a lending institution. Such arrangements would include both outstanding borrowing and the assurance of future credit availability."

The classification of compensating balances on the balance sheet depends on whether the compensation relates to short-term or long-term borrowing. If held for short-term borrowing, it should be presented separately in current assets. If held for long-term borrowing, it should be classified as a noncurrent asset under Investments or Other Assets.

Where compensating balance arrangements exist but do not legally restrict the use of cash, the arrangements and amounts should be disclosed in the footnotes of the financial statements.

(B) ***Other restricted cash.*** Cash balances can be restricted for special purposes such as dividend payments, acquisition of fixed assets, retirement of debt, plant expansion, or deposits made in connection with contracts or bids. Since these cash balances are not immediately available for just any use, they should be presented separately in the balance sheet. Classification as current or noncurrent is dependent upon the date of availability or disbursement.

(C) ***Exclusions from cash.*** Items that should not be presented as cash are postage stamps, postdated checks, travel advances, IOUs, securities, investments in federal funds, and checks deposited and returned because of insufficient funds. Certificates of deposit should be reflected in the temporary investment account, since they are not available for use until the maturity date.

As mentioned earlier, cash includes coins and currency on hand and demand deposits available without restrictions. Cash in a demand deposit account which is being held for the retirement of long-term debts not maturing currently should not be included in the current assets. Instead, it should be shown as a noncurrent investment. The key criterion is management's intention that the cash be available for current purposes (SFAS 6). Cash equivalents include other forms of near-cash as well as demand deposits and liquid, short-term securities. *The key point is that the cash equivalents must be available on demand similar to cash.*

Suggested Disclosures for Cash

- The amount and nature of cash restricted
- The amount and nature of compensating balances
- Overdrafts should be presented as current liabilities

(ii) **Bank reconciliation.** Every organization should prepare a bank reconciliation schedule periodically (e.g., monthly) to reconcile the organization's cash record with the bank's record of the organization's cash. It is unusual that these two sets of records will be the same due to errors and timing differences such as

- Bank or depositor (customer) errors
- Bank credits
- Bank charges
- Deposits in transit
- Outstanding checks

A widely used method reconciles both the bank balance and the book balance to a correct cash balance. This is shown in Exhibit 2.22.

Balance per bank statement

Add:	Deposits in transit
	Undeposited cash receipts
	Bank errors (understating the bank balance)
Deduct:	Outstanding checks
	Bank errors (overstating the bank balance)

Correct cash balance (item 1)

Balance per depositors' books

Add:	Bank credits and collections not yet recorded in the books
	Book errors (understating the book balance)
Deduct:	Bank charges not yet recorded in the books
	Book errors (overstating the book balance)

Correct cash balance (item 2)

The goal is to make item 1 and item 2 equal.

Exhibit 2.22: Reconciliation of bank balance with book balance

Cash requires a good system of internal control, since it is so liquid and easy to conceal and transport. Segregation of duties is an important part of the system of internal control for cash. No one person should both record a transaction and have custody of the asset. Without proper segregation, it is easier for an employee to engage in lapping. **Lapping** is a type of fraud in which an employee misappropriates receipts from customers and covers the shortages in these customers' accounts with receipts from subsequent customers. Therefore, the shortage is never eliminated but transferred to other accounts. Lapping schemes do not require the employee to divert funds for his personal use. The funds can be diverted for other business expenses.

Kiting is a scheme in which a depositor with accounts in two or more banks takes advantage of the time required for checks to clear in order to obtain unauthorized credit. The scheme would be nonexistent if depositors were not allowed to draw against uncollected funds. The use of uncollected funds does not always indicate a kite; such use can be authorized by an officer of the bank. Kiting schemes can be as simple as cashing checks a few days before payday, then depositing the funds to cover checks previously written. Or, they can be as complex as a systematic build-up of uncollected deposits, pyramiding for the "big hit." Kiting can be eliminated or reduced through electronic funds transfer systems. Kiting can be detected when reviewing accounts to determine if a customer or employee is drawing a check against an account in which he has deposited another check that has not yet cleared.

Float is an amount of money represented by items (both check and noncheck) outstanding and in the process of collection. The amount of float incurred is determined by two factors: the dollar volume of checks cleared, and the speed with which the checks are cleared. The relationship between float and these two factors can be expressed as

$$\text{Float} = \text{Dollar volume} \times \text{Collection speed}$$

The cost of float pertains to the potential for earning income from nonearning assets, as represented by items in the process of collection. This cost of float is an opportunity cost—the firm could have fully invested and earned income had the funds been available for investment and not incurred float.

In a financial futures **hedging** transaction, a firm takes a futures position that is opposite to its existing economic, or more commonly called, "cash" position. By taking the opposite position in the financial futures market, the firm can protect itself against adverse interest rate fluctuations by locking in a given yield or interest rate.

(b) **Controls Over Cash.** Cash is a precious resource in any organization. Cash is required to pay employee wages and salaries, buy raw materials and parts to produce finished goods, pay off debt, and pay dividends, among other things. Cash is received from customers for the sale of goods and the rendering of services. Customer payments come into the organization in various forms such as checks, bank drafts, wire transfers, money orders, charge cards, and lockboxes. The cash manager's primary job is to ensure that all customer payments funnel into the company's checking accounts as fast as possible with greater accuracy. Payments received at lockboxes located at regional banks flow into cash concentration accounts, preferably on the same day of deposit.

The cash manager should focus on reducing the elapsed time from customer payment date to the day funds are available for use in the company's bank account. This elapsed time is called the "float."

A major objective of the cash manager is to accelerate the cash inflow and slow the cash outflow without damaging the company's reputation in the industry. To do this, the cash manager needs to find ways to accelerate cash flows into the company which, in turn, reduce investment in working capital. Similarly, the cash manager needs to find ways to slow the outflow of cash by increasing the time for payments to clear the bank. Another major objective is not to allow funds sitting idle without earning interest.

The cash manager needs to focus on the following seven major areas for effective cash management: (1) cash account balances, (2) purchases, (3) payables, (4) manufacturing, (5) sales, (6) receivables, and (7) lockbox systems (see Exhibit 2.23).

- Cash account balances
- Purchases
- Payables
- Manufacturing
- Sales
- Receivables
- Lockbox systems

Exhibit 2.23: Cash control items

(i) **Cash account balances.** The following actions are advised to strengthen controls in cash accounts:

- Take an inventory of cash accounts open. Since each account maintains cash balances, the potential exists to improve control over cash.
- Perform account reconciliations periodically and ensure that the person doing the reconciliation has no cash management duties.
- Review the account of compensating balances held at the banks. Focus on eliminating or reducing the amount of compensating balances.
- Review cash account balances to see if they are kept too high for fear of being overdrawn. Try to bring these balances down to the bare minimum without being overdrawn. This will improve the idle cash situation.
- Review the fees charged by the bank for the number of accounts open and understand the reasons for charging the service fees.

Cash Controls

The more accounts there are, the fewer the controls are over cash balances. Consequently, there is a higher likelihood that there will be significant idle funds sitting in those accounts.

(ii) **Purchases.** The method of payment and the payment date can impact the cash situation. An early payment date demanded by a vendor could add to the interest expense. Payment discounts should be taken by making payment within a specified time. The cash manager should review any purchase contracts containing clauses with unusual late fees and interest rates on unpaid balances.

(iii) **Payables.** The following actions are advised to strengthen controls in payables:

- Establish policies concerning the average payment period. The payment period is calculated by dividing the accounts payable balance by the average daily credit purchases.
- Use remote disbursement banks preferably with zero balance.
- Perform aging of the accounts payable periodically.

(iv) **Manufacturing.** The following actions are advised to strengthen controls in manufacturing:

- Be aware of labor union contract negotiations since their outcome will affect cash balances.
- Be aware of the sale of obsolete or overstocked inventory that will suddenly increase the inflow of cash that must be put to work (i.e., invested).

(v) **Sales.** Credit policies should be balanced. Overly lenient credit policies will cause a rise in payment delinquencies and bad debt. This will create a funding gap in the cash position.

- If bad debts are increasing due to lenient credit policies, see if sales force commission payment policy can be changed from a gross sales basis to a collected balances basis.
- If credit policies are overly stringent, the firm will lose its customers to competition.

(vi) **Receivables.** The following actions are advised to strengthen controls in receivables:

- Review billing and collection policies and procedures.
- Minimize the elapsed time between sale and release of invoice to the customer.
- Reduce the long time between invoice preparation and entry of the invoice into the receivables system.

- Identify receivable backlogs and determine their impact on cash position.
- Minimize the time that is required to record the payment and to remove it from the receivable subledger. If the time lag is too long, collection resources will be wasted pursuing accounts that have already paid.
- Perform aging of receivables.
- Establish procedures related to the types of collection efforts including customer statements, dunning letters, phone calls by trained in-house staff, referral to a collection agency, and so forth.
- Establish policies toward selling the receivables or clarify the policies toward using the receivables as collateral for financing purposes.

(vii) **Lockbox Systems.** Most banks offer both retail and wholesale lockbox services. Wholesale lockboxes collect payments from other companies where the volume of transactions is small and the dollar amount of each transaction is large. Retail lockboxes receive payments from individual customers where the volume of transaction is large and the dollar amount of each transaction is small.

Selection Criteria for Lockbox Banks

If the company has customers scattered around the country and payments are all sent to a single centralized location, use of a lockbox is advisable. Banks servicing the lockboxes are chosen for their proximity to the lockbox, their processing capability, their ability to transfer funds quickly to the cash concentration system, and geographic concentration of customers.

With the lockbox systems, most of the float has been squeezed from the cash management systems of both vendor and customer. These cash acceleration techniques have been referred to as a zero-sum game with no advantage for either side of the transaction (i.e., vendor and customer). Lockbox systems help sellers stay even with their customers in the race to accelerate cash inflow and delay its outflow. *Elimination of float accelerates cash inflow.*

Two types of lockbox systems are in use: manual and electronic. The **manual lockbox** system will collect and process the checks and deposit them into the customer's account. Then the bank sends the money to the cash concentration account and sends the payment information to the customer via a magnetic tape or telecommunication transmission for entry into the accounts receivable system. The funds are transferred from the lockbox account to the cash concentration account through the use of depository transfer checks, wire transfers, or electronic funds transfer through an automated clearinghouse.

Electronic lockboxes eliminate checks and automate the transfer payment data from company to company as a wholesale transaction. When a customer receives a vendor's invoice, the customer calls the third-party computer to make payment. The third party can be a bank or a service bureau, which acts as a payment collector. After the daily cutoff, the payment collector transmits the daily payment receipts file to the vendor's computer for processing by his accounts receivable system automatically.

Some **advantages** of an electronic lockbox system include: acceleration of cash inflow due to no float, misapplied and partial payments do not exist since the payment collector does not accept partial payment, and the customer account is verified prior to payment entry applied properly, information about nonsufficient funds comes back faster than for returned checks, credit controls can be tightened for high-risk or slow-paying customer, and reduces the days of sales outstanding ratio which measures the velocity of collections. **Disadvantages** include high initial system design cost and cost per transaction and service fees by the third-party payment collector.

(c) **Electronic Techniques to Control Cash.** In addition to the electronic lockboxes presented above, two other electronic techniques to control cash need to be mentioned. These include electronic funds transfer (EFT) and electronic data interchange (EDI) systems.

(i) **Electronic funds transfer.** Electronic funds transfer (EFT) systems allow organizations to pay their bills without actually writing checks. EFT eliminates bank float as "good" funds move quickly from customer accounts to vendor accounts at their respective banks. EFT accelerates cash inflow for the company receiving payment.

The EFT system removes several days from the entire payment cycle of cutting a paper check, mailing it, depositing it, clearing it through the bank, recording its payment in the customer's accounts payable system, and recording the cash receipts in the vendor's accounts receivable system. The only cycle time is the time for physically receiving the goods or services through truck, car, by rail, or other.

The automated clearing house (ACH) clears debits and credits created by electronic funds transactions. The ACH clears all transactions each day by properly debiting and crediting to the correct accounts. The ACH then routes these cleared transactions to the proper member banks.

(ii) **Electronic data interchange.** The electronic data interchange (EDI) system is another major step towards a payment acceleration scheme. EDI is not only used to place purchase orders with vendors for raw materials and finished goods, but also is used to send invoices and receive payments. The invoice is automatically created by the EDI system, which is then sent to the customer. After receiving the goods, the customer authorizes an electronic payment with virtually no float. EDI involves a third party as a middleperson to transmit and receive electronic messages between vendors and customers.

The data transferred between vendor and customer contains dollar amount information, invoice number, purchase order number, customer number, discounts taken, shipping instructions, product delivery dates, and payment due dates. Electronic payments are automatically posted to the vendor's accounts receivable system. A major **advantage** of EDI is that the posting is fast, not subject to human errors, and it accelerates cash inflows. A major **drawback** of the EDI system is the need to have a standardized format of data transmitted between vendors and customers. This could limit the flexibility of doing business with many parties.

(d) **Management of Current Assets.** Effective cash management requires a working capital policy, which refers to the firm's policies regarding the desired level for each category of current assets and how current assets will be financed. The components of current assets in the order of liquidity are shown in Exhibit 2.24.

- Cash (most liquid)
- Marketable securities
- Accounts receivable
- Prepaid expenses
- Inventories (least liquid)

Exhibit 2.24: Components of Current Assets

Current assets fluctuate with sales and represent a large portion (usually greater than 40%) of total assets. Working capital management is important for both large and small firms alike.

DEFINITION OF KEY TERMS

- Working capital means current assets (also gross working capital).
- Net working capital is current assets minus current liabilities.
- Working capital management involves the administration of current assets and current liabilities.

For financing current assets, most small firms rely on trade credit and short-term bank loans, both of which affect working capital by increasing current liabilities. Accounts payable represents "free" trade credit when discounts are taken. This is similar to an interest-free loan. However, current liabilities are used to finance current assets and in part represent current maturities of long-term debt. Large firms usually rely on long-term capital markets such as stocks. The components of current liabilities are shown in Exhibit 2.25 with their associated costs.

- Accounts payable (free trade credit)
- Accrued wages
- Accrued taxes
- Notes payable (not free)
- Current maturities of long-term debt

Exhibit 2.25: Components of current liabilities

The relationship between sales and the need to invest in current assets is direct, as shown below: As sales increase, accounts receivable increases, inventory will increase, and cash needs increase. Any increase in an account on the left-hand side of the balance sheet must be matched by an increase on the right-hand side. It involves matching maturities of assets and liabilities. That is, current assets are financed with current liabilities and fixed assets are financed with long-term debt or stock. This is to reduce interest rate risk.

COMPUTATION OF CHANGES IN CASH AND NET WORKING CAPITAL

Example 1: Partial balance sheet information for a company for the years ending December 31, 20X4 and 20X5 is as follows:

	December 31	
	20X5	*20X4*
Current assets (except for cash):		
Accounts receivable	$20,000	$ 5,000
Inventories	50,000	14,000
Prepaid expenses	3,000	6,000
Current liabilities:		
Accounts payable	32,000	16,000
Property tax payable	4,000	3,000

Working capital is assumed to increase in 20X5 by $12,000.

Question: What is the change in cash in 20X5?

Answer: The change is – $19,000, as shown below.

$$
\begin{aligned}
\Delta \text{ Cash } &= \Delta \text{ WC} - \Delta \text{ Noncash CA} + \Delta \text{ CL} \\
&= 12{,}000 - (15{,}000 + 36{,}000 - 3{,}000) \\
&\quad + (16{,}000 + 1{,}000) \\
&= -19{,}000
\end{aligned}
$$

Example 2: The following amounts pertain to the ABC Corporation at December 31, 20X5:

Total current assets	$ 300,000
Total fixed assets	2,200,000
Total assets	2,500,000
Total current liabilities	120,000
Total liabilities	1,600,000
Total paid-in capital	400,000
Total stockholders' equity	900,000

Question: What is the ABC's net working capital at December 31, 20X5?

Answer: It is $180,000. Net working capital is computed by subtracting total current liabilities ($120,000) from total current assets ($300,000), which in this case yields an answer of $180,000.

(i) **Cash conversion cycle model.** The cash conversion model defines the length of time from the payment for the purchase of raw materials to the collection of accounts receivable generated by the sale of the final product. It is an important model since it focuses on the conversion of materials and labor to cash. The model is represented in Exhibit 2.26.

Cash conversion cycle	=	Inventory conversion period (1)	+	Receivables conversion period (2)	–	Payables deferral period (3)

Where: (1) inventory conversion period is the length of time required to convert raw materials into finished goods and then to sell these goods; (2) receivable conversion period is the length of time required to convert the firm's receivables into cash; and (3) payables deferral period is the average length of time between the purchase of raw material and labor and the payment of cash for them.

Exhibit 2.26: Cash conversion model

The cash conversion cycle begins the day a bill for labor and/or supplies is paid and runs to the day receivables are collected. The cycle measures the length of time the firm has funds tied up in working capital. The shorter the cash conversion cycle, the smaller the need for external financing and thus the lower the cost of such financing. This would result in increase in profits.

CALCULATION OF CASH CONVERSION CYCLE

Example: It takes a firm 70 days from the purchase of raw materials to the sale of finished goods, 50 days after a sale to convert a receivable into cash, and 30 days to pay for labor and materials. Its cash conversion cycle is 90 days, as shown below.

70 days + 50 days – 30 days = 90 days or
(Delay in receipt of cash) – (Payment delay) = Net delay

The firm needs to finance the costs of processing for a 90-day period. Its goals should be to shorten its cash conversion cycle without jeopardizing business operations, (i.e., without increasing costs or decreasing sales).

(ii) **Approaches to shorten the cash conversion cycle.** The following list provides approaches to shorten the cash conversion cycle:

- Reduce the inventory conversion period by processing and selling goods more quickly.
- Reduce the receivables conversion period or days sales outstanding by speeding up collections.
- Lengthen the payables deferral period by slowing down payments.

(iii) **Working capital asset investment policies.** Appropriate working capital policies are needed to support various levels of sales. Three such policies include: (1) relaxed, (2) moderate, and (3) restricted (see Exhibit 2.27).

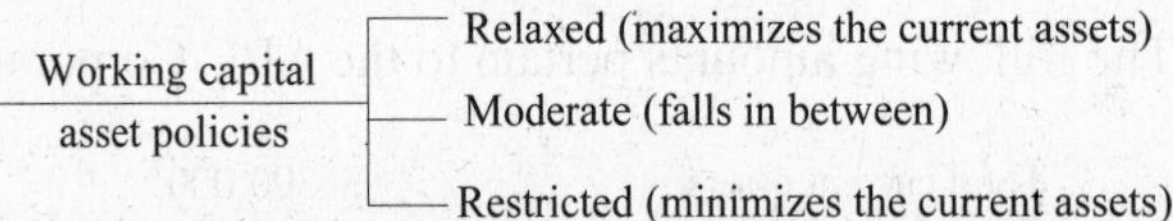

Exhibit 2.27: Working capital asset policies

- **Relaxed (liberal) working capital policy.** Sales are stimulated by the use of a credit policy that provides liberal financing to customers which results in a high level of accounts receivable. This is a policy which maximizes the current assets. Accounts receivable will increase as the credit sales increase for a relaxed policy and the opposite is true for the restricted policy.
- **Moderate working capital policy.** This is a policy which falls between liberal and tight working capital policy.
- **Restricted (tight) working capital policy.** A policy which minimizes current assets. A tight policy lowers the receivables for any given level of sales, or even the risk of a decline in sales. This policy provides the highest expected return of investment and entails the greatest risk. The firm would hold minimal levels of safety stocks for cash and inventories.

CERTAINTY VERSUS UNCERTAINTY OF BUSINESS CONDITIONS

- Under conditions of certainty, the firm knows the sales, costs, order lead times, and collection periods. All firms would hold the same level of current assets. Any larger amounts would increase the need for external funding without a corresponding increase in profits.

Any decrease in amounts would involve late payments to suppliers, lost sales, and production inefficiencies because of inventory shortages.

- Under conditions of uncertainty, the firm does not know the sales, costs, order lead times, and collection periods. The firm requires some minimum amount of cash and inventories based on expected payments, sales, safety stocks, order lead times. Safety stocks help deal with deviations of sales from expected values.

(iv) **Working capital financing policies.** A good working capital financing policy is needed to handle seasonal or cyclical business fluctuations and a strong or weak economy. When the economy is strong, the working capital is built up and inventories and receivables go up. When the economy is weak, the working capital goes down along with inventories and receivables. Current assets are divided into permanent and temporary, and the manner in which these assets are financed constitutes the firm's working capital financing policy.

A firm's working capital asset policy, including the cash conversion cycle, is always established in conjunction with the firm's working capital financing policy. Three financing policies are available to manage working capital, including maturity matching, aggressive approach, and conservative approach.

CALCULATION OF TOTAL ASSETS

Example:

	January 1 (million)	*June 30* (million)
Cash and marketable securities	4	4
Accounts receivable	6	8
Inventories	15	20
Current assets	25 (1)	32 (2)
Fixed assets	40	40
Total assets	65	72

(1) Permanent current assets that are still on hand at the trough of a firm's cycles.
(2) Temporary assets that fluctuate with seasonal or cyclical sales variation which fluctuate from zero to a maximum of $7 million (i.e., 32 – 25 = 7).

Maturity matching or "self-liquidating" approach requires that asset maturities are matched with liability maturities. This means permanent assets are financed with long-term capital to reduce risk. Each loan would be paid off with the cash flows generated by the assets financed by the loan, so loans would be "self-liquidating." Uncertainty about the lives of assets prevents exact matching in an *ex post* sense.

MATURITY MATCHING—ASSETS VERSUS DEBT

- If long-term assets are financed with short-term debt, there might be a problem in making the required loan payments if cash inflows are not sufficient. The loan may not be renewed.
- If long-term assets are financed with long-term debt, the required loan payments would have been matched with cash flows from profits and depreciation. No question of loan renewals will come up.

There are two approaches used in maturity matching: aggressive (nonconservative) approach and conservative approach. Exhibit 2.28 presents characteristics of these two approaches.

Characteristics of aggressive approach to maturity matching	*Characteristics of conservative approach to maturity matching*
• Financing of part of permanent current assets is accomplished with short-term credit. • Financing of all current assets and part of fixed assets is accomplished with short-term credit. • The borrower is exposed to the danger of missing interest payments and loan renewal problems. • There is a trade-off between safety and profits since short-term debt is cheaper than long-term debt. • The length of cash conversion cycle is shorter since the firm holds a minimal level of cash, securities, inventories, and receivables, inventories and receivables conversion periods would be shorter.	• Financing of all permanent assets is accomplished with long-term capital. • The firm uses a small amount of short-term credit to meet its peak requirements. • The length of cash conversion cycle is longer because higher levels of inventories and receivables lengthen the inventory and receivables conversion periods.

Exhibit 2.28: Characteristics of aggressive and conservative approaches to maturity matching

(v) **Advantages and disadvantages of short-term credit.** Short-term credit is generally riskier and cheaper than using long-term credit. There is a trade-off between risk and profits in using short-term credit. The three financing policies discussed above differ in the relative amount of short-term debt financing each uses, as shown in Exhibit 2.29.

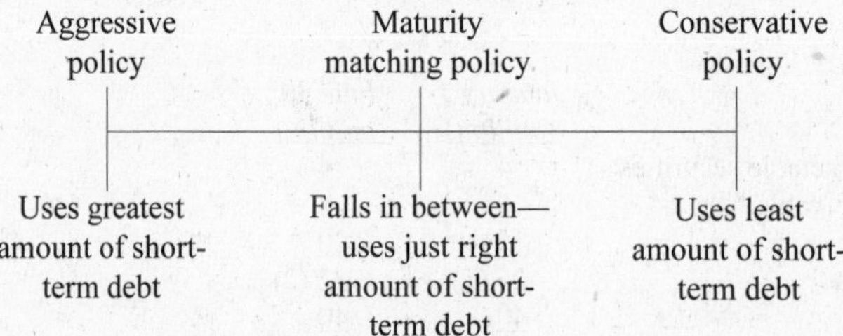

Exhibit 2.29: Advantages and disadvantages of short-term credit

Although short-term credit has disadvantages, it also has some advantages, as shown below.

(vi) **Management of cash.** On one hand, adequate cash serves as protection against a weak economy and can be used to pay off debts and to acquire companies. On the other hand, too much cash makes a firm vulnerable to corporate raiding or takeovers.

Cash = Currency + Bank demand deposits + Near-cash marketable securities
Near-cash marketable securities = US Treasury bills + Bank certificate of deposits, CD

Effective cash management is important to all organizations, whether profit-oriented or not. The scope of cash management encompasses cash gathering (collection) and disbursement techniques and investment of cash. Since cash is a "nonearning" asset until it is put to use, the goal of cash management is to reduce cash holdings to the minimum necessary to conduct normal business. See Exhibit 2.30 for advantages and disadvantages of short-term and long-term credit.

Advantages and disadvantages of short-term credit

Advantages

- A short-term loan can be obtained much more quickly than a long-term loan.
- A short-term loan can accommodate seasonal or cyclical needs for funds.
- It provides flexible repayment schedules.
- It has less restrictive provisions.
- Interest rates are generally lower than on long-term debt due to upward sloping of the yield curve.
- Financing is less expensive than long-term debt.
- Net income and the rate of return on equity will be higher than on long-term debt due to lower interest rates for short-term debt.

Disadvantages

- Short-term debt is subject to more risk (interest-rate risk) than long-term debt due to fluctuating interest expense and the possibility of bankruptcy.
- It runs the risk of having to refinance the short-term debt at a higher interest rate, which would lower the rate of return on equity.
- There is the possibility of being unable to renew the debt when its loans mature thus of facing "maturity risk." Also, tight money supply, labor problems, extreme competition, low demand for products, and higher interest rates will make the creditor raise the interest rates.

Advantages and disadvantages of long-term credit

Advantages

- Interest costs are fixed and stable over time.
- Long-term debt is subject to less risk than short-term debt.
- Temporary changes in either the general level of interest rates or the firm's own financial position do not adversely affect long-term debt.
- Long-run performance can overcome short-run recession.

Disadvantages

- Lenders will require thorough financial examination before granting a long-term loan, which takes time for approval.
- It requires a detailed loan agreement.
- Flotation costs are higher.
- Prepayment penalties can be expensive.
- It can contain provision or covenants that may constrain the firm's future actions.
- Interest rates are higher than on short-term debt due to downward sloping of the yield curve.

Exhibit 2.30: Advantages and disadvantages of short-term and long-term credit

There are four reasons for holding cash by organizations, as shown in Exhibit 2.31.

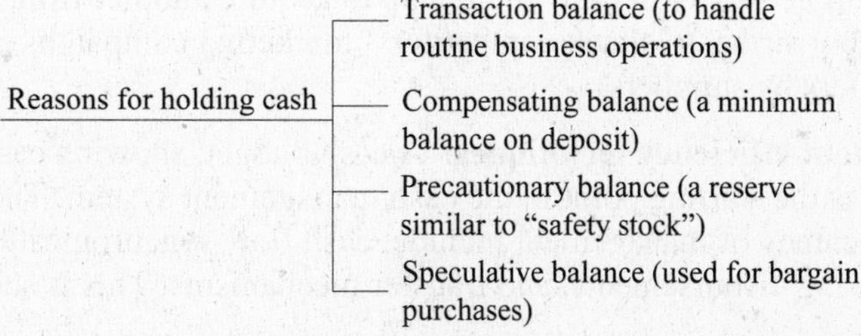

Exhibit 2.31: Reasons for holding cash

1. **Transaction balance.** Payments and collections are handled through cash account. These routine transactions are necessary in business operations.
2. **Compensating balance.** A bank requires the customer to leave a minimum balance on deposit to help offset the costs of providing the banking services. It is a compensation paid to banks for providing loans and services. Some loan agreements also require compensating balances.
3. **Precautionary balance.** Firms hold some cash in reserve to accommodate for random, unforeseen fluctuations in cash inflows and outflows. These are similar to the "safety stocks" used in inventories.

KEY CONCEPTS TO REMEMBER: MANAGEMENT OF CASH

- The less predictable the firm's cash flows, the longer the need for precautionary balance, and vice versa. The easier the access to borrowed funds on short notice, the lower the need to hold cash for precautionary purposes, and vice versa.
- Marketable securities can be an attractive alternative to holding cash for precautionary purposes since the former can provide greater interest income.

4. **Speculative balance.** Cash may be held to enable the firm to take advantage of any bargain purchases that might arise. Similar to precautionary balances, firms could rely on reserve borrowing capacity and on marketable securities than on cash for speculative purposes.

A total desired cash balance for a firm is not simply the addition of cash in transaction, compensating, precautionary, and speculative balances. This is because the same money often serves more than one purpose. For example, precautionary and speculative balances can also be used to satisfy compensating balance requirements. A firm needs to consider these four factors when establishing its target cash position.

(vii) **Advantages of holding adequate cash and near-cash assets.** In addition to the motives for transaction, compensating, precautionary, and speculative balances, firms do have other advantages for holding adequate cash and near-cash assets. These advantages include

- Taking trade discounts. Suppliers offer customers trade discounts—a discount for prompt payment of bills. Cash is needed to take advantage of trade discounts. Cost of not taking trade discounts could be high.
- Keeping current ratios and acid-test ratios in line with those of other firms in the industry requires adequate holdings of cash. Higher ratios give a strong credit rating. A strong credit rating enables the firm both to purchase goods and services from suppliers and provide favorable terms and to maintain an ample line of credit with the bank. A weak credit rating does the opposite.
- Holding ample supply of cash could help to acquire another firm, to handle contingencies such as labor strike, to attack competitors' marketing campaigns, and to take advantages of special offers by suppliers.

(viii) **Cash management efficiency techniques.** A cash budget, showing cash inflows and outflows and cash status, is the starting point in the cash management system. The techniques used to increase the efficiency of management include: cash flow synchronization, use of float, speeding collections, slowing disbursements, and transfer mechanisms. This is shown in Exhibit 2.32.

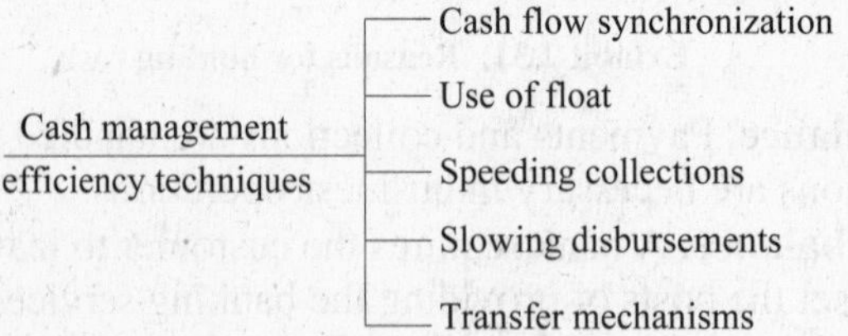

Exhibit 2.32: Cash management efficiency techniques

(A) ***Cash flow synchronization.*** By coinciding cash inflows with cash outflows, the need for transaction balances will be low. The benefits would be to reduce cash balances, decreased bank loan needs, reduced interest expenses, and increased profits.

(B) ***Use of float.*** Two kinds of float exist: disbursement float and collection float. The difference is net float. Disbursement float arises when one makes a payment by a check and is defined as the amount of checks that one has written but that are still being processed and thus have not yet been deducted from one's checking account balances by the bank. Collection float arises when one receives a check for payment and is defined as the amount of checks that one has received but which are in the collection process. It takes time to deposit the check, for the bank to process it, and to credit one's account for the amount collected.

$$\text{Net float} = \text{Disbursement float} - \text{Collection float}$$
$$\text{Net float} = \text{One's checkbook balance} - \text{Bank's book balance}$$

A positive net float is better than a negative net float because the positive net float collects checks written to a firm faster than clearing checks written to others. The net float is a function of the ability to speed up collections on checks received and to slow down collections on checks written. The key is to put the funds received to work faster and to stretch payments longer.

(C) ***Speeding collections.*** Funds are available to the receiving firm only after the check-clearing process has been completed satisfactorily. There is a time delay between a firm processing its incoming checks and its making use of them. Three parties are involved in the check-clearing process: the payer, payee, and the Federal Reserve System (requires a maximum of two days to clear the check). The length of time required for checks to clear is a function of the distance between the payer's and the payee's banks. The greater the distance, the longer the delay due to mail. If the payer's and the payee's bank are the same there is less delay than otherwise.

KEY CONCEPTS TO REMEMBER: TECHNIQUES TO SPEED UP COLLECTIONS

- Lockboxes are used to reduce mail delays and check-clearing delays. Both mail and check collection times are reduced using lockboxes. Lockboxes are mailboxes at the post office.
- Preauthorized debt (checkless transactions) allows funds to be automatically transferred from a customer's account to the firm's account on specified dates. Both mail and check-clearing times are eliminated. Examples include payroll checks, mortgage payments, tax bills, utility bills. The acceptance of a preauthorized debt system by customers is low due to loss of disbursement float and lack of canceled checks as receipt.
- Use of debit cards. Acceptance of debit cards is also low, but predictions are it will pick up in the future.

(D) ***Slowing disbursements.*** Three techniques are available to slow down disbursements. These include delaying payments, writing checks on banks in different locations, and using drafts. Delaying payments has negative consequences such as a bad credit rating. A firm can be sued by a customer for writing checks on banks in distant locations—playing west coast banks against east coast banks in the United States. Speeding the collection process and slowing down disbursements have the same objectives. Both keep cash on hand for longer periods.

Use of draft seems normal. A check is payable on demand, a draft is not. A draft must be transmitted to the issuer who approves it and then deposits funds to cover it, after which it can be collected.

(E) ***Transfer mechanisms.*** A transfer mechanism is a system for moving funds among accounts at different banks. Three types of transfer mechanisms are (1) depository transfer checks, (2) wire transfers, and (3) electronic depository transfer checks. Each is described below.

- A **depository transfer check (DTC)** is restricted for deposit into a particular account at a particular bank. A DTC is payable only to the bank of deposit for credit to the firm's specific account. DTCs provide a means of moving money from local depository banks to regional concentration banks, and to the firm's primary bank, as shown in Exhibit 2.33.

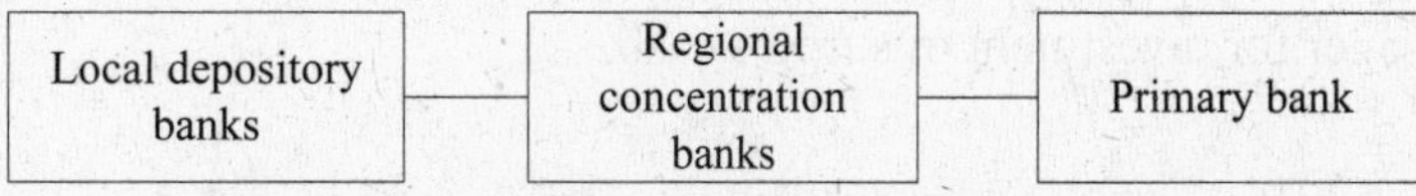

Exhibit 2.33: Movement of depository transfer checks

- **Wire transfer.** A wire transfer is the electronic transfer of funds via a telecommunications network that makes funds collected at one bank immediately available from another bank. The wire transfer eliminates transit float and reduces the required level of transaction and precautionary cash balances.
- The **electronic depository transfer check (EDTC)** is a combination of a wire transfer and a DTC. EDTC provides one-day availability in check clearing-time because it avoids the use of the mail. EDTC is a paperless transaction. EDTC is also called automated clearinghouse (ACH) which is a telecommunication network that provides an electronic means of sending data from one financial institution to another. Magnetic tape files are processed by the ACH and direct computer-to-computer links are also available.

(e) **Management of Marketable Securities.** Two basic reasons for holding marketable securities (e.g., US Treasury bills, commercial paper, and certificates of deposits) are: (1) they are used as a temporary investment, and (2) they serve as a substitute for cash balances. Temporary investment occurs when the firm must finance seasonal or cyclical operations, when the firm must meet some known financial requirements such as new plant construction program, a bond about to mature, quarterly tax payments, and when the proceeds from stocks and bonds are used to pay for operating assets.

Actually, it is a choice between taking out short-term loans or holding marketable securities. There is a trade-off between risks and return. Similar to cash management policy, a firm's marketable security policy should be an integral part of its overall working capital policy. The policy may be conservative, aggressive, or a moderate working capital financing policy (see Exhibit 2.34), as shown below.

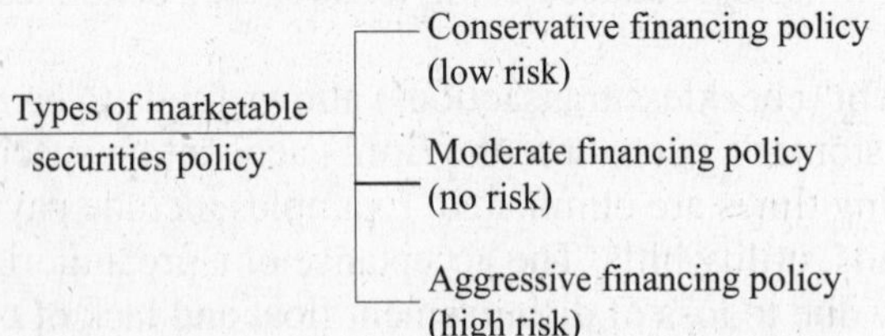

Exhibit 2.34: Types of Marketable Securities Policy

- If the firm has a **conservative working capital financing policy,** its long-term capital will exceed its permanent assets and it will hold marketable securities when inventories and receivables are low. This is a less risky one. There is no liquidity problem since the firm has no short-term debt. However, the firm incurs higher interest rates when borrowing than the return it receives from marketable securities. It is evident that a less risky strategy costs more.
- If the firm has a **moderate working capital financing policy,** the firm will match permanent assets with long-term financing, and meet most seasonal increases in inventories and receivables with short-term loans. The firm also carries marketable securities at certain times. With this policy, asset maturities are matched with those of liabilities. No risk exists, at least theoretically.
- If the firm has an **aggressive working capital financing policy,** it will never carry any securities and will borrow heavily to meet peak needs. This is the riskiest and it will face difficulties in borrowing new funds or repaying the loan, due to its low current ratio. The expected rate of return on both total assets and equity will be higher.

(i) **Criteria for selecting marketable securities.** The selection criteria for a marketable security portfolio include default risk, taxability, and relative yields. Several choices are available for the financial manager in selecting a marketable securities portfolio and they all differ in risk and return. Most financial managers are averse to risk and unwilling to sacrifice safety for higher rates of return. The higher a security's risk, the higher its expected and required return, and vice versa. A trade-off exists between risk and return.

Exhibit 2.35 presents the types of marketable securities that are available to the financial manager for investment of surplus cash.

Securities suitable to hold as near-cash reserve	*Securities not suitable to hold as near-cash reserve*
• Treasury bills	• US Treasury notes and bonds
• Commercial paper	• Corporate bonds
• Negotiable certificates of deposit (CDs)	• Common stock and preferred stock
• Money market mutual funds	• State and local government bonds
• Eurodollar time deposits	• All of the above with more than one year maturity
• All of the above with less than one year maturity	

Exhibit 2.35: Marketable securities available for investment of surplus cash

Large corporations tend to make direct purchases of US Treasury bills, commercial paper, certificate of deposits, and Eurodollar time deposits. Small corporations are more likely to use money market mutual funds as near-cash reserves (because it can be quickly and easily converted to cash). Interest rates on money market mutual funds are lower and net returns are higher than the Treasury bills.

(ii) **Risks in marketable securities.** Let us review the different types of risk (i.e., default risk, interest rate risk, purchasing power risk, and liquidity risk) facing the financial manager in managing the portfolio of marketable securities (see Exhibit 2.36).

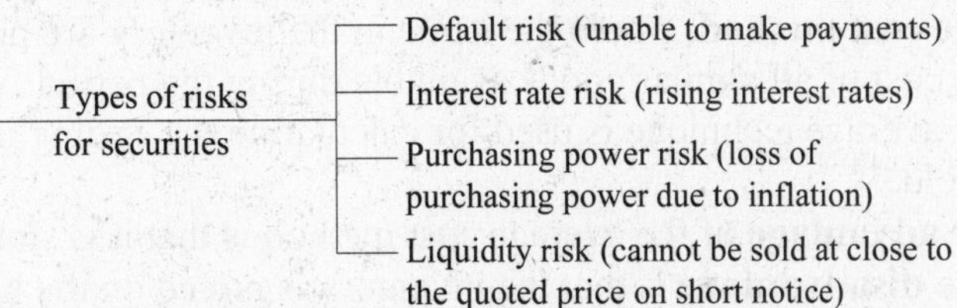

Exhibit 2.36: Risks in marketable securities

(A) ***Default risk.*** The risk that a borrower will be unable to make interest payments or to repay the principal amount upon maturity is known as default risk. For example, the default risk for securities issued by the US Treasury is negligible while securities issued by a corporation and others have some degree of default risk.

The higher the earning power of a firm, the lower its default risk and vice versa.

(B) ***Interest rate risk.*** The risk to which investors are exposed due to rising interest rates is known as interest rate risk. It is the interest rate fluctuations that cause the interest rate risk. Even US Treasury bonds are subject to interest rate risk.

Bond prices vary with changes in interest rates. Long-term bonds have more interest rate risk. Short-term bonds have less interest rate risk.

(C) ***Purchasing power risk.*** The risk that inflation will reduce the purchasing power of a given sum of money is known as purchasing power risk. Purchasing power risk is lower on assets whose returns tend to rise during inflation. Purchasing power risk is higher on assets whose returns are fixed during inflation. So it is the variability of returns during inflation that determines the purchasing power risk.

Real estate, short-term debt, and common stocks are better hedges against inflation. Bonds and other long-term fixed-income securities are not better hedges against inflation.

(D) ***Liquidity (marketability) risk.*** The risk that securities cannot be sold at close to the quoted market price on short notice is known as liquidity risk. For example, securities issued by the US Treasury and larger corporations have little liquidity risk while securities issued by small and unknown companies are subject to liquidity risk. Illiquidity of a firm is the situation where the firm's maturing obligations are greater than the cash immediately available to pay.

An asset that can be sold quickly for close to its quoted price is highly liquid. An asset that cannot be sold quickly and is sold at a reduced price is not highly liquid.

(iii) **Inventory management.** Inventories are least liquid because they take a long time to convert into cash. They can be damaged, spoiled, or stolen.

2.9 Valuation Models

(a) **Inventory Valuation.** ARB 43 defines inventory as "the sum of those items of tangible personal property which are held for sale in the ordinary course of business, in process of production for sale, or to be currently consumed in the production of goods for sale." The three types of manufacturing inventory are raw materials, work in process (WIP), and finished goods, and is the largest current asset. An AICPA committee said "A major objective of accounting for inventories is the proper determination of income through the process of matching appropriate costs against revenues."

(i) **Inventory cost flow methods.** Five inventory costing methods are used based on differing inventory flow assumptions.

1. **Specific identification method,** where the cost of the specific items sold are included in the cost of goods sold, while the costs of the specific items on hand are included in the inventory. This method is used for valuing jewelry, fur coats, automobiles, and high-priced furniture.

   Advantages are accuracy; if done properly, cost flow matches the physical flow of the goods. **Disadvantages** are that it requires detailed recordkeeping, and elaborate manual and/or computer systems.

2. **Average cost method,** where the items in the inventory are priced on the basis of the average cost of all similar goods available during the period. Weighted-average method or moving-average technique is used for calculating the ending inventory and the cost of goods sold.

   The **advantage** of the average cost method is that it is simple to apply and it is objective. The **disadvantage** is that the inventory is priced on the basis of average prices paid which is not realistic.

3. **First-in, first-out (FIFO) method,** where goods are used in the order in which they are purchased; the first goods purchased are the first used. The inventory remaining must represent the most recent purchase. Cost flow matches the physical flow of the goods, similar to the specific identification method.

   An **advantage** of the FIFO method is that the ending inventory is close to current cost and provides a reasonable approximation of replacement cost on the balance sheet when price changes have not occurred since the most recent purchases.

   A **disadvantage** of FIFO is that current costs are not matched against current revenues on the income statement. The oldest costs are charged against the more current revenue, which can lead to distortions in gross profit and net income. This creates transitory or inventory profits ("paper profits").

4. **Last-in, first-out (LIFO) method,** where it matches the cost of the last goods purchased against revenue. The ending inventory would be priced at oldest unit cost. LIFO is the most commonly used method.

   The LIFO method matches the cost of the last goods purchased against revenue, and the ending inventory is costed at the oldest units remaining in the inventory. In other words, in LIFO, the inventory with current costs becomes part of the cost of goods sold for the current period, and this cost of goods sold is matched against revenues and sales for that current period. Ending inventory contains the oldest inventory with the oldest costs.

   LIFO **advantages** include

   - During periods of inflation, current costs are matched against current revenues and inventory profits are thereby reduced. Inventory profits occur when the inventory costs matched against sales are less than the inventory replacement cost. The cost of goods sold is understated and profit is considered overstated.
   - Lower tax payments. The tax law requires that if a firm uses LIFO for tax purposes, it must also use LIFO for financial accounting and reporting purposes.
   - Improved cash flow due to lower tax payments, which could be invested for a return unavailable to those using FIFO.

LIFO **disadvantages** include

- Lower profits reported under inflationary times. The company's stock could fall.
- Inventory is understated on the balance sheet because the oldest costs remain in ending inventory. This understatement of inventory makes the working capital position of the firm appear worse than it really is.
- LIFO does not approximate the physical flow of the items.
- LIFO falls short of measuring current cost (replacement cost) income though not as far as FIFO.
- Manipulation of income at the end of the year could occur by simply altering a firm's pattern of purchases.

5. **Next-in, first-out (NIFO) method,** which is not currently acceptable for purposes of inventory valuation. NIFO uses replacement cost. When measuring current cost income, the cost of goods sold should consist not of the most recently incurred costs but rather of the cost that will be incurred to replace the goods that have been sold.

KEY CONCEPTS TO REMEMBER: INFLATION, LIFO, FIFO, AND TAXES

- During general and prolonged inflation, income tends to be overstated because of holding gains.
- The LIFO method results in a significantly understated value of inventory when prices move up steadily. LIFO helps to exclude inventory profits from the determination of net income, resulting in lower income.
- During a period of rising prices, taxable income and income taxes are reduced through the use of LIFO.
- Under LIFO, the most recent costs of goods acquired are assigned to cost of goods sold, thus resulting in a more realistic matching of costs and revenues.
- Under the FIFO method the inventory is valued at the most recently incurred costs; thus the cost assigned to inventory tends to be relatively close to current replacement cost. Earliest costs are assigned to the cost of goods sold, thus resulting in the reporting of holding gains in net income.
- During a period of rising prices, taxable income and income taxes are increased through the use of FIFO.
- The FIFO method results in a significantly overstated value of inventory when prices move up steadily.
- During inflationary periods, LIFO is usually considered preferable to FIFO. However, with LIFO, in reviewing a company's financial statements, a major problem exists in evaluating inventory on the balance sheet.

(ii) **Inventory valuation methods.** Generally, **historical cost** is used to value inventories and cost of goods sold. In certain circumstances, though, departure from cost is justified. Some other methods of costing inventory include the following:

- **Net realizable value.** Damaged, obsolete, or shopworn goods should never be carried at an amount greater than net realizable value. Net realizable value is equal to the estimated selling price of an item minus all costs to complete and dispose of the item.
- **Lower of cost or market.** If the value of inventory declines below its historical cost, then the inventory should be written down to reflect this loss. A departure from the historical cost principle is required when the future utility of the item is not as great as its original cost. When the purchase price of an item falls, it is assumed that its selling price has fallen or will fall. The loss of the future utility of the item should be charged against the revenues of the period in which it occurred. Market in this context generally means the replacement cost of the item.

However, **market cost is limited by a floor and ceiling cost**. Market cannot exceed net realizable value, which is the estimated selling price minus the cost of completion and disposal (ceiling). Market cannot be less than net realizable value minus a normal profit margin (floor). Lower of cost or market can be applied to each inventory item, each inventory class, or total inventory.

EFFECTS OF INVENTORY ERRORS

- If ending inventory is overstated, assets, gross margin, net income, and owners' equity will be overstated, and cost of goods sold will be understated.
- If ending inventory is understated, assets, gross margin, net income, and owners' equity will be understated, and cost of goods sold will be overstated.

(iii) **Inventory estimation methods.** An organization may estimate its inventory to compare with physical inventories to determine whether shortages exist, to determine the amount of inventory destroyed in a fire or stolen, or to obtain an inventory cost figure to use in monthly or quarterly (interim) financial statements. Two methods of estimating the cost of ending inventory are (1) the gross margin method and (2) the retail inventory method (see Exhibit 2.37).

- Gross margin method (establishes a relationship between gross margin and sales; prior period gross margin rates are used to estimate the current inventory cost)
- Retail inventory method (establishes a relationship between prices and costs; cost/price ratio is used to estimate the current inventory cost)

Exhibit 2.37: Inventory estimation methods

The **gross margin method** is based on the assumption that the relationship between gross margin and sales has been fairly stable. Gross margin rates from prior periods are used to calculate estimated gross margin. The estimated gross margin is deducted from sales to determine estimated cost of goods sold. Estimated cost of goods sold is then deducted from cost of goods available for sale to determine estimated inventory cost.

The **retail inventory method** is used by organizations that mark their inventory with selling prices. These prices are converted to cost using a cost/price (cost-to-retail) ratio. The cost/price ratio is simply what proportion cost is to each sales dollar. This cost/price ratio is applied to ending inventory stated at retail prices to estimate the cost of ending inventory.

The proper treatment of net additional markups and markdowns in the cost-to-retail ratio calculation is to include the net additional markups in the ratio and to exclude net markdowns. This approach approximates the lower-of-average-cost-or-market valuation.

CALCULATION OF INVENTORY LOST DUE TO FIRE

Example: A division of a company experienced a fire in 20X5, which destroyed all but $6,000 of inventory (at cost). Data available is below.

	20X4	*20X5 (to date of fire)*
Sales	$100,000	$40,000
Purchases	70,000	35,000
Cost of goods sold		60,000
Ending inventory		10,000

Question: What is the approximate inventory lost to the fire in 20X5?

Answer: Inventory lost to the fire is $15,000, as shown below.

20X5 sales	$40,000
20X5 cost of goods sold using 20X4 ratio	
($60,000/$100,000) × $40,000 =	$24,000 Cost of goods sold
	$10,000 Beginning inventory 20X5
	$35,000 Purchases in 20X5
	$45,000 Goods available for sale in 20X5
	$24,000 Cost of goods sold in 20X5
	$21,000 Ending inventory in 20X5
	$ 6,000 Undestroyed inventory in 20X5
	$15,000 Destroyed inventory in 20X5

(b) **Financial Asset Valuation.** Policy decisions that are most likely to affect the value of the firm include: investment in a project with large net present value, sale of a risky operating division that will now increase the credit rating of the entire company, and use of more highly leveraged capital structure that results in a lower cost of capital.

Establishing or predicting the value of a firm is an important task of the financial manager since maximizing the value of his firm is a major goal. Here the focus is on maximizing shareholders' wealth. Similar to capital budgeting decisions, the financial manager can use "discounted cash flow" (DCF) techniques to establish the worth of any assets (e.g., stocks, bonds, real estate, equipment) whose value is derived from future cash flows. *The key concept of DCF is that it takes time value of money into account. The value of a firm is a combination of bond valuation, common stock valuation, and preferred stock valuation* (see Exhibit 2.38).

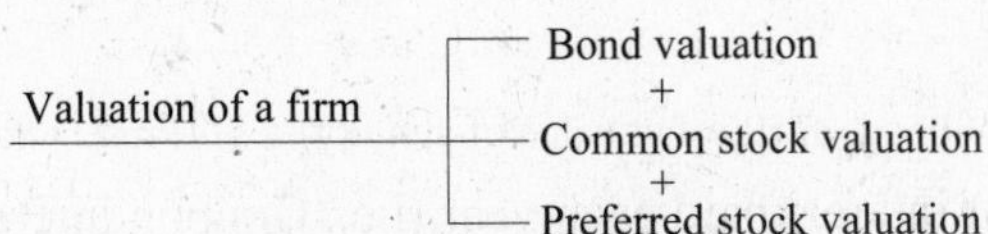

Exhibit 2.38: Valuation of a firm

(i) **Bond valuation.** A bond valuation model shows the mathematical relationships between a bond's market price and the set of variables that determine the price. For example, bond prices and interest rates are inversely related. Corporate bonds are traded in the over-the-counter market.

DEFINITION OF KEY TERMS: BONDS

- Most bonds have a *call provision,* which allows the issuer to pay off (redeem) the bond prior to its maturity date. This gives flexibility to an issuer where he can substitute low-interest-rate bonds for high-interest-rate bonds. When interest rates decline, he can sell a new issue of low-interest-rate bonds and use the proceeds to retire the old high-interest-rate bond.
- The *coupon interest payment* is the specified number of dollars of interest paid each period on a bond.
- *Coupon interest rate* is the coupon interest payment divided by the par value. It is the stated amount rate of interest on a bond and remains fixed.
- The *maturity date* of a bond is a specified date on which the par value must be repaid.
- The *par value* is the stated face value of the bond. The par value represents the amount of money the firm borrows and promises to repay at some future date (i.e., maturity date)
- The bond with shorter (e.g., one year) maturity exposes the buyer to more *reinvestment rate risk* than a bond with longer maturity (e.g., 10 years). It is the risk that income will decline when the funds received from maturing short-term bonds are reinvested.
- *Yield to call* is the rate of return earned on a bond if it is called before the maturity date.
- *Yield to maturity* is the rate of return earned on a bond if it is held to maturity.

Treasuries raise money by issuing bonds, and offering common equity. A bond that has just been issued is known as a new issue. Newly issued bonds are sold close to par value. A bond that has been on the market for a while is called a seasoned issue and is classified as an outstanding bond. The prices of outstanding bonds vary from par value. A bond's market price is determined primarily by its coupon interest payments. The coupon interest payment is set at a level that will cause the market price of the bond to equal its par value.

KEY CONCEPTS TO REMEMBER: BOND VALUATION

- The higher the coupon interest payment, the higher the market price of the bond.
- The lower the coupon interest payment, the lower the market price of the bond.
- At constant coupon interest payment and changing economic conditions, the market price of the bond is more or less equal to its par value.
- A bond's interest rate depends on its riskiness, liquidity, year-to-maturity, and supply and demand conditions of money in the capital markets.

A bond represents an annuity (i.e., interest payments) plus a lump sum (i.e., repayment of the par value), and its value is found as the present value of this payment stream. The equation to find a bond's value is

Value of bond = I (Present value of annuity) + M (Present value of lump sum)

Where I is dollars of interest paid each year (i.e., Coupon interest rate × Par value = Coupon interest payment), and M is par (maturity) value.

Both the present value of the annuity and the lump sum amount are discounted at an appropriate rate of interest (*Kd*) on the bond for a number of years (n) until the bond matures. The value of n declines each year after the bond is issued.

PREMIUM VERSUS DISCOUNT OF A BOND

- When the interest rates fall after bonds are issued, the value of the firm's bonds would increase, and the bond would sell at a premium or above its par value.

  Bond premium = Bond price + Par value
- When the interest rates rise after bonds are issued, the value of the firm's bonds would decline, and the bonds would sell at a discount, below its par value.

  Bond discount = Bond price – Par value

The discount or premium on a bond may be calculated as follows:

Discount or premium = (Interest payment on the old bond – Interest payment on the new bond) × Present value of annuity

The present value is calculated for n years to maturity on the old bond and at current rate of interest (*Kd*) on a new bond. Total rate of return or yield on a bond is equal to Interest (current yield) + Current gains yield.

A graph can be drawn to show the values of a bond in relation to interest rate changes. Note that regardless of what the future interest rates are, the bond's market value will always approach its par value as it nears the maturity date except in bankruptcy. If the firm went bankrupt, the value of the bond might drop to zero.

KEY CONCEPTS TO REMEMBER: INTERRELATIONSHIPS BETWEEN THE COUPON INTEREST RATE, PAR VALUE, AND GOING RATE OF INTEREST

- Whenever the going rate of interest is equal to the coupon interest rate, a bond will sell at its par value.
- Whenever the going rate of interest is greater than the coupon rate, a bond will sell below its par value. This bond is called a discount bond.
- Whenever the going rate of interest is less than the coupon rate, a bond will sell above its par value. This bond is called a premium bond.
- The longer the maturity of the bond, the greater its price changes in response to a given change in interest rates.
- An increase in interest rates will cause the price of an outstanding bond to fall.

- A decrease in interest rates will cause the price of an outstanding bond to rise.
- Those who invest in bonds are exposed to interest rate risk, that is, a risk due to changing interest rates.
- The bond with a longer maturity is exposed to more risk from a rise in interest rates.

(ii) **Common stock valuation.** Investors buy common stock for two main reasons: (1) to receive dividends, and (2) to enjoy capital gain. Dividends are paid to stockholders at management's discretion since there is no legal obligation to pay dividends. Usually stockholders have an expectation to receive dividends even though in reality they may not. If the stock is sold at a price above its purchase price, the investor will receive a capital gain. Similarly, if the stock is sold at a price below its purchase price, the investor will suffer capital losses.

The value of a common stock is calculated at the present value of the expected future cash flow stream (i.e., expected dividends, original investment, and capital gain or loss). Different aspects of these cash flow streams is the determination of the amount of cash flow and the riskiness of the amounts, and knowing what alternative actions affect stock prices.

Next, the stock values are determined using four different scenarios.

(A) ***Scenario 1: Expected dividends as the basis for stock values***

$$\text{Value of stock (Po)} = \sum \frac{Dt}{(1+Ks)^t}$$

Where *Po* is the actual market price of the stock today, *Dt* is the dividend the stockholder expects to receive at the end of year *t* and *t* can vary from one year to infinity and *Ks* is the minimum acceptable or required rate of return on the stock.

(B) ***Scenario 2: Stock values with zero growth.*** A stock reaches a zero growth stage (i.e., $g = 0$) when future dividends are not expected to grow at all (i.e., $D1 = D2 = D3 .. Dn$). Dividends will be constant over time. The value of a zero growth stock is defined as $Po = D/Ks$. Zero growth stock is a perpetuity since it is expected to pay a constant amount of dividend each year.

(C) ***Scenario 3: Stock values with normal growth.*** Most firms experience an increase in earnings and dividends while some firms may not. Dividends growth rate is expected to be equal to nominal gross national product (i.e., real GNP + Inflation). The value of a stock with normal (constant) growth is defined by Myron Gordon as $Po = D1/(Ks - g)$, which is called the Gordon model. The investor's required rate of return on the firm's stock is used in determining the value of a stock when using the Gordon model. This, in turn, is used to calculate the cost of equity.

KEY CONCEPTS TO REMEMBER: COMMON STOCK VALUATION

- A company's stock price decreases as a result of the increase in nominal interest rates.
- Growth in dividends occurs as a result of growth in earnings per share (EPS).
- Earnings growth, in turn, results from the following factors:
  - Inflation. If output is stable and if both sales prices and input costs rise at the inflation rate, then EPS will grow at the inflation rate.
  - The amount of earnings the firm reinvests. EPS will grow as a result of retained earnings.
  - The rate of return the firm earns on its equity.

(D) ***Scenario 4: Stock values with supernormal growth.*** Some companies experience supernormal (non constant) growth where its growth rate is much faster than that of the economy as a whole. The growth rate depends on the actual stage of the company in its business cycle (i.e., introduction, mature).

STOCK PRICES VERSUS GROWTH RATES

- The stock price of a zero growth firm is expected to be constant.
- The stock price of a declining firm is expected to be falling.
- The stock price of a constant growth firm is expected to grow at a constant rate.
- The stock price of a supernormal growth firm is expected to be higher in the beginning and then declines as the growth period ends.

(iii) **Preferred stock valuation.** As mentioned earlier, preferred stock is a hybrid stock—has elements of both bonds and common stock. Most preferred stocks entitle their owners to regular fixed dividend payments. The value of the preferred stock can be found as follows:

$$\text{Vps} = \frac{\text{Dps}}{\text{Kps}}$$

Where Vps is the value of the preferred stock, Dps is the preferred dividend, and Kps is the required rate of return on preferred stock.

(c) **Business Valuation.** Business valuation is valuing the worth of a business entity, whether in whole or part. The value of a business is derived from its ability to generate cash flows consistently period after period over the long term. Business valuation can be performed at various milestones such as new product introduction; mergers, acquisitions, divestitures, recapitalization, and stock repurchases; capital expenditures and improvements; joint venture agreements; and ongoing review of performance of business unit operations.

There are eleven models to help management in making sound decisions during valuation of a business opportunity. These models, in the order of importance and usefulness, include: (1) book value model, (2) liquidation value model, (3) replacement cost model, (4) discounted abnormal earnings model, (5) price multiples model, (6) financial analysis model, (7) economic-value-added model, (8) market-value-added model, (9) economic profit model, (10) net present value model, and (11) discounted cash flow model. Each model will be discussed next.

(i) **Book value model.** The book value (net worth, net assets, or stockholders' equity) of a company's stock represents the total assets of the company less its liabilities. The book value per share has no relation to market value per share, as book values are based on historical cost of assets, not at the current value at which they could be sold. Book values are not meaningful because they are distorted by inflation factors and different accounting assumptions used in valuing assets. One use of book value is to provide a floor value, with the true value of the company being some amount higher. Sales prices of companies are usually expressed as multiples of book values within each industry.

(ii) **Liquidation value model.** Liquidation value of a firm is total assets minus all liabilities and preferred stock minus all liquidation costs incurred. Liquidation value may be a more realistic measure of a firm than its book value in that liquidation price reflects the current market value of the assets and liabilities if the firm is in a growing, profitable industry. Depending on the power of negotiations, the liquidation prices may be set at "fire sale" prices.

(iii) **Replacement cost model.** The replacement cost model is based on the estimated cost to replace a company's assets, which include both tangible (plant, equipment) and intangible assets (patents, copyrights). Only tangible assets are replaceable, not the intangible ones. Because of this, the replacement cost is lower than the market value of the company; sometimes it could be higher than the market value.

(iv) **Discounted abnormal earnings model.** If a firm can earn only a normal rate of return on its book value, then investors will pay no more than the book value. Abnormal earnings are equal to total earnings minus normal earnings. The estimated value of a firm's equity is the sum of the current book values plus the discounted future abnormal earnings.

(v) **Price multiples model.** The value of a firm is based on price multiples of "comparable" firms in the industry. This model requires calculation of the desired price multiples and then applying the multiple to the firm being valued. Examples of price multiples include price-to-earnings (P/E) ratio, price-to-book ratio, price-to-sales ratio, price-to-cash-flow ratio, and market-to-book ratio.

(vi) **Financial analysis model.** Financial analysis includes ratio analysis and cash flow analysis. In ratio analysis, the analyst can compare ratios for a firm over several years, compare ratios for the firm and other firms in the industry, and compare ratios to some benchmark data. While ratio analysis focuses on analyzing a firm's income statement or its balance sheet, the cash flow analysis will focus on operating, investing, and financing policies of a firm by reviewing its statement of cash flows. Cash flow analysis also provides an indication of the quality of the information in the firm's income statement and balance sheet.

(vii) **Economic-value-added model.** Economic-value-added (EVA) is operating profit minus a charge for the opportunity cost of capital. An advantage of the EVA method is its integration of revenues and costs of short-term decisions into long-term capital budgeting process. A disadvantage of EVA is that it focuses only on a single period and that it does not consider risk. The EVA model can be combined with market-value-added model to address this disadvantage. The formula for calculating the EVA is operating profit minus (weighted-average cost of capital multiplied by capital invested).

(viii) **Market-value-added model.** Market-value-added (MVA) model is the difference between the market value of a company's debt and equity and the amount of capital invested since its origin. The MVA measures the amount by which stock market capitalization increases in a period. Market capitalization is simply the number of shares outstanding multiplied by share price. MVA is calculated as follows: present value of debt plus market value of equity minus capital invested.

(ix) **Economic profit model.** According to the economic profit model, the value of a company equals the amount of capital invested plus a premium equal to the present value of the cash flows created each year. Economic profit measures the value created in a company in a single period and it is calculated as follows: invested capital multiplied by (return on invested capital minus weighted-average cost of capital).

(x) **Net present value model.** Basically, the net present value (NPV) model compares the benefits of a proposed project or firm with the costs, including financing costs, and approves those projects or firms whose benefits exceed costs. The NPV model incorporates the time value of money and the riskiness of the cash flows, which are the vital elements of a valuation model. The approach is to calculate the NPV of each alternative and then select the alternative with the highest NPV. NPV is calculated as follows: present value of all cash inflows minus present value of all cash outflows.

(xi) **Discounted cash flow model.** The total value of a firm is value of its debt plus value of its equity. The discounted cash flow (DCF) model goes beyond the NPV model and uses free cash flows. The DCF model focuses on discounting cash flows from operations after investment in working capital, less capital expenditures. The model does not consider interest expenses and cash dividends.

The calculation involves the generation of detailed, multiple-year forecasts of cash flows available to all providers of capital (debt and equity). The forecasts are then discounted at the weighted-average cost of capital to arrive at an estimated present value of the firm. The value of debt is subtracted from the total value of firm to arrive at the value of equity.

(d) **Mergers and Acquisitions.** A merger is defined as the combination of two firms to form a single firm. A merger can be a friendly merger or a hostile merger. In a friendly merger, the terms and conditions of a merger are approved by the management of both companies, while in a hostile merger, the target firm's management resists acquisition. It has been pointed out that many mergers today are designed more for the benefits of managers of the firm than for that of stockholders—who are really the owners of the firm.

Five motives were given to account for the high level of US merger activity: (1) synergy, (2) tax considerations, (3) purchase of assets below their replacement cost, (4) diversification, and (5) maintaining control (see Exhibit 2.39).

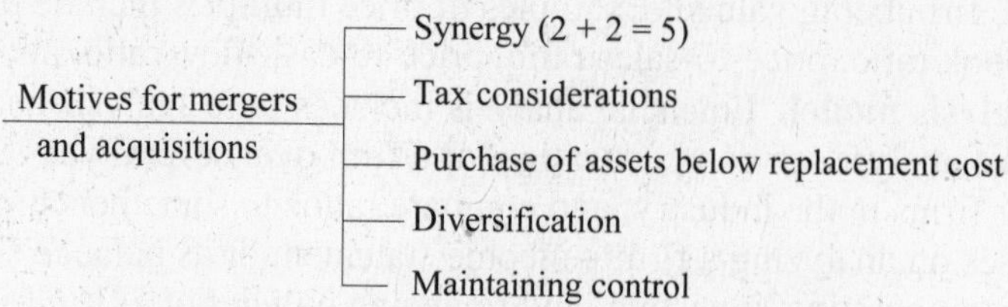

Exhibit 2.39: Motives for mergers and acquisitions

Synergy is seen as the whole is greater than the sum of the parts (i.e., 2 + 2 = 5). It is the basic rationale for any operating merger. Synergistic effects can arise from four sources: (1) operating economies of scale in production or distribution, (2) financial economies, which include a higher price/earnings ratio, a lower cost of debt, or a greater debt capacity, (3) differential management efficiency (one firm's management is seen as inefficient), and (4) increased market power resulting from reduced competition.

Tax considerations include using tax status to the firm's advantage and using excess cash in mergers. Using excess cash to acquire another firm has no immediate tax consequences for either the acquiring firm or its stockholders.

TAXES AND ACQUISITIONS

- A firm which is highly profitable and in the highest tax brackets could acquire a company with large accumulated tax losses, then use those losses to offset its own income. This reduces the total tax bill and that is the one of the motivations.
- A firm with large losses could acquire a profitable firm and minimize the tax bill. Example: A young profitable company acquires an older company in a different industry that has experienced losses recently.

When the **replacement value of a firm's assets** is considerably higher than its market value, the firm becomes an acquisition candidate. Purchase price will be less than the replacement value of the assets.

Diversification was thought to be a stabilizing factor on a firm's earnings and thus reduces risk. There is a controversy about this practice. Stabilization of earnings is beneficial to a firm's employees, suppliers, and customers, but its value to stockholders and debt holders is not clear. This is because investors can diversify their risk on their own; a merger is not the answer.

Maintaining control is a major motivation and based on human psychology. The managers of the acquired companies generally lose their jobs or lose their autonomy. Therefore, managers who own less than 51% of the stock in their firms look to mergers that will lessen the chances of their firm's being taken over. Defensive merger tactics are practiced by using much higher debt to acquire other firms so that it will be hard for any potential acquirer to "digest."

(i) **Types of mergers.** Economists classify mergers into five groups: (1) horizontal, (2) vertical, (3) congeneric, (4) conglomerate, and (5) beachhead merger (see Exhibit 2.40).

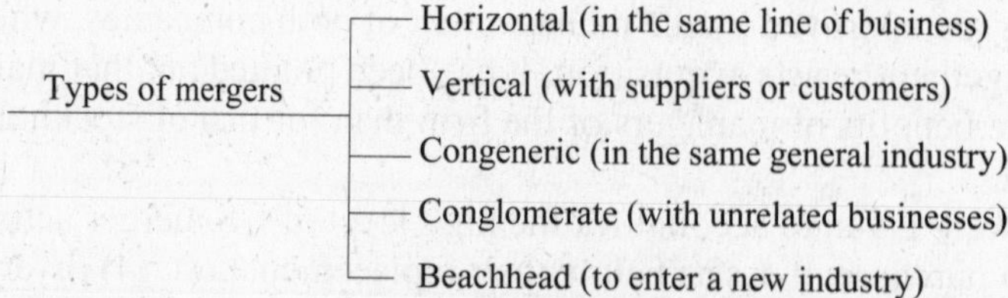

Exhibit 2.40: Types of mergers

A **horizontal merger** occurs when one firm combines with another in its same line of business. It can occur between a producer and another producer in the same industry. This kind of merger provides the greatest synergistic operating benefits and is the target of investigation by the US Department of Justice. It is most likely to be attacked as a restraint of trade.

A **vertical merger** occurs between a firm and one of its suppliers or customers. It can occur between a producer and its supplier. A **congeneric merger** is a merger of firms in the same general industry, but for which no customer or supplier relationship exists. A **conglomerate merger** occurs when unrelated enterprises combine. A **beachhead merger** takes on a new risk and opportunity entering a new industry.

(ii) **Merger analysis.** Whatever type of merger is used, the underlying theory of merger analysis is capital budgeting techniques. The objective is to determine whether the present value of the cash flows expected to result from the merger exceeds the price that must be paid for the target company. The acquiring firm performs the capital budgeting analysis.

CAPITAL BUDGETING TECHNIQUES AND MERGERS

- If the net present value is positive, the acquiring firm acquires the target firm.
- If the net present value is negative, the acquiring firm does not acquire the target firm.

A merger can be either an operating merger or a financial merger or a combination of both. An **operating merger** is a merger in which operations of the firms involved are integrated in the hope of achieving synergistic benefits. Accurate estimates of future cash flows, although difficult to obtain, will be required.

Analytical Techniques Used in Mergers

- Investment analysis (capital budgeting)
- Sensitivity ("what if") analysis
- Scenario analysis
- Simulation analysis
- "Due diligence" reviews

A **financial merger** is one in which the merged companies will be operated independently and from which no significant operating economies are expected. The postmerger cash flows are simply the sum of the expected cash flows of the two companies if they continued to operate independently.

A value of the target firm should be assessed in order to determine an educated price. Both cash flows and a discount rate are essential in valuing the target firm. Cash flows can be developed using a set of pro forma income statements for a number of years (say five years). These net cash flows are discounted at the overall cost of capital, if both debt and equity are used to finance the merger. If only equity is used then the cost of equity should be used. The price paid to acquire the target firm is a summation of the discount net cash flows at the appropriate cost of capital.

REASON FOR ACQUISITION

Example: A company acquired an older and more established competitor in the same industry. The company being acquired had consistently earned lower (but positive) net income and has a low debt-to-equity ratio. The reason for the acquisition probably was to increase financing capacity.

(iii) **Spin-off and divestiture**

(A) ***Spin-off.*** Spin-off is when a company sold one of its operating divisions to its existing shareholders, and the shareholders received new stock representing separate ownership rights in the division.

(B) ***Divestiture.*** Divestiture is when a large US company set up a new corporation based on the assets from one of its divisions. The stock of the new corporation was titled to the stockholders of the original firm.

(iv) **Leveraged buyouts.** Often, a leveraged buyout (LBO) is an alternative to a merger. There is a controversy whether LBOs are a good or a bad idea for a company or the economy as a whole. Some argue that LBOs might destabilize the economy because of the disruptive forces involved in the deal. Others argue that LBOs can stimulate lethargic or complacent management.

The existence of potential bargains, situations in which companies were using insufficient leverage, and the development of the so called "junk bond market" all facilitated the use of leverage in takeovers. LBOs can be initiated in one of two ways.

1. The firm's own managers can set up a new company whose equity comes from the managers themselves plus equity from outside sources. This new company then arranges to borrow a large amount of money by selling junk bonds through an investment-banking firm.
2. A specialized LBO firm will identify a potential target company, go to the management, and suggest that an LBO deal be done.

Whatever method is used in an LBO, the newly formed company will have a high debt ratio ranging from 80 to 98%, hence the term leveraged.

(v) **Holding companies.** A holding company is a company that owns stock in another company and exercises control. The holding company is called the parent company and the controlled companies are called subsidiaries or operating companies. A holding company is taxed on profits, cannot issue tax-free bonds, and is subject to normal government regulations.

Although the holding company has advantages and disadvantages similar to that of large corporations, they differ in the following areas. ***Advantages** of a holding company include* (1) control with fractional ownership (anywhere between 5 and 100% of another company's stock; 10 to 25% of common stock ownership is considered as having a working control), (2) isolation of risk to a single unit, and (3) legal and accounting separation when regulations make such separation desirable.

***Disadvantages** of a holding company include:* partial multiple taxation due to not requiring a consolidated tax return when the ownership is less than 80% of a subsidiary's voting stock, and ease of enforced dissolution by the Justice Department if it finds the ownership of a holding company is unacceptable. The parent company is required to pay tax on dividends from the subsidiary, thus leading to partial multiple taxation.

(vi) **Role of investment bankers in mergers and acquisitions.** An investment banker and a lawyer are usually involved with a merger by helping to arrange mergers, advising target companies in developing and implementing defensive tactics, and helping to value target companies. For these services, a fee and commissions are paid to the investment banker.

DEFINITIONS OF KEY TERMS: MERGERS AND ACQUISITIONS

- A *friendly merger* is a merger whose terms are amicable and approved by the management of both firms.
- A *greenmail* is an acquisition of common stock presently owned by the prospective combinor at a price substantially in excess of the prospective combinor's cost, with the stock thus acquired placed in the treasury or retired stock status.
- A *golden parachute* is a large payment made to the managers of a firm if it is acquired in a hostile takeover.
- A *hostile merger* is a merger in which the target firm's management opposes the proposed acquisition. Examples of defensive tactics include white knight, scorched earth, shark repellent, poison pill, greenmail, and pac-man defense.
- A *pac-man defense* is a threat to undertake a hostile takeover of the prospective combinor.
- A *poison pill* is an action that will seriously damage a company if it is acquired by another firm. It may involve an amendment of the articles of incorporation or bylaws to make it more difficult to obtain stockholders' approval for a hostile takeover.
- A *scorched earth* is the disposal, by sale or by a spin-off to stockholders, of one or more profitable business segments.

- A *shark repellent* is an acquisition of substantial amounts of outstanding common stock for the treasury stock or for retirement of stock, or the incurring of substantial long-term debt in exchange for outstanding common stock.
- A *tender offer* is the offer of one firm to buy the stock of another by going directly to the stockholders, frequently over the opposition of the target firm's management.
- A *white knight* is a friendly company that is more acceptable to the management of a firm under attack in a hostile takeover attempt.

Business mergers can be friendly or hostile. Of particular importance is developing defensive tactics to block hostile mergers. Some commonly used tactics include: changing the bylaws to require a supermajority of directors instead of a simple majority to approve a merger, educating the target firm's stockholders that the price being offered is too low, raising antitrust issues in the hope that the Justice Department will intervene, persuading a white knight more acceptable to the target firm's management that it should compete with the potential acquirer, and taking a "poison pill," which includes management committing suicide to avoid a takeover, borrowing on terms that require immediate repayment of all loans if the firm is acquired, selling off the assets at bargain prices to make the firm less attractive to the potential acquirer, granting lucrative golden parachutes to the firm's executives to drain off some cash, taking on a huge debt, and leaving behind assets of questionable value.

2.10 Business Development Life Cycles

(a) **Overview.** Any nation seeks economic growth, full employment, and price level stability. However, achieving full employment and price level stability is not steady or certain. Both unemployment and inflation in the United States have threatened or interrupted the long-term trend of economic growth.

The business cycle refers to the recurrent ups and downs in the level of economic activity that extends over time. Economists suggest four phases of the business cycle: peak, recession, trough, and recovery (see Exhibit 2.41). The duration and strength of each phase is variable. Some economists prefer to talk of business fluctuations, rather than cycles because cycles imply regularity while fluctuations do not.

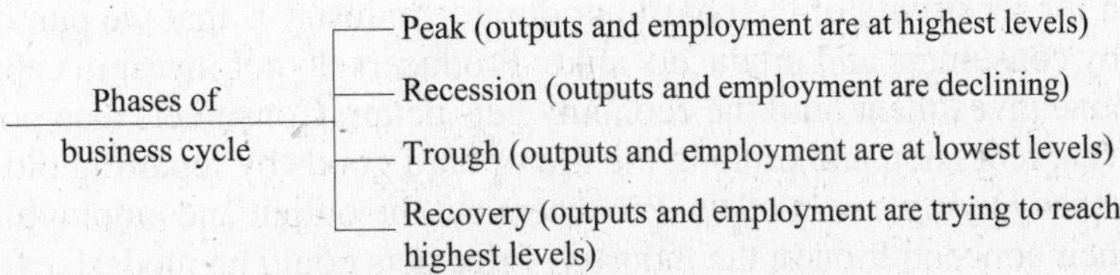

Exhibit 2.41: Phases of business cycle

- **Peak.** The economy is at full employment and the national output is close to capacity. The price level is likely to rise.
- **Recession.** Both output and employment decline, but prices tend to be relatively inflexible in a downward direction. Depression sets in when the recession is severe and prolonged, and prices fall. In an economy experiencing a recession with low inflation, the central bank could stimulate the economy by purchasing securities in the secondary market, which will increase money supply.
- **Trough.** Both output and employment "bottom out" at their lowest levels.
- **Recovery.** Both output and employment expand toward full employment. As recovery intensifies, the price level may begin to rise prior to the realization of full employment and capacity production.

(b) **Causes behind the Business Cycles and Business Activity.** Economists suggest many theories supporting the reasons behind the nature of the four phases of the business cycle and its impact on business activity. Examples include

- Innovations (e.g., computers, drugs, synthetic fibers, automobiles) have greater impact on investment and consumer spending, and therefore upon output, employment, and the price level. This innovation is not regular and continued.
- Political and random events such as war have a major impact on increasing employment and inflation followed by slump when peace returns.
- Monetary policy of the government has a major impact on business activity. When government creates too much money, inflation results. When government restricts money supply, it results in lower output and unemployment.
- The level of total expenditures has a major impact on the levels of output and employment.

KEY CONCEPTS TO REMEMBER: TOTAL EXPENDITURES

- When total expenditure is low, output, employment, and incomes will be low. Less production will be profitable to the business.
- When total expenditure is high, output, employment, and incomes will be high. More production will be profitable to the business.

- Many businesses such as retail, automobile, construction, and agriculture are subject to seasonal variations (e.g., pre-Christmas, pre-Easter).
- Business activity is also subject to a secular trend. The secular trend of an economy is its expansion or contraction over a long period of time (i.e., 25 or more years). Both seasonal variations and secular trends are due to noncyclical fluctuations.

It is important to note that various individuals and various segments of the economy are affected in different ways and in different degrees by the business cycle. For example, consumer durable and consumer nondurable goods industries are affected in different ways, as explained below.

- **Consumer durable.** Those industries producing heavy capital goods and consumer durables (e.g., household appliances, automobiles), called "hard goods" industries, are highly sensitive to the business cycle. Both production and employment will decline during recession and increase during recovery.

The reason for sensitivity of the consumer durable industry is that the purchase of hard goods can be postponed by consumers and producers alike. Producers do not invest in capital goods during recession and postpone investment until the economy gets better. Consumers also postpone the purchase of hard goods during recession and prolong the life of hard goods by repairing old appliances and automobiles rather than buying new models. Producers cut the output and employment instead of lowering prices due to their concentration in the industry. Price cuts could be modest, even if they occur.

- **Consumer nondurables.** Output and employment in nondurable consumer goods industries are less sensitive to the business cycle. This is because food and clothes, which are examples of the consumer nondurable industry, are simply necessities of life. These are called "soft good" industries. Because it is a highly competitive and low concentration industry, prices will be cut instead of production and employment. Production decline would be modest, even if it occurs.

The financial manager needs to develop financial forecasts and capital investment plans according to the phase of the business cycle his firm is going through and the type of industry his firm belongs to (i.e., whether consumer durables or consumer nondurables).

(c) **Growth Concepts.** Another interesting concept is to compare the growth of a firm with that of the economy. Four growth concepts emerge: (1) supernormal growth, (2) normal growth, (3) zero growth, and (4) negative growth (see Exhibit 2.42). Each growth concept is briefly explained below.

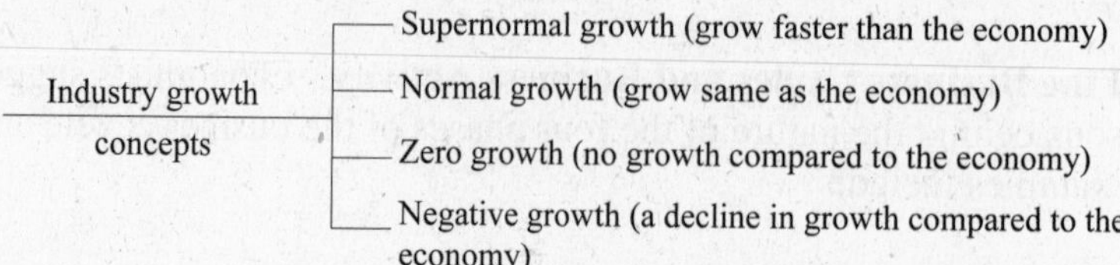

Exhibit 2.42: Industry growth concepts

- **Supernormal growth** is the part of the life cycle of a firm in which its growth is much faster than that of the economy as a whole.
- **Normal growth** is growth that is expected to continue into the foreseeable future at about the same rate as that of the economy as a whole. The growth rate of a firm is equal to the nominal gross national product (GNP), which is real GNP plus inflation.
- **Zero growth** indicates that a firm experiences a zero percent growth compared to the economy as a whole.
- **Negative growth** indicates that a firm experiencing a decline in growth compared to the economy as a whole.

MULTIPLE-CHOICE QUESTIONS (1-545)

Basic Concepts

1. A company uses straight-line depreciation for financial reporting purposes, but uses accelerated depreciation for tax purposes. Which of the following account balances would be lower in the financial statements used for tax purposes than it would be in the general purpose financial statements?

a. Accumulated depreciation.
b. Cash.
c. Retained earnings.
d. Gross fixed assets.

2. The practice of recording advance payments from customers as liabilities is an application of the

a. Going concern assumption.
b. Monetary unit assumption.
c. Historic cost principle.
d. Revenue recognition principle.

3. A newly acquired plant asset is to be depreciated over its useful life. The rationale for this process is the

a. Economic entity assumption.
b. Monetary unit assumption.
c. Materiality assumption.
d. Going concern assumption.

4. Management of a bank concluded that there is no longer reasonable assurance of collection of the full amount of principal and interest from the bank's largest borrower. What is the impact of that conclusion on the bank's financial statements?

a. No accounting or disclosure of a possible loss in value is necessary.
b. A contingency note disclosure of a possible loss in value is required.
c. The carrying amount of the loan should be reduced, with a charge directly to retained earnings.
d. The carrying amount of the loan should be reduced, with a charge to the income statement.

5. A prior period adjustment is charged to the income statement of an earlier period because

a. It is the only way to adjust for an error in previous financial statements.
b. The income statement of the current period portrays only the regular and recurring earnings of the business that are based on normal operations.
c. The income statement of the current period portrays events or estimates arising in the current period only.
d. The income statement of the current period reflects the long-range income-producing ability of the enterprise.

6. What are the effects of an adjusting entry used to accrue revenue from credit sales?

	Assets	*Liabilities*	*Owners' equity*
a.	Decrease	No effect	Decrease
b.	Increase	No effect	Increase
c.	No effect	Decrease	Increase
d.	No effect	Increase	Decrease

Items 7 through 11 are based on the following:

The following information is part of an unadjusted trial balance for an equipment rental company at December 31, 2005:

Cash	$17,400
Prepaid insurance	3,600
Fixed assets	180,000
Accumulated depreciation	32,000
Accounts payable	12,000
Common stock	60,000
Retained earnings	38,000
Rental revenue	171,000
Salaries and wages expense	80,000
Utilities expense	14,000

On October 1, 2005, the company paid $18,000 to renew its only insurance policy for a three-year period beginning on that date. This transaction has not been recorded. Salaries and wages of $1,700 have been incurred but not paid as of December 31, 2005. At December 31, 2005, the balance per bank statement was $12,000. Outstanding checks amounted to $6,900. Interest of $40 was credited to the company's account by the bank during December, but has not yet been entered on the company's books.

7. What amounts should the company report for prepaid insurance and insurance expense in the annual financial statements prepared at December 31, 2005?

	Prepaid insurance	*Insurance expense*
a.	$16,500	$1,500
b.	$16,500	$5,100
c.	$18,000	$3,600
d.	$20,100	$1,500

8. The required adjusting entry at December 31, 2005, related to salaries and wages is

a.	Salaries & wages expense	1,700	
	Income summary		1,700
b.	Salaries & wages payable	1,700	
	Salaries & wages expense		1,700
c.	Salaries & wages expense	1,700	
	Salaries & wages payable		1,700
d.	Income summary	1,700	
	Salaries & wages payable		1,700

9. The journal entry required to close the utilities expense account is

a.	Utilities expense	14,000	
	Income summary		14,000
b.	Income summary	14,000	
	Utilities expense		14,000
c.	Rental revenue	14,000	
	Utilities expense		14,000
d.	Utilities expense	14,000	
	Retained earnings		14,000

10. Assuming no errors exist in the company's cash balance, deposits in transit at December 31, 2005, amount to

a. $ 5,400
b. $12,260
c. $12,300
d. $12,340

11. One of the outstanding checks is a $5,000 check that was written on and dated December 31, 2004, in payment of a vendor invoice. However, the check was locked in the company's vault until it was mailed on January 6, 2005. This situation

a. Involves improper cutoff of cash disbursements.
b. Involves improper cutoff of cash receipts.
c. Is acceptable and often encountered because it improves the working capital position.
d. Is acceptable and often encountered because it improves the working capital (current) ratio.

12. The correct form of the journal entry recorded upon the sale of a plant asset, which was sold for an amount of cash in excess of its net book value, is

a. Debit cash
Debt gain on disposal of machinery
Credit accumulated depreciation—machinery
Credit machinery

b. Debit cash
Debit gain on disposal of machinery
Debit gain on disposal of machinery
Credit machinery

c. Debit cash
Debit machinery
Credit accumulated depreciation—machinery
Credit gain on disposal of machinery

d. Debit cash
Debit accumulated depreciation—machinery
Credit machinery
Credit gain on disposal of machinery

13. Which is the correct order of the following four steps in the accounting cycle?

Step 1 Prepare adjusting journal entries.
Step 2 Take a postclosing trial balance.
Step 3 Prepare an adjusted trial balance.
Step 4 Prepare reversing entries.

a. 1, 3, 2, 4
b. 4, 1, 3, 2
c. 3, 1, 2, 4
d. 1, 2, 3, 4

14. Which adjusting entry should be used at year-end to account for interest expense on the long-term debt?

		Debit	Credit
a.	Interest expense	100,000	
	Interest payable		100,000
b.	Interest expense	50,000	
	Cash		50,000
c.	Interest payable	100,000	
	Interest expense		100,000
d.	Interest expense	50,000	
	Interest payable		50,000

15. Assume that the company reports cost of goods sold of $200,000 and interest expense of $10,000 for the current period. Also assume a 50% tax rate on corporate earnings. The final closing entry required to ensure that current earnings are incorporated into year-end retained earnings is

		Debit	Credit
a.	Income summary	140,000	
	Retained earnings		140,000
b.	Retained earnings	280,000	
	Income summary		280,000
c.	Income summary	240,000	
	Retained earnings		240,000
d.	Retained earnings	240,000	
	Income summary		240,000

16. On January 1, a company establishes a petty cash account and designates one employee as petty cash custodian. The original amount included in the petty cash fund is $500, and it will be used to make small cash disbursements. The fund will be replenished on the first of each month, after the petty cash custodian presents receipts for disbursements to the general cashier.

The following disbursements are made in the month of January:

Office supplies	$173
Postage	$112
Entertainment	$42

The balance in the petty cash box at the end of January is $163. The entry required at the end of January is

		Debit	Credit
a.	Office supplies expense	173	
	Postage expense	112	
	Entertainment expense	42	
	Cash		327
b.	Office supplies expense	173	
	Postage expense	112	
	Entertainment expense	42	
	Petty cash		327
c.	Office supplies expense	173	
	Postage expense	112	
	Entertainment expense	42	
	Cash over and short	10	
	Cash		337
d.	Office supplies expense	173	
	Postage expense	112	
	Entertainment expense	42	
	Cash		317
	Cash over and short		10

17. An entity purchases office equipment for $525,000 on account. Select the appropriate journal entry to record this transaction.

		Debit	Credit
a.	Office expense	525,000	
	Accounts payable		525,000
b.	Office equipment	525,000	
	Accounts payable		525,000
c.	Accounts payable	525,000	
	Office expense		525,000
d.	Accounts payable	525,000	
	Office equipment		525,000

18. ABC Manufacturing Company ships merchandise costing $40,000 on consignment to XYZ Stores. ABC pays $3,000 of freight costs to a transport company, and XYZ pays $2,000 for local advertising costs that are reimbursable from ABC. By the end of the period, three fourths of the consigned merchandise has been sold for $50,000 cash. XYZ notifies

ABC of the sales, retains a 10% commission and the paid advertising costs, and remits the cash due ABC. Select the journal entry that appropriately records the notification of sale and the receipt of cash by ABC.

a. Cash 40,000
Advertising expense 2,000
Commission expense 5,000
Freight expense 3,000
Revenue from consignment sales 50,000

b. Cash 43,000
Advertising expense 2,000
Commission expense 5,000
Revenue from consignment sales 50,000

c. Cash 50,000
Revenue from consignment sales 50,000

d. Cash 45,000
Commission expense 5,000
Revenue from consignment sales 50,000

19. At December 31, a company has total assets at book value of $300,000. Liabilities are $120,000. Also, on December 31, the stock is selling at $20 per share, and there are 10,000 shares outstanding. As a result, the company should take the difference between the book value and fair market value of the stock and

a. Capitalize as an asset (and amortize over the estimated useful life not to exceed 40 years), with the offset to stockholders' equity.
b. Capitalize as an asset (and amortize over the estimated useful life), with the offset to revenue.
c. Capitalize as an asset (and amortize over five years), with the offset to stockholders' equity.
d. Not capitalize any asset, record any revenue nor change stockholders' equity at this time.

20. A company estimates that long-term disability costs as a result of employment during the current period will be $100,000. How should this be accounted for?

a. Disclosure only, with no journal entry.
b. An expense should be recorded for $100,000.
c. An asset of $100,000 should be recognized.
d. A direct reduction to retained earnings of $100,000 should occur.

21. When a perpetual inventory system is used and a difference exists between the perpetual inventory amount balance and the physical inventory count, a separate entry is needed to adjust the perpetual inventory amount. Which of the following demonstrates that adjusting entry?

a. Inventory over and short
Inventory

b. Extraordinary loss due to writedown of inventory
Inventory

c. Extraordinary loss due to writedown of inventory
Allowance for inventory shortages

d. Cost of goods sold
Retained earnings appropriated for shortages

22. On December 1, 2005, a company sold services to a customer and accepted a note in exchange with a $120,000 face value and an interest rate of 10%. The note requires that both the principal and interest be paid at the maturity date, December 1, 2006. The company's accounting period is the calendar year. What adjusting entry (related to this note) would be required at December 31, 2005, on the company's books?

a. Deferred interest income 1,000
Interest receivable 1,000

b. Interest income 1,000
Interest receivable 1,000

c. Interest receivable 1,000
Deferred interest income 1,000

d. Interest receivable 1,000
Interest income 1,000

23. Select the combination below that explains the impact of credit card interest incurred and paid during the period on (1) owners' equity on the balance sheet, and (2) the statement of cash flows.

	(1) *Effect on owners' equity on balance sheet*	*(2)* *Reflected on statement of cash flows as a*
a.	Decrease	Financing outflow
b.	Decrease	Operating outflow
c.	No effect	Financing outflow
d.	No effect	Operating outflow

24. An internal auditor is deriving cash flow data based on an incomplete set of facts. The percentage of credit sales method, at 2%, is used to adjust for bad debt expense. Additional data for this period follows:

Credit sales		$100,000
Accounts receivable beginning balance		5,000
Allowance for bad debts beginning balance		(500)
Accounts receivable written off	$ 1,000	
Increase in net accounts receivable (after subtraction of allowance for bad debts)	30,000	

How much cash was collected this period?

a. $67,000
b. $68,500
c. $68,000
d. $69,000

25. In auditing your organization's records for 2005, the first year of operations, you discover the following errors were made at December 31, 2005:

1. Failed to accrue $50,000 interest expense.
2. Failed to record depreciation expense on office equipment of $80,000.
3. Failed to amortize prepaid rent expense of $100,000.
4. Failed to delay recognition of prepaid advertising expense of $60,000.

The net effect of the above errors was to overstate net income for 2005 by

a. $130,000
b. $170,000
c. $230,000
d. $290,000

26. A company issues bonds payable at a premium. You are analyzing the effects of using the effective interest (constant yield) method in accounting for the bonds over their ten-year life. Which of the following trends related to the reported amounts for (1) interest expense and (2) carrying amount of the bonds would you expect to find?

	Interest expense	Carrying amount
a.	Constant amount	Constant amount
b.	Increasing amount	Decreasing amount
c.	Decreasing amount	Decreasing amount
d.	Decreasing amount	Constant amount

27. Which of the following is a benefit of accounting for inflation in the financial statements?

a. It automatically provides funds for dividends and plant expansion.
b. It preserves the historical cost-based accounting system.
c. It provides for the maintenance of physical capital.
d. It identifies holding gains and losses.

28. In reconciling net income on an accrual basis to net cash provided by operating activities, what adjustment is needed to net income because of (1) an increase during the period in prepaid expenses, and (2) the periodic amortization of premium on bonds payable?

	(1) Increase in prepaid expenses	(2) Amortization of premium on bonds payable
a.	Add	Add
b.	Add	Deduct
c.	Deduct	Add
d.	Deduct	Deduct

29. A company purchased $1,000 gross amount of inventory on account with terms of 2% discount if paid within 10 days, FOB shipping point, with freight of $30 prepaid by the seller. The company records purchases at the net amount. The journal entry to record payment eight days after the invoice date is

		Dr	Cr
a.	Accounts payable	1,010	
	Cash		1,010
b.	Accounts payable	980	
	Freight in	30	
	Cash		1,010
c.	Purchases	1,030	
	Freight in	30	
	Accounts payable		1,060
d.	Purchases	980	
	Freight in	30	
	Accounts payable		1,010

30. What is the purpose of the following entry?

Supplies	xxxx	
Supplies expense		xxxx

a. To recognize supplies used, if purchases of supplies are recorded in supplies.
b. To recognize supplies on hand, if purchases of supplies are recorded in supplies expense.
c. To record the purchase of supplies during or at the end of the period.
d. To close the expense account for supplies at the end of the period.

Items 31 and 32 are based on the following:

An audit of a company has revealed the following four errors that have occurred but have not been corrected:

1. Inventory at December 31, 2004—$40,000, Understated.
2. Inventory at December 31, 2005—$15,000, Overstated.
3. Depreciation for 2004—$ 7,000, Understated.
4. Accrued expenses at December 31, 2005—$10,000, Understated.

31. The errors cause the reported net income for the year ending December 31, 2005 to be

a. Overstated by $72,000.
b. Overstated by $65,000.
c. Understated by $28,000.
d. Understated by $45,000.

32. The errors cause the reported retained earnings at December 31, 2005, to be

a. Overstated by $65,000.
b. Overstated by $32,000.
c. Overstated by $25.000.
d. Understated by $18,000.

33. Company X owns 90% of Company Y. Early in the year Company X loans Company Y $1,000,000. No payments have been made on the debt by year-end. Proper accounting at year-end would

a. Eliminate 100% of both receivable and payable, and related interest.
b. Eliminate 100% of both receivable and payable, but not any related interest.
c. Eliminate 90% of each of receivable, payable, and related interest.
d. Eliminate 90% of each of receivable and payable, but not any related interest.

34. Which of the following statements is **false** regarding disclosure of accounts receivable?

a. Valuation accounts may be deducted from accounts receivable for loss contingencies that exist on the receivables.
b. Valuation accounts may be deducted from accounts receivable for estimated discounts and returns to be granted in the future on existing accounts receivable.
c. Accounts receivable should be reported and identified on the balance sheet as pledged receivables if they are used as security for a loan, which is shown as a liability on the same balance sheet.
d. Accounts receivable from officers and owners should be classified as offsets to owners' equity.

35. Which of the following describes the proper treatment of a loss, which is material, unusual in nature, and infrequent in occurrence?

a. Report as part of continuing operations.
b. Report as part of discontinued operations.
c. Report as an extraordinary item.
d. Report as a prior period item.

36. Which of the following explains the proper treatment of a loss that resulted from the operations and disposal of assets of a segment of business that was terminated during the current period?

a. Report as part of continuing operations.
b. Report as discontinued operations.
c. Report as an extraordinary item.
d. Report as a prior period item.

37. A company decided to sell a line of its business. The assets were sold for $100,000 and had a net book value of $70,000. The applicable tax rate was 20%. The result of this transaction will appear on the

a. Balance sheet as a prior period adjustment.
b. Income statement as an extraordinary item.
c. Income statement as discontinued operations.
d. Income statement as an accounting change.

38. A cable television company receives deposits from customers, which are refunded when service is terminated. The average customer stays with the company eight years. How should these deposits be shown on the financial statements?

a. Operating revenue.
b. Other revenue.
c. Paid-in capital.
d. Liability.

39. At December 31, 2005, a company had the following short-term obligations, which were expected to be refinanced:

17% note payable	$140,000
15% note payable	$200,000

The 17% note payable was issued on October 1, 2005, and matures on July 1, 2006. The 15% note payable was issued on May 1, 2005, and matures on May 1, 2006. On February 1, 2006, the entire $140,000 balance of the 17% note payable was refinanced by issuance of a long-term debt instrument. On February 7, 2006, the company entered into a noncancelable agreement with a lender to refinance the 15% note payable on a long-term basis. On March 1, 2006, the date of issuance of the December 31, 2005 balance sheet, both parties are financially capable of honoring the agreement and there have been no violations of the provisions of the refinancing agreement. The total amount of short-term obligations that may be properly excluded from current liabilities on the company's December 31, 2005 balance sheet is

a. $0
b. $140,000
c. $200,000
d. $340,000

40. Which of the following is a unique reporting problem associated with the determination of the results of operations for an interim period?

a. Advertising and similar costs expensed in one interim period may benefit other interim periods in the same annual period.
b. Cost of goods sold for an interim period reflects only the amount of product cost applicable to sales revenue recognized in the interim period.
c. Depreciation for an interim period represents an estimate.
d. An extraordinary loss occurring in the second quarter must be prorated over the last three interim periods of the year.

41. On January 1, 2005, a company acquired a plant asset for $300,000. Using the straight-line method of depreciation over a service life of 10 years and no salvage value, the company recorded depreciation of $30,000 for the year ending December 31, 2005. The fair value of the asset at December 31, 2005, is $310,000. The balance sheet prepared on December 31, 2005, would

a. Report the excess of the fair value over the book value as goodwill.
b. Report the excess of the fair value over the book value as part of plant and equipment.
c. Report the excess of the fair value over the book value as appraisal capital.
d. Not report the excess of the fair value over the book value.

42. The assets of a liquidating company should be shown on the balance sheet at their

a. Undepreciated historical cost.
b. Fair market value.
c. Net realizable value.
d. Current cost.

43. In December 2005, catalogues were printed for use in a special promotion in January 2006. The catalogues were delivered by the printer on December 13, 2005, with an invoice for $70,000 attached. Payment was made in January, 2006. The $70,000 should be reported as a deferred cost at the December 31, 2005 balance sheet date because of the

a. Matching principle.
b. Revenue realization principle.
c. Objectivity principle.
d. Cost principle.

44. Which of the following should be disclosed in the summary of significant accounting policies?

a. Valuation method used for work in process inventory.
b. Interest capitalized for the period.
c. Adequacy of pension plan assets in relation to vested benefits.
d. Depreciation charges for the period.

45. A company is subject to warranty claims. It is estimated that between $1,000,000 and $3,000,000 will probably be paid out. No estimate of loss within this range is more likely than any other. The company should

a. Make no journal entry at this time.
b. Disclose only a possible loss.
c. Defer a loss of $1,000,000 to 3,000,000 depending on the applicable national accounting standards.
d. Accrue a loss of $1,000,000 to $3,000,000 depending on the applicable national accounting standards.

46. In recording transactions, which of the following best describes the distinction between expense accounts and loss accounts?

a. Losses are extraordinary charges to income whereas expenses are ordinary charges to income.
b. Losses are material items whereas expenses are immaterial items.
c. Expenses are costs related to revenue, losses are not.
d. Expenses can always be prevented whereas losses can never be prevented.

47. Which of the plans for valuation of property, plant, and equipment shown in the table below is required for a company's balance sheet?

Report Disclosures

	Historical cost	*Accumulated depreciation*	*Net realizable value*
Plan A	Yes	Yes	Yes
Plan B	Yes	Yes	No
Plan C	Yes	No	No
Plan D	No	No	Yes

a. Plan A.
b. Plan B.
c. Plan C.
d. Plan D.

48. A company had the following selected per-unit data relating to work in process:

Selling price	$100
Completion costs	10
Historical cost	91
Replacement cost	108
Normal gross profit	20
Selling cost	5

What will be the per-unit impact on gross profit of valuing ending inventory at lower of historical cost or market, in comparison to historical cost?

a. No effect.
b. Reduction of $6.
c. Reduction of $26.
d. Increase of $5.

49. A company with total assets of $100,000,000 and net income of $9,000,000 purchases staplers with an estimated life of 10 years for $1,000. In connection with the purchase, the company debits miscellaneous expense. This scenario is most closely associated with which of the following concepts or principles?

a. Materiality and going concern.
b. Relevance and neutrality.
c. Reliability and comparability/consistency.
d. Materiality and cost/benefit.

50. What are the effects of an adjusting entry used to accrue revenue from credit sales?

	Assets	Liabilities	Owners' equity
a.	Decrease	No effect	Decrease
b.	Increase	No effect	Increase
c.	No effect	Decrease	Increase
d.	No effect	Increase	Decrease

51. The following financial statement notes are extracts from the audited financial statements of public companies. Which note describes a change in accounting estimate?

a. The corporation changed its amortization of capital assets based on a reassessment of the useful lives of the assets. Accordingly, the corporation changed its rate of amortization from 5% and 6%, to 8% and 10%, for machinery and equipment.
b. Prior to 1993, plant and equipment (other than customer service replacement parts) was depreciated on the declining-balance method. Plant and equipment is now depreciated on a straight-line basis.
c. During the year, the company changed its method of accounting for noninterest-bearing, nonrecourse loans due from employees, pursuant to a change in generally accepted accounting principles.
d. Effective January 1, 1994, the company changed to the LIFO method of inventory valuation. Prior to 1994, the FIFO method was used.

52. The purpose of an entry, which contains a debit to prepaid property taxes and a credit to property tax expense, is to recognize a(n)

a. Prepaid expense.
b. Accrued expense.
c. Prepaid revenue.
d. Expired cost.

53. At January 1, 2005, a sole proprietorship's assets totaled $210,000, and its liabilities amounted to $120,000. During 2005, owner investments amounted to $72,000, and owner withdrawals totaled $75,000. At December 31, 2005, assets totaled $270,000, and liabilities amounted to $171,000. The amount of net income for 2005 was

a. $0
b. $ 6,000
c. $ 9,000
d. $12,000

54. Financial accounting standards developed by the International Accounting Standards Committee (IASC)

a. Must be followed by business firms in all developed countries.
b. Must be followed by government enterprises worldwide.
c. Guide the development of accounting principles for government enterprises in centrally planned economies.
d. Are recognized as acceptable "world class" accounting principles for business firms.

55. A company has made all necessary adjusting entries and is now closing its accounts for the period. Dividends of $30,000 were declared and distributed during the year. The entry to close the Dividends account would be

a.	Retained earnings	30,000	
	Dividends		30,000
b.	Dividends	30,000	
	Retained earnings		30,000
c.	Income summary	30,000	
	Dividends		30,000
d.	Dividends	30,000	
	Income summary		30,000

56. A company donated land to the city for a park. The acquisition cost of the land was $75,000, and the market value at the time of the donation was $200,000. The journal entry to record the disposition of the land would be

a.	Donation expense	75,000	
	Land		75,000
b.	Donation expense	200,000	
	Land		75,000
	Paid in capital—land donation		125,000
c.	Donation expense	200,000	
	Land		75,000
	Gain on land disposal		125,000
d.	Donation expense	200,000	
	Land		75,000
	Retained earnings		125,000

57. On January 1, 2005, a company issued a 10-year $500,000 bond at 96% of face value. The bond bears interest at 12%, payable on January 1 and July 1. The entry to record the issuance of the bond on January 1 would be

a.	Cash	480,000	
	Bonds payable		480,000
b.	Cash	500,000	
	Bonds payable		500,000
c.	Cash	480,000	
	Discount on bonds payable		20,000
	Bonds payable		500,000
d.	Cash	500,000	
	Premium on bonds payable		20,000
	Bonds payable		480,000

58. A company issues bonds with a 10% coupon rate at a time when the market interest rate on bonds of similar risk and maturity is 15%. The format of the journal entry that the company would use to record the issuance is

a. Debit cash
Debit premium on bonds payable
Credit bonds payable

b. Debit cash
Credit premium on bonds payable
Credit bonds payable

c. Debit cash
Debit discount on bonds payable
Credit bonds payable

d. Debit cash
Credit discount on bonds payable
Credit bonds payable

59. When financial statements are being prepared, which of the following items requires that accountants estimate the effects of future conditions and events?

a. The purchase price for an acquired building.
b. The price of a marketable security.
c. The amount of recoverable mineral reserves.
d. The physical quantity of inventory.

60. Identify the statement below which represents a required underlying assumption for using the percentage of sales technique to develop pro forma financial statements.

a. Economies of scale exist in the use of assets.
b. Current levels of all assets are optimal for the current sales level.
c. Technological considerations dictate that fixed assets is added in large, discrete amounts.
d. Actual sales-to-asset ratios for the firm in any given period vary with different stages of the economic cycle.

61. Which of the following statements is a correct description of reversing entries?

a. The recording of reversing entries is a mandatory step in the accounting cycle.
b. Reversing entries are made at the end of the next accounting period, after recording regular transactions of the period.
c. Reversing entries are identical to the adjusting entries made in the previous period.
d. Reversing entries are the exact opposite of the adjustments made in the previous period.

62. A company sells a piece of machinery, for cash, prior to the end of its estimated useful life. The sale price is less than the net book value of the asset on the date of sale. The form of the entry that the company would use to record the sale is

a. Debit cash
Debit accumulated depreciation—machinery
Debit loss on disposal of machinery
Credit machinery

b. Debit cash
Debit accumulated depreciation—machinery
Credit gain on disposal of machinery
Credit machinery

c. Debit cash
Debit loss on disposal of machinery
Credit accumulated depreciation—machinery
Credit machinery

d. Debit cash
Debit machinery
Credit accumulated depreciation—machinery
Credit gain on disposal of machinery

63. In the prior accounting period, an organization incorrectly expensed a newly purchased piece of equipment rather than establishing an asset balance and beginning to depreciate it over the estimated useful life of the item. To correct this error in the current period, the organization would record a prior period adjustment of the form

a. Debit equipment
Credit retained earnings
Credit accumulated depreciation—equipment

b. Debit retained earnings
Debit accumulated depreciation—equipment
Credit equipment

c. Debit equipment
Debit retained earnings
Credit accumulated depreciation—equipment

d. Debit equipment
Debit accumulated depreciation—equipment
Credit equipment

64. In the statement of cash flows, the payment of common share dividends appears in the (List A) activities section as a (List B) of cash.

	List A	*List B*
a.	Operating	Source
b.	Financing	Use
c.	Investing	Use
d.	Investing	Source

65. To calculate net sales, (List A) must be (List B) cash receipts from customers.

	List A	*List B*
a.	An increase in accounts receivable	Added to
b.	An increase in accounts receivable	Subtracted from
c.	An increase in accounts payable	Added to
d.	An increase in accounts payable	Subtracted from

66. In the determination of cost of goods sold, (List A) must be (List B) cash payments for goods along with other adjustments.

	List A	*List B*
a.	An increase in accounts payable	Added to
b.	A decrease in accounts payable	Added to
c.	An increase in inventory	Added to
d.	A decrease in inventory	Subtracted from

67. Which of the following steps in the accounting cycle is completed later than the others?

a. Adjustments.
b. Journalization.
c. Posting.
d. Identification and measurement of transactions.

68. A company purchased $50,000 worth of office supplies on January 1 and had $15,000 of office supplies still on hand at year-end. If the initial purchase of supplies entry on January 1 was to debit office supplies expense and to credit cash for $50,000, then the adjusting entry on December 31 will be

a.	Debit office supplies	15,000	
	Credit office supplies expense		15,000
b.	Debit office supplies expense	15,000	
	Credit office supplies		15,000
c.	Debit office supplies	35,000	
	Credit office supplies expense		35,000
d.	Debit office supplies expense	35,000	
	Credit office supplies		35,000

69. In preparing the statement of cash flows, if the payment of cash dividends was omitted, then the net cash provided by (List A) activities will be (List B).

	List A	*List B*
a.	Operating	Understated
b.	Investing	Understated
c.	Investing	Overstated
d.	Financing	Overstated

70. For international investors, which of the following is **not** a potential benefit of the development and adoption of International Accounting Standards?

a. Improved ability to make comparisons across enterprises.
b. Greater freedom in the flow of capital across borders.
c. Greater risk premiums for international investors.
d. Fewer competitive advantages due to varying treatments of items affecting reported earnings.

71. On December 31 a company received a prepayment for the rental of office space for the following year. At the time of the receipt, the entry made was a debit to cash and a credit to rent expense. The books for the year have not yet been closed. To properly record the December 31 receipt, the required additional journal entry would be

a. No entry required.
b. Debit rent expense, credit rent revenue.
c. Debit cash, credit unearned rent revenue.
d. Debit rent expense, credit unearned rent revenue.

72. The amortization of intangible assets over their useful lives is justified by the

a. Economic entity assumption.
b. Going concern assumption.
c. Monetary unit assumption.
d. Historical cost assumption.

73. Which of the following journal entries would correctly record the purchase of advertising services on account by a retail company?

a. Advertising expense
  Prepaid advertising

b. Advertising expense
  Accounts payable

c. Prepaid advertising
  Advertising expense

d. Purchases
  Accounts payable

74. The major distinction made between the multiple-step and single-step income statement format is the separation of

a. Operating and nonoperating data.
b. Income tax expense and administrative expenses.
c. Cost of goods sold expense and administrative expenses.
d. The effect on income taxes due to extraordinary items and the effect on income taxes due to income before extraordinary items.

75. Which financial statement should an investor primarily use to assess the amounts, timing, and uncertainty of investing and financing activities of ABC Company?

a. Statement of operations.
b. Statement of retained earnings.
c. Statement of financial position.
d. Statement of cash flows.

76. Assuming all of the following involve material amounts, which one most likely would properly be classified as an extraordinary item in the income statement?

a. A loss due to an expropriation of assets by a foreign government.
b. A loss due to adjustments of accruals on long-term contracts.
c. A gain due to the disposal of assets associated with a discontinued segment of business.
d. A loss due to a lawsuit that resulted from charges of patent infringement. The company had unsuccessfully defended a similar suit five years ago.

77. Generally accepted accounting principles (GAAP) indicate that a material amount of organization costs should be

a. Expensed in the period the corporation begins operations.
b. Amortized over 60 months from the date of inception of operations.
c. Amortized over the period of their expected useful life, not to exceed 40 years.
d. Capitalized but not amortized because they have an indefinite useful life.

78. An objective of financial reporting is
a. Providing information useful for investor decisions.
b. Assessing the adequacy of internal control.
c. Evaluating management results compared to standards.
d. Providing information on compliance with established procedures.

79. A company disposed of a line of business. The book value of the net assets involved was $450,000; the fair market value of the net assets was $500,000. The assets were sold for $400,000. The company should recognize an
a. Ordinary loss $50,000.
b. Extraordinary loss $50,000.
c. Ordinary loss $100,000.
d. Extraordinary loss $100,000.

80. A company allows customers to redeem 20 coupons for a toy (cost $3.00). Estimates are that 40% of coupons distributed will result in redemption. Since beginning the promotion this year, 4,000,000 coupons were distributed and 1,000,000 coupons redeemed. The adjusting entry to accrue for unredeemed coupons at year-end is

a.	Premium expense	90,000	
	Estimated liability for premiums		90,000
b.	Sales	90,000	
	Estimated liability for premiums		90,000
c.	Premium expense	1,800,000	
	Estimated liability for premiums		1,800,000
d.	Sales	1,800,000	
	Estimated liability for premiums		1,800,000

Intermediate Concepts

81. Which of the following is an example of a contingent liability?
a. A retail store in a shopping mall pays the lessor a minimum monthly rent plus an agreed-upon percentage of sales.
b. A company is refusing to pay the invoice for the annual audit because it seems higher than the amount agreed upon with the public accounting firm's partner.
c. A company accrues income tax payable in its interim financial statements.
d. A lessee agrees to reimburse a lessor for a shortfall in the residual value of an asset under lease.

82. Under a defined contribution pension plan, (List A) is reported on the balance sheet only if the amount the organization has contributed to the pension trust is (List B) the amount required.

	List A	*List B*
a.	An asset	Greater than
b.	An asset	Equal to
c.	A liability	Greater than
d.	A liability	Equal to

83. A company uses the sum-of-the-years' digits method of depreciation. What portion of a four-year asset's depreciable cost will be expensed in the third year of the asset's use?
a. 10%
b. 20%
c. 30%
d. 33.33%

84. On January 1 of year one, a company purchased a machine for $10,000. The estimated useful life was 10 years with no salvage value. The company depreciates its fixed assets using the straight-line method. On January 1 of year five, it was estimated that the machine had a remaining useful life of three years. What is the depreciation expense for the machine in year five?
a. $1,000
b. $2,000
c. $3,000
d. $6,000

Items 85 and 86 are based on the following:

A company estimates warranty costs to be 2% of sales in the year of sale and 1% in the following year. Sales of a new product and actual warranty costs in years one and two were as follows:

	Year 1	*Year 2*
Sales	$3,000,000	$4,000,000
Actual warranty costs	28,000	101,000

85. What is the balance in the estimated warranty liability account at the end of year one?
a. $30,000
b. $32,000
c. $60,000
d. $62,000

86. What amount of warranty expense must the company recognize in year two?
a. $ 80,000
b. $101,000
c. $110,000
d. $120,000

87. If a lease agreement transfers substantially all of the benefits and risks incident to ownership of the asset to the lessee, the asset value is recognized on the lessee's books as (List A) asset and the lease is (List B) lease.

	List A	*List B*
a.	A tangible	A capital
b.	An intangible	A capital
c.	A tangible	An operating
d.	An intangible	An operating

88. During year one, a professional sports team had advance ticket sales of $3,000,000 for games to be played during the period beginning November 1 of year one and ending April 30 of year two. Ten games are played each month. Based on this information, the company should
a. Report a liability for unearned revenue of $2,000,000 on its balance sheet at December 31 of year one.
b. Report a liability for unearned revenue of $3,000,000 on its balance sheet at December 31 of year one.
c. Report revenue of $3,000,000 on its income statement for year one.

d. Report revenue of $1,000,000 on its income statement for year two.

89. A transfer of receivables, with recourse, in exchange for cash should

a. Not be recorded until all of the receivables have been collected.
b. Be recorded as a sale or a borrowing transaction, depending on the provisions of the transfer agreement.
c. Be recorded as a sale of receivables.
d. Be recorded as a borrowing transaction.

90. The measurement basis most often used to report a long-term payable representing a commitment to pay money at a determinable future date is

a. General price level.
b. Current cost.
c. Net realizable value.
d. Present value of future cash flows.

91. Using the cost-recovery method of revenue recognition, profit on an installment sale is recognized as income

a. On the date of the installment sale.
b. As soon as cash collections equal the contribution margin.
c. After cash collections equal to the cost of goods sold have been received.
d. On the date the final cash collection is received.

92. A company purchased a machine on January 1, 1993, for $1,000,000. The machine had an estimated useful life of nine years and a salvage value of $100,000. The company uses straight-line depreciation. On December 31, 1996, the machine was sold for $535,000. The gain or loss that should be recorded on the disposal of this machine is

a. $35,000 gain.
b. $65,000 loss.
c. $365,000 loss.
d. $465,000 loss.

93. If bonds are sold at a discount and the effective interest method of amortization is used, interest expense will

a. Increase from one period to another.
b. Remain constant from one period to another.
c. Equal the cash interest payment each period.
d. Be less than the cash interest payment each period.

94. The following information pertains to the operations of a company that used the installment method of accounting since it began operations at the beginning of the current year:

Installment sales	$1,200,000
Cost of installment sales	840,000
Collections on installment sales	480,000
General and administrative expenses	120,000

The amount of gross profit deferred at the end of the current year should be

a. $144,000
b. $216,000
c. $288,000
d. $600,000

95. Which of the following statements is true for a defined contribution pension plan?

a. The employer is required to contribute a certain amount each period based on the plan's formula.
b. The employer bears the risk of the plan's investment performance.
c. Retirement benefits received by employees are defined by the plan's formula.
d. The employer and employees are required to contribute equal amounts to the pension fund.

96. During 2005, a professional sports team had advance ticket sales of $3,000,000 for games to be played during the period November 2005 through April 2006. Ten games are played each month. Based on this information, the company should

a. Report a liability for unearned revenue of $2,000,000 on its December 31, 2005 balance sheet.
b. Report a liability for unearned revenue of $3,000,000 on its December 31, 2005 balance sheet.
c. Report revenue of $3,000,000 on its 2005 income statement.
d. Report revenue of $1,000,000 on its 2006 income statement.

97. The "percentage-of-completion" and the "completed-contract" methods of accounting for long-term construction projects in progress differ in that

a. It is only under the percentage-of-completion method that progress billings are accumulated in a contra-inventory account called "billings on construction in progress."
b. It is only under the completed-contract method that accumulated construction costs are included in a "construction in progress" inventory account.
c. Only the percentage-of-completion method recognizes all revenues and gross profit on the contract when the contract is completed.
d. It is only under the percentage-of-completion method that gross profit earned to date is accumulated in the "construction in progress" inventory account.

98. A building contractor has a contract to construct a large building. It is estimated that the building will take two years to complete. Progress billings will be sent to the customer at quarterly intervals. Which of the following describes the preferable point for revenue recognition for this contract?

a. After the contract is signed.
b. As progress is made toward completion of the contract.
c. As cash is received.
d. When the contract is completed.

99. There is a material amount due from a customer who declared bankruptcy. This receivable should be classified on the

a. Income statement as a contra revenue item.
b. Income statement as an extraordinary loss.
c. Balance sheet at its face value.
d. Balance sheet at its net realizable value.

100. An airline should recognize revenue from an airline ticket in the period in which the

a. Passenger reservations are booked.
b. Passenger reservations are confirmed.
c. Ticket is issued.
d. Related flight takes place.

101. A company provides fertilization, insect control, and disease control services for a variety of trees, plants, and shrubs on a contract basis. For $50 per month, the company will visit the subscriber's premises and apply appropriate mixtures. If the subscriber has any problems between the regularly scheduled application dates, the company's personnel will promptly make additional service calls to correct the situation. Some subscribers elect to pay for an entire year because the company offers an annual price of $540 if paid in advance. For a subscriber who pays the annual fee in advance, the company should recognize the related revenue

a. When the cash is collected.
b. Evenly over the year as the services are performed.
c. At the end of the contract year after all of the services have been performed.
d. At the end of the fiscal year.

102. The publisher of a popular magazine offers a special discounted price for a three-year subscription. At the balance sheet date, the revenue, which has already been collected but pertains to future periods, is best referred to as

a. Accrued subscriptions revenue (an asset account).
b. Unearned subscriptions revenue (a liability account).
c. Earned subscriptions revenue (a revenue account).
d. Precollected subscriptions receivable (a deferred asset account).

103. Due to inexact estimates of the service life and the residual value of a plant asset, a fully depreciated asset was sold in 1992 at a material gain. This gain should be reported

a. In the "other revenues and gains" section of the 1992 income statement.
b. As part of sales revenue on the 1992 income statement.
c. In the extraordinary item section of the 1992 income statement.
d. As an adjustment to prior periods' depreciation on the statement of retained earnings.

104. On December 1, 2005, a company using the installment sales method sold goods, which cost $1,000, for $1,500. The buyer paid $100 down. Monthly payments start January 1, 2006. Interest accrues at 1% per month on the unpaid balance. To the nearest dollar, the effect on profit for 2005 is

a. $33 increase.
b. $47 increase.
c. $67 increase.
d. $114 increase.

105. To comply with the matching principle, the cost of labor services of an employee who participates in the manufacturing of a product normally should be charged to the income statement in the period in which the

a. Work is performed.
b. Employee is paid.
c. Product is completed.
d. Product is sold.

106. An automobile manufacturer should normally recognize revenue when an

a. Automobile comes off of the assembly line.
b. Order is received from a dealer.
c. Automobile is shipped to a dealer on a nonconsignment basis.
d. Automobile is financed by a dealer to a consumer.

107. At the end of 1990, a company has an unrealized loss account on its trial balance because of the temporary decline in the market value of short-term investments in marketable equity securities. This unrealized loss account should be reported as

a. An "other expense or loss" item on the income statement.
b. An extraordinary loss on the income statement.
c. A separate contra account in the stockholders' equity section of the balance sheet.
d. An adjustment to the beginning balance of retained earnings on the statement of retained earnings.

108. A company offers its customers credit terms of a 2% discount if paid within 10 days, or the full balance is due within 30 days (2/10, n/30). If some customers take advantage of the cash discount and others do not, which of the following accounts will appear on the income statement if the net method of recording receivables is employed?

	Sales discounts	*Sales discounts forfeited*
a.	Yes	Yes
b.	Yes	No
c.	No	No
d.	No	Yes

109. How will net income be affected by the amortization of discount on long-term investment in bonds?

a. Interest revenue is increased so net income is increased.
b. Interest revenue is not affected but net income is increased.
c. Net income is not affected.
d. Net income is decreased.

110. If bonds payable with a carrying value equal to par value are refunded by use of a call provision, the call premium of the refunded issue should be

a. Amortized over the remaining original life of the extinguished issue.
b. Amortized over the life of the new issue.
c. Recognized currently in income as an extraordinary loss.
d. Recognized currently as a loss and reported as a component of income before extraordinary items.

111. A company uses the percentage of completion method and has the following facts:

	20X1	*20X2*
Construction costs	$100	$200
Estimated cost to complete at year-end	$300	-0-

The contract price is $1,000. What is gross profit recognized in 20X2?

a. $150
b. $400
c. $550
d. $800

112. A gain is both unusual and infrequent, and occurs in the second fiscal quarter. How should the gain be accounted for?

a. Recognized in full in the second quarter.
b. Recognized equally over the second, third and fourth quarters.
c. Recognized only in the annual financial statements.

d. Recognized equally in each quarter, by restating the first quarter.

113. A company had $260,000 of net income for 2005. The following data are available from the latest annual report:

	2005	2004
Current assets	$ 220,000	$ 200,000
Plant and equipment	1,780,000	1,700,000
Total assets	2,000,000	1,900,000
Total liabilities	700,000	600,000

The average interest rate on the company's total liabilities is 10%. What is the company's return on equity (rounded to the nearest tenth of a percent)?

a. 20.0%
b. 13.0%
c. 37.1%
d. 16.5%

114. The percentage-of-sales method of financial forecasting is based on an assumption that

a. Future sales are equal to last year's sales.
b. The future sales levels increase each year at a constant percentage rate.
c. Net profits are tied directly to sales.
d. Most balance sheet accounts are tied directly to sales.

Items 115 and 116 are based on the following:

A company with a December 31 year-end purchased $2,000 of inventory on account with terms of FOB shipping point, with freight of $50 paid at destination by the buyer. The invoice date was December 27, 2001, and the goods arrived on January 3, 2002.

115. What is the correct amount of inventory and freight in, respectively, relating to this purchase on the 2001 financial statements?

a. $0, $0
b. $2,050, $0
c. $0, $50
d. $2,000, $50

116. Now assume the terms were FOB destination instead of shipping point. What is the correct amount of inventory and freight in relating to this purchase on the 2001 financial statements?

a. $0, $0
b. $2,050, $0
c. $0, $50
d. $2,000, $50

117. Under which of the following depreciation methods is it possible for depreciation expense to be higher in the later years of an asset's useful life?

a. Straight-line.
b. Activity method based on units of production.
c. Sum-of-the-years' digits.
d. Declining balance.

118. A company has just purchased a machine for $100,000 that has a five-year estimated useful life and a zero estimated salvage value. It is expected to be used to produce 250,000 units of output and 75,000 of those units are expected to be produced in the first year. Which of the following depreciation methods will result in the greatest amount of depreciation expense for this machine in its first year?

a. Straight-line.
b. Activity method based on units of production.
c. Sum-of-the-years' digits.
d. Declining balance method with a 30% depreciation rate.

Items 119 through 121 are based on the following:

A company has the following preclosing trial balance at December 31:

Cash	$ 80,000
Accounts receivable	100,000
Inventory	230,000
Gross fixed assets	600,000
Accumulated depreciation	60,000
Accounts payable	200,000
Long-term debt	1,000,000
Common stock	2,000,000
Retained earnings (Jan. 1)	500,000
Sales revenue	750,000
Purchases	530,000
Administrative expenses	200,000

Additional information

- The balance of opening inventory was $140,000.
- The long-term debt pays interest at a rate of 10% per annum, payable every 12 months. The debt was issued on July 1 of the current year and originally had five years to maturity.
- The fixed assets have a 10-year estimated useful life and were one year old at the start of the current year. Straight-line depreciation is used by the company.

119. The company uses straight-line depreciation for financial reporting purposes, but uses accelerated depreciation for tax purposes. Which of the following account balances would be lower in the financial statements used for tax purposes than it would be in the general-purpose financial statements?

a. Accumulated depreciation.
b. Cash.
c. Retained earnings.
d. Gross fixed assets.

120. On the year-end financial statements, the company will report cost of goods sold of

a. $440,000
b. $620,000
c. $670,000
d. $900,000

121. The company will report year-end total assets of

a. $ 800,000
b. $ 890,000
c. $ 950,000
d. $1,010,000

122. Which of the following is **not** an appropriate basis for measuring the historical cost of fixed assets?

a. The purchase price, freight costs, and installation costs of a productive asset should be included in the asset's cost.
b. Proceeds obtained in the process of readying land for its intended purpose, such as from the sale of cleared timber, should be recognized immediately in income.
c. The costs of improvements to equipment incurred after its acquisition should be added to the asset's cost if they provide future service potential.

d. All costs incurred in the construction of a plant building, from excavation to completion, should be considered as part of the asset's cost.

123. A theme park purchased a new, exciting ride and financed it through the manufacturer. The following facts pertain:

Purchase price	$800,000
Delivery cost	50,000
Installation cost	70,000
Cost of trial runs	40,000
Interest charges for first year	60,000

The straight-line method is to be used. Compute the depreciation on their equipment for the first year assuming an estimated service life of five years.

a. $160,000
b. $184,000
c. $192,000
d. $204,000

124. In making a cash flow analysis of property, plant, and equipment, the internal auditor discovered that depreciation expense for the period was $10,000. Property, plant, and equipment with cost of $50,000 and related accumulated depreciation of $30,000 were sold for a gain of $1,000. If the net book value of property, plant, and equipment increased by $80,000 during the period, how much property, plant, and equipment was purchased this period?

a. $ 91,000
b. $100,000
c. $110,000
d. $119,000

125. An organization purchased a computer on January 1, 2002, for $108,000. It was estimated to have a four-year useful life and a salvage value of $18,000. The double-declining balance method is to be used. The amount of depreciation to be reported for the year ending December 31, 2002, is computed as

a. ($108,000 – $18,000) (25% × 2)
b. ($108,000 – $18,000) (25% × 1/2)
c. ($108,000) (25% × 2)
d. ($108,000) (25% × 1/2)

126. A company with a government contract allocates factory depreciation on the basis of the value of space per square foot.

	First-floor	*Second-floor*
Square feet	20,000	20,000
Value	$216,000	$72,000

If the annual depreciation on the 40,000 square-foot factory is $28,800, what amount would be assigned to a government contract that utilized 10,000 square feet of first-floor space for six months?

a. $ 3,600
b. $ 5,400
c. $ 7,200
d. $10,800

127. An organization acquired a fixed asset with an estimated useful life of five years for $15,000 at the beginning of 2002. For financial statement purposes, how would the depreciation expense calculated using the double-declining balance method compare with that calculated using the sum-of-the-years' digits method in 2002 and 2003 respectively?

	2002	*2003*
a.	Lower	Lower
b.	Lower	Higher
c.	Higher	Lower
d.	Higher	Higher

128. In a statement of cash flows (indirect method), depreciation expense should be presented as

a. An inflow of cash.
b. An outflow of cash.
c. An addition to net income in converting net income to net cash flows from operating activities.
d. A deduction from net income in converting net income to net cash flows from operating activities.

129. A plant asset with an acquisition cost of $450,000 and an estimated salvage value of $60,000 at the end of its estimated five-year service life is to be depreciated using the sum-of-the-years' digits method. What amount of depreciation expense should be reported for the second year of the asset's life?

a. $120,000
b. $104,000
c. $ 60,000
d. $ 52,000

130. A company issues a noninterest-bearing note payable due in one year in exchange for land. Which of the following statements is correct concerning the accounting for the transaction?

a. The land should be recorded at the future value of the note, and interest should be imputed at the prevailing rate on similar notes.
b. No interest should be recognized on the note, and the land should be recorded at the present value of the note.
c. Interest on the note should be imputed at the prime rate and the land recorded at the discounted value of the note.
d. Interest on the note should be imputed at the prevailing rate for similar notes and the land recorded at present value of the note.

131. For an investment in stock to be classified as a temporary investment

	The security must be readily marketable	*There must be a lack of management intent to hold for long-term purposes*
a.	Yes	Yes
b.	Yes	No
c.	No	Yes
d.	No	No

132. From the viewpoint of the investor, which of the following securities provides the least risk?

a. Mortgage bond.
b. Subordinated debenture.
c. Income bond.
d. Debentures.

133. An organization holds the following investments at December 31, 2002, a balance sheet date:

Investment in unconsolidated subsidiary	$200,000
Investment in 90-day Treasury bills	40,000
Redemption (cash surrender) value of life insurance	60,000
Land held for speculation	100,000

The amount to be reported for total long-term investments at December 31, 2002, is

a. $200,000
b. $260,000
c. $360,000
d. $400,000

134. An organization had the following account balances at December 31, 2002:

Common stock, $10 par, 100,000 shares authorized, 80,000 shares issued and outstanding	$800,000
Additional paid-in capital (in excess of par value)	400,000
Retained earnings	500,000

All shares outstanding were issued in a prior period for $15 per share. On January 5, 2003, 1,000 shares were purchased for the treasury for $17 per share. These treasury shares were sold on February 6, 2003, for $18 per share. The effect of the purchase and sale of the 1,000 shares of treasury stock was to

a. Increase stockholders' equity by $1,000.
b. Increase stockholders' equity by $2,000.
c. Increase stockholders' equity by $3,000.
d. Not change stockholders' equity.

135. On April 1, 2001, ABC Company exchanged 10,000 shares of its common stock with a total par value of $20,000 for a piece of land owned by XYZ Company. The shares of stock were treasury shares which were purchased years earlier by ABC for a total of $35,000 and which had a market value of $44,000 on April 1, 2001. The land had a recorded value on XYZ's books of $28,000. What amount should be recorded as the cost of the land by ABC Company?

a. $20,000
b. $28,000
c. $35,000
d. $44,000

136. At December 31, 2003, a company had the following stockholders' equity accounts:

Common stock, $10 par, 100,000 shares authorized, 40,000 shares issued and outstanding	$ 400,000
Paid-in capital in excess of par from issuance of common stock	640,000
Retained earnings	1,000,000
Total stockholders' equity	$2,040,000

Each of the 40,000 shares of common stock outstanding was issued at a price of $26. On January 2, 2004, 2,000 shares were reacquired for $30 per share. The cost method is used in accounting for this treasury stock. Which of the following correctly describes the effect of the acquisition of the treasury stock?

a. Common stock is reduced by $20,000.
b. Paid-in capital in excess of par from issuance of common stock is reduced by $32,000.
c. The retained earnings account balance is reduced by $8,000.
d. Total stockholders' equity is reduced by $60,000.

137. Funds set aside for periodic interest payments on a governmental unit's general obligation bonds would be included in which fund or group of accounts?

a. Special revenue.
b. General long-term debt.
c. Internal service.
d. Debt service.

138. Which of the following is required in order for a company to record an estimated loss contingency as a liability?

a. The exact payee must be known.
b. The exact date payable must be known.
c. It must be considered reasonably possible that a liability has been incurred.
d. It must be possible to reasonably estimate the amount of the loss.

139. An organization has the following contingencies at a balance sheet date:

I. Threat of expropriation of assets; reasonable possibility of loss.
II. Pending litigation; reasonable possibility of loss.
III. Risk of loss or damage of enterprise property by fire, explosion, or other hazards; likelihood of loss is remote.

Which of the above items must be disclosed in the notes to the financial statements?

a. I and II only.
b. II and III only.
c. I and III only.
d. I, II and III.

140. A company issues financial statements in which there is an assumed conversion of warrants and options into common stock. Moreover, there is an assumed repayment of debt relating to the assumed conversion. This scenario is most closely associated with which of the following?

a. Computation of contingent liability disclosures.
b. Computation of primary and fully diluted earnings per share.
c. Extraordinary items and cumulative effect changes.
d. Retroactive-effect changes and common stock equivalents.

141. When a company changes to the last-in-first-out (LIFO) method of inventory valuation, there is no restatement of prior year's income because

a. Restatement would be impractical.
b. Restatement would reduce the usefulness of prior period statements.
c. Restatement would not change the reported result.
d. Restatement would reduce prior year's income.

142. Which of the following errors is **not** self-correcting over two accounting periods?

a. Failure to record accrued wages.
b. Failure to record depreciation.
c. Overstatement of inventory purchases.
d. Failure to record prepaid expenses.

143. Which of the following measures of an employer's pension obligation under a defined benefit plan will result in the largest measurement of the liability?

a. Vested benefits pension obligation.
b. Unvested benefits pension obligation.
c. Projected benefit obligation.
d. Accumulated benefit obligation.

144. A pension fund is projecting the amount necessary today to fund a retiree's pension benefits. The retiree's first annual pension check will be in 10 years. Payments are expected to last for a total of 20 annual payments. Which of the following **best** describes the computation of the amount needed today to fund the retiree's annuity?

a. Present value of $1 for 10 periods, times the present value of an ordinary annuity of 20 payments, times the annual annuity payment.
b. Present value of $1 for 9 periods, times the present value of an ordinary annuity of 20 payments, times the annual annuity payment.
c. Future value of $1 for 10 periods, times the present value of an ordinary annuity of 20 payments, times the annual annuity payment.
d. Future value of $1 for 9 periods, times the present value of an ordinary annuity of 20 payments, times the annual annuity payment.

145. The present value of future benefits payable as a result of work done before the start or change in a pension plan is the definition of

a. Minimum liability.
b. Fair value of plan assets.
c. Projected benefit obligation.
d. Prior service cost.

146. At December 31, 2004 a company had the following data relating to its defined benefit pension plan:

Total fair value of plan assets	$1,800,000
Accumulated benefit obligation	2,600,000
Projected benefit obligation	3,100,000

In its December 31, 2004, balance sheet, the company should report a minimum liability relating to the pension plan of

a. $ 500,000
b. $ 800,000
c. $1,300,000
d. $2,600,000

147. A company that sprays chemicals in residences to eliminate or prevent infestation of insects requires that customers prepay for three months' service at the beginning of each new quarter. Select the term that appropriately describes this situation from the viewpoint of the exterminating company.

a. Unearned revenue.
b. Earned revenue.
c. Accrued revenue.
d. Prepaid expense.

148. The costs of organizing a business, including fees of attorneys and accountants should be

a. Capitalized, but not amortized, due to the indefinite life of the business.
b. Not recorded because they are an expense of the organizer.
c. Capitalized and amortized over their useful life, not to exceed 40 years.
d. Capitalized and deferred until liquidation of the business.

149. MNO Company purchased all 100,000 outstanding shares of XYZ Company's stock for $40 per share on August 31, 2002. On this date, XYZ's balance sheet showed total assets of $5,000,000 and total liabilities of $2,000,000. The fair value of XYZ's identifiable assets on this date was $550,000 greater than their carrying amount. The amount that should be reported on MNO's consolidated balance sheet on August 31, 2002, for goodwill is

a. $0
b. $450,000
c. $550,000
d. $1,000,000

150. A material amount of legal fees and other costs incurred by a holder of a copyright in successfully defending a copyright suit should be

a. Capitalized as part of the cost of the copyright and amortized over the remaining estimated useful life of the copyright, not to exceed 40 years.
b. Charged to an expense account in the period incurred.
c. Charged to a loss account in the period incurred.
d. Capitalized in a separate asset account and amortized over 40 years.

151. A financial statement includes all of the following items: net income, depreciation, operating activities, and financing activities. What financial statement is this?

a. Balance sheet.
b. Income statement.
c. Statement of cash flows.
d. Statement of stockholders' equity.

152. Which of the following is **not** a criterion for classifying and accounting for a noncancelable lease agreement as a capital lease?

a. The lease term is such a large proportion of the economic life of the asset that most of the risks and rewards of ownership are retained by the lessor.
b. The present value of the minimum lease payments is such a large proportion of the fair market value of the asset that the asset is effectively being purchased.
c. The lease transfers ownership of the property to the lessee.
d. The lease contains a bargain purchase option.

153. A company leases a new building. Title to the building will pass to the lessee at the end of the lease. Based on these facts, for the lessee

a. It will be a capital lease, regardless of additional facts.
b. It will be a capital lease, provided other necessary conditions are met.
c. It will be an operating lease, despite any additional facts.
d. It will be an operating lease, provided other necessary conditions are met.

154. Financing (or capital) leases are differentiated from operating leases, in that financing leases normally

a. Provide for maintenance service at no extra cost to the lessee.
b. Are cancelable at any time upon request by the lessee.
c. Have rental payments that are approximately equal to the amortized cost of the equipment.
d. Are used only by financial institutions.

155. A lessee has a lease with the following characteristics:

1. The lessor retains ownership of the leased asset at the end of the lease term. There is no purchase option and no automatic transfer of title.
2. The lease term is 6 years and the economic life of the asset is 10 years.
3. The present value of the minimum lease payments is equal to 75% of the fair value of the leased asset.

This lease should appear on the balance sheet of the lessee as a(n)

a. Asset/liability.
b. Asset/equity.
c. Intangible asset/expense.
d. Does not appear.

156. At the inception of a capital lease the guaranteed residual value should be
a. Included as part of minimum lease payments at present value.
b. Included as part of minimum lease payments at future value.
c. Included as part of minimum lease payments at future value of an annuity due.
d. Ignored since it is not part of the lease contract.

157. The measurement basis most often used to report a long-term payable representing a commitment to pay money at a determinable future date is
a. Historical cost.
b. Current cost.
c. Net realizable value.
d. Present value of future cash flows.

158. Using the cost-recovery method of revenue recognition, profit on an installment sale is recognized as income
a. On the date of the installment sale.
b. In proportion to the cash collections.
c. After cash collections equal to the cost of goods sold have been received.
d. On the date the final cash collection is received.

159. A service company keeps its accounting records on a cash basis. During 1996, the company collected $600,000 from customers. The following information is also available:

	Beginning of year	*End of year*
Accounts receivable	$120,000	$180,000
Unearned revenue	0	15,000

What was the amount of service revenue earned for the year on an accrual basis?
a. $525,000
b. $555,000
c. $645,000
d. $675,000

160. A company has appropriately used the installment method of accounting since it began operations at the beginning of the current year. The following information pertains to its operations for this year:

Installment sales	$1,200,000
Cost of installment sales	840,000
Collections on installment sales	480,000
General and administrative expenses	120,000

The amount of gross profit deferred at the end of the current year should be
a. $720,000
b. $288,000
c. $216,000
d. $144,000

161. A manufacturer receives an advance payment for special-order goods that are to be manufactured and delivered within the next year. The advance payment should be reported in the manufacturer's current year balance sheet as a(n)
a. Current liability.
b. Noncurrent liability.
c. Contra asset amount.
d. Accrued revenue.

162. A company is depreciating an asset with a five-year useful life. It cost $100,000 and has no salvage value. If the (List A) method is used, depreciation expense in the second year will be (List B).

	List A	*List B*
a.	Sum-of-years' digits	$20,000
b.	Sum-of-years' digits	$40,000
c.	Double-declining balance	$16,000
d.	Double-declining balance	$24,000

163. If market rates of interest rise after issuance of a bond
a. The market price of the bond will drop.
b. Interest expense recorded on the bond will rise.
c. Cash interest payments on the bond will rise.
d. The market price of the bond will exceed its face value.

164. In November 2005, the vice president of a local bank reviews the bank's mortgage portfolio prior to the December 31 year-end. The bank's largest client has mortgages on buildings in three cities. The client has incurred net losses for the past three years and is now experiencing serious cash flow problems. For the past six months no payments have been made on any of the three mortgages. The vice president reluctantly concludes that there is no longer reasonable assurance of timely collection of the full amount of principal and interest. What is the impact of this conclusion on the local bank's 2005 financial statements?
a. No accounting or disclosure of a possible loss in value is necessary.
b. Contingency note disclosure of a possible loss in value is required.
c. The carrying amount of the mortgages should be reduced, with a charge directly to retained earnings.
d. The carrying amount of the mortgages should be reduced, with a charge to the income statement.

165. On January 1, 2001, a company purchased a machine for $10,000. The estimated useful life was 10 years, with no salvage value. The company depreciates its fixed assets using the straight-line method. On January 1, 2005, it was estimated that the machine had a remaining useful life of three years. Compute the company's 2005 depreciation expense for the machine.
a. $1,000
b. $2,000
c. $3,000
d. $6,000

166. Which of the following statements is true for a defined-contribution pension plan?
a. The employer is required to contribute a certain amount each period based on the plan's formula.
b. The employer bears the risk of the plan's investment performance.
c. Retirement benefits received by employees are defined by the plan's formula.
d. The employer and employees are required to contribute equal amounts to the pension fund.

167. The accounting treatment for a prior period adjustment revises the income statement of the period to which the event relates. Opening retained earnings are adjusted for the after-tax effect of the prior period adjustment. A prior period adjustment is charged to the income statement of an earlier period because

a. A prior period adjustment indicates that there was an error in previous financial statements; therefore, the previous financial statements are corrected.
b. The income statement of the current period portrays only the regular, recurring earnings of the business, based on normal operations. A prior period adjustment is not a regular, recurring item.
c. The income statement of the current period portrays events or estimates arising in the current period only. A prior period adjustment is a correction for an event or estimate that existed in an earlier period.
d. The income statement of the current period reflects the long-range income-producing ability of the enterprise. A prior period adjustment is not an indication of long-range income producing ability.

168. A company that owns a new professional basketball team sells season tickets to its team's games. The season lasts from November through April, with ten games played each month. In 2005, the company collected $3,000,000 from season-ticket sales for the 2005-2006 season. Its fiscal year end is December 31. Based on this information, the company should

a. Report a liability for unearned revenue of $2,000,000 on its December 31, 2005 balance sheet.
b. Report a liability for unearned revenue of $3,000,000 on its December 31, 2005 balance sheet.
c. Report revenue of $3,000,000 on its 2005 income statement.
d. Report revenue of $1,000,000 on its 2006 income statement.

169. If bonds are initially sold at a discount and the effective interest method of amortization is used

a. Interest expense in the earlier periods will be less than interest expense in the later periods.
b. Interest expense in the earlier periods will be greater than interest expense in the later periods.
c. Interest expense will equal the cash interest payment each period.
d. Interest expense will be less than the cash interest payment each period.

170. A company purchased a machine for $700,000. The machine was depreciated using the straight-line method and had a salvage value of $40,000. The machine was sold on December 31, 2005. The accumulated depreciation related to the machine was $495,000 on that date. The company reported a gain on the sale of the machine of $75,000 in its income statement for the fiscal year ending December 31, 2005. The selling price of the machine was

a. $280,000
b. $240,000
c. $205,000
d. $115,000

171. A company purchased a machine on January 1, 2003, for $1,000,000. The machine had an estimated useful life of nine years and a salvage value of $100,000. The company uses straight-line depreciation. On December 31, 2006, the machine was sold for $535,000. The gain or loss that should be recorded on the disposal of this machine is

a. $35,000 gain.
b. $65,000 loss.
c. $365,000 loss.
d. $465,000 loss.

172. Because of a defect discovered in its seat belts in December 2005, an automobile manufacturer believes it is probable that it will be required to recall its products. The final decision on the recall is expected to be made in March 2006 and is estimated to cost the automobile manufacturer $2,500,000. How should this information be reported in the December 31, 2005 financial statements?

a. As a loss of $2,500,000 and a liability of $2,500,000.
b. As a prior period adjustment of $2,500,000.
c. As an appropriation of retained earnings of $2,500,000.
d. It should not be disclosed because it has not yet happened.

173. The failure to record an accrued expense at year-end will result in which of the following overstatement errors in the financial statements prepared at that date?

	Net income	*Working capital*	*Cash*
a.	No	No	Yes
b.	No	Yes	No
c.	Yes	No	No
d.	Yes	Yes	No

174. A depreciable asset has an estimated 20% salvage value. At the end of the asset's estimated useful life, the accumulated depreciation would equal the original cost of the asset under which of the following depreciation methods?

	Declining balance	*Sum-of-the-years' digits*
a.	Yes	Yes
b.	Yes	No
c.	No	Yes
d.	No	No

175. A company purchased new equipment on July 1, 2005, which had a list price of $52,500. The company traded old equipment, which was being depreciated using the straight-line method, and paid $35,000 in cash. The following information pertains to the old equipment:

Cost on January 1, 2002	$38,900
Estimated useful life	5 years
Residual (salvage) value	$2,900
Fair value on July 1, 2005	$16,000

If the old and new equipment is dissimilar, the company will record the new equipment at

a. $45,100
b. $48,700
c. $51,000
d. $52,500

176. How will net income be affected by the amortization of a premium on bonds payable?

a. Interest expense is decreased so net income is increased.
b. Interest expense is increased so net income is decreased.
c. Interest revenue is increased so net income is increased.
d. Interest revenue is decreased so net income is decreased.

177. Zero coupon bonds
a. Sell for a small fraction of their face value because their yield is much lower than the market rate.
b. Increase in value each year as they approach maturity, providing the owner with the total payoff at maturity.
c. Are redeemable in measures of a commodity such as barrels of oil, tons of coal, or ounces of rare metal (e.g., silver).
d. Are high-interest-rate, high-risk, unsecured bonds which have been used extensively to finance leveraged buyouts.

178. A metropolitan hospital assigns its unpaid patient accounts receivables over 120 days old to a collection agency, with recourse, for 75% of the balance due. The remaining 25% is written off as uncollectible. What is the charge to the hospital's allowance for uncollectible accounts during July 2005 if that month's transactions are summarized as follows?

Accounts assigned	$800,000
Accounts collected	400,000
Accounts returned	100,000

a. $200,000
b. $300,000
c. $400,000
d. $500,000

179. A company presents investments on its financial statements at the lower of cost or market. The company's investment information for the year ended June 30, 2006, was

	Cost	*Market*
Investments at July 1, 2005	$317,000	$335,000
Investments at June 20, 2006	465,000	485,000
Proceeds from sale of investments		209,000
Purchase of investments		352,000
Net gain on investment transactions		3,000
Net losses on investment transactions	8,000	

For the year ended June 30, 2006, what was the company's increase in unrealized appreciation of its investment assets?
a. $147,000
b. $ 12,000
c. $ 7,000
d. $ 5,000

180. If a company employs the sum-of-the-years' digits (SYD) method of depreciation for an asset with an estimated useful life of four years, the percentage of the total depreciable cost that will be expensed in the third year is
a. 10%
b. 25%
c. 20%
d. 75%

181. A vendor sells specialty inks on consignment to a manufacturer of colored paper at a price of $200 per barrel. Payment is made to the vendor in the month the manufacturer uses the barrels in production. The vendor records revenues when the barrels are shipped and makes no adjusting entries to record unearned revenues until the December 31 closing of the books. At the end of July 2005, the manufacturer had 40 barrels of ink on consignment. During August 2005, the vendor consigned 50 barrels and received payment for 30 barrels. Another 5 barrels were returned to the vendor by the manufacturer for credit. At the end of August, what is the amount of unearned revenue contained in the vendor's accounts receivable from the manufacturer?
a. $ 3,000
b. $ 4,000
c. $11,000
d. $12,000

182. On January 1, 2001, a company purchased an abandoned quarry for $1,200,000 to be used as a landfill to service its trash collection contracts with nearby cities for the next twenty years. The company depletes the quarry using the units-of-production method based on a surveyor's measurements of volume of the quarry's pit. This was 500,000 cubic yards when purchased and 350,000 cubic yards at year-end 2005. What is the net amount that should be shown on the company's December 31, 2005 balance sheet for the quarry?
a. $1,200,000
b. $ 900,000
c. $ 840,000
d. $ 360,000

183. An analysis of a company's $150,000 accounts receivable at year-end resulted in a $5,000 ending balance for its allowance for uncollectible accounts and a bad debt expense of $2,000. During the past year, recoveries on bad debts previously written off were correctly recorded at $500. If the beginning balance in the allowance for uncollectible accounts was $4,700, what was the amount of accounts receivable written off as uncollectible during the year?
a. $1,200
b. $1,800
c. $2,200
d. $2,800

184. Which of the following is a noncash charge to earnings?
a. Administrative expense.
b. Interest expense.
c. Income tax expense.
d. Depreciation expense.

Items 185 through 187 are based on the following:

A company sells goods on an installment basis. The table below includes information about the level of installment sales, the cost of the goods sold on installment, and the cash receipts on installment sales for 2003 through 2005. All cash receipt amounts shown are net of any interest charges.

	2003	*2004*	*2005*
Installment sales	$10,000	$5,000	$20,000
Cost of installment sales	6,000	4,000	10,000
Cash receipts on 1993 sales	2,000	4,000	4,000
Cash receipts on 1994 sales		1,000	2,000
Cash receipts on 1995 sales			4,000

185. The company has a rate of gross profit on 2004 installment sales of
a. 20%
b. 40%
c. 50%
d. 80%

186. The amount of gross profit the company will recognize in 2003 on 2003 installment sales is
a. $ 800
b. $2,000
c. $3,200
d. $4,000

187. The company's gross profit amount from 2005 sales to be deferred to future years would be

a. $ 2,000
b. $ 3,000
c. $ 8,000
d. $10,000

188. A company had cash receipts from sales of $175,000 during 2005, of which $30,000 was unearned at the end of 2005. At the end of 2004, the company had $40,000 of unearned revenue, all of which was earned in 2005. The company's sales revenue for 2005 would be

a. $145,000
b. $165,000
c. $175,000
d. $185,000

189. Under the sum-of-the-years' digits (SYD) depreciation method, for an asset with a four-year useful life, the depreciation expense in the first year would be

a. 10%
b. 25%
c. 40%
d. 50%

190. A five-year asset costing $100,000 with no estimated salvage value is being depreciated using the double-declining balance (DDB) method. The book value of this asset at the end of its second year of life would be

a. $24,000
b. $36,000
c. $60,000
d. $64,000

191. The effective interest method and the straight-line method of amortizing a bond discount differ in that the effective interest method results in

a. Higher total interest expense over the term of the bonds.
b. Escalating annual interest expense over the term of the bonds.
c. Shrinking annual interest expense over the term of the bonds.
d. Constant annual interest expense over the term of the bonds.

192. Which one of the following loss contingencies would usually be accounted for by accruing the liability?

a. General or unspecified business risks.
b. Risk of loss from catastrophes that might occur to a manufacturing company.
c. Risk of loss or damage of enterprise property caused by fire, explosion, or other hazards.
d. Premiums offered to customers.

193. On January 1, 2003, a company purchased a piece of equipment for $250,000, which was originally estimated to have a useful life of ten years with no salvage value. Depreciation has been recorded for three years on a straight-line basis.

On January 1, 2006, the estimated useful life was revised so that the equipment is considered to have a total life of 20 years. Assume that the depreciation method and the useful life for financial reporting and tax purposes are the same. The depreciation expense in 2006 on this equipment would be

a. $ 8,750
b. $10,294
c. $12,500
d. $14,706

194. Which of the following leases would be classified as a capital lease by the lessee?

	Lease A	*Lease B*	*Lease C*	*Lease D*
Contains a bargain purchase option?	Yes	No	No	No
Lease term portion of the economic life of the leased property	60%	70%	80%	90%
Present value of the minimum lease payments as a portion of the fair value of the leased property	60%	70%	80%	90%

a. Lease A only.
b. Lease B only.
c. Leases A, C, and D.
d. Leases C and D only.

195. Capital and operating leases differ in that the lessor

a. Only obtains use of the asset under a capital lease.
b. Is using the lease as a source of financing only under an operating lease.
c. Makes rent payments which are actually installment payments constituting a payment of both principal and interest only under a capital lease.
d. Finances the transaction through the leased asset only under a capital lease.

196. In calculating fully diluted earnings per share when a company has convertible bonds outstanding, the number of common shares outstanding must be (List A) to adjust for the conversion feature of the bonds, and the net income must be (List B) by the amount of interest expense on the bonds, net of tax.

	List A	*List B*
a.	Increased	Increased
b.	Increased	Decreased
c.	Decreased	Increased
d.	Decreased	Decreased

197. If a company has outstanding bonds with a sinking fund provision and if interest rates have (List A) since the bonds were issued, then the company would realize a savings in meeting its sinking fund obligations by (List B).

	List A	*List B*
a.	Increased	Buying back bonds in the open market
b.	Remained constant	Calling in a portion of the bonds at face value
c.	Increased	Calling in a portion of the bonds at face value
d.	Decreased	Buying back bonds in the open market

198. If certain goods owned by an organization were not recorded as a purchase and were not counted in ending inventory, in error, then

a. Cost of goods sold for the period will be understated.
b. Cost of goods sold for the period will be overstated.
c. Net income for the period will be understated.

d. There will be no effect on cost of goods sold or net income for the period.

199. If an organization records beginning inventory and purchases correctly, but some items are not included in ending inventory, in error, then

a. Income for the current period is overstated.
b. Income for the following period is understated.
c. Income for the current period plus the following period, in total, is understated.
d. Income for the current period plus the following period, in total, is correct.

200. In the years after mid-service point of a depreciable asset, which of the following depreciation methods will result in the highest depreciation expense?

a. Sum-of-the-years' digits.
b. Declining balance.
c. Double-declining balance.
d. Straight-line.

201. When a right of return exists, all of the following are conditions that must be met for a company to recognize revenue from a sales transaction at the time of sale, **except:**

a. The amount of future returns is known with certainty.
b. The buyer's obligation to the seller would not be changed in the event of theft or physical damage of the product.
c. The seller's price to the buyer is substantially fixed or determinable at the date of sale.
d. The buyer has paid the seller, or the buyer is obligated to pay the seller and the obligation is not contingent on resale of the product.

202. An organization has a long-term construction contract in process. During the current period, the estimated total contract cost has increased sufficiently so that there is a current period loss, even though the contract is still estimated to be profitable overall. Under these circumstances, the (List A) method of revenue recognition would require a (List B) period adjustment of expected gross profit recognized on the contract.

	List A	List B
a.	Percentage-of-completion	Prior
b.	Percentage-of-completion	Current
c.	Completed-contract	Prior
d.	Completed-contract	Current

203. An organization uses the sum-of-the-years' digits (SYD) method of depreciation. In the third year of use of an asset with a four-year estimated useful life, the portion of the depreciable cost for the asset that the organization will expense is

a. 10%
b. 20%
c. 30%
d. 33.33%

204. If the market rate of interest is (List A) the coupon rate when bonds are issued, then the bonds will sell in the market at a price (List B) the face value and the issuing firm will record a (List C) on bonds payable.

	List A	List B	List C
a.	Equal to	Equal to	Premium
b.	Greater than	Greater than	Premium
c.	Greater than	Less than	Discount
d.	Less than	Greater than	Discount

205. Under a defined contribution pension plan, a(n) (List A) is reported on the balance sheet only if the amount the organization has contributed to the pension trust is (List B) the amount required.

	List A	List B
a.	Asset	Greater than
b.	Asset	Equal to
c.	Liability	Greater than
d.	Liability	Equal to

206. If a lease agreement transfers substantially all of the benefits and risks incident to ownership of the asset to the lessee, then the asset value is recognized on the lessee's records as a(n) (List A) asset and the lease is referred to as a(n) (List B) lease.

	List A	List B
a.	Tangible	Capital
b.	Intangible	Capital
c.	Tangible	Operating
d.	Intangible	Operating

207. Convertible bonds and bonds issued with warrants differ in that

a. Convertible bonds have lower coupon rates than straight bonds while bonds issued with warrants have higher coupon rates than straight bonds.
b. Convertible bonds have higher coupon rates than straight bonds while bonds issued with warrants have lower coupon rates than straight bonds.
c. Convertible bonds remain outstanding after the bondholder exercises the right to become a common shareholder, while bonds that are issued with warrants do not.
d. Bonds that are issued with warrants remain outstanding after the bondholder exercises the right to become a common shareholder, while convertible bonds do not.

208. If depreciation was materially overstated in error in the prior year, the correction in the following year when the error is detected will involve

a. Increasing reported earnings for the current year.
b. Decreasing reported earnings for the current year.
c. Increasing the opening balance of retained earnings for the current year.
d. Decreasing the opening balance of retained earnings for the current year.

209. Suppose that the company has paid one of its liabilities twice during the year, in error. The effects of this mistake would be

a. Assets, liabilities, and owners' equity are understated.
b. Assets, net income, and owners' equity are unaffected.
c. Assets and liabilities are understated.
d. Assets, net income, and owners' equity are understated, and liabilities are overstated.

210. Which of the following is **not** an appropriate basis for measuring the historical cost of fixed assets?

a. The purchase price, freight costs, and installation costs of a productive asset should be included in the asset's cost.
b. Proceeds obtained in the process of readying land for its intended purpose, such as from the sale of cleared timber, should be recognized immediately in income.
c. The costs of improvements to equipment incurred after its acquisition should be added to the asset's cost if they provide future service potential.
d. All costs incurred in the construction of a plant building, from excavation to completion, should be considered as part of the asset's cost.

211. If sales are accounted for using the installment method, which of the following is (are) only recognized in proportion to the cash collected on the sales during the period?

a. Sales.
b. Sales and cost of sales.
c. Sales, cost of sales, and selling expenses.
d. Sales, cost of sales, and administrative expenses.

212. A company sells inventory for $80,000 that had an inventory cost of $40,000. The terms of the sale involve payments receivable of $10,000 in the first year, $45,000 in the second year, and $25,000 in the third year. The buyer of the inventory is a new firm with no credit history. If the cost recovery method of revenue recognition is used, then the amount of gross profit the company will recognize in the second year is

a. $0
b. $ 5,000
c. $15,000
d. $45,000

213. A company is depreciating an asset with a five-year useful life. It cost $100,000 and has no salvage value. If the (List A) method is used, depreciation expense in the second year will be (List B).

	List A	*List B*
a.	Sum-of-years' digits	$20,000
b.	Sum-of-years' digits	$40,000
c.	Double-declining-balance	$16,000
d.	Double-declining-balance	$24,000

214. The Accumulated Pension Obligation of a company includes benefit obligations to (List A) employees at (List B) salary levels.

	List A	*List B*
a.	Vested	Current
b.	Vested	Future
c.	Vested and nonvested	Current
d.	Vested and nonvested	Future

215. A company sold a depreciable asset in the middle of the fifth year of its estimated 10-year useful life. The original cost of the asset was $100,000 and it was being depreciated on the straight-line basis. If the asset was sold for $80,000, the reported gain on the sale will be

a. $20,000
b. $25,000
c. $30,000
d. $35,000

216. A company issues 10-year bonds with a face value of $1,000,000, dated January 1, 2004, and bearing interest at an annual rate of 12% payable semiannually on January 1 and July 1. The full interest amount will be paid each due date. The market rate of interest on bonds of similar risk and maturity, with the same schedule of interest payments, is also 12%. If the bonds are issued on February 1, 2004, the amount the issuing company receives from the buyers of the bonds on that date is

a. $ 990,000
b. $1,000,000
c. $1,010,000
d. $1,020,000

217. Which of the following is **not** a factor, with respect to pending or threatened litigation, that must be considered in determining whether a liability should be recorded?

a. The time period in which the underlying cause for action occurred.
b. The probability of an unfavorable outcome.
c. The ability to make a reasonable estimate of the amount of loss.
d. The number of parties involved in the litigation.

218. Which of the following is **not** considered to be an intangible asset?

a. Goods on consignment.
b. Patents.
c. Copyrights.
d. Goodwill.

219. A company has $100 of current assets, $100 of fixed assets, $100 of debt, and $100 of equity. If it then leases a $75 asset in a(n) (List A) lease agreement, the debt to assets ratio of the company will then be (List B)

	List A	*List B*
a.	Operating	64%
b.	Operating	100%
c.	Capital	50%
d.	Capital	64%

220. Which of the following statements is **not** true of a "capital" lease?

a. The lessor "capitalizes" the present value of the future rental payments.
b. The lessor records the leased item as an asset.
c. The lessee records depreciation or "capital" cost allowance on the leased asset.
d. The lease arrangement represents a form of financing.

Items 221 through 223 are based on the following:

On January 1, 2003, a construction company signed a contract with a property management firm involving the construction of a large urban office tower. The total price of constructing the tower was agreed to be $10 million with $2 million being paid on the date of the agreement. Construction began immediately upon the signing of the contract and was expected to take three years to complete. The original estimate of total construction costs was $8 million.

During the year ended December 31, 2003, $4 million of construction costs were incurred, and engineering estimates indicated that the office tower was 30% complete at year-end. At year-end the revised estimate of total construction costs was $8.5 million and the property management firm had been billed a further $4 million, although only $1 million of that amount had been collected by year-end.

221. If the construction company uses the completed-contract method of revenue recognition, the December 31, 2003 financial statements will report (List A) of revenue from the long-term contract and (List B) will be the balance of the construction in progress account.

	List A	List B
a.	$0	$4 million
b.	$1 million	$4 million
c.	$2 million	$8 million
d.	$3 million	$8.5 million

222. If the construction company uses the percentage-of-completion (cost-to-cost basis) method of revenue recognition, then in 2003 the amount of revenue it will recognize on the long-term contract will be

a. $3,000,000
b. $4,705,882
c. $5,000,000
d. $6,000,000

223. Without prejudice to the previous two questions and answers, assume that the construction company recognizes $2 million of revenue for the long-term contract in 2003. If the company uses the percentage-of-completion method (cost-to-cost basis), then the unbilled contract price at the end of 2003 will be shown on the December 31, 2003 balance sheet as a (List A) of (List B).

	List A	List B
a.	Current asset	$1,000,000
b.	Current asset	$4,000,000
c.	Current liability	$1,000,000
d.	Current liability	$4,000,000

224. A new machine has an initial cost of $ 300,000, an estimated useful life of 2,000 hours of use over a three-year period and an estimated salvage value of $70,000. Usage rates are estimated as 500 hours in the first year, 700 hours in the second year, and 800 hours in the third year. Depreciation expense in year two under the activity method of depreciation will be

a. $ 57,500
b. $ 75,000
c. $ 80,500
d. $105,000

225. If a company employs the sum-of-the-years' digits method of depreciation for an asset with an estimated useful life of four years, then the percentage of the total depreciable cost that will be expensed in the third year is

a. 10%
b. 25%
c. 20%
d. 75%

226. Which of the following correctly describes how prior period adjustments are accounted for?

a. They are included in the determination of net income for the current period.
b. Prior period financial statements are adjusted and reissued.
c. They are charged or credited directly to the opening balance of retained earnings for the current period.
d. They are charged or credited directly to the closing balance of retained earnings for the prior period.

227. The straight-line and the effective interest methods are two ways to amortize bond discounts and premiums. The (List A) method results in constant interest revenue for the investing firm and the (List B) method results in a varying rate of return on the book value of the long-term bond investment.

	List A	List B
a.	Straight-line	Straight-line
b.	Straight-line	Effective interest
c.	Effective interest	Straight-line
d.	Effective interest	Effective interest

228. In what type of pension plan does the employee get the benefit of gain or the risk of loss from contributed assets?

a. Mutual fund.
b. Real estate trust.
c. Defined benefit.
d. Defined contribution.

Items 229 through 232 are based on the following:

On January 1 a new landscaping firm acquired a fleet of vehicles, all the necessary tools and equipment, and a parking and storage facility. It began operations immediately. It is now the end of the first year of operations and the first set of year-end financial statements is being prepared. Several decisions have to be made regarding the appropriate accounting and reporting practices for this company. Relevant information for several of these items is described in the following list of transactions and events.

At year-end, the parking and storage facility that was purchased for $150,000 has a market value of $250,000. The physical flow of inventory is first-in-first-out (FIFO), and the cost of materials has risen steadily over the year. In order to promote sales for the coming year, maintenance contracts were sold in December at very reasonable prices, provided that the customers paid cash. On April 1, the company arranged a $100,000, 10% bank loan. Interest payments of $5,000 are due on October 1 and April 1 of each year during the five-year term of the loan.

During the first year of operations, the company experienced a 5% bad-debt rate on credit sales. None of the bad debts are expected to be recovered, since this is the industry average level of bad debts. Total credit sales for the year were $400,000. The year-end balance of accounts receivable, which includes uncollected overdue accounts, is $100,000. Half of the uncollected overdue amounts are estimated to be uncollectible.

229. The company will recognize revenue from the December sale of the maintenance contracts in the (List A) year if it selects (List B) basis reporting.

	List A	List B
a.	First	Cash
b.	First	Accrual
c.	Second	Cash
d.	Third	Accrual

230. The company will report a value of (List A) for the parking and storage facility if it prepares financial reports consistent with the (List B) principle.

	List A	List B
a.	$150,000	Matching
b.	$150,000	Historic cost
c.	$250,000	Going concern
d.	$250,000	Revenue recognition

231. If the company uses the (List A) approach to estimate bad debt expense, the estimated bad debt expense will be (List B).

	List A	List B
a.	Balance sheet	$20,000
b.	Balance sheet	$100,000
c.	Income statement	$20,000
d.	Income statement	$50,000

232. If the company reports expenses on an accrual basis, interest expense for the first year of operations is

a. $ 5,000
b. $ 7,500
c. $10,000
d. $12,500

233. The ABC Company operates a catering service, which specializes in business luncheons for large corporations. ABC requires customers to place their orders two weeks in advance of the scheduled events. ABC bills its customers on the tenth day of the month following the date of service and requires that payment be made within 30 days of the billing date. Conceptually, ABC should recognize revenue from its catering services at the date when a

a. Customer places an order.
b. Luncheon is served.
c. Billing is mailed.
d. Customer's payment is received.

234. In performing an audit you encounter an adjusting journal entry recorded at year-end which contains a debit to rental revenue and a credit to unearned rental revenue. The purpose of this journal entry is to record a(n)

a. Accrued revenue.
b. Unexpired cost.
c. Expired cost.
d. Deferred revenue.

235. A company provides monitoring services for home security systems. It collects the quarterly monitoring fees in advance. During 2005, the company collected $400,000 for fees that pertain to 2006. On the financial statements, these advance receipts should be classified as

a. Revenues on the income statement.
b. Unearned revenues on the balance sheet.
c. Accrued revenues on the balance sheet.
d. Accrued liabilities on the balance sheet.

236. DEF is the consignee for 1,000 units of product X for ABC Company. ABC should recognize the revenue from these 1,000 units when

a. The agreement between DEF and ABC is signed.
b. ABC ships the goods to DEF.
c. DEF receives the goods from ABC.
d. DEF sells the goods and informs ABC of the sale.

237. On December 31, 2001, XYZ Company issued five-year bonds with a face amount of $1,000,000. The bonds carry a stated interest rate of 10% and were sold at par. Interest is payable annually on December 31. According to the provisions of the bond indenture, XYZ is to make annual deposits into a bond sinking fund (beginning December 31, 2002) in order to accumulate the funds necessary to retire the bonds at their maturity. On December 31, 2005, all required interest payments and sinking fund payments due to-date have been made on schedule. If it has been determined that sinking fund assets are to be reported in the long-term investment classification on the balance sheet, how should the balance of bonds payable be classified on the December 31, 2005 balance sheet?

a. Current liability.
b. Long-term liability.
c. Contra to long-term investments.
d. Deferred credit.

238. At December 31, 2005, the balance of a customer's account is $500,000, which represents a material amount to the reporting company. The customer has recently declared bankruptcy. How should the company report the $500,000 receivable on its financial statements for 2005?

a. As an extraordinary loss on the income statement
b. As a reduction of sales on the income statement
c. At its face amount on the balance sheet
d. At its estimated net realizable value on the balance sheet

239. On January 1, 2005, ABC Company purchased a piece of equipment, which is expected to have an estimated service life of four years and a salvage value of $200,000. The following expenditures relate to the acquisition of that equipment:

Purchase price	$500,000
Shipping charges	50,000
Set-up costs	120,000

Assuming the sum-of-the-years' depreciation (SYD) method is used to calculate depreciation, what amount of depreciation should be reported for 2005?

a. $120,000
b. $188,000
c. $200,000
d. $268,000

240. On January 1, 2005, the XYZ Corporation purchased a new machine at a price of $400,000. A down payment of $100,000 was made at the date of purchase and six monthly installments of $50,000 each were made beginning on February 1. Interest at a rate of 12% per annum was also due and paid monthly on the unpaid balance. The interest charges amounted to $10,500 over the six-month period. Installation charges of $25,000 were also paid on January 1, 2005. The machine is estimated to have a service life of five years and no salvage value. The appropriate base for depreciation is

a. $400,000
b. $410,500
c. $425,000
d. $435,500

241. A company, using the cost method, reacquired 100 shares of its $10 par common stock for $1,000. The company later sold 40 of these shares at $12 per share and another 40 shares at $9 per share. The net effect of these three transactions on stockholders' equity is a

a. $160 decrease.
b. $200 increase.
c. $200 decrease.
d. $160 increase.

242. A material gain on the sale of a fully depreciated asset should be classified on the income statement as part of

a. Discontinued operations.
b. Extraordinary income.
c. Income from operations.
d. Other revenues and gains.

243. A company needs $84,000 in a bond sinking (retirement) fund at the end of five years. Deposits are made at the end of each year. The future amount of 1 for an ordinary annuity is 6.0 and the future amount of 1 for an annuity due is 7.0. The annual contribution to the sinking fund should be

a. $16,800
b. $12,000
c. $14,000
d. $13,800

244. A company purchased the following for $120,000:

	Seller's book	*Estimated fair market*
Land	$ 50,000	$60,000
Building	$100,000	$90,000

Land should be recorded as

a. $40,000
b. $48,000
c. $50,000
d. $60,000

245. A major difference between operating and financial leases is that

a. Operating leases usually do not provide for maintenance while financial leases do.
b. Operating lease contracts are written for a period that exceeds the economic life of the leased equipment.
c. Operating leases frequently contain a cancellation clause, while financial leases are not cancelable.
d. The lessee finances the assets leased for an operating lease.

246. On February 1, 2004, a computer software firm agrees to program a software package. Twelve payments of $10,000 on the first of each month are to be made, with the first payment March 1, 2004. The client accepted the software on June 1, 2005. How much 2004 revenue should be recognized?

a. $0
b. $100,000
c. $110,000
d. $120,000

247. A company uses the sum-of-the-year's digits (SYD) depreciation method. Proper 2005 financial statements disclosure relating to a $100,000 cost depreciable asset with $10,000 salvage value and five-year life purchased January 1, 2003 will include

a. Depreciation expense $20,000.
b. Depreciation expense $24,000.
c. Accumulated depreciation $54,000.
d. Accumulated depreciation $72,000.

248. A corporation purchases equipment, which costs $100,000. Transportation costs amount to $8,000 and installation costs are $13,000. The corporation finances the purchase of this equipment with a 12%, five-year, $100,000 note. The principal and interest on the note are due at the end of year 5. The appropriate base for depreciating this equipment is

a. $121,000
b. $113,000
c. $181,000
d. $108,000

249. In 2004, a construction company agreed to build a bridge for $3,000,000. Given

	2004	*2005*
During the year		
Costs incurred	$ 720,000	$ 995,000
Customer billings	900,000	1,000,000
Collections of billings	750,000	1,100,000
Estimated costs to complete, December 31	1,680,000	735,000

Gross profit recognized in 2005 under the percentage-of-completion method is

a. $205,000
b. $223,367
c. $240,000
d. $385,000

250. When a lease meets certain criteria it is to be capitalized for financial reporting purposes. A capitalized lease will result in reporting items on financial statements that differ from the items that get reported for an operating lease. Which of the following groups represents items that will be reported by a lessee with a piece of equipment under capital lease?

a. Rent expense and prepaid rent.
b. Interest expense and prepaid rent.
c. Depreciation expense and interest expense.
d. Depreciation expense and rent expense.

251. A Company which sponsors a defined benefit plan for its employees should disclose the (a) Fair market value of plan assets available for benefits. (b) Amount of unrecognized prior service cost.

a. Both the (a) and the (b).
b. The (a) but not the (b).
c. The (b) but not the (a).
d. Neither the (a) nor the (b).

Advanced Concepts

252. An US company and a German company purchased the same stock on the German stock exchange and held the stock for one year. If the value of the German mark weakened against the US dollar during the period, in comparison with the German company's return, the US company's return will be

a. Lower.
b. Higher.
c. The same.
d. Indeterminate from the information provided.

253. When a business is acquired, the purchasing company calculates goodwill associated with the acquisition as the difference between the purchase price and the

a. Book value of the identifiable net assets acquired.
b. Fair market value of the identifiable net assets acquired.
c. Book value of the net tangible assets acquired.
d. Fair market value of the net tangible assets acquired.

254. A business combination during 2002 resulted in purchased goodwill of $200,000. Subsequently, the combined entity spent an additional $80,000 during 2002 on activities that were designed to maintain the collective goodwill of the combined entity. Management looks upon goodwill as having an indefinite life. The amount of goodwill which can be capitalized during 2002 amounts to

a. $0
b. $80,000
c. $200,000
d. $280,000

255. A corporation acquires an ownership interest in the common stock of another corporation. The ownership acquired is 30% of the outstanding common stock. In this situation, the long-term investment is generally accounted for on the investor corporation's books using which of the following reporting methods?

a. Lower of cost or market.
b. Cost.
c. Consolidated.
d. Equity.

256. If a company has a long-term investment in (List A) percent of the outstanding common stock of another company, it would generally report this investment using the (List B) method.

	List A	*List B*
a.	80	Cost
b.	40	Equity
c.	15	Consolidation
d.	5	Equity

257. In which legal form of business organization do the owners of the business enjoy limited liability?

a. Sole proprietorship.
b. Partnership.
c. Corporation.
d. Oligopoly.

258. A corporation has gathered the following data in order to compute the purchasing power gain or loss to be included in its supplementary information for the year ended December 31, 2005:

	Amount in nominal dollars	
	December 31, 2004	*December 31, 2005*
Net monetary assets	$800,000	$943,000
		Index number
Consumer price index at December 31, 2004		200
Consumer price index at December 31, 2005		230
Average consumer price index for 2005		220

The purchasing power gain or loss on net monetary items (expressed in average-for-the-year dollars for 1990) should be reported at what amount for the year ended December 31, 2005?

a. $121,000 purchasing power loss.
b. $121,000 purchasing power gain.
c. $126,500 purchasing power loss.
d. $126,500 purchasing power gain.

259. A conglomerate company acquired 100% of the net assets of a target company for $900 cash. The target company's balance sheet just prior to the acquisition is presented below.

Target Company (as of acquisition date)

	Book value	*Fair value*
Cash	$ 100	$100
Receivables	200	200
Inventory	150	200
Property, plant, and equipment (net)	600	400
Total assets	$1,050	$900
Current liabilities	$ 200	$200
Capital stock	200	
Retained earnings	650	
Total liabilities and equity	$1,050	

The amount of goodwill to be recorded by the conglomerate company related to its purchase of the target company would be

a. $(200)
b. $ 50
c. $ 200
d. None of the above.

260. The effect of amortizing a positive amount of goodwill would be to

a. Decrease reported earnings.
b. Increase other income.
c. Decrease operating expenses.
d. Increase reported cost of goods sold.

261. Company A acquired Company B for $1,000,000. At the time of the acquisition, Company B's net assets had a book value of $900,000 and a fair market value of $800,000. The amount of goodwill Company A recorded on the acquisition date was

a. $0
b. $100,000
c. $200,000
d. $300,000

Financial Statement Analysis

262. Which of the following is true about the impact of price inflation on financial ratio analysis?

a. Inflation impacts only those ratios computed from balance sheet accounts.
b. Inflation impacts financial ratio analysis for one firm over time, but not comparative analysis of firms of different ages.
c. Inflation impacts financial ratio analysis for one firm over time, as well as comparative analysis of firms of different ages.
d. Inflation impacts comparative analysis of firms of different ages, but not financial ratio analysis for one firm over time.

263. The times-interest-earned ratio is primarily an indication of a company's

a. Solvency.
b. Liquidity.
c. Asset management.
d. Degree of financial leverage.

264. What conclusion should a financial analyst draw if a company has a high fixed assets turnover ratio?

a. The company may be overcapitalized.
b. The company may have a problem with employees converting inventory to personal use.
c. The company may be undercapitalized.
d. The company has favorable profitability.

265. Which combination of ratios can be used to derive return on equity?

a. Market value to book value ratio and total debt to total assets ratio.
b. Price to earnings ratio, earnings per share, and net profit margin.
c. Price to earnings ratio and return on assets.
d. Net profit margin, asset turnover, and equity multiplier.

266. What conclusion should a financial analyst draw from the following ratios?

	Company average	*Industry average*
Return on assets	7.9%	9.2%
Return on equity	15.2%	12.9%

a. The company's product has a high market share, leading to higher profitability.
b. The company uses more debt than does the average company in the industry.
c. The company's profits are increasing over time.
d. The company's stock has a higher market value to book value ratio than does the rest of the industry.

267. A company's receivables collection period is equal to

a. The inventory conversion period.
b. Average daily sales divided by total assets.
c. Days sales outstanding.
d. Inventory divided by average daily sales.

268. When comparing two companies, if all else is equal, the company that has a higher dividend payout ratio will have a

a. Higher marginal cost of capital.
b. Lower debt ratio.
c. Higher investment opportunity schedule.
d. Higher price to earnings ratio.

Items 269 and 270 are based on the following:

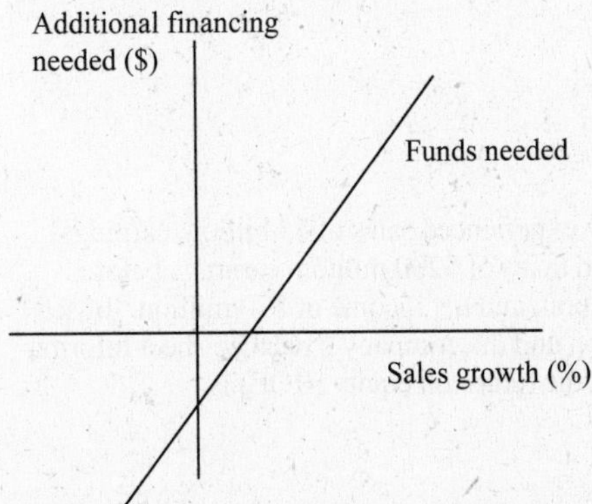

269. If all else is equal, firms with higher profit margins require less additional financing for any sales growth rate. If the profit margin of a company increased, the funds needed line would shift

a. Up and become less steep.
b. Up and become more steep.
c. Down and become less steep.
d. Down and become more steep.

270. The funds needed line does not pass through the origin unless the firm has a

a. 100% dividend payout policy.
b. 0% dividend payout policy.
c. 100% sales growth rate.
d. 0% sales growth rate.

271. All other things held constant, external capital requirements are lower for companies with which of the following characteristics?

a. Lower retention ratios.
b. Higher sales growth rates.
c. Lower capital intensity ratios.
d. Lower profit margins.

Items 272 through 277 are based on the following:

A company reports the following account balances at year-end:

Account	*Balance*
Long-term debt	$200,000
Cash	$ 50,000
Net sales	$600,000
Fixed assets (net)	$320,000
Tax expense	$ 67,500
Inventory	$ 25,000
Common stock	$100,000
Interest expense	$ 20,000
Administrative expense	$ 35,000
Retained earnings	$150,000
Accounts payable	$ 65,000
Accounts receivable	$120,000
Cost of goods sold	$400,000
Depreciation expense	$ 10,000

Additional information

The opening balance of common stock was $100,000.
The opening balance of retained earnings was $82,500.
The company has 10,000 common shares outstanding all year.
No dividends were paid during the year.

272. If cash dividends were paid, which of the following accounts would be affected?

a. Accounts receivable.
b. Retained earnings.
c. Fixed assets (net).
d. Inventory.

273. For the year just ended, the company has times-interest-earned of

a. 3.375 times.
b. 6.75 times.
c. 7.75 times.
d. 9.5 times.

274. At year end, the company has a book value per share, to the nearest cent, of

a. $10.00
b. $15.00
c. $21.63
d. $25.00

275. For the year just ended, the company had a rate of return on common equity, rounded to two decimals, of

a. 31.21%
b. 58.06%
c. 67.50%
d. 71.68%

276. Suppose that the company has paid one of its liabilities twice during the year, in error. The effects of this mistake would be

a. Assets, liabilities, and owners' equity are understated.
b. Assets, net income, and owners' equity are unaffected.
c. Assets and liabilities are understated.
d. Assets, net income, and owners' equity are understated, and liabilities are overstated.

277. Suppose that the opening balance of inventory was overstated due to errors in the physical count taken at the end of the prior year. The error has not been detected, but the physical count taken this year was conducted correctly. Which of the following accounts is overstated for the current year-end?

a. Cost of goods sold.
b. Net sales.
c. Fixed assets (net).
d. Net income.

Items 278 and 279 are based on the following:

A company has a current ratio of 1.4, a quick, or acid test, ratio of 1.2, and the following partial summary balance sheet:

Cash	$10	Current liabilities	$
Accounts receivable		Long-term liabilities	40
Inventory			
Fixed assets		Stockholders' equity	30
Total assets	$100	Total liabilities and equity	$

278. The company has an accounts receivable balance of

a. $12
b. $26
c. $36
d. $66

279. The company has a fixed assets balance of

a. $0
b. $16
c. $58
d. $64

280. A city's financial condition can be analyzed by looking at financial ratios. A high ratio on which of the following indicators suggests that the city has sufficient cash to pay its short-term obligations?

a. $\frac{\text{Total general fund cash and investments}}{\text{Total general fund liabilities}}$

b. $\frac{\text{Total general fund liabilities}}{\text{Total general fund revenues}}$

c. $\frac{\text{Unreserved general fund balance}}{\text{Total general fund revenues}}$

d. $\frac{\text{Debt service}}{\text{Total revenues}}$

281. The following account balances represent the December 31, 2002 balance sheet of a company:

Accounts payable	$ 67,000
Accounts receivable (net)	115,000
Accumulated depreciation – building	298,500
Accumulated depreciation – equipment	50,500
Cash	27,500
Common stock ($10 par value)	100,000
Deferred income taxes payable	37,500
Equipment	136,000
Income taxes payable	70,000
Inventory	257,000
Land and building	752,000
Long-term notes payable	123,000
Marketable securities	64,000
Notes payable within one year	54,000
Other current liabilities	22,500
Paid-in capital in excess of par	150,000
Prepaid expenses	27,000
Retained earnings	403,500

The company's quick ratio for 2002 is

a. 1.42
b. 1.08
c. 0.96
d. 0.82

Items 282 through 284 are based on the following:

EXHIBIT A
Company's Balance Sheet

	2002 (millions of dollars)
Assets	
Cash	$ 300
Marketable securities	400
Accounts receivable	200
Inventories	400
Net plant and equipment	1,700
Total assets	$3,000
Liabilities and equity	
Accounts payable	$ 300
Notes payable	400
Accrued wages	50
Accrued taxes	150
Debentures	600
Common stock	500
Retained earnings	1,000
Total liabilities and equity	$3,000

282. Based on the balance sheet shown in Exhibit A, the quick ratio is

a. 0.55
b. 1.00
c. 1.28
d. 1.44

283. Based on the balance sheet shown in Exhibit A, the debt ratio is

a. 20%
b. 40%
c. 50%
d. 100%

284. A company experienced sales of $5 billion, earnings before interest and taxes of $200 million, earnings before taxes of $100 million, and net income of $70 million. Based on this information and the company's balance sheet information in Exhibit A, the return on equity (ROE) is

a. 4.67%
b. 6.67%
c. 13.33%
d. 14%

Items 285 and 286 are based on the following:

Balance Sheet A

Assets (in millions)	Jan. 1	June 30
Cash	$ 3	$ 4
Accounts receivable	5	4
Inventories	8	10
Fixed assets	10	11
Total assets	26	29

Liabilities and stockholders' equity (in millions)	*Jan. 1*	*June 30*
Accounts payable	$ 2	$ 3
Notes payable	4	3
Accrued wages	1	2
Long-term debt	9	11
Stockholders' equity	10	10
Total liabilities and stockholders' equity	26	29

285. From January 1 to June 30, the net working capital

a. Decreased by $1 million.
b. Stayed the same.
c. Increased by $1 million.
d. Increased by $2 million.

286. From January 1 to June 30, the current ratio _____, and the quick ratio _____.

a. Increased, increased.
b. Increased, decreased.
c. Decreased, increased
d. Decreased, decreased.

287. Which of the following financial statement analyses is most useful in determining whether the various expenses of a given company are higher or lower than industry averages?

a. Horizontal.
b. Vertical.
c. Activity ratio.
d. Defensive-interval ratio.

288. A condensed comparative balance sheet for a company appears below.

	12/31/01	*12/31/02*
Cash	$ 40,000	$ 30,000
Accounts receivable	120,000	100,000
Inventory	200,000	300,000
Property, plant, and equipment	500,000	550,000
Accumulated depreciation	(280,000)	(340,000)
Total assets	$580,000	$640,000
Current liabilities	$ 60,000	$100,000
Long-term liabilities	390,000	420,000
Stockholders' equity	130,000	120,000
Total liabilities and equity	$580,000	$640,000

In looking at liquidity ratios at both balance sheet dates, what happened to the (1) current ratio and (2) acid-test (quick) ratio?

	(1) *Current ratio*	*(2)* *Acid-test ratio*
a.	Increased	Increased
b.	Increased	Decreased
c.	Decreased	Increased
d.	Decreased	Decreased

289. The management of ABC Corporation is analyzing the financial statements of XYZ Corporation because ABC is strongly considering purchasing a block of XYZ common stock that would give ABC significant influence over XYZ. Which financial statement should ABC primarily use to assess the amounts, timing, and uncertainty of future cash flows of XYZ Company?

a. Income statement.
b. Statement of retained earnings.
c. Statement of cash flows.
d. Balance sheet.

290. A reader of a statement of cash flows wishes to analyze the major classes of cash receipts and cash payments from operating activities. Which methods of reporting cash flows from operating activities will supply that information?

a. Both the direct and indirect methods.
b. Only the direct method.
c. Only the indirect method.
d. Neither method.

291. The following data have been extracted from the records of the ABC Company for the year ending December 31, 2002:

Cash balance, January 1, 2002	$ 85,000
Proceeds from the sale of common stock	80,000
A stock dividend distribution of 50%	60,000
Cash provided by operations	36,000
Purchase of land and building	120,000
Purchase of short-term investments	8,000

Based on the above, the cash balance at December 31, 2002, would be

a. $13,000
b. $37,000
c. $73,000
d. $81,000

Items 292 and 293 are based on the following:

A company had the following selected data:

Accounts receivable	$ 200
Average total assets	80,000
Cash	100
Current liabilities	500
Inventory	400
Marketable securities, short-term	50
Net income	1,000
Prepaid expenses	70
Sales	50,000
Selling, general and administrative expenses	5,000
Total liabilities	30,000

292. What is the quick ratio?

a. 0.03
b. 0.70
c. 1.50
d. 1.64

293. What is the asset turnover ratio?

a. 0.38
b. 0.63
c. 1.60
d. 2.67

294. A company issued long-term bonds and used the proceeds to repurchase 40% of the outstanding shares of its stock. This financial transaction will likely cause the

a. Total assets turnover ratio to increase.
b. Current ratio to decrease.
c. Times-interest-earned ratio to decrease.
d. Fixed charge coverage ratio to increase.

Items 295 through 301 are based on the following:

RST Corporation
COMPARATIVE INCOME STATEMENTS
For the Years Five and Six

	Year six	*Year five*
Sales (all are credit)	$285,000	$200,000
Cost of goods sold	150,000	120,000
Gross profit	135,000	80,000
Selling and administrative expenses	65,000	36,000
Income before interest and income taxes	70,000	44,000
Interest expense	3,000	3,000
Income before income taxes	67,000	41,000
Income tax expense	27,000	16,000
Net income	$ 40,000	$ 25,000

RST Corporation
COMPARATIVE BALANCE SHEETS
End of Years Five and Six

Assets	*Year six*	*Year five*
Current assets:		
Cash	$ 5,000	$ 4,000
Short-term marketable investments	3,000	2,000
Accounts receivable (net)	16,000	14,000
Inventory	30,000	20,000
Total current assets	54,000	40,000
Noncurrent assets		
Long-term investments	11,000	11,000
Property, plant, and equipment	80,000	70,000
Intangibles	3,000	4,000
Total assets	$148,000	$125,000
Liabilities and stockholders' equity		
Current liabilities:		
Accounts payable	$ 11,000	$ 7,000
Accrued payables	1,000	1,000
Total current liabilities	12,000	8,000
10% bonds payable, due in year 12	30,000	30,000
Total liabilities	42,000	38,000
Stockholders' equity		
Common stock, 2,400 shares, $10 par	24,000	24,000
Retained earnings	82,000	63,000
Total stockholders' equity	106,000	87,000
Total liabilities and stockholders' equity	$148,000	$125,000

The market value of RST's common stock at the end of year six was $100.00 per share.

295. RST's current ratio at the end of year six is
a. 4.5 to 1
b. 2.4 to 1
c. 2.0 to 1
d. 1.5 to 1

296. RST's acid-test (or quick) ratio at the end of year six is
a. 2.40 to 1
b. 2.18 to 1
c. 2.00 to 1
d. 1.50 to 1

297. Based on a comparison of RST's quick ratio in year five and year six, what is a likely conclusion?
a. RST has improved its management of long-term investments in year six.
b. RST has written off obsolete inventory in year six.
c. RST's ability to meet short-term financing needs has declined since year five.
d. RST's ability to meet short-term financing needs has improved since year five.

298. RST's accounts receivable turnover for year six is
a. 19 times.
b. 16 times.
c. 10 times.
d. 6 times.

299. RST's times-interest-earned ratio at the end of year six is
a. 23.33 times.
b. 14.33 times.
c. 13.33 times.
d. 10.00 times.

300. Based on a comparison of RST's times-interest-earned ratio in year five and year six, what is a likely conclusion?
a. RST's long-run solvency has declined.
b. RST's long-run solvency has improved.
c. RST's liquidity has improved.
d. RST's liquidity has declined.

301. RST's payout ratio for year six is
a. 52.50%
b. 34.29%
c. 21.76%
d. 6 times

Items 302 through 304 are based on the following:

A company whose balance sheet is presented in Table A had the following results of operations for the year ended December 31, 2005:

Sales	$15,000,000
Cost of goods sold	11,500,000
Net operating income	1,750,000
Net income	1,000,000

The company has 175,000 shares of common stock outstanding.

Table A—Balance Sheet, 2005
(in thousands)

Assets	
Cash	$ 450
Marketable securities	50
Accounts receivable	650
Inventories	1,350
Total current assets	2,500
Gross plant and equipment	7,000
Less: depreciation	2,000
Net plant and equipment	5,000
Goodwill	500
Total assets	8,000
Liabilities and equity	
Accounts payable	250
Notes payable	550
Accrued wages	100
Accrued taxes	200
Total current liabilities	1,100
Long-term debt	3,500
Common stock	1,000
Additional paid-in capital	900
Retained earnings	1,500
Total stockholders' equity	3,400
Total liabilities and equity	8,000

302. The fixed assets turnover or utilization ratio for the year ended 12/31/05 is
a. 1.88
b. 3.00
c. 5.18
d. 11.11

303. Based on the information provided, the company's earnings per share is
a. $ 5.71
b. $ 8.57
c. $10.00
d. $20.00

304. Based on the information provided, the company's return on operating assets is
a. 21.88%
b. 35.00%
c. 23.33%
d. 12.50%

305. An unexpected decrease in which of the following ratios could indicate that fictitious inventory has been recorded?
a. Average collection period.

b. Total asset turnover.
c. Price/earnings.
d. Current.

Items 306 through 308 are based on the following:

Assume a company's 2005 cost of goods sold was $1.8 million, its sales were $3.2 million, and its net income was $190,000. Table A provides a balance sheet for the company for 2005.

Table A
Balance Sheet of December 31, 2005

Assets	
Cash	$20,000
Marketable securities	30,000
Accounts receivable	200,000
Inventories	540,000
Total current assets	$790,000
Gross plant and equipment	1,400,000
Less: depreciation	400,000
Net plant and equipment	$1,000,000
Total assets	$1,790,000
Liabilities and Equity	
Accounts payable	$70,000
Notes payable	150,000
Accrued wages	30,000
Accrued taxes	20,000
Total current liabilities	$270,000
Long-term debt	$840,000
Common stock	200,000
Additional paid-in capital	180,000
Retained earnings	300,000
Total stockholders' equity	$680,000
Total liabilities and equity	$1,790,000

306. What was the company's quick ratio?
a. 0.18
b. 0.93
c. 2.18
d. 2.93

307. What was the company's fixed assets turnover ratio?
a. 1.8
b. 1.28
c. 2.28
d. 3.2

308. What was the company's profit margin?
a. 5.94%
b. 10.55%
c. 10.61%
d. 27.94%

309. A company has a high fixed-asset turnover ratio. What conclusion can a financial analyst draw from this?
a. The company may be overcapitalized.
b. The company may have a problem with employees converting inventory to personal use.
c. The company may be undercapitalized.
d. The company has favorable profitability.

310. The times-interest-earned ratio is primarily an indication of a company's
a. Solvency.
b. Liquidity.
c. Asset management.
d. Profitability.

311. Which of the following is true about the impact of price inflation on financial ratio analysis?
a. Inflation has no impact on financial ratio analysis.
b. Inflation impacts financial ratio analysis for one firm over time, but not comparative analysis of firms of different ages.
c. Inflation impacts financial ratio analysis for one firm over time, as well as comparative analysis of firms of different ages.
d. Inflation impacts comparative analysis of firms of different ages, but not financial ratio analysis for one firm over time.

312. An investor has been given several financial ratios for a company but none of the financial reports. Which combination of ratios can be used to derive return on equity?
a. Market to book value ratio and total debt to total assets.
b. Price to earnings ratio, earnings per share, and net profit margin.
c. Price to earnings ratio and return on assets.
d. Net profit margin, asset turnover, and equity multiplier.

313. Assume that a company's debt ratio is presently 50%. It plans to purchase fixed assets by either using borrowed funds for the purchase or entering into an operating lease. The company's debt ratio as measured by the balance sheet
a. Will increase whether the assets are purchased or leased.
b. Will increase if the assets are purchased, and remain unchanged if the assets are leased.
c. Will increase if the assets are purchased and decrease if the assets are leased.
d. Will remain unchanged whether the assets are purchased or leased.

314. The formula for calculating the times-interest-earned ratio is

a. $\frac{\text{Earnings before interest and taxes}}{\text{Interest expense}}$

b. $\frac{\text{Earnings before taxes}}{\text{Interest expense}}$

c. $\frac{\text{Interest expense}}{\text{Earnings before interest and taxes}}$

d. $\frac{\text{Interest expense}}{\text{Earnings before taxes}}$

Items 315 through 317 are based on the following:

A company has the following income statements. Assume a 365-day year in any calculations.

	Income statements 2005	Income statements 2004
Sales	$1,500,000	$1,400,000
Cost of goods sold	700,000	750,000
Gross profit	800,000	650,000
Selling and administrative expenses	62,000	60,000
Depreciation expenses	50,000	50,000
Earnings before interest and taxes (EBIT)	688,000	540,000
Interest expenses	100,000	100,000
Earnings before tax	588,000	440,000
Income tax (50%)	294,000	220,000
Net income	$294,000	$220,000

Selected balance sheet items are as follows:

	2005 year-end	2004 year-end
Accounts receivable	$300,000	$200,000
Accounts payable	250,000	275,000

315. In 2005 the company had cash provided by operations of

a. $219,000
b. $244,000
c. $344,000
d. $469,000

316. Based on the 2005 year-end balance of accounts receivable and the 2005 income statement, the company had an average collection period for 2005 of

a. 49 days.
b. 52 days.
c. 73 days.
d. 78 days.

317. The company had an interest-coverage ratio in 2004 of

a. 2.20 times.
b. 2.94 times.
c. 5.40 times.
d. 6.88 times.

318. All else being equal, a company with a higher dividend-payout ratio will have a (List A) debt-to-assets ratio and a (List B) current ratio.

	List A	*List B*
a.	Higher	Higher
b.	Higher	Lower
c.	Lower	Higher
d.	Lower	Lower

Items 319 and 320 are based on the following:

A company has the following partially completed balance sheet:

Cash	$240	Accounts payable	$140
Accounts receivable	?	Long-term debt	?
Inventory	?	Capital stock	330
Net fixed assets	400	Retained earnings	?
Total	?	Total	$1,250

Additional information:
The quick ratio is 4.0
The total debt-to-assets ratio is 0.60

319. The accounts receivable balance of the company would be

a. $35
b. $320
c. $290
d. $560

320. The long-term debt balance of the company would be

a. $100
b. $240
c. $610
d. $750

Items 321 and 322 are based on the following:

A company had the following opening and closing inventory balances in 2005:

	January 1, 2005	*December 31, 2005*
Finished goods	$ 90,000	$260,000
Raw materials	105,000	130,000
Work in process	220,000	175,000

The following transactions and events occurred during 2005:

- $300,000 of raw materials was purchased, of which $20,000 was returned because of defects.
- $600,000 of direct labor costs was incurred.
- $750,000 of manufacturing overhead costs was incurred.

321. The company's cost of goods sold for the year ended December 31, 2005, would be

a. $1,480,000
b. $1,500,000
c. $1,610,000
d. $1,650,000

322. Without prejudice to your answer to previous question above, assume that cost of goods sold for the year ended December 31, 2005, is $2,000,000. Inventory turnover on total inventory for the company would be

a. 2.04 times.
b. 3.54 times.
c. 4.08 times.
d. 4.82 times.

Items 323 through 327 are based on the following:

A company's financial statements for the current year are presented below.

BALANCE SHEET

Cash	$100
Accounts receivable	200
Inventory	50
Net fixed assets	600
Total	$950
Accounts payable	$140
Long-term debt	300
Capital stock	260
Retained earnings	250
Total	$950

STATEMENT OF INCOME AND RETAINED EARNINGS

Sales	$3,000
Cost of goods sold	1,600
Gross profit	$1,400
Operations expenses	970
Operating income	$ 430
Interest expense	30
Income before tax	$ 400
Income tax	200
Net income	$ 200
Plus Jan. 1 retained earnings	150
Less dividends	100
Dec. 31 retained earnings	$ 250

323. The company has a dividend-payout ratio of

a. 19.6%
b. 28.6%
c. 40.0%
d. 50.0%

324. The company has net working capital of

a. $160
b. $210
c. $350
d. $490

325. The company has return on assets of

a. 21.1%
b. 39.2%
c. 42.1%
d. 45.3%

326. The company has a times-interest-earned ratio of

a. 6.67 times.
b. 13.33 times.

c. 14.33 times.
d. 100.0 times.

327. The company has a profit margin of
a. 6.67%
b. 13.33%
c. 14.33%
d. 46.67%

Items 328 and 329 are based on the following:

A company had the following account balances in the preclosing trial balance:

Opening inventory	$100,000
Closing inventory	$150,000
Purchases	$400,000
Transportation in	$6,000
Purchase discounts	$40,000
Purchase allowances	$15,000
Returned purchases	$5,000
Less returned purchases	(5,000)
Net Purchases	$340,000

328. The company had net purchases for the period of
a. $340,000
b. $346,000
c. $370,000
d. $376,000

329. Without prejudice to your answer to previous question, if net purchases for the company are $500,000 for the period, then cost of goods sold is
a. $250,000
b. $450,000
c. $550,000
d. $750,000

330. An organization offers its customers credit terms of 5/10 net 20. One-third of the customers take the cash discount and the remaining customers pay on day 20. On average, 20 units are sold per day, priced at $10,000 each. The rate of sales is uniform throughout the year. Using a 360-day year, the organization has days sales outstanding, to the nearest full day, of
a. 13 days.
b. 15 days.
c. 17 days.
d. 20 days.

Items 331 through 333 are based on the following:

At the end of the accounting period, a company has the following partially completed financial statements:

INCOME STATEMENT	
Sales	
Cost of goods sold	
Gross profit	
Administrative expense	$40,000
Depreciation expense	
Earnings before interest and tax	
Interest expense	
Earnings before tax	
Tax expense	
Net income	$100,000

BALANCE SHEET	
Current assets	
Other assets	$300,000
Total assets	
Current liabilities	
Long-term debt	$1,000,000
Equity	
Total liabilities and equity	

Additional information
Gross profit percentage = 30%
Corporate tax rate = 40%
Annual interest cost on long-term debt = 10%
Return on total assets = 3%
Fixed assets originally cost $500,000 and are being depreciated over 10 years on a straight-line basis
Working capital = $2,000,000

331. The company had sales for the period of
a. $ 891,667
b. $1,100,000
c. $1,188,890
d. $1,466,667

332. The company has current assets of
a. $1,000,000
b. $3,033,333
c. $3,333,333
d. $3,633,333

333. The company has times-interest-earned of
a. 1.667 times.
b. 2.5 times.
c. 2.667 times.
d. 3.5 times.

334. A company has 100,000 outstanding common shares with a market value of $20 per share. Dividends of $2 per share were paid in the current year and the company has a dividend payout ratio of 40%. The price to earnings ratio of the company is
a. 2.5
b. 4
c. 10
d. 50

335. An organization has total asset turnover of 3.5 times and a total debt to total assets ratio of 70%. If the organization has total debt of $1,000,000, then it has a sales level of
a. $5,000,000.00
b. $2,450,000.00
c. $ 408,163.26
d. $ 200,000.00

336. Which of the following financial ratios is used to assess the liquidity of a company?
a. Days sales outstanding.
b. Total debt to total assets ratio.
c. Profit margin on sales.
d. Current ratio.

337. Assume that employees confessed to a $500,000 inventory theft, but are not able to make restitution. How should this material fraud be shown in the company's financial statements?
a. Classified as a loss and shown as a separate line item in the income statement.
b. Initially classified as an accounts receivable because the employees are responsible for the goods. Since they cannot pay, the loss would be recognized as a write-off of accounts receivable.
c. Included in cost of goods sold because the goods are not on hand, losses on inventory shrinkage are ordinary, and it would cause the least amount of attention.
d. Recorded directly to retained earnings since it is not an income-producing item.

Items 338 through 343 are based on the following:

Presented below are partial year-end financial statement data for companies A and B.

BALANCE SHEET

	Company A	*Company B*
Cash	$100	$200
Accounts receivable	unknown	100
Inventories	unknown	100
Net fixed assets	200	100
Accounts payable	100	50
Long-term debt	200	50
Common stock	100	200
Retained earnings	150	100

INCOME STATEMENT

	Company A	*Company B*
Sales	$600	$5,800
Cost of goods sold	300	5,000
Administrative expenses	100	500
Depreciation expense	100	100
Interest expense	20	10
Income tax expense	40	95
Net income	40	95

338. If Company A has a quick ratio of 2, then it has an accounts receivable balance of

a. $100
b. $200
c. $300
d. $500

339. Company B has a return on equity, to the nearest full percentage point, of

a. 16%
b. 32%
c. 48%
d. 95%

340. Based on 365 days per year, company B has days sales outstanding to the nearest full day of

a. 0 days
b. 3 days
c. 6 days
d. 7 days

341. Company A has a times-interest-earned ratio of

a. 4 times.
b. 5 times.
c. 10 times.
d. 15 times.

342. The degree of financial leverage of Company B, to two decimal places, is

a. 1.03
b. 1.05
c. 1.12
d. 1.25

343. If Company A has 60 common shares outstanding, then it has a book value per share, to the nearest cent, of

a. $1.67
b. $2.50
c. $4.17
d. $5.00

Items 344 through 349 are based on the following:

During the year ended December 31, 2003, a company had $500,000 in sales revenue and purchased $150,000 of inventory. The cost of goods sold was $250,000 for the year and the company incurred $25,000 of general and administrative expenses. The January 1, 2003 opening balance sheet was as follows:

Cash		$120,000
Accounts receivable		100,000
Inventory		200,000
Fixed assets (gross)	600,000	
Accumulated depreciation	(100,000)	
Net fixed assets		500,000
Total assets		$920,000
Accounts payable		$220,000
Long-term debt		400,000
Common stock		100,000
Retained earnings		200,000
Total liabilities and equity		$920,000

- The cost of long-term debt financing is 10% per annum, payable in one installment on December 31 of each year.
- The company has a 50% corporate tax rate.
- The company has a dividend payout ratio of 25%.
- The fixed assets were one year old at the start of the current year, were originally estimated to have a six-year useful life, and are being depreciated on a straight-line basis.

344. The company has a closing inventory balance of

a. $100,000
b. $250,000
c. $300,000
d. $350,000

345. If the company had purchased a larger amount of inventory during the year, with the additional items being purchased on December 31, 2003, what is the effect on cost of goods sold and on net earnings for the year?

	Cost of goods sold	*Net earnings*
a.	Increase	Decrease
b.	Increase	Increase
c.	Decrease	Increase
d.	No effect	No effect

346. The company would pay dividends for the year of

a. $10,625
b. $21,250
c. $23,125
d. $42,500

347. If the company were to reduce its dividend payout percentage, the effect would be to (List A) its ending cash balance and to (List B) its ending retained earnings balance.

	List A	*List B*
a.	Increase	Increase
b.	Increase	Decrease
c.	Decrease	Increase
d.	Decrease	Decrease

348. If the company were able to speed up the collection of accounts receivable without affecting the level of sales, what is the effect on its cash balance and its level of total assets?

	Cash balance	*Total assets*
a.	Increase	Increase
b.	Increase	No effect
c.	Decrease	Decrease
d.	Decrease	No effect

349. What would be the effect of a lower tax rate on the ending balance of common stock and on dividends paid for the year?

	Ending balance of common stock	*Dividends paid*
a.	Increase	Increase
b.	Decrease	Decrease
c.	No effect	Increase
d.	No effect	Decrease

350. A company has $400 of current assets, composed of $200 of cash, $100 of accounts receivable and $100 of inventory. The company has $200 of long-term debt, $100 of accounts payable, and $75 of notes payable. The notes payable are due in six months. The acid-test ratio for this company, to two decimal places, is

a. 0.80
b. 1.29
c. 1.71
d. 2.29

351. If Company A has a higher rate of return on assets than Company B, this could be because Company A has a (List A) profit margin on sales, or a (List B) asset turnover ratio, or both.

	List A	*List B*
a.	Higher	Higher
b.	Higher	Lower
c.	Lower	Higher
d.	Lower	Lower

352. Given an acid-test ratio of 2, current assets of $5,000 and inventory of $2,000; the value of current liabilities is

a. $1,500
b. $2,500
c. $3,500
d. $6,000

353. Which of the outcomes represented in the following table would result from a company's retirement of debt with excess cash?

	Total assets turnover ratio	*Following period's interest earned ratio*
a.	Increase	Increase
b.	Increase	Decrease
c.	Decrease	Increase
d.	Decrease	Decrease

Items 354 through 356 are based on the following:

The following selected data pertains to PQR Company at December 31, 2005:

Quick assets	$208,000
Acid-test ratio	2.6 to 1
Current ratio	3.5 to 1
Net sales for 1990	$1,800,000
Cost of sales for 1990	$990,000
Average total assets for 2005	$1,200,000

354. Based on the above, the PQR Company's current liabilities at December 31, 2005, amount to

a. $ 59,429
b. $ 80,000
c. $134,857
d. $187,200

355. Based on the above data, the PQR Company's inventory balance at December 31, 2005, is

a. $ 72,000
b. $187,200
c. $231,111
d. $282,857

356. Based on the above, the PQR Company's asset turnover for 2005 is

a. 0.675
b. 0.825
c. 1.21
d. 1.50

Cost of Capital Evaluation

357. A company will finance next year's capital projects through debt rather than additional equity. The benchmark cost of capital for these projects should be

a. The before-tax cost of new-debt financing.
b. The after-tax cost of new-debt financing.
c. The cost of equity financing.
d. The weighted-average cost of capital.

358. A company has $650,000 of 10% debt outstanding and $500,000 of equity financing. The required return of the equity holders is 15% and there are no retained earnings currently available for investment purposes. If new outside equity is raised, it will cost the firm 16%. New debt would have a before-tax cost of 9%, and the corporate tax rate is 50%. When calculating the marginal cost of capital, the company should assign a cost of (List A) to equity capital and (List B) to the after-tax cost of debt financing.

	List A	*List B*
a.	15%	4.5%
b.	15%	5.0%
c.	16%	4.5%
d.	16%	5.0%

359. When calculating the cost of capital, the cost assigned to retained earnings should be

a. Zero.
b. Lower than the cost of external common equity.
c. Equal to the cost of external common equity.
d. Higher than the cost of external common equity.

360. When a company is at its optimal capital structure, its (List A) will be (List B).

	List A	*List B*
a.	Weighted-average cost of capital	Minimized
b.	Earnings per share	Minimized
c.	Earnings per share	Maximized
d.	Weighted-average cost of capital	Maximized

Items 361 through 364 are based on the following:

A new company requires $1 million of financing and is considering two arrangements as shown in the table below.

Arrangement	*Amount of equity raised*	*Amount of debt financing*	*Before-tax cost of debt*
#1	$700,000	$300,000	8% per annum
#2	$300,000	$700,000	10% per annum

In the first year of operations, the company is expected to have sales revenues of $500,000, cost of sales of $200,000, and general and administrative expenses of

$100,000. The tax rate is 30%, and there are no other items on the income statement. All earnings are paid out as dividends at year-end.

361. If the cost of equity is 12%, then the weighted-average cost of capital under arrangement #1, to the nearest full percentage point, would be

a. 8%
b. 10%
c. 11%
d. 12%

362. Which of the following statements comparing the two financing arrangements is true?

a. The company will have a higher expected gross margin under arrangement #1.
b. The company will have a higher degree of operating leverage under arrangement #2.
c. The company will have higher interest expense under arrangement #1.
d. The company will have higher expected tax expense under arrangement #1.

363. Under financing arrangement #2 the degree of financial leverage (DFL), rounded to two decimal places, would be

a. 1.09
b. 1.14
c. 1.32
d. 1.54

364. The return on equity will be (List A) and the debt ratio will be (List B) under arrangement # 2, as compared with arrangement #1.

	List A	*List B*
a.	Higher	Higher
b.	Higher	Lower
c.	Lower	Higher
d.	Lower	Lower

365. The marginal cost of debt for a firm is defined as the interest rate on (List A) debt minus the (List B).

	List A	*List B*
a.	New	Firm's marginal tax rate
b.	Outstanding	Firm's marginal tax rate
c.	New	Interest rate times the firm's marginal tax rate
d.	Outstanding	Interest rate times the firm's marginal tax rate

366. A company has 10,000 outstanding shares with a market value of $25 each. It just paid a $1 per share dividend. Dividends are expected to grow at a constant rate of 10%. If flotation costs are 5% of the selling price, the cost of new equity financing is calculated by the following formula:

a. $$\text{Cost of equity} = \frac{\text{Dividend at time zero}}{\text{Market price}} + \text{Dividend growth rate}$$
$$= \$1/\$25 + .10$$
$$= .04 + .10 = 14.00\%$$

b. $$\text{Cost of equity} = \frac{\text{Dividend at time zero}}{\text{Net proceeds}} + \text{Dividend growth rate}$$
$$= \$1/\$23.75 + .10$$
$$= .0421 + .10 = 14.21\%$$

c. $$\text{Cost of equity} = \frac{\text{Expected dividend at end of period}}{\text{Market price}} + \text{Dividend growth rate}$$
$$= \$1.10/\$25 + .10$$
$$= .044 + .10 = 14.40\%$$

d. $$\text{Cost of equity} = \frac{\text{Expected dividend at end of period}}{\text{Net proceeds issuing one share}} + \text{Dividend growth rate}$$
$$= \frac{\$1(1 + \text{dividend growth rate})}{\$25(1 - .05)} + \text{Dividend growth rate}$$
$$= \$1(1.1)/\$23.75 + .10$$
$$= .0463 + .10 = 14.63\%$$

367. Assume that the risk-free interest rate is 8%, the required rate of return on the market portfolio (containing all stocks) is 15%, and the beta coefficient of a particular stock is .9. According to the capital asset pricing model, the required rate of return on that particular stock is

a. 6.3%
b. 14.3%
c. 15.0%
d. 21.5%

368. According to the capital asset pricing model (CAPM), the relevant risk of a security is its

a. Company-specific risk.
b. Diversifiable risk.
c. Systematic risk.
d. Total risk.

369. A firm's optimal capital structure is that which

a. Minimizes the firm's tax liability.
b. Minimizes the firm's risk.
c. Maximizes the firm's degree of financial leverage.
d. Maximizes the price of the firm's stock.

370. The capital structure decision involves the proportions of financing with

a. Long-term debt versus short-term debt.
b. Debt versus equity.
c. Short-term assets versus long-term assets.
d. Retained earnings versus the issuance of new stock.

371. A firm seeking to optimize its capital budget has calculated its marginal cost of capital and projected rates of return on several potential projects. The optimal capital budget is determined by

a. Calculating the point at which marginal cost of capital meets the projected rate of return, assuming that the most profitable projects are accepted first.
b. Calculating the point at which average marginal cost meets average projected rate of return, assuming the largest projects are accepted first.
c. Accepting all potential projects with projected rates of return exceeding the lowest marginal cost of capital.
d. Accepting all potential projects with projected rates of return lower than the highest marginal cost of capital.

372. An investor uses the capital asset pricing model (CAPM) to evaluate the risk/return relationship on a portfolio of stocks held as an investment. Which of the following would **not** be used to estimate the portfolio's expected rate of return?

a. Expected risk premium on the portfolio of stocks.
b. Interest rate for the safest possible investment.
c. Expected rate of return on the market portfolio.
d. Standard deviation of the market returns.

373. A company uses portfolio theory to develop its investment portfolio. If the company wishes to obtain optimum risk reduction through the portfolio effect, it should make its next investment in

a. An investment that correlates negatively to the present portfolio holdings.
b. An investment that is uncorrelated to the present portfolio holdings.
c. An investment that is highly correlated to the present portfolio holdings.
d. An investment that is perfectly correlated to the present portfolio holdings.

Types of Debt and Equity

374. If a high percentage of a firm's total costs are fixed, the firm's operating leverage will be

a. High.
b. Low.
c. Unchanged.
d. Unable to be determined.

375. A company with a present debt ratio of 50% plans to purchase fixed assets by either using borrowed funds or entering into an operating lease. The company's debt ratio as measured by the balance sheet will

a. Increase whether the assets are purchased or leased.
b. Remain unchanged if the assets are leased and increase if the assets are purchased.
c. Increase if the assets are purchased and decrease if the assets are leased.
d. Remain unchanged whether the assets are purchased or leased.

376. Common shareholders with preemptive rights are entitled to

a. Vote first at annual meetings.
b. First right of refusal for bonds sold by the firm.
c. Purchase any additional shares sold by the firm.
d. Gain control of the firm in a proxy fight.

377. Which of the following represent(s) the value of the common stock of a firm with no expected dividend growth?

I. The present value of all expected future dividends.
II. The current dividend divided by the cost of equity.
III. The dividend divided by the current share price.

a. II only.
b. I and II only.
c. I and III only.
d. I, II, and III.

378. In the distribution of liquidation proceeds for a bankrupt firm, which of the following claimants has highest priority?

a. Preferred stock.
b. Common stock.
c. Bonds payable.
d. Taxes payable.

379. The difference between the required rate of return on a given risky investment and that of a risk-free investment with the same expected return is the

a. Risk premium.
b. Coefficient of variation.
c. Standard error of measurement.
d. Beta coefficient.

380. Capital structure decisions involve determining the proportions of financing from

a. Short-term or long-term debt.
b. Debt or equity.
c. Short-term or long-term assets.
d. Retained earnings or common stock.

381. If two companies, Company X and Company Y, are alike in all respects except that Company X employs more debt financing and less equity financing than Company Y does, which of the following statements is true?

a. Company X has more net earnings variability than Company Y.
b. Company X has more operating earnings variability than Company Y.
c. Company X has less operating earnings variability than Company Y.
d. Company X has less financial leverage than Company Y.

382. A company is arranging debt financing for the purchase of a new piece of equipment that has a five-year expected useful life. Which of the following alternative financing arrangements has the **lowest** effective annual percentage rate if each has a quoted nominal rate of 9.5%?

a. A five-year term loan with interest compounded annually.
b. A ten-year term loan with interest compounded semiannually.
c. A five-year term loan with interest compounded quarterly.
d. A ten-year term loan with interest compounded monthly.

383. Bondholders are assured of protection against inflation if they hold

a. Income bonds.
b. Convertible bonds.
c. Mortgage bonds.
d. Indexed bonds.

384. Compared to another bond with the same risk and maturity but without a conversion feature, a convertible bond has a

a. Higher face value.
b. Lower face value.
c. Higher coupon rate.
d. Lower coupon rate.

385. A one-year, $20,000 loan with a 10% nominal interest rate provides the borrower with the use of (List A) if interest is charged on a (List B) basis

	List A	*List B*
a.	$18,000	Simple
b.	$20,000	Simple
c.	$20,000	Discount
d.	$22,000	Discount

386. Which of the following is a characteristic of a bond that is issued at a discount?

a. The coupon rate exceeds the market rate on bonds of similar risk and maturity.
b. Interest is paid semiannually rather than annually.

c. The market value of the bond approaches its par value as the maturity date approaches.
d. The market value of the bond falls between the date of issue and the maturity date.

387. A plot of land is acquired in exchange for $250,000 cash and a noninterest-bearing note with a face amount of $1,000,000 on January 1, 2002. The $1,000,000 is payable in installments of $250,000 each, with the first installment due December 31, 2002. With regard to imputing interest on this note, (1) what market rate should be used to account for interest for 2002, and (2) what should be done in future years when there is a change in prevailing interest rates?

	(1) Market rate to use to compute interest expense for 2002	*(2) Impact of change in prevailing interest rates in future periods on rate used to account for this note*
a.	Rate prevailing at January 2, 2002	Ignore change in rate
b.	Rate prevailing at January 2, 2002	Use new market rate
c.	Rate prevailing at December 31, 2002	Ignore change in rate
d.	Rate prevailing at December 31, 2002	Use new market rate

388. Which of the following scenarios would encourage a company to use short-term loans to retire its ten-year bonds that have five years until maturity?
a. The company expects interest rates to increase over the next five years.
b. Interest rates have increased over the last five years.
c. Interest rates have declined over the last five years.
d. The company is experiencing cash flow problems.

389. Zero coupon bonds issued by corporations
a. Are initially sold at par value (a zero discount).
b. Are initially sold for a price above par value.
c. Are tax-free.
d. Require no cash outlay from the issuer until the bonds mature.

390. An investor is presently holding income bonds, debentures, subordinated debentures, and first-mortgage bonds. Which of these securities traditionally is considered to have the least risk?
a. Income bonds.
b. Debentures.
c. Subordinated debentures.
d. First-mortgage bonds.

391. On **August 1, 2001,** a company issued five-year bonds with a face amount of $10,000,000. The bonds carry a stated interest rate of 10% and interest is payable annually on July 31. Which of the following are the appropriate classification of bonds payable and the related accrued interest payable on the **December 31, 2005** balance sheet?

Classification Table

	Bonds payable	*Interest payable*
Classification A	Current liability	Current liability
Classification B	Current liability	Long-term liability
Classification C	Long-term liability	Current liability
Classification D	Long-term liability	Long-term liability

a. Classification A.
b. Classification B.
c. Classification C.
d. Classification D.

392. A bond backed by fixed assets is known as a(n)
a. Income bond.
b. Subordinated debenture.
c. Debenture.
d. Mortgage bond.

393. Participating preferred stockholders are entitled to
a. Monitor any sinking funds for the purchase and retirement of debt.
b. Vote at all annual meetings.
c. Convert the shares into common stock.
d. Share in the firm's earnings beyond the stated dividend level.

394. In which stage of a firm's development is it most likely to seek and obtain external equity financing in the form of venture capital?
a. Formation.
b. Rapid growth.
c. Growth to maturity.
d. Maturity and industry decline.

395. The market value of a firm's outstanding common shares will be higher, everything else equal, if
a. Investors have a lower required return on equity.
b. Investors expect lower dividend growth.
c. Investors have longer expected holding periods.
d. Investors have shorter expected holding periods.

396. A call option on a share of common stock is more valuable when there is a lower
a. Market value of the underlying share.
b. Exercise price on the option.
c. Time to maturity on the option.
d. Variability of market price on the underlying shares.

397. If a firm identifies (or creates) an investment opportunity with a present value (List A) its cost, then the value of the firm and the price of its common stock will (List B).

	List A	*List B*
a.	Greater than	Increase
b.	Greater than	Decrease
c.	Equal to	Increase
d.	Equal to	Decrease

398. Which of the following is usually **not** a feature of cumulative preferred stock?
a. Has priority over common stock with regard to earnings.
b. Has priority over common stock with regard to assets.
c. Has voting rights.
d. Has the right to receive dividends in arrears before common stock dividends can be paid.

399. Preferred stock is a security with characteristics of both common stock and bonds. Preferred stock has (List A) like common stock and (List B) like bonds.

	List A	List B
a.	A maturity date	A fixed periodic payment
b.	No maturity date	No fixed periodic payment
c.	A maturity date	No fixed periodic payment
d.	No maturity date	A fixed periodic payment

400. A company issued $10 par value convertible preferred stock at face value. The convertible preferred stock can be converted into two shares of common stock. This convertible preferred stock would have a minimal conversion price of

a. $2
b. $5
c. $10
d. $20

401. Preferred and common stock differ in that

a. Failure to pay dividends on common stock will not force the firm into bankruptcy while failure to pay dividends on preferred stock will force the firm into bankruptcy.
b. Common stock dividends are a fixed amount while preferred stock dividends are not.
c. Preferred stock has a higher priority than common stock with regard to earnings and assets in the event of bankruptcy.
d. Preferred stock dividends are deductible as an expense for tax purposes while common stock dividends are not.

402. The market value of a firm's outstanding common shares will be higher, everything else equal, if

a. Investors have a lower required return on equity.
b. Investors expect lower dividend growth.
c. Investors have longer expected holding periods.
d. Investors have shorter expected holding periods.

403. A firm has liabilities of $200,000, a value equal to 40% of its total assets. What will the firm's return on common equity (ROE) equal if net income available to common stockholders is $450,000?

a. 0.40
b. 0.44
c. 1.50
d. 2.25

404. A company uses the cost method of accounting for treasury stock transactions. The company purchases 100 treasury shares at $10 per share, and then sells 40 treasury shares for $12. The effect on stockholders' equity of these transactions is

a. Increase $600.
b. Decrease $1,000.
c. Increase $480.
d. Decrease $520.

405. A company has $1,500,000 of outstanding debt and $1,000,000 of outstanding common equity. Management plans to maintain the same proportions of financing from each source if additional projects are undertaken. If the company expects to have $60,000 of retained earnings available for reinvestment in new projects in the coming year, what dollar amount of new investments can be undertaken without issuing new equity?

a. $0
b. $ 24,000
c. $ 90,000
d. $150,000

406. A company has previously issued preferred stock, common stock, and bonds. For shareholders, preferred stock has an advantage in that

a. Its dividend payments must be made for the company to avoid bankruptcy.
b. Its dividend payments typically rise as interest rates rise.
c. It has a higher priority claim than common stock.
d. It has a higher priority claim than bonds.

407. Issues of preferred stock which specify redemption of the issues over relatively short periods such as five to ten years are called

a. Transient preferreds.
b. Short-term preferreds.
c. Preferred stock obligations.
d. Temporary preferreds.

408. A firm must select from among several methods of financing arrangements when meeting its capital requirements. To acquire additional growth capital while attempting to maximize earnings per share, a firm should generally

a. Attempt to increase both debt and equity in equal proportions, which preserves a stable capital structure and maintains investor confidence.
b. Select debt over equity initially, even though increased debt is accompanied by interest costs and a degree of risk.
c. Select equity over debt initially, which minimizes risk and avoids interest costs.
d. Discontinue dividends and utilize current cash flow, which avoids the cost and risk of increased debt and the dilution of earnings per share through increased equity.

409. Which of the following brings in additional capital to the firm?

a. Two for one stock split.
b. Conversion of convertible bonds to common stock.
c. Exercise of warrants.
d. Exercise of option purchased through option exchange.

410. When the equity method is used to account for the investment in common stock of another corporation, the recording of the receipt of a cash dividend from the investee will result in

a. The recognition of investment income.
b. A reduction in the investment account.
c. An increase in a liability account.
d. An increase in a special owners' equity account.

411. The following excerpt was taken from a company's financial statements: "...10% convertible participating... $10,000,000." What is most likely being referred to?

a. Bonds.
b. Common stock.
c. Stock options.
d. Preferred stock.

412. The degree of operating leverage (DOL) is

a. Constant at all levels of sales.
b. A measure of the change in earnings available to common stockholders associated with a given change in operating earnings.

c. A measure of the change in operating income resulting from a given change in sales.
d. Lower if the degree of total leverage is higher, other things held constant.

413. Everything else being equal, a (List A) highly leveraged firm will have (List B) earnings per share.

	List A	*List B*
a.	More	Lower
b.	More	Less volatile
c.	Less	Less volatile
d.	Less	Higher

414. A company is considering the early retirement of its 10%, 10-year bonds payable. Before retiring the bonds, the company's capital structure was

Current liabilities	$125,000
Long-term liabilities:	
Notes payable (due in 5 years)	200,000
Bonds payable	300,000
Premium on bonds payable	25,000
Owners' equity:	
Common stock ($5 par value)	150,000
Paid-in capital in excess of par	50,000
Retained earnings	450,000

If the bonds can be retired at 103.5%, then the
a. Debt/equity ratio will increase.
b. Financial leverage will decrease.
c. Asset turnover ratio will decrease.
d. Return on owners' equity will decrease.

415. Companies experience changes in interest expenses, variable cost per unit, quantity of units sold, and fixed costs. Their degree of operating leverage is not affected by the change in
a. Interest expenses.
b. Variable cost per unit.
c. Quantity of units sold.
d. Fixed costs.

416. Which class of leverage causes earnings before interest and taxes to be more sensitive to changes in sales?
a. Credit.
b. Financial.
c. Operating.
d. Intrinsic.

417. Which of the changes in leverage would apply to a company that substantially increases its investment in fixed assets as a proportion of total assets and replaces some of its long-term debt with equity?

	Financial leverage	*Operating leverage*
a.	Increase	Decrease
b.	Decrease	Increase
c.	Increase	Increase
d.	Decrease	Decrease

418. During 2005, a company's balance sheet accounts increased by the following amounts:

Assets	$180,000
Liabilities	50,000
Capital stock	90,000
Additional paid-in capital	15,000

Net income for 2005 was $42,000. The only other change in retained earnings was for the declaration of cash dividends. The amount of dividends declared was
a. $ 2,000
b. $17,000
c. $33,000
d. $67,000

419. If a company has a higher dividend payout ratio, then if all else is equal it will have
a. A higher marginal cost of capital.
b. A lower marginal cost of capital.
c. A higher investment opportunity schedule.
d. A lower investment opportunity schedule.

420. The correct sequence of events in the actual payment of cash dividends on common shares is
a. Declaration date, ex-dividend date, holder of record date, payment date.
b. Declaration date, holder of record date, ex-dividend date, payment date.
c. Holder of record date, declaration date, ex-dividend date, payment date.
d. Ex-dividend date, declaration date, holder of record date, payment date.

421. Stock dividends and stock splits differ in that
a. Stock splits involve a bookkeeping transfer from retained earnings to the capital stock account.
b. Stock splits are paid in additional shares of common stock, whereas in a stock dividend, outstanding shares are replaced with a new issue of shares.
c. In a stock split, a larger number of new shares replace the outstanding shares.
d. A stock dividend results in a decline in the par value per share.

422. A company following a residual dividend payout policy will pay higher dividends when, everything else equal, it has
a. Less attractive investment opportunities.
b. Lower earnings available for reinvestment.
c. A lower targeted debt to equity ratio.
d. A lower opportunity cost of retained earnings.

423. All else being equal, a company with a higher dividend-payout ratio will have a (List A) debt-to-assets ratio and a (List B) current ratio.

	List A	*List B*
a.	Higher	Higher
b.	Higher	Lower
c.	Lower	Higher
d.	Lower	Lower

424. On May 28, 2005, a company announced that its directors had met on May 26, 2005, declared a dividend of 25 cents per share, payable to stockholders of record on June 20, 2005, with payment to be made on July 5, 2005. The date on which the declared dividend becomes a liability of the company is
a. May 26, 2005.
b. May 28, 2005.
c. June 20, 2005.
d. July 5, 2005.

425. If the form of the distribution to shareholders does not affect future earnings of the company, then stock repurchases provide stockholders with (List A) and cash dividends provide stockholders with (List B).

	List A	List B
a.	Capital gain income	Capital gain income
b.	Capital gain income	Ordinary income
c.	Ordinary income	Capital gain income
d.	Ordinary income	Ordinary income

426. A company declares and pays both a $200,000 cash dividend and a 10% stock dividend. The effect of the (List A) dividend is to (List B).

	List A	List B
a.	Cash	Increase retained earnings
b.	Cash	Decrease retained earnings and increase stockholders' equity
c.	Stock	Decrease retained earnings
d.	Stock	Decrease retained earnings and decrease stockholders' equity

427. Which of the following types of dividends do **not** reduce the stockholders' equity in the corporation?

a. Cash dividends.
b. Property dividends.
c. Liquidating dividends.
d. Stock dividends.

428. A company in a 40% tax bracket needs (List A) of operating income to pay $1 of interest and (List B) of pretax income to pay $1 of dividends.

	List A	List B
a.	$0.60	$0.60
b.	$1.00	$1.00
c.	$1.00	$1.67
d.	$1.67	$1.00

429. All else being equal, a company with a higher dividend payout ratio will have a (List A) debt to assets ratio and a (List B) current ratio.

	List A	List B
a.	Higher	Higher
b.	Higher	Lower
c.	Lower	Higher
d.	Lower	Lower

Items 430 and 431 are based on the following:

A company has 1,000 shares of $10 par value common stock and $5,000 of retained earnings. Two proposals are under consideration. The first is a stock split giving each stockholder two new shares for each share formerly held. The second is to declare and distribute a 50% stock dividend.

430. The stock split proposal will (List A) earnings per share by (List B) than will the stock dividend proposal.

	List A	List B
a.	Increase	More
b.	Increase	Less
c.	Decrease	More
d.	Decrease	Less

431. Under the stock (List A), the par value per outstanding share will (List B).

	List A	List B
a.	Dividend	Increase
b.	Split	Increase
c.	Dividend	Decrease
d.	Split	Decrease

432. A profitable company is following a residual dividend policy. It will pay (List A) dividends if it has (List B) positive net present value investment opportunities.

	List A	List B
a.	Higher	Few
b.	Higher	Many
c.	Lower	Few
d.	Zero	Zero

433. The date when the right to a dividend expires is called the

a. Declaration date.
b. Ex-dividend date.
c. Holder-of-record date.
d. Payment date.

434. Assume that nominal interest rates just increased substantially, but that the expected future dividends for a company over the long run were not affected. As a result of the increase in nominal interest rates, the company's stock price should

a. Increase.
b. Decrease.
c. Stay constant.
d. Change, but in no obvious direction.

435. If a company uses the residual dividend policy, it will pay

a. A fixed cash dividend each quarter and use the residual as retained earnings.
b. A fixed stock dividend each quarter and retain all earnings as a residual.
c. All earnings as dividends each year.
d. Dividends only if earnings exceed the amount needed to support an optimal capital budget.

436. A corporation issued a property dividend to its shareholders. The dividend was distributed in the form of 100% of the common stock of a subsidiary. This is known as a

a. Spin off.
b. Split up.
c. Scrip dividend.
d. Reverse split up.

Financial Instruments

437. Foreign bonds and Eurobonds differ in that

a. Foreign bonds are always issued by foreign governments while Eurobonds are not.
b. Foreign bonds are sold outside the country of the borrower while Eurobonds are not.
c. Less disclosure is required for issuers of foreign bonds.
d. Foreign bonds are denominated in the currency of the country in which they are sold, while Eurobonds are not.

438. A company has a foreign-currency-denominated trade payable, due in 60 days. In order to eliminate the foreign exchange risk associated with the payable, the company could

a. Sell foreign currency forward today.
b. Wait 60 days and pay the invoice by purchasing foreign currency in the spot market at that time.
c. Buy foreign currency forward today.
d. Borrow foreign currency today, convert it to domestic currency on the spot market, and invest the

funds in a domestic bank deposit until the invoice payment date.

439. If the exchange rate has changed from 1 US dollar being worth 5 French francs to a rate of 1 US dollar being worth 5.5 French francs, then

a. The US dollar has appreciated by 10%.
b. The US dollar has depreciated by 10%.
c. The French franc has appreciated by 20%.
d. The French franc has depreciated by 20%.

440. Assuming that the real rate of interest is the same in both countries, if Country A has a higher nominal interest rate than Country B, then the currency of Country A will likely be selling at a

a. Forward discount relative to the currency of Country B.
b. Forward premium relative to the currency of Country B.
c. Spot discount relative to the currency of Country B.
d. Spot premium relative to the currency of Country B.

441. Which of the following financial instruments can be traded in international money markets?

a. Mortgages.
b. Preferred stocks.
c. Government Treasury bills.
d. Government Treasury bonds.

442. Which of the following is a characteristic of Eurobonds?

a. Are always denominated in Eurodollars.
b. Are always sold in some country other than the one in whose currency the bond is denominated.
c. Are sold outside the country of the borrower but are denominated in the currency of the country in which the issue is sold.
d. Are generally issued as registered bonds.

443. Two countries have flexible exchange rate systems and an active trading relationship. If incomes (List A) in Country 1, everything else equal, then the currency of Country 1 will tend to (List B) relative to the currency of Country 2.

	List A	*List B*
a.	Rise	Remain constant
b.	Fall	Depreciate
c.	Rise	Depreciate
d.	Remain constant	Appreciate

444. In an interest rate swap, the first company

a. Sells its right to low interest rate financing at a financial institution to the second company that is seeking to borrow funds.
b. Agrees to service the debt of the second company by making interest payments directly to the bank of the second company, while the second company agrees in exchange to make interest payments to the bank of the first company.
c. Buys the outstanding public debt of the second company and swaps the interest payments it receives on that debt for the interest payments it must make on its own debt.
d. Agrees to exchange with the second company the difference between the interest charges on its own borrowings and the interest charges on the borrowings of the second company.

445. A US company and a German company purchased the same stock on the German stock exchange and held the stock for one year. The value of the German mark weakened against the dollar over this period. Comparing the returns of the two companies, the United States company's return will be

a. Lower.
b. Higher.
c. The same.
d. Indeterminate from the information provided.

446. A company has recently purchased some stock of a competitor as part of a long-term plan to acquire the competitor. However, it is somewhat concerned that the market price of this stock could decrease over the short run. The company could hedge against the possible decline in the stock's market price by

a. Purchasing a call option on that stock.
b. Purchasing a put option on that stock.
c. Selling a put option on that stock.
d. Obtaining a warrant option on that stock.

447. The risk that securities cannot be sold at a reasonable price on short notice is called

a. Default risk.
b. Interest rate risk.
c. Purchasing power risk.
d. Liquidity risk.

Cash Management

448. Why would a company maintain a compensating cash balance?

a. To make routine payments and collections.
b. To pay for banking services.
c. To provide a reserve in case of unforeseen fluctuations in cash flows.
d. To take advantage of bargain purchase opportunities that may arise.

449. An imprest bank account is

a. A difference between the amount on deposit according to the company's records and the amount of collected cash according to the bank record.
b. The principal bank account through which most companies' cash transactions are cycled.
c. An account used to make a specific amount of cash available for a limited purpose.
d. A local post office box from which a local bank is authorized to pick up and deposit remittances.

Items 450 and 451 are based on the following:

On January 1, a company establishes a petty cash account and designates one employee as petty cash custodian. The original amount included in the petty cash fund is $500, and it will be used to make small cash disbursements. The fund will be replenished on the first of each month, after the petty cash custodian presents receipts for disbursements to the general cashier.

The following disbursements are made in the month of January:

Office supplies	$173
Postage	112
Entertainment	42

The balance in the petty cash box at the end of January is $163.

450. Who is responsible, at all times, for the amount of the petty cash fund?

a. The president of the company.
b. The general office manager.
c. The general cashier.
d. The petty cash custodian.

451. Which of the following is **not** an appropriate procedure for controlling the petty cash fund?

a. The petty cash custodian files receipts by category of expenditure after their presentation to the general cashier, so that variations in different types of expenditures can be monitored.
b. Surprise counts of the fund are made from time to time by a superior of the petty cash custodian to determine that the fund is being accounted for satisfactorily.
c. The petty cash custodian obtains signed receipts from each individual to whom petty cash is paid.
d. Upon receiving petty cash receipts as evidence of disbursements, the general cashier issues a company check to the petty cash custodian, rather than cash, to replenish the fund.

452. For good internal control over the disbursement of payroll checks, a company makes a specific amount of cash available in a checking account for this limited purpose. The type of account used for this purpose is called a(n)

a. General checking account.
b. Imprest bank account.
c. Lockbox account.
d. Compensatory account.

453. On a company's December 31, 2004 balance sheet, which of the following items should be included in the amount reported as cash?

I. A check payable to the company, dated January 2, 2005, in payment of a sale made in December 2004.
II. A check drawn on the company's account, payable to a vendor, dated and recorded in the company's books on December 31, 2004, but not mailed until January 10, 2005.

a. I only.
b. II only.
c. I and II only.
d. Neither I nor II.

454. The following information pertains to a checking account of a company at July 31, 2005:

Balance per bank statement	$40,000
Interest earned for July	100
Outstanding checks	3,000
Customers' checks returned or insufficient funds	1,000
Deposit in transit	5,000

At July 31, 2005, the company's correct cash balance is

a. $41,100
b. $41,000
c. $42,100
d. $42,000

455. A company shows a cash balance of $35,000 on its bank statement dated November 1. As of November 1, there are $11,000 of outstanding checks and $7,500 of deposits in transit. The correct cash balance on the company books as of November 1 would be

a. $24,000
b. $31,500
c. $42,500
d. $53,500

456. An organization is reconciling its bank statement with internal records. The cash balance per the bank statement is $10,000 while the cash balance per the organization's books is $9,000. There are $1,000 of bank charges not yet recorded, $1,500 of outstanding checks, $2,500 of deposits in transit, and $3,000 of bank credits and collections not yet recorded in the organization's books. If there are no bank or book errors, what is the organization's correct cash balance?

a. $10,000
b. $11,000
c. $12,000
d. $14,500

457. An organization borrows funds from its bank for a one-year period. The bank charges interest at a nominal rate of 15% per annum, on a discount basis, and requires a 10% compensating balance. The effective annual interest rate on the loan is

a. 16.67%
b. 17.65%
c. 20.00%
d. 25.00%

458. The correct equation for calculating the approximate percentage cost, on an annual basis, of not taking trade discounts is

a. $\dfrac{\text{Discount \%}}{100 - \text{Discount \%}} \times \dfrac{360}{[\text{Days credit is outstanding} - \text{Discount period}]}$

b. $\dfrac{\text{Discount \%}}{100} \times \dfrac{360}{[\text{Days credit is outstanding} - \text{Discount period}]}$

c. $\dfrac{100 - \text{Discount \%}}{\text{Discount \%}} \times \dfrac{360}{[\text{Days credit is outstanding} - \text{Discount period}]}$

d. $\dfrac{\text{Discount \%}}{100 - \text{Discount \%}} \times \dfrac{[\text{Days credit is outstanding} - \text{Discount period}]}{360}$

459. Everything else being equal, the balance of cash reported in a customer's bank statement will be less than the balance shown in the customer's own records if there are

a. Deposits in transit.
b. Outstanding checks.
c. Interest payments to the customer that are not yet recorded in the customer books.
d. Credits to the customer's account that incorrectly include deposits from another customer.

Items 460 and 461 are based on the following:

A company sells 10,000 skateboards a year at $66 each. All sales are on credit, with terms of 3/10, net 30, which means 3% discount if payment is made within 10 days; otherwise full payment is due at the end of 30 days. One-half of the customers are expected to take advantage of the discount and pay on day 10. The other half are expected to pay on day 30. Sales are expected to be uniform throughout the year for both types of customers.

460. What is the expected average collection period for the company?

a. 10 days.
b. 15 days.

c. 20 days.
d. 30 days.

461. Without prejudice to your answer for the previous question, assume that the average collection period is 25 days. After the credit policy is well established, what is the expected average accounts receivable balance for the company at any point in time, assuming a 365-day year?

a. $ 684.93
b. $ 1,808.22
c. $27,123.30
d. $45,205.48

462. A manufacturing firm wants to obtain a short-term loan and has approached several lending institutions. All of the potential lenders are offering the same nominal interest rate but the terms of the loans vary. Which of the following combinations of loan terms will be **most** attractive for the borrowing firm?

a. Simple interest, no compensating balance.
b. Discount interest, no compensating balance.
c. Simple interest, 20% compensating balance required.
d. Discount interest, 20% compensating balance required.

463. A service company's working capital at the beginning of January 2005 was $70,000. The following transactions occurred during January:

Performed services on account	$30,000
Purchased supplies on account	5,000
Consumed supplies	4,000
Purchased office equipment for cash	2,000
Paid short-term bank loan	6,500
Paid salaries	10,000
Accrued salaries	3,500

What is the amount of working capital at the end of January?

a. $80,500
b. $78,500
c. $50,500
d. $47,500

464. A company considers a project that will generate cash sales of $50,000 per year. Fixed costs will be $10,000 per year, variable costs will be 40% of sales, and depreciation of the equipment in the project will be $5,000 per year. Taxes are 40%. The expected annual cash flow to the company resulting from the project is

a. $15,000
b. $ 9,000
c. $19,000
d. $14,000

465. A company plans to produce a new product, which will typically be sold to other firms on credit. The cash conversion cycle resulting from this new product can be measured as the length of time from

a. Cash purchases of raw materials to the collection of accounts receivable.
b. Cash purchases of raw materials to the time the final product is completed.
c. Cash purchases of raw materials to the sale of the product.
d. When the product is completed to the sale of the product.

466. Determining the amount and timing of conversions of marketable securities to cash is a critical element of a financial manager's performance. In terms of the rate of return foregone on converted securities and the cost of such transactions, the optimal amount of cash to be raised by selling securities is

a. Inversely related to the rate of return foregone and directly related to the cost of the transaction.
b. Directly related to the rate of return foregone and directly related to the cost of the transaction.
c. Directly related to the rate of return foregone and inversely related to the cost of the transaction.
d. Inversely related to the rate of return foregone and inversely related to the cost of the transaction.

467. A company serves as a distributor of products by ordering finished products once a quarter and using that inventory to accommodate the demand over the quarter. If it plans to ease its credit policy for customers, the amount of products ordered for its inventory every quarter will be

a. Increased to accommodate higher sales levels.
b. Reduced to offset the increased cost of carrying accounts receivable.
c. Unaffected if safety stock is part of the current quarterly order.
d. Unaffected if the ABC inventory control system is used.

468. The following transactions occurred during a company's first year of operations:

I. Purchased a delivery van for cash.
II. Borrowed money by issuance of short-term debt.
III. Purchased treasury stock.

Which of the items above caused a change in the amount of working capital?

a. I only.
b. II and III only.
c. I and III only.
d. I, II, and III.

469. If a company was experiencing cash flow problems, it could attempt a reorganization that would involve

a. A shortening of the maturity on existing debt.
b. Replacing some of the debt outstanding with common stock.
c. Replacing some of the common stock outstanding with debt.
d. Replacing some of the debt outstanding with preferred stock.

470. A company has accounts payable of $5 million with terms of 2% discount within 15 days, net 30 days (2/15 net 30). It can borrow funds from a bank at an annual rate of 12% or it can wait until the 30th day when it will receive revenues to cover the payment. If it borrows funds on the last day of the discount period in order to obtain the discount, its total cost would be

a. $51,000 less.
b. $75,500 less.
c. $100,000 less.
d. $24,500 more.

471. A company plans to purchase a machine with the following conditions:

- Purchase price = $300,000
- The down payment = 10% of purchase price with remainder financed at an annual interest rate of 16%

- The financing period is 8 years with equal annual payments made every year
- The present value of an annuity of $1 per year for 8 years at 16% is 4.3436
- The present value of $1 due at the end of 8 years at 16% is .3050

The annual payment (rounded to the nearest dollar) is
a. $39,150
b. $43,200
c. $62,160
d. $82,350

472. A given company offers credit terms of a 2% discount if paid within 10 days, or the full balance is due within 30 days (2/10, net 30). Eighty percent of customers take discounts and pay on day 10, while the other 20% pay on day 30. The average collection period is equal to
a. 14 days.
b. 20 days.
c. Average daily sales divided by average inventory.
d. Average daily sales divided by receivables.

473. An example of secured short-term financing is
a. Commercial paper.
b. A warehouse receipt.
c. A revolving credit agreement.
d. Trade credit.

474. A company is in need of a short-term source of funds. Local banks and a finance company have offered the needed funds under each of the following sets of terms. All involve a one-year note.

- Bank one: $100,000 note, 12% interest.
- Bank two: $100,000 note, 10% interest, 20% compensating balance required.
- Bank three: $110,000 noninterest-bearing note, discounted at 11%.
- Finance company: $100,000 note, 11% interest, with an up-front charge of six points (6%).

Which option is the most cost-efficient alternative?
a. Bank one.
b. Bank two.
c. Bank three.
d. Finance company.

475. Which of the following is true regarding the assignment and factoring of accounts receivable for a manufacturing firm?
a. The lender has recourse to the manufacturing firm under factoring but not under the assignment of accounts receivable.
b. The factoring of accounts receivable provides collateral for the manufacturing firm while the assignment of receivables provides direct financing.
c. The assignment of accounts receivable involves the invoice from the manufacturing firm to its customer being stamped with a notification that payment is to be made directly to the other party, while the factoring of accounts receivable does not.
d. The factoring of accounts receivable involves the invoice from the manufacturing firm to its customer being stamped with a notification that payment is to be made directly to the other party, while the assignment of accounts receivable does not.

476. A transfer of receivables with recourse in exchange for cash should
a. Not be recorded until all of the receivables have been collected.
b. Be recorded as a sale or a borrowing, depending on the provisions of the transfer agreement.
c. Be recorded as a sale of receivables.
d. Be recorded as a borrowing transaction.

477. A company's receivables collection period is equal to
a. The inventory conversion period.
b. The cash conversion cycle.
c. The days sales outstanding.
d. The inventory divided by average daily sales.

478. A company obtaining short-term financing with trade credit will pay a higher percentage financing cost, everything else being equal, when
a. The discount percentage is lower.
b. The items purchased have a higher price.
c. The items purchased have a lower price.
d. The supplier offers a longer discount period.

479. At the end of September, a company has outstanding accounts receivable of $350 on third-quarter credit sales, composed as follows:

Month	*Credit sales*	*Still outstanding at the end of September*
July	$600	$100
August	900	170
September	500	80

The percentage of receivables in the 31-to-60-day age group at the end of September is
a. 21.43%
b. 28.57%
c. 48.57%
d. 71.43%

480. A firm sells on terms of 2/10 net 60. It sells 1000 units per day at a unit price of $10. On 60% of sales, customers take the cash discount. On the remaining 40% of sales, customers pay, on average, in 70 days. What would be the impact on the balance of accounts receivable if the firm initiates a more aggressive collection policy and is able to reduce the average payment period to 60 days for those customers not taking the cash discount? (Assume sales levels are unaffected by the change in policy.)
a. Decrease by $4,000.
b. Decrease by $40,000.
c. Decrease by $240,000.
d. Decrease by $280,000.

481. A short-term bank loan will have a higher effective financing cost if it has which combination of characteristics?
a. A 10% compensating balance and regular interest.
b. A 10% compensating balance and discount interest.
c. A 20% compensating balance and regular interest.
d. A 20% compensating balance and discount interest.

482. The comparative balance sheet for a company that had net income of $150,000 for the year ended December 31, 2005, and paid $125,000 of dividends during 2005 is as follows:

	12/31/05	*12/31/04*
Cash	$150,000	180,000
Accounts receivable	200,000	220,000
Total assets	$350,000	400,000
Payables	$ 80,000	160,000
Capital stock	130,000	125,000
Retained earnings	140,000	115,000
Total	$350,000	400,000

The amount of net cash provided by operating activities during 2005 was

a. $ 70,000
b. $ 90,000
c. $150,000
d. $210,000

483. The credit instrument known as a banker's acceptance

a. Calls for immediate payment upon delivery of the shipping documents to the bank's customer and acceptance of goods by the bank.
b. Involves an invoice being signed by the banker upon receipt of goods, after which both the banker and the seller record the transaction on their respective books.
c. Is a time draft payable on a specified date and guaranteed by the bank.
d. Is a method of sales financing in which the bank retains title to the goods until the buyer has completed payment.

484. A growing company is assessing current working capital requirements. An average of 58 days is required to convert raw materials into finished goods and to sell them. Then an average of 32 days is required to collect on receivables. If the average time the company takes to pay for its raw materials were 15 days after they are received, then the total cash conversion cycle for this company would be

a. 11 days.
b. 41 days.
c. 75 days.
d. 90 days.

485. Which is **not** a correct description of the assignment of accounts receivable?

a. The lender has a claim against the receivables and has recourse to the borrower.
b. The risk of default on the pledged accounts receivable remains with the borrower.
c. In a general assignment of receivables, the borrower can substitute new receivables for accounts receivable that are collected in cash.
d. In a specific assignment of receivables, the borrower can substitute new receivables for accounts receivable that are collected in cash.

Items 486 and 487 are based on the following:

A company has a 10% cost of borrowing and incurs fixed costs of $500 for obtaining a loan. It has stable, predictable cash flows and the estimated total amount of net new cash needed for transactions for the year is $175,000. The company does not hold safety stocks of cash.

486. When the average cash balance of the company is higher, the (List A) the cash balance is (List B).

	List A	*List B*
a.	Opportunity cost of holding	Higher
b.	Total transactions costs associated with obtaining	Higher
c.	Opportunity cost of holding	Lower
d.	Total costs of holding	Lower

487. If the average cash balance for the company during the year is $20,916.50 then the opportunity cost of holding cash for the year will be

a. $ 2,091.65
b. $ 4,183.30
c. $ 8,750.00
d. $17,500.00

488. The amount of cash that a firm keeps on hand in order to take advantage of any bargain purchases that may arise is referred to as its

a. Transactions balance.
b. Compensating balance.
c. Precautionary balance.
d. Speculative balance.

Items 489 and 490 are based on the following:

Effective September 1, a company initiates seasonal dating as a component of its credit policy, allowing wholesale customers to make purchases early but not requiring payment until the retail selling season begins. Sales occur as follows:

Date of sale	*Quantity sold*
September 1	300 units
October 1	100 units
November 1	100 units
December 1	150 units
January 1	50 units

- Each unit has a selling price of $10, regardless of the date of sale.
- The terms of sale is 2/10 net 30, January 1 dating.
- All sales are on credit.
- All customers take the discount and abide by the terms of the discount policy.
- All customers take advantage of the new seasonal dating policy.
- The peak selling season for all customers is mid-November to late December.

489. For the selling firm, which of the following is **not** an expected advantage of initiating seasonal dating?

a. Reduced storage costs.
b. Reduced credit costs.
c. Attractive credit terms for customers.
d. Reduced uncertainty about sales volume.

490. For sales after the initiation of the seasonal dating policy on September 1, total collections on or before January 11 will be

a. $0
b. $6,370
c. $6,860
d. $7,000

491. The following amounts pertain to the ABC Corporation at December 31, 2005:

Total current assets	$ 300,000
Total fixed assets	2,200,000
Total assets	2,500,000
Total current liabilities	120,000

Total liabilities	1,600,000
Total paid-in capital	400,000
Total stockholder's equity	900,000

ABC's working capital at December 31, 2005, amounts to

a. $180,000
b. $400,000
c. $500,000
d. $900,000

492. A firm desires a finished goods ending inventory equal to 25% of the following month's budgeted sales. January sales are budgeted at 10,000 units and February at 12,000 units. Each unit requires two pounds of Material X, which costs $4 per pound. The company has a just-in-time system and materials are delivered daily just prior to use, so no raw material inventories are maintained. Materials are paid for in the month following purchase. The January 1 finished goods inventory is 2,500 units. In February, what amount should the company expect to pay as a cash outflow for raw materials?

a. $40,000
b. $42,000
c. $80,000
d. $84,000

493. Factoring refers to

a. Selling of accounts receivable by one company to another.
b. Selling of inventory by one company to another.
c. Conversion of accounts receivable to bad debt on financial statements for accounts that are long overdue.
d. Adjustment of inventories on financial statements for supplies that have become obsolete.

494. A company had $30 million in total sales last year and expects $40 million in total sales this year. Ten percent of each year's sales are on credit that will be paid the following year. The company anticipates the following expenses for this year:

- Depreciation of $5 million.
- Labor, material, taxes, and other expenses of $51 million.

Assume the company begins with a zero cash balance. At the end of this year, the company will have a cash deficit of

a. $8 million.
b. $12 million.
c. $15 million.
d. $17 million.

495. A company is preparing its cash budget for the coming month. All sales are made on account. Given the following:

	Beginning balances	Budgeted amounts
Cash	$ 50,000	--
Beginning accounts receivable	$180,000	--
Sales	--	$800,000
Cash disbursements	--	$780,000
Depreciation	--	$ 25,000
Ending accounts receivable	--	$210,000

What is the expected cash balance of the company at the end of the coming month?

a. $15,000
b. $40,000
c. $45,000
d. $70,000

496. Partial balance sheet information for a company for the years ending December 31, 2004 and 2005 is as follows:

	December 31 2005	2004
Current assets (except for cash)		
Accounts receivable	$ 20,000	$ 5,000
Inventories	50,000	14,000
Prepaid expenses	3,000	6,000
Current liabilities		
Accounts payable	$ 32,000	$16,000
Property tax payable	4,000	3,000

Working capital increased in 2005 by $12,000. The change in cash in 2005 was

a. $ 12,000
b. $ 43,000
c. $(19,000)
d. $(36,000)

497. MKT Corporation's assets on December 31, 2005, include the following:

I. US Treasury bills, acquired on October 15, 2005. These securities mature on April 15, 2006.
II. Shares of PF Company. PF has been very profitable and MKT Corporation plans to increase its ownership in PF as it believes PF has strong growth potential.
III. Bonds of ABC Corporation, which matures in 3 years. These bonds will be sold, as needed, to meet MKT Corporation's current financing needs.

Which of the above should be classified as temporary investments?

a. I and III only.
b. I only.
c. I and II only.
d. I, II, and III.

Valuation Models

498. The cost of materials has risen steadily over the year. The company uses its newest materials first when removing items from inventory. Which of the following methods of estimating the ending balance of the materials inventory account will result in the highest net income, all other variables held constant?

a. Last-in-first-out (LIFO).
b. First-in-first-out (FIFO).
c. Weighted-average.
d. Specific identification.

Items 499 and 500 are based on the following:

On January 1, a company has no opening inventory balance. The following purchases are made during the year:

	Units purchased	Unit cost
January 1	5,000	$10.00
April 1	5,000	9.00
July 1	5,000	8.00
October 1	5,000	7.50

There are 10,000 units in inventory on December 31.

499. If the company uses the first-in, first-out (FIFO) method of inventory valuation, the ending inventory balance will be

a. $77,500
b. $85,000
c. $86,250
d. $95,000

500. If the company uses the last-in, first-out (LIFO) method of inventory valuation, cost of goods sold for the year will be

a. $77,500
b. $86,250
c. $87,500
d. $95,000

501. The following information (for the current year) is for a retail company that maintains a markup of 25% based on cost:

Purchases of merchandise	$690,000
Freight-in on purchases	25,000
Sales	900,000
Ending inventory	80,000

Beginning inventory was

a. $40,000
b. $85,000
c. $110,000
d. $265,000

502. A company's beginning inventory for year 5 was understated by $13,000 and the ending inventory for year 5 was overstated by $26,000. These errors will cause the year 5 net income to be

a. Understated by $13,000.
b. Understated by $39,000.
c. Overstated by $26,000.
d. Overstated by $39,000.

503. A merchandising company had the following inventory related transactions in its first year of operations:

Date	Purchases in units	Sales in units	Balance in units
Jan. 1	10,000 @ $5		10,000
March 1	6,000 @ $6		16,000
May 1		3,000	13,000
July 1	8,000 @ $6.25		21,000
Sept. 1		12,000	9,000
Nov. 1	5,000 @ $7		14,000
Dec. 1		2,000	12,000

If the company uses the first-in-first-out (FIFO) method of inventory valuation, its ending inventory balance, to the nearest dollar, will be

a. $62,000
b. $70,759
c. $78,750
d. $84,000

504. A physical inventory count showed a company had inventory costing $1,000,000 on hand at December 31, 2004. Excluded from this amount were the following:

- Goods costing $82,000, shipped to a customer free on board (FOB) shipping point on December 28, 2004. They were expected to be received by the customer on January 4, 2005.
- Goods costing $122,000 shipped to a customer free on board (FOB) destination December 30, 2004. They were expected to be received by the customer on January 5, 2005.

Compute the correct ending inventory to be reported on the shipper's balance sheet at December 31, 2004.

a. $1,000,000
b. $1,082,000
c. $1,122,000
d. $1,204,000

505. An organization uses the retail method of inventory estimation for interim reporting purposes. Management knows to expect some normal shrinkage in the inventory due to theft. What effect will the failure to consider this shrinkage have on the computation of (1) the cost/retail ratio, and (2) the estimated ending inventory at retail?

	(1) *Effect on cost/ retail ratio*	(2) *Effect on estimated ending inventory at retail*
a.	No effect	No effect
b.	No effect	Overstatement
c.	Overstatement	Overstatement
d.	Overstatement	Understatement

506. The following amounts relate to a company:

Beginning inventory	$ 50,000
Purchases	170,000
Sales	180,000
Gross margin	60,000

The amount of ending inventory is

a. $60,000
b. $100,000
c. $120,000
d. $160,000

507. A retail company maintains a markup of 25% based on cost. The company has the following information for 1996:

Purchases of merchandise	$690,000
Freight-in on purchases	25,000
Sales	900,000
Ending inventory	80,000

Beginning inventory was

a. $ 40,000
b. $ 85,000
c. $110,000
d. $265,000

508. Which inventory pricing method generally approximates current cost for each of the following?

	Ending inventory	*Cost of goods sold*
a.	FIFO	FIFO
b.	LIFO	FIFO
c.	FIFO	LIFO
d.	LIFO	LIFO

509. The following information is available for a company for the quarter ended March 31, 1995:

Merchandise inventory, as of January 1, 2005	$ 30,000
Sales	200,000
Purchases	190,000

The gross profit margin is normally 20% of sales. What is the estimated cost of the merchandise inventory at March 31, 2005?

a. $ 20,000
b. $ 40,000
c. $ 60,000
d. $180,000

510. The following data are available from the records of a department store for the year ended December 31, 2005:

	At cost	*At retail*
Merchandise inventory, as of January 1, 2005	$ 9,000	$13,000
Purchases	33,000	46,000
Markups (net)		1,000
Markdowns (net)		4,000
Sales		48,000

Using the retail method to approximate valuation at lower of average cost or market, the department store's merchandise inventory at December 31, 2005, is

a. $8,400
b. $8,000
c. $6,000
d. $5,600

Items 511 and 512 are based on the following:

A Company started in 2005 with 200 scented candles on hand at a cost of $3.50 each. These candles sell for $7.00 each. The following schedule represents the purchases and sales of candles during 2005:

Transaction number	*Quantity purchased*	*Unit cost*	*Quantity sold*
1	--	--	150
2	250	$3.30	--
3	--	--	100
4	200	$3.10	--
5	--	--	200
6	350	$3.00	--
7	--	--	300

511. If the company uses perpetual LIFO inventory pricing, the cost of goods sold for 2005 would be

a. $2,320
b. $2,370
c. $2,375
d. $2,380

512. If the company uses periodic FIFO inventory pricing, the gross profit for 2005 would be

a. $2,755
b. $2,805
c. $2,854
d. $2,920

Items 513 and 514 are based on the following:

Illustrated below is a perpetual inventory card for 2005.

Date	*Units purchased*	*Units sold*	*Units balance*
January 1			0
January 12	1,000 @ $2.00		1,000
March 15		300	700
May 5	500 @ $2.20		1,200
July 8		500	700
November 24	1,000 @ $1.65		1,700

Additional information

- The company had no opening inventory.
- The items sold on March 15 were purchased on January 12.
- The items sold on July 8 were purchased on May 5.

513. The ending inventory balance, under the first-in-first-out (FIFO) method of inventory valuation, would be

a. $3,050
b. $3,150
c. $3,230
d. $3,430

514. The cost of goods sold, under the specific identification method of inventory valuation, would be

a. $1,320
b. $1,520
c. $1,600
d. $1,700

Items 515 and 516 are based on the following:

An organization has 8,000 units in inventory on January 1, valued at $10 per unit. During the year, the organization sold 25,000 units and purchased additional inventory as follows:

Date	*Quantity purchased*	*Unit price*
April 1	15,000 units	$ 8
July 1	10,000 units	$ 9
October 1	12,500 units	$10

515. If the organization uses the first-in-first-out (FIFO) method of inventory valuation, what is the value of ending inventory?

a. $180,000
b. $197,000
c. $218,000
d. $235,000

516. If the organization uses the weighted-average cost method of inventory valuation, cost of goods sold for the period will be

a. $186,978
b. $197,000
c. $228,023
d. $235,000

517. A company had 1000 units of opening inventory that cost $10 per unit. On May 1, 1000 units were purchased at a cost of $11 each, and on September 1 another 1000 units were purchased at a cost of $12 each. If 2000 units were sold during the year, the company will report cost of goods sold of (List A) if the (List B) method of inventory valuation is used.

	List A	*List B*
a.	$22,000	LIFO
b.	$23,000	Weighted-average
c.	$21,000	FIFO
d.	$22,000	FIFO

518. A company had 500 units of opening inventory that cost $5 per unit. On March 1, the company purchased 300 units at a cost of $7 each. On September 1 another 300 units were purchased. During the year 700 units were sold and the balance of ending inventory is $2,500. If the company uses the first-in-first-out (FIFO) method of inventory valuation, then the per unit cost of the items purchased on September 1, to the nearest cent, was

a. $3.67
b. $6.00
c. $6.67
d. $7.58

519. If ending inventory is underestimated due to an error in the physical count of items on hand, then cost of goods sold for the period will be (List A) and net earnings will be (List B).

	List A	*List B*
a.	Underestimated	Underestimated
b.	Underestimated	Overestimated
c.	Overestimated	Underestimated
d.	Overestimated	Overestimated

Items 520 and 521 are based on the following:

On January 1, a company has no opening inventory balance. The following purchases are made during the year:

Date	Units purchased	Unit cost
January 1	5,000	$10.00
April 1	5,000	$ 9.00
July 1	5,000	$ 8.00
October 1	5,000	$ 7.50

There are 10,000 units in inventory on December 31.

520. If the company uses the first-in-first-out (FIFO) method of inventory valuation, the ending inventory balance will be

a. $77,500
b. $85,000
c. $86,250
d. $95,000

521. Cost of goods sold for the year, if the company uses the last-in-first-out (LIFO) method of inventory valuation, will be

a. $77,500
b. $86,250
c. $87,500
d. $95,000

522. XYZ Company took a physical inventory on December 31, 2004, and determined that merchandise with a cost of $1,000,000 was on hand at that date. The following facts were also established:

- Excluded from the $1,000,000 was merchandise of $90,000 shipped by a vendor FOB destination on December 29, 2004, and received by XYZ on January 4, 2005.
- Excluded from the $1,000,000 was merchandise of $60,000 shipped by a vendor FOB shipping point on December 28, 2004, and received by XYZ on January 7, 2005.
- Excluded from the $1,000,000 was merchandise of $64,000 shipped by XYZ FOB destination to a customer on December 31, 2004. The customer received the merchandise on January 5, 2005.
- Excluded from the $1,000,000 was merchandise of $100,000 held by XYZ on consignment.

The consignor is ABC Company. The amount to be reported for inventory on XYZ's balance sheet at December 31, 2004, is

a. $1,000,000
b. $1,090,000
c. $1,124,000
d. $1,224,000

523. The following information relates to the merchandise inventory of a company:

	Units	Cost/unit
Inventory, June 1	1,000	$10.00
Purchases, June 12	4,000	$12.00
Purchases, June 23	5,000	$11.30

Sales during June amounted to 8,000 units. If the company uses a periodic inventory system and the weighted-average method, the cost of inventory on June 30 is

a. $22,200
b. $22,600
c. $22,000
d. $22,900

524. A division experienced a 2005 fire, which destroyed all but $6,000 of inventory (at cost). Data available is below.

	2004	2005 (to date of fire)
Sales	$100,000	$40,000
Purchases	70,000	35,000
Cost of goods sold	60,000	
Ending inventory	10,000	

What is the approximate inventory lost to the fire?

a. $10,000
b. $15,000
c. $16,000
d. $21,000

525. Management of a new retail sales company has asked for your advice in the selection of an appropriate inventory-costing method. The business carries 20 lines of homogeneous products, the turnover rate is expected to be high, purchase prices are expected to increase continuously and inventory quantities on hand at the end of each accounting period are expected to remain constant or increase. Management seeks an inventory-cost method that would defer holding gains (or losses) arising from specific price changes. Which of the following methods would best meet this objective?

a. First-in-first-out (FIFO).
b. Weighted-average with a periodic system.
c. Weighted-average with a perpetual system.
d. Last-in-first-out (LIFO).

526. The economic value of a firm will rise following an increase in

a. Net cash flow.
b. Systematic risk.
c. Unsystematic risk.
d. The discount rate.

527. The maximum acquisition value of an inefficiently managed corporation is the discounted net present value of the

a. Current market value of the corporation.
b. Current earnings before interest and taxes.
c. Current net profit.
d. Expected future cash flows.

528. The policy decision that by itself is **least** likely to affect the value of the firm is the

a. Investment in a project with a large net present value.
b. Sale of a risky division that will now increase the credit rating of the entire company.
c. Distribution of stock dividends to shareholders.
d. Use of a more highly leveraged capital structure that resulted in a lower cost of capital.

529. The long-term goal of financial management is to

a. Avoid risk.
b. Maximize shareholders' wealth.
c. Maximize profits.
d. Maximize the book value of assets.

530. Which of the following is directly applied in determining the value of a stock when using the constant growth (Gordon) model?

a. The firm's capital structure.
b. The firm's cash flows.
c. The firm's liquidity.
d. The investor's required rate of return on the firm's stock.

531. Which of the following statements is **not** correct about business valuation models?

a. The corporate valuation model can be used even for a company that does not pay dividends.
b. The corporate valuation model discounts free cash flows by the required return on equity.
c. The corporate valuation model can be used to find the value of a division.
d. An important step in applying the corporate valuation model is forecasting the pro forma financial statements.

532. Which of the following is **not** always a way to increase the value of a business?

a. Increase the growth rate of sales.
b. Increase the operating profitability.
c. Decrease the capital requirement.
d. Decrease the weighted-average cost of capital.

533. A company's earnings are $60 million, $35 million in cost of goods sold, and $15 million in operating expenses. It invested $40 million in long-term capital and has a weighted-average cost of capital of 10%. What is the economic value added (EVA) for this company?

a. $4.0 million.
b. $5.0 million.
c. $6.0 million.
d. $7.0 million.

534. A firm has 3 million common shares outstanding at a market price of $50 per share. Its debt is valued at $60 million and it employed a capital of $100 million. How much market value is added to the firm?

a. $100 million.
b. $110 million.
c. $150 million.
d. $160 million.

535. A company forecasts free cash flow in one year to be $10 million and free cash flow in two years to be $20 million. After the second year, free cash flow will grow at a constant rate of 4% per year forever. If the overall cost of capital is 14%, what is the current value of operations, to the nearest million?

a. $150 million.
b. $167 million.
c. $200 million.
d. $208 million.

536. Which of the following is the major determinant of the value of a firm?

a. Net income.
b. Dividends.
c. Cash flows.
d. Net sales.

537. Which of the following determines the value of a company's assets?

I. Higher cash flows.
II. Higher required return.
III. Higher net income.
IV. Lower required return.

a. I and II.
b. II and III.
c. I and IV.
d. III and IV.

Business Development Life Cycles

538. Which of the following threatens a nation's long-term trend of economic growth?

I. Full employment.
II. Price level stability.
III. Unemployment.
IV. Inflation.

a. I and II.
b. III only.
c. IV only.
d. III and IV.

539. Some economists prefer to use which of the following terms to refer to economic growth of a nation?

a. Business fluctuations.
b. Business cycles.
c. Business interruptions.
d. Business trends.

540. In which of the following phases of business development life cycle will both outputs and employment be declining?

a. Peak.
b. Recession.
c. Trough.
d. Recovery.

541. When an economy is experiencing a recession with low inflation, the central bank could stimulate the economy by

a. Purchasing securities.
b. Selling securities.
c. Purchasing stocks only.
d. Selling stocks only.

542. When a government restricts the money supply, it results in which of the following?

a. Higher income and higher inflation.
b. Lower output and lower employment.
c. Higher profits and higher production.
d. Lower income and higher production.

543. In a normal growth pattern, the growth rate of a firm is equal to the

a. Nominal gross national product (GNP).
b. Real GNP plus deflation.
c. Real GNP minus inflation.
d. Nominal GNP plus real gross domestic product (GDP).

544. During recession, which of the following characterizes consumer durable goods industry?

I. Low production.
II. Low employment.
III. Low prices.
IV. High investment in capital goods.

a. I only.
b. II only.
c. I and II.
d. III and IV.

545. In business activity, both seasonal variations and secular trends are due to which of the following?

a. Cyclical fluctuations.
b. Noncyclical fluctuations.
c. Business expansions.
d. Business contractions.

MULTIPLE-CHOICE ANSWERS AND EXPLANATIONS

1. c	63. a	125. c	187. c	249. a	311. c
2. d	64. b	126. b	188. d	250. c	312. d
3. d	65. a	127. c	189. c	251. a	313. b
4. d	66. a	128. c	190. b	252. a	314. a
5. c	67. a	129. b	191. b	253. b	315. a
6. b	68. a	130. d	192. d	254. c	316. c
7. b	69. d	131. a	193. b	255. d	317. c
8. c	70. c	132. a	194. c	256. b	318. b
9. b	71. d	133. c	195. d	257. c	319. b
10. d	72. b	134. a	196. a	258. a	320. c
11. d	73. b	135. d	197. a	259. c	321. a
12. d	74. a	136. d	198. d	260. a	322. c
13. a	75. d	137. d	199. d	261. c	323. d
14. d	76. a	138. d	200. d	262. c	324. b
15. a	77. c	139. a	201. a	263. a	325. a
16. c	78. a	140. b	202. b	264. c	326. c
17. b	79. a	141. a	203. b	265. d	327. a
18. b	80. a	142. b	204. c	266. b	328. b
19. d	81. d	143. c	205. a	267. c	329. b
20. b	82. a	144. b	206. a	268. a	330. c
21. a	83. b	145. d	207. d	269. c	331. c
22. d	84. b	146. b	208. c	270. a	332. b
23. b	85. d	147. a	209. c	271. c	333. c
24. c	86. d	148. c	210. b	272. b	334. b
25. b	87. a	149. b	211. b	273. c	335. a
26. c	88. a	150. a	212. c	274. d	336. d
27. b	89. b	151. c	213. d	275. a	337. a
28. d	90. d	152. a	214. c	276. c	338. a
29. a	91. c	153. a	215. b	277. a	339. b
30. b	92. b	154. c	216. c	278. b	340. c
31. b	93. a	155. d	217. d	279. c	341. b
32. b	94. b	156. a	218. a	280. a	342. b
33. a	95. a	157. d	219. d	281. c	343. c
34. d	96. a	158. c	220. c	282. b	344. a
35. c	97. d	159. c	221. a	283. c	345. d
36. b	98. b	160. c	222. b	284. a	346. a
37. c	99. d	161. a	223. d	285. c	347. a
38. d	100. d	162. d	224. c	286. d	348. b
39. d	101. b	163. a	225. c	287. b	349. c
40. a	102. b	164. d	226. c	288. d	350. c
41. d	103. a	165. b	227. a	289. c	351. a
42. c	104. b	166. a	228. d	290. b	352. a
43. a	105. d	167. c	229. a	291. c	353. a
44. a	106. c	168. a	230. b	292. b	354. b
45. d	107. a	169. a	231. c	293. b	355. a
46. c	108. d	170. a	232. b	294. c	356. d
47. b	109. a	171. b	233. b	295. a	357. d
48. b	110. c	172. a	234. d	296. c	358. c
49. d	111. c	173. d	235. b	297. c	359. b
50. b	112. a	174. d	236. d	298. a	360. a
51. a	113. a	175. c	237. b	299. a	361. b
52. a	114. d	176. a	238. d	300. b	362. d
53. d	115. d	177. b	239. b	301. a	363. d
54. d	116. a	178. b	240. c	302. b	364. a
55. a	117. b	179. b	241. a	303. a	365. c
56. c	118. c	180. c	242. d	304. c	366. d
57. c	119. c	181. c	243. c	305. b	367. b
58. c	120. a	182. c	244. b	306. b	368. c
59. c	121. b	183. c	245. c	307. d	369. d
60. b	122. b	184. d	246. a	308. a	370. b
61. d	123. c	185. a	247. d	309. c	371. a
62. a	124. c	186. a	248. a	310. a	372. a

373. a __ __	403. c __ __	433. b __ __	463. a __ __	493. a __ __	523. d __ __
374. a __ __	404. d __ __	434. b __ __	464. d __ __	494. b __ __	524. b __ __
375. b __ __	405. d __ __	435. d __ __	465. a __ __	495. b __ __	525. d __ __
376. c __ __	406. c __ __	436. a __ __	466. a __ __	496. c __ __	526. a __ __
377. b __ __	407. a __ __	437. d __ __	467. a __ __	497. a __ __	527. d __ __
378. d __ __	408. b __ __	438. c __ __	468. c __ __	498. b __ __	528. c __ __
379. a __ __	409. c __ __	439. a __ __	469. b __ __	499. a __ __	529. b __ __
380. b __ __	410. b __ __	440. a __ __	470. b __ __	500. a __ __	530. d __ __
381. a __ __	411. d __ __	441. c __ __	471. c __ __	501. b __ __	531. b __ __
382. a __ __	412. c __ __	442. b __ __	472. a __ __	502. d __ __	532. a __ __
383. d __ __	413. c __ __	443. c __ __	473. b __ __	503. c __ __	533. c __ __
384. d __ __	414. b __ __	444. d __ __	474. a __ __	504. c __ __	534. b __ __
385. b __ __	415. a __ __	445. a __ __	475. d __ __	505. b __ __	535. b __ __
386. c __ __	416. c __ __	446. b __ __	476. b __ __	506. b __ __	536. c __ __
387. a __ __	417. b __ __	447. d __ __	477. c __ __	507. b __ __	537. c __ __
388. c __ __	418. b __ __	448. b __ __	478. d __ __	508. c __ __	538. d __ __
389. d __ __	419. a __ __	449. c __ __	479. c __ __	509. c __ __	539. a __ __
390. d __ __	420. a __ __	450. d __ __	480. b __ __	510. d __ __	540. b __ __
391. a __ __	421. c __ __	451. a __ __	481. d __ __	511. c __ __	541. a __ __
392. d __ __	422. a __ __	452. b __ __	482. b __ __	512. b __ __	542. b __ __
393. d __ __	423. b __ __	453. b __ __	483. c __ __	513. b __ __	543. a __ __
394. b __ __	424. a __ __	454. d __ __	484. c __ __	514. d __ __	544. c __ __
395. a __ __	425. b __ __	455. b __ __	485. d __ __	515. b __ __	545. b __ __
396. b __ __	426. c __ __	456. b __ __	486. a __ __	516. c __ __	
397. a __ __	427. d __ __	457. c __ __	487. a __ __	517. c __ __	
398. c __ __	428. c __ __	458. a __ __	488. d __ __	518. b __ __	
399. d __ __	429. b __ __	459. a __ __	489. b __ __	519. c __ __	
400. b __ __	430. c __ __	460. c __ __	490. c __ __	520. a __ __	
401. c __ __	431. d __ __	461. d __ __	491. a __ __	521. a __ __	1st: __/545 = __%
402. a __ __	432. a __ __	462. a __ __	492. d __ __	522. c __ __	2nd: __/545 = __%

Basic Concepts

1. (c) Under accelerated depreciation, depreciation expense is higher and net income is lower. Retained earnings would therefore be lower for tax-reporting purposes than for general-purpose financial reporting based on straight-line depreciation. Choice (a) is incorrect. The balance of accumulated depreciation would be higher in the financial statements for tax purposes, since higher depreciation expense would be reported under accelerated depreciation than under straight-line depreciation. Choice (b) is incorrect. Depreciation expense is a noncash charge. The cash balance is unaffected by the depreciation method used. Choice (d) is incorrect. The historic cost of fixed assets is recorded in the gross fixed assets account. The historic cost of the assets is unaffected by the depreciation method used.

Subject Area: Financial accounting and finance—basic concepts. Source: CIA Model Exam 2002, IV-7.

2. (**d**) Since the amount received in cash has not yet been earned, it is appropriate to record the advance payment as a liability of the company. This is an example of the revenue recognition principle, which states that revenue, should not be recognized until it is earned. Choice (a) is incorrect. The going concern assumption is that the business will have a long life. This does not relate directly to the practice of recording unearned revenues as liabilities. Choice (b) is incorrect. The monetary unit assumption is that money is the common denominator by which economic activity is conducted, and that the monetary unit provides an appropriate basis for accounting measurement and analysis. It does not relate directly to the practice of recording unearned revenues as liabilities. Choice (c) is incorrect. The historic cost principle is the requirement that most assets and liabilities be accounted for and reported on the basis of acquisition price. It does not relate directly to the practice of recording unearned revenues as liabilities.

Subject Area: Financial accounting and finance—basic concepts. Source: CIA Model Exam 2002, IV-9.

3. (**d**) The going concern assumption provides that the accountant assumes unless there is evidence to the contrary, that the reporting entity will have a life long enough to fulfill its objectives and commitments. "Only if we assume some permanence to the enterprise are depreciation and amortization policies justifiable and appropriate." Choice (a) is incorrect because the economic entity assumption provides that economic activity can be identified with a particular unit of accountability. Choice (b) is incorrect because the monetary unit assumption provides that all transactions and events can be measured in terms of a common denominator, for instance, the dollar. Choice (c) is incorrect because the materiality assumption simply implies that items of insignificant value can be expensed.

Subject Area: Financial accounting and finance—basic concepts. Source: CIA 1192, IV-26.

4. (**d**) The carrying amount of the loan should be reduced, with a charge to the income statement. Choice (a) is incorrect because this is only appropriate if the situation is determined to be temporary. Choice (b) is incorrect because this is not required if the situation is determined to be temporary and is insufficient if the situation is determined to be other than temporary. Choice (c) is incorrect because the carrying amount should be reduced, but this is not charged directly to retained earnings.

Subject Area: Financial accounting and finance—basic concepts. Source: CIA Model Exam 2002, IV-21.

5. **(c)** The income statement of the current period portrays events or estimates arising in the current period only. The events or estimates may be disclosed outside normal operations (for example, discontinued operations, extraordinary items). A prior period adjustment is a correction for an event or estimate that existed in an earlier period. Choice (a) is incorrect. Correction of an error is not a prior period adjustment, although the accounting treatment is the same. Choice (b) is incorrect. The income statement of the current period portrays events or estimates that may not recur, for example, gains or losses on disposal of capital assets. Response (b) describes the current operating performance income statement approach. Choice (d) is incorrect. A prior period adjustment may be an indication of long-range income-producing ability. Advocates of the all-inclusive income statement approach would include prior period adjustments in the current year's income statement.

Subject Area: Financial accounting and finance—basic concepts. Source: CIA Model Exam 2002, IV-25.

6. **(b)** The journal entry to accrue revenue involves a debit to a receivable account and a credit to a revenue account. Thus, the accrual of revenue increases assets and owners' equity. Choice (a) is incorrect because the accrual of revenue increases assets and owners' equity. Choice (c) is incorrect because the accrual of revenue increases assets, increases owners' equity, and has no effect on liabilities. Choice (d) is incorrect because the accrual of revenue increases assets, increases owners' equity, and has no effect on liabilities.

Subject Area: Financial accounting and finance—basic concepts. Source: CIA Model Exam 1998, IV-3.

7. **(b)** Calculations follow:

$18,000/36 months = $500 per month
36 months – 3 months (Oct., Nov., & Dec. 2005) = 33 months
$500 × 33 months = $16,500 prepaid at Dec. 31, 2005

Beginning prepaid balance	$ 3,600
Payments in 1997	18,000
Subtotal	21,600
Ending prepaid	16,500
Insurance expense	$ 5,100

Choice (a) is incorrect. This answer incorrectly ignores the existing balance of $3,600 in the prepaid insurance account. Choice (c) is incorrect. This answer ignores the expiration of insurance cost for October, November, and December 2005 at $500 per month. Choice (d) is incorrect. This answer does not properly handle the unadjusted balance in the prepaid insurance account. The facts clearly indicate that the cost of the unexpired insurance at the balance sheet date is $16,500. Thus, all other insurance cost reflected on the trial balance should be accounted for as expired cost.

Subject Area: Financial accounting and finance—basic concepts. Source: CIA Model Exam 1998, IV-4.

8. **(c)** An expense incurred but not yet paid is an accrued expense. The adjusting entry to record an accrued expense involves a debit to an expense account and a credit to a liability account. Choice (a) is incorrect because no adjusting entry involves the income summary account. The income summary account is used in closing entries. A liability account should be credited in the required adjusting entry. Choice (b) is incorrect because the accounts in this entry are reversed from what they should be for the adjusting entry required in this case. The entry shown is a reversing entry that could be made at the beginning of the subsequent period. Choice (d) is incorrect because the debit should be to an expense account.

Subject Area: Financial accounting and finance—basic concepts. Source: CIA Model Exam 1998, IV-5.

9. **(b)** All income statement account balances are closed either to a summary account (such as income summary or revenue and expense summary) or to retained earnings. The normal balance of an expense account is a debit; therefore, an expense account is credited in a closing entry. Choice (a) is incorrect because the normal balance of an expense account is a debit. Therefore, an expense account should be credited in a closing entry, and the income summary account should be debited. Choice (c) is incorrect because an expense account should not be closed to a revenue account. Such offsetting is not good practice. Choice (d) is incorrect because the normal balance of an expense account is a debit; therefore, the expense account should be credited in a closing entry.

Subject Area: Financial accounting and finance—basic concepts. Source: CIA Model Exam 1998, IV-6.

10. **(d)** Computations follow:

Balance per bank statement	$12,000
Outstanding checks, December 31	(6,900)
Interest credited by bank, not yet recorded on the books	(40)
Deposits in transit	X
Balance per books before adjustment	$17,400

Solving for X

X = $17,400 – $12,000 + $6,900 + $40
X = $12,340

Choice (a) is incorrect. This answer is simply the difference between the cash balance per ledger ($17,400) and the balance per bank ($12,000). This answer incorrectly ignores the outstanding checks and the interest credited by the bank. Choice (b) is incorrect. This answer incorrectly adds the $40 unrecorded interest earned to the cash balance per bank. Computations follow:

Balance per bank statement	$12,000
Outstanding checks, December 31	(6,900)
Interest credited by bank, not yet recorded on the books	40
Deposits in transit	X
Balance per books before adjustment	$17,400

Solving for X

X = $17,400 – $12,000 + $6,900 – $40
X = $12,260

Choice (c) is incorrect. This answer incorrectly ignores the $40 interest credited by the bank. Computations follow:

Balance per bank statement	$12,000
Outstanding checks, December 31	(6,900)
Deposits in transit	X
Balance per books before adjustment	$17,400

Solving for X

X = $17,400 – $12,000 + $6,900
X = $12,300

Subject Area: Financial accounting and finance—basic concepts. Source: CIA Model Exam 1998, IV-7.

11. **(a)** The check must be disbursed to the payee for it to be considered a cash payment. Thus, the check must at least be in the mail, not in the vault or otherwise in the possession of the payor company. Proper cutoff of cash receipts and disbursements is important; improper cutoff will affect

the computation of the current ratio. Choice (b) is incorrect because this situation involves the improper cutoff of cash disbursements. Choice (c) is incorrect because this practice is not acceptable, although it may be frequently encountered. It will not affect the working capital amount; however, it will affect the working capital ratio. Choice (d) is incorrect because this practice is not acceptable, although it may be frequently encountered.

Subject Area: Financial accounting and finance—basic concepts. Source: CIA Model Exam 1998, IV-8.

12. **(d)** The correct entry is as follows:

1. The cash account should be debited to record sale proceeds received.
2. Accumulated depreciation should be eliminated by debiting by an amount equal to depreciation accumulated up to the start of the current accounting period plus any depreciation that has accumulated between the start of the current period and the date of disposal.
3. The machinery account must be credited to eliminate the original cost of the asset.
4. The gain should be recorded as a credit entry.

Choice (a) is incorrect because the gain is a credit. Accumulated depreciation is a debit. Choice (b) is incorrect because the gain should be recorded as a credit, not a debit. Choice (c) is incorrect because the machinery account should be credited, not debited, and accumulated depreciation should be debited, not credited.

Subject Area: Financial accounting and finance—basic concepts. Source: CIA Model Exam 1998, IV-23.

13. **(a)** The correct order of the four listed steps is

1. Prepare adjusting journal entries
3. Prepare an adjusted trial balance
2. Take a postclosing trial balance
4. Prepare reversing entries

Choice (b) is incorrect. The preparation of reversing entries is the last step in the accounting cycle. Choice (c) is incorrect. The adjusted trial balance is prepared after adjusting entries are made. Choice (d) is incorrect. The post-closing trial balance is prepared after adjusting entries and the adjusted trial balances are completed.

Subject Area: Financial accounting and finance—basic concepts. Source: CIA 594, IV-3.

14. **(d)** There is $50,000 of accrued interest at year-end that should be recognized as an expense of the current period with an adjusting entry that debits interest expense and credits interest payable by this amount. Choice (a) is incorrect. The debt has been outstanding for only 6 months so accrued interest is only $50,000.

$1,000,000 (.10)(6/12) = $50,000.

Choice (b) is incorrect. The debt pays annual interest and no cash outlay is required at year-end. Choice (c) is incorrect. The debt has been outstanding for only 6 months so accrued interest is only $50,000 (see choice a) and because this entry debits interest payable (which should be credited) and credits interest expense (which should be debited).

Subject Area: Financial accounting and finance—basic concepts. Source: CIA 594, IV-4.

15. **(a)** Net earnings, after tax, for the current period is calculated as follows:

Sales revenue	$750,000
– Cost of goods sold	(200,000)
– Depreciation expense	(60,000)
– Interest expense	(10,000)
– Administrative expenses	(200,000)
Earnings before tax	$280,000
Tax (50%)	140,000
Earnings after tax	$140,000

Current period revenues and expenses are closed to the income summary account, which is then closed to retained earnings by debiting the income summary and crediting retained earnings.

Choice (b) is incorrect. This answer is obtained by omitting income taxes and by crediting the income summary (which should be debited) and debiting retained earnings (which should be credited). See choice (a) for the correct solution.

Sales revenue	$750,000
– Cost of goods sold	(200,000)
– Depreciation expense	(60,000)
– Interest expense	(10,000)
– Administrative expenses	(200,000)
Earnings before tax	$280,000

Choice (c) is incorrect. This answer is obtained by omitting administrative expenses. See choice (a) for the correct solution.

Sales revenue	$750,000
– Cost of goods sold	(200,000)
– Depreciation expense	(60,000)
– Interest expense	(10,000)
Earnings before tax	$480,000
Tax (50%)	240,000
Earnings after tax	$240,000

Choice (d) is incorrect. This answer is obtained if administrative expenses are omitted (see the solution to choice (c) for supporting calculations) and if the income summary is credited, rather than debited and if retained earnings are debited, rather than credited. See choice (a) for the correct solution.

Subject Area: Financial accounting and finance—basic concepts. Source: CIA 594, IV-6.

16. **(c)** Each expense item is recognized, cash is credited for the total expenditures plus the cash shortage ($173 + $112 + $42 + $10 = $337) and the discrepancy is debited to the "cash over and short" account. The discrepancy is the original balance of the fund less total documented expenditures less the ending balance of the fund: $500 – $327 – $163 = $10. The petty cash fund is short $10 so the cash over and short account is debited by this amount. Choice (a) is incorrect because this entry does not recognize that $10 is missing from the petty cash fund (see choice c). Choice (b) is incorrect because this entry credits petty cash rather than cash and because it does not recognize that $10 is missing from the petty cash fund (see choice c). Choice (d) is incorrect because this entry credits the cash account for the wrong amount ($317 rather than $337) and because it credits the cash over and short account rather than debiting it (see choice c).

Subject Area: Financial accounting and finance—basic concepts. Source: CIA 594, IV-10.

17. **(b)** The purchase of office equipment represents the acquisition of an asset. An increase in an asset is recorded by a debit. The purchase on account increases liabilities. An increase in a liability is recorded by a credit. Choice (a) is incorrect. The charge should be to an asset account rather than an expense account. Choice (c) is incorrect. An increase in accounts payable is recorded by a credit. The purchase of equipment results in an asset, which is recorded by a debit to an asset account. Choice (d) is incorrect. An increase in a liability is recorded by a credit. An increase in an asset is recorded by a debit.

Subject Area: Financial accounting and finance—basic concepts. Source: CIA 1193, IV-29.

18. **(b)** The commission cost of $5,000 (10% × $50,000) and the advertising charges of $2,000 are deducted from the $50,000 by the consignee to determine the $43,000 that is remitted to the consignor. Choice (a) is incorrect. The freight was paid earlier in the period and would have been recorded then by a credit to Cash and a debit to Inventory. Therefore, the freight costs will be released to income via cost of goods sold. Choice (c) is incorrect. The 10% commission and the advertising costs are ignored in this answer. Choice (d) is incorrect. The reimbursable advertising costs are ignored in this answer.

Subject Area: Financial accounting and finance—basic concepts. Source: CIA 1193, IV-37.

19. **(d)** For a company which is not being acquired, the fact that the stock price is more (or less) than the book value of the underlying net assets of the company is an everyday occurrence which does not result in any journal entry. Therefore, by definition, choices (a), (b), and (c) would be incorrect.

Subject Area: Financial accounting and finance—basic concepts. Source: CIA 1193, IV-45.

20. **(b)** Disability benefits should be accrued, as they are similar to vacation benefits, which are also accrued, to match with revenues. The journal entry is debit expense and credit estimated liability. Choice (a) is incorrect. Disability benefits should be accrued, as they are similar to vacation benefits, which are also accrued, to match with revenues. Choice (c) is incorrect. A liability rather than an asset is recognized. Choice (d) is incorrect. The expense goes to the income statement rather than directly to retained earnings.

Subject Area: Financial accounting and finance—basic concepts. Source: CIA 1191, IV-41.

21. **(a)** The entry to record the necessary writedown is a debit to inventory over and short (reported as an adjustment of cost of goods sold or as an other expense on the income statement) and a credit to Inventory. Choice (b) is incorrect. It is very common to have a difference between a physical count and a perpetual inventory balance (reasons include normal and expected shrinkage, breakage, shoplifting, and incorrect recordkeeping). It is, therefore, not an extraordinary item. Choice (c) is incorrect. It is very common to have a difference between a physical count and a perpetual inventory balance (reasons include normal and expected shrinkage, breakage, shoplifting, and incorrect recordkeeping). It is, therefore, not an extraordinary item. Also, the credit should be to the Inventory account rather than to a valuation account. Choice (d) is incorrect. Although the debit to cost of goods sold is acceptable, the credit should be to the inventory account. Any appropriation of retained earnings would also have to involve the unappropriated retained earnings account.

Subject Area: Financial accounting and finance—basic concepts. Source: CIA 1191, IV-31.

22. **(d)** This entry correctly increases a receivable account and an earned income account because of the accrued interest (interest earned but not received). Choice (a) is incorrect. This entry incorrectly reduces a liability account and an asset account whereas the correct entry will increase an asset account and an earned income account. Choice (b) is incorrect. This entry incorrectly reduces an income account and an asset account whereas the correct entry will increase an income account and an asset account. Choice (c) is incorrect. This entry incorrectly increases an unearned income account whereas the correct entry increases an earned income account.

Subject Area: Financial accounting and finance—basic concepts. Source: CIA 591, IV-32.

23. **(b)** Credit card interest incurred is classified as interest expense on the income statement, which in turn reduces owners' equity on the balance sheet. Credit card interest payments are to be classified on the statement of cash flows as an outflow of cash due to operating activities. Choice (a) is incorrect. Credit card interest payments are to be reflected as an operating outflow on the statement of cash flows. Choice (c) is incorrect. Credit card interest charges reduce owners' equity and interest payments are classified as an operating outflow on the statement of cash flows. Choice (d) is incorrect. Credit card interest charges are reflected as interest expense, which reduces owners' equity.

Subject Area: Financial accounting and finance—basic concepts. Source: CIA 1193, IV-33.

24. **(c)**

Accounts receivable beginning balance		$ 5,000
Allowance for bad debts beginning balance		(500)
Net accounts receivable beginning balance		$ 4,500
Credit sales	100,000	
Bad debt expense .02 × $100,000	(2,000)	$98,000
Net accounts receivable ending balance, **before** considering cash collections this period		$102,500

Actual net accounts receivable ending balance

$4,500 beginning balance (above) + $30,000 increase = $ 34,500
Cash collections this period $102,500 – $34,500 = $ 68,000

Choice (a) is incorrect. The $1,000 write-off does not affect the answer and should not be considered. Choice (b) is incorrect. Ignore the $500 beginning balance in allowance for bad debts in part of the solution. Choice (d) is incorrect. The $1,000 write-off does not affect the answer and should not be considered.

Subject Area: Financial accounting and finance—basic concepts. Source: CIA 1193, IV-41.

25. **(b)** The computation is as follows:

Error	*Effect on 2005 expense*	*Effect on 2005 net income*
Failure to accrue interest expense	Understate $ 50,000	Overstate $ 50,000
Failure to record depreciation	Understate $ 80,000	Overstate $ 80,000
Failure to amortize prepaid rent expense	Understate $100,000	Overstate $100,000
Failure to recognize prepaid advertising	Overstate $ 60,000	Understate $ 60,000
Totals	Understate $170,000	Overstate $170,000

Choice (a) is incorrect. This selection incorrectly ignores the effect of errors (3) and (4). Choice (c) is incorrect. This answer selection incorrectly ignores error (4). Choice (d) is incorrect. This answer selection incorrectly handles error (4). The failure to recognize prepaid expense will overstate expense for the current period.

Subject Area: Financial accounting and finance—basic concepts. Source: CIA 593, IV-36.

26. **(c)** When the interest method is used, interest expense is computed each period by multiplying the effective rate (a constant rate) times the carrying amount at the beginning of the period. (Carrying amount is par value minus the balance of the unamortized premium.) The difference between the amount of interest expense and the stated amount of interest is the amount of premium amortization for the period. The premium amortization for the period is deducted from the beginning carrying amount to determine the carrying amount at the end of the period. The carrying amount decreases each period because of the premium amortization and the interest expense is a decreasing amount each period because of the constant rate applied to a decreasing carrying amount. Choice (a) is incorrect. The interest expense is a decreasing amount each period because it is computed by a constant rate applied to a decreasing carrying amount. Choice (b) is incorrect. The interest expense is a decreasing amount each period because it is computed by a constant rate applied to a decreasing carrying amount. Choice (d) is incorrect. The carrying value decreases each period because of the periodic amortization of the premium.

Subject Area: Financial accounting and finance—basic concepts. Source: CIA 593, IV-37.

27. **(b)** The reason for accounting for inflation in statements is to eliminate the effects of general price level changes. One advantage of accounting for inflation without current cost measurements is that the historical cost-based accounting system (which is currently used and understood) is maintained. Choice (a) is incorrect. Neither constant dollar nor current cost financial statements will automatically provide funds for special purposes. Choice (c) is incorrect. Only current cost-based statements provide for the maintenance of physical capital. Choice (d) is incorrect. Only current cost-based statements will identify and measure holding gains and losses.

Subject Area: Financial accounting and finance—basic concepts. Source: CIA 593, IV-38.

28. **(d)** An increase in prepaid expenses indicates cash outlays for expense exceeded the related expense incurred; thus, net income exceeded net cash provided by operating activities and a deduction is needed in the reconciliation. Also, the amortization of premium on bonds payable causes a reduction of interest expense but does not increase cash; therefore, net income exceeds net cash from operating activities and a deduction is needed in the reconciliation. Choice (a) is incorrect. An increase in prepaid expenses indicates cash outlays for expense exceeded the related expense incurred; thus, net income exceeded net cash provided by operating activities and a deduction is needed in the reconciliation. Also, the amortization of premium on bonds payable causes a reduction of interest expense but does not increase cash; therefore, net income exceeds net cash from operating activities and a deduction is needed in the reconciliation. Choice (b) is incorrect. An increase in prepaid expenses indicates that cash outlays for expenses exceeded the amount of expenses incurred; therefore, net income exceeds net cash provided by operating activities and a deduction is needed in the reconciliation. Choice (c) is incorrect. The amortization of premium on bonds payable causes a reduction of interest expense but does not increase cash; therefore, net income exceeds net cash from operating activities and a deduction is needed in the reconciliation.

Subject Area: Financial accounting and finance—basic concepts. Source: CIA 593, IV-44.

29. **(a)** This entry is at the payment date under the net method. The amount is [$1,000 × (1 – .02)] + $30 = $1,010. Choice (b) is incorrect. Freight in was debited earlier, at the invoice date. Accounts payable needs to be debited for the entire amount (including freight of $30) owed to the seller. Choice (c) is incorrect. This is the entry at the invoice date if the gross method had been used. Choice (d) is incorrect. This is the correct entry at the invoice date, but the entry on the payment date was called for.

Subject Area: Financial accounting and finance—basic concepts. Source: CIA 592, IV-30.

30. **(b)** Because Supplies Expense was debited when supplies were purchased, Supplies Expense must be credited and Supplies debited at the end of the period for the amount of supplies on hand. Choice (a) is incorrect. The correct entry for the situation described is

Supplies expense
  Supplies

Choice (c) is incorrect. The correct entry for the situation described is

Supplies or supplies expense
  Cash or accounts payable

Choice (d) is incorrect. The correct entry for the situation described is

Income summary
  Supplies expense

Subject Area: Financial accounting and finance—basic concepts. Source: CIA 592, IV-31.

31. **(b)** Computations

1.	Overstated	$40,000
2.	Overstated	15,000
3.	No effect	--
4.	Overstated	10,000
	Overstated	$65,000

Choice (a) is incorrect. Computations

1.	Overstated	$40,000	OK
2.	Overstated	15,000	OK
3.	Overstated	7,000	Should be no effect
4.	Overstated	10,000	OK
	Overstated	$72,000	

Choice (c) is incorrect. Computations

1.	Understated	$40,000	Should be overstated $40,000
2.	Overstated	15,000	OK
3.	Overstated	7,000	Should be no effect
4.	Understated	10,000	Should be overstated $10,000
	Understated	$28,000	

Choice (d) is incorrect. Computations

1.	Understated	$40,000	Should be overstated $40,000
2.	Understated	15,000	Should be overstated $15,000
3.	No effect	--	OK
4.	Overstated	10,000	OK
	Understated	$45,000	

Subject Area: Financial accounting and finance—basic concepts. Source: CIA 591, IV-45.

32. **(b)** Computations follow:

1.	No effect		
2.	Overstated	$15,000	
3.	Overstated	7,000	
4.	Overstated	10,000	
	Overstated	$32,000	

Choice (a) is incorrect. Computations

1.	Overstated	$40,000	Should be no effect
2.	Overstated	15,000	OK
3.	No effect	--	Should be overstated 7,000
4.	Overstated	10,000	OK
	Overstated	$65,000	

Choice (c) is incorrect. Computations

1.	No effect	--	OK
2.	Overstated	$15,000	OK
3.	No effect	--	Should be overstated $7,000
4.	Overstated	10,000	OK
	Overstated	$25,000	

Choice (d) is incorrect. Computations

1.	No effect	--	OK
2.	Understated	$15,000	Should be overstated 15,000
3.	Overstated	7,000	OK
4.	Understated	10,000	Should be overstated 10,000
	Understated	$18,000	

Subject Area: Financial accounting and finance—basic concepts. Source: CIA 591, IV-46.

33. **(a)** All aspects of this intercompany transaction must be eliminated, as there is a consolidated entity. Choice (b) is incorrect. The interest must be eliminated. Choices (c) and (d) are incorrect because 100% of the transaction must be eliminated.

Subject Area: Financial accounting and finance—basic concepts. Source: CIA 1191, IV-46.

34. **(d)** Receivables from officers and owners are assets and should be presented in the balance sheet as assets, not as offsets to owners' equity. If material, they should be segregated from the other categories of receivables. Choices (a), (b), and (c) are incorrect because each one is a correct statement regarding the disclosure of accounts receivable.

Subject Area: Financial accounting and finance—basic concepts. Source: CIA 591, IV-31.

35. **(c)** A material gain or loss which is unusual in nature and infrequent in occurrence meets the criteria to be classified as an extraordinary item. By definition, choices (a), (b), and (d) would be incorrect.

Subject Area: Financial accounting and finance—basic concepts. Source: CIA 1193, IV-32.

36. **(b)** Discontinued operations are reported separate from continuing operations and extraordinary items. Therefore, by definition, choices (a), (c), and (d) would be incorrect.

Subject Area: Financial accounting and finance—basic concepts. Source: CIA 1193, IV-34.

37. **(c)** Gain or loss from discontinued operations appears on the income statement as a separate component. Therefore, by definition, choices (a), (b), and (d) will be incorrect.

Subject Area: Financial accounting and finance—basic concepts. Source: CIA 592, IV-36.

38. **(d)** The money given by customers is a deposit and hence must be returned or credited to the customers' accounts. It is therefore a liability. Therefore, by definition, choices (a), (b), and (c) will be incorrect.

Subject Area: Financial accounting and finance—basic concepts. Source: CIA 592, IV-38.

39. **(d)** An enterprise is required to exclude a short-term obligation from current liabilities if the entity has the intent and ability to refinance it on a long-term basis. The ability to consummate the refinancing may be demonstrated either by (1) actually refinancing the short-term obligation by issuance of a long-term obligation or equity securities after the date of the balance sheet but before it is issued, or (2) entering into a financing agreement that clearly permits the enterprise to refinance the debt on a long-term basis. The ability to refinance the 17% note payable of $140,000 is demonstrated by the actual refinancing after the balance sheet date but before the date of issuance of the balance sheet. The ability to refinance the 15% note payable of $200,000 is demonstrated by the financing agreement that exists at the date the balance sheet is issued. Choice (a) is incorrect because both the $140,000 and $200,000 may properly be excluded from current liabilities. Choice (b) is incorrect because the $200,000 may also properly be excluded from current liabilities. Choice (c) is incorrect because the $140,000 may also properly be excluded from current liabilities.

Subject Area: Financial accounting and finance—basic concepts. Source: CIA 591, IV-36.

40. **(a)** The general guidelines are that costs such as advertising should be deferred in an interim period if the benefits extend beyond that period; otherwise they should be expensed as incurred. But such a determination is difficult, and even if deferred, there is the question of how the deferred costs should be allocated between quarters. Therefore, many companies expense the costs as incurred even though they may benefit other interim periods in the same annual period. Choice (b) is incorrect. The only product costs appropriate to expense in an interim period are the ones related to the revenue transactions recognized in the same interim period so this is not a problem. Choice (c) is incorrect. The annual depreciation amount is an estimate. The depreciation amount for an interim period is simply a pro rata amount of the annual estimate so this is not a unique problem. Choice (d) is incorrect. An extraordinary item is to be reported in the interim period in which it occurs rather than allocated to multiple interim periods. This approach is consistent with the way extraordinary items are handled on an annual basis.

Subject Area: Financial accounting and finance—basic concepts. Source: CIA 591, IV-38.

41. **(d)** According to the historical cost principle and the matching principle, the plant asset would be reported at its book value of $270,000. An excess of fair value over book value of plant assets is not reflected in conventional financial statements. Choice (a) is incorrect because an excess of fair value over book value of plant assets is not reflected in conventional financial statements. Choice (b) is incorrect. According to the historical cost principle and the matching principle, the plant asset would be reported at its book value of $270,000. An excess of fair value over book value of plant assets is not reflected in conventional financial statements. Choice (c) is incorrect because an excess of fair value over book value of plant assets is not reflected in conventional financial statements.

Subject Area: Financial accounting and finance—basic concepts. Source: CIA 591, IV-43.

42. (c) When liquidation of a company is imminent the most appropriate valuation method for assets is the net realizable value method. Net realizable value refers to the estimated selling price upon disposal less costs of disposal. Choice (a) is incorrect. A going concern should report assets at their undepreciated historical cost. When liquidation appears imminent, historical cost is inappropriate for balance sheet reporting. Choice (b) is incorrect. A company facing liquidation is expected to dispose of its assets in a "forced" or "distressed" sale situation and is unlikely to realize the fair market value amount. The net realizable value of the assets is the appropriate amount for reporting purposes. Choice (d) is incorrect. Current cost is only appropriate when the going concern is applicable and when the effects of changing prices are to be measured and reported in the financial statements.

Subject Area: Financial accounting and finance—basic concepts. Source: CIA 591, IV-44.

43. (a) The matching principle dictates that expenses should be matched with the revenues that they help to create. Because the catalogues are still on hand at the balance sheet date, they will not contribute to the revenue generating process until the next period. Hence, the cost should be deferred and matched with the revenues of the following period. Choice (b) is incorrect. The revenue realization principle is used to determine in what period to recognize revenue. Once the revenues are allocated to the proper periods, the matching principle directs us to match expenses with the revenues they helped to create. Choice (c) is incorrect. The objectivity principle indicates that to the extent possible, accounting data should be unbiased and verifiable. Choice (d) is incorrect. The cost principle states that cost is to be measured by the fair value of the consideration given or the fair value of the consideration received, whichever is the more objectively determinable.

Subject Area: Financial accounting and finance—basic concepts. Source: CIA 593, IV-25.

44. (a) All significant accounting principles and methods that involve selection from among alternatives or those that are peculiar to a given industry should be specifically identified and described in an initial note to the financial statements. This summary of significant accounting policies should not duplicate other facts to be disclosed elsewhere in the statements. The valuation method for inventory is one example of an accounting method (policy) that should be disclosed. Choice (b) is incorrect. The amount of interest capitalized during a period should be disclosed; however, this disclosure does not relate to an accounting policy disclosure. Choice (c) is incorrect. The summary of significant accounting policies should not duplicate facts required to be disclosed elsewhere in the financial statements. Choice (d) is incorrect. Although the amount of depreciation charges for the period should be disclosed, this disclosure is not part of the summary of significant accounting policies.

Subject Area: Financial accounting and finance—basic concepts. Source: CIA 593, IV-26.

45. (d) Because accounting standards differ from one country to another, an accrual will have to be made for a loss between $1 and $3 million. Choice (c) is incorrect because the loss is not deferred, it is accrued.

Subject Area: Financial accounting and finance—basic concepts. Source: CIA 1192, IV-45.

46. (c) The distinction between expenses and losses depends on the typical activities of the reporting enterprise. Expenses are decreases in net assets which result from delivering goods or producing goods, rendering services, or carrying out other activities that constitute the entity's ongoing major or central operations. Losses are decreases in net assets from peripheral or incidental transactions of an entity and from all other transactions and other events and circumstances affecting the entity during a period except those that result from expenses or distributions to owners. Choice (a) is incorrect because not all losses are extraordinary items. Choice (b) is incorrect because losses may be immaterial and most expenses are material. Choice (d) is incorrect because some expenses cannot be "prevented," or at least not in the short run. Some losses can be prevented.

Subject Area: Financial accounting and finance—basic concepts. Source: CIA 1192, IV-38.

47. (b) The basis of valuation for property, plant, and equipment (which is usually historical cost) must be disclosed. Accumulated depreciation, either by major classes of depreciable assets or in total, must be disclosed. The net realizable value of property, plant, and equipment does not generally get disclosed. The general accounting standard of lower of cost or market does not apply to property, plant, and equipment. Even when fixed assets have suffered partial obsolescence, accountants are reluctant to write them down to a net realizable value. Because the assets are expected to continue in use with the entity, some people believe that the current net realizable value has no significance. Choice (a) is incorrect. The net realizable value of property, plant, and equipment does not generally get disclosed. The general accounting standard of lower of cost or market does not apply to property, plant, and equipment. Even when fixed assets have suffered partial obsolescence, accountants are reluctant to write them down to a net realizable value. Because the assets are expected to continue in use with the entity, some people believe that the current net realizable value has no significance. Choice (c) is incorrect. Accumulated depreciation, either by major classes of depreciable assets or in total, must also be disclosed. Choice (d) is incorrect. The basis of valuation for property, plant, and equipment (which is usually historical cost) must be disclosed. Accumulated depreciation, either by major classes of depreciable assets or in total, must be disclosed. The net realizable value of property, plant, and equipment does not generally get disclosed.

Subject Area: Financial accounting and finance—basic concepts. Source: CIA 1192, IV-28.

48. (b) Market is the replacement cost, but market cannot exceed ceiling nor be lower than floor. Ceiling is $100 – $5 – $10 = $85. Floor is ceiling less normal gross profit, or $85 – $20 = $65. Thus, market is $85, which is a reduction of $6 in comparison to the $91 historical cost. This is also the effect on gross profit. Choice (a) is incorrect. This implies market is at least as high as cost. See choice (b). Choice (c) is incorrect. If market were incorrectly thought to be floor, then $91 – $65 = $26 would be the impact on gross profit. Choice (d) is incorrect. The effect was incorrectly thought to be caused by selling costs of $5.

Subject Area: Financial accounting and finance—basic concepts. Source: CIA 1192, IV-43.

49. **(d)** With regard to materiality, see choice (a). The cost/benefit concept is tied to materiality, and relates to the cost of information. Specifically, the cost of producing the information (such as depreciation expense numbers over 10 years for the staplers) probably is higher than the benefits in useful information for decision making. Therefore, it is not worth it to generate the depreciation numbers, and the expedient procedure of merely expensing the $1,000 should be followed. Choice (a) is incorrect. The relatively small amount of the transaction, $1,000 in comparison to the total assets of $100,000,000 and net income of $9,000,000 indicates that there is no material difference on the financial statements between expensing and the more theoretically correct depreciating. Therefore, materiality is a concept being applied. Going concern relates more to circumstances in which there is doubt as to the viability of the enterprise. Choice (b) is incorrect. Relevance relates to using accounting principles, which are relevant to economic decisions such as whether to buy the company's stock. Neutrality relates to using unbiased accounting principles. Choice (c) is incorrect. Reliability relates to using reproducible accounting numbers, such as historical cost to record assets. Comparability/consistency relates to using the same accounting principles from period to period.

Subject Area: Financial accounting and finance—basic concepts. Source: CIA 592, IV-29.

50. **(b)** The journal entry to accrue revenue involves a debit to a receivable account and a credit to a revenue account. Thus, the accrual of revenue increases assets and owners' equity. Choice (a) is incorrect because the accrual of revenue increases assets and owners' equity. Choice (c) is incorrect because the accrual of revenue increases assets, increases owners' equity, and has no effect on liabilities. Choice (d) is incorrect because the accrual of revenue increases assets, increases owners' equity, and has no effect on liabilities.

Subject Area: Financial accounting and finance—basic concepts. Source: CIA 597, IV-3.

51. **(a)** A change in the estimate of the service lives of depreciable assets is a change in accounting estimate. Choice (b) is incorrect because a change from declining-balance depreciation to straight-line depreciation is a change in accounting policy. Choice (c) is incorrect because this is a change in accounting policy due to a change in generally accepted accounting principles. Choice (d) is incorrect because a change from FIFO to LIFO inventory valuation is a change in accounting policy.

Subject Area: Financial accounting and finance—basic concepts. Source: CIA 597, IV-22.

52. **(a)** The adjusting entry reduces an expense and increases a prepaid expense. This type of entry is necessary when payments are recorded to an expense account and there is a prepaid amount at the balance sheet date. The adjusting entry defers the expense recognition to a future period for which the property taxes apply. Choice (b) and (c) are incorrect because the adjusting entry records a prepaid (deferred) expense. Choice (d) is incorrect because the adjusting entry records an unexpired cost.

Subject Area: Financial accounting and finance—basic concepts. Source: CIA 1196, IV-4.

53. **(d)** Using the basic accounting equation and reasons for changes in owners' equity, the computations are shown below. Choice (a) is incorrect because the answer is one-half of the correct answer. Choice (b) is incorrect because this answer incorrectly deducts the $72,000 and incorrectly adds the $75,000 in the computation illustrated. Choice (c) is incorrect because this answer reflects the net difference between beginning owners' equity ($90,000) and ending owners' equity ($99,000).

Supporting computations

A = L + OE

$210,000 = $120,000 + $90,000[a] Balance at 1/1/95

+	72,000	Owner investments
–	75,000	Owner withdrawal
+	X	Net income

$270,000 = $171,000 + $99,000[b] Balance at 12/31/95

[a]$210,000 – $120,000 = $90,000

[b]$270,000 – $171,000 = $99,000

Solving for X

$90,000 + $72,000 – $75,000 + X = $99,000
$90,000 + $72,000 – $75,000 = $99,000 –X
$90,000 + $72,000 – $75,000 – $99,000 = –X
– $12,000 = –X
$12,000 = X

Subject Area: Financial accounting and finance—basic concepts. Source: CIA 1196, IV-5.

54. **(d)** The IASC is widely recognized as establishing "world-class" accounting principles for business firms. Choice (a) is incorrect because international accounting standards of the IASC are followed by voluntary compliance. Choice (b) is incorrect because international accounting standards of the IASC are followed by voluntary compliance and are for business enterprises. Choice (c) is incorrect because international accounting standards of the IASC are developed for use by profit oriented, business enterprises. They are not designed as a guide for government accounting practices and are not specifically designed for a type of political system.

Subject Area: Financial accounting and finance—basic concepts. Source: CIA 1196, IV-75.

55. **(a)** The dividends account is closed directly to retained earnings. The effect of dividends is to reduce retained earnings, so the entry is a debit to retained earnings and a credit to close the dividends account. Choice (b) is incorrect because the effect of dividends is to reduce retained earnings. The closing entry should credit dividends and debit retained earnings. Choice (c) is incorrect because the dividends account is closed directly to retained earnings and does not flow through the income summary. Choice (d) is incorrect because the dividends account is closed directly to retained earnings and does not flow through the income summary. Also, the entry that closes the dividends account must credit, not debit, dividends.

Subject Area: Financial accounting and finance—basic concepts. Source: CIA 596, IV-5.

56. **(c)** The fair market value of the donation is the basis for the amount of donation expense recorded. The land account is credited for the carrying value of the donated land, and the difference is recorded as a gain on disposal. Choice (a) is incorrect. The fair market value of the donation must be recognized when the land is disposed of. The amount of donation expense should be based on the fair market value, not on the book value, and any difference between the fair value and the carrying value should be recorded as a gain or loss. Choice (b) is incorrect. The amount of the donation expense should be based on the fair market value of the land. The land account should be credited for the carrying value of the land. However, the gain on disposal should not be recorded as additional paid-in capital. Choice (d) is incorrect. This entry is correct except for the credit to retained earnings. Donations would not be credited directly to retained earnings.

Subject Area: Financial accounting and finance—basic concepts. Source: CIA 596, IV-22.

57. **(c)** The company received $480,000 cash on the issuance of the bonds. The face value of the issue is $500,000, which must be paid at maturity so this is the amount of the credit to bonds payable. The difference is recorded as a discount on bonds payable and is amortized over the life of the issue. Choice (a) is incorrect. Bonds payable is based on the face, or maturity, value of the bonds issued. The difference between the amount received on issuance and the face value of the bonds is recorded as a premium or discount on bonds payable. Choice (b) is incorrect. Bonds payable is based on the face, or maturity, value of the bonds. The amount of cash recorded in this entry is incorrect, however. The company received only .96($500,000) = $480,000 from bond investors at the time of issue. The difference between bonds payable and the cash received for the issue is recorded as a discount. Choice (d) is incorrect. The company received $480,000, not $500,000, of cash on the issuance of the bonds. Also, the face, or maturity value of the bonds is $500,000 and this is recorded as bonds payable, not the $480,000 received. Finally, the $20,000 difference is a discount, not a premium.

Subject Area: Financial accounting and finance—basic concepts. Source: CIA 596, IV-23.

58. **(c)** Bonds sold with coupon rates below the market rate on comparable bonds are sold at a discount from face value. Cash will be debited for the amount received, which will be below the face value reflected in the bonds payable account. The difference between the face value of the issued bonds and the cash received is debited to the discount on bonds payable account, and the bonds payable account is credited for the face value. Choice (a) is incorrect. Bonds sold with coupon rates below the market rate on comparable bonds are sold at a discount from face value. This entry includes a premium on the bond issue. Further, if it were a premium bond issue, the premium on bonds payable would be a credit entry, reflecting the premium over face value received by the company. Choice (b) is incorrect. This is the entry for the issuance of premium bonds. Choice (d) is incorrect. The discount on bonds payable account should be debited not credited. It includes the difference between the face value of the issued bonds and the cash received.

Subject Area: Financial accounting and finance—basic concepts. Source: CIA 595, IV-18.

59. **(c)** The value of recoverable mineral reserves must be estimated. The value will be determined by future conditions and events. Choice (a) and (b) are incorrect. In both of these situations, the transaction value can be calculated with certainty. No estimate is required. Choice (d) is incorrect. The physical quantity of inventory as of the financial statement date can be measured. While some estimation of the correct amount may be required, the estimates will not depend on future conditions and events but on current conditions and measurement methods.

Subject Area: Financial accounting and finance—basic concepts. Source: CIA 596, IV-28.

60. **(b)** The asset-to-sales ratio must be constant when applying the percentage of sales forecasting method. If the current level of all assets is considered to be optimal for the current sales level, then the asset-to-sales ratio is constant. Choice (a) is incorrect because if economies of scale exist in the use of assets, the ratios of assets to sales are not constant and the percentage of sales method is inappropriate. Choice (c) is incorrect because if fixed assets must be added in large, discrete amounts, the ratios of assets to sales are not constant and the percentage-of-sales method is inappropriate. Choice (d) is incorrect because if sales-to-assets ratios vary with economic cycles then the percentage of sales method is inappropriate.

Subject Area: Financial accounting and finance—basic concepts. Source: CIA 596, IV-56.

61. **(d)** In order for the reversing entries to reverse the prior adjustments, the reversing entries must be the exact opposite of the adjustments made in the previous period. Choice (a) is incorrect because the recording of reversing entries is an optional step in the accounting cycle. Choice (b) is incorrect because reversing entries are made at the beginning of the next accounting period, before recording the regular transactions of the period. Choice (c) is incorrect because reversing entries are the exact opposite of the adjustments made in the previous period; they are not identical to those adjusting entries.

Subject Area: Financial accounting and finance—basic concepts. Source: CIA 1195, IV-4.

62. **(a)** The cash account is debited with the amount of the sale proceeds. The machinery and the accumulated depreciation—machinery accounts are eliminated by crediting and debiting, respectively. Since the sale price was less than the net book value of the asset on the date of sale, there has been a loss on disposal of the machinery and this is a debit entry. Choice (b) is incorrect. There has been a loss on the disposal of the machinery, since the sale price was below the net book value of the asset on the date of sale. Choice (c) is incorrect. To eliminate accumulated depreciation—machinery, the account must be debited, not credited. Choice (d) is incorrect. There has been a loss on the disposal of the machinery, since the sale price was below the net book value of the asset on the date of sale. Also, to eliminate accumulated depreciation—machinery, the account must be debited, not credited.

Subject Area: Financial accounting and finance—basic concepts. Source: CIA 1195, IV-22.

63. **(a)** To correct the prior error, the company must debit the equipment account with the cost of the newly purchased equipment and credit the accumulated depreciation—equipment account with the depreciation expense appropriate for the first year of the estimated useful life of the equipment. The retained earnings account must also be credited, with the difference between the equipment cost and the first year depreciation expense, since this is the income error from the prior period. Choice (b) is incorrect because this is the reverse of the correct entry. Choice (c) is incorrect because the retained earnings account should be credited, not debited. In the prior period, too large an amount (the full cost of the equipment) was expensed. The correction therefore involves increasing retained earnings. Choice (d) is incorrect because the accumulated depreciation—equipment account should be credited, not debited, with the first year of depreciation expense for the new equipment.

Subject Area: Financial accounting and finance—basic concepts. Source: CIA 1195, IV-23.

64. **(b)** The payment of cash dividends to providers of common equity financing is a use of cash that appears in the financing section of the statement of cash flows. Choice (a) is incorrect because the payment of cash dividends is not a cash flow impact of the operating activities of the company, so it does not appear in the operating section of the statement of cash flows. Choices (c) and (d) are incorrect. The payment of cash dividends is not a cash flow impact of the investing activities of the company, so it does not appear in the investing section of the statement of cash flows as either a use or a source of cash.

Subject Area: Financial accounting and finance—basic concepts. Source: CIA 1195, IV-34.

65. **(a)** Net sales are the sum of cash receipts from customers and the increase in accounts receivable. To calculate net sales beginning with cash receipts, the increase in accounts receivable must be added. Choices (b), (c), and (d) are incorrect because changes in accounts payable are not included in the calculation of net sales.

Subject Area: Financial accounting and finance—basic concepts. Source: CIA 595, IV-1.

66. **(a)** An increase in accounts payable must be added to cash payments for goods to calculate cost of goods sold. Choice (b) is incorrect because decreases in accounts payable must be subtracted from, not added to, cash payments to calculate cost of goods sold. Choice (c) is incorrect because an increase in inventory must be subtracted from, not added to, cash payments to calculate cost of goods sold. Choice (d) is incorrect because a decrease in inventory must be added to, not subtracted from, cash payments to calculate cost of goods sold.

Subject Area: Financial accounting and finance—basic concepts. Source: CIA 595, IV-2.

67. **(a)** The order of the listed steps in the accounting cycle is

1. Identification and measurement of transactions
2. Journalization
3. Posting
4. Adjustments

Adjustments are the latest step in the accounting cycle of those listed. Choice (b) is incorrect because of the steps listed, journalization occurs second. Choice (c) is incorrect because of the steps listed, posting occurs third. Choice (d) is incorrect because the identification and measurement of transactions is the first step in the accounting cycle.

Subject Area: Financial accounting and finance—basic concepts. Source: CIA 595, IV-3.

68. **(a)** Since the initial entry recorded the entire purchase as office supplies expense, the year-end adjusting entry must debit office supplies to reflect the remaining supplies on hand of $15,000. Also, since the initial entry recorded the entire purchase as office supplies expense of the current period, the adjusting entry must credit (reduce) office supplies expense for the $15,000 of supplies that were not used during the period. Choice (b) is incorrect. Office supplies expense was initially recorded at the full amount of the purchase, or $50,000 so this entry would incorrectly result in office supplies expense of $65,000 for the current period when only $35,000 was used. The correct form of the entry is to debit office supplies and to credit office supplies expense. Choice (c) is incorrect. This entry has the correct form but is for the wrong amount. The remaining value of office supplies from the January 1st purchase is $15,000, not $35,000. Choice (d) is incorrect. Office supplies expense was initially recorded at the full amount of the purchase, or $50,000, so this entry would incorrectly result in office supplies expense of $85,000 for the current period when only $35,000 was used. The correct form of the entry is to debit office supplies and to credit office supplies expense. The correct amount of the entry is the remaining value of office supplies from the January 1 purchase or $15,000, not $35,000.

Subject Area: Financial accounting and finance—basic concepts. Source: CIA 595, IV-4.

69. **(d)** Cash flows from financing activities involve liability and owners' equity items and include (1) obtaining capital from owners and providing them with a return on and of their investment and (2) borrowing from and repaying creditors. This category of cash flows will be overstated if the use of cash to pay dividends to equity holders is omitted from the statement of cash flows. Choice (a) is incorrect because cash flows from operating activities are those regarding the cash effects of transactions that enter into the determination of net income. Cash dividends do not affect the cash flows from operating activities. Choice (b) and (c) are incorrect because cash flows from investing activities are those regarding the making and collecting of loans and the acquisition and disposal of investments (both debt and equity) and property, plant, and equipment. Cash dividends do not affect the cash flows from investing activities.

Subject Area: Financial accounting and finance—basic concepts. Source: CIA 595, IV-6.

70. **(c)** It is widely believed that with more comparable financial measurement and disclosure practices, international investors will require lower, not higher, risk premiums. Higher risk premiums result in higher costs of equity financing, so higher risk premiums would not be considered to be an advantage of developing and adopting International Accounting Standards. Choices (a) and (b) are incorrect because increased comparability and greater freedom in international capital flows are both potential benefits of the development and adoption of International Accounting Standards. Choice (d) is incorrect because the elimination of unfair competitive advantages due to differences in reporting standards is a potential benefit of International Accounting Standards.

Subject Area: Financial accounting and finance—basic concepts. Source: CIA 595, IV-65.

71. **(d)** The rent expense must be debited to correct the original error and the unearned rent revenue account should be credited instead. Choice (a) is incorrect because the original entry credited rent expense in error. The credit should have been to the unearned rent revenue account. Choice (b) is incorrect because this entry eliminates the incorrect credit to rent expense but the credit should be to unearned rent revenue, not to rent revenue. Choice (c) is incorrect because the debit should be to rent expense, not to cash.

Subject Area: Financial accounting and finance—basic concepts. Source: CIA 1194, IV-42.

72. **(b)** The going concern assumption provides that the accountant assumes unless there is evidence to the contrary, that the reporting entity will have a life long enough to fulfill its objectives and commitments. "Only if we assume some permanence to the enterprise are depreciation and amortization policies justifiable and appropriate." Choice (a) is incorrect because the economic entity assumption provides that economic activity can be identified with a particular unit of accountability. Choice (c) is incorrect because the monetary unit assumption provides that all transactions and events can be measured in terms of a common denominator—the dollar. Choice (d) is incorrect because the historical cost assumption simply states that cost has an advantage over other validations; it is reliable.

Subject Area: Financial accounting and finance—basic concepts. Source: CIA 590, IV-25.

73. (b) The purchase of advertising services on account will result in an increase in liabilities, which is reflected in this entry as a credit to accounts payable. The debit can be initially made either to advertising expense or prepaid advertising. In the entry given, the debit was made to advertising expense, which assumes the benefits of the cost will be consumed in the period of acquisition. If, at the end of the accounting period, there are benefits from this expenditure that extend beyond the current period, an adjusting entry will be required to defer an appropriate portion of the related cost. Choice (a) is incorrect because this entry is an adjusting entry to transfer advertising cost from an asset account to an expense account as the benefits expire for which a prepayment had been made and previously recorded as a deferred cost. Choice (c) is incorrect because this entry is an adjusting entry to transfer unexpired cost from an expense account to an asset account. Choice (d) is incorrect because the purchases account is one which is to be used to record the acquisition of goods to be held for resale to customers. The purchases account is used to record the acquisition of inventory items when the periodic inventory system is used.

Subject Area: Financial accounting and finance—basic concepts. Source: CIA 590, IV-27.

74. (a) With the single-step format, two categories exist: revenues and expenses. The expenses are deducted from the revenues to arrive at the income or loss before extraordinary items. In a multiple-step format for the income statement, the basic division is between operating and nonoperating activities, and both revenues and expenses are subdivided into these groups. The multiple-step format "recognizes a separation of operating transactions from nonoperating transactions and matches costs and expenses with related revenues." Choice (b) is incorrect because both formats separate income tax expense and administrative expenses. Choice (c) is incorrect because both formats separate cost of goods sold expense and administrative expenses. Choice (d) is incorrect because intraperiod income tax allocation procedures must be applied to both formats and thus an extraordinary item must be reported net of its related tax effect regardless of the choice of formats referred to in the question.

Subject Area: Financial accounting and finance—basic concepts. Source: CIA 590, IV-32.

75. (d) The primary purpose of a statement of cash flows is to provide relevant information about the cash receipts and cash payments of an enterprise during a period. "The information provided in a statement of cash flows, if used with related disclosures and information in the other financial statements, should help investors, creditors, and others to assess the enterprise's ability to generate future net cash flows." Choice (a) is incorrect because the statement of operations is another name for the statement of income or statement of earnings. The statement of income is prepared on an accrual basis and is not meant to report cash flows. Choice (b) is incorrect because the statement of retained earnings merely shows the reasons for changes in retained earnings during the reporting period. Choice (c) is incorrect because the statement of financial position is another name for the balance sheet. The balance sheet reports on the financial position at a point in time.

Subject Area: Financial accounting and finance—basic concepts. Source: CIA 590, IV-33.

76. (a) According to APB Opinion 30, extraordinary items are events and transactions that are distinguished by their unusual nature and by the infrequency of their occurrence. Gains or losses from the sale or abandonment of property, plant, or equipment used in the business constitute extraordinary items only if they are a direct result of a major casualty, an expropriation, or a prohibition under a newly enacted law or regulation that clearly meets the criteria of unusual and infrequent. Therefore, assuming the criteria of unusual in nature and infrequency in occurrence are met in this situation, this would be classified as an extraordinary item. Choice (b) is incorrect because the effects of adjustments of accruals on long-term contracts are expressly denied extraordinary treatment under APB Opinion 30. Choice (c) is incorrect because gains or losses on disposal of a segment of business are expressly denied extraordinary treatment under APB Opinion 30. Choice (d) is incorrect because the description of the situation indicates the criterion of infrequency is not met.

Subject Area: Financial accounting and finance—basic concepts. Source: CIA 590, IV-35.

77. (c) According to generally accepted accounting principles (GAAP), all intangible assets should be amortized over their useful lives, but the amortization period should not exceed 40 years. "The 40-year requirement is based on the premise that only a few, if any, intangibles last for a lifetime." Choice (a) is incorrect because this answer would violate the matching principle. Choice (b) is incorrect because although income tax regulations require the amortization of organization costs over a period of at least 60 months, the emphasis in financial statement reporting is on the expected useful life of the benefits derived from the costs. Choice (d) is incorrect because organization costs are capitalized because they are of benefit to a number of periods but they should be amortized because APB Opinion 17 requires that all intangible assets must be amortized over a period not to exceed 40 years.

Subject Area: Financial accounting and finance—basic concepts. Source: CIA 590, IV-40.

78. (a) This is the major objective of financial reporting. Choice (b) is incorrect because this deals with internal control, not external financial reporting. Choice (c) is incorrect because this deals with management accounting, not financial accounting. Choice (d) is incorrect because this deals with auditing, not financial accounting.

Subject Area: Financial accounting and finance—basic concepts. Source: CIA 1190, IV-27.

79. (a) Net book value – Sales price = $50,000 loss. The loss is an ordinary loss. Choices (b) and (d) are both incorrect because extraordinary losses must be both unusual and nonrecurring. The disposal of a line of business is not unusual. Choice (c) is incorrect because loss is calculated as the difference between net book value and sales price.

Subject Area: Financial accounting and finance—basic concepts. Source: CIA 1190, IV-30.

80. **(a)** An expense should be accrued for the coupons still outstanding that are expected to be redeemed. Of the 4,000,000 boxes sold, 40% estimated redeemable is 1,600,000. Of those, 1,000,000 have already been redeemed, thus 600,000 more are expected to be redeemed. The promotion requires 20 coupons to receive one toy, so 30,000 (600,000/20) more toys are expected to be required. Each toy costs \$3.00, creating a liability of 30,000 × \$3.00 = \$90,000. Choice (b) is incorrect because sales should not be reduced as an offset to an expense. Choice (c) is incorrect. Although an expense should be accrued, the amount is incorrect. Consideration of the fact that 20 coupons are required to receive a toy is ignored. (600,000 × \$3.00 = \$1,800,000). Choice (d) is incorrect because sales should not be reduced as an offset to an expense and the amount is the incorrect amount in choice (c) above.

Subject Area: Financial accounting and finance—basic concepts. Source: CIA 1190, IV-37.

Intermediate Concepts

81. **(d)** This is a guarantee. The liability is contingent on the lessor not receiving the full residual value from a third party. Choice (a) is incorrect. There is no uncertainty regarding the amount of rent. Rent expense can be accrued as sales occur. Choice (b) is incorrect. A service was received and the company owes an amount. The amount is not contingent on a future event. The company can accrue the amount it expected the invoice to show. Choice (c) is incorrect. As of the date of the interim financial statements, the income tax is payable because earnings have occurred. There is no uncertainty regarding the amount or the timing of the payment as of the date of the interim financial statements.

Subject Area: Financial accounting and finance—intermediate concepts. Source: CIA Model Exam 2002, IV-6.

82. **(a)** Under a defined contribution plan, the company reports an asset on the balance sheet only if the contribution to the pension trust is greater than the defined, required contribution. Choice (b) is incorrect. An asset is reported only if the contribution is in excess of the required contribution. If the actual contribution is equal to that required, no asset is reported. Choice (c) is incorrect. The company would report a liability on the balance sheet only if the contribution was less than the required amount, not greater than the required amount. Choice (d) is incorrect. The company would not report a liability on the balance sheet if it contributed the required amount to the pension trust.

Subject Area: Financial accounting and finance—intermediate concepts. Source: CIA Model Exam 2002, IV-16.

83. **(b)** Under the sum-of-the-years' digits method, the portion of depreciable cost to expense in any given year is calculated as: the number of years of estimated life remaining as of the beginning of the year divided by the sum of the years of estimated useful life. Therefore, the portion to expense in the third year of an asset with a four-year estimated useful life = 2/(1+2+3+4) = 2/10 = 20%. Choice (a) is incorrect. This solution results from calculating the portion of depreciable cost to expense in any given year using the end of the current year in the numerator, as follows: the number of years of estimated life remaining as of the end of the year divided by the sum of the years of estimated useful life. Portion to expense = 1/(1+2+3+4) = 1/10 = 10%. Choice (c) is incorrect. This solution uses the digit of the current year in the numerator, as follows: depreciation year divided by the sum of the years of estimated useful life. Therefore, the portion to expense in the third year of an asset with a four-year estimated useful life = 3/(1+2+3+4) = 3/10 = 30%. Choice (d) is incorrect. This solution incorrectly calculates the denominator as the sum of the years up to the end of the current year, as follows: the number of years of estimated life remaining as of the beginning of the year divided by the sum of the years of use as of the end of the year. Therefore, the portion to expense in the third year of an asset with a four-year estimated useful life = 2/(1+2+3) = 2/6 = 33.33%.

Subject Area: Financial accounting and finance—intermediate concepts. Source: CIA Model Exam 2002, IV-19.

84. **(b)** The machine's net book value at January 1 of year five is \$6,000 (Cost – Accumulated depreciation of \$1,000 per year). A change in accounting estimate is applied prospectively. Therefore, depreciation expense is \$2,000 per year (\$6,000/3) for the next three years.

Subject Area: Financial accounting and finance—intermediate concepts. Source: CIA Model Exam 2002, IV-22.

85. **(d)** Calculations follow:

Estimated warranty liability = Beginning balance in estimated liability
+ Warranty expense – Actual warranty cost
= 0 + [3,000,000 × (0.02 + 0.01)] – 28,000
= \$62,000.

Choice (a) is incorrect.

\$3,000,000 × 0.01 = \$30,000.

Choice (b) is incorrect.

(\$3,000,000 × 0.02) – \$28,000 = \$32,000.

Choice (c) is incorrect.

\$3,000,000 × 0.02 = \$60,000

Subject Area: Financial accounting and finance—intermediate concepts. Source: CIA Model Exam 2002, IV-23.

86. **(d)** Warranty expense must be matched with revenue in the year of sale. Warranty expense related to year two sales

= \$4,000,000(0.02 + 0.01) = \$120,000

Choice (a) is incorrect.

\$4,000,000 × 0.02 = \$80,000.

Choice (b) is incorrect. Actual warranty cost in year two = \$101,000.

Choice (c) is incorrect.

(\$4,000,000 × 0.02) + (\$3,000,000 × 0.01) = \$110,000

Subject Area: Financial accounting and finance—intermediate concepts. Source: CIA Model Exam 2002, IV-24.

87. (a) Leased assets are recognized as tangible assets. When lease agreements transfer the risks and benefits of ownership of the asset to the lessee, the lease is referred to as a capital lease since it is essentially a form of financing, or capital, for the lessee. Choice (b) is incorrect because leased assets are not recognized as intangibles. Choice (c) is incorrect. If substantially all of the risks and benefits of ownership of the asset are transferred to the lessee, then the lease is referred to as a capital lease, not an operating lease. Choice (d) is incorrect. See responses given for choices (b) and (c).

Subject Area: Financial accounting and finance—intermediate concepts. Source: CIA Model Exam 2002, IV-26.

88. (a) The company should recognize $1,000,000 as revenue in year one because it has earned 1/3 (two out of six months) of the $3,000,000 in season-ticket collections. The remaining $2,000,000 should be reported as a liability on the balance sheet at December 31 of year one, because it is unearned at that time. Choices (b), (c), and (d) are incorrect. See response given for choice (a).

Subject Area: Financial accounting and finance—intermediate concepts. Source: CIA Model Exam 2002, IV-29.

89. (b) If (1) the transferor surrenders control of the future economic benefits embodied in the receivables, (2) the transferor's obligation under the recourse provisions can be reasonably estimated, and (3) the transferee cannot require the transferor to repurchase the receivables except pursuant to the recourse provisions, then the transfer is accounted for as a sale of receivables. If the foregoing three conditions are not met, the transaction is accounted for as a borrowing transaction. Choice (a) is incorrect because both the receipt of cash and its source (either sale or borrowing transaction) must be recorded. Choice (c) is incorrect because the transfer is properly recorded as a sale only if the three conditions listed in response for choice (b) are met. Choice (d) is incorrect because the transfer is properly recorded as a borrowing transaction if the conditions listed in response for choice (b) are not met.

Subject Area: Financial accounting and finance—intermediate concepts. Source: CIA Model Exam 2002, IV-39.

90. (d) The measurement basis most commonly adopted by enterprises in preparing their financial statements are historical cost. This, however, is usually combined with other measurement bases. For example, inventories are usually carried at the lower of cost or net realizable value, marketable securities may be carried at market value, and pension liabilities are carried at their present value. A long-term payable that represents a commitment to pay money at a determinable future date should be valued at the present value of its future interest and principal cash flows.

Subject Area: Financial accounting and finance—intermediate concepts. Source: CIA Model Exam 1998, IV-1.

91. (c) Under the cost-recovery method, no profit is recognized until cash payments by the buyer exceed the seller's cost of the merchandise sold. This method is appropriate when there is great uncertainty surrounding the collection of the revenue. Choice (a) is incorrect because this answer describes the accrual basis of revenue recognition. Choice (b) is incorrect because the contribution margin (Selling price – Total variable costs) does not have any relationship to the amount at risk. Choice (d) is incorrect because as soon as the cash collections equal the cost of sales, gross profit is to be recognized for any further collections.

Subject Area: Financial accounting and finance—intermediate concepts. Source: CIA Model Exam 1998, IV-10.

92. (b) Calculations follow:

Annual depreciation	=	(Cost – Salvage value)/Estimated useful life
	=	(1,000,000 – 100,000)/9
	=	$100,000
Book value on 12/31/96	=	Cost – Accumulated depreciation
	=	1,000,000 – 400,000
	=	$600,000
Loss on disposal	=	Book value – Proceeds
	=	600,000 – 535,000
	=	$65,000 loss

Choice (a) is incorrect. This response incorrectly calculates the gain/loss as

Selling price – Book value + Salvage value
= 535,000 – 600,000 + 100,000
= $35,000 gain

Choice (c) is incorrect. This response incorrectly calculates the gain/loss as

Cost – Selling price – Salvage value
= 1,000,000 – 535,000 – 100,000
= $365,000 loss

Choice (d) is incorrect. This response incorrectly calculates the gain/loss as

Cost – Selling price
= $1,000,000 – 535,000
= $465,000 loss

Subject Area: Financial accounting and finance—intermediate concepts. Source: CIA Model Exam 1998, IV-11.

93. (a) Interest expense equals the carrying value of the liability at the beginning of the period times the effective interest rate. The carrying value of the liability equals the face value of the bond minus the discount. As the discount is amortized over the life of the bond, the carrying value increases. Consequently, the interest expense increases over the life of the bond. Choice (b) is incorrect. See response given for choice (a). Choices (c) and (d) are incorrect because interest expense exceeds the cash interest payment. The excess is the amount of discount amortized each period.

Subject Area: Financial accounting and finance—intermediate concepts. Source: CIA Model Exam 1998, IV-13.

94. (b) Computations follow:

Installment sales for the year	$ 1,200,000
Cost of installment sales	(840,000)
Gross profit on installment sales	360,000
Divided by sales of	÷ 1,200,000
Equals the gross profit percentage	30%
Installment sales for the year	$ 1,200,000
Collections on installment sales	(480,000)
Installment receivables, end of year	720,000
Gross profit percentage	× 30%
Deferred gross profit, end of year	$ 216,000

General and administrative expenses have no effect on the computation of realized gross profit or the computation of deferred gross profit; they are to be classified as operating expenses on the income statement in the period in which they are incurred. Choice (a) is incorrect. This answer incorrectly treats general and administrative expenses as a component of deferred gross profit. ($1,200,000 – $840,000 – $120,000 = $240,000 gross profit; $240,000 ÷ $1,200,000 = 20%; 20% × $720,000 receivables = $144,000). Choice (c) is incorrect. This answer incorrectly applies the gross profit percentage (30%) to the sum of cost of sales and general and administrative expenses ($840,000 + $120,000). Choice (d) is incorrect. This answer represents the balance of installment accounts receivable at the end of the year ($1,200,000 – $480,000) less general and administrative expenses ($120,000).

Subject Area: Financial accounting and finance—intermediate concepts. Source: CIA Model Exam 1998, IV-15.

95. **(a)** This is the definition of a defined contribution plan. Choice (b) is incorrect because the employees bear the risk of the plan's investment performance. Choice (c) is incorrect because this is the definition of a defined benefit plan. Choice (d) is incorrect because this is not required for a defined contribution plan.

Subject Area: Financial accounting and finance—intermediate concepts. Source: CIA Model Exam 1998, IV-21.

96. **(a)** The company should recognize $1,000,000 as revenue in 2005 because it has earned 1/3 (two out of six months) of the $3,000,000 in season-ticket collections. The remaining $2,000,000 should be reported as a liability on the December 31, 2005, balance sheet because it is unearned at that time.

Subject Area: Financial accounting and finance—intermediate concepts. Source: CIA Model Exam 1998, IV-28.

97. **(d)** The completed-contract method does not recognize any gross profit until the contract is completed, while the percentage-of-completion method recognizes a portion of revenues and gross profit each period, based upon the percentage of completion. Accumulated gross profit and accumulated construction costs are included in the "construction in progress" inventory account under the percentage-of-completion method. Choice (a) is incorrect. Progress billings are accumulated in the "billings on construction in progress" account under both methods. Choice (b) is incorrect. Accumulated construction costs are included in the "construction in progress" inventory account under both methods. Choice (c) is incorrect. The percentage-of-completion method recognizes a percentage of revenues and gross profit each period.

Subject Area: Financial accounting and finance—intermediate concepts. Source: CIA 594, IV-26.

98. **(b)** There are two methods used for revenue recognition for long-term construction contracts—the percentage-of-completion method and the completed-contract method. Under the percentage-of-completion method, revenues and gross profit are recognized each period based upon the progress of the construction. The presumption is that the percentage-of-completion approach is the better method and that the completed-contract method should be used only when the percentage-of-completion method is inappropriate. Choice (a) is incorrect. Revenue is not earned until progress has been made toward completion. Choice (c) is incorrect. The cash basis is inappropriate. An accrual method—the percentage-of-completion method—should be used. Choice (d) is incorrect. The completed-contract method should be used only if conditions for using the percentage-of-completion method cannot be met or when there are inherent hazards in the contract beyond the normal, recurring business risks.

Subject Area: Financial accounting and finance—intermediate concepts. Source: CIA 1193, IV-28.

99. **(d)** When there is uncertainty about the collection of receivables, they should be reported at their net realizable value—the amount expected to be received in cash. Choices (a) and (b) are incorrect because the receivable should be reported as an asset on the balance sheet. Choice (c) is incorrect because receivables should be classified at their net realizable value.

Subject Area: Financial accounting and finance—intermediate concepts. Source: CIA 1193, IV-35.

100. **(d)** The critical event in the earnings process for the airline is the delivery of the service to the customer, which is the flight for the passenger. The revenue should be recognized in the period it is earned. Choice (a) is incorrect. The revenue should not be recognized until it is earned. The earnings process is not complete at the point when the reservations are booked. Choice (b) is incorrect. The revenue should not be recognized until it is earned. The earnings process is not complete at the point when the reservations are confirmed. Choice (c) is incorrect. The revenue should not be recognized until it is earned. The earnings process is not complete at the point when the ticket is issued.

Subject Area: Financial accounting and finance—intermediate concepts. Source: CIA 593, IV-27.

101. **(b)** The revenue recognition principle provides that revenue is generally recognized when (1) realized or realizable and (2) earned. Revenue is realized when goods or services are exchanged for cash or claims to cash. Revenue is considered earned when the entity has substantially accomplished what it must do to be entitled to the benefits represented by the revenue. In the situation presented, the performance of the service (monthly spraying) is so significant to completing the earning process that revenue should not be recognized until "delivery" occurs. At the point of performing the service (monthly spraying and any special visits), the revenue has been realized and earned and should be recognized at that point. Choice (a) is incorrect. The revenue has not been earned at this point. Choice (c) is incorrect. Revenue from services rendered is recognized when the services have been performed. A portion of the services is performed monthly and, therefore, a portion of the related revenue should be recognized monthly rather than waiting until the entire contract year is complete. Choice (d) is incorrect. See choice (b).

Subject Area: Financial accounting and finance—intermediate concepts. Source: CIA 1192, IV-27.

102. **(b)** Unearned revenue is revenue which has been received but not earned. The amount unearned (received in advance) is considered a liability because it represents an obligation to perform a service in the future arising from a past transaction. As dictated by the "revenue recognition principle," revenue is recognized (reported as earned revenue) in the period in which it is earned; therefore, when it is received in advance of its being earned, the amount applicable to future periods is deferred to future periods. Choice (a) is incorrect.

An accrued revenue is a revenue that has been earned but not received. In the situation described, the revenue has been received but not earned. Choice (c) is incorrect. The revenue has not been earned and should not be reported as revenue until it has been earned. It will be earned in future periods when forthcoming issues of the magazine are published and distributed to the subscribers. Choice (d) is incorrect. There is no such thing as a precollected receivable. Precollected revenue would refer to unearned revenue, which is revenue that has been received but not earned (classified as a liability). A subscription receivable (an asset) would arise from accrued revenue, which is revenue which has been earned but not received.

Subject Area: Financial accounting and finance—intermediate concepts. Source: CIA 1192, IV-29.

103. (a) The sale of the plant asset is a peripheral or incidental transaction of the entity and the resulting gain, therefore, should be classified as an "other" item. The asset sold was not stock in trade so the proceeds should not be classified as sales revenue. The transaction is not infrequent in occurrence so it does not meet the criteria to be classified as an extraordinary item. The gain should never be accounted for by an adjustment of prior periods. Choice (b) is incorrect. The asset sold was not stock in trade and the sale of plant assets does not constitute the entity's major or central operations so the proceeds should not be classified as sales revenue. Choice (c) is incorrect. The transaction does not meet the criteria to be classified as an extraordinary item. Choice (d) is incorrect. The transaction does not represent a prior period adjustment.

Subject Area: Financial accounting and finance—intermediate concepts. Source: CIA 1192, IV-37.

104. (b)

100 + .01(1,500 – 100)	= $114 revenue
(100/1,500) × 1,000	= $ 67 costs
	$ 47 profit

Choice (a) is incorrect. This is the net income effect excluding interest revenue of .01(1,500 – 100). Choice (c) is incorrect. This is only the cost of goods sold of (100/1,500) × 1,000. Choice (d) is incorrect. This is only the revenue of 100 + .01 (1,500 – 100).

Subject Area: Financial accounting and finance—intermediate concepts. Source: CIA 592, IV-34.

105. (d) The revenue is earned at this point and should be recognized. The matching principle dictates that the related expenses should be recognized in the same time period as the revenue. The expense recognition is tied to the revenue recognition. Choices (a), (b), and (c) are incorrect because each one has occurred prior to the point of earning the revenue and the expense recognition is tied to the revenue recognition.

Subject Area: Financial accounting and finance—intermediate concepts. Source: CIA 1191, IV-29.

106. (c) The revenue recognition principle dictates that revenue be recognized when it is (1) realized or realizable and (2) earned. Revenue is considered earned when the entity has substantially accomplished what it must do to be entitled to the benefits represented by the revenue. In the case of an automobile manufacturer, the critical event in the revenue generating process is the sale and transfer of the automobile by the manufacturer to a dealer. The point of sale would be at the time of shipment to a dealer and the point of sale would be the time to recognize the revenue. Choices (a) and (b) are incorrect because the revenue has not been earned at this point and should not be recognized until it is earned. Choice (d) is incorrect. The revenue of the manufacturer should be recognized at the point of sale by the manufacturer rather than waiting until the point of sale by the dealer.

Subject Area: Financial accounting and finance—intermediate concepts. Source: CIA 1191, IV-30.

107. (a) A temporary decline in the market value of the current portfolio of investment in marketable equity securities is to be reported by a charge to income. By the process of elimination, this unrealized loss is classified as an "other" item on a multiple-step income statement. Choice (b) is incorrect. This loss does not meet the criteria to be classified as extraordinary. Choice (c) is incorrect. This unrealized loss is to be charged to the current income statement. Unrealized losses on the noncurrent portfolio of investment in marketable equity securities are to be classified as a contra stockholders' equity item. Choice (d) is incorrect. This unrealized loss is to flow through the current income statement. It is not a prior period adjustment as suggested by this distracter.

Subject Area: Financial accounting and finance—intermediate concepts. Source: CIA 1191, IV-33.

108. (d) The sales discounts forfeited account will report the amount of discounts offered but not taken when the net method is used. The sales discounts account will only appear on the books when the gross method is employed and it accumulates the total amount of discounts taken. Choice (a) is incorrect. The sales discounts account will appear on the books only when the gross method of recording accounts receivable is employed. Choice (b) is incorrect. The sales discounts forfeited account should appear and the sales discounts account should not appear when the net method is used. Choice (c) is incorrect. The sales discounts forfeited account should appear when the net method is used and some customers do not take advantage of the discount offered.

Subject Area: Financial accounting and finance—intermediate concepts. Source: CIA 1191, IV-34.

109. (a) The amortization of a discount on investment in bonds will cause an increase in the carrying value of the investment and an increase in interest revenue. The increase in interest revenue causes an increase in net income. Choice (b) is incorrect because the amount of interest revenue is increased. Choices (c) and (d) are incorrect because net income is increased.

Subject Area: Financial accounting and finance—intermediate concepts. CIA 1191, IV-37.

110. (c) The amount paid on redemption before maturity, including any call premium, is called the reacquisition price. An excess of the reacquisition price over the carrying amount is a loss from extinguishment of debt. Gains and losses from extinguishment of debt are to be classified as extraordinary items on the income statement in the period of extinguishment. Choices (a) and (b) are incorrect because the excess of reacquisition price over net carrying amount of the old bonds is recognized as a loss from extinguishment of debt in the period of refunding. Choice (d) is incorrect because gains and losses from extinguishment of debt are to be classified as extraordinary items on the income statement in the period of extinguishment.

Subject Area: Financial accounting and finance—intermediate concepts. Source: CIA 1191, IV-39.

111. (c) Calculations follow:

$1000 – $250 (20X1 revenue) = $750 (20X2 revenue)
– $200 (19X2 cost)
= $550 (19X2 gross profit)

Choice (a) is incorrect.

[$100/($100 + $300)] × $1000 = $250 (20X1 revenue)
– $100 (20X1 cost)
= $150 (20X1 gross profit)

Choice (b) is incorrect.

[$1000 – ($100 + $300 + $200)] = $400

Revenue less all costs including estimated cost to complete.

Choice (d) is incorrect.

$1000 – $200 = $800

Forgot to subtract $250 (20X1 revenue).

Subject Area: Financial accounting and finance—intermediate concepts. Source: CIA 1191, IV-40.

112. (a) Extraordinary gains, which are both unusual and infrequent, should be recognized in the period in which they occur. Therefore, by definition, choices (b), (c), and (d) will be incorrect.

Subject Area: Financial accounting and finance—intermediate concepts. Source: CIA 1191, IV-42.

113. (a) The $260,000 of net income is divided by the $1,300,000 of stockholders' equity giving 20%. The beginning equity was the same as the year-end equity. Therefore, by definition, choices (b), (c), and (d) will be incorrect.

Subject Area: Financial accounting and finance—intermediate concepts. Source: CIA 591, IV-59.

114. (d) There is a certain relationship between balance sheet accounts and sales that assumes that past relationships will hold true for estimating future items. Choice (a) is incorrect because future sales are not assumed equal to last year's sales. Choice (b) is incorrect because future sales are not assumed to increase at a constant percentage rate. Choice (c) is incorrect because net profits are not tied directly to sales.

Subject Area: Financial accounting and finance—intermediate concepts. Source: CIA 593, IV-51.

115. (d) The FOB terms indicate the purchase took place at the shipping point. Therefore, the 2001 ending inventory would include the cost of this purchase. Also, the buyer would be responsible for the freight regardless of which party initially paid the freight. Therefore, by definition, choices (a), (b), and (c) will be incorrect.

Subject Area: Financial accounting and finance—intermediate concepts. Source: CIA 592, IV-32.

116. (a) The FOB terms indicate the purchase took place at the destination. The 2001 ending inventory would exclude the cost of this purchase. Therefore, by definition, choices (b), (c), and (d) will be incorrect.

Subject Area: Financial accounting and finance—intermediate concepts. Source: CIA 592, IV-33.

117. (b) If the estimated activity level is higher in later years of the asset's useful life, depreciation expense will also be higher in later years under the activity method based on units of production. Choice (a) is incorrect because depreciation expense is constant for all years of the useful life of the asset under the straight-line method. Choice (c) is incorrect because depreciation expense declines under the sum-of-the-years' digits method. Choice (d) is incorrect because depreciation expense declines under the declining balance method.

Subject Area: Financial accounting and finance—intermediate concepts. Source: CIA 594, IV-19.

118. (c) Sum-of-the-years' digits method will result in depreciation expense in the first year of

5/15 × $100,000 = $33,333.33

Choice (a) is incorrect. Straight-line depreciation expense will be

$100,000/5 = $20,000 per year.

Choice (b) is incorrect. Activity method based on units of production will result in depreciation expense in the first year of

75,000/250,000 × $100,000 = $30,000

Choice (d) is incorrect. Declining balance method with a 30% depreciation rate will result in depreciation expense in the first year of

.30 × $100,000 = $30,000

Subject Area: Financial accounting and finance—intermediate concepts. Source: CIA 594, IV-20.

119. (c) Under accelerated depreciation, depreciation expense is higher and net income is lower. Retained earnings would therefore be lower for tax reporting purposes than for general-purpose financial reporting based on straight-line depreciation. Choice (a) is incorrect. The balance of accumulated depreciation would be higher in the financial statements for tax purposes, since higher depreciation expense would be reported under accelerated depreciation than under straight-line depreciation. Choice (b) is incorrect. Depreciation expense is a noncash charge. The cash balance is unaffected by the depreciation method used. Choice (d) is incorrect. The historic cost of fixed assets is recorded in the gross fixed assets account. The historic cost of the assets is unaffected by the depreciation method used.

Subject Area: Financial accounting and finance—intermediate concepts. Source: CIA 594, IV-1.

120. (a) The cost of goods sold is calculated as

Opening inventory + Purchases – Closing inventory
= $140,000 + $530,000 – $230,000 = $440,000

Choice (b) is incorrect. This answer is obtained by reversing the opening and closing inventory figures.

Closing inventory + Purchases – Opening inventory
= $230,000 + $530,000 – $140,000 = $ 620,000

Choice (c) is incorrect. This answer is obtained by omitting closing inventory from the calculation.

Opening inventory + Purchases
= $140,000 + $530,000 = $670,000

Choice (d) is incorrect. This answer is obtained by adding, rather than subtracting, closing inventory.

Opening inventory + Purchases + Closing inventory
= $140,000 + $530,000 + $230,000 = $900,000

Subject Area: Financial accounting and finance—intermediate concepts. Source: CIA 594, IV-2.

121. (b) After adjusting for depreciation expense for the current period, the balance of accumulated depreciation will be $120,000.

Asset cost/Useful Life = $600,000/10 = $60,000 per year

Total accumulated depreciation at the end of the second year

= \$60,000 × 2 = \$120,000

Total assets is then calculated as

Cash	\$ 80,000
Accounts receivable	100,000
Inventory (closing)	230,000
Gross fixed assets	600,000
Accumulated depreciation	(120,000)
Total assets	\$ 890,000

Choice (a) is incorrect. Solution if opening inventory is used rather than closing inventory

Cash	\$ 80,000
Accounts receivable	100,000
Inventory (opening)	140,000
Gross fixed assets	600,000
Accumulated depreciation	(120,000)
Total assets	\$ 800,000

Choice (c) is incorrect. Answer if no adjustment is made for depreciation for the current year

Cash	\$ 80,000
Accounts receivable	100,000
Inventory (closing)	230,000
Gross fixed assets	600,000
Accumulated depreciation	(60,000)
Total assets	\$ 950,000

Choice (d) is incorrect. Answer if accumulated depreciation is not deducted at all

Cash	\$ 80,000
Accounts receivable	100,000
Inventory (closing)	230,000
Gross fixed assets	600,000
Total Assets	\$1,010,000

Subject Area: Financial accounting and finance—intermediate concepts. Source: CIA 594, IV-5.

122. (b) It would be inappropriate to recognize such proceeds immediately in income. They should be treated as reductions in the price of the land. Choices (a), (c), and (d) are incorrect because each choice is an appropriate action.

Subject Area: Financial accounting and finance—intermediate concepts. Source: CIA 594, IV-30.

123. (c) The cost of the depreciable asset includes all costs necessary to get the asset in the place and condition for its intended purpose. Interest charges during construction may be capitalizable under certain conditions, but all interest charges incurred after the asset is ready for operations are a period cost.

Computations

Purchase price	\$800,000
Delivery cost	50,000
Installation cost	70,000
Cost of trial runs	40,000
Depreciable cost	\$ 960,000

\$960,000 ÷ 5 years = \$192,000 depreciation per year

Choice (a) is incorrect because this answer incorrectly omits the delivery cost (\$50,000), installation cost (\$70,000), and cost of trial runs (\$40,000) from the depreciable base. Choice (b) is incorrect because this answer incorrectly omits the cost of trial runs (\$40,000) from the depreciable base. Choice (d) is incorrect because this answer incorrectly includes the interest charges of \$60,000 in the depreciable base. Interest charges during construction may be capitalizable under certain conditions, but all interest charges incurred after the asset is ready for operations are a period cost.

Subject Area: Financial accounting and finance—intermediate concepts. Source: CIA 1193, IV-38.

124. (c) Choice (c) is the correct answer.

Book value of property, plant, and equipment sold (\$50,000 cost – \$30,000 accumulated depreciation)	\$ 20,000
Depreciation expense	10,000
Gross decrease in book value of property plant and equipment	30,000
Net increase in book value of property plant and equipment	80,000
Gross increase in book value of property plant and equipment (caused by purchase of property plant and equipment)	\$110,000

Choice (a) is incorrect. Wrongly used the 1,000 gain (which should be ignored). The 30,000 accumulated depreciation on asset sold was not combined with the 50,000 cost of asset sold. Choice (b) is incorrect. Ignored the 10,000 depreciation expense, which should be considered. Choice (d) is incorrect. Wrongly used the 10,000 depreciation expense twice, and considered the 1,000 gain, which should be ignored.

Subject Area: Financial accounting and finance—intermediate concepts. Source: CIA 1193, IV-42.

125. (c) When using a declining-balance method, a constant rate is applied to the changing carrying value of the asset. The carrying value for the first period's calculation is the acquisition cost. The constant rate for the double-declining balance method is twice the straight-line rate. The straight-line rate is 100% divided by the service life. Choice (a) is incorrect. The salvage value is ignored in computing depreciation by use of a declining-balance method until the later years of the life. The asset should not be depreciated below its residual value. Choice (b) is incorrect. The salvage value is ignored in computing depreciation by use of a declining-balance method until the later years of the life. The asset should not be depreciated below its residual value. The rate should be twice the straight-line rate. Choice (d) is incorrect. The rate should be double (twice) the straight-line rate.

Subject Area: Financial accounting and finance—intermediate concepts. Source: CIA 593, IV-30.

126. (b) The first step is to divide the \$28,800 into the part attributable to the first floor and part attributable to the second floor. Since the first floor is three times more valuable than the second floor, the allocation would be \$21,600 and \$7,200. Since the contract project occupied half of the first floor, the annual depreciation for that portion would be \$10,800. For half a year, the charge would be \$5,400. Therefore, by definition, choices (a), (c), and (d) will be incorrect.

Subject Area: Financial accounting and finance—intermediate concepts. Source: CIA 1192, IV-4.

127. (c) Double-declining balance

Year 1992 = \$15,000(.4) = \$6,000
Year 1993 = \$ 9,000(.4) = \$3,600

Sum-of-the-years' digits

Year 2002 = \$15,000(5/15) = \$5,000
Year 2003 = \$15,000(4/15) = \$4,000

Therefore, by definition, choices (a), (b), and (d) will be incorrect.

Subject Area: Financial accounting and finance—intermediate concepts. Source: CIA 592, IV-27.

128. **(c)** Depreciation is a noncash charge to income. Therefore, in a reconciliation of net income and net cash provided by operations, depreciation is added back to net income to arrive at net cash provided by operations. Choice (a) is incorrect because the recording of depreciation expense does not involve an inflow or outflow of cash. Choice (b) is incorrect because the purchase and the sale of property, plant, and equipment constitute investing activities. The process of depreciating such assets is not defined as an investing activity. Choice (d) is incorrect because depreciation should be added to rather than deducted from net income when converting net income from an accrual to a cash basis.

Subject Area: Financial accounting and finance—intermediate concepts. Source: CIA 1191, IV-32.

129. **(b)** Computations follow:

4/15 × ($450,000 – $60,000) = $104,000.

Choice (a) is incorrect because this answer incorrectly ignores the estimated salvage value in its computations. Computations

4/15 × $450,000 = $120,000.

Choice (c) is incorrect because this answer incorrectly ignores the estimated salvage value and uses an incorrect numerator for the fraction. Computations

2/15 × $450,000 = $60,000.

Choice (d) is incorrect because this answer uses an incorrect numerator for the fraction. Computations

2/15 × ($450,000 – $60,000) = $52,000.

Subject Area: Financial accounting and finance—intermediate concepts. Source: CIA 1191, IV-36.

130. **(d)** Notes without a stated interest rate should be recorded at present value, with a discount rate the same as that of similar risk and maturity notes. Because the note is at present value, the land should reflect this and not the overstated future value. Choice (a) is incorrect. The value of the land will be overstated if it is recorded at future value; present value is the correct valuation. Choice (b) is incorrect. Interest should be recognized on the note. Choice (c) is incorrect. The proper discount rate is the prevailing rate for similar notes, not the prime rate.

Subject Area: Financial accounting and finance—intermediate concepts. Source: CIA 1193, IV-44.

131. **(a)** Temporary investments must be (1) readily marketable, and (2) intended to be converted into cash as needed within one year or the operating cycle, whichever is longer. Generally, intention to convert is substantiated when the invested cash is considered a contingency fund to be used whenever a need arises. Therefore, there must be a lack of management intent to hold the security for a long-term reason. Choice (b) is incorrect. For an investment to be classified as temporary, there must be a lack of management intent to hold it for some long-term reason. Choice (c) is incorrect. For an investment to be classified as temporary, it must also be readily marketable. Choice (d) is incorrect. For an investment to be classified as temporary it must be readily marketable and there must be a lack of management intent to hold the security for some long-term reason.

Subject Area: Financial accounting and finance—intermediate concepts. Source: CIA 593, IV-29.

132. **(a)** A mortgage bond is secured with real property. Choice (b) is incorrect because a subordinated debenture is unsecured and would contain more risk than a mortgage bond. Choice (c) is incorrect because an income bond is also unsecured. Choice (d) is incorrect because a debenture is also unsecured.

Subject Area: Financial accounting and finance—intermediate concepts. Source: CIA 1191, IV-50.

133. **(c)** The computation is as follows:

Investment in unconsolidated subsidiary	$200,000
Cash surrender value of life insurance	60,000
Land held for speculation	100,000
Total long-term investments	$360,000

The investment in 90-day Treasury bills should be classified as a temporary (short-term) investment. Choice (a) is incorrect because this response is the result of one of two wrong combinations of the items. It reflects either the failure to include the third and fourth items or the failure to include the first one and omit the second. Choice (b) is incorrect because this answer incorrectly omits the land held for speculation. Choice (d) is incorrect because this answer incorrectly includes the investment in 90-day Treasury bills, which should be classified as a temporary (short-term) investment.

Subject Area: Financial accounting and finance—intermediate concepts. Source: CIA 593, IV-31.

134. **(a)** Using the cost method of accounting, the journal entry to record the purchase of the treasury shares would be

Treasury stock	17,000	
Cash		17,000

The journal entry to record the sale of the treasury stock would be

Cash	18,000	
Treasury stock		17,000
Paid-in capital from treasury stock		1,000

Therefore, the effect of the purchase of the treasury shares was to reduce stockholders' equity by the $17,000 cost of the shares. The effect of the sale of the treasury shares was to increase stockholders' equity by the $18,000 proceeds from the sale. The net effect was an increase in stockholders' equity of $1,000. Choice (b) is incorrect. The purchase of treasury stock will reduce stockholders' equity by the cost of the shares. The sale of treasury stock will increase stockholders' equity by the sales price of the treasury shares. Choice (c) is incorrect. The purchase of treasury stock will reduce stockholders' equity by the cost of the shares. The sale of treasury stock will increase stockholders' equity by the sales price of the treasury shares. Choice (d) is incorrect. The purchase of treasury stock will reduce stockholders' equity by the cost of the shares. The sale of treasury stock will increase stockholders' equity by the sales price of the treasury shares.

Subject Area: Financial accounting and finance—intermediate concepts. Source: CIA 593, IV-34.

135. **(d)** An asset is to be recorded at historical cost when it is acquired. Historical cost is measured by the cash or cash equivalent of the consideration given or by the cash equivalent of the consideration received whichever is the more objectively determinable. Therefore, the market value of the treasury stock ($44,000) would be used for measuring the cost of the land in this exchange. Choice (a) is incorrect. $20,000 represents the par value of the stock given in the exchange. The par value does not have significance in the valuation process. The par value of these shares will not be used in the entry to record the exchange unless the treasury stock is accounted for by the par value method rather than the cost method. Choice (b) is incorrect. $28,000 represents the seller's cost. It does not affect the determination of the buyer's cost. Choice (c) is incorrect. $35,000 represents the cost of the treasury shares. It was used to record the acquisition of the treasury shares when they were acquired and it has no relevance to determining the cost of the land.

Subject Area: Financial accounting and finance—intermediate concepts. Source: CIA 1191, IV-28.

136. **(d)** Using the cost method, the journal entry to record the acquisition of the treasury stock includes a debit to treasury stock for $60,000. The balance of the treasury stock account is classified as a contra stockholders' equity item. Therefore, the acquisition of the treasury stock reduces total stockholders' equity by $60,000 ($30 × 2,000 shares = $60,000). Choice (a) is incorrect because the Common Stock account balance is not affected when treasury stock is acquired. Choice (b) is incorrect because no additional paid-in capital account balance is affected when treasury stock is acquired and the cost method is used. Choice (c) is incorrect because the retained earnings account balance is not affected by treasury stock acquisitions when the cost method is used.

Subject Area: Financial accounting and finance—intermediate concepts. Source: CIA 591, IV-37.

137. **(d)** Funds set aside for periodic interest payments on a governmental unit's general obligation bonds are included in the debt service fund. Choice (a) is incorrect because special revenue funds account for the proceeds of specific revenue sources. Choice (b) is incorrect because the general long-term debt account group reflects certain debt having maturity dates of more than one year. Choice (c) is incorrect because internal service funds account for costs of service departments by charging them back to user departments.

Subject Area: Financial accounting and finance—intermediate concepts. Source: CIA 591, IV-40.

138. **(d)** In order to record a liability it must be possible to develop a reasonable estimate of the amount of the loss. Choice (a) is incorrect. The exact payee does not have to be known. Choice (b) is incorrect. The exact date payable does not have to be known. Choice (c) is incorrect. It must be "probable" [defined as the future event(s) are likely to occur] before a liability is recorded, not just "reasonably possible" [defined as the chance of the future event(s) occurring is more than remote but less than likely].

Subject Area: Financial accounting and finance—intermediate concepts. Source: CIA 594, IV-22.

139. **(a)** All contingencies that have a reasonable probability of loss are to be disclosed (items I and II). Contingencies that have a remote possibility of loss need not be disclosed (item III). Therefore, choices (b), (c), and (d) are incorrect.

Subject Area: Financial accounting and finance—intermediate concepts. Source: CIA 593, IV-33.

140. **(b)** The modified treasury stock method used to compute primary and fully diluted earnings per share assumes conversion of options and warrants (which are considered common stock equivalents because they have no yield) into common stock. The assumed conversion results in assumed cash for the company, which is used to purchase treasury shares, but only up to 20% of ending outstanding common shares. Excess cash is used first to pay off debt. Choice (a) is incorrect because the computation of contingent liabilities is unrelated to the scenario. Choice (c) is incorrect because these concepts or principles are unrelated to the scenario. Choice (d) is incorrect because retroactive-effect changes are unrelated to the scenario.

Subject Area: Financial accounting and finance—intermediate concepts. Source: CIA 592, IV-25.

141. **(a)** The data will probably not be available for restatement because information would be needed regarding the costs and quantities of layers of inventory established in prior periods. Choice (b) is incorrect because it would be easier to compare prior period statements with current statements if they were restated. Choice (c) is incorrect because restatement is likely to change reported results. Choice (d) is incorrect because restatement could reduce, increase, or leave constant, prior year's income.

Subject Area: Financial accounting and finance—intermediate concepts. Source: CIA 594, IV-24.

142. **(b)** A failure to record depreciation must be corrected as it does not correct itself over two periods. It is a noncounterbalancing error. Choice (a) is incorrect because a failure to record accrued wages will correct itself over two periods. It therefore represents a counterbalancing error. Choice (c) is incorrect because the overstatement of purchases will correct itself over two periods and is therefore a counterbalancing error. Choice (d) is incorrect because a failure to record prepaid expenses will correct itself over two periods and is therefore a counterbalancing error.

Subject Area: Financial accounting and finance—intermediate concepts. Source: CIA 594, IV-23.

143. **(c)** The projected benefit obligation measure bases the computation of deferred compensation on both vested and nonvested service using future salary levels, which can be expected to be higher than current salary levels. Choice (a) is incorrect because this measure includes only the entitlement of employees based on past service. Choice (b) is incorrect. If such a measure were used, it would result in a smaller estimate of pension obligations than would approaches that include both vested and unvested obligations, such as the projected benefit obligation. Choice (d) is incorrect. The accumulated benefit obligation measure bases the computation of deferred compensation on all years of service, both vested and unvested, but uses current salary levels.

Subject Area: Financial accounting and finance—intermediate concepts. Source: CIA 594, IV-25.

144. **(b)** The name of the pattern of cash flows in the stem and correct answer (b) is the present value of an ordinary annuity of twenty payments deferred nine additional periods. For example, assume that the problem had a 10% interest rate. The present value of $1 factor for nine periods would be .424098. The present value of an ordinary annuity of twenty payments would be 8.513564. If each of the retiree's twenty retirement payments were to be $10,000, the correct calculation of the amount needed today to fund the retirement annuity would be .424098 × 8.513564 × $10,000 = $36,106. An alternative way to get the correct answer would be to use as the interest factor, the present value of an ordinary annuity of twenty-nine payments, minus the present value of an ordinary annuity of the "missing" nine payments: (9.369606 – 5.759024) × $10,000 = $36,106. Choice (a) is incorrect. Note that the present value of an ordinary annuity assumes payments start at the end of the first period. Therefore, there is a "built in" one-period delay, so only nine periods (not ten as in choice a.) are used in the present value of $1 part of the equation. Choices (c) and (d) are incorrect because no future values, instead only present values, are used in the correct answer.

Subject Area: Financial accounting and finance—intermediate concepts. Source: CIA 1193, IV-40.

145. (d) The definition given is of prior service cost. Choice (a) is incorrect because this phrase, used in pension accounting, refers to required recognition of a liability in some circumstances. Choice (b) is incorrect because this phrase, used in pension accounting refers to the pension plan assets. Choice (c) is incorrect because this phrase, used in pension accounting refers to all future benefits payable.

Subject Area: Financial accounting and finance—intermediate concepts. Source: CIA 1191, IV-45.

146. (b) The minimum liability related to the defined pension plan is equal to the excess of the accumulated benefit obligation over the fair value of plan assets.

Computations

$2,600,000 – $1,800,000 = $800,000.

Choice (a) is incorrect. The minimum liability related to the defined pension plan is equal to the excess of the accumulated benefit obligation over the fair value of plan assets. This answer selection was determined incorrectly by taking the excess of the projected benefit obligation over the accumulated benefit obligation. Choice (c) is incorrect. The minimum liability related to the defined pension plan is equal to the excess of the accumulated benefit obligation over the fair value of plan assets. This answer selection was determined incorrectly by taking the excess of the projected benefit obligation over the total fair value of plan assets. Choice (d) is incorrect. The minimum liability related to the defined pension plan is equal to the excess of the accumulated benefit obligation over the fair value of plan assets. This answer selection was determined incorrectly by considering only the amount of the accumulated benefit obligation.

Subject Area: Financial accounting and finance—intermediate concepts. Source: CIA 591, IV-30.

147. (a) Revenue that has been received but not earned is referred to as unearned revenue or deferred revenue. It is reported as a liability on the balance sheet. Choice (b) is incorrect. The revenue is not earned yet because the exterminator has not performed the related services for the customer. Choice (c) is incorrect. Accrued revenue is revenue that has been earned but not received. The exterminator has revenue that has been received but not earned. Choice (d) is incorrect. The customer has a prepaid expense (expense paid but not incurred); the exterminator has unearned revenue (revenue received but not earned).

Subject Area: Financial accounting and finance—intermediate concepts. Source: CIA 1193, IV-30.

148. (c) Organization costs are usually classified as an intangible asset. All intangible assets are to be amortized over their useful lives, but the amortization period is not to exceed 40 years. Choice (a) is incorrect. Organization costs are usually classified as an intangible asset. All intangible assets are to be amortized over their useful lives, but the amortization period is not to exceed 40 years. Choice (b) is incorrect. They are an expense of the organization. Choice (d) is incorrect. The costs should be matched with the periods benefitted; however, the amortization period is not to exceed 40 years.

Subject Area: Financial accounting and finance—intermediate concepts. Source: CIA 593, IV-32.

149. (b) The computation is as follows: The cost of $4,000,000 ($40 × 100,000 = $4,000,000) is in excess of the $3,550,000 ($5,000,000 + $550,000 – $2,000,000 = $3,550,000) fair value of the net identifiable assets by $450,000. This excess is due to an unidentifiable asset and is reported as goodwill.

Choice (a) is incorrect. Cost in excess of fair value of the net identifiable assets is to be reported as goodwill. Choice (c) is incorrect. The $550,000 excess of fair value over carrying amount of net identifiable assets on the seller's books will be recorded as part of the acquisition cost of the identifiable assets on the buyer's books. Choice (d) is incorrect. The purchase price of $4,000,000 exceeds the seller's $3,000,000 carrying value of net identifiable assets by $1,000,000. Of this difference, $550,000 is attributed to an excess of the fair value of net identifiable assets over the seller's carrying value. Therefore, only $450,000 is attributed to an unidentifiable asset.

Subject Area: Financial accounting and finance—intermediate concepts. Source: CIA 593, IV-43.

150. (a) The accounting for copyrights is similar to accounting for patents. Legal fees and other costs incurred in successfully defending a patent suit are to be charged to the Patent account because such a suit establishes the legal rights of the holder of the patent. This same guideline can be applied to accounting for the costs of successfully defending a copyright suit. The balance in the copyright account is then amortized over the remaining estimated useful life of the copyright to comply with the matching principle. The total amortization period for any intangible asset should not exceed 40 years, even though the legal life and useful life may exceed 40 years. The legal life of a copyright is the life of the author plus 70 years. Choices (b) and (c) are incorrect because the costs should be capitalized and amortized over the remaining useful life of the copyright. The total amortization period should not exceed 40 years. Choice (d) is incorrect. The costs should be charged to the Copyright account and amortized over the remaining useful life of the copyright.

Subject Area: Financial accounting and finance—intermediate concepts. Source: CIA 591, IV-35.

151. (c) Operating, financing and investing activities are major components of the statement of cash flows. Using the indirect approach, net income will be a part of operating activities. Therefore, by definition, choices (a), (b), and (d) will be incorrect.

Subject Area: Financial accounting and finance—intermediate concepts. Source: CIA 592, IV-35.

152. (a) In a capital lease, if the lease term is sufficiently long relative to the economic life of the asset, ownership has effectively been transferred to the lessee. Choice (b) is incorrect. One of the criteria for classifying a noncancelable lease agreement as a capital lease is if the present value of the minimum lease payments is such a large proportion of the fair market value of the asset that the asset is effectively being purchased. Choice (c) is incorrect. One of the criteria for classifying a noncancelable lease agreement as a capital lease is if the lease transfers ownership of the property to the lessee. Choice (d) is incorrect. One of the criteria for classifying a noncancelable lease agreement as a capital lease is if the lease contains a bargain purchase option.

Subject Area: Financial accounting and finance—intermediate concepts. Source: CIA 594, IV-28.

153. (a) Because title to the new building passes to the lessee at the end of the lease, the lease will be a capital lease and recorded by the lessee with a debit to the leased building asset and credit to a lease liability. Choice (b) is incorrect. No other conditions are necessary for the lessee to account for the lease as a capital lease because title to the asset will go to the lessee. Choice (c) is incorrect. An operating lease, also known as a rental contract, does not pass to the lessee the risks and benefits of ownership. Because the lessee will retain title to the building, the lessee will have the risks and benefits of ownership. Thus, a capital lease is appropriate. Choice (d) is incorrect. Additional conditions will not change the lessee's proper accounting for the lease as a capital lease, because the lessee will get to keep the leased asset after the end of the lease.

Subject Area: Financial accounting and finance—intermediate concepts. Source: CIA 1193, IV-43.

154. (c) For financing leases, rental payments are equal to the full price of the leased equipment. Choice (a) is incorrect because financing leases do not normally provide for maintenance service. Choice (b) is incorrect because financing leases are not normally cancelable. Choice (d) is incorrect because financing leases are used by companies in various industries.

Subject Area: Financial accounting and finance—intermediate concepts. Source: CIA 592, IV-52.

155. (d) From the viewpoint of the lessee, any lease which is not a capital lease, is an operating lease. To be a capital lease, the lease must meet at least one of the following criteria:

1. The lease transfers economic ownership of the asset to the lessee.
2. The lease contains a bargain purchase option.
3. The lease term is equal to 75% or more of the estimated economic life of the leased property.
4. The present value of the minimum lease payments (excluding executory costs) equals or exceeds 90% of the fair value of the leased property.

The lease in question meets none of the above criteria; therefore, it is classified as an operating lease. Choices (a), (b) and (c) are incorrect because the lease does not meet the criteria to be classified as an asset capital lease.

Subject Area: Financial accounting and finance—intermediate concepts. Source: CIA 592, IV-47.

156. (a) Guaranteed residuals are considered part of minimum lease payments, and must be discounted to present value to arrive at correct asset and liability amounts. Choice (b) is incorrect because the guaranteed residual must be discounted to present value. Choice (c) is incorrect because guaranteed residual values are accounted for at both start and end of the lease. Choice (d) is incorrect because guaranteed residuals are part of the lease contract.

Subject Area: Financial accounting and finance—intermediate concepts. Source: CIA 1191, IV-44.

157. (d) The measurement basis most commonly adopted by enterprises in preparing their financial statements is historical cost. This, however, is usually combined with other measurement bases. For example, inventories are usually carried at the lower of cost or net realizable value, marketable securities may be carried at market value, and pension liabilities are carried at their present value. A long-term payable that represents a commitment to pay money at a determinable future date should be valued at the present value of its future interest and principal cash flows. Choices (a), (b), and (c) are incorrect due to GAAP.

Subject Area: Financial accounting and finance—intermediate concepts. Source: CIA 597, IV-1.

158. (c) Under the cost-recovery method, no profit is recognized until cash payments by the buyer exceed the seller's cost of the merchandise sold. This method is appropriate when there is great uncertainty surrounding the collection of the revenue. Choice (a) is incorrect because this answer describes the accrual basis of revenue recognition. Choice (b) is incorrect because this answer describes the installment basis of revenue recognition. Choice (d) is incorrect. As soon as the cash collections equal the cost of sales, gross profit is to be recognized for any further collections.

Subject Area: Financial accounting and finance—intermediate concepts. Source: CIA 597, IV-10.

159. (c) Computations follow:

Cash collections	$600,000
Increase in receivables	60,000
Increase in unearned revenue	(15,000)
Service revenue earned	$645,000

Choice (a) is incorrect. This answer deducts rather than adds the $60,000 increase in receivables. Computations follow:

Cash collections	$600,000
Increase in receivables	(60,000)
Increase in unearned revenue	(15,000)
Service revenue earned	$525,000

Choice (b) is incorrect. This answer incorrectly deducts the increase in receivables ($60,000) and adds the increase in unearned revenue ($15,000). Computations follow:

Cash collections	$600,000
Increase in receivables	(60,000)
Increase in unearned revenue	15,000
Service revenue earned	$555,000

Choice (d) is incorrect. This answer incorrectly adds the $15,000 increase in unearned revenue. Computations follow:

Cash collections	$600,000
Increase in receivables	60,000
Increase in unearned revenue	15,000
Service revenue earned	$675,000

Subject Area: Financial accounting and finance—intermediate concepts. Source: CIA 597, IV-12.

160. (c) Computations follow:

Installment sales for the year	$1,200,000
Cost of installment sales	(840,000)
Gross profit on installment sales	360,000
Divided by sales of	1,200,000
Equals the gross profit percentage	30%
Installment sales for the year	$1,200,000
Collections on installment sales	(480,000)
Installment receivables, end of year	720,000
Gross profit percentage	x 30%
Deferred gross profit, end of year	$ 216,000

General and administrative expenses have no effect on the computation of realized gross profit or the computation of deferred gross profit; they are to be classified as operating expenses on the income statement in the period in which they are incurred. Choice (a) is incorrect. This answer represents the balance of installment accounts receivable at the end of the year ($1,200,000 – $480,000). Choice (b) is incorrect. This answer incorrectly applies the gross profit percentage (30%) to the sum of cost of sales and general and administrative expenses ($840,000 + $120,000). Choice (d) is incorrect. This answer incorrectly treats general and administrative expenses as a component of deferred gross profit. ($1,200,000 – $840,000 – $120,000 = $240,000 gross profit; $240,000 ÷ $1,200,000 = 20%; 20% × $720,000 receivables = $144,000).

Subject Area: Financial accounting and finance—intermediate concepts. Source: CIA 597, IV-13.

161. **(a)** The revenue has been realized but not earned. The company has an obligation to deliver goods or to refund the customer's money. The delivery of goods is to take place within a year of the balance sheet date; therefore, the obligation is expected to require the use of current assets and meets the definition of a current liability. Choice (b) is incorrect. The obligation is expected to require the use of current assets; therefore, it is a current liability. Choice (c) is incorrect. Contra asset accounts are used to show the estimated expenditure of a portion of an asset. Choice (d) is incorrect. The revenue has not been earned.

Subject Area: Financial accounting and finance—intermediate concepts. Source: CIA 597, IV-14.

162. **(d)** The double-declining balance method uses twice the straight-line rate for the asset, and depreciation expense in year two is calculated as follows:

In the first year of the asset life, depreciation expense is

(2)(Straight-line rate)(Cost)
= (2)(1/Number of years of useful life)(Cost)
= 2/5(100,000) = $40,000 in year one

In the second year, the depreciation base is reduced by the amount of depreciation expense already taken in the first year, so depreciation expense in year two is

= 2/5(100,000 – 40,000) = $24,000

Choice (a) is incorrect. Depreciation in year two will be $20,000 under the straight-line method of depreciation. Under the sum-of-years' digits method, it will be

(Years remaining/Sum of years)(Cost – Salvage value)
= 4/15(100,000 – 0) = $26,667

Choice (b) is incorrect. See response (a) for the correct solution for the sum-of-years'-digits method. Choice (c) is incorrect. This is the answer if the straight-line rate, rather than double the straight-line rate, of depreciation is used.

In the first year of the asset life, depreciation expense is

(Straight line rate)(Cost)
= (1/Number of years of useful life)(Cost)
= 1/5(100,000 – 0) = $20,000 in year one

In the second year, the depreciation base is reduced by the amount of depreciation expense already taken in the first year, so depreciation expense in year two is

= 1/5(100,000 – 20,000) = $16,000

Subject Area: Financial accounting and finance—intermediate concepts. Source: CIA 597, IV-17.

163. **(a)** The market price of the bond at any point in its life equals the present value of the future cash payments discounted at the market rate of interest at that time. As the market rate increases, the present value decreases. Therefore, the market price of the bond will decrease. Choice (b) is incorrect. The interest expense equals the carrying value of the liability times the market rate of interest at the time of bond issuance. The interest expense, therefore, is unaffected by changes in the market rate subsequent to bond issuance. Choice (c) is incorrect. The cash interest payment is determined by the contractual terms of the bond, which are unaffected by future market interest rate changes. Choice (d) is incorrect. Whether the market price of the bond is less than or greater than its face value at any point in the life of the bond depends on the relation between the market interest rate at that time and the stated rate of interest on the bond. The rise in market rates of interest, therefore, does not imply that the bond will have a market price above its face value.

Subject Area: Financial accounting and finance—intermediate concepts. Source: CIA 597, IV-18.

164. **(d)** The carrying amount of the mortgage should be reduced, with a charge to the income statement. Choice (a) is incorrect because this is only appropriate if the situation is determined to be temporary. Choice (b) is incorrect because this is not required if the situation is determined to be temporary and is insufficient if the situation is determined to be other than temporary. Choice (c) is incorrect because the carrying amount should be reduced, but this is not charged directly to retained earnings.

Subject Area: Financial accounting and finance—intermediate concepts. Source: CIA 597, IV-19.

165. **(b)** The machine's net book value at January 1, 2005, is $6,000 (Cost – Accumulated depreciation). A change in accounting estimate is applied prospectively. Therefore, depreciation expense is $2,000 per year for the next three years. By definition, choice (a), (c), and (d) are incorrect.

Subject Area: Financial accounting and finance—intermediate concepts. Source: CIA 597, IV-20.

166. **(a)** This is the definition of a defined-contribution plan. Choice (b) is incorrect because the employees bear the risk of the plan's investment performance. Choice (c) is incorrect because this is the definition of a defined-benefit plan. Choice (d) is incorrect because this is not required for a defined-contribution plan.

Subject Area: Financial accounting and finance—intermediate concepts. Source: CIA 597, IV-21.

167. **(c)** The income statement of the current period portrays events or estimates arising in the current period only. The events or estimates may be disclosed outside normal operations (for example, discontinued operations, extraordinary items). A prior period adjustment is a correction for an event or estimate that existed in an earlier period. Choice (a) is incorrect. Correction of an error is not a prior period adjustment, although the accounting treatment is the same. Choice (b) is incorrect. The income statement of the current period portrays events or estimates that may not recur, for example, gains or losses on disposal of capital assets. Choice (b) describes the current operating performance income statement approach. Choice (d) is incorrect. A prior period adjustment may be an indication of long-range income-producing ability. Advocates of the all-inclusive income statement approach would include prior period adjustments in the current year's income statement.

Subject Area: Financial accounting and finance—intermediate concepts. Source: CIA 597, IV-25.

168. (a) The company should recognize $1,000,000 as revenue in 2005 because it has earned 1/3 (2 out of 6 months) of the $3,000,000 in season-ticket collections. The remaining $2,000,000 should be reported as a liability on the December 31, 2005 balance sheet because it is unearned at that point in time.

Subject Area: Financial accounting and finance—intermediate concepts. Source: CIA 597, IV-28.

169. (a) Interest expense equals the carrying value of the liability at the beginning of the period times the effective interest rate. The carrying value of the liability equals the face value of the bond minus the discount. As the discount is amortized over the life of the bond, the carrying value increases. Consequently, the interest expense increases over the life of the bond. Choices (c) and (d) are incorrect because interest expense exceeds the cash interest payment. The excess is the amount of discount amortized each period.

Subject Area: Financial accounting and finance—intermediate concepts. Source: CIA 597, IV-30.

170. (a) Computations follow:

Selling price – Book value of machine = Gain (loss)
Book value = Cost – Accumulated depreciation
= $700,000 – 495,000
= $205,000

Therefore, selling price

= $205,000 + $75,000 = $280,000

Choice (b) is incorrect because this response incorrectly calculates the selling price as

Book value + Gain – Salvage value
= $205,000 + 75,000 – 40,000
= $240,000

Choice (c) is incorrect because this is the book value. Choice (d) is incorrect because this response incorrectly calculates the selling price as

Gain + Salvage value
= 75,000 + 40,000
= $115,000

Subject Area: Financial accounting and finance—intermediate concepts. Source: CIA 597, IV-33.

171. (b) Calculations follow:

Annual depreciation = (Cost – Salvage value)/Estimated useful life
= (1,000,000 – 100,000)/9
= $100,000

Book value on 12/31/96 = Cost – Accumulated depreciation
= 1,000,000 – 400,000
= $600,000

Loss on disposal = Book value – Proceeds
= 600,000 – 535,000
= $65,000 loss

Choice (a) is incorrect because this response incorrectly calculates the gain/loss as

Selling price – Book value + Salvage value
= 535,000 – 600,000 + 100,000
= $35,000 gain

Choice (c) is incorrect because this response incorrectly calculates the gain/loss as

Cost – Selling price – Salvage value
= 1,000,000 – 535,000 – 100,000
= $365,000 loss

Choice (d) is incorrect because this response incorrectly calculates the gain/loss as

Cost – Selling price
= $1,000,000 – 535,000
= $465,000 loss

Subject Area: Financial accounting and finance—intermediate concepts. Source: CIA 597, IV-34.

172. (a) A loss contingency must be accrued when it is probable that a liability has been incurred at the date of the financial statements and the amount of the loss can be reasonably estimated.

Subject Area: Financial accounting and finance—intermediate concepts. Source: CIA 597, IV-36.

173. (d) An accrued expense is an expense that has been incurred but not paid. The appropriate adjusting entry to record an accrued expense will (1) increase an expense account and (2) increase a liability account. The failure to record an accrued expense will result in an understatement of expenses, an overstatement of net income, an understatement of current liabilities, an overstatement of working capital, and no effect on cash. Choice (a) is incorrect because the failure to record an accrued expense will result in an overstatement of net income in the period the error originates, an overstatement of working capital, and no effect on cash. Choice (b) is incorrect because the failure to record an accrued expense will result in an overstatement of net income in the period the error occurs. Choice (c) is incorrect because the failure to record an accrued expense will result in an overstatement of working capital.

Subject Area: Financial accounting and finance—intermediate concepts. Source: CIA 1196, IV-3.

174. (d) At the end of the estimated useful life of a depreciable plant asset, the amount of accumulated depreciation should equal the depreciable cost of the plant asset (original cost less estimated salvage value), regardless of the depreciation method used. By definition, choice (a), (b), and (c) are incorrect.

Subject Area: Financial accounting and finance—intermediate concepts. Source: CIA 1196, IV-10

175. (c) The dissimilar assets are recorded at the fair value of the old asset ($16,000) plus cash paid ($35,000), which is the actual outlay for the equipment. Choice (a) is incorrect because book value of old equipment after being depreciated for 4.0 years is ($10,100) + Cash paid ($35,000). Choice (b) is incorrect because the correct book value of old equipment after being depreciated for 3.5 years is ($13,700) + Cash paid ($35,000). Choice (d) is incorrect because list price of the new equipment is ($52,500)

Subject Area: Financial accounting and finance—intermediate concepts. Source: CIA 1196, IV-18.

176. (a) The amortization of a premium on bonds payable reduces the interest expense, thereby decreasing the deductions from sales and increasing net income. Choice (b) is incorrect because this would be true for the amortization of a discount on bonds payable. Choice (c) is incorrect because this answer refers to an investment asset that was purchased at a discount. Choice (d) is incorrect because this answer refers to an investment asset that was purchased at a premium.

Subject Area: Financial accounting and finance—intermediate concepts. Source: CIA 1196, IV-19.

177. (b) This is one of the features of zero coupon bonds attractive to the issuer. Choice (a) is incorrect because deep discount and zero coupon bonds sell for a small fraction of their face value but deep discount bonds pay interest (based on an interest rate that is significantly below the market rate) while zero coupon bonds do not. Choice (c) is incorrect because this is the definition for "commodity-backed" bonds, which are also called "asset-linked" bonds. Choice (d) is incorrect because this is the definition for "junk bonds."

Subject Area: Financial accounting and finance—intermediate concepts. Source: CIA 1196, IV-20.

178. (b) Computations follow:

(800,000 × 1/4) + 100,000

Choice (a) is incorrect.

(800,000 × 1/4)

Choice (c) is incorrect.

[(800,000 – 400,000] × 0.75) – 100,000

Choice (d) is incorrect.

(800,000 – 400,000) + 100,000

Subject Area: Financial accounting and finance—intermediate concepts. Source: CIA 1196, IV-27.

179. (b) Computations follow:

(485,000 – 465,000) – (335,000 – 327,000)

Choice (a) is incorrect.

(485,000 – 335,000) – 3,000

Choice (c) is incorrect.

(485,000 – 465,000) – (335,000 – 327,000) – (8,000 – 3,000)

Choice (d) is incorrect

(352,000-209,000) – (465,000-327,000)

Subject Area: Financial accounting and finance—intermediate concepts. Source: CIA 1196, IV-28.

180. (c) Under the sum-of-the-years' digits method, the amount of the depreciable cost that is expensed each year is the remaining useful life at the beginning of that year divided by the sum of the years of useful life. For the third year, the portion expensed is calculated as

2/(1 + 2 + 3 + 4) = 2/10 = 20%

Choice (a) is incorrect because this solution is the amount that would be expensed in the last year. It is one divided by the sum of the years of useful life.

1/(1+2+3+4) = 1/10 = 10%

Choice (b) is incorrect because this is the portion of the depreciable cost that would be expensed each year for four years under the straight-line method. Choice (d) is incorrect because this is the number of the third year divided by the number of years of useful life: 3/4 = 75%.

Subject Area: Financial accounting and finance—intermediate concepts. Source: CIA 1196, IV-29.

181. (c) Computations follow:

(40 + 50 – 30 – 5) × $200

Choice (a) is incorrect.

(50 – 30 – 5) × $200

Choice (b) is incorrect.

(50 – 30) × $200

Choice (d) is incorrect

(40 + 50 – 30) × $200

Subject Area: Financial accounting and finance—intermediate concepts. Source: CIA 1196, IV-30.

182. (c) Computations follow:

(350,000/500,000) × $1,200,000

Choice (a) is incorrect.

$1,200,000 historic cost

Choice (b) is incorrect.

$1,200,000 – (5/20) × $1,200,000

Choice (d) is incorrect.

(500,000 – 350,000/500,000) × $1,200,000

Subject Area: Financial accounting and finance—intermediate concepts. Source: CIA 1196, IV-32.

183. (c) Computations follow:

(4,700 + 500) – (5,000 – 2,000)

Choice (a) is incorrect.

(4,700 – 500) – (5,000 – 2,000)

Choice (b) is incorrect.

5,000 – (4,700 + 500 – 2,000)

Choice (d) is incorrect.

(5,000+ 500) – (4,700 – 2,000)

Subject Area: Financial accounting and finance—intermediate concepts. Source: CIA 1196, IV-33.

184. (d) Depreciation expense is a noncash charge. It represents the allocation of the historical cost of assets to the time periods in which they are used to generate revenues. Choices (a), (b), and (c) are incorrect because administrative, interest, and income tax expenses are all cash charges.

Subject Area: Financial accounting and finance—intermediate concepts. Source: CIA 1196, IV-36.

185. (a) The rate of gross profit on 2004 installment sales is calculated as

(2004 installment sales – Cost of 2004 installment sales)/2004 installment sales
= (5,000 – 4,000)/5,000 = 20%

Choice (b) is incorrect. This is the gross profit on the 2003 installment sales.

(2003 installment sales – Cost of 2003 installment sales)/2003 installment sales
= (10,000 – 6,000)/10,000 = 40%

Choice (c) is incorrect. This is the gross profit on the 2005 installment sales.

= (2005 installment sales – Cost of 2005 installment sales)/2005 installment sales
= (20,000 – 10,000)/20,000 = 50%

Choice (d) is incorrect. This is the ratio of the cost of 2004 installment sales to the level of 2004 installment sales.

Cost of 2004 installment sales/2004 installment sales
= 4,000/5,000 = 80%

Subject Area: Financial accounting and finance—intermediate concepts. Source: CIA 596, IV-1.

186. (a) In 2003, the company collects cash receipts of $2,000 on its 2003 installment sales. The gross profit realized is the gross profit on the portion of sales for which payment has been received. This is the gross profit percentage on the sales multiplied by the cash receipts on the sales received during the period.

(Gross profit percentage)(Collection)
= [(2003 installment sales – Cost of 2003 installment sales]/2003 installment sales)($2,000)
= [($10,000 – $6,000]/$10,000)($2,000) = (.40)($2,000) = $800

Choice (b) is incorrect. This is the amount of cash receipts during 2003 on the 2003 installment sales. The cash receipts should be multiplied by the gross profit percentage. Choice (c) is incorrect. This is the amount of the total gross profit on 2003 installment sales that is deferred to future periods, rather than being realized in 2003. The total gross profit on 2003 installment sales is $4,000 ($10,000 – $6,000). Of this total, it is the collected portion, or $800, that should be realized in 2003 while the remaining $3,200 should be deferred. Choice (d) is incorrect. This is the total amount of gross profit on 2003 installment sales. The company should recognize gross profit in 2003 only on the portion of these sales for which payment is received during the period.

Subject Area: Financial accounting and finance—intermediate concepts. Source: CIA 596, IV-2.

187. (c) This represents total gross profit from 2005 sales reduced by cash receipts received in 2005 from 2005 sales.

[(20,000 – 10,000]/20,000) × (20,000 – 4,000) = $8,000

Choice (a) is incorrect. This represents gross profit on 2005 sales collected in 2005.

[(20,000 – 10,000]/20,000) × $4,000 = $2,000

Choice (b) is incorrect. This represents net profit from 2005 sales reduced by cash received in 2005 from 2005 sales.

[(20,000 – 10,000]/20,000) × (10,000 – 4,000) = $3,000

Choice (d) is incorrect. This represents total gross margin on 2005 sales with no recognition of the amounts collected in 2005.

Subject Area: Financial accounting and finance—intermediate concepts. Source: CIA 596, IV-3.

188. (d) The sales revenue earned in 2005 is the cash receipts less any receipts in 2005 for which the revenue has not yet been earned plus the revenues earned from cash receipts in 2004.

2005 receipts – 2005 unearned revenue + 2004 receipts for which revenue was earned in 2005
= 175,000 – 30,000 + 40,000 = $185,000

Choice (a) is incorrect because this calculation of sales revenue neglects to add to cash receipts the receipts from 2004 sales earned in 2005.

2005 sales revenue = 2005 receipts – 2005 unearned revenue
= 175,000 – 30,000 = $145,000

Choice (b) is incorrect because this calculation adds, rather than subtracts, the 2005 unearned revenue and subtracts, rather than adds, the 2004 receipts for which revenue was earned in 2005.

2005 receipts + 2005 unearned revenue – 2004 receipts for which revenue was earned in 2005
= 175,000 + 30,000 – 40,000 = $165,000

Choice (c) is incorrect because this is the cash receipts for 2005, not the sales revenue earned.

Subject Area: Financial accounting and finance—intermediate concepts. Source: CIA 596, IV-4.

189. (c) The fraction of the depreciation base charged to depreciation expense in the first year is

Fraction depreciated = Number of years remaining at start of year/Sum of the years in first year of a 4-year asset
= 4/(1 + 2 + 3 + 4)
= 4/10 = 40%

Choice (a) is incorrect. It is in the final year that 10% of the depreciation base of the asset will be charged to depreciation expense.

Fraction depreciated = Number of years remaining at start of year/Sum of the years in 4th year of a 4-year asset
= 1/(1 + 2 + 3 + 4)
= 1/10 = 10%

Choice (b) is incorrect. This is the fraction of the asset cost that will be charged to depreciation expense under the straight-line method.

Straight-line depreciation rate = 1/Number of years = 1/4 = 25%

Choice (d) is incorrect. This is the fraction of the asset cost that will be charged to depreciation expense under the double-declining balance method.

DDB method = Two times the straight-line method
= 2(25%) = 50%

Subject Area: Financial accounting and finance—intermediate concepts. Source: CIA 596, IV-19.

190. (b) Under the double-declining balance method, the depreciation rate is double the straight-line rate. The straight-line rate on an asset with a five-year life is one-fifth or 20%, so the double-declining rate is 40%. Depreciation expense each year is the 40% rate multiplied by the carrying value of the asset.

Depreciation expense in year 1
= .40($100,000) = $40,000

Depreciation expense in year 2
= .40($100,000 – $40,000) = $24,000

Depreciation expenses in years 1 and 2 = $64,000.
Carrying value at end of year 2
= $100,000 – $64,000 = $36,000

Choice (a) is incorrect because this is the amount of depreciation expense in the second year. Choice (c) is incorrect because this is the book value of the asset at the end of the second year under the straight-line method of depreciation or the book value of the asset at the end of the first year under the double-declining method of depreciation.

Depreciation expense in year 1
= $100,000/5 = $20,000

Depreciation expense in year 2
= $100,000/5 = $20,000

Depreciation expenses in years 1 and 2 = $40,000
Carrying value at end of year 2
= $100,000 – $40,000 = $60,000

Double-declining balance
Depreciation expense in year 1
= .40($100,000) = $40,000

Carrying value at end of year 1
= $100,000 – $40,000 = $60,000

Choice (d) is incorrect because these are the total depreciation expenses in years 1 and 2.

Subject Area: Financial accounting and finance—intermediate concepts. Source: CIA 596, IV-20.

191. (b) Interest expense for each period is the effective-interest rate multiplied by the carrying value of the bond issue. As the discount is amortized, the carrying value rises and the interest expense increases. Choice (a) is incorrect. Both methods of bond discount amortization result in the same total interest expense over the term of the bonds. Choice (c) is incorrect. As the discount is amortized, the carrying value rises, rather than falls, so that the interest expense is increasing, not decreasing, over time. Choice (d) is incorrect. Interest expense rises during the life of the bonds. It does not remain constant under the effective-interest method. It is under the straight-line method that interest expense is constant.

Subject Area: Financial accounting and finance—intermediate concepts. Source: CIA 596, IV-24.

192. (d) The amount of the loss on premiums offered to customers can be reasonably estimated as of the issuance of the financial statements and whether it is probable that a liability has been incurred is also known at that time. Premiums offered to customers can therefore be accrued. Choices (a), (b), and (c) are incorrect because none of these loss contingencies are accrued. In each of these cases, it is unknown whether it is probable that a liability has been incurred. Also, the amount of the liability is unknown.

Subject Area: Financial accounting and finance—intermediate concepts. Source: CIA 596, IV-25.

193. (b) In 2006 the book value at the start of the period will be amortized over the revised estimated number of years of useful life.

Book value at start of 2006

= Original book value (7/10)
= $250,000 (7/10) = $175,000

Revised estimate of remaining useful life

= 20 – 3 = 17 years

2006 depreciation

= Book value at start of 2006/Remaining years of useful life
= $175,000/17 = $10,294

Choice (a) is incorrect. This is the result of depreciating the remaining carrying value over the full 20 years of estimated useful life, rather than on the remaining 17 years.

Book value at start of 2006/years of estimated life
= $175,000/20 = $8,750

Choice (c) is incorrect. This solution treats the revision retroactively; depreciating in each year from the first year the asset was in use.

Original book value/Revised useful life
= $250,000/20 = $12,500

Revisions in accounting estimates are accounted for prospectively.

Choice (d) is incorrect. This solution depreciates the original book value over the revised estimate of remaining useful life.

Original book value/Revised remaining useful life
= $250,000/17 = $14,706

Subject Area: Financial accounting and finance—intermediate concepts. Source: CIA 596, IV-27.

194. (c) Lease A is a capital lease because the terms of the lease include a bargain purchase option. Leases C and D pass the economic life (75%) test, and lease D also passes the recovery of investment (90%) test. Choice (a) is incorrect because lease A is a capital lease, because the terms of the lease include a bargain purchase option, but lease A is not the only capital lease in the set. Choice (b) is incorrect because lease B is the only operating lease in the set. The terms of the lease do not include a bargain purchase option and this lease also fails both the economic life (75%) test and the recovery of investment (90%) test. Choice (d) is incorrect because leases C and D are capital leases, but so is lease A. Lease A contains a bargain purchase option, so it classifies as a capital lease even though it does not pass either the economic life (75%) test or the recovery of investment (90%) test.

Subject Area: Financial accounting and finance—intermediate concepts. Source: CIA 596, IV-31.

195. (d) In a capital lease transaction, the lessee is using the lease as a financing source and the lessor is financing the transaction (providing the investment capital) through the leased asset. Choice (a) is incorrect because it is the lessee that obtains use of the asset in a lease transaction, whether it is an operating or a capital lease. Choice (b) is incorrect because it is the lessee that uses the lease as a source of financing, but under a capital lease rather than under an operating lease. Choice (c) is incorrect because it is the lessee that makes payments to the lessor. These payments are actually installment payments under a capital lease.

Subject Area: Financial accounting and finance—intermediate concepts. Source: CIA 596, IV-32.

196. (a) The weighted-average number of shares outstanding must be increased to reflect the shares the bonds could be converted into. Also, the effect of the bond interest on net income must be eliminated. In this way, an earnings per share is calculated as if the bonds had been converted into common shares as of the start of the year. Choice (b) is incorrect because the net income must be increased to reflect what earnings would have been; had there been no interest expense on the convertible bonds. Choices (c) and (d) are incorrect because the weighted-average number of shares outstanding must be increased, not decreased, to reflect the number of shares that would have been outstanding, had the bonds been converted into common shares at the start of the year.

Subject Area: Financial accounting and finance—intermediate concepts. CIA 596, IV-34.

197. (a) If interest rates have increased, then the bonds will be selling at a discount, below face value, in the open market. It will be cheaper for the company to retire a portion of the outstanding bonds by buying them back in the open market at the discounted price, rather than calling in a portion of the bonds at face value. Choice (b) is incorrect because if interest rates have remained constant, the bonds will still be selling at face value in the open market. The cost of buying bonds back on the open market will be the same as the cost of calling in a portion of the bonds at face value. Choice (c) is incorrect because if interest rates have increased, then the bonds will be selling at a discount in the open market. Buying back bonds in the open market will therefore be the cheaper alternative, not calling in a portion of the bonds at face value. Choice (d) is incorrect because if interest rates have decreased, then the bonds will be selling at a premium in the open market. It will be more costly, not less costly, to retire a portion of the outstanding bond issue by purchasing bonds on the open market. It will be cheaper to meet the sinking fund obligations by calling in a portion of the bonds at face value.

Subject Area: Financial accounting and finance—intermediate concepts. Source: CIA 596, IV-57.

198. (d) The error offsets itself in cost of goods sold because purchases and closing inventory are both understated by the same amount. Neither cost of goods sold nor net income is affected. Choices (a) and (b) are incorrect. The errors offset each other so that cost of goods sold is not understated or overstated for the period. Cost of goods sold equals opening inventory plus purchases minus closing inventory. If the goods are not recorded as a purchase, then purchases are understated. If the goods are also not counted in closing inventory, then closing inventory is understated by the same amount and the two errors offset each other. Choice (c) is incorrect because cost of goods sold is unaffected by the error so net income is also unaffected.

Subject Area: Financial accounting and finance—intermediate concepts. Source: CIA 1195, IV-1.

199. (d) Income for the current period will be understated and income for the following period will be overstated by the same amount. Taken together, the total income for the two periods will be correct. Choice (a) is incorrect because income for the current period is understated, not overstated, since if closing inventory is too low, cost of goods sold will be too high. Choice (b) is incorrect because income for the following period is overstated, not understated, since if opening inventory is too low, cost of goods sold will be too low. Choice (c) is incorrect because the errors in the two years sum to zero.

Subject Area: Financial accounting and finance—intermediate concepts. Source: CIA 1195, IV-2.

200. (d) Under the straight-line depreciation method the same amount of depreciation expense is charged in each year of the estimated useful life of the asset. This average amount will be greater than the depreciation charge under decreasing charge methods in the later years of the life of the asset. Choices (a), (b), and (c) are incorrect. Accelerated depreciation methods, such as sum-of-the-years' digits, declining balance and double-declining balance, charge higher depreciation cost in the early years of the asset life and lower depreciation cost in the later years. These decreasing charge methods will therefore charge less depreciation expense in the later years of the asset life than would the straight-line method, which charges the same amount to depreciation expense each year.

Subject Area: Financial accounting and finance—intermediate concepts. Source: CIA 1195, IV-11.

201. (a) The amount of future returns does not have to be known with certainty before a company can recognize sales revenue at the time of sale. It is only necessary that the amount of future returns can be reasonably estimated. Choices (b), (c), and (d) are incorrect because these are all conditions that must be met before a company can recognize sales revenue at the time of sale.

Subject Area: Financial accounting and finance—intermediate concepts. Source: CIA 1195, IV-15.

202. (b) Under the percentage-of-completion method, a current period loss on a profitable contract is treated, as a change in accounting estimate and a current period adjustment is required. Choice (a) is incorrect. Under the percentage-of-completion method, a current period loss on a profitable contract is treated as a change in accounting estimate and a current period adjustment, not a prior period adjustment, is required. Choices (c) and (d) are incorrect. Under the completed-contract method, no profit is recognized until the contract is completed. Cost estimate adjustments while the contract is in process do not result in profit recognition prior to completion unless an overall loss is expected on the contract.

Subject Area: Financial accounting and finance—intermediate concepts. Source: CIA 1195, IV-16.

203. (b) Under the sum-of-the-years' digits method, the portion of depreciable cost to expense in any given year is calculated as follows:

$$\frac{\text{Number of years of estimated life remaining at the beginning of the year}}{\text{The sum of the years of estimated useful life}}$$

So in the third year for an asset with a four-year estimated useful life portion to expense

= 2/(1+2+3+4) = 2/10 = 20%

Choice (a) is incorrect. This solution results from calculating the portion of depreciable cost to expense in any given year using the end of the current year in the numerator, as follows:

$$\frac{\text{Number of years of estimated life remaining at the end of the year}}{\text{The sum of the years of estimated useful life}}$$

So in the third year for an asset with a four-year estimated useful life portion to expense

= 1/(1+2+3+4) = 1/10 = 10%

Choice (c) is incorrect. This solution uses the digit of the current year in the numerator as follows:

Depreciation year/Sum of the years of estimated useful life

So in the third year for an asset with a four-year estimated useful life portion to expense

= 3/(1+2+3+4) = /10 = 30%

Choice (d) is incorrect. This solution incorrectly calculates the denominator as the sum of the years up to the end of the current year, as follows:

$$\frac{\text{Number of years of estimated life remaining at the beginning of the year}}{\text{The sum of the years of use as of the end of the year}}$$

So in the third year for an asset with a four-year estimated useful life portion to expense

= 2/(1+2+3) = 2/6 = 33.33%

Subject Area: Financial accounting and finance—intermediate concepts. Source: CIA 1195, IV-19.

204. (c) If the market rate exceeds the coupon rate, then the bonds will sell in the market at a price below the face value and the issuing company will record the difference between the face value and the market price as a discount. Choice (a) is incorrect. If the market rate equals the coupon rate and the bonds sell in the market at a price equal to face value, this is a par bond issue and there is no premium for the issuing company to record. Choice (b) is incorrect. If the market rate exceeds the coupon rate then the bond issue will sell at a discount, not a premium. Choice (d) is incorrect. If the market rate is less than the coupon rate then the bonds will sell at a price in excess of the face value. The issuing company will then have a premium, rather than a discount, to record.

Subject Area: Financial accounting and finance—intermediate concepts. Source: CIA 1195, IV-21.

205. (a) Under a defined contribution plan, the company reports an asset on the balance sheet only if the contribution to the pension trust is greater than the defined, required contribution. Choice (b) is incorrect. An asset is reported only if the contribution is in excess of the required contribution. If the actual contribution is equal to that required, no asset is reported. Choice (c) is incorrect. The company would report a liability on the balance sheet only if the contribution was less than the required amount, not greater than the required amount. Choice (d) is incorrect. The company would not report a liability on the balance sheet if it contributed the required amount to the pension trust.

Subject Area: Financial accounting and finance—intermediate concepts. Source: CIA 1195, IV-26.

206. (a) Leased assets are recognized as tangible assets. When lease agreements transfer the risks and benefits of ownership of the asset to the lessee, the lease is referred to as a capital lease since it is essentially a form of financing, or capital, for the lessee. Choice (b) is incorrect because leased assets are not recognized as intangibles. Choices (c) and (d) are incorrect. If substantially all of the risks and benefits of ownership of the asset are transferred to the lessee, then the lease is referred to as a capital lease, not an operating lease.

Subject Area: Financial accounting and finance—intermediate concepts. Source: CIA 1195, IV-28.

207. (d) Warrants are detachable. The bonds remain outstanding if the warrants are exercised. Choices (a) and (b) are incorrect because both bonds issued with warrants and convertible bonds have lower coupon rates than straight bonds. Choice (c) is incorrect because if the bondholder elects to convert bonds into common shares, the convertible bonds are exchanged for the common stock and do not remain outstanding after conversion.

Subject Area: Financial accounting and finance—intermediate concepts. Source: CIA 1195, IV-46.

208. (c) If depreciation was overstated in the prior year then net income was understated. The correction involves increasing the opening balance of retained earnings for the current year. Choices (a) and (b) are incorrect. The correction of an error in the prior year is charged or credited directly to the opening balance of retained earnings for the current year and is excluded from the determination of net income for the current year. Choice (d) is incorrect. If depreciation was overstated in the prior year then net income was understated. The correction involves increasing, not decreasing, the opening balance of retained earnings for the current year.

Subject Area: Financial accounting and finance—intermediate concepts. Source: CIA 595, IV-7.

209. (c) If a liability is paid for twice, assets and liabilities are both understated by the amount of the liability. Choice (a) is incorrect. The double payment of a liability does not affect expenses of the period so it does not affect net income and owners' equity. Choice (b) is incorrect. While net income and owners' equity are unaffected, the double payment of a liability does reduce assets. Choice (d) is incorrect. Net income and owners' equity are unaffected and because liabilities are understated, not overstated, if a liability is paid for twice.

Subject Area: Financial accounting and finance—intermediate concepts. Source: CIA 595, IV-8.

210. (b) It would be inappropriate to recognize such proceeds immediately in income. They should be treated as reductions in the price of the land. Choices (a), (c), and (d) are incorrect because they are appropriate.

Subject Area: Financial accounting and finance—intermediate concepts. Source: CIA 595, IV-10.

211. (b) Sales less cost of sales equals gross profit. The gross profit on the sales is recognized only when the cash is collected. The proportion of gross profit that is deferred equals the proportion of sales revenue that is uncollected at the end of the accounting period. Choice (a) is incorrect. Under the installment method, the gross profit on sales is not recognized until the cash is collected. The proportion of cash collected on the sales during the accounting period determines the proportion of the gross profit on those sales that is recognized during the period. Since both sales and cost of sales are deferred, answer (a) is incorrect. Choices (c) and (d) are incorrect because only the gross profit is deferred on sales for which cash has not yet been collected.

Subject Area: Financial accounting and finance—intermediate concepts. Source: CIA 595, IV-11.

212. (c) The profit recognized in the second year is calculated as follows:

Profit in second year = Payments received by end of year 2 – Seller's cost
= ($10,000 + $45,000) – $40,000 = $15,000

Choice (a) is incorrect. Under the cost recovery method, profit is recognized when cash payments by the buyer exceed the seller's cost of merchandise. By the end of the second year, $55,000 has been collected and this is in excess of the cost of merchandise so some profit will be recognized.

Choice (b) is incorrect because this is the answer if profit to be recognized is calculated without consideration of the payment received in the first year.

Profit in second year = Payments received in year 2 – Seller's cost
= $45,000 – $40,000 = $5,000

Choice (d) is incorrect because this is the payment received in the second year.

Subject Area: Financial accounting and finance—intermediate concepts. Source: CIA 595, IV-12.

213. (d) The double-declining balance method uses twice the straight-line rate for the asset and depreciation expense in year two is calculated as follows: In the first year of the asset life, depreciation expense is

(2)(Straight-line rate)(Cost)
= (2)(1/Number of years of useful life)(Cost)
= 2/5(100,000) = $40,000 in year one

In the second year, the depreciation base is reduced by the amount of depreciation expense already taken in the first year, so depreciation expense in year two is

= 2/5(100,000 – 40,000) = $24,000

Choice (a) is incorrect. Depreciation in year two will be $20,000 under the straight-line method of depreciation. Under the sum-of-the-years' digits method, it will be

(Years remaining/Sum of years)(Cost – Salvage value)
= 4/15(100,000 – 0) = $26,667

Choice (b) is incorrect. See choice (a) for correct solution for sum of the years' digits method. Choice (c) is incorrect. This is the answer if the straight-line rate, rather than double the straight-line rate of depreciation, is used.

In the first year of the asset life, depreciation expense is

(Straight line rate)(Cost) = (1/Number of years of useful life)(Cost)
= 1/5(100,000 – 0) = $20,000 in year one

In the second year, the depreciation base is reduced by the amount of depreciation expense already taken in the first year, so depreciation expense in year two is

= 1/5(100,000 – 20,000) = $16,000

Subject Area: Financial accounting and finance—intermediate concepts. Source: CIA 595, IV-15.

214. (c) The accumulated benefit obligation of a company includes both vested and nonvested employees and is calculated at current salary levels. Choice (a) is incorrect. The measure of pension obligations that includes benefits only to vested employees at current salary levels is called the vested benefit obligation. Most pension plans require a certain minimum number of years of service to the employer before an employee achieves vested benefits status. Vested benefits are those the employee is entitled to receive under the plan even if the employee renders no additional services. Choice (b) is incorrect. The accumulated benefit obligation of a company includes both vested and nonvested employees and is calculated at current, not future, salary levels. Choice (d) is incorrect. The measure of pension obligations that includes benefits to both vested and nonvested employees at future salary levels is called the projected benefit obligation.

Subject Area: Financial accounting and finance—intermediate concepts. Source: CIA 595, IV-16.

215. (b) The gain on the sale is the difference between the sale proceeds and the undepreciated cost of the asset. Depreciation must be taken up to the point of sale. The gain is calculated as follows:

Depreciation per year = Asset cost/Estimated useful life

= $100,000/10 = $10,000

Depreciation taken to end of 4th year

= 4($10,000) = $40,000

Depreciation for additional 6 months to account for use in the first half of the fifth year

= Depreciation per year (6/12)
= $10,000/2 = $5,000

Total depreciation to time of sale

= $40,000 + $5,000 = $45,000

Undepreciated cost at time of sale

= Original cost – Depreciated cost
= $100,000 – $45,000 = $55,000

Gain on sale

= Sale proceeds – Undepreciated cost at time of sale
= $80,000 – $55,000 = $25,000

Choice (a) is incorrect. This is the answer if depreciation is not taken for the first half of the fifth year. The gain is then calculated as follows: Depreciation per year

= Asset cost/Estimated useful life
= $100,000/10 = $10,000

Depreciation taken to end of 4th year

= 4 ($10,000) = $40,000

Undepreciated cost at time of sale

= Original cost – Depreciated cost
= $100,000 – $40,000 = $60,000

Gain on sale

= Sale proceeds – Undepreciated cost at time of sale
= $80,000 – $60,000 = $20,000

Choice (c) is incorrect. This is the answer if five full years of depreciation are taken, rather than four and a half years. The gain is then calculated as follows: Depreciation per year

= Asset cost/Estimated useful life
= $100,000/10 = $10,000

Depreciation taken to end of 5th year

= 4($10,000) = $50,000

Undepreciated cost at time of sale

= Original cost – Depreciated cost
= $100,000 – $50,000 = $50,000

Gain on sale

= Sale proceeds – Undepreciated cost at time of sale
= $80,000 – $50,000 = $30,000

Choice (d) is incorrect. This is the answer if one calculates gain on sale as sale proceeds minus book value at time of sale. The book, or undepreciated, value at the time of sale is $55,000 (see b.) The gain on sale would be calculated as follows: Gain on sale

= Sale proceeds – Undepreciated cost at time of sale
= $80,000 – $45,000 = $35,000

Subject Area: Financial accounting and finance—intermediate concepts. Source: CIA 595, IV-17.

216. (c) The amount the issuing company receives on February 1, 2004, is the face value of the issue plus one month of accrued interest.

Face value + One month of accrued interest
= $1,000,000 + $1,000,000(.12)(1/12) = $1,010,000

The buyers of the bond must pay the seller the interest accrued from the last interest payment date to the date of issuer, in advance. In effect they are paying for the portion of the first full 6-month interest payment that they are not entitled to because they did not hold the bonds for the full 6-month period.

Choice (a) is incorrect. This is the answer if one month of accrued interest is deducted from, rather than added to, the amount the bond buyers pay.

Face value – One month of accrued interest
= $1,000,000 – $1,000,000(.12)(1/12) = $990,000

Choice (b) is incorrect. The bond buyers must pay more than the face value of the bonds. In addition, they must pay for the accrued interest from the last date of interest to the issue date, since they will receive 6 months' interest but did not hold the bonds for the entire first six months.

Choice (d) is incorrect. This is the answer if two months of accrued interest are added to the face value.

Face value + Two months of accrued interest
= $1,000,000 + $1,000,000(.12)(2/12) = $1,020,000

Subject Area: Financial accounting and finance—intermediate concepts. Source: CIA 595, IV-19.

217. (d) The number of parties involved in the litigation is irrelevant. For example, the same recording treatment is applied whether an individual brings a claim or whether it is a class action suit. Choices (a), (b), and (c) are incorrect because these are all factors that must be considered when determining whether to record a liability with respect to pending or threatened litigation. Note that the time period in which the underlying cause for action occurred must be on or before the financial statement date for a liability to be recorded in the financial statements.

Subject Area: Financial accounting and finance—intermediate concepts. Source: CIA 595, IV-20.

218. (a) Goods on consignment are not considered to be intangible. The distinguishing feature of an intangible asset is the high degree of uncertainty regarding the future benefits the organization will derive from it. Lack of physical substance is not a distinguishing feature of intangible assets. Choices (b), (c), and (d) are incorrect because patents, copyrights and goodwill are all considered to be intangible assets.

Subject Area: Financial accounting and finance—intermediate concepts. Source: CIA 595, IV-25.

219. (d) If the lease is a capital lease, both the asset and the obligation for future payments are recorded. The company would have the following balance sheet after recording the new leased asset:

Current assets	$100	Debt	$175
Fixed assets	$175	Equity	$100

Debt ratio = Debt/(Current assets + Fixed assets)
= $175/ ($100 + $175) = 64%

Choice (a) is incorrect because this would be the debt to assets ratio if the lease were recorded as a capital lease. Choice (b) is incorrect because this is the debt to equity ratio for an operating lease. Operating leases are treated like rental agreements and neither the asset nor the obligation for future payments is recorded on the balance sheet. The balance of debt remains at $100 so the debt to equity ratio is $100/$100 or 100%. Choice (c) is incorrect because this is the debt to assets ratio for an operating lease. The balance of debt remains at $100 and the balance of total assets remains at $200 ($100 of current assets and $100 of fixed assets), since neither the asset or the obligation for future payments are recorded on the balance sheet. The debt to assets ratio then remains at $100/$200 or 50%.

Subject Area: Financial accounting and finance—intermediate concepts. Source: CIA 595, IV-26.

220. (c) It is the lessor, not the lessee, who records depreciation on the leased asset under a capital lease so this statement does not describe a capital lease. Choices (a) and (b) are incorrect because the lessor does capitalize the present value of the future rental payments and the leased asset is recorded as a capital asset on the balance sheet. Choice (d) is incorrect because this statement does describe a capital lease. For all intents and purposes, the leased asset is being purchased and a financial lease is identical to a loan to purchase the asset. Hence the lease agreement represents a form of financing or "capital" and should be recorded as such.

Subject Area: Financial accounting and finance—intermediate concepts. Source: CIA 595, IV-27.

221. (a) Under the completed-contract method no revenue is recognized until the contract is complete. The balance in the construction in progress account equals the total construction costs incurred to date of $4 million. Choice (b) is incorrect because under the completed-contract method, no revenue is recognized until the contract is complete. The $1 million figure is the amount the property management firm paid to the construction firm at the end of 1993. This would not be recognized as revenue. Choice (c) is incorrect because the $2 million initial contract payment would not be recognized as revenue and the original estimate of total construction costs is not the correct balance in the construction in progress account. Choice (d) is incorrect because the $3 million collected to date would not be recognized as revenue and the revised estimate of total construction costs is not the correct balance in the construction in progress account.

Subject Area: Financial accounting and finance—intermediate concepts. Source: CIA 1194, IV-7.

222. (b) The cost-to-cost approach to the percentage-of-completion method calculates percentage completion as costs incurred to date divided by the most recent estimate of total construction costs. The calculation of revenue to be recognized in 2003 is

= (Costs incurred to date/Most recent estimate of total cost)(Estimated total revenue)
= ($4,000,000/$8,500,000)($10,000,000) = $4,705,882

Choice (a) is incorrect because this solution employs the engineering estimate of percentage of completion rather than the cost-to-cost approach.

(Percent complete)(Estimated total revenue)
= (.30)($10,000,000) = $3,000,000

Choice (c) is incorrect because this solution employs the original estimate of total construction costs.

($4,000,000/$8,000,000)($10,000,000) = $5,000,000

Choice (d) is incorrect because this solution employs the percentage of total revenue billed to date, rather than the proportion of estimated total costs incurred, to calculate percentage of completion.

($6,000,000/$10,000,000)($10,000,000) = $6,000,000

Subject Area: Financial accounting and finance—intermediate concepts. Source: CIA 1194, IV-8.

223. (d) At the end of 2003, the construction company had recognized $2 million of revenue and billings to date were $6 million. Unbilled contract price is the difference between revenue recognized to date and billings to date, or $2 million minus $6 million = minus $4 million. If the amount is negative it is listed as a current liability on the balance sheet. Choice (a) is incorrect. Unbilled contract price is calculated as the difference between revenue recognized to date and receipts to date or $2 million minus $3 million = negative $1 million. This solution also incorrectly lists this negative amount as a current asset. Choice (b) is incorrect. If the unbilled contract revenue is a positive amount, then it is listed on the balance sheet as a current asset. Choice (c) is incorrect. Unbilled contract price is calculated as the difference between revenue recognized to date and receipts to date or $2 million minus $3 million = minus $1 million.

Subject Area: Financial accounting and finance—intermediate concepts. Source: CIA 1194, IV-9.

224. (c) Depreciation expense in year two is calculated as follows:

(Cost – Salvage)(Estimated hours of use in year two)/Total estimated hours of use
= ($300,000 – $70,000)(700 hours)/2,000 hours = $80,500

Choice (a) is incorrect because this solution uses the estimated hours of use in year one rather than in year two.

(Cost – Salvage)(Estimated hours of use in year one)/Total estimated hours of use
= ($300,000 – $70,000)(500 hours)/2,000 hours

Choice (b) is incorrect because this solution fails to deduct the estimated salvage value and uses the estimated hours of use in the first year.

(Cost)(Estimated hours of use in year one)/Total estimated hours of use
($300,000)(500 hours)/2,000 hours = $75,000

Choice (d) is incorrect because this solution fails to deduct the salvage value in calculating the depreciable asset cost.

(Cost)(Estimated hours of use in year 2)/Total estimated hours of use
($300,000)(700 hours)/2000 hours = $105,000

Subject Area: Financial accounting and finance—intermediate concepts. Source: CIA 1194, IV-19.

225. (**c**) Under the sum-of-the-years' digits method, the amount of the depreciable cost that is expensed each year is the remaining useful life at the beginning of that year divided by the sum of the years of useful life. For the third year, the portion expensed is calculated as

2/(1 + 2 + 3 + 4) = 2 / 10 = 20%

Choice (a) is incorrect because this solution is the amount that would be expensed in the last year. It is one divided by the sum of the years of useful life.

1/(1+2+3+4) = 1/10 = 10%

Choice (b) is incorrect because this is the portion of the depreciable cost that would be expensed each year for four years under the straight-line method.

Choice (d) is incorrect because this is the number of the third year divided by the number of years of useful life.

3/4 = 75%

Subject Area: Financial accounting and finance—intermediate concepts. Source: CIA 1194, IV-20.

226 (**c**) Prior period adjustments are charged or credited directly to the opening balance of retained earnings for the current period. Choice (a) is incorrect because prior period adjustments are excluded from the determination of current period net income. Choice (b) is incorrect because prior period financial statements are not reissued. The numbers may be updated to facilitate comparison with future periods. Choice (d) is incorrect because prior period adjustments are not accounted for by adjusting the closing retained earnings balance of the prior period.

Subject Area: Financial accounting and finance—intermediate concepts. Source: CIA 1194, IV-22.

227. (**a**) The straight-line method results in constant interest revenue, since the same adjustment to interest revenue is made each period. The constant interest revenue provides a varying rate of return on the book value of the bond investment, since the carrying value changes as the discount or premium is amortized. Choice (b) is incorrect. The effective interest method results in a constant rate of return on the book value of the bond investment since the effective interest rate computed at the time of the bond investment is applied to its beginning carrying value each period to calculate interest revenue. Choice (c) is incorrect. The effective interest method results in varying interest revenue on the bond investment since a constant effective interest rate is applied to a changing carrying value each period. Choice (d) is incorrect. The effective interest method results in varying interest revenue and in a constant rate of return on the book value of the bond investment.

Subject Area: Financial accounting and finance—intermediate concepts. Source: CIA 1194, IV-23.

228. (**d**) Employees get the benefit of gain or the risk of loss when pension contributions are defined but benefits are not. Choice (a) is incorrect because a mutual fund is not a pension plan. Choice (b) is incorrect because a real estate trust is not a pension plan. Choice (c) is incorrect because in defined benefit plans the employees are entitled to a defined level of benefits. They do not get the benefit of gain or the risk of loss from assets contributed to the pension plan.

Subject Area: Financial accounting and finance—intermediate concepts. Source: CIA 1194, IV-41.

229. (**a**) Cash-basis reporting involves revenue recognition upon the receipt of cash. Since the cash was received in year one, this is the year it would be recognized. Choice (b) is incorrect because accrual-basis reporting would recognize the revenue from the maintenance contracts in the second year since this is the year that the services are performed and the revenue is earned. Choice (c) is incorrect because cash-basis reporting would recognize the revenue in year one since that is when the cash was received. Choice (d) is incorrect because accrual-basis reporting would recognize the revenue in year two since this is the year the revenue is earned.

Subject Area: Financial accounting and finance—intermediate concepts. Source: CIA 1194, IV-25.

230. (**b**) If the company follows the historic cost principle, the fixed assets will be reported on the basis of their original purchase price rather than on the basis of market value on the reporting date. Choice (a) is incorrect because the matching principle is related to the recognition of related revenues and expenses in the same accounting period, not to the valuation basis for fixed assets. Choices (c) and (d) are incorrect because the going concern and revenue recognition principles are not related to the valuation basis for fixed assets.

Subject Area: Financial accounting and finance—intermediate concepts. Source: CIA 1194, IV-26.

231. (**c**) Under the income statement approach, bad debt expense is estimated as a portion of total credit sales for the period as follows:

(Credit sales)(Estimated bad debt rate)
= $400,000 (.05) = $20,000

Choice (a) is incorrect because the bad debt expense estimate is $20,000 under the income statement approach. Choice (b) is incorrect because this is the total amount of overdue accounts. The balance sheet approach would estimate bad debt expense as only the portion of overdue accounts that is estimated to be uncollectible. Choice (d) is incorrect because this is the estimated bad debt expense under the balance sheet approach. It is calculated as the portion of total overdue accounts that are estimated to be uncollectible as follows:

(Overdue accounts)(Estimated uncollectible portion)
($100,000)(.50) = $50,000

Subject Area: Financial accounting and finance—intermediate concepts. Source: CIA 1194, IV-27.

232. (**b**) Interest expense would include the $5,000 cash payment on October 1 of year one plus half of the $5,000 payment due on April 1 of year two, which has accrued by year-end. Choice (a) is incorrect because it is under cash-basis reporting that $5,000 of interest expense would be attributed to the first year of operations, since only one interest payment date occurs in the first year. Choice (c) is incorrect because the interest expense would be $10,000 for the year if the loan had been outstanding for the full year, but it was not arranged until April 1 so only 9 months of the term of the loan have passed by year-end. Choice (d) is incorrect because interest expense of $12,500 would imply that the loan had been outstanding for 15 months during the first year of operations.

Subject Area: Financial accounting and finance—intermediate concepts. Source: CIA 1194, IV-28.

233. **(b)** The revenue recognition principle provides that revenue is generally recognized when (1) realized or realizable and (2) earned. Revenue is realized when goods or services are exchanged for cash or claims to cash. Revenue is considered earned when the entity has substantially accomplished what it must do to be entitled to the benefits represented by the revenue. In the situation presented, the performance of the service (serving a luncheon) is so significant to completing the earning process that revenue should not be recognized until "delivery" occurs. At the point of delivery (serving the luncheon), the revenue has been realized and earned and should be recognized at that point. Choice (a) is incorrect because the revenue has not been earned at this point. Choice (c) is incorrect because the date selected for billing is one of administrative procedure and convenience. The revenue was earned at the date the service was performed and should be recognized at that point. Choice (d) is incorrect because at the point of performance of the service, the revenue has been realized and earned and should be recognized at that point. To wait until the receivable is collected would be to ignore the accrual basis of accounting and constitute a cash basis of accounting which is not in accordance with generally accepted accounting principles (unless the amount of potentially uncollectible accounts is not reasonably estimable).

Subject Area: Financial accounting and finance—intermediate concepts. Source: CIA 590, IV-26.

234. **(d)** A deferred revenue is a revenue item which has been received but not earned. The journal entry described in the question is an adjusting entry to transfer an amount from the earned revenue account to an unearned (deferred) revenue account. It is apparent that the collection of cash in advance from the tenant was initially recorded by a credit to the earned revenue account. Therefore, at the end of the accounting period, an adjusting entry is required to transfer any remaining unearned amount from the earned revenue account to a deferred revenue account. Choice (a) is incorrect because accrued revenue is revenue, which has been earned but not received. The journal entry described in the stem of the question indicates that collection has been made but the revenue has not yet been earned. Choice (b) is incorrect because the situation described in the stem of the question relates to a revenue type transaction rather than a cost or expense type transaction. Choice (c) is incorrect because the situation described in the stem of the question relates to a revenue-type transaction rather than a cost or expense-type transaction.

Subject Area: Financial accounting and finance—intermediate concepts. Source: CIA 590, IV-28.

235. **(b)** As dictated by the "revenue recognition principle," revenue is recognized (reported as revenue) in the period in which it is earned; therefore, when it is received in advance of its being earned, the amount applicable to future periods is deferred to future periods. The amount unearned (received in advance) is considered a liability because it represents an obligation to perform a service in the future arising from a past transaction. Unearned revenue is revenue which has been received but not earned. Choice (a) is incorrect because revenue should not be recognized until it is (1) realized or realizable and (2) earned. The advance receipts represent unearned revenue. Choice (c) is incorrect because accrued revenue is revenue which has been earned but not received. In the situation given, the revenue has been received but not earned. Choice (d) is incorrect because an accrued liability arises from an accrued expense, which is an expense incurred but not paid. The situation given deals with revenue received but not earned.

Subject Area: Financial accounting and finance—intermediate concepts. Source: CIA 590, IV-30.

236. **(d)** Under a consignment arrangement, the consignor (ABC) ships merchandise to the consignee (DEF) who is to act as an agent for the consignor in selling the merchandise. "A modified version of the sales basis of revenue recognition is used by the consignor. That is, revenue is recognized only after the consignor receives notification of sale and the cash remittance from the consignee." "The consignor periodically receives from the consignee an account of sales that shows the merchandise received, merchandise sold, expenses chargeable to the consignment, and the cash remitted. Revenue is then recognized by the consignor." Choices (a), (b), and (c) are incorrect because the revenue has not been realized nor earned at this point and should not be recognized yet.

Subject Area: Financial accounting and finance—intermediate concepts. Source: CIA 590, IV-31.

237. **(b)** Current liabilities are "obligations whose liquidation is reasonably expected to require the use of existing assets properly classified as current assets or the creation of other current liabilities." At the balance sheet date of December 31, 2005, the bonds will be coming due within a year of the balance sheet date but a special fund has been used to accumulate the necessary funds for retirement and the assets in the fund are classified in a noncurrent category. "Long-term debts maturing currently should not be included as current liabilities if they are to be retired by assets accumulated for this purpose that properly have not been shown as current assets." Choice (a) is incorrect because the bonds should be classified as a long-term liability because the bonds will not require the use of current assets within a year after the December 31, 2005 balance sheet date. Choice (c) is incorrect because there are very limited cases in which it is acceptable to offset assets and liabilities and this is not one of them. Choice (d) is incorrect because the bonds are a liability and should not be put in some ambiguous category such as deferred credits.

Subject Area: Financial accounting and finance—intermediate concepts. Source: CIA 590, IV-34.

238. **(d)** Short-term receivables are valued and reported at net realizable value which is the net amount expected to be received in cash, which is not necessarily the amount legally receivable. An allowance account (valuation account) related to the Account Receivable control account should be adjusted to allow for the estimated losses on the particular account and the rest of the company's trade accounts receivable. The expense to be recorded in making this adjustment is normally reported as an operating expense on the income statement. Choice (a) is incorrect. Even if the entire amount were estimated to be uncollectible, it would not be reported as an extraordinary item. APB Opinion 30 expressly denies extraordinary treatment to the write-down or write-off of receivables. Choice (b) is incorrect. Even if the entire amount were estimated to be uncollectible, it would not be reported as a reduction of sales on the income statement. In providing an adequate allowance account, the related debit is normally reported as an operating expense on the income statement. Choice (c) is incorrect. Receivables are initially recorded at their face value. For reporting purposes they should be valued at their net realizable value.

Subject Area: Financial accounting and finance—intermediate concepts. Source: CIA 590, IV-36.

239. (b) The acquisition cost of the asset includes the purchase price, shipping and installation charges, and other set-up costs (which includes the cost of labor and materials for trial runs) necessary to get the asset in the condition and location for its intended use. Salvage value is deducted from the acquisition cost in computing depreciation.

Computation

($500,000 + $50,000 + $120,000 – $200,000) × 4/10 = $188,000.

Choice (a) is incorrect because this answer incorrectly ignores the shipping charges of $50,000 and the set-up costs of $120,000.

Computation

($500,000 – $200,000) × 4/10 = $120,000.

Choice (c) is incorrect because this answer incorrectly ignores the shipping charges, set-up costs, and salvage value in calculating depreciation.

Computation

$500,000 × 4/10 = $200,000.

Choice (d) is incorrect because this answer incorrectly ignores the salvage value.

Computation

($500,000 + $50,000 + $120,000) × 4/10 = $268,000

Subject Area: Financial accounting and finance—intermediate concepts. Source: CIA 590, IV-38.

240. (c) The cost (and resulting depreciable base) of the asset should be its purchase price (cash equivalent purchase price) of $400,000 plus all costs to get the asset in the location and condition for its intended use. The installation charges of $25,000 are part of the asset's cost because they are necessary to prepare the asset for its intended use. The interest charges of $10,500 were not necessary to prepare the asset for its intended use. The interest charges were incurred after the asset was ready to be used in operations. The interest charges do not qualify for capitalization in this case and should be accounted for as interest expense in the period they are incurred. Choice (a) is incorrect because this answer incorrectly excludes the $25,000 of installation charges. Choice (b) is incorrect because this answer incorrectly includes the interest (financing costs) of $10,500 and incorrectly excludes the installation charges of $25,000. Choice (d) is incorrect because this answer incorrectly capitalizes the financing costs (interest of $10,500). The $10,500 should be accounted for as interest expense rather than as a component of cost of the asset.

Subject Area: Financial accounting and finance—intermediate concepts. Source: CIA 590, IV-39.

241. (a) These treasury stock transactions decrease equity by $160.

Choice (b) is incorrect because a $200 decrease does not consider the net $40 increase to paid-in capital which increases equity. Choice (c) is incorrect because a $200 increase does not consider the $40 increase to paid-in capital and does not deduct treasury from equity. Choice (d) is incorrect because the treasury stock transactions decrease equity.

Subject Area: Financial accounting and finance—intermediate concepts. Source: CIA 590, IV-42.

242. (d) Gain on the sale of an asset should be presented as other revenues and gains. Choice (a) is incorrect because gain on the sale of one asset would not represent a discontinued operation. Choice (b) is incorrect because gain on the sale of an asset is not unusual and infrequent. Choice (c) is incorrect because gain on the sale of an asset should be presented separately from operating income.

Subject Area: Financial accounting and finance—intermediate concepts. Source: CIA 590, IV-43.

243. (c) The annual contribution of an ordinary annuity is $84,000/6. Choice (a) is incorrect because this amount does not consider any time value of the money invested. Choice (b) is incorrect because this amount represents the annual contribution of an annuity due ($84,000/7) but the deposits are made at the end of each year. Choice (d) is incorrect because this amount falls between the contribution based on the two annuity concepts.

Subject Area: Financial accounting and finance—intermediate concepts. Source: CIA 590, IV-44.

244. (b) The $48,000 is 40% of $150,000, which is an allocated share for land based on fair market value. Choice (a) is incorrect because the $40,000 results from an allocation based on book value but fair market value should be used. Choice (c) is incorrect because the $50,000 represents an arbitrary amount equal to book value. Choice (d) is incorrect because the $60,000 is just 50% of the purchase price and does not consider an allocation based on fair market value.

Subject Area: Financial accounting and finance—intermediate concepts. Source: CIA 590, IV-45.

245. (c) This is the official difference. Choice (a) is incorrect because operating leases usually provide for maintenance while financial leases do not. Choice (b) is incorrect because operating lease contracts are written for a period less than the economic life. Choice (d) is incorrect because the lessor finances the assets leased for an operating lease.

Subject Area: Financial accounting and finance—intermediate concepts. Source: CIA 590, IV-53.

246. (a) Ordinarily no revenue is recognized until goods or services are delivered. Delivery took place in 2005.

Choice (b) is incorrect. March through December payment (10 × $10,000).

Choice (c) is incorrect. February through December payment (11 × $10,000).

Choice (d) is incorrect. All 12 payments (12 × $10,000).

Subject Area: Financial accounting and finance—intermediate concepts. Source: CIA 1190, IV-28.

247. (d) Accumulated depreciation at year-end 2005 is computed as follows:

[(5/15) + (4/15) + (3/15)] × ($100,000 – $10,000) = $72,000.

Choice (a) is incorrect. The 2005 depreciation expense is computed without considering salvage value.

$$(3/15) \times \$100{,}000 = \$20{,}000$$

Choice (b) is incorrect. The 2004 depreciation expense is computed

$$(4/15) \times (\$100{,}000 - \$10{,}000) = \$24{,}000$$

Choice (c) is incorrect. Accumulated depreciation at year-end 2004 is computed

$$[(5/15) + (4/15)] \times (\$100{,}000 - \$10{,}000) = \$54{,}000$$

Subject Area: Financial accounting and finance—intermediate concepts. Source: CIA 1190, IV-29.

248. **(a)** The appropriate base should include all expenditures incurred in acquiring the equipment and preparing it for use. This includes the purchase price of $100,000, transportation cost of $8,000 and installation cost of $13,000. The interest cost, which is a financing cost, should not be included in the depreciable cost of the equipment. Therefore, by definition, choices (b), (c), and (d) will be incorrect.

Subject Area: Financial accounting and finance—intermediate concepts. Source: CIA 1190, IV-34.

249. **(a)** Choice (a) is correct.

$$(\$720{,}000 + 995{,}000)/(\$720{,}000 + \$995{,}000 + \$735{,}000) \times [\$3{,}000{,}000 - (720{,}000 + \$995{,}000 + \$735{,}000)] - (\$720{,}000)/(\$720{,}000 + \$1{,}680{,}000) \times [\$3{,}000{,}000 - (\$720{,}000 + \$1{,}680{,}000)] = \$205{,}000$$

Choice (b) is incorrect because the expense is based on 2005 results only.

$$[\$995{,}000/(\$720{,}000 + \$995{,}000 + \$735{,}000)] \times [\$3{,}000{,}000 - (\$720{,}000 + \$995{,}000 + \$735{,}000)] = \$223{,}367$$

Choice (c) is incorrect because the estimate of gross profit is not changed.

$$(\$720{,}000 + \$995{,}000)/(\$720{,}000 + \$995{,}000 + \$735{,}000) \times [\$3{,}000{,}000 - (\$720{,}000 + \$1{,}680{,}000)] - (\$720{,}000)/(\$720{,}000 + \$1{,}680{,}000) \times [\$3{,}000{,}000 - (\$720{,}000 + \$1{,}680{,}000)] = \$240{,}000$$

Choice (d) is incorrect because the 2004 gross profit recognized was not deducted.

$$(\$720{,}000 + \$995{,}000)/(\$720{,}000 + \$995{,}000 + \$735{,}000) \times [\$3{,}000{,}000 - (\$720{,}000 + \$995{,}000 + \$735{,}000)] = \$385{,}000$$

Subject Area: Financial accounting and finance—intermediate concepts. Source: CIA 1190, IV-36.

250. **(c)** Interest expense is calculated and reported based on a rate applied to an obligation balance. Depreciation expense is calculated and reported based on a method applied to an asset balance. Choice (a) is incorrect because rent expense would not appear. Interest expense and depreciation expense would be in its place. Prepaid rent would not appear. Any rent payments in advance of their due date would simply reduce the obligation under capital lease account balance. Choice (b) is incorrect because prepaid rent would not appear. Any rent payments in advance of their due date would be recorded as a reduction of the lease obligation rather than as an asset. Choice (d) is incorrect because rent expense would not appear but interest expense would appear.

Subject Area: Financial accounting and finance—intermediate concepts. Source: CIA 1190, IV-44.

251. **(a)** There are a number of items which are to be disclosed with regard to the reporting of pension plans in financial statements. The items listed are two of the required disclosures. Choices (b), (c), and (d) are incorrect since both are required disclosures.

Subject Area: Financial accounting and finance—intermediate concepts. Source: CIA 1190, IV-45.

Advanced Concepts

252. **(a)** Since the return to the US company is adversely affected and the return to the German company is unaffected, the return to the US company will definitely be lower than the return to the German company. Choice (b) is incorrect because the return to the US company is adversely affected by the exchange rate movement. Choice (c) is incorrect because the return to the US company is directly affected by the exchange rate movement, while the return to the German company is not. Choice (d) is incorrect. See response given for choice (a).

Subject Area: Financial accounting and finance—advanced concepts. Source: CIA Model Exam 2002, IV-41.

253. **(b)** Goodwill is the difference between the purchase price and the fair market value of identifiable net assets acquired. Choice (a) is incorrect because goodwill is calculated as the difference between the purchase price and the fair market value, not the book value, of identifiable net assets acquired. Choice (c) is incorrect because it is the fair market value of identifiable net assets that is used in calculating goodwill. Further, both tangible and intangible assets are included. Choice (d) is incorrect because the values of both tangible and intangible acquired net assets are included in the goodwill calculation.

Subject Area: Financial accounting and finance—advanced concepts. Source: CIA Model Exam 1998, IV-42.

254. **(c)** Goodwill is recorded only when an entire business is purchased. Thus, the $200,000 is to be capitalized as goodwill but the $80,000 should not be capitalized. Choice (a) is incorrect because this answer selection incorrectly reflects no capitalization of any of the expenditures mentioned. Choice (b) is incorrect because goodwill is recorded only when an entire business is purchased. Thus, the $200,000 is to be capitalized as goodwill but the $80,000 should not be capitalized. Choice (d) is incorrect because this answer selection incorrectly reflects the capitalization of the internally generated goodwill of $80,000. That $80,000 should be expensed in 2002 rather than be capitalized.

Subject Area: Financial accounting and finance—advanced concepts. Source: CIA 1192, IV-35.

255. **(d)** Long-term investments in the 20 to 50% ownership range are generally accounted for using equity basis reporting. Choices (a) and (b) are incorrect because cost basis or lower of cost or market reporting is generally used to account for passive investments where less than 20% of the stock of the investee is owned by the investor. Choice (c) is incorrect because consolidated reporting is generally used to account for long-term investments when more than 50% of the stock of the investee is owned by the investor.

Subject Area: Financial accounting and finance—advanced concepts. Source: CIA 596, IV-26.

256. **(b)** A 40% ownership interest is usually sufficient to ensure that the investor has significant influence over the financial and operating policies of the investee. Such investments are reported using the equity method. Choice (a) is incorrect. An 80% ownership interest is generally sufficient to classify the investee as a subsidiary of the investor and the investment is accounted for on a consolidated basis. Choice (c) is incorrect. An ownership level of 15% is generally not sufficient to allow the investor to control the investee. Consolidated reporting would therefore not be appropriate. Choice (d) is incorrect. Intercorporate share investments of 5% are generally considered to be passive investments and the cost method of reporting is used.

Subject Area: Financial accounting and finance—advanced concepts. Source: CIA 1195, IV-20.

257. (c) Owners (stockholders) of corporations have limited liability. They risk only what they pay for the stock purchased and not their other assets. Choice (a) is incorrect because sole proprietors do not enjoy limited liability. Choice (b) is incorrect because partners do not enjoy limited liability. Choice (d) is incorrect because an oligopoly is not a legal form of business organization.

Subject Area: Financial accounting and finance—advanced concepts. Source: CIA Model Exam 2002, IV-70.

258. (a) The net monetary asset position at the beginning of the period ($800,000) is restated to $880,000 average constant dollars ($800,000 × 220/200 = $880,000). The actual increase in net monetary assets ($943,000 – $800,000 = $143,000) is assumed to have occurred evenly throughout the year so it is already stated in terms of average-for-the-year dollars. The restated beginning balance ($880,000) plus the increase ($143,000) yields a subtotal of $1,023,000. This subtotal is compared with the ending balance restated to an average basis ($943,000 × 220/230 = $902,000) to yield a purchasing power loss of $121,000. Choice (b) is incorrect because there is a purchasing power loss rather than a gain. Choice (c) is incorrect because this $126,500 answer selection results from restating the beginning balance and the increase to an end-of-the-year basis rather than an average-for-the-year basis. Choice (d) is incorrect because there is a purchasing power loss rather than a gain. Also, the amount of $126,500 was calculated based on end-of-the-year dollars whereas average-for-the-year-dollars should be used.

Subject Area: Financial accounting and finance—advanced concepts. CIA 1190, IV-39.

259. (c) Goodwill is the difference between the purchase price and the fair value of the acquired net assets. Fair value of net assets

= Cash + Receivables + Inventory + Property – Liabilities
= 100 + 200 + 200 + 400 – 200 = $700

Goodwill

= Purchase price – Fair value of net assets = 900 – 700 = $200

Choice (a) is incorrect. If the fair value of the net assets of the acquired company is incorrectly calculated as $1100, then negative goodwill of $200 results. The net assets could be incorrectly estimated at $1100 by adding, rather than subtracting, the fair value of the current liabilities from the fair value of all of the assets. Fair value of net assets

= Cash + Receivables + Inventory + Property + Liabilities
= 100 + 200 + 200 + 400 + 200 = $1100

Goodwill

= Purchase price – Fair value of net assets = 900 – 1100 = $(200)

Choice (b) is incorrect. If the fair value adjustment for the current liabilities is subtracted from the book value of net assets, then goodwill will be incorrectly calculated as follows: Book value of net assets

= Cash + Receivables + Inventory + Property – Fair value for liabilities
= 100 + 200 + 150 + 600 – 200 = $850

Goodwill

= Purchase price – Fair value of net assets = 900 – 850 = $50

Subject Area: Financial accounting and finance—advanced concepts. Source: CIA 596, IV-30.

260. (a) The amortization of a positive amount of goodwill represents an additional expense. Reported earnings will be reduced as a result. Choice (b) is incorrect because amortizing goodwill would result in an increase of operating expenses and would have no relationship to other income. Choice (c) is incorrect because the amortization of positive goodwill would result in a charge, or increase, to operating expenses. Thus, this response is exactly opposite of a correct response. Choice (d) is incorrect because the amortization of goodwill does not affect cost of goods sold. Cost of goods sold includes opening inventory plus purchases less closing inventory.

Subject Area: Financial accounting and finance—advanced concepts. Source: CIA 1195, IV-45.

261. (c) Goodwill equals the excess of the acquisition cost over the fair market value of acquired assets.

Goodwill

= $1,000,000 – $ 800,000 = $ 200,000

Choice (a) is incorrect. Goodwill equaling the excess of the acquisition cost over the fair market value of identifiable net assets acquired must be recorded on the acquisition date.

Choice (b) is incorrect. This is the answer if goodwill is calculated as the excess of the acquisition cost over the book value of net assets acquired.

Goodwill

= $1,000,000 – $ 900,000 = $ 100,000

Choice (d) is incorrect. This is the answer if goodwill is calculated as the acquisition cost less the book value of the acquired net assets plus the increment of fair value over book value.

Goodwill

= $1,000,000 – $ 200,000 + ($900,000 – $ 800,000) = $300,000

Subject Area: Financial accounting and finance—advanced concepts. Source: CIA 1196, IV-23.

Financial Statement Analysis

262. (c) Choice (c) is the correct answer. Inflation impacts both aspects. Choice (a) is incorrect because inflation also distorts depreciation charges, inventory costs, and profits. Choices (b) and (d) are incorrect because inflation impacts both aspects.

Subject Area: Financial accounting and finance—financial statement analysis. Source: CIA Model Exam 2002, IV-5.

263. (a) The times-interest-earned ratio is earnings before taxes and interest divided by the interest charges. It measures the extent to which operating income can decline before the firm is unable to meet its annual interest cost, a measure of debt-paying capacity.

Subject Area: Financial accounting and finance—financial statement analysis. Source: CIA Model Exam 2002, IV-8.

264. (c) This high ratio could be an indicator that the company cannot afford to buy enough assets. Choice (a) is incorrect because the ratio may indicate just the opposite. Choice (b) is incorrect because the fixed assets turnover ratio is sales divided by net fixed assets; fluctuations in inventory do not affect the ratio. Choice (d) is incorrect because the fixed assets turnover ratio is not a profitability indicator. It is sales divided by net fixed assets.

Subject Area: Financial accounting and finance—financial statement analysis. Source: CIA Model Exam 2002, IV-20.

265. (d) These three ratios comprise the simple Du Pont equation.

$$\frac{\text{Net income available to stockholders}}{\text{Sales}} \times \frac{\text{Sales}}{\text{Total assets}} \times \frac{\text{Total assets}}{\text{Common equity at book value}} = \text{Return on equity}$$

The total assets and sales cancel out in multiplication, leaving net income available to stockholders divided by common equity at book value, which equals return on equity. Choice (a) is incorrect. The market value to book value ratio is the market value of common equity per share derived by dividing the book value of common equity by the average number of shares outstanding. Neither this ratio nor the total debt to total assets ratio provides any information about net income available to stockholders, which is necessary to calculate the return on equity. Choice (b) is incorrect. The price to earnings ratio is the ratio of the stock's market price divided by earnings per share; the earnings per share is the net income available to stockholders divided by the average number of shares outstanding; and the net profit margin is net profit divided by sales. While all three ratios contain much information about the equity account, none of them provides information about the book value of common equity, which is necessary to calculate the return on equity. Choice (c) is incorrect. The price to earnings ratio is the ratio of the stock's market price divided by earnings per share, and the return on assets ratio is net income divided by assets. Neither of these two ratios provides information about the book value of common equity, which is necessary to calculate the return on equity.

Subject Area: Financial accounting and finance—financial statement analysis. Source: CIA Model Exam 1998, IV-2.

266. (b) The use of debt as financial leverage has a multiplier effect on return on assets to yield return on equity. The Du Pont formula illustrates this point by showing that return on equity is the return on assets times the equity multiplier. The greater use of debt increases the equity multiplier, because it is calculated as total assets divided by common equity at book value. In this example, the company's equity multiplier is 1.92 and the industry average is 1.40.

The company	*The industry average*
7.9% × 1.92 = 15.2%	9.2% × 1.40 = 12.9%

The higher equity multiplier indicates that the company has greater use of debt than the industry average. Choice (a) is incorrect. The question gave no information about market share, nor can the reader necessarily infer any. The question provides two measures of profitability, one of which is higher than that of the industry, one of which is lower. Choice (c) is incorrect. This comparison is with an industry average, not over time. The reader can infer no conclusions about the company's profits over time. Choice (d) is incorrect. The stock market responds to different situations in different ways. Just because the company has a higher return on equity than the industry average does not mean that the company has a more favorable market-to-book-value.

Subject Area: Financial accounting and finance—financial statement analysis. Source: CIA Model Exam 1998, IV-17.

267. (c) The day's sales outstanding is the accounts receivable balance divided by average credit sales per day. Its result is the average length of time required to convert the firm's receivables into cash, which is also the definition of the receivables collection period. Choice (a) is incorrect because the inventory conversion period is the average length of time required to convert materials into finished goods and then to sell those goods. This period typically occurs before the receivables collection period, and the amount of time in each of the periods does not necessarily bear any relationship to the other. Choice (b) is incorrect because average daily sales divided by total assets describes return on assets, a profitability ratio. Choice (d) is incorrect because the inventory divided by the sales per day is the average length of time required to convert materials into finished goods and then to sell those goods. This result is the same as the inventory conversion period, not the receivables collection period.

Subject Area: Financial accounting and finance—financial statement analysis. Source: CIA Model Exam 1998, IV-27.

268. (a) The higher the dividend payout ratio, the sooner retained earnings are exhausted and the company must seek more costly, outside equity financing. This drives up the marginal cost of capital. Choice (b) is incorrect because the debt ratio is computed by dividing total debts by total assets. The dividend payout ratio has no impact on the debt ratio. Choice (c) is incorrect because the investment opportunities available to the company are not determined by the level of dividend payout. Choice (d) is incorrect because the opposite is true. The price to earnings ratio is computed by dividing price per share by earnings per share, so a company with a higher dividend payout ratio would have a lower price to earnings ratio.

Subject Area: Financial accounting and finance—financial statement analysis. Source: CIA Model Exam 1998, IV-30.

269. (c) A higher profit margin would reduce the additional financing needed, shifting the funds-needed line down. Choices (a) and (b) are incorrect because a higher profit margin would reduce the additional financing needed, as stated in the question. The result would be a downward, not an upward, shift in the funds-needed line. Choice (d) is incorrect because the line would become less, not more steep if the firm had a higher profit margin.

Subject Area: Financial accounting and finance—financial statement analysis. Source: CIA Model Exam 1998, IV-44.

270. (a) If all earnings are paid out as dividends, then there is no earnings retention. All sales growth must be financed from spontaneous or external sources. Choice (b) is incorrect because the funds-needed line only passes through the origin in the special case where all earnings are paid out as dividends. Choice (c) is incorrect because the funds-needed line is a graph of the relationship between sales growth and additional financing needs. It is not drawn for just one point, or one level of sales growth. Choice (d) is incorrect because while the sales growth rate would be zero at the point where the funds-needed line passed through the origin, funds needed may be nonzero when sales growth is zero.

Subject Area: Financial accounting and finance—financial statement analysis. Source: CIA Model Exam 1998, IV-45.

271. **(c)** The capital intensity ratio is the amount of assets required per dollar of sales. External financial requirements are lower if the capital intensity ratio is low, because this means sales can grow rapidly without much outside capital, other things held constant. Choice (a) is incorrect. If earnings retention is low (that is, if dividend payout is high), more external capital is needed, other things held constant. Choice (b) is incorrect. Higher sales growth means higher capital requirements, other things held constant. Choice (d) is incorrect. Firms with lower profit margins require more external capital, other things held constant.

Subject Area: Financial accounting and finance—financial statement analysis. Source: CIA Model Exam 1998, IV-62.

272. **(b)** When a cash dividend is paid, the balances of the cash and the retained earnings accounts are reduced. Choice (a) is incorrect. Dividend payments do not affect the balance of accounts receivable. Choice (c) is incorrect. Dividend payments do not affect the balance of the fixed assets (net) account. Choice (d) is incorrect. Dividend payments do not affect the inventory account.

Subject Area: Financial accounting and finance—financial statement analysis. Source: CIA 594, IV-11.

273. **(c)** Times-interest-earned is calculated as

Earnings before interest and taxes/Interest expense
(Sales – Cost of goods sold – Admin. expense
– Depreciation expense)/Interest expense
= (600,000 – 400,000 – 35,000 – 10,000)/20,000
= 155,000/20,000 = 7.75 times

Choice (a) is incorrect. Answer if used net income in numerator.

155,000 – 20,000 – 67,500/20,000 = 3.375 times

Choice (b) is incorrect. Answer if deduct interest expense when calculating earnings before interest and tax.

155,000 – 20,000/20,000 = 6.75 times

Choice (d) is incorrect. Answer if neglect to deduct administrative expenses when calculating earnings before interest and tax.

(600,000 – 400,000 – 10,000)/20,000 = 9.5 times

Subject Area: Financial accounting and finance—financial statement analysis. Source: CIA 594, IV-12.

274. **(d)** Book value per share is calculated as

Book value of common equity/Outstanding shares
= (Common stock + Retained earnings)/Outstanding shares
= (100,000 + 150,000)/10,000 = $25

Choice (a) is incorrect. Calculation if retained earnings is excluded (see d.).

100,000/10,000 = $10

Choice (b) is incorrect. Calculation if common stock is excluded (see d.):

150,000/10,000 = $15

Choice (c) is incorrect. Calculation based on average shareholder equity

Average equity = 182,500 + 250,000/2 = 216,250
216,250/10,000 = $21.63

Subject Area: Financial accounting and finance—financial statement analysis. Source: CIA 594, IV-13.

275. **(a)** Rate of return on equity is calculated as

Net income/Average shareholders' equity
= (Sales – Cost of goods sold – Administrative expense
– Depreciation expense – Interest expense
– Tax expense)/[(Beginning equity + Ending equity)/2]
= (600,000 – 400,000 – 35,000 – 10,000 – 20,000 – 67,500)/
[(182,500 + 250,000)/2]
= 67,500/216,250 = 31.21%

Choice (b) is incorrect. Answer if common stock is excluded from denominator (see a.)

Average retained earnings = (82,500 + 150,000)/2 = 116,250
Return on equity = 67,500/116,250 = 58.06%

Choice (c) is incorrect. Answer if retained earnings is excluded from denominator (see a.).

Average common stock = 100,000
Return on equity = 67,500/100,000 = 67.5%

Choice (d) is incorrect. Answer if earnings before interest and tax is used in the numerator (see a.)

Earnings before interest and tax = Sales – Cost of goods sold
– Administrative expense – Depreciation expense
= 600,000 – 400,000 – 35,000 –10,000 = 155,000
Return on equity = 155,000/216,250 = 71.68%

Subject Area: Financial accounting and finance—financial statement analysis. Source: CIA 594, IV-14.

276. **(c)** If a liability is paid for twice, assets and liabilities are both understated by the amount of the liability. Choice (a) is incorrect. The double payment of a liability does not affect expenses of the period so it does not affect net income and owners' equity. Choice (b) is incorrect. While net income and owners' equity are unaffected, the double payment of a liability does reduce assets. Choice (d) is incorrect. Net income and owners' equity are unaffected and because liabilities are understated, not overstated, if a liability is paid for twice.

Subject Area: Financial accounting and finance—financial statement analysis. Source: CIA 594, IV-15.

277. **(a)** Cost of goods sold is first-in-first-out as: Opening inventory + Purchases – Closing inventory so the overstatement of inventory at the start of the current period will result in cost of goods sold being overstated in the second period. Choice (b) is incorrect because an inventory error does not affect net sales. Choice (c) is incorrect because an inventory error does not affect the balance of the net fixed assets account. Choice (d) is incorrect because the overstatement of opening inventory will result in an overstatement of cost of goods sold, so current earnings will be understated.

Subject Area: Financial accounting and finance—financial statement analysis. Source: CIA 594, IV-16.

278. **(b)** The correct method of filling in the missing account balances on the partial summary balance sheet for the company is presented below.

Cash	$ 10	(given)	Current liabilities	$ 30	(see 2)
Accounts receivable	26	(see 6)	Long-term liabilities	40	(given)
Inventory	6	(see 5)			
Current assets	$ 42	(see 3)	Stockholders' equity	30	(given)
Fixed assets	58	(see 4)			
Total assets	$100	(given)	Total liabilities and equity	$100	(see 1)

Supporting calculations

1. Total liabilities and equity = Total assets
$100 = $100
2. Current liabilities = Total liabilities and equity – Equity – Long-term liabilities
$30 = $100 – $30 – $40
3. Current ratio = Current assets/Current liabilities so Current assets = Current ratio × Current liabilities
$42 = 1.4 (30)
4. Fixed assets = Total assets – Current assets
58 = 100 – 42
5. Quick ratio = (Current assets – Inventory)/Current liabilities so Inventory = Current assets – Quick ratio (Current liabilities)
$6 = $42 – 1.2 (30)
6. Accounts receivable = Current assets – Inventory – Cash
$26 = $42 – $6 – $10

Choice (a) is incorrect because this answer is the result of having incorrectly calculated the quick ratio as (Current assets – Accounts receivable)/Current liabilities. Choice (c) is incorrect because this answer is the result of neglecting to subtract the cash balance in calculation (6) above. Choice (d) is incorrect because this answer is the result of neglecting to subtract the equity balance when calculating the current liability balance in (2) above.

Subject Area: Financial accounting and finance—financial statement analysis. Source: CIA 594, IV-33.

279. (c) Supporting calculations to fill in the missing account balances in the partial summary balance sheet of the company are provided in the solution to the previous question. Choice (a) is incorrect because this is a distracter. Choice (b) is incorrect because this answer is the result of neglecting to subtract the equity balance when calculating the current liability balance in (2) above. Choice (d) is incorrect because this answer is the result of having mixed up the two ratios (i.e., taking the current ratio as 1.2 and the quick ratio as 1.4).

Subject Area: Financial accounting and finance—financial statement analysis. Source: CIA 594, IV-34.

280. (a) This is the measure defined in the question. Choice (b) is incorrect because a low ratio for this measure suggests that short-term obligations can easily be serviced by the normal flow of annual revenues. Choice (c) is incorrect because a high ratio for this measure suggests the presence of resources that can be used to overcome a revenue shortfall. Choice (d) is incorrect because a low ratio for this measure suggests an ability to pay debt service requirements when due.

Subject Area: Financial accounting and finance—financial statement analysis. Source: CIA 596, III-97.

281. (c) The "quick" assets for this company are Cash ($27,500), Marketable Securities ($64,000), and Accounts receivable ($115,000). The current liabilities include Accounts payable ($67,000), Notes payable—Current portion ($54,000), Income taxes payable ($70,000), and Other current liabilities ($22,500). Dividing the sum of the quick assets by the sum of the current liabilities equals .958. Choice (a) is incorrect because it does not include the Income taxes payable in the current liabilities. Choice (b) is incorrect because it includes Prepaid expenses in the quick assets and does not include Income taxes payable in the current liabilities. Choice (d) is incorrect because it includes Deferred income taxes payable in the current liabilities.

Subject Area: Financial accounting and finance—financial statement analysis. Source: CIA 1193, IV-46.

282. (b) This answer

= (Cash + MS + AR)/Current liabilities = $900m / $900m = 1.00.

Choice (a) is incorrect. This answer

= (Cash + MS + AR – Inv.)/Current liabilities

Choice (c) is incorrect. This answer

= (Current assets – Inventory)/(AP + NP).

Choice (d) is incorrect. This answer

= All current assets/Current liabilities

Subject Area: Financial accounting and finance—financial statement analysis. Source: CIA 1193, IV-57.

283. (c) This answer

= Total debt/Total assets = $1500m/$3000m = 50%

Choice (a) is incorrect. This answer

= LT debt/Total assets

Choice (b) is incorrect. This answer

= LT debt/Total equity

Choice (d) is incorrect. This answer

= Total debt/Total equity

Subject Area: Financial accounting and finance—financial statement analysis. Source: CIA 1193, IV-58.

284. (a) This answer

= Net income/Total equity = $70m/$1500m = 4.67%.

Choice (b) is incorrect. This answer

= EBT/(Total equity).

Choice (c) is incorrect. This answer

= EBIT/(Total equity).

Choice (d) is incorrect. This answer

= Net income/Common stock.

Subject Area: Financial accounting and finance—financial statement analysis. Source: CIA 1193, IV-59.

285. (c)

January 1 = (3+5+8) – (2+4+1) = 9; June 30 = (4+4+10) – (3+3+2) = 10

Choice (a) is incorrect. This answer leaves out inventories.

January 1 = (3+5) – (2+4+1) = 1
June 30 = (4+4) – (3+3+2) = 0

Choice (b) is incorrect. This answer includes all assets and all liabilities.

January 1 = (26 – 26) = 0
June 30 = (29-29) = 0

Choice (d) is incorrect. This answer leaves out accrued wages.

January 1 = (3+5+8) – (2+4) = 10
June 30 = (4+4+10) – (3+3) = 12

Subject Area: Financial accounting and finance—financial statement analysis. Source: CIA 1192, IV-52.

286. **(d)** The current ratio is decreased as follows:

January 1 = (3+5+8)/(2+4+1) = 16/7 = 2.29
June 30 = (4+4+10)/(3+3+2) = 18/8 = 2.25

The quick ratio is decreased as follows:

January 1 = (3+5)/(2+4+1) = 8/7 = 1.14
June 30 = (4+4)/(3+3+2) = 8/8 = 1.00

Choices (a), (b), and c) are incorrect. The current ratio decreased from 2.29 to 2.25, while the quick ratio decreased from 1.14 to 1.00.

Subject Area: Financial accounting and finance—financial statement analysis. Source: CIA 1192, IV-53.

287. **(b)** Vertical analysis is the expression of each item on a financial statement in a given period to a base figure; on the income statement, each item is stated as a percentage of sales. Thus, the percentages for the company in question can be compared with industry norms. Choice (a) is incorrect because a horizontal analysis indicates the proportionate change over a period of time and is useful in trend analysis of an individual entity in comparing the entity with itself in other periods. Choice (c) is incorrect because activity ratio analysis would include the preparation of turnover ratios such as for receivables, inventory, and total assets. Choice (d) is incorrect because the defensive-interval ratio is part of a liquidity analysis.

Subject Area: Financial accounting and finance—financial statement analysis. Source: CIA 593, IV-39.

288. **(d)** The current ratio is determined by dividing current assets by current liabilities. The acid-test ratio is determined by dividing quick assets by current liabilities. At December 31, 2001, the current ratio is ($40,000 + $120,000 + $200,000) divided by $60,000 which equals 6:1. At December 31, 2002, the current ratio is ($30,000 + $100,000 + $300,000) divided by $100,000 which is 4.3:1. Hence, there was a decrease in the current ratio from 6 to 4.3. At December 31, 2001, the acid-test ratio is ($40,000 + $120,000) divided by $60,000 which equals 2.7:1. At December 31, 2002, the acid-test ratio is ($30,000 + $100,000) divided by $100,000 which equals 1.3:1. Therefore, the acid-test ratio also declined from 2.7 to 1.3. Choice (a), (b), and (c) are incorrect because both ratios decreased.

Subject Area: Financial accounting and finance—financial statement analysis. Source: CIA 593, IV-40.

289. **(c)** The primary purpose of a statement of cash flows is to provide relevant information about the cash receipts and cash payments of an enterprise during a period. "The information provided in a statement of cash flows, if used with related disclosures and information in the other financial statements, should help investors, creditors, and others to assess the enterprise's ability to generate future net cash flows." Choice (a) is incorrect because the statement of income is prepared on an accrual basis and is not meant to report cash flows. Choice (b) is incorrect because the statement of retained earnings merely shows the reasons for changes in retained earnings during the reporting period. Choice (d) is incorrect because the balance sheet reports on the financial position at a point in time.

Subject Area: Financial accounting and finance—financial statement analysis. Source: CIA 1192, IV-30.

290. **(b)** The direct method reports major classes of gross cash receipts and gross cash payments from operating activities and their arithmetic sum—the net cash flow from operating activities. The indirect method adjusts net income to reconcile it to net cash from operating activities. The indirect method does not report individually the major classes of cash receipts and cash payments from operations. Choice (a) is incorrect. Only the direct method will supply information about individual classes of gross cash receipts and gross cash payments related to operating activities. Choice (c) is incorrect. The direct method, rather than the indirect method, supplies information about individual classes of gross cash receipts and gross cash payments related to operating activities. Choice (d) is incorrect. The direct method reports major classes of gross cash receipts and gross cash payments from operating activities.

Subject Area: Financial accounting and finance—financial statement analysis. Source: CIA 1192, IV-32.

291. **(c)** The computation is as follows:

Cash balance, January 1, 2002	$ 85,000
Proceeds from the sale of common stock	80,000
Distribution of a 50% stock dividend	--
Cash provided by operations	36,000
Purchase of land and building	(120,000)
Purchase of short-term investments	(8,000)
Cash balance, December 31, 2002	$ 73,000

Neither the declaration nor distribution of a stock dividend has any effect on cash.

Choice (a) is incorrect because the computation to yield this answer incorrectly includes a deduction for $60,000 for the distribution of a stock dividend. A stock dividend involves the distribution of additional shares of stock to existing shareholders for no consideration. There is no effect on cash of a stock dividend. Choice (b) is incorrect because the computation to yield this answer incorrectly omits the $36,000 of cash provided by operations. Choice (d) is incorrect because the computation for this answer incorrectly omits the deduction of $8,000 for the purchase of short-term investments.

Subject Area: Financial accounting and finance—financial statement analysis. Source: CIA 1192, IV-33.

292. **(b)** This is

Cash + Marketable securities + Receivables/Current liabilities
= $200 + $100 + $50/$500 = $350/$500 = 0.7

Choice (a) is incorrect. This is

Net Income/Total liabilities = $1,000/$30,000 = 0.03

Choice (c) is incorrect. This is

Cash + Marketable securities + Receivables + Inventory/Current liabilities
= $200 + $100 + $50 + $400/$500 = $750/$500 = 1.5

Choice (d) is incorrect. This is

Cash + Marketable securities + Receivables + Inventory
+ Prepaid expenses/Current liabilities
= $200 + $100 + $50 + $400 + $70/$500 = $820/$500 = 1.64.

Subject Area: Financial accounting and finance—financial statement analysis. Source: CIA 1192, IV-40.

293. **(b)** This is

Sales/Total assets = $50,000/$80,000 = 0.63.

Choice (a) is incorrect. This is

Total liabilities/Total assets = $30,000/$80,000 = 0.38.

Choice (c) is incorrect. This is the inverse of choice (b)

$80,000/$50,000 = 1.6.

Choice (d) is incorrect. This is the inverse of choice (a) $80,000/$30,000 = 2.67.

Subject Area: Financial accounting and finance—financial statement analysis. Source: CIA 1192, IV-41.

294. **(c)** The TIE ratio is = EBIT/interest charges. The denominator will increase with additional bonds issued. Choice (a) and (b) are incorrect because these ratios are unaffected. Choice (d) is incorrect because this ratio would decrease.

Subject Area: Financial accounting and finance—financial statement analysis. Source: CIA 1192, IV-60.

295. **(a)** The formula for the current ratio is

$$\frac{\text{Current assets}}{\text{Current liabilities}}$$

$54,000/$12,000 = 4.5.

Choice (b) is incorrect. This selection was derived by dividing current liabilities ($12,000) by the amount of cash ($5,000) which produces no meaningful ratio. Choice (c) is incorrect. This selection was derived by dividing the total of cash, short-term marketable investments, and net receivables by total current liabilities, which is called the acid-test or quick ratio.

$5,000 + $3,000 + $16,000 = $24,000
$24,000/ $12,000 = 2.0.

Choice (d) is incorrect. This selection was derived by dividing total current liabilities by the sum of cash and short-term marketable investments, which produces no meaningful ratio.

$12,000/($5,000 + $3,000) = 1.5.

Subject Area: Financial accounting and finance—financial statement analysis. Source: CIA 592, IV-40.

296. **(c)** The formula for the acid-test ratio is

$$\frac{\text{Cash + Short-term investments + Accounts receivable}}{\text{Current liabilities}}$$

$$\frac{\$5,000 + \$3,000 + \$16,000}{\$12,000}$$

Choice (a) is incorrect because this selection was derived by dividing total current liabilities ($12,000) by the amount of cash ($5,000) which produces no meaningful ratio. Choice (b) is incorrect because this selection was derived by dividing quick assets ($5,000 + $3,000 + 16,000) by accounts payable ($11,000). The denominator should also include current liabilities other than accounts payable. Choice (d) is incorrect because this selection was derived by dividing total current liabilities ($12,000) by the sum of cash ($5,000) and short-term marketable investments ($3,000) which produces no meaningful ratio.

Subject Area: Financial accounting and finance—financial statement analysis. Source: CIA 592, IV-41.

297. **(c)** RST's quick ratio has decreased from 2.5 in year five [($40,000 – $20,000)/$8,000] to 2.0 in year six [($54,000 – $30,000)/$12,000]. RST has fewer assets that are easily convertible to cash available to meet current liabilities and, therefore, its ability to meet its short term financing needs has declined. Choice (a) is incorrect because the quick ratio compares current assets (less inventory) to current liabilities; conclusions about long term investments cannot be made. Choice (b) is incorrect because the quick ratio compares current assets (less inventory) to current liabilities; the existence of inventory write-offs cannot be determined. Inventory write-offs would tend to make the quick ratio increase, not decrease. Choice (d) is incorrect. See choice (c).

Subject Area: Financial accounting and finance—financial statement analysis. Source: CIA 592, IV-42.

298. **(a)** The formula for the accounts receivable turnover is

$$\frac{\text{Net credit sales}}{\text{Average trade receivables (net)}}$$

$$\frac{\$285,000}{(\$16,000 + \$14,000) \times 1/2}$$

Choice (b) is incorrect because this selection was derived by dividing average sales of years 5 and 6 [($285,000 + $200,000) × ½] by average receivables ($15,000) which produces no meaningful ratio. Choice (c) is incorrect because this selection was derived by dividing cost of goods sold ($150,000) for year 6 by average accounts receivable ($15,000) which produces no meaningful ratio. Choice (d) is incorrect because this selection was derived by dividing cost of goods sold for year 6 ($150,000) by average inventory ($25,000) which produces the inventory turnover ratio.

Subject Area: Financial accounting and finance—financial statement analysis. Source: CIA 592, IV-43.

299. **(a)** The formula for the times-interest-earned ratio is

$$\frac{\text{Income before taxes and interest charges}}{\text{Interest charges}}$$

$$\frac{\$70,000}{\$3,000} = 23.33 \text{ times}$$

Choice (b) is incorrect because this selection was derived by dividing the sum of the net income ($40,000) and the interest charges ($3,000) by the amount of interest charges ($3,000) which produces no meaningful ratio. Choice (c) is incorrect because this selection was derived by dividing net income ($40,000) by the interest charges ($3,000) which produces no meaningful ratio. Choice (d) is incorrect because this selection was derived by dividing the sum of the interest charges ($3,000) and income taxes ($27,000) by the amount of interest charges ($3,000) which yields no meaningful ratio.

Subject Area: Financial accounting and finance—financial statement analysis. Source: CIA 592, IV-44.

300. **(b)** The times-interest-earned ratio increased from 14 times in year five ($44,000/$3,000) to 23.33 times in year six ($70,000/$3,000). This indicates that RST has more income available to meet the interest payments on its debt, and the long-run solvency has improved. Choice (c) is incorrect because liquidity refers to a firm's ability to meet current liabilities with current assets by converting assets to cash. It is not related to the times-interest-earned ratio, which compares income before interest and taxes to interest expense associated with long term investments.

Subject Area: Financial accounting and finance—financial statement analysis. Source: CIA 592, IV-45.

301. **(a)** First, the amount of cash dividends paid on common stock must be computed. Beginning retained earnings for year five ($63,000) plus net income for year six ($40,000) minus ending retained earnings for year six ($82,000) equals the cash dividends declared during year six of $21,000. The payout ratio is the ratio of cash dividends on common stock to the net income available to common stockholders. The payout ratio for RST for year six is therefore computed as follows:

$$\frac{\$21,000}{\$40,000} = 52.50\%$$

Choice (b) is incorrect because this selection was derived by dividing the sum of the dividends ($21,000) and interest ($3,000) by the amount of income before interest and taxes ($70,000) which produces no meaningful ratio. Choice (c) is incorrect because this selection was derived by dividing the sum of the dividends ($21,000) by the average amount of stockholders' equity [($87,000 + $106,000) × ½] which yields no meaningful ratio. Choice (d) is incorrect because this selection was derived by dividing the market price of the stock ($100) by the earnings per share figure ($40,000 net income divided by 2,400 shares outstanding = $16.67 EPS) which equals 6 times and is called the price earnings ratio.

Subject Area: Financial accounting and finance—financial statement analysis. Source: CIA 592, IV-46.

302. **(b)** The fixed-assets turnover or utilization ratio is defined as the ratio of sales divided by net fixed assets (gross plant and equipment minus depreciation) and is equal to 3.0. Choice (a) is incorrect because the ratio of sales divided by the value of total assets is called the total asset turnover ratio and is equal to 1.8 times. Choice (c) is incorrect because the ratio of gross plant and equipment divided by inventory is equal to 5.18. Choice (d) is incorrect because the inventory turnover ratio, also called the inventory utilization ratio, is defined as sales divided by inventories and is equal to 11.11.

Subject Area: Financial accounting and finance—financial statement analysis. Source: CIA 592, IV-56.

303. **(a)** Computed as net income of $1 million/175,000 shares = $5.71. Choice (b) is incorrect. This answer reflects retained earnings divided by number of shares. Choice (c) is incorrect. This answer reflects net operating income divided by number of shares. Choice (d) is incorrect. This answer reflects (net sales minus cost of goods sold) divided by number of shares.

Subject Area: Financial accounting and finance—financial statement analysis. Source: CIA 592, IV-57.

304. **(c)** Computed as net operating income ($1,750,000) divided by net operating assets of $7,500,000. Choice (a) is incorrect because this answer reflects net operating income divided by total assets. Choice (b) is incorrect because this answer reflects net operating income divided by net plant and equipment. Choice (d) is incorrect because this answer reflects net income divided by total assets.

Subject Area: Financial accounting and finance—financial statement analysis. Source: CIA 592, IV-58.

305. **(b)** The total asset turnover ratio is sales/total assets. An increase in the reported inventory figure will increase total assets, which would decrease the ratio. Choice (a) is incorrect. The average collection period is (receivables)\(sales/360). An increase in the reported inventory figure would not affect it. Choice (c) is incorrect. The price/earnings ratio is price per share/earnings per share. Fictitious inventory would not directly affect it. Choice (d) is incorrect. The current ratio is current assets/current liabilities. Fictitious inventory would cause it to increase.

Subject Area: Financial accounting and finance—financial statement analysis. Source: CIA 1191, IV-50.

306. **(b)** This ratio is determined as (current assets-inventory)/current liabilities. ($790,000 – $540,000)/$270,000 = 0.93. Choice (a) is incorrect. This ratio is determined by excluding both accounts receivable and inventory from the numerator. ($790,000 – $540,000 – $200,000)/$270,000 = 0.18. Choice (c) is incorrect. This ratio is determined by excluding accounts receivable (rather than inventory) from the numerator. ($790,000 – $200,000)/$270,000 = 2.18. Choice (d) is incorrect. This ratio is the current ratio. $790,000/$270,000 = 2.93.

Subject Area: Financial accounting and finance—financial statement analysis. Source: CIA 591, IV-55.

307. **(d)** This answer is determined as sales divided by net plant and equipment. $3,200,000/$1,000,000 = 3.2. Choice (a) is incorrect. This answer is derived from dividing the cost of goods sold (instead of sales) by net plant and equipment. $1,800,000/$1,000,000 = 1.8. Choice (b) is incorrect. This answer is derived from dividing the cost of goods sold (instead of sales) by gross (instead of net) plant and equipment. $1,800,000/$1,400,000 = 1.28. Choice (c) is incorrect. This answer is derived from dividing the sales by gross (instead of net) plant and equipment. $3,200,000/$1,400,000 = 2.28.

Subject Area: Financial accounting and finance—financial statement analysis. Source: CIA 591, IV-56.

308. **(a)** Determined as net income divided by sales.

($190,000/$3,200,000) × 100% = 5.94%.

Choice (b) is incorrect because this answer was determined as net income divided by cost of goods sold.

($190,000/$1,800,000) × 100% = 10.55%.

Choice (c) is incorrect because this answer represents the return on assets, determined as net income divided by total assets.

($190,000/$1,790,000) × 100% = 10.61%.

Choice (d) is incorrect because this answer represents the return on equity, determined as net income divided by total stockholders' equity.

($190,000/$680,000) × 100% = 27.94%.

Subject Area: Financial accounting and finance—financial statement analysis. Source: CIA 591, IV-57.

309. **(c)** This high ratio could be an indicator that the company cannot afford to buy enough assets. Choice (a) is incorrect because it may indicate just the opposite. Choice (b) is incorrect because the fixed-asset turnover ratio is sales divided by net fixed assets; fluctuations in inventory do not affect the ratio. Choice (d) is incorrect because the fixed-asset turnover ratio is not a profitability indicator. It is sales divided by net fixed assets.

Subject Area: Financial accounting and finance—financial statement analysis. Source: CIA 597, IV-24.

310. **(a)** The times-interest-earned ratio is earnings before taxes and interest divided by the interest charges. It measures the extent to which operating income can decline before the firm is unable to meet its annual interest cost, a measure of debt-paying capacity.

Subject Area: Financial accounting and finance—financial statement analysis. Source: CIA 597, IV-31.

311. **(c)** Inflation impacts both aspects. Choice (a) is incorrect because inflation badly distorts firms' balance sheets, depreciation charges, inventory costs, and profits. Choices (b) and (d) are incorrect because inflation impacts both aspects.

Subject Area: Financial accounting and finance—financial statement analysis. Source: CIA 597, IV-35.

312. (d) These three ratios comprise the simple Du Pont equation.

$$\frac{\text{Net income available to stockholders}}{\text{Sales}} \times \frac{\text{Sales}}{\text{Total assets}} \times \frac{\text{Total assets}}{\text{Common equity at book value}} = \text{Return on equity}$$

The total assets and sales cancel out in multiplication, leaving net income available to stockholders divided by common equity at book value, which equals return on equity. Choice (a) is incorrect. The market-to-book-value ratio is the market value of common equity per share derived by dividing the book value of common equity by the average number of shares outstanding. Neither this ratio nor the total debt to total assets ratio provides any information about net income available to stockholders, which is necessary to calculate the return on equity. Choice (b) is incorrect. The price to earnings ratio is the ratio of the stock's market price divided by earnings per share; the earnings per share is the net income available to stockholders divided by the average number of shares outstanding; and the net profit margin is net profit divided by sales. While all three ratios contain much information about the equity account, none of them provides information about the book value of common equity, which is necessary to calculate the return on equity. Choice (c) is incorrect. The price-to-earnings ratio is the ratio of the stock's market price divided by earnings per share, and the return on assets ratio is net income divided by assets. Neither of these two ratios provides information about the book value of common equity, which is necessary to calculate the return on equity.

Subject Area: Financial accounting and finance—financial statement analysis. Source: CIA 597, IV-37.

313. (b) Operating leases do not increase the debt or assets since the assets are not included on the balance sheet. Choices (a) and (c) are incorrect because if the assets are leased, the debt ratio will remain unchanged. Choice (d) is incorrect because if the assets are purchased, the debt ratio will increase.

Subject Area: Financial accounting and finance—financial statement analysis. Source: CIA 1190, IV-55.

314. (a) The times-interest-earned ratio equals operating income divided by interest expense. Choice (b) is incorrect because the numerator should be net of interest expense. Choice (c) is incorrect because this is the reciprocal of the correct formula. Choice (d) is incorrect because operating income, not earnings before tax, should be used and the numerator and denominator are reversed in this formula.

Subject Area: Financial accounting and finance—financial statement analysis. Source: CIA 1196, IV-26.

315. (a) Cash provided by operations is calculated as follows:

Net income + Depreciation – Increase in accounts receivable
– Decrease in accounts payable
= 294,000 + 50,000 – (300,000 – 200,000) – (275,000 – 250,000)
= 294,000 + 50,000 – 100,000 – 25,000
= $219,000

An increase in receivable constitutes a use of cash because additional credit is extended to customers. A decrease in accounts payable constitutes a use of cash because less credit is extended to the firm by its suppliers. Choice (b) is incorrect. This solution does not consider the changes in accounts receivable and payable during 1995 and subtracts depreciation charges from net income, rather than adding depreciation charges to net income, as follows:

Net income – Depreciation = 294,000 – 50,000 = $244,000

Choice (c) is incorrect. This solution does not consider the changes in accounts receivable and payable during 1995 and calculates cash provided by operations as

Net Income + Depreciation = 294,000 + 50,000 = $344,000.

Choice (d) is incorrect. This solution adds, rather than subtracts, the increase in receivable and the decrease in payable as follows:

Net income + Depreciation + Increase in accounts receivable
+ Decrease in accounts payable
= 294,000 + 50,000 + (300,000 – 200,000) + (275,000 – 250,000)
= 294,000 + 50,000 + 100,000 + 25,000
= $469,000

Subject Area: Financial accounting and finance—financial statement analysis. Source: CIA 1196, IV-37.

316. (c) The average collection period for 1995 is calculated as follows:

= Accounts receivable/Average daily sales
= Accounts receivable/(Annual sales/365)
= 300,000/(1,500,000/365) = 300,000/4109.59 = 73 days

Choice (a) is incorrect. This solution incorrectly uses the accounts receivable balance from 1994 and calculates the average collection period as

= Prior accounts receivable/Average daily sales
= Prior accounts receivable/(Annual sales/365)
= 200,000/(1,500,000/365) = 200,000/4109.59 = 49 days

Choice (b) is incorrect. This solution incorrectly uses both the accounts receivable balance and the annual sales from 1994 and calculates the average collection period as

= Prior accounts receivable/Prior average daily sales
= Prior accounts receivable/(Prior annual sales/365)
= 200,000/(1,400,000/365) = 200,000/3835.62 = 52 days

Choice (d) is incorrect. This solution incorrectly uses the annual sales from the prior period and calculates 1995 average collection period as follows:

= Accounts receivable/Prior average daily sales
= Accounts receivable/(Prior annual sales/365)
= 300,000/(1,400,000/365) = 300,000/3835.62 = 78 days

Subject Area: Financial accounting and finance—financial statement analysis. Source: CIA 1196, IV-38.

317. (c) Interest coverage for 2004 is calculated as follows:

Prior earnings before interest and taxes/Interest charges
= 540,000/100,000 = 5.40 times

Choice (a) is incorrect. This solution incorrectly uses net income, rather than earnings before interest and taxes, and calculates interest coverage as

Prior net income/Interest charges = 220,000/100,000 = 2.20 times

Choice (b) is incorrect. This solution incorrectly uses net income, rather than earnings before interest and taxes. It also uses 2005 income statement information rather than 2004 information as required in the question.

2005 net income/Interest charges
= 294,000/100,000 = 2.94 times

Choice (d) is incorrect. This solution incorrectly uses 2005 rather than prior year data as follows:

2004 earnings before interest and taxes/Interest charges
= 688,000/100,000 = 6.88 times

Subject Area: Financial accounting and finance—financial statement analysis. Source: CIA 1196, IV-39.

318. (b) A company with a higher dividend payout ratio is paying out more of its earnings as dividends to common shareholders. It will have less cash and less total assets than a comparable firm with a lower payout ratio. The debt-to-assets ratio will be higher, since total assets are lower, and the current ratio will be lower, since cash is lower, than for the lower dividend payout firm. Choice (a) is incorrect because the higher dividend payout company will have less cash and a lower current ratio than a comparable firm with a lower payout policy. Choice (c) is incorrect because this is opposite to the correct solution. Choice (d) is incorrect because the higher dividend payout company will have less cash and less total assets, and hence a higher debt-to-assets ratio, than a comparable company with a lower payout policy.

Subject Area: Financial accounting and finance—financial statement analysis. Source: CIA 1196, IV-53.

319. (b) The quick ratio is current assets excluding inventories divided by current liabilities.

(Current assets – Inventories)/Current liabilities = 4.0
(Cash + Receivables)/Payables = 4.0
Receivables = 4.0 (Payables) – Cash
= 4.0 (140) – 240
= 560 – 240 = $320

Choice (a) is incorrect. This calculation incorrectly calculates the quick ratio as the ratio of payables to receivables.

Accounts payable/Accounts receivable = 4.0
Receivables = Payables/4.0 = $140/4 = $35

Choice (c) is incorrect. This is the inventory balance, not the balance of receivables. The inventory balance is calculated by first calculating the receivables balance to be $320. Then total assets equals total liabilities and equities so total assets are $1250. Inventories are then calculated as

Inventory = Total assets – Net fixed assets – Cash – Receivables
= 1,250 – 400 – 240 – 320 = $290

Choice (d) is incorrect. This calculation does not include the cash balance in the numerator of the quick ratio.

(Current assets – Inventories)/Current liabilities = 4.0
Receivables/Payables = 4.0
Receivables = 4.0(Payables)
= 4.0(140)
= $560

Subject Area: Financial accounting and finance—financial statement analysis. Source: CIA 596, IV-8.

320. (c) The total debt-to-assets ratio was given to be .60, so the balance of the long-term debt account can be calculated as follows:

(Current liabilities + Long-term debt)/Total assets = .60
Long-term debt = .60(Total assets) – Current liabilities
= .60(1250) – 140 = $750 – 140 = $610

Choice (a) is incorrect. This calculation uses net fixed assets, rather than total assets, in the denominator of the total debt-to-assets ratio.

(Current liabilities + Long-term debt)/Net fixed assets = .60
Long-term debt = .60(Net fixed assets) – Current liabilities
= .60(400) – 140 = $100

Choice (b) is incorrect. This calculation uses net fixed assets, rather than total assets, in the denominator and long-term debt, rather than total debt, in the numerator of the total debt-to-assets ratio.

Long-term debt/Net fixed assets = .60
Long-term debt = .60(Net fixed assets)
= .60(400) = $240

Choice (d) is incorrect. This calculation uses long-term debt, rather than total debt, in the numerator of the total debt-to-assets ratio.

Long-term debt/Total assets = .60
Long-term debt = .60(Total assets)
= .60(1250) = $750

Subject Area: Financial accounting and finance—financial statement analysis. Source: CIA 596, IV-9.

321. (a) Cost of goods sold for 2005 is calculated as follows:

Calculation of cost of goods manufactured during the year	
Raw materials opening balance	$105,000
Plus purchases	300,000
Less returns	20,000
Raw materials available for use	$385,000
Less Dec. 31 balance	130,000
Raw materials used	$255,000
Plus direct labor costs	600,000
Plus manufacturing overhead	750,000
Plus work in process opening balance	220,000
Less Dec. 31 balance	175,000
Cost of goods manufactured during the year	$1,650,000
Calculation of cost of goods sold during the year:	
Finished goods opening balance	$ 90,000
Plus cost of goods manufactured during the year	$1,650,000
Cost of goods available for sale	$1,740,000
Less Dec. 31 finished goods inventory	260,000
Cost of goods sold	$1,480,000

Choice (b) is incorrect. In this incorrect calculation, the purchase returns are not deducted when calculating raw materials available for use.

Calculation of cost of goods manufactured during the year	
Raw materials opening balance	$105,000
Plus purchases	300,000
Raw materials available for use	$405,000
Less Dec. 31 balance	130,000
Raw materials used	$275,000
Plus direct labor costs	600,000
Plus manufacturing overhead	750,000
Plus work in process opening balance	220,000
Less Dec. 31 balance	175,000
Cost of goods manufactured during the year	$1,670,000

Calculation of cost of goods sold during the year	
Finished goods opening balance	$ 90,000
Plus cost of goods manufactured during the year	$1,670,000
Cost of goods available for sale	$1,760,000
Less Dec. 31 finished goods inventory	260,000
Cost of goods sold	$1,500,000

Choice (c) is incorrect. This calculation fails to deduct the ending balance of raw materials when calculating raw materials used during the year.

Calculation of cost of goods manufactured during the year	
Raw materials opening balance	$105,000
Plus purchases	300,000
Less returns	20,000
Raw materials available for use	$385,000
Raw materials used	$385,000
Plus direct labor costs	600,000
Plus manufacturing overhead	750,000
Plus work in process opening balance	220,000
Less Dec. 31 balance	175,000
Cost of goods manufactured during the year	$1,780,000

Calculation of cost of goods sold during the year	
Finished goods opening balance	$ 90,000
Plus cost of goods manufactured during the year	$1,780,000
Cost of goods available for sale	$1,870,000
Less Dec. 31 finished goods inventory	260,000
Cost of goods sold	$1,610,000

Choice (d) is incorrect. This is the cost of goods manufactured during the year, not the cost of goods sold.

Subject Area: Financial accounting and finance—financial statement analysis. Source: CIA 596, IV-14.

322. (c) Inventory turnover is the ratio of cost of goods sold to the average inventory balance.

Average inventory balance

= (Opening inventory + Closing inventory)/2
= (90,000 + 105,000 + 220,000 + 260,000 + 130,000 + 175,000)/2
= $490,000

Inventory Turnover

= Cost of goods sold/Average inventory
= $2,000,000/$490,000 = 4.08 times

Choice (a) is incorrect. This calculation adds all inventory balances, opening and closing, to obtain the inventory figure for the denominator of the turnover ratio as follows:

Inventory

= 90,000 + 105,000 + 220,000 + 260,000 + 130,000 + 175,000
= 415,000 + 565,000 = $980,000

Inventory turnover

= Cost of goods sold/Inventory
= $2,000,000/$980,000 = 2.04 times

Choice (b) is incorrect. This calculation uses the year-end inventory balances, rather than the average inventory level for the year.

Inventory

= 260,000 + 130,000 + 175,000 = $ 565,000

Inventory turnover

= Cost of goods sold/Inventory
= $2,000,000/$565,000 = 3.54 times

Choice (d) is incorrect. This calculation uses the opening inventory balances, rather than the average inventory level for the year.

Inventory

= 90,000 + 105,000 + 220,000 = $ 415,000

Inventory Turnover

= Cost of goods sold/Inventory
= $2,000,000/$415,000 = 4.82 times

Subject Area: Financial accounting and finance—financial statement analysis. Source: CIA 596, IV-15.

323. (d) The dividend-payout ratio is the ratio of dividends paid to net income for the period.

Dividends/Net income = 100/200 = 50%

Choice (a) is incorrect. This is the ratio of dividends paid to the December 31 book value of common equity.

Dividends/(Capital stock + December 31 retained earnings)
= 100/(260 + 250) = 100/510 = 19.6%

Choice (b) is incorrect. This is the ratio of dividends paid to the sum of opening retained earnings and net income.

Dividends/(January 1 retained earnings + Net income)
= 100/(150 + 200) = 100/ 350 = 28.6%

Choice (c) is incorrect. This is the ratio of dividends paid to the December 31 retained earnings.

Dividends/ + December 31 retained earnings
= 100/+ 250 = 100/250 = 40.0%

Subject Area: Financial accounting and finance—financial statement analysis. Source: CIA 596, IV-36.

324. (b) Net working capital is current assets minus current liabilities.

= Cash + Receivables + Inventories – Payables
= 100 + 200 + 50 – 140
= $210

Choice (a) is incorrect. This is net quick assets or cash plus receivables minus current liabilities.

= Cash + Receivables – Payables
= 100+ 200 – 140
= $160

Choice (c) is incorrect. This is gross working capital, or current assets.

= Cash + Receivables + Inventories
= 100 + 200 + 50
= $350

Choice (d) is incorrect. This is current assets plus current liabilities.

= Cash + Receivables + Inventories + Payables
= 100 + 200 + 50 + 140
= $490

Subject Area: Financial accounting and finance—financial statement analysis. Source: CIA 596, IV-37.

325. (a) Return on assets is the ratio of net income to total assets.

Net income/Total assets = 200/950 = 21.052 = 21.1%

Choice (b) is incorrect. This is the ratio of net income to common equity.

Net income/(Capital stock + Retained earnings)
= 200/(260 + 250)
= 200/510 = 39.2%

Choice (c) is incorrect. This is the ratio of income before tax to total assets.

Income before tax/Total assets = 400/950 = 42.1%

Choice (d) is incorrect. This is the ratio of income before interest and tax to total assets.

Income before interest and tax/Total assets = 430/950 = 45.3%

Subject Area: Financial accounting and finance—financial statement analysis. Source: 0CIA 596, IV-38.

326. (c) Times-interest-earned is the ratio of income before interest and tax to interest charges.

Income before interest and tax/Interest expense = 430/30 = 14.33 times

Choice (a) is incorrect. This is the ratio of net income to interest charges.

Net income/Interest expense = 200/30 = 6.67 times

Choice (b) is incorrect. This is the ratio of income before tax to interest charges.

Income before tax/Interest expense = 400/30 = 13.33 times

Choice (d) is incorrect. This is the ratio of sales to interest charges.

Sales/Interest expense = 3,000/30 = 100 times

Subject Area: Financial accounting and finance—financial statement analysis. Source: CIA 596, IV-39.

327. (a) The profit margin is the ratio of net income to sales.

Net income/Sales = 200/3000 = 6.67%

Choice (b) is incorrect. This is the ratio of income before tax to sales.

Income before tax/Sales = 400/3000 = 13.33%

Choice (c) is incorrect. This is the ratio of income before interest and tax to sales.

Income before interest and tax/Sales = 430/3000 = 14.33%

Choice (d) is incorrect. This is the ratio of gross profit to sales.

Gross profit/Sales = 1,400/3000 = 46.67%

Subject Area: Financial accounting and finance—financial statement analysis. Source: CIA 596, IV-40.

328. (b) Net purchases for the period is calculated as follows:

Purchases	$400,000
Less purchase discounts	(40,000)
Less purchase allowances	(15,000)
Less returned purchases	(5,000)
Plus transportation-in	6,000
Net purchases	$346,000

Choice (a) is incorrect. This solution is obtained if transportation-in is omitted from the calculation of net purchases as follows:

Purchases	$400,000
Less purchase discounts	(40,000)
Less purchase allowances	(15,000)
Less returned purchases	(5,000)
Net purchases	$340,000

Choice (c) is incorrect. This solution omits transportation-in and adds, rather than subtracts, purchase allowances as follows:

Purchases	$400,000
Less purchase discounts	(40,000)
Plus purchase allowances	15,000
Less returned purchases	(5,000)
Net purchases	$370,000

Choice (d) is incorrect. This solution adds, rather than subtracts, purchase allowances as follows:

Purchases	$400,000
Less purchase discounts	(40,000)
Plus purchase allowances	15,000
Less returned purchases	(5,000)
Plus transportation-in	6,000
Net purchases	$376,000

Subject Area: Financial accounting and finance—financial statement analysis. Source: CIA 1195, IV-5.

329. (b) Cost of goods sold for the period is calculated as follows:

Cost of goods sold = Opening inventory
+ Purchases – Closing inventory
= $100,000 + $500,000 – $150,000 = $450,000

Choice (a) is incorrect. This solution subtracts, rather than adds opening inventory as follows:

Cost of goods sold = – Opening inventory
+ Purchases – Closing inventory
= –$100,000 + $500,000 – $150,000 = $250,000

Choice (c) is incorrect. This solution subtracts, rather than adds, opening inventory and adds, rather than subtracting, closing inventory as follows:

Cost of goods sold = – Opening inventory
+ Purchases + Closing inventory
= –$100,000 + $500,000 + $150,000 = $550,000

Choice (d) is incorrect. This solution adds, rather than subtracts, closing inventory as follows:

Cost of goods sold = Opening inventory
+ Purchases + Closing inventory
= $100,000 + $500,000 + $150,000 = $750,000

Subject Area: Financial accounting and finance—financial statement analysis. Source: CIA 1195, IV-6.

330. (c) One-third of the customers take advantage of the 5% cash discount and pay on day 10. The remaining two-thirds of the customers pay on day 20. Average days sales outstanding is calculated as

Days sales outstanding = (1/3)(10 days) + (2/3)(20 days) = 17 days

Choice (a) is incorrect because this solution includes only the day's sales outstanding for customers that do not take the cash discount.

Days sales outstanding = (Proportion of customers)(Days till payment)
= (2/3)(20 days) = 13 days

Choice (b) is incorrect because this solution uses five days till payment, rather than ten, for the customers that do take the cash discount.

Days sales outstanding = (1/3)(5 days) + (2/3)(20 days) = 15 days

Choice (d) is incorrect because this solution uses the 20-day collection period for customers not taking the cash discount as the days sales outstanding, rather than the average days till payment of all customers.

Subject Area: Financial accounting and finance—financial statement analysis. Source: CIA 1195, IV-7.

331. (c) Sales for the period can be calculated as follows:

Sales	$1,118,890	= Gross profit/(.30)
Cost of goods sold		
Gross profit	$356,667	= EBIT + Depreciation and administrative expense
Administrative expense	$40,000	
Depreciation expense	$50,000	= $500,000 (1/10)
Earnings before interest and tax	$266,666	= EBT + Interest
Interest expense	$100,000	= $1,000,000 (10%)
Earnings before tax	$166,667	= $100,000/(1 – Tax rate)
Tax expense		
Net income	$100,000	

Choice (a) is incorrect because this solution uses a gross profit percentage equal to the tax rate, of 40%, rather than 30% as stated. Sales are then calculated as follows:

Sales	$891,667	= Gross profit/(.40)
Cost of goods sold		
Gross profit	$356,667	= EBIT + Depreciation and administrative expense
Administrative expense	$40,000	
Depreciation expense	$50,000	= $500,000 (1/10)
Earnings before interest and tax	$266,666	= EBT + Interest
Interest expense	$100,000	= $1,000,000 (10%)
Earnings before tax	$166,667	= $100,000/(1 – Tax rate)
Tax expense		
Net income	$100,000	

Choice (b) is incorrect because this solution incorrectly calculates Earnings Before Tax as Net Income divided by the tax rate and also incorrectly calculates Sales as Gross Profit divided by the tax rate percentage, as follows:

Sales	$1,100,000	= Gross profit/(.40)
Cost of goods sold		
Gross profit	$440,000	= EBIT + Depreciation and administrative expense
Administrative expense	$40,000	
Depreciation expense	$50,000	= $500,000 (1/10)
Earnings before interest and tax	$350,000	= EBT + Interest
Interest expense	$100,000	= $1,000,000 (10%)
Earnings before tax	$250,000	= $100,000/(Tax rate)
Tax expense		
Net income	$100,000	

Choice (d) is incorrect because this solution incorrectly calculates Earnings Before Tax as Net Income divided by the tax rate, as follows:

Sales	$1,466,667	= Gross profit/(.30)
Cost of goods sold		
Gross profit	$440,000	= EBIT + Depreciation and administrative expense
Administrative expense	$40,000	
Depreciation expense	$50,000	= $500,000 (1/10)
Earnings before interest and tax	$350,000	= EBT + Interest
Interest expense	$100,000	= $1,000,000 (10%)
Earnings before tax	$250,000	= $100,000/(tax rate)
Tax expense		
Net income	$100,000	

Subject Area: Financial accounting and finance—financial statement analysis. Source: CIA 1195, IV-12.

332. (b) The calculation of current assets is done in two parts. First, total assets is calculated using the return on assets ratio as follows:

Return on total assets = Net income/Total assets = .03
$100,000/Total assets = .03
Total assets = $100,000/.03 = $3,333,333

Then current assets are calculated by deducting fixed assets from total assets.

Current assets + Other assets = Total assets
Current assets = Total assets – Other assets
Current assets = $3,333,333 – $300,000 = $3,033,333

Choice (a) is incorrect. This solution is obtained by incorrectly defining working capital as current assets minus long term debt, as follows:

Working capital = Current assets – Long term debt
$2,000,000 = Current assets – $1,000,000
Current assets = $2,000,000 – $1,000,000 = $1,000,000

Choice (c) is incorrect because this is the amount of total assets. Choice (d) is incorrect because this solution is the result of incorrectly calculating current assets as the sum of total and other assets, as follows:

Current assets + Other assets = Total assets
Current assets = Total assets + Other assets
Current assets = $3,333,333+ $300,000 = $3,633,333

Subject Area: Financial accounting and finance—financial statement analysis. Source: CIA 1195, IV-13.

333. (c). Times-interest-earned is calculated by dividing earnings before tax and interest charges by the amount of the interest charges.

Earnings before tax = Net income/(1 – tax rate)
= $100,000/.6= $166,667
Interest = Amount of debt × Interest cost percentage
= 1,000,000(.10) = $100,000
Earnings before interest and tax = Earnings before tax + Interest
= $166,667 + $100,000 = $266,667
Times-interest-earned = Earnings before interest and tax/Interest
= $266,667/$100,000 = 2.667 times

Choice (a) is incorrect. This solution uses earnings before tax, rather than earnings before interest and tax, in the calculation of times-interest-earned as follows:

Earnings before tax = Net income/(1 – tax rate)
= $100,000/.6 = $166,667
Interest = Amount of debt × Interest cost percentage
= $1,000,000(.10) = $100,000
Times-interest-earned = Earnings before tax/Interest
= $166,667/$100,000 = 1.667 times

Choice (b) is incorrect. This solution calculates earnings before tax as net income divided by the tax rate and also uses earnings before tax rather than earnings before interest and tax in calculating times-interest-earned as follows:

Earnings before tax = Net Income/(Tax rate) = $100,000/.4 = $250,000
Interest = Amount of debt × Interest cost percentage
= $1,000,000(.10) = $100,000
Times-interest-earned = Earnings before tax/Interest
= $250,000/$100,000 = 2.5 times

Choice (d) is incorrect. This solution calculates earnings before tax as net income divided by the tax rate, as follows:

Earnings before tax = Net income/(Tax rate) = $100,000/.4 = $250,000
Interest = Amount of debt × Interest cost percentage
= $1,000,000(.10) = $100,000
Earnings before interest and tax = Earnings before tax + Interest
= $250,000 + $100,000 = $350,000
Times-interest-earned = Earnings before interest and tax/Interest
= $350,000/$100,000 = 3.5 times

Subject Area: Financial accounting and finance—financial statement analysis. Source: CIA 1195, IV-14.

334. (b) The price-earnings ratio is the share price divided by the earnings per share.

Share price/Earnings per share
= Share price/(Dividends per share/Payout percentage)
= $20/($2/.40) = $20/$5 = 4

Choice (a) is incorrect. This solution calculates the price-to-earnings ratio incorrectly as earnings per share divided by dividends per share as follows:

Earnings per share/Dividends per share
= (Dividends per share/Payout percentage)/Dividends per share
= 1/Payout percentage = ($2/.40)/$2 = 1/.40 = 2.5

Choice (c) is incorrect. This solution is obtained by calculating the price-to-earnings ratio incorrectly as a price-to-dividends ratio as follows:

Price per share/Dividend per share = $20/$2 = 10

Choice (d) is incorrect. This solution is obtained by incorrectly calculating the price-to-earnings ratio as the price per share divided by the dividend payout percentage.

Price per share/Payout percentage = 20/.40 = 50

Subject Area: Financial accounting and finance—financial statement analysis. Source: CIA 1195, IV-32.

335. (a) The level of sales for the company is calculated using both ratios as follows:

Total assets = Total debt/.70 = $1,000,000/.70 = $1,428,571.4
Sales = 3.5 (Total assets) = 3.5(1,428,571.4) = $5,000,000.00

Choice (b) is incorrect. This solution is obtained if total assets is calculated as total debt multiplied by .70, rather than divided by .70, as follows:

Total assets = Total debt(.70) = $1,000,000(.70) = $700,000
Sales = 3.5(Total assets) = 3.5(700,000) = $2,450,000

Choice (c) is incorrect. This solution is obtained if sales is calculated by dividing total assets by 3.5, rather than multiplying by 3.5, as follows:

Total assets = Total debt/.70 = $1,000,000/.70 = $1,428,571.4
Sales = Total assets/3.5 = 1,428,571.4/3.5 = $408,163.26

Choice (d) is incorrect. This solution is obtained by misinterpreting both ratios as their reciprocal, so that in the first part of the calculation total assets is calculated as total debt multiplied by .70 and in the second part of the calculation sales is calculated by dividing total assets by 3.5, as follows:

Total assets = Total debt (.70) = $1,000,000(.70) = $700,000
Sales = Total assets/3.5 = 700,000/3.5 = $200,000

Subject Area: Financial accounting and finance—financial statement analysis. Source: CIA 1195, IV-35.

336. (d) The current ratio is a measure of the liquidity of a company. It is the ratio of the current assets to the current liabilities. Liquidity is the ability of a company to meet its current obligations. Choice (a) is incorrect because days sales outstanding is used to assess the efficiency of asset management, not the liquidity of a company. Choice (b) is incorrect because the debt-to-assets ratio is used to assess the debt management activities of a company. Choice (c) is incorrect because profit margin is an indicator of the profitability of a company.

Subject Area: Financial accounting and finance—financial statement analysis. Source: CIA 1195, IV-36.

337. (a) The item is not an expense. It is appropriately recorded as a loss. Choice (b) is incorrect because the scenario already indicates that no restitution will be made. Thus, recording the item as a receivable, then writing it off, is not consistent with the substance of the event that has taken place. Choice (c) is incorrect because it would not be proper to classify the loss as a cost of goods sold. While some inventory shrinkage is expected in the normal course of processing, fraud is not expected. Therefore, the item should be recorded as a loss. Choice (d) is incorrect because it is not properly recorded to retained earnings.

Subject Area: Financial accounting and finance—financial statement analysis. Source: CIA 595, IV-29.

338. (a) Given that the quick ratio is equal to 2, the balance of accounts receivable can be calculated as follows:

$$\text{Quick ratio} = \frac{\text{Cash + Accounts receivable}}{\text{Current liabilities}}$$

$$2 = \frac{\text{Cash + Accounts receivable}}{\text{Accounts payable}}$$

$$2 = \frac{\text{100 + Accounts receivable}}{100}$$

Accounts receivable = 2(100) – 100 = 100

Choice (b) is incorrect. This is the answer if cash is excluded from the numerator.

$$\text{Quick ratio} = \frac{\text{Accounts receivable}}{\text{Current liabilities}}$$

$$2 = \frac{\text{Accounts receivable}}{\text{Accounts payable}}$$

$$2 = \frac{\text{Accounts receivable}}{100}$$

Accounts receivable = 2(100) = 200

Choice (c) is incorrect. This is the answer if long-term debt is used in the denominator rather than current liabilities:

$$\text{Quick ratio} = \frac{\text{Cash + Accounts receivable}}{\text{Long-term debt}}$$

$$2 = \frac{\text{100 + Accounts receivable}}{200}$$

Accounts receivable = 2(200) – 100 = 300

Choice (d) is incorrect. This is the answer if total liabilities is used in the denominator rather than current liabilities.

$$\text{Quick ratio} = \frac{\text{Cash + Accounts receivable}}{\text{Total liabilities}}$$

$$2 = \frac{\text{100 + Accounts receivable}}{\text{Long-term debt + Accounts payable}}$$

$$2 = \frac{\text{100 + Accounts receivable}}{200 + 100}$$

Accounts receivable = 2(300) – 100 = 500

Subject Area: Financial accounting and finance—financial statement analysis. Source: CIA 595, IV-31.

339. (b) The return on equity for Company B is calculated as follows:

$$\text{Return on equity} = \frac{\text{Net income}}{\text{Common stock + Retained earnings}}$$

95/(200 + 100) = 32%

Choice (a) is incorrect. This is the answer if the return on equity is calculated for Company A rather than for Company B.

$$\text{Return on equity} = \frac{\text{Net income}}{\text{Common stock + Retained earnings}}$$

= 40/(100 + 150) = 16%

Choice (c) is incorrect. This is the answer if retained earnings is omitted from the denominator.

$$\text{Return on equity} = \frac{\text{Net income}}{\text{Common stock}}$$

95/200 = 48%

Choice (d) is incorrect. This is the answer if common stock is omitted from the denominator.

$$\text{Return on equity} = \frac{\text{Net income}}{\text{Retained earnings}}$$

= 95/100 = 95%

Subject Area: Financial accounting and finance—financial statement analysis. Source: CIA 595, IV-32.

340. (c) Days sales outstanding for Company B is calculated as follows:

$$\text{Days sales outstanding} = \frac{\text{Accounts receivable}}{\text{Average sales/Day}}$$

$$= \frac{\text{Accounts receivable}}{\text{Sales/365}}$$

= 100/(5800/365) = 100/15.89 = 6 days

Choice (a) is incorrect. This is the answer if sales is used in the denominator rather than average sales per day.

$$\text{Days sales outstanding} = \frac{\text{Accounts receivable}}{\text{Sales}}$$

= 100/5800 = 0

Choice (b) is incorrect. This is the answer if accounts payable is used in the numerator rather than accounts receivable.

$$\text{Days sales outstanding} = \frac{\text{Accounts receivable}}{\text{Average sales/Day}}$$

$$= \frac{\text{Accounts payable}}{\text{Sales/365}}$$

$$= 50/(5800/365) = 50/15.89 = 3 \text{ days}$$

Choice (d) is incorrect. This is the answer if average cost of goods sold per day is used in the denominator rather than average sales per day.

$$\text{Days sales outstanding} = \frac{\text{Accounts receivable}}{\text{Average cost of goods sold/Day}}$$

$$= \frac{\text{Accounts receivable}}{\text{Cost of goods sold/365}}$$

$$= 100/(5000/365) = 100/13.699 = 7 \text{ days}$$

Subject Area: Financial accounting and finance—financial statement analysis. Source: CIA 595, IV-33.

341. (**b**) The times-interest-earned ratio for Company A is calculated as follows:

$$\text{Times-interest-earned} = \frac{\text{Earnings before interest and tax}}{\text{Interest expense}}$$

where earnings before interest and tax is calculated as

Sales – Cost of goods sold – Administrative expense
– Depreciation expense
= 600 – 300 – 100 – 100 = 100
Times-interest-earned = 100/20 = 5 times

Choice (a) is incorrect. This is the answer if earnings before tax rather than earnings before interest and tax is used in the formula as follows:

$$\text{Times-interest-earned} = \frac{\text{Earnings before tax}}{\text{Interest expense}}$$

where earnings before tax is calculated as

Sales – Cost of goods sold – Administrative expense
– Depreciation expense – Interest expense
= 600 – 300 – 100 – 100 – 20 = 80
Times-interest-earned = 80/20 = 4 times

Choice (c) is incorrect. This is the answer if depreciation expense is not deducted in calculating earnings before interest and tax.

$$\text{Times-interest-earned} = \frac{\text{Earnings before tax}}{\text{Interest expense}}$$

where earnings before interest and tax is calculated incorrectly as

Sales – Cost of goods sold – Administrative expense
= 600 – 300 – 100 = 200
Times-interest-earned = 200/20 = 10 times

Choice (d) is incorrect. This is the answer if gross margin is used in the numerator rather than earnings before interest and tax.

$$\text{Times-interest-earned} = \frac{\text{Sales – Cost of goods sold}}{\text{Interest expense}}$$

$$= (600 - 300)/20 = 15 \text{ times}$$

Subject Area: Financial accounting and finance—financial statement analysis. Source: CIA 595, IV-34.

342. (**b**) The degree of financial leverage for Company B is calculated as follows:

$$\text{Degree of financial leverage} = \frac{\text{EBIT}}{\text{EBIT – Interest expense}}$$

where EBIT is calculated as

EBIT = Sales – Cost of goods sold – Administrative expense
– Depreciation expense
= 5800 – 5000 – 500 – 100 = 200
Degree of financial leverage = 200/(200 – 10) = 1.05

Choice (a) is incorrect. This is the answer if depreciation expense is omitted from the calculation of earnings before interest and taxes (EBIT).

$$\text{Degree of financial leverage} = \frac{\text{EBIT}}{\text{EBIT – Interest expense}}$$

where EBIT is calculated incorrectly as

EBIT = Sales – Cost of goods sold – Administrative expense
= 5800 – 5000 – 500 = 300
Degree of financial leverage = 300/(300 – 10) = 1.03

Choice (c) is incorrect. This is the answer if net income is used instead of EBIT in the formula as follows:

$$\text{Degree of financial leverage} = \frac{\text{Net income}}{\text{Net income – Interest expense}}$$

Degree of financial leverage = 95/(95 – 10) = 1.12

Choice (d) is incorrect. This is the answer if the degree of financial leverage is calculated for Company A rather than for Company B.

$$\text{Degree of financial leverage} = \frac{\text{EBIT}}{\text{EBIT – Interest expense}}$$

where EBIT is calculated as

EBIT = Sales – Cost of goods sold – Administrative expense
– Depreciation expense
= 600 – 300 – 100 – 100 = 100
Degree of financial leverage = 100/(100 – 20) = 1.25

Subject Area: Financial accounting and finance—financial statement analysis. Source: CIA 595, IV-35.

343. (**c**) The book value per share for Company A is calculated as follows:

$$\text{Book value per share} = \frac{\text{Common stock + Retained earnings}}{\text{No. of shares}}$$

$$= (100 + 150)/60 = 4.17$$

Choice (a) is incorrect. This is the answer if retained earnings are omitted from the numerator.

$$\text{Book value per share} = \frac{\text{Common stock}}{\text{No. of shares}} = 100/60 = 1.67$$

Choice (b) is incorrect. This is the answer if common stock is omitted from the numerator.

$$\text{Book value per share} = \frac{\text{Retained earnings}}{\text{No. of shares}} = 150/60 = 2.50$$

Choice (d) is incorrect. This is the answer if the book value per share is calculated for Company B rather than for Company A.

$$\text{Book value per share} = \frac{\text{Common stock + Retained earnings}}{\text{No. of shares}}$$

$$= (200 + 100)/60 = 5.00$$

Subject Area: Financial accounting and finance—financial statement analysis. Source: CIA 595, IV-36.

344. (**a**) Given that the cost of goods sold for the year was \$250,000, purchases totaled \$150,000 and opening inventory was $200,000, the balance of closing inventory can be calculated as follows:

Cost of goods sold = Opening inventory + Purchases
– Closing inventory
Closing inventory = Opening inventory + Purchases
– Cost of goods sold
= $200,000 + $150,000 – $250,000 = $100,000

Choice (b) is incorrect. The cost of goods sold is $250,000. Choice (c) is incorrect. This solution calculates cost of goods sold incorrectly, reversing the signs for opening and closing inventory as follows:

Cost of goods sold = Closing inventory + Purchases
– Opening inventory
Closing inventory = Cost of goods sold – Purchases
+ Opening inventory
= $250,000 – $150,000 + $200,000 = $300,000

Choice (d) is incorrect. This solution calculates cost of goods sold incorrectly, omitting closing inventory from the calculation as follows:

Cost of goods sold = Purchases + Opening inventory
= $150,000 + $200,000 = $350,000

Subject Area: Financial accounting and finance—financial statement analysis. Source: CIA 1194, IV-1.

345. (d) Both cost of goods sold and net earnings are unaffected by an increase in purchases at year-end. There would be no additional carrying costs if the additional purchase occurred on December 31. Choice (a) is incorrect. All else equal, if purchases are greater but the level of sales does not change, then purchases and closing inventory will increase by the same amount. Since cost of goods sold is equal to opening inventory plus purchases minus closing inventory, cost of goods sold will not increase if purchases and closing inventory increase by the same amount. Net income will not be affected. Choice (b) is incorrect. Cost of goods sold is unaffected if purchases for the year increase, since closing inventory will increase by the same amount. Further, if cost of goods sold did increase, the net earnings would decline rather than increase. Choice (c) is incorrect. Cost of goods sold is unaffected if purchases for the year increase, since closing inventory will increase by the same amount.

Subject Area: Financial accounting and finance—financial statement analysis. Source: CIA 1194, IV-2.

346. (a) Dividends for the year will be 25% of net income.

Sales	$500,000
Cost of sales	250,000
General & admin. expense	25,000
Interest expense (.10)(400,000)	40,000
Depreciation expense (600,000/6)	100,000
Earnings before tax	$ 85,000
Tax (50%)	42,500
Net income	$ 42,500
Dividend payout (25%)	10,625

Choice (b) is incorrect. This solution uses a 50% payout ratio.

Dividends = .5 Net income = .5(42,500) = $21,250

Choice (c) is incorrect. This solution omits depreciation expense.

Sales	$500,000
Cost of sales	250,000
General & admin. expense	25,000
Interest expense (.10)(400,000)	40,000
Earnings before tax	$185,000
Tax (50%)	92,500
Net income	$ 92,500
Dividend payout (25%)	23,125

Choice (d) is incorrect. This solution uses a 50% payout ratio and ignores income taxes.

Dividends = .5 Earnings before tax = .5 (85,000) = $42,500

Subject Area: Financial accounting and finance—financial statement analysis. Source: CIA 1194, IV-3.

347. (a) If the company pays out less of its earnings as dividends and retains more of its earnings for reinvestment, then both the cash balance and the retained earnings balance will increase. Choice (b) is incorrect. Retained earnings will be higher if dividend payout is lower. Choice (c) is incorrect. The cash balance will be higher if dividend payout is lower. Choice (d) is incorrect. Both the cash balance and the retained earnings balances will be higher if the company has a lower dividend payout percentage.

Subject Area: Financial accounting and finance—financial statement analysis. Source: CIA 1194, IV-4.

348. (b) Faster collection of receivables would shift assets from the receivables to the cash account and the total asset level would not change. Choice (a) is incorrect because faster collection of receivables would increase the cash balance and there would be an equal, offsetting reduction in the accounts receivable balance so total assets would be unaffected. Choice (c) is incorrect because faster collection of receivables would increase, not decrease, the cash balance and the level of total assets would not be affected. Choice (d) is incorrect because faster collection of receivables would increase, not decrease, the cash balance.

Subject Area: Financial accounting and finance—financial statement analysis. Source: CIA 1194, IV-5.

349. (c) The common stock is not affected by a change in tax rate since it represents contributed capital. Dividends paid will increase because they are a percentage of after-tax earnings. Choices (a), (b), and (d) are incorrect because the common stock is not affected and dividends will increase.

Subject Area: Financial accounting and finance—financial statement analysis. Source: CIA 1194, IV-6.

350. (c) Accounts payable and notes payable are current liabilities. The acid-test ratio is calculated as

(Current assets – Inventories)/Current liabilities
= ($400 – $100)/$175 = 1.71

Choice (a) is incorrect. This solution uses total liabilities, rather than current liabilities, in the denominator as follows:

Total liabilities = Accounts payable + Notes payable
+ Long term debt = $100 + $75 + $200 = $375
(Current assets – Inventory)/Total liabilities
= ($400 – $100)/$375 = .80

Choice (b) is incorrect. This solution calculates the ratio using working capital in the numerator as follows:

(Current assets – Current liabilities)/Current liabilities
= ($400 – $175)/$175 = 1.29

Choice (d) is incorrect. This solution uses the current ratio, rather than the acid-test ratio, as follows:

Current assets/Current liabilities = $400/$175 = 2.29

Subject Area: Financial accounting and finance—financial statement analysis. Source: CIA 1194, IV-12.

351. (a) The relationship between return on assets, profit margin and asset turnover is as follows:

Return on assets = Profit margin × Asset turnover

So if one company has higher return on assets than the other does, it must have higher profit margin, higher asset turnover, or both. Choice (b) is incorrect. Higher, not lower, asset turnover would contribute to a higher return on assets. Choice (c) is incorrect. Higher, not lower, profit margin on sales would contribute to a higher return on assets. Choice (d) is incorrect. Higher profit margin and higher asset turnover would contribute to higher return on assets.

Subject Area: Financial accounting and finance—financial statement analysis. Source: CIA 1194, IV-14.

352. (a) The acid-test ratio equals (Current assets – Inventories)/Current liabilities. Therefore, if the acid-test ratio equals 2, current assets equal $5,000 and inventory equals $2,000; the value of current liabilities is $1,500(2 = ($5,000 – $2,000)/$1,500). Choice (b) is incorrect because current liabilities of $2,500 indicate a current ratio (Current assets/Current liabilities) of 2, not an acid-test ratio of 2. Choice (c) is incorrect because current assets plus inventory divided by current liabilities of $3,500 equals 2, but this is not the acid-test ratio. Choice (d) is incorrect because current liabilities of $6,000 divided by current assets minus inventory equals 2, but this is not the acid-test ratio.

Subject Area: Financial accounting and finance—financial statement analysis. Source: CIA 590, IV-47.

353. (a) Because total assets will decline without any impact on sales, the total assets turnover ratio will increase. In addition, a reduced debt level should cause a reduction in annual interest payments paid on debt, so that the times-interest-earned ratio should increase. Choice (b) is incorrect because the times-interest-earned ratio will decrease. Choice (c) is incorrect because the total assets turnover ratio will increase. Choice (d) is incorrect because the total assets turnover ratio will increase and the times-interest-earned ratio will increase.

Subject Area: Financial accounting and finance—financial statement analysis. Source: CIA 590, IV-59.

354. (b) Computations follow:

$$\frac{\text{Quick assets}}{\text{Current liabilities}} = \text{Acid-test ratio}$$

$$\frac{\$208{,}000}{\text{Current liabilities}} = 2.6$$

$$\text{Current liabilities} = \frac{\$208{,}000}{2.6} = \underline{\$80{,}000}$$

Choice (a) is incorrect because this answer selection incorrectly reflects the computation quick assets ($208,000) divided by the current ratio (3.5). Choice (c) is incorrect because this answer selection reflects the incorrect computation of average total assets ($1,200,000) divided by the current ratio (3.5). Choice (d) is incorrect because this answer selection reflects the incorrect computation of quick assets ($208,000) multiplied by the excess of the current ratio (3.5) over the acid-test ratio (2.6).

Subject Area: Financial accounting and finance—financial statement analysis. Source: CIA 1190, IV-40.

355. (a) Computations follow:

$$\frac{\$208{,}000}{\text{Current liabilities}} = 2.6$$

$$\frac{\$208{,}000}{2.6} = \text{Current liabilities} = \underline{\$80{,}000}$$

$$\frac{\text{Current assets}}{\text{Current liabilities}} = \text{Current ratio}$$

$$\frac{\text{Current assets}}{\$80{,}000} = 3.5$$

$$\text{Current assets} = 3.5 \times \$80{,}000 = \$280{,}000$$

$$\text{Current assets} - \text{Quick assets} = \text{Inventory}$$
$$\$280{,}000 \quad \$208{,}000 \quad \$72{,}000$$

Choice (b) is incorrect because this answer selection reflects the incorrect computation of the current ratio (3.5) minus the acid-test ratio (2.6) multiplied by quick assets ($208,000). Choice (c) is incorrect because this answer selection reflects the incorrect computation of quick assets ($208,000) divided by the excess of the current ratio (3.5) over the quick ratio (2.6). Choice (d) is incorrect because this answer selection reflects the incorrect computation of cost of sales ($990,000) divided by the current ratio (3.5).

Subject Area: Financial accounting and finance—financial statement analysis. Source: CIA 1190, IV-41.

356. (d) Computations follow:

$$\frac{\text{Net sales}}{\text{Average total assets}} = \frac{\$1{,}800{,}000}{\$1{,}200{,}000} = 1.5$$

Choice (a) is incorrect because this answer reflects the incorrect computation of gross profit ($1,800,000 – $990,000) divided by average total assets ($1,200,000). Choice (b) is incorrect because this answer reflects the incorrect computation of cost of sales ($990,000) divided by average total assets ($1,200,000). Choice (c) is incorrect because this answer reflects the incorrect computation of average total assets ($1,200,000) divided by cost of sales ($990,000).

Subject Area: Financial accounting and finance—financial statement analysis. Source: CIA 1190, IV-42.

Cost of Capital Evaluation

357. (d) A weighted-average of the costs of all financing sources should be used, with the weights determined by the usual financing proportions. The terms of any financing raised at the time of initiating a particular project does not represent the cost of capital for the firm. Choice (a) is incorrect because the cost of capital is a composite, or weighted-average, of all financing sources in their usual proportions. The cost of capital should also be calculated on an after-tax basis. Choices (b) and (c) are incorrect because the cost of capital is a composite, or weighted-average, of all financing sources in their usual proportions. It includes both the after-tax cost of debt and the cost of equity financing.

Subject Area: Financial accounting and finance—cost of capital evaluation. Source: CIA Model Exam 2002, IV-52.

358. (c) The marginal cost of equity financing is 16% and the after-tax cost of new debt financing is 9% (1 – .5) or 4.5%. Choice (a) is incorrect because 15% is the cost of existing equity financing. Choice (b) is incorrect because these are the costs of existing debt and equity financing and the question asks for the incremental costs of both financing sources. Choice (d) is incorrect because 5% is the after-tax cost of existing debt financing.

Subject Area: Financial accounting and finance—cost of capital evaluation. Source: CIA 1196, IV-46.

359. (b) Newly issued or "external" common equity is more costly than retained earnings because the company incurs issuance costs when raising new, outside funds. Choice (a) is incorrect because the cost of retained earnings is the rate of return stockholders require on equity capital the firm obtains by retaining earnings. The opportunity cost of retained funds will be positive. Choices (c) and (d) are incorrect because retained earnings will always be less costly than external equity financing because earnings retention does not require the payment of issuance costs.

Subject Area: Financial accounting and finance—cost of capital evaluation. Source: CIA 1195, IV-43.

360. (a) When a company is at its optimal capital structure it has minimized its weighted-average cost of capital. Choices (b) and (c) are incorrect because the optimal capital structure always calls for a debt ratio which is lower than the one that maximizes expected earnings per share, so a company at its optimal capital structure will **not** have maximized or minimized its earnings per share. Choice (d) is incorrect because a firm at its optimal capital structure will have minimized, not maximized, its weighted-average cost of capital.

Subject Area: Financial accounting and finance—cost of capital evaluation. Source: CIA 595, IV-58.

361. (b) The weighted-average cost of capital is calculated as follows:

= (Weight of equity)(Cost of equity) +
(Weight of debt)(Before-tax cost of debt)(1 – Tax rate)
= (.7)(.12) + (.3)(.08)(1 – .3) = .084 + .0168 = 10%

Choice (a) is incorrect because 8% is the before-tax cost of debt. Choice (c) is incorrect because this solution uses the before-tax cost of debt rather than the after-tax cost of debt.

= (Weight of equity)(Cost of equity) +
(Weight of debt)(Before-tax cost of debt)
= (.7)(.12) + (.3)(.08) = .084 + .024 = 11%

Choice (d) is incorrect because 12% is the cost of equity.

Subject Area: Financial accounting and finance—cost of capital evaluation. Source: CIA 1194, IV-35.

362. (d) Taxes payable will be higher under arrangement # 1 because with lower interest expense, taxable income will be higher.

	#1	#2
Sales revenue	$500,000	$500,000
Cost of sales	200,000	200,000
General & admin. expense	100,000	100,000
Interest expense	24,000	70,000
Taxable income	$176,000	$130,000
Taxes payable (30%)	52,800	39,000

Choice (a) is incorrect because expected gross margin is unaffected by the choice of financing arrangement. Choice (b) is incorrect because the degree of operating leverage is lower under arrangement #2. Choice (c) is incorrect because interest expense will be higher under arrangement #2. Under arrangement #1 interest expense will be $300,000(0.08) = $24,000, while under arrangement # 2 interest expense will be $700,000 (0.10) =$70,000 per annum.

Subject Area: Financial accounting and finance—cost of capital evaluation. Source: CIA 1194, IV-36.

363. (d) The degree of financial leverage for financial arrangement #2 is calculated as follows. Note: EBIT is an acronym for earnings before interest and taxes.

$$\frac{\text{EBIT}}{\text{EBIT} - \text{Interest}} = \frac{\$200{,}000}{\$200{,}000 - \$70{,}000} = 1.54$$

Choice (a) is incorrect because this solution uses the after-tax interest cost in the denominator of the formula and includes the interest expense under arrangement #1 rather than arrangement #2.

$$\frac{\text{EBIT}}{\text{EBIT} - \text{Interest}\ (1 - \text{Tax rate})} = \frac{\$200{,}000}{\$200{,}000 - \$24{,}000(.7)} = 1.09$$

Choice (b) is incorrect because this is the degree of financial leverage for financial arrangement # 1.

$$\frac{\text{EBIT}}{\text{EBIT} - \text{Interest}} = \frac{\$200{,}000}{\$200{,}000 - \$24{,}000} = 1.14$$

Choice (c) is incorrect because this solution uses the after-tax interest cost in the denominator of the formula:

Subject Area: Financial accounting and finance—cost of capital evaluation. Source: CIA 1194, IV-37.

$$\frac{\text{EBIT}}{\text{EBIT} - \text{Interest}\ (1 - \text{Tax rate})} = \frac{\$200{,}000}{\$200{,}000 - \$70{,}000(.7)} = 1.32$$

364. (a) Return on equity is calculated as net income divided by the amount of equity invested. The debt ratio is the amount of debt financing divided by the total assets. Calculations of the two ratios for both financing arrangements are as follows:

	#1	#2
Sales revenue	$500,000	$500,000
Cost of sales	200,000	200,000
General & admin. expense	100,000	100,000
Interest expense	24,000	70,000
Taxable income	$176,000	$130,000
Tax payable (30%)	52,800	39,000
Net income	$123,200	$ 91,000
Equity invested	$700,000	$300,000
Return on equity	123,200 / 700,000	91,000 / 300,000
	17.6%	30.3%
Debt ratio	300,000 / 1,000,000	700,000 / 1,000,000
	03	0.7

Therefore, by definition, choices (b), (c), and (d) are incorrect.

Subject Area: Financial accounting and finance—cost of capital evaluation. Source: CIA 1194, IV-38.

365. (c) The marginal cost of debt is calculated as

(Cost of new debt) × (1 – Marginal tax rate)

or

$$K_d(1 - T) = K_d - K_dT$$

Choice (a) is incorrect because the marginal cost of debt financing is the interest rate on new debt less the firm's marginal tax rate multiplied by the interest rate. Choice (b) is incorrect because the marginal or incremental cost of debt to the firm is based on the cost of newly issued debt, not on the cost of outstanding debt. Choice (d) is incorrect. (1) The marginal or incremental cost of debt to the firm is based on the cost of newly issued debt, not on the cost of outstanding debt and because (2) the marginal cost of debt financing is the interest rate on new debt less the firm's marginal tax rate multiplied by the interest rate.

Subject Area: Financial accounting and finance—cost of capital evaluation. Source: CIA 594, IV-48.

366. (d) The cost of new equity is calculated by adding the expected dividend yield, based on the net proceeds of the new issue, to the expected dividend growth rate. The expected dividend at the end of the period equals the dividend at time zero times one plus the expected dividend growth rate. Net proceeds received by the firm when issuing one common share is the market price of a share times one minus the flotation cost percentage. Flotation costs include items such as underwriting fees, printing, and advertising costs.

The calculation of the cost of new equity is as follows:

$$\text{Cost of equity} = \frac{\text{Expected dividend at end of period}}{\text{Net proceeds issuing one share}} + \text{Dividend growth rate}$$
$$= \frac{\$1(1 + \text{Dividend growth rate})}{\$25(1 - .05)} + \text{Dividend growth rate}$$
$$= \$1(1.1)/\$23.75 + .10$$
$$= .0463 + .10 = 14.63\%$$

Choice (a) is incorrect because this solution does not use the end of period expected dividend or the net proceeds of the issue in calculating the dividend yield:

$$\text{Cost of equity} = \frac{\text{Dividend at time zero}}{\text{Market price}} + \text{Dividend growth rate}$$
$$= \$1/\$25 + .10$$
$$= .04 + .10 = 14.00\%$$

Choice (b) is incorrect because this solution does not use the end of period expected dividend in calculating the dividend yield.

$$\text{Cost of equity} = \frac{\text{Dividend at time zero}}{\text{Net proceeds}} + \text{Dividend growth rate}$$
$$= \$1/\$23.75 + .10$$
$$= .0421 + .10 = 14.21\%$$

Choice (c) is incorrect because this solution does not use net proceeds in calculating the dividend yield.

$$\text{Cost of equity} = \frac{\text{Expected dividend at end of period}}{\text{Market price}} + \text{Dividend growth rate}$$
$$= \$1.10/\$25 + .10$$
$$= .044 + .10 = 14.40\%$$

Subject Area: Financial accounting and finance—cost of capital evaluation. Source: CIA 594, IV-80.

367. (b) Determined as the risk-free rate + (Beta times the difference between the market return and risk-free rate). That is, (8) + [0.9 × (15 – 8)] = 14.3%. Choice (a) is incorrect because this answer results when excluding the risk-free rate portion of the equation. That is, (15 – 8) × 0.9 = 6.3%. Choice (c) is incorrect because this answer results from excluding the stock's beta. That is, (8) + (15 – 8) = 15.0%. Choice (d) is incorrect because this answer results when excluding the risk-free rate in computing the risk premium of the stock. That is, (8) + (0.9 × 15) = 21.5%.

Subject Area: Financial accounting and finance—cost of capital evaluation. Source: CIA 1191, IV-52.

368. (c) Systematic risk is the component of the total risk of a security that cannot be eliminated through diversification and is relevant to valuation. Choice (a) is incorrect because "company-specific" risk can be eliminated through portfolio diversification and is not relevant to the valuation of the security. Choice (b) is incorrect because "diversifiable" risk can be eliminated through portfolio diversification and is not relevant to the valuation of the security. Choice (d) is incorrect because only the systematic component of total risk is relevant to security valuation.

Subject Area: Financial accounting and finance—cost of capital evaluation. CIA 1194, IV-53.

369. (d) Maximizing a firm's stock price is analogous to maximizing shareholder wealth. Choice (a) is incorrect because a very high debt ratio could minimize the firm's tax liability but may not maximize shareholder wealth, because the risk level would be unacceptable. Choice (b) is incorrect because a very low debt ratio could minimize the firm's risk but may not maximize shareholder wealth, because the potential return to shareholders would be unacceptable. Choice (c) is incorrect because a maximum degree of financial leverage may result in excessive risk and therefore would not maximize shareholder wealth.

Subject Area: Financial accounting and finance—cost of capital evaluation. Source: CIA 590, IV-49.

370. (b) The optimal capital structure for a company is that which maximizes shareholder wealth. It requires selecting the best mix of preferred stock, common stock, and long-term debt. Choice (a) is incorrect because this answer ignores equity. Choice (c) is incorrect because the decision does not directly involve assets. Choice (d) is incorrect because the decision involves equity, but does not focus on the type of equity used.

Subject Area: Financial accounting and finance—cost of capital evaluation. Source: CIA 1192, IV-49.

371. (a) The optimal capital budget is determined by calculating the point where marginal cost of capital (which increases as capital requirements increase) and projected rates of return (which decrease as the most profitable projects are accepted first) intersect. Choice (b) is incorrect because the intersection of average marginal cost with average projected rates of return when the largest (not most profitable) projects are accepted first offers no meaningful capital budgeting conclusion. Choice (c) is incorrect because optional capital budgeting assumes that the most profitable projects will be accepted first. Since the marginal cost of capital increases as capital requirements increase, it is entirely possible for the optimal capital budgeting point to exclude less profitable projects as lower-cost capital goes first to projects with higher rates of return. Thus, the optimal capital budget is not determined by accepting all projects with rates of return exceeding the lowest marginal cost of capital. Choice (d) is incorrect because accepting projects with rates of return lower than the cost of capital makes no business sense.

Subject Area: Financial accounting and finance—cost of capital evaluation. Source: CIA 1191, IV-57.

372. (a) The expected risk premium on the portfolio of stocks held as an investment is **not** used to compute the portfolio's expected rate of return. The expected risk premium is the difference between the expected rate of return and the risk-free rate of return. The expected rate of return must be computed before the expected risk premium can be computed. Choice (b) is incorrect because it was directly used in the capital asset pricing model. Choice (c) is incorrect because it was used in the CAPM mode. Choice (d) is incorrect because it was used to compute the beta coefficients for each security held in the investment portfolio and the beta coefficient for the market portfolio.

Subject Area: Financial accounting and finance—cost of capital evaluation. Source: CIA 1193, IV-47.

373. (**a**) Negatively correlated investments result in reduced risk. Choice (b) is incorrect because uncorrelated investments are more risky than negatively correlated investments. Choices (c) and (d) are incorrect because correlated investments are very risky.

Subject Area: Financial accounting and finance—cost of capital evaluation. CIA 591, IV-48.

Types of Debt and Equity

374. (**a**) In business terminology, a high degree of operating leverage, other things held constant, means that a relatively small change in sales will result in a large change in operating income. Therefore, if a high percentage of a firm's total cost is fixed, the firm is said to have a high degree of operating leverage. Choice (b) is incorrect. The opposite is true; see response given for choice (a). Choices (c) and (d) are incorrect. See responses given for choices (a) and (b).

Subject Area: Financial accounting and finance—types of debt and equity-leveraging. Source: CIA Model Exam 2002, IV-30.

375. (**b**) If the assets are purchased, the debt ratio will increase. If the assets are leased, the debt ratio will remain unchanged. Choice (a) is incorrect because if the assets are leased, the debt ratio will remain unchanged. Choice (c) is incorrect because if the assets are leased, the debt ratio will remain unchanged. Choice (d) is incorrect because if the assets are purchased, the debt ratio will increase.

Subject Area: Financial accounting and finance—types of debt and equity. Source: CIA Model Exam 2002, IV-37.

376. (**c**) Preemptive rights protect the proportion of ownership of common shareholders against dilution, by giving them the first opportunity to purchase any additional shares sold by the firm. Choice (a) is incorrect because preemptive rights do not entitle shareholders to vote first at annual meetings. There is no prescribed order of shareholder voting. Choice (b) is incorrect because preemptive rights do not entitle shareholders to purchase any additional bonds sold by the firm. It is protection against dilution of equity ownership that the rights provide. Choice (d) is incorrect because preemptive rights do not allow common shareholders to gain control of the firm in a proxy fight. It is the proportion of ownership that determines the ability to gain control in a control contest.

Subject Area: Financial accounting and finance—types of debt and equity. Source: CIA Model Exam 2002, IV-45.

377. (**b**) Items I and II are correct. The present value of all expected future dividends (item I) equals the current dividend divided by the cost of equity (item II). This calculation provides the value of outstanding common equity, per share. Item III is incorrect because the dividend divided by the current share price is just the dividend yield. It is not the value of the equity.

Subject Area: Financial accounting and finance—types of debt and equity. Source: CIA Model Exam 2002, IV-48.

378. (**d**) Taxes payable is a priority claim. Priority claims are paid in full before any liquidation proceeds are distributed to general claimants or shareholders. Choice (a) is incorrect because preferred shareholders are not among the high priority claimants of a bankrupt firm, ranking ahead of only the common shareholders. Choice (b) is incorrect because common shareholders are the residual claimants of a bankrupt firm. They receive a portion of the liquidation proceeds only after all other claims have been satisfied in full. Choice (c) is incorrect because bonds payable are general, unsecured claims. They share in liquidation proceeds only after all priority claimants are satisfied.

Subject Area: Financial accounting and finance—types of debt and equity. Source: CIA Model Exam 1998, IV-29.

379. (**a**) The risk premium is the portion of expected return attributed to the increased risk. Choice (b) is incorrect because the coefficient of variation represents the standard deviation of an investment's returns divided by the mean returns. Choice (c) is incorrect because the standard error represents a measure of variability in the investment's returns. Choice (d) is incorrect because the beta coefficient represents the sensitivity of the investment's returns to the market returns.

Subject Area: Financial accounting and finance—types of debt and equity. Source: CIA Model Exam 1998, IV-32.

380. (**b**) Both debt and equity are factors in a company's capital structure. Choice (a) is incorrect because this answer ignores equity. Choice (c) is incorrect because the decision does not directly involve assets. Choice (d) is incorrect because the decision involves equity, but does not focus on the type of equity used.

Subject Area: Financial accounting and finance—types of debt and equity. Source: CIA Model Exam 1998, IV-33.

381. (**a**) Since Company X has more debt financing, it has greater fixed financing charges than Company Y. Interest payments are fixed financing charges while common share dividends are not. As a result, Company X will have a more volatile net income stream than Company Y, all else equal. Choice (b) is incorrect because the level of fixed financing charges does not affect operating income variability. Choice (c) is incorrect because the level of fixed financing charges does not affect operating income variability. Choice (d) is incorrect because Company X has greater, not less, financial leverage than Company Y. Greater use of debt financing means that a company has greater financial leverage.

Subject Area: Financial accounting and finance—types of debt and equity. Source: CIA 1196, IV-49.

382. (**a**) For any given quoted nominal rate, the least frequent compounding is associated with the lowest effective annual percentage cost. Annual compounding is less frequent than semiannual, quarterly or monthly. Note that the term of the loan is not relevant to the calculation of the effective annual percentage cost of financing. Choices (b), (c), and (d) are incorrect because the more frequent the interest compounding, the more costly the loan. Semiannual, quarterly and monthly compounding is more frequent than annual compounding.

Subject Area: Financial accounting and finance—types of debt and equity. Source: CIA 1196, IV-45.

383. (**d**) Indexed bonds have interest payments based on an inflation index, such as the consumer price index, so as to protect the holder from inflation. Interest paid rises automatically when the inflation rate rises. Choice (a) is incorrect because income bonds pay interest to the holder only if the interest is earned. The interest paid is not inflation adjusted. Choice (b) is incorrect because convertible bonds can be redeemed for the common stock of the company at the option of the holder. Interest payments are not inflation adjusted. Choice (c) is incorrect because mortgage bonds are secured and offer senior priority to bondholders in the event of liquidation. Interest payments are not inflation adjusted.

Subject Area: Financial accounting and finance—types of debt and equity. Source: CIA 595, IV-39.

384. (d) Convertible bonds have a lower coupon rate than nonconvertible bonds because they offer investors a chance for capital gains in exchange for the lower coupon rate. Choices (a) and (b) are incorrect because the face value is not a distinguishing feature of convertible bonds. Choice (c) is incorrect because convertible bonds have lower, not higher, coupon rates.

Subject Area: Financial accounting and finance—types of debt and equity. Source: CIA 595, IV-40.

385. (b) If interest is charged on a simple basis, then the full face value of the loan is made available to the borrower. Choice (a) is incorrect because if interest is charged on a simple basis, then the full face value of the loan is made available to the borrower. It is when interest is charged on a discount basis that the nominal interest charge for the year, or $2,000 in this example, is deducted from the face value of the loan before the borrower obtains use of the funds. Choice (c) is incorrect because if interest is charged on a discount basis, the borrower obtains the use of only the face value less the nominal interest charge, or $20,000 less $2,000 in this example. The borrower does not receive the full face value of the loan. Choice (d) is incorrect. It is when interest is charged on an add-on basis that the face value of the loan initially equals the borrowed amount plus the nominal interest charge for the year. When interest is charged on a discount basis the borrower obtains use of only the face value less the nominal interest charge.

Subject Area: Financial accounting and finance—types of debt and equity. Source: CIA 595, IV-50.

386. (c) The market value of all bonds (discount, premium and par bonds) will approach face value as the maturity date approaches. Choice (a) is incorrect because the coupon rate on discount bonds is below the market rate on bonds of similar risk and maturity. Choice (b) is incorrect because discount bonds can offer semiannual, annual or any other pattern of coupon payments. Choice (d) is incorrect because in the case of discount bonds, the market value will rise, not fall, between the issue date and the maturity date.

Subject Area: Financial accounting and finance—types of debt and equity. Source: CIA 594, IV-53.

387. (a) Determination of the imputed interest rate is made at the time the debt instrument is issued; any subsequent changes in prevailing interest rates are ignored. Choice (b) is incorrect because any subsequent changes in prevailing interest rates are ignored. Choice (c) is incorrect because determination of the imputed interest rate is made at the time the debt instrument is issued. Choice (d) is incorrect because determination of the imputed interest rate is made at the time the debt instrument in issued; any subsequent changes in prevailing interest rates are ignored.

Subject Area: Financial accounting and finance—types of debt and equity. Source: CIA 593, IV-42.

388. (c) The company benefits from short-term loans if interest rates are expected to fall. Choice (a) is incorrect because the company would not benefit from short-term loans if interest rates are expected to rise. Choice (b) is incorrect because the company would rather maintain the existing debt if prevailing interest rates were higher. Choice (d) is incorrect because the company does not solve the cash flow problem by shifting to short-term loans.

Subject Area: Financial accounting and finance—types of debt and equity. Source: CIA 593, IV-56.

389. (d) These bonds are sold at a discount below par and provide compensation to investors in the form of appreciation. Choices (a) and (b) are incorrect because these bonds are sold at a discount. Choice (c) is incorrect because these bonds are subject to taxes.

Subject Area: Financial accounting and finance—types of debt and equity. Source: CIA 1192, IV-56.

390. (d) First-mortgage bonds are backed by fixed assets. Choice (a) is incorrect because income bonds only pay interest if interest is earned. Choice (b) is incorrect because debentures are unsecured bonds. Choice (c) is incorrect because subordinated debentures are subordinated to other debt.

Subject Area: Financial accounting and finance—types of debt and equity. Source: CIA 1192, IV-57.

391. (a) Current liabilities are "obligations whose liquidation is reasonably expected to require the use of existing assets properly classified as current assets or the creation of other current liabilities." At the balance sheet date of December 31, 2005, both the principal of the bonds and the interest accrued at the balance sheet date will be coming due within a year of the balance sheet date. These amounts are expected to require the use of current assets (because there is no evidence to the contrary) and, therefore, should both be classified as current liabilities. Choice (b) is incorrect because the interest payable should be classified as a current liability because it is coming due within a year after the December 31, 2005 balance sheet date and, therefore, will require the use of assets properly classifiable as current assets at the balance sheet date. Choice (c) is incorrect because the balance of bonds payable should be classified as a current liability because the bonds are becoming due within a year after the December 31, 2005 balance sheet date and, therefore, will require the use of current assets. Choice (d) is incorrect because both the balance of bonds payable and interest payable should be classified as current liabilities.

Subject Area: Financial accounting and finance—types of debt and equity. Source: CIA 1192, IV-31.

392. (d) A company pledges certain assets as security. Choice (a) is incorrect because an income bond pays interest to the holder only if the interest is earned. Choice (b) is incorrect because subordinated debentures have a claim on assets only after the senior debt has been paid off in the event of liquidation. Choice (c) is incorrect because debentures are not secured by a mortgage on specific property; it is an unsecured bond.

Subject Area: Financial accounting and finance—types of debt and equity. Source: CIA 1191, IV-53.

393. (d) Participating preferred stockholders would be entitled to share in the earnings of the firm. They participate in earnings distributions under set terms and conditions. Choice (a) is incorrect because the participation privilege is unrelated to monitoring privileges. Choice (b) is incorrect because preferred stockholders do not have voting rights except in circumstances where the firm has not paid the preferred share dividends for a specified period. Choice (c) is incorrect because a conversion feature, not a participation feature, allows conversion to common stock.

Subject Area: Financial accounting and finance—types of debt and equity. Source: CIA 597, IV-49.

394. (b) At the rapid growth stage, if a company is reasonably profitable it will experience financing needs in excess of funds available either internally or from trade credit or bank credit. Additional debt financing would often result in an unreasonable amount of financial leverage at this stage of development and public equity financing is not yet available to the company. This is the stage at which the company is most likely to seek and obtain venture capital financing. Choice (a) is incorrect. During the formation stage, personal savings, trade credit and government agencies are the main sources of financing. Prior to demonstrating initial success, a company is not likely to easily attract venture capital financing. Choice (c) is incorrect. In the growth to maturity stage of development, the company is able to access formal markets for debt and equity because it has a track record of success and a better balance between cash in and outflows than it had in the rapid growth stage. Formal capital markets provide financing at lower cost than venture capitalists, so venture capital is not likely to be sought at this stage. Choice (d) is incorrect. The decline phase is characterized by more than adequate cash flows, relative to available investment opportunities, so venture capital is not likely to be sought at this stage of development.

Subject Area: Financial accounting and finance—types of debt and equity. Source: CIA 1196, IV-51.

395. (a) Investors value common shares more highly if they have a lower required return because then they apply a lower discount rate to the expected future dividend stream of the company. Choice (b) is incorrect because lower expected dividend growth would reduce, not increase, the market value of the outstanding common shares of the company. Choice (c) is incorrect because expected holding periods of investors are not relevant to market valuation of the outstanding common shares of the company. Choice (d) is incorrect because expected holding periods of investors are not relevant to market valuation of the outstanding common shares of the company.

Subject Area: Financial accounting and finance—types of debt and equity. Source: CIA 1196, IV-25.

396. (b) The lower the exercise price, the more valuable the call option. The exercise price is the price at which the call holder has the right to purchase the underlying share. Choice (a) is incorrect because a call option is the right to purchase a share of common stock at a set price for a set time period. If the underlying share has a lower market value, then all else equals and the call option is less, not more, valuable. Choice (c) is incorrect because a call option is less, not more, valuable if there is less time to maturity. When the option has less time to expire, there is less of a chance that the share price will rise further. Choice (d) is incorrect because a call option is less, not more, valuable if there is less variation in the price of the underlying share. Less variability means there is a less of a chance of a price increase on the underlying share.

Subject Area: Financial accounting and finance—types of debt and equity. Source: CIA 1196, IV-58.

397. (a) Investments with present values in excess of their costs (that is, positive net present values) that can be identified or created by the capital budgeting activities of the firm will have a positive impact on firm value and on the price of the common stock of the firm. Choice (b) is incorrect because positive net present value (NPV) investments will increase, not decrease, firm value and share prices for a firm. Choices (c) and (d) are incorrect because investments with present values equal to their costs have a zero net present value and neither increase nor decrease firm value and share price.

Subject Area: Financial accounting and finance—types of debt and equity. Source: CIA 1195, IV-44.

398. (c) Preferred stock does not usually have voting rights. Preferred shareholders are generally given the right to vote for directors of the company only if the company has not paid the preferred dividend for a specified period of time, such as ten quarters. Choice (a) is incorrect because preferred stock does have priority over common stock with regard to earnings, so dividends must be paid on preferred stock before they can be paid on common stock. Choice (b) is incorrect because preferred stock does have priority over common stock with regard to assets, so in the event of bankruptcy, the claims of preferred shareholders must be satisfied in full before the common shareholders receive anything. Choice (d) is incorrect because cumulative preferred stock does have the right to receive any dividends in arrears before common stock dividends are paid.

Subject Area: Financial accounting and finance—types of debt and equity. Source: CIA 1195, IV-47.

399. (d) Like common stock (but unlike bonds), preferred stock has no maturity date. Like bonds (but unlike common stock), preferred stock has a fixed periodic payment. The fixed payment is in the form of a stated dividend in the case of the preferred stock and is in the form of interest payments in the case of bonds. Choice (a) is incorrect because preferred stock does not have a maturity date. Choice (b) is incorrect because preferred stock does have fixed periodic dividend payments. Choice (c) is incorrect because preferred stock does not have a maturity date and does have fixed periodic dividend payments.

Subject Area: Financial accounting and finance—types of debt and equity. Source: CIA 596, IV-46.

400. (b) The conversion price is the effective price paid for the common stock obtained by converting the convertible security. The conversion price is calculated as the par value of the convertible security divided by the conversion ratio. For this preferred stock issue the par value is $10 and the conversion ratio is 2, so the conversion price is $5. Choice (a) is incorrect because the conversion ratio is two shares of common stock for one share of preferred. The conversion price is not $2. It is based on the par value of the preferred stock and on the conversion ratio. Choice (c) is incorrect because this is the par value of the convertible preferred stock. Choice (d) is incorrect because this is the par value of the preferred stock multiplied by the conversion ratio ($10 times 2). The conversion price is calculated by dividing the par value of the preferred by the conversion ratio.

Subject Area: Financial accounting and finance—types of debt and equity. Source: CIA 596, IV-47.

401. (c) In the event of bankruptcy, the claims of preferred stockholders must be satisfied before common stockholders receive anything. Choice (a) is incorrect because failure to pay dividends will not force the firm into bankruptcy, whether the dividends are for common or preferred stock. Only failure to pay interest will force the firm into bankruptcy. Choice (b) is incorrect because the opposite is true. Choice (d) is incorrect because neither common nor preferred dividends are tax deductible.

Subject Area: Financial accounting and finance—types of debt and equity. Source: CIA 595, IV-48.

402. (a) Investors value common shares more highly if they have a lower required return because then they apply a lower discount rate to the expected future dividend stream of the company. Choice (b) is incorrect because lower expected dividend growth would reduce, not increase, the market value of the outstanding common shares of the company. Choice (c) is incorrect because expected holding periods of investors are not relevant to market valuation of the outstanding common shares of the company. Choice (d) is incorrect because expected holding periods of investors are not relevant to market valuation of the outstanding common shares of the company.

Subject Area: Financial accounting and finance—types of debt and equity. Source: CIA 1194, IV-46.

403. (c) Choice (c) is correct.

ROE = Net income available to common stockholders ($450,000)/Common equity [1 – .4(200,000/.4)].

Choice (a) is incorrect because ROE is not equal to the ratio of liabilities to total assets. Choice (b) is incorrect because ROE is not equal to the ratio of liabilities to net income available to common stockholders. Choice (d) is incorrect because ROE is not equal to the ratio of net income available to common stockholders to liabilities.

Subject Area: Financial accounting and finance—types of debt and equity. Source: CIA 590, IV-46.

404. (d) Decreases by $520 = (100 × $10) – (40 × $12). The decrease in stockholders' equity is the buyback cost less the proceeds from resale of treasury shares. Choice (a) is incorrect. Increases by $600 = (100 – 40) × $10. The $12 resale price has not been used, but has instead been replaced with the $10 buyback price. Choice (b) is incorrect. Decreases by 1000 = 100 × $10. Only buyback cost of treasury shares has been considered. Choice (c) is incorrect. Increases by 480 = 40 × $12. Only resale of treasury shares has been considered.

Subject Area: Financial accounting and finance—types of debt and equity. Source: CIA 1190, IV-35.

405. (d) The proportion of equity in the financial structure of the firm is the value of outstanding equity divided by the total value of all financing sources.

$$\frac{\text{Value of equity}}{\text{Value of debt + Value of equity}} = \frac{1{,}000{,}000}{1{,}000{,}000 + 1{,}500{,}000} = .40$$

Since the question states that the firm will maintain the same weight of each financing source, each dollar invested is composed of 40 cents of equity and 60 cents of debt. The first $60,000 of equity used in financing new projects is sourced from retained earnings. This source of equity is exhausted when the firm reaches an investment level of: $60,000/.4 = $150,000. When the level of investment exceeds this amount; equity financing must be raised externally. Choice (a) is incorrect because the company has retained earnings to use as one source of project financing. Choice (b) is incorrect because this answer multiplies, rather than divides by the weight equity represents in the financial structure. This solution is calculated as ($60,000)(.40) = $24,000. Choice (c) is incorrect because this answer calculates the proportion of equity financing incorrectly as value of equity/value of debt = 1,000,000/1,500,000 = .667, so the investment level at which retained earnings would be exhausted is $60,000/.667 = $90,000.

Subject Area: Financial accounting and finance—types of debt and equity. Source: CIA 594, IV-47.

406. (c) Dividends on preferred stock must be paid before common stock dividends. Choice (a) is incorrect because lack of payments does not force bankruptcy. Choice (b) is incorrect because the dividends do not rise. Choice (d) is incorrect because preferred stock does not have a priority claim over bonds.

Subject Area: Financial accounting and finance—types of debt and equity. Source: CIA 1193, IV-54.

407. (a) The term "transient preferreds" is used to refer to preferred stock issues, which specify redemption over relatively short periods such as five to ten years. There have been an increasing number of such issuances recently. Choices (b), (c), and (d) are incorrect because there is no such term in common usage, and are distracters.

Subject Area: Financial accounting and finance—types of debt and equity. Source: CIA 1192, IV-36.

408. (b) Earnings per share (EPS) will generally be higher if debt is used to raise capital instead of equity, provided that the firm isn't over-leveraged. However, the prospect of higher EPS is accompanied by greater risk to the firm resulting from required interest costs, creditors' liens on the firm's assets and the possibility of proportionately lower EPS if sales volume fails to meet projections. Choice (a) is incorrect because earnings per share are not a function of investor confidence and are not maximized by concurrent proportional increases in both debt and equity. EPS are generally higher if debt is used instead of equity to raise capital, at least initially. Choice (c) is incorrect because equity capital will not satisfy the stated goal of maximizing earnings per share. EPS are generally higher if debt is used to raise capital, at least initially. Choice (d) is incorrect because utilizing only current cash flow to raise capital is usually too conservative an approach for a growth oriented firm. Management is expected to be willing to take acceptable risks in order to be competitive and attain an acceptable rate of growth.

Subject Area: Financial accounting and finance—types of debt and equity. Source: CIA 1191, IV-58.

409. (c) Warrants are options which permit the holder to buy stock for a stated price. Its exercise results in cash to the firm accompanied by additional outstanding common stock. Choice (a) is incorrect because a stock split is merely an accounting action which increases (or occasionally decreases) the number of shares outstanding. It does not bring in additional capital. Choice (b) is incorrect because conversion of convertible bonds to common stock simply replaces debt with outstanding common stock. It does not bring in additional capital. Choice (d) is incorrect because options purchased and exercised through option exchanges are transactions between individual investors not affecting the firm whose stock is involved. Transactions involving such options do not bring additional capital to the firm.

Subject Area: Financial accounting and finance—types of debt and equity. Source: CIA 1191, IV-59.

410. (b) When the equity method is used, the investment account on the investor's books is adjusted each period for changes in the net assets of the investee. That is, the investment's carrying amount is periodically increased (decreased) by the investor's share of the earnings (losses) of the investee and decreased by all dividends received by the investor from the investee. Choice (a) is incorrect because when the equity method is used, investment income (loss) is recognized for the investee's share of earnings (losses) of the investee. Dividends received by the investee are recorded as a reduction of the investment account. Choice (c) is incorrect because the receipt of dividends will result in a credit to the investment account rather than to a liability account. Choice (d) is incorrect because the receipt of dividends will result in a credit to the investment account rather than to an owners' equity account.

Subject Area: Financial accounting and finance—types of debt and equity. Source: CIA 591, IV-34.

411. (d) Preferred stock can have any or all of these described features. Choice (a) is incorrect because bonds normally have a coupon yield stated in percent and may be convertible but are not participating. Choice (b) is incorrect because common stock is not described as convertible or participating on the financial statements. Choice (c) is incorrect because common stock options are not participating and do not have a stated yield rate.

Subject Area: Financial accounting and finance—types of debt and equity. Source: CIA 592, IV-39.

412. (c) The degree of operating leverage (DOL) is a measure of the change in earnings available to common stockholders associated with a given change in operating earnings. It is calculated, for a particular level of sales, as

$$\frac{\text{Sales revenue} - \text{Variable costs}}{\text{Sales revenue} - \text{Variable costs} - \text{Fixed operating costs}}$$

Choice (a) is incorrect because DOL is specific to the initial sales level and varies with the initial sales level. Choice (b) is incorrect because the statement describes the degree of financial leverage (DFL), not the degree of operating leverage (DOL). Choice (d) is incorrect because the degree of total leverage is the multiple of the degree of operating leverage and the degree of financial leverage. Other things equal, DOL is higher if the degree of total leverage is higher.

Subject Area: Financial accounting and finance—types of debt and equity. Source: CIA 594, IV-52.

413. (c) Earnings per share is less volatile in less highly leveraged firms. Lower fixed interest costs result in less variable earnings. Choice (a) is incorrect because higher leverage is associated with higher, not lower, earnings per share. Choice (b) is incorrect because earnings per share is more volatile in more highly leveraged firms, since higher fixed interest costs result in more variable earnings. Choice (d) is incorrect because less leverage is associated with lower, not higher, earnings per share.

Subject Area: Financial accounting and finance—types of debt and equity. Source: CIA 595, IV-51.

414. (b) The act of borrowing creates financial leverage. In general, the use of debt increases the financial risk to the shareholders and therefore, their financial leverage. Choice (a) is incorrect because the retirement of debt will decrease the debt-to-equity ratio. The relative amount of equity outstanding increases as the amount of debt decreases. Choice (c) is incorrect because the total assets will decrease (assets will be used to retire the debt) and the net income will increase (reduced interest expenses) resulting an increased asset turnover ratio. Choice (d) is incorrect because the interest expense being saved will increase net income and thus, the return on stockholders' equity.

Subject Area: Financial accounting and finance—types of debt and equity. Source: CIA 1193, IV-48.

415. (a) The degree of operating leverage (DOL) is equal to the percentage change in earnings before interest and taxes (EBIT) divided by the percentage change in sales. Since interest expenses are not included in EBIT, the DOL is not affected by a change in interest expense. Choice (b) is incorrect because variable cost per unit affects EBIT and therefore affects the DOL. Choice (c) is incorrect because quantity of units sold affects EBIT and therefore affects the DOL. Choice (d) is incorrect because fixed costs affect EBIT and therefore affect the DOL.

Subject Area: Financial accounting and finance—types of debt and equity. Source: CIA 1193, IV-53.

416. (c) Degree of operating leverage is the percentage change in EBIT resulting from a given percentage change in sales. Choice (a) is incorrect because the term "credit" is not applicable. Choice (b) is incorrect because "financial" refers to the sensitivity of earnings per share (EPS) to earnings before interest and taxes (EBIT). Choice (d) is incorrect because the term "intrinsic" is not applicable.

Subject Area: Financial accounting and finance—types of debt and equity. CIA 593, IV-57.

417. (b) Because the proportion of long-term debt relative to equity is decreasing, financial leverage is decreasing. Because the proportional investment in fixed assets is increasing, operating leverage is increasing. Choice (a) is incorrect because financial leverage is decreasing and operating leverage is increasing. Choice (c) is incorrect because financial leverage is decreasing. Choice (d) is incorrect because operating leverage is increasing.

Subject Area: Financial accounting and finance—types of debt and equity. Source: CIA 590, IV-56.

418. (b) Computations follow:

Increase in assets	$180,000
Increase in liabilities	(50,000)
Increase in owners' equity	130,000
Increase in common stock	(90,000)
Increase in additional paid-in capital	(15,000)
Increase in retained earnings	25,000

Dividends declared = Net income – Increase in retained earnings = $42,000 – 25,000 = $17,000.

Choice (a) is incorrect because this answer incorrectly ignores the $15,000 increase in net assets due to an increase in additional paid-in capital. Choice (c) is incorrect. This answer incorrectly deducts the sum of the increase in paid-in capital accounts ($90,000 + $15,000) and net income ($42,000) from the increase in assets ($180,000). Choice (d) is incorrect. This answer incorrectly adds net income ($42,000) and the increase in net assets other than from owner contributions [($180,000 – $50,000) – ($90,000 + $15,000)].

Subject Area: Financial accounting and finance—types of debt and equity. Source: CIA 597, IV-2.

419. (a) The higher the dividend payout ratio, the sooner retained earnings are exhausted and the company must seek more costly, outside equity financing. This drives up the marginal cost of capital. Choice (b) is incorrect because the opposite is true. Choice (c) and (d) are incorrect because the level of dividend payout does not determine the investment opportunities available to the company.

Subject Area: Financial accounting and finance—types of debt and equity. Source: CIA 597, IV-53.

420. (a) After cash dividends are declared, there is a date when the shares go ex-dividend and a new purchaser of the shares will not receive the dividend. The holder of record date determines the identity of dividend recipients and occurs a few days after the shares go ex-dividend, since there is a lag between the sale of shares and the transfer of title on the company records. The final date is the actual date the dividend payments are distributed to shareholders of record. Choice (b) is incorrect because the ex-dividend date occurs prior to the holder of record date. Choice (c) is incorrect because the ex-dividend date occurs prior to the holder of record date, and the dividend declaration date must proceed both. Choice (d) is incorrect because the dividend declaration date must occur prior to the date when the shares go ex-dividend.

Subject Area: Financial accounting and finance—types of debt and equity. Source: CIA 597, IV-53.

421. (c) A stock split involves a larger number of new shares being issued to replace and retire all outstanding shares. Choice (a) is incorrect because it is stock dividends that involve this bookkeeping transfer. Stock splits do not involve a change in the capital accounts. Choice (b) is incorrect because it is stock dividends that are paid in additional shares of common stock. In stock splits all outstanding shares are replaced with a new issue of shares. Choice (d) is incorrect because in a stock split there is a large decline in the book value, and in the market value, per share. A stock dividend does not affect the par value of stock.

Subject Area: Financial accounting and finance—types of debt and equity. Source: CIA 1196, IV-55.

422. (a) A company with less attractive investment opportunities will have a lower optimal capital budget. Under a residual dividend policy, a lower optimal capital budget will result in a higher dividend payout ratio, everything else equal. Choice (b) is incorrect because when fewer earnings are available for reinvestment, any level of capital expenditures will require, everything else equal, a greater proportion of available internal funds. The dividend payout ratio will then be lower, not higher, under a residual payout policy. Choice (c) is incorrect because the lower the debt-to-equity ratio, the higher the proportion of new investments financed with equity. Under a residual dividend payout policy, this will result in a lower, not a higher, dividend payout, as more internally available funds are retained for reinvestment. Choice (d) is incorrect because the lower the opportunity cost of funds, the lower the discount rate used to evaluate capital projects and the more attractive the investment opportunities, everything else equal. Under a residual payout policy, more internally generated funds will be required to finance the optimal capital budget and the dividend payout will be lower, not higher.

Subject Area: Financial accounting and finance—types of debt and equity. Source: CIA 1195, IV-49.

423. (b) A company with a higher dividend payout ratio is paying out more of its earnings as dividends to common shareholders. It will have less cash and less total assets than a comparable firm with a lower payout ratio. The debt-to-assets ratio will be higher, since total assets are lower, and the current ratio will be lower, since cash is lower, than for the lower dividend-payout firm. Choice (a) is incorrect because the higher dividend-payout company will have less cash and a lower current ratio than a comparable firm with a lower payout policy will. Choice (c) is incorrect because this is opposite to the correct solution given in choice (b). Choice (d) is incorrect because the higher dividend-payout company will have less cash and less total assets, and hence a higher debt-to-assets ratio, than a comparable company with a lower payout policy.

Subject Area: Financial accounting and finance—types of debt and equity. Source: CIA 596, IV-35.

424. (a) The dividend becomes a liability of the company on the declaration date. Choice (b) is incorrect because this is the announcement date. The dividend becomes a liability of the company as soon as it is declared. Choice (c) is incorrect because this is the holder of record date, on which the list of stockholders owning the shares who will receive the dividend payments is determined. The dividend becomes a liability of the company much earlier, when it was first declared. Choice (d) is incorrect because this is the dividend payment date. The declared dividend is no longer a liability after the payment is made. The date the dividend becomes a liability is on the declaration date.

Subject Area: Financial accounting and finance—types of debt and equity. Source: CIA 596, IV-54.

425. (b) Stock repurchases provide capital gain in place of cash dividends. If the form of the distribution does not affect future earnings, then after the stock repurchase earnings per share and share price will be higher for the remaining shares. This share price appreciation provides capital gains for stockholders in place of a cash dividend. Cash dividends provide ordinary income. Choice (a) is incorrect because stock repurchases provide capital gain income since they result in share price appreciation. Cash dividends provide ordinary income, not capital gain income. Choice (c) is incorrect because stock repurchases provide capital gains, not ordinary income. Cash dividends provide ordinary income, not capital gain income. Choice (d) is incorrect because stock repurchases provide capital gains, not ordinary income. Cash dividends provide ordinary income.

Subject Area: Financial accounting and finance—types of debt and equity. Source: CIA 596, IV-55.

426. (c) Stock dividends result in a transfer from retained earnings to paid-in-capital. Choice (a) is incorrect because cash dividends reduce retained earnings. Choice (b) is incorrect because cash dividends decrease both retained earnings and stockholders' equity. Choice (d) is incorrect because stock dividends have no net impact on stockholders' equity.

Subject Area: Financial accounting and finance—types of debt and equity. Source: CIA 1195, IV-10.

427. (d) With a stock dividend, the company just issues additional shares of stock to each stockholder and nothing more. Stockholders' equity is not reduced because the corporation does not pay out assets or incur a liability. Choices (a), (b), and (c) are incorrect because cash, property and liquidating dividends all reduce stockholders' equity in the corporation since they all involve an immediate or promised future distribution of assets.

Subject Area: Financial accounting and finance—types of debt and equity. Source: CIA 595, IV-30.

428. **(c)** Interest is deductible from operating income to obtain taxable income but dividends are not. While it takes only $1 of pretax income to pay $1 of interest, it takes $1.67 of pretax income to pay $1 of dividends for a firm in a 40% tax bracket. This is calculated as follows:

Required pretax income = Dividend payment/(1 – Tax rate)
= $1/(1 – .4) = $1.67

Choice (a) is incorrect because at least $1 of operating income will be needed to pay $1 of either interest or dividends. Choice (b) is incorrect because if both were tax deductible then $1 of pretax income would be needed to pay $1 of either interest or dividends. Dividends are not deductible for tax purposes, however. Choice (d) is incorrect because the opposite is true.

Subject Area: Financial accounting and finance—types of debt and equity. Source: CIA 595, IV-66.

429. **(b)** A company with a higher dividend payout ratio is paying out more of its earnings as dividends to common shareholders. It will have less cash and less total assets than a comparable firm with a lower payout ratio. The debt-to-assets ratio will be higher, since total assets are lower, and the current ratio will be lower, since cash is lower, than for the lower dividend payout firm. Choice (a) is incorrect because the higher dividend payout company will have less cash and a lower current ratio than a comparable firm with a lower payout policy will. Choice (c) is incorrect because this is opposite to the correct solution given in choice (b). Choice (d) is incorrect because the higher dividend payout company will have less cash and less total assets, and hence a higher debt-to-assets ratio, than a comparable company with a lower payout policy.

Subject Area: Financial accounting and finance—types of debt and equity. Source: CIA 1194, IV-11.

430. **(c)** The proposed two-for-one stock split will double the number of outstanding shares to 2,000 while the proposed 50% stock dividend will increase the number of outstanding shares by 50% to 1,500. Since the stock split results in a larger increase in the number of outstanding shares, it will cause a greater decline in earnings per share. Choices (a) and (b) are incorrect because both the stock split and the stock dividend will increase the number of outstanding shares and will therefore reduce, not increase, earnings per share. Choice (d) is incorrect because the stock split results in a larger increase in the number of outstanding shares, it will cause a greater, not a lesser, decline in earnings per share.

Subject Area: Financial accounting and finance—types of debt and equity. Source: CIA 1194, IV-50.

431. **(d)** The par value per share decreases following a stock split since the number of shares increases but the total par value of outstanding shares does not change. Choice (a) is incorrect because par value per share does not change following a stock dividend. Choice (b) is incorrect because the par value per share decreases, rather than increases, following a stock split, since the number of shares increases but the total par value of outstanding shares does not change. Choice (c) is incorrect because par value per share does not change following a stock dividend.

Subject Area: Financial accounting and finance—types of debt and equity. Source: CIA 1194, IV-51.

432. **(a)** When a residual dividend policy is followed, dividends are paid only if earnings available to common shareholders are not used for undertaking positive net present value investment opportunities. Dividend payments will be higher when few investment opportunities are available. Choice (b) is incorrect because dividend payments will be lower when a firm has many investment opportunities and a residual dividend policy is followed. Choice (c) is incorrect because dividend payments will be higher when a firm has few investment opportunities and a residual dividend policy is followed. Choice (d) is incorrect. If there are no positive net present value investment opportunities and the company is profitable, dividends will be paid if a residual dividend policy is followed.

Subject Area: Financial accounting and finance—types of debt and equity. Source: CIA 1194, IV-52.

433. **(b)** The ex-dividend date is four days prior to the holder-of-record date, and is the date when the right to a dividend leaves a stock. Choice (a) is incorrect because the declaration date is the earliest date pertaining to dividend payment. Choice (c) is incorrect because the holder-of-record date is subsequent to the declaration and ex-dividend dates, and is the date at which stockholder eligibility for dividends is determined. Choice (d) is incorrect because the payment date is when the company actually mails dividend checks.

Subject Area: Financial accounting and finance—types of debt and equity. Source: CIA 590, IV-48.

434. **(b)** A less-than-expected dividend increase would result in a stock price decline. As the nominal interest rates increase, expenses increase, profits decrease, and cash available for dividends would decrease. Also, interest rates create a competition between stocks and bonds. Investors switch to bonds when interest rates increase, forcing them to sell stocks, which further depresses the stock price. Choices (a), (c), and (d) are incorrect because a higher interest rate raises the required return of investors, which results in a lower stock price.

Subject Area: Financial accounting and finance—types of debt and equity. Source: CIA 593, IV-49.

435. **(d)** Residual dividend policy implies that dividends should be paid only out of "leftover" earnings. Choice (a) is incorrect because its cash dividend would not be stable, but a residual. Choice (b) is incorrect because all earnings are not retained. Choice (c) is incorrect because all earnings are not distributed as dividends.

Subject Area: Financial accounting and finance—types of debt and equity. Source: CIA 593, IV-58.

436. **(a)** A spin-off is accomplished by distributing stock of another corporation to shareholders, who then become shareholders of both corporations. Choice (b) is incorrect because a corporation issuing additional shares of its own stock to shareholders accomplishes a split-up. Choice (c) is incorrect because a scrip dividend is one that is payable in the form of notes payable. Choice (d) is incorrect because a reverse split-up is where a corporation reduces the number of shares outstanding.

Subject Area: Financial accounting and finance—types of debt and equity. Source: CIA 591, IV-54.

Financial Instruments

437. **(d)** Foreign bonds are denominated in the currency of the country of sale, while Eurobonds are sold in a country other than the one in whose currency the bond is denominated. Choice (a) is incorrect because foreign bonds are bonds sold by a foreign borrower but denominated in the currency of the country in which they are sold. A government need not issue them. Choice (b) is incorrect because all international bonds are sold outside the country of the borrower, so this is not a distinguishing feature of either foreign bonds or Eurobonds. Choice (c) is incorrect because the opposite is true.

Subject Area: Financial accounting and finance—financial instruments. Source: CIA 597, IV-69.

438. **(c)** The company can arrange today for the exchange rate at which it will purchase the foreign currency in 60 days' time by buying the currency in the forward market. This will eliminate the exchange risk associated with the trade payable. Choice (a) is incorrect because the company needs to arrange to buy the foreign currency in order to make payment to the supplier. This cannot be accomplished by a forward market sale of foreign currency. Choice (b) is incorrect because waiting to convert the currency in 60 days' time does not eliminate the risk of exchange rate movements. Choice (d) is incorrect because this strategy would be comparable to a future sale of the foreign currency at a rate known today, which would not provide the currency needed to pay the invoice. The opposite strategy would be an effective money market hedge however. If the company converted domestic currency to foreign currency in the spot market today and invested in a foreign bank deposit or Treasury bill, it could then use the proceeds from the foreign investment to pay the invoice in 60 days' time.

Subject Area: Financial accounting and finance—financial instruments. Source: CIA 1196, IV-64.

439. **(a)** The exchange rate in the question is expressed as the external value of the US dollar, using the US dollar as the numerator. The percentage change in the external value of the US dollar is calculated as

$$(\text{New rate} - \text{Prior rate})/\text{Prior rate} = (5.5 - 5)/5 = 10\%$$

Choice (b) is incorrect because the US dollar is appreciating, since one US dollar will now purchase more French francs. Choice (c) is incorrect because the French franc is depreciating, not appreciating. Also, the rate of depreciation is not 20%. Choice (d) is incorrect because the French franc has depreciated by

$$(.454545 - .5)/.5 = 9.09\%.$$

To calculate the rate of appreciation or depreciation of a currency you must express the exchange rate using that currency as the numerator. In this question the external value of the French franc in terms of US dollars is the reciprocal of the US dollar exchange rate given.

Subject Area: Financial accounting and finance—financial instruments. Source: CIA 1196, IV-73.

440. **(a)** If the real rates of interest are the same, the country with the higher nominal interest rate is expected to experience a higher rate of inflation. A higher rate of inflation is associated with a devaluing currency so the currency of the country with the higher nominal interest rate will likely be selling at a forward discount. Choice (b) is incorrect because the currency of Country A will be selling at a forward discount. Choice (c) is incorrect due to spot discount. Choice (d) is incorrect because the spot relationship between two currencies cannot be identified from the information given.

Subject Area: Financial accounting and finance—financial instruments. Source: CIA 1196, IV-74.

441. **(c)** Government Treasury bills are debt securities maturing in less than one year and are traded in international money markets, the largest such markets being in New York and London. Choice (a) and (b) are incorrect because mortgages and preferred stocks are long-term, capital market securities and are not traded in money markets. Choice (d) is incorrect because Treasury bonds are long-term, capital market securities and are not traded in money markets.

Subject Area: Financial accounting and finance—financial instruments. Source: CIA 1195, IV-65.

442. **(b)** Eurobonds are, by definition, always sold in some country other than the one in whose currency the bond issue is denominated. Choice (a) is incorrect because Eurobonds are not always denominated in Eurodollars. Choice (c) is incorrect because this statement describes a foreign bond, not a Eurobond. Choice (d) is incorrect because Eurobonds are generally issued not as registered bonds but as bearer bonds, so names and nationalities of the investors are not recorded.

Subject Area: Financial accounting and finance—financial instruments. Source: CIA 1195, IV-66.

443. **(c)** If incomes in Country 1 rise, then consumers in Country 1 will increase their imports from Country 2. The resulting increase in the supply of currency 1 will result in a tendency for it to depreciate relative to the currency of Country 2. Choice (a) is incorrect because if incomes in Country 1 rise, then consumers in Country 1 will increase their imports from Country 2. The resulting increase in the supply of currency 1 will result in a tendency to devalue, not to remain constant, relative to the currency of Country 2. Choice (b) is incorrect because if incomes in Country 1 fall, then consumers in Country 1 will reduce their imports from Country 2. The resulting decrease in the supply of currency 1 will result in a tendency to appreciate, not depreciate, relative to the currency of Country 2. Choice (d) is incorrect because if incomes in Country 1 remain constant, then everything else equal, the currency of Country 1 will not tend to appreciate or depreciate relative to the currency of Country 2.

Subject Area: Financial accounting and finance—financial instruments. Source: CIA 1195, IV-67.

444. **(d)** In an interest rate swap, two companies exchange their debt servicing obligations on some notional amount of debt principal. The actual exchange of funds during the agreement is in the form of a net payment, from the party owing the greater amount for the period. Choice (a) is incorrect because an interest rate swap is not a sale of a right to borrow at a preferential rate from a financial institution. Choice (b) is incorrect because the parties to an interest rate swap deal only with each other. They do not make payments on the debt of the counterparty directly to the bank of the counterparty. Choice (c) is incorrect because an interest rate swap is not the exchange of interest income of bond investments for the interest expense on the borrowings of the company.

Subject Area: Financial accounting and finance—financial instruments. Source: CIA 596, IV-29.

445. (a) It is the relative change in the exchange rates that determines whether one currency is higher or lower than the others. Here, the returns on the US currency is lower compared to Germany since the US dollar got stronger. Choice (b) is incorrect because the exchange rate movement adversely affects the return to the US company. Choice (c) is incorrect because the exchange rate movement directly affected the return to the US company, while the return to the German company was not affected. Choice (d) is incorrect. Since the return to the US company is adversely affected and the return to the German stock is unaffected, the return to the US company will definitely be lower than the return to the German company.

Subject Area: Financial accounting and finance—financial instruments. Source: CIA 1190, IV-58.

446. (b) A put option provides the right to sell the stock at a specified price. Choice (a) is incorrect because a call option would only provide the right to purchase more shares. Choice (c) is incorrect because selling a put option would possibly force the company to purchase additional stock if the option is exercised. Choice (d) is incorrect because a warrant give the holder a right to purchase stock (it is usually distributed along with debt).

Subject Area: Financial accounting and finance—financial instruments. Source: CIA 590, IV-57.

447. (d) Liquidity (marketability) risk is the risk that securities cannot be sold at a reasonable price on short notice. Choice (a) is incorrect. Default risk is the risk that a borrower will not pay the interest or principal on a loan. Choice (b) is incorrect. Interest rate risk is the risk to which investors are exposed due to changing interest rates. Choice (c) is incorrect. Purchasing power risk is the risk that inflation will reduce the purchasing power of a given sum of money.

Subject Area: Financial accounting and finance—financial instruments. Source: CIA 1190, IV-51.

Cash Management

448. (b) The cash balance called the compensating balance is the money left in a checking account in the bank in order to compensate the bank for services that it provides. Choice (a) is incorrect because the cash balance maintained for making routine payments and collections is called the transactions balance. Choice (c) is incorrect because the cash balance maintained as a reserve for unforeseen cash flow fluctuations is called the precautionary balance. Choice (d) is incorrect because it is the speculative cash balance that is maintained in order to enable the firm to take advantage of any bargain purchase opportunities that may arise.

Subject Area: Financial accounting and finance—cash management. Source: CIA Model Exam 2002, IV-36.

449. (c) Imprest bank accounts are used to make a specific amount of cash available for a limited purpose. Choice (a) is incorrect because this is the definition of a collection float, not an imprest bank account. Choice (b) is incorrect because this is a description of a general checking account. Choice (d) is incorrect because this is a description of a lockbox account.

Subject Area: Financial accounting and finance—cash management. Source: CIA 594, IV-7.

450. (d) The petty cash custodian is responsible, at all times, for the amount of the petty cash fund. Choice (a) is incorrect. The president of the company is not directly responsible for the amount of the petty cash fund. Choice (b) is incorrect. The general office manager is not directly responsible for the amount of the petty cash fund. Choice (c) is incorrect. The general cashier is not directly responsible for the amount of the petty cash fund.

Subject Area: Financial accounting and finance—cash management. Source: CIA 594, IV-8.

451. (a) It would be inappropriate to retain the petty cash receipts. They should be canceled or mutilated after they have been submitted for reimbursement, so that they cannot be used to secure a second reimbursement. Choice (b) is incorrect because surprise counts of the fund are an appropriate control procedure. Choice (c) is incorrect because requiring signed receipts is an appropriate control procedure. Choice (d) is incorrect because reimbursement by company check is an appropriate control procedure.

Subject Area: Financial accounting and finance—cash management. Source: CIA 594, IV-9.

452. (b) An impest bank account is used to make a specific amount of cash available for a limited purpose. The account acts as a clearing account for a large volume of checks or for a specific type of check. Choice (a) is incorrect. An amount is removed from the general checking account and deposited in an imprest bank account to be used for a specific type of check. Choice (c) is incorrect. Lockbox accounts are frequently used by large, multilocation companies to make collections in cities within areas of heaviest customer billing. The company rents a local post office box and authorizes a local bank to pick up the remittances mailed to that box number. Choice (d) is incorrect. There is no such thing as a compensatory account, unless the term is used to refer to a cash account maintained under a compensating balance agreement with a bank and associated with a loan acquired from that bank.

Subject Area: Financial accounting and finance—cash management. Source: CIA 597, IV-9.

453. (b) Because the check payable to the company is dated after the balance sheet date, the amount of the check should be reported as a receivable in the company December 31, 2004 balance sheet. Because the check drawn on the company's account was dated and recorded in the company books in 2004 but not mailed out until after the financial statement date, the amount of the check should be included in both the amount reported as cash and the amount reported as accounts payable in the company's December 31, 2004 balance sheet. In the control of cash, there must be a proper cutoff of cash receipts and cash disbursements. Choice (a) is incorrect because the check payable to the company is dated after the balance sheet date; the amount of the check should be reported as a receivable in the company's December 31, 2004 balance sheet. Because the check drawn on the company's account was dated and recorded in the company's books in 2004 but not mailed out until after the financial statement date; the amount of the check should be included in both the amount reported as cash and the amount reported as accounts payable in the company December 31, 2004 balance sheet. Choice (c) is incorrect because the check payable to the company is dated after the balance sheet date, the amount of the check should be reported as a receivable in the company's December 31, 2004 balance sheet. Choice (d) is incorrect because the check drawn on the company's account was dated and recorded in the company's books in 2004 but not mailed out until after the financial statement date; the amount of the check should be included in both the amount reported as cash and the amount reported as accounts payable in the company's December 31, 2004 balance sheet.

Subject Area: Financial accounting and finance—cash management. Source: CIA 1196, IV-6.

454. (d) The company's correct cash balance at July 31, 2005, is computed as follows:

Cash balance per bank statement, July 31, 2005	$40,000
Deposit in transit, July 31, 2005	5,000
Outstanding checks, July 31, 2005	(3,000)
Correct cash balance, July 31, 2005	$42,000

The bank statement already reflects the interest earned and NSF check.

Choice (a) is incorrect. The customer's check returned for insufficient funds is erroneously subtracted from the balance per bank statement at July 31, 2005. The interest earned for July is mistakenly added to the balance per bank statement at July 31, 2005.

Cash balance per bank statement, July 31,2005	$40,000
Deposit in transit, July 31, 2005	5,000
Outstanding checks, July 31, 2005	(3,000)
Return of customer's check for insufficient funds	(1,000)
Interest earned for July 2005	100
Incorrect cash balance, July 31, 2005	$41,100

Choice (b) is incorrect. The amount of the customer's check returned for insufficient funds is erroneously subtracted from the balance per bank statement at July 31, 2005.

Cash balance per bank statement, July 31, 2005	$40,000
Deposit in transit, July 31, 2005	5,000
Outstanding checks, July 31, 2005	(3,000)
Return of customer's check for insufficient funds	(1,000)
Incorrect cash balance, July 31, 2005	$41,000

Choice (c) is incorrect. The interest earned for July is erroneously added to the balance per bank statement at July 31, 2005.

Cash balance per bank statement, July 31, 2005	$40,000
Deposit in transit, July 31, 2005	5,000
Outstanding checks, July 31, 2005	(3,000)
Interest earned for July 2005	100
Incorrect cash balance, July 31, 2005	$42,100

Subject Area: Financial accounting and finance—cash management. Source: CIA 1196, IV-7.

455. (b) The correct cash balance for the company is calculated as follows:

Cash balance = Balance per bank statement
+ Deposits in transit – Outstanding checks
= $35,000 + $7,500 – $11,000
= $31,500

Deposits in transit must be added to the bank statement balance because these are deposits made by the company at the bank that do not yet show up in the statement. Outstanding checks must be deducted because these are payments made by the company and already recorded by the company in its own books that will reduce the bank account balance when the recipients cash the checks. Choice (a) is incorrect. The correct cash balance is calculated as the bank statement balance plus the deposits in transit less outstanding checks. This solution neglects to add deposits in transit and calculates the cash balance as

Cash balance = Balance per bank statement – Outstanding checks
= $35,000 – $11,000
= $24,000

Choice (c) is incorrect. This calculation does not deduct outstanding checks when calculating the correct cash balance.

Cash balance = Balance per bank statement + Deposits in transit
= $35,000 + $7,500
= $42,500

Choice (d) is incorrect. This calculation adds outstanding checks, which should be subtracted when calculating the correct cash balance.

Cash balance = Balance per bank statement
+ Deposits in transit + Outstanding checks
= $35,000 + $7,500 + $11,000 = $53,500

Subject Area: Financial accounting and finance—cash management. Source: CIA 596, IV-6.

456. (b) There are two ways to calculate the correct cash balance of the company.

Balance per bank statement	$10,000
+ Deposits in transit	2,500
– Outstanding checks	(1,500)
Correct cash balance	$11,000
Balance per depositors' books	$ 9,000
+ Bank credits and collections not yet recorded in the books	3,000
– Bank charges not yet recorded in the books	(1,000)
Correct cash balance	$11,000

Choice (a) is incorrect because this is the balance per the bank statement. It is not the correct cash balance of the company.

Choice (c) is incorrect because this solution results from an incorrect combination of the approaches shown in b., where the balance per the bank statement is adjusted for items not recorded on the books of the company.

Balance per bank statement	$10,000
+ Bank credits and collections not yet recorded in the books	3,000
– Bank charges not yet recorded in the books	(1,000)
Correct cash balance	$12,000

Choice (d) is incorrect because $10,000 solution results from incorrectly adjusting the balance per the bank statement as follows:

Balance per bank statement	$10,000
+ Bank credits and collections not yet recorded in the books	3,000
+ Deposits in transit	2,500
– Bank charges not yet recorded in the books	(1,000)
Correct cash balance	$14,500

Subject Area: Financial accounting and finance—cash management. Source: CIA 1195, IV-8.

457. (c) The effective annual interest rate is increased by both the discount interest arrangement and by the compensating balance requirement. It is calculated as

$$\text{Effective rate} = \frac{\text{Nominal rate (fraction)}}{1 - \text{Nominal rate (fraction)} - \text{Compensating balance (fraction)}}$$

$$= .15/(1 - .15 - .1) = .20 \text{ or } 20.00\%$$

Choice (a) is incorrect. This solution does not adjust for the discount interest arrangement on the loan but does adjust the nominal rate for the compensating balance requirement as follows:

$$\text{Effective annual interest rate} = \frac{\text{Nominal rate (fraction)}}{1 - \text{Compensating balance (fraction)}}$$

$$= .15/(1 - .1) = .1667 \text{ or } 16.67\%$$

Choice (b) is incorrect. This solution adjusts for the discount interest arrangement, but does not adjust the nominal rate for the compensating balance requirement, as follows:

$$\text{Effective annual interest rate} = \frac{\text{Nominal rate (fraction)}}{1 - \text{Nominal rate (fraction)}}$$

$$= .15/(1 - .15) = .1765 \text{ or } 17.65\%$$

Choice (d) is incorrect because this is the sum of the nominal rate and the compensating balance requirement, not the effective annual interest rate.

Subject Area: Financial accounting and finance—cash management. Source: CIA 1195, IV-52.

458. (a) The first term of the formula represents the periodic cost of the trade discount, calculated as the cost per unit of trade credit (discount percent) divided by the funds made available by not taking the discount (100 – Discount percent). The second term represents the number of times per year this cost is incurred. The multiple of these terms is the approximate percentage cost, on an annual basis, of not taking the trade discount. A precise formula would incorporate the effects of compounding when calculating the annual cost. Choice (b) is incorrect because the denominator of the first term should be 100 minus the discount percentage, representing the funds made available by not taking the discount. Choice (c) is incorrect because the first term should be the reciprocal of that presented. The periodic cost of the trade discount is the discount percentage divided by 100 minus the discount percentage. Choice (d) is incorrect because the second term should be the reciprocal of that presented. It should be 360 divided by the difference between the days credit is outstanding and the length of the discount period, to measure the number of times per year the cost is incurred.

Subject Area: Financial accounting and finance—cash management. Source: CIA 1195, IV-53.

459. (a) Deposits in transit are end-of-month deposits of cash recorded on the customer's books in one month that are received and recorded by the bank in the following month. Deposits in transit are not yet reflected in the bank statement, so the balance of cash reported in the bank statement is below the balance shown in the books of the customer. Choice (b) is incorrect. If there are outstanding checks, the amounts of the checks have been deducted in the books of the customer but are not reflected in the bank statement. The result will be that the balance of cash reported in the bank statement is above, not below, the balance shown in the books of the customer. Choice (c) is incorrect. If there are interest payments reflected in the bank statement that have not yet been recorded in the books of the customer, the result will be that the cash balance in the bank statement is above, not below, the balance shown in the books of the customer. Choice (d) is incorrect. If the bank has credited the customer with deposits made by another customer, then the result will be that the cash balance in the bank statement is above, not below, the balance shown in the books of the customer.

Subject Area: Financial accounting and finance—cash management. Source: CIA 595, IV-5.

460. (c) The average collection period is calculated as

$$5(10 \text{ days}) + .5(30 \text{ days}) = 5 + 15 = 20 \text{ days.}$$

Choice (a) is incorrect because it is based on 100% of the customers taking the discount. Choice (b) is incorrect because it is based on half of the customers paying on day thirty but ignores the remaining half of the customers who are paying on day 10. Choice (d) is incorrect because it is based on 100% of the customers paying on day 30.

Subject Area: Financial accounting and finance—cash management. Source: CIA 594, IV-35.

461. (d) The average accounts receivable balance is calculated as

$$\text{Credit sales per day} \times \text{Average collection period}$$
$$= (10{,}000 \text{ units} \times \$66 \text{ unit price})\ 365 \times 25 \text{ days}$$
$$= \$45{,}205.48$$

Note that it would be incorrect to deduct the expected discounts from the accounts receivable balance, since discounts are not realized until taken by the customers.

Choice (a) is incorrect because it is based on credit sales of $10,000 per annum rather than 10,000 × $66.

$$(\$10{,}000/365) \times 25 = \$684.93$$

Choice (b) is incorrect because it is the credit sales per day

$$(10{,}000 \times \$66)/365 = \$1808.22$$

Choice (c) is incorrect because the calculation is based on a 15-day average collection period

$$\$1808.22 \times 15 = \$27{,}123.30$$

Subject Area: Financial accounting and finance—cash management. Source: CIA 594, IV-36.

462. (a) The most desirable set of terms are those that result in the lowest cost of borrowing. Discount interest results in a higher effective borrowing cost than simple interest because the bank deducts interest in advance so the borrower receives less than the face value of the loan. A compensating balance results in a higher effective borrowing cost because the compensating balance is an amount of cash that the firm is unable to use. The cheapest terms, given that all options have the same nominal interest rate, will be simple interest with no compensating balance. Choice (b) is incorrect because these loan terms include discount interest. Choice (c) is incorrect because these loan terms include a compensating balance. Choice (d) is incorrect because these loan terms include both discount interest and a compensating balance.

Subject Area: Financial accounting and finance—cash management. Source: CIA 594, IV-51.

463. (a) Working capital is the excess of total current assets over total current liabilities. Computations:

Beginning working capital	$70,000	
Performed services on account	30,000	CA increase, CL no effect
Purchased supplies on account	--	CA increase, CL increase
Consumed supplies	(4,000)	CA decrease, CL no effect
Purchased office equipment	(2,000)	CA decrease, CL no effect
Paid short-term bank loan	--	CA decrease, CL decrease
Paid salaries	(10,000)	CA decrease, CL no effect
Accrued salaries	(3,500)	CA no effect, CL increase
Working capital, end of January	$80,500	

Choice (b) is incorrect. Computations follow:

Beginning working capital	$70,000
Performed services on account	30,000
Purchased supplies on account	(5,000)
Consumed supplies	--
Purchased office equipment	--
Paid short-term bank loan	(6,500)
Paid salaries	(10,000)
Accrued salaries	--
Working capital, end of January	$78,500

Choice (c) is incorrect. Computations follow:

Beginning working capital	$70,000
Performed services on account	--
Purchased supplies on account	--
Consumed supplies	(4,000)
Purchased office equipment	(2,000)
Paid short-term bank loan	--
Paid salaries	(10,000)
Accrued salaries	(3,500)
Working capital, end of January	$50,500

Choice (d) is incorrect. Computations follow:

Beginning working capital	$70,000
Performed services on account	--
Purchased supplies on account	--
Consumed supplies	(4,000)
Purchased office equipment	(2,000)
Paid short-term bank loan	(6,500)
Paid salaries	(10,000)
Accrued salaries	--
Working capital, end of January	$47,500

Subject Area: Financial accounting and finance—cash management. Source: CIA 1193, IV-36.

464. (d) (50,000 – 10,000 – .4(50,000) – 5,000)0.6 = 9,000 after-tax income. 9,000 + 5,000 = $14,000 with depreciation added back. Choice (a) is incorrect because this answer reflects the pretax income from the project. Choice (b) is incorrect because this answer reflects all cash flows, but also includes depreciation as a cash outflow. Choice (c) is incorrect because this answer reflects pretax income plus depreciation.

Subject Area: Financial accounting and finance—cash management. Source: CIA 1193, IV-50.

465. (a) The entire cash conversion cycle is included. Choices (b), (c), and (d) are incorrect because cash inflows have not yet been received.

Subject Area: Financial accounting and finance—cash management. Source: CIA 1193, IV-52.

466. (a) It can be related to a formula similar to EOQ,

$$C^* = \sqrt{\frac{2(F)(T)}{k}}$$

1 where: C^* = cash to be raised, T = total cash needed for the period, F = fixed cost of making a securities trade, and k = opportunity cost of holding cash.

Choice (b) is incorrect because a high opportunity cost results in lower optimal cash balance. Choice (c) is incorrect because a high opportunity cost results in a lower optimal cash balance, while high transactions costs result in higher cash balances. Choice (d) is incorrect because high transaction costs result in higher cash balances.

Subject Area: Financial accounting and finance—cash management. Source: CIA 593, IV-52.

467. (a) Inventory levels directly depend upon sales levels. Receivables arise after sales have been made while inventory must be acquired or produced ahead of sales. Choice (b) is incorrect because its inventory should be increased to accommodate higher sales levels. Choice (c) is incorrect because its inventory should be increased to accommodate higher sales levels. Safety stock is based on expected sales and they are expected to rise. Choice (d) is incorrect because the ABC system is not the solution to this scenario.

Subject Area: Financial accounting and finance—cash management. Source: CIA 593, IV-53.

468. (c) Working capital is computed by deducting total current liabilities from total current assets. The purchase of a delivery van for cash will reduce current assets and have no effect on current liabilities; hence working capital will be reduced. The borrowing of cash by short-term debt will increase current assets by the same amount as it increases current liabilities; hence, it will have no effect on working capital. The purchase of treasury stock will decrease current assets but have no effect on current liabilities; hence it will reduce working capital. Choice (a) is incorrect because the purchase of treasury stock will decrease working capital. Choice (b) is incorrect because the purchase of a noncurrent asset by use of a current asset will decrease working capital. The borrowing of cash by use of short-term debt will not change working capital. Choice (d) is incorrect because borrowing cash by the use of short-term debt will leave working capital unchanged.

Subject Area: Financial accounting and finance—cash management. Source: CIA 593, IV-28.

469. (b) A reorganization would involve keeping the organization alive. This is a situation where cash flows are a problem and includes replacing some of the debt outstanding with common stock. The courts and the Securities and Exchange Commission (SEC) will determine the fairness and the feasibility of the proposed reorganization plan. Choice (a) is incorrect because shortening the debt maturity would make cash flow problems worse. Choice (c) is incorrect because replacing common stock by debt would make cash flow problems worse. Choice (d) is incorrect because replacing debt by preferred stock would make cash flow problems worse.

Subject Area: Financial accounting and finance—cash management. Source: CIA 593, IV-59.

470. (b) Cost to borrow funds for 15 days to obtain discount is

$$\$4.9M \times \frac{12}{100} \times \frac{15}{360} = 24,500 = \text{Interest}$$

Total cost of accounts payable if funds are borrowed

$$\$4,900,000 + 24,500 = \$4,924,500.$$

Total cost of accounts payable if funds are not borrowed: $5,000,000 – $4,924,500 = $75,500 less cost to borrow funds than to pay on 30th day of month.

Choice (a) is incorrect because this answer uses a 30-day borrowing period. Choice (c) is incorrect because this answer accounts for the discounted price but ignores the interest paid. Choice (d) is incorrect because this answer reflects interest paid, but ignores the discounted price.

Subject Area: Financial accounting and finance—cash management. Source: CIA 1192, IV-54.

471. (c) Choice (c) is the correct answer.

$$\$270,000 \div 4.3436 = \$62,160.42 = \$62,160$$

Choice (a) is incorrect because this answer is based on dividing (270,000 × 1.16) by 8 (years). Choice (b) is incorrect because this answer is 16% of the $270,000. Choice (d) is incorrect because this answer results from multiplying the present value of a sum due (.305) instead of dividing by the present value of an annuity (4.3436).

Subject Area: Financial accounting and finance—cash management. Source: CIA 1192, IV-55.

472. (a) The average collection period is the *weighted-average* time period within which the value of receivables is collected. This value is calculated as: 14 days = 0.8(10) + 0.2(30). Choice (b) is incorrect because the average collection period is the weighted-average time period within which the value of receivables is collected. In this problem, 20 days is the simple average of the discount period of 10 days and the full-price collection period of 30 days. Choices (c) and (d) are incorrect because the average collection period is equal to the total value of receivables divided by average daily sales.

Subject Area: Financial accounting and finance—cash management. Source: CIA 1191, IV-55.

473. (b) Warehouse receipts use inventory as security. Choice (a) is incorrect because commercial paper is a type of unsecured promissory note issued by large firms to other firms, insurance companies, mutual funds, and so on. Choice (c) is incorrect because a revolving credit agreement is a formal line of credit, usually with a bank, that large firms often use. Choice (d) is incorrect because accounts payable, or trade credit, is the most prominent source of unsecured short-term financing.

Subject Area: Financial accounting and finance—cash management. Source: CIA 1191, IV-56.

474. (a) The $12,000 of interest, divided by the $100,000 received produces an effective interest rate of 12%. Choice (b) is incorrect because dividing the $10,000 of interest by the $80,000 available for use produces an effective interest rate of 12.5%. Choice (c) is incorrect because dividing the $12,100 of interest by the 97,900 available for use produces an effective interest rate of 12.36%. Choice (d) is incorrect because dividing the $17,000 of interest and points by the $93,000 available for use produces an effective interest rate of 18.28%.

Subject Area: Financial accounting and finance—cash management. Source: CIA 591, IV-60.

475. (d) In a factoring arrangement, the customers of the manufacturing firm are notified that they are to pay the factor directly to settle their invoice. Choices (a) and (b) are incorrect because the reverse is true. Choice (c) is incorrect because the assignment of receivables does not affect the relationship between the manufacturing firm and its customers. Customers continue to make payment to the manufacturing firm.

Subject Area: Financial accounting and finance—cash management. Source: CIA 594, IV-29.

476. (b) If (1) the transferor surrenders control of the future economic benefits embodied in the receivables, (2) the transferor's obligation under the recourse provisions can be reasonably estimated, and (3) the transferee cannot require the transferor to repurchase the receivables except pursuant to the recourse provisions, then the transfer is accounted for as a sale of receivables. If the foregoing three conditions are not met, the transaction is accounted for as a borrowing. Choice (a) is incorrect because both the receipt of cash and its source (either sale or borrowing transaction) must be recorded. Choice (c) is incorrect because the transfer is properly recorded as a sale only if the following three conditions are met: (1) the transferor surrenders control of the future economic benefits embodied in the receivables, (2) the transferor's obligation under the recourse provisions can be reasonably estimated, and (3) the transferee cannot require the transferor to repurchase the receivables except pursuant to the recourse provisions. Choice (d) is incorrect because the transfer is properly recorded as a sale if three conditions are met.

Subject Area: Financial accounting and finance—cash management. Source: CIA 591, IV-33.

477. (c) The days sales outstanding is the accounts receivable balance divided by average credit sales per day. Its result is the average length of time required to convert the firm's receivables into cash, which is also the definition of the receivables collection period. Choice (a) is incorrect because the inventory conversion period is the average length of time required to convert materials into finished goods and then to sell those goods. This period typically occurs before the receivables collection period, and the amount of time in each of the periods does not necessarily bear any relationship to the other. Choice (b) is incorrect because the cash conversion cycle is a combination of the inventory conversion period plus the receivables collection period minus the payables deferral period. It estimates the length of time between when the company makes payments and when it receives cash inflows. Choice (d) is incorrect because the inventory divided by the sales per day is the average length of time required to convert materials into finished goods and then to sell those goods. This result is the same as the inventory conversion period, not the receivables conversion period.

Subject Area: Financial accounting and finance—cash management. Source: CIA 597, IV-27.

478. (d) If the discount period is longer, the days of extra credit obtained by foregoing the discount are fewer. This makes the trade credit more costly. Choice (a) is incorrect because the lower the discount percentage, the lower the opportunity cost of foregoing the discount and using the trade credit financing. Choices (b) and (c) are incorrect because percentage financing cost is unaffected by the purchase price of the items.

Subject Area: Financial accounting and finance—cash management. Source: CIA 597, IV-51.

479. (c) Receivables on August sales still outstanding at the end of September are in the 31- to 60-day age group. As a proportion of total receivables, the 31- to 60-day age group represents 170/350 = 48.57%. Choice (a) is incorrect because this is the proportion of receivables in the 0- to 30-day age group at the end of September. Receivables on September sales still outstanding at the end of September are in the 0- to 30-day age group and represent 75/350 = 21.43% of total outstanding receivables at that time. Choice (b) is incorrect because this is the proportion of receivables in the 61- to 90-day age group at the end of September. Receivables on July sales still outstanding at the end of September are in the 61- to 90-day age group and represent 100/350 = 28.57% of total outstanding receivables at that time. Choice (d) is incorrect because this is the proportion of outstanding receivables that are from 0 to 60 days old and that arose from both August and September sales. As a proportion of total receivables, those that are 0 to 60 days old represent (170 + 80)/350 = 250/350 = 71.43%.

Subject Area: Financial accounting and finance—cash management. Source: CIA 1196, IV-42.

480. (b) On the 40% of sales to customers not taking the cash discount, a 10-day reduction in the average collection period will reduce the accounts receivable balance as follows:

.4(Daily unit sales)(Unit price)(Reduction in days outstanding)
= .4(1,000)($10)(10) = $40,000

Choice (a) is incorrect because this solution does not multiply the unit sales volume by the price per unit and calculates the reduction in accounts receivable as

.4(Daily unit sales) × (Reduction in days outstanding)
= .4(1,000)(10) = 4,000

Choice (c) is incorrect because this is the total balance of accounts receivable under the new collection policy.

.4(Daily unit sales)(Unit price)(Average collection period)
.4(1,000)($10)(60 days) = $240,000

Choice (d) is incorrect because this is the total balance of accounts receivable under the old collection policy.

.4(Daily unit sales)(Unit price)(Average collection period)
.4(1,000)($10)(70 days) = $280,000

Subject Area: Financial accounting and finance—cash management. Source: CIA 1196, IV-44.

481. (d) The most costly combination of characteristics is a higher compensating balance and discount interest. The higher the compensating balance, the higher the portion of the loan funds that must be left on deposit with the lender. Hence the interest paid is charged on a smaller amount of funds available to be used by the borrower and the effective cost is higher. Also, discount interest is deducted from the loan funds in advance, resulting in a further increase in the effective financing cost. Choice (a) is incorrect because lower compensating balances and regular interest rates are less costly. Choice (b) is incorrect because a lower compensating balance is cheaper than a higher compensating balance, since with a higher compensating balance, less of the loan funds is available for use by the borrower. Choice (c) is incorrect because regular interest is less costly because it is not paid in advance and it is therefore not deducted from the loaned funds that the borrower can use.

Subject Area: Financial accounting and finance—cash management. Source: CIA 1196, IV-52.

482. (b) The net cash provided by operations is calculated as follows:

Net income + Reduction in receivables – Reduction in payables
= $150,000 + (220,000 – 200,000) – (160,000 – 80,000)
= $150,000 + 20,000 – 80,000
= $90,000

A reduction in receivables represents a source of cash and a reduction in payables represents a use of cash.

Choice (a) is incorrect because this calculation fails to add to net income the reduction in accounts receivable for the year, which represents an increase in cash.

Cash provided by operations = Net income – Reduction in payables
= 150,000 – (160,000 – 80,000) = $70,000

Choice (c) is incorrect because this is net income for the year, not the amount of cash provided by operating activities. Choice (d) is incorrect because this calculation subtracts, rather than adds, the reduction in receivables and adds, rather than subtracts, the reduction in payables during the year.

Net income – Reduction in receivables + Reduction in payables
= $150,000 – (220,000 – 200,000) + (160,000 – 80,000)
= $150,000 – 20,000 + 80,000
= $210,000

Subject Area: Financial accounting and finance—cash management. Source: CIA 596, IV-10.

483. (c) A banker's acceptance is a time draft, payable on a specified future date, with the bank guaranteeing the payment. Choice (a) is incorrect because the description is of a sight draft, except that with a sight draft it is the buyer that accepts the goods, not the bank. Choice (b) is incorrect because the description is of an open account for any buyer/seller relationship. Choice (d) is incorrect because the description is of a conditional sales contract except that with a conditional sales contract it is the seller, not the bank, who retains title to the goods until the buyer has completed payment.

Subject Area: Financial accounting and finance—cash management. Source: CIA 596, IV-41.

484. (c) The cash conversion cycle is the length of time between paying for purchases and receiving cash from the sale of finished goods. It is calculated as follows:

Cash conversion cycle = Inventory conversion period
+ Receivables collection period – Payables deferral period
= 58 days + 32 days – 15 days = 75 days

Choice (a) is incorrect because this solution subtracts, rather than adds, the receivables collection period.

Cash conversion cycle = Inventory conversion period
– Receivables collection period – Payables deferral period
= 58 days – 32 days – 15 days = 11 days

Choice (b) is incorrect because this solution subtracts, rather than adds, the receivables collection period and also adds, rather than subtracts, the payables deferral period.

Cash conversion cycle = Inventory conversion period – Receivables collection period + Payables deferral period
= 58 days – 32 days + 15 days = 41 days

Choice (d) is incorrect because this calculation omits the subtraction of the payables deferral period.

Cash conversion cycle = Inventory conversion period
+ Receivables collection period
= 58 days + 32 days = 90 days

Subject Area: Financial accounting and finance—cash management. Source: CIA 596, IV-53.

485. (d) In a specific assignment of receivables the lender and borrower have agreed on which specific accounts receivable represent collateral against the loan. As receivables are collected, the borrower cannot unilaterally substitute different receivables as security against the loan. Choice (a) is incorrect because lenders with claims against assigned receivables do have recourse to the borrower. Choice (b) is incorrect because the risk of default on pledged accounts receivable does remain with the borrower. Choice (c) is incorrect because in a general assignment of receivables the borrower can substitute new receivables for the ones collected. That is, when a customer of the borrower pays in cash and the receivable is eliminated, the borrower can provide a different, new account receivable as collateral against the loan.

Subject Area: Financial accounting and finance—cash management. Source: CIA 595, IV-28.

486. (a) The opportunity cost of holding cash balances is calculated by multiplying the average cash balance by the opportunity cost percentage. The opportunity cost of holding cash balances is higher if the average cash balance is higher. Choice (b) is incorrect because everything else equal, if the average cash balance is higher, fewer replenishing transactions are needed and the total transactions costs associated with obtaining cash balances for the period are lower. Choice (c) is incorrect because the opposite is true. Choice (d) is incorrect because the total costs of holding cash balances are the sum of the opportunity costs and transactions costs. When the size of each cash transaction is suboptimal, total costs decrease if the average cash balance is increased. When the size of each cash transaction is too large, total costs increase with an increase in the average cash balance. There is an optimal average cash balance that minimizes the total costs of holding cash balances for the company. Whether total costs are lower when the average cash balance is higher depends on whether the cash balance is below, at, or above the optimal average cash balance for the company.

Subject Area: Financial accounting and finance—cash management. Source: CIA 595, IV-45.

487. (a) The opportunity cost of holding cash balances for the year is calculated as the average cash balance multiplied by the opportunity cost percentage.

Opportunity cost
= (Average cash balance)(Opportunity cost percentage)
= (20,916.50)(.10) = 2,091.65

Choice (b) is incorrect because this is the answer if the optimal cash transfer, or twice the average cash balance, in calculating the opportunity cost of holding cash for the year is used.

Opportunity cost = (Cash transfer)(Opportunity cost percentage)
= (2 × average cash balance)(Opportunity cost percentage)
= (2)(20,916.50)(.10) = 4,183.30

Choice (c) is incorrect because this is the answer if half the total cash requirement for the year, rather than the average cash balance, in calculating the opportunity cost of holding cash for the year is used.

Opportunity cost = (Total cash required/2)(Opportunity cost percentage)
= (175,000/2)(.10) = 8,750

Choice (d) is incorrect because this is the answer if the total cash required for the year, rather than the average cash balance, in calculating the opportunity cost of holding cash for the year is used.

Opportunity cost
= (Total cash required for the year)(Opportunity cost percentage)
= (175,000)(.10) = 17,500

Subject Area: Financial accounting and finance—cash management. Source: CIA 595, IV-46.

488. (d) Speculative cash balances are held to enable the firm to take advantage of any bargain purchases that might arise. Choice (a) is incorrect because transaction balances are those associated with routine payments and collections. Choice (b) is incorrect because compensating balances are minimum amounts left on deposit at the bank to compensate the bank for providing loans and services. Choice (c) is incorrect because precautionary balances are reserves for random, unforeseen fluctuations in inflows and outflows.

Subject Area: Financial accounting and finance—cash management. Source: CIA 1194, IV-15.

489. (b) Seasonal dating is a procedure for inducing customers to buy early by not requiring payment until the customers' selling season, regardless of when the merchandise is shipped. Under seasonal dating the selling firm incurs higher credit costs as customers take longer to pay. This is not an advantage of seasonal dating. Choice (a) is incorrect because under seasonal dating, customers buy earlier and the selling firm incurs lower storage costs. This is an advantage of seasonal dating. Choice (c) is incorrect because providing attractive credit terms for customers is an advantage of a seasonal dating policy. Choice (d) is incorrect because reduced uncertainty about sales volume is an advantage of a seasonal dating policy.

Subject Area: Financial accounting and finance—cash management. Source: CIA 1194, IV-29.

490. (c) If all customers take advantage of seasonal dating and all customers take the discount, then collections on or before January 11 will be

= (Number of units sold)(Unit selling price) (1 – Discount percentage)
= (700 units) @ \$10 (1 – .02) = \$7,000(.98) = \$6,860

Choice (a) is incorrect because all customers take the discount and abide by the terms of the discount policy, so they will pay on or before January 11 (see choice c). Choice (b) is incorrect because this solution omits the collection of the January 1 sales revenue (see c. for the correct solution).

Collections = (300 + 100 + 100 + 150) @ \$10(.98)
= (650) @\$9.80 = \$ 6,370

Choice (d) is incorrect because this solution does not take the discount into account (see c. for the correct solution).

Collections = (300 + 100 + 100 + 150 + 50) @\$10
= (700) @ 10 = \$7,000

Subject Area: Financial accounting and finance—cash management. Source: CIA 1194, IV-30.

491. (a) Working capital is computed by subtracting total current liabilities (\$120,000) from total current assets (\$300,000) which in this case yields an answer of \$180,000. Choice (b) is incorrect because this answer could have been obtained from the data given by deducting total liabilities (\$1,600,000) from total fixed assets (\$2,000,000) or by looking just at the total paid-in capital (\$400,000), neither of which is the way to compute working capital. Choice (c) is incorrect because this answer could be obtained from the data given either by deducting total fixed assets (\$2,000,000) from total assets (\$2,500,000) or by subtracting total paid-in capital (\$400,000) from total stockholders' equity (\$900,000), neither of which will yield the amount of working capital. Choice (d) is incorrect because the answer was obtained by deducting total liabilities (\$1,600,000) from total assets (\$2,500,000) which is not the correct procedure to calculate working capital.

Subject Area: Financial accounting and finance—cash management. Source: CIA 590, IV-37.

492. (d) The firm will need 10,000 units for January sales plus 3,000 for inventory. Subtract the 2,500 in beginning inventory, leaving a production quota for January of 10,500. Each unit requires two pounds of materials, or 21,000 pounds. At \$4 per pound, the materials will cost \$84,000, which will be paid in February. Therefore, by definition, choice (a), (b), and (c) will be incorrect.

Subject Area: Financial accounting and finance—cash management. Source: CIA 590, IV-12.

493. (a) This is the definition of factoring. Choice (b) is incorrect because factoring does not refer to inventory. Choice (c) is incorrect because factoring does not refer to an accounting adjustment for overdue accounts. Choice (d) is incorrect because factoring does not refer to an accounting adjustment for obsolete inventory.

Subject Area: Financial accounting and finance—cash management. Source: CIA 590, IV-50.

494. (b) This answer is based on the \$3 million cash inflows from last year's credit sales, the \$35 million cash inflows from next year's cash sales and the \$50 million cash outflows from next year's cash expenses. Choice (a) is incorrect because this answer results from including next year's credit sales in the estimation of next year's cash inflows. Choice (c) is incorrect because this answer results from excluding the \$3 million cash inflows that result from last year's credit sales. Choice (d) is incorrect because this answer results from including depreciation when estimating cash outflows.

Subject Area: Financial accounting and finance—cash management. Source: CIA 590, IV-55.

495. (b) Collections on account are beginning accounts receivable of \$180,000 plus sales on account of \$800,000 less budgeted ending balance of accounts receivable of \$210,000 equals \$770,000. The beginning cash balance of \$50,000 plus cash collections on account of \$770,000 less budgeted cash disbursements of \$780,000 equals \$40,000. Depreciation of \$25,000 is excluded as it is a noncash expense. Choice (a) is incorrect because this is the beginning cash balance of \$50,000 plus cash collections on account of \$770,000 less total expenses of \$805,000. Depreciation of \$25,000 should be excluded as it is a noncash expense. Choice (c) is incorrect because this is the beginning cash balance of \$50,000 plus budgeted sales on account of \$800,000 less total expenses of \$805,000. Choice (d) is incorrect because this is the beginning cash balance of \$50,000 plus sales on account of \$800,000 less budgeted cash disbursements of \$780,000.

Subject Area: Financial accounting and finance—cash management. Source: CIA 1190, IV-16.

496. (c)

Change in cash = Change in working capital – Change in noncash current assets + Change in current liabilities
=12,000 – (15,000 + 36,000 – 3,000) + (16,000 + 1,000)
= –19,000

Therefore, by definition, choices (a), (b), and (d) will be incorrect.

Subject Area: Financial accounting and finance—cash management. Source: CIA 1190, IV-31.

497. (a) Temporary investments are held temporarily in place of cash and can be readily converted into cash when needed. They must be (1) readily marketable, and (2) intended to be converted into cash as needed within one year or the operating cycle, whichever is longer. Items I and III satisfy these two criteria. Item II does not. Therefore, by definition, choices (b), (c), and (d) will be incorrect.

Subject Area: Financial accounting and finance—cash management. Source: CIA 1190, IV-32.

Valuation Models

498. (b) The first-in-first-out (FIFO) method assumes that the oldest and hence least costly units have been removed from inventory. This method will result in the highest inventory balance if costs rise steadily during the accounting period. This then results to the lowest cost of goods sold and therefore the highest net income. Choice (a) is incorrect because the last-in-first-out (LIFO) method assumes that the most recent and hence costliest units have been removed from inventory. This method will result in the lowest inventory balance if costs rise steadily during the accounting period, the highest cost of good sold and the lowest net income. Choice (c) is incorrect because the weighted-average cost method will average the cost of all inventory items and will result in a lower inventory balance and net income than does the FIFO method. Choice (d) is incorrect because specific identification charges the actual cost of each unit to cost of goods sold each period, leaving as inventory the actual cost of all items still in inventory. Since the question states that the newest and most costly items are removed from inventory first, the inventory balance and net income will be lower than that obtained using FIFO estimation.

Subject Area: Financial accounting and finance—valuation models (inventory). Source: CIA 594, IV-17.

499. (a) Under FIFO inventory valuation, the 10,000 units in ending inventory are assumed to have been the most recent items purchased. The cost of the most recent 10,000 units purchased is

5,000 units @ \$7.50 + 5,000 units @ \$8
= \$37,500 + \$40,000 = \$77,500.

Choice (b) is incorrect. This solution is the ending inventory balance under the specific identification method if the units remaining in inventory at year-end were identified as having been purchased on April 1 and July 1.

5,000 units @ \$9 + 5,000 units @ \$8 = \$45,000 + \$40,000 = \$85,000.

Choice (c) is incorrect. This solution is the ending inventory balance under the average cost method. The average cost of all items purchased is used to calculate the ending inventory balance. The average cost of items purchased is

[\$10(5,000) + \$9(5,000) + \$8(5,000) + \$7.50(5,000)]/20,000
= \$8.625 per unit

So 10,000 units are assigned a value of \$86,250.

Choice (d) is incorrect. This solution is the ending inventory balance under the last-in, first-out (LIFO) method of inventory valuation. The most recent items purchased are assumed to be sold first, so the items remaining in inventory are assigned the cost of the earliest purchases.

5,000 units @ \$10 + 5,000 units @ \$9 = \$50,000 + \$45,000
= \$95,000

Subject Area: Financial accounting and finance—valuation models (inventory). Source: CIA Model Exam 2002, IV-27.

500. (a) Under last-in, first-out (LIFO), the 10,000 units sold during the year are assumed to have been those purchased most recently. The cost of goods sold for the year is calculated as

5,000 units @ \$7.50 + 5,000 units @ \$8
= \$37,500 + \$40,000 = \$77,500.

Choice (b) is incorrect. This is the solution if the average cost method is used. The average cost of all items purchased is \$8.625 per unit so the 10,000 units sold are assigned a cost of $86,250. Choice (c) is incorrect. This is the solution if the specific identification method is used and if the units remaining in inventory at yearend were identified as having been purchased on April 1 and July 1. The sold items would then have been purchased on January 1 and October 1, and cost of goods sold for the year is calculated as

5,000 units @ $10 + 5,000 units @ $7.50
= $50,000 + $37,500 = $87,500.

Choice (d) is incorrect. This is the solution if the first-in, first-out (FIFO) method is used. Under FIFO, the oldest items are assumed to have been sold, so cost of goods sold for the year is calculated as

5,000 units @ $10 + 5,000 units @ $9 = $50,000 + $45,000 = $95,000

Subject Area: Financial accounting and finance—valuation models (inventory). Source: CIA Model Exam 2002, IV-28.

501. (b) Computations follow: Markup on cost 25%, that is, Cost + Markup on cost = 20% markup on sales.

Sales	$900,000
Cost of sales ratio (100% – 20%)	80%
Estimated cost of goods sold	$720,000
Beginning inventory	$ X
Purchases	690,000
Freight-in on purchases	25,000
Goods available for sale	Y
Ending inventory	(80,000)
Cost of goods sold (estimated)	$720,000

Solving for goods available for sale

Y – 80,000 = 720,000
Y = $720,000 + $80,000 = $800,000

Solving for beginning inventory

X + $690,000 + $25,000 = $800,000
X = $85,000 = Beginning inventory

Choice (a) is incorrect. This answer incorrectly uses 25%, rather than 20%, as the markup on sales. Computations follow:

Sales	$900,000
Cost of sales ratio (100% – 25%)	75%
Estimated cost of goods sold	$675,000
Beginning inventory	$ X
Purchases	690,000
Freight-in on purchases	25,000
Goods available for sale	Y
Ending inventory	(80,000)
Cost of goods sold (estimated)	$675,000

Solving for goods available for sale

Y – 80,000 = 675,000
Y = $675,000 + $80,000 = $755,000

Solving for beginning inventory

X + $690,000 + $25,000 = $755,000
X = $40,000 = Beginning inventory

Choice (c) is incorrect. This answer incorrectly omits the freight-in from the computation of cost of goods available for sale. Computations follow: Markup on cost 25%, that is, Cost + Markup on cost = 20% markup on sales.

Sales	$900,000
Cost of sales ratio (100% – 20%)	80%
Estimated cost of goods sold	$720,000
Beginning inventory	$ X
Purchases	690,000
Goods available for sale	Y
Ending inventory	(80,000)
Cost of goods sold (estimated)	$720,000

Solving for goods available for sale

Y – 80,000 = 720,000
Y = $720,000 + $80,000 = $800,000

Solving for beginning inventory

X + $690,000 = $800,000
X = $110,000 = Beginning inventory

Choice (d) is incorrect. This answer incorrectly uses the sales figure for cost of goods sold; it therefore ignores the markup of 20% on sales. Computations follow:

Beginning inventory	$ X
Purchases	690,000
Freight-in on purchases	25,000
Goods available for sale	Y
Ending inventory	(80,000)
Cost of goods sold	$900,000

Solving for goods available for sale

Y – 80,000 = 900,000
Y = $900,000 + $80,000 = $980,000

Solving for beginning inventory

X + $690,000 + $25,000 = $980,000
X = $265,000 = Beginning inventory

Subject Area: Financial accounting and finance—valuation models (inventory). Source: CIA Model Exam 1998, IV-14.

502. (d) The understatement of the beginning inventory will cause an understatement in the cost of goods sold expense, which will cause an overstatement of net income, by $13,000. The overstatement of the ending inventory will cause an understatement in the cost of goods sold expense, which will cause an overstatement of net income, by $26,000. The total effect is an overstatement of net income by $39,000. Choice (a) is incorrect. The understatement of the beginning inventory will cause an understatement in the cost of goods sold expense, which will cause an overstatement of net income, by $13,000. The overstatement of the ending inventory will cause an understatement in the cost of goods sold expense, which will cause an overstatement of net income, by $26,000. The total effect is an overstatement of net income by $39,000. Choice (b) is incorrect. Net income of Year 5 will be overstated. Choice (c) is incorrect. The understatement of the beginning inventory will cause an understatement in the cost of goods sold expense, which will cause an overstatement of net income, by $13,000. The overstatement of the ending inventory will cause an understatement in the cost of goods sold expense, which will cause an overstatement of net income, by $26,000. The total effect is an overstatement of net income by $39,000.

Subject Area: Financial accounting and finance—valuation models (inventory). Source: CIA 1191, IV-35.

503. (c) Computations follow:

(5,000 units @ $7) + (7,000 units @ $6.25)
= $35,000 + $43,750 = $78,750.

Choice (a) is incorrect. This would be the ending inventory balance under the last-in-last-out (LIFO) method of inventory valuation.

(10,000 units @$5) + (2,000 units @$6) = $50,000 + $12,000 = $62,000.

Choice (b) is incorrect. This would be the ending inventory balance under the weighted-average valuation method.

10,000 units @ $5	Cost $50,000
6,000 units @ $6	Cost $36,000
8,000 units @ $6.25	Cost $50,000
5,000 units @ $7	Cost $35,000

Totals 29,000 units at a total cost of $171,000
Average cost per unit = $171,000/29,000 = $5.89655
Ending inventory = (12,000 units @ $5.89655) = $70,759

Choice (d) is incorrect. This is 12,000 units at the most recent price of $7 per unit.

Subject Area: Financial accounting and finance—valuation models (inventory). Source: CIA 594, IV-18.

504. **(c)** The $122,000 should be included because with freight terms of free on board (FOB) destination, title to the goods will not pass until the customer receives the goods. The $82,000 should not be included in the inventory because with freight terms of free on board (FOB) shipping point, title to the goods passed when the goods left the shipper's dock. Choice (a) is incorrect because the inventory should include the $122,000 shipped to a customer free on board (FOB) destination. Choice (b) is incorrect because the inventory should not include the $82,000 but it should include the $122,000. Choice (d) is incorrect because the $82,000 should not be included in the inventory.

Subject Area: Financial accounting and finance—valuation models (inventory). Source: CIA 1193, IV-31.

505. **(b)** The model for the retail method of inventory estimation is as follows:

	Cost	Retail
Beginning inventory	XXX	YYY
Purchases	XXX	YYY
Freight-in	XX	
Goods available for sale	XXXX	YYYY
Ratio = XXXX/YYYY		
Sales		(YYY)
Estimated shrinkage		(YY)
Sales returns		YY
Ending inventory at retail		YYY
Ending inventory at cost	XXX	

Ratio × Ending inventory at retail = Ending inventory at cost.

Shrinkage has no effect on the cost/retail ratio computation but it should be deducted in arriving at the estimated ending inventory at retail. An overstatement of the ending inventory at retail will result if shrinkage is ignored. Choice (a) is incorrect because the estimated shrinkage at retail should be deducted from the goods available at retail to arrive at the estimated ending inventory at retail. Choice (c) is incorrect because shrinkage has no effect on the cost/retail ratio calculation. Choice (d) is incorrect because shrinkage has no effect on the cost/retail ratio computation but it should be deducted in arriving at the estimated ending inventory at retail. An overstatement of the ending inventory at retail will result if shrinkage is ignored.

Subject Area: Financial accounting and finance—valuation models (inventory). Source: CIA 593, IV-35.

506. **(b)** Computations follow:

Sales	$180,000
Cost of goods sold	(X)
Gross margin	$ 60,000

Solving for X

$180,000 – $60,000 = $120,000, or cost of goods sold

Beginning inventory	$ 50,000
Purchases	170,000
Goods available for sale	220,000
Ending inventory	(Y)
Cost of goods sold	120,000

Solving for Y

$220,000 – $120,000 = $100,000 Ending inventory

Choice (a) is incorrect. This answer incorrectly subtracts the gross margin ($60,000) from the cost of goods sold ($120,000). Choice (c) is incorrect. This answer represents the cost of goods sold ($180,000 – $60,000). Choice (d) is incorrect. This answer incorrectly deducts the gross margin ($60,000) from the goods available for sale ($50,000 + $170,000).

Subject Area: Financial accounting and finance—valuation models (inventory). Source: CIA 597, IV-11.

507. **(b)** Computations follow: Markup on cost 25%, that is, Cost + Markup on cost = 20% markup on sales

Sales	$900,000
Cost of sales ratio (100% – 20%)	80%
Estimated cost of goods sold	$720,000
Beginning inventory	$ X
Purchases	690,000
Freight-in on purchases	25,000
Goods available for sale	Y
Ending inventory	(80,000)
Cost of goods sold (estimated)	$720,000

Solving for goods available for sale

Y – 80,000 = 720,000
Y = $720,000 + $80,000 = $800,000

Solving for beginning inventory

X + $690,000 + $25,000 = $800,000
X = $85,000 = Beginning inventory

Choice (a) is incorrect. This answer uses 25%, rather than 20%, as the markup on sales. Computations follow:

Sales	$900,000
Cost of sales ratio (100% – 25%)	75%
Estimated cost of goods sold	$675,000
Beginning inventory	$ X
Purchases	690,000
Freight-in on purchases	25,000
Goods available for sale	Y
Ending inventory	(80,000)
Cost of goods sold (estimated)	$675,000

Solving for goods available for sale

Y – 80,000 = 675,000
Y = $675,000 + $80,000 = $755,000

Solving for beginning inventory

X + $690,000 + $25,000 = $755,000
X = $40,000 = Beginning inventory

Choice (c) is incorrect. This answer incorrectly omits the freight-in from the computation of cost of goods available for sale. Computations follow: Markup on cost 25%, that is, Cost + Markup on cost = 20% markup on sales.

Sales	$900,000
Cost of sales ratio (100% – 20%)	80%
Estimated cost of goods sold	$720,000
Beginning inventory	$ X
Purchases	690,000
Goods available for sale	Y
Ending inventory	(80,000)
Cost of goods sold (estimated)	$720,000

Solving for goods available for sale

Y – 80,000 = 720,000
Y = $720,000 + $80,000 = $800,000

Solving for beginning inventory

X + $690,000 = $800,000
X = $110,000 = Beginning inventory

Choice (d) is incorrect. This answer incorrectly uses the sales figure for cost of goods sold; it therefore ignores the markup of 20% on sales. Computations follow:

Beginning inventory	$ X
Purchases	690,000
Freight-in on purchases	25,000
Goods available for sale	Y
Ending inventory	(80,000)
Cost of goods sold	$900,000

Solving for goods available for sale

Y – 80,000 = 900,000
Y = $900,000 + $80,000 = $980,000

Solving for beginning inventory

X + $690,000 + $25,000 = $980,000
X = $265,000 = Beginning inventory

Subject Area: Financial accounting and finance—valuation models (inventory). Source: CIA 597, IV-15.

508. (c) FIFO assigns the most recent purchase prices to ending inventory and the earliest purchase prices to cost of goods sold. LIFO uses the earliest acquisition costs to price the ending inventory. Thus, FIFO approximates current cost for ending inventory, and LIFO approximates current cost of goods sold. Choice (a) is incorrect. LIFO (last-in, first-out) generally approximates current cost of goods sold. Choice (b) is incorrect. FIFO (first-in, first-out) generally approximates current cost for ending inventory. LIFO generally approximates current cost of goods sold. Choice (d) is incorrect. FIFO approximates current cost for ending inventory.

Subject Area: Financial accounting and finance—valuation models (inventory). Source: CIA 597, IV-16.

509. (c) The gross profit (margin) percentage is given as a percentage of sales and therefore does not require an adjustment. The estimated cost of the merchandise inventory at March 31, 2005, is computed as follows:

Merchandise inventory, January 1, 2005		$ 30,000
Purchases from January 1, 2005, to March 31, 2005		190,000
Cost of goods available for sale, March 31, 2005		220,000
Estimated cost of goods sold		
Sales from January 1, 2005, to March 31, 2005	$200,000	
Estimated gross profit (margin) ($200,000 × 20%)	(40,000)	(160,000)
Estimated cost of merchandise inventory at March 31, 2005		$ 60,000

Choice (a) is incorrect. This answer is derived by subtracting the period's sales from the period's cost of goods available for sale.

Merchandise inventory, January 1, 2005	$ 30,000
Purchases from January 1, 2005, to March 31, 2005	190,000
Cost of goods available for sale, March 31, 2005	220,000
Sales from January 1, 2005, to March 31, 2005	(200,000)
Incorrect estimate of cost of merchandise inventory at March 31, 2005	$ 20,000

Choice (b) is incorrect. This answer is derived by multiplying the period's sales by the period's gross profit (margin) percentage.

Sales from January 1, 2005, to March 31, 2005	$200,000
Gross profit (margin) percentage on sales	x 20%
Incorrect estimate of cost of merchandise inventory at March 31, 2005	$ 40,000

Choice (d) is incorrect. This answer is derived by subtracting the period's estimated gross profit (margin) from the period's cost of goods available for sale.

Merchandise inventory, January 1, 2005	$ 30,000
Purchases from January 1, 1995, to March 31, 2005	190,000
Cost of goods available for sale, March 31, 2005	220,000
Estimated gross profit (margin) ($200,000 × 20%)	(40,000)
Incorrect estimate of cost of merchandise inventory at March 31, 2005	$180,000

Subject Area: Financial accounting and finance—valuation models (inventory). Source: CIA 1196, IV-8.

510. (d) Using the retail method to approximate a lower of average cost or market valuation, the cost of the merchandise inventory at December 31, 2005, is computed as follows:

	Cost	*Retail*
Merchandise inventory, January 1, 2005	$ 9,000	$13,000
Purchases	33,000	46,000
Markups, net	--	1,000
	$42,000	60,000
Sales		(48,000)
Markdowns, net		(4,000)
Merchandise inventory at retail, December 31, 2005		8,000
Cost-to-retail ratio ($42,000 $60,000)		x 70%
Merchandise inventory at cost, December 31, 2005		$ 5,600

Choice (a) is incorrect. This answer neglects to subtract the net markdowns to compute the merchandise inventory at retail at December 31, 2005.

	Cost	*Retail*
Merchandise inventory, January 1, 2005	$ 9,000	$13,000
Purchases	33,000	46,000
Markups, net	--	1,000
	$42,000	60,000
Sales		(48,000)
Erroneous estimate of merchandise inventory at retail, December 31, 2005		12,000
Cost-to-retail ratio ($42,000 $60,000)		× 70%
Incorrect estimate of merchandise inventory at cost, December 31, 2005		$ 8,400

Choice (b) is incorrect. This answer is the merchandise inventory at retail at December 31, 2005.

	Cost	*Retail*
Merchandise inventory, January 1, 2005	$ 9,000	$13,000
Purchases	33,000	46,000
Markups, net	--	1,000
	$42,000	60,000
Sales	(48,000)	
Markdowns, net	(4,000)	
Merchandise inventory at retail, December 31, 2005	$ 8,000	

Choice (c) is incorrect. This answer is computed by erroneously including the net markdowns in the cost-to-retail ratio.

	Cost	*Retail*
Merchandise inventory, January 1, 2005	$ 9,000	$13,000
Purchases	33,000	46,000
Markups, net		1,000
Markdowns, net		(4,000)
	$42,000	56,000
Sales		(48,000)
Merchandise inventory at retail, December 31, 2005	8,000	
Erroneous cost-to-retail ratio ($42,000 $56,000)	× 75%	
Incorrect estimate of merchandise inventory at cost at December 31, 2005	$ 6,000	

Subject Area: Financial accounting and finance—valuation models (inventory). Source: CIA 1196, IV-9.

511. (c) Choice (c) is the correct answer.

Beginning inventory (200 units @ $3.50) + Purchases [(250 units @ $3.30) + (200 units @ $3.10) + (350 units @ $3.00)] – Ending inventory [(150 units @ $3.30) + (50 units @ $3.00) + (50 units @ $3.50)]

Choice (a) is incorrect. Correct answer using periodic LIFO inventory pricing

Beginning inventory (200 units @ $3.50) + Purchases [(250 units @ $3.30) + (200 units @ $3.10) + (350 units @ $3.00)] – Ending inventory [(200 units @ $3.50) + (50 units @ $3.30)]

Choice (b) is incorrect. Ignores beginning inventory when determining the value of ending inventory

Beginning inventory = (200 units @ $3.50) + Purchase [(250 units @ $3.30) + (200 units @ $3.10) + (350 units @ $3.00)] – Ending inventory (250 units $3.30)

Choice (d) is incorrect.

Beginning inventory = (200 units $3.50) + Purchases [(250 units @ $3.30) + (200 units @ $3.10) + (350 units @ $3.00)] – Ending inventory [(50 units @ $3.50) + (150 units @ $3.30) + (50 units @ $3.10)]

Subject Area: Financial accounting and finance—valuation models (inventory). CIA 1196, IV-21.

512. (b) Sales (750 units @ $7.00) less cost of good sold {beginning inventory (200 units @ $3.50) plus purchases [(250 units @ $3.30) + (200 units @ $3.10) + (350 units @ $3.00)] less ending inventory (250 units @ $3.00)}. Choice (a) is incorrect. This answer is sales (750 units @ $7.00) less purchase [(250 units @ $3.30) + (200 units @ $3.00)]. Choice (c) is incorrect. This answer is the same as (b) except it uses a weighted-average ending inventory value (250 units @ $3.195). Choice (d) is incorrect. This answer is the same as (b) except is uses a periodic LIFO inventory value.

Subject Area: Financial accounting and finance—valuation model (inventory). Source: CIA 1196, IV-22.

513. (b) Under the FIFO method, the 1,700 units of ending inventory are valued at the most recent prices. Ending inventory is valued as if it includes

1,000 units purchased November 24 @ $1.65 = $1,650
500 units purchased May 5 @ $2.20 = $1,100
200 units purchased January 12 @ $2.00 = $400

So the ending inventory balance

= $1,650 + $1,100 + $400 = $3,150

Choice (a) is incorrect. This is the ending inventory balance under the specific identification method. The 1,700 items remaining in ending inventory include

700 units purchased January 12 @ $2.00 = $1,400
1,000 units purchased November 24 @ $1.65 = $1,650

So the ending inventory balance

= $1,400 + $1,650 = $3,050

Choice (c) is incorrect. This is the ending inventory balance under the weighted-average cost method of inventory valuation.

Total inventory costs = 1000 @ $2.00 + 500 @ $2.20 + 1,000 @ $1.65 = $2,000 + $1,100 + $1,650 = $4,750
Weighted-average unit cost = $4,750 / 2,500 units = $1.90 per unit
Ending inventory balance = 1,700 units @ $1.90 = $3,230

Choice (d) is incorrect. This is the ending inventory balance under the last-in-first-out (LIFO) method of inventory valuation. Under the LIFO method, the 1,700 units of ending inventory are valued at the unit costs of the items purchased the longest time ago. Ending inventory is valued as if it includes

1000 units purchased January 12 @ $2.00 = $2,000
500 units purchased May 5 @ $2.20 = $1,100
200 units purchased November 24 @ $1.65 = $330

So the ending inventory balance

= $2,000 + $1,100 + $330 = $3,430

Subject Area: Financial accounting and finance—valuation models (inventory). Source: CIA 596, IV-17.

514. (d) Of the 800 units sold during the period, the 300 units sold on March 15 were purchased on January 12 at a cost of $2.00 per unit and the remaining 500 units were purchased on May 5 at a cost of $2.20 per unit. The cost of goods sold under the specific identification method is therefore

300 units @ $2.00 + 500 units @ $2.20 = $600 + $1,100 = $1,700

Choice (a) is incorrect. This is the cost of goods sold under the last-in, first-out (LIFO) method of inventory valuation. Under LIFO, the 800 units sold are assigned the cost of the most recent purchases.

800 units @ $1.65 cost on November 24 = $1,320

Choice (b) is incorrect. This is the cost of goods sold under the weighted-average method of inventory valuation.

Total inventory costs = 1000 @ $2.00 + 500 @ $2.20 + 1,000 @ $1.65 = $2,000 + $1,100 + $1,650 = $4,750
Weighted-average unit cost = $4,750/2,500 units = $1.90 per unit
Cost of goods sold = 800 units @ $1.90 = $1,520

Choice (c) is incorrect. This is the cost of goods sold under the first-in, first-out (FIFO) method of inventory valuation. Under FIFO, the items sold are assigned the cost of the oldest items in inventory during the period.

800 units @ $2.00 cost on January 12 = $1,600

Subject Area: Financial accounting and finance—valuation models (inventory). Source: CIA 596, IV-18.

515. (b) The value of ending inventory under the first-in, first-out (FIFO) method of inventory valuation is calculated as follows: Value of 20,500 units in ending inventory if they are the most recent purchases

= 12,500 units purchased October 1 @ $10 per unit
+ 8,000 units purchased July 1 @ $9 per unit = $197,000

Choice (a) is incorrect. This is the value of ending inventory under the last-in, first-out (LIFO) method of inventory valuation, calculated as follows:

Total units available for sale = Opening units + Purchased units = 8,000 + 15,000 + 10,000 + 12,500 = 45,500

Units in ending inventory = Units available – Units sold = 45,500 – 25,000 = 20,500

Value of 20,500 units in ending inventory if they are the least recent purchases

= 8,000 opening inventory @ $10 per unit
+ 12,500 units purchased April 1 @ $8 per unit
= $80,000 + $100,000 = $180,000
= 125,000 + $72,000 = $197,000

Choice (c) is incorrect. This is the cost assigned to the 25,000 units sold under the FIFO method, calculated as follows: Cost of the 25,000 units sold, if they are the least recent purchases

= 8,000 units in opening inventory @ $10 per unit
+ 15,000 units purchased April 1 @ $8 per unit
+ 2,000 units purchased July 1 @ $9 per unit
= $80,000 + $120,000 + $18,000 = $218,000

Choice (d) is incorrect. This is the cost assigned to the 25,000 units sold under the LIFO method, calculated as follows: Cost of the 25,000 units sold, if they are the most recent purchases

= 12,500 units purchased October 1 @ $10 per unit
+ 10,000 units purchased July 1 @ $9 per unit

Subject Area: Financial accounting and finance—valuation models (inventory). Source: CIA 1195, IV-17.

516. (c) Under the weighted-average cost method, the weighted-average cost per unit is multiplied by the number of units sold to determine the cost of goods sold for the period. Total units available for sale

= Opening units + Purchased units
= 8,000 + 15,000 + 10,000 + 12,500 = 45,500

Total cost of all units available for sale

= 8,000($10) + 15,000($8) + 10,000($9) + 12,500($10) = $415,000

Weighted-average cost per unit of inventory

= $415,000/45,500 = $ 9.1209

Cost of goods sold

= 25,000 units × $9.1209 = $ 228,023

Choice (a) is incorrect. This is the value of ending inventory under the weighted-average cost method, calculated as follows: Total units available for sale

= Opening units + Purchased units
= 8,000+ 15,000 + 10,000 + 12,500 = 45,500

Units in ending inventory

= Units available – units sold = 45,500 – 25,000 = 20,500

Value of 20,500 units at average cost of $9.1209 (see c.)

= 20,500($9.1209) = $186,978

Choice (b) is incorrect. This is the ending inventory under the first-in, first-out method of inventory valuation, calculated as follows: Value of 20,500 units in ending inventory if they are the most recent purchases

= 12,500 units purchased October 1 @ $10 per unit
+ 8,000 units purchased July 1 @ $9 per unit
= $125,000 + $72,000 = $197,000

Choice (d) is incorrect. This is the cost of goods sold under the last-in, first-out (LIFO) method of inventory valuation, calculated as follows: Cost of the 25,000 units sold, if they are the most recent purchases

= 12,500 units purchased October 1 @ $10 per unit
+ 10,000 units purchased July 1 @ $9 per unit
+ 2,500 units purchased April 1 @ $8 per unit
= $125,000 + $90,000 + $20,000 = $235,000
+ 2,500 units purchased April 1 @ $8 per unit
= $125,000 + $90,000 + $20,000 = $235,000

Subject Area: Financial accounting and finance—valuation models (inventory). Source: CIA 1195, IV-18.

517. (c) Under the first-in, first-out (FIFO) method of inventory valuation, the oldest items in inventory are presumed to have been sold. These are the 1000 items that were in inventory at the start of the period, which cost $10,000, and the items purchased on May 1 for $11,000, for total cost of goods sold of $21,000. Choice (a) is incorrect. It is under the weighted-average method of inventory valuation that cost of goods sold will be $22,000. The weighted-average cost of all items available for sale is ($10,000 + $11,000 + $12,000)/3000 = $11 per unit. Since 2000 units were sold, cost of goods sold would be 2000 ($11) = $22,000 under this method. Choice (b) is incorrect. Cost of goods sold would be $22,000 under the weighted-average method of inventory valuation. It is under the last-in, first-out (LIFO) method that cost of goods sold would be $23,000, since the 2000 most recently purchased units would be presumed to have been sold and they cost $12,000 plus $11,000 or $23,000. Choice (d) is incorrect. It is under the first-in, first-out (FIFO) method of inventory valuation that cost of goods sold would be $21,000. Under the weighted-average method, cost of goods sold would be $22,000.

Subject Area: Financial accounting and finance—valuation models (inventory). Source: CIA 595, IV-13.

518. (b) Since 700 units were sold during the year, the ending inventory which is valued at $2500 includes 400 units, 100 purchased on March 1 for $7 each and 300 units with an unknown cost purchased on September 1.

$2500 = 100 ($7) + 300 (unknown cost)
Unknown cost = ($2500 – $700)/300 = $6.00

Choice (a) is incorrect. If calculations are based on the company having sold 600, rather than 700, units during the year. The ending inventory which is valued at $2500 includes 500 units, 200 purchased on March 1 for $7 each and 300 units with an unknown cost purchased on September 1.

$2500 = 200 ($7) + 300 (unknown cost)
Unknown cost = ($2500 – $1400)/300 = $3.67

Choice (c) is incorrect. This is the answer if the units purchased on March 1 are assigned a cost of $5 each (the per unit cost of the opening inventory).

$2500 = 100 ($5) + 300 (unknown cost)
Unknown cost = ($2500 –$500)/300 = $6.67

Choice (d) is incorrect. This is the answer if the weighted-average method of inventory valuation is used rather than first-in, first-out. The cost of the 400 units remaining in inventory, that have been assigned a value of $2500, is calculated as

$2500 = (Average cost per unit)(400)
$2500 = (Total cost of all units available for sale/Number of units available for sale)(400)

$$\$2500 = \left[\frac{500\,(\$5) + 300\,(\$7) + 300\,(\text{unknown})}{1100}\right](400)$$

$2500 (1100) /400 = $2500 + $2100 + 300 (unknown)
$6875 = $4600 + 300 (unknown)
Unknown = ($6875 – $4600)/300 = $ 7.58

Subject Area: Financial accounting and finance—valuation models (inventory). Source: CIA 595, IV-14.

519. (c) Cost of goods sold equals opening inventory plus purchases less closing inventory. If closing inventory is underestimated, cost of goods sold will be overestimated for the period. If cost of goods sold is overestimated, the net earnings for the period will be underestimated. Choice (a) is incorrect because if closing inventory is underestimated, cost of goods sold for the period will be overestimated, not underestimated. Choice (b) is incorrect because the opposite is correct. Cost of goods sold will be overestimated and net earnings will be underestimated. Choice (d) is incorrect because if cost of goods sold is overestimated in error, then earnings for the period will be underestimated, not overestimated.

Subject Area: Financial accounting and finance—valuation models (inventory). Source: CIA 1194, IV-10.

520. (a) Under FIFO inventory valuation, the 10,000 units in ending inventory are assumed to have been the most recent items purchased. The cost of the most recent 10,000 units purchased is

5,000 units @ $7.50 + 5,000 units @ $8 = $37,500 + $40,000 = $77,500

Choice (b) is incorrect. This solution is the ending inventory balance under the specific identification method if the units remaining in inventory at year-end were identified as having been purchased on April 1 and July 1.

5,000 units @ $9 + 5,000 units @ $8 = $45,000 + $40,000 = $85,000

Choice (c) is incorrect. This solution is the ending inventory balance under the average cost method. The average cost of all items purchased is used to calculate the ending inventory balance. The average cost of items purchased is

[$10(5,000) + $9 (5,000) + $8 (5,000) + $7.50(5,000)]/20,000
= $8.625 per unit so 10,000 units are assigned a value of $86,250.

Choice (d) is incorrect. This solution is the ending inventory balance under the last-in, first-out (LIFO) method of inventory valuation. The most recent items purchased are assumed to be sold first, so the items remaining in inventory are assigned the cost of the earliest purchases.

5,000 units @ $10 + 5,000 units @ $9 = $50,000 + $45,000 = $95,000

Subject Area: Financial accounting and finance—valuation models (inventory). Source: CIA 1194, IV-17.

521. (a) Under last-in, first-out (LIFO), the 10,000 units sold during the year are assumed to have been those purchased most recently. The cost of goods sold for the year is calculated as

5,000 units @ $7.50 + 5,000 units @ $8 = $37,500 + $40,000 = $77,500

Choice (b) is incorrect because this is the solution if the average cost method is used. The average cost of all items purchased is $8.625 per unit so the 10,000 units sold are assigned a cost of $86,250. Choice (c) is incorrect because this is the solution if the specific identification method is used and if the units remaining in inventory at year-end were identified as having been purchased on April 1 and July 1. The sold items would then have been purchased on January 1 and October 1 and cost of goods sold for the year is calculated as

5,000 units @ $10 + 5,000 units @ $7.50
= $50,000 + $37,500 = $87,500

Choice (d) is incorrect because this is the solution if the first-in, first-out (FIFO) method is used. Under FIFO, the oldest items are assumed to have been sold, so cost of goods sold for the year is calculated as

5,000 units @ $10 + 5,000 units @ $9 = $50,000 + $45,000 = $95,000.

Subject Area: Financial accounting and finance—valuation models (inventory). Source: CIA 1194, IV-18.

522. (c) The goods costing $90,000 were properly excluded from the inventory because title for these goods will not pass to XYZ until they are received by XYZ. The goods in transit of $60,000 must be added to the $1,000,000 to get the proper balance of inventory at the end of the year. Due to the shipping terms of FOB shipping point, title to the goods passed when they were shipped by the seller on December 28, 2004. Therefore, XYZ should include the $60,000 in the inventory balance to be reported at December 31, 2004. The goods in transit costing $64,000 must be added to the $1,000,000 to get the proper balance of inventory at the end of the year. Due to the shipping terms of FOB destination, title to the goods will not pass to the buyer until the buyer receives them, which will be in the following accounting period. The sale and the related cost of goods sold should not be recorded until 2005. The $100,000 of goods held on consignment were properly excluded from the $1,000,000 because those goods are the property of the consignor and not XYZ who is the consignee. Choice (a) is incorrect because this answer incorrectly excludes $60,000 of goods in transit shipped by a vendor FOB shipping point. This answer also incorrectly excludes the $64,000 of goods in transit shipped to a customer FOB destination. Choice (b) is incorrect because this answer incorrectly includes the $90,000 of goods in transit shipped FOB destination by a vendor. This answer also incorrectly excludes the $60,000 of goods in transit shipped FOB shipping point by a vendor and the $64,000 of goods in transit shipped to a customer FOB destination. Choice (d) is incorrect because this answer improperly includes the $100,000 of goods on consignment.

Subject Area: Financial accounting and finance—valuation models (inventory). Source: CIA 590, IV-29.

523. (d) Weighted-average cost per unit

$$= \frac{1{,}000 \times \$10 + 4{,}000 \times \$12 + 5{,}000 \times \$11.30}{10{,}000}$$

$$= \$11.45/\text{Unit}$$

The cost of inventory on June 30

$$= (1{,}000 + 4{,}000 + 5{,}000 - 8{,}000) \times \$11.45 = \$22{,}900$$

Therefore, by definition, choices (a), (b), and (c) will be incorrect.

Subject Area: Financial accounting and finance—valuation models (inventory). Source: CIA 1190, IV-33.

524. (b) Computations follow:

2005 cost of goods sold = (2004 cost of goods sold/1990 sales) × 2005 year-to-date sales
$24,000 = ($60,000/$100,000) × $40,000

$40,000	(2005 year-to-date sales)
$24,000	Less cost of goods sold
$16,000	Gross profit

Choice (c) is incorrect

$10,000	Beginning inventory
$35,000	Plus purchases
$45,000	Goods available for sale
$24,000	Less cost of goods sold
$21,000	Ending inventory
$6,000	Less undestroyed inventory
$15,000	Destroyed inventory

Therefore, by definition, choices (a), (c), and (d) will be incorrect.

Subject Area: Financial accounting and finance—valuation models (inventory). Source: CIA 1190, IV-47.

525. (d) During inflation, LIFO the latest purchases are expensed first. Beginning inventories consist of the lower cost items. Holding gains are avoided. Choice (a) is incorrect because first-in, first-out (FIFO) would accumulate holding gains since the most recent (and most costly purchases) are assumed to be in inventory. Choices (b) and (c) are incorrect because average inventory costs would be higher than LIFO, thus some holding gains would occur.

Subject Area: Financial accounting and finance—valuation models (inventory). Source: CIA 1190, IV-48.

526. (a) The value of the firm is given by the expression

$$V = \sum_{t=1}^{N} \frac{CF_t}{(1+k)^t}$$

Where V is value, CF is net cash flow, k is the discount rate (cost of capital), and t is time. It follows that value will rise as CF increases. Choice (b) is incorrect. An increase in systematic (or market) risk will increase the overall cost of capital and thereby increase k, the discount rate. As a result, the value of the firm will fall. Choice (c) is incorrect. An increase in unsystematic (or firm-specific) risk is diversifiable and will have no effect on the value of the firm. Choice (d) is incorrect. An increase in the discount rate will reduce the value of the firm.

Subject Area: Financial accounting and finance—valuation models (business). Source: CIA Model Exam 2002, IV-38.

527. (d) The discounted net present value of expected future cash flows reflects the favorable effects of enhanced operating efficiency after the acquisition, and provides a measure of the maximum value of the firm to an acquirer. Choice (a) is incorrect because the current market value of the corporation reflects, in part, the inefficient manner in which it is run. This value understates its acquisition value to an acquirer that would subsequently increase operating efficiency. Choice (b) is incorrect because the discounted net present value of earnings before interest and taxes (EBIT) is reduced by inefficiency, and thus provides only a partial measure of acquisition value to an acquirer that would subsequently enhance operating efficiency. Choice (c) is incorrect because the discounted net present value of current net profit is reduced by inefficiency, and thus provides only a partial measure of acquisition value to an acquirer that would subsequently enhance operating efficiency.

Subject Area: Financial accounting and finance—valuation models (business). Source: CIA Model Exam 1998, IV-35.

528. (c) The market value of the stock dividend is transferred from retained earnings to common stock and additional paid-in capital. Choice (a) is incorrect because a positive NPV project should increase the value of the firm. Choice (b) is incorrect because the higher credit rating should reduce the required rate of return, and therefore increase the value of the firm. Choice (d) is incorrect because the lower cost of capital should reduce the required rate of return, and therefore increase the value of the firm.

Subject Area: Financial accounting and finance—valuation models (business). Source: CIA 593, IV-46.

529. (b) The goal of financial management is to maximize the value of the firm for present stockholders. That is, stockholders' wealth. Choice (a) is incorrect because management, which simply avoids risk even when the possible gains to stockholders are sufficient to warrant taking the gamble, will turn down investment projects which are beneficial to stockholders. Choice (c) is incorrect because value maximization is broader than profit maximization in that it involves both risk and time period considerations. Choice (d) is incorrect because maximizing the book value of assets could simply involve increasing firm size, or the selective use of accounting policy. Neither is necessarily in the interest of current stockholders.

Subject Area: Financial accounting and finance—valuation models (business). Source: CIA 592, IV-50.

530. (d) The Gordon Model uses the growth rate in dividends and the investor's required rate of return. Choices (a), (b), and (c) are incorrect because they do not talk about dividends and rate of returns. Choice (a) talks about the amount of debt and equity in the firm's capital structure. Choices (b) and (c) talk about cash flows and liquidity, which have nothing to do with in determining the value of a stock.

Subject Area: Financial accounting and finance—valuation models (business). Source: CIA 1190, IV-53.

531. (b) The discounted cash flow (DCF) model goes beyond the net present value (NPV) model and uses free cash flows. The DCF model focuses on discounting cash flows from operations after investment in working capital, less capital expenditures.

Subject Area: Financial accounting and finance—valuation models (business). Source: CBM, Volume 4.

532. (a) The value of a business is determined by its profitability and growth rates, which are influenced by its marketing and finance strategies. Therefore, operating profits, capital requirement, and cost of capital, not sales, is important to increase the value of a business. Choice (b) deals with net operating profit after taxes/sales. Choice (c) deals with capital/sales.

Subject Area: Financial accounting and finance—valuation models (business). Source: CBM, Volume 4.

533. (c) First, we need to compute the operating profit and then apply the EVA formula.

Operating profit = Revenue – Cost of goods sold – Operating expenses = \$60 – \$35 – \$15 = \$10 million

EVA = Operating profit – (Weighted-average cost of capital × Capital invested) = \$10 – (0.01 × \$40) = \$6.0 million

Subject Area: Financial accounting and finance—valuation models (business). Source: CBM, Volume 4.

534. (b) Choice (b) is the correct answer.

Market value of equity = Number of common shares outstanding × Market price per share = 3 million × \$50 per share = \$150 million

Market-value-added (MVA) = Present value of debt + Market value of equity – Capital invested = \$60 + 150 – \$100 = \$110 million

Subject Area: Financial accounting and finance—valuation models (business). Source: CBM, Volume 4.

535. (b) First, find the horizon or terminal value. Horizon value in second year

= [Free cash flows in second year (1+ g)]/(r-g)
= \$20 (1.04)/(0.14 – 0.04) = 20.8/0.10 = \$208 million

Next find the present value of the free cash flows and the horizon value.

Value of operations = (Free cash flows in one year/1.14) + (Free cash flows in second year + horizon value)/(1.14) × (1.14)

Value of operations = (–\$10/1.14) + (\$20 +\$208)/(1.14) × (1.14)
= –8.772 + \$175.439 = \$166.67 = \$167 million

Subject Area: Financial accounting and finance—valuation models (business). Source: CBM, Volume 4.

536. (c) It is the cash flows (both inflows and outflows) that are the major determinant of the value of a firm. "Cash is King" is true here.

Subject Area: Financial accounting and finance—valuation models (business). Source: CBM, Volume 4.

537. (c) The higher the expected cash flows, the greater the asset's value; also, the lower the required return, the greater the asset's value. Net income is not the same as the cash flows.

Subject Area: Financial accounting and finance—valuation models (business). Source: CBM, Volume 4.

Business Development Life Cycles

538. (d) Any nation seeks economic growth, full employment, and price level stability. However, achieving full employment and price level stability is not steady or certain. Both unemployment and inflation can threaten or interrupt the long-term trends of any nation's economic growth.

Subject Area: Financial accounting and finance—business development life cycles. Source: Author.

539. (a) Some economists prefer to talk of business fluctuations rather than business cycles because cycles imply regularity while fluctuations do not.

Subject Area: Financial accounting and finance—business development life cycles. Source: Author.

540. (b) Economists suggest four phases of the business cycle: peak, recession, trough, and recovery. During the recession phase, both output and employment will decline, but prices tend to be relatively inflexible in a downward direction.

Subject Area: Financial accounting and finance—business development life cycles. Source: Author.

541. (a) In an economy experiencing a recession with low inflation, the central bank could stimulate the economy by purchasing securities in the secondary market, which will increase the money supply. Securities include stock and bonds.

Subject Area: Financial accounting and finance—business development life cycles. Source: Author.

542. (b) When a government restricts the money supply, meaning total expenditures are low, it results in lower output, lower employment, and lower income. Less production will be profitable to the business.

Subject Area: Financial accounting and finance—business development life cycles. Source: Author.

543. (a) One needs to compare the growth of a firm with that of the economy. Normal growth rate of a firm is about the same as the economy as a whole. The growth rate of a firm is equal to the nominal gross national product (GNP), which is real GNP plus inflation.

Subject Area: Financial accounting and finance—business development life cycles. Source: Author.

544. (c) Consumer durable "hard goods" industries are highly sensitive to the business cycle. Producers cut the production and employment instead of lowering prices due to their concentration in the industry. Price cuts could be modest, even if they occur. Also, producers do not invest in capital goods during recession.

Subject Area: Financial accounting and finance—business development life cycles. Source: Author.

545. (b) Both seasonal variations and secular trends are due to noncyclical fluctuations. Many businesses such as retail, automobile, construction, and agriculture are subject to seasonal variations such as pre-Christmas and pre-Easter holidays. Business activity is also subject to a secular trend. The secular trend of an economy is its expansion or contraction over a long period of time (i.e., 25 or more years).

Subject Area: Financial accounting and finance—business development life cycles. Source: Author.

3 MANAGERIAL ACCOUNTING (10–20%)

THEORY

3.1 Cost Concepts

(a) **Absorption and Variable Costing Methods.** The cost of goods sold, which is larger than all of the other expenses combined in a product cost, can be determined under either the absorption costing or variable costing method.

Under absorption costing, all manufacturing costs are included in finished goods and remain there as an inventory asset until the goods are sold. Management could misinterpret increases or decreases in income from operations, due to mere changes in inventory levels, to be the result of business events, such as changes in sales volume, prices, or costs. Absorption costing is necessary in determining historical costs for financial reporting to external users and for tax reporting.

Variable costing may be more useful to management in making decisions. In variable costing (direct costing), the cost of goods manufactured is composed only of variable manufacturing costs—costs that increase or decrease as the volume of production rises or falls. These costs are the direct materials, direct labor, and only those factory overhead costs that vary with the rate of production. The remaining factory overhead costs, which are fixed or nonvariable costs, are generally related to the productive capacity of the manufacturing plant and are not affected by changes in the quantity of product manufactured. Thus the fixed factory overhead does not become a part of the cost of goods manufactured but is treated as an expense of the period (period cost) in which it is incurred.

The income from operations under variable costing can differ from the income from operations under absorption costing. This difference results from change in the quantity of the finished goods inventory, which are caused by differences in the levels of sales and production.

The following decision rules apply:

- If units sold are less than units produced, then variable costing income is less than absorption costing income.
- If units sold are greater then units produced, then variable costing income is greater than the absorption costing income.

Many accountants believe that variable costing method should be used for evaluating operating performance because absorption costing encourages management to produce inventory. This is because producing inventory absorbs fixed costs and causes the income from operations to appear higher. In the long run, building inventory without the promise of future sales may lead to higher costs such as handling, storage, financing, and obsolescence costs.

(b) **Management's Use of Absorption and Variable Costing Methods.** Management's use of variable costing and absorption costing includes controlling costs, pricing products, planning production, analyzing market segments (sales territory and product profitability analysis), and analyzing contribution margin. Preparing comparative reports under both concepts provides useful insights.

Controlling Costs

All costs are controllable in the long run by someone within a business, but they are not all controllable at the same level of management. For example, plant supervisors, as members of operating management, are responsible for controlling the use of direct materials in their departments. They have no control, however, of insurance costs related to the buildings housing their departments. For a specific level of management, **controllable costs** are costs that can be influenced by management at that level, and **noncontrollable costs** are costs that another level of management controls. This distinction is useful in fixing the responsibility for incurring costs and for reporting costs to those responsible for their control.

Variable manufacturing costs are controlled at the operating level. If the product's cost includes only variable manufacturing costs, operating management can control these costs. The fixed factory overhead costs are normally the responsibility of a higher level of management. When the fixed factory overhead costs are reported as a separate item in the variable costing income statement, they are easier to identify and control than when they are spread among units of product, as they are under absorption costing.

As in the case with the fixed and variable manufacturing costs, the control of the variable and fixed operating expenses is usually the responsibility of different levels of management. Under variable costing, the variable selling and administrative expenses are reported separately from the fixed selling and administrative expenses. Because they are reported in this manner, both types of operating expenses are easier to identify and control than is the case under absorption costing.

Pricing Products

Many factors enter into determining the selling price of a product. The cost of making the product is clearly significant. Microeconomic theory states that income is maximized by expanding output to the volume where the revenue realized by the sale of an additional unit (marginal revenue) equals the cost of that unit (marginal cost). Although the degree of accuracy assumed in economic theory is rarely achieved, the concepts of marginal revenue and marginal cost are useful in setting selling prices.

In the short run, a business is committed to its existing manufacturing facilities. The pricing decision should be based upon making the best use of such capacity. The fixed costs cannot be avoided, but the variable costs can be eliminated if the company does not manufacture the product. The selling price of a product, therefore, should at least be equal to the variable costs of making and selling it. Any price above this minimum selling price contributes an amount toward covering fixed costs and providing income. Variable costing procedures yield data that emphasize these relationships.

In the long run, plant capacity can be increased or decreased. If a business is to continue operating, the selling prices of its products must cover all costs and provide a reasonable income. Hence, in establishing pricing policies for the long run, information provided by absorption costing procedures is needed. The results of a research study indicated that the companies studied used absorption costing in making routine pricing decisions. However, these companies regularly used variable costing as a basis for setting prices in many short-run situations.

Planning Production

Planning production also has both short-run and long-run implications. In the short run, production is limited to existing capacity. Operating decisions must be made quickly before opportunities are lost. For example, a company manufacturing products with a seasonal demand may have an opportunity to obtain an off-season order that will not interfere with its production schedule nor reduce the sales of its other products. The relevant factors for such a short-run decision are the additional revenues and the additional variable costs associated with the off-season order. If the revenues from the special order will provide a contribution margin, the order should be accepted because it will increase the company's income from operations. For long-run planning, management must also consider the fixed costs.

Analyzing Market Segments

Market analysis is performed by the sales and marketing function in order to determine the profit contributed by market segments. A **market segment** is a portion of business that can be assigned to a manager for profit responsibility. Examples of market segments include sales territories, products, salespersons, and customer distribution channels. Variable costing can provide significant insight to decision making regarding such segments.

Analyzing Contribution Margins

Another use of the contribution margin concept to assist management in planning and controlling operations focuses on differences between planned and actual contribution margins. However, mere knowledge of the differences is insufficient. Management needs information about the causes of the differences. The systematic examination of the differences between planned and actual contribution margins is termed **contribution margin analysis**.

Since contribution margin is the excess of sales over variable costs, a difference between the planned and actual contribution margin can be caused by (1) an increase or decrease in the amount of sales or (2) an increase or decrease in the amount of variable costs. An increase or decrease in either element may in turn be due to (1) an increase or decrease in the number of units sold (quantity factor) or (2) an increase or decrease in the unit sales price or unit cost (unit price or unit cost factor). The effect of these two factors on either sales or variable costs may be stated as follows:

1. Quantity factor—the effect of a difference in the number of units sold, assuming no change in unit sales price or unit cost. The quantity factor is the difference between the actual quantity sold and the planned quantity sold, multiplied by the planned unit sales price or unit cost.
2. Unit price factor or unit cost factor—the effect of a difference in unit sales price or unit cost on the number of units sold. The unit price or unit cost factor is the difference between the actual unit price or unit cost and the planned unit price or unit cost, multiplied by the actual quantity sold.

(c) **Technical Aspects of Absorption and Variable Costing Methods.** An understanding of the inventory costing method is important for several reasons such as: (1) in measuring product costs and inventories,

(2) determining income, (3) deciding between making or buying a product, (4) setting prices, and (5) planning product mix to produce or sell.

Two major methods of inventory costing are absorption costing and variable costing (see Exhibit 3.1), and they differ in whether fixed manufacturing overhead is an "inventoriable" cost (i.e., whether such overhead is included in the inventory or not). Other names used for fixed manufacturing overhead are fixed factory overhead or indirect manufacturing cost.

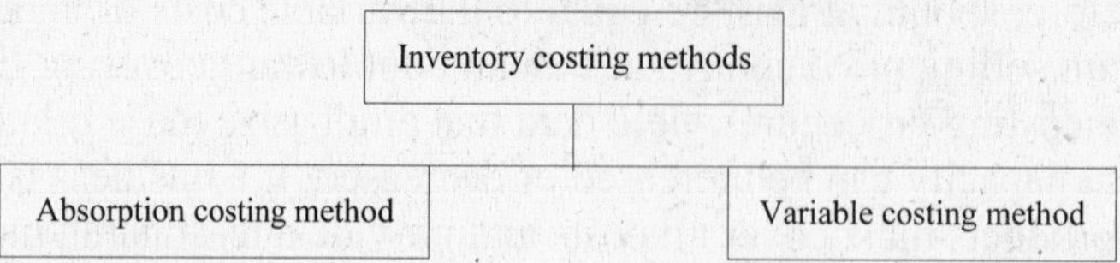

Characteristics of absorption costing method

- Also called full costing method.
- Includes all direct manufacturing costs and both variable and fixed indirect manufacturing costs as inventoriable costs.
- Production volume variance exists.
- All nonmanufacturing costs are expensed.
- Greater incentive to build inventory levels.
- Fixed manufacturing cost is held back in inventory.
- Income statement classifies cost by business function (i.e., marketing, manufacturing).
- Gross margin is different from contribution margin.
- Variable marketing and administrative costs are expensed (i.e., become period costs) in the period incurred along with fixed components, and deducted from gross margin to arrive at operating income.

Characteristics of variable costing method

- Also called direct or marginal costing method.
- Includes all direct manufacturing costs and variable indirect manufacturing costs only as inventoriable cost (fixed indirect manufacturing costs are excluded from the inventoriable costs).
- No production volume variance exists.
- All nonmanufacturing costs are expensed.
- No incentive to build up inventory levels.
- Fixed manufacturing cost is expensed in the period incurred.
- Income statement classifies cost by cost behavior (i.e., fixed, variable).
- Contribution is different from gross margin.
- Variable marketing and administrative costs are expensed (i.e., become period costs) in the period incurred. However, they are included to compute contribution margin.
- All fixed indirect costs including manufacturing, marketing, and administrative costs are deducted from the contribution margin to arrive at operating income.

Exhibit 3.1: Two methods of inventory costing

OPERATING INCOME UNDER THE ABSORPTION AND VARIABLE COSTING METHODS

Absorption costing method		*Variable costing method*	
Sales	$xxx	Sales	$xxx
Less variable manufacturing costs	xxx	Less variable manufacturing cost of goods sold	xxx
Less fixed manufacturing costs	xxx		
Deduct ending inventory	xxx	Less variable marketing costs	xxx
Equals **gross margin**	xxx	Less variable administrative costs	xxx
Deduct total marketing and administrative costs including variable costs	xxx	Total variable costs	xxx
		Contribution margin	xxx
		Deduct all fixed costs	xxx
Operating income	xxx	Operating income	xxx

The difference in operating income between these two methods arises from the difference in the amount of inventories. The contribution margin and gross margin highlight the conflict of the underlying concepts of variable cost and absorption cost. Both methods can operate in conjunction with actual, normal, or standard costing systems.

The following are the arguments for and against variable costing method:

Arguments for	Fixed portion of factory overhead is relevant to overall plant capacity, not to the production of a specific product. Hence, focus should be on all variable costs.
Arguments against	Inventories should contain fixed costs in addition to variable costs since both are needed to produce goods. Hence, all costs should be inventoried.

KEY CONCEPTS TO REMEMBER: RELATIONSHIPS BETWEEN VARIABLE COSTING AND ABSORPTION COSTING METHODS

- If inventories increase during a period, the variable costing method will generally report less operating income than will absorption costing method.
- If inventories decrease, the variable costing method will report more operating income than the absorption costing method.
- The differences in operating income are due solely to moving fixed overhead in and out of inventories.

Absorption costing operating income – Variable costing operating income = Fixed overhead in ending inventory in absorption cost – Fixed overhead in beginning inventory in absorption costing

- The difference between variable costing and absorption cost incomes is a matter of timing. Under the variable costing method, fixed overhead is expensed in the period incurred. Under the absorption costing method, fixed overhead is inventoried and is expensed when the related units are sold.
- Under the variable costing method, operating income is drawn by fluctuations in sales volume. Operating income should increase as sales increase and vice versa. Operating income rises at the rate of the contribution margin per unit. This dovetails precisely with cost-volume-profit analysis, and the breakeven point can easily be calculated. Temptations are not available to manipulate income.
- Under the absorption costing method, both sales volume and production volume drives the operating income. Changes in inventory levels and choosing a production schedule and volume can dramatically affect income. Temptations are great to manipulate income.
- Under the absorption costing method, it is possible to report a lower operating income even though sales volume was increased due to unusually large amounts of fixed overhead being charged to a single accounting period.
- If the number of units produced exceeds the number of units sold, ending inventory increases. Since absorption defers some fixed overhead in the increased ending inventory, absorption costing income is generally higher than variable costing income.
- A manager whose performance bonus is based on absorption costing income could increase production levels to obtain favorable production volume variance by hiding fixed overhead expenses as inventoriable costs in order to increase income. A manager can also choose to decrease absorption costing income by decreasing inventory if he has met this year's targeted income. Thus, managers are tempted to make short-run decisions at the expense of long-run objectives of the organization.
- To balance the negative effects of the absorption costing method (such as build up the inventory), a manager's performance should be based on both financial and nonfinancial criteria. Examples of nonfinancial performance criterion include meeting inventory levels, meeting product delivery dates, adhering to plant maintenance schedules, and meeting or exceeding product quality and customer service levels.
- Variable cost is not acceptable for tax or external financial reporting purposes. Variable cost is heavily used for internal management reporting.
- Generally accepted accounting principles (GAAP) require that all manufacturing overhead is inventoried. Some firms may choose not to include depreciation on factory equipment as part of inventory cost.
- The US Internal Revenue Code requires that all manufacturing and some marketing, distribution, and administrative costs are included in inventory.

APPLICATION OF ABSORPTION AND VARIABLE COSTING METHODS

During the first year of operations, a company produced 275,000 units and sold 250,000 units. The following costs were incurred during the year:

Variable costs per unit	
Direct material	$ 15.00
Direct labor	10.00
Manufacturing overhead	12.50
Selling and administrative	2.50
Total fixed costs	
Manufacturing overhead	$ 2,200,000
Selling and administrative	1,375,000

What would be the difference between operating income calculated on the absorption (full) costing basis and on the variable (direct) costing basis?

a. Absorption costing operating income would be greater than variable costing operating income by $200,000.
b. Absorption costing operating income would be greater than variable costing operating income by $220,000.
c. Absorption costing operating income would be greater than variable costing operating income by $325,000.
d. Variable costing operating income would be greater than absorption costing operating income by $62,500.

Choice (a) is the correct answer. Absorption costing operating income will exceed variable costing operating income because production exceeds sales resulting in a deferral of fixed manufacturing overhead in the inventory under absorption. The amount of difference is the fixed manufacturing overhead per unit ($2,200,000/275,000 = $8.00) times the difference between production and sales (275,000 – 250,000 = 25,000 units; this could also be stated as the inventory change in units). That is, $8.00 × 25,000 units = $200,000.

Choice (b) is incorrect. Same reasoning as response choice (a) except fixed manufacturing overhead per unit is calculated by using unit sales rather than production units ($2,200,000/250,000 = $8.80; $8.80 × 25,000 = $220,000).

Choice (c) is incorrect. Same reasoning as response choice (a) except all fixed costs treated as being inventoriable under absorption costing and production units used as the base [($2,200,000 + 1,375,000)/275,000 = $13.00; $13.00 × 25,000 = $325,000)].

Choice (d) is incorrect. This response assumes that the difference between variable and absorption costing is that variable selling and administrative costs are inventoriable for variable costing and not inventoriable for absorption costing; thus, a portion of the variable selling and administrative expenses would be deferred in the inventory meaning variable operating income would exceed absorption operating income ($2.50 × 25,000 = $62,500).

(d) **Other Cost Concepts.** The following list provides a brief description about cost concepts other than absorption or variable costs:

- **Actual costs.** The amounts determined on the basis of cost incurred for making a product or delivering a service to customers.
- **Average costs.** The total cost divided by the activity, that is, number of units.
- **Budgeted costs.** Costs that were predetermined for managerial planning and controlling purposes.
- **Common costs.** Costs of facilities and services shared by several functional departments. It is a cost incurred for the benefit of more than one cost objective.
- **Conversion costs.** A combination of direct labor costs, indirect material costs, and factory overhead. Assembly workers' wages in a factory are an example of conversion costs since their time is charged to direct labor.
- **Current costs.** Costs that represent fair market value at current date.
- **Direct costs.** Costs that can be directly identified with or traced to a specific product, service, or activity (e.g., direct labor and direct materials). In a manufacturing operation, direct material costs would include wood in a furniture factory since it is a basic raw material of furniture. Direct labor costs are wages paid to workers.

Examples include insurance on the corporate headquarters building since it is not a cost of production, depreciation on salespersons' automobiles, salary of a sales manager, commissions paid to sales personnel, and advertising and rent expenses.

- **Expired costs.** It is the portion of cost that is expensed. An expired cost is a period cost and it is either an expense or loss.
- **Fixed costs.** Costs that remain constant in total, but change per unit, over a relevant range of production or sales volume (e.g., rent, depreciation). It is a unit cost that decreases with an increase in activity. A fixed cost is constant in total but varies per unit in direct proportion to changes in total activity or volume. It is a cost that remains unchanged in total for a given period despite fluctuations in volume or activity.

  A fixed cost remains constant in total for a given period despite variations in activity as long as the production is within the relevant range. A fixed cost may change in total between different periods or when production is outside the relevant range. Therefore, unit fixed cost decreases as output increases at a given relevant range.
- **Full costs.** A combination of direct costs and a fair share of the indirect costs for a cost objective. Full costs refer to a unit of finished product. They consist of prime costs and overhead. It is the entire sacrifice related to a cost objective.
- **Historical costs.** Costs that were incurred at the time of occurrence of a business transaction. They represent what costs were.
- **Indirect costs.** Costs that cannot be identified with or traced to a specific product, activity, or department (e.g., salaries, taxes, utilities, machine repairs). An example is a factory manager's salary. Another term for indirect costs is factory overhead. It consists of all costs other than direct labor and direct materials associated with the manufacturing process.
- **Joint costs.** Costs of manufactured goods of relatively significant sales values that are simultaneously produced by a process.
- **Long-run costs.** Costs that vary as plant capacity changes over a long period of time.
- **Marginal costs.** The cost to make an additional unit or the last unit. It is the incremental or variable costs of producing an additional or extra unit.
- **Mixed costs.** Costs that fluctuate with volume, but not in direct proportion to production or sales. Mixed costs (semivariable or semifixed costs) have elements of both fixed and variable costs. (e.g., supervision and inspection). A salesperson's compensation is an example of mixed costs since salary is fixed and commissions are variable.
- **Period costs.** Costs that can be associated with the passage of time, not the production of goods. Period costs are always expensed to the same period in which they are incurred, not to a particular product. Period costs are not identifiable with a product and are not inventoried. Only product costs are included in manufacturing overhead. Period costs are those costs deducted as expenses during the current period without having been previously classified as costs of inventory.
- **Prime costs.** A combination of direct labor and direct material costs. Overhead is not a part of it. Prime costs refer to a unit of finished product. They can be identified with and physically traceable to a cost objective.
- **Product costs.** Costs that can be associated with production of certain goods or services. Product costs are those that are properly assigned to inventory when incurred. Inventoriable costs are those costs incurred to produce the inventory and stays with the inventory as an asset until they are sold. Product costs are expensed (as cost of goods sold) in the period the product is sold.

  Examples include property taxes on a factory in a manufacturing company, direct materials, direct labor, and factory overhead. Product costs include direct labor, direct material, and plant manufacturing overhead.
- **Short-run costs.** Costs that vary as output varies for a short period or for a given production capacity.
- **Standard costs.** Predetermined or engineered costs that should be attained under normal conditions of operations. They represent what costs should be.
- **Step costs.** A step cost is constant over small ranges of volume (output) but increases in discrete steps as volume increases. A supervisor of the second shift is an example of step cost. If the step is narrow, it is equal to variable cost and fixed cost of a wider step.

- **Sunk costs.** A past cost that has already been incurred (e.g., installed factory machinery and equipment) or committed to be incurred. It is not relevant to most future costs and decisions since it cannot be changed by any decision made now or in the future. It is irreversible. It cannot be affected by the choices made.
- **Unexpired costs.** The portion of cost that remains as assets, and continues to generate future benefits.
- **Variable costs.** Costs that fluctuate in total, but remain constant per unit, as the volume of production or sales changes. A variable cost is constant per unit produced but varies in total in direct proportion to changes in total activity or volume. The cost of fabricator wages should be considered variable because they change in total in direct proportion to the number of similar cables fabricated. General and administrative and other indirect costs can be either fixed or variable. In general, variable costs vary directly with volume or activity. For example, if indirect materials vary directly with volume, then indirect materials can be classified as variable costs.

APPLICATION OF A SUNK COST CONCEPT

A company has an old machine with a book value of $75,000, with no salvage value, and an estimated remaining life of 12 years. A new machine is available at a cost of $190,000. It has the same estimated remaining life and the same capacity as the old machine, but it would reduce operating costs by $17,000 per year. Which of the following amounts is a sunk cost in the decision whether or not to replace the old machine?

a. $0
b. $17,000
c. $75,000
d. $190,000

Choice **(c)** is the correct answer. The old machine's book value of $75,000 is an outlay made in the past that cannot be changed. Choice (a) is incorrect. The salvage value does not dictate sunk costs. Choice (b) is incorrect. The $17,000 is a future cost which can be avoided. Choice (d) is incorrect. The $190,000 is a future cost which can be avoided.

- **Avoidable costs.** Costs that will not be incurred or costs that may be saved if an ongoing activity is discontinued, changed, or deleted such as in a make or buy decision. These costs are relevant costs.
- **Unavoidable costs.** Opposite of avoidable costs. Costs that are irrelevant; they are sunk costs.
- **Controllable costs.** Costs that can be definitely influenced by a given manager within a given time span. Examples include office supplies purchased by an office manager. In the long run, all costs are controllable. In the short run, costs are controllable too but they are controlled at different management levels. The higher the management level, the greater the possibility of control.
- **Noncontrollable costs.** Opposite of the controllable costs. Costs that are unaffected by a manager's decision (e.g., plant rent expense by a plant foreman).
- **Out-of-pocket costs.** Costs that require the consumption of current economic resources (e.g., taxes, insurance). It is the current or near-future expenditure that will require a cash outlay to execute a decision.
- **Embodied costs.** It measures sacrifices in terms of their origins, reflecting what was originally given up to acquire and convert the object being costed.
- **Displaced costs.** It measures sacrifices in terms of their ultimate effects upon the group making the sacrifice, reflecting the opportunity lost by, or the adverse consequences resulting from, the sacrifice in question. It is also called opportunity costs.
- **Discretionary costs.** Costs that arise from periodic budgeting decisions and which have no strong input/output relationship.
- **Opportunity costs.** The maximum net benefit that is foregone by the choice of one course of action over another course of action. It is the economic sacrifice attributable to a given decision. It is the loss associated with choosing the alternative that does not maximize the benefit.

- **Incremental costs.** The increase in total sacrifice identifiable with the specific object, or group of objects, being costed, recognizing that fixed and otherwise joint sacrifices may be increased little, if at all, because of what was done to or for the specific object being costed. It is also called differential costs.
- **Differential costs.** The difference in total costs between alternatives.

APPLICATION OF A DIFFERENTIAL COST CONCEPT

ABC Company receives a onetime special order for 5,000 units of Kleen. Variable costs per unit are as follows: direct materials $1.50, direct labor $2.50, variable overhead $0.80, and variable selling $2.00. Fixed costs per year include fixed overhead of $100,000 and fixed selling and administrative cost of $50,000. Acceptance of this special order will not affect the regular sales of 80,000 units. Variable selling costs for each of these 5,000 units will be $1.00.

Question: What is the differential cost to the company of accepting this special order?

Answer: The differential cost is $29,000, as shown below.

We need to consider all differential or incremental costs that would change as a result of the changes in production operations. It should include all variable manufacturing costs and variable selling costs. That is, $1.50 (materials) + $2.50 (direct labor) + $0.80 (variable overhead) + $1.00 (new variable selling cost for 5,000 units) = $5.80. This is multiplied by 5,000 units gives $29,000. Here, fixed costs and variable selling costs for sales of 80,000 units are not relevant.

- **Replacement costs.** The cost that would have to be incurred to replace an asset.
- **Implicit costs.** Implicit costs are imputed costs, and used in the analysis of opportunity costs.
- **Imputed costs.** Costs that can be associated with an economic event when no exchange transaction has occurred (e.g., the rent for a building when a company "rents to itself" a building).
- **Committed costs.** Two types: (1) manageable and (2) unmanageable. Manageable committed costs are sacrifices influenced to an important degree by managers' decisions and actions but these influences have already had most of their effect, setting in motion the chain of events that largely determine the sacrifice in question. Most fixed costs are committed costs. Unmanageable committed costs are sacrifices largely influenced by factors or forces outside managers' control and already set in motion to such an extent that influences have had most of their effect.
- **Uncommitted costs.** Two types: (1) manageable and (2) unmanageable. Manageable uncommitted costs are sacrifices influenced to an important degree by managers' decisions and actions with plenty of time for these influences to have their effect. Unmanageable uncommitted costs are sacrifices largely influenced by factors or forces outside managers' control with plenty of time for these influences to have their effect.
- **Rework costs.** Costs incurred to turn an unacceptable product into an acceptable product and sold as normal finished good.
- **Engineered costs.** Costs resulting from a measured relationship between inputs and outputs.

(e) **Cost Behavior.** Costs have a behavior pattern. For example, costs vary with volumes of production, sales, or service levels, with the application of the amount of resources, and with the timeframe used. Knowing the cost-behavior information helps in developing budgets, interpreting variances from standards, and making critical decisions. The manager who can predict costs and their behavior is a step ahead in planning, budgeting, controlling, product pricing, nonroutine decisions (i.e., make or buy, keep or drop), and in separating cost into its components (i.e., fixed, variable, and mixed costs). In order to make more accurate cost predictions, the manager needs superior cost estimates at his disposal.

COST ESTIMATION VERSUS COST PREDICTION

- In cost estimation, an equation is formulated to measure and describe past cost relationships.

- In cost prediction, future costs are forecasted using the cost estimation equation. Here, the behavior of past costs will help in predicting future costs.

Two **assumptions** are made in the estimation of cost functions: (1) cost behavior is a linear function within the relevant range, and (2) variations in the total cost level can be explained by variations in a single cost driver. A cost driver is any factor whose change causes a change in the total cost of a related cost object. Machine hours and direct labor hours are examples of cost drivers in a manufacturing firm.

A cost function is an equation showing the cost behavior pattern for all changes in the level of the cost driver. A linear cost function is described below.

$$y = a + bx$$

where *y* is the estimated value, *a* equals constant or intercept (does not vary with changes in the level of the cost driver within a relevant range), *b* is slope coefficient (the amount of change in total cost (*y*) for each unit change in the cost driver (*x*) within the relevant range). The intercept includes "fixed costs" that cannot be avoided even at shutdown of the operations. The relevant range is the range of the cost driver in which a valid relationship exists between total cost and the level of the cost driver.

Three types of linear cost functions exist: (1) variable cost function where its total cost changes in direct proportion to changes in "*x*" within the relevant range because the intercept "*a*" is zero, (2) fixed cost function where the total cost will be constant regardless of the changes in the level of the cost driver, and (3) mixed cost function, also known as semivariable cost, which has both fixed and variable elements. The total costs in the mixed cost function changes as the number of units of the cost driver changes, not proportionately.

Techniques to Separate Costs

- Statistics (regression analysis, scatter graphs, and least squares methods)
- The high-low method
- Spreadsheet analysis
- Sensitivity analysis
- Managerial judgment

(i) **Assumptions underlying cost classifications.** The classification of costs into their variable cost or fixed cost components is based on three assumptions.

1. The cost object must be specified since costs are variable or fixed with respect to a chosen cost object. Cost objects can be product-based or activity-based.
2. The time span must be specified. Costs are affected by the time span. The longer the time span, the higher the proportion of total costs that are variable and the lower the fixed costs. Costs that are fixed in the short run may be variable in the long run. There should be a cause-and-effect relationship between the cost driver and the resulting costs. Cost driver may be either an input (e.g., direct labor hour or machine hour) or an output (finished goods). For example, fixed manufacturing costs decline as a proportion of total manufacturing costs as the time span is lengthened from the short run to the medium-run to the long run.
3. The relevant range for changes in the cost driver must be specified. Each of the cost-behavior patterns such as variable cost, fixed cost, or mixed cost has a relevant range within which the specified cost relationship will be valid. Constraints such as labor agreements and plant capacity levels set the relevant range. If volume exceeds the relevant range, total fixed costs would increase if a new plant is built, and unit variable costs would increase if overtime must be paid.

(ii) **Cost estimation approaches.** Four approaches are available to estimate costs including: (1) industrial engineering method, (2) conference method, (3) account analysis method, and (4) quantitative analysis method of current or past cost relationships (see Exhibit 3.2). The first three methods require less historical data than do most quantitative analyses. Therefore, cost estimations for a new product will begin with one or more of the first three methods. Quantitative analysis may be adopted later, after experience is gained. These cost estimation approaches, which are not mutually exclusive, differ in the cost of conducting the analysis, the assumptions they make, and the evidence they yield about the accuracy of the estimated cost function.

1. Industrial engineering method (analyzes relationships between inputs and outputs in physical terms)
2. The conference method (incorporates analysis and opinions gathered from various departments of the firm)
3. The account analysis method (classifies cost accounts in the ledger as variable, fixed, or mixed costs)
4. Quantitive analysis method (uses time-series data based on past cost relationships, regression analysis)

Exhibit 3.2: Four methods to cost estimation

1. **The industrial engineering method** analyzes the relationship between inputs and outputs in physical terms. Using time and motion studies, physical measures are transformed into standard or budgeted costs. The drawbacks of this method are that it can be time-consuming and costly. This method is most often used for significant costs such as direct labor and direct material costs that are relatively easy to trace to the products. This method is less often used or not used for indirect cost categories such as manufacturing overhead due to difficulty in specifying physical relationships between inputs and outputs.
2. The **conference method** develops cost estimates based on analysis and opinions gathered from various departments of an organization. Product costs are developed on consensus of the relevant departments. The advantages of this method include the speed at which cost estimates can be developed, the pooling of knowledge from experts in the functional area, and the resulting credibility of the cost estimates. The disadvantage of this method is that the accuracy of the cost estimates depends on the care and detail taken by those people providing the inputs.
3. The **account analysis method,** which is widely used, classifies cost accounts in the ledger as variable, fixed, or mixed costs. It can be thought of as a first step in cost classification and estimation. The conference method is used as a supplement to the account analysis method, which improves the credibility of the latter.
4. **Quantitative analysis methods,** such as time-series data or cross-sectional data based on past cost relationships, are often used to estimate cost functions. Time-series data pertain to the same entity over a sequence of past time periods, while cross-sectional data pertain to different entities for the same time period.

STEPS IN ESTIMATING COST FUNCTION

Six steps in estimating cost function based on an analysis of current or past cost relationships include

1. Choosing the dependent variable (the variable to be predicted). It is guided by the purpose for estimating a cost function.
2. Choosing the cost driver that is economically plausible (logical and common sense) and accurately measurable. There should be a cause-and-effect relationship between the cost driver and the resulting costs. For example, number of employees is a cost driver for measuring health benefit costs.
3. Collecting data on the dependent variable and on the cost driver. The time period (e.g., daily, weekly) used to measure the dependent variable and the cost driver should be identical.
4. Plotting the data. The general relationship between the dependent variable and the cost driver (i.e., correlation) can be observed in a plot of the data. A plot of data will reveal whether the cost relation is linear or whether there are outliers. Extreme observations, or outliers, can occur due to error in recording the data or from an unusual event such as a labor strike, fire, or flood.
5. Estimating the cost function either by using regression analysis or the high-low method.
6. Evaluating the estimated cost function. The relationship between the dependent variable and the cost driver should be economically plausible. The closer the actual cost observations are to the values predicted by a cost function, the better the goodness of fit

of the cost function. In other words, the cost function should be economically plausible and fit the data.

Let us review the quantitative methods such as regression analysis and high-low methods used to estimate cost function.

(iii) **Regression analysis.** Regression analysis provides a model for estimating a cost function and probable error for cost estimates. It measures the average amount of change in the dependent variable, Y', that is associated with a unit change in the amount of one or more independent (or explanatory) variable x. x is also called the cost driver.

$Y' = a + bx$, Where a is constant or intercept and b is slope coefficient

When only one independent variable (e.g., machine hours) is used, the analysis is called simple regression; when more than one independent variable is used (e.g., machine hours, direct labor hours), it is called multiple regression.

Regression analysis offers a structured approach, based on past data relationships, for identifying cost drivers. All independent variables in a regression model should satisfy the following four selection criteria for qualifying as a cost driver:

1. **Economic plausibility.** The relationship between the dependent variable and the independent variable(s) should make economic sense and be intuitive.
2. **Goodness of fit.** The coefficient of determination, r square, measures the extent to which the independent variable(s) accounts for the variability in the dependent variable. The range of r square is from zero to one, where zero implies no explanatory ability and one implies perfect explanatory ability. The goal of maximizing r square is called data mining and should not be done at the expense of economic plausibility. A balance is required.
3. **Significance of independent variable(s).** The t-value is computed by dividing the slope coefficient by its standard error. The t-value of a slope coefficient (b) measures the significance of the relationship between changes in the dependent variable and changes in the independent variable. The coefficient of the chosen independent variable(s) should be significantly different from zero for that independent variable to be considered a possible cost driver.
4. **Specification analysis.** Cost function models make assumptions such as linearity within the relevant range, constant variance of residuals, independence of residuals, and normality of residuals. When these assumptions are met, the sample values of "a" and "b" from a regression model are the best available linear, unbiased estimates of the population parameters, alpha and beta. Testing the assumptions underlying regression analysis is termed specification analysis.

Multicollinearity can exist in a multiple regression when two or more independent variables are highly correlated with each other. This is indicated when a coefficient of correlation (r) is greater than 0.70. Multicollinearity has the effect of increasing the standard error of the coefficients of the individual independent variable(s) thus increasing their uncertainty.

Regression analysis and interviews with operating personnel are used to identify cost drivers. For example: number of products is a cost driver in product design function, number of suppliers can be a cost driver in a manufacturing operation, and number of advertisements can be a cost driver in a marketing function.

(iv) **High-low method.** The high-low method uses two extreme data points (i.e., highest, lowest) to calculate the formula for a line. These two data points could be outliers or may not be representative of all the observations. This method ignores information on all but two observations when estimating the cost function.

APPLICATION OF HIGH-LOW METHOD

Example

	Machine hour	*Indirect manufacturing costs*
Highest observation of cost driver	5,000	\$400,000
Lowest observation of cost driver	2,000	\$190,000
Difference	3,000	\$210,000

Slope coefficient (b) = \$210,000/3,000 = \$70 per machine hour
Constant (a) can be calculated using either highest or lowest observations.
Using the highest observation = \$400,000 – \$70 (5,000) = \$50,000
The high-low estimate of the cost function is $Y' = a + bx$ = \$50,000 + \$70 (machine hours)

(v) **Nonlinearity and cost functions.** A nonlinear cost function is a cost function in which a single constant and a single slope coefficient do not describe in an additive manner the behavior of costs for all changes in the level of the cost driver. For example, even direct materials costs are not always linear variable costs due to quantity discounts. The cost per unit decreases with large orders, but the total costs increase slowly as the cost driver increases.

Step function cost is a situation where the cost of the input is constant over various small ranges of the cost driver, but the cost increases by discrete amounts (in steps) as the cost driver moves from one relevant range to the next. This step-pattern behavior occurs when the input is acquired in discrete quantities, but is used in fractional quantities (e.g., vehicle-leasing costs for a package-delivery company).

Batch costs are increased when products are made in batches and a changeover (setup) cost is needed to run a different type of batch. These batch costs are incurred regardless of the size of each batch and have no linear relationship with the number of items in a batch.

(vi) **Learning curves and cost functions.** A learning curve is a function that shows how labor hours per unit decline as units of output increase. The learning curve helps managers predict how labor hours or costs will change as more units are produced. The idea behind the learning curve is that workers handling repetitive tasks will become more efficient as they become more familiar with the operation.

Management must be cautious in using the learning curve in establishing standards. A steady state condition can be reached when the effect of the learning curve ceases, and the standard costs would be lower per unit. The corresponding standard cost for the learning curve phase will be higher per unit. If the steady-state standards are imposed during the learning-curve phase, an unfavorable efficiency variance between standards and actual performance may persist, and the employees might reject the standards as unattainable. This situation will lead to low morale and low productivity.

The benefit of the learning curve can be clearly seen with new products, new workers, and new machines. Learning curves are more frequently applied to direct labor and overhead, and less frequently to direct materials. In addition to volume as a driver of learning, product design and process configuration are being researched as possible drivers of learning.

APPLICATION OF LEARNINGCURVE PRINCIPLE

Example: Sun Corporation has received an order to supply 240 units of a product. The average direct labor cost was estimated to be \$40,000 per unit for the first lot of 30 units. The direct labor is subject to a 90% learning curve.

Question: What is the cumulative average unit cost of labor for production of 240 units?

Answer: The cumulative average unit cost of labor for production of 240 units is \$29,160, as shown below.

Cumulative number of lots	*Cumulative number of units*	*Cumulative average unit cost of labor*
1	30	($40,000 × 1) = $40,000
2	60	($40,000 × .9) = 36,000
4	120	($36,000 × .9) = 32,400
8	240	($32,400 × .9) = 29,160

The term **experience curve** describes the broader application of the learning curve to include not only manufacturing cost but also marketing, distribution, and customer service areas. An experience curve is a function that shows how full costs per unit decline as units of output increase.

(vii) **Learning-curve models.** Two learning-curve models exist: (1) the cumulative average-time learning model and (2) the incremental unit-time learning model.

(A) ***Cumulative average-time learning model.*** The cumulative average time per unit is reduced by a constant percentage each time the cumulative quantity of units produced is doubled. Learning occurs at a faster rate with this method, as compared to the incremental unit-time model.

(B) ***Incremental unit-time learning model.*** The time needed to produce the last unit is reduced by a constant percentage each time the cumulative quantity of units produced is doubled. This method requires a higher cumulative total time to produce two or more units as compared with cumulative average-time model.

The deciding factor between the cumulative average-time and incremental unit-time learning model is the ability to approximate the behavior of labor hour usage as output levels increase.

3.2 Capital Budgeting

Capital budgeting decisions deal with the long-term future of a firm's course of action. Capital budgeting is the process of analyzing investment projects and deciding whether they should be included in the capital budget which, in turn, outlines the planned expenditures on fixed assets such as buildings, plant, machinery, equipment, warehouses, and offices.

CURRENT ASSETS VERSUS FIXED ASSETS

- Working capital decisions focus on increasing current assets.
- Investment decisions focus on increasing fixed assets.

A firm needs to develop capital budget plans several years in advance to synchronize the timing of funds availability with the timing of fixed asset acquisitions. Capital budgeting projects are initiated and selected by the company's management to be in line with the strategic business plan (e.g., mergers and acquisitions, introduction of new products). Generally, the larger the required investment, the more detailed the analysis, and the higher the level of management approval required to authorize the expenditure.

Simulation and Capital Budgeting

A firm is evaluating a large project; it desires to develop not only the best guess of the outcome of the project, but also a list of outcomes that might occur. The firm would best achieve its objective by using simulation as applied to capital budgeting.

The process of capital budgeting is similar to securities valuation (i.e., stocks and bonds) in that the value of the firm increases when the asset's present value exceeds its cost. A link between capital budgeting and stock values exists in that the more effective the firm's capital budgeting procedures, the higher the price of its stock. From an economics point of view, an optimal capital budget is determined by the point where the marginal cost of capital is equal to the marginal rate of return on investment.

(a) **Methods to Rank Investment Projects.** Four methods used to rank investment projects and to decide whether or not they should be accepted for inclusion in the capital budget are: (1) payback method (regular and discounted), (2) net present value method, (3) regular internal rate of return, and (4) modified internal rate of return (see Exhibit 3.3).

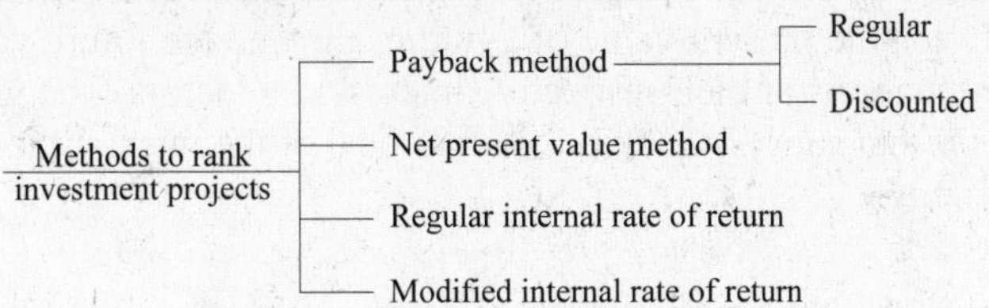

Exhibit 3.3: Methods to rank investment projects

(b) **Payback Method.** The payback period is investment divided by after-tax cash flows. It is the expected number of years required to recover the original investment in a capital budgeting project. The procedure calls for accumulating the project's net cash flows until the cumulative total becomes positive. The shorter the payback period, the greater the acceptance of the project and the greater the project's liquidity. Risk can be minimized by selecting the investment alternative with the shortest payback period. Initial investment money can be recouped quickly.

A variation of the regular payback method is the discounted payback period, where the expected cash flows are discounted by the project's cost of capital or the required rate of return for the project. A comparison between regular payback and discounted payback is

- A regular payback period is the number of years required to recover the investment from the project's net cash flows. It does not take account of the cost of capital. The cost of debt and equity used to finance the project is not reflected in the cash flows.
- A discounted payback period is the number of years required to recover the investment from discounted cash flows. It does take into account the cost of capital. It shows the breakeven years after covering debt and equity costs.
- Both methods are deficient in that they do not consider the time value of money.
- Both methods ignore cash flows after the payback period.

It is possible for the regular payback and the discounted payback methods to produce conflicting ranking of projects. The payback method is often used as a rough measure of both the liquidity and the riskiness of a project since longer-term cash flows are riskier than near-term cash flows. This method is used as a screening device to weed out projects with high and marginal payback periods. A low payback period is preferred. The payback method can be used to reduce the uncertainty surrounding a capital budgeting decision, and is often used in conjunction with net present value and internal rate of return methods.

(c) **Net Present Value Method.** A simple method to accommodate the uncertainty inherent in estimating future cash flows is to adjust the minimum desired rate of return. Discounted cash flow (DCF) techniques, which consider the time value of money, were developed to compensate for the weakness of the payback method. *Two examples of DCF techniques include (1) the net present value (NPV) method and (2) the internal rate of return (IRR) method.*

NPV is equal to the present value of future net cash flows, discounted at the marginal cost of capital. The approach calls for finding the present value of cash inflows and cash outflows, discounted at the project's cost of capital, and adding these discounted cash flows to give the project's NPV. The rationale for the NPV method is that the value of a firm is the sum of the values of its parts.

$$\text{NPV} = (\text{After-tax cash flows}) \times (\text{Present value of annuity}) - (\text{Initial investment})$$

The NPV index or profitability index is the present value of after-tax cash flows divided by initial investment. Accounting rate of return is annual after-tax net income divided by initial or average investment. When the profitability index or cost-benefit ratio is one, the NPV is zero.

Decision Rules

- If the NPV is positive, the project should be accepted since the wealth of the current stockholders would be increased.

Present Values and Future Values

The relationship between the present value of a future sum and the future value of a present sum can be expressed in terms of their respective interest rate factors. The interest factor for the future value of a present sum is equal to the reciprocal of the interest factor for the present value of a future sum.

- If the NPV is negative, the project should be rejected since the wealth of the current stockholders would be reduced.
- If the NPV is zero, the project should be accepted even though the wealth of the current stockholders is unchanged (the firm's investment base increases but the value of its stock remains constant).
- If two projects are mutually exclusive, the one with the higher positive NPV should be chosen.
- If two projects are independent, there is no conflict in selection. Capital rationing is the only limiting factor.
- If money is available, invest in all projects in which the NPV is greater than zero.
- If a project's return exceeds the company's cost of capital, select the combination of projects that will fully utilize the budget and maximize the sum of the net present values.

(d) **Regular Internal Rate of Return.** In the regular IRR method, the discount rate that equates the present value of future cash inflows to the investment's cost is found. In other words, the IRR method is defined as the discount rate at which a project's NPV equals zero. Similarities and differences between the NPV and IRR methods follow.

Similarities

- Both NPV and IRR methods consider the time value of money.
- Both methods use the same basic mathematical equation for solving the project's problems.

Differences

- In the NPV method, the discount rate is specified, and the NPV is found.
- In the IRR method, the NPV is specified to equal zero and the value of IRR that forces this equality is determined.
- The NPV method assumes reinvestment of project cash flows at the cost of capital.
- The IRR method assumes reinvestment of project cash flows at the internal rate of return.

When a project's IRR is greater than its marginal cost of capital, it increases the value of the firm's stock since a surplus remains after paying for the capital. Similarly, when a project's IRR is less than its marginal cost of capital, it decreases the value of the firm's stock since the project reduces the profits of the existing stockholders.

Evaluating Capital Projects

The payback method, NPV method, and IRR method all show an investment "break-even" point for the project in an accounting sense, which would be useful in evaluating capital projects. The IRR method, NPV method, and NPV index consider risk only indirectly through the selection of a discount rate used in the present value computations.

Two kinds of projects exist: (1) normal and (2) nonnormal. A normal project is one that has one or more cash outflows followed by a series of cash inflows. No difficulties are encountered when evaluated by the IRR method. However a nonnormal project (i.e., a project that calls for a large cash outflow either sometime during or at the end of its life) can give unique difficulties when evaluated by the IRR method.

(e) **Which Method Is Best: Payback, NPV, or IRR?** Any capital budgeting method should meet the following three criteria in order to produce consistent and correct investment decisions:

1. The method must consider all cash flows throughout the entire life of a project. The payback method does not meet this property while the NPV and IRR methods do.

2. The method must consider the time value of money. A dollar received today is more valuable than a dollar received tomorrow. The payback method does not meet this property while the IRR and NPV methods do.
3. The method must choose the project that maximizes the firm's stock price when faced with selecting from a set of mutually exclusive projects. The payback method and the IRR methods do not meet this property while the NPV method does meet this property all the time.

The NPV method is better for evaluating mutually exclusive projects. However, when two projects are independent, both the NPV and the IRR criteria always lead to the same accept or reject decision.

The critical issue in resolving the NPV/IRR conflicts between mutually exclusive projects is the different reinvestment rate assumptions made. The reinvestment rate is the opportunity cost rate at which a firm can invest differential early year's cash flows generated from NPV or IRR methods.

The following list presents assumptions in NPV and IRR methods:

- **NPV assumptions.** The cash flows generated by a project can be reinvested at the cost of capital. The NPV method discounts cash flows at the cost of capital.
- **IRR assumptions.** The cash flows generated by a project can be reinvested at the IRR. The IRR method discounts cash flows at the project's IRR.

It has been demonstrated that the best assumption is that projects' cash flows are reinvested at the cost of capital. Therefore, the NPV method is better.

(f) **Modified Internal Rate of Return.** Academics prefer the NPV method, while business executives favor the IRR method. The reason business executives prefer the IRR method is that they find IRR "more natural" to analyze investments in terms of percentage rates of return rather than dollars of NPV.

The regular IRR method can be modified to make it a better indicator of relative profitability and hence better for use in capital budgeting. The new measure is called the modified IRR (MIRR) and it is the discount rate at which the present value of a project's cost is equal to the present value of its terminal value. The terminal value is the sum of the future values of the cash inflows, compounded at the firm's cost of capital. In other words, the MIRR is the discount rate that forces the present value of the costs to equal the present value of the terminal value.

The modified IRR method is better than the regular IRR method because MIRR assumes that cash flows from all projects are reinvested at the firm's cost of capital, whereas the regular IRR method assumes that the cash flows from each project are reinvested at the project's own IRR. Therefore, the modified IRR method is better indicator of a project's true profitability.

MODIFIED INTERNAL RATE OF RETURN (MIRR) VERSUS NET PRESENT VALUE (NPV)

- If the two projects are of equal size, NPV and MIRR will always lead to the same project selection decision. No conflict is present.
- If the projects differ in size, conflicts can occur similar to NPV and regular IRR. NPV is better because it provides a better indicator of how much each project will cause the value of the firm to increase.
- The MIRR method is superior to the regular IRR method as an indicator of a project's "true" rate of return.

(g) **Postaudit of Capital Projects.** A postaudit is a comparison of the actual and expected results (both costs and savings) for a given capital project and explanation of variances, if any. A postaudit is a good learning exercise and is practiced by most successful organizations. The lessons learned from the postaudit can be used to fine-tune forecasts of costs and benefits and to improve business operations.

The postaudit is a complicated process to review since factors such as demand uncertainty and unexpected deviations from plans occur, which are beyond the control of most managers in the firm. Actual savings may not materialize as expected due to unexpected costs. Despite these problems, it is a good approach to conduct a postaudit of capital projects as long as the blame is on the process, not on the people involved.

(h) **Project Cash Flows and Risk Assessment.**

(i) **Project cash flows.** It is important to note that capital budgeting decisions must be based on annual cash flows, not accounting income, and that only incremental cash flows are relevant to the accept or reject decision. Cash flows and accounting income can be different due to depreciation expense, which is a noncash expense. Since we are interested in net cash flows, it is obtained by adding depreciation expense to the net income after taxes.

Incremental cash flows represent the changes in the firm's total cash flows that occur as a direct result of accepting or rejecting the project. It is the net cash flow that can be traceable to an investment project.

Four special problems occur in determining incremental cash flows: (1) sunk costs, (2) opportunity costs, (3) externalities, and (4) shipping and installation costs (see Exhibit 3.4).

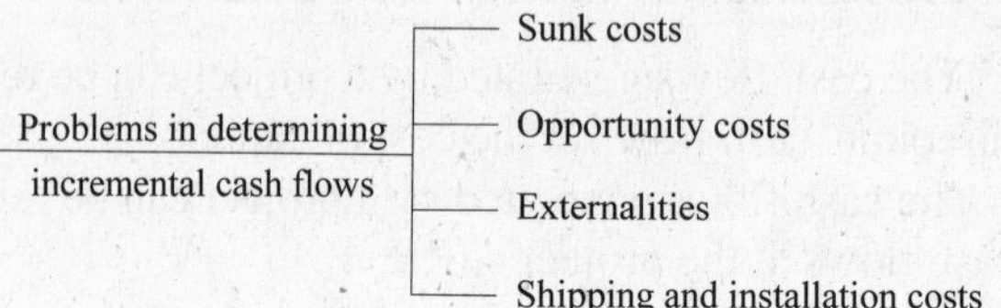

Exhibit 3.4: Problems in determining incremental cash flows

Sunk costs are not incremental costs, and they should not be included in the project analysis. A sunk cost is an outlay that has already been committed or has already occurred and hence is not affected by the "accept" or "reject" decision under consideration. Only incremental cash flows should be compared with the incremental investment.

Opportunity costs are the cash flows that can be generated from assets the firm already owns provided they are not used for the project in question. It is the return on the best alternative use of an asset, which is foregone due to funds invested in a particular project. Opportunity costs are not incremental costs.

Externalities are the indirect effects of a project on cash flows in other parts of the firm. Revenues produced from the effects of externalities should not be treated as incremental income.

Shipping and installation costs incurred on a new fixed asset (e.g., equipment) should be added to the invoice price of the fixed asset. The depreciation base for calculating the depreciation expense is the total invoice price including the shipping and installation costs. Therefore, shipping and installation costs should not be treated as incremental cash flows since they would be double-counted.

(ii) **Project risk assessment**. Risk analysis is important to capital budgeting decisions. Three separate and distinct types of project risk include (1) the project's own stand-alone risk, (2) corporate risk (within-firm risk), and (3) market risk (beta risk) (see Exhibit 3.5).

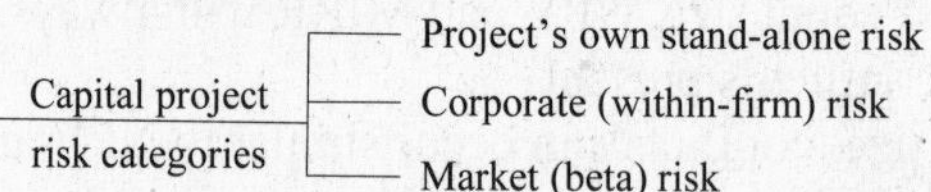

Exhibit 3.5: Capital project risk categories

A **project's stand-alone risk** is measured by the variability of the project's expected returns. A project's **corporate risk** is measured by the project's impact on the firm's earnings variability. It does not consider the effects of stockholders' diversification.

A project's **market (beta) risk** is measured by the project's effect on the firm's beta coefficient. Market risk cannot be eliminated by diversification. If the project has highly uncertain returns, and if those are highly correlated with those of the firm's other assets and also with most other assets in the economy, the project will have a high degree of all types of risk. A company whose beta value has decreased due to a change in its marketing strategy would apply lower discount rate to expected cash flows of potential projects.

Market risk is important because of its direct effect on a firm's stock prices. It has been found that both market risk and capital risk affect stock prices. Corporate risk for weak firms increases significantly compared to strong firms. This is because weak firms would have difficulty in borrowing money at reasonable interest rates, which, in turn, would decrease profits. The decrease in profits would be reflected in the price of the stock.

KEY CONCEPTS TO REMEMBER: CAPITAL PROJECT RISKS

- It is much easier to estimate a project's stand-alone risk than its corporate risk.
- It is far easier to measure stand-alone risk than market risk.
- Stand-alone risk, corporate risk, and market risk are highly correlated.

The Economy → The Firm → The Project

If the economy is good, both the firm and the projects are good, and vice versa.

- The stand-alone risk is a good proxy for hard-to-measure market risk.

Risk to a company is affected by both project variability and how project returns correlate with those of the company's prevailing business. Overall company risk will be lowest when a project's returns exhibit low variability and negative correlation.

(i) **Techniques for Measuring Stand-Alone Risk.** Here we are interested in determining the uncertainty inherent in the project's cash flows. Three techniques are available for assessing a project's stand-alone risk: sensitivity analysis, scenario analysis, and Monte Carlo simulation (see Exhibit 3.6).

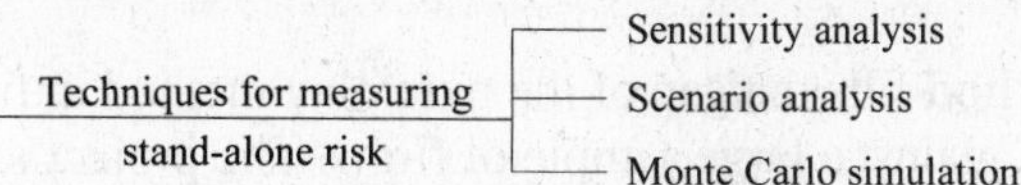

Exhibit 3.6: Techniques for measuring stand-alone risk

Sensitivity analysis can provide useful insights into the riskiness of a project. It is a technique that indicates exactly how much the NPV will change in response to a given change in an input variable, other things held constant. For example, if each input variable can be changed by several percentage points above and below the expected value, then a new NPV can be calculated for each of those values. Finally, the set of NPVs can be plotted against the variable that was changed. The slope of the lines in the graphs show how sensitive NPV is to changes in each of the inputs; the steeper the slope, the more sensitive the NPV is to a change in the variable.

Scenario analysis is a risk analysis technique that considers both the sensitivity of NPV to changes in key variables and the range of likely variable values. NPV under bad conditions (i.e., low sales, high variable cost per unit) and good conditions (i.e., high sales and low variable cost per unit) are calculated and compared to the expected (i.e., base case) NPV. The following are the highlights of these relationships:

Bad condition → Worst case scenario → (all input variables are set at their worst forecasted values)
Good condition → Best case scenario → (all input variables are set at their best forecasted values)
Base case condition → Most likely scenario → (all input variables are set at their most likely values)

The results of the scenario analysis are used to determine the expected NPV, the standard deviation of NPV, and the coefficient of variation. Even though scenario analysis provides useful information about a project's stand-alone risk, it is limited in that it only considers a few discrete NPV outcomes for the project. In reality, there are an infinite number of outcomes.

Monte Carlo simulation ties together sensitivities and input variable probability distributions. Probability distributions of each uncertain cash flow variable are specified. The computer chooses at random a value for each uncertain variable based on the variable's specified probability distributions. The model then determines the net cash flows for each year which, in turn, are used to determine the project's NPV in the first run. Since this is a simulation technique, this model is repeated many times to yield a probability distribution.

The primary advantage of simulation is that it shows a range of possible outcomes along with their attached probabilities. The scenario analysis shows only a few point estimates of the NPV. Both the standard deviation of the NPV and the coefficient of variation are calculated providing additional information in assessing the riskiness of a project.

It is difficult to obtain valid estimates of probability distributions and correlations among the variables. From both scenario analysis and simulation analysis, no clear-cut decision rule emerges. Both techniques ignore the effects of the project as well as the investor diversification—which is the major drawback.

(j) **Market or Beta Risk.** As mentioned earlier, beta risk is that part of a project's risk that cannot be eliminated by diversification. It is measured by the project's beta coefficient. Two methods are available to estimate the betas of individual projects: (1) the pure play method and (2) the accounting beta method.

In the **pure play method,** the company tries to find several single-product firms in the same line of business as the project being evaluated, and it then applies these betas to determine the cost of capital for its own project. A major drawback of the pure play method is that the approach can only be applied for major assets such as whole divisions, not individual projects. Therefore, it is difficult to find comparable business firms of the size in question.

Capital Asset Pricing Model to Measure Risk

Capital asset pricing model (CAPM) can be used to measure market (beta) risk. A major drawback of CAPM is that it ignores bankruptcy costs. The probability of bankruptcy depends on a firm's corporate risk, not on its market risk. Therefore, management should give careful consideration to corporate risk instead of concentrating entirely on market risk.

The **accounting beta method** fills the gap of the pure play method in finding single-product, publicly traded firms by applying against a large sample of firms. The project's beta is determined by regressing the returns of a particular company's stock against returns on a stock market index. Betas determined by using accounting data rather than stock market data are called accounting betas. In practice, accounting betas are normally calculated for divisions or other large units, not for single assets, and divisional betas are then imputed to the asset.

(k) **Project Risks and Capital Budgeting.** Capital budgeting can affect a firm's market risk, its corporate risk, or both. It is difficult to develop a good measure of project risk due to difficulty in quantifying either risk.

Two methods for incorporating project risk into the capital budgeting decision process include (1) certainty equivalent approach and (2) risk-adjusted discount rate approach.

Under the **certainty equivalent approach,** the expected cash flows are adjusted to reflect project risk. All unknown cash flows will have low certainty equivalent values. This approach is difficult to implement in practice despite its theoretical appeal.

Under the **risk-adjusted discount rate approach,** differential project risk is dealt with by changing the discount rate. Risk adjustments are subjective and take the following decision paths:

- Average-risk projects are discounted at the firm's average cost of capital.
- Above-average-risk projects are discounted at a higher cost of capital.
- Below-average-risk projects are discounted at a rate below the firm's average.

(l) **Capital Rationing.** The amount of funds available to a firm is limited even though acceptable capital budget projects are many. A firm will approve an independent project if its NPV is positive. It selects the project with the highest NPV when faced with mutually exclusive projects. Management cannot or would not want to raise whatever funds are required to finance all of the acceptable projects. When capital budget must be limited, this situation is called capital rationing.

Capital rationing is a constraint placed on the total size of the firm's capital investment. A drawback of capital rationing is that it is not maximizing a firm's stock value since it deliberately forgoes profitable projects. Because of this negative effect, only a few firms ration their capital.

(m) **Key Principles and Practices in Capital Budgeting.** The following are key principles and practices to be employed during capital budgeting decision-making process:

- Principle 1. Integrate organizational goals into the capital decision-making process.
  - Practice 1a. Conduct comprehensive assessment of needs to meet results-oriented goals and objectives.
  - Practice 1b. Identify current capabilities including the use of an inventory of assets and their condition, and determine if there is a gap between current and needed capabilities.

- Practice 1c. Decide how best to meet the gap by identifying and evaluating alternative approaches.
- Principle 2. Evaluate and select capital assets using an investment approach.
  - Practice 2a. Establish review and approval framework.
  - Practice 2b. Rank and select projects based on established criteria.
  - Practice 2c. Decide a long-term capital plan that defines capital asset decisions.
- Principle 3. Balance budgetary control and managerial flexibility when funding capital projects.
  - Practice 3a. Budget for projects in useful segments.
  - Practice 3b. Consider innovative approaches to full up-front funding.
- Principle 4. Use project management techniques to optimize project success.
  - Practice 4a. Monitor project performance and establish incentives for accountability.
  - Practice 4b. Use cross-functional teams to plan for and manage projects.
- Principle 5. Evaluate results and incorporate lessons learned into the decision-making process.
  - Practice 5a. Evaluate results to determine if organization-wide goals have been met.
  - Practice 5b. Evaluate the decision-making process; reappraise and update to ensure those organization-wide goals are met.

(n) **International Capital Budgeting.** The techniques presented in this section for domestic capital budgeting are equally applicable to the international capital budgeting process. However, three types of risks exist in the international area: (1) cash flow risk, that is, cash flow estimation is much more difficult, (2) exchange rate risk, that is, exchange rate fluctuations add to the riskiness of the foreign investment, and (3) sovereignty risk, that is, the possibility of deliberate foreign government acts that reduce or eliminate cash flows.

In terms of cash flows, the relevant cash flows are the dollar cash flows that the subsidiary can turn over to the parent. Since the foreign currency cash flows turned over to the parent must be converted to the US dollar values by translating them at expected future exchange rates, an exchange rate premium should be added to the domestic cost of capital. This is done to reflect the exchange rate risk inherent in the investment. The exchange rate risk can be minimized by hedging, which adds to the cost of the project.

Sovereignty risk includes the possibility of expropriation or nationalization without adequate compensation, and also the possibility of unanticipated restrictions of cash flows to the parent company, such as tighter controls on repatriation of dividends or higher taxes. Generally, sovereignty risk premiums are not added to the cost of capital to adjust for sovereignty risk. Companies can take steps to reduce the potential loss from expropriation in three major ways: (1) by financing the subsidiary with local sources of capital, (2) by structuring operations so that the subsidiary has value only as a part of the integrated corporate system, and (3) by obtaining insurance against economic losses from expropriations. When the insurance is taken, its cost should be added to the project's cost.

3.3 Operating Budgets

A budgeting system includes both expected results and historical or actual results. A budgeting system builds on historical, or actual, results and expands to include consideration of future, or expected, results. A budgeting system guides the manager into the future.

Budget system → Forward looking
Historical cost system → Backward looking

A budget is a quantitative expression of a plan of action. It will aid in the coordination of various activities or functions throughout the organization. The master budget by definition summarizes the objectives of all subunits of an organization. The master budget helps in coordinating activities, implementing plans, authorizing actions, and evaluating performance (see Exhibit 3.7).

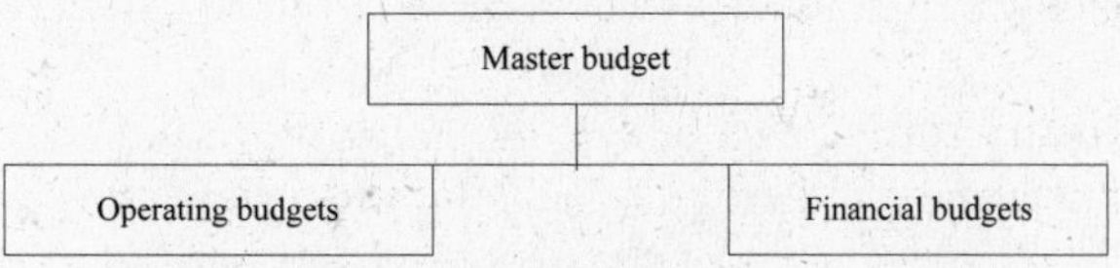

Exhibit 3.7: Master budget and its components

- Sales budget
- Manufacturing budget
- Marketing expense budget
- Administrative expense budget
- Budgeted income statement
- Cash budget
- Capital budget
- Budgeted balance sheet
- Budgeted statement of cash flows

The master budget captures the financial impact of all the firm's other budgets and plans. Although the master budget itself is not a strategic plan, it helps managers to implement the strategic plans. The master budget focuses on both operating decisions and financing decisions. Operating decisions concentrate on the acquisition and use of scarce resources.

Financing decisions center on how to get the funds to acquire resources. This section focuses on operating decisions and budgets.

(a) **Benefits of Operating Budgets.** The following is a list of benefits to be derived from budgets:

- Budgets are planning "tools." Budgets force managers to look into the future and make them prepare to meet uncertainties and changing business conditions.
- Budgets provide a starting point for discussing business strategies. In turn, these strategies direct long-term and short-term planning. Therefore, strategic plans and budgets are interrelated and affect one another.

Budget Alerts

Be alert to: (1) communication breakdown, (2) empire-building (self-centered) efforts of managers during the budgeting process, and (3) behavioral implication of budgets.

- Budgeted performance is better than historical data for judging or evaluating employee performance. This is because employees know what is expected of their performance. A major drawback of using historical data is that inefficiencies and bad decisions may be buried in past actions.
- Budgets can be a valuable vehicle for communication with interested parties. Budgets help coordinate activities of various functions within the organization to achieve overall goals and objectives.
- Budgets are control systems. Budgets help to control waste of resources and to search out weaknesses in the organizational structure.
- A budget should be implemented so as to gain acceptance by employees. This requires a "buy-in" by employees, senior management support, and lower-level management involvement.
- A budget should be set tight, but attainable and flexible. A budget should be thought of as a means to an end, not the end in itself.
- A budget should not prevent a manager from taking prudent action. Nonetheless, he should not disregard the budget entirely.

(b) **Different Dimensions in Operating Budgets.** The time period for budgets varies from one year to five or more years. The common budget period is one year and broken down by quarters and months. Four types of budgets emerge from the time coverage and update point of view: short-term, long-term, static, and continuous budgets.

- Short-term budgets (operating budgets) have a time frame of one to two years.
- Long-term budgets (strategic budgets) have a time frame of three to five or more years.
- Static budgets are the original budgeted numbers, which are not changed. The time frame does not change.
- Continuous budgets are also called rolling budgets, where a twelve-month forecast is always available by adding a month in the future as the month just ended is dropped. The time frame keeps changing in the continuous budgets.

LENGTH OF THE BUDGET AND CHOICE OF THE BUDGET

- The length of the budget period depends on the nature of the business, that is, stable versus unstable. Stable firms will have a longer budget period than unstable firms.
- The choice of budget periods depends on the objectives, uses, and reliability of the budget data.

Budgets should be viewed positively, not negatively. Although budget preparation is mechanical, its administration and interpretation require patience, education, and people skills. Budgets are a positive device designed to help managers choose and accomplish objectives. However, budgets are not a substitute for bad management or poor accounting system.

(c) **How Operating Budgets Are Prepared.** The **master budget** (static budget) is developed after the goals, strategies, and long-range plans of the organization have been determined. It summarizes the goals of the subunits or segments of an organization. This information summarizes, in a financial form, expectations regarding future income, cash flows, financial position, and supporting plans. The functions of budgets include planning, coordinating activities, communicating, evaluating performance, implementing plans, motivating, and authorizing actions. It contains the operating budget.

A detailed budget is prepared for the coming fiscal year along with some less-detailed amounts for the following years. Budgets may be developed from the **top-down or the bottom-up approach**. With the top-down approach, upper management determines what it expects from subordinate managers. Subordinate managers may then negotiate with upper management concerning the items they feel are unreasonable. With the bottom-up approach, lower-level managers propose what they expect to accomplish and the required resources. Upper management then makes suggestions and revisions. Budgets may be used for long-range planning, but the typical planning-and-control budget period is one year. This annual budget may be broken down into months or quarters and continuously updated.

HOW MANY BUDGETS ARE THERE?

- **Budgeted balance sheet.** This budget reflects the expected balance sheet at the end of the budget period. The budgeted balance sheet is determined by combining the estimate of the balance sheet at the beginning of the budget period with the estimated results of operations for the period obtained from the budgeted income statements and estimating changes in assets and liabilities. These changes in assets and liabilities result from management's decisions regarding capital investment in long-term assets, investment in working capital, and financing decisions.
- **Budgeted income statement or operating budget.** This budget reflects the income expected for the budget period.
- **Budgets for other expenses.** These budgets may be broken down according to expense category depending on the relative importance of the types of expenses (i.e., selling, administrative, research and development, etc.).
- **Cash budget.** The cash budget summarizes cash receipts and disbursements and indicates financing requirements. This budget is important in assuring an organization's solvency, maximizing returns from cash balances, and determining whether the organization is generating enough cash for current and future operations.
- **Cash disbursements budget.** This budget is dependent on the pattern of payments for expenses. Cash disbursements do not typically match costs in a period, since expenses are typically paid later than they are incurred.
- **Cash receipts budget.** The collection of sales depends on an organization's credit policies and its customer base. Most organizations must obtain cash to pay current bills while waiting for payment from customers. This cash represents an opportunity cost to the organization.
- **Labor budget.** This budget may be broken down by type of worker required in hours or number of workers.
- **Production cost budget.** This budget may be broken down by product or plant.

- **Production budget.** This budget may be broken down by product or plant. Production must meet current sales demand and maintain sufficient inventory levels for expected activity levels during the budget period and on into the next period. This budget is reviewed with the production managers to determine if the budget is realistic. If the budget is not attainable, management may revise the sales forecast or try to increase capacity. If production capacity will exceed requirements, other uses of the idle capacity may be considered.
- **Purchases budget.** This budget is typically broken down by raw materials and parts. An organization's inventory policy determines its level of purchases.
- **Sales budget.** This budget may be broken down by product, territory, plant, or other segment of interest.

(d) **Operating Budgeting Techniques.** Budgets are a necessary component of financial decision making because they help provide an efficient allocation of resources. A budget is a profit-planning and a resource-controlling tool. It is a quantitative expression of management's intentions and plans for the coming year(s) to meet their goals and objectives within the resource constraints. Budgets are prepared at the beginning of each year. Departmental or functional budgets are summarized and compared with revenue forecasts, and revised as necessary.

Five budgeting techniques are available: (1) incremental budgeting, (2) flexible budgeting, (3) zero-base budgeting, (4) program planning budgeting, and (5) performance budgeting (see Exhibit 3.8). Each budget is presented briefly.

- Incremental budgeting (adds a percentage or fixed amount to the previous budget)
- Flexible budgeting (reflects variation in activity levels)
- Zero-based budgeting (uses "decision packages" to specify objectives and workloads)
- Program planning budgeting (presents budget choices more explicitly in terms of objectives)
- Performance budgeting (links performance levels with specific budget amounts)

Exhibit 3.8: Budgeting techniques

- **Incremental budgeting** is a traditional approach to budgeting focusing on incremental changes in detailed categories of revenues and expenses, called line items, to represent sales, salaries, travel, supplies, and so forth. The incremental approach to budgeting does not take variation in volume or change in activity levels into account. It operates on the principle of management by exception.
- **Flexible budgeting** (variable or dynamic budgeting) is a budget that is adjusted for changes in the unit level of the cost or revenue. It is also called a variable budget. The flexible budget is based on the knowledge of how revenues and costs should behave over a range of activity. Thus, it is appropriate for any relevant level of activity. The master budget is not adjusted after it is developed, regardless of changes in volume, cost, or other conditions during the budget period.
- **Zero-based budgeting,** especially in the public sector, attempts to analyze the incremental change in a program's output at different levels of funding. For each program, a "decision package" would specify objectives and measures of efficiency, effectiveness, and workload for alternate levels of funding.
- **Planning, programming, and budgeting systems (PPBS)** attempt to further advance budgeting techniques, especially in the public sector, by presenting budget choices more explicit in terms of public objectives. With PPBS budgets, the cost and effectiveness of programs would be evaluated in a multiyear framework and alternate approaches would be considered.
- **Performance budgeting,** again focusing on the public sector, links performance measures directly to agency missions and program objectives. Under the performance budgeting model, budgets would be developed based on unit costs and service expectations followed by analysis of actual work performed compared with budget estimates.

Budget Purposes

The main purpose of a budget is to forecast and control the expenditures for a certain activity. A budget is an aid to planning and control. It helps managers to allocate resources efficiently and to achieve objectives effectively. A budget does not allow managers to estimate a firm's beta coefficient, which is a measure of stock market volatility.

(e) **Advantages of Operating Budgets.** Budgets are more commonly used in both large and small organizations. No matter what the size of the organization, typically the benefits of budgeting exceed the costs. The **advantages** of budgets are that they

- **Compel planning.** Management must have targets, and budgets reflect expected perfor-mance. Budgets affect strategies that are the relatively general and permanent plans of an organization that change as conditions and/or objectives change. Budgets can give direction to operations, point out problems, and give meaning to results.
- **Provide performance criteria.** The budget allows employees to know what is expected of them. Comparing actual results to budgeted amounts instead of past performance provides more useful information. Comparison with past performance may be hampered by past inefficiencies or changes in technology, personnel, products, or general economic conditions.
- **Promote communication and coordination.** Coordination deals with the interests of the organization as a whole, meshing and balancing the factors of production and other departments and functions so that objectives can be achieved. Budgets aid coordination because they require well-laid plans and isolate any problems.

(f) **Limitations of Operating Budgeting Techniques.** There are many limitations of budgets, which should be interpreted carefully. The following is a list of peculiarities and limitations of budgets:

- Be aware that budgeted items are a mixture of fixed and variable cost components. Accordingly, mixed costs cannot be used for linear projection.
- Be aware that budgeted items include some direct costs and some allocated costs. Direct costs are more useful for decision making than allocated costs. Responsibility accounting favors direct and controllable costs, not allocated and uncontrollable costs.
- The nature of volume levels needs to be understood. Most budgets are based on a single level of volume (point estimates) while multiple volume levels (range estimates) would be better for decision making.
- The kind of assumptions made during the budget development process need to be known. Understand the budget preparer's state of mind: optimistic, most likely, or pessimistic outcomes. Each of these outcomes would bring a different type of realism to the budget numbers.
- The variances from budgets need to be analyzed very carefully. Performance reports show the variations between the actual and the budgets—an element of control. Corrective action requires determination of underlying causes of variation. Variation could be favorable or unfavorable.

3.4 Transfer Pricing

Transfer pricing involves inter- or intracompany transfers, whether domestic or international. A transfer price is the price one unit of a corporation charges for a product or service supplied to another unit of the same corporation. The units involved could be either domestic or international, and the products involved could be intermediate products or semifinished goods.

The following are **reasons** for establishing transfer pricing in either domestic or international operations:

- Performance evaluation of decentralized operations
- Overall minimization of taxes to a corporation
- Minimization of custom duties and tariffs
- Minimization of risks associated with movements in foreign currency exchange rates
- Circumventing restrictions on profit remittance to the corporate headquarters
- Motivation of unit managers

KEY CONCEPTS TO REMEMBER: SUPPLYING UNIT AND RECEIVING UNIT

Supplying unit (seller)	Receiving unit (buyer)
Domestic	Domestic
Domestic	International
International	International
International	Domestic

- If the seller is a profit or investment center, transfer pricing is most likely to cause conflicts.
- If the seller is a cost center, it has less (no) incentive to maximize sales revenues. Hence, there is little or no conflict.

(a) **Transfer Pricing Methods.** Three methods are available for determining transfer prices: (1) Market-based, (2) cost-based, and (3) negotiated (see Exhibit 3.9).

Transfer pricing methods
- Market-based (trade journals, outside sources)
- Cost-based (actual or standard costs)
- Negotiated (no relation to cost or market price)

Exhibit 3.9: Transfer pricing methods

- **Market-based transfer prices.** The price appearing in a trade journal or other independent (outside) sources establishes the transfer price of a product or service. Difficulty in obtaining market price forces corporations to resort to cost-based transfer prices. This method is widespread in use.

Transfer Prices Alert

There is no single "best" method in determining transfer prices. Ideally, the chosen method should help the unit manager to make optimal decisions for the organization as a whole.

- **Cost-based transfer prices.** The costs used could be either actual costs or standard costs, and include variable manufacturing costs, or absorption (full) costs. Use of full cost-based prices leads to suboptimal decisions in the short run for the company as a whole. This method is also widespread in use. Standard costs are used more widely than actual costs to motivate the seller to produce efficiently. If transfer prices are based on actual costs, sellers can pass along costs of inefficiency to the buyers.
- **Negotiated transfer prices.** These are the negotiated prices between units of a corporation and may not have any relation to either cost or market-price data. Unit autonomy is preserved. Drawbacks include time-consuming and drawn-out negotiations, which may not lead to goal congruence. Weak bargaining units may lose out to the strong.

The choice of a transfer pricing method affects the operating income of individual units. Next, we will discuss how the criteria of goal congruence, managerial effort, and unit autonomy affect the choice of transfer-pricing methods.

(b) **Transfer Pricing Management. Goal congruence** exists when individual goals, group goals, and senior management goals coincide. Under these conditions, each unit manager acts in his own best interest, and the resulting decision is in the long-term best interest of the company as a whole. A transfer price method should lead to goal congruence.

A sustained high level of **managerial effort** can lead to achievement of goals. A transfer price method promotes management effort if sellers are motivated to hold down costs and buyers are motivated to use the purchased inputs efficiently.

Senior management should allow a high level of **unit autonomy** in decision making in a decentralized organization. This means that a transfer price method should preserve autonomy if unit managers are free to make their own decisions and are not forced to buy or sell products at a price that is unacceptable to them.

KEY CONCEPTS TO REMEMBER: TRANSFER PRICING

- If no incremental fixed costs are incurred, variable costs are a "floor" transfer price since the seller will not sell for less than the incremental costs incurred to make the product.
- Market price is a "ceiling" transfer price since the buyer will not pay more than market price.
- Therefore, the final transfer price usually falls between variable cost and market price.
- Corporations may use different transfer price methods for different items (i.e., market-based pricing for big-ticket items, variable cost-plus for low-value items, and negotiated prices for mid-range items).

(c) **Dual Pricing.** Dual pricing uses two separate transfer-pricing methods to price each inter-unit transaction. This is because seldom does a single transfer price meet the criteria of goal congruence, managerial effort, and unit autonomy. An example of dual pricing is when the selling unit receives a full-cost plus markup-based price and the buying unit pays the market price for the internally transferred products.

The dual pricing method reduces the goal-congruence problems associated with a pure cost-plus-based transfer-pricing method. Some of the drawbacks of dual pricing include

- The manager of the supplying unit may not have sufficient incentives to control costs.
- It does not provide clear signals to unit managers about the level of decentralization senior managers are seeking.
- It tends to insulate managers from the frictions of the marketplace, that is, knowledge of units' buying and selling market forces.

(d) **International Transfer Pricing.** The multinational corporation (MNC) must deal with transfer pricing and international taxation, and therefore, a knowledge of international laws related to these areas is important. A transfer is a substitute for a market price and is recorded by the seller as revenue and by the buyer as cost of goods sold. The transfer pricing system should motivate unit managers not to make undesirable decisions at the expense of the corporation as a whole. The ideal manager would act in the best interests of the company as a whole, even at the expense of the reported profits of his own unit. For this to happen, the manager must be rewarded when he chooses companywide goal congruence over his unit performance.

APPLICATION OF TRANSFER PRICING METHOD

Example 1: Unit A sells 500 units of product X to Unit B for $5 per unit. The $5 selling price is the transfer price.

Example 2: Unit A sells 500 units of product X to Unit B for $6 per unit. The normal market price is $4 per unit. Unit A shows increased sales of $2 per unit and a higher profit. Unit B shows the cost of goods sold has increased by $2 per unit and therefore has a lower profit. This example clearly violates the goal congruence principle since Unit A's decision to charge an inflated transfer price for products transferred to Unit B.

GOAL CONGRUENCE AND DECISION MAKING

- Desirable decisions enhance goal congruence.
- Undesirable decisions stifle goal congruence.
- Undesirable decisions can be minimized when the performance evaluation system is compatible with the transfer system.

According to Mueller[1], the international transfer pricing system must also attempt to accomplish objectives that are irrelevant in a purely domestic operation. These objectives include: worldwide income tax minimization, minimization of worldwide import duties, avoidance of financial restrictions, managing currency fluctuations, and winning host-country government approval. Each objective is discussed briefly.

- **Objective 1: Worldwide income tax minimization.** The transfer pricing system can be used to shift taxable profits from a country with a higher tax rate to a country with a lower tax rate; the result is that the MNC retains more profit after taxes. For example, the Cayman Islands have long been considered a tax haven for MNCs due to the zero corporate income tax rate and Pakistan being the highest at 50%.
- **Objective 2: Minimization of worldwide import duties.** Transfer prices can reduce tariffs. Import duties are normally applied to intracompany transfers as well as sales to unaffiliated buyers. If the goods are transferred in at low prices, the resulting tariffs will be lower.

  Tariffs interact with income taxes. Two associations exist: (1) low import duties and high income tax rates, and (2) high import duties and low income tax rates. There is a trade-off between income taxes and tariffs. The MNC has to evaluate the benefits of a lower (higher) income tax in the importing country against a higher (lower) import tariff as well as the potentially higher (lower) income tax paid by the MNC in the exporting country.
- **Objective 3: Avoidance of financial restrictions.** Foreign governments place certain types of economic restrictions on MNC operations with respect to the amount of cash transferred between the countries, and the amount of a tax credit or subsidy allowed. A subsidy is a payment from the government to the subsidiary unit and the nondeductibility of certain expenses provided by the parent against taxable income. This includes research and development expenses, general and administrative expenses, and royalty fees.

  Some ways to avoid these financial restrictions include setting a high transfer price on goods imported into the country, which would facilitate the desired movement of cash because the importing subsidiary must remit payment; charging a high transfer price on exported products, which will be followed by a larger tax credit or higher subsidy; or inflating the transfer price of imports to the subsidiary so that the nondeductibility of certain expenses can be recovered.

  The following options are available to a MNC:

  - If the goal is to show lower profitability, high transfer prices on imports to subsidiaries can be used. This objective is appropriate to discourage potential competitors from entering the market or takeover by outsiders.
  - If the goal is to show higher profitability, lower transfer prices on imports to subsidiaries can be used. Higher profits may trigger the subsidiary's employees to demand higher wages or profit-sharing plans or takeover by outsiders. Lower transfer prices on imports could improve the subsidiary's financial position, which facilitates local financing and enjoys a competitive edge during its initial stages of growth.

- **Objective 4: Managing currency fluctuations.** A country suffering from balance-of-payments problems may decide to devalue its national currency. Losses from such a devaluation may be avoided by using inflated transfer prices to transfer funds from the country to the parent or to some other affiliate unit.

  Balance-of-payments problems often result from an inflationary environment. Inflation erodes the purchasing power of the MNC's monetary assets. Using inflated transfer prices on goods imported to such an environment may offer a timely cash removal method.
- **Objective 5: Winning host-country government approval.** Maintaining positive relations with the host government is a good idea since the government is concerned about (1) intercorporate pricing and its effect on reported profits and (2) continually changing and manipulating transfer prices. For example, using unfavorable transfer prices to a country's economic detriment could result in the loss of goodwill. It is a trade-off between sacrificing some profits and satisfying foreign government authorities. Factors such as tax rates, tariffs, inflation, foreign exchange controls, gov-

[1] ***Accounting: An International Perspective****, by Mueller, Gernon, and Meek, (Burr Ridge, Illinois: Irwin), 1994.*

ernment price controls, and government stability need to be considered when analyzing the trade-offs.

(e) **Transfer Pricing Choices.** Basically, two choices exist in transfer pricing: (1) market-based pricing and (2) cost-based pricing. The benefits of using market-based pricing would be: divisional profitability approaches the real economic contribution of the subsidiary to the total MNC, creates a sense of competition among various subsidiaries, facilitates better evaluation of a subsidiary's performance, and incurs less scrutiny from foreign government tax authorities.

Pitfalls of using market-based pricing would be: subsidiaries need not be autonomous profit centers, subsidiary managers may not have the authority to make autonomous decisions, there may not be an intermediate market in order to establish a free competitive market price, and the MNC may not have much flexibility to manipulate profits and cash flows.

If market prices are either unavailable or cannot be reasonably estimated, then cost-based transfer prices are conveniently determined because the information on costs is available. Cost may be the full cost, a variable cost, or marginal cost with a markup added to allow the selling subsidiary some percentage of profit.

Disadvantages of cost-based transfer pricing include loss of incentive on the selling party to control costs or to operate efficiently; since the inefficiencies can be passed along to the purchasing subsidiary, undesirable behavior may result in the form of poor decision making.

KEY CONCEPTS TO REMEMBER: TRANSFER PRICING CHOICES

- A highly decentralized MNC would be expected to use market-based transfer prices. Smaller firms favor decentralized operations to achieve their objectives and to avoid foreign government scrutiny.
- A centralized MNC would control the setting of cost-based transfer prices. Large firms are generally more centralized due to worldwide optimization of objectives. Cost-based transfer pricing provides flexibility and control.
- The nationality of the parent company's management also affects whether the MNC uses market prices or costs in establishing a transfer price.

(f) **Taxes and Transfer Pricing.** Intercompany transactions from an MNC point of view are subject to Section 482 of the Internal Revenue Code of the United States. Section 482 gives the Internal Revenue Service (IRS) the authority to reallocate income and deductions among subsidiaries if it determines that this is necessary to prevent tax evasion, the illegal reduction of taxes. The key test is whether intercompany sales of goods or services appear to be priced at arm's-length market values. Among items the IRS will scrutinize include trademarks, patents, research and development cost, and management services.

The IRS allows three pricing methods considered arm's-length: (1) the comparable uncontrolled price method (i.e., market-based transfer pricing), (2) the resale price method (i.e., sales price less markup), and (3) the cost-plus method (i.e., cost-based transfer pricing).

TAX OBJECTIVES AT CONFLICT: IRS VERSUS MNC

- The IRS's objective is to determine the MNC's tax liability.
- The MNC's objective is after-tax profit maximization.
- These two objectives conflict.
- It is possible that a US MNC may use one transfer price for internal financial reporting and another for computing its US tax liability.

3.5 Cost-Volume-Profit Analysis

Cost-volume-profit (CVP) analysis helps managers who are making decisions about short-term duration and for specific cases where revenue and cost behaviors are linear and where volume is assumed to be the only cost and revenue driver. CVP is an approximation tool and low-cost tool.

KEY CONCEPTS TO REMEMBER: WHAT ARE COST OR REVENUE DRIVERS?

- A cost driver is any factor whose change causes a change in the total cost of a related cost object.
- A revenue driver is any factor whose change causes a change in the total revenue of a related product or service.
- There are many cost drivers and revenue drivers besides volume of units produced or sold. Examples affecting total cost and revenue include changes in quantity of materials and changes in setting prices, respectively.

CVP analysis is a straightforward, simple-to-apply, widely used management tool. CVP analysis answers questions such as, how will costs and revenues be affected if sales units are up or down by *x* percent? If price is decreased or increased by *x* percent? A decision model can be built using CVP relationships for choosing among courses of action. *CVP analysis tells management what will happen to financial results if a specific level of production or sales volume fluctuates or if costs change.*

An example of a decision model is the breakeven point (BEP), which shows the interrelationships of changes in costs, volume, and profits. It is the point of volume where total revenues and total costs are equal. No profit is gained or loss incurred at the BEP.

(a) **Methods for Calculating BEP.** Three methods available for calculating the BEP are shown in Exhibit 3.10.

Breakeven point methods
- The equation method
- The contribution-margin method
- The graphic method

Exhibit 3.10: Breakeven point methods

An increase in the BEP is a "red flag" for management to analyze all its CVP relationships more closely.

(i) **Equation method.** The equation method is more general and thus is easier to apply with multiple products, with multiple costs and revenue drivers, and with changes in the cost structure. At breakeven point, the operating income is zero.

Formula: (Unit sales price × number of units) – (Unit variable cost × number of units) – Fixed costs = Operating income or Sales – Variable costs – Fixed costs = Operating income

Example: Price is $100, variable cost is $60, fixed costs are $2,000. What is the breakeven units?

$$100\text{ N} - 60\text{ N} - 2{,}000 = 0$$
$$40\text{ N} = 2{,}000$$
$$\text{N} = 2{,}000/40 = 50 \text{ units}$$

(ii) **Contribution-margin method.** Contribution-margin (CM) is equal to sales minus all variable costs. BEP is calculated as follows:

BEP = Fixed costs/ Unit contribution margin

Using the same example, BEP = 2,000/(100 – 60) = 2,000/40 = 50 units

A desired target operating income can be added to the fixed costs to give a new BEP which tells how many units must be sold to generate enough CM to cover total fixed costs plus target operating income.

The BEP tells how many units of product must be sold to generate enough contribution margin to cover total fixed costs. The CM method is valid only for a single product and a single cost driver. The CM method is a restatement of the equation method in a different form. Either method can be used to calculate the BEP.

(iii) **Graphic method.** A CVP chart results when units are plotted on the x-axis and dollars on the y-axis. The break-even point is where the total-sales line and total-cost line intersect. The total sales line begins at the origin because if volume is zero, sales revenue will be zero, too.

VOLUME VERSUS COSTS VERSUS SALES

- As volume increases, total fixed costs remain the same over the entire volume range.
- As volume increases, both total variable costs and sales increase.

The total fixed-cost line will be flat because fixed costs are constant across a wide range of volumes. Linear CVP analysis is approximate under perfect competition thus showing the link between cost accounting and economics. In economics, the slope of the total revenue (TR) function equals marginal revenue (MR), which equals sales per unit. The slope of the total cost (TC) function is marginal cost (MC), which equals variable cost per unit. The sales price per unit and variable cost per unit are constant across a wide range of volumes only if there is perfect competition in input and output markets. However, this is not true for imperfect competition, where sales price must be reduced to increase volume.

Use the following cost-volume-profit (CVP) chart for examples 1 and 2.

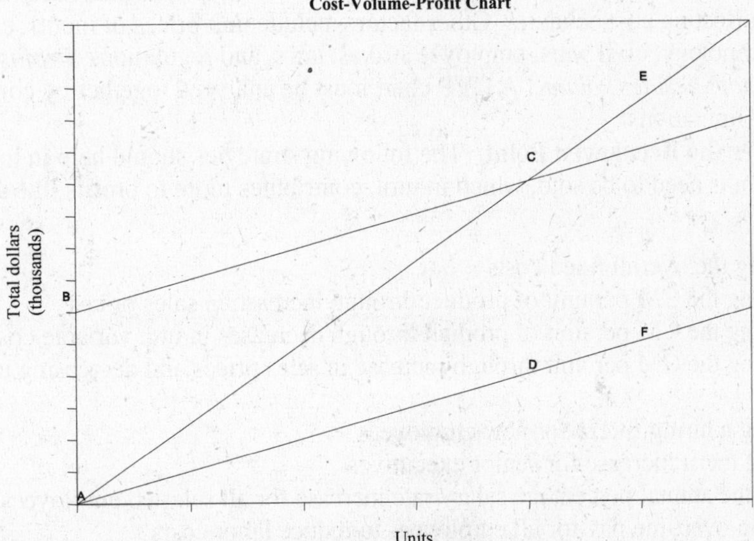

Example 1: Which of the following labeled points on this chart is the breakeven point?

a. Point A
b. Point B
c. Point C
d. Point D

Choice **(c)** is the correct answer. Point C is the intersection of the total cost line and the total revenue line, which is the breakeven point. Choice (a) is incorrect. Point A is the origin, where total revenues are zero and there is a loss equal to the amount of fixed costs. Choice (b) is incorrect. Point B is the total cost line at zero activity, which is the amount of total fixed costs. Choice (d) is incorrect. Point D is on the total variable cost curve, and represents the total variable costs at the breakeven point.

Example 2: Which of the following items is graphically represented on the cost-volume-profit chart as the difference between labeled points E and F?

a. Total profit
b. Total variable costs
c. Total fixed costs
d. Total contribution margin

Choice **(d)** is the correct answer. The difference between labeled Points E (which is on the total revenue line) and Point F (which is on the total variable cost line) is total contribution margin. Choice (a) is incorrect because it is on Point C. Choice (b) is incorrect because it is on Point D. Choice (c) is incorrect because it is on Point B. Choices (a), (b), and (c) are not between Points E and F.

(b) **CVP Assumptions and Their Limitations.**

Assumptions. We already learned that the CVP relationships hold true for only a limited range of production or sales volume levels. This means that these relationships would not hold if volume fell below or rose above a certain level. The following is a list of assumptions:

- The behavior of total revenues and total costs is linear over the relevant range of volume.
- Selling prices, total fixed costs, efficiency, and productivity are constant.
- All costs can be divided neatly into fixed and variable components. Variable cost per unit remains constant.
- A greater sales mix will be maintained as total volume changes.
- Volume is the only driver of costs.
- The production volume equals sales volume, or changes in beginning and ending inventory levels are zero.

Limitations. There are many limitations to the CVP assumptions made above. Volume is only one of the factors affecting cost behavior. Other factors include unit prices of inputs, efficiency, changes in production technology, civil wars, employee strikes, laws, and regulations. *Profits are affected by changes in factors besides volume.* A CVP chart must be analyzed together by considering all assumptions and their limitations.

(c) **Ways to Lower the Breakeven Point.** The following strategies should help in lowering the BEP, which means fewer units need to be sold, which in turn, contributes more to profits (the strategies are not order-ranked).

- Reducing the overall fixed costs
- Increasing the CM per unit of product through increase in sales prices
- Increasing the CM per unit of product through decreases in unit variable costs
- Increasing the CM per unit through increase in sales prices and decreasing unit variable costs together
- Selecting a hiring freeze for new employees
- Limiting merit increase for senior executives
- Cutting the annual percentage salary rate increase for all salaried employees
- Reducing overtime pay for all employees to reduce labor costs
- Reducing the number of employees on payroll
- Improving employee productivity levels
- Increasing machine utilization rates

(d) **Sensitivity Analysis in CVP.** A CVP model developed in a dynamic environment determined that the estimated parameters used may vary between limits. Subsequent testing of the model with respect to all possible values of the estimated parameters is termed a sensitivity analysis.

Sensitivity analysis is a management tool that will answer questions such as: What will operating income be if volume changes from the original prediction? What will operating income be if variable costs per unit decrease or increase by x percent? If sales drop, how far can they fall below budget before the BEP is reached? The last question can be answered by the margin of safety tool. The margin of safety is a tool of sensitivity analysis and is the excess of budgeted sales over the break-even volume.

Sensitivity analysis is a "what-if" technique aimed at asking how a result will be changed if the original predicted data are not achieved or if an underlying assumption changes. It is a measure of changes in outputs resulting from changes in inputs. It reveals the impact of changes in one or more input variables on the output or results.

(e) **Changes in Variable and Fixed Costs.** Organizations often face a trade-off between fixed and variable costs. Fixed costs can be substituted for variable costs and vice versa. This is because variable costs and fixed costs are subject to various degrees of control at different volumes—boom or slack. For example, when a firm invests in automated machinery to offset increase in labor rates, its fixed costs increase, but unit variable costs decrease.

(f) **Contribution Margin and Gross Margin. Contribution margin** (CM) is the excess of sales over all variable costs, including variable manufacturing, marketing, and administrative categories. **Gross margin** (GM), also called gross profit, is the excess of sales over the cost of the goods sold. Both CM and GM would be different for a manufacturing company. They will be equal only when fixed manufacturing costs included in cost of goods sold are the same as the variable nonmanufacturing costs, which is a highly unlikely event.

- Variable manufacturing, marketing, and administrative costs are subtracted from sales to get CM, but not GM.
- Fixed manufacturing overhead is subtracted from sales to get GM, but not CM.
- Both the CM and GM can be expressed as totals, as an amount per unit, or as percentages of sales in the form of ratios.
- An example of CM and GM is

Gross margin		*Contribution margin*	
Sales	$50,000	Sales	$50,000
Manufacturing		Variable manufacturing costs	$20,000
cost of goods sold	$30,000	Variable nonmanufacturing costs	$ 5,000
Gross margin	$20,000	Total variable costs	$25,000
		Contribution margin	$25,000

APPLICATION OF CONTRIBUTION MARGIN CONCEPT

Example: A department store prepares segmented financial statements. During the past year, the income statement for the perfume department located near the front entrance appeared as follows:

Sales	$200,000
Cost of goods sold	120,000
Gross profit	80,000
Janitorial expense	5,000
Sales commissions	40,000
Heat and lighting	4,000
Depreciation	3,000
Income before taxes	$ 28,000

Janitorial expense, heat and lighting, and depreciation are allocated to the department based on square footage. Sales personnel work for only one department and are paid on commission. What is the perfume department's contribution margin?

a. $28,000
b. $31,000
c. $37,000
d. $40,000

Choice **(d)** is the correct answer. Contribution margin is the gross profit of $80,000 minus the $40,000 of sales commissions, that is, $40,000. Choice (a) is incorrect. This is net income, as given. Choice (b) is incorrect. Janitorial and heat and light are fixed costs ($80,000 – $40,000 – $5,000 – $4,000). Choice (c) is incorrect. Depreciation is a fixed cost, hence not a part of contribution margin ($80,000 – $40,000 – $3,000).

(g) **Profit-Volume Chart.** The profit-volume (PV) chart is preferable to the CVP chart because it is simpler to understand. The PV chart shows a quick, condensed comparison of how alternatives on pricing, variable costs, or fixed costs affect operating income as volume changes. The operating income is drawn on the y-axis and the x-axis represents volume (units or dollars).

Due to operating leverage, profits increase during high volume because more of the costs are fixed and do not increase with volume. Profits decrease during low volume because fixed costs cannot be avoided despite the lower volume.

(h) **Effect of Sales Mix and Income Taxes**. Sales mix is the relative combination of quantities of products that constitute total sales. A change in sales mix will cause actual profits to differ from budgeted profits.

It is the combination of low-margin or high-margin products that causes the shift in profits, despite achievement of targeted sales volume.

There will be a different breakeven point for each different sales mix. A higher proportion of sales in high contribution margin products will reduce the BEP. A lower proportion of sales in small contribution margin products will increase the BEP. Shifting marketing efforts to high contribution margin products can increase the operating income and profits.

Management is interested in the effect of various production and sales strategies on the operating income, not so much of BEP. Both the operating income and BEP are dependent on the assumptions made (i.e., if the assumptions change, the operating income and the BEP will also change).

The impact of income taxes is clear. The general equation method can be changed to allow for the impact of income taxes, as shown below.

Target operating income = (Target net income) divided by (1 – Tax rate)

Each unit beyond the BEP adds to net income at the unit contribution margin multiplied by (1 – Tax rate). However, the BEP itself is unchanged. This is because no income tax is paid at a level of zero income. In other words, an increase in income tax rates will not affect the BEP.

3.6 Relevant Costs

(a) **Differential Analysis.** Managers must consider the effects of alternative decisions on their businesses. We discuss differential analysis, which reports the effects of alternative decisions on total revenues and costs. Planning for future operations involves decision making. For some decisions, revenue and cost data from the accounting records may be useful. However, the revenue and cost data for use in evaluating courses of future operations or choosing among competing alternatives are often not available in the accounting records and must be estimated. These estimates include relevant revenues and costs. The relevant revenues and costs focus on the differences between each alternative. Costs that have been incurred in the past are not relevant to the decision. These costs are called **sunk costs.**

FOCUS OF RELEVANT COSTS

The relevant revenues and costs focus on the difference between each alternative.

Differential revenue is the amount of increase or decrease in revenue expected from a course of action as compared with an alternative. To illustrate, assume that certain equipment is being used to manufacture calculators, which are expected to generate revenue of $150,000. If the equipment could be used to make digital clocks, which would generate revenue of $175,000, the differential revenue from making and selling digital clocks is $25,000.

Differential cost is the amount of increase or decrease in cost that is expected from a course of action as compared with an alternative. For example, if an increase in advertising expenditures from $100,000 to $150,000 is being considered, the differential cost of the action is $50,000.

Differential income or loss is the difference between the differential revenue and the differential costs. Differential income indicates that a particular decision is expected to be profitable, while a differential loss indicates the opposite.

Differential analysis focuses on the effect of alternative courses of action on the relevant revenues and costs. For example, if a manager must decide between two alternatives, differential analysis would involve comparing the differential revenues of the two alternatives with the differential costs.

Differential analysis can be used in analyzing the following alternatives:

1. Leasing or selling equipment
2. Discontinuing an unprofitable segment
3. Manufacturing or purchasing a needed part (make-or-buy analysis)
4. Replacing usable fixed assets
5. Processing further or selling an intermediate product
6. Accepting additional business at a special price

(b) **Application of Relevant Cost Concept.** When deciding whether to accept a special order from a customer, the best thing to do is to compare the total revenue to be derived from this order with the total relevant costs incurred for this order. The key terms are incremental relevant costs and incremental relevant revenues. The relevant costs are those that vary with the decision.

The long-term fixed costs should be excluded from the analysis since they will be incurred regardless of whether the order is accepted. Direct labor, direct materials, variable manufacturing overhead, and variable selling and administrative costs are relevant because they will not be incurred if the special order is not accepted. Incremental fixed costs would be relevant in short-term decision making under certain situations.

3.7 Costing Systems

Product cost control systems can be viewed in terms of target costing and traditional costing a product.

(a) **Target Costing.** Target costing is a new way of controlling a product's cost. A target cost is the allowable amount of cost that can be incurred on a given product and still earn the required profit margin. It is a market-driven cost in which cost targets are set by considering customer requirements and competitive environment. Cost targets are achieved by focusing and improving both process design and product design. Market research indicates the target price customers are willing to pay.

$$\text{Target price} - \text{Profit margin} = \text{Target cost}$$

The need for target costing arises due to sophisticated customers demanding better quality products with more features and functions at an affordable price. This is made real by aggressive competitors who are willing to take risks and provide a product at target price with the hope of achieving efficiencies in cost management and production operations.

Target costing is not the same as "design to cost" or "design for manufacturability," which are the issues for engineering and manufacturing management respectively. Target costing integrates strategic business planning with cost/profit planning. To achieve this integration, a target-costing system requires cross-functional teams to take ownership and responsibility for costs. These teams consist of representatives from finance/accounting, marketing, engineering, manufacturing, and other functions.

(b) **Traditional Costing.** Traditional costing systems use a cost plus approach, where production costs are first estimated, then a profit margin is added to it to obtain a product price that the market is going to pay for it. If the price is too high, cost reductions are initiated. It is a cost-driven approach where customer requirements and competitive environment are not considered.

$$\text{Traditional production cost} + \text{Profit margin} = \text{Traditional product price}$$

The cost to manufacture a product is necessary for external reporting (e.g., inventory valuation and cost of goods sold determination) and internal management decisions (e.g., price determination, product mix decisions, and sensitivity analysis). One of the goals of cost accounting is to provide information for management planning and control and determination of product or service costs. This is achieved through the accumulation of costs by department and/or by product. Although the terminology differs between manufacturing and service industries, the principles of cost accounting are the same.

Two methods exist to accumulate product costs: (1) job order costing system and (2) process (operations) costing system. Both methods help management in planning and control of business operations. A job order cost system provides a separate record for the cost of each quantity of product that passes through the factory. A job order cost system is best suited to industries that manufacture custom goods to fill special orders from customers or that produce a high variety of products for stock (job shops). Under a process cost system, costs are accumulated for each of the departments or processes within the factory. A process cost system is best suited for manufacturers of units of products that are not distinguishable from each other during a continuous production process (e.g., oil refineries and food processing).

TRADITIONAL COST SYSTEMS VERSUS TARGET COST SYSTEMS

- Traditional cost systems are closed systems where the focus is on internal measures of efficiency. Suppliers are involved after the product is designed. Cost reduction is initiated after the fact based on product standards or budgets with the aim of reducing or eliminating waste and inefficiency. Costs determine price.

- Target cost systems are open systems where the focus is on external market demands. Suppliers are involved before the product is designed. Cost reduction is initiated before the fact based on continuous improvement opportunities with the aim of enhancing the product's design. Prices determine costs.

Exhibit 3.11 compares these two product cost systems.

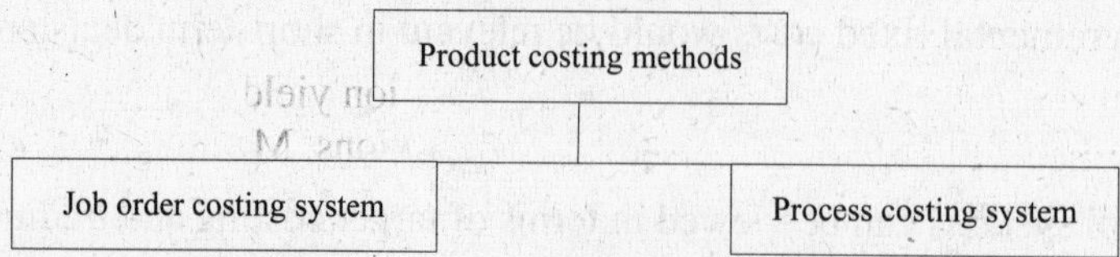

Exhibit 3.11: Product costing methods

Characteristics of job order costing system

- Unlike (heterogeneous) products are manufactured.
- Products tends to be special and unique.
- Costs are allocated to a specific unit or to a small batch of products or services.
- A production job retains its identity from start to finish.
- Costs are averaged (i.e., total costs divided by small number of units of production).
- Only one work in process (WIP) account is involved and units move from WIP to finished goods.
- Costs are collected separately for each job.
- Systems are complex and more expensive than the process costing method.
- Examples include printing jobs and construction jobs.

Characteristics of process costing systems

- Like (homogeneous) products are manufactured.
- Products tend to be common and generic.
- Costs are allocated to large number of units that proceed in a continuous fashion.
- A production job does not retain its identity due to byproducts, joint products, and main products.
- Costs are averaged (i.e., total costs divided by large number of units of production).
- Several WIP accounts are involved and units move from one department's WIP account to the next.
- Costs are collected separately for each process and then summed up.
- Systems are simpler and less expensive than the job order costing method.
- Examples include oil refinery, food products, and soft drinks.

(c) **Activity-Based Costing.** Activity-based costing (ABC) is a management system that focuses on activities as the fundamental cost objects and uses the costs of these activities as building blocks for compiling the costs of other cost objects. ABC helps management in controlling costs through its focus on cost drivers. ABC can provide more accurate product cost data by using multiple cost drivers that more accurately reflect the causes of costs. Inaccurate product cost information can lead to cross-subsidization of products. This results in systematic under-costing of products due to lower overhead rate. These cost drivers can be both non-volume-based as well as volume-based drivers.

KEY CONCEPTS TO REMEMBER: ACTIVITY-BASED COSTING

- The key focus of ABC is on activities, not on products. This is in line with the philosophy of executives in managing costs. The scope of activities may range from start to finish for a product or service (i.e., from research and development to customer service).
- If the manufacturing process is described as machine-paced, then machine hours should be used as the cost driver.

- If the manufacturing process is described as labor-paced, then direct labor hours should be used as the cost driver.
- If direct labor is a small percentage (e.g., 5%) of total manufacturing costs, it should be regarded as a part of indirect costs, not direct costs.
- The ABC can be a part of a job-costing or process-costing system.

ABC builds the cost of a product from the bottom up for all activities involved (A1 through An) in all departments (D1 through Dn) in a manufacturing function yielding to inventoriable cost. The full cost of a product is obtained similarly by adding costs for functions. Manufacturing and nonmanufacturing (e.g., research and development, product design, marketing, customer service) costs are accumulated for each activity as a separate cost object. The costs collected at each cost object can be variable costs of the activity or both variable and fixed costs of the activity.

(i) **Benefits of activity-based costing system.** Major benefits of an activity-based costing system include

- Better cost control
- Accurate product cost information
- Lower information processing costs
- Individual costs allocated to products via several cost drivers
- Better make-or-buy decisions
- Focus on activities where costs are incurred and accumulated instead of products

(ii) **When to use activity-based costing system.** The presence of the following characteristics indicate the use of an ABC system:

- Companies with high overhead costs
- Companies with a widely diverse range of products and operating activities
- Companies with wide variation in number of production runs and costly setups
- Companies with the accounting system lagging behind the production system's advancements

(iii) **Comparison of traditional accounting system with activity-based costing system.** A better appreciation of an activity-based costing system can be made when it is compared with the traditional, typical accounting system (see Exhibit 3.12).

Traditional accounting system	*Activity-based costing system*
Functions are divided into departments.	Departments are dividend into activities.
Fails to highlight the interrelationships among activities in different departments or functions.	Highlights the interrelationships among activities in different departments or functions.
Accountants need not possess interpersonal skills to interact with production staff	Accountants need to possess interpersonal skills to interact with production staff.
Accountants need not become knowledgeable in production operations.	Accountants need to become knowledgeable in production operations.
One or few indirect cost pools for each department or whole plant is used.	Many indirect cost pools, because of many activity areas, are used.
Indirect cost application bases are often financial, such as direct labor costs or direct material costs.	Indirect cost application bases are often nonfinancial variables, such as number of parts in a product or hours of test time.
Indirect costs are allocated to products using a single overhead rate.	Indirect costs are allocated to products using multiple cost drivers, preferably the same as the indirect cost application bases.

Exhibit 3.12: Comparison of traditional accounting system with activity-based costing system

(d) **Standard Costing.** Standard costs are predetermined costs or estimated costs requiring a startup investment to develop them. Ongoing costs for maintenance of standards can be lower than for an actual-cost system. Standard costs should be attainable and are expressed on a per-unit basis. Without standard costs, there is no flexible budgeting system since the latter is developed at different volumes of production using standard costs per unit.

Standard costs, flexible budgets, and standards are equally applicable to manufacturing and non-manufacturing firms. Standard costs and flexible budgets are interrelated. Flexible budget is a budget that is adjusted for changes in the unit level of the cost driver or revenue driver. In a standard cost system, the concept of flexible budget is key to the analysis of variances.

A powerful benefit of standard costing is its feedback mechanism where actual costs are compared with standard costs resulting in variances. This feedback helps explore better ways of adhering to standards, modifying standards, and of accomplishing production goals. Standard costs can be developed for material, labor, and overhead. One drawback of a standard cost system is that actual direct material costs and actual direct labor costs cannot be traced to individual products.

STANDARD COST VERSUS BUDGETED COST

- Standard cost refers to the cost of a single unit of output (e.g., $50 per unit).
- Budgeted cost refers to a total amount ($500,000 at 10,000 units).
- A standard amount and a budgeted amount are the same when standards are attainable.

Major purposes of standard costs, in decreasing order of importance, would include the following:

- Cost management
- Price-making policy
- Budgetary planning and control
- Financial statement preparation
- Lower recordkeeping costs

Line management is responsible for standard setting and the budget-development process whereas the accounting department, which is a staff function, is responsible for expressing the physical standard in monetary terms, for coordinating the budgeting process throughout the firm, and for reporting operating performance in comparison with standards and budgets.

Standards help in evaluating the performance of responsibility centers. Most recently established standards should be used in variance analysis. Variances, differences between standards and actuals, can be developed, reported, and tracked for control purposes in a number of ways, as shown in the Exhibit 3.13.

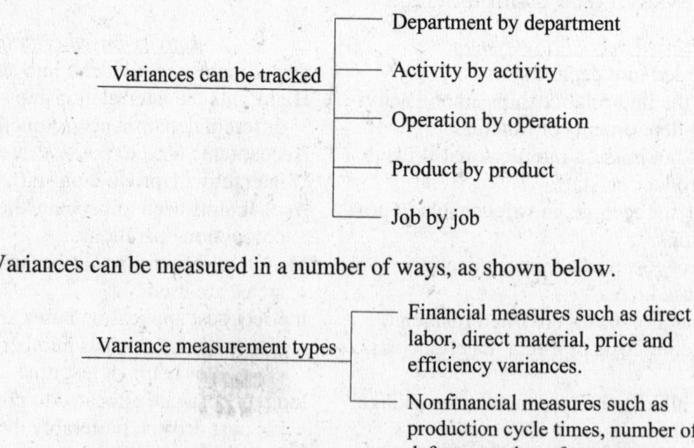

Exhibit 3.13: Different ways of tracking and measuring variances

Organizations are moving away from financial measures to nonfinancial measures for better focus on the problem at hand. For example, one reason for moving away from direct labor as a measurement of variance is its minor role in total cost for firms with automated production operations.

(i) **Types of standards.** Two concepts prevail in standards: (1) perfection (ideal or theoretical) standards, and (2) currently attainable standards. Their features are shown in the Exhibit 3.14.

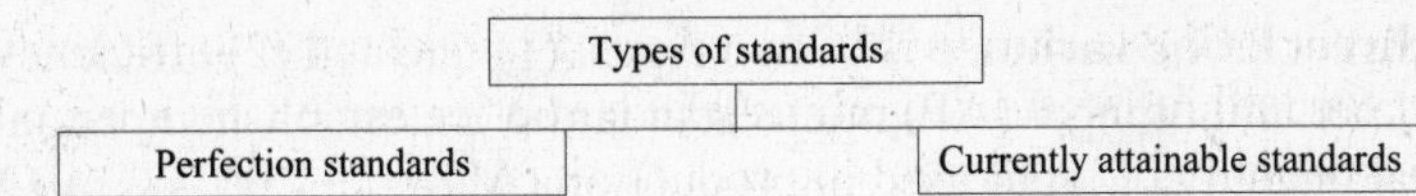

Characteristics of perfection standards

- Leads to the absolute minimum possible costs operating under the best conditions.
- No provisions are made for waste, spoilage, machine breakdowns, fatigue.
- In line with continual improvement quality and operating efficiency.
- Results in "unreasonable" standards.
- Cannot be used for cash budgeting or for product costing due to their impracticality. Results will be inaccurate.
- Does not motivate employees and variances will be larger.
- Used for compiling performance reports.

Characteristics of currently attainable standards

- Achievable by a specified level of effort.
- Provision is made for normal waste, spoilage, and nonproductive time.
- The standards are "expected actuals," prediction of what will likely occur.
- Accommodates anticipated inefficiency. Results in "reasonable" standards.
- Managers use it for costing products, budgeting cash, and budgeting departmental performance.
- Motivates employees, and variances will be small.
- Major unfavorable variances could signal a problem requiring management's attention.

Exhibit 3.14: Characteristics of standards

(ii) **Types of Variances.** In general, **price variance** is the difference between actual unit prices and budgeted unit prices multiplied by the actual quantity of goods sold, used, or purchased.

Price variance = (Actual unit price – Standard unit price) × Actual inputs purchased

Companies that use fewer suppliers and longer-term contracts are less likely to have significant material price variances. This is because (1) contracts specify unchanging prices for fixed time spans, and (2) the buying firm has leverage against the selling firm.

Companies that use several suppliers and short-term contracts are more likely to have significant material price variances. This is because (1) contracts are frequently changed or canceled, and (2) the buying firm has little or no leverage against the selling firm.

Due to labor union contracts, labor price variance is relatively insignificant since management knows the future labor rates, unlike material prices.

The purchasing manager is responsible for the price variance. Price variance is rate variance with respect to direct labor. The purchasing manager can help control price variance by: (1) getting many price quotations, (2) buying in economical lot sizes, (3) taking advantage of cash discounts, and (4) selecting the most economical means of material delivery. This could result in favorable price variance depending on how standards are set.

In general, **efficiency variance** is of two types: material efficiency and labor efficiency. Possible reasons for material efficiency variances include (1) quality of materials (2) workmanship, (3) choice of materials, (4) mix of materials, and (5) incorrect standards.

Efficiency variance is the difference between the quantity of actual inputs used and the quantity of inputs that should have been used multiplied by the budgeted price.

Efficiency variance = (Inputs actually used – Inputs that should have been used) × Standard unit price of inputs

The factory supervisor is responsible for the efficiency variance. Efficiency variance is quantity or usage variance with respect to direct materials.

Specifically, **direct materials variance** is of two types: (1) price and (2) quantity. The price variance is actual price paid per unit of input (AP) minus standard price established per unit of input (SP) multiplied by actual quantity of input used in production (AQ).

$$\text{Direct materials price variance} = (AP - SP) \times AQ$$

The materials price variance is unfavorable if AP is greater than SP and favorable if AP is less than SP.

The quantity variance is actual quantity of input used in production (AQ) minus standard quantity of input that should have been used in production (SQ) multiplied by standard price established per unit of input (SP).

$$\text{Direct materials quantity variance} = (AQ - SQ) \times SP$$

The materials quantity variance is unfavorable if AQ is greater than SQ and favorable if AQ is less than SQ.

Specifically, **direct labor variance** is of two types: (1) rate and (2) efficiency. The rate variance is actual price paid per unit of input (AP) minus standard price established per unit of input (SP) multiplied by actual quantity of input used in production (AQ).

$$\text{Direct labor rate variance} = (AP - SP) \times AQ$$

The labor rate variance is unfavorable if AP is greater than SP and favorable if AP is less than SP.

The efficiency variance is actual quantity of input used in production (AQ) minus standard quantity of input that should have been used in production (SQ) multiplied by standard price established per unit of input (SP).

$$\text{Direct labor efficiency variance} = (AQ - SQ) \times SP$$

The labor efficiency variance is unfavorable if AQ is greater than SQ and favorable if AQ is less than SQ.

Specifically, **overhead variance** is of four types: (1) spending variance, (2) efficiency variance, (3) budget variance, and (4) volume variance. Variances (1) and (2) are part of variable overhead variances while variances (3) and (4) are part of fixed overhead variances.

$$\text{Spending variance} = \text{Actual variable overhead} - (\text{Actual hours} \times \text{Budget rate})$$
$$\text{Efficiency variance} = \text{Budget rate} \times (\text{Actual hours} - \text{Standard hours})$$

The budget variance is sometimes called the fixed overhead spending variance. It is calculated as the difference between actual fixed costs and budget fixed costs.

The volume variance is sometimes called the idle capacity variance. This is computed as Budget fixed cost – (Standard hours allowed for actual output at standard rate).

CALCULATION OF VARIANCES

Example 1: A manager prepared the following table by which to analyze labor costs for the month:

Actual hours at actual rate	*Actual hours at standard rate*	*Standard hours at standard rate*
$10,000	$9,800	$8,820

What variance was $980? It is the labor efficiency variance, which is the difference between actual and standard hours multiplied times standard wages. That is, $9,800 – $8,820 = $980.

Example 2: A firm's budget showed planned sales of 20,000 units at a $20 contribution margin each, or $400,000. Actual sales totaled 21,000 units. There were no variable cost variances. What was the sales volume variance for the period? It is $20,000, as shown below.

The sales volume variance is the difference between actual results (21,000 units) and planned results (20,000 units) at planned contribution margin ($20), or $20,000.

Example 3: The exhibit below reflects a summary of performance for a single item of a retail store's inventory for the month ended April 30, 2004.

	Actual results	*Flexible budget variances*	*Flexible budget*	*Static (master) budget*
Sales (units)	11,000		11,000	12,000
Revenue (sales)	$208,000	$12,000 U	$220,000	$240,000
Variable costs	121,000	11,000 U	110,000	120,000
Contribution margin	$121,000	$23,000 U	$110,000	$120,000
Fixed costs	72,000	——	72,000	72,000
Operating income	49,000	$23,000 U	$38,000	$48,000

What is the sales volume variance? It is $10,000 U, as shown below. Sales volume variance is defined as the difference between the flexible-budget amounts and the static (master)-budget amounts ($38,000 – $48,000 = $10,000 U).

KEY CONCEPTS TO REMEMBER: PRICE AND EFFICIENCY VARIANCE

- A manager has less control over price variance because of outside influences. Variance is the difference in price multiplied by actual inputs purchased.
- A manager has better control over efficiency variance because the quantity of inputs used is affected by factors inside the firm. Efficiency variance is the difference in quantity multiplied by the standard unit price.
- Price and efficiency variances are either written off immediately to cost of goods sold or prorated among the inventories and cost of goods sold.

A performance measurement and reward system for a firm should emphasize total organizational objectives, not individual departments' variances. The goal is to reduce the total costs of the company as a whole, not price variance or efficiency variance (i.e., single performance measure).

Although labor rates are known from the union contract, unfavorable labor price variance can occur due to

- The use of a "single average standard labor rate" for a given activity that requires different labor rates (the averaging effect)
- The assignment of a high-skilled worker earning more money to an activity that should have been assigned to a less-skilled worker earning less money

The control of direct labor is more important to firms with less automation and less important to firms with more automation. The source documents for variance reports are time tickets showing the actual time used. Codes are used to indicate the departmental responsibility and causes of the variance. Employee absenteeism can affect labor efficiency.

Variance analysis should be subjected to the same cost-benefit test as any other managerial decision. No fixed guidance can be given as to how much unfavorable or favorable variance ought to be analyzed. However, it is important to separate variances caused by random events (uncontrollable) from variances that are controllable. Random variances are attributable to chance rather than to management's implementation decisions.

KEY CONCEPTS TO REMEMBER: WHAT IS A STANDARD?

- A standard is not a single acceptable measure.
- A standard is a range of possible acceptable outcomes.
- Variances are expected to fluctuate randomly within some normal limits. A random variance per se is within this range, and requires no corrective action. Only nonrandom variance requires corrective action by management.

(iii) **Effects of variance prorations.** Generally accepted accounting principles and income tax laws require that financial statements show actual costs of inventories and cost of goods sold. Consequently, variance prorations are required if they result in a material change in inventories or operating income. Variance is the difference between actual costs and standard costs. A good benefit of proration is that it prevents managers from setting standards aimed at manipulating income. By setting loose standards, managers can take the resulting favorable variance into current income. If managers do not have to prorate variances, they can more easily affect a year's operating income by how they set standards. The relevant questions are

- **How should variances occurring during the first stages of new operations be accounted for?** Standards might initially be set at a "loose" level to allow for start-up inefficiencies and later they should be tightened. If the standards are currently attainable, variances should be carried forward as assets and written off in future periods.
- **How should variances be prorated?** First, a decision should be made whether proration should occur, and it usually depends on whether the variances are material in amount.

Decision rules: 1. Immaterial variances should be written off immediately and adjusted to cost of goods sold.

2. Material variances should be prorated as follows: (a) to affect current incomes by posting to cost of goods sold and income accounts, (b) to affect inventories by apportioning among work in process, finished goods, and cost of goods sold.

Some contend that variances are measures of inefficiency and should be completely written off to the accounting period instead of being prorated among inventories and cost of goods sold. They argue that inventory costs will be more representative of desirable and attainable costs.

KEY CONCEPTS TO REMEMBER: VARIANCES

- Variance proration tends to carry costs of inefficiency as assets.
- Variances need not be prorated to inventories as long as standards are currently attainable.
- If ideal or obsolete standards are used, variances should be split: (1) the portion of the variance that reflects departures from currently attainable standards should be written off as period costs, and (2) the portion that does not reflect departure from currently attainable standards should be prorated to inventories and cost of goods sold.

Adjustments to inventory accounts is made to satisfy external reporting requirements as follows:

- **Converting** a variable-costing inventory valuation to absorption-costing valuation
- **Prorating variances.** The journal entry to accomplish this adjustment would be to **debit** finished goods inventory adjustment account and to **credit** either fixed factory overhead or cost variance accounts (e.g., direct material price variance).

(iv) **Reporting of variances.** Interim reporting of variance differs in that some firms write off all variances monthly or quarterly to cost of goods sold while others prorate the variances among inventories and cost of goods sold. Most firms will follow the same reporting practices for both interim and annual financial statements.

The interim overhead variances are often called "planned" variances and deferred. These variances include direct material price variances and factory overhead production volume variances. The rationale is that these variances are expected to disappear by the end of the year through the use of averaging as costs are applied to the product. The "unplanned," unanticipated, underapplied, or overapplied overhead should be reported at the end of an interim period following the same procedures used at the end of a fiscal year (according to Accounting Principles Board, [APB] Opinion 28).

UNDERAPPLIED VERSUS OVERAPPLIED MANUFACTURING OVERHEAD

- If underapplied manufacturing overhead is carried forward during the year, it would appear on an interim balance sheet as a current asset, a prepaid expense.
- If overapplied manufacturing overhead is carried forward during the year, it would appear on an interim balance sheet as a current liability, a deferred credit.

3.8 Responsibility Accounting

(a) **Overview.** Managers are responsible and accountable for their decisions and actions in planning and controlling the resources of the organization. Resources include physical, human, and financial resources. Resources are used to achieve the organization's goals and objectives. Budgets help to quantify the resources required to achieve goals.

The concept of responsibility accounting emerged since a few senior managers at the top cannot run all parts of a business effectively. To improve performance, the organization is divided into centers, product lines, divisions, and units so that a lower-level manager is responsible for a specific center, product line, division, or a unit.

(b) **Definition of Responsibility Accounting.** Each manager is in charge of a responsibility center and is accountable for a specified set of activities and operations within a segment of the organization. The degree of responsibility varies directly with the level of the manager. Responsibility accounting is a system that measures the plans and actions of each responsibility center. Four types of responsibility centers are common, as shown in Exhibit 3.15.

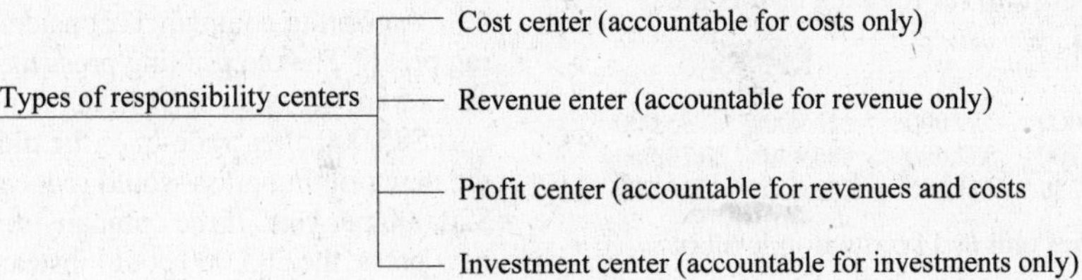

Exhibit 3.15: Types of responsibility centers

In a **cost center,** a manager is accountable for costs only (e.g., a manufacturing plant). In a **revenue center,** a manager is accountable for revenues only (e.g., a product manager or brand manager). In a **profit center,** a manager is accountable for revenues and costs (e.g., a division). In an **investment center,** a manager is accountable for investment (e.g., a division revenues and costs).

A major **advantage** of the responsibility accounting approach is that costs can be traced to either (1) the individual who has the best knowledge about the reasons for cost increase, or (2) the activity that caused the cost increase. A major **disadvantage** is its behavioral implications on managers whose performance is to be evaluated.

A manager should be held accountable for the costs that he has control over. Controllability is the degree of influence that a specific manager has over costs, revenues, and investment. A controllable cost is any cost that is subject to the influence of a given manager of a given responsibility center for a given time span. Controllable costs should be separated from uncontrollable costs in a manager's performance report.

KEY CONCEPTS TO REMEMBER: RESPONSIBILITY ACCOUNTING

- Most managers have partial control over their costs; their rewards depend on factors they cannot control.
- Managers should be compensated according to risk taking regardless of who controls the costs. Otherwise, management turnover, frustration, and low motivation will set in.
- A manager should be able to influence activities even though he does not have full control over costs.
- A manager's behavior can be changed by switching from cost center to profit center if it helps the organization.

In responsibility accounting, feedback is crucial. When budgets are compared with actual results, variances occur. The key is to use variance information to raise questions and seek answers from the right party. Variance information should not be abused—in other words, it should not be used to "fix the blame" on others. *Variances invoke questions as to why and how, not who.*

MULTIPLE-CHOICE QUESTIONS (1-239)

Cost Concepts

1. Total production costs of prior periods for a company are listed below. Assume that the same cost behavior patterns can be extended linearly over the range of 3,000 to 35,000 units and that the cost driver for each cost is the number of units produced.

Production in units per month	3,000	9,000	16,000	35,000
Cost X	$23,700	$52,680	$86,490	$178,260
Cost Y	47,280	141,840	252,160	551,600

What is the average cost per unit at a production level of 8,000 units for cost X?

a. $5.98
b. $5.85
c. $7.90
d. $4.83

2. Many companies recognize three major categories of costs of manufacturing a product. These are direct material, direct labor, and overhead. Which of the following is an overhead cost in the production of an automobile?

a. The cost of small tools used in mounting tires on each automobile.
b. The cost of the tires on each automobile.
c. The cost of the laborers who place tires on each automobile.
d. The delivery costs for the tires on each automobile.

3. Which of the following is the definition of the term "conversion cost" in a manufacturing environment?

a. Direct materials plus overhead.
b. Direct labor plus overhead.
c. Direct labor plus direct materials.
d. Direct materials plus indirect materials.

4. During the current accounting period, a manufacturing company purchased $70,000 of raw materials, of which $50,000 of direct materials and $5,000 of indirect materials was used in production. The company also incurred $45,000 of total labor costs and $20,000 of other factory overhead costs. An analysis of the work in process control account revealed $40,000 of direct labor costs. Based upon the above information, what is the total amount accumulated in the factory overhead control account?

a. $25,000
b. $30,000
c. $45,000
d. $50,000

5. A company experienced a machinery breakdown on one of its production lines. As a consequence of the breakdown, manufacturing fell behind schedule, and a decision was made to schedule overtime in order to return manufacturing to schedule. Which one of the following methods is the proper way to account for the overtime paid to the direct laborers?

a. The overtime hours times the sum of the straight-time wages and overtime premium would be charged entirely to manufacturing overhead.
b. The overtime hours times the sum of the straight-time wages and overtime premium would be treated as direct labor.
c. The overtime hours times the overtime premium would be charged to repair and maintenance expense, while the overtime hours times the straight-time wages would be treated as direct labor.
d. The overtime hours times the overtime premium would be charged to manufacturing overhead while the overtime hours times the straight-time wages would be treated as direct labor.

6. A printing company is considering replacing an old printing press. The old printing press has a book value of $24,000 and a trade-in value of $14,000. A new printing press would cost $85,000 after trade-in of the old press. It is estimated that the new printing press would reduce operating costs by $20,000 per year. If the company decides not to purchase the new press, the $85,000 could instead be used to retire debt, which is currently costing $9,000 per year in interest. Which of the above is an example of a sunk cost?

a. The book value of the old printing press.
b. The trade-in value of the new printing press.
c. The estimated reduction in operating costs.
d. The interest on the existing debt.

Items 7 and 8 are based on the following:

A company is contemplating opening a new manufacturing plant, but is concerned as to whether the plant will be able to produce at a break-even level. The major costs that will be incurred under three alternative levels of production are

<u>Cost categories</u>	<u>Production levels</u>		
	1,000	**2,000**	**3,000**
Indirect materials	$4,550	$9,100	$13,650
Indirect labor	7,500	15,000	22,500
Factory rent	7,000	7,000	7,000
Electricity expense	13,000	16,000	19,000

7. Based on the above data, it can be determined that indirect materials is a

a. Variable cost.
b. Fixed cost.
c. Mixed cost.
d. Sunk cost.

8. Based on the above data, electricity expense would be an example of a

a. Variable cost.
b. Fixed cost.
c. Mixed cost.
d. Sunk cost.

9. That portion of a product's unit cost that decreases as the number of units produced increases is the

a. Variable cost.
b. Fixed cost.
c. Step-function cost.
d. Sunk cost.

10. Controllable costs are those which

a. Arise from periodic appropriation decisions and have no well-specified function relating inputs to outputs.
b. Are primarily subject to the influence of a given manager of a given responsibility center for a given time span.
c. Arise from having property, plant, and equipment, and a functioning organization.
d. Result specifically from a clearcut measured relationship between inputs and outputs.

11. Management of a bookkeeping company observed that the average time spent to perform identical tasks using a new software package decreases as the number of tasks performed increases. The following information on the utilization of the new software was collected.

Number of tasks performed	*Total time to perform all tasks*	*Average time to perform each task*
1	10 minutes	10 minutes
2	18 minutes	9 minutes
4	32.4 minutes	8.1 minutes

If this learning effect continues, what is the average time to perform each of the first eight tasks?

a. 7.29 minutes.
b. 8.1 minutes.
c. 6.83 minutes.
d. 7.75 minutes.

12. A company has observed that the average amount of time spent by new employees to produce a given product decreases as the number of units produced increases. A supervisor collected the following information on an employee who was hired recently.

Total number of units produced	*Average time to produce each unit to date (in minutes)*	*Total time to produce all units to date (in minutes)*
1	500	500
2	400	800
4	320	1,280

If the learning effect continues, what is the total time (in minutes) to produce the first eight units?

a. 2,048 minutes.
b. 2,560 minutes.
c. 2,080 minutes.
d. 1,960 minutes.

Items 13 and 14 are based on the following:

A professional organization is planning to conduct a series of one-day continuing education programs in various cities. The projected costs related to these programs are

Promotional advertising	$1,250 per program
Instructor's fee	$750 per program
Instructional materials	$12 per participant
Hotel charges	
Room rental and set-up fee	$400 per program
Continental breakfast	$10 per participant
Lunch	$25 per participant
Refreshment breaks	$8 per participant

The hotel requires a $200 nonrefundable deposit on the room rental and set-up fee 75 days prior to the program. At about the same time, the promotional advertising materials are developed, prepared, and mailed to potential participants and a 20% payment is made to ensure the services of an instructor. The instructor keeps this 20% payment even if the program is canceled and receives the balance of the fee at the conclusion of the program. The remaining hotel fees and charges, as well as the cost of instructional materials, are paid at the conclusion of the program. The capacity for each program is 100 persons, but past attendance for similar programs has averaged 80 persons.

13. The cost-estimating equation for calculating the costs for a one-day continuing education program is

a. $79 times the number of participants.
b. $85 times the number of participants.
c. $800 plus ($55 times the number of participants).
d. $2,400 plus ($55 times the number of participants).

14. Approximately ten days before the scheduled date of one program, only 25 individuals had registered for the program. All fees had been paid as scheduled. The director of the program decided to review the costs to determine whether the program should be canceled. Which of the following cost-estimation equations should be used to determine the additional costs that would be incurred if the program were **not** canceled?

a. $119 times the number of participants.
b. $800 plus ($55 times the number of participants).
c. $1,600 plus ($55 times the number of participants).
d. $2,400 plus ($55 times the number of participants).

15. A company is attempting to determine if there is a cause-and-effect relationship between scrap value and output produced. The following exhibit presents the company's scrap data for the last fiscal year:

Scrap Value as a Percent of Standard Dollar Value of Output Produced

Month	*Standard dollar value of output*	*Percent scrap (%)*
Nov 04	$1,500,000	4.5
Dec 04	$1,650,000	2.5
Jan 05	$1,600,000	3
Feb 05	$1,550,000	2.5
Mar 05	$1,650,000	1.5
Apr 05	$1,500,000	4
May 05	$1,400,000	2.5
Jun 05	$1,300,000	3.5
Jul 05	$1,650,000	5.5
Aug 05	$1,000,000	4.5
Sep 05	$1,400,000	3.5
Oct 05	$1,600,000	2.5

Based on the above data, the company's scrap value in relation to the standard dollar value of output produced appears to be

a. A variable cost.
b. A fixed cost.
c. A semifixed cost.
d. Unrelated to the standard dollar value of output.

Items 16 and 17 are based on the following:

A company wants to determine its marketing costs for budgeting purposes. Activity measures and costs incurred for four months of the current year are presented in the table below. Advertising is considered to be a discretionary cost. Salespersons are paid monthly salaries plus commissions. The sales force was increased from 20 to 21 individuals during the month of May.

	March	*April*	*May*	*June*
Activity measures:				
Sales orders	2,000	1,800	2,400	2,300
Units sold	55,000	60,000	70,000	65,000
Dollar sales	$11,150,000	$1,200,000	$1,330,000	$1,275,000
Marketing costs:				
Advertising	$190,000	$200,000	$190,000	$190,000
Sales salaries	20,000	20,000	21,000	21,000
Commissions	23,000	24,000	26,600	26,500
Shipping costs	93,000	100,000	114,000	107,000
Total marketing costs	$326,000	$344,000	$351,600	$343,500

16. Which of the following most appropriately describes the classification and behavior of shipping costs?

	Classification	*Behavior*
a.	Variable cost	\$1.66 per unit sold
b.	Mixed cost	\$16,000 per month plus \$1.40 per unit sold
c.	Mixed cost	\$30,000 per month plus \$35.00 per sales order
d.	Mixed cost	\$58,000 per month plus \$23.33 per sales order

17. In relation to the dollar amount of sales, which of the following cost classifications is appropriate for advertising and sales salaries costs?

	Advertising	*Sales salaries*
a.	Mixed cost	Fixed cost
b.	Fixed cost	Variable cost
c.	Mixed cost	Mixed cost
d.	Fixed cost	Fixed cost

18. A company produces stereo speakers for automobile manufacturers. The automobile manufacturers emphasize total quality control (TQC) in their production processes and reject approximately 3% of the stereo speakers received as being of unacceptable quality. The company inspects the rejected speakers to determine which ones should be reworked and which ones should be discarded. The discarded speakers are classified as

a. Waste.
b. Scrap.
c. Spoilage.
d. Rework costs.

19. An assembly plant accumulates its variable and fixed manufacturing overhead costs in a single cost pool, which is then applied to work in process using a single application base. The assembly plant management wants to estimate the magnitude of the total manufacturing overhead costs for different volume levels of the application activity base using a flexible budget formula. If there is an increase in the application activity base that is within the relevant range of activity for the assembly plant, which one of the following relationships regarding variable and fixed costs is correct?

a. The variable cost per unit is constant, and the total fixed costs decrease.
b. The variable cost per unit is constant, and the total fixed costs increase.
c. The variable cost per unit and the total fixed costs remain constant.
d. The variable cost per unit increases, and the total fixed costs remain constant.

20. The production engineer's salary should be classified as

a. Overhead cost.
b. Direct labor cost.
c. Variable cost.
d. Engineered cost.

21. Production that does not meet standards and is junked or sold for disposal value is classified as

a. Defective (reworked) units.
b. Spoilage.
c. Waste.
d. Scrap.

22. A hospital's monthly cost of laundry was \$2,600 when the average patient count was 325. The monthly cost jumped to \$3,360 during a month when the average patient count was 420. Within the relevant range of 325–420, this cost could properly be called a

a. Variable cost.
b. Fixed cost.
c. Mixed cost.
d. Semivariable cost.

23. Internal auditors must often distinguish between product costs and period costs. Product costs are those that are properly assigned to inventory when incurred. Period costs are always expensed in the same period in which they are incurred. Which of the following items is a product cost for a manufacturing company?

a. Insurance on the corporate headquarters building.
b. Property taxes on a factory.
c. Depreciation on salespersons' automobiles.
d. Salary of a sales manager.

24. A company has an old machine with a book value of \$75,000, with no salvage value, and an estimated remaining life of 12 years. A new machine is available at a cost of \$190,000. It has the same estimated remaining life and the same capacity as the old machine, but it would reduce operating costs by \$17,000 per year. Which of the following amounts is a sunk cost in the decision whether or not to replace the old machine?

a. \$0
b. \$ 17,000
c. \$ 75,000
d. \$190,000

25. In a traditional manufacturing operation, direct costs would normally include

a. Machine repairs in an automobile factory.
b. Electricity in an electronics plant.
c. Wood in a furniture factory.
d. Commissions paid to sales personnel.

26. Overhead costs usually include

a. Abnormal spoilage.
b. Overtime premiums.
c. Prime costs.
d. Material price variances.

27. Input material that does not become part of the finished product and has relatively minor economic value is classified as

a. Scrap.
b. Spoilage.
c. Defective product.
d. Waste.

28. For which type of product is it appropriate for the seller to accept any price that exceeds the storage and delivery costs for the product?

a. By-product.
b. Optional product.
c. Captive product.
d. Product bundle.

29. When using absorption costing, manufacturing overhead costs are best described as

a. Direct period costs.
b. Indirect period costs.
c. Direct product costs.
d. Indirect product costs.

30. Abnormal spoilage is
a. Not expected to occur when standard costs are used.
b. Not usually controllable by the production supervisor.
c. The result of unrealistic production standards.
d. Not expected to occur under efficient operating conditions.

31. The units that failed inspection during the current month would be classified as
a. Abnormal spoilage.
b. Normal scrap.
c. Normal reworked units.
d. Normal waste.

32. A manufacturing company properly classifies and accounts for one product as a by-product rather than as a main product because it
a. Can never be developed into a main product by this or any other manufacturer.
b. Has no sales value to the manufacturing company.
c. Has low physical volume when compared to the other main products.
d. Has low sales value when compared to the main products.

Capital Budgeting

33. If the net present value profiles for two mutually exclusive capital projects are shaped as in the graph below, which of the following statements is true?

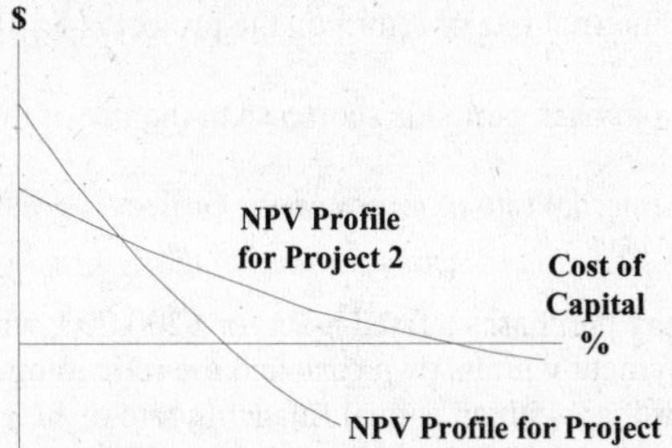

a. Project 2 has a higher internal rate of return than Project 1.
b. Project 1 has a higher internal rate of return than Project 2.
c. Project 1 has a higher net present value than Project 2.
d. Project 2 has a higher net present value than Project 1.

Items 34 through 36 are based on the following:

A company that annually reviews its investment opportunities and selects appropriate capital expenditures for the coming year is presented with two projects, called project A and project B. Best estimates indicate that the investment outlay for project A is $30,000 and for project B is $1 million. The projects are considered to be equally risky. Project A is expected to generate cash inflows of $40,000 at the end of each year for two years. Project B is expected to generate cash inflows of $700,000 at the end of the first year and $500,000 at the end of the second year. The company has a cost of capital of 8%.

34. What is the net present value (NPV) of each project when the cost of capital is zero?

	Project A	Project B
a.	$ 30,000	$1,000,000
b.	$ 50,000	$ 200,000
c.	$ 80,000	$1,200,000
d.	$110,000	$2,200,000

35. The internal rate of return of project A, to the nearest full percentage point, is
a. 10%
b. 15%
c. 25%
d. 100%

36. Net present value (NPV) and internal rate of return (IRR) differ in that
a. NPV assumes reinvestment of project cash flows at the cost of capital while IRR assumes reinvestment of project cash flows at the internal rate of return.
b. NPV and IRR make different accept or reject decisions for independent projects.
c. IRR can be used to rank mutually exclusive investment projects but NPV cannot.
d. NPV is expressed as a percentage while IRR is expressed as a dollar amount.

Items 37 and 38 are based on the following:

The financial management team of a company is assessing an investment proposal involving a $100,000 outlay today. Manager number one expects the project to provide cash inflows of $20,000 at the end of each year for six years. She considers the project to be of low risk, requiring only a 10% rate of return. Manager number two expects the project to provide cash inflows of $5,000 at the end of the first year, followed by $23,000 at the end of each year in years two through six. He considers the project to be of medium risk, requiring a 14% rate of return. Manager number three expects the project to be of high risk, providing one large cash inflow of $135,000 at the end of the sixth year. She proposes a 15% rate of return for the project.

37. According to the net present value criterion, which of the following is true?
a. Manager one will recommend that the project be accepted.
b. Manager two will recommend that the project be accepted.
c. All three managers will recommend acceptance of the project.
d. All three managers will recommend rejection of the project.

38. Which manager will assess the project as having the shortest payback period?
a. Manager one.
b. Manager two.
c. Manager three.
d. All three managers will agree on the payback period.

Items 39 through 41 are based on the following:

A company purchased a new machine to stamp the company logo on its products. The cost of the machine was $250,000 and it has an estimated useful life of five (5) years with an expected salvage value at the end of its useful life of $50,000. The company uses the straight-line depreciation method.

The new machine is expected to save $125,000 annually in operating costs. The company's tax rate is 40% and it uses a 10% discount rate to evaluate capital expenditures.

Year	Present value of $1	Present value of an ordinary annuity of $1
1	.909	.909
2	.826	1.736
3	.751	2.487
4	.683	3.170
5	.621	3.791

39. What is the traditional payback period for the new stamping machine?

a. 2.00 years.
b. 2.35 years.
c. 2.75 years.
d. 3.38 years.

40. What is the simple rate of return based on the average investment in the new stamping machine?

a. 20.4%
b. 34.0%
c. 45.0%
d. 51.0%

41. What is the net present value of the new stamping machine?

a. $125,940
b. $200,000
c. $250,000
d. $375,940

42. A company has analyzed seven new projects, each of which has its own internal rate of return (IRR). It should consider each project whose internal rate of return is _____ its marginal cost of capital and accept those projects in _____ order of their internal rate of return.

a. Below; decreasing.
b. Above; decreasing.
c. Above; increasing.
d. Below; increasing.

43. An actuary has determined that a company should have $90,000,000 accumulated in its pension fund twenty years from now in order for the fund to be able to meet its obligations. An interest rate of 8% is considered appropriate for all pension fund calculations involving an interest component. The company wishes to calculate how much it should contribute to the pension fund at the end of each of the next twenty years in order for the pension fund to have its required balance in twenty years. Assume you are given the following two factors from present value/future value tables:

(1) Factor for present value of an ordinary annuity for n = 20, i = 8%
(2) Factor for future value of an ordinary annuity for n = 20, i = 8%

Which of the following sets of instructions correctly describes the procedures necessary to compute the annual amount the company should contribute to the fund?

a. Divide $90,000,000 by the factor for present value of an ordinary annuity for n = 20, i = 8%.
b. Multiply $90,000,000 by the factor for present value of an ordinary annuity for n = 20, i = 8%.
c. Divide $90,000,000 by the factor for future value of an ordinary annuity for n = 20, i = 8%.
d. Multiply $90,000,000 by the factor for future value of an ordinary annuity for n = 20, i = 8%.

44. An existing machine with estimated remaining life of five years and which cost $100,000 can be sold for $20,000. The variable cost of output from this machine has been $1 per unit with 100,000 units per year produced. A new machine will cost $90,000 and is estimated to lower the variable cost to $.70 per unit over its five-year life. The most appropriate term for the decision process involved in this scenario is

a. Capital budgeting.
b. Economic order quantity.
c. Flexible budgeting.
d. Sensitivity analysis.

45. The relationship between the present value of a future sum and the future value of a present sum can be expressed in terms of their respective interest factors. If the present value of $100,000 due at the end of eight years, at 10%, is $46,650, what is the approximate future value of $100,000 invested for the same length of time and at the same rate?

a. $ 46,650
b. $100,000
c. $146,650
d. $214,360

46. At a company's cost of capital (hurdle rate) of 15%, a prospective investment has a positive net present value. Based on this information, it can be concluded that

a. The accounting rate of return on the project is greater than 15%.
b. The internal rate of return on the project is less than 15%.
c. The payback period is shorter than the life of the asset.
d. The internal rate of return on the project is greater than 15%.

47. A company purchases a fixed asset for $200,000, with a 10% down payment with its own cash and the remaining 90% from a 20-year loan with an annual financing rate of 12%. For an interest rate of 12% and a time period of 20 years, the present value interest factor (PVIF) is .1037, the future value interest factor is 9.6463, and the present value interest factor of an annuity is 7.4694. The annual payment required on the loan, assuming equal payments on the loan in each of the 20 years is

a. $18,660
b. $20,740
c. $24,098
d. $26,776

48. A project is expected to result in the following adjustments over the next year:

Cash sales increase by $400,000.
Expenses (except depreciation) increase by $180,000.
Depreciation increases by $80,000.

Assume the corporate tax rate is 34%. The total relevant net cash flows during that year are

a. $ 92,400
b. $145,200
c. $172,400
d. $220,000

49. A company is considering a capital budgeting decision involving a risky foreign investment. Risk can best be minimized by selecting the investment alternative with the

a. Shortest payback period.
b. Highest internal rate of return (IRR).
c. Highest net present value (NPV).
d. Highest net present value index.

50. In response to competitive pressures, management has proposed an ambitious capital expenditures program to enhance production facilities. The internal auditor should know that the inherent feasibility of this program is dependent upon
a. Coordination with the long-term financing needs of the company.
b. Approval by the appropriate governmental agencies.
c. Ratification of the board of directors.
d. The working capital position of the company.

Items 51 and 52 are based on the following:

A firm, with an 18% cost of capital, is considering the following projects (on January 1, 1996).

	Jan. 1, 1996 Cash outflow (000's omitted)	*Dec. 31, 2000 Cash outflow (000's omitted)*	*Project internal rate of return*
Project A	$3,500	$7,400	15%
Project B	4,000	9,950	?

Present Value of $1 Due at the End of "N" Periods

N	12%	14%	15%	16%	18%	20%	22%
4	.6355	.5921	.5718	.5523	.5158	.4823	.4230
5	.5674	.5194	.4972	.4761	.4371	.4019	.3411
6	.5066	.4556	.4323	.4104	.3704	.3349	.2751

51. Using the net-present-value method, project A's net present value is
a. $ 316,920
b. $0
c. $(265,460)
d. $(316,920)

52. Project B's internal rate of return is closest to:
a. 15%
b. 18%
c. 20%
d. 22%

53. An organization is using capital budgeting techniques to compare two independent projects. It could accept one, both, or neither of the projects. Which of the following statements is true about the use of net-present-value (NPV) and internal-rate-of-return (IRR) methods for evaluating these two projects?
a. NPV and IRR criteria will always lead to the same accept or reject decision for two independent projects.
b. If the first project's IRR is higher than the organization's cost of capital, the first project will be accepted but the second project will not.
c. If the NPV criterion leads to accepting or rejecting the first project, one cannot predict whether the IRR criterion will lead to accepting or rejecting the first project.
d. If the NPV criterion leads to accepting the first project, the IRR criterion will never lead to accepting the first project.

Items 54 and 55 are based on the following:

Investment project	*Cash outlay*	*Present value of cash inflows*
A	$1,100,000	$980,000
B	250,000	600,000
C	1,400,000	1,830,000
D	650,000	790,000

The company has $2,000,000 of financing available for new investment projects.

54. The investment project with the highest profitability index is
a. Project A.
b. Project B.
c. Project C.
d. Project D.

55. If only one project may be selected, which should the company undertake?
a. Project A.
b. Project B.
c. Project C.
d. Project D.

56. An individual is to receive $137,350 in four years. Using the correct factor, determine the current investment if interest of 10% is assumed.

# of Periods	*FVIF*	*PVIF*	*FVIFA*	*PVIFA*
1	1.1000	.9091	1.0000	.9091
2	1.2100	.8264	2.1000	1.7355
3	1.3310	.7513	3.2781	2.4869
4	1.4641	.6830	4.5731	3.1699
5	1.6105	.6029	5.9847	3.7908

a. $ 30,034.33
b. $ 43,329.44
c. $ 93,810.05
d. $201,094.14

Items 57 through 60 are based on the following:

An organization has four investment proposals with the following costs and expected cash inflows:

Expected Cash Inflows

Project	*Cost*	*End of year 1*	*End of year 2*	*End of year 3*
A	unknown	$10,000	$10,000	$10,000
B	$20,000	$ 5,000	$10,000	$15,000
C	$25,000	$15,000	$10,000	$ 5,000
D	$30,000	$20,000	unknown	$20,000

Additional information

Discount rate	*Number of periods*	*Present value of $1 due at the end of n periods [PVIF]*	*Present value of an annuity of $1 per period for n periods [PVIFA]*
5%	1	0.9524	0.9524
5%	2	0.9070	1.8594
5%	3	0.8638	2.7232
10%	1	0.9091	0.9091
10%	2	0.8264	1.7355
10%	3	0.7513	2.4869
15%	1	0.8696	0.8696
15%	2	0.7561	1.6257
15%	3	0.6575	2.2832

57. If project A has an internal rate of return (IRR) of 15%, then it has a cost of
a. $ 8,696
b. $22,832

c. $24,869
d. $27,232

58. If the discount rate is 10%, the net present value (NPV) of project B is
a. $ 4,079
b. $ 6,789
c. $ 9,869
d. $39,204

59. The payback period of project C is
a. 0 years.
b. 1 year.
c. 2 years.
d. 3 years.

60. If the discount rate is 5% and the discounted payback period of project D is exactly two years, then the year two cash inflow for project D is
a. $ 5,890
b. $10,000
c. $12,075
d. $14,301

61. Everything else being equal, the internal rate of return (IRR) of an investment project will be lower if
a. The investment cost is lower.
b. Cash inflows are received later in the life of the project.
c. Cash inflows are larger.
d. The project has a shorter payback period.

62. If the investment projects listed below are mutually exclusive, which alternative should be accepted?

Project	Net present value
A	$100,000
B	($20,000)
C	$60,000
D	$30,000

a. Project A.
b. Project B.
c. Projects A and C.
d. Projects A, C, and D.

Items 63 through 66 are based on the following:

A company is evaluating three investment projects.

Project A costs $100,000, has a 10% cost of capital, and has equal end-of-period cash inflows each year for five years.

Project B costs $50,000 and has equal end-of-period cash inflows of $40,000 per year for two years.

Project C costs $60,000 and has cash inflows of $20,000 at the end of year one, $35,000 at the end of year two, and an unknown cash inflow at the end of year three.

Number of years	Discount rate (percent)	Present value of $1 due at the end of n periods (PVIF)	Present value of an annuity of $1 per period for n periods (PVIFA)
1	10	0.9091	0.9091
1	12	0.8929	0.8929
2	10	0.8264	1.7355
2	12	0.7972	1.6901
3	10	0.7513	2.4869
3	12	0.7118	2.4018
4	10	0.683	3.1699
4	12	0.6355	3.0373
5	10	0.6209	3.7908
5	12	0.5674	3.6048

63. If the net present value of project A is $12,405, then the size of each equal, end-of-period cash inflow, to the nearest dollar, is
a. $19,979
b. $21,863
c. $29,652
d. $31,182

64. If the cost of capital is 12%, the net present value of Project B, to the nearest dollar, is
a. $(18,112)
b. $(16,944)
c. $ 17,604
d. $ 19,420

65. If Project C has an internal rate of return of 12% then the cash inflow at the end of year three, to the nearest dollar, is
a. $17,162
b. $20,006
c. $24,126
d. $24,981

66. Without prejudice to your answer to question 65, if the year three cash inflow for Project C is $46,000, then the Payback Period for (List A) is (List B) year(s)

	List A	List B
a.	Project B	one
b.	Project B	two
c.	Project C	one
d.	Project C	two

Items 67 through 70 are based on the following:

A company is evaluating two investment proposals. Project A costs $700,000 and Project B costs $500,000. Expected cash inflows for the two projects are as follows:

Year	Cash Inflow at end of year for Project A	Cash Inflow at end of year for Project B
1	$400,000	$250,000
2	$300,000	$250,000
3	$600,000	$250,000

Both projects are assessed as being equally risky and having an appropriate cost of capital of 10%.

For a 10% cost of capital, the following present value factors apply:

Number of years	Present value of $1 received at end of year n [PVIF]	Present value of an annuity of $1 received at end of each year for n years [PVIFA]
1	.9091	.9091
2	.8264	1.7355
3	.7513	2.4873

For a three-year annuity, the following present value factors apply:

Discount rate	Present value of a three-year annuity of $1 [PVIFA]
16%	2.2459
20%	2.1065
24%	1.9813
28%	1.8684

67. Project A has a payback period of
a. 0 years.
b. 1 year.
c. 2 years.
d. 3 years.

68. Project A has a net present value (to the nearest dollar) of

a. $ 362,340
b. $1,062,340
c. $1,676,670
d. $2,376,670

69. Which of the following most closely approximates the internal rate of return of Project B?

a. 16%
b. 20%
c. 24%
d. 28%

70. If projects A and B are independent, the company will undertake

a. Both projects.
b. Only Project A.
c. Only Project B.
d. Neither project.

71. The phrase "The process of choosing projects by considering the present value of cash flows and deciding how to raise the funds required by the project" best defines

a. Full absorption costing.
b. Payback.
c. Capital rationing.
d. Capital budgeting.

72. A company plans to purchase a machine for $300,000 that will require a 20% down payment. The remainder will be financed over a ten-year period at an annual interest rate of 9%. The present value interest factor of an annuity at 9% over ten years is 6.4177. The future value interest factor of an annuity at 9% over ten years is 14.487. The annual payment on the amortized loan is

a. $46,746
b. $16,567
c. $37,397
d. $45,600

73. On January 1, 1990, a company recorded the purchase of an asset correctly at $275,132. A down payment of $200,000 was made with the balance of $100,000 due in three years at an imputed annual interest rate of 10%. What is the 1990 interest to record on the payable?

a. $ 7,513
b. $ 8,289
c. $10,000
d. $27,513

74. A company purchased a new machine on an installment payment plan and is to make equal annual payments beginning on the date of purchase. Using an interest rate of 10%, the cost of the machine can be determined by multiplying one payment by the

a. Future value of one dollar.
b. Future value of an annuity due of one dollar.
c. Present value of one dollar.
d. Present value of an annuity due of one dollar.

75. If a prospective investment has a positive net present value at a company's cost of capital of 15%, it can be concluded that

a. The accounting rate of return of the project is greater than 15%.
b. The internal rate of return of the project is equal to the accounting rate of return.
c. The payback period of the associated asset is shorter than its life.
d. The internal rate of return of the project is greater than 15%.

76. If a firm identifies an investment opportunity with a present value (List A) its cost, the value of the firm and the price of its common stock will (List B).

	List A	*List B*
a.	Greater than	Increase
b.	Greater than	Decrease
c.	Equal to	Increase
d.	Equal to	Decrease

Operating Budget

77. A master budget

a. Shows forecasted and actual results.
b. Contains only controllable costs.
c. Can be used to determine manufacturing cost variances.
d. Contains the operating budget.

78. Budgets are generally classified as both planning documents and control devices. An important difference between the budget planning information needed and the budget control information needed is that planning information is more

a. Likely to be generated using external data.
b. Detailed.
c. Likely to be quantifiable.
d. Likely to be more accurate.

79. A flexible budget is a quantitative expression of a plan that

a. Is developed for the actual level of output achieved for the budget period.
b. Is comprised of the budgeted income statement and its supporting schedules for a budget period.
c. Focuses on the costs of activities necessary to produce and sell products and services for a budget period.
d. Projects costs on the basis of future improvements in existing practices and procedures during a budget period.

80. A company has budgeted sales of 24,000 finished units for the forthcoming six-month period. It takes four pounds of direct materials to make one finished unit. Given the following:

	Finished units	*Direct material (pounds)*
Beginning inventory	14,000	44,000
Target ending inventory	12,000	48,000

How many pounds of direct material should be budgeted for purchase during the six-month period?

a. 88,000
b. 92,000
c. 96,000
d. 100,000

81. A company reported a significant material efficiency variance for the month of January. All of the following are possible explanations for this variance **except:**

a. Cutbacks in preventive maintenance.
b. An inadequately trained and supervised labor force.

c. Processing a large number of rush orders.
d. Producing more units than planned for in the master budget.

82. A company uses two major material inputs in its production. To prepare its manufacturing operations budget, the company has to project the cost changes of these material inputs. The cost changes are independent of one another. The purchasing department provides the following probabilities associated with projected cost changes:

Cost change	*Material 1*	*Material 2*
3% increase	.3	.5
5% increase	.5	.4
10% increase	.2	.1

The probability that there will be a 3% increase in the cost of both material 1 and material 2 is

a. 15%
b. 20%
c. 60%
d. 80%

83. A company is formulating its plans for the coming year, including the preparation of its cash budget. Historically, 30% of the company's sales are cash sales. The remaining 70% are credit sales with the following collection pattern:

Collections on account	*Percentage*
In the month of sale	40%
In the month following the sale	58
Uncollectible	2

Sales for the first five months of the coming year are forecast as follows:

January	$3,500,000
February	3,800,000
March	3,600,000
April	4,000,000
May	4,200,000

For the month of April, the total cash receipts from sales and collections on account would be

a. $3,729,968
b. $3,781,600
c. $4,025,200
d. $4,408,000

84. Budgets are generally classified as both planning documents and control devices. An important difference between the budget planning information needed and the budget control information needed is that planning information is more

a. Likely to be generated using external data.
b. Detailed.
c. Likely to be quantifiable.
d. Likely to be more accurate.

85. The auditor found that budgetary controls were functioning effectively to control sales expenses. In addition to the preparer's signature, each of the 75 weekly expense reports showed a signature for budgetary approval, and at least four other signatures, providing evidence of review and approval of expenses by various levels of sales management. Sales calls and related performance information were reported separately to the sales person's immediate supervisor and keyed into the sales database for information and reporting purposes. The auditor should

a. Recommend that approval of expense reports be limited to the person with budgetary responsibility for the related expenses.
b. Trace all amounts on the expense reports to the designated general ledger account to ensure accurate posting.
c. Send special confirmations to customers to determine that sales calls were made on the reported dates.
d. Determine whether performance information includes the accurate and timely presentation of expenses to sales department management.

86. The primary purpose of budgets is to

a. Move a company toward its short-term and long-term strategic goals.
b. Define a company's mission.
c. Identify new markets for a company's products.
d. Provide an informal communication network.

87. The major feature of zero-based budgeting is that it

a. Takes the previous year's budgets and adjusts them for inflation.
b. Questions each activity and determines whether it should be maintained as it is, reduced, or eliminated.
c. Assumes all activities are legitimate and worthy of receiving budget increases to cover any increased costs.
d. Focuses on planned capital outlays for property, plant, and equipment.

88. A manufacturing company is preparing the schedules that comprise its master budget. The forecasted production in units of finished goods for the first four months of the coming year are as follows:

Month	*Production (in units)*
January	400,000
February	380,000
March	420,000
April	440,000

Additional details regarding inventory requirements and direct material purchases are as follows. The company pays for the direct material purchases in the month of the purchase and takes all discounts.

Item	*Requirement*
Month-end direct materials inventory requirement	25% of the next month's production requirements
Direct material required per unit of finished good	One (1) pound of direct material
Invoice price (cost) of direct material	$5 per pound
Purchase terms for direct material	2/10, n/30

The cash that would be required to pay for direct material purchases during the month of February would be

a. $1,813,000
b. $1,862,000
c. $1,911,000
d. $1,950,000

89. The major objectives of any budget system are to

a. Define responsibility centers, provide a framework for performance evaluation, and promote communication and coordination among organization segments.
b. Define responsibility centers, facilitate the fixing of blame for missed budget predictions, and ensure goal congruence between superiors and subordinates.

c. Foster the planning of operations, provide a framework for performance evaluation, and promote communication and coordination among organization segments.
d. Foster the planning of operations, facilitate the fixing of blame for missed budget predictions, and ensure goal congruence between superiors and subordinates.

90. The procedure employed in **zero-base budgeting** is to
a. Budget from the ground up whereby every proposed expenditure for every unit is reviewed as though the budget was being prepared for the very first time.
b. Review the prior period's budget along with actual results for that period and the expectations for the coming period to develop more realistic budget amounts for the coming period.
c. Require managers to establish priorities by including a description of what activities or changes would occur if the budget were increased and decreased by a fixed percentage amount.
d. Ascertain the outputs that are desired and work backward to determine the amount of inputs that will be required to generate the desired outputs.

91. A company has budgeted sales for the upcoming quarter as follows:

	January	*February*	*March*
Units	15,000	18,000	16,500

The ending finished goods inventory for each month equals 50% of the next month's budgeted sales. Additionally, three pounds of raw material are required for each finished unit produced. The ending raw materials inventory for each month equals 200% of the next month's production requirements. If the raw materials cost $4.00 per pound and must be paid for in the month purchased, the budgeted raw materials purchases (in dollars) for January are
a. $216,000
b. $207,000
c. $198,000
d. $180,000

92. There are many different budget techniques or processes which business organizations can employ. One of these techniques or processes is zero-base budgeting which is
a. Budgeting from the ground up as though the budget process was being initiated for the first time.
b. Budgeting for cash inflows and outflows in order to time investments and borrowings in a way to maintain a bank account with a minimum balance.
c. Using the prior year's budget as a base year and adjust it for the experiences gained from the prior year and the expectations for the coming year to develop the coming year's budget.
d. Developing budgeted costs from clear-cut measured relationships between inputs and outputs.

93. Many service industries utilize a budgeting process to identify major programs and develop short-term operating budgets, such as expected revenues and expected direct expenses, for the identified programs. For example, a nursing home may develop one-year revenue and expense budgets for each of its different programs, such as day care for the elderly or meals-on-wheels. Which of the following is a major advantage of short-term program planning and budgeting?
a. It eliminates the need for periodic program evaluation.
b. It provides a rigid basis for periodic program evaluation.
c. It promotes communication and coordination within an organization.
d. It provides an important basis for strategic analysis of the goals of the organization.

94. Actual and projected sales of a company for September and October are as follows:

	Cash sales	*Credit sales*
September (actual)	$20,000	$50,000
October (projected)	30,000	55,000

All credit sales are collected in the month following the month in which the sale is made. The September 30 cash balance is $23,000. Cash disbursements in October are projected to be $94,000. To maintain a minimum cash balance of $15,000 on October 31, the company will need to borrow
a. $0
b. $ 6,000
c. $11,000
d. $16,000

95. A firm uses zero-base budgeting (ZBB) to develop its annual master budget. The customer relations department had a budget last year of $190,000. Inflation has been 10% during the past year. Similarly, sales are expected to increase 10% next year. Under the concept of zero-base budgeting, which would be next year's probable budget for the customer relations department?
a. An amount that is dependent, in part, upon the level of service to be rendered.
b. The same as last year ($190,000).
c. Equal to last year's adjusted for sales increase ($209,000).
d. Equal to last year's adjusted for both inflation and sales increase ($229,900).

96. One of the primary advantages of budgeting is that it
a. Does not take the place of management and administration.
b. Bases the profit plan on estimates.
c. Is continually adapted to fit changing circumstances.
d. Requires departmental managers to make plans in conjunction with the plans of other interdependent departments.

97. The exhibit below reflects a summary of performance for a single item of a retail store's inventory for the month ended April 30, 1991.

	Flexible budget			
	Actual results	*Variances*	*Flexible budget*	*Static (master) budget*
Sales (units)	11,000	--	11,000	12,000
Revenue (sales)	$208,000	$12,000 U	$220,000	$240,000
Variable costs	121,000	11,000 U	110,000	120,000
Contribution margin	$121,000	$23,000 U	$110,000	$120,000
Fixed costs	72,000	--	72,000	72,000
Operating income	49,000	$23,000 U	$38,000	$48,000

The sales volume variance is
a. $ 1,000 F
b. $10,000 U
c. $11,000 F
d. $12,000 U

Items 98 and 99 are based on the following:

The operating results in summarized form for a retail computer store for 1994 are

Revenue:	
Hardware sales	$4,800,000
Software sales	2,000,000
Maintenance contracts	1,200,000
Revenue total	$8,000,000
Costs and expenses	
Cost of hardware sales	3,360,000
Cost of software sales	1,200,000
Marketing expenses	600,000
Customer maintenance costs	640,000
Administrative expenses	1,120,000
Total costs and expenses	$6,920,000
Operating income	$1,080,000

The computer store is in the process of formulating its operating budget for 1995 and has made the following assumptions:

- The selling prices of hardware are expected to increase 10% but there will be no selling price increases for software or maintenance contracts.
- Hardware unit sales are expected to increase 5% with a corresponding 5% growth in the number of maintenance contracts; growth in units software sales is estimated at 8%.
- The cost of hardware and software is expected to increase 4%.
- Marketing expenses will be increased 5% in the coming year.
- Three technicians will be added to the customer maintenance operations in the coming year, increasing the customer maintenance costs by $120,000.
- Administrative costs will be held at the same level.

98. The retail computer store's budgeted total revenue for 1995 would be

a. $8,804,000
b. $8,460,000
c. $8,904,000
d. $8,964,000

99. The retail computer store's budgeted total costs and expenses for the coming year would be

a. $7,252,400
b. $7,526,960
c. $7,558,960
d. $7,893,872

100. A defense contractor for a government space project has incurred $2,500,000 in actual design costs to date for a guidance system whose total budgeted design cost is $3,000,000. If the design phase of the project is 60% complete, what is the amount of the contractor's current overrun/savings on this design work?

a. $300,000 savings.
b. $500,000 overrun.
c. $500,000 savings.
d. $700,000 overrun.

Items 101 and 102 are based on the following:

Operational budgets are used by a retail company for planning and controlling its business activities. Data regarding the company's monthly sales for the last six months of the year and its projected collection patterns are

Forecasted sales	
July	$775,000
August	750,000
September	825,000
October	800,000
November	850,000
December	900,000
Types of sales	
Cash sales	20%
Credit sales	80%
Collection pattern for credit sales	
In the month of sale	40%
In the first month following the sale	57%
Uncollectible	3%

The cost of merchandise averages 40% of its selling price. The company's policy is to maintain an inventory equal to 25% of the next month's forecasted sales. The inventory balance at cost is $80,000 as of June 30.

101. The budgeted cost of the company's purchases for the month of August would be

a. $302,500
b. $305,000
c. $307,500
d. $318,750

102. The company's total cash receipts from sales and collections on account that would be budgeted for the month of September would be

a. $757,500
b. $771,000
c. $793,800
d. $856,500

Transfer Pricing

103. Which of the following is **not** true about international transfer prices for a multinational firm?

a. Allows firms to attempt to minimize worldwide taxes.
b. Allows the firm to evaluate each division.
c. Provides each division with a profit-making orientation.
d. Allows firms to correctly price products in each country in which it operates.

104. One department of an organization, Final Assembly, is purchasing subcomponents from another department, Materials Fabrication. The price that will be charged to Final Assembly by Materials Fabrication is to be determined. Outside market prices for the subcomponents are available. Which of the following is the most correct statement regarding a market-based transfer price?

a. Marginal production cost transfer prices provide incentives to use otherwise idle capacity.
b. Market transfer prices provide an incentive to use otherwise idle capacity.
c. Overall long-term competitiveness is enhanced with a market-based transfer price.
d. Corporate politics is more of a factor in a market-based transfer price than with other methods.

105. The Eastern division sells goods internally to the Western division of the same company. The quoted external price in industry publications from a supplier near Eastern is $200 per ton plus transportation. It costs $20 per ton to transport the goods to Western. Eastern's actual market cost per ton to buy the direct materials to make the transferred product is

$100. Actual per ton direct labor is $50. Other actual costs of storage and handling are $40. The company president selects a $220 transfer price. This is an example of

a. Market-based transfer pricing.
b. Cost-based transfer pricing.
c. Negotiated transfer pricing.
d. Cost plus 20% transfer pricing.

106. Which of the following is the most significant disadvantage of a cost-based transfer price?

a. Requires internally developed information.
b. Imposes market effects on company operations.
c. Requires externally developed information.
d. May not promote long-term efficiencies.

107. The price charged by one subunit of an organization for a product or service supplied to another subunit of the same organization is called the

a. Direct (cost) price.
b. Shadow (cost) price.
c. Transfer price.
d. Dual price.

108. Division Z of a company produces a component which it currently sells to outside customers for $20 per unit. At its current level of production, which is 60% of capacity, Division Z's fixed cost of producing this component is $5 per unit and its variable cost is $12 per unit. Division Y of the same company would like to purchase this component from Division Z for $10. Division Z has enough excess capacity to fill Division Y's requirements. The managers of both divisions are compensated based upon reported profits. Which of the following transfer prices would maximize total company profits and be most equitable to the managers of Division Y and Division Z?

a. $10 per unit.
b. $12 per unit.
c. $18 per unit.
d. $20 per unit.

109. A carpet manufacturer maintains a retail division consisting of stores stocking its brand and other brands, and a manufacturing division, which makes carpets and pads. An outside market exists for carpet padding material in which all padding produced can be sold. The proper transfer price for padding transferred from the manufacturing division to the retail division is

a. Variable manufacturing division production cost.
b. Variable manufacturing division production cost plus allocated fixed factory overhead.
c. Variable manufacturing division production cost plus variable selling and administrative cost.
d. The market price at which the retail division could purchase padding.

110. A company's independent manufacturing division sells 50,000 units to outsiders and transfers 3,000 units to another division. The product has a perfectly competitive market price of $7.00. Variable unit cost is $4.00, fixed costs are $110,000, and manufacturing capacity is 55,000 units. The optimal transfer price for the company is

a. $4.00
b. $6.00
c. $6.08
d. $7.00

111. A multinational company operates a production facility in country A and a distribution outlet in country B. The tax rates are 40% in country A and 50% in country B. The production facility sells the goods to the distribution outlet, both of which are wholly owned by the multinational company. The internal sale of goods occurs at a "transfer" price set by the multinational company. Assuming no nontax considerations and no interference from the tax authorities of the two countries, the company should

a. Maximize the transfer price.
b. Minimize the transfer price.
c. Establish a transfer price that results in the same profit margin for both operations.
d. Use a transfer price based on the market price for the product that other producers charge.

112. A large manufacturing company has several autonomous divisions that sell their products in perfectly competitive external markets as well as internally to the other divisions of the company. Top management expects each of its divisional managers to take actions that will maximize the organization's goals as well as their own goals. Top management also promotes a sustained level of management effort of all of its divisional managers. Under these circumstances, for products exchanged between divisions, the transfer price that will generally lead to optimal decisions for the manufacturing company would be a transfer price equal to the

a. Full cost of the product.
b. Full cost of the product plus a markup.
c. Variable cost of the product plus a markup.
d. Market price of the product.

Items 113 and 114 are based on the following:

A company has two foreign sales divisions, one in Country X and the other in Country Y. The company sells only one product, which costs $20 per unit to produce. There are no trade barriers or tariffs among the three countries. The corporate income tax rate, product selling prices, quantity sold, and level of additional costs in each of the three countries are indicated below.

Country	*Corporate tax rate*	*Before-tax selling price*	*Quantity sold*	*Additional costs*
Home	50%	$30	1,500	$10,000
X	60%	$40	1,000	$12,500
Y	40%	$35	2,000	$11,000

113. When selling items to its sales division in (List A), the company should set the (List B) allowable transfer price.

	List A	*List B*
a.	Countries X and Y	Highest
b.	Countries X and Y	Lowest
c.	Country X	Highest
d.	Country Y	Highest

114. The company earns the (List A) total profit from sales in (List B).

	List A	*List B*
a.	Greatest	The home country
b.	Lowest	The home country
c.	Greatest	Country X
d.	Lowest	Country Y

115. A company produces a good in Country A and sells some of its output in Country B. Selling prices are identical in the two countries. The corporate tax rates are 40% in Country A and 20% in Country B. Assuming that the company does not increase or decrease production, the company should (List A) sales in Country B and set as (List B) a transfer price as possible, in order to minimize global taxes.

	List A	*List B*
a.	Maximize	High
b.	Maximize	Low
c.	Minimize	High
d.	Minimize	Low

116. It would be appropriate to use market price as an intracompany transfer price when

a. There is a perfectly competitive external market for the transferred component.
b. The selling division is operating at less than full capacity.
c. There is a monopolistic external market for the transferred component.
d. There are no alternative uses for idle capacity.

117. A limitation of transfer prices based on actual cost is that they

a. Charge inefficiencies to the department that is transferring the goods.
b. Can lead to suboptimal decisions for the company as a whole.
c. Must be adjusted by some markup.
d. Lack clarity and administrative convenience.

Cost-Volume-Profit Analysis

Items 118 and 119 are based on the following:

The following data pertains to a company.

	Total cost	*Unit cost*
Sales (40,000 units)	$1,000,000	$25
Raw materials	160,000	4
Direct labor	280,000	7
Factory overhead:		
Variable	80,000	2
Fixed	360,000	
Selling and general expenses:		
Variable	120,000	3
Fixed	225,000	

118. How many units does the company need to produce and sell to make a before-tax profit of 10% of sales?

a. 65,000 units.
b. 36,562 units.
c. 90,000 units.
d. 29,250 units.

119. Assuming that the company sells 80,000 units, what is the maximum that can be paid for an advertising campaign while still breaking even?

a. $ 135,000
b. $1,015,000
c. $ 535,000
d. $ 695,000

120. A company's management wants to choose a selling price for each of its products that will maximize the contribution margin from sales of the product. Variable cost of one product is $7 per unit. The probabilities of demand for both 10,000 units and 15,000 units at each of four selling prices are given below.

	Demand in units	
Selling price	**10,000**	**15,000**
$20	0.20	0.80
21	0.45	0.55
22	0.60	0.40
23	0.80	0.20

At which selling price will the company earn the highest expected contribution margin?

a. $20
b. $21
c. $22
d. $23

121. A retail company determines its selling price by marking up variable costs 60%. In addition, the company uses frequent selling price markdowns to stimulate sales. If the markdowns average 10%, what is the company's contribution margin ratio?

a. 27.5%
b. 30.6%
c. 37.5%
d. 41.7%

122. A company is concerned about its 2005 operating performance, as summarized below.

Sales ($12.50 per unit)	$300,000
Variable costs	180,000
Net operating loss	(40,000)

How many additional units should have been sold in order for the company to break even in 2005?

a. 32,000
b. 24,000
c. 16,000
d. 8,000

123. Data from the duplicating department of a company for the last two months are as follows:

	Number of copies made	*Duplicating dept.'s costs*
January	100,000	$8,500
February	150,000	9,500

What is total variable cost at 110,000 copies?

a. $ 1,100
b. $ 2,200
c. $ 5,500
d. $22,000

124. A company has sales of $500,000, variable costs of $300,000 and pretax profit of $150,000. If the company increased the sales price per unit by 10%, reduced fixed costs by 20%, and left variable cost per unit unchanged, what would be the new breakeven point in sales dollars?

a. $ 88,000
b. $100,000
c. $110,000
d. $125,000

125. A company has the following 2003 budget data:

Beginning finished goods inventory	40,000 units
Sales	70,000 units
Ending finished goods inventory	30,000 units
Direct materials	$10 per unit
Direct labor	$20 per unit
Variable factory overhead	$5 per unit
Selling costs	$2 per unit
Fixed factory overhead	$80,000

What will be 2003 total budgeted production costs?

a. $2,100,000
b. $2,180,000
c. $2,240,000
d. $2,320,000

Items 126 and 127 are based on the following:

A company had sales revenue of $400,000 in 2001. Expenses for 2001, which are classified as variable or fixed, are presented below.

Expense	*Classification*	*Amount*
Sales commission	Variable	$20,000
Sales salaries	Fixed	42,000
Selling expense	Variable	12,000
Cost of goods sold	Variable	140,000
Cost of goods sold	Fixed	55,000
Administrative expense	Fixed	33,000

126. The contribution margin in 2001 amounted to
a. $205,000
b. $228,000
c. $240,000
d. $260,000

127. The gross profit in 2001 amounted to
a. $ 98,000
b. $143,000
c. $205,000
d. $260,000

128. Two manufacturers sell similar products in a highly competitive market. There are differentiating characteristics between the two products. In addition, the first manufacturer has a more labor-oriented manufacturing process while the second manufacturer is more automated. Data regarding the selling prices and costs for the two manufacturers are presented below.

	First manufacturer	*Second manufacturer*
Selling price per unit	$40.00	$30.00
Variable costs per unit		
Manufacturing	14.00	7.50
Selling	8.00	4.50
Total variable costs per unit	$22.00	$12.00
Annual fixed costs		
Manufacturing	411,840	540,000
Selling	110,800	100,000
Administrative	95,120	98,000
Total fixed costs	$617,760	$738,000

The breakeven point for the first manufacturer will be
a. The same as the second manufacturer in terms of units because the contribution margins are the same for both manufacturers.
b. 6,680 units lower than the second manufacturer.
c. 8,160 units lower than the second manufacturer.
d. 33,420 units lower than the second manufacturer.

129. Data regarding four different products manufactured by an organization are presented below. Direct material and direct labor are readily available from the respective resource markets. However, the manufacturer is limited to a maximum of 3,000 machine hours per month.

	Product A	*Product B*	*Product C*	*Product D*
Selling price/unit	$15	$18	$20	$25
Variable cost/unit	$ 7	$11	$10	$16
Units produced per machine hour	3	4	2	3

The product that is the most profitable for the manufacturer in this situation is
a. Product A.
b. Product B.
c. Product C.
d. Product D.

130. A company with $280,000 of fixed costs has the following data:

	Product A	*Product B*
Sales price per unit	$5	$6
Variable costs per unit	$3	$5

Assume 3 units of A are sold for each unit of B sold. How much will be sales in dollars of product B at the breakeven point?
a. $200,000
b. $240,000
c. $600,000
d. $840,000

131. The ABC Company manufactures components for use in producing one of its finished products. When 12,000 units are produced, the full cost per unit is $35, separated as follows:

Direct material	$ 5
Direct labor	$15
Variable overhead	$10
Fixed overhead	$ 5

The XYZ Company has offered to sell 12,000 components to ABC for $37 each. If ABC accepts the offer, some of the facilities presently being used to manufacture the components can be rented as warehouse space for $40,000. However, $3 of the fixed overhead currently applied to each component would have to be covered by ABC's other products. What is the differential cost to the ABC Company of purchasing the components from the XYZ Company?
a. $ 8,000
b. $20,000
c. $24,000
d. $44,000

132. A company produces and sells three products, as follows:

	Products		
	C	J	P
Sales	$200,000	$150,000	$125,000
Separable (product) fixed costs	60,000	35,000	40,000
Allocated fixed costs	35,000	40,000	25,000
Variable costs	95,000	75,000	50,000

The company lost its lease and must move to a smaller facility. As a result, total allocated fixed costs will be reduced by 40%. However, one of its products must be discontinued in order for the company to fit in the new facility. Since the company's objective is to maximize profits, what is its expected net income after the appropriate product has been discontinued?
a. $10,000
b. $15,000
c. $20,000
d. $25,000

Items 133 through 139 are based on the following:

A company manufactures and sells a single product. Demand for this product, which depends solely on the selling price charged, is as follows:

$$Q = 30{,}000 - 50P,$$

where Q is the number of units demanded and P is the selling price per unit.

Because it can predict exactly what demand will be, the company produces exactly as many units as are demanded. Total fixed costs are $2,800,000 and variable costs are $80 per unit.

Select the appropriate value from the table of alternative choices to respond to the following:

Alternative choices	
A	$195
B	$270
C	$290
D	$300
E	$320
F	$360
G	$390
H	$400
I	$410
J	$480
K	$535
L	$580

133. What is the contribution margin per unit if selling price is $370 per unit?

134. If the sales of 14,000 units are the goal, what selling price should be charged?

135. What is the average cost per unit when its selling price is $400 per unit?

136. What selling price must be charged to maximize total revenue?

137. By what amount (in thousands of dollars) will revenue change if the selling price is lowered from $410 per unit to $350 per unit?

138. What is the profit (in thousands of dollars) when its selling price is $370 per unit?

139. Given the demand and cost functions, what is the maximum profit (in thousands of dollars) that can be earned?

140. The following data relate to a retail sales organization:

Fixed cost = $30,000
Selling price = $5
Variable costs = $3.20 per unit

What is the breakeven point in sales?

a. $ 9,375
b. $16,667
c. $46,875
d. $83,335

141. The following data relate to a retail sales organization:

Fixed costs = $36,000
Desired profit before taxes = $24,000
Selling price = $8
Variable costs = $5

What level of sales is required to achieve the stated profit before taxes?

a. $ 7,500
b. $ 20,000
c. $ 96,000
d. $160,000

Items 142 and 143 are based on the following:

An entrepreneur wishes to determine if it would be profitable to sell souvenir T-shirts at a two-night rock concert. The shirts would cost $3 each, and booth space and exclusive rights can be obtained for $5,000. The concert is already sold out for both nights, 12,000 tickets each night. Past experience has shown that approximately one in ten ticket holders buys a shirt.

142. What would be the pretax sales breakeven point if the sales price of the shirts were $8 each?

a. $1,000
b. $5,000
c. $6,000
d. $8,000

143. How many T-shirts in total would have to be sold to generate a pretax profit of $1,000 **per night** ($2,000 for the concerts)?

a. 1,200 shirts.
b. 1,400 shirts.
c. 2,400 shirts.
d. 11,200 shirts.

Items 144 through 146 are based on the following:

A company is attempting to determine the optimum sales price for a new product and knows that to be competitive the new product must sell for $75 or less per unit. Fixed expenses are estimated at $150,000 for production levels up to 4,000 units, and variable expenses at 4,000 units are projected at $40,000.

144. At what sales price will each unit sold contribute $50 toward fixed expenses?

a. $40
b. $60
c. $65
d. $75

145. What is the pretax breakeven point in units assuming a $50 unit contribution margin?

a. 2,308 units.
b. 3,000 units.
c. 3,800 units.
d. 5,000 units.

146. What is the margin of safety in sales dollars if the sales price for 3,500 units is $70 per unit?

a. $35,000
b. $60,000
c. $70,000
d. $95,000

147. The following information relates to a new product that an organization plans to introduce:

Selling price	$80 per unit
Variable cost	$60 per unit
Fixed cost	$200,000 per year

How many units of this product must be sold each year to break even?

a. 2,500 units.
b. 3,333 units.
c. 10,000 units.
d. 20,000 units.

Items 148 and 149 are based on the following:

A company has the following data regarding one of its products, which currently sells 10,000 units annually.

	Per unit
Price	$10
Direct materials	$ 4
Direct labor	$ 2
Variable overhead	$ 1

148. If per unit direct materials cost increases by 25%, what will the new total contribution margin be?

a. $(30,000)
b. $ 20,000
c. $ 30,000
d. $ 40,000

149. If instead, volume of sales were reduced by 10%, what would be the new total contribution margin?

a. $20,000
b. $27,000
c. $30,000
d. $33,000

150. The following data pertains to a company's four major products.

Product	*A*	*B*	*C*	*D*
Price per unit	$10	$20	$ 5	$15
Variable costs per unit	$ 7	$18	$ 4	$11
Sales volume, in units	1000	2000	3000	500

A 10% increase in unit sales volume would have the greatest impact on profit from which product?

a. A
b. B
c. C
d. D

151. A company is considering selling 10,000 units of a new product, which has the following estimated data:

	Per unit
Revenue	$20.00
Direct materials	3.00
Direct labor	4.00
Variable factory overhead	2.00
Sales commission	1.00
Allocated fixed overhead	5.00

Adding the product will not increase total fixed costs, but will increase profits by

a. $ 50,000
b. $100,000
c. $110,000
d. $140,000

152. A company makes a product which sells for $30. During the coming year, fixed costs are expected to be $180,000 and variable costs are estimated at $26 per unit. How many units must the company sell in order to break even?

a. 6,000
b. 6,924
c. 45,000
d. 720,000

Items 153 and 154 are based on the following:

A company makes a product which has variable costs, estimated at $4.00 per unit and which sells for $6.00 per unit. Fixed costs for the coming year are estimated to be $130,000.

153. How many units must the company sell in order to generate pretax income of $30,000?

a. 26,667
b. 50,000
c. 65,000
d. 80,000

154. Assume that the actual unit sales were 30% below the level required to earn $50,000 pretax income. Under those conditions, the pretax income or (loss) would be

a. $ 39,000
b. $ 35,000
c. $ (4,000)
d. $126,000

155. In its first year of operations, a firm had $50,000 of fixed operating costs. It sold 10,000 units at a $10 unit price and incurred variable costs of $4 per unit. If all prices and costs will be the same in the second year and sales are projected to rise to 25,000 units, what will the degree of operating leverage (the extent to which fixed costs are used in the firm's operations) be in the second year?

a. 1.25
b. 1.50
c. 2.0
d. 6.0

Items 156 through 160 are based on the following:

Data regarding a company's current year operations are as follows:

Sales revenue (150,000 units)	$9,000,000
Variable costs:	
Direct material	1,800,000
Direct labor	720,000
Manufacturing overhead	1,080,000
Selling expenses	450,000
Fixed costs:	
Manufacturing overhead	600,000
Administrative expenses	567,840
Selling expenses	352,800
Income tax rate	40%

The company estimates that in the coming year direct material costs will increase by 10% and direct labor costs will increase by $0.60 per unit to $5.40 per unit. In addition, fixed selling expenses will increase by $29,520. All other costs will be incurred at the same rates or amounts as the current year.

156. The company's total contribution margin for the current year is

a. $2,970,000
b. $4,950,000
c. $5,400,000
d. $6,030,000

157. The gross profit for the current year is

a. $3,429,360
b. $4,232,160
c. $4,350,000
d. $4,800,000

158. The company's breakeven point in unit sales for the current year is

a. 36,495 units.
b. 42,240 units.
c. 46,080 units.

d. 56,320 units.

159. What dollar sales volume, to the nearest dollar, would be required by the company in the coming year to earn the same net income as in the current year?

a. $ 6,938,031
b. $ 8,736,000
c. $ 9,576,000
d. $10,374,000

160. What selling price would the company have to charge for its product in the coming year if it wants to maintain the same contribution margin percentage rate as in the current year?

a. $61.80
b. $64.00
c. $64.50
d. $72.00

161. A manufacturing company's primary goals include product quality and customer satisfaction. The company sells a product, for which the market demand is strong, for $50 per unit. Due to the capacity constraints in the production department, only 300,000 units can be produced per year. The current defective rate is 12% (i.e., of the 300,000 units produced; only 264,000 units are sold and 36,000 units are scrapped). There is no revenue recovery when defective units are scrapped. The full manufacturing cost of a unit is $29.50, including

Direct material	$17.50
Direct labor	4.00
Fixed manufacturing overhead	8.00

The company's designers have estimated that the defective rate can be reduced to 2% by using a different direct material. However, this will increase the direct material cost by $2.50 per unit to $20 per unit. The net benefit of using the new material to manufacture the product would be

a. $ (120,000)
b. $ 120,000
c. $ 750,000
d. $ 1,425,000

Items 162 and 163 are based on the following:

A company that sells its single product for $40 per unit uses cost/volume/profit analysis in its planning. The company's after-tax net income for the past year was $1,188,000 after applying an effective tax rate of 40%. The projected costs for manufacturing and selling its single product in the coming year are as follows:

Variable costs per unit:		
Direct material	$5.00	
Direct labor	4.00	
Manufacturing overhead	6.00	
Selling and administrative costs	3.00	
Total cost per unit	$18.00	
Annual fixed operating costs:		
Manufacturing overhead		$6,200,000
Selling and administrative costs		3,700,000
Total annual fixed cost		$9,900,000

162. The dollar sales volume required in the coming year to earn the same after-tax net income as the past year is

a. $20,160,000
b. $21,600,000
c. $23,400,000
d. $26,400,000

163. The company has learned that a new direct material is available that will increase the quality of its product. The new material will increase the direct material costs by $3 per unit. The company will increase the selling price of the product to $50 per unit and increase its marketing costs by $1,575,000 to advertise the higher quality product. The number of units the company has to sell in order to earn a 10% before-tax return on sales would be

a. 337,500 units
b. 346,875 units
c. 425,000 units
d. 478,125 units

164. A company produced and sold 100,000 units of a component with a variable cost of $20 per unit. First quality components have a selling price of $50. The component's specifications require its weight to be 20 kg. with a tolerance of ∀1 kg. Unfortunately, 1,200 of the units produced failed the company's tolerance specifications. These 1,200 units were reworked at a cost of $12 per unit and sold as factory seconds at $45 each. Had the company had a quality assurance program in place such that all units produced conformed to specifications, the increase in the company's contribution margin from this component would have been

a. $14,400
b. $20,400
c. $21,600
d. $39,600

Items 165 and 166 are based on the following:

An organization sells a single product for $40 per unit, which it purchases for $20. The salespeople receive a salary plus a commission of 5% of sales. Last year the organization's net income (after taxes) was $100,800. The organization is subject to an income tax rate of 30%. The fixed costs of the organization are

Advertising	$124,000
Rent	60,000
Salaries	180,000
Other fixed costs	32,000
Total	$396,000

165. The breakeven point in unit sales for the organization is

a. 8,800 units.
b. 18,000 units.
c. 19,800 units.
d. 22,000 units.

166. The organization is considering changing the compensation plan for sales personnel. If the organization increases the commission to 10% of sales and reduces salaries by $80,000, what dollar sales volume must the organization have in order to earn the same net income as last year?

a. $1,042,000
b. $1,100,000
c. $1,150,000
d. $1,630,000

Items 167 and 168 are based on the following:

A mail-order confectioner sells fine candy in one-pound boxes. It has the capacity to produce 600,000 boxes annually, but forecasts that it will produce and sell only 500,000 boxes in the coming year. The costs to manufacture and distribute the candy are detailed below. The organization has invested capital of $6,750,000.

Variable costs per pound:	
Manufacturing	$4.85
Packaging	.35
Distribution	1.80
Total	$7.00
Annual fixed costs:	
Manufacturing overhead	$810,000
Marketing and distribution	270,000

167. The selling price per pound that the confectioner should charge for a one-pound box of candy to obtain a 20% rate of return on invested capital is

a. $ 9.70
b. $11.05
c. $11.50
d. $11.86

168. The confectioner has been asked by a retailer to submit a bid for a special order of 40,000 one-pound boxes of candy; this is a onetime order that will not be repeated. While the candy would be almost identical, the candy ingredients would be $0.45 less. The total distribution costs for the entire order would be $32,000. Special setup costs required by this order would amount to $60,000. There would be no other changes in costs, rates, or amounts. The minimum selling price per one-pound box that the confectioner would bid on this special order would be

a. $7.05
b. $8.85
c. $9.05
d. $9.55

Items 169 and 170 are based on the following:

A company manufactures and sells a single product. Fixed expenses are $40, 000 per month, selling price is $100 per unit, and the contribution margin percentage is 20%.

169. How many units must this company sell to break even?

a. 1,000 units.
b. 2,000 units.
c. 4,000 units.
d. 5,000 units.

170. What dollar volume of sales must the company have to earn a profit of $20,000?

a. $ 60,000
b. $200,000
c. $240,000
d. $300,000

Items 171 and 172 are based on the following:

A wholesale distributing company has budgeted its before-tax profit to be $643,500 for 2004. The company is preparing its annual budget for 2005 and has accumulated the following data:

2005 data		
Projected annual dollar sales	$6,000,000	
Variable costs as a percent of sales:		
Cost of merchandise		30%
Sales commissions		5%
Shipping expenses		10%
Annual fixed operating costs:		
Selling expenses	$ 772,200	
Administrative expenses	$1,801,800	

171. If the wholesale distributing company wants to earn the same before-tax profit in 2005 as budgeted for 2004, the annual dollar sales volume would not be the projected $6,000,000 but would have to be

a. $4,950,000
b. $5,362,500
c. $5,850,000
d. $7,150,000

172. Using the original $6,000,000 projection, the wholesale distributing company's margin of safety in dollar sales volume for 2005 would be

a. $ 82,500
b. $ 150,000
c. $ 280,000
d. $1,320,000

173. A company produces golf balls. One dozen golf balls sell for $5 and have variable costs of $4. The firm's fixed costs are $30,000 per year. How many dozen-golf balls must the company sell to earn a profit equal to 10% of sales revenue?

a. 60,000 dozen.
b. 70,000 dozen.
c. 50,000 dozen.
d. 30,000 dozen.

174. A company has $450,000 per year of fixed production costs, of which $150,000 is noncash outlays. The variable cost per unit is $15, and the unit selling price is $25. The breakeven volume in sales units for this company would be:

a. 18,000 units.
b. 30,000 units.
c. 45,000 units.
d. 60,000 units.

175. A company has a 50% gross margin, general and administrative expenses of $50, interest expense of $20, and net income of $10 for the year just ended. If the corporate tax rate is 50%, the level of sales revenue for the year just ended was

a. $ 90
b. $135
c. $150
d. $180

176. All else being equal, the breakeven point in units will be higher if

a. Sales revenue is higher
b. Fixed costs are lower
c. Unit variable costs are higher
d. More units are sold

177. The correct formula for calculating contribution margin in dollars is

a. Sales revenue – Total variable costs – Fixed operating costs.
b. Sales revenue – Variable costs per unit.
c. Sales revenue – Total variable costs.
d. Selling price – Variable cost per unit – Fixed operating costs.

178. A new product will sell at $40 per unit. Variable costs are $24 per unit and fixed costs are $50,000 per year. The company expects to sell 50,000 units in the coming year. What is the contribution margin per unit?

a. $15
b. $16
c. $24
d. $40

179. Assuming a contribution margin per unit of $30, fixed costs of $93,750, and a selling price of $100, what is the breakeven point in units?

a. 938
b. 1,340
c. 3,000
d. 3,125

180. A department store prepares segmented financial statements. During the past year, the income statement for the perfume department located near the front entrance appeared as follows:

Sales	$ 200,000
Cost of goods sold	120,000
Gross profit	80,000
Janitorial expense	5,000
Sales commissions	40,000
Heat and lighting	4,000
Depreciation	3,000
Income before taxes	$ 28,000

Janitorial expense, heat and lighting, and depreciation are allocated to the department based on square footage. Sales personnel work for only one department and are paid on commission. What is the perfume department's contribution margin?

a. $28,000
b. $31,000
c. $37,000
d. $40,000

181. A company has excess capacity in production-related fixed assets. If in a given year these fixed assets were being used to only 80% of capacity and the sales level in that year was $2,000,000, the full capacity sales level is

a. $ 1,600,000
b. $ 2,000,000
c. $ 2,500,000
d. $10,000,000

Relevant Costs

182. A company manufactures a product that is sold to wholesalers for $37.95. The company employs an absorption cost system. The plant capacity for manufacturing this product is 750,000 units annually, but normal volume is 500,000 units. The unit and total costs at normal volume are given below.

	Unit cost	*Total cost*
Direct material	$ 9.80	$ 4,900,000
Direct labor	4.50	2,250,000
Manufacturing overhead	12.00	6,000,000
Selling and administrative costs:		
Variable	2.50	1,250,000
Fixed	4.20	2,100,000
Total costs	$33.00	$16,500,000

The manufacturing overhead includes both variable and fixed costs; the fixed manufacturing overhead for the current year is budgeted at $4,500,000.

The company has been approached by a prospective customer who wants to use the company's product as a component in merchandise the customer is manufacturing. The customer has offered to purchase 100,000 units at $25.00 each. The customer wants the product packaged in large cartons rather than the normal individual containers, and it will pick up the units in its own trucks. This will decrease the variable selling and administrative expenses by 60%.

When deciding whether the company should accept this special order from the customer, the company will compare the total revenue of $2,500,000 to be derived from this order with the total relevant costs of

a. $1,830,000
b. $1,880,000
c. $2,930,000
d. $3,150,000

183. A company has 7,000 obsolete toys, which are carried in inventory at a manufacturing cost of $6 per unit. If the toys are reworked for $2 per unit, they could be sold for $3 per unit. If the toys are scrapped, they could be sold for $1.85 per unit. Which alternative is more desirable (rework or scrap) and what is the total dollar amount of the advantage of that alternative?

a. Scrap, $5,950
b. Rework, $36,050
c. Scrap, $47,950
d. Rework, $8,050

Items 184 through 186 are based on the following:

A company has had the following production experience over the last 10 quarters for product P1:

Quarterly production	*Frequency*
1,000 units	2
1,500	3
2,000	4
2,500	1
	10

Additional information for P1:

Unit variable costs	$7
Quarterly unavoidable allocated fixed costs	$4,000

A unit of P1 can be purchased from an outside supplier for $8.75. If P1 is purchased, the plant facilities now used for its manufacture can be used to produce another product that will generate a quarterly contribution margin of $5,500.

184. Assuming that P1 is to be produced internally, what is the expected quarterly production?

a. 700
b. 1,000
c. 1,700
d. 2,000

185. Assume future sales can be predicted with complete accuracy. Up to what amount should the company be willing to pay for this information?

a. The difference between the profit that would be expected to be lost if too few are produced and the additional carrying costs that would be expected if too many are produced.
b. The sum of the profit that would be expected to be lost if too few are produced and the additional carrying costs that would be expected if too many are produced.
c. The expected profit from the sales of P1 less the expected additional carrying costs if too many of P1 were manufactured.
d. The difference between the expected profit with perfect information and the highest expected profit with existing information.

186. Assume that 2,500 units of P1 will be sold next quarter. Should P1 be purchased next quarter from the outside supplier?

a. Yes. Outside purchase would reduce total costs by $1,125.

b. Yes. Outside purchase would reduce total costs by $5,125.
c. No. Outside purchase would increase total costs by $4,375.
d. No. Outside purchase would increase total costs by $9,875.

Items 187 and 188 are based on the following:

A manufacturing company is considering a new product for the coming year, an electric motor, which the company can purchase from a reliable vendor for $21.00 per unit. The alternative is to manufacture the motor internally. The company has excess capacity to manufacture the 30,000 motors needed in the coming year except for manufacturing space and special machinery. The machinery can be leased for $45,000 annually. Finished goods warehouse space adjoining the main manufacturing facility, leased for $39,000 annually, can be converted and used to manufacture the motors. Additional off-site space can be leased at an annual cost of $54,000 to replace the finished goods warehouse. The estimated unit costs for manufacturing the motors internally, exclusive of the leasing costs itemized above, are

Direct materials	$8.00
Direct labor	4.00
Variable manufacturing overhead	3.00
Allocated fixed manufacturing overhead	5.00
Total manufacturing cost per unit	$20.00

187. A cost/benefit analysis would show that the manufacturing company would save
a. $54,000 by purchasing the motors from the outside vendor.
b. $69,000 by purchasing the motors from the outside vendor.
c. $81,000 by making the motors internally.
d. $96,000 by making the motors internally.

188. If the manufacturing company decides to use its excess manufacturing capacity for the motors, then the contribution or net benefit that could have been obtained from other alternative uses is referred to as
a. Residual income.
b. Sunk costs.
c. Separable costs.
d. Opportunity costs.

Items 189 and 190 are based on the following:

A company manufactures and sells a single product. It takes two machine hours to produce one unit. Annual sales are expected to be 75,000 units. Annual production capacity is 200,000 machine hours. Expected selling price is $10 per unit.

Cost data for manufacturing and selling the product are as follows:

Variable costs (per unit)	
Direct materials	$3.00
Direct labor	1.00
Variable manufacturing overhead	0.80
Variable selling	2.00
Fixed costs (per year)	
Fixed manufacturing overhead	$90,000
Fixed selling	60,000

189. The company receives a special order for 10,000 units at $7.60. Variable selling cost for each of these 10,000 units will be $1.20. This special order will not affect regular sales of 75,000 units. If the company accepts this special order, its profit will
a. Increase by $8,000.
b. Increase by $16,000.
c. Decrease by $4,000.
d. Decrease by $12,000.

190. The company estimates that by reducing its selling price to $9.30 per unit, it can increase sales to 90,000 units annually. Fixed costs per year and unit variable costs will remain unchanged. If the company reduces its selling price to $9.30 per unit, its profit will
a. Decrease by $5,000.
b. Decrease by $15,000.
c. Decrease by $45,000.
d. Increase by $15,000.

Items 191 and 192 are based on the following:

A business organization needs a computer application that can be either developed internally or purchased from an outside vendor. The organization plans to use a cost-benefit approach in making this decision.

The cost of a suitable software package from a reputable outside vendor would be $29,000. Any minor modifications and testing required to adapt the package to the organization's current system can be conducted by the organization's existing systems staff as part of their regular scheduled workload.

If the software were developed internally, one of the organization's regular systems analysts would be assigned to the project full time while an independent contractor would be hired to assume the responsibilities of the regular systems analyst. The hourly labor rate for the regular systems analyst is $25, and the hourly charge for the independent contractor would be $22. The independent contractor would occupy one of the organization's empty offices. All offices are 100 square feet in size, and the organization's occupancy costs are estimated at $45 per square foot.

Other related data regarding this project are presented below. The Information Systems Department charges all users for computer time using predetermined standard rates. The organization has sufficient excess computer capacity for either the software development or the modification/testing of the purchased software package.

	Internal development	*Purchased software*
Systems analyst time in hours		
Development	1,000	N/A
Modifications and testing	N/A	40
Computer charges	$800	$250
Additional hardware purchases	$3,200	N/A
Incidental supplies	$500	$200

191. When applying the cost-benefit approach to a decision situation, the primary criterion is how well management goals will be achieved in relation to costs. In the cost-benefit approach, costs would include all expected
a. Variable costs for the alternative courses of action but not expected fixed costs because only the expected variable costs are relevant.
b. Incremental out-of-pocket costs as well as all expected continuing costs that are common to all the alternative courses of action.
c. Future costs that differ among the alternative courses of action plus all qualitative factors that cannot be measured in numerical terms.

d. Historical and future costs relative to the alternative courses of action including all qualitative factors that cannot be measured in numerical terms.

192. Based solely on the cost figures presented, the cost of developing the computer application will be
a. $3,500 less than acquiring the purchased software package.
b. $500 less than acquiring the purchased software package.
c. $1,550 more than acquiring the purchased software package.
d. $3,550 more than acquiring the purchased software package.

Costing Systems

193. Which of the following statements about activity-based costing is **not** true?
a. Activity-based costing is useful for allocating marketing and distribution costs.
b. Activity-based costing is more likely to result in major differences from traditional costing systems if the firm manufactures only one product rather than multiple products.
c. In activity-based costing, cost drivers are what cause costs to be incurred.
d. Activity-based costing differs from traditional costing systems in that products are not cross-subsidized.

194. Which of the following would be a reasonable basis for allocating the material handling costs to the units produced in an activity-based costing system?
a. Number of production runs per year.
b. Number of components per completed unit.
c. Amount of time required producing one unit.
d. Amount of overhead applied to each completed unit.

195. When the executive management of an organization decided to form a team to investigate the adoption of an activity-based costing (ABC) system, an internal auditor was assigned to the team. The best reason for including an internal auditor would be the auditor's knowledge of
a. Activities and cost drivers.
b. Information processing procedures.
c. Current product cost structures.
d. Internal controls alternatives.

196. Unlike the traditional full-absorption cost system, activity-based costing (ABC) assigns
a. Costs to individual products based only on nonfinancial variables.
b. Costs to individual products based on various activities involved.
c. Overhead to individual products based on some common measure of production volume.
d. Only costs that can be directly traced to individual products.

Items 197 and 198 are based on the following:

Believing that its traditional cost system may be providing misleading information, an organization is considering an activity-based costing (ABC) approach. It now employs a full cost system and has been applying its manufacturing overhead on the basis of machine hours.

The organization plans on using 50,000 direct labor hours and 30,000 machine hours in the coming year. The following data show the manufacturing overhead that is budgeted:

Activity	*Cost driver*	*Budgeted activity*	*Budgeted cost*
Material handling	Number of parts handled	6,000,000	$720,000
Setup costs	Number of setups	750	315,000
Machining costs	Machine hours	30,000	540,000
Quality control	Number of batches	500	225,000
Total manufacturing overhead cost			$1,800,000

Cost, sales, and production data for one of the organization's products for the coming year are as follows:

Prime costs:	
Direct material cost per unit	$4.40
Direct labor cost per unit .05 DLH @ $15.00/DLH	0.75
Total prime cost	$5.15

Sales and production data:	
Expected sales	20,000 units
Batch size	5,000 units
Number of setups	2 per batch
Total parts per finished unit	5 parts
Machine hours required	80 MH per batch

197. If the organization uses the traditional full cost system, the cost per unit for this product for the coming year would be
a. $5.39
b. $5.44
c. $6.11
d. $6.95

198. If the organization employs an activity-based costing system, the cost per unit for the product described for the coming year would be
a. $6.00
b. $6.08
c. $6.21
d. $6.30

Items 199 through 201 are based on the following:

A company has identified the following overhead costs and cost drivers for the coming year:

Overhead item	*Cost driver*	*Budgeted cost*	*Budgeted activity level*
Machine setup	Number of setups	$ 20,000	200
Inspection	Number of inspections	$130,000	6500
Material handling	Number of material moves	$ 80,000	8000
Engineering	Engineering hours	$ 50,000	1000
		$280,000	

The following information was collected on three jobs that were completed during the year.

	Job 101	*Job 102*	*Job 103*
Direct materials	$5,000	$12,000	$8,000
Direct labor	$2,000	$2,000	$4,000
Units completed	100	50	200
Number of setups	1	2	4
Number of inspections	20	10	30
Number of material moves	30	10	50
Engineering hours	10	50	10

Budgeted direct labor cost was $100,000 and budgeted direct material cost was $280,000.

199. If the company uses activity-based costing, how much overhead cost should be allocated to Job 101?
a. $1,300
b. $1,900

c. $5,000
d. $5,600

200. If the company uses activity-based costing, compute the cost of each unit of Job 102.
a. $340
b. $392
c. $440
d. $520

201. The company prices its products at 140% of cost. If the company uses activity-based costing, the price of each unit of Job 103 would be
a. $ 98
b. $112
c. $148
d. $240

202. Typical product costing systems synchronize the recording of accounting-system entries with the physical sequence of purchases and production. The alternative (which is normally used in high-speed automated production environments) of delaying journal entries until after the physical sequences have occurred is referred to as
a. Backflush costing.
b. Direct costing.
c. Operation costing.
d. Process costing.

Items 203 and 204 are based on the following:

A company harvests, packs, and ships all of its own produce. The company operates three packing lines. A summary of completed inventory costs is as follows:

Packing-line employee salary expense	150,000
Packing-line supervision salary expense	90,000
Quality control salary expense	30,000
Packing crates expense	15,000
Electricity expense	3,000
Depreciation expense	66,000

203. Costs for the packing lines would be accumulated in part by
a. Recording payroll expense by employee job category.
b. Computing depreciation expense.
c. Producing monthly financial statements.
d. Forecasting monthly material shortages.

204. At the end of the reporting period, 600,000 units had been packed and shipped. No inventory remained on hand. If the company used process costing, the cost per unit would be
a. $0.197
b. $0.275
c. $0.315
d. $0.590

Items 205 and 206 are based on the following:

The standard direct labor cost to produce one pound of output for a company is presented below. Related data regarding the planned and actual production activities for the current month for the company are also given below.

NOTE: DLH = Direct labor hours.

Direct labor standard:	0.4 DLH @ $12.00 per DLH = $4.80
Planned production	15,000 pounds
Actual production	15,500 pounds
Actual direct labor costs (6,250 DLH)	$75,250

205. The company's direct labor rate variance for the current month would be
a. $10 unfavorable.
b. $240 unfavorable.
c. $248 unfavorable.
d. $250 unfavorable.

206. The company's direct labor efficiency variance for the current month would be
a. $600 unfavorable.
b. $602 unfavorable.
c. $2,400 unfavorable.
d. $3,000 unfavorable.

Items 207 through 209 are based on the following:

A company harvests, packs, and ships all of its own produce. The company operates three packing lines. A summary of completed inventory costs is as follows:

Packing-line employee salary expense	$150,000
Packing-line supervision salary expense	$90,000
Quality control salary expense	$30,000
Packing crates expense	$15,000
Electricity expense	$3,000
Depreciation expense	$66,000

207. Costs for the packing lines would be accumulated in part by
a. Recording payroll expense by employee job category.
b. Computing depreciation expense.
c. Producing monthly financial statements.
d. Forecasting monthly material shortages.

208. At the end of the reporting period, 600,000 units had been packed and shipped. No inventory remained on hand. If the company used process costing, the cost per unit would be
a. $0.197
b. $0.275
c. $0.315
d. $0.59

209. If the company used variable costing for its produce packing, what would be the total cost of inventory prior to shipping?
a. $165,000
b. $273,000
c. $288,000
d. $354,000

210. A manufacturing company has a continuous flow cycle that employs simplified activities in a short manufacturing cycle. The company produces a single product with a minimal defect rate. The product costing system that this company would most likely use for its manufacturing operations is
a. Activity-based costing.
b. Job-order costing.
c. Operation costing.
d. Process costing.

211. A corporation manufactures two qualities (brands) of barbed wire fencing for sale to wholesalers and large ranchers. Which of the following would be the best type of costing system for such a company to use?
a. EOQ system.
b. Job-order system.
c. Process system.
d. Retail inventory system.

212. The loan department of a financial corporation makes loans to businesses. The costs of processing these loans are often several thousand dollars. The costs for each loan, which include labor, telephone and travel, are significantly different across loans. Some loans require the use of outside services such as appraisals, legal services and consulting services, whereas other loans do not require these services. The most appropriate cost accumulation method for the loan department of the corporation is

a. Job-order costing.
b. Process costing.
c. Differential costing.
d. Joint product costing.

Items 213 and 214 are based on the following:

The materials standard per unit of finished goods is 3 pounds of raw materials at $5.00 per pound. During July the company purchased 3,700 pounds of raw material at a total cost of $18,130, and placed 3,600 pounds into production producing 1,220 units of finished goods.

213. The direct materials usage variance for July was

a. $294 favorable.
b. $200 unfavorable.
c. $300 favorable.
d. $300 unfavorable.

214. The company accounts for materials price variances during production. The direct materials price variance for July was

a. $122 favorable.
b. $360 favorable.
c. $366 favorable.
d. $370 favorable.

215. The sales volume variance is

a. The difference between actual and master budgeted sales volume times actual sales price.
b. The difference between flexible budgeted and actual sales volume times actual sales price.
c. The difference between flexible budgeted and actual sales volume times master budgeted sales price.
d. The difference between flexible budgeted and master budgeted sales volume times master budgeted sales price.

Items 216 and 217 are based on the following:

A manufacturer has the following direct material standard for one of its products.

Direct material 3 pounds @ $1.60/pound = $4.80

The company records all inventory at standard cost. Data for the current period regarding the manufacturer's budgeted and actual production for the product as well as direct material purchases and issues to production for manufacture of the product are presented below.

Budgeted production for the period is 8,000 units

Actual production for the period	7,500 units
Direct material purchases:	
Pounds purchased	25,000 pounds
Total cost	$38,750

Direct material issued to production is 23,000 pounds.

216. The material price variance for this direct material for the current period would be

a. $1,125 favorable.
b. $1,150 favorable.
c. $1,200 favorable.
d. $1,250 favorable.

217. The material efficiency variance for this direct material for the current period would be

a. $775 unfavorable.
b. $800 unfavorable.
c. $1,600 favorable.
d. $3,200 favorable.

218. The following is a standard cost variance analysis report on direct labor cost for a division of a manufacturing company.

Job	*Actual hours at actual wages*	*Actual hours at standard wages*	*Standard hours at standard wages*
213	$ 3,243	$ 3,700	$ 3,100
215	$15,345	$15,675	$15,000
217	$ 6,754	$ 7,000	$ 6,600
219	$19,788	$18,755	$19,250
221	$ 3,370	$ 3,470	$ 2,650
Totals	$48,500	$48,600	$46,600

What is the total flexible budget direct labor variance for the division?

a. $100 favorable.
b. $1,900 unfavorable.
c. $1,900 favorable.
d. $2,000 unfavorable.

219. The total budgeted direct labor cost of a company for the month was set at $75,000 when 5,000 units were planned to be produced. The following cost standard, stated in terms of direct labor hours (DLH), was used to develop the budget for direct labor cost:

1.25 DLH @ $12.00/DLH = $15.00/unit produced

The actual operating results for the month were as follows:

Actual units produced	5,200
Actual direct labor hours worked	6,600
Actual direct labor cost	$77,220

The direct labor efficiency variance for the month would be

a. $4,200 unfavorable.
b. $3,000 unfavorable.
c. $2,220 unfavorable.
d. $1,200 unfavorable.

220. A company producing a single product employs the following direct material cost standard for each unit of output:

3 pounds of material @ $4.00/pound = $12.00/output unit

Data regarding the operations for the current month are as follows:

Planned production	26,000 units
Actual production	23,000 units
Actual purchases of direct materials (75,000 pounds)	$297,000

Direct material used in production is 70,000 pounds

What would be the amount of the direct material purchase price variance and direct material quantity variance that the company would recognize for the month?

	Purchase price variance	*Quantity variance*
a.	$3,120 favorable	$32,000 favorable
b.	$3,000 favorable	$24,000 unfavorable
c.	$3,000 favorable	$4,000 unfavorable
d.	$2,800 favorable	$4,000 unfavorable

221. The following information is available from the records of a manufacturing company that applies factory overhead based on direct labor hours:

Estimated overhead cost	$500,000
Estimated labor hours	200,000 hours
Actual overhead cost	$515,000
Actual labor hours	210,000 hours

Based on this information, overhead would be
- a. Underapplied by $9,524.
- b. Overapplied by $10,000.
- c. Overapplied by $15,000.
- d. Overapplied by $40,750.

Responsibility Accounting

222. Which of the following is **not** true of responsibility accounting?
- a. Managers should only be held accountable for factors over which they have significant influence.
- b. The focus of cost center managers will normally be narrower than that of profit center managers.
- c. In the presence of a suitable responsibility accounting system, managers will be more attuned to the financial consequences of their behavior than they otherwise would be.
- d. Every factor that affects a firm's financial performance is ultimately controllable by someone, even if that someone is the person at the top of the firm.

223. An organization employs a system of internal reporting, which furnishes departmental managers with revenue and cost information on only those items that are subject to their control. Items not subject to the manager's control are not included in the performance reports. This method of accounting is known as
- a. Contribution margin reporting.
- b. Segment reporting.
- c. Absorption accounting.
- d. Responsibility accounting.

224. The receipt of raw materials used in the manufacture of products and the shipping of finished goods to customers is under the control of the warehouse supervisor. The warehouse supervisor's time is spent approximately 60% on receiving activities and 40% on shipping activities. Separate staffs for the receiving and shipping operations are employed. The labor-related costs for the warehousing function are as follows:

Warehouse supervisor's salary	$ 40,000
Receiving clerks' wages	75,000
Shipping clerks' wages	55,000
Employee benefit costs (30% of wage & salary costs)	51,000
	$221,000

The company employs a responsibility accounting system for performance reporting purposes. The costs are classified on the report as period or product costs. The total labor-related costs that would be listed on the responsibility accounting performance report as product costs under the control of the warehouse supervisor for the warehousing function would be
- a. $ 97,500
- b. $128,700
- c. $130,000
- d. $221,000

225. Which of the following techniques would be **best** for evaluating the management performance of a department that is operated as a cost center?
- a. Return on assets ratio.
- b. Return on investment ratio.
- c. Payback method.
- d. Variance analysis.

226. A company segment that is accountable for revenues and costs is a(n)
- a. Cost center.
- b. Investment center.
- c. Profit center.
- d. Revenue center.

227. When comparing the residual income of several investment centers, the validity of comparisons may be destroyed by
- a. Peculiarities of each investment center.
- b. Differences in the relative amount of income.
- c. Consistent use of an imputed interest rate.
- d. Common amounts of invested capital for each investment center.

Items 228 through 230 are base on the following:

Segmented statements, prepared in a responsibility accounting reporting format, can be useful in performance evaluation and in operational decision making. An outline of a segmented income statement prepared in responsibility accounting format and segmented by product line is presented below.

	Total company	*Product Line A*	*Product Line B*
Revenue from sales	$ xxx	$ xxx	$ xxx
Variable production costs	xxx	xxx	xxx
Margin I	$ xxx	$ xxx	$ xxx
Variable selling and administrative costs	xxx	xxx	xxx
Margin II	$ xxx	$ xxx	$ xxx
Traceable discretionary fixed costs	xxx	xxx	xxx
Margin III	$ xxx	$ xxx	$ xxx
Traceable committed (infrastructure) fixed costs	xxx	xxx	xxx
Margin IV	$ xxx	$ xxx	$ xxx
Common fixed costs	xxx		
Margin V	$ xxx		

228. In the above segmented income statement, a product line manager, such as the manager of product line A, would be able to exercise control over all of the revenue and/or cost components, which appear above
- a. Margin I.
- b. Margin II.
- c. Margin III.
- d. Margin V.

229. The appropriate margin line to use to decide whether to accept a onetime special order when there is excess plant capacity is
- a. Margin I.
- b. Margin II.
- c. Margin III.
- d. Margin IV.

230. The common fixed costs that appear on this segmented income statement refer to costs that
- a. Are due to the production of finished goods.
- b. Are incurred by each of the individual segments in the conduct of normal business.
- c. Are incurred at one level for the benefit of two or more segments.

d. Can be influenced by a single segment manager over a short-term time period.

231. Residual income is a performance evaluation that is used in conjunction with return on investment (ROI) or instead of ROI. In many cases, residual income is preferred over ROI because

a. Residual income is a measure over time while ROI represents the results for a single time period.
b. Residual income concentrates on maximizing absolute dollars of income rather than a percentage return as with ROI.
c. The imputed interest rate used in calculating residual income is more easily derived than the target rate that is compared to the calculated ROI.
d. Average investment is employed with residual income while year-end investment is employed with ROI.

232. Return on investment (ROI) is a very popular measure employed to evaluate the performance of corporate segments because it incorporates all of the major ingredients of profitability (revenue, cost, investment) into a single measure. Under which one of the following combination of actions regarding a segment's revenues, costs, and investment would a segment's ROI always increase?

	Revenue	*Costs*	*Investment*
a.	Increase	Decrease	Increase
b.	Decrease	Decrease	Decrease
c.	Increase	Increase	Increase
d.	Increase	Decrease	Decrease

233. Making segment disclosures is an advantage to a company because it

a. Facilitates evaluation of company management by providing data on particular segments.
b. Eliminates the interdependence of segments.
c. Masks the effect of intersegment transfers.
d. Provides competitors with comparative information on the company's performance.

234. A firm prepared a segmented income statement that included the following data for its suburban marketing segment:

Fixed costs controllable by the suburban marketing segment manager	150,000
Fixed suburban marketing costs controllable by corporate management	250,000
Fixed manufacturing costs allocated to the suburban marketing segment	110,000
Variable manufacturing costs	200,000
Variable selling costs	100,000
Variable administrative costs	130,000
Net sales	950,000

The best measure of the economic performance of the suburban marketing segment is

a. $370,000
b. $ 10,000
c. $520,000
d. $120,000

Items 235 and 236 are based on the following:

A and B are autonomous divisions of a corporation. They have no beginning or ending inventories, and the number of units produced is equal to the number of units sold. Following is financial information relating to the two divisions.

	Division A	Division B
Sales	$150,000	$400,000
Other revenue	10,000	15,000
Direct materials	30,000	65,000
Direct labor	20,000	40,000
Variable factory overhead	5,000	15,000
Fixed factory overhead	25,000	55,000
Variable selling and administrative expense	15,000	30,000
Fixed selling and administrative expense	35,000	60,000
Central corporate expenses (allocated)	12,000	20,000

235. What is the total contribution to corporate profits generated by Division A before allocation of central corporate expenses?

a. $18,000
b. $20,000
c. $30,000
d. $90,000

236. What is the contribution margin of Division B?

a. $150,000
b. $205,000
c. $235,000
d. $265,000

Items 237 and 238 are based on the following:

The following information was reported by a company for its most recent operating period (in thousands):

	Division A	*Division B*
Revenues	$1,000	$2,000
Variable manufacturing cost of goods sold	400	1,160
Variable selling and administrative costs	200	240
Fixed costs controllable by division manager	220	160
Fixed costs controllable by company headquarters	40	100

237. The total operating income (in thousands) by Division A is

a. $140
b. $180
c. $400
d. $600

238. The contribution margin (in thousands) for Division B is

a. $340
b. $440
c. $600
d. $840

239. A company plans to implement a bonus plan based on segment performance. In addition, the company plans to convert to a responsibility accounting system for segment reporting. The following costs, which have been included in the segment performance reports that have been prepared under the current system, are being reviewed to determine if they should be included in the responsibility accounting segment reports.

I. Corporate administrative costs allocated on the basis of net segment sales
II. Personnel costs assigned on the basis of the number of employees in each segment
III. Fixed computer facility costs divided equally among each segment
IV. Variable computer operational costs charged to each segment based on actual hours used times a predetermined standard rate; any variable cost efficiency or inefficiency remains in the computer department

Of these four cost items, the only item which could logically be included in the segment performance reports prepared on a responsibility accounting basis would be the

a. Corporate administrative costs.
b. Personnel costs.
c. Fixed computer facility costs.
d. Variable computer operational costs.

MULTIPLE-CHOICE ANSWERS AND EXPLANATIONS

1. a __ __	50. a __ __	99. b __ __	148. b __ __	197. c __ __
2. a __ __	51. c __ __	100. d __ __	149. b __ __	198. d __ __
3. b __ __	52. c __ __	101. c __ __	150. b __ __	199. a __ __
4. b __ __	53. a __ __	102. b __ __	151. b __ __	200. a __ __
5. d __ __	54. b __ __	103. d __ __	152. c __ __	201. a __ __
6. a __ __	55. c __ __	104. c __ __	153. d __ __	202. a __ __
7. a __ __	56. c __ __	105. a __ __	154. c __ __	203. a __ __
8. c __ __	57. b __ __	106. d __ __	155. b __ __	204. d __ __
9. b __ __	58. a __ __	107. c __ __	156. b __ __	205. d __ __
10. b __ __	59. c __ __	108. c __ __	157. d __ __	206. a __ __
11. a __ __	60. c __ __	109. d __ __	158. c __ __	207. a __ __
12. a __ __	61. b __ __	110. d __ __	159. c __ __	208. d __ __
13. d __ __	62. a __ __	111. a __ __	160. b __ __	209. c __ __
14. b __ __	63. c __ __	112. d __ __	161. c __ __	210. d __ __
15. d __ __	64. c __ __	113. c __ __	162. b __ __	211. c __ __
16. b __ __	65. b __ __	114. b __ __	163. d __ __	212. a __ __
17. d __ __	66. b __ __	115. b __ __	164. b __ __	213. c __ __
18. c __ __	67. c __ __	116. a __ __	165. d __ __	214. b __ __
19. c __ __	68. a __ __	117. b __ __	166. c __ __	215. d __ __
20. a __ __	69. c __ __	118. c __ __	167. d __ __	216. d __ __
21. b __ __	70. a __ __	119. a __ __	168. a __ __	217. b __ __
22. a __ __	71. d __ __	120. a __ __	169. b __ __	218. b __ __
23. b __ __	72. c __ __	121. b __ __	170. d __ __	219. d __ __
24. c __ __	73. a __ __	122. d __ __	171. c __ __	220. c __ __
25. c __ __	74. d __ __	123. b __ __	172. d __ __	221. b __ __
26. b __ __	75. d __ __	124. a __ __	173. a __ __	222. d __ __
27. a __ __	76. a __ __	125. b __ __	174. c __ __	223. d __ __
28. a __ __	77. d __ __	126. b __ __	175. d __ __	224. a __ __
29. d __ __	78. a __ __	127. c __ __	176. c __ __	225. d __ __
30. d __ __	79. a __ __	128. b __ __	177. c __ __	226. c __ __
31. b __ __	80. b __ __	129. b __ __	178. b __ __	227. a __ __
32. d __ __	81. d __ __	130. b __ __	179. d __ __	228. c __ __
33. a __ __	82. a __ __	131. b __ __	180. d __ __	229. b __ __
34. b __ __	83. b __ __	132. d __ __	181. c __ __	230. c __ __
35. d __ __	84. a __ __	133. c __ __	182. a __ __	231. b __ __
36. a __ __	85. a __ __	134. e __ __	183. a __ __	232. d __ __
37. d __ __	86. a __ __	135. f __ __	184. c __ __	233. a __ __
38. a __ __	87. b __ __	136. d __ __	185. d __ __	234. d __ __
39. a __ __	88. c __ __	137. j __ __	186. a __ __	235. c __ __
40. b __ __	89. c __ __	138. k __ __	187. c __ __	236. d __ __
41. a __ __	90. a __ __	139. l __ __	188. d __ __	237. a __ __
42. b __ __	91. a __ __	140. d __ __	189. b __ __	238. c __ __
43. c __ __	92. a __ __	141. d __ __	190. b __ __	239. d __ __
44. a __ __	93. c __ __	142. d __ __	191. c __ __	
45. d __ __	94. b __ __	143. b __ __	192. a __ __	
46. d __ __	95. a __ __	144. b __ __	193. b __ __	
47. c __ __	96. d __ __	145. b __ __	194. b __ __	
48. c __ __	97. b __ __	146. c __ __	195. d __ __	1st: __/239 = __%
49. a __ __	98. d __ __	147. c __ __	196. b __ __	2nd: __/239 = __%

Cost Concepts

1. **(a)** Cost X is a mixed cost (part variable and part fixed). We use the high-low method to determine the fixed portion and the variable portion, calculate the total cost at the 8,000-unit level, and then calculate the average cost at 8,000 units.

(178,260 – 23,700)/(35,000 – 3,000) = 4.83 per unit

Total cost = (Variable cost per unit)(Number of units) + Fixed cost
178,260 = (4.83)(35,000) + FC
FC = 9,210
TC = (4.83)(8,000) + 9,210
TC = 47,850

Average cost = TC/Number of units
AC = 47,850/8,000 = $5.98

Choice (b) is incorrect. $5.85 = 52,680/9,000. Choice (c) is incorrect. $7.90 = 23,700/3,000. Choice (d) is incorrect. $4.83 is only the variable cost per unit (exclude the fixed cost portion of the mixed cost).

Subject Area: Managerial accounting—cost concepts. Source: CIA 594, III-99.

2. **(a)** The cost of small tools used in mounting tires cannot be identified solely with the manufacture of a specific automobile; rather, this cost is overhead as it is identifiable to

the production process. Choice (b) is incorrect because tire costs are readily and directly identifiable with each automobile, and thus are direct material cost. Choice (c) is incorrect because the cost of the laborers who place tires on each automobile are readily and directly identifiable with each automobile, and thus are direct labor cost. Choice (d) is incorrect because delivery costs are readily and directly identifiable with the tires delivered, and thus are direct material cost.
Subject Area: Managerial accounting—cost concepts. Source: CIA 1193, IV-1.

3. **(b)** Conversion costs are all manufacturing costs other than direct materials. Choice (a) is incorrect because this is neither a common term nor a common classification of manufacturing costs. Choice (c) is incorrect because this is the definition of prime costs. Choice (d) is incorrect because this is neither a common term nor a common classification of manufacturing costs.
Subject Area: Managerial accounting—cost concepts. Source: CIA 1193, IV-2.

4. **(b)** The factory overhead control account should have the following costs:

Indirect materials	$5,000
Indirect labor ($45,000 – $40,000)	5,000
Other factory overhead	20,000
Total overhead	$30,000

Choice (a) is incorrect. The $25,000 amount includes only two of the three factory overhead costs.
Choice (c) is incorrect. The $45,000 amount includes additional costs, which are not classified as factory overhead costs. Choice (d) is incorrect. The $50,000 amount also includes additional costs, which are not classified as factory overhead costs.
Subject Area: Managerial accounting—cost concepts. Source: CIA 1193, IV-4.

5. **(d)** This treatment is appropriate because the overtime premium cost is a cost that should be borne by all production. Choice (a) is incorrect. This treatment is inappropriate because only the overtime premium times the overtime hours is charged to overhead. The straight-time wages times the overtime hours should still be treated as direct labor. Choice (b) is incorrect. This treatment is inappropriate because only the straight-time wages times the overtime hours should still be treated as direct labor. The overtime premium times the overtime hours is charged to overhead. Choice (c) is incorrect. While the second part of this response is correct, the first part is inappropriate. There is no way that the overtime hours times the premium can be charged to repair and maintenance expense because this cost is not related to any repairs. This work is production work—not repairs.
Subject Area: Managerial accounting—cost concepts. Source: CIA 1193, IV-5.

6. **(a)** The book value of the old press is a past (sunk) cost, which has no relevance to the replacement decision. Choice (b) is incorrect because the trade-in value of the old press affects the out-of-pocket cost of the new printing press. Choice (c) is incorrect because the estimated reduction in operating costs is a differential cost between keeping the old press and buying the new press. Choice (d) is incorrect because the interest on the current debt is an opportunity cost of buying the new printing press.
Subject Area: Managerial accounting—cost concepts. Source: CIA 1193, IV-15.

7. **(a)** The materials cost increases in direct proportion to increases in production. Choices (b) and (c) are incorrect because material is a variable cost. Choice (d) is incorrect because materials costs are not the result of a past irrevocable decision.
Subject Area: Managerial accounting—cost concepts. Source: CIA 1192, IV-1.

8. **(c)** The electricity cost increases as production increases, but not in direct proportion to the increases in production. Thus, there is apparently some element of fixed cost included in the total for electricity cost. Choice (a) is incorrect because the cost is not variable because there would still be $10,000 of cost even with zero production. Choice (b) is incorrect because the cost is not fixed because it increases as production increases. Choice (d) is incorrect because the cost for electricity is not the result of a past irrevocable decision.
Subject Area: Managerial accounting—cost concepts. Source: CIA 1192, IV-2.

9. **(b)** The fixed cost per unit decreases as volume increases. Choice (a) is incorrect because the variable cost per unit does not change as volume increases. Choice (c) is incorrect because the step-function cost is not an element of product cost, but rather is a function whereby the cost of input is constant over small ranges of output, but the costs increase in discrete amounts (steps) as production increases. Choice (d) is incorrect because mixed cost is not itself an element of product cost, but rather is a function containing both variable and fixed elements.
Subject Area: Managerial accounting—cost concepts. Source: CIA 591, IV-15.

10. **(b)** Controllable costs are those that are primarily subject to the influence of a given manager of a given responsibility center for a given time span. Choice (a) is incorrect because discretionary, not controllable, costs arise from periodic appropriation decisions and have no well-specified function relating inputs to outputs. Choice (c) is incorrect because committed costs, not controllable costs, arise from having property, plant, and equipment, and a functioning organization. Choice (d) is incorrect because engineered, not controllable costs, result specifically from a clear-cut measured relationship between inputs and outputs.
Subject Area: Managerial accounting—cost concepts. Source: CIA 591, IV-21.

11. **(a)**

$$\text{Learning rate} = \frac{\text{Average time to perform 2X tasks}}{\text{Average time to perform X tasks}}$$

$$= \frac{\text{Average time to perform 2 tasks}}{\text{Average time to perform 1 task}} \text{ or } \frac{\text{Avg. time to perform 4 tasks}}{\text{Avg. time to perform 2 tasks}}$$

$$= \frac{9}{10} \text{ 1 or } \left(\frac{8.1}{9}\right) \text{ 2}$$

$$= 0.9$$

$$= \frac{\text{Average time to perform 8 tasks}}{\text{Average time to perform 4 tasks}}$$

$$0.9 = \frac{\text{Average time to perform 8 tasks}}{8.1}$$

Average time to perform 8 tasks = 0.9 × 8.1 = 7.29 minutes. Therefore, by definition, choices (b), (c), and (d) would be incorrect.

Subject Area: Managerial accounting—cost concepts. Source: CIA 1193, III-69.

12. (a)

$$\text{Learning rate} = \frac{\text{Average time to produce 2X units}}{\text{Average time to produce X units}}$$

Average time to produce 4 units = 320 minutes
Average time to produce 2 units = 400 minutes
Average time to produce 1 unit = 500 minutes

$$\text{Therefore, learning rate} = \frac{320}{400} = \frac{400}{500} = 0.8$$

Therefore, average time to produce 8 units = 0.8 × 320 = 256 minutes.

Therefore, total time to produce 8 units = 8 × 256 = 2,048 minutes. By definition, choices (b), (c), and (d) will be incorrect.

Subject Area: Managerial accounting—cost concepts. Source: CIA 592, III-67.

13. (d) This response incorporates the appropriate fixed cost amount and variable cost amount for the one-day program. See supporting calculations below. Choice (a) is incorrect. This response represents the average cost for the maximum number of participants (100) attending the program {[$2400 + (55 × 100)]/100}. See supporting calculations below. Choice (b) is incorrect. This response represents the average cost for the average number of participants (80) that have attended similar programs in the past {[$2400 + (55 × 80)]/80}. See supporting calculations below. Choice (c) is incorrect. This response omits the promotional advertising ($1,250), the 20% down payment to the instructor ($750 × .2 = $150), and the nonrefundable room rental and set-up fee ($200) from the fixed cost calculations [$2400 – ($1250 + 150 + 200)]. The variable cost figure is correct. See supporting calculations below.

Supporting calculations

Fixed costs:	
Promotional advertising	$1,250
Instructor's fee	750
Room rental and set-up fee	400
Total fixed costs	$2,400
Variable costs per participant:	
Continental breakfast	$10
Lunch	25
Refreshment breaks	8
Instructional materials	12
Total variable costs	$55

Subject Area: Managerial accounting—cost concepts. Source: CIA 597, III-92.

14. (b) This response appropriately omits the costs which have already been incurred—promotional advertising ($1,250), the 20% down payment to the instructor ($750 × .2 = $150), and the nonrefundable room rental and set-up fee ($200)—from the fixed cost calculations [$2400 – ($1250 + 150 + 200) = 800] because they are sunk costs. The variable cost figure is still relevant and, thus, is unchanged. See supporting calculations below. Choice (a) is incorrect. This response represents the average costs for the 25 persons already registered if sunk costs are used in place of additional fixed costs {[$1600 + ($55 × 25)]/25 = $119}. See supporting calculations below. Choice (c) is incorrect. This response includes only the incurred (sunk) costs—promotional advertising ($1,250), the 20% down payment to the instructor ($750 × .2 = $150), and the nonrefundable room rental and set-up fee ($200)—as the fixed costs ($1250 + 150 + 200 = 1600). The variable cost figure is still relevant and, thus, is unchanged. See supporting calculations below. Choice (d) is incorrect. This response represents the original cost function, which is not correct because it includes the costs, which have already been incurred and are now sunk costs. The variable cost figure is still relevant and, thus, is unchanged. See supporting calculations below.

Supporting calculations

	Total	*Sunk*	*Additional*
Fixed costs:			
Promotional advertising	$1,250	$1,250	$ -0-
Instructor's fee	750	150	600
Room rental and set-up fee	400	200	200
Total fixed costs	$2,400	$1,600	$800
Variable costs per participant:			
Continental breakfast	$10	$ -0-	$10
Lunch	25	-0-	25
Refreshment breaks	8	-0-	8
Instructional materials	12	-0-	12
Total variable costs	$55	$ -0-	$55

Subject Area: Managerial accounting—cost concepts. Source: CIA 597, III-93.

15. (d) There is no systematic relationship between standard dollars shipped and the percent of scrap. Choice (a) is incorrect because a variable cost would remain a constant percentage of standard dollars shipped. Choice (b) is incorrect because a fixed cost would be a lower percentage when standard dollars shipped were high than when they were low. Choice (c) is incorrect because a semifixed cost, as a percentage would move up and down with standard dollars shipped with a base level higher than 0%.

Subject Area: Managerial accounting—cost concepts. Source: CIA 596, III-94.

16. (b) This solution employs the high-low method based on units sold to determine the variable cost rate and the y-intercept (fixed cost component) for shipping costs (see supporting calculations on the next page). Note that the shipping costs for the two months not employed in the calculations (April and June) will prove out using these amounts.

Choice (a) is incorrect. This alternative calculates the total shipping costs for the four months ($414,000) and divides the total by the total of the units shipped for the same four months (250,000) to get an average cost of $1.656 per unit sold. This average cost is neither a variable cost nor an appropriate description of the shipping costs.

Choice (c) is incorrect. This solution employs the high-low method based on orders to determine the variable cost rate and the y-intercept (fixed cost component) for shipping costs (see supporting calculations on the next page). However, while the high and low independent variable is employed in the calculations, paired points for shipping costs are not used (the low shipping cost of $93,000 is used in the calculation rather than $100,000, the shipping cost for the April when 1,800 units were shipped). Note that the shipping costs for three months (March, April, and June) will not prove out using these amounts. Choice (d) is incorrect. This solution employs the high-low method based on orders to determine the variable cost rate and the y-intercept (fixed cost component) for shipping costs (see supporting calculations on the next page). Note that the shipping costs for the two months not employed in the calculations (March and June) will not prove out using these amounts.

Supporting calculations

Variable cost component b = $\frac{\text{Change in cost (dependent variable)}}{\text{Change in volume (independent variable)}}$

Fixed cost component (y-intercept):

(Total cost at either the high or low volume) – (Variable cost at volume level) = Fixed cost

	Alternative b	*Alternative c*	*Alternative d*
Change in cost	114,000 – 93,000	114,000 – 93,000	114,000 – 100,000
Change in volume	70,000 – 55,000	2,400 – 1,800	2,400 – 1,800
VC component (b)	1.4	35.00	23.3333
Total costs at high	114,000	114,000	114,000
Variable cost at high			
70,000 × 1.40	98,000		
2400 × 35		84,000	
2400 × 23.333			56,000
Fixed cost component	16,000	30,000	58,000

Shipping cost calculations using calculated variables:

March			
(1.40 × 55,000) + 16,000 =	93,000		
(35 × 2,000) + 30,000 =		100,000	
(23.3333 × 2,000) + 58,000 =			104,667
April			
(1.40 × 60,000) + 16,000 =	100,000		
(35 × 1,800) + 30,000 =		93,000	
(23.3333 × 1,800) + 58,000 =			100,000
May			
(1.40 × 70,000) + 16,000 =	114,000		
(35 × 2,400) + 30,000 =		114,000	
(23.3333 × 2,400) + 58,000 =			114,000
June			
(1.40 × 65,000) + 16,000 =	107,000		
(35 × 2,300) + 30,000 =		110,500	
(23.3333 × 2,300) + 58,000 =			111,667

Subject Area: Managerial accounting—cost concepts. Source: CIA 1196, III-82.

17. (d) The classification of the costs is appropriate in this alternative. The advertising is the same for three of the four months and would be considered a fixed cost in terms of dollar sales (the April amount of $200,000 would be considered a discretionary increase). Sales salaries appear to vary by $1,000 per salesperson, but in terms of dollar sales, this would be considered a fixed cost. Choice (a) is incorrect. The only correct classification in this alternative is fixed cost for sales salaries; sales salaries appear to vary by $1,000 per salesperson, but in terms of dollar sales, this would be considered a fixed cost. The advertising is the same for three of the four months and would be considered a fixed cost in terms of dollar sales (the April amount of $200,000 would be considered a discretionary increase).

Choice (b) is incorrect. The only correct classification in this alternative is fixed cost for advertising which is the same for three of the four months; it would be considered a fixed cost in terms of dollar sales (the April amount of $200,000 would be considered a discretionary increase). Sales salaries appear to vary by $1,000 per salesperson, but in terms of dollar sales, this would be considered a fixed cost—not a variable cost. Choice (c) is incorrect. The advertising is the same for three of the four months and would be considered a fixed cost in terms of dollar sales and not a mixed cost (the April amount of $200,000 would be considered a discretionary increase). Sales salaries appear to vary by $1,000 per salesperson, but in terms of dollar sales, this would be considered a fixed cost—not a mixed cost.

Subject Area: Managerial accounting—cost concepts. Source: CIA 1196, III-83.

18. (c) Output units that are discarded as defective are classified either as abnormal spoilage (defective units were not expected as part of the normal operating conditions) or normal spoilage (an inherent result of the normal production process). Choice (a) is incorrect because waste is input material that either lost in the production process or has no sales value. Choice (b) is incorrect because scrap is input material that has a relatively minor sales value at the end of the production process. Choice (d) is incorrect because rework costs are costs incurred to make unacceptable units appropriate for sale or use. They may be normal or abnormal.

Subject Area: Managerial accounting—cost concepts. Source: CIA 1194, III-46.

19. (c) This solution is correct because both parts of the solution are stated correctly. Within the relevant range for the application activity base, the total variable costs in the flexible budget formula should increase while the total fixed cost would be constant. A *variable cost* is a cost that changes in total indirect proportion to changes in activity level within the relevant range. The cost per unit for a *variable cost* is constant per activity level unit. Thus, if the activity volume increases (decreases) within the relevant range, then total variable costs would increase (decrease). A *fixed cost* is a cost that does not change in total despite volume changes in the activity level within the relevant range. If the activity volume increases or decreases within the relevant range, then total fixed costs would remain unchanged. If fixed cost per activity unit (i.e., total fixed cost divided by activity volume) were calculated, then the fixed cost per unit would increase (decrease) as the activity volume decreased (increased). Choice (a) is incorrect. This solution is incorrect because the second part of the solution is stated incorrectly. The fixed cost per unit of activity would decrease (cost is spread over more units), but total fixed cost in the flexible budget would be constant within the relevant range for the application activity base. The first part of the solution (variable cost per unit is constant) is correctly stated resulting in the total variable cost increasing with an increase in volume. Choice (b) is incorrect. This solution is incorrect because the second part of the solution is stated incorrectly. The fixed cost per unit of activity would decrease (cost is spread over more units), but total fixed cost in the flexible budget would be constant within the relevant range for the application activity base. The first part of the solution (variable cost per unit is constant) is correctly stated resulting in the total variable cost increasing with an increase in volume. Choice (d) is incorrect. This solution is incorrect because the first part of the solution is stated incorrectly. The variable cost per unit does not increase (it is constant); rather, total variable cost would increase. The second part (the total fixed cost remains constant) of the solution is correctly stated because the total fixed cost in the flexible budget would be constant within the relevant range for the application activity base.

Subject Area: Managerial accounting—cost concepts. Source: CIA 1194, III-50.

20. (a) All manufacturing costs other than direct labor and direct material costs are classified as overhead cost. Choice (b) is incorrect because direct labor cost is the cost of labor that can be directly identified with the production of the finished product. The production engineer's salary cannot be directly identified with the production of the finished product. Choice (c) is incorrect because a variable cost is a cost that changes in total in direct proportion to changes in activity. The production engineer's salary does not vary in direct proportion with changes in activity. Choice (d) is incorrect because an engineered cost is a cost that has an explicit, specified relationship with a selected measure of activity. The production engineer's salary does not fit this definition.

Subject Area: Managerial accounting—cost concepts. Source: CIA 590, IV-1.

21. (b) This is the definition of spoilage. Choice (a) is incorrect because defective units are defined as production that does not meet dimensional or quality standards and that is subsequently reworked and sold through regular channels as first or seconds. Choice (c) is incorrect because waste is material that is lost, evaporates or shrinks in a manufacturing process, or is residue that has no measurable recovery value. Choice (d) is incorrect because scrap is material residue from a manufacturing process that has measurable but relatively minor recovery value.

Subject Area: Managerial accounting—cost concepts. Source: CIA 590, IV-5.

22. (a) The cost was a uniform $8 per patient during each month. Choice (b) is incorrect because the cost varied with activity. Choice (c) is incorrect because there was no fixed element to the cost; it was always $8 per average patient. Choice (d) is incorrect because there was no fixed element to the cost.

Subject Area: Managerial accounting—cost concepts. Source: CIA 590, IV-9.

23. (b) Property taxes on a factory are a product cost. Choice (a) is incorrect because insurance on the corporate headquarters building is not a cost of production and is therefore a period cost. Choice (c) is incorrect because depreciation on salespersons' automobiles is not a cost of production and is therefore a period cost. Choice (d) is incorrect because the salary of sales manager is not a cost of production and is therefore a period costs.

Subject Area: Managerial accounting—cost concepts. Source: CIA 1190, IV-1.

24. (c) The old machine's book value of $75,000 is an outlay made in the past, which cannot be changed. Choice (a) is incorrect. The salvage value does not dictate sunk costs. Choice (b) is incorrect. The $17,000 is a future cost, which can be avoided. Choice (d) is incorrect. The $190,000 is a future cost which can be avoided.

Subject Area: Managerial accounting—cost concepts. Source: CIA 1190, IV-2.

25. (c) Wood is a raw material (a direct cost) of furniture. Choice (a) is incorrect because machine repairs are usually an overhead (indirect) cost. Choice (b) is incorrect because electricity is usually an overhead (indirect) cost. Choice (d) is incorrect because sales commissions are period costs. They are neither direct nor indirect costs with regard to products.

Subject Area: Managerial accounting—cost concepts. Source: CIA 1190, IV-5.

26. (b) Overtime premiums are usually considered a part of overhead. Choice (a) is incorrect because abnormal spoilage is not charged to overhead, but rather is expensed. Choice (c) is incorrect because prime costs include direct labor and direct materials, which are not part of overhead. Choice (d) is incorrect because material price variances are charged or credited, as appropriate, to a material price variance account, not to overhead.

Subject Area: Managerial accounting—cost concepts. Source: CIA 1190, IV-6.

27. (a) Scrap is material residue from a manufacturing process that has measurable but relatively minor recovery value. Choice (b) is incorrect because spoilage is unacceptable units of production that are discarded or sold for disposal value. Choice (c) is incorrect because defective units are defined as production that does not meet dimensional or quality standards and that is subsequently reworked and sold through regular channels as firsts or seconds. Choice (d) is incorrect because waste is material that is lost, evaporates, or shrinks in a manufacturing process, or is residue that has no measurable recovery value.

Subject Area: Managerial accounting—cost concepts. Source: CIA Model Exam 2002, IV-54.

28. (a) Any amount received above the storage and delivery costs for a by-product allows the seller to reduce the main product's price to make it more competitive. Choice (b) is incorrect. Optional products are those offered for sale along with the main product. They are unlikely to have a zero production cost so the seller must receive a price above the storage and delivery costs for such products. Choice (c) is incorrect. Captive products are those that must be used along with the main product, such as film for use with a camera. Sellers often make their money on the captive products rather than on the main product, which is sold at a low price. The captive products therefore will be priced well above the storage and delivery costs. Choice (d) is incorrect. Product bundles are combinations of products sold together at a reduced price, such as season tickets for a theater. Products are bundled in order to promote the sale of certain items that consumers might not otherwise purchase. The combined price of the bundle must be low enough to encourage consumers to buy the bundle, but must recover production costs and provide some profit for the seller, so the price must exceed storage and delivery costs.

Subject Area: Managerial accounting—cost concepts. Source: CIA Model Exam 2002, IV-63.

29. (d) Manufacturing overhead costs are indirect product costs because they are necessary for production and cannot be directly traced to a specific unit produced. Choice (a) is incorrect because manufacturing overhead costs are neither direct nor period costs. Choice (b) is incorrect because manufacturing overhead costs are product costs, not period costs. Choice (c) is incorrect because manufacturing overhead costs are indirect costs, not direct costs.

Subject Area: Managerial accounting—cost concepts. Source: CIA Model Exam 2002, IV-67.

30. (d) Abnormal spoilage is not expected under efficient operating conditions. It is not an inherent part of the production process. Choice (a) is incorrect because abnormal spoilage is not a function of the costing system; it is a function of the production process. Choice (b) is incorrect because abnormal spoilage may result from any of a variety of conditions or circumstances, which are generally controllable by first-line supervisors. Choice (c) is incorrect because abnormal spoilage may result from any of a variety of conditions or circumstances, which are not necessarily related to standards.

Subject Area: Managerial accounting—cost concepts. Source: CIA Model Exam 1998, IV-54.

31. **(b)** If the lost units have minimal value and can be sold as is without any rework, then they are classified as scrap. Scrap can be sold, disposed of, or reused. Choice (c) is incorrect because reworked units are defective units which require further processing to make them acceptable units that can be sold as seconds or first rate good units. Choice (a) is incorrect. In order to be classified as abnormal spoilage, the amount of spoilage has to exceed the normal limit. Choice (d) is incorrect because waste is considered any type of residue, evaporation, or shrinkage. Waste has no monetary value and may actually have a disposal cost to have it removed.

Subject Area: Managerial accounting—cost concepts. Source: CIA 1196, III-86.

32. **(d)** This is the correct reason for treating a product generated from a joint process as a by-product. Choice (a) is incorrect. A by-product may be developed into a main product. Some manufacturers choose not to develop a by-product into a main product due to the lack of facilities, cost, lack of fit with other main products, etc. However, this does not preclude others from taking the by-product and developing it into a salable finished product (e.g., sawdust and wood chips manufactured into particleboard). Choice (b) is incorrect. This alternative is incorrect because it describes scrap, whereas a by-product provides sales value to the manufacturer. Choice (c) is incorrect because the physical volume of the by-product may be significant.

Subject Area: Managerial accounting—cost concepts. Source: CIA 1196, III-87.

Capital Budgeting

33. **(a)** The internal rate of return is the cost of capital percentage at which the net present value profile crosses the horizontal axis. The net present value profile for Project 2 intersects the horizontal axis at a higher cost of capital percentage than does the net present value profile for Project 1. Choice (b) is incorrect. The net present value profile for Project 1 intersects the horizontal axis at a lower cost of capital percentage than does the net present value profile for project 2. Choices (c) and (d) are incorrect. The net present value profiles of projects 1 and 2 intersect. Neither project will have a higher net present value than the other at all cost of capital percentages. To the left of the intersection point, Project 1 has a higher net present value and to the right of the intersection point, Project 2 has a higher net present value.

Subject Area: Managerial accounting—capital budgeting. Source: CIA 594, IV-39.

34. **(b)** At a zero cost of capital, the NPV is simply the sum of a project's undiscounted cash flows.

NPV for A = –$30,000 + $ 40,000 + $ 40,000 = $50,000
NPV for B = –$1,000,000 + $700,000 + $500,000 = $200,000

Choice (a) is incorrect because these amounts are only the initial investment outlays and do not incorporate the cash inflows from the projects. Choice (c) is incorrect because these amounts are the sums of cash inflows without deducting the initial investment outlays. Choice (d) is incorrect because these amounts are calculated by adding the initial outlays to the sum of the cash inflows rather than by subtracting the initial outlays from the sum of the cash inflows.

Subject Area: Managerial accounting—capital budgeting. Source: CIA 594, IV-40.

35. **(d)** The internal rate of return is the discount rate that sets the projects' net present value equal to zero. In the case of project A, the internal rate of return is 100%.

NPV = 0 for project A when
$\$30{,}000 = \$40{,}000/(1 + IRR) + \$40{,}000/(1+IRR)^2$
which occurs at an IRR of 100%

Choice (a) is incorrect because applying a discount rate of 10% to the cash flows of project A results in a net present value of $69,421. Choice (b) is incorrect because applying a discount rate of 15% to the cash flows of project A results in a net present value of $65,028. Choice (c) is incorrect because applying a discount rate of 25% to the cash flows of project A results in a net present value of $57,600.

Subject Area: Managerial accounting—capital budgeting. Source: CIA 594, IV-41.

36. **(a)** NPV assumes that cash inflows from the investment project can be reinvested at the cost of capital while IRR assumes that cash flows from each project can be reinvested at the IRR for that particular project. This underlying assumption is considered to be a weakness of the IRR technique. Choice (b) is incorrect because NPV and IRR make consistent accept/reject decisions for independent projects. When NPV is positive, IRR exceeds the cost of capital and the project is acceptable. Choice (c) is incorrect because it is the NPV method that can be used to rank mutually exclusive projects while IRR cannot be used for this purpose. The reinvestment rate assumption causes IRR to make faulty project rankings under some circumstances. Choice (d) is incorrect because IRR is expressed as a percentage while NPV is expressed in dollar terms.

Subject Area: Managerial accounting—capital budgeting. Source: CIA 594, IV-42.

37. **(d)** All three managers will reject the project. Manager one will calculate a net present value of –$12,894 (see choice (a) above), Manager two will calculate a net present value of –$26,349 (see choice b. above) and Manager three will calculate a net present value of –$41,640.

NPV = –$100,000 + $135,000[PVIF (6 years, 15%)]
= –$100,000 + $135,000 (0. 4323)
= –$41,636

Choice (a) is incorrect. Manager one will calculate the net present value to be minus $12,894 and will recommend that the project be rejected.

–$100,000 + $20,000 [PVIFA (6 years, 10%)]
–$100,000 + $20,000 (4.3553) = –$12,894

Choice (b) is incorrect. Manager two will calculate the net present value to be minus $26,350 and will recommend that the project be rejected.

NPV = –$100,000
+ $5,000[PVIF(1 year, 14%)]
+ $23,000 [PVIFA(5 years,14%)] [PVIF(1 year, 14%)]
= –$100,000 + $5,000(.8772) + $23,000(3.4331)(0.8772)
= –$26,349

Choice (c) is incorrect. All three managers will calculate a negative net present value for the project. None will recommend acceptance.

Subject Area: Managerial accounting—capital budgeting. Source: CIA 594, IV-45.

38. **(a)** Manager one will calculate a five-year payback period. Payback period is the number of periods it takes before the cash flows from the project repay the original investment outlay. Manager one expects inflows of $20,000 per year so it will take exactly five years for the project to repay the original $100,000 invested.

Choice (b) is incorrect. Manager two will calculate a payback period of more than five years. Only $5,000 is expected at the end of year one, followed by inflows of $23,000 at the end of each year in years two through six. At the end of year five only $97,000 will have been received, based on these expectations. Choice (c) is incorrect. Manager three will calculate a payback period of six years. She estimates one inflow of $135,000 at the end of year six. Choice (d) is incorrect. All three managers will derive a different payback period for the project.

Subject Area: Managerial accounting—capital budgeting. Source: CIA 594, IV-46.

39. **(a)** This is the traditional payback period.

$250,000/125,000 = 2.0 years.

Choice (b) is incorrect. This is the discounted traditional payback period.

Year	PV of cash savings	Balance
1	125,000 (.909) = 113,625	113,625
2	125,000 (.826) = 103,250	216,875
3	125,000 (.751) = 93,875	310,750

1+1 +33,125/93,875 = 2.35

Choice (c) is incorrect. This is the cash flow payback period.

$$\frac{\$250{,}000}{125{,}000\,(1-.40)+\left[\dfrac{250{,}000-50{,}000}{5}\right](.40)}=250{,}000/91{,}000=2.75 \text{ years}$$

Choice (d) is incorrect. This is the discounted payback period.

Year	PV of cash flow amount	Balance
1	91,000 (.909) = 82,719	82,719
2	91,000 (.826) = 75,166	157,885
3	91,000 (.751) = 68,341	226,226
4	91,000 (.683) = 62,153	288,379

1 + 1 + 1 + 23,774/62,153 = 3.38 years.

Subject Area: Managerial accounting—capital budgeting. Source: CIA 593, IV-22.

40. **(b)** This is the simple rate of return using the average investment.

$$\frac{(\$125{,}000-40{,}000)\,(1-.40)}{\left(\dfrac{250{,}000+50{,}000}{2}\right)}=\frac{51{,}000}{150{,}000}=34.0\%$$

Choice (a) is incorrect. This is the simple rate of return using the original investment.

$$\frac{(125{,}000-40{,}000)\,(1-.40)}{250{,}000}=20.4\%$$

Choice (c) is incorrect. This answer uses an incorrect calculation of depreciation and the average investment.

$$\frac{(125{,}000-50{,}000)\,(1-.40)}{\left(\dfrac{250{,}000-50{,}000}{2}\right)}=45.0\%$$

Choice (d) is incorrect. This answer uses an incorrect calculation of the average investment.

$$\frac{(125{,}000-40{,}000)\,(1-.40)}{\left(\dfrac{250{,}000-50{,}000}{2}\right)}=\frac{51{,}000}{100{,}000}=51.0\%$$

Subject Area: Managerial accounting—capital budgeting. Source: CIA 593, IV-23.

41. **(a)** This answer ignores the salvage value.

Year	Cash flow amount	PV factor	PV of cash flow
0	(250,000)	1.000	(250,000)
1	125,000 (.60) + 40,000 (.40)	.909	82,719
2	125,000 (.60) + 40,000 (.40)	.826	75,166
3	125,000 (.60) + 40,000 (.40)	.751	68,341
4	125,000 (.60) + 40,000 (.40)	.683	62,153
5	125,000 (.60) + 40,000 (.40) + 50,000	.621	87,561
	Net present value		125,940

Therefore, by definition, choice (b), (c), and (d) will be incorrect.

Subject Area: Managerial accounting—capital budgeting. Source: CIA 593, IV-24.

42. **(b)** When a project's IRR is greater than its marginal cost, it increases the value of the firm's stock since a surplus remains after paying for the capital. Choice (a) is incorrect because it only accepts projects whose IRR exceeds the MCC. Choice (c) is incorrect because it should rank IRRs from highest to lowest. Choice (d) is incorrect because it should rank IRRs from highest to lowest and should only accept projects whose IRR exceeds the MCC.

Subject Area: Managerial accounting—capital budgeting. Source: CIA 593, IV-55.

43. **(c)** $90,000,000 represents the future value of the funding payments. The amount of each funding payment can be calculated by dividing the future value of the funding payments by the factor for future value of an ordinary annuity for n = 20, I = 8%.

Choice (a) is incorrect because the $90,000,000 is a future value figure. The factor to be used for the division process should be a future value factor, not a present value factor. Choice (b) is incorrect because the $90,000,000 is a future value figure. The factor to be used should, therefore, be a future value factor. That factor should be used in a division, rather than a multiplication process, in this case. Choice (d) is incorrect because the $90,000,000 should be divided by the appropriate factor.

Subject Area: Managerial accounting—capital budgeting. Source: CIA 1192, IV-39.

44. **(a)** This is the term for deciding on long-term investments such as described. Choice (b) is incorrect because this deals with the quantity of goods to order at a time, which will minimize the total of order and storage costs during the period. Choice (c) is incorrect because this deals with short-term adjustments of a budget to conform to actual production or sales. Choice (d) is incorrect because this deals with any instance in which a range of outcome is possible and is not restricted to long-term investment decisions.

Subject Area: Managerial accounting—capital budgeting. Source: CIA 592, IV-24.

45. **(d)** The interest factor for the future value of a present sum is equal to the reciprocal of the interest factor for the present value of a future sum. Thus, 100,000/ 46,650 = 2.14362 × 100,000 = 214,360. Choice (a) is incorrect because if $46,650 were invested at 10%, it would be worth $100,000 at the end of 8 years. Choice (b) is incorrect because it is the present value of $100,000. Choice (c) is incorrect because the addition of the present and future values is a nonsense answer.

Subject Area: Managerial accounting—capital budgeting. Source: CIA 592, IV-53.

46. **(d)** The NPV method compares the initial outflow of cash to the present value of future cash flows to calculate the NPV. Choice (a) is incorrect because the accounting rate of return equals net income divided by initial investment. Choice (b) is incorrect because the IRR exceeds (not is less than) 15%. Choice (c) is incorrect because the payback method ignores the time value of money.

Subject Area: Managerial accounting—capital budgeting. Source: CIA 591, IV-50.

47. **(c)** The answer is determined as: $180,000/7.4694 = $24,098. Choice (a) is incorrect because this answer uses PVIF × $180,000 rather than $180,000/PVIFA. Choice (b) is incorrect because this answer uses PVIF × $200,000 rather than $180,000/PVIFA. Choice (d) is incorrect because this answer is based on $200,000 rather than $180,000.

Subject Area: Managerial accounting—capital budgeting. Source: CIA 591, IV-51.

48. **(c)** Inflows = cash sales of $400,000, while outflows = expenses other than depreciation of $180,000 plus taxes of $47,600. Thus, relevant cash flows = $400,000 – $227,600 = $172,400. Choice (a) is incorrect because this answer includes a noncash expense as a cash outflow. Choice (b) is incorrect because this answer ignores the tax benefit of depreciation in estimating relevant cash flows. Choice (d) is incorrect because this answer ignores the tax effects on cash flows. Subject Area: Managerial accounting—capital budgeting. Source: CIA 591, IV-52.

49. **(a)** The payback period measures how quickly the initial investment will be recovered. Management could best manage risk by getting its money back quickly. Choices (b), (c), and (d) are incorrect because they tell nothing about risk or the time period when funds will be recovered.

Subject Area: Managerial accounting—capital budgeting. Source: CIA 1191, IV-26.

50. **(a)** The capital expenditures budget must be coordinated with long-term financing needs to assure availability of financing. Choice (b) is incorrect because no approvals are required by federal agencies for investments in production facilities. Choice (c) is incorrect because while ratification of the program may be required, this does not relate to the inherent feasibility of the program per se. Choice (d) is incorrect because long-term capital expenditures relate to long-term financing not the current working capital position.

Subject Area: Managerial accounting—capital budgeting. Source: CIA 591, I-24.

51. **(c)** The December 31, 2000 cash inflow is five years from the present cash outflow, and the net present value method uses the firm's cost of capital of 18%. The present value factor for 18% for 5 years is .4371, and $7,400,000 times .4371 equals $3,234,540, which is $265,460 less than the present cash outflow of $3,500,000. Choice (a) is incorrect because this answer discounts the cash inflow at the correct discount rate (18%), but for four years instead of five. Choice (b) is incorrect because this answer discounts the cash inflow at 15% (the project's internal rate of return) instead of at 18% (the cost of capital), which the net present value method uses. Choice (d) is incorrect because this answer discounts the cash inflow at the correct discount rate (18%), but for four years instead of five, and also subtracts the cash outflow from the cash inflow, instead of vice versa.

Subject Area: Managerial accounting—capital budgeting. Source: CIA 597, IV-40.

52. **(c)** Twenty percent is the rate of return that equates the cash inflows with the cash outflows. The present value of 20% for five years is .4019, which multiplied by $9,950,000 equals $3,998,905. Therefore, the net present value of the project approximates $0 using the 20% rate.

Subject Area: Managerial accounting—capital budgeting. Source: CIA 597, IV-41.

53. **(a)** NPV and IRR criteria will always lead to the same accept or reject decision. Choice (b) is incorrect because if the second project's internal rate of return is higher than the first project's, the organization would accept the second project based on IRR. Choices (c) and (d) are incorrect. See response given for choice (a).

Subject Area: Managerial accounting—capital budgeting. Source: CIA 597, IV-41.

54. **(b)** Project B has the highest profitability index, equal to 2.4 as calculated below. Choice (a) is incorrect because the profitability index of Project A is only .891. The profitability index is the present value of the cash inflows divided by the investment outlay. The calculations for all four projects are as follows:

Project	Profitability index
A	980,000/1,100,000 = .891
B	600,000/250,000 = 2.400
C	1,830,000/1,400,000 = 1.307
D	790,000/650,000 = 1.215

Choices (c) and (d) are incorrect because Projects C and D have profitability indices of 1.307 and 1.215 respectively (see choice a.), which are both lower than the profitability index for Project B.

Subject Area: Managerial accounting—capital budgeting. Source: CIA 1196, IV-40.

55. **(c)** Project C has the highest net present value of the available projects and would be ranked as the best. Choice (a) is incorrect. Mutually exclusive investment projects must be ranked using the net present value technique. The best project is that which provides the greatest present value of cash flows less the present value of the investment outlays. The project with the highest net present value contributes the most to the value of the firm and to the wealth of shareholders. Project A does not have the highest net present value of the available projects:

Project	Net present value
A	980,000 – 1,100,000 = –120,000
B	600,000 – 250,000 = 350,000
C	1,830,000 – 1,400,000 = 430,000
D	790,000 – 650,000 = 140,000

Choice (b) is incorrect. While Project B does have the highest relative profitability, as measured using the profitability index in question 54 above, it does not have the highest absolute profitability as measured using net present value. When ranking mutually exclusive projects, net present value must be used. An exception is if there is a capital rationing constraint, but no such constraint exists in this case since the company has sufficient financing available for any of the four projects. Choice (d) is incorrect. Project D does not have the highest net present value of the available projects. It would not be undertaken.

Subject Area: Managerial accounting—capital budgeting. Source: CIA 1196, IV-41.

56. **(c)** $137,350(.6830) = $93,810.05 (present value of a future payment). Therefore, by definition, choices (a), (b), and (d) will be incorrect.

Subject Area: Managerial accounting—capital budgeting. Source: CIA 1190, III-44.

57. **(b)** The internal rate of return is the discount rate that sets the net present value of the project to zero, so the present value of the costs equals the present value of the cash inflows. The cost of Project A can be calculated as follows:

Present value (costs) = Present value (inflows)
Cost = $10,000 [PVIFA (15%, 3)] = $10,000 (2.2832) = $22,832

Choice (a) is incorrect. This solution uses the present value interest factor for 15%, three periods rather than the present value interest factor for an annuity.

Present value (costs) = Present value (inflows)
Cost = 10,000 [PVIF (15%, 3)] = 10,000 (.8696) = $8,696

Choice (c) is incorrect. This solution is obtained using a 10% discount rate, rather than 15%.

Present value (costs) = Present value (inflows)
Cost = $10,000 [PVIFA (10%, 3)] = $10,000 (2.4869) = $24,869

Choice (d) is incorrect. This solution is obtained using a 5% discount rate, rather than 15%.

Present value (costs) = Present value (inflows)
Cost = $10,000 [PVIFA (5%, 3)] = $10,000 (2.7232) = $27,232

Subject Area: Managerial accounting—capital budgeting. Source: CIA 1195, IV-38.

58. (a) The net present value is the present value of the cash inflows less the cost of the project.

= $5,000 [PVIF (1,10%)] + $10,000 [PVIF (2,10%)] + $15,000 [PVIF (3, 10%)] – $20,000

= $5,000 [.9091] + $10,000 [.8264] + $15,000 [.7513] – $20,000

= 4,545.5 + 8264 + 11,269.5 – 20,000 = $4,079

Choice (b) is incorrect. This solution is obtained using a 5%, rather than a 10%, discount rate.

= $5,000 [PVIF (1,5%)] + $10,000 [PVIF (2,5%)] + $15,000 [PVIF (3, 5%)] – $20,000

= $5,000 [.9524] + $10,000 [.9070] + $15,000 [.8638] – $20,000

= 4762+ 9070 + 12,957 – 20,000 = $6,789

Choice (c) is incorrect. This is the net present value of Project A at a 10% discount rate.

= $10,000 [PVIFA (10%, 3)] – $15,000 = $10,000 (2.4869) – $15,000 = $9,869

Choice (d) is incorrect. This solution is obtained using the present value interest factor for annuities (PVIFA) rather than the present value interest factors (PVIF):

= $5,000 [PVIFA (1,10%)] + $10,000 [PVIFA (2,10%)] + $15,000 [PVIFA (3, 10%)] – $20,000

= $5,000 [.9091] + $10,000 [1.7355] + $15,000 [2.4869] – $20,000

= 4,545.5 + 17,355 + 37,303.5 – 20,000 = $39,204

Subject Area: Managerial accounting—capital budgeting. Source: CIA 1195, IV-39.

59. **(c)** After two years, the cumulative cash inflows for project C are exactly equal to the initial investment outlay.

Investment cost = Year 1 cash inflow + Year 2 cash inflow
$25,000 = $15,000 + $10,000

Choice (a) is incorrect. The payback period would be zero only if a project had no cost or provided immediate cash inflows in excess of the investment outlay. Project C does not provide an immediate payback of its investment cost. Choice (b) is incorrect. After one year, the cumulative cash inflows for Project C are only $15,000 versus an initial investment outlay of $25,000. The project has not yet recovered its cost. Choice (d) is incorrect. Project C pays back its initial investment outlay in only two years (see choice c.)

Subject Area: Managerial accounting—capital budgeting. Source: CIA 1195, IV-40.

60. **(c)** The discounted payback period is the length of time required for discounted cash flows to recover the cost of the investment. The year two cash inflow for Project D, which is consistent with a discounted payback period of two years, can be calculated as follows:

Investment cost = Present value of year 1 and 2 cash inflows

$30,000 = $20,000 [PVIF (5%, 1)] + year 2 cash inflow [PVIF (5%, 2)]

$30,000 = $20,000 (.9524) + year 2 cash inflow (.9070)

Year 2 cash inflow = [$30,000 – $20,000 (.9524)]/.9070 = $12,074.97

Choice (a) is incorrect. This solution is obtained using present value interest factors for annuities (PVIFA) rather than present value interest factors (PVIF). See choice (c) for the correct solution.

Investment cost = Present value of year 1 and 2 cash inflows

$30,000 = $20,000 [PVIFA (5%, 1)] + year 2 cash inflow [PVIFA (5%, 2)]

$30,000 = $20,000 (.9524) + year 2 cash inflow (1.8594)

Year 2 cash inflow = [$30,000 – $20,000 (.9524)]/1.8594 = $5,890.07

Choice (b) is incorrect. This solution is based on the regular payback period. Since the cash inflow in year one is $20,000, Project D pays back its $30,000 cost in two years if the cash inflow in year two is $10,000. Choice (d) is incorrect. This solution is obtained using a 10%, rather than a 5%, discount rate.

Investment cost = Present value of year 1 and 2 cash inflows

$30,000 = $20,000 [PVIF (10%, 1)] + year 2 cash inflow [PVIF (10%, 2)]

$30,000 = $20,000 (.9091) + year 2 cash inflow (.8264)

Year 2 cash inflow = [$30,000 – $20,000 (.9091)] / .8264 = $14,300.58

Subject Area: Managerial accounting—capital budgeting. Source: CIA 1195, IV-41.

61. **(b)** Choice (b) is the correct answer. Cash inflows that occur later in the project have a lower present value than cash inflows that occur earlier, since the present value of a dollar is higher the sooner it is received. Projects with later cash flows will have lower net present values, for any given discount rate, than will projects with earlier cash flows, everything else equal. Hence, projects with later cash flows will have a lower internal rate of return. Choice (a) is incorrect. The IRR is the discount rate that sets the net present value of a project equal to zero. Net present value is calculated as follows:

Net present value = – Investment cost + Present value of cash inflows

The present value of the cash inflows is inversely related to the discount rate. That is, if the discount rate is higher, the present value of the cash inflows is lower. If the investment cost is lower, then a higher discount rate will be required to set the net present value to zero, not a lower discount rate. Choice (c) is incorrect. The larger the cash inflows, the higher will be the internal rate of return. Higher cash inflows have a higher present value at any given discount rate. A higher discount rate will be required to set the net present value to zero, not a lower discount rate. Choice (d) is incorrect. Projects with shorter payback periods have higher cash inflows early in the life of the project. Projects with earlier cash flows have higher internal rates of return.

Subject Area: Managerial accounting—capital budgeting. Source: CIA 595, IV-37.

62. **(a)** With mutually exclusive projects only one can be accepted. The decision rule is to accept the project with the highest net present value, and this is Project A. Choice (b) is incorrect because Project B has a negative net present value and would not be accepted. Choices (c) and d) are incorrect because only one mutually exclusive project can be accepted.

Subject Area: Managerial accounting—capital budgeting. Source: CIA 595, IV-38.

63. **(c)** The size of the end-of-period cash inflows is calculated as follows:

Net present value = – Investment cost + Cash inflow (PVIFA [k,n])

12,405 = –100,000 + Cash inflow (PVIFA [10%, 5])

12,405 + 100,000 = Cash inflow (3.7908)

Cash inflow = 112,405/3.7908 = 29,652

Choice (a) is incorrect. This is the answer if the investment cost is omitted from the calculation and if the PVIF is used rather than the PVIFA:

12,405 = Cash inflow (PVIF [10%, 5])

12,405 = Cash inflow (.6209)

Cash inflow = 12,405/.6209 = 19,979

Choice (b) is incorrect. This is the answer if the investment cost is omitted from the calculation, if a 12% discount rate is used and if the PVIF is used rather than the PVIFA:

12,405 = Cash inflow (PVIF [12%, 5])

12,405 = Cash inflow (.5674)

Cash inflow = 12,405/.5674 = 21,863

Choice (d) is incorrect. This is the answer if a 12% discount rate is used rather than 10%.

12,405 = –100,000 + Cash inflow (PVIFA [12%, 5])

112,405 = Cash inflow (3.6048)

Cash inflow = 112,405/3.6048 = 31,182

Subject Area: Managerial accounting—capital budgeting. Source: CIA 595, IV-41 to 44.

64. **(c)** The net present value of Project B is calculated as follows:

NPV = –Investment cost + Cash inflow (PVIFA [k, n])

NPV = –50,000 + 40,000 (PVIFA [12%, 2])

NPV = –50,000 + 40,000 (1.6901) = 17,604

Choice (a) is incorrect. This is the answer if the PVIF for 12%, 2 periods is used instead of the PVIFA:

NPV = –50,000 + 40,000 (PVIF [12%, 2])

NPV = –50,000 + 40,000 (.7972) = –18,112

Choice (b) is incorrect. This is the answer if the PVIF is used instead of the PVIFA and if a 10% discount rate is used.

NPV = –50,000 + 40,000 (PVIF [10%, 2])

NPV = –50,000 + 40,000 (.8264) = –16,944

Choice (d) is incorrect. This is the answer if a 10% discount rate is used instead of 12%.

NPV = –50,000 + 40,000 (PVIFA [10%, 2])

NPV = –50,000 + 40,000 (1.7355) = 19,420

Subject Area: Managerial accounting—capital budgeting. Source: CIA 595, IV-41 to 44.

65. **(b)** The internal rate of return (IRR) is the discount rate that sets the net present value (NPV) of the project equal to zero. The NPV of Project C will equal zero when

Investment cost = Present value of cash inflows

60,000 = 20,000 [PVIF (IRR, 1)] + 35,000 [PVIF (IRR, 2)] + year 3 cash inflow [PVIF (IRR, 3)]

if IRR equals 12%, then

60,000 = 20,000 (.8929) + 35,000 (.7972) + Year 3 cash inflow (.7118)

Year 3 cash inflow = (60,000 – 17,858 – 27,902) / .7118 = 20,006

Choice (a) is incorrect. This is the answer if a 10% internal rate of return is used.

60,000 = 20,000 [PVIF (10%,1)] + 35.000 [PVIF (10%,2)] + Year 3 cash inflow [PVIF (10%,3)]

60,000 = 20,000 (.9091) + 35,000 (.8264) + Year 3 cash inflow (.7513)

Year 3 cash inflow = (60,000 – 18,182 – 28,924) / .7513 = 17,162

Choice (c) is incorrect. This is the answer if the project cash inflows are treated as a level annuity and if a 10% discount rate is used rather than 12%.

60,000 = Level cash inflow [PVIFA (10%, 3)]

Cash inflow = 60,000 / 2.4865 = 24,126

Choice (d) is incorrect. This is the answer if the project cash inflows are treated as a level annuity.

60,000 = Level cash inflow [PVIFA (12%, 3)]

Cash inflow = 60,000 / 2.4018 = 24,981

Subject Area: Managerial accounting—capital budgeting. Source: CIA 595, IV-41 to 44.

66. **(b)** After two years, the cash inflows for Project B sum to $80,000, so the investment outlay of $50,000 has been fully recovered. Choice (a) is incorrect. After one year, Project B has had a $50,000 outflow but only $40,000 of inflows, so the investment outlay has not been fully recovered. Choices (c) and (d) are incorrect. It takes three years for the cash inflows from Project C to repay the investment outlay. After two years, $55,000 of inflows is expected but the investment outlay is $60,000.

Subject Area: Managerial accounting—capital budgeting. Source: CIA 595, IV-41 to 44.

67. **(c)** Choice (c) is the correct answer. After two years, cash inflows for Project A ($400,000 + $300,000) are expected to exactly equal the initial cash outlay of $700,000. Choice (a) is incorrect. The payback for Project A is not immediate. It takes two years for the cash inflows from the project to repay the initial cash outlay. Choice (b) is incorrect. After one year, Project A has recovered only $400,000 of the initial cash outlay. Choice (d) is incorrect. After three years, expected cash inflows for Project A are expected to be in excess of the initial cash outlay. The initial cash outlay is expected to have been recovered after only two years.

Subject Area: Managerial accounting—capital budgeting. Source: CIA 1194, IV-31.

68. **(a)** The net present value of Project A is calculated by subtracting the initial cash outlay from the present value of the expected cash inflows:

–$700,000 + $400,000 [PVIF(10%,1)] + $300,000[PVIF(10%,2)] + $600,000[PVIF(10%,3)]

–$700,000 + $400,000 (.9091) + $300,000 (.8264) + $600,000 (.7513)

–$700,000 + $363,640 + $247,920 + $450,780 = $362,340

Choice (b) is incorrect. This solution does not subtract the initial cash outlay.

$400,000[PVIF(10%,1)] + $300,000[PVIF(10%,2)] + $600,000[PVIF(10%,3)]

$400,000 (.9091) + $300,000 (.8264) + $600,000 (.7513)

$363,640 + $247,920 + $450,780 = $1,062,340

Choice (c) is incorrect. This solution applies PVIFAs, present value factors for annuities, to the calculation.

–$700,000 + $400,000 [PVIFA(10%,1)] + $300,000[PVIFA(10%,2)] + $600,000[PVIFA(10%,3)]

–$700,000 + $400,000 (.9091) + $300,000 (1.7355) + $600,000 (2.4873)

–$700,000 + $363,640 + $520,650 + $1,492,380 = $1,676,670

Choice (d) is incorrect. This solution applies PVIFAs, present value factors for annuities, to the calculation and also does not subtract the initial cash outlay.

$400,000[PVIFA(10%,1)] + $300,000[PVIFA(10%,2)] + $600,000[PVIFA(10%,3)]

$400,000 (.9091) + $300,000 (1.7355) + $600,000 (2.4873)

$363,640 + $520,650 + $1,492,380 = $2,376,670

Subject Area: Managerial accounting—capital budgeting. Source: CIA 1194, IV-32.

69. **(c)** At a discount rate of 24%, the net present value of Project B is

– $500,000 + $250,000 [PVIFA (3 years, 24%)]

= – $500,000 + $250,000 (1.9813)

= $4,675

Of the discount rates given, this one most closely approximates the internal rate of return on Project B. The internal rate of return is the discount rate that sets the net present value of a project equal to zero.

Choice (a) is incorrect. At a discount rate of 16%, the net present value of Project B is

–$500,000 + $250,000 [PVIFA (3 years, 16%)]

= –$500,000 + $250,000 (2.2459)

= $61,475

This is not as close to zero as the net present value calculated at a 24% discount rate (see c.).

Choice (b) is incorrect. At a discount rate of 20%, the net present value of Project B is

–$500,000 + $250,000 [PVIFA (3 years, 20%)]

= –$500,000 + $250,000 (2.1065)

= $26,625

This is not as close to zero as the net present value calculated at a 24% discount rate (see c.).

Choice (d) is incorrect. At a discount rate of 28%, the net present value of Project B is

–$500,000 + $250,000 [PVIFA (3 years, 28%)]

= –$500,000 + $250,000 (1.8684)

= –$32,900

This is not as close to zero as the net present value calculated at a 24% discount rate (see c.).

Subject Area: Managerial accounting—capital budgeting. Source: CIA 1194, IV-33.

70. **(a)** When investment projects are independent, the company can select any or all of them. All positive net present value projects will be undertaken. Project A has a net present value of $362,340 (see solution to question 36). The net present value of Project B is

–$500,000 + $250,000 [PVIFA (10%, 3 years)]

–$500,000 + $250,000 [2.4873] = –$500,000 + $621,825 = $121,825

Since both projects have positive net present values, both will be undertaken.

Choices (b), (c), and (d) are incorrect because projects A and B both have positive net present values.

Subject Area: Managerial accounting—capital budgeting. Source: CIA 1194, IV-34.

71. **(d)** This fits the definition of capital budgeting. Chapter (a) is incorrect because absorption costing refers to the assigning of all types of manufacturing costs, including fixed manufacturing overhead, to units produced. Choice (b) is incorrect because payback does not use present values. Choice (c) is incorrect because capital rationing imposes constraints on the amount of total capital expenditures in each period.

Subject Area: Managerial accounting—capital budgeting. Source: CIA 590, IV-24.

72. **(c)** The amount to be financed represents a present value, which should be divided by the present value interest factor of an annuity payment. Choice (a) is incorrect because this answer used $300,000 instead of $240,000 as the amount to be financed. Choice (b) is incorrect because this answer used the future value of an annuity rather than the present value of an annuity. Choice (d) is incorrect because this answer is based on payment of annual interest plus an equal fraction of the principal in every year.

Subject Area: Managerial accounting—capital budgeting. Source: CIA 590, IV-54.

73. **(a)** Computations follow.

$275,132 cost of machine
–200,000 down payment
$ 75,132 × .1 = $7,513

Choice (b) is incorrect. $100,000 – 75,132 = 24,868/3 = $8,289. Choice (c) is incorrect. $100,000 × .1 = $10,000 (1990 "interest" on down payment). Choice (d) is incorrect. $275,132 × .1 = $27,513 (1990 "interest" on cost of machine).

Subject Area: Managerial accounting—capital budgeting. Source: CIA 1190, IV-46.

74. (d) The cost of the equipment equals the present value of all of the payments, which can be calculated by multiplying one payment by the present value of an annuity due of one dollar. Choice (a) is incorrect because the situation described in the stem involves discounting rather than accumulation and an annuity rather than a single sum. Choice (b) is incorrect because the situation described in the stem involves the discounting of cash flows rather than the accumulation of cash flows. Choice (c) is incorrect because the situation described in the stem involves an annuity rather than a single sum.

Subject Area: Managerial accounting—capital budgeting. Source: CIA Model Exam 2002, IV-42.

75. (d) The net present value method compares the initial outflow of cash to the present value of future cash flows, discounted at the rate of return required by the company, to calculate the net present value. Choice (a) is incorrect. The accounting rate of return does not consider the time value of money. It simply equals net income divided by initial investment, and therefore cannot be determined from the information provided. Choice (b) is incorrect. The internal rate of return exceeds the cost of capital (15%) if the investment has a positive net present value. The accounting rate of return, however, cannot be determined from the information provided. Choice (c) is incorrect. The payback method ignores the time value of money and the company's required rate of return. The payback period therefore cannot be determined from the information provided.

Subject Area: Managerial accounting—capital budgeting. Source: CIA Model Exam 1998, IV-37.

76. (a) Investments with present values in excess of their costs (that is, positive net present values) that can be identified or created by the capital budgeting activities of the firm will have a positive impact on firm value and on the price of the common stock of the firm. Choice (b) is incorrect because positive net present value investments will increase, not decrease, firm value and share prices for a firm. Choice (c) is incorrect because investments with present values equal to their costs have a zero net present value and neither increase nor decrease firm value and share price. Choice (d) is incorrect. See response given for choice (c).

Subject Area: Managerial accounting—capital budgeting. Source: CIA Model Exam 1998, IV-43.

Operating Budget

77. (d) The operating budget is a major element of the master budget. Choice (a) is incorrect because the master budget does not contain actual results. Choice (b) is incorrect because (b) the master budget reflects all applicable expected costs, whether controllable by individual managers or not. Choice (c) is incorrect because the master budget is not structured to allow determination of manufacturing cost variances. This is accomplished using the flexible budget and actual results.

Subject Area: Managerial accounting—operating budget. Source: CIA Model Exam 2002, IV-56.

78. (a) Because planning is impacted more strongly by the organization's environment, the planning information is more likely to be generated using external data. Choice (b) is incorrect because control information is more detailed. Choice (c) is incorrect because both types of information need to be quantifiable, but planning is likely to require less quantification. Choice (d) is incorrect because this is more likely to be true of control information.

Subject Area: Managerial accounting—operating budget. Source: CIA Model Exam 2002, III-23.

79. (a) This is the definition of a flexible budget. Choice (b) is incorrect because this is the definition of an operating budget. Choice (c) is incorrect because this is the definition of activity-based budgeting. Choice (d) is incorrect because this is the definition of Kaizen budgeting.

Subject Area: Managerial accounting—operating budget. Source: CIA Model Exam 1998, III-21.

80. (b) Required production of finished units is 22,000 (target ending inventory of 12,000 + sales of 24,000 less beginning inventory of 14,000). This is 88,000 pounds of direct material (times 4 per unit). Required purchases of direct material is 92,000 (target ending inventory of 48,000 + usage of 88,000 less beginning inventory of 44,000). Choice (a) is incorrect because this is required production of finished units (22,000) times 4 pounds per unit, and does not allow for the planned increase of 4,000 pounds in target ending direct materials inventory. Choice (c) is incorrect because this is budgeted sales of finished units (24,000) times 4 pounds per unit, and does not allow for any of the planned inventory changes. Choice (d) is incorrect because this is budgeted sales of finished units (24,000) times 4 pounds per unit, plus the 4,000 unit planned increase in ending direct materials inventory.

Subject Area: Managerial accounting—operating budget. Source: CIA 1190, IV-15.

81. (d) Producing more units than planned in the master budget will not affect the efficiency of the materials used for each unit. Choice (a) is incorrect because poorly functioning machines will have more material waste and spoilage. Choice (b) is incorrect because an inadequately trained and supervised labor force will have more material waste and spoilage than an adequately trained and supervised labor force. Choice (c) is incorrect because rush orders disrupt the manufacturing process by interfering with normal work routines, practices, and procedures. These disruptions will adversely affect each of the manufacturing processes, including the efficient use of material, labor, and overhead.

Subject Area: Managerial accounting—operating budget. Source: CIA 597, III-18.

82. (a) The joint probability of occurrence of two independent events equals the product of their individual probabilities. Prob (cost of Material 1 increases 3% and cost of Material 2 increases 3%) = Prob (cost of Material 1 increases 3%) × Prob (cost of Material 2 increases 3%) = 0.3 × 0.5 = 0.15. Therefore, by definition, choices (b), (c), and (d) would be incorrect.

Subject Area: Managerial accounting—operating budget. Source: CIA 597, III-99.

83. (b) See supporting calculations below. Choice (a) is incorrect because the April cash sales are correct in this response, but collection of April and March credit sales are incorrectly calculated. The 2% uncollectible amount is taken out of the credit sales before the collection pattern is applied. The calculations for these two amounts are as follows: collection of April credit sales, 4,000,000 × .7 × .98 × .40 = 1,097,600;

collection of March credit sales, 3,600,000 × .7 × .98 × .58 = 1,432,368. Choice (c) is incorrect because the April cash sales and the collection of April credit sales are correct in this response, but this response includes the collection of May credit sales (4,200,000 × .7 × .58 = 1,705,200) rather than the collection of March credit sales. Choice (d) is incorrect because the April cash sales and the collection of April credit sales are correct in this response, but collection of March credit sales are incorrectly calculated. The collection of March credit sales omits the 70% ratio that represents the credit sales [3,600,000 × .58 = 2,088,000].

Supporting calculations ($000's)

Correct—choice (b)		*Choice (a)*	*Choice (c)*	*Choice (d)*
April cash sales 4,000 × .3 =1,200.0		1,200.0	1,200.0	1,200.0
Collections a/c:				
April 4,000 × .7 × .4 = 1,120.0		1,097.6	1,120.0	1,120.0
March 3,600 × .7 × .58 = 1461.6		1,432.3		2,088.0
February None—not coll.				
May, 4,200 × .7 × .58			1,705.2	
Total	3,781.6	3,729.9	4,025.2	4,408.0

Subject Area: Managerial accounting—operating budget. Source: CIA 595, III-97.

84. **(a)** Answer is arrived at by deduction. Choice (b) is incorrect because control information is more detailed. Choice (c) is incorrect because both types of information need to be quantifiable, but planning is likely to require less quantification. Choice (d) is incorrect because statement is more likely to be true of control information.

Subject Area: Managerial accounting—operating budget. Source: CIA 1190, III-58.

85. **(a)** Review and approval of expense report forms by sales management other than the person with budgetary responsibilities does not add control and is not an efficient use of their time. Choice (b) is incorrect because there is no indication that this procedure is necessary for all transactions. Choice (c) is incorrect because there is no basis in the given information for performing extensive confirmation procedures in this audit. Choice (d) is incorrect. Based on the functioning of budgetary controls, there is no basis for identifying this performance criterion.

Subject Area: Managerial accounting—operating budget. Source: CIA 595, III-17.

86. **(a)** Budgets provide a tight, goal-oriented, rational linkage with the strategic plan. Choice (b) is incorrect because strategic planning defines the company's mission. Choice (c) is incorrect because too specific, one of many opportunities that may exist for the company. Choice (d) is incorrect because budgets are a formal communication device.

Subject Area: Managerial accounting—operating budget. Source: CIA 595, III-19.

87. **(b)** Zero-based budgeting requires each responsibility manager to justify every activity and its cost. Choices (a) and (c) are incorrect because each one is a feature of traditional or incremental budgeting. Choice (d) is incorrect because this is a definition of a capital budget.

Subject Area: Managerial accounting—operating budget. Source: CIA 595, III-20.

88. **(c)** This response is payment for February purchases net of discount ($1,950,000 × .98 = $1,911,000). Please refer to the supporting calculations, which follow the explanation of the responses for the correct calculation.

Supporting calculations

February	
Forecasted production	380,000
DM pounds/FG unit	1.0
Total DM pounds for prod	380,000
+Ending DM requirements	105,000
Total DM needs	485,000
–Beg DM inventory	95,000
Total DM unit purchases	390,000
Invoice cost per pound	$5
Total DM purchases in $	$1,950,000
Less 2% cash discount	39,000
February CD for DM purchases	$1,911,000

Choice (a) is incorrect because this response reverses the inventory adjustments for determining the amount of direct materials that need to be purchased during February. The 2% cash discount is included in the calculations (refer to supporting calculations for choice c.).

Total DM pound for prod	380,000
+Beginning DM inventory	95,000
Total DM needs	475,000
–Ending DM requirements	105,000
Total DM unit purchases	370,000
Invoice cost per pound	$5
Total DM purchases in $	$1,850,000
Less 2% cash discount	37,000
February CD for DM purchases	$1,813,000

Choice (b) is incorrect because this response ignores any adjustment for beginning and ending direct materials inventories by using the total direct material pounds for February production of 380,000. The dollar amounts are as follows:

January	
Total RM pound for production	380,000
Invoice cost per pound	$5
Total DM cost in $	$1,900,000
Less 2% cash discount	38,000
	$1,862,000

Choice (d) is incorrect because this response represents the payment for February purchases ($1,950,000) but does not consider the 2% cash discount (refer to supporting calculations for choice c).

Subject Area: Managerial accounting—operating budget. Source: CIA 1194, III-53.

89. **(c)** These three items are all generally considered and accepted as being objectives of budgets. Choice (a) is incorrect because the first item in this list is incorrect. Responsibility centers really have to be defined before a budget can be prepared. The other two items are appropriate objectives. Choice (b) is incorrect because none of these items are considered appropriate objectives of budgets. Responsibility centers really have to be defined before a budget can be prepared. The purpose of a budget should never be to fix blame; rather, it should be used to evaluate performance to determine why performance was or was not obtained so that the cause of the performance can be promoted or corrected as necessary. A budget can never really assure that goal congruence will occur between superiors and subordinates. Choice (d) is incorrect because item one of this list is correct, but the last two are not. The purpose of a budget should never be to fix blame; rather, it should be used to evaluate performance to determine why performance was or was not obtained so that the cause of the performance can be promoted or corrected as necessary. A budget can never really assure that goal congruence will occur between superiors and subordinates.

Subject Area: Managerial accounting—operating budget. Source: CIA 1194, III-54.

90. **(a)** This is the correct explanation for zero-base budgeting. Choice (b) is incorrect because this is the explanation for ordinary incremental budgets. Choice (c) is incorrect because this is the explanation for priority incremental budgets. Choice (d) is incorrect because this is the explanation for input/output procedure for budget development.

Subject Area: Managerial accounting—operating budget. Source: CIA 1194, III-55.

91. **(a)** Computations follow:

	January	*February*
Sales (finished units)	15,000	18,000
Desired ending finished goods inventory		
(.50 × 18,000)	9,000	8,250
	24,000	26,250
Est. beginning finished goods inventory		
(.50 × 15,000)	(7,500)	(9,000)
Production requirements (units)	16,500	17,250
Material per finished unit	3	3
Materials required for production	49,500	51,750
Desired ending raw mat'l inventory		
(2.0 × 51,750)	103,500	
Est. beginning raw mat'l inventory	153,000	
(2.0 × 49,500)	(99,000)	
Purchases (pounds)	54,000	
Cost per pound	$ 4	
Purchases (in dollars)	$216,000	

Choice (b) is incorrect because it represents the cost of the materials required for February's production ($4 × 51,750). Choice (c) is incorrect because it represents the cost of the materials required for January's production ($4 × 49,500). Choice (d) is incorrect because it represents the cost of the materials required for January's sales (15,000 × 3 × $4).

Subject Area: Managerial accounting—operating budget. Source: CIA 1193, IV-13.

92. **(a)** Zero-base budgeting is a budget technique whereby the budgeting process begins with the decision units at the lowest level of the organization and all activities have to be identified and justified. Choice (b) is incorrect because this response attempts to describe a zero-balance bank account as a form of budgeting. Choice (c) is incorrect because this response describes an incremental budget process. Choice (d) is incorrect because this response is an adaptation of the definition of engineered costs, which forms the basis for the input/output approach to budgeting.

Subject Area: Managerial accounting—operating budget. Source: CIA 1192, IV-19.

93. **(c)** Promotion of communication and coordination is a major advantage of short-term program planning and budgeting. Choice (a) is incorrect because short-term program planning and budgeting provides the basis for periodic program evaluation. Choice (b) is incorrect because the administration of budgets should never be rigid, as changed conditions call for changes in the budget. Choice (d) is incorrect because strategic analysis is long-term rather than short-term in nature, and usually precedes the development of short-term budgets.

Subject Area: Managerial accounting—operating budget. Source: CIA 592, IV-17.

94. **(b)** Ending cash balance = Beginning cash balance + Cash collections – Cash disbursements = $23,000 + (50,000 + 30,000) – 94,000 = $ 9,000

Borrowing = $15,000 – 9,000 = $6,000

Therefore, by definition, choices (a), (c), and (d) will be incorrect.

Subject Area: Managerial accounting—operating budget. Source: CIA 1191, IV-14.

95. **(a)** Under zero-base budgeting (ZBB), each year's budget is independent of previous years. Every dollar is justified from a zero base. Thus, from the information given there is no way to determine the budget for next year. This is in contrast to incremental budgeting, which justifies only additions to previous cost levels. Therefore, by definition, choices (b), (c), and (d) will be incorrect.

Subject Area: Managerial accounting—operating budget. Source: CIA 590, IV-13.

96. **(d)** This is one of the major advantages of budgeting. Choice (a) is incorrect because this is a disadvantage. Choice (b) is incorrect because this is a disadvantage. Choice (c) is incorrect because the need for continual change is a disadvantage.

Subject Area: Managerial accounting—operating budget. Source: CIA 590, IV-14.

97. **(b)** Sales-volume variance is defined as the difference between the flexible-budget amounts and the static (master)-budget amounts ($38,000 – 48,000 = $10,000 U). Choice (a) is incorrect because actual minus static budget (49,000 – 48,000) is a static-budget variance. Choice (c) is incorrect because actual minus flexible-budget amount is the flexible-budget variance ($49,000 – $38,000 = $11,000 F). Choice (d) is incorrect because actual sales-budgeted sales ($209,000 – 220,000 = $11,000 U).

Subject Area: Managerial accounting—operating budget. Source: CIA 1190, IV-18.

98. **(d)** This is the correct calculation as shown below. Choice (a) is incorrect because this response is correct except the growth in software sales is omitted. Software sales are included at only $2,000,000 as compared to the correct amount shown in the correct calculation below. Thus, the revenue components are $5,544,000 + 2,000,000 + 1,260,000. Choice (b) is incorrect because this response is correct except the increase in hardware selling price is omitted. Hardware sales are included at only $5,040,000 as compared to the correct amount shown in the correct calculation below. Thus, the revenue components are: $5,040,000 + 2,160,000 + 1,260,000. Choice (c) is incorrect because this response is correct except the growth in maintenance contracts is omitted. Maintenance contracts are included at only $1,200,000 as compared to the correct amount shown in the correct calculation below. Thus, the revenue components are: $5,544,000 + 2,160,000 + 1,200,000.

Calculation of correct response

Hardware sales	$4,800,000 × 1.10 × 1.05	$5,544,000
Software sales	2,000,000 × 1.08	2,160,000
Maintenance contracts	1,200,000 × 1.05	1,260,000
Total		$8,964,000

Subject Area: Managerial accounting—operating budget. Source: CIA 1195, III-89.

99. **(b)** The correct amounts and how they are calculated are shown in the first column below. Choice (a) is incorrect because all of the amounts are correct in this response except for the hardware and software cost of sales. In both of these, the volume increase of 5% and 8% respectively were omitted. The amounts were calculated as: 3,360,000 × 1.04 for hardware; 1,200,000 × 1.04 for software. The remaining amounts are as shown below. Choice (c) is incorrect because all of the amounts are correct in this response except for the amount for customer maintenance costs. The amount for customer maintenance cost was increased incorrectly by 5% before the $120,000 for technicians was added [(640,000 × 1.05) + 120,000]. The remaining amounts are as shown below. Choice (d) is incorrect because all of the amounts are correct in this response except for the hardware cost of sales. The selling price increase of 10% was incorrectly included in the calculation. The amount was calculated as: 3,360,000 × 1.04 × 1.05 × 1.10. The remaining amounts are as shown below.

Supporting calculations

	Correct – choice (b)	Choice (a)	Choice (c)	Choice (d)
Hardware				
,360,000 × 1.05 × 1.04 =	$3,669,120	3,494,400	3,669,120	4,036,032
Software				
1,200,000 × 1.08 × 1.04 =	1,347,840	1,248,000	1,347,840	1,347,840
Marketing				
600,000 × 1.05 =	630,000	630,000	630,000	630,000
Cust. maint.				
640,000+120,000 =	760,000	760,000	792,000	760,000
Admin. (no change)	1,120,000	1,120,000	1,120,000	1,120,000
Total	$7,526,960	7,252,400	7,558,960	7,893,872

Subject Area: Managerial accounting—operating budget. Source: CIA 1195, III-90.

100. (d) 2,500,000 – (3,000,000)(0.6). Choice (a) is incorrect. (3,000,000 – 2,500,000)(0.6). Choice (b) is incorrect. (2,500,000 – 3,000,000). Choice (c) is incorrect. (3,000,000 – 2,500,000)

Subject Area: Managerial accounting—operating budget. Source: CIA 596, III-87.

101. (c) This response calculates the purchases needed for the current month (40% of August sales) correctly, the 25% ending inventory requirement (September sales times 40% times 25%) correctly, and correctly deducts as the beginning inventory balance what the ending inventory should be as of July 31 based on the sales figures (750,000 × .4 × .25). Refer to the supporting calculations. Choice (a) is incorrect because this response calculates the purchases needed for the current month (40% of August sales) correctly and the 25% ending inventory requirement (September sales times 40% times 25%) correctly but deducts as the beginning inventory balance the balance given in the problem for June 30 rather than the inventory balance as of July 31. Refer to the supporting calculations. Choice (b) is incorrect because this response calculates the purchases needed for the current month (40% of August sales) correctly and the 25% ending inventory requirement (September sales times 40% times 25%) correctly but deducts as the beginning inventory balance what the ending inventory should be as of June 30 based on the sales figures (775,000 × .4 × .25) rather than what the balance should be on July 31. Refer to the supporting calculations. Choice (d) is incorrect because this response calculates the purchases needed for the current month (40% of August sales) correctly and uses the correct sales figures for determining the 25% ending and beginning inventory requirements but the sales figures used in the inventory calculations are not adjusted by the cost percentage of 40%. Refer to the supporting calculations.

Supporting calculations

	Choice (a)	Choice (b)	Choice (c)	Choice (d)
Purchases to meet sales				
750,000 × .4	$300,000	$300,000	$300,000	$300,000
Plus end inv requirement				
825,000 × .4 × .25	82,500	82,500	82,500	
825,000 × .25				206,250
Less beg inv 6/30 inv	(80,000)			
775,000 × .4 × .25		(77,500)		
750,000 × .4 × .25			(75,000)	
750,000 × .25				(187,500)
Net budgeted purchases	$302,500	$305,000	$307,500	$318,750

Subject Area: Managerial accounting—operating budget. Source: CIA 596, III-88.

102. (b) This response recognizes that 20% of the September sales are cash sales that would be collected in the month, 40% of the September credit sales (80% of the total sales) would be collected in the month, and 57% of the August credit sales (80% of the total sales) would be collected in September. Refer to the supporting calculations. Choice (a) is incorrect because this response ignores the September cash sales that would be collected in the month, incorrectly calculates the collection from September credit sales collected in the month as 40% of the total sales (rather than 80% of the total sales), and incorrectly calculates the collection in September from August credit sales as 57% of total sales (rather than 80% of the total sales). Refer to the supporting calculations. Choice (c) is incorrect because this response recognizes that 20% of the September sales are cash sales that would be collected in the month and 40% of the September credit sales (80% of the total sales) would be collected in the month but incorrectly uses 57% of the October credit sales (80% of the total sales) as being collected in September rather than collections on August credit sales. Refer to the supporting calculations. Choice (d) is incorrect because this response recognizes that 20% of the September sales are cash sales that would be collected in the month and 40% of the September credit sales (80% of the total sales) would be collected in the month but incorrectly calculates the collection in September from August credit sales as 57% of total sales (rather than 80% of the total sales). Refer to the supporting calculations.

Supporting calculations

	Choice (a)	Choice (b)	Choice (c)	Choice(d)
Cash sales				
825,000 × .2	$	$165,000	$165,000	$165,000
Ignored	-0-			
Coll on A/C-September				
825,000 × .8 × .4		264,000	264,000	264,000
825,000 × .4	330,000			
Coll on A/C-August				
750,000 × .8 × .57		342,000		
800,000 × .8 × .57			364,800	
750,000 × .57	427,500			427,500
Total cash receipts-Sept	$757,500	$771,000	$793,800	$856,500

Subject Area: Managerial accounting—operating budget. Source: CIA 596, III-89.

Transfer Pricing

103. (d) The calculation of transfer prices in the international arena must be systematic. A scheme for calculating transfer prices for a firm may correctly price the firm's product in Country A but not in Country B. The product may be overpriced in Country B and sales will be lower than anticipated. Alternatively, the product may be underpriced in Country B and the authorities in Country B may allege that the firm is dumping their product in Country B. Choice (a) is incorrect because properly chosen transfer prices allow firms to attempt to minimize worldwide taxes by producing various parts of the products in different countries and strategically transferring the parts at various systematically calculated prices. Choice (b) is incorrect because properly chosen transfer prices allocate revenues and expenses to divisions in various countries. These numbers are used as part of the input for the performance evaluation of each division. Choice (c) is incorrect because transfer prices motivate division managers to buy parts and products (from either internal or external suppliers) at the lowest possible prices and to sell their products (to either internal or external customers) at the highest possible prices. This provides each division with a profit-making orientation.

Subject Area: Managerial accounting—transfer pricing. Source: CIA 594, III-40.

104. (c) Market-based prices provide market discipline and hence inefficient internal suppliers will tend to wither, while efficient ones prosper, enhancing the overall long-term competitiveness of the firm. Choice (a) is incorrect because marginal production cost does not relate to market-based transfer prices. Choice (b) is incorrect because marginal cost based transfer prices provide more of an incentive to the purchasing division to buy internally and thus use idle facilities of the selling division than the usually higher market-based transfer price. Choice (d) is incorrect because corporate politics is less of a factor than in other methods such as a negotiated transfer price, because market-based prices are objective.

Subject Area: Managerial accounting—transfer pricing. Source: CIA 1193, IV-18.

105. (a) 200 + 20 = 220. Choice (b) is incorrect. Cost would be 100 + 50 + 40 + 20 = 210. Choice (c) is incorrect. No negotiations took place. Choice (d) is incorrect. This would be (210 × 1.2) = 252.

Subject Area: Managerial accounting—transfer pricing. Source: CIA 1193, IV-19.

106. (d) By ignoring relevant alternative market prices, a company may pay more than is necessary to produce goods and services internally compared to a potentially lower price from an outside supplier. Choice (a) is incorrect because this is necessary to a cost-based transfer price but is not much of a disadvantage. Choice (b) is incorrect because this is a characteristic of a market-based transfer price. Choice (c) is incorrect because this is a characteristic of a market-based transfer price.

Subject Area: Managerial accounting—transfer pricing. Source: CIA 593, IV-16.

107. (c) A transfer price is the price charged for the exchange of products or services between subunits of an organization. Choice (a) is incorrect because direct cost represents the cost of an item that can be identified specifically with a single cost objective. This is not appropriate use of this term in this situation. Choice (b) is incorrect because shadow (cost) price is a concept used in linear programming applications. Choice (d) is incorrect because dual price relates to the use of two separate transfer-pricing methods to price each interdivision transaction (i.e., the buyer uses one price point while the seller uses another). This is not appropriate use of this term in this situation.

Subject Area: Managerial accounting—transfer pricing. Source: CIA 1192, IV-23.

108. (c) $18 because it saves the purchasing division money over purchasing at the market price and gives the supplier a profit. Choice (a) is incorrect because $10 is not equitable to the supplier, Division Z, because it doesn't cover the variable costs. Choice (b) is incorrect because $12 is not equitable to the supplier, Division Z, because it would not make money. Choice (d) is incorrect because $20 is the market price.

Subject Area: Managerial accounting—transfer pricing. Source: CIA 592, IV-19.

109. (d) Market transfer prices reduce arguments between divisions as to the best transfer price, and result in optimal allocation of company resources in the long run. Therefore, by definition, choices (a), (b), and (c) will be incorrect.

Subject Area: Managerial accounting—transfer pricing. Source: CIA 1191, IV-19.

110. (d) Use of the market price generally leads to optimal decisions when the market is perfectly competitive and where interdependencies of organizational subunits are minimal. Choice (a) is incorrect because this is the cost-based minimum transfer price. Generally, the market price is the optimal transfer price when the market is perfectly competitive and where interdependencies of organizational subunits are minimal. (Explanation of $4.00 price: This minimum transfer price consists of the outlay costs [which in this case are the variable costs only] plus any opportunity cost. In this case there is sufficient available capacity to produce the 3,000 transferred units without affecting other production and therefore no opportunity costs are involved.) Choice (b) is incorrect because this is based on full costs (it is also incorrectly computed). The use of full costs as the basis for transfer prices may lead to suboptimal decisions for the company as a whole. (Explanation of $6.00 price: This average unit full cost [$4.00 variable costs plus ($110,000 fixed cost/55,000 unit capacity)] is based on the production capacity of 55,000 units and therefore does not represent the correct unit full cost). Choice (c) is incorrect because this is based on full costs. The use of full costs as the basis for transfer prices may lead to suboptimal decisions for the company as a whole. (Explanation of $6.08 price: This average unit full costs is based on 53,000 units ($4.00 variable cost plus [$110,000/53,000] = $6.08).

Subject Area: Managerial accounting—transfer pricing. Source: CIA 591, IV-22.

111. (a) The country where the producer is located has the lower tax rate so the overall tax burden is lowered by maximizing the transfer price. This will maximize reported taxable income in the lower tax country (by maximizing revenue) and minimize reported taxable income in the lower tax country (by maximizing expenses). Choice (b) is incorrect. A low transfer price results in higher total taxes paid. The country where the producer is located has the lower tax rate, so the overall tax burden is higher when the minimum transfer price is used. With a lower transfer price, reported taxable income will be lower in the lower tax country and reported taxable income will be maximized in the higher tax country, since expenses there will be minimized. Choice (c) is incorrect. Establishing a transfer price that results in the same profit margin for both operations will not minimize taxes. As explained in choice (a), any transfer price lower than the maximum will result in higher total taxes paid. Choice (d) is incorrect. Market-based pricing will not minimize total taxes and the question states that there are no nontax considerations to be taken into account in making this decision.

Subject Area: Managerial accounting—transfer pricing. Source: CIA 594, IV-72.

112. (d) A market price transfer price will lead to goal congruence and a sustained level of management effort while maintaining autonomy of divisions when there is a competitive marketplace. Choice (a) is incorrect. A transfer at full cost means that the selling division will never make a profit on the product. In addition, the selling division may be foregoing profits that could be obtained by selling to outside customers. Thus, full-cost based transfer prices can lead to suboptimal decisions. Choice (b) is incorrect. A transfer price of full cost plus markup results in no incentive for the selling division to hold its costs down. This means a sustained level of management effort may not be maintained. Again, suboptimal decisions can take place. Choice (c) is incorrect. A transfer price of variable cost plus markup has the same weaknesses as a full cost plus markup. There is no incentive for the selling division to hold its costs down which does not promote a sustained level of management effort. In addition, suboptimal decisions can take place.

Subject Area: Managerial accounting—transfer pricing. Source: CIA 1195, III-96.

113. (c) Country X has a higher tax rate than the home country, so the incentive is to transfer profits out of country X. The sales division in country X will be less profitable if it is charged a high transfer price. Choices (a) and (b) are incorrect. Country X has a higher tax rate than the home country and country Y has a lower tax rate. The transfer pricing incentives will be different for the two sales divisions. Choice (d) is incorrect. Country Y has a lower tax rate than the home country, so the incentive is to transfer profits into country Y by charging that sales division a low transfer price.

Subject Area: Managerial accounting—transfer pricing. Source: CIA 596, IV-72.

114. (b) The total after-tax profit in each of the three countries is calculated as follows:

Per unit profit = [(Sales price – Unit cost)(Quantity sold) – Additional costs] (1 – Tax rate)

Home = [($30 – $20)(1500) – 10,000] (1 – .5) = $2,500

Country X = [($40 – $20)(1000) – 12,500] (1 – .6) = $3,000

Country Y = [($35 – $20)(2000) – 11,000] (1 – .4)= $11,400

Hence the total profit is lowest for the sales in the home country.

Choice (a) is incorrect because the total after-tax profit from sales in the home country is the lowest, not the highest, available. Choice (c) is incorrect because sales in Country X do not provide the greatest total after-tax profit. It is sales in Country Y that provide the greatest after-tax profit. Choice (d) is incorrect because sales in Country Y provide the greatest, not the lowest, total after-tax profit.

Subject Area: Managerial accounting—transfer pricing. Source: CIA 596, IV-73.

115. (b) The tax minimizing strategy involves maximizing sales in Country B and minimizing the reported cost of goods sold in Country B. Choice (a) is incorrect. If selling prices are identical, the tax minimizing strategy does involve maximizing sales in Country B. However, to report the highest possible profits in the lower tax country, input costs must be minimized in the lower tax country. The transfer price paid to the production facility in Country A must therefore be set as low as possible, rather than as high as possible. Choice (c) is incorrect. A strategy of minimizing sales in Country B and maximizing reported cost of goods sold in Country B would result in the lowest reported profit in the lower tax country, thus maximizing taxes paid. Choice (d) is incorrect. The tax minimizing strategy involves maximizing sales revenue in the lower tax country, not minimizing it.

Subject Area: Managerial accounting—transfer pricing. Source: CIA 595, IV-68.

116. (a) Market is the best transfer price when there is a competitive external market. Choice (b) is incorrect because idle capacity would lead to a preference for a negotiated price. Choice (c) is incorrect because monopolistic markets charge higher prices by restricting output. Choice (d) is incorrect because an idle capacity would lead to a preference for a negotiated price.

Subject Area: Managerial accounting—transfer pricing. Source: CIA 590, IV-17.

117. (b) Cost-based transfer prices lead to suboptimal decisions for the company as a whole. Choice (a) is incorrect because inefficiencies are charged to the buying department. Choice (c) is incorrect because cost-based transfer prices need not be adjusted by some markup. Choice (d) is incorrect because cost-based transfer prices provide clarity and administrative convenience.

Subject Area: Managerial accounting—transfer pricing. Source: CIA 1190, IV-20.

Cost-Volume-Profit Analysis

118. (c) Revenue – Variable expense – Fixed expense = Net income

25X – 16X – 585,000 = (10%)(25X)
X = 90,000 units

Choice (a) is incorrect. 25X – 16X – 585,000 = 0. Choice (b) is incorrect. 25X – 9X – 585,000 = 0. Choice (d) is incorrect. 25X – 5X – 585,000 = 0

Subject Area: Managerial accounting—cost-volume-profit analysis. Source: CIA 594, III-42.

119. (a) Revenue – Variable expense – Fixed expense = Net income

(25)(80,000) – (16)(80,000) – 585,000 – X = 0
X = $135,000

Choice (b) is incorrect. (25)(80,000) – (5)(80,000) – 585,000 – X = 0. Choice (c) is incorrect. (25)(80,000) – (11)(80,000) – 585,000 – X = 0. Choice (d) is incorrect. (25)(80,000) – (9)(80,000) – 585,000 – X = 0

Subject Area: Managerial accounting—cost-volume-profit analysis. Source: CIA 594, III-43.

120. (a) Choice (a) is correct.

Selling price	*Expected CM*
$20	($20 – 7) × (0.2 × 10,000 + 0.8 × 15,000) = $182,000
$21	($21 – 7) × (0.45 × 10,000 + 0.55 × 15,000) = $178,500
$22	($22 – 7) × (0.6 × 10,000 + 0.4 × 15,000) = $180,000
$23	($23 – 7) × (0.8 × 10,000 + 0.2 × 15,000) = $176,000

Therefore, by definition, choices (b), (c), and (d) would be incorrect.

Subject Area: Managerial accounting—cost-volume-profit analysis. Source: CIA 1193, 1II-66.

121. (b) Assume that the variable costs average $10 per unit. The average selling price is therefore $16 (1.60 × $10).

However, the 10% markdown implies that the actual average selling price is $14.40 (.90 × $16). The contribution margin is 30.6% [($14.40 – $10.00)/ $14.40]. Choice (a) is incorrect because it represents the contribution margin per unit divided by the selling price before considering any markdowns ($4.40/$16). Choice (c) is incorrect because it does not consider the markdowns. Choice (d) is incorrect because it represents the contribution margin before the markdowns divided by the selling price after the markdowns.

Subject Area: Managerial accounting—cost-volume-profit analysis. Source: CIA 1193, 1V-11.

122. (d)

(1) Prepare a contribution margin income statement in order to determine the annual fixed costs.

	Total	*Per unit*
Sales	$300,000	$12.50
Variable costs	(180,000)	(7.50)
Contribution margin	120,000	5.00
Fixed costs	(160,000)	
Net loss	$(40,000)	

(2) Compute the sales volume (units) required to break even in 2005.

Fixed costs/Contribution margin per unit = $160,000/$5.00 = 32,000 units

(3) Compute the difference between the actual sales volume and the breakeven sales volume.

Actual sales volume $300,000/$12.50 = 24,000
Break even sales volume = 32,000
Additional units 8,000

Choice (a) is incorrect because it represents the 2005 breakeven sales volume. Choice (b) is incorrect because it represents the actual sales volume for 2005. Choice (c) is incorrect because it represents the breakeven point if the candidate treats the net operating loss as a net operating profit.

Subject Area: Managerial accounting—cost-volume-profit analysis. Source: CIA 1193, 1V-12.

123. (b)

$$\frac{\$9,500 - \$8,500}{150,000 - 100,000} = \frac{\$1,000}{50,000} = \$.02 \text{ per copy; x } 110,000 = \$2,200$$

Choice (a) is incorrect because the answer is less by 50%.

$$\frac{\$9,500 - \$8,500}{100,000} = \frac{\$1,000}{100,000} = \$.01 \text{ per copy; x } 110,000 = \$1,100$$

Choice (c) is incorrect because the answer is off by a factor of 2.5. Choice (d) is incorrect because the answer is off by a factor of 10.

Subject Area: Managerial accounting—cost-volume-profit analysis. Source: CIA 593, 1V-10.

124. (a)

$$\frac{\text{Fixed costs } (\$50,000 \text{ x } .8) + \text{Desired pretax profit } 0}{\text{Sales } [(\$500,000 \text{ x } 1.1) - \text{Variable costs } \$300,000] / \text{Sales } (\$500,000 \text{ x } 1.1)} = \text{Sales } \$88,000$$

Choice (b) is incorrect because it ignored 10% sales price increase.

$$\frac{\text{Fixed costs } (\$50,000 \text{ x } .8) + \text{Desired pretax profit } 0}{\text{Sales } (\$500,000 - \text{Variable costs } \$300,000) / \text{Sales } \$500,000} = \text{Sales } \$100,000$$

Choice (c) is incorrect because it ignored 20% decrease in fixed costs.

$$\frac{\text{Fixed costs } (\$50,000) + \text{Desired pretax profit } 0}{\text{Sales } [(\$500,000 \text{ x } 1.1) - \text{Variable costs } \$300,000] / \text{Sales } (\$500,000 \text{ x } 1.1)} = \text{Sales } \$110,000$$

$$\frac{\text{Fixed costs } (\$50,000) + \text{Desired pretax profit } 0}{\text{Sales } (\$500,000 - \text{Variable costs } \$300,000) / \text{Sales } \$500,000} = \text{Sales } \$125,000$$

Choice (d) is incorrect because it ignored both 10% and 20% changes above.

Subject Area: Managerial accounting—cost-volume-profit analysis. Source: CIA 593, 1V-11.

125. (b)

Beginning inventory	40,000
+ Production (plug #2)	60,000
= Subtotal (plug #1)	100,000
– Ending inventory	30,000
= Sales	70,000

Direct materials	60,000 × $10 = $ 600,000
Direct labor	60,000 × $20 = 1,200,000
Variable overhead	60,000 × $ 5 = 300,000
Fixed overhead	80,000
Total budgeted production costs	$2,180,000

Choice (a) is incorrect because it ignored fixed overhead.

Direct materials	60,000 × $10 = $ 600,000
Direct labor	60,000 × $20 = 1,200,000
Variable overhead	60,000 × $ 5 = 300,000
Total budgeted production costs	$2,100,000

Choice (c) is incorrect because it included selling costs and excluded fixed overhead.

Direct materials	60,000 × $10 = $ 600,000
Direct labor	60,000 × $20 = 1,200,000
Variable overhead	60,000 × $ 5 = 300,000
Selling costs	140,000
Total budgeted production costs	$2,240,000

Choice (d) is incorrect because it included selling costs.

Direct materials	60,000 × $10 = $ 600,000
Direct labor	60,000 × $20 = 1,200,000
Variable overhead	60,000 × $ 5 = 300,000
Selling costs	140,000
Fixed overhead	80,000
Total budgeted production costs	$2,320,000

Subject Area: Managerial accounting—cost-volume-profit analysis. Source: CIA 593, 1V-12.

126. (b) Contribution margin is the difference between sales and variable expenses.

CM = 400,000 – (20,000 + 12,000 + 140,000) = $228,000

Therefore, by definition, choices (a), (c), and (d) will be incorrect.

Subject Area: Managerial accounting—cost-volume-profit analysis. Source: CIA 1192, 1V-11.

127. (c) Gross profit is the difference between sales and cost of goods sold.

GP = 400,000 – (140,000 + 55,000) = $205,000

Therefore, by definition, choices (a), (b), and (d) will be incorrect.

Subject Area: Managerial accounting—cost-volume-profit analysis. Source: CIA 1192, 1V-12.

128. (b) The breakeven point in units is calculated by dividing the total fixed costs by the contribution margin per unit. The calculations are summarized as follows: (41,000 – 34,200 = 6,680).

	First manufacturer	*Second manufacturer*
Selling price	$40.00	$30.00
Total variable costs	22.00	12.00
Contribution margin	18.00	18.00
Total fixed costs	$617,760	$738,000
Breakeven in units [FC/CM]	34,320	41,000

Choice (a) is incorrect because the breakeven point in terms of unit sales dollars depends upon the contribution margin and the total fixed costs. Thus, while the contribution margins ($18) are the same, the breakeven points in units will not be the same because the fixed costs are different. Choice (c) is incorrect because this response ignores all selling and administrative costs, both variable and fixed. Thus, the breakeven points are calculated by dividing the fixed manufacturing costs by the manufacturing margin (selling price less variable manufacturing cost). The incorrect breakeven calculation for the first manufacturer is 15,840 units [$411,840/(40 – 14)] and 24,000 for the second manufacturer [$540,000/(30 – 7.50)] for the difference of 8,160 units. Choice (d) is incorrect because this response divides the total fixed costs by the variable costs per unit rather than the contribution margin. The incorrect breakeven calculation for the first manufacturer is 28,080 units [$617,760/(22)] and 61,500 for the second manufacturer [$738,000/(12.00)] for the difference of 33,420 units.

Subject Area: Managerial accounting—cost-volume-profit analysis. Source: CIA 1192, 1V-13.

129. (b) When resources are limited, maximum profits are achieved by maximizing dollar contribution margin per limited or constraining factor. In this situation, machine hours are the constraining factor. Product B has a contribution margin per machine hour of $28 [4 × (18 – 11)], which is greater than Product A [3 × (15 – 7)) = 24], Product C [2 × (20 – 10 = 20] or Product D [3 × (25 – 16) = 27]. Choice (a) is incorrect because Product A does have the greatest contribution margin ratio (53%), but when resources are limited, maximum profits are achieved by maximizing dollar contribution margin per limited or constraining factor which in this case is machine hours. Choice (c) is incorrect because Product C does have the greatest dollar contribution margin ($10), but when resources are limited, maximum profits are achieved by maximizing dollar contribution margin per limited or constraining factor, which in this case is machine hours. Choice (d) is incorrect because Product D does have the greatest selling price per unit ($25), but when resources are limited, maximum profits are achieved by maximizing dollar contribution margin per limited or constraining factor, which in this case is machine hours.

Subject Area: Managerial accounting—cost-volume-profit analysis. Source: CIA 1192, 1V-17.

130. (b) Because 1 unit of B is sold for every 3 units of A,

Units of B at breakeven = Fixed costs/combined contribution margin

$$= \frac{\$280,000}{3(\$2)+1(\$1)} = \frac{\$280,000}{\$7} = 40,000 \text{ units.}$$

Sales = 40,000 × $6 = $240,000

Choice (a) is incorrect. B units at A price. 40,000 × $5 = $200,000. Choice (c) is incorrect. A units not B. 120,000 × $5 = $600,000. Choice (d) is incorrect. A + B. $240,000 + $600,000 = $840,000.

Subject Area: Managerial accounting—cost-volume-profit analysis. Source: CIA 593, 1V-17.

131. (b)

Cost to purchase:	
$37 × 12,000 =	$444,000
Plus fixed overhead 12,000 × $3 =	36,000
Less rent income	40,000
	440,000
Cost to manufacture:	
35 × 12,000 =	420,000
Price differential:	
440,000 – 420,000 = $20,000 in favor of manufacture	

Choice (a) is incorrect because this answer uses the $3 as the relevant direct fixed cost. 444,000 – (360,000 + 36,000 + 40,000) = 8,000. Choice (c) is incorrect because this answer compares the full cost of manufacturing with cost to purchase. 444,000 – (35 × 12,000) = 24,000. Choice (d) is incorrect because this answer ignores the opportunity cost. 44,000

Subject Area: Managerial accounting—cost-volume-profit analysis. Source: CIA 593, 1V-19.

132. (d) See the following income statement before discontinuing a product:

	C	*J*	*P*	*Total*
Sales	$200,000	$150,000	$125,000	$475,000
Variable costs	95,000	75,000	50,000	220,000
Contribution margin	105,000	75,000	75,000	255,000
Separable (product) fixed costs	60,000	35,000	40,000	135,000
Product margin	45,000	40,000	35,000	120,000
Allocated fixed costs				100,000
Net income				$ 20,000

Eliminate Product P, based on lowest margin. Income statement after eliminating product P:

	C	*J*	*Total*
Sales	$200,000	$150,000	$350,000
Variable costs	95,000	75,000	170,000
Contribution margin	105,000	75,000	180,000
Separable (product) fixed costs	60,000	35,000	95,000
Product margin	45,000	40,000	85,000
Allocated fixed costs			60,000
Net income			$ 25,000

Choice (a) is incorrect because see choice (d) by definition. Choice (b) is incorrect because this is net income if Product C is eliminated. Choice (c) is incorrect because this is net income if Product J is eliminated.

Subject Area: Managerial accounting—cost-volume-profit analysis. Source: CIA 593, 1V-20.

133. (c)

Unit contribution margin = Selling price – Unit variable cost
= $370 – 80
= $290

Therefore, by definition, all the other choices will be incorrect.

Subject Area: Managerial accounting—cost-volume-profit analysis. Source: CIA 592, III-94.

134. (e) Choice (e) is correct.

Q = 30,000 – 50P
14,000 = 30,000 – 50P
P = $320

Therefore, by definition, all the other choices will be incorrect.

Subject Area: Managerial accounting—cost-volume-profit analysis. Source: CIA 592, III-95.

135. (f) When P = 400,

Q = 30,000 – 50 × 400 = 10,000 units
C = 2,800,000 + 80Q
= 2,800 = 80 × 10,000
= 3,600,000

$$\text{Average unit cost} = \frac{3{,}600{,}000}{10{,}000} = \$360$$

Therefore, by definition, all the other choices will be incorrect.

Subject Area: Managerial Accounting—Cost-Volume-Profit & Breakeven Analysis. Key concept(s) or skill(s) tested: the ability to compute the total cost first using the demand equation and then calculating the average cost per unit (UL). CIA 592, III-96. Cross-reference to theory section(s) 4630.

136. (d) Revenue = P × Q = 30,000P – 50P^2. Revenue is maximum when the first derivative of revenue equals 0.

that is, 30,000 – 100P = 0
P = $300

Therefore, by definition, all the other choices will be incorrect.

Subject Area: Managerial accounting—cost-volume-profit analysis. Source: CIA 592, III-97.

137. (j) When P = 410, Revenue = PQ = 30,000 × 410 – 50 × (410)^2 = $3,895,000

When P = 350, Revenue = PQ = 30,000 × 350 – 50 × (350)^2 = $4,375,000

Difference in revenue = 4,375,000 – 3,895,000 = $480,000 = $480 (in thousands). Therefore, by definition, all the other choices will be incorrect.

Subject Area: Managerial accounting—cost-volume-profit analysis. Source: CIA 592, III-98.

138. (k) Profit = Revenue – Cost
When P = 370,

Q = 30,000 – 50 × 370 = 11,500 units
Revenue = 370 × 11,500 = $4,255,000
Cost = 2,800,000 + 80 × 11,500 = <u>3,720,000</u>
Profit $535,000 or $535 (in thousands)

Therefore, by definition, all the other choices will be incorrect.

Subject Area: Managerial accounting—cost-volume-profit analysis. Source: CIA 592, III-99.

139. (l) Profit = Revenue – Cost
= PQ – C
= PQ – (2,800,000 + 80Q)
Q = 30,000 – 50P

Therefore, profit = P(30,000 – 50P) – [2,800,000 + 80(30,000 – 50P)] = 34,000P – 50P^2 – 5,200,000.

Profit is maximum when the first derivative of profit equals 0.

that is., 34,000 – 100P = 0

Therefore, P = $340.

When P = 340,

Q = 13,000 units
Revenue = 340 × 13,000 = $4,420,000
Cost = 2,800 + 80 × 13,000 = <u>3,840,000</u>
Profit $580,000 or $580 (in thousands)

Therefore, by definition, all the other choices will be incorrect.

Subject Area: Managerial accounting—cost-volume-profit analysis. Source: CIA 592, III-100.

140. (d) Q = $30,000/($5 – $3.20) = 16,667: Sales = P ≅ Q = 5 ≅ 16,667 = 83,335.
Therefore, by definition, choices (a), (b), and (c) will be incorrect.

Subject Area: Managerial accounting—cost-volume-profit analysis. Source: CIA 592, III-72.

141. (d) Q = $36,000+24,000/($8 – $5) = 20,000: Sales = P ≅ Q = 8 ≅ 20,000 = $160,000.

Therefore, by definition, choices (a), (b), and (c) will be incorrect.

Subject Area: Managerial accounting—cost-volume-profit analysis. Source: CIA 592, III-73.

142. (d) Using the equation method

u = Units sold
Sales = Variable expenses + Fixed expenses + Net income
$8u = $3u + $5,000 + $0
$5u = $5,000
u = 1,000 units sold
1,000 units @ $8 = $8,000 in sales for $0 profit (i.e., break-even point)

Therefore, by definition, choices (a), (b), and (c) will be incorrect.

Subject Area: Managerial accounting—cost-volume-profit analysis. Source: CIA 592, IV-12.

143. (b) Using the equation method

u = Units sold
Sales = Variable expenses + Fixed expenses + Net income
$8u = $3u + $5,000 + 2($1,000)
$5u = $7,000
u = 1,400 tee shirts

Therefore, by definition, choices (a), (c), and (d) will be incorrect.

Subject Area: Managerial accounting—cost-volume-profit analysis. Source: CIA 592, IV-13.

144. (b) The problem requires that the unit contribution margin be $50. The unit contribution margin is equal to unit sales price minus unit variable expenses, which are $10 per unit ($40,000 divided by 4,000 units). Therefore

$50 = Unit sales price – $10.
$60 = Unit sales price.

Therefore, by definition, choices (a), (c), and (d) will be incorrect.

Subject Area: Managerial accounting—cost-volume-profit analysis. Source: CIA 592, IV-14.

145. (b) The breakeven point in units equals fixed expenses plus desired net income divided by the unit contribution margin. Therefore, ($150,000 + $0 profit) divided by $50 equals 3,000 units. Or, using the equation method and the $60 per unit selling price from problem 14

u = Units sold; variable expenses are $40,000 / 4,000 units, or $10 per unit
Sales = Variable expenses + Fixed expenses + Net income
$60u = $10u + $150,000 + $0
$50u = $150,000
u = 3,000 units

Therefore, by definition, choices (a), (c), and (d) will be incorrect.

Subject Area: Managerial accounting—cost-volume-profit analysis. Source: CIA 592, IV-15.

146. (c) The margin of safety is the excess of sales over breakeven sales volume. Using the equation method to calculate the breakeven point in units:

> u = Units sold; variable expenses remain $10 per unit (i.e., $40,000 divided by 4,000 units);
> Fixed expenses = $150,000.
> Sales = Variable expenses + Fixed expenses + Net income
> $70u = $10u + $150,000 + $0 (i.e., breakeven)
> $60u = $150,000
> u = 2,500 units breakeven point

Or, using the unit contribution method

> Unit contribution margin equals the unit sales price minus unit variable expenses. $70 – $10 = $60 unit contribution margin. The breakeven point in units equals fixed expenses plus desired net income ($0) divided by the unit contribution margin.
>
> ($150,000 + $0) divided by $60 equals 2,500 units breakeven point.
> Sales at 3,500 units @ $70 = $245,000
> Breakeven at 2,500 units @ $70 = $175,000
> Margin of safety = $ 70,000

Therefore, by definition, choices (a), (b), and (d) will be incorrect.

Subject Area: Managerial accounting—cost-volume-profit analysis. Source: CIA 592, IV-16.

147. (c) The breakeven point in units (X_{BE}) can be computed as $X_{BE} = \frac{F}{p-v}$ where F = Fixed costs, p = Selling price, v = variable cost per unit.

Using this formula, $X_{BE} = \frac{200{,}000}{80-60} = 10{,}000$ units.

Therefore, by definition, choices (a), (b), and (d) will be incorrect.

Subject Area: Managerial accounting—cost-volume-profit analysis. Source: CIA 1191, IV-13.

148. (b) [$10 – (($4 × 1.25) + $2 + $1)] × 10,000 = $20,000

Choice (a) is incorrect. [$10 – (($4 × 2.5) + $2 + $1)] × 10,000 = ($30,000)

Direct Materials increased to 2.5 times original $4, rather than being increased by 25%. Choice (c) is incorrect. [$10 – ($4 + $2 + $1)] × 10,000 = $30,000. Direct Materials unchanged from original $4, rather from being increased by 25%. Choice (d) is incorrect. [$10 – (($4 × .75) + $2 + $1)] × 10,000 = $40,000. Direct Materials reduced by 25%, rather than increased.

Subject Area: Managerial accounting—cost-volume-profit analysis. Source: CIA 1191, IV-20.

149. (b) [$10 – ($4 + $2 + $1)] × 10,000 × .9 = $27,000

Choice (a) is incorrect. [($10 × .9) – ($4 + $2 + $1)] × 10,000 = $20,000. Sales price per unit reduced by 10%, rather than sales volume. Choice (c) is incorrect. [$10 – ($4 + $2 + $1)] × 10,000 = $30,000. No change made to sales volume, or anything else. Choice (d) is incorrect. [$10 – ($4 + $2 + $1)] × 10,000 × 1.1 = $33,000. Sales volume increased, rather than reduced, by 10%.

Subject Area: Managerial accounting—cost-volume-profit analysis. Source: CIA 1191, IV-21.

150. (b) .1 × 2000 × ($20 – $18) = $400. Choice (a) is incorrect. .1 × 1000 × ($10 – $7) = $300. Choice (c) is incorrect. .1 × 3000 × ($5 – $4) = $300. Choice (d) is incorrect. .1 × 500 × ($15 – $11) = $200.

Subject Area: Managerial accounting—cost-volume-profit analysis. Source: CIA 1191, IV-22.

151. (b) ($20 – $10) × 10,000 = $100,000. Correctly included all costs except already incurred fixed costs of $5 per unit. Choice (a) is incorrect. ($20 – $15) × 10,000 = $50,000. Erroneously included already incurred fixed costs of $5 per unit. Choice (c) is incorrect. ($20 – $9) × 10,000 = $110,000. Erroneously ignored sales commission of $1 per unit. Choice (d) is incorrect. ($20 – $6) × 10,000 = $140,000. Erroneously ignored variable overhead of $4 per unit.

Subject Area: Managerial accounting—cost-volume-profit analysis. Source: CIA 1191, IV-23.

152. (c) The contribution to overhead for each unit is $4.00. Fixed costs of $180,000 divided by the contribution of $4.00 produces the answer. Choice (a) is incorrect because this ignores variable costs. Total unit sales needed to cover fixed costs only are $180,000 / $30. Choice (b) is incorrect because this is total fixed costs divided by variable costs per unit. Choice (d) is incorrect because this is total fixed costs multiplied by the contribution to overhead of $4.00 per unit instead of divided by it.

Subject Area: Managerial accounting—cost-volume-profit analysis. Source: CIA 591, IV-17.

153. (d) Each unit contributes $2.00 to fixed costs. Fixed costs plus desired profit divided by contribution per unit produces answer. ($130,000 + $30,000)/$2.00 = 80,000. Choice (a) is incorrect because this is fixed costs plus the desired profit ($130,000 + $30,000 = $160,000) divided by the sales price. Choice (b) is incorrect because this is the quantity, which result in a loss of $30,000. ($130,000 – $30,000)/ $2.00 = $50,000. Choice (c) is incorrect because this is the quantity required to break even. Each unit contributes $2.00 to fixed costs. $130,000/$2.00 = 65,000.

Subject Area: Managerial accounting—cost-volume-profit analysis. Source: CIA 591, IV-18.

154. (c) Sales for 50,000 before tax income = ($130,000 + $50,000)/$2 = 90,000. (.7) 90,000 = 63,000 ($2) = 126,000—130,000 = (4,000). Choice (a) is incorrect because this is 30% of fixed costs .3($130,000) = $39,000. Choice (b) is incorrect because this is 30% less than the desired profit 50,000 – (.3 × $50,000) = $35,000. Choice (d) is incorrect because this is the total contribution margin, but the question requires the pretax income (or loss).

Subject Area: Managerial accounting—cost-volume-profit analysis. Source: CIA 591, IV-19.

155. (b) The projected degree of operating leverage would be calculated as follows:

> DOL = Q(P – V) / [Q(P – V) – F]
> = 25,000($10 – $4)/ [25,000($10 – $4) – $50,000]
> = 150,000/100,000 = 1.50

Where DOL = degree of operating leverage

> Q = Units sold
> P = Unit price
> V = Unit variable cost
> F = Fixed operating costs

Choice (a) is incorrect because this solution incorrectly uses total revenue, rather than contribution to fixed costs, in the degree of operating leverage formula as follows:

> DOL = Q(P) / [Q(P) – F]
> = 25,000($10)/ [25,000($10) – $50,000]
> = 250,000/200,000 = 1.25

Choice (c) is incorrect because this solution uses the year one sales level of 10,000 units and also uses total revenue, rather than the contribution to fixed costs, in calculating the degree of operating leverage as follows:

DOL = Q(P) / [Q(P) – F]
= 10,000($10)/ [10,000($10) – $50,000]
= 100,000/50,000 = 2.00

Choice (d) is incorrect because this solution incorrectly uses the year one sales level of 10,000 units in calculating the degree of operating leverage as follows:

DOL Q(P – V) / [Q(P – V) – F]
10,000($10 – $4)/ [10,000($10 – $4) – $50,000]
60,000/10,000 = 6.00

Subject Area: Managerial accounting—cost-volume-profit analysis. Source: CIA 597, IV-52.

156. (b) This response correctly calculates the contribution margin as the sales revenue less the variable costs. See supporting calculations below. Choice (a) is incorrect because this response correctly calculates the contribution margin as the sales revenue less the variable costs, but then takes this amount net of the income tax rate. See supporting calculations below. Choice (c) is incorrect because this response calculates the contribution margin as sales revenue less the sum of direct material, direct labor, and variable manufacturing overhead; variable selling expenses are incorrectly omitted. See supporting calculations below. Choice (d) is incorrect because this response calculates the contribution margin as sales revenue less the sum of direct material, direct labor, and variable selling expenses; variable manufacturing overhead is incorrectly omitted. See supporting calculations below.

Supporting calculations

	Choice (a)	*Correct Choice (b)*	*Choice (c)*	*Choice (d)*
Revenue	$9,000,000	$9,000,000	$9,000,000	$9,000,000
DM	$1,800,000	$1,800,000	$1,800,000	$1,800,000
DL	720,000	720,000	720,000	720,000
VOH	1,080,000	1,080,000	1,080,000	
Var. Sell	450,000	450,000		450,000
Total costs	$4,050,000	$4,050,000	$3,600,000	$2,970,000
Total CM	$4,950,000	$4,950,000	$5,400,000	$6,030,000
Income tax (.40)	1,980,000			
CM net of tax	$2,970,000			

Subject Area: Managerial accounting—cost-volume-profit analysis. Source: CIA 597, III-84.

157. (d) This response deducts all of the appropriate product costs (direct material, direct labor, variable and fixed manufacturing overhead) from revenue to obtain gross profit. See supporting calculations below. Choice (a) is incorrect because this response represents the calculation of operating income before taxes. See supporting calculations below. Choice (b) is incorrect because this response includes all of the appropriate product costs (direct material, direct labor, variable and fixed manufacturing overhead) but incorrectly includes fixed administrative expenses. See supporting calculations below. Choice (c) is incorrect because this response includes all of the appropriate product costs (direct material, direct labor, variable and fixed manufacturing overhead) but incorrectly includes variable selling expenses. See supporting calculations below.

Supporting calculations

	Choice (a)	*Choice (b)*	*Choice (c)*	*Correct Choice (d)*
Revenue	$9,000,000	$9,000,000	$9,000,000	$9,000,000
DM	$1,800,000	$1,800,000	$1,800,000	$1,800,000
DL	720,000	720,000	720,000	720,000
VOH	1,080,000	1,080,000	1,080,000	1,080,000
FOH	600,000	600,000	600,000	600,000
Var. sell	450,000		450,000	
Fix. sell	352,800			
Fix. admin	567,840	67,840		
Total costs	$5,570,640	$4,767,840	$4,650,000	$4,200,000
Gross profit	$3,429,360	$4,232,160	$4,350,000	$4,800,000

Subject Area: Managerial accounting—cost-volume-profit analysis. Source: CIA 597, III-85.

158. (c) This response divides the correct total fixed costs ($1,520,640) by the correct contribution margin per unit of $33. See supporting calculations below. Choice (a) is incorrect because this response treats fixed manufacturing overhead as a variable cost and omits variable selling expense, making the contribution margin figure incorrect. Then, the total fixed costs are calculated as only the fixed manufacturing overhead plus fixed administrative expenses ($600,000 + 567,840 = 1,167,840). This incorrect fixed cost amount is divided by the incorrect contribution margin per unit of $32. See supporting calculations below. Choice (b) is incorrect because this response omits variable selling expenses from the contribution margin per unit calculation. The correct total fixed costs ($1,520,640) are divided by an incorrect contribution margin per unit of $36. See supporting calculations below. Choice (d) is incorrect because this response divides the correct total fixed costs ($1,520,640) by the total variable costs per unit of $27. See supporting calculations below.

Supporting calculations
Total fixed cost calculation:

Manufacturing overhead	$ 600,000
Selling expenses	352,800
Administrative expenses	567,840
Total fixed costs	$1,520,640

	Choice (a)	*Choice (b)*	*Correct Choice (c)*	*Choice (d)*
Sell price/ unit*	$60.00	$60.00	$60.00	<ignored>
Variable costs/unit				
DM	$12.00	$12.00	$12.00	$12.00
DL	4.80	4.80	4.80	4.80
VOH	7.20	7.20	7.20	7.20
FOH	4.00			
Var sell			3.00	3.00
Total VC	$28.00	$24.00	$27.00	
CM per unit	$32.00	$36.00	$33.00	$27.00

**Selling price and variable costs per unit figures are derived by dividing the respective total dollar amounts given in the problem by the sales volume of 150,000 units.*

Subject Area: Managerial accounting—cost-volume-profit analysis. Source: CIA 597, III-86.

159. (c) This response incorporates the original fixed costs, additional fixed costs for the coming year, and the operating income before taxes in the calculation. The correct contribution margin rate is employed. ($4,979,520/.52). See supporting calculations below. Choice (a) is incorrect because this response incorporates the original fixed costs and additional fixed costs for the coming year but uses net income instead of operating income before taxes in the calculation. The correct contribution margin rate is employed. ($3,607,776/.52). See supporting calculations below.

Choice (b) is incorrect because this response incorporates the original fixed costs, additional fixed costs for the coming year, and the operating income before taxes in the calculation. However, the variable selling expenses are omitted from the contribution margin rate calculation. ($4,979,520/.57). See supporting calculations below. Choice (d) is incorrect because this response incorporates the original fixed costs, additional fixed costs for the coming year, and the operating income before taxes in the calculation. However, the variable cost ratio is incorrectly employed. ($4,979,520/.48). See supporting calculations below.

Supporting calculations

Calculation of numerator (fixed cost plus profit):

	Choice (a)	*Choices (b), (c) & (d)*
Total fixed costs	$1,520,640	$1,520,640
Additional fixed costs in current year	29,520	29,520
Operating income		3,429,360
Net income [$3,429,360 *(1 – .4)]	2,057,616	______
Numerator for calculation [FC + Profit]	$3,607,776	$4,979,520

Calculation of denominator (contribution margin rate):

	Choice (a) & (c)	*Choice (b)*	*Choice (d)*
Sell price/unit* (SP)	$60.00	$60.00	<ignored>
Variable costs/unit			
DM	$13.20	$13.20	$13.20
DL	5.40	5.40	5.40
VOH	7.20	7.20	7.20
Var sell	3.00	____	3.00
Total VC (TotVC)	$28.80	$25.80	$28.80
CM per unit (SP – TotVC)	$31.20	$34.20	
CM rate= CM/SP	52%	57%	
VC ratio (28.80/60)			48%

**Selling price and variable costs per unit figures are derived by dividing the respective total dollar amounts given in the problem by the sales volume of 150,000 units.*

Subject Area: Managerial accounting—cost-volume-profit analysis. Source: CIA 597, III-87.

160. (b) This response divides current variable costs ($28.80) by the original variable cost rate (45%) yielding a selling price ($64.00) that will have the same contribution margin percentage rate as originally (($64.00 – 28.80)/64.00 = 55%). See supporting calculations below. Choice (a) is incorrect because this response adds the increase in the total variable costs ($28.80 – 27.00 = $1.80) to the original selling price ($60.00 + 1.80 = 61.80). While this new selling price will yield the same contribution margin of $33.00 ($61.80 – 28.80 = 33.00), the contribution margin percentage rate is less than the original rate of 55% [(61.80 – 28.80)/61.80 = 53.4%]. See supporting calculations below. Choice (c) is incorrect because this response omits the variable selling expenses from the current variable costs and employs the original variable cost ratio when selling expenses are also omitted from the calculation. Thus, there are two errors in this calculation ($25.80/0.40 = $64.50). See supporting calculations below. Choice (d) is incorrect because this response divides current variable costs ($28.80) by the original variable cost ratio when selling expenses are omitted from the calculation (28.80/.40 = $72.00). See supporting calculations below.

Supporting calculations

Calculation: $\frac{\text{SP} - \text{New VC}}{\text{SP}}$ = Orig CM% with SP calculated as: New VC/(1– Orig CM%)

	New VC used in a, b, d	*New VC used in c*	*Orig VC used in a & b*	*Orig VC used in c & d*
Sell price/unit	$60.000	$60.000	$60.000	$60.000
Variable costs/unit				
DM	$13.20	$13.20	$12.00	$12.00
DL	5.40	5.40	4.80	4.80
VOH	7.20	7.20	7.20	7.20
Var sell	3.00		3.00	
Total VC	$28.80	$25.80	$27.00	$24.00
CM per unit [SP – TotVC]	$31.20	$34.20	$33.00	$36.00
CM rate [CM/SP]			55%	60%
VC ratio [VC/SP or 1 – CM%]		45%	40%	

**Selling price and variable costs per unit figures are derived by dividing the respective total dollar amounts given in the problem by the sales volume of 150,000 units.*

Subject Area: Managerial accounting—cost-volume-profit analysis. Source: CIA 597, III-88.

161. (c) Choice (c) is the correct answer. This solution includes the variable cost of the 300,000 units produced as well as the $2.50 incremental variable cost for the new direct material. See supporting calculations. Choice (a) is incorrect because this solution only considers the production costs of the good units sold and excludes the scrap cost of the defective units. A full 300,000 units would be produced with direct material so that the cost of the total units produced must be included in the costs. The solution also includes fixed manufacturing overhead, which is inappropriate; the fixed manufacturing overhead will be the same regardless of what direct material is used, and thus, it can be omitted from the solution. See supporting calculations. Choice (b) is incorrect because this solution only considers the variable costs of the good units produced and excludes the variable cost of the defective units produced. A full 300,000 units would be produced with direct material so that the variable cost of all 300,000 units produced must be included in the costs; this includes the additional $2.50 incremental cost for the new direct material. See supporting calculations. Choice (d) is incorrect because this solution is the same as alternative (c) except for the incremental cost of the new material. In this solution, the incremental cost of the new direct material is included only for the increase in the number of good units produced (294,000 – 264,000 = 30,000) which is not appropriate—the new material cost would be incurred for all 300,000 units. See supporting calculations.

Supporting calculations

	Choice (a)	*Choice (b)*	*Correct Choice (c)*	*Choice (d)*
Original:				
Units produced	300,000	300,000	300,000	300,000
Good units (88%)	264,000	264,000	264,000	264,000
Revenue				
264,000 × $50	13,200,000	13,200,000	13,200,000	13,200,000
Prod dept costs				
264,000 × $29.50	(7,788,000)			
264,000 × $21.50		(5,676,000)		
300,000 × $21.50			(6,450,000)	(6,450,000)
Margin	5,412,000	7,524,000	6,750,000	6,750,000

	Choice (a)	Choice (b)	Correct Choice (c)	Choice (d)
New material:				
Units produced	300,000	300,000	300,000	300,000
Good units (98%)	294,000	294,000	294,000	294,000
Revenue				
294,000 × $50	14,700,000	14,700,000	14,700,000	14,700,000
Prod dept costs				
294,000 × $29.50	(8,673,000)			
300,000 × $21.50			(6,450,000)	(6,450,000)
300,000 × $2.50			(750,000)	
294,000 × $21.50		(6,321,000)		
294,000 × $2.50	(735,000)	(735,000)		
30,000 × $2.50				(75,000)
Margin	5,292,000	7,644,000	7,500,000	8,175,000
Increase (decrease)	(120,000)	120,000	750,000	1,425,000

NOTE: The fixed manufacturing overhead is really irrelevant because it will be incurred in full under both situations. The inclusion of fixed manufacturing overhead in choice (a) is inappropriate because this solution is attempting to treat the overhead as a variable cost.

Subject Area: Managerial accounting—cost-volume-profit analysis. Source: CIA 596, III-80.

162. (b) This response uses the appropriate contribution margin rate, the correct annual fixed operating costs, and the correct adjustment of after-tax net income to a before-tax basis. Refer to the supporting calculations. Choice (a) is incorrect because this response does not include an adjustment to convert after-tax net income to before-tax income. Otherwise, the substitution and calculations are appropriate. Refer to the supporting calculations. Choice (c) is incorrect because this response uses the appropriate contribution margin rate and the correct annual fixed operating costs, but adjusts the after-tax net income to a before-tax basis incorrectly. The after-tax net income is divided by the tax rate of 40% rather than one minus the tax rate (1 – 40% = 60%). Refer to the supporting calculations. Choice (d) is incorrect because this response uses the correct annual fixed operating costs and the correct adjustment of after-tax net income to a before-tax basis, but uses the variable cost percentage (45%) rather than the contribution margin rate (55%). Refer to the supporting calculations.

Supporting calculations

The formula employed to calculate the dollar sales volume required to earn the same after-tax net income as the past year would be a derivation of the following:

Profit = Sales – Variable costs – Fixed costs

Because the response is to be in dollar sales volume, the sales less variable costs, which is the contribution margin, should be stated as a percentage of sales. In addition, the after-tax net income has to be converted to a before tax profit because the right side of the equation is before-tax. This can be accomplished by dividing net income by the factor "one minus the tax rate." The correct numbers to be used in the calculations are as follows:

	Per unit	Percent of sales
Selling price per unit	$40	100.0%
Variable costs per unit:		
Direct material	$ 5	12.5%
Direct labor	4	10.0
Manufacturing overhead	6	15.0
Selling and administrative costs	3	7.5
Total variable costs per unit	$18	45.0%
Contribution margin	$22	55.0%
Annual fixed operating costs:		
Manufacturing overhead		$6,200,000
Selling and administrative costs		3,700,000
Total annual fixed operating costs		$9,900,000

The substitutions into the basic C/V/P formula given above to derive the numerical answer for each of the four alternatives are as follows (S = Dollar sales volume):

Choice (a): $1,188,000 = 1.00S – .45S – $9,900,000; S = $20,160,000.

Choice (b): $1,188,000/(1 – .4) = 1.00S – .45S – $9,900,000; S = $21,600,000.

Choice (c): $1,188,000/.4) = 1.00S – .45S – $9,900,000; S = $23,400,000.

Choice (d): $1,188,000/(1 – .4) = .45S – $9,900,000; S = $26,400,000.

Subject Area: Managerial accounting—cost-volume-profit analysis. Source: CIA 596, III-84.

163. (d) This response makes the appropriate substitutions for the profit (10% return on sales), unit contribution (selling price less variable costs), and fixed costs (original plus additional marketing). Refer to the supporting calculations.

Choice (a) is incorrect because this response makes the appropriate substitutions for unit contribution (selling price less variable costs) and fixed costs (original plus additional marketing) but uses the wrong sign for the profit (10% return on sales), making the calculation incorrect. Refer to the supporting calculations. Choice (b) is incorrect because this response makes the appropriate substitutions for the profit (10% return on sales), unit contribution (selling price less variable costs), and original fixed costs but the additional marketing is added into the right side of the equation rather than being subtracted. Refer to the supporting calculations. Choice (c) is incorrect because this response makes the appropriate substitutions for the profit (10% return on sales) and fixed costs (original plus additional marketing). However, the unit contribution substitution is incorrect (selling price less variable costs); the contribution margin per unit is off by $3.00 which can represent ignoring the $3.00 increase in direct material or ignoring the variable selling and administrative cost, either of which is incorrect. Refer to the supporting calculations.

Supporting calculations

The formula employed to calculate the dollar sales volume required to earn the same after-tax net income as the past year would be a derivation of the following:

Profit = Sales – Variable costs – Fixed costs

Because the response is to be in unit sales volume, the sales less variable costs, which is the contribution margin, should be stated in unit figures. The correct numbers to be used in the calculations are as follows:

Selling price per unit (revised)		$50
Variable costs per unit:		
Direct material (revised)		$ 8
Direct labor		4
Manufacturing overhead		6
Selling and administrative costs		3
Total variable costs per unit		21
Contribution margin		$29
Annual fixed operating costs:		
Manufacturing overhead	$ 6,200,000	
Selling and administrative costs	3,700,000	
Additional marketing costs	1,575,000	
Total annual fixed operating costs	$11,475,000	

The substitutions into the basic C/V/P formula given above to derive the numerical answer for each of the four alternatives are as follows (X = unit sales volume):

Choice (a): –0.10 × ($50X) = $50X – $21X – $11,475,000; X = 337,500.

Choice (b): 0.10 × ($50X) = $50X – $21X – $9,900,000 + 1,575,000; X = 346,875.

Choice (c): 0.10 × ($50X) = $50X – $18X – $11,475,000; X = 425,000.

Choice (d): 0.10 × ($50X) = $50X – $21X – $11,475,000; X = 478,125.

Subject Area: Managerial accounting—cost-volume-profit analysis. Source: CIA 596, III-85.

164. (b) [$12 + ($50 – $45)] × 1,200. Choice (a) is incorrect. $12 × 1,200. Choice (c) is incorrect. [$50 – ($20 + $12)] × 1,200. Choice (d) is incorrect. ($45 – $12) × 1,200.

Subject Area: Managerial accounting—cost-volume-profit analysis. Source: CIA 596, III-96.

165. (d) This solution correctly divides the total fixed costs by contribution margin per unit ($396,000/18). See supporting calculations below. Choice (a) is incorrect because this solution divides the total fixed costs by the contribution margin rate, but ignores the decimal point resulting in an inappropriate amount ($396,000/45). See supporting calculations below. Choice (b) is incorrect because this solution divides the total fixed costs by the total variable costs ($396,000/22). See supporting calculations below. Choice (c) is incorrect because this solution divides the total fixed costs by the variable cost of sales (or unit contribution margin if the commission is ignored) ($396,000/20). See supporting calculations below.

Supporting calculation:

	Dollar amount	*Percent*
Selling price	$40	100%
Variable costs		
Cost of sales	$20	50%
Commission (5%)	2	5
Total variable costs	$22	55%
Contribution margin	$18	45%
Total fixed costs: $396,000		

$$\frac{\text{Total fixed costs}}{\text{Unit cont. margin}} = \frac{396{,}000}{18} = 22{,}000$$

Subject Area: Managerial accounting—cost-volume-profit analysis. Source: CIA 1195, III-87.

166. (c) This solution correctly adjusts the net income to before-tax profits by dividing net income by one minus the tax rate. The fixed costs include salaries at $80,000, rather than reducing the fixed costs by $80,000, resulting in an incorrect amount of $296,000. The new contribution margin rate of 40% is employed. Thus, the calculation is: [$100,800/(1 – .3)] = .40S-$296,000, where S = Dollar sales volume. See supporting calculations below. Choice (a) is incorrect because this solution does not adjust the net income to before-tax profits; all other calculations are appropriate ($100,800 = .40S – $316,000, where S = Dollar sales volume). See supporting calculations below. Choice (b) is incorrect because this solution correctly adjusts the net income to before-tax profits by dividing net income by one minus the tax rate. The fixed costs are decreased by $80,000 to $316,000 and the new contribution margin rate of 40% is employed. Thus, the correct calculation is: [$100,800/(1 – .3)] = .40S-$316,000, where S = Dollar sales volume. See supporting calculations below. Choice (d) is incorrect because this solution incorrectly adjusts the net income to before-tax profits by dividing net income by the tax rate; all other calculations are appropriate [($100,800/.3) = .40S – $316,000, where S = Dollar sales volume]. See supporting calculations below.

Supporting calculations

	Dollar amount	*Percent*
Selling price	$40	100%
Variable costs		
Cost of sales	$20	50%
Commission (10%)	4	10%
Total variable costs	$24	60%
Contribution margin	$16	40%
Fixed costs:		
Advertising	$124,000	
Rent	60,000	
Salaries (adjusted)	100,000	
Other fixed	32,000	
Total	$316,000	

Sales volume = (Net income before taxes + Fixed costs)/ Contribution margin
Sales volume = (144,000 + 316,000)/0.4 = 1,150,000
Net income before taxes = 100,800/(1.00-0.30) = 100,800/0.7 = 144,000

Subject Area: Managerial accounting—cost-volume-profit analysis. Source: CIA 1195, III-88.

167. (d) This response is correct because the fixed cost per unit and the target return on investment per unit are based on the planned volume for the year. See supporting calculations below. Choice (a) is incorrect because this response includes the correct variable costs per unit and the appropriate calculated target return on investment per unit (based on 500,000 units), but omits all of the fixed costs. See supporting calculations below.

Choice (b) is incorrect because this response includes the correct variable costs per unit. While the fixed costs and the target return on investment are included, the cost per unit is based on 600,000 units rather than the correct amount of 500,000 [Fixed costs: ($810,000 + 270,000)/600,000 = $1.80; Target return: ($6,750,000 × 2)/600,000 = $2.25]. See supporting calculations below. Choice (c) is incorrect because this response includes the correct variable costs per unit and the appropriately calculated target return on investment per unit. However, the fixed cost per unit is based on 600,000 units rather than the correct amount of 500,000 [Fixed costs: ($810,000 + 270,000)/600,000 = $1.80]. See supporting calculations below.

Supporting calculations

	Correct Choice (d)	*Choice (a)*	*Choice (b)*	*Choice (c)*
Variable mfg. cost	$ 4.85	$ 4.85	$ 4.85	$ 4.85
Variable packaging cost	.35	.35	.35	.35
Variable distribution cost	1.80	1.80	1.80	1.80
Total variable costs	$ 7.00	$ 7.00	$ 7.00	$ 7.00
Fixed costs				
MOH 810,000/500,000	1.62		1.35	1.35
Packaging and distribution 270,000/500,000	.54		.45	.45
Target return (6,750,000 × .2)/500,000	2.70	2.70	2.25	2.70
Total	$11.86	$ 9.70	$11.05	$11.50

Subject Area: Managerial accounting—cost-volume-profit analysis. Source: CIA 1195, III-91.

168. (a) The confectioner manufacturer's minimum bid selling price would include its variable manufacturing costs, variable marketing and packaging costs, distribution costs, and the special setup costs. Fixed costs are capacity costs that do not change because the manufacturer has excess capacity. See supporting calculations below. Choice (b) is incorrect because this solution is incorrect because the additional distribution costs are added to the original distribution costs ($1.80+.80). See supporting calculations below. Choice (c) is incorrect because this solution incorrectly adds an amount for the fixed costs to the relevant costs. See supporting calculations below. Choice (d) is incorrect because this solution incorrectly adds an amount for the target return on investment to the relevant costs. See supporting calculations below.

Supporting calculations

	Correct Choice (a)	*Choice (b)*	*Choice (c)*	*Choice (d)*
Variable mfg. cost ($4.85 – .45)	$4.40	$4.40	$4.40	$4.40
Variable packaging cost	.35	.35	.35	.35
Variable dist. cost ($32,000/40,000)	.80	2.60	.80	.80
Setup ($60,000/40,000)	1.50	1.50	1.50	1.50
Relevant costs	$7.05	$8.85	$7.05	$7.05
Fixed costs 1,080,000/540,000	N/R	N/R	2.00	N/R
Target return (6,750,000 × .2)/540,000	N/R	N/R	N/R	2.50
Total	$7.05	$8.85	$9.05	$9.55

Subject Area: Managerial accounting—cost-volume-profit analysis. Source: CIA 1195, III-92.

169. (b) Contribution margin per unit = CM% × Selling price = 0.2 × 100 = $20

$$\text{Breakeven units} = \frac{\text{Fixed expenses}}{\text{CM per unit}} = \frac{40{,}000}{20} = 2{,}000 \text{ units.}$$

Therefore, choices (a), (c), and (d) are incorrect.

Subject Area: Managerial accounting—cost-volume-profit analysis. Source: CIA 595, III-83.

170. (d)

$$\text{Sales} = \frac{\text{Fixed expenses + Profit}}{\text{CM\%}} = \frac{40{,}000 + 20{,}000}{0.2} = \$300{,}000$$

Therefore, by definition choices (a), (b,) and (c) are incorrect.

Subject Area: Managerial accounting—cost-volume-profit analysis. Source: CIA 595, III-84.

171. (c) This solution divides the sum of the annual fixed operating costs ($772,200 + 1,801,800 = $2,574,000) and the projected profit in 2005 ($643,500), or $3,217,500, by the correct contribution margin percentage of .55 calculated by subtracting the sum of the variable cost percentages for merchandise (.30), commissions (.05), and shipping (.10) from 1.00. Choice (a) is incorrect because this solution divides the sum of the annual fixed operating costs ($772,200 + 1,801,800 = $2,574,000) and the projected profit in 2005 ($643,500), or $3,217,500, by an incorrect contribution margin percentage of .65 calculated by subtracting the sum of the variable cost percentages for merchandise (.30) and commissions (.05) from 1.00. Choice (b) is incorrect because this solution divides the sum of the annual fixed operating costs ($772,200 + 1,801,800 = $2,574,000) and the projected profit in 2005 ($643,500), or $3,217,500, by an incorrect contribution margin percentage of .60 calculated by subtracting the sum of the variable cost percentages for merchandise (.30) and shipping (.10) from 1.00. Choice (d) is incorrect because this solution divides the sum of the annual fixed operating costs ($772,200 + 1,801,800 = $2,574,000) and the projected profit in 2005 ($643,500), or $3,217,500, by an incorrect contribution margin percentage of .45 which is really the sum of the variable cost percentages for merchandise (.30), commissions (.05), and shipping (.10).

Subject Area: Managerial accounting—cost-volume-profit analysis. Source: CIA 1194, III-51.

172. (d) This solution represents the difference between the projected annual dollar sales for 2005 of $6,000,000 and the correct calculation of breakeven sales for 2005 calculated by dividing the annual fixed operating costs ($772,200 + 1,801,800 = $2,574,000) by a contribution margin percentage of 0.55 obtained by subtracting the sum of the variable cost percentages for merchandise (.30), commissions (.05), and shipping (.10) from 1.00. Choice (a) is incorrect because this solution represents the difference between the before-tax profit that would be earned on 2005 sales [($6,000,000 × .55) – (772,200 + 1,801,800) = $726,000] and the projected before-tax profit for 2004 ($643,500). Choice (b) is incorrect because this solution represents the difference between the projected annual dollar sales for 2005 of $6,000,000 and the sales volume required to earn the same before-tax profit in 2005 as projected for 2004 (solution for item 51; $3,217,500/.55 = $5,850,000). Choice (c) is incorrect because this solution represents the difference between the projected annual dollar sales for 2005 of $6,000,000 and an incorrect calculation of breakeven sales for 2005 calculated by dividing the annual fixed operating costs ($772,200 + 1,801,800 = $2,574,000) by an incorrect contribution margin percentage of .45 which is the sum of the variable cost percentages for merchandise (.30), commissions (.05), and shipping (.10).

Subject Area: Managerial accounting—cost-volume-profit analysis. Source: CIA 1194, III-52.

173. (a) Computations follow:

Revenue – Variable cost – Fixed cost = Profit. Let X = Number of dozen golf balls.

5X – 4X = 30,000 + 0.1 (5X)
X = 60,000 dozen

Therefore, choices (b), (c), and (d) are incorrect.

Subject Area: Managerial accounting—cost-volume-profit analysis. Source: CIA 590, III-50.

174. (c) The breakeven volume is calculated as follows:

Breakeven volume = Fixed costs/(Price – Unit variable costs)
= 450,000/($25 – $15) = 450,000/($10) = 45,000 units

Choice (a) is incorrect because this answer is calculated with only price in the denominator, rather than price less unit variable costs, as follows:

Breakeven volume = Fixed costs / Price
= 450,000 / ($25) = 18,000 units

Choice (b) is incorrect because this answer is calculated with only unit variable costs in the denominator, rather than price less unit variable costs, as follows:

Breakeven volume = Fixed costs / Unit variable costs

= 450,000 / ($15) = 30,000 units

Choice (d) is incorrect because this answer is calculated by adding the $150,000 noncash outlays to the fixed production costs and dividing this amount by price less unit variable costs, as follows:

Breakeven volume = (Fixed costs + Noncash outlays)/(Price – Unit variable costs)

= (450,000 + 150,000)/($25 – $15)

= 600,000/($10) = 60,000 units

Subject Area: Managerial accounting—cost-volume-profit analysis. Source: CIA 596, IV-43.

175. (d) Sales revenue is calculated as follows:

Earnings before tax = Net income/ (1 – Tax rate) = $10/.5 = $20

Earnings before interest and tax = Earnings before tax + Interest

= $20 + $20 = $40

Sales – Cost of goods sold – General & admin. expense = $40

Sales – Cost of goods sold – $50 = $40

Sales – Cost of goods sold = $90

and using the gross margin percentage of .5,

Sales = 2 (Cost of goods sold)

So 2 (cost of goods sold) – Cost of goods sold = $90
Cost of goods sold = $90 and sales = $180

Choice (a) is incorrect because this is the gross profit or sales minus cost of goods sold. Choice (b) is incorrect because this solution uses the 50% gross margin figure incorrectly in deriving the figure for sales revenue as follows:

Sales – Cost of goods sold = $90

and using the gross margin percentage of .5,

Sales = (1 + .5) (Sales – Cost of goods sold)

Sales = 1.5 ($90) = $135

Choice (c) is incorrect because this solution calculates earnings before tax as .5 times net income rather than 2 times net income and calculates sales revenue as follows:

Earnings before tax = .5 (Net income) = .5 ($10) = $5

Earnings before interest and tax = Earnings before tax + Interest
= $5 + $20 = $25

Sales – Cost of goods sold – General & admin. expense = $25

Sales – Cost of goods sold – $50 = $25

Sales – Cost of goods sold = $75

and since the gross margin = .5 , Sales = 2 (cost of goods sold)

So 2 (Cost of goods sold) – Cost of goods sold = $75

So Cost of goods sold = $75 and Sales = 2 (Cost of goods sold) = $150

Subject Area: Managerial accounting—cost-volume-profit analysis. Source: CIA 596, IV-44.

176. (c) If unit variable costs are higher, the unit contribution margin will be lower and the breakeven point in units will be higher. Choice (a) is incorrect because the breakeven point in units is that point of sales volume where total revenues equal total costs. It is calculated as follows:

$$\frac{\text{Fixed costs}}{\text{Unit contribution margin}} = \frac{\text{Fixed costs}}{\text{Unit price} - \text{Unit variable costs}}$$

If sales revenue is higher, all else equal, then the unit price must be higher and the breakeven point in units will be lower. Choice (b) is incorrect because if fixed costs are lower then the breakeven point in units will be lower. Choice (d) is incorrect because the number of units sold does not affect the breakeven point in units.

Subject Area: Managerial accounting—cost-volume-profit analysis. Source: CIA 1194, IV-44.

177. (c) Contribution margin in dollars is sales revenue minus total variable costs. Choice (a) is incorrect because this formula calculates operating income. Choice (b) is incorrect because the calculation of contribution margin in dollars involves subtracting total variable costs, not variable costs per unit, from sales revenue. Choice (d) is incorrect. When calculating contribution margin in dollars, total variable costs are subtracted rather than variable costs per unit and fixed operating costs are not subtracted from sales revenue.

Subject Area: Managerial accounting—cost-volume-profit analysis. Source: CIA 1194, IV-45.

178. (b) The contribution margin is the selling price ($40) less the variable cost ($24), or $16. Choice (a) is incorrect because this includes fixed costs. Choice (c) is incorrect because this is the variable cost. Choice (d) is incorrect because this is the selling price.

Subject Area: Managerial accounting—cost-volume-profit analysis. Source: CIA 590, IV-10.

179. (d) Breakeven point is equal to fixed costs divided by contribution margin.

93,750/30 = 3,125 units.

Therefore, by definition, choices (a, b, and c) will be incorrect.

Subject Area: Managerial accounting—cost-volume-profit analysis. Source: CIA 590, IV-11.

180. (d) Contribution margin is the gross profit of $80,000 minus the $40,000 of sales salaries. Choice (a) is incorrect because this is net income. Choice (b) is incorrect because janitorial and heat and light are fixed costs. Choice (c) is incorrect because depreciation is a fixed cost.

Subject Area: Managerial accounting—cost-volume-profit analysis. Source: CIA 590, IV-18.

181. **(c)** Full capacity sales can be calculated as follows:

Actual sales/Percent of capacity at which fixed assets were operated

= $2,000,000/.80

= $2,500,000

Choice (a) is incorrect because this is 80% of the actual sales, calculated as .80 ($2,000,000) = $1,600,000. Choice (b) is incorrect because this is the actual sales. Choice (d) is incorrect because this is actual sales divided by the proportion of unused, rather than used, capacity, or $2,000,000/.2 = $10,000,000.

Subject Area: Managerial accounting—cost-volume-profit analysis. Source: CIA Model Exam 2002, IV-55.

Relevant Costs

182. **(a)** Includes the relevant costs of direct material, direct labor, variable overhead, and variable selling and administrative at 40% of the original amount. All fixed costs are irrelevant because they will be unchanged. See supporting calculations. Choice (b) is incorrect because it includes the relevant costs of direct material, direct labor, variable overhead, and variable selling and administrative but the variable selling and administrative is at 60% of the original amount which is incorrect. The fixed costs were not included. See supporting calculations. Choice (c) is incorrect because it includes the relevant costs of direct material, direct labor, variable overhead, and variable selling and administrative at 40% of the original amount. The fixed costs were inappropriately included (they will not change as a consequence of the order) but the total fixed costs were spread over a volume level of 600,000 units. See supporting calculations. Choice (d) is incorrect because it includes the relevant costs of direct material, direct labor, variable overhead, and variable selling and administrative at 40% of the original amount. The fixed costs were inappropriately included (they will not change as a consequence of the order) at the full absorption unit cost. See supporting calculations.

Supporting calculations

	Choice (a)	Choice (b)	Choice (c)	Choice (d)
Direct material	$ 9.80	$ 9.80	$ 9.80	$ 9.80
Direct labor	4.50	4.50	4.50	4.50
Variable overhead (.25 × 12.00)	3.00	3.00	3.00	3.00
Fixed overhead	N/R	N/R	7.50[3]	9.00[4]
Variable S & A	1.00[1]	1.50[2]	1.00[1]	1.00[1]
Fixed S & A	N/R	N/R	3.50[3]	4.20[4]
Total unit costs	$18.30	$18.80	$29.30	$31.50
Total cost @ volume of 100,000 (000 omitted)	$1,830	$1,880	$2,930	$3,150

N/R = Not Relevant.

[1] *Original unit cost reduced by the savings [$2.50 × (1 – .6)].*

[2] *Original cost times the savings (incorrect) ($2.50 × .6).*

[3] *Fixed cost components divided by the new total volume:*

Fixed overhead: (.75×$6,000,000)/(500,000 + 100,000).
Fixed S & A: $2,100,000/(500,000 + 100,000).

[4] *Fixed cost components at their original unit cost for a volume of 500,000 units.*

Subject Area: Managerial accounting—relevant costs. Source: CIA 592, IV-10.

183. **(a)** Choice (a) is correct.

(3 – 2)(7,000) = $ 7,000 for rework
(1.85)(7,000) = $12,950 for scrap
Advantage SCRAP by $5,950

Choice (b) is incorrect. (6 + 3 – 2)(7,000) – (1.85)(7,000). Choice (c) is incorrect. (1.85 + 6)(7,000) – (3 – 2)(7,000). Choice (d) is incorrect. (3)(7,000) – (1.85)(7,000).

Subject Area: Managerial accounting—relevant costs. Source: CIA 594, III-45.

184. **(c)** Choice (c) is correct.

Sales	Probability	Expected Value
1,000	.2	200
1,500	.3	450
2,000	.4	800
2,500	.1	250
		1,700

Choice (a) is incorrect because this is the incorrectly computed simple average of the past quarters: (1,000 + 1,500 + 2,000 + 2,500)/10 = 700. Choice (b) is incorrect because this is the minimum number of P1 manufactured during the past quarters; it does not represent expected requirements for P1 for the following quarter. Choice (d) is incorrect because this number represents the quantity of P1 sold that occurred with the greatest frequency; it does not represent expected requirements of P1 in the following quarter.

Subject Area: Managerial accounting—relevant costs. Source: CIA 591, IV-25.

185. **(d)** Perfect information is the difference between the expected profit with perfect information and the highest expected profit with existing information. Choice (a) is incorrect. The difference between lost profits (a cost of underproduction) and additional carrying costs (a cost of overproduction) does not represent the value of perfect information. Choice (b) is incorrect. The sum of lost profits and additional carrying costs does not represent the value of perfect information. Choice (c) is incorrect. The expected profit from sales of P1 less the expected carrying costs if too many are produced does not represent the value of perfect information.

Subject Area: Managerial accounting—relevant costs. Source: CIA 591, IV-26.

186. **(a)** Choice (a) is correct.

	Make	Buy
Variable costs ($7.00 × 2,500)	$17,500	--
Fixed costs $4,000	$4,000	
Outside purchase ($8.75 × 2,500)	--	21,875
Contribution from otherwise unused facilities		(5,500)
Total costs	$21,500	$20,375

Difference: $21,500 – $20,375 = $1,125.

Choice (b) is incorrect because this solution ignores the fact that fixed costs of $4,000 will continue to be experienced even if the parts are purchased:

Make: $17,500 + $4,000 = $21,500.
Buy: $21,875 – $5,500 = $16,375.
Difference (incorrect): $21,500 – $16,375 = $5,125.

Choice (c) is incorrect because this solution ignores the $5,500 contribution made by production of the alternate product:

Make: $17,500 + $4,000 = $21,500.
Buy: $21,875 + $4,000 = $25,875.
Difference (incorrect): $21,500 – $25,875 = $(4,375).

Choice (d) is incorrect because this solution incorrectly adds the $5,500 contribution from production of the alternate product to the purchase and fixed costs of the buy alternative:

Make: $17,500 + $4,000 = $21,500.

Buy: $21,875 + $4,000 + $5,500 = $31,375.

Difference (incorrect): $21,500 – $31,375 = $(9,875).

Subject Area: Managerial accounting—relevant costs. Source: CIA 591, IV-27.

187. (c) Besides the relevant direct material, direct labor, variable manufacturing overhead, and rental costs of the special machinery, this solution excludes the irrelevant fixed manufacturing overhead capacity and uses the rental costs of the new warehouse which has to be rented as a consequence of deciding to manufacture the motor internally. The cost of the current warehouse space is not relevant to the decision because it will be incurred regardless of the decision; it is a sunk cost. See the supporting calculations below. Choice (a) is incorrect. Besides the relevant direct material, direct labor, variable manufacturing overhead, and rental costs of the special machinery, this solution includes fixed manufacturing overhead that is not relevant to capacity and uses the rental costs of the current warehouse space (sunk cost that is not relevant) rather than the cost of the new warehouse which has to be rented as a consequence of deciding to manufacture the motor internally. See the supporting calculations below. Choice (b) is incorrect. Besides the relevant direct material, direct labor, variable manufacturing overhead, and rental costs of the special machinery, this solution includes fixed manufacturing overhead that is not relevant to capacity and uses the rental costs of the new warehouse which has to be rented as a consequence of deciding to manufacture the motor internally. The cost of the current warehouse space is not relevant to the decision because it will be incurred regardless of the decision; it is a sunk cost. See the supporting calculations below. Choice (d) is incorrect. Besides the relevant direct material, direct labor, variable manufacturing overhead, and rental costs of the special machinery, this solution includes the rental costs of the current warehouse space (sunk cost that is not relevant) rather than the cost of the new warehouse, which has to be rented as a consequence of deciding to manufacture the motor internally. See the supporting calculations below.

Supporting calculations

	Choice (a)	*Choice (b)*	*Choice (c)*	*Choice (d)*
Direct material	$ 8.00	$ 8.00	$ 8.00	$ 8.00
Direct labor	4.00	4.00	4.00	4.00
Variable mfg. overhead	3.00	3.00	3.00	3.00
Fixed mfg. overhead	5.00	5.00		
Current space rental (39,000/30,000)	1.30			1.30
New space rental (54,000/30,000)		1.80	1.80	
Machinery rental (45,000/30,000)	1.50	1.50	1.50	1.50
Internal cost/unit	$ 22.80	$ 23.30	$ 18.30	$ 17.80
Outside cost/unit	21.00	21.00	21.00	21.00
Advantage: Make/<Buy>	$ (1.80)	$ (2.30)	$ 2.70	$ 3.20
Volume	30,000	30,000	30,000	30,000
Advantage: Make/<Buy>	$(54,000)	$(69,000)	$81,000	$96,000

Subject Area: Managerial accounting—relevant costs. Source: CIA 1195, III-68.

188. (d) The stem defines opportunity cost, which is the contribution that is foregone (rejected) by not using a limited resource for another alternative. Choice (a) is incorrect because residual income is the net operating income of a segment/project less an imputed interest charge for the investment base; this is not an appropriate use of the term in this setting. Choice (b) is incorrect because sunk costs are past costs that are unavoidable because they cannot be changed regardless of the action that is taken; this is not an appropriate use of the term in this setting. Choice (c) is incorrect because separable costs arise in a joint process setting and are those costs incurred beyond the split-off point that are assigned to individual products; this is not an appropriate use of the term in this setting.

Subject Area: Managerial accounting—relevant costs. Source: CIA 1195, III-69.

189. (b) If the company accepts the special order, its revenue will increase by $76,000 ($7.60 × 10,000 units). Its incremental cost will include only the variable costs. Fixed manufacturing and fixed selling costs will remain unchanged. The increase in cost from accepting the special order

= ($3.00 + 1.00 + 0.80 + 1.20) × 10,000 units
= $60,000.

Therefore, acceptance of the special order will increase profit by $76,000 – 60,000 = $16,000. By definition, choices (a), (c), and (d) are incorrect.

Subject Area: Managerial accounting—relevant costs. Source: CIA 595, III-85.

190. (b) Since total fixed costs are unaffected, the change in profit can be computed by computing the change in contribution margin.

Contribution margin at current selling price
= ($10 – 3 – 1 – 0.80 – 2) × 75,000 units
= $240,000.

Contribution margin at $9.30 selling price
= ($9.30 – 3 – 1 – 0.80 – 2) × 90,000 units
= $225,000.

Therefore, profit will be reduced by $15,000 if the selling price is lowered to $9.30. By definition, choices (a), (c), and (d) are incorrect.

Subject Area: Managerial accounting—relevant costs. Source: CIA 595, III-86.

191. (c) This item is correct because it includes the quantitative costs that are relevant (expected future costs that differ among the alternative courses of action) and the qualitative factors, which cannot be measured in numerical terms. Choice (a) is incorrect because one of the pitfalls of cost-benefit analysis is to assume that all variable costs are relevant to decisions and all fixed costs are irrelevant. This is not the case; variable costs can be relevant or irrelevant and so can fixed costs. Choice (b) is incorrect because only expected incremental out-of-pocket costs would be relevant in cost-benefit analysis; common costs would not be relevant. Choice (d) is incorrect because expected historical costs would not be relevant in cost-benefit analysis; these costs would include any sunk costs, which should have no impact on the decision.

Subject Area: Managerial accounting—relevant costs. Source: CIA 1194, III-56.

192. (a) This solution is correct because it considers only the relevant costs of this decision. The systems development cost is valued at the cost of the independent contractor because this is the out-of-pocket expenditure required for the project. The hardware and the incremental supplies cost are also incremental expenditures. The computer time is irrelevant because the organization has excess time. The occupancy cost will be incurred whether this person is working or not. Please refer to the supporting calculations for all four alternatives, which follow the explanation of responses. Choice (b) is incorrect because it values the development cost at the rate of the internal systems analyst. These are not incremental out-of-pocket costs. Choice (c) is incorrect because it includes the irrelevant computer charges and occupancy costs. Choice (d) is incorrect because this solution includes the incremental development hours for the internal systems analyst value at the internal hourly charge—both of which are incorrect. The out-of-pocket rate is $22 and a full 1,000 hours are needed for developing the internal software. Computer charges and occupancy costs are irrelevant.

Supporting calculations

	Choice (a)	*Choice (b)*	*Choice (c)*	*Choice (d)*
System analyst		25,000[1]		24,000[2]
Outside contractor	22,000[3]		22,000[3]	
Computer charges			550[4]	550[4]
Hardware	3,200	3,200	3,200	3,200
Supplies	300[5]	300[5]	300[5]	300[5]
Occupancy			4,500[6]	4,500[6]
Subtotal	25,500	28,500	30,550	32,550
Cost of outside package	29,000	29,000	29,000	29,000
Differential costs	–3,500	–500	+1,550	+3,550

[1] *1,000 × 25=25,000*
[2] *(1000 – 40) × 25=24,000*
[3] *1000 × 22=22,000*
[4] *800 – 250=550*
[5] *500 – 200=300*
[6] *100 × 45=4,500*

Subject Area: Managerial accounting—relevant costs. Source: CIA 1194, III-57.

Costing Systems

193. (b) When there is only one product, the allocation of costs to the product is trivial. All of the cost is assigned to the one product; the particular method used to allocate the costs does not matter. Choices (a), (c), and (d) are incorrect because each one is a true statement.

Subject Area: Managerial accounting—costing systems. Source: CIA 594, III-47.

194. (b) There is a direct causal relationship between the number of components in a finished product and the amount of material handling costs incurred. Choice (a) is incorrect because this allocation basis is related to batch costs and not to individual unit costs. Choice (c) is incorrect because this allocation basis is the traditional basis for allocating overhead costs to the units produced when the production process is labor-intensive. Choice (d) is incorrect because this is not an allocation basis but rather the result of the allocation process when determining product costs.

Subject Area: Managerial accounting—costing systems. Source: CIA 597, III-80.

195. (d) An internal auditor is concerned with management being able to rely on the information contained in the company's operating reports. Choice (a) is incorrect because an engineer would have the best knowledge on activities and cost drivers. Choice (b) is incorrect because an information systems expert would have the best knowledge of information needs and information processing procedures. Choice (c) is incorrect because a management accountant would have the best knowledge of a company's current product cost.

Subject Area: Managerial accounting—costing systems. Source: CIA 596, III-22.

196. (b) Cost drivers provide direct tracing from support activities to products. Choice (a) is incorrect because both financial and nonfinancial cost drivers are employed in ABC. Choice (c) is incorrect because traditional full-absorption costing does this. Choice (d) is incorrect because both full-absorption and ABC assign direct costs to products as well as indirect costs using some application basis.

Subject Area: Managerial accounting—costing systems. Source: CIA 596, III-79.

197. (c) The traditional full cost system can be a standard cost or absorption cost system. It adds all costs to produce a product. This solution adds the total manufacturing overhead ($1,800,000) applied on the basis of total machine hours (30,000) to the total prime costs ($4.40 + 0.75 = $5.15). The manufacturing overhead rate employed in this case is $60 times the number of machine hours required [(20,000 units/5,000 per batch) × 80 MH per batch = 320]. See supporting calculations below. Choice (a) is incorrect because this solution employs the appropriate manufacturing overhead (MOH) rate ($60), but ignores the fact that there are four batches; thus only 80 machine hours are used. The inappropriate MOH per unit is added to the total prime costs ($4.40 + 0.75 = $5.15). See supporting calculations below. Choice (b) is incorrect because this solution employs only the machining overhead rate ($18), but does use the correct machine hours [(80MH/batch) × (4 batches) = 320]. The inappropriate MOH per unit is added to the total prime costs ($4.40 + 0.75 = $5.15). See supporting calculations below. Choice (d) is incorrect because this solution employs a direct labor hour manufacturing overhead rate ($36), which is inappropriate. The inappropriate MOH per unit (.05 × $36 = $1.80) is added to the total prime costs ($4.40 + 0.75 = $5.15). See supporting calculations below.

Supporting calculations

Alternative manufacturing overhead rates:

Choices (a) & (c):	(Total MOH)/(Total MH) = $1,800,000/30,000 = $60
Choice (b):	(Machining cost)/(Total MH) = $540,000/30,000 = $18
Choice (d):	(Total MOH)/(Total DLH) = $1,800,000/50,000 = $36

	Correct Choice (c)	*Choice (a)*	*Choice (b)*	*Choice (d)*
MOH rate used	$60	$60	$18	$36
Basis	MH 4 × 80 = 320	MH= 80	MH 4 × 80 = 320	DLH .05 × 20,000 = 1,000
Total MOH	$19,200	$4,800	$5,760	$36,000
MOH/unit (divide by 20,000)	$ .96	$ .24	$ .288	$1.80
Prime costs	5.15	5.15	5.15	5.15
Total unit cost	$6.11	$5.39	$5.438	$6.95

Subject Area: Managerial accounting—costing systems. Source: CIA 1195, III-93.

198. (d) This solution uses the correct cost per driver and the appropriate number of parts, batches, and setups. See supporting calculations below. Choice (a) is incorrect. This solution is correct except the two setups per batch are omitted from the setup cost calculation and only 80 machine hours are used for machining cost calculation (the four batches are ignored). See supporting calculations below. Choice (b) is incorrect. This solution is correct except only 80 machine hours are used for machining cost calculation (the four batches are ignored). See supporting calculations below. Choice (c) is incorrect. This solution is correct except the two setups per batch are omitted from the setup cost calculation. See supporting calculations below.

Supporting calculations

Activity	Budgeted activity	Budgeted cost	Cost per driver
Material handling	6,000,000	$ 720,000	$0.12/part
Setup costs	750	315,000	$420/setup
Machining costs	30,000	540,000	$18/MH
Quality control	500	225,000	$450/batch
Total MOH cost		$1,800,000	

	Correct choice (d)	Choice (a)	Choice (b)	Choice (c)
Mat hand 5 pts × 20,000 × $.12	$12,000	$12,000	$12,000	$12,000
Setup 4btch × 2Stup × $420	3,360	1,680	3,360	1,680
Machining 4btch × 80MH × $18	5,760	1,440	1,440	5,760
Qual cntrl 4btch × $450	1,800	1,800	1,800	1,800
Total MOH cost applied	$22,920	$16,920	$18,600	$21,240
MOH/unit (divide by 20,000)	$1.146	$ .846	$ .930	$1.062
Prime costs	5.150	5.150	5.150	5.150
Total unit cost	$6.296	$5.996	$6.080	$6.212

Subject Area: Managerial accounting—costing systems. Source: CIA 1195, III-94.

199. (a) The costs per unit of each activity are as follows:

Machine setups $\frac{\$20{,}000}{200}$ = $100/setup

Inspections $\frac{\$130{,}000}{6{,}500}$ = $20/inspection

Material moves $\frac{\$80{,}000}{8{,}000}$ = $10 material move

Engineering hours $\frac{\$50{,}000}{1{,}000}$ = $50/engineering hour

Overhead allocated to Job 101

= 1 setup × $100/setup + 20 inspections × $20 per inspection + 30 material moves × $10/move + 10 engineering hours × $50/hour = $1,300

Therefore, choices (b), (c), and (d) are incorrect.

Subject Area: Managerial accounting—costing systems. Source: CIA 595, IV-90.

200. (a) The costs per unit of each activity are as follows:

Machine setups $\frac{\$20{,}000}{200}$ = $100/setup

Inspections $\frac{\$130{,}000}{6{,}500}$ = $20/inspection

Material moves $\frac{\$80{,}000}{8{,}000}$ = $10 material move

Engineering hours $\frac{\$50{,}000}{1{,}000}$ = $50/engineering hour

Overhead allocated to Job 102

= 2 setups × $100/setup + 10 inspections × $20 per inspection + 10 material moves × $10/move + 50 engineering hours × $50/hour
= $3,000

Production cost of Job 102 =DM + DL + OH
= 12,000 + 2,000 + 3,000
= $17,000

Cost/unit $\frac{\$17{,}000}{50}$ = $340

Therefore, by definition choices (b), (c), and (d) are incorrect.

Subject Area: Managerial accounting—costing systems. Source: CIA 595, IV-91.

201. (a) The costs per unit of each activity are as follows:

Machine setups $\frac{\$20{,}000}{200}$ = $100/setup

Inspections $\frac{\$130{,}000}{6{,}500}$ = $20/inspection

Material moves $\frac{\$80{,}000}{8{,}000}$ = $10 material move

Engineering hours $\frac{\$50{,}000}{1{,}000}$ = $50/engineering hour

Overhead allocated to job 103

= 4 setups × $100/setup + 30 inspections × $20/inspection + 50 material moves × $10/move + 10 engineering hours × $50/hour
= $2,000

Production cost of Job 103 = DM + DL + OH
= 8,000 + 4,000 + 2,000
= 14,000

Cost/unit $\frac{\$14{,}000}{200}$ = $70

Price = 140% of $70
= $98

Therefore, by definition, choices (b), (c), and (d) are incorrect.

Subject Area: Managerial accounting—costing systems. Source: CIA 595, IV-92.

202. (a) Backflush refers to accounting for component parts in a pull system (as a unit is completed), rather than keeping track of parts on a daily basis. Choice (b) is incorrect because direct or variable costing is a method of inventory costing in which all variable product costs are treated as inventoriable costs and fixed manufacturing overhead is treated as a period cost. Choice (c) is incorrect because operation costing refers to a hybrid costing system that blends characteristics of both job and process costing systems. Operation costing is usually applied to batches of similar products where each batch of product is a variation of a single design and requires a sequence of selected operations/activities. An operation costing system would track work in process inventory. Choice (d) is incorrect because process costing is a sequential costing system in which the cost of a product or service is obtained by assigning costs to masses of similar units as they are produced and then computing unit costs on an average basis. There would be a tracking of work in process inventory with a process costing system.

Subject Area: Managerial accounting—costing systems. Source: CIA Model Exam 1998, III-2.

203. (a) Cost accumulation is performed by accounting systems that organize data by an appropriate catalog. Actual costs, rather than predicted costs, are accumulated. Choice (b) is incorrect because computing depreciation expense would not organize data into categories. Choice (c) is incorrect because producing financial statements would not organize data into categories. Choice (d) is incorrect because forecasting material shortages would not organize data into categories.

Subject Area: Managerial accounting—costing systems. Source: CIA Model Exam 1998, IV-64.

204. (d) Process costing is the average cost per unit produced, or total cost ÷ number of units. ($150,000 + 90,000 + 30,000 + 15,000 + 3,000 + 66,000 = $354,000/ 600,000 = $.59). Choice (a) is incorrect because process costing does not allocate costs per packing line. ($150,000 + 90,000 + 30,000 + 15,000 + 3,000 + 66,000 = $354,000/ 600,000 = .59/3 = $.197). Choice (b) is incorrect because process costing includes all costs. ($150,000 + 15,000 = 165,000/600,000 = $.275). Choice (c) is incorrect because process costing includes all costs. ($90,000 + 30,000 + 3,000 + 66,000 = 189,000/600,000 = $.315).

Subject Area: Managerial accounting—costing systems. Source: CIA Model Exam 1998, IV-65.

205. (d) This response multiplies the actual direct labor hours (6,250) times the difference between the standard direct labor rate ($12.00) and the actual direct labor rate ($75,250/6,250 = $12.04). [(6,250) × ($12.00 – 12.04) = $250]. Choice (a) is incorrect because this response multiplies the difference between the planned direct labor hours (15,000 × .4 = 6,000) and the actual direct labor hours (6,250) times the difference between the standard direct labor rate ($12.00) and the actual direct labor rate ($75,250/6,250 = $12.04). [(6,000 – 6,250) × ($12.00 – 12.04) = $10]. Choice (b) is incorrect because this response multiplies the planned direct labor hours (15,000 × .4 = 6,000) times the difference between the standard direct labor rate ($12.00) and the actual direct labor rate ($75,250/6,250 = $12.04). [(6,000) × ($12.00 – 12.04) = $240]. Choice (c) is incorrect because this response multiplies the direct labor hours allowed for actual production (15,500 × .4 = 6,200) times the difference between the standard direct labor rate ($12.00) and the actual direct labor rate ($75,250/6,250 = $12.04). [(6,200) × ($12.00 – 12.04) = $248].

Subject Area: Managerial accounting—costing systems. Source: CIA Model Exam 1998, IV-67.

206. (a) This response multiplies the difference between the direct labor hours allowed for the output achieved (15,500 × .4 = 6,200) and the actual hours worked (6,250) times the standard direct labor rate ($12.00). Calculation: [(6,200 – 6,250) × $12]. Choice (b) is incorrect because this response multiplies the difference between the direct labor hours allowed for the output achieved (15,500 × .4 = 6,200) and the actual hours worked (6,250) times the actual direct labor rate ($75,250/6,250 = $12.04). Calculation: [(6,200 – 6,250) × $12.04]. Choice (c) is incorrect because this response multiplies the difference between the direct labor hours allowed for the planned production (15,000 × .4 = 6,000) and the direct labor hours allowed for the output achieved (15,500 × .4 = 6,200) times the standard direct labor rate ($12.00). Calculation: [(6,000 – 6,200) × $12]. Choice (d) is incorrect because this response multiplies the difference between the direct labor hours allowed for the planned production (15,000 × .4 = 6,000) and the actual hours worked (6,250) times the standard direct labor rate ($12.00). Calculation: [(6,000 – 6,250) × $12].

Subject Area: Managerial accounting—costing systems. Source: CIA Model Exam 1998, IV-68.

207. (a) Cost accumulation is performed by accounting systems that organize data by an appropriate catalog. Actual costs, rather than predicted costs, are accumulated. Choice (b) is incorrect because computing depreciation expense would not organize data into categories. Choice (c) is incorrect because producing financial statements would not organize data into categories. Choice (d) is incorrect because forecasting material shortages would not organize data into categories.

Subject Area: Managerial accounting—costing systems. Source: CIA 597, III-81.

208. (d) Process costing is the average cost per unit produced (that is, total cost ÷ number of units) ($150,000 + 90,000 + 30,000 + 15,000 + 3,000 + 66,000 = $354,000 600,000 = $.59). Choice (a) is incorrect because process costing does not allocate costs per packing line. ($150,000 + 90,000 + 30,000 + 15,000 + 3,000 + 66,000 = $354,000/ 600,000 = .59/3 = $.197). Choice (b) is incorrect because process costing includes all costs. ($150,000 + 15,000 = 165,000/600,000 = $.275). Choice (c) is incorrect because process costing includes all costs. ($90,000 + 30,000 + 3,000 + 66,000 = 189,000/600,000 = $.315).

Subject Area: Managerial accounting—costing systems. Source: CIA 597, III-82.

209. (c) Variable costing for inventory includes all direct and variable overhead costs. ($150,000 + 90,000 + 30,000 + 15,000 +3,000 = $288,000). Choice (a) is incorrect because variable costing for inventory includes all direct and variable overhead costs. ($150,000 + 15,000 = $165,000). Choice (b) is incorrect because variable costing for inventory includes all direct and variable overhead costs. ($150,000 + 90,000 + 30,000 + 3,000 = $273,000). Choice (d) is incorrect because variable costing for inventory does not include fixed overhead costs. ($150,000 + 90,000 + 30,000 + 15,000 +3,000 + 66,000 = $354,000).

Subject Area: Managerial accounting—costing systems. Source: CIA 597, III-83.

210. (d) The situation describes a mass-produced product in a continuous flow environment; this is the classic application of a process cost system. Choice (a) is incorrect because activity-based costing is not a product costing system but rather a method of assigning overhead costs within a product costing system such as job order, operation, or process costing. Furthermore, activity-based costing would most likely be employed when there are a variety of different activities employed to produce different products. This does not fit the situation described above of a mass-produced product in a continuous flow environment with simplified activities. Choice (b) is incorrect because job-order costing would be employed in a situation where a company would be producing heterogeneous products on a custom-order basis. This does not fit the situation described above of a mass-produced product in a continuous flow environment. Choice (c) is incorrect because operation costing is employed in a hybrid costing system when batches of similar products are being manufactured. This does not fit the situation described above of a mass-produced product in a continuous flow environment.

Subject Area: Managerial accounting—costing systems. Source: CIA 1196, III-84.

211. (c) A process costing system is used in those cases where a company produces a standardized product, which is sold to many different customers. The production department becomes the cost center. Choice (a) is incorrect because an EOQ system is an inventory control tool, not a cost system. Choice (b) is incorrect because a job-order system is used where products are differentiated from one customer to the next. Each job (customer) is a separate cost center. Choice (d) is incorrect because a retail inventory system cannot be used in a manufacturing company due to the way the inventory is handled by these companies.

Subject Area: Managerial accounting—costing systems. Source: CIA 595, III-93.

212. (a) Job-order costing is used by companies whose products or services are readily identified by individual units, each of which receives varying amounts of inputs. Choice (b) is incorrect because process costing is used by companies whose products or services are relatively uniform and are produced in series of production steps called processes. Choice (c) is incorrect because differential costing is not a cost accumulation method. It is useful for decision making. Choice (d) is incorrect because joint product costing is not a cost accumulation method. It is a method of allocating joint costs to joint products.

Subject Area: Managerial accounting—costing systems. Source: CIA 590, IV-3.

213. (c) (3,600 – 3,660) × $5.00 = $300 favorable

1,220 × 3 = 3,660 standard quantity for units produced
3,600 actual quantity used
$18,130 ÷ 3,700 lbs. = 4.90 price per pound

Choice (a) is incorrect. (3,600 – 3,660) × $4.90 = $294. Choice (b) is incorrect. (3,700 – 3,660) × $5.00 = $200. Choice (d) is incorrect. (3,600 – 3,660) × $5.00 = $300 unfavorable.

Subject Area: Managerial accounting—costing systems. Source: CIA 1193, IV-16.

214. (b) (4.90 – 5.00) × 3,600 = $360

$18,130/3,700 = $4.90 per lb. actual price.

Choice (a) is incorrect. (4.90 – 5.00) × 1,220 = $122. Choice (c) is incorrect. (4.90 – 5.00) × 3,660 = $366. Choice (d) is incorrect. (4.90 – 5.00) × 3,700 = $370.

Subject Area: Managerial accounting—costing systems. Source: CIA 1193, IV-17.

215. (d) This is the definition of the sales volume variance. Choice (a) is incorrect. Budgeted, not actual sales price is used in the sales volume variance. Choice (b) is incorrect. The flexible budgeted volume **is** the actual volume, resulting in a zero variance. Choice (c) is incorrect. It is the master budgeted sales volume, not actual sales volume, that is used in the computation.

Subject Area: Managerial accounting—costing systems. Source: CIA 593, IV-14.

216. (d) The direct material price variance is calculated using the formula AQ × (SP – AP) where AQ is the actual quantity purchased during the period. This response multiplies the direct materials purchased (25,000 pounds) times the difference between standard price and actual price [($1.60 – 1.55) = $0.05]. That is, 25,000 × $0.05 = $1,250 F.

Choice (a) is incorrect. The direct material price variance is calculated using the formula AQ × (SP – AP) where AQ is the actual quantity purchased during the period. This response multiplies the standard direct materials which should have been used by production [(3x7,500) = 22,500 pounds] times the difference between standard price and actual price [($1.60 – 1.55) = $0.05].

Choice (b) is incorrect. This response multiplies the direct materials issued to production (23,000 pounds) times the difference between standard price and actual price [($1.60 – 1.55) = $0.05].

Choice (c) is incorrect. This response multiplies the direct materials that should have been used for budgeted production [(3 × 8,000) = 24,000 pounds] times the difference between standard price and actual price [($1.60 – 1.55) = $0.05].

Subject Area: Managerial accounting—costing systems. Source: CIA 1192, IV-20.

217. (b) The direct material efficiency (usage) variance is calculated using the formula (SQ – AQ) × SP where SQ is the standard quantity which should have been used for the actual production achieved during the period. This response multiplies the difference between standard quantity [(3 × 7,500) = 22,500] and actual quantity used (23,000) times the standard price ($1.60). That is, (23,000 – 22,500) × $1.60 = 800 U.

Choice (a) is incorrect. The direct material efficiency (usage) variance is calculated using the formula (SQ – AQ) × SP where SQ is the standard quantity which should have been used for the actual production achieved during the period. This response multiplies the difference between standard quantity [(3 × 7,500) = 22,500] and actual quantity used (23,000) times the actual price ($1.55).

Choice (c) is incorrect. This response multiplies the difference between standard quantity which should have been used for budgeted production [(3 × 8,000) = 24,000] and actual quantity used (23,000) times the standard price ($1.60).

Choice (d) is incorrect. This response multiplies the difference between the actual quantity purchased (25,000) and actual quantity used (23,000) times the standard price ($1.60).

Subject Area: Managerial accounting—costing systems. Source: CIA 1192, IV-21.

218. (b) This is the total flexible budget direct labor variance. $48,500 – $46,600 = $1,900(U). Choice (a) is incorrect. This amount is the direct labor price (rate) variance. Choice (c) is incorrect. The dollar amount is correct, but the flexible budget variance is unfavorable, not favorable, as total actual cost exceeds the total flexible budget amount. Choice (d) is incorrect. This amount is the direct labor efficiency (usage) variance.

Subject Area: Managerial accounting—costing systems. Source: CIA 592, IV-18.

219. (d) The direct labor efficiency (or quantity) variance is based on the formula (SQ – AQ) × SP; in this case the standard quantity (SQ) is based on the actual output, or 5,200 units. Thus the standard direct labor allowed for this level of output is 6,500 DLH (5,200 units × 1.25DLH/unit). The variance calculation is (6,500 – 6,600) × 12 = 1,200 U.

Choice (a) is incorrect. This variance compares the 6,600 actual direct labor hours worked for 5,200 actual units of output with the 6,250 budgeted direct labor hours for 5,000 units of budgeted output (5,000 units × 1.25 DLH/unit = 6,250

DLH). This variance calculation is: (6,250 DLH – 6,600 DLH) × $12/DLH = $4,200 U.

Choice (b) is incorrect. This variance is based upon the difference between the budgeted units to be produced and the actual units produced. The variance can be derived using either one of the following calculations: [(5,000 – 5,200 units) × $15/unit = $3,000 U] or [(5,000 – 5,200 units) × 1.25DLH × $12/DLH = $3,000 U].

Choice (c) is incorrect. This calculation compares the actual direct labor cost with the budgeted direct labor cost ($75,000 – $77,220), which is an inappropriate comparison.

Subject Area: Managerial accounting—costing systems. Source: CIA 1191, IV-15.

220. (c) Direct material (DM) purchase price variance is the difference between the DM standard price per pound ($4.00) and actual price per pound ($297,000/75,000 = $3.96) times the pounds of direct material purchased for the month (75,000 pounds) that is, ($4.00 – 3.96) × 75,000 = $3,000 F; the DM quantity variance is the difference between actual usage of direct material (70,000 pounds) and standard usage of direct material for actual output (23,000 × 3 = 69,000 pounds) valued at the DM standard price per pound ($4.00), that is, (70,000 – 69,000) × $4 = $4,000 U. Therefore, by definition, choices (a), (b), and (d) will be incorrect.

Subject Area: Managerial accounting—costing systems. Source: CIA 1191, IV-16.

221. (b) Applied overhead would be the actual labor hours times the estimated application rate ($2.50 per direct labor hour) or $525,000. This amount is $10,000 higher than the actual overhead cost incurred.

Choice (a) is incorrect. This reflects overhead application based on the estimated volume times an application rate based on the actual overhead over the actual volume. The application rate would be $2.45238 and the applied overhead would be $490,476.

Choice (c) is incorrect. This is simply the actual overhead cost less the estimated overhead cost and does not reflect any application.

Choice (d) is incorrect. This reflects overhead application based on the actual volume times an application rate based on the actual overhead over the estimated volume. The application rate would be $2.575 per hour and the applied overhead would be $540,750.

Subject Area: Managerial accounting—costing systems. Source: CIA 591, IV-11.

Responsibility Accounting

222. (d) This is not a premise of responsibility accounting. Choices (a), (b), and (c) are incorrect because each choice is a premise of responsibility accounting.

Subject Area: Managerial accounting—responsibility accounting. Source: CIA 594, III-71.

223. (d) Including figures for items over which a manager can exercise control is a characteristic of responsibility accounting. Choice (a) is incorrect because contribution margin reporting separates costs by behavior (i.e., variable costs are listed first followed by fixed costs). While some responsibility accounting systems use a contribution-margin-reporting format, contribution margin reporting may include costs not controllable by a manager. Choice (b) is incorrect because segment reporting is preparation of performance reports by reportable segments. Segment reports often include allocated costs, which are not controllable by managers. Choice (c) is incorrect because absorption accounting is a method of accounting which treats direct material, direct labor, variable manufacturing overhead, and fixed manufacturing overhead as product costs. Thus, this type of reporting may include some costs which are not controllable by a manager.

Subject Area: Managerial accounting—responsibility accounting. Source: CIA 1192, IV-22.

224. (a) First, the responsibility accounting report would only list the costs over which the warehousing supervisor exercises control. This would exclude his own salary, because this would not be controlled by the warehouse supervisor but by the warehouse supervisor's superior. Secondly, only the product costs are to be considered. This would exclude the shipping clerks' wages and fringe benefits because these are period costs (shipping is a selling expense). Thus the only product cost under the control of the warehouse supervisor is the receiving clerks' wages ($75,000) and the related fringe benefits (.3 × $75,000 = $22,500) or a total of $97,500. Choice (b) is incorrect because this solution correctly includes the receiving clerks' wages and related benefits ($97,500) but incorrectly includes 60% of the warehouse supervisor's salary and related fringe benefits [(.6 × $40,000) + .3 × (.6 × $40,000) = $31,200]. Choice (c) is incorrect because this solution correctly includes the receiving clerks' wages ($75,000) but incorrectly includes the shipping clerks' wages ($55,000), which are a period expense. This solution also ignores any employee benefits. Choice (d) is incorrect because this solution includes all of the listed costs, which is incorrect because the warehouse supervisor's salary (and related employee benefits) is not under the control of the warehouse supervisor and the shipping clerks' wages (and related employee benefits) are a period cost.

Subject Area: Managerial accounting—responsibility accounting. Source: CIA 1191, IV-17.

225. (d) Of the alternatives given, variance analysis is the only one that can be used in a cost center. Variance analysis involves comparing actual costs with predicted or standard costs. Choice (a) is incorrect because return on assets cannot be computed for a cost center because there is no revenue (no return), nor is the manager responsible for the assets available. Choice (b) is incorrect because return on investment cannot be computed for a cost center because there is no revenue, nor is the manager responsible for the investment available. Choice (c) is incorrect because the payback method is not a means of evaluating management performance, but a means of evaluating alternative investment proposals.

Subject Area: Managerial accounting—responsibility accounting. Source: CIA 595, III-96.

226. (c) A profit center is accountable for costs and revenues. Choice (a) is incorrect because a cost center is accountable for costs only. Choice (b) is incorrect because an investment center is accountable for costs, revenues, and investments. Choice (d) is incorrect because a revenue center is accountable for revenues only.

Subject Area: Managerial accounting—responsibility accounting. Source: CIA 1190, IV-19.

227. (a) Peculiarities of each investment center may destroy the validity of comparisons. Choice (b) is incorrect because comparisons are valid if adjustments are made for relative investment bases. Choice (c) is incorrect because use of the same imputed interest rate provides a consistent objective against which each investment can be measured. Choice (d) is incorrect because common amounts of invested capital would eliminate a major factor causing differences in residual income.

Subject Area: Managerial accounting—responsibility accounting. Source: CIA 1190, IV-21.

228. (**c**) The product line manager can control the revenue from sales, variable production costs, variable selling and administrative costs, and the traceable discretionary fixed costs. The committed (infrastructure) fixed costs would not be controllable by the product line manager because these costs arise from having property, plant, equipment, and a functioning organization structure, which would be beyond the realm of control of the product line manager. The common fixed costs are those costs that arise from operating a facility, operation, or activity that is shared by two or more managers; thus, these costs would not be controllable by a single product line manager. Choice (a) is incorrect because the product line manager can control more than the revenue from sales and variable production costs. The product line manager can also control the variable selling and administrative costs and the variable discretionary fixed costs. Choice (b) is incorrect because the product line manager can control more than the revenue from sales, variable production costs, and variable selling and administrative costs. The product line manager can also control the traceable discretionary fixed costs. Choice (d) is incorrect because it includes committed (infrastructure) fixed costs and common fixed costs as a controllable. The committed (infrastructure) fixed costs arise from having property, plant, equipment, and a functioning organization structure. The common fixed costs are those costs that arise from operating a facility, operation, or activity that is shared by two or more managers. Neither of these two cost categories would be within the realm of control of the product line manager.

Subject Area: Managerial accounting—responsibility accounting. Source: CIA 596, III-91.

229. (**b**) It considers the incremental revenue and incorporates all of the relevant variable costs that would be involved in making the decision to accept the onetime special order. The fixed cost categories should not be considered because the situation indicates that there is excess plant capacity; this implies that there would be no additional fixed costs. Choice (a) is incorrect because it does not include the variable selling and administrative costs, which might arise in a onetime special order. The fixed cost categories should not be considered because the situation indicates that there is excess plant capacity; this implies that there would be no additional fixed costs. Choice (c) is incorrect because it includes the discretionary fixed costs as well as the incremental revenue and all of the relevant variable costs that would be involved in making the decision to accept the onetime special order. The discretionary fixed costs should not be considered because the situation indicates that there is excess plant capacity; this implies that there would be no additional fixed costs. Choice (d) is incorrect. This response is incorrect because it includes the fixed costs.

Subject Area: Managerial accounting—responsibility accounting. Source: CIA 596, III-92.

230. (**c**) This is the correct definition of common cost. A common cost arises from operating a facility, operation, or activity that is shared by two or more managers. Choice (a) is incorrect because the first part of the response is not correct. While common fixed costs cannot be traced to the production process directly (correct statement), they may include period as well as production costs. Choice (b) is incorrect. This response is incorrect because if the costs were incurred by each of the individual segments in the conduct of their normal business then they would be traceable to the individual segments (i.e., they would not be included in the common fixed cost category). Choice (d) is incorrect because if the cost arises from operating a facility, operation, or activity that is shared by two or more managers, then the cost cannot be influenced by a single segment manager.

Subject Area: Managerial accounting—responsibility accounting. Source: CIA 596, III-93.

231. (**b**) Residual income concentrates on earnings in excess of the minimum desired return. With ROI, a segment may reject a project that exceeds the minimum return if the project will decrease the segment's overall ROI. For example, a project that earns ROI of 22%, which is greater than the target rate of 20%, might be rejected if the segment is currently earning 25%, because the project will decrease the segment's ROI. This would not occur with residual income. Choice (a) is incorrect because both measures represent the results for a single time period. Choice (c) is incorrect because the target rate for ROI is the same as the imputed interest rate used in the residual income calculation. Choice (d) is incorrect because average investment should be employed in both methods. At any rate, the investment base employed for both methods would be the same.

Subject Area: Managerial accounting—responsibility accounting. Source: CIA 1195, III-79.

232. (**d**) The increase in revenue coupled with a decrease in costs will increase the numerator of ROI. The decrease in investment will decrease the denominator. Thus, the ROI would increase in this situation. Choice (a) is incorrect. The increase in revenue and decrease in costs would cause the numerator of ROI to be larger, but the increase in investment would increase the denominator. The ROI would only increase if the numerator increased more than the denominator increased. Thus, this combination is not conclusive. Choice (b) is incorrect. The decrease in revenue coupled with a decrease in costs may or may not increase the numerator of ROI. The decrease in investment would decrease the denominator. The ROI would only increase if the decrease in costs were sufficient to cause the numerator to increase. Thus, this combination is not conclusive. Choice (c) is incorrect. The increase in revenue coupled with an increase in costs may or may not increase the numerator of ROI. The increase in investment would increase the denominator. The ROI would only increase if the increase in revenues were sufficient to cause the numerator to increase more than the denominator. Thus, this combination is not conclusive.

Subject Area: Managerial accounting—responsibility accounting. Source: CIA 1195, III-67.

233. (**a**) Segment reporting does facilitate evaluation of company management by providing specific data on management's efforts with particular segments. Choice (b) is incorrect because interdependence of segments is not affected by reporting methods. Choice (c) is incorrect because this is a disadvantage of segment reporting. Choice (d) is incorrect because this is a disadvantage of segment reporting.

Subject Area: Managerial accounting—responsibility accounting. Source: CIA 595, III-95.

234. (**d**) Variable costs – Fixed costs controllable by mkt. mgr. – Fixed costs controllable by corporate management.

950,000 – 430,000 – 150,000 – 250,000 = 120,000

Choice (a) is incorrect because this measures the performance of the marketing segment manager (950,000 – 430,000 – 150,000). Choice (b) is incorrect because this incorrectly includes allocated costs (950,000 – 430,000 – 150,000 – 250,000 – 110,000). Choice (c) is incorrect because this is the contribution margin (950,000 – 430,000).

Subject Area: Managerial accounting—responsibility accounting. Source: CIA 594, III-44.

235. (**c**) 150,000 + 10,000 – 30,000 – 20,000 – 5,000 – 25,000 – 15,000 – 35,000 = 30,000. Choice (a) is incorrect because it subtracted central corporate expenses. Choice (b) is incorrect because it did not add other revenue. Choice (d) is incorrect because it did not subtract fixed expenses.

Subject Area: Managerial accounting—responsibility accounting. Source: CIA 1193, IV-20.

236. (**d**) 400,000 + 15,000 – 65,000 – 40,000 – 15,000 – 30,000 = 265,000. Choice (a) is incorrect because it subtracted fixed expenses. Choice (b) is incorrect because it subtracted fixed selling and administrative expense. Choice (c) is incorrect because it subtracted fixed selling and administrative expense and did not subtract variable selling and administrative expense.

Subject Area: Managerial accounting—responsibility accounting. Source: CIA 1193, IV-21.

237. (**a**) The operating income by a segment is the revenues minus variable manufacturing cost of goods sold, variable selling and administrative costs, fixed costs controllable by the division manager, and fixed costs controllable by others ($1,000 – $400 – $200 – $220 – $40 = $140). Choice (b) is incorrect because the $180 figure incorrectly excludes the fixed costs controllable by company headquarters ($40). These costs must be deducted to arrive at the division contribution. Choice (c) is incorrect because the $400 figure incorrectly excludes the fixed costs controllable by company headquarters ($40) and the fixed cost controllable by the division manager ($220). These costs must be deducted to arrive at the division contribution. Choice (d) is incorrect because the $600 figure incorrectly excludes the fixed costs controllable by others ($40), the fixed costs controllable by the division manager ($220), and the variable selling and administrative costs ($200). These costs must be deducted to arrive at the division contribution.

Subject Area: Managerial accounting—responsibility accounting. Source: CIA 591, IV-23.

238. (**c**) The contribution margin is revenues minus variable manufacturing cost of goods sold and variable selling and administrative costs ($2,000 – $1,160 – $240 = $600).

Choice (a) is incorrect because the figure $340 represents the division contribution ($2,000 – $1,160 – $240 – $160 – $100 = $340). Choice (b) is incorrect because the figure $440 represents the contribution controllable by the division manager ($2,000 – $1,160 – $240 – $160 = $440). Choice (d) is incorrect because the figure $840 represents the manufacturing contribution margin, calculated as revenues minus variable manufacturing cost of goods sold ($2,000 – $1,160 = $840).

Subject Area: Managerial accounting—responsibility accounting. Source: CIA 591, IV-24.

239. (**d**) This cost can be included. First, the segments are being charged for actual usage, which is under each segment's control. The predetermined standard rate is set at the beginning of the year which is known by the segment managers and the efficiencies and inefficiencies of the Computer Department are not being passed on to the segments; both of these procedural methods promote a degree of control by the segments. Choice (a) is incorrect. This cost should be excluded from the performance report because the segments have no control over the cost incurrence, or the allocation basis, that is, the allocation depends upon the segment sales (controllable) as well as the sales of other segments (uncontrollable). Choice (b) is incorrect. This cost should be excluded from the performance report because the segments have no control over the cost incurrence nor the method of assignment,(i.e., the assignment depends upon the number of employees in the segment (controllable) in proportion to the total number of employees in all segments (not controllable). Choice (c) is incorrect. This cost should be excluded from the performance report because the segments have no control over the cost and the equal assignment is arbitrary bearing no relation to usage.

Subject Area: Managerial accounting—responsibility accounting. Source: CIA 1191, IV-18.

4 REGULATORY, LEGAL, AND ECONOMICS (5-15%)

THEORY

4.1 Impact of Government Legislation and Regulation on Business

Government impacts business in many ways. This impact is felt through regulations to control environment, labor practices, safety at workplace, product liability, import and export laws, banking practices, and other areas. Government also impacts business through depreciation laws and tax credits to control investment levels in the economy by the private sector. Using fiscal and monetary policies, government controls employment, production, inflation, interest rates, government spending, and money supply in the economy.

For example, Consumer Product Safety Commission enforces the Consumer Product Safety Act, which covers safety of any consumer product not addressed by other regulatory agencies. The Food and Drug Administration agency enforces laws and develops regulations to prevent distribution and sale of adulterated foods, drugs, cosmetics, and hazardous consumer products. The manufacturer is usually liable for dangerous and unsafe products. Government laws and regulations can appear as a constraint on business behavior. Another way to view them is an opportunity to provide safer and more efficient products to consumers. Recent events such as deregulation in the airlines and telecommunications industries have helped both producers and consumers alike.

(a) **Governmental Legislation and Regulation.** Governmental legislation and regulation includes both state and federal government. The scope of state regulation includes pricing by public utility companies while the scope of federal regulation covers price fixing, deceptive pricing, price discrimination, and promotional pricing. Examples include: the Sherman Antitrust Act, the Clayton Act, Federal Trade Commission Act, the Robinson-Patman Act, Wheeler-Lea Act, and Celler Antimerger Act. These federal statutes when combined with state legislation intend to promote and preserve competition in a free enterprise system and to prevent monopoly power. The coverage of these acts extends to interstate commerce among the several states, but not intrastate activity. All states have antitrust statutes applicable to intrastate activity.

(i) **Sherman Act.** The Sherman Act of 1880 is the primary, first tool of antitrust enforcement. The Act declared any combination, contract, or conspiracy in restraint of trade made among the states or with foreign countries illegal. The Act also made it illegal to monopolize, attempt to monopolize, or conspire to monopolize any portion of interstate commerce or any portion of trade with foreign nations. However, the Sherman Act did not state exactly what types of action were prohibited. Two substantial provisions as defined in the Sections 1 and 2 of the Act are described below.

- **Section 1:** "Every contract, combination in the form of trust or otherwise, or conspiracy, in restraint of trade or commerce among the several States, or with foreign nations, is declared to be illegal."

  Section 1 is concerned with contract, combination, and conspiracies in restraint of trade. Two or more persons working together (i.e., combination) to fix prices or divide market to achieve the anticompetitive results, for example, constitute a violation of the Act. On the other hand, conspiracy is concerned with the conduct of an individual firm (e.g., predatory pricing) to create or maintain a monopoly.

  Restraint of trade consists of horizontal and vertical types. **A horizontal restraint** is an agreement among competitors such as manufacturers, retailers, wholesalers. Examples of horizontal restraints include division of markets, price fixing, group boycotts, and exchange of market information. **A vertical restraint** is an agreement between persons standing in a buyer-seller relationship (a manufacturer and a retailer in the same line of products). Examples of vertical restraint include: resale price maintenance, location, territory, and customer restrictions, tying arrangements, and exclusive dealing contracts.
- **Section 2:** "Every person who shall monopolize, or attempt to monopolize, or combine or conspire with any other person or persons, to monopolize any part of the trade or commerce among the several States, or with foreign nations, shall be deemed guilty of a felony."

  The wording of the Act is too broad and general and leaves much discretion to federal courts for interpretation. These two sections complement each other in achieving the goal of preventing monopoly and anticompetitiveness. *The Sherman Act requires proof of actual and substantial anticompetitive effect.*

  Labor unions, agricultural cooperatives, fisherman's organizations, and export trade associations enjoy limited **antitrust exemption**.

Violations of the Sherman Act

Violations of both Sections 1 and 2 are felonies punishable by imprisonment of up to three years and fines up to $100,000, or both, for individuals, and fines up to $1 million for corporations. Civil actions are more common than criminal proceedings.

Approximately 75% of civil suits are settled through consent decrees (a compromise between the government and the defendant). The Sherman Act also contains the seldom-used forfeiture remedy, where the property may be seized.

Conduct that would violate the Sherman Act in the absence of union involvement is not immunized by the participation of the union. For example, a union may not band together with a nonlabor party, such as a contractor or manufacturer, to achieve a result forbidden by the antitrust laws.

(ii) **Clayton Act.** The Clayton Act of 1914 was designed to strengthen and clarify the provisions of the Sherman Act. It defines specifically what constitutes monopolistic or restrictive practices, whereas the Sherman Act does not.

The Clayton Act makes price discrimination illegal unless it can be justified because of differences in costs. The Clayton Act prohibits the use of exclusive or tying contracts when their use "substantially lessens competition or tends to create a monopoly." Exclusive or tying contracts are contracts in which the seller agrees to sell a product to a buyer on the condition that the buyer will not purchase products from the seller's competitors. The Clayton Act also made intercorporate stockholdings illegal if they tend to greatly reduce competition or to create a monopoly. In addition, the Clayton Act makes interlocking directorates (having the same individual on two or more board of directors) illegal if the corporations are competitive and if at least one of the corporations is of a certain minimum size.

Four provisions (sections 2, 3, 7, and 8) that are of importance include

- Section 2 prohibits certain types of price discrimination.
- Section 3 prohibits certain sales made on condition that the buyer not deal with the seller's competitors.

Violations of the Clayton Act

No criminal sanctions are imposed for violations of the Clayton Act. Private remedies, and legal and equitable relief are available. Legal relief is a private action for money damages.

In a private action, the plaintiff must ordinarily prove both the existence of an antitrust violation and damages resulting from that violation.

- Section 7 prohibits certain corporate mergers.
- Section 8 prohibits a person serving on the board of directors of two competing companies (an "interlocking directorate) if one or both companies are larger than a given size.

The goal of the Clayton Act is to curb anticompetitive practices in their incipiency. Under the Clayton Act, by simply showing a probable, rather than actual, anticompetitive effect would be enough cause for a violation of the act. This means the Clayton Act is more sensitive to anticompetitive practices than the Sherman Act.

The scope of the Clayton Act in mergers includes both asset and stock acquisitions. The Act now covers both mergers between actual competitors and vertical and conglomerate mergers having the requisite anti-competitive effect.

RULES OF MERGERS

- A horizontal merger is one between former competitors.
- A vertical merger occurs when a firm acquires a supplier or customer.
- If a business acquires a supplier, it is said to vertically integrate "backward" or "upstream."
- If a business acquires a customer, it is said to vertically integrate "forward" or "downstream."
- A conglomerate merger involves parties who were neither former competitors nor in the same supply chain.

(iii) **Federal Trade Commission Act.** Like the Clayton Act, the Federal Trade Commission Act was designed to prevent abuses and to sustain competition. The Federal Trade Commission Act declared as unlawful "unfair methods of competition in commerce."

The Act also established the Federal Trade Commission (FTC) in 1914 and gave it the power and the resources to investigate unfair competitive practices. The FTC Act authorizes the FTC to issue "cease and desist" orders prohibiting "unfair methods of competition" and "unfair or deceptive acts or practices." These orders provide injunctive relief by preventing or restraining unlawful conduct. *One of the goals of the FTC is to enforce antitrust laws and to protect consumers.*

Violations of the FTC Act

No criminal sanctions are imposed for violations of the FTC Act. Most FTC investigations are settled by a consent order procedure.

Although no criminal sanctions or private damage remedies are imposed for FTC act violations, a $10,000 per day civil penalty is imposed for violating cease and desist orders.

The FTC has a dual role in prohibiting unfair methods of competition and anticompetitive practices. *The FTC Act supplements the Sherman and the Clayton Acts.* The FTC protects consumers who are injured by practices such as deceptive advertising or labeling without regard to any effect on competitors.

Although not explicitly empowered to do so, the FTC frequently enforces the Sherman Act indirectly and enjoins conduct beyond the reach of either the Sherman or Clayton Acts.

(iv) **Robinson-Patman Act.** Congress passed the Robinson-Patman Act in 1936 to protect small competitors by amending the Clayton Act. It is often called the "chain store act." The Robinson-Patman Act amended the price discrimination section of the Clayton Act. It was aimed at protecting independent retailers and wholesalers from "unfair discriminations" by large chain stores and mass distributors, which were supposedly obtaining large and unjustified price discounts because of their purchasing power and bargaining position.

Both the Department of Justice and the FTC can proceed against violators of the Robinson-Patman Act. The Robinson-Patman Act prohibits price discrimination (where a seller charges one buyer more than another for the same product). It makes it unlawful for sellers to grant concessions to buyers unless concessions are granted to all buyers on terms that are proportionally equal. The Act reaches the quantity discount, a major form of price discrimination.

The Robinson-Patman Act made it illegal

- To discriminate by granting unjustified quantity discounts which greatly reduce competition or tend to create a monopoly among sellers or buyers
- To pay brokerage fees if no broker is involved in a transaction
- To grant or obtain larger discounts than those available to competitors who purchase the same goods in the same amounts
- For sellers to grant concessions to buyers unless concessions are created to all buyers on terms that are proportionally equal

The Act applies only to sales, not to leases, agency/consignment arrangements, licenses, or refusals to deal (selling to one firm while refusing to deal with another). The scope of the Robinson-Patman Act applies to tangible personal property (commodities) and in the sale of services or intangibles such as advertising.

Violations of the Robinson-Patman Act

To violate the statute, the discrimination in price must be "between different purchasers." A mere showing of different prices charged is enough to violate.

A mere showing that competing buyers were charged different prices is generally sufficient to establish a prima facie Robinson-Patman Act violation. Proof of a prima facie case of price discrimination does not necessarily result in a liability.

The seller may avoid the consequences of the discrimination by proving one of three defenses: (1) the "cost justification" defense, (2) the "meeting competition" defense, and (3) the "changing conditions." The burden of proving a defense is on the discriminating seller.

(v) **Wheeler-Lea Act.** In 1938, the Wheeler-Lea Act was passed as an amendment to the FTC Act. The Wheeler-Lea Act makes "unfair or deceptive acts or practices" in interstate commerce illegal;

thus, it is designed to protect consumers rather than competitors. Now, the FTC has the authority to prohibit false and misleading advertising and product misrepresentation.

(vi) **Celler Antimerger Act.** The Celler Antimerger Act of 1950 also amended the Clayton Act by making it illegal for a corporation to acquire the assets, as well as the stock, of a competing corporation if the effect is to greatly reduce competition or to tend to create a monopoly.

(b) **Government's Monitoring of Environmental Issues.** The US Environmental Protection Agency (EPA) protects and enhances the environment today and for future generations to the fullest extent possible under the laws enacted by the US Congress. The agency's mission is to control and abate pollution in the areas of air, water, solid waste, pesticides, radiation, and toxic substances. Its mandate is to mount an integrated, coordinated attack on environmental pollution in cooperation with state and local governments.

The Council on Environmental Quality was established within the Executive Office of the President by the national Environmental Policy Act of 1969 to formulate and recommend national policies to promote the improvement of the quality of the environment.

The council develops and recommends to the president national policies that further environmental quality; performing a continuing analysis of changes or trends in the national environment; reviews and reappraises programs of the federal government to determine their contributions to sound environmental policy; conducts studies, research, and analysis relating to ecological systems and environmental quality; assists the president in the preparation of the annual environmental quality report to the Congress; and oversees implementation of the national environmental policy act.

(i) **Air and radiation.** The air activities of the Agency include: development of national programs, technical policies, and regulations for air pollution control, enforcement of standards, development of national standards for air quality, emission standards for new stationary and mobile sources, and emission standards for hazardous pollutants, technical direction, support, and evaluation of regional air activities, and provision of training in the field of air pollution control.

Related activities include technical assistance to states and agencies having radiation protection programs, including radon mitigation program; a national surveillance and inspection program for measuring radiation levels in the environment.

(ii) **Water.** The Agency's water quality activities represent a coordinated effort to restore the nation's waters. The functions of this program include: development of national programs, technical policies, and regulations for water pollution control and water supply, ground water protection, marine and estuarine protection, enforcement of standards, water quality standards and effluent guidelines development, technical direction, support, and evaluation of regional water activities, development of programs for technical assistance and technology transfer, and provision of training in the field of water quality.

(iii) **Solid waste and emergency response.** The Office of Solid Waste and Emergency Response provides policy, guidance, and direction for the agency's hazardous waste and emergency response programs. The functions of these programs include: development of policies, standards, and regulations for hazardous waste treatment, storage, and disposal, national management of the Superfund toxic waste cleanup program, development of guidelines for the emergency preparedness and "community right to know" programs, development of guidelines and standards for underground storage tanks, enforcement of applicable laws and regulations, analysis of technologies and methods for the recovery of useful energy from solid waste, and provision of technical assistance in the development, management, and operation of waste management activities.

(iv) **Pesticides and toxic substances.** The Office of Pesticides and Toxic Substances is responsible for: developing national strategies for the control of toxic substances, directing the pesticides and toxic substances enforcement activities, developing criteria for assessing chemical substances, standards for test protocols for chemicals, rules, and procedures for industry reporting and regulations for the control of substances deemed to be hazardous to man or the environment, and evaluating and assessing the impact of existing chemicals, new chemicals, and chemicals with new uses to determine the hazard and, if needed, develop appropriate restrictions.

Additional activities include control and regulation of pesticides and reduction in their use to ensure human safety and protection of environmental quality. This includes: establishment of tolerance levels for pesticides that occur in or on food, monitoring of pesticide residue levels in food, humans, and nontarget fish and wildlife and their environments, and investigation of pesticide accidents. It also coordinates activities under its statutory responsibilities with other agencies for the assessment and control of toxic substances and pesticides.

4.2 Trade Legislation and Regulations

(a) **Tied Aid Practices.** Tied aid refers to foreign assistance that is linked to the purchase of exports from the country extending the assistance. Tied aid can consist of foreign aid grants alone, grants mixed with commercial financing or official export credits (mixed credits), or concessional (low-interest-rate) loans.

Mixed Credits

Mixed credits are a combination of subsidized loans and commercial loans, which, in effect, subsidize the purchase of a country's exports.

Competitors' tied aid practices are of concern to the United States because US exporters can be put at a competitive disadvantage in bidding on overseas projects when competitor countries make tied aid available. The effect is the same for any exporting country.

The Organization for Economic Cooperation and Development (OECD) is a forum for monitoring economic trends and coordinating economic policy among its 24 member countries, which include the economically developed free-market democracies of North America, Western Europe, and the Pacific. Negotiators representing countries in the OECD have agreed to curb the use of tied aid for commercial purposes and are taking steps to reduce the use of mixed credits.

(b) **US Export-Import Bank.** Exports play a vital role in any economy by creating jobs and generating economic growth. Most industrialized nations have programs to help companies export, that is, sell their products abroad. These programs, collectively referred to as "export promotion," include offering business counseling and training and giving representational assistance, as well as providing market research information, trade fair opportunities, and export financing assistance. These programs can play an important role in increasing the exports of a country's goods and services in sectors of the economy in which it is competitive.

Budget Deficit

Budget deficit reduction and liberalized trade are important to the long-term health of any economy.

The US Export-Import Bank (Eximbank) is one of ten federal government agencies that offers programs to assist exporters. The Eximbank offers a wide range of export financing assistance, including direct loans, loan guarantees, and export insurance covering credit and political risks. Credit risk is the probability that a loan will not be repaid by a foreign country. Political risk is the probability that a foreign country's political system is unstable. Although the Eximbank was created to facilitate the financing of both US exports and imports, it has been used almost exclusively to finance US exports.

The Eximbank is required to "counter" competitors' use of tied aid and mixed credits. In 1986 the US Congress authorized the Eximbank to create a "war chest" fund as a means of overmatching or outbidding other countries that have repeatedly used tied aid and mixed credits to increase their exports. However, war chest funds have not been used extensively.

The export promotion programs will be effective in the following situations:

- When US firms lack export awareness because markets have failed to give the right information to producers who otherwise would export
- When US businesses are aware of export opportunities but need additional technical assistance to consummate export sales
- When US firms need representational assistance from the US government in opening doors overseas

- When US businesses need competitive financing, loan guarantees, or insurance to close an export deal

KEY CONCEPTS TO REMEMBER: IMPORTS AND EXPORTS

- Import quotas differ from tariffs because quotas discriminate on the basis of quantity, whereas tariffs directly increase prices.
- Gross national product (GNP) will fall following an increase in imports.
- A deficit in the balance of payments occurs when imports exceed exports.

(c) **Methods, Restrictions, and Barriers of International Trade.** A country will have a trade deficit when it consumes more than it produces and imports the difference from other countries. A country will become a debtor nation when there is a huge trade deficit and when it borrows to finance the domestic budget deficit.

A country should strike a balance between the national savings rate and the budget deficit, specifically by reducing the deficit without endangering long-term economic growth. An imbalance is created when the savings rate is declining and the budget deficit is increasing. The national savings rate should be sufficient to meet the needs of both private sector investments and government borrowing. A country should focus on long-term investment as a way to enhance its competitiveness in the global marketplace.

A government's economic policies require a difficult balancing of domestic goals with international economic objectives and constraints. For example, at the macroeconomic level, a government may adopt policies that: support private sector investment by keeping the cost of capital at reasonable levels; support rising productivity in the private sector by improving infrastructure and a better educated and trained labor force; and encourage private sector firms to improve their own goals, policies, and management control and information systems as their critical contribution to enhancing their country's competitiveness.

(i) **Methods of restricting the trade.** Tariffs, import quotas, and domestic content laws are examples of restricting foreign trade (see Exhibit 4.1).

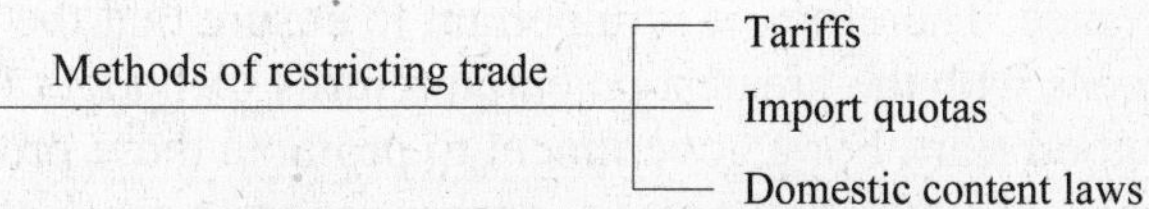

Exhibit 4.1: Methods of restricting trade

(A) ***Tariffs.*** A tariff is a tax imposed on imported goods, usually as a percentage of the product's value. Import duties, or tariffs, have been a source of government revenue far longer than income and value-added taxes. Goods entering a country are taxed at an *ad valorem* (percent of value) basis. Many foreign countries prefer to use tariffs since it is relatively easy to check and control as goods come through designated ports.

Another popularity of tariffs is its incentive feature to relocate manufacturing production facilities and be competitive. If an American firm exporting to Brazil finds that its products are priced much higher in Brazil because of tariffs, it may build a manufacturing plant in Brazil to produce for the Brazilian market. This strategy has dual benefits: it not only avoids the tariffs to be paid but also makes the American firm's products more competitive in Brazil.

The imposition of a tariff against an imported good raises its cost relative to what it would have been in the tariff's absence. Importers, therefore, need to charge a higher price to their customers. As a consequence, tariffs tend to worsen an imported product's competitive position compared with similar items produced domestically.

Because of high prices of imported goods due to tariffs, more sales will go to local manufacturers. Thus, tariffs offer a degree of market protection to local sellers whose life has been made competitively difficult by imports in their markets. For this reason, when imports become an important factor in a market, domestic manufacturers frequently will ask the government for tariff protection. The usual argument is that imports are injuring the local industry and causing unemployment.

(B) ***Import quotas.*** A quota is simply a quantitative restriction applied to imports. Under GATT, import quotas are supposed to be banned, but there are so many exceptions that the ban is not that useful. In fact, as tariffs have been reduced as an instrument of protection, the tendency has been to replace them with quotas.

(C) ***Domestic content laws.*** Another way many countries have attempted to assure the participation of domestic producers has been through domestic content laws. These laws stipulate that when a product is sold in the marketplace, it must incorporate a specified percentage of locally made components. These laws must meet "local content requirements."

KEY CONCEPTS TO REMEMBER: TRADE

- Consumption taxes on imported goods are an example of a tariff.
- Import tariffs have the same economic effect as a consumption tax plus a production subsidy. A direct effect of imposing a protective tariff on an imported product is lower domestic consumption of the item.
- The merchandise trade balance (or balance of trade) does not reflect capital outflows.
- The point price elasticity of demand for imports will become larger following an increase in import prices.
- A nation experiencing chronic trade deficits might consider trade quotas. Unemployment and productivity rates will decline as a result of trade quotas.
- Increased total world output provides the best justification for reducing trade barriers between nations.
- An embargo creates the most restrictive barrier to exporting to a country, and often results from political actions. It is a total ban on some kind of imports, which is an extreme form of import quota.

(ii) **Methods of international trade.** Export promotion programs, trade agreements, and technology policies set the stage for international trade to occur.

(A) ***Export promotion programs.*** As each country's economic advancement is dependent on its success in trading with other countries, the way that country promotes its exports will be of great importance. Therefore, it is important to ensure that the funds allocated are being channeled into areas with the greatest potential returns. A budget for export promotion programs would be a good start. For a government to promote these programs requires good internal controls, program evaluation criteria, proper program accountability, enhanced planning and decision making. *Export promotion programs, export loans, credit guarantees, and insurance are some examples of promoting international trade.*

(B) ***Trade agreements.*** Two popular trade agreements are: (1) World Trade Organization (WTO), formally known as General Agreement on Tariffs and Trade (GATT), and (2) North American Free Trade Agreement (NAFTA). The aim of US trade negotiations is to remove foreign barriers to imports and unfair governmental incentives to exports, thus encouraging the free flow of international trade. The principal multinational trade regime has been the WTO, which requires the negotiations of concerned countries in liberalizing the trade and removing tariffs and other barriers—which is not an easy thing to accomplish. More is said about WTO later.

Trade Agreements

A vigorous and effective system for monitoring and enforcing agreements is essential to avoid violations, delaying tactics, and drawn-out dispute settlements.

More recently, the United States, Mexico, and Canada concluded negotiations and signed the North American Free Trade Agreement (NAFTA), which became effective in 1994. The most significant aspect of NAFTA is that it binds Mexico's recent market-oriented economic reforms to international obligations, thereby making these reforms more permanent. Though NAFTA will likely have only a modest net effect on the US economy, much controversy remains as to the scope and extent of social and economic adjustments that will be caused by its implementation, such as effects on employment, immigration, and the environment. More is said about NAFTA later.

(C) ***Technology policies.*** Technology policies, the financial market structures, and the business/government relationships of other nations will receive greater significance in the more closely integrated global marketplace.

The United States International Trade Commission furnishes studies, reports, and recommendations involving international trade and tariffs to the president, the Congress, and other government agencies. In this capacity, the Commission conducts a variety of investigations, public hearings, and research projects pertaining to the international policies of the United States.

EXERCISE ON TRADE BARRIERS

The United States imposed many barriers to international trade during the 1920s and 1930s. However, the United States has become much less protectionist in more recent times and has eliminated or lessened numerous former barriers to trade. Yet, in the last several years, as a result of increased foreign competition in some historically strong US industries, some observers have become concerned that the US will extend protection to other industries.

Question: Describe the basic types of trade barriers.

Answer: *The three basic types of trade barriers include tariffs, quotas, and other nontariff barriers.* A **tariff** is an import tax that may be used as a source of revenue for the government.

A **quota** is a physical or dollar value limitation on the volume of imports of a particular commodity. A quota generates no revenue for the government, but it generates monopoly profits for the protected industry. A quota also increases the burden of adjustment of prices relative to tariffs. **Other nontariff barriers** include an array of government practices and regulations that interfere with the free flow of goods between countries. Some of the most common nontariff barriers include: export subsidies and taxes, differences in product standards, domestic subsidies and aids, and dumping regulations and customs valuations procedures.

Question: For each type, describe the impact on the protectionist country (importer) imposing the barrier.

Answer: All of the trade barriers are designed to decrease the quantity of imported goods supplied either by increasing prices or directly restricting quantities causing subsequent price increases. A tariff works by raising prices and hence cutting the demand for imports, while quotas restrict the supply of imports forcing prices up. The increase in price associated with a tariff does not directly benefit the seller; it becomes a source of revenue for the importing country. The increase in price associated with a quota does not become a source of revenue for the importing country, but the benefits become the property rights of some participant in the market yielding monopoly profits. The degree of protection that is achieved is determined by: (1) the demand elasticity of the product and (2) whether or not the exporting country imposes retaliatory trade barriers.

Question: Describe the impact on producer nations (exporter) facing the barrier.

Answer: Tariffs, quotas, and other nontariff barriers cause the volume of trade to decline. Since products can no longer be exported as profitably, prices will decline in the exporting country. Production will decrease in the exporting country resulting in a loss of income.

Question: Describe the impact on international trade in the year-end balance of payments between the protectionist and the producer.

Answer: In the importing country, the balance of payments improves. In the exporting country, the balance of payments worsens.

SOURCE: CIA Examination, May 1986, Part IV, Question No. 42. The Institute of Internal Auditors (IIA) Altamonte Springs, Florida.

(d) **Theory of Comparative Advantage.** Increased total world output is a good argument for free trade between countries. Incentives exist for trade to develop along the lines of comparative advantage. Countries achieve comparative advantage in certain goods due to international differences in demand or supply.

The law of comparative advantage explains how mutually beneficial trade can occur when one country is less efficient than another county in the production of all commodities. The less efficient country should specialize in and export the commodity in which its absolute disadvantage is smallest, and should import the other commodity.

Countries should specialize when they have their greatest absolute advantage or in their least absolute disadvantage. This rule is known as the law of comparative advantage. An absolute advantage is the ability to produce a good using less input than is possible anywhere in the world.

Production of the good with the lower price expands, and the country with a lower relative price of a product has comparative advantage in that product. Therefore, production and trade follow the line of comparative advantage. For trade to occur along the lines of comparative advantage, the relative wage ratio must lie between the extremes of the differences in relative productive advantages.

The **HO theorem** states that a country will have a comparative advantage in, and therefore will export that good whose production is relatively intensive in the factor with which that country is relatively well endowed. For example, a country that is relatively capital-abundant compared with another country will have a comparative advantage in the good that requires more capital per worker to produce.

In a competitive environment, trade flows are determined by profit-seeking firms. If a product is relatively cheap in one country, it will tend to be exported to those places where it is relatively expensive. This practice supports the assumption that trade will flow in the direction of comparative advantage. *Each country exports its comparative advantage good and imports its comparative disadvantage good.*

EXAMPLES OF COMPARATIVE ADVANTAGE THEORY

Example 1

Country A		*Country B*	
Good X	*Good Y*	*Good X*	*Good Y*
100	0	60	0
60	20	30	10
20	40	0	20
0	50		

The above table represents production possibilities for Country A and Country B for two goods, X and Y. Based on the principle of comparative advantage, Country B should produce Good X.

Example 2

	Country A	*Country B*
Cotton	3	12 labor hours per unit of output
Automobile	6	8

Note that country A is four times (that is 12 to 3) more efficient in the production of cotton relative to country B. However, country A is only 4/3 (that is 8/6) more efficient in the production of automobiles relative to country B. Because country A's greatest absolute advantage is in the production of cotton, it is said to have a comparative advantage in cotton. Because country B's least absolute disadvantage is in the production of automobiles, it is said to have a comparative advantage in automobiles.

Example 3

Assume a simple economy consisting of only two nations—Nation A and Nation B. The countries produce and consume only two products: rice and cars. The comparative costs of production in each country are

	Nation A	*Nation B*
Rice (per ton)	10,000	20,000
Cars	15,000	16,000

Given this cost structure and a fixed supply of inputs, what can be said with respect to comparative advantage and international trade?

a. Nation B has a comparative advantage with respect to the production of cars and will export cars to Nation A.
b. Nation B has a comparative advantage with respect to rice and will export rice to Nation A.
c. Nation A has a comparative advantage with respect to cars and will export cars to Nation B.
d. There will be no overall advantage to international trade.

Choice (a) is the correct answer. Nation B has a comparative advantage in cars because the within-country price comparison between cars and rice is lower for Nation B (16,000/20,000 = 0.8) than for Nation A (15,000/10,000 = 1.5). Nation A has an absolute advantage, but Nation B has the comparative advantage. Choice (b) is incorrect. Nation A has the comparative advantage for rice because its cost relationship (10,000/15,000 = 0.667) is lower than in Nation B (20,000/16,000 = 1.25). Choice (c) is incorrect. Nation B has the comparative advantage for cars. Choice (d) is incorrect. Total output will be maximized when each nation specializes in the products in which it has the greatest comparative advantage.

(e) **International Laws.** Laws regarding WTO, NAFTA, The European Union, and other regional groups are discussed in this section.

(i) **World Trade Organization.** The Final Act resulting from the Uruguay Round of negotiations of the GATT was signed in April 1994. The Final Act created a new World Trade Organization (WTO) as a successor to GATT. WTO would bring all 117 member countries under more of the multilateral trade disciplines.

Implementation of the Uruguay Round agreement is meant to further open markets by reducing tariffs worldwide by one-third; improve GATT procedures over unfair trade practices; broaden GATT coverage by including areas of trade in services, intellectual property rights, and trade-related investment that previously were not covered; and provide increased coverage to the areas of agriculture, textiles and clothing, government procurements, and trade and the environment.

WORLD TRADE ORGANIZATION STRUCTURE

The agreement establishing the World Trade Organization (WTO) would, for the first time, create a formal organization encompassing all GATT disciplines. WTO membership would be open only to countries that agree to adhere to all of the Uruguay Round agreements and submit schedules of market access commitments for industrial goods, agricultural goods, and services. As such, this agreement would resolve the "free rider" problem and permit members to "cross-retaliate" by suspending concessions under any of these agreements when authorized to impose sanctions. Adherence to the four "plurilateral agreements" would not be mandatory.

The free rider problem. Due to the WTO's Most-Favored-Nation (MFN) requirements, member countries that adhere to a given code and provide concessions in accordance with its obligations are required to accord the same benefits to all WTO members, including those countries that did not adhere to the code and, thus, do not reciprocate.

The inability to cross-retaliate. When a WTO member country is authorized to impose sanctions against another member for violating its obligations under a given code, it may only suspend concessions provided under that code. This restriction limits the plaintiff country's options and may make it difficult for that country to devise a sanction that is effective.

The agreement also makes provision for improved cooperation with other multilateral organizations with responsibilities and concerns similar to WTO, such as the World Bank and International Monetary Fund (IMF), as well as the OECD. It also would establish within WTO a Trade Policy Review Board comprised of the members. This review body would examine, on a regular basis, national trade policies and other economic policies affecting the international trading environment.

(A) ***Agreement for market access.*** The market access for goods agreement is a key part of the Uruguay Round's overall goal of liberalizing international trade by further opening markets among WTO countries. It is essentially a tariff schedule that reflects the concessions agreed upon by the WTO signatories. The main contribution of the market access agreements would be to significantly lower, or eliminate, tariff and nontariff barriers and to expand the extent of tariff bindings, on industrial products among WTO signatories. The global economic impact of this agreement is substantial.

(B) ***Provisions for subsidies and countervailing duties.*** Subsidies essentially lower a producer's costs or increase its revenues. Consequently, producers may sell their products at lower prices than their competitors from other countries. Subsidies to firms that produce or sell internationally traded products can distort international trade flows.

The United States has historically provided fewer industrial subsidies than most countries, and it has sought to eliminate trade-distorting subsidies provided by foreign governments.

Countervailing duty laws can address some of the adverse effects that subsidies can cause. Countervailing duties are special customs duties imposed to offset subsidies provided on the manufacture, protection, or export of a particular good.

The agreement would create for the first time three categories of subsidies and remedies: (1) prohibited subsidies (known as the "red light" category); (2) actionable subsidies (known as the "yellow light" category), and (3) nonactionable subsidies (known as the "green light" category) (see Exhibit 4.2).

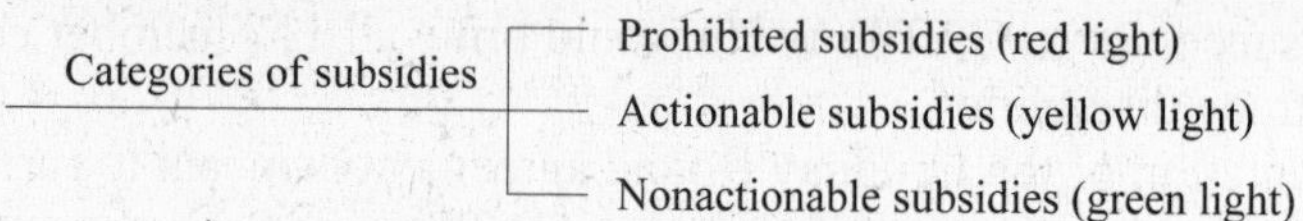

Exhibit 4.2: Categories of subsidies

Prohibited subsidies include subsidies to encourage exports, including de facto export subsidies, and subsidies contingent on the use of local content.

Actionable subsidies are domestic subsidies against which remedies can be sought if they are shown to distort trade. Trade distortion occurs if subsidized imports cause injury to a domestic industry (e.g., depress prices or threaten to do so); subsidies nullify or impair benefits owed to another country under WTO (e.g., the benefits of bound tariff concessions); or subsidized products displace or impede imports from another country or another country's exports to a third-country market.

There is also a special category of actionable subsidies that have a high likelihood of being trade distorting. These subsidies are presumed to cause "serious prejudice" to the trade interests of other countries when any of the following conditions are met: the total ad valorem subsidization of a product exceeds 5% of the value of the firm's or industry's output of a product (calculate on the basis of cost to the subsidizing government), subsidies are provided to forgive debts, or subsidies cover a firm's or an industry's operating losses. In cases where serious prejudice is presumed, the burden is on the subsidizing government to demonstrate that serious prejudice did not result from the subsidy in question.

Nonactionable subsidies include those that are not "specific" (i.e., not limited to an enterprise or industry or group of enterprises or industries). Subsidies also are nonactionable if they fall into three classes: (1) certain government assistance for research and precompetitive development activity, (2) certain government assistance for disadvantaged regions, and (3) certain government assistance to adapt existing plants and equipment to new environmental requirements.

(C) ***Provision for antidumping.*** Dumping is generally considered to be the sale of an exported product at a price lower than that charged for the same or a like product in the "home" market of the exporter. This practice is thought of as a form of price discrimination that can potentially harm the importing nation's competing industries.

Dumping may occur as a result of exporter business strategies that include: trying to increase an overseas market share, temporarily distributing products in overseas markets to offset slack demand in the home market, lowering unit costs by exploiting large-scale production, and attempting to maintain stable prices during periods of exchange rate fluctuations.

International trade rules, as defined by WTO, take political as well as economic concerns into account and view dumping and its potential harm broadly. Article VI of the WTO agreement notes that the contracting parties recognize that dumping "is to be condemned if it causes or threatens material injury to an established industry in the territory of a contracting party or materially retards the establishment of a domestic industry." The rules allow for the imposition of antidumping duties, or fees, to neutralize the injurious effect of these pricing practices.

Some trade economists view dumping as harmful only when it involves the use of "predatory" practices that intentionally try to eliminate competition and gain monopoly power in a market. They believe that predatory dumping rarely occurs and that antidumping enforcement is a protectionist tool whose cost to consumers and import-using industries exceeds the benefits to the industries receiving protection. Moreover, they believe that increased use of antidumping protection effectively reduces the anticipated gains that trade liberalization through tariff reduction will realize for the national economy.

(D) ***Provision for safeguards.*** A safeguard is a temporary import control or other trade restriction a country imposes to prevent injury to domestic industry caused by increased imports. Article 19 of the current GATT agreement, known as the "safeguard clause," allows contracting parties to obtain emergency relief from import surges. It is designed to help the domestic industries adjust to an influx of fairly traded imports.

The new Safeguard Agreement would require that safeguard measures be limited to an eight-year period for developed countries and ten years for developing countries. It provides for suspending the automatic right to retaliate to a safeguard measure for the first three years. However, it would maintain the requirement that safeguards be applied on a most-favored-nation (MFN) basis rather than being applied selectively (applied to just the country or countries causing injury to the domestic industry).

(E) ***Agreement on trade-related aspects of intellectual property rights.*** The World Intellectual Property Organizations (WIPO), a UN specialized agency, is a world body whose mission is to (1) promote the protection of intellectual property rights throughout the world through cooperation among countries and, where appropriate, in collaboration with international organizations; and (2) ensure administrative cooperation among the intellectual property unions. WIPO administers a number of international agreements on intellectual property protection, including in particular the Berne Convention for the Protection of Literary and Artistic Works, which provides for copyright protection; and the Paris Convention for the Protection of Industrial Property, which provides protection for patents, trademarks, and industrial designs and the repression of unfair competition.

According to US officials, these conventions do not contain specific commitments in important areas. For example, the Paris Convention does not contain a required minimum length of time for patent protection nor specify the subject matter to be covered by patents, and the Berne Convention does not provide copyright protection for newer creations such as sound recordings. Further, they do not provide for meaningful enforcement measures, an area long considered crucial by US interests; the Industry Functional Advisory Committee on intellectual property rights has pointed out that standards of protection are useless unless they are enforced.

(F) ***Agreement on trade in services.*** Service industries dominate the US economy and are important contributors to US exports. The US service industry is also the world's largest exporter of services. International trade in services takes place through various channels, including

- Cross-border transactions, such as transmission of voice, video, data, or other information and the transportation of goods and passengers from one country to another
- Travel of individual consumers to another country (e.g., services provided to nonresident tourists, students, and medical patients)
- Sales of services (e.g., accounting, advertising, and insurance) through foreign branches or other affiliates established in the consuming country
- Travel of individual producers to another country (e.g., services provided to foreign clients by business consultants, engineers, lawyers, etc.)

The Uruguay Round meetings created General Agreement on Trade in Services (GATS), which is the first multilateral, legally enforceable agreement covering trade and investment in the services sector.

(G) ***Agreement on trade-related investment measures.*** There is consensus among many, primarily developed, countries that foreign direct investment can have a favorable effect on a host country's economy. The foreign direct investment can create jobs, increase tax revenues, and introduce new technologies. It also increases the host country wages and productivity and seems to have a net positive effect on the competitiveness of the host economy.

According to the US Department of Commerce review of foreign direct investment, firms choose to expand their activities overseas for a variety of reasons. These reasons include a desire to: maintain profitability while reducing prices when faced with lower competitors' prices; maintain an increased worldwide market share; gain access to or retain access in an overseas market, especially in periods when trade restrictions are threatened; exploit, and maintain control over, an advantage specific to a company such as management, marketing, and/or technology, or a comparative advantage in producing in the foreign market; and improve the company's ability to meet the overseas market's needs by providing a special product design and/or service.

WTO created trade-related investment measures (TRIMs), which have economic effects that are comparable to those of traditional instruments of commercial policy, such as quotas, tariffs, and subsidies. TRIMs exist in many forms. TRIMs include local content requirements (obliging an investor to purchase or use a specified amount of inputs from local suppliers). Local content requirements are the most common form of TRIM, and are used in an attempt to ensure that the investment increases local employment and develops physical and human capital. TRIMs also include trade-balancing requirements. TRIMs are placed on foreign direct investment by governments in an effort to influence investment decisions such as sourcing, production, and market locations; to increase the likelihood that the host nation will capture the benefits expected from the investment; and to redistribute the investment benefits from the investor to the host country.

TRIMs can be implemented in different ways. TRIMs can be mandatory, that is, enforceable under domestic law or administrative rulings. An example of this type of mandatory TRIM would be a law that states that investors must include a certain percentage of local content in their production. In addition, TRIMs can be actions that are necessary for an investor to undertake in order to obtain some type of advantage (investment incentive)—a quid pro quo approach. For example, a host government might approach an investor with a proposal that allows the investor to receive a tax exemption in return for including a certain percentage of local content in the company's production.

(H) ***Agriculture provisions of the Uruguay Round.*** The Uruguay Round represented the first time that WTO contracting parties undertook to substantially reform agricultural trade. The Punta del Este ministerial declaration recognized an urgent need to stabilize the world agriculture market and liberalize trade by reducing import barriers, discipling the use of direct and indirect subsidies that affect trade, and minimizing the adverse effect of sanitary and phytosanitary regulations and barriers. The declaration recognized that other negotiating areas were likely to improve agricultural trade as well, such as efforts to strengthen the dispute resolution process. The sanitary and phytosanitary regulations and barriers are measures taken to protect human, animal, or plant life or health.

(ii) **North American Free Trade Agreement.** North American Free Trade Agreement (NAFTA), which went into effect on January 1, 1994, was intended to facilitate trade and investment throughout North America (United States, Canada, and Mexico). It incorporates features such as the elimination of tariff and nontariff barriers. NAFTA also supports the objective of locking in Mexico's self-initiated, market-oriented reforms. By removing barriers to the efficient allocation of economic resources, NAFTA was projected to generate overall, long-term economic gains for member countries—modest for the United States and Canada, and greater for Mexico. For the United States, this is due to the relatively small size of Mexico's economy and because many Mexican exports to the United States were already subject to low or no duties. Under NAFTA, intra-industry trade and coproduction of goods across the borders were expected to increase, enhancing specialization and raising productivity.

NAFTA also included procedures first to avoid, and then to resolve, disputes between parties to the agreement. Separately, the three NAFTA countries negotiated and entered into two supplemental agreements designed to facilitate cooperation on environment and labor matters among the three countries. NAFTA will create the largest free trade zone in the world, with 360 million people and an annual gross national product totaling over six trillion dollars.

(A) ***Major provisions of NAFTA.*** Major provisions include "rules of origin"; import/export quotas and licenses; technical standards and certification; escape clauses; telecommunications networks; cross-border trade in services; antidumping and subsidy laws; cross-subsidization; investments; performance requirements; right to convert and transfer local currencies; disputes; intellectual property rights; due process, temporary entry visas, and the side agreements.

Rules of origin. The NAFTA trade is subject to "rules of origin" that determine whether goods qualify for its tariff preferences. These include goods wholly originating in the free trade area. A general waiver of the NAFTA rules of origin requirements is granted if their nonregional value consists of no more than 7% of the price or total cost of the goods. Regional value may be calculated in most cases either by a "transaction value" or a "net cost" method. The former avoids costly accounting systems. The latter is based upon the total cost of the goods less royalties, sales promotion, packing and shipping, and allowable interest. Either method will require manufacturers to trace the source of non-NAFTA components and maintain source records.

Import/export quotas and licenses. Import and export quotas, licenses and other restrictions will gradually be eliminated under NAFTA subject to limited rights to restrain trade, for example to protect human, animal or plant health, or to protect the environment.

Technical standards and certification. Technical standards and certification procedures for products are classic examples of nontariff trade barriers. Mutual recognition of professional license is encouraged (notably for legal consultants and engineers), but not made automatic. All three countries have agreed not to lower existing environmental, or health and safety standards in order to attract investments and will attempt to "upwardly harmonize" them. Environmental impact statements for foreign investments are required.

Escape clauses. Escape clause rules and procedures are applicable to United States–Mexico trade under the NAFTA. These permit temporary trade relief against import surges subject to a right of compensation in the exporting nation.

Telecommunications and networks. Public telecommunications networks and services must be opened on reasonable and nondiscriminatory terms for firms and individuals who need the networks to conduct business.

Cross-border trade in services. Cross-border trade in services is subject to national treatment, including no less favorable treatment than that most favorably given at federal, state, or local government levels. Existing cross-border restraints on the provision of financial services are frozen and no new restraints may be imposed. Providers of financial services in each NAFTA nation will receive both national and most favored nation treatment. This includes equality of competitive opportunity, which is defined as avoidance of measures that pose a disadvantage to foreign providers relative to domestic providers.

Various procedural transparency rules are established to facilitate the entry and equal opportunity of NAFTA providers of financial services. The host nation may legislate reasonable prudential requirements for such companies and, under limited circumstances, protect their balance of payments in ways that restrain financial providers.

Antidumping and subsidy laws. Antidumping and subsidy laws and countervailing duties are applicable. A special committee may be invoked if the opportunity for independent judicial review on a dumping or subsidy determination has been denied.

Cross-subsidization. Cross-subsidization between public transport services is not prohibited, nor are monopoly providers of public networks or services.

Investments. Investment in the industrial and services sectors of the NAFTA nations is promoted through rules against nondiscriminatory and minimum standards of treatment that even benefit non-NAFTA investors with substantial business operations in a NAFTA nation.

Performance requirements. Performance requirements, for example, specific export levels, minimum domestic content, domestic sources preferences, trade balancing, technology transfer, and product mandates are disallowed in all areas except government procurement, export promotion, and foreign aid.

Senior management positions may not be reserved by nationality, but NAFTA states may require that a majority of the board of directors or committees thereof be of a designated nationality of residence provided this does not impair the foreign investor's ability to exercise control.

Right to convert and transfer local currencies. A general right to convert and transfer local currency at prevailing market rates for earnings, sale proceeds, loan repayments and other investment transactions has been established. Direct and indirect expropriations of investments by NAFTA investors are precluded except for public purposes and if done on a nondiscriminatory basis following due process of law. A right of compensation without delay at fair market value plus interest is created.

Disputes. In the event of a dispute, a NAFTA investor may elect monetary (but not punitive) damages through binding arbitration in the home state of the investor or pursue judicial remedies in courts of the host state.

Investment, dumping, and subsidy, financial services, environmental-investment and standards disputes are subject to special dispute resolution procedures. A right of consultation exists when one country's rights are affected.

Intellectual property rights. The NAFTA mandates adequate and effective intellectual property rights in all countries, including national treatment and effective internal and external environment rights.

For copyright, the NAFTA obligates protection for computer programs, database, computer program and sound recording rentals, and a 50-year term of protection for sound recordings. For patents, the NAFTA mandates a minimum 20 years of coverage of nearly all products and processes including pharmaceuticals and agricultural chemicals. Compulsory licensing is limited, notably regarding pharmaceuticals in Canada. Service marks are traded equally with trademarks. Satellite signal poaching is illegal and trade secrets are generally protected. The NAFTA details member states' duties to provide damages, injunctive, antipiracy and general due process remedies in the intellectual property field.

Due process. An agreement exists that deals with general duty of legal transparency, fairness, and due process regarding all laws affecting traders and investors with independent administrative or judicial review of governmental action. Generalized exceptions to the agreement cover actions to protect national security and national interests such as public morals, health, national treasures, natural resources, or to enforce laws against deceptive or anticompetitive practices, short of arbitrary discriminations or disguised restraints on trade.

Balance of payments trade restraints are governed by the rules of the International Monetary Fund. Taxation issues are subject to bilateral double taxation treaties, including a new one between Mexico and the United States.

Temporary entry visas. Entry rights cover businesspersons, traders, investors, intracompany transferees, and 63 designated professionals. White-collar businesspersons will only need proof of citizenship and documentation of business purpose to work in another NAFTA country for up to five years. However, an annual limit of 5,500 additional Mexican professionals may temporarily enter the United States during the first 10 years of the NAFTA. Apart from these provisions, no common market for the free movement of workers is undertaken.

Side agreements. The side agreements on labor and the environment commit each country to creation of environmental and labor commissions that monitor compliance with the adequacy and the enforcement of domestic law. These commissions are empowered to receive complaints. Negotiations to resolve complaints would first ensue. Absent a solution, an arbitral panel of experts from the three nations would be convened to evaluate the complaint.

(B) ***Impacts and implementation of NAFTA.*** Assessment of NAFTA's effects is a complex undertaking since the provisions last ten to fifteen years. While NAFTA is not yet fully implemented, US trade with NAFTA members has accelerated, and is in accordance with pre-NAFTA expectations.

At the sector level, there are diverse impacts from NAFTA. Within sectors, these may include increases or decreases in trade flows, hourly earnings, and employment. Economic efficiency may improve from this reallocation of resources, but it creates costs for certain sectors of the economy and labor force, including job dislocation.

In general, NAFTA or broader trade policies cannot be expected to substantially alter overall US employment levels, which are determined largely by demographic conditions and macroeconomic factors such as monetary policy.

While there is wide conceptual agreement on the contribution to trade liberalization to improvement in the standard of living through increased productivity and lower prices, estimating the extent to which NAFTA specifically furthers these goals presents a major empirical challenge. For example, there are no estimates of NAFTA's direct impact on productivity. However, growth in shared production activity and two-way trade suggests that increases in sector specialization, a mechanism through which productivity may be improved, have occurred.

NAFTA's system for avoiding and settling disputes among the member countries is a critical element of the agreement. The agreement includes mechanisms such as the establishment of committees and working groups and an early consultation process to help the parties avoid disputes. These mechanisms have helped the governments resolve important trade issues and have kept the number of formal dispute settlement cases relatively low.

Trade laws agreed to under NAFTA have helped members improve the transparency (openness) of their antidumping and countervailing duty administrative processes, thus reducing the potential for arbitrariness in their application.

It is too early to determine what definitive effect the supplemental agreements will have on the North American environment and labor. However, the two commissions created to implement the agreements have been acknowledged by some government and private sector officials for several positive achievements to date.

(iii) **European Union.** The European Union (EU), often called the Common Market, is a supranational legal regime with its own legislative, administrative, treaty-making, and judicial procedures. To create this regime, fifteen or more European nations have surrendered substantial sovereignty to the EU. European Union law has replaced national law in many areas and the EU legal system operates as an umbrella over the legal systems of the member states. The EU law is vast and intricate. The EU has an aggregate population exceeding 375 million and a gross national product exceeding $7,000 billion. EU is the largest market for exports from the United States.

The tasks of EU include creation of an economic and monetary union with emphasis upon price stability with the goal of establishing a Europe "without internal frontiers."

(A) ***The Council, the Commission, the Parliament, the Court of Justice.*** **The Council** consists of representatives of the ruling governments of the member states. The European Community Treaty requires the Council to act by a qualified majority on some matters and with unanimity on others.

The Commission is independent of the member states. Its twenty commissioners are selected by council appointment. They do not represent member states or take orders from member state governments. The Commission is charged with the duty by acting only in the best interests of the Union, and serves as the guardian of the Treaties. The Commission largely maintains EU relations with GATT and WTO. The Commission proposes and drafts EU legislation and submits to the Council for adoption.

The Parliament historically played an advisory role. The European Parliament has the power to put questions to the Commission and the Council concerning Union affairs. It also has the power, so far unused, to censure the Commission, in which event all the Commissioners are required to resign as a body. As a minimum, the Parliament has a right to be consulted and to give an "opinion" as part of the EU legislative process. The opinion is not binding upon the Commission or Council.

The Court of Justice is to ensure that in the interpretation and application of Treaty "the law" is observed. There are fifteen Justices (one from each state) that make up the European Court of Justice. If a conflict arises between Union law and the domestic law of a member state, the Court of Justice has held that the former prevails. When there is no conflict, both Union law and domestic law can coexist.

(B) ***Major provisions of the European Union.*** The major provisions of the European Union laws include free movement of goods, free movement of workers, free movement of capital, free movement of payments, establishment of a monetary system, a tax system, and trade rules with nonmember states.

Free movement of goods. The Treaty attempts to achieve free movement of goods by establishment of a Customs Union to eliminate, between the member states, customs duties and all other charges having "equivalent effect." It has established a Common Customs Tariff with the outside world. Quantitative restriction on imports between member states and measures having an equivalent effect are also prohibited. Nontariff trade barriers are frequently the subject of intense negotiation within the Union and remain the most troublesome feature of the Customs Union.

Free movement of workers. The Treaty distinguishes the "free movement of workers" (blue collar workers and artisans) from the "right of establishment" and "freedom to provide services." Regarding free movement of workers, the Treaty prohibits "any discrimination, based on nationality, between workers of the member sates as regards employment, remuneration and other conditions of work and employment." Free movement of self-employed persons and of services across member state boundaries are aided by the right of establishment. Restrictions on the freedom to provide services across borders without local establishment are being abolished progressively.

Free movement of capital. The Treaty requires the removal of national restrictions on the free movement of capital belonging to persons of member states "to the extent necessary to insure the proper functions of the Common Market."

Free movement of payments. The "free" movement of workers and capital should be distinguished from the free movement of payments necessary to EU trade. Current payments are, as a rule, treated more liberally under Union law and indeed are essential to the free movement of goods and services in the Common Market.

Monetary system. In movement toward a monetary Union, the member states have created the European Monetary System (EMS) and the European Exchange Rate Mechanism (ERM). The ERM is similar in concept and form to the currency basket, and allows limited fluctuations on national exchange rates from agreed parities.

The states have also established a joint credit facility for giving short- and medium-term financial support to EMS currencies under pressure. The European Currency Unit (ECU) is the basis of definition of the basket parities. ECUs, although not a tangible currency, are used as the basis of settlement between banks within the EMS, for budgetary purposes, to calculate agricultural subsidies, and levy fines and penalties. ECUs are increasingly used as reference values in private transactions.

Tax system. With considerable effort the EU nations have adopted a common tax system called value-added taxation (VAT). But different revenue needs and tax policies cause different levels of VAT to apply to like items in the various member states.

The tax frontiers will be eliminated by imposing VAT reporting and collection duties on importers and exporters using the "destination principle" on VAT rates.

Trade rules. The Treaty requires member states to coordinate and implement a common commercial policy toward nonmember states. This policy is based upon uniform principles regarding tariff and trade agreements, fishing rights, export policy, and other matters of external concern to the Union.

WTO VS. NAFTA VS. EU

- 117 or more nations are involved in WTO, 3 in NAFTA, and 15 or more in EU.
- The provisions of WTO have more far-reaching long-term effects on the world economy than NAFTA or EU due to its focus on reducing trade barriers.
- When there is a conflict between WTO and NAFTA, the latter prevails.
- NAFTA is better streamlined politically, legislatively, and judicially than EU.
- There is no NAFTA Council of Ministers, Court of Justice, no Parliament when compared to EU.
- The EU Commission is more powerful than NAFTA's Trade Commission.
- NAFTA goals and techniques are strikingly limited while they are strikingly ambitious for EU.
- NAFTA's goals are more achievable than those of EU due to EU's grand-scale nature.
- NAFTA's treaty is for a limited duration (ten to fifteen years) while it is unlimited for EU. Any nation in the NAFTA may withdraw on six months notice and other nations can be admitted to the NAFTA.
- NAFTA's economic integration can advance to greater degrees than EU due to several, different, complex nations involved in EU.
- The EU has legal foundation while NAFTA has economic foundation.

(iv) **Other regional groups.** Many nations are contemplating or have already formed regional economic integration to capture the economic gains and international negotiating strength that regionalization can bring. The following list provides some regions or groups:

- Several groups have been formed in Africa including UDEA, CEAO, and ECOWAS. The purpose is to establish a common customs and tariff approach toward the rest of the world and to formulate a common foreign investment trade.
- Regional groups have been established in Latin America and the Caribbean (CARICOM, CACM, LAFTA/LAIA). The Latin American Free Trade Association (LAFTA) had small success in reducing tariffs and developing the region through cooperative industrial sector programs. These programs allocated industrial production among the participating states. In 1994 some 37 nations signed the Association of Caribbean States agreement with long-term economic integration goals.
- Gulf Cooperations Council (GCC) was formed between Bahrain, Kuwait, Oman, Qatar, Saudi Arabia, and United Arab Emirates with objectives to establish freedom of movement, a regional armaments industry, common banking and financial systems, a unified currency policy, a customs union, a common foreign aid program, and a joint, international investment company, the Gulf Investment Corporation. The GCC has already implemented trade and investment rules concerning tariffs on regional and imported goods, government contracts, communications, transportation, real estate investment, freedom of movement of professionals, and development of a Uniform Commercial Code. In 1987, the GCC entered into negotiations with the EU that resulted in a major 1990 trade and cooperation agreement.
- The Andean Common Market (ANCOM) was founded by Bolivia, Chile, Colombia, Ecuador, and Peru in 1969 primarily to counter the economic power of Argentina, Brazil, and Mexico and to reduce dependency upon foreign capital. Later, Venezuela joined and Chile left the group. ANCOM Commission has not been an activist on behalf of regional integration like the EU Commission. It mostly reacts to proposals put forth by the Junta, the administrative arm of ANCOM.
- The Association of South East Asian Nations (ASEAN) was formed in 1967 by Indonesia, Malaysia, the Philippines, Singapore, and Thailand. Brunei joined in 1984, Vietnam in 1995. The Bangkok Declaration establishing ASEAN as a cooperative association is a broadly worded document, but with little supranational legal machinery, to implement its stated goals.
- East Asian Integration, ranging from Japan in the north to Indonesia in the south, has formed Asia-Pacific Economic Cooperation (APEC) consisting of 18 Asian-Pacific nations including the United States. East Asia, unlike Europe, has not developed a formal Common

Market with uniform trade, licensing, and investment rules. Late in 1994, the APEC nations targeted free trade and investment for developed countries by the year 2010 and developing countries by the year 2020.

OPTIONS FOR NATIONS

Nations in the world have options to consider prior to joining a group of countries for economic integration. These include free trade areas, customs unions, common market, economic communities, and economic unions.

Free trade areas. In free trade areas, tariffs, quotas and other barriers to trade among participating states are reduced or removed while individual national trade barriers vis-à-vis third-party states are retained.

Customs unions. Customs unions not only remove trade barriers among participating states, but they also create common trade barriers for all participating states as regards third-party states.

Common markets. Common markets go further than customs unions by providing for the free movement of factors of production (e.g., capital, labor, technology, enterprise) among participating states.

Economic communities. Economic communities build on common markets by introducing some harmonization of basic national policies related to the economy of the community (e.g., transport, taxation, corporate structure, monetary matters, and regional growth).

Economic unions. Economic unions embrace a more or less complete harmonization of national policies related to the economy of the union (e.g., company laws, commercial treaties, social welfare, currencies, and governmental subsidies). The difference between an economic community and an economic union relates only to the number and importance of harmonized national policies.

4.3 Taxation Schemes

Taxes are assessed for various purposes such as: (1) to collect revenues, (2) to encourage or discourage different kinds of investments, (3) to redistribute income among citizens. Different types of taxes are in place where they differ in: (1) the classes of income that are taxable, (2) which expenses are allowed for deduction from revenues and how they are to be calculated, (3) what kind of taxes (e.g., direct or indirect) are to be collected, and (4) the extent to which companies report income honestly. Exhibit 4.3 presents different types of taxes.

- Sales
- Use
- Value-added
- Income
- Property
- Ad valorem
- Accumulated earnings
- Capital stock
- Unrelated business income
- Gift
- Estate
- Excise
- Unified transfer

Exhibit 4.3: Different types of taxes

(a) **Sales Tax.** A sales tax is a state-level or local-level (e.g., county, city) tax on the retail sale of specified property. Generally, the purchaser pays the tax, but the seller collects it, as an agent for the government. Various taxing jurisdictions allow exemptions for purchases of specific items, including certain food, services, and manufacturing equipment. If the purchaser and seller are in different states, a use tax usually applies.

THREE CONCEPTS OF AN INCOME TAX SYSTEM

A tax system should be equitable and nondistorting. Three different concepts of equity as it applies to the tax system include: (1) the "ability-to-pay" principle, (2) the benefit principle, and (3) "equal treatment of those equally situated."

Ability-to-pay principle. Under this concept, people with higher incomes should pay more than those with lower incomes. It is based on the assumption that a more equal distribution of income would be more equitable. The real question is at what rate should different incomes be taxed? Some argue that the tax rate should be **proportional**—that is, the same percentage of each person's income.

Some argue that the tax rate should be **progressive**—that is, a higher percentage tax on high incomes than on low incomes. All ability-to-pay advocates argue against **regressive** taxation, which takes a larger percentage of income from the lower-income groups. Regressive taxes will not take a larger absolute amount of income as income rises. There is no objective way of deciding whether tax rates should be proportional or progressive, or, if progressive, how steeply progressive.

Benefit principle. This concept proposes that people should be taxed only to pay for the benefits they choose to buy from the government. This concept is more revolutionary in that each individual should have the income that he earns by helping to produce what consumers choose to buy. A direct sale of government services to the user would prevent redistribution of income.

Equal treatment of those equally situated. This concept states that persons equally situated should be taxed equally. The term "equally situated" is not clear and may have many meanings. Are two people with the same income always equally situated? What about the differences among disabled people, or retired men and healthy young men with the same income?

(b) **Use Tax.** A use tax is a sales tax that is collectible by the seller when the purchaser is domiciled in a different state.

(c) **Value-Added Tax.** A value-added tax (VAT) is a form of sales tax. Many European countries use VATs. The firm pays a percentage of tax based on the value that its production process adds to the final product. VAT is less complex and easier to calculate than an income tax, and is easier to monitor. VAT encourages honesty whereas income tax does not.

(d) **Income Tax.** Income tax is a tax imposed on income earned after deducting allowable expenses from all sources of revenues. Income tax rates vary depending on the amount of income earned. Corporations are subject to an alternative minimum tax (AMT), which has a more expansive tax base than does the regular tax. The corporation is required to apply a minimum tax rate to the expanded base and pay the difference between the AMT tax liability and the regular tax.

(e) **Property Tax.** An ad valorem tax, usually levied by a city or county government, on the value of real or personal property that the taxpayer owns on a specified date. Most states exclude intangible property and assets owned by exempt organizations from the tax base, and some exclude inventory, pollution control or manufacturing equipment, and other items to provide relocation or retention incentives to the taxpayer.

(f) **Ad Valorem Tax.** Ad valorem tax is a tax imposed on the value of property. The most common ad valorem tax is that imposed by states, counties, and cities on real estate. Ad valorem taxes can, however, be imposed on personal property as well.

(g) **Accumulated Earnings Tax.** A special tax imposed on corporations that accumulate (rather than distribute) their earnings beyond the reasonable needs of the business. The accumulated earnings tax and related interest are imposed on accumulated taxable income in addition to the corporate income tax.

(h) **Capital Stock Tax.** A state-level tax is usually imposed on out-of-state corporations for the privilege of doing business in the state. The tax may be based on the entity's apportionable income or payroll, or on its apportioned net worth as of a specified date.

(i) **Unrelated Business Income Tax.** Unrelated business income tax is levied on the unrelated business taxable income of an exempt organization.

(j) **Gift Tax.** A gift tax is a tax imposed on the transfer of property by gift. Such tax is imposed upon the donor of a gift and is based on the fair market value of the property on the date of the gift.

(k) **Estate Tax.** An estate tax is a tax imposed on the right to transfer property by death. Thus, an estate tax is levied on the decedent's estate and not on the heir receiving the property.

(l) **Excise Tax.** An excise tax is a tax on the manufacture, sale, or use of goods or on the carrying on of an occupation or activity, or a tax on the transfer of property. Thus, the federal estate and gift taxes are, theoretically, excise taxes.

(m) **Unified Transfer Tax.** Unified transfer tax is a set of tax rates applicable to transfers by gift and death made after 1976. It is a tax imposed upon the transfer of property.

(n) **Differences between Tax Reporting and Financial Reporting.** The net income computed for financial accounting purposes will be different from taxable income reported on the corporation's income tax return, and therefore, reconciliation between these two types of income is essential to ensure accuracy. The starting point for the reconciliation is net income per books, which is the financial accounting net income. Additions and subtractions are entered for items that affect net income per books and taxable income differently.[1]

Net income per books
+ additions
– subtractions
= Taxable income

The following items are added *to the net income per books:*

- Federal income tax liability (deducted in computing net income per books but not deductible in computing taxable income)
- The excess of capital losses over capital gains (deducted for financial accounting purposes but not deductible by corporations for income tax purposes)
- Income that is reported in the current year for tax purposes that is not reported in computing net income per books (e.g., prepaid income)
- Various expenses that are deducted in computing net income per books but not allowed in computing taxable income (e.g., charitable contributions in excess of the 10% ceiling applicable to corporations)

The following items are subtracted *from the net income per books:*

- Income reported for financial accounting purposes but not included in taxable income (e.g., tax-exempt interest)
- Expenses deducted on the tax return but not deducted in computing net income per books (e.g., a charitable contributions carryover deducted in a prior year for financial accounting purposes but deductible in the current year for tax purposes

The result is taxable income before net operating loss deduction and the dividends received deduction.

4.4 Contracts

(a) **Definition of a Contract.** Contracts are governed by state common law. A contract is a binding agreement that the courts will enforce. It is a promise or a set of promises for the breach of which the law gives a remedy, or the performance of which the law in some way recognizes a duty. A promise manifests or demonstrates the intention to act or to refrain from acting in a specified manner.

Those promises that meet all of the essential requirements of a binding contract are contractual and will be enforced. All other promises are not contractual, and usually no legal remedy is available for a breach of, or a failure to properly perform, these promises. The remedies provided for breach of

[1] ***Corporations, Partnerships, Estates, and Trusts*** *by Hoffman, Raabe, and Smith, (St.Paul, MN: West's Federal Taxation, West Publishing Company), 1993.*

contract include compensatory damages, equitable remedies, reliance damage, and restitution. Thus, a promise may be contractual (and therefore binding) or noncontractual. In other words, all contracts are promises, but not all promises are contracts.

(b) **Requirements of a Contract.** The four basic requirements of a contract include: (1) mutual assent, (2) consideration, (3) legality of object and subject matter, and (4) capacity (competent parties).

- **Mutual assent.** The parties to a contract must manifest by words or conduct that they have agreed to enter into a contract. The usual method of showing mutual assent is by offer and acceptance. An offer is a proposal or expression by one person that he is willing to do something for certain terms. A contract does not exist until the offer is formally accepted, either verbally or in written form. The offer and acceptance have to match. If they match, there is an agreement leading up to a contract. If they do not, it is more like a negotiation, to which someone responds with a counteroffer rather than an acceptance, which continues until both parties reach an agreement or a "meeting of the minds."
- **Consideration.** Each party to a contract must intentionally exchange a legal benefit or incur a legal detriment as in inducement to the other party to make a return exchange. Consideration is a form of "mutual obligation." In the business world, mutual promises in a contract of sale, whether express or implied, are generally sufficient consideration.
- **Legality of object and subject matter.** The purpose of a contract must not be criminal, tortious, or otherwise against public policy. If the purpose is illegal, the resulting contract is null and void. The performance of a party in regard to the contract must not be an unlawful act if the agreement is to be enforceable. However, if the primary purpose of a contract is legal, but some terms contained within the agreement are not, then the contract may or may not be itself be illegal depending on the seriousness of the illegal terms and the degree to which the legal and illegal terms can be separated.
- **Capacity (competent parties).** The parties to a contract must have contractual capacity. Certain persons, such as adjudicated incompetents, have no legal capacity to contract, while others, such as minors, incompetent persons, and intoxicated persons, have limited capacity to contract. All others have full contractual capacity. The parties can be principals or qualified agents. The parties cannot engage in any fraudulent activities. The use of force or coercion to reach an agreement is not acceptable in signing a contract because both parties must enter into the agreement on their own free will. Both parties must indicate a willingness to enter into the agreement and be bound by its terms.

In addition, though in a limited number of instances a contract must be evidenced in writing to be enforceable, in most cases an oral contract is binding and enforceable. Moreover, there must be an absence of invalidating conduct, such as duress, undue influence, misrepresentation, or mistake. A promise meeting all of these requirements is contractual and legally binding. However, if any requirement is unmet, the promise is noncontractual.

(c) **Classification of Contracts.** Contracts can be classified according to various characteristics, such as method of formation, content, and legal effect. The standard classifications are express or implied contracts; bilateral or unilateral contracts; valid, void, voidable, or unenforceable contracts; and executed or executory contracts. These classifications are not mutually exclusive. For example, a contract may be express, bilateral, valid, executory, and informal.

- **Express and implied contracts.** A contract formed by conduct, is an implied or, more precisely, an implied in fact contract. In contrast, a contract in which the parties manifest assent in words is an express contract. Both are contracts, equally enforceable. The difference between them is merely the manner in which the parties manifest their assent.
- **Bilateral and unilateral contracts.** When each party is both a promisor (a person making a promise) and a promisee (the person to whom a promise is made), it is called a bilateral contract. A unilateral contract is one where only one of the parties makes a promise.
- **Valid, void, voidable, and unenforceable contracts.** A valid contract is one that meets all of the requirements of a binding contract. It is an enforceable promise or an agreement. A void contract is an agreement that does not meet all of the requirements of a binding contract. It has no legal effect and it is merely a promise or agreement. An example is an agreement entered by a person whom the courts have declared incompetent. A contract that is neither void nor void-

able may nonetheless be unenforceable. An unenforceable contract is one for the breach of which the law provides no remedy. After the statutory time period has passed, a contract is referred to as unenforceable, rather than void or voidable.

- **Executed and executory contracts.** A contract that has been fully carried out and completed by all of the parties to it is an executed contract. By comparison, the term executory contract applies to contracts that are still partially or entirely unperformed by one or more of the parties.

(d) **Other Types of Contracts.** Two other types of contracts that occur in common include the doctrine of promissory estoppel and quasi contracts.

(i) **Doctrine of promissory estoppel.** In certain circumstances, the courts enforce noncontractual promises under the doctrine of promissory estoppel in order to avoid injustice. A noncontractual promise is enforceable when it is made under circumstances that should lead the promisor reasonably expect that the promisee, in reliance on the promise, would be induced by it to take definite and substantial action or to forbear, and the promisee does take such action or does forbear.

(ii) **Quasi contracts.** Quasi (meaning "as if") contract is not a contract at all. A quasi contract is based neither on an express nor on an implied in fact contract. Rather, quasi contract is a contract implied in law, which is an obligation imposed by law to avoid injustice. Not frequently, quasi contracts are used to provide a remedy when the parties enter into a void contract, an unenforceable contract, or a voidable contract that is avoided. In such a case, the law of quasi contracts will determine what recovery is permitted for any performance rendered by the parties under the invalid, unenforceable, or invalidated agreements.

4.5 Nature and Rules of Legal Evidence

Eight types of legal evidence exist, which are described below[2] (see Exhibit 4.4). Both legal evidence and audit evidence have common objectives of providing proof and fostering an honest belief about the truth or falsity of any proposition at issue. The focus of audit evidence differs somewhat from that of legal evidence. Legal evidence relies heavily on oral testimony. Audit evidence relies more on documentary evidence. Legal evidence permits certain presumptions. Audit evidence is not bound by any presumptions. This requires auditors to question all evidence until they, themselves, are satisfied with its truth or falsity.

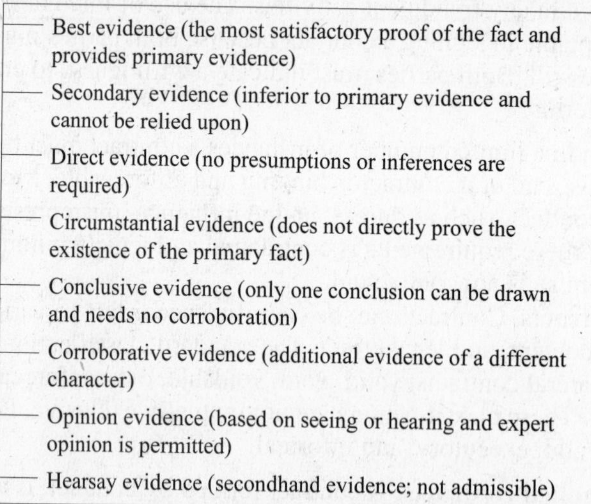

Exhibit 4.4: Eight forms of legal evidence

(a) **Best Evidence.** Best evidence is often referred to as primary evidence and is the evidence that is the most natural and reliable. It is confined to documentary evidence and applies to proof of the content in writing. Oral evidence may not be used to dispute a written instrument such as a contract or a deed; however, oral evidence can be used to explain the meaning of the instrument where such an instrument is capable of more than one interpretation.

Examples of best evidence include

[2] ***Sawyer's Internal Auditing*** *by Lawrence B. Sawyer, (Altamonte Springs, FL: The Institute of Internal Auditors [IIA]), 1988.*

- The audit procedure providing the best evidence about the collectibility of notes receivable would be an examination of cash receipts records to determine promptness of interest and principal payments.
- "Reconciling shipping records to recorded sales" is a substantive fieldwork procedure providing best evidence about the completeness of recorded revenues.
- The best evidence in assessing the acceptability of various benefit programs to employees is to evaluate program participation ratios and their trends during an audit of the personnel function, where participation in some of these benefit programs is optional.
- In testing the write-off of a deteriorated piece of equipment, the best evidence of the condition of the equipment would be a physical inspection of the actual piece of equipment.

(b) **Secondary Evidence.** Secondary evidence is inferior to primary evidence and cannot be given the same reliance. Examples include a copy of a writing or oral evidence of its contents. A copy of writing is permissible when it is lost, destroyed, or controlled by a public entity.

(c) **Direct Evidence.** Direct evidence proves a fact without having to use presumptions or inference to establish that proof. The testimony of a witness to a fact is direct evidence. The most likely source of evidence indicating employee theft of inventory would be a warehouse employee's verbal charge of theft.

(d) **Circumstantial Evidence.** Circumstantial evidence proves an intermediate fact(s) from which one can infer the existence of some primary fact that is significant to the issue under consideration. It provides a logical inference that it exists.

(e) **Conclusive Evidence.** Conclusive evidence is incontrovertible evidence, irrespective of its nature. It is so strong that it overbears all other evidence. It cannot be contradicted and needs no corroboration.

(f) **Corroborative Evidence.** Corroborative evidence is additional evidence of a different character concerning the same point. It is evidence supplementary to that already given and tends to strengthen or confirm it.

Examples of corroborative evidence include

- Salespersons often order inventory for stock without receiving the approval of the vice president of sales and a detail testing showed that there are no written approvals on purchase orders for replacement parts. The detail testing is a good example of "corroborative evidence."
- Interviews should be corroborated by gathering objective data.

(g) **Opinion Evidence.** The opinion rule holds that a witness must ordinarily testify to fact only—to what they actually saw or heard. Opinions may be biased, self-serving, or uninformed. However, experts are permitted to offer an opinion based on the facts.

(h) **Hearsay Evidence.** The hearsay rule renders objectionable any statements made by someone, other than a witness, to prove the truth of the matter stated. It refers to any oral or written evidence brought into court and offered as proof of things said out of court.

Business documents (e.g., sales slips, purchase orders) made during regular business routines are admissible. Photographs represent hearsay evidence, but are considered admissible if properly authenticated by witnesses who are familiar with the subject.

4.6 Key Economic Indicators

(a) **Nature of Key Economic Indicators.** Business conditions relate to business cycles. Decisions such as ordering inventory, borrowing money, increasing staff, and spending capital are dependent on the current and predicted business cycle. For example, decision making in preparation for a recession, such as cost reduction and cost containment is especially different and difficult. Also, during a recession, defaults on loans can increase due to bankruptcies and unemployment.

Timing is everything when it comes to making good cycle-sensitive decisions. Managers need to make appropriate cutbacks prior to the beginning of a recession. Similarly, managers cannot get caught short during a period of rapid expansion. Economic forecasting is a necessity for predicting business cycles and swings. Trend analysis, economic surveys, opinions, and simulation techniques are quite useful to managers trying to stay abreast of the latest economic developments.

Businesses use economic forecasts in making investment and production decisions. When they foresee an economic downturn, inventories may be reduced. When prices are expected to rise quickly, they buy goods in advance and add to equipment and plant.

Statistical models are most successful when past circumstances can be used to predict future events. Economic models use historical data to develop predictive models. Current input to the model provides a meaningful production only if the important factors retain the same proportional significance. During the energy crisis of the early 1970s, most economic models performed very poorly. This occurred because key relationships had changed. Thus, predictive models improved once new historical patterns emerged.

The opposite of forecasting economic events is measuring economic events. This historical information is important in evaluating and providing information for predicting the future. The business cycle is the up and down movement of an economy's ability to generate wealth. Historical economic data show a clear pattern of alternating recessions and expansions. In between there have been peaks and troughs of varying magnitude and duration. The business cycles have a predictable structure but variable timing.

(b) **Specific Types of Key Economic Indicators.** Three types of economic indicators are used in forecasting, including leading indicators, coincident indicators, and lagging indicators (see Exhibit 4.5).

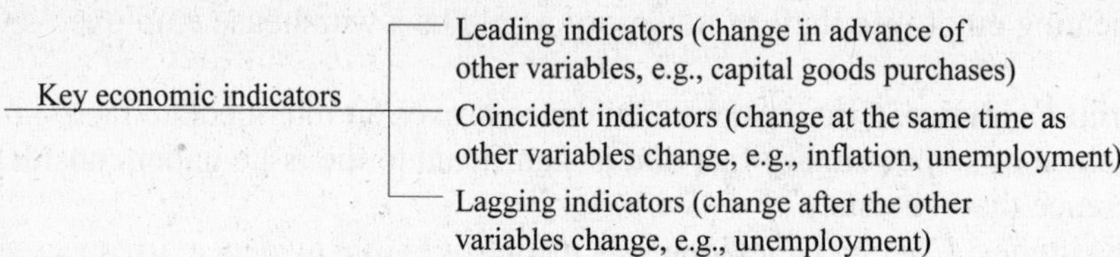

Exhibit 4.5: Key economic indicators

1. **Leading indicators** change in advance of other variables. These are the least likely to be accurate. However, they are the most useful for business planning, because they provide information for action. Example: capital goods purchases are a leading indicator for recession. The consumer price index is often used in making plans for inflation and wages because it is a leading economic indicator.
2. **Coincident indicators** change at the same time as other variables change. Example: inflation, unemployment, and consumer confidence are coincident indicators.
3. **Lagging indicators** change after the other variables change. These are more accurate, but the information is much less useful for decision making. Example: unemployment figures are lagging indicators of recession.

(c) **Other Types of Key Economic Indicators.** Other types of key economic indicators include gross national product (GNP), gross domestic product (GDP), net national product (NNP), consumer price index (CPI), and producer price index (PPI). These are discussed below.

(i) **Gross national product and gross domestic product.** A measure of the change in prices for all final goods and services produced in the economy is the gross national product (GNP) price deflator. This inflation index can be used to estimate the inflation rate on all goods and services over a recent time period.

The following list provides relationships between GNP, GDP, NNP, CPI, and PPI:

- The two main variables that contribute to increases in a nation's real gross domestic product (GDP) are labor productivity and total worker hours.
- Net national product (NNP) is composed of the total market value of all final goods and services produced in the economy in one year minus the capital consumption allowance.
- The basic source of improvements in real wage rates and in the standard of living is productivity growth.
- Under the income approach, gross national product (GNP) is measured as follows: Depreciation charges + Indirect business taxes + Wages, rents, interest, and profits.
- In the output (expenditures) approach to measuring a country's GNP, it is calculated as follows: Consumption + Investments + Government purchases + Expenditures by foreigners.
- When gross investment is less than depreciation, the capital stock of the economy is shrinking.
- An increase in the average hours worked per week of production workers would provide a leading indicator of a future increase in gross national product (GNP).

- The sale of final goods is included in the GNP and the sale of intermediate goods is excluded from the GNP.
- GNP price deflator is the price index for all final goods and services used to adjust the money (or nominal) GNP to measure the real GNP.

(ii) **Consumer price index and producer price index.** Consumer price index (CPI) is a statistic used to measure the changes in prices in a market basket of selected items. The CPI is one factor in setting cost of living adjustments in a country. Critics of CPI argue that it overstates increases in the cost of living. This is due to the constant composition of the market basket of items whose prices are measured. The producer price index (PPI) measures the price of a basket of commodities at the point of their first commercial sale.

APPLICATION OF CPI, REAL INCOME, AND INFLATION

Example

Assume that in 1990 an internal auditor is making $40,000 per year and five years later his income has risen to $90,000, but the CPI has increased from 100 to 250. The real income (in 1990 prices) for the later year is calculated as follows:

The inflation rate is (250 – 100)/250 = 150/250 = 0.60, that is, 60%.

Real income is nominal income minus inflation rate, that is, 100% – 60 % = 40%.

Therefore, real income is $90,000 × 0.40 = $36,000.

(d) **Methods of Measuring Economic Performance.** The basic goals of the public and private sectors are to achieve both the full employment of resources and a stable price level. *Two major methods exist to measure economic performance of a country: (1) unemployment and (2) inflation.*

(i) **Unemployment.** The key point is that the level of output depends directly upon total or aggregate expenditures. A high level of total spending means: it will be profitable for the various industries to produce large outputs, and it will be profitable for various resource suppliers to be employed at high levels. Hence,

Total spending = Private sector spending + Public sector spending

Private sector spending alone is not enough to keep the economy at full employment. The government's obligation (public spending) is to augment private sector spending sufficient enough to generate full employment. *Government has two basic economic tools with which to accomplish public spending: (1) spending programs and (2) taxes.* Specifically, government should increase its own spending on public goods and services on the one hand, and reduce taxes in order to stimulate private sector spending on the other. Unemployment results when either private sector spending or public sector spending does not measure up to expectations.

There are four variations of unemployment: (1) full employment, (2) frictional unemployment, (3) cyclical employment, and (4) structural unemployment (see Exhibit 4.6).

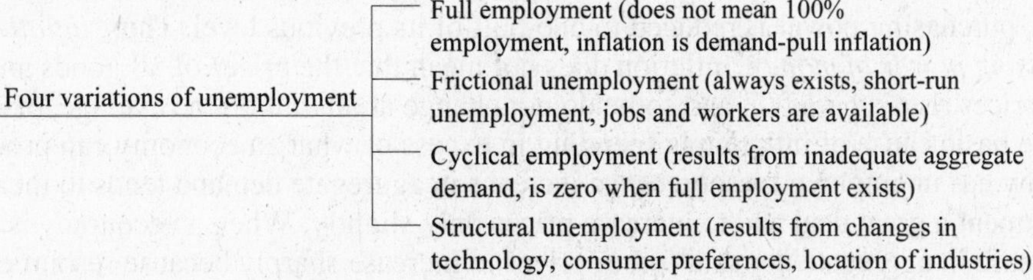

Exhibit 4.6: Four variations of unemployment

Full employment means that all people sixteen years of age or older are employed or are actively seeking employment or that cyclical unemployment is zero. Inflation occurring during a period of full employment is most likely to be a demand-pull inflation. In an economy that is near full employment, a decrease in the money supply is likely to decrease the price level.

Types of Employment/Unemployment

- Full employment means that all people available to produce goods and services are employed.
- Frictional unemployment is short-run and caused by people voluntarily changing jobs.
- Cyclical employment results from inadequate aggregate demand.
- Structural unemployment results from an economy's failure to adjust to changes in technology, consumer preferences, or locations of industries.

Frictional unemployment will always exist in a dynamic economy. It is short-run unemployment that is caused by people voluntarily changing jobs or by frictions that result from lack of knowledge about job opportunities and lack of labor mobility.

Thus, full employment means that only frictional unemployment exists. In other words, there is no cyclical or structural unemployment when the economy is operating at full employment. There always will be some unemployment at all times caused by workers changing jobs. Frictional unemployment occurs when both jobs and the workers qualified to fill them are available. It is equal to about 5 or 6%.

Cyclical employment is unemployment that results from inadequate aggregate demand during the recession and depression phases of the business cycle.

Structural unemployment is unemployment that results from an economy's failure to adjust completely and efficiently to basic structural changes such as changes in technology, changes in consumer preferences, and changes in the geographical locations of certain industries. It is equal to about 5 or 6%.

Structural changes prevent certain people from obtaining jobs because of their geographical location, race, age, inadequate education, or lack of training. *People who are structurally unemployed are often referred to as the hard-core unemployed.*

(ii) **Inflation and deflation.** If aggregate spending exceeds the full-employment output, the excess spending will have the effect of increasing the price level. Therefore, excessive aggregate spending is inflationary. Government intervenes to eliminate the excess spending by cutting its own expenditures and by raising taxes so as to curtail private spending. The inverse relationship between unemployment and inflation is embodied in the Phillips curve.

UNEMPLOYMENT AND INFLATION DILEMMA

- Total spending should increase to generate full employment.
- Excessive aggregate spending leads to inflation.
- An increase in the price level would tend to decrease consumption.

Inflation is a rise in the general level of prices; deflation is a decline in the general level of prices. However, inflation has been the prevailing condition in the United States in recent decades.

When prices rise, purchasing power or the ability to buy goods and services declines. If prices double, purchasing power is reduced to one-half of its previous level. Thus, *inflation reduces the purchasing power of money.* Inflation does not mean that the prices of all goods and services rise. Some prices rise, others fall, and some do not change at all, but on the average, prices rise.

The basic cause of inflation is spending in excess of what an economy can produce. If an economy has unemployed resources, an increase in aggregate demand tends to increase output and employment a great deal and to increase prices only slightly. When an economy is fully employed, an increase in aggregate demand forces prices to increase sharply because resources are scarce and output cannot be increased.

(e) **Types of Inflation.** In reality, there are seven types of inflation, which are presented below (see Exhibit 4.7).

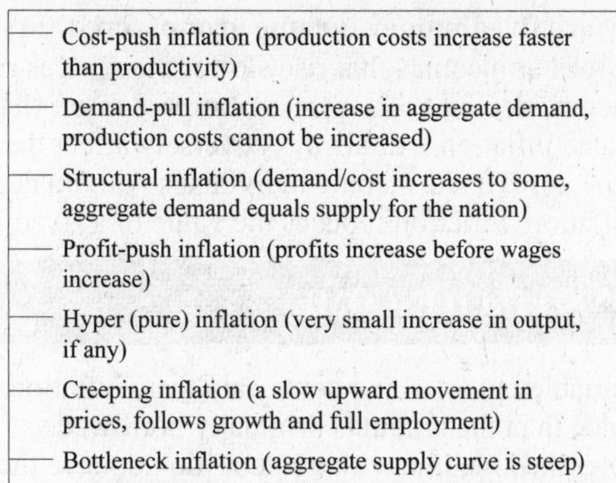

Exhibit 4.7: Seven types of inflation

- **Cost-push inflation** is a rise in prices brought about by production costs increasing faster than productivity. Since labor is usually the largest cost of production, cost-push inflation is often called wage-push inflation. The expected impact is an increase in unemployment.
- **Demand-pull inflation** is a rise in prices that is caused by an increase in aggregate demand when an economy's resources are fully employed and production cannot be increased. The expected impact is a decrease in unemployment.
- **Structural inflation** results when demand increases or costs increase in certain industries even though aggregate demand equals aggregate supply for the nation as a whole.

Types of Inflation

- Cost-push inflation is caused by increase in wages and prices.
- Demand-pull inflation is caused by increase in aggregate demand.
- Structural inflation results when demand increases or cost increases in certain industries.
- Profit-push inflation occurs when corporate profits increase before wages increase.
- Hyperinflation or pure inflation is a rise in prices with a very small increase in output.
- Creeping inflation is a slow upward movement in prices over a period of several years.
- Bottleneck inflation occurs when the aggregate supply curve is steep.

- **Profit-push inflation** occurs when corporate profits increase before wages increase. An increase in corporate profits can result from increases in prices or from improvements in productivity that reduce the labor cost per unit.
- **Hyperinflation or pure inflation** is a rise in prices with a very small, if any, increase in output.
- **Creeping inflation** is a slow upward movement in prices over a period of several years. Creeping inflation is usually defined as a 1, 2, or 3% increase in the general price level each year. Creeping inflation generally accompanies growth and full employment. Many economists prefer creeping inflation to price stability accompanied by unemployment and lack of economic growth.
- **Bottleneck inflation** can be associated with an aggregate supply curve that is steep.

Before the redistribution effects of inflation can be discussed, a distinction must be made between money income and real income. **Money income** is the amount of money or number of dollars a person receives for the work he does; real income is the amount of goods and services the money income will buy or the purchasing power of the money income. **Real income** is thus a function of money income and the prices of goods and services.

(f) **Effects of Inflation.** *If nominal income increases faster than the price level, then real income will rise. Three classes of people generally suffer from inflation, and three classes of people generally benefit from inflation.*

1. **Those who suffer are fixed money income groups, creditors, and savers.** People who have **fixed money incomes** or incomes that rise slower than prices rise suffer from inflation because their real income declines when prices increase faster than their money incomes increase. Unanticipated inflation will always adversely affect the wealth of lenders with fixed rate mortgage loans. Low-fixed-income individuals with no debts would likely suffer most adversely from inflation. Inflation reduces the value of a fixed income.

VARIABLE INCOME VS. FIXED INCOME

- Individuals with variable incomes and debts gain from inflation by paying them with dollars of lesser value than the amounts originally borrowed.
- Individuals with low fixed income with no debts do not have the advantage enjoyed by middle to upper middle class and rich individuals.

Creditors suffer from inflation because the loans they make are paid back with dollars of less purchasing power than the dollars they lent. **Savers** suffer just like creditors, since the money people save declines in purchasing power as prices rise.

2. **Those who benefit are flexible money income groups, debtors, and speculators. Flexible money income groups** or people whose incomes rise faster than prices rise benefit from inflation because they experience an increase in their real incomes. **Debtors** benefit because they pay off their loans with dollars that are "cheaper" (worth less) than the dollars they borrowed. **Speculators**—people who buy goods in anticipation of making profits when prices change—can increase their real wealth if they borrow money to buy goods during inflation.

It is interesting to note that inflation redistributes wealth and income unevenly by penalizing some groups and bestowing benefits on other groups (assuming full employment). Inflation is often called the "cruelest tax" because it penalizes those who are the most vulnerable to it. A higher inflation rate generally results in higher nominal interest rates.

(g) **Nature of Deflation.** Deflation is a decrease in prices. Deflation can be induced through contractionary monetary and fiscal policies. If deflation occurs in the United States, it becomes cheaper for other countries to buy US goods. Deflation can arise automatically due to an excess of imports over exports.

MULTIPLE-CHOICE QUESTIONS (1-200)

Impact of Government Legislation

1. The Sherman Act specifically prohibits which of the following?

a. Monopolizing.
b. Asset acquisitions that reduce competition.
c. Price discrimination.
d. Mergers that reduce competition.

2. The Clayton Act specifically prohibits which of the following?

a. Monopolies.
b. Asset acquisitions that reduce competition.
c. Exclusive dealings.
d. Conspiracies in restraint of trade.

3. The US Federal Trade Commission (FTC) enforces antitrust laws by

a. Sentencing individuals up to three years imprisonment.
b. Awarding triple damages.
c. Issuing cease-and-desist orders.
d. Imposing fines on corporations up to $1 million.

4. Which of the following forbids conspiracies in restraint of trade?

a. Sherman Act.
b. Clayton Act.
c. FTC Act.
d. Robinson-Patman Act.

5. Boycotts that are in violation of the Sherman Act include which of the following?

a. A seller's refusal to deal with any particular buyer.
b. A manufacturer who refuses to sell to a retailer who persists in selling below the manufacturer's suggested retail price.
c. When two or more firms agree not to deal with a third party.
d. Cooperative agreements designed to increase economic efficiency and render markets more competitive.

6. The definition of price-fixing includes which of the following?

a. Agreements that may, among other things, lower prices.
b. Agreements that stabilize prices.
c. Agreements that raise prices.
d. All of the above.

7. Which of the following describes an arrangement by which the seller or lessor of a product agrees with conditions upon which the buyer's or lessee's promise **not** to work with a competitor's goods?

a. Tying arrangements.
b. Exclusive dealing arrangements.
c. Monopoly arrangements.
d. Monopsony arrangements.

8. A merger involving firms producing unrelated goods and services is termed a

a. Tying arrangement.
b. Vertical merger.
c. Conglomerate merger.
d. Horizontal merger.

9. The process of entering a new industry to exploit perceived opportunities is called a

a. Beachhead merger.
b. Vertical merger.
c. Conglomerate merger.
d. Horizontal merger.

10. The acquisition of a bottle manufacturer by a soft-drink producer is an example of a

a. Horizontal merger.
b. Vertical merger.
c. Congeneric merger.
d. Conglomerate merger.

11. A company sold one of its divisions to its existing shareholders, and the shareholders received new stock representing separate ownership rights in the division. This process is referred to as a

a. Liquidation.
b. Spin-off.
c. Leveraged buyout.
d. Managerial buyout.

12. In a two-tier merger offer, shareholders receive a higher amount per share if they

a. Agree to purchase newly issued bonds in the combined firm.
b. Agree to sell back to the firm any bonds they currently own.
c. Tender their stock later.
d. Tender their stock earlier.

13. Which of the following is correct regarding the Clayton Act?

a. It eased the burden of proving some antitrust violations.
b. It added criminal sanctions to the Sherman Act.
c. It repealed the Robinson-Patman Act.
d. It required that actual injury be proven.

14. Under Section 1 of the Sherman Act, which of the following is illegal per se?

a. Vertical market restrictions.
b. Horizontal market allocations.
c. Vertical price-fixing.
d. Both (b) and (c).

15. To determine "market share," one would require knowledge of which of the following?

a. What other products compete with the product.
b. Where the product is sold.
c. How much of the product is sold.
d. All of the above.

16. In order for there to be a violation of Section 2 of the Sherman Act, in addition to monopoly power, the courts must find which of the following?

a. Unfair conduct.
b. Concerted action.
c. Competitive behavior.
d. Economic advantage.

17. If a seller conditions a product's sale upon the buyer's purchasing a second product from the seller, this is known as which of the following?

a. A tying arrangement.
b. A vertical restraint.
c. A horizontal restraint.
d. A disparagement.

18. In an attempt to limit the power of large purchasers, the US Congress amended Section 2 of the Clayton Act by adopting the

a. Sherman Act.
b. Federal Trade Commission.
c. Robinson-Patman Act.
d. Celler-Kefauver Act.

19. The rule of reason test, under the Sherman Antitrust Act

a. Considers the makeup of a relevant industry.
b. Does not consider the defendant's position in that industry.
c. Considers the defendant's need for the financial gain from the restraint of trade.
d. Does not consider competitor's ability to respond to the challenged practice of restraint of trade.

20. Monopoly power would most likely be found where a market share is greater than which of the following of the overall market for that product or service?

a. 25%
b. 30%
c. 50%
d. 75%

21. Failure to comply with Sections 1 or 2 of the Sherman Act

a. Is a felony and can result in imprisonment.
b. May subject an individual to a fine of up to $350,000 per violation under the 1990 amendments.
c. May subject a corporation to a fine of $10,000,000 per violation.
d. All of the above.

22. Which of the following provisions deal with the Clayton Act?

a. Supply price discrimination.
b. Tying arrangements and mergers.
c. Interlocking ties.
d. Price mergers.

23. Which of the following prohibits price discrimination in interstate commerce?

a. The Sherman Act.
b. The Federal Trade Commission.
c. The Robinson-Patman Act.
d. The Celler-Kefauver Act.

24. All of the following organizations are exempt from the provisions of the Clayton Act **except:**

a. Labor.
b. Manufacturing.
c. Agricultural.
d. Horticultural.

25. Conglomerate mergers have been challenged only where

a. One of the merging firms would be highly likely to enter the market of the other firm.
b. The merged company would be disproportionately large.
c. Both (a) and (b).
d. The merged company is a supplier.

26. Price-fixing was made illegal under which of the following US legislation?

a. Clayton Act.
b. Sherman Antitrust Act.
c. Robinson-Patman Act.
d. Federal Trade Commission Act.

27. Price discrimination was made illegal under which of the following US legislation?

a. Clayton Act.
b. Sherman Antitrust Act.
c. Robinson-Patman Act.
d. Federal Trade Commission Act.

28. Price discrimination is illegal in which of the following situations?

a. When the seller realizes cost differences between buyers.
b. When the seller is trying to match a competitor's lower price.
c. When different customers purchase different volumes.
d. When the seller favors certain customers over others.

29. When a manufacturer and retailers agree upon some minimum price to be charged to consumers, it is called

a. Margin setting.
b. Price fixing.
c. Resale price maintenance.
d. Base-level pricing.

30. The practice of driving rivals out of business by pricing at such a low level that the rival cannot make money is called

a. High/low pricing.
b. Predatory pricing.
c. Price penetration.
d. Price skimming.

31. With regard to government regulation

a. Regulation is increasing throughout the world.
b. Many organizations do not have to face government regulation.
c. Utility companies do not face much regulation.
d. Deregulation and privatization are increasing worldwide.

32. Which of the following pricing behaviors is most likely to be perceived as unfair by consumers?

a. Frequent price promotions.
b. Raising price when demand decreases.
c. Comparative price advertising.
d. Raising price when demand increases.

33. Which of the following does **not** represent a legally permissible reason for charging different prices to competitive customers?

a. We are hoping to develop a stronger relationship with one customer.
b. There is no harm to competition.
c. We are selling to end consumers.
d. We are matching competitors' prices for some customers.

34. Regulatory costs are borne by workers when

a. Demand is perfectly inelastic.
b. Demand is perfectly elastic.
c. Supply is perfectly inelastic.
d. Supply is perfectly efficient.

35. The view of regulation as a government-imposed means of private-market control is called
a. Capture theory.
b. Public choice theory.
c. Public interest theory.
d. Public efficient theory.

36. For a given level of tax collections, prices, and interest rates, a decrease in government purchases will result in a (n)
a. Increase in aggregate demand.
b. Increase in aggregate supply.
c. Decrease in aggregate demand.
d. Decrease in aggregate supply.

37. Implementation of a government's monetary policy in most major industrial countries is managed by
a. The central bank.
b. The federal government.
c. Commercial banks.
d. Bond market traders.

38. The money supply will grow following
a. Open-market purchases by the Federal Reserve.
b. An increase in the required reserve ratio.
c. An increase in excess reserves.
d. An increase in the discount rate.

39. Which of the following is a tool of monetary policy that a nation's central bank could use to stabilize the economy during an inflationary period?
a. Sale of government securities.
b. Lower bank reserve requirements.
c. Lower bank discount rates.
d. Encourage Congress to raise tax rates.

40. Which of the following instruments of monetary policy is the **most** important means by which the money supply is controlled?
a. Changing the reserve ratio.
b. Open market operations.
c. Manipulation of government spending.
d. Changing the discount rate.

41. The money supply in a nation's economy will decrease following
a. Open-market purchases by the nation's central bank.
b. A decrease in the discount rate.
c. An increase in the reserve ratio.
d. A decrease in the margin requirement.

42. An increase in excess reserves by the Board of Governors of the Federal Reserve Banks has the effect of
a. Reducing the money supply.
b. Reducing aggregate demand.
c. Increasing the availability of credit.
d. Increasing interest rates.

43. Government spending is known to affect the economy. The "crowding out effect" refers to the (list A) impact of an expansionary fiscal policy on (list B).

	List A	List B
a.	Positive	The money multiplier
b.	Positive	Investment
c.	Negative	The money multiplier
d.	Negative	Investment

44. An expansionary (list A) policy will have (list B) effect on net exports.

	List A	List B
a.	Fiscal	A negative
b.	Fiscal	No
c.	Monetary	A negative
d.	Monetary	No

45. Given a balanced budget multiplier equal to one, a $1 billion increase in both taxes and government spending will
a. Reduce the savings rate.
b. Reduce aggregate supply.
c. Reduce aggregate demand.
d. Increase the budget deficit.

46. If a government were to use only fiscal policy to stimulate the economy from a recession it would
a. Raise consumer taxes and increase government spending.
b. Lower business taxes and government spending.
c. Increase the money supply and increase government spending.
d. Lower consumer taxes and increase government spending.

Trade Legislation

47. Which of the following measures creates the most restrictive barrier to exporting to a country?
a. Tariffs.
b. Quotas.
c. Embargoes.
d. Exchange controls.

48. In the law of comparative advantage, the country, which should produce a specific product is determined by
a. Opportunity costs.
b. Profit margins.
c. Economic order quantities.
d. Tariffs.

49. Assume a simple economy consisting of only two nations—Nation A and Nation B. The countries produce and consume only two products: rice and cars. The comparative costs of production in each country are

	Nation A	Nation B
Rice (per ton)	10,000	20,000
Cars	15,000	16,000

Given this cost structure and a fixed supply of inputs, what can be said with respect to comparative advantage and international trade?
a. Nation B has a comparative advantage with respect to the production of cars and will export cars to Nation A.
b. Nation B has a comparative advantage with respect to rice and will export rice to Nation A.
c. Nation A has a comparative advantage with respect to cars and will export cars to Nation B.
d. There will be no overall advantage to international trade.

50. Suppose two countries (Country A and Country B) currently produce the same two goods (good X and good Y) and do not engage in international trade. Their unit production costs are as outlined in the table below.

	Country A	*Country B*
Unit cost of producing X	$30	$10
Unit cost of producing Y	$20	$ 6

According to the theory of comparative advantage, which of the following patterns of production and trade could increase, or at least not reduce, the wealth of both countries?

a. Country A should produce and export good X.
b. Country A should produce and export good Y.
c. Country A should refuse to trade with Country B.
d. Country B should refuse to trade with Country A.

51. Which of the following provides the **best** justification for reducing trade barriers between nations?

a. The military self-sufficiency argument.
b. Diversification for stability.
c. The infant industry argument.
d. Increased total world output.

52. Which of the following provides the **best** argument for free trade between nations?

a. The infant industry argument.
b. Increased total world output.
c. National defense.
d. Increased diversification within the economies of individual nations.

53. In international economics, the theory of comparative advantage proposes that total worldwide output will be greatest when

a. Each nation's imports approximately equal its exports.
b. Each good is produced by that nation which has the lowest opportunity cost for that good.
c. Goods that contribute to a nation's balance of payments deficit are no longer imported.
d. International trade is unrestricted and tariffs are not imposed.

54. A nation experiencing chronic trade deficits might consider trade quotas. Some accompanied effects from this course of action would be that

a. Unemployment and productivity rates will rise.
b. Unemployment will rise and productivity rates will decline.
c. Unemployment will fall and productivity rates will rise.
d. Unemployment and productivity rates will decline.

55. Which of the following is a direct effect of imposing a protective tariff on an imported product?

a. Lower domestic prices on the product.
b. Lower domestic consumption of the product.
c. Reduced domestic production of the product.
d. Higher sales revenues for foreign producers of the product.

56. A direct effect of imposing a protective tariff on an item for which there are both foreign and domestic producers is that domestic producers will sell (list A) of the item while domestic consumers consume (list B) of the item.

	List A	*List B*
a.	More	More
b.	More	Less
c.	Less	More
d.	Less	Less

57. Which of the following is a direct effect of imposing a protective tariff on an imported product?

a. Lower domestic prices on the imported item.
b. Lower domestic consumption of the item.
c. Reduced domestic production of the item.
d. Higher sales revenues for foreign producers of the item.

58. Which of the following is a tariff?

a. Licensing requirements.
b. Consumption taxes on imported goods.
c. Unreasonable standards pertaining to product quality and safety.
d. All of the above.

59. A domestic company looking to do business abroad must understand the international trade system. In attempting to sell to another country, a firm will face various trade restrictions. The most common is a tariff, which is defined as a

a. Tax levied by a foreign government against certain imported products.
b. Limit on the amount of goods that the importing country will accept in certain product categories.
c. A restriction in which imports in prescribed categories are totally banned.
d. Arrangements between nations that prevent corporate and individuals from being double taxed.

60. If a country uses trade quotas to overcome chronic trade deficits, the most likely outcome is

a. Unemployment and productivity rates will rise.
b. Unemployment rates will rise and productivity rates will decline.
c. Unemployment rates will decline and productivity rates will rise.
d. Unemployment and productivity rates will decline.

61. Revenue tariffs are designed to

a. Develop new export opportunities.
b. Provide the government with tax revenues.
c. Restrict the amount of a commodity that can be imported in a given period.
d. Encourage foreign companies to limit the amount of their exports to a particular country.

62. Which of the following creates the most restrictive barrier to exporting to a country?

a. Tariffs.
b. Quotas.
c. Embargoes.
d. Exchange controls.

Taxation Schemes

63. Which of the following correctly describes the introduction of a government tax credit on investments?

a. Corporate investments will have higher net present values, all else being equal, than without the tax credit.
b. Tax credits on investments are designed to restrain inflation.
c. Tax credits on investments increase investment costs and, all else being equal, reduce the level of corporate investment.
d. Tax credits on investments are taxes that are typically levied on individual projects rather than on groups of projects.

64. General sales taxes tend to be regressive with respect to income because

a. A larger portion of a poor person's income is subject to the tax.
b. A smaller portion of a poor person's income is subject to the tax.
c. The tax rate is higher for the poor.
d. The tax claims an increasing amount of income as income rises.

65. A value-added tax is collected on the basis of

a. The difference between the value of a company's sales and the value of its purchases from other domestic companies.
b. The difference between the selling price of real property and the price the company originally paid for the property.
c. The value of a company's sales to related companies.
d. The profit earned on a company's sales.

66. Which of the following refers to taxes that do not necessarily take a larger absolute share of an increase in income?

a. Progressive.
b. Proportional.
c. Regressive.
d. Regenerative.

67. Temporary and permanent differences between taxable income and pretax financial income differ in that

a. Temporary differences do not give rise to future taxable or deductible amounts.
b. Only permanent differences have deferred tax consequences.
c. Only temporary differences have deferred tax consequences.
d. Temporary differences include items that enter into pretax financial income but never into taxable income.

68. A company purchases $150,000 of inputs from other firms and incurs $500,000 of labor costs in manufacturing its products. It also incurs $100,000 of interest expense. The company sells all of its output for $2,500,000. Rather than paying income tax, the company must pay a 25% value-added tax. How much tax will be due for this year's activities?

a. $437,500
b. $462,500
c. $587,500
d. $625,000

69. In order to index a progressive tax system to inflation, the government must

a. Adjust only tax deductions and exemptions.
b. Adjust only tax brackets.
c. Adjust deductions, exemptions, and tax brackets.
d. Ensure that nominal tax receipts grow more slowly than inflation.

70. In most countries (list A) taxes tend to be (list B) with respect to income.

	List A	*List B*
a.	General sales	Proportional
b.	Property	Regressive
c.	Personal income	Proportional
d.	Personal income	Regressive

71. An increase in excise taxes will generate (list A) tax revenue if it is levied on products for which demand is (list B) elastic.

	List A	*List B*
a.	More	More
b.	More	Less
c.	Negative	Less
d.	Less	Less

72. The part of corporate income which is paid out as dividends may be taxed twice, first under the (list A) tax and then again under the (list B) tax.

	List A	*List B*
a.	Sales income	Corporate income
b.	Property	Personal income
c.	Corporate income	Value added
d.	Corporate income	Personal income

73. An individual had taxable income of $23,000 per year and paid $8,000 in income tax. The individual's taxable income then increased to $30,000 per year resulting in a $10,000 income tax liability. The personal tax system being applied to this individual is

a. Progressive.
b. Regressive.
c. Marginal.
d. Proportional.

74. Which one of the following statements describes the asset-liability method of accounting for deferred income taxes?

a. The amount of deferred income tax is based on tax rates in effect when temporary differences originate.
b. The amount of deferred income tax is based on the tax rates expected to be in effect during the periods in which the temporary differences reverse.
c. The tax effects of temporary differences are not reported separately but are reported as adjustments to the amounts of specific assets and liabilities and the related revenues and expenses.
d. The appropriate tax rate to be reported on the income statement is the tax actually levied in that year, meaning no deferred taxes would be reported.

75. In a (list A) personal tax system, an individual's marginal tax rate is normally (list B) their average tax rate.

	List A	*List B*
a.	Progressive	Greater than
b.	Progressive	Equal to
c.	Regressive	Equal to
d.	Regressive	Greater than

76. If the government were to increase corporate tax rates, then after-tax cost-volume-profit relationships for individual firms would change as follows:

a. Breakeven points would increase.
b. Breakeven points would decrease.
c. There would be no change in the breakeven points.
d. There would be no change whatsoever in cost-volume-profit relationships.

77. A nation has a progressive tax structure where income tax brackets are not indexed to inflation. An individual taxpayer experiences an income increase just equal to the general inflation rate and moves into a higher tax bracket. The individual taxpayer will then experience (list A) nominal taxes payable and (list B) real taxes payable.

	List A	List B
a.	Increasing	Increasing
b.	Increasing	Decreasing
c.	Decreasing	Increasing
d.	Decreasing	Decreasing

78. A taxpayer who earns $50,000 during the year and pays a 15% tax rate on the first $30,000 of income and a 30% tax rate on all earnings over $30,000, has a

a. Marginal tax rate of 15%.
b. Marginal tax rate of 21%.
c. Average tax rate of 21%.
d. Average tax rate of 22.5%.

79. Which of the following is the best example of supply-side economics?

a. Increased government spending.
b. An easy money policy.
c. Increased excise taxes.
d. Reduced marginal tax rates on earned income.

Items 80 and 81 are based on the following:

A company purchases an asset with a 10-year useful life. It will use an accelerated depreciation method for tax purposes. For reporting purposes it will use straight-line depreciation since this is believed to reflect better the usage of the asset over its economic life.

80. During the 10-year life of the asset, the company will report as deferred tax an amount that

a. Increases steadily for the 10 years.
b. Is constant.
c. Increases and then decreases.
d. Decreases and then increases.

81. When calculating cash flows accruing to the firm, using financial statements prepared for tax purposes would result in

a. No effect on cash flow calculations.
b. An overstatement of cash flows throughout the economic life of the asset.
c. An understatement of cash flows throughout the economic life of the asset.
d. An overstatement of cash flows in the early years and then an understatement of cash flows in the later years of the economic life of the asset.

Contracts

82. In addition to the four basic requirements of a contract, which of the following must also occur in order to have a valid contract?

a. The agreement must always be in writing.
b. There must be evidence of undue influence.
c. There must be an absence of invalidating contract.
d. A legal remedy need not be available for there to be a breach.

83. The requirement that each party to a contract must intentionally exchange something of value as an inducement to the other party to make a return exchange is known as

a. Mutual assent.
b. Consideration.
c. Legality of object.
d. Contractual capacity.

84. Which of the following is **not** always necessary in order for a valid contract to be formed?

a. Mutual assent.
b. Legality of purpose.
c. A writing.
d. Competent parties.

85. According to common law, informing someone of an intention to do an act or an intention to refrain from acting in a specified manner is considered to be a(n)

a. Implied in fact contract.
b. Express contract.
c. Promise.
d. Quasi contract.

86. Which of the following is **not** generally required in order to have a valid contract?

a. Mutual assent.
b. A lawful purpose.
c. Fairness of the bargain.
d. Parties who have contractual capacity.

87. An obligation imposed by law where there has been no agreement or expression of assent by word or act on the part of either party involved is

a. Implied in fact contract.
b. Express contract.
c. Void contract.
d. Quasi contract.

88. The Uniform Commercial Code (UCC) applies to which of the following?

a. Employment contracts.
b. Service contracts.
c. Insurance contracts.
d. Personal property contracts.

89. The doctrine of promissory estoppel is which of the following?

a. A doctrine enforcing noncontractual promises.
b. Includes as a requirement within the doctrine that there has been justifiable reliance on the promise.
c. A doctrine relying on justice and not contractual rights.
d. All of the above.

90. In order for a full warranty to be given for a consumer product, the manufacturer must provide

a. That the product will be repaired for free.
b. That the warranty lasts for at least 10 days.
c. That the consumer can opt for refund rather than repair.
d. That consequential damage cannot be excluded.

91. What are the remedies available for the Federal Trade Commission?

a. Affirmative exemption.
b. Corrective advertising and multiple products order.
c. Impounding inventory.
d. Fines and monetary penalties.

92. What reported warranty problems caused US Congress to enact the Magnuson-Moss Warranty Act?

a. Most warranties were not understandable.
b. Most warrantors disclaimed implied warranties.
c. Most warranties were unfair.
d. All of the above.

93. Warranties that are **not** included in a sales contract but exist by "operation of the law," are called

a. Express warranties.
b. Exclusive warranties.
c. Quasi warranties.
d. Implied warranties.

94. The warranty of title for the sale of goods found in Article 2 of the Uniform Commercial Code (UCC)

a. May be excluded with the phrase "as is."
b. Will vest title in a bona fide purchaser for value when the seller is a merchant.
c. May not be excluded or modified by the seller.
d. Will apply regardless of whether it is provided for in the contract unless the parties have specifically excluded it.

95. An express warranty within the meaning of the Uniform Commercial Code (UCC) is best described by which of the following?

a. A sample.
b. A description.
c. A promise.
d. All of the above.

96. Which of the following is true with regard to implied warranties under the Uniform Commercial Code (UCC)?

a. They may arise from course of dealing or usage of trade.
b. They are a result of specific language in the sales contract.
c. They continue the common law rule of caveat emptor.
d. They are intended to protect the seller rather than the buyer.

97. Which of the following is **not** an express warranty?

a. Restating facts or market figures about a product.
b. The opinion of an expert in a certain field regarding a product in that field.
c. A statement of the product specifications.
d. The seller's opinion of the value of goods.

98. An obligation of the merchant-seller that the goods are reasonably fit for general purposes for which they are manufactured and sold and that the goods are of fair average quality is known as

a. Warranty of merchantability.
b. Strict liability.
c. Express warranty.
d. Warranty of fitness for a particular purpose.

99. Whether an implied warranty arises out of the circumstances under which the parties enter into a contract may depend on the following factor(s):

a. The type of contract entered into.
b. The seller's merchant or nonmerchant status.
c. Applicability of other statutes.
d. All of the above.

100. If the buyer inspects the goods before entering into the contract, then implied warranties

a. Still apply.
b. Will in no circumstances be applicable.
c. Do not apply to defects that are apparent upon reasonable inspection.
d. None of the above.

101. Manufacturers can avoid strict liability in tort under which of the following conditions?

a. When the seller uses due care and diligence in preparing the goods.
b. When the seller produces this type of goods on a regular basis.
c. When the seller gives notice of the defect to the buyer.
d. When the product was not in the same condition when the consumer was injured as it was when the seller or manufacturer sold it.

102. A warranty that may arise out of the mere existence of a sale, any affirmation of fact, or promise made by the seller to the buyer, or out of the circumstances under which the sale is made is the description of

a. Warranty of title.
b. Express warranty.
c. Implied warranty.
d. All of the above.

Legal Evidence

103. Legal evidence relies heavily on which of the following?

a. Oral evidence.
b. Documentary evidence.
c. Circumstantial evidence.
d. Corroborative evidence.

104. Which of the following cannot be used to dispute a written instrument?

a. Oral evidence.
b. Documentary evidence.
c. Circumstantial evidence.
d. Corroborative evidence.

105. Which of the following is referred to as primary evidence?

a. Direct evidence.
b. Best evidence.
c. Circumstantial evidence.
d. Hearsay evidence.

106. Which of the following is secondhand evidence?

a. Testimonial evidence.
b. Secondary evidence.
c. Opinion evidence.
d. Hearsay evidence.

107. Which of the following provides additional evidence?

a. Conclusive evidence.
b. Direct evidence.
c. Corroborative evidence.
d. Secondary evidence.

108. Photographs represent what type of evidence?

a. Circumstantial evidence.
b. Direct evidence.
c. Corroborative evidence.
d. Hearsay evidence.

109. Cross-examination of a witness is used in what type of evidence?

a. Opinion evidence.
b. Hearsay evidence.
c. Best evidence.
d. Circumstantial evidence.

110. Which of the following evidence cannot be contradicted?

a. Corroborative evidence.
b. Conclusive evidence.
c. Hearsay evidence.
d. Circumstantial evidence.

111. Which of the following is an example of legal evidence?

a. Subjective evidence.
b. Objective evidence.
c. Direct evidence.
d. Indirect evidence.

112. Which of the following evidence needs no corroboration?

a. Opinion evidence.
b. Conclusive evidence.
c. Hearsay evidence.
d. Circumstantial evidence.

113. Best evidence is a(n)

a. Documentary evidence.
b. Oral evidence.
c. Copy of a writing.
d. Corroborative evidence.

114. During interviews with the inventory management personnel, the auditor learned that salespersons often order inventory for stock without receiving the approval of the vice president of sales. Also, detail testing showed that there are no written approvals on purchase orders for replacement parts. The detail testing is a good example of a(n)

a. Indirect evidence.
b. Circumstantial evidence.
c. Corroborative evidence.
d. Subjective evidence.

Key Economic Indicators

115. Which of the following is **not** a major category of the consumer price index (CPI)?

a. Food and beverages.
b. Housing.
c. Income taxes.
d. Sales taxes.

116. Which of the following is a major category of the consumer price index (CPI)?

a. Stocks and bonds.
b. Medical care.
c. Real estate.
d. Life insurance.

117. Which of the following is **not** a major category of the consumer price index (CPI)?

a. Apparel.
b. Transportation.
c. Social security taxes.
d. Recreation.

118. The consumer price index includes which of the following populations?

a. Urban residents.
b. Farm residents.
c. Military personnel.
d. Rural residents.

119. Which of the following is the best definition of the consumer price index (CPI)?

a. It is a cost-of-living index.
b. It is defined in absolute dollars.
c. It is a measure of the average change in prices.
d. It compares intercity cost of living.

120. The producer price index (PPI) does **not** include which of the following?

a. Manufacturer rebates.
b. Manufacturer promotions.
c. Taxes.
d. Actual transaction prices.

121. Which of the following is a lagging economic indictor?

a. Consumer price index.
b. Producer price index.
c. Purchasing manager's index.
d. Gross domestic product.

122. Net national product (NNP) is equal to gross national product (GNP)

a. Minus depreciation.
b. Minus capital expenditures.
c. Plus US capital.
d. Plus US labor.

123. Gross domestic product (GDP) deflators include which of the following?

I. Exports.
II. Imports.
III. Real GDP.
IV. Nominal GDP.

a. I and III.
b. II and IV.
c. III and IV.
d. I, II, III, and IV.

124. Which of the following is a leading economic indicator?

a. Average prime rate charged by banks.
b. Commercial and industrial loans outstanding.
c. New building permits issued.
d. Ratio of constant dollar inventories to sales for manufacture and trade.

125. In economics, a diffusion index that registers 40% indicates that

a. Leading indicators on average have fallen by 60%.
b. 40% of the leading indicators have fallen.
c. 60% of the leading indicators have fallen.
d. All leading indicators have risen by 40%.

126. Economic forecasting methods do which of the following?

a. They require explicit assumptions about the relations among economic variables.
b. They can estimate the direction but not the magnitude of change for forecasted variables.
c. They can estimate the magnitude but not the direction of change for forecasted variables.
d. They always remain the same from period to period with some exceptions.

127. Which of the following is a lagging economic indicator?

a. Average prime rate charged by banks.
b. New orders for nonmilitary capital goods.
c. New money supply.
d. New orders for consumer goods.

128. Which of the following is an example of a leading economic indicator of business cycle?
a. The average duration of unemployment.
b. The change in prices for consumer services.
c. Personal income minus transfer payments.
d. An index of sock prices for 500 stocks.

129. The composite economic index does **not** include which of the following?
a. Leading indicators.
b. Independent indicators.
c. Lagging indicators.
d. Coincident indicators.

130. Which of the following is a coincident economic indicator?
a. Manufacturing and trade sales.
b. Average prime rates.
c. Commercial and industrial loans.
d. Index of consumer expectations.

131. All of the following are economic indicators that might indicate that full employment has been reached **except:**
a. Low number of new unemployment claims.
b. No bottlenecks arise in certain sectors of the economy.
c. High number of hours in the average workweek.
d. High level of manufacturing capacity utilization.

132. The difference between a normal profit and an economic profit is that an economic profit includes an amount
a. To cover all appropriate labor costs.
b. To cover the risk taken by an entrepreneur.
c. To cover most, though not all, labor costs.
d. To cover labor, capital, and land costs.

133. Some economic indicators lead the economy into a recovery or recession, and some lag it. An example of a lag variable would be
a. Chronic unemployment.
b. Orders for consumer and producer goods.
c. Housing starts.
d. Consumer expectations.

134. The two main variables that contribute to increases in a nation's real gross domestic product (GDP) are labor productivity and
a. Definition of the labor force.
b. Inflation rate.
c. Quality of output.
d. Total worker hours.

135. Total union membership has declined in recent years in many industrialized countries. Which of the following is least likely to explain that decline?
a. A shift in consumer demand and employment patterns.
b. An increase in the proportion of part-time workers.
c. The shift from craft unionism to industrial unionism.
d. The substitution of machines for workers.

136. When gross investment (list A) depreciation, the capital stock of the economy is (list B).

	List A	List B
a.	Exceeds	Shrinking
b.	Equals	Shrinking
c.	Equals	Growing
d.	Is less than	Shrinking

137. Net national product (NNP) is composed of the total market value of
a. All final goods and services produced in the economy in one year.
b. All goods and services produced in the economy in one year.
c. All final goods and services produced in the economy in one year minus the capital consumption allowance.
d. All goods and services produced in the economy in one year minus the capital consumption allowance.

138. The formula for calculating a price index for the year 2003, using the year 2000 as a reference period, is

a. $\frac{\text{Price of 2003 market basket in 2003}}{\text{Price of 2003 market basket in 2000}} \times 100$

b. $\frac{\text{Price of 2000 market basket in 2003}}{\text{Price of 2000 market basket in 2000}} \times 100$

c. $\frac{\text{Price of 2003 market basket in 2003}}{\text{Price of 2000 market basket in 2000}} \times 100$

d. $\frac{\text{Price of 2000 market basket in 2000}}{\text{Price of 2000 market basket in 2003}} \times 100$

139. In the output or "expenditures" approach to measuring a country's gross national product, which of the following calculations is used?
a. Consumption + Investment + Government purchases + Expenditures by foreigners.
b. Consumption + Investment + Government purchases – Expenditures by foreigners.
c. Consumption + Investment – Government purchases – Expenditures by foreigners.
d. Consumption – Investment – Government purchases – Expenditures by foreigners.

140. Craft unions achieve higher wages for their members by
a. Increasing the demand for labor.
b. Decreasing the demand for labor.
c. Increasing the supply of labor.
d. Decreasing the supply of labor.

141. If indirect business taxes were subtracted from net national product (NNP) the result would be
a. Disposable personal income.
b. Personal income.
c. National income.
d. Gross national product.

142. Critics of the consumer price index (CPI) argue that it overstates increases in the cost of living. This is due to
a. The inclusion of qualitative improvements in available goods and services.
b. The constant composition of the market basket of items whose prices are measured.
c. The use of the same techniques as those used to measure the gross national product (GNP) deflator.
d. The inclusion of changes in consumer preferences from year to year.

143. The Gross National Product (GNP) will fall following an increase in

a. Consumption expenditures.
b. Imports.
c. Exports.
d. Inflation.

144. A nation's unemployment rate increased from 4% to 6%. The economic cost of this increase in unemployment can be described as the amount by which

a. Actual gross national product falls short of potential gross national product.
b. Aggregate expenditures fall short of the full-employment level of net national product.
c. Aggregate spending exceeds the full-employment level of net national product.
d. Merchandise imports exceed exports.

145. If an oil embargo increased prices it would be termed ________ inflation, however if excessive consumer spending increased prices it would be termed ________ inflation.

a. Cost-push, a wage-price.
b. Supply short, a wage-price.
c. Cost-push, demand-pull.
d. Shock created, a wage-price.

146. Which of the following would tend to benefit from the effect of unanticipated inflation?

a. Borrowers.
b. Lenders.
c. Savers.
d. Fixed-income recipients.

147. Macroeconomic stability theory includes the concepts of full employment and price stability. Which of the following are generally considered unavoidable factors preventing the achievement of 100% employment?

a. Frictional, structural, and cyclical unemployment.
b. Effects of demand-pull and cost-push inflation.
c. Decisions of employable persons to voluntarily remain unemployed or to cease seeking employment.
d. International specialization and resource allocation.

148. The natural rate of unemployment, or total unavoidable unemployment, is equal to

a. Cyclical unemployment.
b. Frictional unemployment.
c. Structural unemployment.
d. Frictional plus structural unemployment.

149. A developed country that has an increasing rate of secondary school dropouts and declining standardized test scores might be expected to experience an increase in

a. Cyclical unemployment.
b. Structural unemployment.
c. Frictional unemployment.
d. Productivity rates.

Basic Economics

150. Incremental profit is which of the following?

a. The changes in profit that result from a unitary change in output.
b. Total revenue minus total cost.
c. The change in profit caused by a given managerial decision.
d. The change in profits earned by the firm over a brief period of time.

151. The incremental profit earned from the production and sale of a new product will be higher if

a. The costs of materials needed to produce the new product increase.
b. Excess capacity can be used to produce the new product.
c. Existing facilities used to produce the new product must be modified.
d. The revenues earned from existing products decrease.

152. Which of the following short-run strategies should a manager select to obtain the highest degree of sales penetration?

a. Maximize revenues.
b. Minimize average costs.
c. Minimize total costs.
d. Maximize profits.

153. If total revenue increases at a constant rate as output increases, marginal revenue

a. Is greater than average revenue.
b. Is less than average revenue.
c. Is greater than average revenue at low levels of output and less than average revenue at high levels of output.
d. Equals average revenue.

154. The comprehensive impact resulting from a decision is the

a. Gain or loss associated with a given managerial decision.
b. Change in total cost.
c. Change in total profit.
d. Incremental change.

155. Total revenue is maximized at the point where

a. Marginal revenue equals zero.
b. Marginal cost equals zero.
c. Marginal revenue equals marginal cost.
d. Marginal profit equals zero.

156. Marginal profit equals

a. The change in total profit following a one-unit change in output.
b. The change in total profit following a managerial decision.
c. Average revenue minus average cost.
d. Total revenue minus total cost.

157. Marginal cost is the

a. Change in output following a one-dollar change in cost.
b. Change in cost following a one-unit change in output.
c. Change in average cost following a one-unit change in output.
d. Change in cost following a managerial decision.

158. Total revenue increases at a constant rate as output increases when average revenue

a. Increases as output increases.
b. Increases and then decreases as output increases.
c. Exceeds price.
d. Is constant.

159. Marginal profit equals average profit when

a. Marginal profit is maximized.

b. Average profit is maximized.
c. Marginal profit equals marginal cost.
d. The profit maximizing output is produced.

160. If average profit increases with output, marginal profit must be
a. Decreasing.
b. Greater than average profit.
c. Less than average profit.
d. Increasing.

161. At the profit-maximizing level of output
a. Marginal revenue equals marginal cost.
b. Marginal cost equals zero.
c. Average profit equals zero.
d. Marginal profit equals average profit.

162. When marginal profit equals zero
a. The firm can increase profits by increasing output.
b. The firm can increase profits by decreasing output.
c. Marginal revenue equals average revenue.
d. Profit is maximized.

163. If marginal profit is positive, as output increases
a. Total profit must decrease.
b. Total profit must increase.
c. Average and total profit must increase.
d. Average profit must increase.

164. If profit is to rise as output expands, then marginal profit must be
a. Falling.
b. Constant.
c. Positive.
d. Rising.

165. A firm will earn normal profits when price
a. Equals average total cost.
b. Equals average variable cost.
c. Equals marginal cost.
d. Exceeds minimum average total cost.

166. Which of the following applies to a firm in a perfectly competitive market equilibrium?
a. MR < AR.
b. P > AC.
c. P > MR.
d. P = MC.

167. Which of the following applies to a firm in a perfectly competitive market equilibrium?
a. MC < AC.
b. MR > AR.
c. P < AC.
d. MR = MC.

168. Which of the following applies to a monopoly firm in equilibrium?
a. MC < AC.
b. MR > AR.
c. P < AC.
d. MR = MC.

169. In long-run equilibrium, monopoly prices are set at a level where
a. Price exceeds marginal revenue.
b. Industry demand equals industry supply.
c. Industry demand is less than industry supply.
d. Price exceeds average revenue.

170. A monopsony is a market with
a. Many sellers.
b. One buyer.
c. Many buyers.
d. One seller.

171. In a perfectly competitive market
a. Sellers and buyers have perfect information.
b. Entry and exit are difficult.
c. Sellers produce similar, but not identical products.
d. Each seller can affect the market price by changing output.

172. Any limit on asset redeployment from one line of business or industry to another is called a
a. Barrier to mobility.
b. Barrier to entry.
c. Barrier to exit.
d. Capacity constraint.

173. In both monopolistic competition and oligopoly market structures
a. There is an easy entry and exit.
b. Consumers perceive differences among the products of various competitors.
c. Economic profits may be earned in the long run.
d. There are many sellers.

174. When prices in monopolistically competitive markets exceed those in a perfectly competitive equilibrium, this difference is the cost of
a. Information.
b. Market power.
c. Inefficiency.
d. Product differentiation.

175. Monopolistic competition is characterized by
a. Homogeneous products.
b. Barriers to entry and exit.
c. Perfect dissemination of information.
d. Few buyers and sellers.

176. In a monopolistically competitive industry, firms
a. Offer products that are not perfect substitutes.
b. Make decisions in light of expected reactions from other firms.
c. Set price equal to marginal cost.
d. Are price takers.

177. Oligopolistic firms
a. Seldom earn economic profits.
b. Always produce differentiated products.
c. Always produce homogenous products.
d. Make decisions expecting reactions from competitors.

178. The kinked demand curve theory of oligopoly assumes that rival firms
a. React to price increases.
b. React to price increases and decreases.
c. Do not react to price changes.
d. React to price decreases.

179. Demand for consumption of goods and services is
a. Derived demand.
b. Direct demand.
c. Product demand.
d. Utility.

180. Derived demand is the
a. Demand for inputs used in production.
b. Demand for products other than raw materials.
c. First derivative of the demand function.
d. Demand for consumption products.

181. The supply of a product does **not** depend on which of the following?
a. Raw material costs.
b. Wage rates.
c. Consumer incomes.
d. Technology.

182. If the production of two goods is complementary, a decrease in the price of one will
a. Increase supply of the other.
b. Increase the quantity supplied of the other.
c. Decrease the price of the other.
d. Decrease supply of the other.

183. The supply curve expresses the relation between the aggregate quantity supplied and
a. Price, holding constant the effects of all other variables.
b. Aggregate quantity demanded, holding constant the effects of all other variables.
c. Profit, holding constant the effects of all other variables.
d. Each factor that affects supply.

184. The equilibrium market price of a good is the
a. Price that buyers are willing and able to pay.
b. Price where shortages exceed surpluses.
c. Price that maximizes profit for sellers.
d. Price where the quantity demanded equals the quantity supplied.

185. If the market price is higher than the equilibrium price
a. A shortage exists and the equilibrium price will rise until it equals the market price and the shortage is eliminated.
b. A surplus exists and the market price will fall until it equals the equilibrium price and the surplus is eliminated.
c. A surplus exists and the equilibrium price will rise until it equals the market price and the surplus is eliminated.
d. A shortage exists and the market price will fall until it equals the equilibrium price and the shortage is eliminated.

186. The concept of point advertising elasticity reveals the
a. Percentage change in demand following a change in advertising.
b. Percentage change in the quantity demanded following a change in advertising.
c. Percentage change in advertising following a change in the quantity demanded.
d. Percentage change in advertising following a change in demand.

187. The concept of cross-price elasticity is used to examine the responsiveness of demand
a. To changes in income.
b. For one product to changes in the price of another.
c. To changes in "own" price.
d. To changes in income.

188. Elasticity is the
a. Percentage change in a dependent variable, *Y*, resulting from a 1% change in the value of an independent variable, *X*.
b. Change in a dependent variable, *Y*, resulting from a change in the value of an independent variable, *X*.
c. Change in an independent variable, *X*, resulting from a change in the value of a dependent variable, *Y*.
d. Percentage change in an independent variable, *X*, resulting from a 1% change in the value of a dependent variable, *Y*.

189. Point elasticity measures elasticity
a. Over a given range of a function.
b. At a spot on a function.
c. Along an arc.
d. Before nonprice effects.

190. A direct relation between the price of one product and the demand for another holds for all
a. Complements.
b. Substitutes.
c. Normal goods.
d. Inferior goods.

191. A utility function is a descriptive statement that relates total utility to
a. Income.
b. The production of goods and services.
c. The consumption of goods and services.
d. Prices.

192. Two products are complements if the
a. Cross-price elasticity of demand is less than zero.
b. Cross-price elasticity of demand equals zero.
c. Cross-price elasticity of demand is greater than zero.
d. Price elasticity of demand for each good is greater than zero.

193. A product that enjoys rapidly growing demand over time is likely to be
a. A noncyclical normal good.
b. A cyclical normal good.
c. Neither a normal nor an inferior good.
d. An inferior good.

194. A firm supplying a single product to two distinct submarkets will maximize profits by equating
a. Average revenue in each market to average cost.
b. Average revenue in each market to marginal cost.
c. Marginal revenue in each market to marginal cost.
d. Price in each market to marginal cost.

195. Unemployment between jobs is called
a. Frictional unemployment.
b. Structural unemployment.
c. Cyclical unemployment.
d. Deficit demand unemployment.

196. The rate of unemployment in a full employment environment is
a. Frictional unemployment plus structural unemployment.
b. Cyclical unemployment plus structural unemployment.

c. Deficit demand unemployment plus frictional unemployment.
d. Cyclical unemployment plus deficit demand unemployment.

197. Which of the following is **not** a characteristic of a purely competitive market?
a. Differentiated products.
b. Lack of control over product price by individual firms.
c. No barriers to market entry for new firms.
d. A very large number of producing firms.

198. Which of the following is typically an advantage of a monopoly from the viewpoint of the consumer?
a. Costs of production may be lower because of quantities of scale.
b. Prices charged to the public are lower because there is no need for advertising.
c. Quantities produced are greater.
d. Products produced are of higher quality.

199. Which of the following is a tool of monetary policy that a nation's central bank could use to stabilize the economy during an inflationary period?
a. Selling government securities.
b. Lowering bank reserve requirements.
c. Lowering bank discount rates.
d. Encouraging higher tax rates.

200. Inflation caused by an increase in costs is referred to as which of the following?

I. Cost-push inflation.
II. Supply-side inflation.
III. Demand-pull inflation.
IV. Demand-side inflation.

a. I only.
b. I and II.
c. III only.
d. III and IV.

MULTIPLE-CHOICE ANSWERS AND EXPLANATIONS

1. a __ __	42. c __ __	83. b __ __	124. c __ __	165. a __ __
2. c __ __	43. d __ __	84. c __ __	125. c __ __	166. d __ __
3. c __ __	44. a __ __	85. c __ __	126. a __ __	167. d __ __
4. a __ __	45. a __ __	86. c __ __	127. a __ __	168. d __ __
5. c __ __	46. d __ __	87. d __ __	128. d __ __	169. a __ __
6. d __ __	47. c __ __	88. d __ __	129. b __ __	170. b __ __
7. b __ __	48. a __ __	89. d __ __	130. a __ __	171. a __ __
8. c __ __	49. a __ __	90. a __ __	131. b __ __	172. c __ __
9. a __ __	50. a __ __	91. b __ __	132. b __ __	173. b __ __
10. b __ __	51. d __ __	92. d __ __	133. a __ __	174. d __ __
11. b __ __	52. b __ __	93. d __ __	134. d __ __	175. c __ __
12. d __ __	53. b __ __	94. d __ __	135. c __ __	176. a __ __
13. a __ __	54. d __ __	95. d __ __	136. d __ __	177. d __ __
14. d __ __	55. b __ __	96. a __ __	137. c __ __	178. d __ __
15. d __ __	56. b __ __	97. d __ __	138. a __ __	179. b __ __
16. a __ __	57. b __ __	98. a __ __	139. a __ __	180. a __ __
17. a __ __	58. b __ __	99. b __ __	140. d __ __	181. c __ __
18. c __ __	59. a __ __	100. c __ __	141. c __ __	182. d __ __
19. a __ __	60. d __ __	101. d __ __	142. b __ __	183. a __ __
20. d __ __	61. b __ __	102. d __ __	143. b __ __	184. d __ __
21. d __ __	62. c __ __	103. a __ __	144. a __ __	185. b __ __
22. b __ __	63. a __ __	104. a __ __	145. c __ __	186. a __ __
23. c __ __	64. a __ __	105. b __ __	146. a __ __	187. b __ __
24. b __ __	65. a __ __	106. d __ __	147. a __ __	188. a __ __
25. c __ __	66. c __ __	107. c __ __	148. d __ __	189. b __ __
26. b __ __	67. c __ __	108. d __ __	149. b __ __	190. b __ __
27. c __ __	68. c __ __	109. b __ __	150. c __ __	191. c __ __
28. d __ __	69. c __ __	110. b __ __	151. b __ __	192. a __ __
29. c __ __	70. b __ __	111. c __ __	152. a __ __	193. b __ __
30. b __ __	71. b __ __	112. b __ __	153. d __ __	194. c __ __
31. d __ __	72. d __ __	113. a __ __	154. d __ __	195. a __ __
32. d __ __	73. b __ __	114. c __ __	155. a __ __	196. a __ __
33. a __ __	74. b __ __	115. c __ __	156. a __ __	197. a __ __
34. b __ __	75. a __ __	116. b __ __	157. b __ __	198. a __ __
35. c __ __	76. c __ __	117. c __ __	158. d __ __	199. a __ __
36. c __ __	77. a __ __	118. a __ __	159. b __ __	200. b __ __
37. a __ __	78. c __ __	119. c __ __	160. b __ __	
38. a __ __	79. d __ __	120. c __ __	161. a __ __	
39. a __ __	80. c __ __	121. d __ __	162. d __ __	
40. b __ __	81. a __ __	122. a __ __	163. b __ __	1st: __/200 = __%
41. c __ __	82. c __ __	123. d __ __	164. c __ __	2nd: __/200 = __%

Impact of Government Legislation

1. **(a)** Section 1 of the Sherman Act prohibits contracts, combinations, and conspiracies that restrict trade, while Section 2 outlaws both monopolies and attempts to monopolize.

Subject Area: Regulatory, legal, and economics—impact of government legislation. Source: Author.

2. **(c)** The major provisions of the Clayton Act deal with tying contracts, exclusive dealings, and mergers. The Act no longer deals with price discrimination.

Subject Area: Regulatory, legal, and economics—impact of government legislation. Source: Author.

3. **(c)** Although the FTC most frequently enters a cease-and-desist order having the effect of an injunction, it may order other relief, such as affirmative disclosure, corrective advertising, and the granting of patent licenses on a reasonable royalty basis.

Subject Area: Regulatory, legal, and economics—impact of government legislation. Source: Author.

4. **(a)** Section 1 of the Sherman Act provides that "every contract, combination in the form of trust or otherwise, or conspiracy, in restraint of trade or commerce among the several states or with foreign nations is hereby declared to be illegal."

Subject Area: Regulatory, legal, and economics—impact of government legislation. Source: Author.

5. **(c)** When two or more firms agree not to deal with a third party, their agreement represents a concerted refusal to deal, or a group boycott, which may violate Section 1 of the Sherman Act. Such a boycott may be clearly anticompetitive, eliminating competition or reducing market entry.

Subject Area: Regulatory, legal, and economics—impact of government legislation. Source: CBM, Volume two.

6. (d) Price-fixing is an agreement with the purpose or effect of inhibiting price competition; such agreements may, among other things, raise, depress, fix, peg, or stabilize prices.

Subject Area: Regulatory, legal, and economics—impact of government legislation. Source: CBM, Volume two.

7. (b) Exclusive dealing arrangements are agreements by which the seller or lessor of a product conditions the agreement upon the buyer's or lessee's promise not to deal in a competitor's goods.

Subject Area: Regulatory, legal, and economics—impact of government legislation. Source: CBM, Volume two.

8. (c) A conglomerate merger is an acquisition by one company of another that is not a competitor, customer, or supplier.

Subject Area: Regulatory, legal, and economics—impact of government legislation. Source: CBM, Volume two.

9. (a) Beachhead merger takes on a new risk and opportunity in entering a new industry. Horizontal merger means two firms in the same industry are merged. Vertical merger means both manufacturer and supplier are merged. Conglomerate merger means a firm in one industry acquires a firm in another industry.

Subject Area: Regulatory, legal, and economics—impact of government legislation. Source: Author.

10. (b) A vertical merger is a merger between a firm and one of its suppliers or customers. A bottle manufacturer can supply bottles to be used by a soft-drink producer. Choice (a) is incorrect because a horizontal merger is a combination of two firms producing the same type of good or service. Choice (c) is incorrect because a congeneric merger is a merger of firms in the same industry, but the two firms do not have a customer or supplier relationship (as in a vertical merger). Choice (d) is incorrect because a conglomerate merger is a merger of companies in totally different industries.

Subject Area: Regulatory, legal, and economics—impact of government legislation. Source: CIA Model Exam 1998, IV-46.

11. (b) This is a definition of a spin-off. Choice (a) is incorrect. In a liquidation, assets are sold piecemeal. Choice (c) is incorrect. In a leveraged buyout, the managers become the owners. Choice (d) is incorrect. In a managerial buyout, the managers become the owners.

Subject Area: Regulatory, legal, and economics—impact of government legislation. Source: CIA Model Exam 2002, IV-43.

12. (d) In a two-tier offer, shareholders are enticed to sell to the bidder early by a higher stock price offer for those who tender their stock earlier. Choices (a) and (b) are incorrect. An offer that is "two-tier" involves two different offer prices for the shares acquired. The terms of the share acquisition do not relate to the issuance or repurchase of bonds in the company. Choice (c) is incorrect. This is the opposite of the correct answer.

Subject Area: Regulatory, legal, and economics—impact of government legislation. Source: CIA Model Exam 2002, IV-44.

13. (a) In 1914, the US Congress strengthened the Sherman Act by adopting the Clayton Act, which was expressly designed "to supplement existing laws against unlawful restraints and monopolies."

Subject Area: Regulatory, legal, and economics—impact of government legislation. Source: CBM, Volume two.

14. (d) All horizontal price-fixing agreements are illegal per se. Similarly, it is illegal per se for a seller to fix the price at which its purchasers must resell its product. This vertical form of price-fixing—usually called retail price maintenance—is considered a per se violation of Section 1 of the Sherman Act.

Subject Area: Regulatory, legal, and economics—impact of government legislation. Source: CBM, Volume two.

15. (d) Market share is a firm's fractional share of the total relevant products and geographic markets.

Subject Area: Regulatory, legal, and economics—impact of government legislation. Source: CBM, Volume two.

16. (a) If sufficient monopoly power has been proven, the law must then show that the firm has engaged in unfair conduct.

Subject Area: Regulatory, legal, and economics—impact of government legislation. Source: CBM, Volume two.

17. (a) Section 3 of the Clayton Act prohibits tying arrangements and exclusive dealing, selling, or leasing arrangements that prevent purchasers from dealing with the seller's competitors when such arrangements may substantially lessen competition or tend to create a monopoly.

Subject Area: Regulatory, legal, and economics—impact of government legislation. Source: CBM, Volume two.

18. (c) The major provisions of the Clayton Act deal with price discrimination, tying contracts, exclusive dealings, and mergers. Section 2, which deals with price discrimination, was amended and rewritten by the Robinson-Patman Act. The Celler-Kefauver Act specifically prohibits asset acquisitions that reduce competition.

Subject Area: Regulatory, legal, and economics—impact of government legislation. Source: CBM, Volume two.

19. (a) The rule of reason test is a flexible standard under which the courts, in determining whether a challenged practice unreasonably restricts competition, consider a variety of factors, including the makeup of the relevant industry, the defendants' position within that industry, the ability of the defendants' competitors to respond to the challenged practice, and the defendants' purpose in adopting the restraint.

Subject Area: Regulatory, legal, and economics—impact of government legislation. Source: CBM, Volume two.

20. (d) A market share greater than 75% generally indicates monopoly power, while a share less than 50% does not.

Subject Area: Regulatory, legal, and economics—impact of government legislation. Source: CBM, Volume two.

21. (d) The act subjects individual offenders to imprisonment of up to three years and fines of up to $350,000, while corporate offenders are subject to fines of up to $10,000,000 per violation.

Subject Area: Regulatory, legal, and economics—impact of government legislation. Source: CBM, Volume two.

22. (b) Section 3 of the Clayton Act prohibits tying arrangements and exclusive dealing, selling, or leasing arrangements that prevent purchasers from dealing with the seller's competitors when such arrangements may substantially lessen competition or tend to create a monopoly. Section 7 of the Clayton Act prohibits a corporation from merging or acquiring another corporation's stock or assets when such an action would substantially lessen competition or would tend to create a monopoly.

Subject Area: Regulatory, legal, and economics—impact of government legislation. Source: CBM, Volume two.

23. (c) The Robinson-Patman Act prohibits price discrimination in interstate commerce concerning commodities of like grade and quality. The Sherman Act specifically prohibits monopolizing. The Federal Trade Commission enforces antitrust laws. The Celler-Kefauver Act specifically prohibits asset acquisitions that reduce competition.

Subject Area: Regulatory, legal, and economics—impact of government legislation. Source: CBM, Volume two.

24. (b) The Clayton Act exempts labor, agricultural, and horticultural organizations from all antitrust laws.

Subject Area: Regulatory, legal, and economics—impact of government legislation. Source: Author.

25. (c) A conglomerate merger is a catchall category that covers all acquisitions not involving a competitor, customer, or supplier.

Subject Area: Regulatory, legal, and economics—impact of government legislation. Source: CBM, Volume two.

26. (b) Price-fixing was made illegal under the Sherman Antitrust Act.

Subject Area: Regulatory, legal, and economics—impact of government legislation. Source: Author.

27. (c) Price discrimination was made illegal under the Robinson-Patman Act.

Subject Area: Regulatory, legal, and economics—impact of government legislation. Source: Author.

28. (d) Price discrimination is illegal when the seller favors certain customers over others.

Subject Area: Regulatory, legal, and economics—impact of government legislation. Source: Author.

29. (c) When a manufacturer and retailers agree upon some minimum price to be charged to consumers, it is called resale price maintenance.

Subject Area: Regulatory, legal, and economics—impact of government legislation. Source: CBM, Volume two.

30. (b) The practice of driving rivals out of business by pricing at such a low level that the rival cannot make money is called predatory pricing.

Subject Area: Regulatory, legal, and economics—impact of government legislation. Source: CBM, Volume two.

31. (d) With regard to government regulation, deregulation and privatization are increasing worldwide.

Subject Area: Regulatory, legal, and economics—impact of government legislation. Source: Author.

32. (d) Raising prices when demand increases is most likely to be perceived as unfair by consumers.

Subject Area: Regulatory, legal, and economics—impact of government legislation. Source: Author.

33. (a) "We are hoping to develop a stronger relationship with one customer" does NOT represent a legally permissible reason for charging different prices to competitive customers. Legally permissible reasons include (1) there is no harm to competition, (2) we are selling to end consumers, and (3) we are matching competitors' prices for some customers.

Subject Area: Regulatory, legal, and economics—impact of government legislation. Source: Author.

34. (b) The regulatory system can increase consumer prices and cut profits when dispute resolution is slow, litigation costs are high, and the outcomes of legal proceedings are risky. When product prices are high, demand for that product will be lower if the demand is perfectly elastic (sensitive to price changes). Companies will lay off workers due to lower demand. Eventually, workers will pay for regulatory costs.

Subject Area: Regulatory, legal, and economics—impact of government legislation. Source: CBM, Volume two.

35. (c) Capture theory is in stark contrast to more traditional public interest theory, which sees regulation as a government-imposed means of private-market control.

Subject Area: Regulatory, legal, and economics—impact of government legislation. Source: CBM, Volume two.

36. (c) Aggregate demand includes government purchases. A decrease in government purchases will decrease aggregate demand. Choice (a) is incorrect because government purchases are a component of aggregate demand. If government purchases decrease, aggregate demand also decreases. Choices (b) and (d) are incorrect because government purchases do not have an effect on aggregate supply.

Subject Area: Regulatory, legal, and economics—impact of government legislation. Source: CIA 1196, IV-72.

37. (a) It is the central bank that is responsible for managing implementation of the nations' monetary policy. Choice (b) is incorrect because the federal government establishes monetary policy but implementation is managed by the central bank. Choice (c) is incorrect because actions of the central bank affect commercial bank reserves and the level of interest rates charged to, and by, commercial banks. The implementation of monetary policy is not managed by the commercial banks. Choice (d) is incorrect. One instrument that the central bank can use to implement monetary policy is open market bond transactions, but it is the central bank that manages this process and not the bond market traders.

Subject Area: Regulatory, legal, and economics—impact of government legislation. Source: CIA 595, IV-63.

38. (a) When the Federal Reserve Banks buy securities in the open market, commercial bank reserves are increased and the money supply will grow. Choice (b) is incorrect because an increase in the required reserve ration will reduce the money supply. Choice (c) is incorrect because an increase in excess reserves means a reduction in bank lending and a fall in the money supply. Choice (d) is incorrect because an increase in the discount rate will reduce commercial bank borrowing to meet reserve requirements and thereby reduce the money supply.

Subject Area: Regulatory, legal, and economics—impact of government legislation. Source: CIA 590, IV-69.

39. (a) Selling government securities is contractional because it takes money out of circulation. Choice (b) is incorrect because lower reserve requirements would fuel the economy because banks could lend more money. Choice (c) is incorrect because lower discount rates would fuel the economy because borrowing would be encouraged. Choice (d) is incorrect because this is fiscal policy—not monetary policy.

Subject Area: Regulatory, legal, and economics—impact of government legislation. Source: CIA 1190, IV-69.

40. (b) Open market operations through bond sales and purchases are flexible (government securities can be purchased or sold in large or small amounts), cause prompt changes in bank reserves and are more subtle than reserve ratio changes. Choice (a) is incorrect because reserve ratio changes are infrequent, offer less flexibility and have less prompt effects than open market operations. Choice (c) is incorrect because manipulation of government spending is an instrument of fiscal policy, not monetary policy. Choice (d) is incorrect because the amount of commercial bank reserves obtained by borrowing from the central bank is small and because whether a change in the discount rate has much impact depends on whether the change occurs at a time when the commercial banks are inclined to alter their central bank borrowings.

Subject Area: Regulatory, legal, and economics—impact of government legislation. Source: CIA 594, IV-69.

41. (c) An increase in the reserve ratio decreases the money supply by increasing the amount of required reserves a bank must keep thereby reducing the amount available for lending. Choice (a) is incorrect because open-market purchases by the central bank increase the money supply by increasing commercial banks' reserves. Choice (b) is incorrect because a decrease in the discount rate has the effect of increasing the money supply by increasing bank reserves. Choice (d) is incorrect because a decrease in the margin requirement decreases the minimum down payment which purchasers of stock must make. This is a credit control, which affects the stock market and has no direct impact on the money supply.

Subject Area: Regulatory, legal, and economics—impact of government legislation. Source: CIA 1193, IV-66.

42. (c) An increase in excess reserves has the effect of increasing the availability of credit. Choice (a) is incorrect because an increase in excess reserves has the effect of increasing the money supply. Choice (b) is incorrect because an increase in excess reserves has the effect of increasing the money supply, which in turn has the effect of increasing aggregate demand. Choice (d) is incorrect because an increase in excess reserves has the effect of increasing the availability of credit and leads to a decrease in interest rates.

Subject Area: Regulatory, legal, and economics—impact of government legislation. Source: CIA 1191, IV-67.

43. (d) As the government borrows to finance greater spending under an expansionary fiscal policy, interest rates rise. Higher interest rates choke off or "crowd out" private investment, which cancels or weakens the stimulus of the fiscal policy. Choices (a) and (c) are incorrect because fiscal policy has no direct effect on the money multiplier. Choice (b) is incorrect because expansionary fiscal policy results in higher interest rates as the government borrows money to finance greater spending levels. Higher interest rates will have a negative, not a positive, effect on investment levels.

Subject Area: Regulatory, legal, and economics—impact of government legislation. Source: CIA 596, IV-71.

44. (a) A fiscal expansion causes an increase in domestic interest rates and international capital inflows. These capital inflows cause the domestic currency to appreciate, which has a negative effect on net exports. Choice (b) is incorrect because a fiscal expansion does influence net exports since it has an effect on the external value of the domestic currency. Choice (c) is incorrect because a monetary expansion causes a reduction in domestic interest rates and hence international capital outflows. These capital outflows cause the domestic currency to depreciate, which has a positive, not a negative, effect on net exports. Choice (d) is incorrect because a monetary expansion does influence net exports since it has an effect on the external value of the domestic currency.

Subject Area: Regulatory, legal, and economics—impact of government legislation. Source: CIA 1196, IV-71.

45. (a) A $1 billion increase in government spending will increase aggregate demand by $1 billion. The taxes will cause disposable income to decline accompanied by a decline in both consumption and savings. Choice (b) is incorrect. Given a balanced budget multiplier equal to one, a $1 billion increase in both taxes and government spending will increase aggregate demand by $1 billion, and result in an increase in aggregate supply. Choice (c) is incorrect. Given a balanced budget multiplier equal to one, a $1 billion increase in both taxes and government spending will increase aggregate demand by $1 billion. Choice (d) is incorrect. A $1 billion increase in both taxes and government spending will have no effect on the budget deficit, defined as government spending minus taxes.

Subject Area: Regulatory, legal, and economics—impact of government legislation. Source: CIA 1191, IV-66.

46. (d) During a recessionary period the government would want to increase its own spending and increase consumers' and business spending by decreasing taxes. Choice (a) is incorrect because the government would not want to raise consumers' taxes. Choice (b) is incorrect because the government would not want to lower government spending. Choice (c) is incorrect because flexible (liberal) money policy involves monetary and not fiscal policy.

Subject Area: Regulatory, legal, and economics—impact of government legislation. Source: CIA 1192, IV-68.

Trade Legislation

47. (c) An embargo is a total ban on some kinds of imports. As such, it is an extreme form of the import quota. Embargoes have the effect of totally excluding the exporting firm from selling in that country and are the most restrictive type of import/export law. Choice (a) is incorrect because a tariff is a tax levied by a foreign government against certain imported products. A firm exporting to a country must accept lower profits, absorbing the tariff, or increase selling prices in the foreign country to compensate. This reduces profitability and/or competitiveness in the foreign market but does not exclude the firm from exporting to that country. Choice (b) is incorrect because a quota is a limit set by a foreign government on the amount of goods that the importing country will accept in certain product categories. The effect of a quota is to restrict the quantity the firm can export to that country, but not to exclude the firm from selling in that market. The effect on revenues and profitability depends on market conditions in that country. Choice (d) is incorrect because exchange controls limit the amount of foreign exchange that can be transacted and/or the exchange rate against other currencies. These controls limit the ability of a firm selling in the country to repatriate its export earnings, but do not exclude the firm from selling in that market.

Subject Area: Regulatory, legal, and economics—trade legislation. Source: CIA 597, IV-75.

48. (a) The respective opportunity costs determine which country will produce which product. Choice (b) is incorrect because profit margins do not enter into the decision. Choice (c) is incorrect because economic order quantity determines optimum inventory levels. Choice (d) is incorrect because tariffs would only come into play after each country produced its respective products.

Subject Area: Regulatory, legal, and economics—trade legislation. Source: CIA 597, IV-61.

49. (a) Nation B has a comparative advantage in cars because the within-country price comparison between cars and rice is lower for Nation B (16,000/20,000 = .8) than for Nation A (15,000/10,000 = .5). Nation A has an absolute advantage, but Nation B has the comparative advantage. Choice (b) is incorrect because Nation A has the comparative advantage for rice because its cost relationship (10,000/15,000 = .667) is lower than in Nation B (20,000/16,000 = 1.25). Choice (c) is incorrect because Nation B has the comparative advantage for cars. Choice (d) is incorrect because total output will be maximized when each nation specializes in the products in which it has the greatest comparative advantage.

Subject Area: Regulatory, legal, and economics—trade legislation. Source: CIA 1190, IV-70.

50. (a) Country A has a comparative advantage in producing good X. The cost of producing X is only $30/$10 = 3 times higher in A while the cost of producing Y is $20/$6 = 3.333 times higher in A. Choice (b) is incorrect because Country A is relatively better at producing X, not Y. Choice (c) is incorrect. Since the relative costs of production favor A producing good X, there could be gains from trade if A produces X and exports it to B, while B produces Y and exports it to A. Choice (d) is incorrect. Although Country B is absolutely more efficient at producing both goods, it is relatively better at producing Y. If the terms of trade are favorable, the wealth of B will also increase under the more efficient allocation of production prescribed by the theory of comparative advantage.

Subject Area: Regulatory, legal, and economics—trade legislation. Source: CIA 594, IV-63.

51. (d) According to the principle of comparative advantage, world output can be maximized by each country specializing in and exporting what it can produce most efficiently. Choice (a) is incorrect because military self-sufficiency is an argument for increasing trade barriers to strengthen industries producing strategic goods and materials essential for defense. Choice (b) is incorrect because the diversification for stability is an argument for increasing trade barriers by promoting industrial diversification and less dependence on other nations for certain products. Choice (c) is incorrect because the infant industry argument is an argument for increasing trade barriers for the purpose of allowing new domestic industries to establish themselves.

Subject Area: Regulatory, legal, and economics—trade legislation. Source: CIA 1193, IV-68.

52. (b) Free trade, combined with specialization according to comparative advantage, can increase total world output and thus benefit all trading countries. Choice (a) is incorrect because the infant industry argument is a basis for protection rather than free trade. Choice (c) is incorrect because national defense is an argument for protection since free trade implies increase specialization in production. However, specialization in production is risky since a nation must depend upon others for what it consumes. Choice (d) is incorrect. For free trade to be advantageous, economies must specialize rather than diversify.

Subject Area: Regulatory, legal, and economics—trade legislation. Source: CIA 593, IV-70.

53. (b) The theory of comparative advantage states that the total worldwide output will be greatest when each good is produced by that nation which has the lowest opportunity cost (the amount of other goods, which must be foregone to produce the product desired). Choice (a) is incorrect because the theory of comparative advantage does not suggest that a situation in which each nation's imports are equal to its exports will maximize worldwide output. It is unlikely that any nation would voluntarily adopt such a policy, and economic theory does not suggest a correlation between import-export equality and worldwide output maximization. Choice (c) is incorrect because the theory of comparative advantage does not suggest that goods, which contribute to a nation's balance of payments deficit should not be imported. Such a deficit is a function of volume, not specific goods, and such a policy is not related to maximization of worldwide output. Choice (d) is incorrect. While unrestricted trade policies are compatible with implementation of the theory of comparative advantage, the key component of the theory is lowest opportunity cost, not unrestricted trade.

Subject Area: Regulatory, legal, and economics—trade legislation. Source: CIA 1191, IV-70.

54. (d) With trade quotas home jobs will be saved, hence unemployment will decline. Since jobs will be saved for inefficient industries (less efficient than foreign competitors) productivity rates will decline because they will not be specializing on those goods with which they have a comparative advantage. Therefore, by definition, choices (a), (b), and (c) will be incorrect.

Subject Area: Regulatory, legal, and economics—trade legislation. Source: CIA 591, IV-70.

55. (b) The tariff will increase the price of the product to domestic consumers, resulting in the reallocation of expenditures to other products. Choice (a) is incorrect because protective tariffs increase domestic prices of the product. Choice (c) is incorrect because domestic production of the product will expand because domestic producers are not subject to the tariff and therefore receive a higher price per unit. Choice (d) is incorrect because foreign producers receive the same unit price (net of the tariff, which is paid to the government), but their sales volume falls. Revenue is calculated as price multiplied by quantity so foreign producers receive lower revenues after the tariff is imposed.

Subject Area: Regulatory, legal, and economics—trade legislation. Source: CIA 597, IV-71.

56. (b) Domestic producers are not subject to the tariff and are protected from foreign competition. The domestic price of the item will be higher, so domestic producers will sell more of the item and at a higher price. Domestic consumers will consume less of the item following the price increase. Choice (a) is incorrect because domestic consumers will consume less of the item, since the protective tariff will result in a higher domestic price for the item. Choices (c) and (d) are incorrect because domestic producers will sell more, not less, of the item following the imposition of a protective tariff.

Subject Area: Regulatory, legal, and economics—trade legislation. Source: CIA 1195, IV-68.

57. (b) The tariff will increase the price of the item to domestic consumers, resulting in the reallocation of expenditures to other products. Choice (a) is incorrect because protective tariffs increase domestic prices of the item. Choice (c) is incorrect because domestic production of the item will expand because domestic producers are not subject to the tariff so they receive a higher price per unit. Choice (d) is incorrect because foreign producers receive the same unit price (net of the tariff, which is paid to the government), but their sales volume falls. Revenue is calculated as price multiplied by quantity so foreign producers receive lower revenues after the tariff is imposed.

Subject Area: Regulatory, legal, and economics—trade legislation. Source: CIA 595, IV-61.

58. (b) Consumption taxes are tariffs. Choice (a) is incorrect because licensing requirements are nontariff trade barriers. Choice (c) is incorrect because unreasonable standards pertaining to product quality and safety are nontariff trade barriers. Choice (d) is incorrect because licensing requirements and unreasonable standards are not tariffs.

Subject Area: Regulatory, legal, and economics—trade legislation. Source: CIA 594, IV-64.

59. (a) A tax levied by the foreign government against certain imported products is known as a tariff. Choice (b) is incorrect because a limit on the amount of goods that the reporting country will accept in certain products is a quota. Choice (c) is incorrect because a restriction in which imports in prescribed categories are totally banned is a quota. Choice (d) is incorrect because arrangements between nations that prevent corporate and individual income from being double taxed is refereed to as tax treaty.

Subject Area: Regulatory, legal, and economics—trade legislation. Source: Transition Question No.1, IIA 1994.

60. (d) With trade quotas, home jobs will be saved, hence unemployment will decline. Since jobs will be saved for inefficient industries (less efficient than foreign competitors), productivity rates will decline because they will not be specializing in those goods with which they have a comparative advantage.

Subject Area: Regulatory, legal, and economics—trade legislation. Source: CIA Model Exam 1998, IV-69.

61. (b) Revenue tariffs are usually applied to products that are not produced domestically. Their purpose is to provide the government with tax revenues. Import quotas are designed to restrict the amount of a commodity, which can be imported in a period of time (choice c.). Voluntary export restrictions, which have the same effect as import quotas, encourage foreign firms to limit their exports to a particular country (choice d.).

Subject Area: Regulatory, legal, and economics—trade legislation. Source: CIA Model Exam 1998, IV-73.

62. (c) An embargo is a total ban on some kinds of imports. As such, it is an extreme form of the import quota. Embargoes have the effect of totally excluding the exporting firms from selling in that country and are the most restrictive type of import/export law. A tariff is a tax levied by a foreign government against certain imported products. Firms exporting to that country must accept lower profits, absorbing the tariff, or increase selling prices in the foreign country to compensate. This reduces profitability and/or competitiveness in the foreign market but does not exclude the firm from exporting to that country (choice a.). A quota is a limit set by a foreign government on the amount of goods that the importing country will accept in certain product categories. The effect of a quota is to restrict the quantity the firm can export to that country, but not to exclude the firm from selling in that market. The effect on revenues and profitability depends on market conditions in that country (choice b.). Exchange controls limit the amount of foreign exchange that can be transacted and/or the exchange rate against other currencies. These controls limit the ability of a firm selling in the country to repatriate its export earnings but do not exclude the firm from selling in that market (choice d.).

Subject Area: Regulatory, legal, and economics—trade legislation. Source: CIA Model Exam 1998, IV-75.

Taxation Schemes

63. (a) Investment tax credits are deductions from the corporate tax bill. The result is lower investments cost and higher project net present values, all else equal. Tax credits are deductions from the actual corporate tax bill, and since more of profits are available for dividends, inflation is not restrained (choice b.). Choice (c) is incorrect because the opposite is true. Investment tax credits are not taxes levied on projects (choice d.).

Subject Area: Regulatory, legal, and economics—taxation schemes. Source: CIA Model Exam 1998, IV-74.

64. (a) A rich person avoids the general sales tax on the portion of their income that is saved, whereas the poor person is unable to save. Choice (b) is incorrect because the opposite is true. Choice (c) is incorrect because the tax rate is uniform for all taxpayers in a general sales tax. Choice (d) is incorrect because general sales tax does not claim an increasing amount of income as income rises. This statement is a description of a progressive, not a regressive, tax.

Subject Area: Regulatory, legal, and economics—taxation schemes. Source: CIA Model Exam 1998, IV-76.

65. (a) A value-added tax is collected on the basis of the value created by the firm. This is measured as the difference between the value of its outputs and its inputs. Choice (b) is incorrect because this is a description of how to calculate capital gains tax. Choice (c) is incorrect because this is a description of an internal transfer price. Choice (d) is incorrect because this is a description of how to calculate income tax.

Subject Area: Regulatory, legal, and economics—taxation schemes. Source: CIA Model Exam 1998, IV-77.

66. (c) Regressive taxes are those for which the average tax rate falls as income rises. They take a smaller percentage of income as income rises, so they will not necessarily take a larger absolute amount of income as income rises. Progressive taxes, for which the average tax rate rises as income rises, take both a larger percentage of income and a larger absolute amount of income as income rises (choice a.). Proportional taxes, for which the average tax rate is constant for all income levels, always take a larger absolute amount of income as income rises (choice b.). "Regenerative" is not a term used to designate types of taxes (choice d.).

Subject Area: Regulatory, legal, and economics—taxation schemes. Source: CIA Model Exam 1998, IV-79.

67. (c) Permanent differences have no deferred tax consequences because they affect only the period in which they occur. Permanent differences include (1) items that enters into pretax financial income but never into taxable income and (2) items that enter into taxable income but never into pretax financial income. In contrast, temporary differences result in taxable or deductible amounts in some future year(s), when the reported amounts of assets are recovered and the reported amounts of liabilities are settled. Temporary differences therefore do have deferred tax consequences while permanent differences do not. Choice (a) is incorrect. It is temporary differences that result in taxable or deductible amounts in some future year(s), when the reported amounts of assets are recovered and the reported amounts of liabilities are settled. Choice (b) is incorrect. Temporary differences have deferred tax consequences while the permanent differences do not. Permanent differences affect only the period in which they occur. Choice (d) is incorrect. Permanent differences, not temporary differences, include items that enter into pretax financial income but never into taxable income.

Subject Area: Regulatory, legal, and economics—taxation schemes. Source: CIA Model Exam 1998, IV-80.

68. (c) The value added is the difference between the value of the output and the value of the purchased inputs. Value added tax payable is calculated as follows:

(Value-added tax rate) (Value-added)
= (.25) (Sales – Purchased inputs)
= (.25) (2,500,000 – 150,000) = $587,500

Choice (a) is incorrect. This is 25% of earnings before tax, calculated as follows:

Earnings before tax = Sales	$2,500,000
– Purchased inputs	150,000
– Labor costs	500,000
– Interest expense	100,000
Earnings before tax	$1,750,000

(.25) (1,750,000) = $437,500

Choice (b) is incorrect. This calculation of the value added tax measures value added incorrectly, deducting both purchased inputs and labor costs, as follows:

(Value-added tax rate) (Value-added)
= (.25) (Sales – Purchased inputs – Labor costs)
= (.25) (2,500,000 – 150,000 – 500,000) = $462,500

Choice (d) is incorrect. This is the value added tax rate multiplied by the output of the firm.

(Value-added tax rate) (Sales) = (.25) (2,500,000) = $625,000

Subject Area: Regulatory, legal, and economics—taxation schemes. Source: CIA 1196, IV-76.

69. (c) It is necessary to adjust the deductions, exemptions and tax brackets in order to maintain the same real level of taxes in a progressive tax system. Nominal taxes will then keep place with inflation and real taxes will remain constant, or invariant to inflation. Choice (a) is incorrect because if only deductions and exemptions are indexed to inflation, real taxes will still increase with inflation as taxpayers' experience "bracket creep." That is, the same real income level will pay taxes based on a higher tax rate. Choice (b) is incorrect because if only tax brackets are adjusted, deductions and exemptions will have less real value. Real taxes will rise. Choice (d) is incorrect because indexing does not result in nominal tax receipts growing more slowly than the rate of inflation. Rather, indexing maintains the same real rate of taxation by ensuring that nominal tax receipts just keep pace with inflation.

Subject Area: Regulatory, legal, and economics—taxation schemes. Source: CIA 1195, IV-69.

70. (b) Property taxes tend to be regressive, like sales taxes. Families with lower incomes must pay a higher portion of their income for housing and hence property taxes tend to be a larger percentage of their income. Choice (a) is incorrect because general sales taxes tend to be regressive with respect to income. A larger portion of a poor person's income is exposed to the tax, since low-income individuals are unable to save as high a portion of their income. High-income individuals are less exposed to general sales taxes since they avoid the tax on the portion of their income that is saved. Choices (c) and (d) are incorrect because personal income taxes tend to be progressive, since higher tax rates are charged on higher income.

Subject Area: Regulatory, legal, and economics—taxation schemes. Source: CIA 1195, IV-70.

71. (b) A higher excise tax will cause an increase in the selling price of the product. This price increase will have a less negative effect on sales volume for products with less elastic demand. Examples of products with low elasticity of demand include gasoline, tobacco and alcohol. The tax revenue generated by an increase in excise taxes is therefore higher if the tax is levied on products with less elastic demand. Choice (a) is incorrect because the more price elastic the demand for a product, the more demand will fall as a result of the tax induced price increase. The reduction in sales volume will reduce the tax revenues generated on sales of the product. Choice (c) is incorrect because an increase in excise taxes will result in a decrease in tax revenue only if demand for the product on which it is levied is extremely elastic. Choice (d) is incorrect because the less price elastic the demand for a product, the less demand will fall as a result of the tax induced price increase. The smaller reduction in sales volume will increase, not reduce, the tax revenues generated on sales of the product.

Subject Area: Regulatory, legal, and economics—taxation schemes. Source: CIA 1195, IV-71.

72. (d) The part of corporate income which is paid out as dividends is taxed first as corporate income and then may be taxed again, as personal income to stockholders. Choice (a) is incorrect because corporate income is not subject to sales tax. Choice (b) is incorrect because property tax is not based on corporate earnings. Choice (c) is incorrect because after paying corporate income tax, value-added tax is not imposed on the part of corporate earnings paid out as dividends. A value-added tax is paid on the difference between a firm's sales and the value of its purchases from other firms.

Subject Area: Regulatory, legal, and economics—taxation schemes. Source: CIA 1195, IV-72.

73. (b) The average tax rate of the individual has decreased from

$8,000/$23,000 = 34.8%

to $10,000/$30,000 = 33.3%.

Under a regressive tax system, the average tax rate falls as income rises, although the amount of tax paid may rise. Choice (a) is incorrect because both the amount of tax and the percentage of income paid in tax (the average tax rate) rise under a progressive tax system as income increases. In the case described, the individual pays a higher amount of tax, but a lower percentage of income in tax. Choice (c) is incorrect because "marginal" is not a type of tax system, but a type of tax rate. The marginal tax rate is the tax rate paid on incremental income. Choice (d) is incorrect because under a proportional income tax system, the average tax rate is invariant to the level of income. The average tax rate of this individual falls as income rises.

Subject Area: Regulatory, legal, and economics—taxation schemes. Source: CIA 596, IV-74.

74. (b) Deferred taxes are viewed as economic liabilities for taxes payable and as assets for prepaid tax. This is a balance-sheet oriented approach and is referred to as the "asset-liability" approach to accounting for deferred income taxes. Choice (a) is incorrect because this statement describes the "deferred" method of accounting for deferred income taxes. Choice (c) is incorrect because this is the "net of tax" method, which recognizes that future taxability and tax deductibility are important factors in the valuation of individual assets and liabilities. Choice (d) is incorrect because this is the "nonallocation" or "flow-through" approach, which does not support the calculation and reporting of deferred income tax at all.

Subject Area: Regulatory, legal, and economics—taxation schemes. Source: CIA 596, IV-75.

75. (a) The marginal tax rate is the tax applicable to the last unit of income while the average tax rate is the total tax paid divided by taxable income. In a progressive tax system, higher incomes attract higher tax rates so the marginal tax rate paid on the last unit of income exceeds the average tax rate. Choices (b) and (c) are incorrect because in both progressive and regressive tax systems, the tax rate varies with the level of income so the marginal and average tax rates differ. Choice (d) is incorrect because in a regressive tax system the marginal tax rate is less than, not greater than, the average tax rate.

Subject Area: Regulatory, legal, and economics—taxation schemes. Source: CIA 595, IV-70.

76. (c) The breakeven point for each individual firm is unaffected by an increase in corporate tax rates. Choices (a) and (b) are incorrect because the breakeven point is at the point of zero profit where there is no income tax since the income level is zero. At the breakeven point, the corporate tax rate has no impact. Choice (d) is incorrect because the contribution margin per unit will be lower if the corporate tax rate is higher, for all companies operating above their breakeven point.

Subject Area: Regulatory, legal, and economics—taxation schemes. Source: CIA 1194, IV-65.

77. (a) As the nominal income of the taxpayer increases, the taxpayer will be in a higher tax bracket and will face a higher marginal tax rate, even though no real increase in income has occurred. The taxpayer will experience increasing nominal and increasing real taxes payable. Choice (b) is incorrect because real taxes payable also increase. Choice (c) is incorrect because nominal taxes payable also increase. Choice (d) is incorrect because both real and nominal taxes payable will increase.

Subject Area: Regulatory, legal, and economics—taxation schemes. Source: CIA 1194, IV-71.

78. (c) Her average tax rate is calculated as: $(0.15 \times 3/5) + (0.30 \times 2/5) = 0.21 = 21\%$. Choices (a) and (b) are incorrect because her marginal tax rate is 30%. Choice (d) is incorrect because this response was calculated as a simple numerical average, not a valid computation. $(0.15 + 0.30)/2 = 0.225 = 22.5\%$

Subject Area: Regulatory, legal, and economics—taxation schemes. CIA 594, IV-71.

79. (d) Supply-side economics consists of policies intended to stimulate incentives to work, save and invest, and undertake entrepreneurial risk. Lower marginal tax rates increase the attractiveness of work and simultaneously increase the opportunity cost of leisure. Choice (a) is incorrect because fiscal policies of this type are demand management policies. Choice (b) is incorrect because monetary policies are of the demand-management type. An increase in the money supply is used to increase aggregate demand. Choice (c) is incorrect because it is a part of Keynesian economic theory. Choices (a), (b), and (c) are part of demand-side economics.

Subject Area: Regulatory, legal, and economics—taxation schemes. CIA 1191, IV-61.

80. (c) The cumulative deferred tax increases (peaks) and then decreases to zero at the end of the useful life of the asset if accelerated depreciation is used for tax purposes while straight-line depreciation is used for reporting purposes. In the early years, the asset is being depreciated more quickly for tax purposes than it is for financial reporting purposes and vice versa in the later years. Hence in the early years, actual taxes payable will be less than those reported for bookkeeping purposes, giving rise to deferred taxes. By the end of the useful life of the asset, cumulative actual taxes payable equals cumulative reported taxes payable, so the deferred tax balance is zero. Choice (a) is incorrect because the difference between accumulated depreciation for tax and for reporting purposes will only increase for the first few years of the life of the asset. Choice (b) is incorrect because the amount of deferred taxes is not constant over the life of the asset. Choice (d) is incorrect because the opposite is true

Subject Area: Regulatory, legal, and economics—taxation schemes. Source: CIA 1194, IV-69.

81. **(a)** Cash flows are calculated as: Net income + Depreciation + Deferred tax for the current period. Hence cash flows are the same regardless of the depreciation method used for reporting purposes. Choices (b), (c), and (d) are incorrect because cash flows are unaffected by the method of depreciation used for reporting purposes.

Subject Area: Regulatory, legal, and economics—taxation schemes. Source: CIA 1194, IV-70.

Contracts

82. **(c)** There must be an absence of an invalidating contract, such as duress, undue influence, misrepresentation, or mistake. That is, the purpose should be legal. The four basic requirements include mutual assent, consideration, legality of object, and capacity.

Subject Area: Regulatory, legal, and economics—contracts. Source: CBM, Volume two.

83. **(b)** Consideration occurs when each party to a contract must intentionally exchange a legal benefit or incur a legal detriment as an inducement to the other party to make a return exchange.

Subject Area: Regulatory, legal, and economics—contracts. Source: CBM, Volume two.

84. **(c)** Though in a limited number of instances a contract must be evidenced by a writing to be enforceable, in most cases an oral contract is binding and enforceable.

Subject Area: Regulatory, legal, and economics—contracts. Source: CBM, Volume two.

85. **(c)** A promise is between two individuals: a promisor (a person making a promise) and a promisee (the person to whom a promise is made).

Subject Area: Regulatory, legal, and economics—contracts. Source: CBM, Volume two.

86. **(c)** The four basic requirements of a contract are as follows: (1) mutual assent, (2) consideration, (3) legality of object, and (4) capacity.

Subject Area: Regulatory, legal, and economics—contracts. Source: CBM, Volume two.

87. **(d)** A quasi contract is an obligation not based upon contract that is imposed to avoid injustice.

Subject Area: Regulatory, legal, and economics—contracts. Source: CBM, Volume two.

88. **(d)** The UCC applies to personal property contacts and does not apply to employment, service, or insurance contracts.

Subject Area: Regulatory, legal, and economics—contracts. Source: CBM, Volume two.

89. **(d)** As a general rule, promises are not enforceable if they do not meet all the requirements of a contract. Nevertheless, in certain circumstances, the courts enforce noncontractual promises under the doctrine of promissory estoppel in order to avoid injustice.

Subject Area: Regulatory, legal, and economics—contracts. Source: CBM, Volume two.

90. **(a)** Under a warranty designated as full, the warrantor must agree to repair the product, without charge, to conform with the warranty; no limitation must be placed on the duration of any implied warranty; the consumer must be given the option of a refund or replacement if repair is unsuccessful; and consequential damages may be excluded only if the warranty conspicuously indicates their exclusion.

Subject Area: Regulatory, legal, and economics—contracts. Source: Author.

91. **(b)** The FTC has employed three remedies: (1) affirmative disclosure, (2) corrective advertising, and (3) multiple products order.

Subject Area: Regulatory, legal, and economics—contracts. Source: CBM, Volume two.

92. **(d)** The Magnuson-Moss Warranty Act provides for (1) disclosure in clear and understandable language of the warranty that is to be offered, (2) a description of the warranty as either "full" or "limited," (3) a prohibition against disclaiming implied warranties if a written warranty is given, and (4) an optional informal settlement mechanism.

Subject Area: Regulatory, legal, and economics—contracts. Source: CBM, Volume two.

93. **(d)** An implied warranty, unlike an express warranty, is not found in the language of the sales contract or in a specific affirmation or promise by the seller. Instead, it exists by operation of law. An implied warranty arises out of the circumstances under which the parties enter into their contract and depends on factors such as the type of contract or sale entered into the seller's merchant or nonmerchant status, the conduct of the parties, and the applicability of other statutes.

Subject Area: Regulatory, legal, and economics—contracts. Source: CBM, Volume two.

94. **(d)** Under the Code's warranty of title, the seller implicitly warrants (1) that the title conveyed is good and its transfer rightful and (2) that the goods are subject to no security interest or other lien of which the buyer did not know at the time of contracting. A warranty of title may be excluded only by specific language or by certain circumstances.

Subject Area: Regulatory, legal, and economics—contracts. Source: Author.

95. **(d)** An express warranty is an explicit undertaking by the seller with respect to the quality, description, condition, or performability of the goods. The undertaking may consist of an affirmation of fact or a promise that relates to the goods, a description of the goods, or a sample or model of the goods.

Subject Area: Regulatory, legal, and economics—contracts. Source: CBM, Volume two.

96. **(a)** An implied warranty, unlike an express warranty, is not found in the language of the sales contract or in a specific affirmation or promise by the seller. Instead, it exists by operation of law. An implied warranty arises out of the circumstances under which the parties enter into their contract and depends on factors such as the type of contract or sale entered into, the seller's merchant or nonmerchant status, the conduct of the parties, and the applicability of other statutes.

Subject Area: Regulatory, legal, and economics—contracts. Source: CBM, Volume two.

97. (d) An express warranty is an explicit undertaking by the seller with respect to the quality, description, condition, or performability of the goods. The undertaking may consist of an affirmation of fact or a promise that relates to the goods, a description of the goods, or a sample or model of the goods.

Subject Area: Regulatory, legal, and economics—contracts. Source: Author.

98. (a) The implied warranty of merchantability provides that the goods are reasonably fit for the ordinary purposes for which they are used, pass without objection in the trade under the contract description, and are of fair, average quality.

Subject Area: Regulatory, legal, and economics—contracts. Source: CBM, Volume two.

99. (b) A merchant-seller makes an implied warranty of the merchantability of goods that are of the kind in which he deals. Unlike the warranty of merchantability, the implied warranty of fitness for a particular purpose applies to any seller, whether or not he is a merchant.

Subject Area: Regulatory, legal, and economics—contracts. Source: Author.

100. (c) If the buyer inspects the goods before entering into the contract, implied warranties do not apply to defects that are apparent on examination. Moreover, there is no implied warranty on defects that an examination ought to have revealed not only when the buyer has examined the goods as fully as desired, but also when the buyer has refused to examine the goods.

Subject Area: Regulatory, legal, and economics—contracts. Source: CBM, Volume two.

101. (d) Under the strict liability in tort cases, the manufacturer is liable (1) when there is a defect in design or manufacturing or (2) when the seller or manufacturer failed to warn the consumer about the defect. However, the manufacturer or seller is not liable if the condition of the product at the time of injury is substantially changed from the condition in which the manufacturer or seller sold the product to the consumer.

Subject Area: Regulatory, legal, and economics—contracts. Source: Author.

102. (d) A warranty may arise out of the mere existence of a sale (a warranty of title), out of any affirmation of fact or promise made by the seller to the buyer (an express warranty), or out of the circumstances under which the sale is made (an implied warranty).

Subject Area: Regulatory, legal, and economics—contracts. Source: CBM, Volume two.

Legal Evidence

103. (a) Legal evidence relies heavily on oral testimony.

Subject Area: Regulatory, legal, and economics—legal evidence. Source: Author.

104. (a) Oral evidence cannot be used to dispute a written instrument since the instrument is considered the best evidence.

Subject Area: Regulatory, legal, and economics—legal evidence. Source: Author.

105. (b) Best evidence is the primary evidence since it is the most natural and satisfactory proof of the fact under investigation.

Subject Area: Regulatory, legal, and economics—legal evidence. Source: Author.

106. (d) Hearsay evidence is secondhand evidence since someone other than the witness is making the statement.

Subject Area: Regulatory, legal, and economics—legal evidence. Source: Author.

107. (c) Corroborative evidence is additional evidence of a different character concerning the same point or issue.

Subject Area: Regulatory, legal, and economics—legal evidence. Source: Author.

108. (d) Photographs are hearsay evidence and are admissible in the court if properly authenticated.

Subject Area: Regulatory, legal, and economics—legal evidence. Source: Author.

109. (b) Cross-examination is hearsay evidence, which is done by putting the witnesses under oath and questioning them about what they saw or heard.

Subject Area: Regulatory, legal, and economics—legal evidence. Source: Author.

110. (b) Conclusive evidence cannot be contradicted since it is incontrovertible.

Subject Area: Regulatory, legal, and economics—legal evidence. Source: Author.

111. (c) Direct evidence is one of the eight types of legal evidence, and it does not require inference to prove the fact or falsity.

Subject Area: Regulatory, legal, and economics—legal evidence. Source: Author.

112. (b) Conclusive evidence needs no corroboration since it is very strong by itself.

Subject Area: Regulatory, legal, and economics—legal evidence. Source: Author.

113. (a) Best evidence is confined to documentary evidence (writings or documents). Oral evidence and a copy of writing are examples of secondary evidence.

Subject Area: Regulatory, legal, and economics—legal evidence. Source: Author.

114. (c) Corroboration occurs whenever evidence collected from two separate sources confirm each other. Here sources include interviews and detail testing. Choice (a) is incorrect because this is direct evidence due to detail testing. Choice (b) is incorrect because this is not a circumstantial evidence as it is direct evidence. Subjective evidence is generally opinion oriented, is not dependable for reaching audit conclusions, and it is not relevant here (choice d).

Subject Area: Regulatory, legal, and economics—legal evidence. Source: CIA 592, II-25.

Key Economic Indicators

115. (c) Eight categories of the consumer price index (CPI) include food and beverages, housing, apparel, transportation, medical care, recreation, education and communication, and other goods and services (e.g., haircuts, college tuition, and bank fees). Taxes that are directly associated with the prices of specific goods and services, such as sales and excise taxes, are also included. The CPI includes various governmental charged user fees, such as water and sewage charges, auto registration fees, and vehicle tolls. Taxes not directly associated with the purchase of consumer goods and services, such as income taxes and social security taxes, are excluded. In addition, the CPI does not include investment items, such as stocks, bonds, real estate, and life insurance, because they relate to savings not daily living expenses.

Subject Area: Regulatory, legal, and economics—key economic indicators. Source: Author.

116. (b) Medical care is included in the calculation of the consumer price index (CPI). Stocks and bonds, real estate, and life insurance are not included in the CPI.

Subject Area: Regulatory, legal, and economics—key economic indicators. Source: Author.

117. (c) Both income taxes and social security taxes are not included in the calculation of the consumer price index (CPI).

Subject Area: Regulatory, legal, and economics—key economic indicators. Source: Author.

118. (a) Only urban residents (consumers) are included in the CPI calculation. Excluded from the population are rural residents outside metropolitan areas, all farm residents, the military personnel, and individuals in institutions.

Subject Area: Regulatory, legal, and economics—key economic indicators. Source: Author.

119. (c) The CPI is a measure of the average change in prices paid by urban consumers for a fixed basket of goods and services. The CPI is not a cost-of-living index, since it is not defined in absolute dollars. Intercity or interregional cost-of-living comparisons are not possible with the CPI data. The CPI simply measures the cost of maintaining the same purchases over time or each geographic area. The CPI data do not show base year figures for each geographic area in dollar terms.

Subject Area: Regulatory, legal, and economics—key economic indicators. Source: Author.

120. (c) By definition, the producer price index (PPI) actually measures changes in net unit revenues received by US producers. Taxes received by the government are not included. It includes sales promotions and rebates offered by manufacturers but do not include car dealer rebates offered to a customer. The PPI attempts to capture actual transaction prices, not list prices.

Subject Area: Regulatory, legal, and economics—key economic indicators. Source: Author.

121. (d) Gross domestic product (GDP) is the broadest measure of the health of the US economy. Real GDP is defined as the output or total value of all goods and services produced by labor and investment in the US GDP data release date generally lags other economic indicators' release date. As such, other indicators "build up" to the market's anticipation of how the GDP numbers describe the state of the economy. GDP data reflect income as well as expenditure flows, and it is a lagging indicator. Both PPI and CPI are leading economic indicators. The purchasing managers' index a composite index used by financial analysts to help project government-produced economic indicators related to manufacturing and industrial production. The composite index leads the business cycle, but the lead varies significantly from cycle to cycle (peaks and troughs).

Subject Area: Regulatory, legal, and economics—key economic indicators. Source: Author.

122. (a) Gross national product (GNP) is a measure of national output related to GDP; it includes production with inputs owned by US citizens but not production from domestic inputs that are foreign owned. Net national product (NNP) is a measure of the national economy that is equal to GNP minus depreciation. GNP is more of a measure of income since it reflects income from domestic production (GDP) plus net income from abroad.

Subject Area: Regulatory, legal, and economics—key economic indicators. Source: Author.

123. (d) GDP deflator is a measure of the average price level in the US economy. Exports and imports, as well as all components of nominal and real GDP, enter the calculations for GDP deflators. Two most commonly used GDP deflators are the implicit GDP deflator and the fixed-weighted GDP deflator. The implicit GDP deflator is the ratio of nominal GDP to real GDP. The fixed-weighted GDP deflator has fixed weights for the components based on expenditure shares in the base year. Sharp swings in quarterly GDP deflators are often caused by changes in prices for oil, apparel, and computers as well as by annual wage increases for government employees and occasionally by drought or other disasters affecting crops and commodities.

Subject Area: Regulatory, legal, and economics—key economic indicators. Source: Author.

124. (c) Examples of leading indicators include: average workweek of production workers in manufacturing; average initial weekly claims for state unemployment insurance; new orders for consumer goods and materials, adjusted for inflation; vendor performance; new orders for nonmilitary capital goods, adjusted for inflation; new building permits issued; index of stock prices; money supply; spread between rates on 10-year Treasury bonds and federal funds; and index of consumer expectations.

Subject Area: Regulatory, legal, and economics—key economic indicators. Source: CBM, Volume two.

125. (c) Diffusion indices are highly correlated with growth rates expressed by leading indicators. That is, a low diffusion index is associated with low growth rates, and a high diffusion index is associated with high growth rates. When a diffusion index is 40%, it means that 60% of the leading indicators have fallen.

Subject Area: Regulatory, legal, and economics—key economic indicators. Source: CBM, Volume two.

126. (a) Econometric models force the forecaster to make explicit assumptions about the linkages among the variables in the economic system being examined. In other words, the forecaster must deal with causal relations. This produces logical consistency in the forecast model and increase reliability.

Subject Area: Regulatory, legal, and economics—key economic indicators. Source: CBM, Volume two.

127. (a) The average prime rate charged by banks is an example of lagging economic indicator. The other choices are examples of leading economic indicators.

Subject Area: Regulatory, legal, and economics—key economic indicators. Source: Author.

128. (d) Stock price is an example of leading indicator of business cycle.

Subject Area: Regulatory, legal, and economics—key economic indicators. Source: CBM, Volume two.

129. (b) The term "independent indicators" is meaningless here. Leading, lagging, and coincident indicators are relevant to the composite economic index. The purchasing managers' index is a composite index based on data from a monthly report.

Subject Area: Regulatory, legal, and economics—key economic indicators. Source: CBM, Volume two.

130. (a) The coincident economic indicator is primarily used as a tool for dating the business cycle, that is, determining turning points such as cyclical peaks and troughs. Manufacturing and trade sales will determine whether a business cycle is turning into peaks or troughs. Average prime rates and commercial and industrial loans are examples of lagging indicators while the index of consumer expectations is an example of leading economic indicators.

Subject Area: Regulatory, legal, and economics—key economic indicators. Source: CBM, Volume two.

131. (b) Possible economic indicators that might indicate that full employment has been reached in the economy include: (1) low number of new unemployment claims filed, (2) rise of bottlenecks and imbalances in labor markets in certain sectors of the economy, (3) high number of hours in the average workweek, (4) high level of manufacturing capacity utilization, and (5) labor shortages, which can increase wages in certain sectors of the economy.

Subject Area: Regulatory, legal, and economics—key economic indicators. Source: Author.

132. (b) Economic profits include what is needed to compensate the risk of an entrepreneur. Choice (a) is incorrect because labor costs are already included in both. Choice (c) is incorrect because all labor costs are already included in both. Choice (d) is incorrect because all labor, capital, and land costs are already included in both.

Subject Area: Regulatory, legal, and economics—key economic indicators. Source: CIA 597, IV-57.

133. (a) Initial claims of unemployment is a lead indicator but chronic unemployment is a lag variable. Choice (b) is incorrect because orders for consumer and producer goods lead the economy. Choice (c) is incorrect because housing starts lead the economy. Choice (d) is incorrect because consumer expectations lead the economy.

Subject Area: Regulatory, legal, and economics—key economic indicators. Source: CIA 597, IV-58.

134. (d) The major components of real GDP are total worker hours and labor productivity. Choice (a) is incorrect because the definition of the labor force would not affect the total hours worked. Choice (b) is incorrect because the word "real" means discounting for inflation. Choice (c) is incorrect because national income accounts do not address the quality of output.

Subject Area: Regulatory, legal, and economics—key economic indicators. Source: CIA 597, IV-59.

135. (c) When the emphasis changed in the 1930s, union membership grew. Choice (a) is incorrect because the shift from manufactured goods to services has reduced strong union areas. Choice (b) is incorrect because part-time workers are not as dedicated to the workforce and are thus harder for unions to recruit. Choice (d) is incorrect because as union wage demands increase, manufacturers reduce costs by automating.

Subject Area: Regulatory, legal, and economics—key economic indicators. Source: CIA 597, IV-57.

136. (d) If gross investment is less than depreciation, new investment is insufficient to replace the usage of existing capital and the capital stock of the economy is shrinking. Choice (a) is incorrect. When gross investment exceeds depreciation, new investment is greater than the usage of existing capital and the capital stock is growing, not shrinking. Choices (b) and (c) are incorrect. When gross investment equals depreciation, new investment is just sufficient to replace the usage of existing capital and the capital stock is constant.

Subject Area: Regulatory, legal, and economics—key economic indicators. Source: CIA 597, IV-73.

137. (c) Net national product is calculated as the market value of all final goods and services less capital consumption allowance. Choice (a) is incorrect because net national product is calculated net of capital consumption allowance. Choice (b) is incorrect because net national product includes only final goods since the inclusion of intermediate goods would involve double counting. Also, net national product is calculated net of capital consumption allowance. Choice (d) is incorrect because net national product does not include intermediate goods since this would involve double counting.

Subject Area: Regulatory, legal, and economics—key economic indicators. Source: CIA 1196, IV-59.

138. (a) The 2003 price index using 2000 as a reference period is the price of the 2003 market basket in 2003 relative to the price of the same basket of goods and services in 2000. In general, the price index in a given year is calculated as: (Price of market basket in a given year/Price of the same market basket in the base year) x 100. Choice (b) is incorrect because it is the 2003 market basket that is used to calculate the 2003 price index, not the 2000 market basket. Choice (c) is incorrect because the 2003 market basket is used in both the numerator and the denominator. The price index compares the 2003 and 2000 prices of the same market basket. Choice (d) is incorrect because it should be the 2003 market basket that is used to calculate the 2000 price index and the convention is to calculate the 2003 price relative to the 2000 price.

Subject Area: Regulatory, legal, and economics—key economic indicators. Source: CIA 1195, IV-55.

139. (a) Under the output approach, all four items are added to obtain the gross national product. Choices (b), (c), and (d) are incorrect because under the output approach, all four items are added, none are subtracted, in calculating gross national product.

Subject Area: Regulatory, legal, and economics—key economic indicators. Source: CIA 1195, IV-57

140. (d) Craft unions achieve higher wages for their members by decreasing the supply of labor. This is accomplished through the use of restrictive membership policies. Choices (a) and (b) are incorrect because craft unions do not affect the demand for labor. Choice (c) is incorrect because craft unions decrease, rather than increase, the supply of labor.

Subject Area: Regulatory, legal, and economics—key economic indicators. Source: CIA 1195, IV-60.

141. (c) This is the official definition. Choices (a), (b), and (d) are incorrect because they are distractors. Answer is definitional in nature.

Subject Area: Regulatory, legal, and economics—key economic indicators. Source: CIA 590, IV-67.

142. (b) The CPI is based on a fixed market basket of consumer goods and services purchased by a "typical" urban consumer. It measures changes in the costliness of a constant standard of living since the market basket weights are fixed. It therefore ignores changes in consumption patterns in response to changes in relative prices. Choice (a) is incorrect because the CPI does not take qualitative improvements into account. Choice (c) is incorrect because the GNP deflator is not a "fixed weight" index. Rather, the GNP deflator is calculated by first establishing the market basket on the basis of output in a particular year and then determining what the price of that composition of goods would have been in the base year. Choice (d) is incorrect because the CPI is based on a fixed market basket of consumer goods and services and does not incorporate changes in consumer preferences from year to year.

Subject Area: Regulatory, legal, and economics—key economic indicators. Source: CIA 594, IV-56.

143. (b) A rise in imports will cause a fall in net exports and gross national product (GNP). Choice (a) is incorrect. By definition, GNP = C + I + G + X where C is consumption, I is investment, G is government, and X is net exports (exports-imports). Therefore, GNP will rise with an increase in consumption. Choice (c) is incorrect because an increase in exports will increase GNP. Choice (d) is incorrect because an increase in inflation will increase GNP.

Subject Area: Regulatory, legal, and economics—key economic indicators. Source: CIA 1193, IV-64.

144. (a) The economic cost of unemployment can be described by the amount by which actual GNP falls short of potential GNP. This is known as the GNP gap. Choice (b) is incorrect because the amount by which aggregate expenditures fall short of the full-employment level of net national product describes a recessionary gap. Choice (c) is incorrect because the amount by which aggregate spending exceeds the full-employment level of net national product describes an inflationary gap. Choice (d) is incorrect because the amount by which merchandise imports exceed exports describes a trade deficit.

Subject Area: Regulatory, legal, and economics—key economic indicators. Source: CIA 1193, IV-67.

145. (c) Cost-push inflation results from a decrease in aggregate supply and is accompanied by decreased in real output and employment. Demand-pull inflation is the result of an increase in aggregate demand. Choices (a), (b), and (d) are incorrect because they would not be involved with a wage-price inflation.

Subject Area: Regulatory, legal, and economics—key economic indicators. Source: CIA 1192, IV-69.

146. (a) Inflation tends to benefit borrowers at the expense of lenders because the dollars repaid have less purchasing power than those borrowed. Lenders attempt to anticipate the cost of inflation and include the effect in their interest rates. However, unanticipated inflation would tend to benefit the borrower. Choice (b) is incorrect because inflation tends to benefit borrowers, not lenders, because the dollars repaid have less purchasing power than those borrowed. Choice (c) is incorrect because as inflation causes prices to rise, the purchasing power of savings decreases. Therefore, savers do not benefit from inflation. Choice (d) is incorrect because as inflation causes prices to rise, the purchasing power of a fixed income decreases. Therefore, fixed-income recipients do not benefit form inflation.

Subject Area: Regulatory, legal, and economics—key economic indicators. Source: CIA 1191, IV-69.

147. (a) Frictional unemployment (whereby at any time some workers are in the process of voluntarily switching jobs), structural unemployment (whereby changes in technology and demand alter the needed work force composition) and cyclical unemployment (caused by inevitable business cycles) are generally considered unavoidable factors preventing the achievement of 100% employment of the workforce. Choice (b) is incorrect. Though cost-push inflation may lead to cyclical unemployment, many economists feel that demand-pull inflation is more closely associated with increased employment. Therefore, these types of inflation are not generally considered factors preventing the achievement of 100% employment. Choice (c) is incorrect. Measurements of employment levels are generally made after excluding those not considered actively in the potential labor force, such as those voluntarily unemployed or not seeking employment. Therefore, even though such individuals inevitably exist, they are not unavoidable factors preventing the achievement of 100% employment. Choice (d) is incorrect. International specialization and resource allocation are factors of the concept of comparative advantage, by which countries strive to produce those products that they are best suited to produce in the international marketplace. Successful application of these factors would tend to reduce unemployment in the exercising country, and therefore, would not be considered factors preventing the achievement of 100% employment.

Subject Area: Regulatory, legal, and economics—key economic indicators. Source: CIA 592, IV-69.

148. (d) The natural rate of unemployment (or "full-employment unemployment") is defined as total unavoidable unemployment or the sum of frictional plus structural unemployment. Choice (a) is incorrect because cyclical unemployment is avoidable unemployment caused by the recession phase of the business cycle. Choice (b) is incorrect because frictional (or "search") unemployment is unavoidable unemployment caused by the process of workers voluntarily switching jobs. Choice (c) is incorrect because structural unemployment is the unavoidable unemployment caused by important changes in the structure of consumer demand over time.

Subject Area: Regulatory, legal, and economics—key economic indicators. Source: CIA 1191, IV-68.

149. (b) Structural unemployment is impacted by the quality of labor. Choice (a) is incorrect because cyclical unemployment is affected by upturns and downturns in the economy. Choice (c) is incorrect because frictional unemployment relates to individuals in transition between jobs. Choice (d) is incorrect because productivity rates would be expected to drop as the quality of labor drops.

Subject Area: Regulatory, legal, and economics—key economic indicators. Source: CIA 591, IV-69.

Basic Economics

150. (c) Incremental profit refers to a gain or loss associated with a given managerial decision.
Subject Area: Regulatory, legal, and economics—basic economics. Source: Author.

151. (b) Manufacturing capacity has an opportunity cost. Excess capacity that is not utilized is a waste of valuable resources. If the excess capacity is put to good use such as manufacturing a new product, then the incremental profit will be positive.
Subject Area: Regulatory, legal, and economics—basic economics. Source: CBM, Volume two.

152. (a) Revenue is the driving force and results from increasing sales. Profits will be maximized when revenues are maximized and costs are minimized.
Subject Area: Regulatory, legal, and economics—basic economics. Source: CBM, Volume two.

153. (d) When the marginal revenue is greater than the average revenue, the average must be increasing. At some output level, the marginal revenue equals the average revenue.
Subject Area: Regulatory, legal, and economics—basic economics. Source: Author.

154. (d) The incremental change is the change resulting from a given managerial decision.
Subject Area: Regulatory, legal, and economics—basic economics. Source: CBM, Volume two.

155. (a) Total revenue increases as long as the marginal revenue increases. When the marginal revenue equals zero, the total revenue is not going to increase reaching its maximum level.
Subject Area: Regulatory, legal, and economics—basic economics. Source: CBM, Volume two.

156. (a) Marginal profit is the change in total profit due to a one-unit change in output.
Subject Area: Regulatory, legal, and economics—basic economics. Source: Author.

157. (b) Marginal cost is the change in total cost following a one-unit change in output.
Subject Area: Regulatory, legal, and economics—basic economics. Source: CBM, Volume two.

158. (d) When the marginal is greater than the average, the average must be increasing. If total revenue increases at a constant rate, then the average revenue acts the same.
Subject Area: Regulatory, legal, and economics—basic economics. Source: Author.

159. (b) At some output level, average profit will be equal to marginal profit, and the average profit is maximized.
Subject Area: Regulatory, legal, and economics—basic economics. Source: Author.

160. (b) When marginal profit is positive, total profit is increasing; when marginal profit is negative, total profit is decreasing. The marginal profit increases greater than the average profit.
Subject Area: Regulatory, legal, and economics—basic economics. Source: Author.

161. (a) The optimal output level is determined when marginal revenue is equal to marginal cost, marginal profit is zero, and total profit is maximized.
Subject Area: Regulatory, legal, and economics—basic economics. Source: Author.

162. (d) Maximization of the profit function occurs at the point where the marginal switches from positive value to negative value.
Subject Area: Regulatory, legal, and economics—basic economics. Source: CBM, Volume two.

163. (b) When marginal profit is positive, total profit is increasing; when marginal profit is negative, total profit is decreasing.
Subject Area: Regulatory, legal, and economics—basic economics. Source: Author.

164. (c) When marginal profit is positive, total profit is increasing; when marginal profit is negative, total profit is decreasing.
Subject Area: Regulatory, legal, and economics—basic economics. Source: CBM, Volume two.

165. (a) Normal profit is sales minus all costs, where cost equals average total cost.
Subject Area: Regulatory, legal, and economics—basic economics. Source: CBM, Volume two.

166. (d) Profit maximization requires that a firm operate at the output level at which marginal revenue and marginal cost are equal. With price constant, average revenue equals marginal revenue. Therefore, maximum profits result when market price is set equal to marginal cost for firms in a perfectly competitive industry.
Subject Area: Regulatory, legal, and economics—basic economics. Source: CBM, Volume two.

167. (d) Profit maximization requires that a firm operate at the output level at which marginal revenue and marginal cost are equal.
Subject Area: Regulatory, legal, and economics—basic economics. Source: CBM, Volume two.

168. (d) When a monopoly equates marginal revenue and marginal cost, it simultaneously determines the output level and the market price for its product.
Subject Area: Regulatory, legal, and economics—basic economics. Source: CBM, Volume two.

169. (a) In monopoly markets, barriers to entry or exit can allow above normal profits, even over the long run. Under these conditions, price exceeds marginal revenue.
Subject Area: Regulatory, legal, and economics—basic economics. Source: CBM, Volume two.

170. (b) A monopsony is a market with one buyer.
Subject Area: Regulatory, legal, and economics—basic economics. Source: Author.

171. (a) In a perfectly competitive market, cost, price, and product quality information is known by all buyers and all sellers.
Subject Area: Regulatory, legal, and economics—basic economics. Source: CBM, Volume two.

172. (c) A barrier to exit is any restriction on the ability of incumbents to redeploy assets from one industry or line of business to another.

Subject Area: Regulatory, legal, and economics—basic economics. Source: CBM, Volume two.

173. (b) Products are perceived to be heterogeneous or unique in both monopolistic and oligopolistic market structures.

Subject Area: Regulatory, legal, and economics—basic economics. Source: CBM, Volume two.

174. (d) Monopolistic competition exists when individual producers have moderate influence over product prices, where each product enjoys a degree of uniqueness in the perception of consumers.

Subject Area: Regulatory, legal, and economics—basic economics. Source: CBM, Volume two.

175. (c) There is perfect dissemination of information in monopolistic competition. Cost, price, and product quality information are known by all buyers and all sellers.

Subject Area: Regulatory, legal, and economics—basic economics. Source: CBM, Volume two.

176. (a) In a monopolistic competitive industry, there is product heterogeneity. The output of each firm is perceived to be essentially different from, though comparable with, the output of other firms in the industry.

Subject Area: Regulatory, legal, and economics—basic economics. Source: Author.

177. (d) In an oligopoly, if one firm changes its price, other firms react by changing their prices. The demand curve for the initial firm shifts position so that instead of moving along a single demand curve as it changes price, the firm moves to an entirely new demand curve.

Subject Area: Regulatory, legal, and economics—basic economics. Source: CBM, Volume two.

178. (d) A kinked demand curve results from different competitor reactions to price changes.

Subject Area: Regulatory, legal, and economics—basic economics. Source: Author.

179. (b) Known as the theory of consumer behavior, direct demand relates to personal consumption products. This model is appropriate for analyzing individual demand for goods and services that directly satisfy consumer desires.

Subject Area: Regulatory, legal, and economics—basic economics. Source: Author.

180. (a) Derived demand is the demand for inputs used in production. Inputs could be raw materials, parts, components, labor, capital, and energy.

Subject Area: Regulatory, legal, and economics—basic economics. Source: CBM, Volume two.

181. (c) Individual firms will expand or reduce supply based on the expected impact of profits. Factors that influence supply include price of the product itself, prices of related products, technology, and changes in input prices such as raw material costs and labor wage rates.

Subject Area: Regulatory, legal, and economics—basic economics. Source: CBM, Volume two.

182. (d) When the price of one product increases, there is a reduction in demand for another. Goods that are inversely related in this manner are known as complements; they are used together rather than in place of each other.

Subject Area: Regulatory, legal, and economics—basic economics. Source: Author.

183. (a) The supply curve expresses the relation between the price charged and the quantity supplied, holding constant the effects of all other variables.

Subject Area: Regulatory, legal, and economics—basic economics. Source: CBM, Volume two.

184. (d) The market equilibrium price, or the market-clearing price, clears the market of all supplied products. In other words, market equilibrium describes a condition of perfect balance in the quantity demanded and the quantity supplied at a given price.

Subject Area: Regulatory, legal, and economics—basic economics. Source: Author.

185. (b) A surplus is created when producers more of a product at a given price than buyers demand. Surplus describes a condition of excess supply. Prices tend to decline as firms recognize that consumers are unwilling to purchase the quantity of product available at prevailing prices.

Subject Area: Regulatory, legal, and economics—basic economics. Source: CBM, Volume two.

186. (a) Point elasticity measures elasticity at a given point on a function. The point elasticity concept is used to measure the effect on a dependent variable Y, in this case advertising, of a very small or marginal change in an independent variable X, in this case demand.

Subject Area: Regulatory, legal, and economics—basic economics. Source: Author.

187. (b) The concept of cross-price elasticity is used to examine the responsiveness of demand for one product to changes in the price of another.

Subject Area: Regulatory, legal, and economics—basic economics. Source: CBM, Volume two.

188. (a) Elasticity is defined as the percentage change in a dependent variable, Y, resulting from a one percent change in the value of an independent variable, X.

Subject Area: Regulatory, legal, and economics—basic economics. Source: CBM, Volume two.

189. (b) Point elasticity measures elasticity at a given point on a function.

Subject Area: Regulatory, legal, and economics—basic economics. Source: CBM, Volume two.

190. (b) In general, a direct relation between the price of one product and the demand for a second product holds for all substitutes. A price increase for a given product will increase demand for substitutes; a price decrease for a given product will decrease demand for substitutes.

Subject Area: Regulatory, legal, and economics—basic economics. Source: Author.

191. (c) Individuals are viewed as attempting to maximize the total utility or satisfaction provided by the goods and services they acquire and consume.

Subject Area: Regulatory, legal, and economics—basic economics. Source: CBM, Volume two.

192. (a) The cross-price elasticity is negative for complements; price and quantity move in opposite directions for complementary goods and services.

Subject Area: Regulatory, legal, and economics—basic economics. Source: CBM, Volume two.

193. (b) Goods that have positive elasticity are referred to as cyclical normal goods. Accordingly, demand is strongly affected by changing economic conditions.
Subject Area: Regulatory, legal, and economics—basic economics. Source: CBM, Volume two.

194. (c) Peak and off-peak pricing, price discrimination, and joint product pricing practices are efficient means for operating so that marginal revenue is equal to marginal cost for each customer or customer group and product class.
Subject Area: Regulatory, legal, and economics—basic economics. Source: Author.

195. (a) Frictional unemployment refers to those individuals who are either searching for jobs or are waiting to take jobs in the near future. It is unemployment between jobs or by taking time to find a new job. Structural unemployment refers to those individuals who are unemployed because they lack the requisite skills to find employment in the marketplace. Their skills do not match those needed by employers without retraining, additional education, or possible relocation. Cyclical unemployment (deficit demand unemployment) is the result of a general slowdown in economic activity from a recession or depression, and it is a long-term situation.
Subject Area: Regulatory, legal, and economics—basic economics. Source: Author.

196. (a) In a full employment environment, the natural rate of unemployment is the total of frictional and structural unemployment, with no cyclical unemployment. This situation is said to exist when the labor market is in balance because the total number of job seekers is equal to the total number of job vacancies.
Subject Area: Regulatory, legal, and economics—basic economics. Source: Author.

197. (a) Product differentiation is not a characteristic of a purely competitive market. It is a characteristic of monopolistically competitive markets and may characterize an oligopolistic market. The characteristics listed in the other choices are an indication of a purely competitive market.
Subject Area: Regulatory, legal, and economics—basic economics. Source: CIA Model Exam 1998, IV-78.

198. (a) This is why regulated utilities are permitted. Costs are lower and prices charged to the public could be lower because of quantities of scale. A lack of advertising does not necessarily mean lower prices (choice b.). Quantities are typically lower (choice c.). There is no need for higher quality since there is no competition (choice d.).
Subject Area: Regulatory, legal, and economics—basic economics. Source: CIA Model Exam 2002, IV-71.

199. (a) Selling government securities is contractional because it takes money out of circulation. Lower reserve requirements would fuel the economy because banks could lend more money (choice b.). Lower discount rates would fuel the economy because borrowing would be encouraged (choice c.). Choice (d) is fiscal policy, not monetary policy.
Subject Area: Regulatory, legal, and economics—basic economics. Source: CIA Model Exam 1998, IV-72.

200. (b) Inflation caused by an increase in costs is called cost-push or supply-side inflation. Inflation that is initiated by an increase in aggregate demand is called demand-pull inflation.
Subject Area: Regulatory, legal, and economics—basic economics. Source: Author.

5 INFORMATION TECHNOLOGY (30–40%)

THEORY

5.1 Control Frameworks

Seven types of information technology (IT)-related control frameworks will be discussed in this section. They include: (1) the IIA's system assurance and control (eSAC), (2) ISACF's control objectives for information and related technology (COBIT), (3) ISACF's control objectives for net centric technology (CONCT), (4) AICPA/CICA's SysTrust Principles and Criteria for Systems Reliability, (5) British Standard 7799, A Code of Practice for Information Security Management, (6) OECD's Guidelines for the Security of Information Systems, and (7) IFAC's Managing Security of Information.

(a) **IIA's Systems Assurance and Control.** Electronic systems assurance and control (eSAC) sets the stage for effective technology risk management by providing a framework for evaluating the e-business control environment. Within the context of an organization's mission, values, objectives, and strategies, the different SAC modules will assist in gaining an objective perspective on the organization's IT culture. This knowledge will then aid in providing assurance to customers, regulators, management, and boards that IT risks are understood and managed.

SAC brings executive management, corporate governance entities, and auditors new information to understand, monitor, assess, and mitigate IT risks. It will examine and assess risks that accompany each organizational component, including customers, competitors, regulators, community at large, and owners and investors. The SAC title is enhanced by changing "Auditability" to "Assurance" to recognize the important perspectives of governance and the alliances—both within an organization and between business partners—needed to assure effective security, auditability, and control of information.

(i) **Components of technology challenge.** Components of technology challenge include open systems, technology complexity, information security, privacy concerns, and development and distribution processes.

(A) ***Open systems.*** Internet-based distributed systems have very different characteristics from internally focused, closed private computer information systems. Open systems that use the Internet are the first truly pubic systems, and as such are exposed to more and different risks. Never before have organizations been so accessible to so many. The Internet (the World Wide Web, or Web) is a global client/server environment that evolved due to low-cost powerful computers with large storage capacity, mass communications, and user-friendly software.

(B) ***Technology complexity.*** Dispersion of technology into every department, division, or business unit will provide new challenges to control and assurance. Over both proprietary and Internet connections, organizational system boundaries will blur into those of allies, partners, suppliers, and end users. Such widespread distribution will challenge already inadequate abilities to provide security, control, and privacy.

Control migration from application code to the environment is a growing trend. Traditional applications—accounting, purchasing, scheduling, manufacturing, inventory, sales, delivery, and collection—are often integrated into enterprise resource planning (ERP) systems. Data resides in one central database, with more responsibility for control. The human resources system and its database may support all employee-related activities, such as payroll, evaluations, training and skills, benefits, and retirement benefits. Customer relationship management (CRM) is a relatively new system made practical by advances in technology.

Proliferation of computers and the Internet has brought technology services into even the smallest of businesses and organizations. Common applications offer enormous economies of scale, and even niche applications can thrive well. Software size and complexity has consumed new capability faster than computer chips can make it available. As more people acquire computers and access spreads to more countries, the current Web will expand to even more products, services, and languages, challenging controls over users' interaction while providing the information and services they seek.

(C) ***Information security.*** Effective security is not only a technology problem, it is a business issue. It must address people's awareness and actions, training, and especially the corporate culture, influenced by management's security consciousness and the tone at the top.

Access to computer system is not an issue, rather the issue is how much access is enough. When access exists, there is the potential for inappropriate access, introduction of errors, possible disclosure, corruption, and destruction of information. Since security is a moving target, there must be a continual risk assessment and management process to examine changing vulnerabilities and consequences, and to prioritize risks and probabilities. This will focus security resources on things that must be protected and threats that can be mitigated at appropriate cost based on cost benefit analysis.

(D) ***Privacy concerns.*** Countries treat privacy matters differently based on their cultures, treaties, and practices. Globalization of business due to the Internet has meant many new laws and regulations to address concerns over specific rights to control personal information. Privacy provisions range from confidentiality of communications to specific access rights. The global privacy landscape involves legislative, regulatory, and cultural considerations of overlapping or conflicting requirements that range from generally acceptable use to more restriction in certain countries.

(E) ***Development and distribution processes.*** The design and development process has changed. Formerly, systems were developed to facilitate existing business operations, but today are frequently seen as a new line of business. E-business and the need to get to market faster often mean expansion of the IT infrastructure outside the organization. Hardware and software, telecommunications, and Web hosting are often outsourced to Internet service providers (ISPs). Providing control, and assurance that controls are deserving of reliance placed on them, grows exponentially more complex as the number of parties and layers grows.

(F) ***Responses to the technology challenge.*** Risk assessment, internal control, and e-assurance are suggested as responses to the technology challenge.

Risk assessment. Functional and technology managers must reject the "silo" attitude or inept behavior towards risks. An organization may do its strategic planning too quickly or not at all, it may not align strategy and enterprise design with market requirements, managers may not look beyond strict areas of their authority, compensating controls may not be designed to mitigate local risks, or teamwork among cross functions may not exist to communicate the nature and severity of risks to senior management.

There is no standard way to measure risks and associated losses since e-commerce risks affect businesses differently. Therefore, each business unit should conduct its own risk assessment, addressing such questions as

- What are the risks?
- How large is the adverse effect of an exposure?
- Are preventive, detective, and corrective controls in place, and are they effective?
- How much security protection against risks is justified?
- Which risks threaten survivability of the business?
- Which risks can be mitigated at relatively low cost?

Internal control. Internal control comprises the activities an organization uses to reduce risks that can affect its mission. The "tone at the top" determines the focus for the entire organization, including the system of internal control. Management has direct responsibility for control and must coordinate efforts to achieve objectives. Although changes in technology present new risks and require different control techniques, basic control objectives remain essentially unchanged.

While definitions of internal control vary, they address the same objectives. The system of internal control is processes and procedures to provide reasonable assurance that goals and objectives are achieved and assure that risk is reduced to an acceptable level of risk.

A cost-benefit analysis should decide which controls—internal or external—mitigate the risks most effectively. To devise an IT risk strategy, management must decide which risks are serious, which can be insured, which controls they can rely on, and which risks require compensating controls. Monitoring for compliance and constant update are essential.

E-assurance. Systems are imperfect, things go wrong, and people seek assurance that prudent controls minimize risk. Assurance services check the degree to which a system deviates from industry standards or management requirements for reliability. Whenever one party makes an assertion that requires review before others can rely on it, there must be an agreed-upon set of criteria against which to measure it, and a process to collect such evidence. When there are few agreed-upon standards, attaining such a goal becomes difficult at best.

Traditional assurance services are being revamped to meet the new challenges. The problem is the ever-shifting nature of risks and controls. As a body of data is developed, these services, along with improvements in firewalls and intelligence being built into routers, third-party certifications, trusted certificate authorities, digital signatures, and encryption using public key infrastructure (PKI) and the like will combine to improve controls over e-business.

An issue exists as to whether the marketplace—internal or external—will accept that internally provided assurance by internal auditors is effective in enhancing trust. The visible trust marks and Web site seals that external assurance service providers can provide are increasingly seen as viable methods to reassure the users of e-business services. For most organizations, an appropriate balance between using internal and external assurance is the best path.

(ii) **eSAC model.** The eSAC model's assurance objectives or control attributes, such as availability, capability, functionality, protectability, and accountability, are integrated with the COSO's objectives, such as effectiveness and efficiency of operations, financial and other management reporting, compliance with laws and regulations, and safeguarding of assets. Privacy concerns are discussed under protectability and accountability. Next, we will discuss the five assurance objectives of the eSAC model.

(A) ***Availability.*** Information, processes, and services must be available when needed. Specifically, the organization must be able to receive, accept, process, and support transactions in a manner acceptable to its customers. Access via the Internet can mean availability 24/7/365. To ensure availability, the auditor evaluates controls that deal with potential causes of business interruption. These might include

- Physical and logical security of system resources
- Mechanical failure of computer file storage devices
- Malfunction of software or unexpected incompatibilities
- Inadequate computer capacity planning

In the event of a problem, controls must provide for swift recovery to the normal position.

(B) ***Capability.*** Capability means end-to-end reliable and timely completion and fulfillment of all transactions. This means that the system has adequate capacity, communications, and other aspects to consistently meet needs even at peak demand. For systems to provide such services, monitoring of usage, service-level agreements with ISPs, application service providers (ASPs), and others are important controls. It is critical that system and process bottlenecks be identified and eliminated or carefully managed—the goal is to achieve and maintain an efficient and effective balance across the organization.

Efficiency of systems is an aspect of capability that leads to effective use of resources. A key is controlling system development and acquisition methodologies to prevent cost overruns and systems that do not perform as required. To help ensure efficiency of IT, the auditor evaluates controls that deal with causes and risks of excessive costs, characterized as waste and inefficiency. Some of the problems might include

- Weaknesses in controls that result in excessive correction of errors; prevention is usually more efficient
- Controls that consume more resources than the benefits they deliver

Systems that are inefficient may foster user creation of shadow systems that work around the official system. Such duplicate costs are clearly inefficient. The unreliable system must be fixed before the shadow system is halted. The objectives of system development controls are to avoid such issues. Methodologies should result in efficient and appropriate design and development of an application, and ensure that controls, auditability, and security are built into the system.

An information system that is not maintained effectively becomes unreliable. Controls over system maintenance, often called change controls, provide continuity while hardware or software changes are made, and ensure that all changes are documented, approved, and confirmed. System maintenance controls include things like adequate user involvement in requesting, testing, and approving program changes; creating appropriate audit trails, including program change history logs; IT and user personnel approval; and sufficient documentation of program changes. Once complete, controlled production transfer procedures reduce the risk of programmers having the ability to introduce unapproved test versions of programs into production environment.

(C) ***Functionality.*** Functionality means the system provides the facilities, responsiveness, and ease-of-use to meet user needs. Good functionality goes well beyond the minimum transaction processing. It should also provide for recording control information and other issues of concern to management. Preventing problems in functionality includes considering the perspective of untrained, possibly unknown online users. Users can become impatient and may quit without completing a transaction or may resubmit input causing duplicates. To help ensure functionality, the auditor evaluates controls that monitor and provide feedback. Some of these might include

- The display of progress indicators following input
- Positive confirmation of transactions

- Monitoring user abandonment of transactions
- Monitoring system "hang-ups"

Effective information is relevant to the business process, delivered by a functional system. Relevance of information is based on system design, which requires user and management participation to reach functionality. Problems often stem from inadequate specifications due to lack of user involvement in system development, which usually means the resulting application will be ineffective.

To help ensure effectiveness, the auditor evaluates controls over timely, correct, consistent, and usable information. The system should permit flexible display and reports that can be tailored to different audiences. The format in which information is delivered can have a substantial impact on effective communication.

(D) ***Protectability.*** Protectability includes protection of hardware, software, and data from unauthorized access, use, or harm. Robust security is difficult to maintain due to the vast access possible via the Internet, which structure has inherent weaknesses. Controls are needed to safeguard IT assets against loss, and identify when such loss has occurred. Many current controls focus on reducing risks of catastrophic damage, internal fraud, or embezzlement. To ensure protectability, the auditor evaluates general controls over IT that are often grouped as follows:

- **Data security and confidentiality.** Access to data, an important asset, should be limited to those authorized to process or maintain specific data or records. Protecting organizational data is the key responsibility of the information security function and its administrators. The security functions may include restricting access to data through various logical access paths, based on user requirements; restricting access to program libraries and data files on a "need-to-know" basis; and providing the ability to hold users accountable for activities performed.
- **Program security.** Access to program files and libraries should be restricted to authorized personnel through the use of access control and other security software. Program updates should be monitored and controlled using library management software. Appropriate segregation of duties should ensure that the programming function does not have unrestricted access to production programs.
- **Physical security.** Access to computer processors and storage devices should be limited to those (e.g., data center management and computer operations staff) requiring access to perform job functions. Access to the host server computer room should be monitored and controlled (e.g., card access control systems). Physical control over reports containing confidential data should be implemented (e.g., report distribution procedures). Physical safeguards include fire prevention, preventive maintenance, backup of data files, and property insurance.

Many protectability objectives are designed to ensure that data retains its integrity. In other words, that data is complete, accurate, and up-to-date, and cannot be changed on an unauthorized basis. To help ensure integrity, the auditor evaluates controls over causes of erroneous data, often characterized as application controls, complemented by general controls over access. More detailed integrity control objectives include

- Authorized transactions are initially and completely recorded.
- All transactions are completely and accurately entered into the system for processing.
- Approved transactions entered are accepted by the system and processed to completion.
- All transactions are processed only once; no duplicate transactions are processed.
- All transactions are processed accurately, updating the correct files and records.

Procedures should minimize the opportunity for application programmers and users to make unauthorized changes to production programs. Access to system software should be controlled to avoid direct compromise of the integrity of program code, data on file, or results of processing.

Confidentiality and privacy are issues of accountability in compliance, and protectability in making it possible. There is no privacy without security. Confidentiality refers to intellectual property, trade secrets, and strategic plans. Privacy is usually viewed in the context of personal information, including customers, employees, and stockholders, but not corporate entities.

(E) ***Accountability.*** Accountability identifies individual roles, actions, and responsibilities. It includes the concepts of data ownership, identification, and authentication, all fundamental to being able to identify who or what caused a transaction. The audit or transaction trail should have enough information—and be retained long enough—for transactions to be confirmed, if necessary.

Accountability also includes the concept of nonrepudiation. This means that once authenticated, a user cannot disclaim a transaction, as might happen when an online brokerage user seeks to break a trade that turned out to be a bad idea that they nonetheless actually caused.

Accountability also includes issues in granting traceable access to restricted information and software functions. This is a particular problem in IT, where systems analysts, programmers, system administrators, and the like resist controls over their own activities. In some cases, monitoring of such use, while seemingly appropriate, can be turned off by the very system administrator it is designed to watch.

Organizations need to authenticate the identity of people entrusted with authority to change data files or software. Similarly, an organization holding private information has an obligation to authenticate the identity of inquiries before disclosing information. In such cases, accountability and privacy may appear to be in conflict. Accountability means identifying the source of a transaction, while privacy might deny meaningful identification. These objectives can be reconciled with care. Accountability protects everyone, for example where a seller has a legitimate need to authenticate the identity of a buyer for credit purposes, while the holder of the credit card has a legitimate need to authenticate the seller to prevent fraudulent misrepresentation.

To support accountability, information must be sufficient, accurate, timely, and available to management to meet its responsibilities. To help ensure reliability of information, the auditor evaluates controls over unacceptable processing and reporting. These might include

- Information can be supported irrefutably. Controls that provide support are variously known as transaction trails or audit trails.
- Information should be timely. It must be available when decisions are made. This is a common criticism of financial statements issued months after the events.
- Information must be consistent, in accordance with applicable policies. Errors of inappropriate processing, whether programmed or not, are common causes of this effect. Management override can be another.

(b) **Control Objectives for Information and Related Technology.** Control objectives for information and related technology (COBIT) is issued by the Information Systems Audit and Control Foundation (ISACF) is aimed at addressing business objectives. The control objectives make a clear and distinct link to business objectives in order to support significant use outside the audit community. Control objectives are defined in a process-oriented manner following the principle of business reengineering.

An internal control system or framework must be in place to support business processes, and it must be clear how each individual control activity satisfies the information requirements and impacts the resources. Impact on IT resources is highlighted in the COBIT framework together with the business requirements for effectiveness, efficiency, confidentiality, integrity, availability, compliance, and reliability of information that need to be satisfied. Control, which includes policies, organizational structures, practices, and procedures, is management's responsibility. Management, through its corporate governance, must ensure that due diligence is exercised by all individuals involved in the management, use, design, development, maintenance, or operation of information systems.

Business orientation is the main theme of COBIT. It is designed not only to be employed by users and auditors but also—and more importantly—as a comprehensive checklist for business process owners. Increasingly, business practice involves the full empowerment of business process owners as they have total responsibility for all aspects of the business process. In particular, this includes providing adequate controls. The COBIT framework provides a tool for the business process owner that facilitates the discharge of this responsibility.

The COBIT framework starts from a simple and pragmatic premise: in order to provide the information that the organization needs to achieve its objectives, IT resources need to be managed by a set of naturally grouped processes.

The COBIT framework includes: the classification of domains where high-level control objectives apply (domains and processes), an indication of the business requirements for information in that domain, and the IT resources primarily impacted by the control objectives.

COBIT continues with a set of 34 high-level control objectives, one for each of the IT processes, grouped into four domains: (1) planning and organization, (2) acquisition and implementation, (3) delivery and support, and (4) monitoring. It has identified 318 detailed control objectives.

In establishing the list of business requirements, COBIT combines the principles embedded in existing and known reference models.

- Quality requirements cover quality, cost, and delivery.
- Fiduciary requirements (COSO report) cover effectiveness and efficiency of operations, reliability of information, and compliance with laws and regulations.
- Security requirements cover confidentiality, integrity, and availability.

The COBIT framework consists of high-level control objectives and an overall structure for their classification. The underlying theory of the classification is that there are, in essence, three levels of IT efforts when considering the management of IT resources (see Exhibit 5.1). Starting at the bottom, there are activities and tasks needed to achieve a measurable result. Activities have a life-cycle concept while tasks are more discrete. The life-cycle concept has typical control requirements that are different from discrete activities. Processes are then defined one layer up as a series of joined activities or tasks with natural (control) breaks. At the highest level, processes are naturally grouped together into domains.

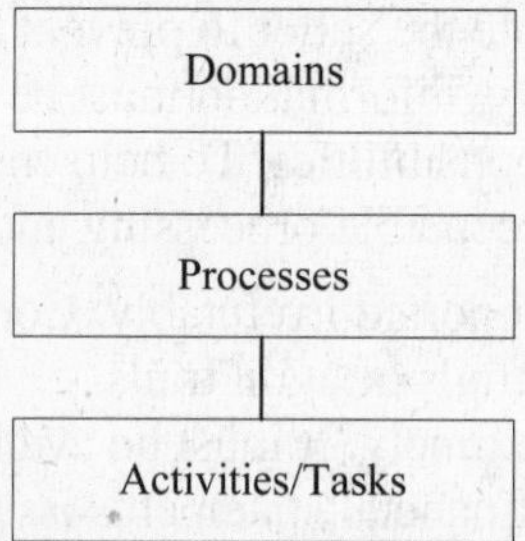

Exhibit 5.1: COBIT classification system

The conceptual framework can be approached from three vantage points: (1) information criteria, (2) IT resources, and (3) IT processes. Four domains were identified: (1) planning and organization, (2) acquisition and implementation, (3) delivery and support, and (4) monitoring.

- **Domain 1: Planning and organization.** This domain covers strategy and tactics and concerns the identification of the ways IT can best contribute to the achievement of business objectives. Furthermore, the realization of the strategic vision needs to be planned, communicated, and managed for different perspectives. Finally, a proper organization as well as a technological infrastructure must be put in place.
- **Domain 2: Acquisition and implementation.** To realize the IT strategy, IT solutions need to be identified, developed, or acquired, as well as implemented and integrated into the business process. In addition, changes in and maintenance of existing systems are covered by this domain to make sure that the life cycle is continued for these systems.
- **Domain 3: Delivery and support.** This domain is concerned with the actual delivery of required services, which range from traditional operations of security to the continuity of training. In order to deliver services, the necessary support processes must be set up. This domain includes the actual processing of data by application systems, often classified under application controls.
- **Domain 4: Monitoring.** All IT processes need to be regularly assessed over time for their quality and compliance with control requirements. This domain thus addresses management's oversight of the organization's control process and independent assurance provided by internal and external audit or obtained from alternative sources.

In summary, in order to provide the information that the organization needs to achieve its objectives, IT governance must be exercised by the organization to ensure that IT resources are managed by a set of naturally grouped IT processes.

DEFINITIONS ACCORDING TO COBIT

General Definitions

Control is defined as the policies, procedures, practices, and organizational structures designed to provide reasonable assurance that business objectives will be achieved and that undesired events will be prevented or detected and corrected.

IT control objective is defined as a statement of the desired result or purpose to be achieved by implementing control procedures in a particular IT activity.

IT governance is defined as a structure of relationships and processes to direct and control an enterprise in order to achieve the enterprise's goals by adding value, while balancing risk versus return, to IT and its processes. COBIT is the model for IT governance.

COBIT's management guidelines are generic and action-oriented for the purpose of answering the following types of management questions: How far should we go, and is the cost justified by the benefit? What are the indicators of good performance? What are the critical success factors? What are the risks of not achieving our objectives? What do others do? How do we measure and compare?

Business Requirements for Information

Effectiveness deals with information being relevant and pertinent to the business process as well as being delivered in a timely, correct, consistent, and usable manner.

Efficiency concerns the provision of information through the optimal (most productive and economical) use of resources.

Confidentiality concerns the protection of sensitive information from unauthorized disclosure.

Integrity is related to the accuracy and completeness of information as well as to its validity in accordance with business values and expectations.

Availability relates to information being available when required by the business process both now and in the future. It also concerns the safeguarding of necessary resources and associated capabilities.

Compliance deals with complying with those laws, regulations, and contractual arrangements to which the business process is subject (i.e., externally imposed business criteria).

Reliability of information relates to the provision of appropriate information for management to operate the entity and for management to exercise its financial and compliance reporting responsibilities.

IT Resources

Data are objects in the widest sense (i.e., external and internal), including structured and nonstructured, graphics, sound, and other forms of data.

Application systems are understood to be the sum of manual and programmed procedures.

Technology covers hardware, operating systems, database management systems, networking, multimedia, and so forth.

Facilities are all the resources used to house and support information systems.

People include staff skills, awareness, and the productivity needed to plan, organize, acquire, deliver, support, and monitor information systems and services.

Money or **capital** was not retained as an IT resource, because it can be considered as an investment into any of the above resources.

(c) **Control Objectives for Net Centric Technology Framework.** Control objectives for net centric technology (CONCT), issued by the ISACF, focus on the following activities: intranet, extranet, internet; data warehouses; and online transaction processing systems. CONCT provides well-structured ways of understanding and assessing the very complex centric technology environment that exists.

The IT governance model for the centric technology has three dimensions. They are: IT control objectives for information services, IT activities, and the IT resources required for the accomplishment of these activities.

(d) **AICPA/CICA SysTrust Principles and Criteria for Systems Reliability.** Several organizations such as AICPA/CICA provide guidance on information security in terms of principles, standards, management, assurance, and measurement.

SysTrust is an assurance service designed to increase the comfort of management, customers, and business partners with the systems that support a business or a particular activity. The SysTrust service entails a public accountant providing an assurance service in which he or she evaluates and tests whether a system is reliable when measured against four essential principles: availability, security, integrity, and maintainability. For each of the four principles, 58 reliability criteria have been established against which a system can be evaluated.

Potential users of this service are shareholders, creditors, bankers, business partners, third-party users who outsource functions to other entities, stakeholders, and anyone who in some way relies on the continued availability, integrity, security, and maintainability of a system. The SysTrust service will help differentiate entities from their competitors because entities that undergo the rigors of a SysTrust engagement will presumably be better service providers—attuned to the risks posed by their environment and equipped with the controls that address those risks.

(e) **British Standard 7799: A Code of Practice for Information Security Management: Specification for Information Security Management Systems.** BS 7799-1 was first issued in 1995 to provide a comprehensive set of controls comprising best practices in information security. It is intended to serve as a single reference point for identifying the range of controls needed for most situations where information systems are used in industry and commerce, and is to be used by large, medium, and small organizations.

BS 7799 treats information as an asset that, like other important business assets, has value to an organization and consequently needs to be suitably protected. Information security protects information from a wide range of threats in order to ensure business continuity, minimize business damage, and maximize return on investments and business opportunities.

Information security is characterized within BS 7799 as the preservation of

- **Confidentiality.** Ensuring that information is accessible only to those authorized to have access
- **Integrity.** Safeguarding the accuracy and completeness of information and processing methods
- **Availability.** Ensuring that authorized users have access to information and associated assets when required

Information security is achieved by implementing a suitable set of controls from BS 7799, which can be policies, practices, procedures, organizational structures, and software functions. These controls help ensure that the specific security objectives of the organization are met.

(f) **OECD's Guidelines for the Security of Information Systems.** The Guidelines for the Security of Information Systems, which are issued by the Organization for Economic Cooperation and Development (OECD), are designed to provide a foundation from which countries and the private sector, acting singly and in concert, may construct a framework for security of information systems. The framework will include laws, codes of conduct, technical measures, management and user practices, and public education and awareness activities. It is hoped that the Guidelines will serve as a benchmark against which the public sector, the private sector, and society can measure their progress.

The Guidelines are intended to

- Raise awareness of risks to information systems and the safeguards available to meet those risks.
- Create a general framework to assist those responsible, in the public and private sectors, for the development and implementation of coherent measures, practices, and procedures for the security of information systems.
- Promote cooperation between the public and private sectors in the development and implementation of such measures, practices, and procedures.
- Foster confidence in information systems and the manner in which they are provided and used.
- Facilitate development and use of information systems, nationally and internationally.
- Promote international cooperation in achieving security of information systems.

Eight principles include

1. Computer security supports the mission of the organization.
2. Computer security is an integral element of sound management.
3. Computer security should be cost-effective.
4. Systems owners have security responsibilities outside their own organizations.

5. Computer security responsibilities and accountability should be made explicit.
6. Computer security requires a comprehensive and integrated approach.
7. Computer security should be periodically reassessed.
8. Computer security is constrained by societal factors.

(g) **IFAC's Managing Security of Information.** International Information Technology Guidelines are issued by the International Federation of Accountants (IFAC), Information Technology Committee, New York, 1998.

Threats to information systems may arise from intentional or unintentional acts and may come from internal or external sources. Threats may emanate from, among others, technical conditions (program bugs, disk crashes), natural disasters (fires, floods), environmental conditions (electrical surges), human factors (lack of training, errors, and omissions), unauthorized access (hacking), or viruses. In addition to these, other threats such as business dependencies (reliance on third-party communications carriers, outsourced operations) that can potentially result in a loss of management control and oversight are increasing in significance.

The objective of information security is "the protection of the interest of those relying on information, and the information systems and communications that deliver the information, from harm resulting from failures of availability, confidentiality, and integrity." For any organization, the security objective is met when

- Information systems are available and usable when required (availability objective).
- Data and information are disclosed only to those who have a right to know it (confidentiality objective).
- Data and information are protected against unauthorized modification (integrity objective).

The relative priority and significance of availability, confidentiality, and integrity vary according to the data within the information systems and the business context in which it is used. Core information security principles presented by the IFAC are derived from the Guidelines published by the OECD.

5.2 Data and Network Communications and Connections

(a) **Computer Network Types.** There are **seven types** of computer networks available today: (1) virtual networks (VNs), (2) wide area networks (WANs), (3) metropolitan area networks (MANs), (4) value-added networks (VANs), (5) local area networks (LANs), (6) multicorporate networks, and (7) integrated services digital network (ISDN) (see Exhibit 5.(2).

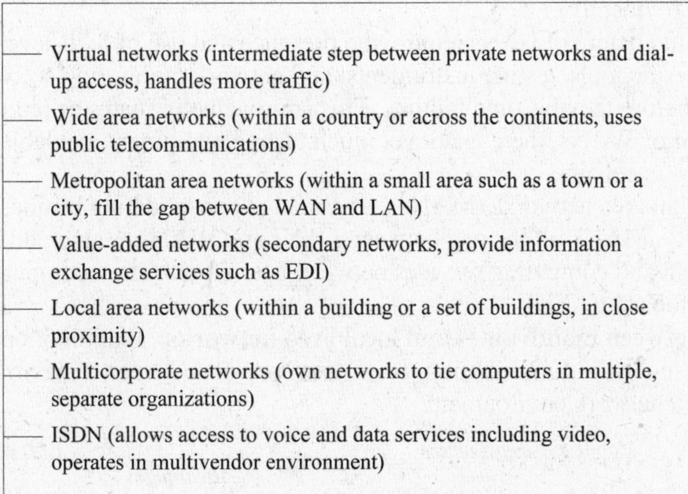

Virtual networks (intermediate step between private networks and dial-up access, handles more traffic)
Wide area networks (within a country or across the continents, uses public telecommunications)
Metropolitan area networks (within a small area such as a town or a city, fill the gap between WAN and LAN)
Value-added networks (secondary networks, provide information exchange services such as EDI)
Local area networks (within a building or a set of buildings, in close proximity)
Multicorporate networks (own networks to tie computers in multiple, separate organizations)
ISDN (allows access to voice and data services including video, operates in multivendor environment)

Exhibit 5.2: Network types

(i) **Virtual networks.** Long-distance telephone carriers are offering virtual network (VN) services, controlled by software, as a good intermediate step between private networks and dial-up access. The benefits of VN are that it allows carriers to route more traffic over existing facilities, offer volume discounts, support ISDN, and control remote access.

(ii) **Wide area networks.** Wide area networks (WANs) connect system users who are geographically dispersed through public telecommunication facilities. WANs provide system users with access to any connected computer for fast interchange of information among the users of the network. Major components of WANs include mainframe computers, mid-range computers, minicomputers, microcomputers, intelligent terminals, modems, front-end processors, and communication controllers. WANs cover a distance of greater than 30 miles or 50 km. More is said about WANs later in this section.

(iii) **Metropolitan area networks.** Metropolitan area networks (MANs) link an organization's factory or office buildings within a small geographic area such as a town or a city. MANs cover a distance up to 50 km (30 miles) and fill the technical or operational gap between WANs and LANs. More is said about MANs later in this section.

Network Interconnectivity Practices

A LAN can be connected to a WAN. A WAN can be used as an intermediary to interconnect two separate LANs. A WAN can be used to geographically disperse subnetworks, some of which can be LANs and others could be MANs. LANs can be interconnected directly or through higher-level MANs or WANs. The MANs can be used to interconnect groups of LANs.

(iv) **Value-added networks.** Value-added network (VAN) vendors operate in a secondary network market. They lease communication facilities from primary, common carriers. They add equipment such as multiplexors and computers and provide time-sharing, routing, and information exchange services. A packet-switched network is an example of VANs. More is said about VANs later in this section.

(v) **Local area networks.** Local area networks (LANs) connect computers with other computers, peripherals (e.g., printers) and workstations that are fairly close in proximity. It is a type of network that is used to support interconnections within a building or set of buildings (e.g., a campus). More is said about LANs later in this section.

(vi) **Differences between WANs, LANs, MANs, and VANs.** WANs, used across geographical locations, are usually static in nature in that changes to them mean that maintenance crews have to go out and climb telephone poles, reroute lines, install new modems, and the like. But LAN topologies, used across and within buildings, are reconfigured in real time (i.e., lines go up and down more easily, gateways to host computers are installed often, system users change frequently, and departments reroute cables frequently).

The dynamic nature of LANs require the presence and use of high-level protocol analyzers, problem diagnostic tools, testing instruments, and network monitoring software to recognize potential problems before they become failures. This approach eliminates or reduces the need for trial and error practice. For WANs, there is not yet much testing equipment available in the way of control logic, recovery, or repairs.

Metropolitan area networks (MANs) are aimed at consolidating business operations spread out in a town or city. MANs fill the gap between LANs and WANs. Value-added networks (VANs) provide networking and computing services between user organization computers and third-party service organizations (e.g., EDI).

(vii) **Differences between mainframes and local area networks.** Exhibit 5.3 presents advantages and disadvantages in terms of information, costs, and controls between a mainframe computer system and a local area network environment.

Mainframe environment	LAN environment
Advantages	***Advantages***
• Avoids loss of control due to data fragmentation	• Increases speed of access to system data
• Facilitates compiling of summary data	• Greater local control over computing resources
Disadvantages	***Disadvantages***
• Increases communication costs and access time	• High data transfer charges to communicate with the host computer
• Cannot accommodate all users' needs	• Increases the difficulty of compiling summary data

Exhibit 5.3: Advantages and disadvantages of mainframe and LAN environments

(viii) **Multicorporate networks.** Certain kinds of organizations operating in specific industries, such as banks and airlines, have developed their own networks to tie computers in multiple, separate organizations. Examples are: SITA network for passing messages between airline computers around the world and SWIFT network for transferring electronic funds between banks. The SWIFT system uses a message switching network. Transactions can be entered into the system regardless of whether or not the recipient bank's terminals are busy.

The integration of WANs, MANs, VANs, LANs and PBX to the backbone network is becoming an absolute requirement. Modern networks can be interconnected through **gateways**. Typically, gateways are located between the backbone network and other subnetworks (e.g., WANs, LANs). A gateway translates the address and document content to conform to the standards of the receiving environment. The gateway's job is to receive a message and translate it into a form that the next message-handling service can understand.

(ix) **Integrated services digital networks.** An integrated services digital network (ISDN) may be defined as an end-to-end digital network that provides customer services using existing subscriber loops. The development of ISDN is an evolving international movement, which pledges to provide digital transmission to customer premises and to allow integrated access to voice and data services including video and other types of services by using circuit and/or packet switching services.

The main feature of ISDN is the provision of a wide range of service capabilities with the promise of great potential in future applications. ISDN is intended to provide easier access both to knowledge and to distributed processing, including better customer service applications. ISDN operates in a multivendor environment.

Digital technologies provide greater benefit for data communications. This is because the digital data signals do not have to be converted from their original digital form into analog signals for transmission or for switching, and because very high bit rates can be sent economically over digital transmission facilities.

The ISDN standards define two types of services: (1) basic and (2) supplementary. The supplementary services can be implemented in conjunction with basic services to increase the number of features and functions available to the end user. Call waiting, call transfer, and call pick-up are examples of supplementary services.

The ultimate goal of ISDN is to combine voice, video, image, text, graphics, and data calls all in the same telephone line to all customers of a common telephone carrier. The user can connect any desired equipment to the network, as long as that equipment is capable of generating a digital bit stream that conforms to ISDN standards.

The ISDN will be able to detect the nature of the terminals that are connected to it and will automatically be able to supply the type of services that are required by the user. The ISDN will be able to perform functions such as maintenance, system control, network management, malicious call blocking, detailed billing information, electronic mail, electronic funds transfer, automatic dialing and call answering, facsimile services, restricting outgoing toll calls, videotext and teletext services, and local voice telephone service.

The goal of ISDN network management is similar to the goal of OSI management, that is, to have a single system that manages all network components, such as terminal adapters, switches, work stations, digital phones, and network services that include, for example, telephone connections and supplementary services. Network control and management will be vital to the operation of integrated digital networks. Usage and application of ISDN services will be affected by the availability and effectiveness of the network's management system.

Adoption of ISDN necessitates new equipment such as telephones, terminals, and central office line modules. One example of specific network management requirements for ISDN applications concerns the management of ISDN terminal profiles. Consider the situation in which a customer service agent transfers a customer's call to another customer service agent. In such a situation, should access to management information about this customer be transferred to the new agent? The management information in question may include the customer's terminal profile, which defines the functionality of the terminal that the customer is using. When the new agent has a choice to supply more than one type of service in response to the customer's request, then the new agent wants to know what types of services this customer's terminal supports.

Access to the information contained in the user's terminal profile may be restricted to network management personnel such as the administrator, who may be solely responsible for updating customers' terminal profiles. However, some customers may require access rights to update their terminal profile(s) and to change their terminal configurations themselves. These issues need to be addressed by affected parties.

Network management users want to see a consolidated set of standards, which allow the development of integrated management systems that monitor and control both ISDN and OSI networks.

(b) **Network Management, Changes, Interoperability, and Architecture.**

(i) **Network management.** Network management deals with six categories.

1. Network architecture specifies network management functions that are essential building elements for a network management system from an architectural point of view.
2. Configuration management is concerned with initializing a network and gracefully shutting down part or all of the network.
3. Fault management encompasses fault detection, isolation, and the correction of abnormal operations.
4. Security management supports the application of security policies.
5. Performance management allows evaluation of the behavior of resources in the open system and of the effectiveness of communication activities.
6. Accounting management enables charges to be established for the use of resources in the open system and for costs to be identified for the use of those resources.

(ii) **Network changes.** Network changes are many and common in any computer center. Unauthorized, incomplete, or incorrect network changes can have an adverse effect on a computer center's security, integrity, and operations. Adequate and timely procedures are needed to define clearly who should do what, when, and how. The following are some examples of network changes:

- Adding, changing, or deleting a user to access computer systems and data files (e.g., application systems, databases, electronic mail, utility programs)
- Adding, changing, or removing a VDU/CRT terminal, printer, or a PC connection or its location
- Adding, changing, or removing network data lines and circuits
- Adding, changing, or removing a modem (dial-in) connection to inter- and intraorganization computers
- Adding a person to use the voice-mail and voice-answering telephone system
- Adding, changing, or removing other related network devices, connections (e.g., gateways, LANs, WANs, MANs, and VANs), and their definitions

A network change request can from many sources, either on paper or phone, or other media. Regardless of request media, basic information such as user name, user/terminal/controller ID, hardware device model/serial number and location, modem type (external/ internal), network port number, logical address of the hardware device, control unit address, request date, and date service needed, is required for effective and timely service.

If the current paper-based network change request mechanism is slow and ineffective, a computer-based approach should be considered. The change request can be entered electronically by the requestor, can be routed to various personnel that process the request, and can be updated by the person who completed it, and the status (e.g., closed, open, deferred, pending, and waiting) can be inquired by the requestor or other interested parties.

(iii) **Network interoperability.** Many organizations' computing environment today consists of hardware, systems software, applications software, printers, protocols, and terminals acquired from different vendors with different platforms. Problems abound in terms of computers' ability to talk to each other. Data cannot be extracted from these systems easily and quickly, so management can get a consolidated view of the business operations and performance. Decisions are made without complete information, and available information is normally out-of-date.

The question is how to integrate data from a vast array of dissimilar systems of mainframe, midrange, mini, and microcomputers acquired from different vendors. Interoperability of systems is becoming a prerequisite to operate and manage in local and global markets and to handle competition. A major stumbling point in the struggle towards interoperability today is the lack of a global, distributed naming standards and directory services that would help users find services in geographically dispersed networks.

The ideal goal for the network management in providing network interoperability is to

- Minimize the costs of handling data
- Minimize the learning curve in accessing new data
- Increase data integrity
- Increase system reliability

(iv) **Network architecture.** Network architecture is a plan describing the design of software, firmware, and hardware components that make up a data communication system. The functions performed by software or firmware are divided into independent **layers.** Each layer isolates the layers above it from the complexities below. The network architecture also defines protocols, rules, standards, and message formats to which different hardware and software vendors must conform in order to achieve given customer data communication needs and objectives.

Basically, network architectures are developed by three organizations: standards organizations such as American National Standards Institute (ANSI), International Organization for Standardization (ISO), International Telegraph and Telephone Consultative Committee (CCITT); common carriers such as AT&T and Western Union; and computer manufacturers such as IBM and DEC. **Gateways** are used to interconnect dissimilar network architectures from competing computer network manufacturers such as IBM and DEC.

The two most popular network architecture methods are discussed here briefly: (1) Open Systems Interconnect (OSI) model and (2) IBM's Systems Network Architecture (SNA). The goal of the OSI model is to serve as a universal standard for communicating from one computer to another in a standardized and flexible manner using the concept of software layers. The OSI model was developed by ISO. The major goals of network architecture are ease of use, reliability, connectivity, modularity, and ease of implementation and maintenance.

There are **seven software layers** in the **OSI model**. The outermost layer, **application layer 7** consists of query software where a person could request a piece of information and the system displays the answer. **Presentation layer 6** consists of software that might compress, encrypt, and expand data. **Session layer 5** software helps users interact with the system and other users. **Transport layer 4** software is responsible for transmitting a message between one network user and another.

Network layer 3 software is responsible for transmitting a message from its source to its destination. **Data link layer 2** software or hardware handles the physical transmission of frames over a single data link. A high-level data link control specifies the rules that must be followed in transmitting a single frame between one device and another over a single data link. The innermost **physical layer 1** software handles the electrical interface between a terminal and a modem. Exhibit 5.4 presents seven layers of the ISO/OSI model.

There are **seven software layers** in the IBM's **SNA** model. The top layer, **transaction services layer 7** provides application services to end users of the network. It provides service to the layers below it. The **presentation service layer 6** is responsible for formatting data for different presentation media used in a session. The **data flow control layer 5** is concerned with the overall integrity of the flow of data during a session between two network users. **Transmission control layer 4** monitors the status of sessions between users, data are sent and received in the proper sequence, and provides data encryption/decryption options.

Path control layer 3 is responsible for routing data from one node to the next in the path that a message takes through the network. The **data link control layer 2** is comparable to the layer 2 in the OSI model. It is responsible for the transmission of data between two nodes over a physical link, to detect transmission errors, and to recover from such errors. The lower level, **physical control layer 1** handles the transmission of bits over a physical circuit. Today, the OSI model and SNA model are not compatible at higher-level layers. However, they are compatible at the lower-level layers—physical and data link layers.

One-to-one correspondence between the layers of OSI and SNA architectures does not exist. This incompatibility could change in the future. IBM's SNA is compatible with internetworking standard x.25. Exhibit 5.5 presents the seven layers of the SNA model.

Layer name	*Layer no.*	*Layer functions*
Application	7	Data flow modeling; file management; distributed processing/databases, and operating systems; electronic mail; virtual terminals
Presentation	6	Security and privacy; data conversion, cryptography; encryption, public keys
Session	5	Dialog management; data exchange; exception reporting; connections and disconnections
Transport	4	Protocols; buffering; crash recovery; voice communications
Network	3	Datagrams; virtual circuits; routing; deadlock; gateways; internetworking
Data link	2	Protocols; error detection and correction; models; efficiency analysis
Physical	1	Transmission media; switching (circuit, packet); ISDN; computer terminals; medium access; data rates; noises; electronic signals; multiplexing and concentration

Exhibit 5.4: Seven layers of the ISO/OSI model

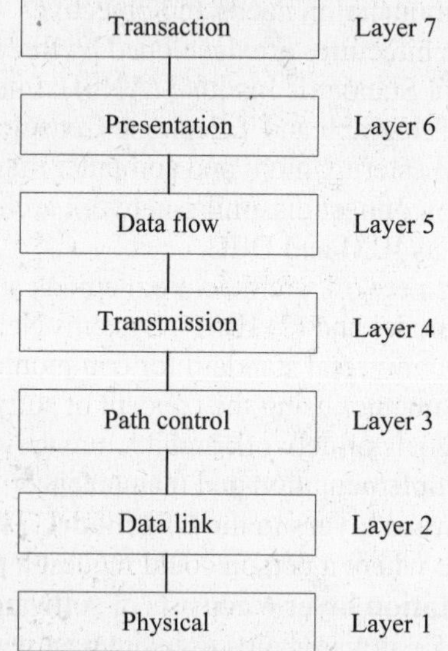

Exhibit 5.5: The seven layers of SNA model

(c) **Data Communications Connectivity Hardware.** Bridges and routers are lower level network interconnection devices. Typically network interconnection strategies will involve some combination of bridges and routers. The decision about when to use a bridge and when to use a router is a difficult one.

(i) **Bridges.** A bridge is a device that connects similar or dissimilar LANs together to form an extended LAN (see Exhibit 5.6). It can also connect LANs and WANs. Bridges are protocol-independent devices and are designed to store and then forward frames destined for another LAN. Bridges are transparent to the end-stations that are connecting through the bridge. Bridges can reduce total traffic on the extended LAN by filtering unnecessary traffic from the overall network. A bridge functions in a MAC/Data Link layer of the OSI Reference Model.

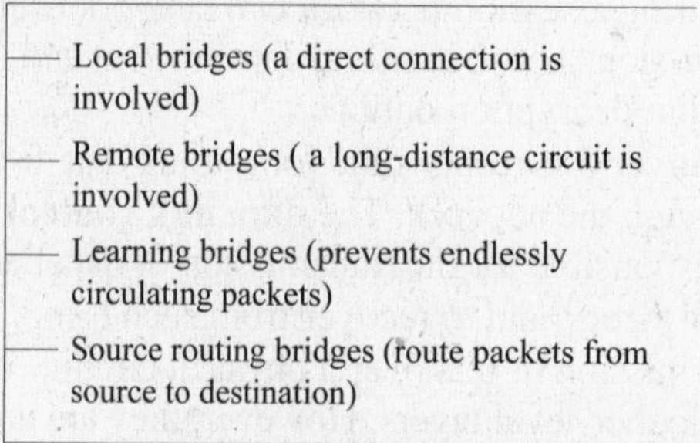

Exhibit 5.6: Types of bridges

Local bridges connect to LANs together directly at one bridge. **Remote bridges** connect two distant LANs through a long-distance circuit (which is invisible to the stations on the LANs).

Learning bridges learn whether they must forward packets by observing the source addresses of packets on the networks to which they are connected. The bridge maintains a table of source addresses for each subnetwork. Learning bridges generally participate in a spanning tree algorithm, in which the bridges communicate with each other to establish a tree through the extended LAN, so that there is one and only one path between any two stations, preventing endlessly circulating packets.

With **source routing bridges,** the source and destination stations explicitly participate in the routing through the bridges. The source station inserts the route through the bridges to the information field of the packet. The bridge, in turn, just uses the routing information supplied by the source station to route packets.

(ii) **Routers.** Routers offer a complex form of interconnectivity. The router keeps a record of node addresses and current network status. Routers are known to the end-stations as they are device dependent. LANs connect personal computers, terminals, printers, and plotters within a limited geographical area. An extended LAN is achieved through the use of bridges and routers. In other words, the capabilities of a single LAN are extended by connecting LANs at distant locations. A router functions in a Network Layer of the ISO/OSI Reference Model.

Routers convert between different data link protocols and resegment transport level protocol data units (PDUs) as necessary to accomplish this. These PDUs are reassembled by the destination end point transport protocol entity.

There are several routing protocols in common use. Routers must have more detailed knowledge than bridges about the protocols that are used to carry messages through internetwork. When routers are used to connect FDDI to other networks, it is important to be certain that the routers support the needed network level protocols.

BRIDGES VS. ROUTERS

- Bridges are generally considered to be faster than routers since the processing they perform is simpler.
- Routers are limited to particular routing protocols, while bridges may be transparent to most routing protocols.
- Bridging protocols are semiautomatic. Routers are automatic and depend on routing tables, which typically must be maintained.
- Bridge protocols limit the size of any extended LAN network while routers do not.
- Routers are used to connect LANs and WANs.

(iii) **Brouters.** Brouters are routers that can also bridge; they route one or more protocols and bridge all other network traffic. Routing bridges are those capable of maintaining the protocol transparency of a standard bridge while also making intelligent path selections, just like a router. Brouters merge the capabilities of bridges and routers into a single, multifunctional device.

Brouters = Bridges + Routers

(iv) **Repeaters.** Repeaters offer the simplest form of interconnectivity (See Exhibit 5.7). They merely generate or repeat data packets or electrical signals between cable segments. Repeaters perform data insertion and reception functions. They receive a message and then retransmit it, regenerating the signal at its original strength. In their purest form, repeaters physically extend a network. They also provide a level of fault tolerance by isolating networks electrically, so problems on one cable segment do not affect other segments. However, repeaters exert stress on a network's bandwidth due to difficulty in isolating network traffic. Repeaters are independent of protocols and media. A repeater functions in a Physical Layer of the ISO/OSI Reference Model and performs no Data Link Level functions.

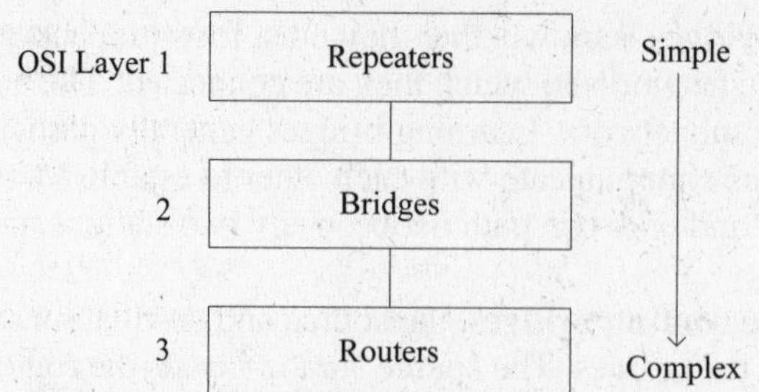

Exhibit 5.7: Complexity of network interconnecting devices

(v) **Gateways/protocol converters.** Protocol converters are devices that change one type of coded data to another type of coded data for computer processing. Conversion facilities allow an application system conforming to one network architecture to communicate with an application system conforming to some other network architecture. A gateway, a hardware device, is an example of a protocol converter operating in the Application Layer of the ISO/OSI Reference Model. A gateway performs three major functions: message format conversion, address translation, and protocol conversion.

Gateways are used to connect LANs to host computers. Gateways act as translators between networks using incompatible transport protocols. A gateway is used to interconnect networks that may have different architectures. Gateways offer the greatest flexibility in network interconnections. The gateway's job is to receive a message and translate it into a form that the next message-handling service can understand. The gateway can be a potential bottleneck considering the number of stations to handle and the amount of traffic going through the gateway. To overcome performance limitations, an organization might need more than one gateway, which, in turn, complicates the station software. There are trade-offs associated with gateways. On extended LANs and networks, they can introduce substantial packet-queuing delays, which could be longer than in either a bridge or router. This is due to traffic passing up one protocol stack and out another. Simple checksums are calculated at each gateway to ensure data integrity. See Exhibit 5.8 for major features of network connecting devices.

REPEATERS, BRIDGES, ROUTERS, AND SWITCHES VS. GATEWAYS

- Repeaters, bridges, routers, and switches are used to interconnect LANs to form a larger network. They are internetworking devices.
- Gateways are used to convert one set of communication protocols to some other set of communication protocols. They are protocol conversion devices.

Device feature	Repeaters	Bridges	Routers	Gateways
Simple form of interconnectivity between the same type	X			
Repeats data packets	X			
Provides fault tolerance mechanism	X			
Used in bus/ring topology	X	X		
Handles complex tasks		X		
Handles mixed protocols		X		
Balances network loads		X		
Handles different protocols			X	
Provides LAN-to-LAN links		X	X	X
Provides LAN-to-WAN links			X	X
Powerful and complex			X	
Complex and expensive network				X
Provides LAN-to-host link		X	X	X
Introduces packet-queuing delays				X
Handles incompatible transport protocols				X

Exhibit 5.8: Major features of network connecting devices

(vi) **Backbone.** A backbone network is a central network to which other networks connect. Users are not attached directly to the backbone network; they are connected to the access networks, which in turn connect to the backbone. A backbone network provides connection between LANs and WANs. Dumb terminals can be attached directly to the backbone through terminal servers.

The backbone network is a high-speed connection within a network that connects shorter, usually slower circuits. It is also used in reference to a system that acts as a "hub" for activity, but it is not common now.

(vii) **Collapsed backbone.** A LAN hub is a device that facilitates wiring LANs as stars or trees. Users may contemplate converting to FDDI to provide more bandwidth. In some cases, the ability of hubs to switch 10-Base-T links will mean that a more expensive FDDI workstation port is not required. In other cases, the hubs may make it possible to dispense with even an FDDI backbone, and the bus of the hub becomes what is sometimes called a "collapsed backbone."

What is Connectivity Hardware?

Connectivity hardware includes concentrators, repeaters, bridges, and routers. Bridges, repeaters, and routers connect networks together. They are examples of interconnecting devices.

(viii) **Concentrators.** The major function of concentrators is to gather together several lines in one central location. Concentrators are the foundation of an FDDI network and are attached directly to the FDDI dual ring. Concentrators provide highly fault tolerant connections to the FDDI rings.

The concentrator allows stations to be inserted and removed with minimal effect on the operation of the ring. One of the functions of the concentrator is to ensure ports (stations) are automatically bypassed in response to a detected fault connection, a high error rate, or when a user powers down the station. This bypass function of the concentrator enhances the reliability of the FDDI ring.

(ix) **Ethernet switches.** Bridges and repeaters share the same physical transmission medium to interconnect or extend a LAN. Switches and hardware devices are designed for the opposite purpose of bridges and repeaters. Switches, in the form of routers, interconnect when the systems forming one workgroup are physically separated from the systems forming other workgroups. Switches do not extend LANs as bridges and repeaters do. Switches are primarily used to implement multiple, parallel transmission medium segments to which different groups of workstations can be connected, and provide full network bandwidth to multiple groups of systems.

In a switched network, connections are established by closing switches through dialing. Ethernet switches establish a data link in which a circuit or a channel is connected to an Ethernet network.

(x) **Network interface cards.** Network interface cards (NIC) are circuit boards used to transmit and receive commands and messages between a PC and a LAN. When the network interface card fails, workstations and file servers also fail.

Network adapters establish a connection to other computers or peripherals, such as a printer in the network. Network adapters function similarly to NIC.

(d) **More on Local Area Networks.** A local area network (LAN) refers to a network that interconnects systems located in a small geographic area, such as a building or a complex of buildings (campus). LANs can be classified in a number of different ways. Four commonly used classifications are in terms of topology, transmission control, transmission/ communications medium, and the way they are implemented—architectural scope.

(i) **LAN applications.** Three types of applications provided by a local area network (LAN) include: (1) distributed file storing, (2) remote computing, and (3) messaging.

(A) ***Distributed file storing.*** Distributed file storing provides users transparent access to part of the mass storage of a remote server. Distributed file storing provides capabilities such as remote filing and remote printing. Remote filing allows users to access, retrieve, and store files. Generally, remote filing is provided by allowing a user to attach to part of a remote mass storage device (a file server) as though it were connected directly. This virtual disk is then used as though it were a disk drive local to the workstation.

Remote printing allows users to print to any printer attached to any component on the LAN. Remote printing addresses two user needs: ongoing processing while printing, and shared use of expensive printers. LAN print servers can accept files immediately; users continue to work on their local workstations, instead of waiting for the print job to be completed. Many users utilizing the same printer can justify the cost of fast, high-quality printers.

(B) ***Remote computing.*** Remote computing refers to the concept of running an application or applications on remote components. Remote computing allows users to: remotely log in to another component on the LAN; remotely execute an application that resides on another component; or remotely run an application on one or more components while having the appearance, to the user, of running locally. Remote login allows users to log in to a remote system (such as a multiuser system) as though the user were directly connected to the remote system. The ability to run an application on one or more components allows the user to utilize the processing power of the LAN as a whole.

(C) ***Messaging.*** Messaging applications are associated with electronic mail and conferencing capabilities. Electronic mail has been one of the most-used capabilities available on computer systems and across networks. Mail services act as local post offices, providing users the ability to send and receive messages across a LAN. A conferencing capability, analogous to the telephone, allows users to actively communicate with each other.

(ii) **LAN topologies.** Topology refers to the manner in which a network is physically connected. It shows the physical layout of system resources such as workstations, servers, and printers on the entire network. Each end-unit of the network is referred to as a node (see Exhibit 5.9).

The interaction between various network topologies and protocols is very important in choosing the right combination. A wrong combination affects the network performance negatively. The three most common topologies are the star, bus, and ring. At a higher level, the choice of topology depends on reliability, performance, expandability, and other factors. At a lower level, the selection of a topology depends on many factors, such as

- The type of application system being used on the network
- Availability of existing wiring in the area suitable for LAN installation
- Physical location and distance of the nodes being serviced

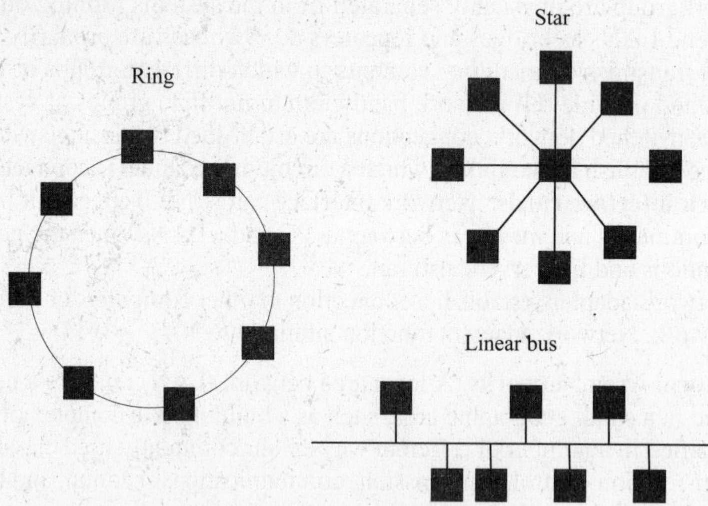

Exhibit 5.9: Topologies for LANs

(A) ***Star topology.*** The star topology uses a central hub connecting workstations and servers. Depending on the type of network, this central hub may be at the server or a separate wire connection unit. The star topology facilitates the sharing of resources such as hard disks, communications devices, printers, or common data files that are located at the central node.

The star topology may not be optimal for a large number of nodes because of the throughput limitation of the central node. Communication between any two stations is via circuit switching, and readily integrates voice with data. It is good at handling devices with low data-transfer rates. The star topology is good for a small, low-cost network. It is used in dial-up telephone services and private branch exchanges (PBXs). See Exhibit 5.10 for advantages and disadvantages of star topology.

Advantages of star topology	*Disadvantages of star topology*
• When one workstation fails, other workstations do not fail, because of the central hub. • It eliminates a number of lengthy cable runs, due to proper positioning of the central hub. • Troubleshooting network problems becomes easier due to the shorter length of cable. • Fewer problems are caused by cut cabling, because all cables run to a central hub.	• There is the potential for the central hub to become inactive, thereby forcing the entire network down. • Remote troubleshooting of problems may not be possible, due to lack of built-in fault tolerance mechanisms such as disk mirroring or disk duplexing.

Exhibit 5.10: Advantages and disadvantages of star topology

(B) ***Bus topology.*** **Bus topology** uses a single cable running the entire length of the network, from one end to the other. Nodes are physically attached to the bus at drop points. Two variations exist: (1) linear topology and (2) tree topology.

Linear bus topology is also useful for sharing devices as well as for facilitating communication between any of the nodes. There are no switches or repeaters. Each station makes a determination whether to accept, process, or ignore the message. The linear bus is used in medium- and large-sized local area networks.

Tree topology, which is another variation of the bus, is complex where all stations receive all transmissions. The bus/tree topology appears to be the most flexible one in terms of handling a number of devices, data rates, and data types, and in achieving high bandwidth. See Exhibit 5.11 for advantages and disadvantages of bus topology.

Bandwidth refers to a relative range of frequencies, that is, the difference between the highest and lowest frequencies transmitted. The greater the range, the higher the available bandwidth and the higher the bandwidth, the more information can be carried. A channel's bandwidth has a direct relationship to its data rate.

Advantages of bus topology	*Disadvantages of bus topology*
• It allows for easy expandability of nodes due to the installation of the long, single, main cable.	• If one workstation fails, all other workstations fail, because of their interdependence. • More problems are caused by cut cabling, because all cable do not run to a central hub, as in the star topology. • It is susceptible to a single point of failure, due to reliance on a single cable. • It uses point-to-point topology, and thus is susceptible to cut cable risks.

Exhibit 5.11: Advantages and disadvantages of bus topology

(C) ***Ring topology.*** The ring topology interconnects nodes in a circular fashion where personal computers are connected successively to form a ring. Each node is dependent on the physical connection of the preceding and succeeding nodes on the network.

Unlike the star topology, there is no central hub through which all traffic flows. All data packets traveling on the LAN pass through each workstation on the ring.

In a ring topology, each member of the network gets access to the communication channel for a set time, at predefined intervals. Two variations of ring topology are available: (1) token ring and (2) token bus. See Exhibit 5.12 for advantages and disadvantages of physical ring topology. See Exhibit 5.13 for a comparison of LAN topologies.

Advantages of physical ring topology	*Disadvantages of physical ring topology*
• No central wiring is required. • The point-to-point layout lends itself to easier wiring in a small network.	• In simple networks, if one workstation fails, all other workstations fail because of their interdependence. • More problems are caused by cut cabling because all cables do not run to a central hub, as in a star topology.

Exhibit 5.12: Advantages and disadvantages of physical ring topology

WHAT CAN GO WRONG IN LOCAL AREA NETWORKS?

- Failure of either the star or the bus node could make the network unavailable.
- In ring topology, duplicate address (two stations think it is their turn) and broken ring (no station thinks that it is its turn) can occur, leading to errors.
- A single-link failure, a repeater failure, or a break in the cable could disable a large part or all of the network.
- When two or more stations transmit at the same time, data frames will collide, leading to unpredictable results and garbled transmission. Neither one gets through. "Who goes next?" is the problem to be resolved. The number of **collisions** will increase as the channel's load increases. When two frames collide, the medium remains unusable for the duration of transmission of both damaged frames. Collision detectors are needed to resolve collision.
- There may not be a backup person for the LAN administrator.
- The backup person, even though designated, may not have been trained adequately to take over the LAN administrator's job duties when needed.
- Changes made to the LAN network may not be transparent to end users.

LAN feature	Star topology	Bus/tree topology	Ring/bus topology
Size of network (number of nodes)	Small	Medium/large	Large
Stability/secure	Low/medium	Low/medium	High
Transmission control	Centralized	Random	Distributed
Connectivity/communication links	Point-to-point	Multipoint	Point-to-point
Data transmission	One at a time	In packets	In packets
Communications between stations is via:	Circuit/central switching	Tap, cable, no repeaters, no switches	Repeaters
Collision	Possible	Not possible	Not possible
Fault isolation and recovery	Complex	Complex	Simpler
Throughput	Lower	Lower	Greater

Exhibit 5.13: Comparison of LAN topologies

(iii) **Building technology infrastructure and cabling.** Building a technology infrastructure involves transmission control, a transmission medium, and topology. Transmission control refers to where in the network the access control function to the transmission medium is performed. Three possibilities exist: (1) random control, where any station can transmit without any permission; (2) distributed control, where only one station can transmit at a time; and (3) centralized control, where one station controls the entire network and other stations must receive permission from the central station. Random control is used on a bus/tree-structured network. Distributed control is used on a ring-structured network. Centralized control is used on a star-structured network.

The transmission medium describes the nature of the links between nodes. It is the physical path between transmitter and receiver in a communications network, and includes twisted-pair wire, coaxial cable, fiber-optics, and infrared and radio.

(A) ***Twisted-pair wire.*** Twisted-pair wire is the most commonly used medium, and its application is limited to a single building or a few buildings. Lower-performance systems use twisted-pair links, that is, copper-based cable wire. This cable is vulnerable to interference and noise, and radiates signals that allow easy eavesdropping. Two types of wires exist: shielded and unshielded. Shielded twisted cable is subject to less electrical interference than unshielded (see Exhibit 5.14).

Advantages of twisted-pair wire	Disadvantages of twisted-pair wire
• Used extensively in residential telephone systems	• Relatively low information capacity
• Inexpensive and widespread	• Susceptible to electronic interference
• Easy to connect and disconnect devices	

Exhibit 5.14: Advantages and disadvantages of twisted-pair wire

(B) ***Coaxial cable.*** Higher-performance systems use coaxial cable and radio frequency-type communications because they are less subject to electrical interferences. A coaxial cable is a solid copper wire with an inner insulation over this core, a braided metallic ground shield, and an outer insulation. A coaxial cable is similar to the one used in cable television connections—a thin cable. However, a thicker cable is available for Ethernet installations that have a high rate of data transmitted under this protocol (see Exhibit 5.15).

Advantages of coaxial cable	*Disadvantages of coaxial cable*
• Used extensively for cable television • Sufficient capacity to handle most advanced telecommunication applications • Less susceptible to electrical interferences	• Used primarily in one-way networks • Requires additional switching equipment in most cable networks to permit two-way communication

Exhibit 5.15: Advantages and disadvantages of coaxial cable

Two types of transmission techniques are available over twisted-pair and coaxial cable: (1) **baseband,** in which devices can share a single transmission channel, and (2) **broadband,** in which devices can communicate with each other on dedicated frequencies and support multiple channels. Broadband will allow more data to be transmitted per unit of time. Baseband, using digital signaling, can be employed on twisted-pair or coaxial cable. Broadband, using analog signaling in the radio-frequency range, employs coaxial cable. Coaxial cables and twisted-pair cables can be damaged by excessive bending, crimping, stapling, or stretching.

(C) ***Fiberoptic cable.*** Optical fibers, the newest communication link, allow the highest data transfer rates and solve many of the problems associated with electrical signals (e.g., power surges, noise, radio frequency interferences from electric motors). It is difficult to eavesdrop over optical fiber, which makes it more secure. Optical fiber is more reliable, smaller, lightning-fast, and lighter than the others. However, it is the most difficult and expensive communication medium to install, especially in attaching connectors to the fiberoptic cable (see Exhibit 5.16). See Exhibit 5.17 for a comparison of transmission or communication media.

Advantages fiberoptic cable	*Disadvantages of fiberoptic cable*
• Very high information capacity • Relatively secure • Not susceptible to electronic interference	• Expensive to install support equipment • Not installed in most areas

Exhibit 5.16: Advantages and disadvantages of fiberoptic cable

Comparative item	*Twisted-pair wire*	*Coaxial cable*	*Optical fiber*
Size, weight	Thick, heavy	Thick, heavy	Thin, light
Cost	Low	Medium	High
Performance	Low	High	High
Security	Low	Medium	High
Data rates, speed (Mbps)	1-10, low	1-10, low	Up to 500, high
Installation	Easy	Medium	Difficult
Cable reliability	Poor	Poor	Good
Connectivity/communication links	Point-to-point, multipoint	Point-to-point, multipoint	Point-to-point
Bandwidth	Low	Medium	High
Testing	Easy, not critical	Easy, not critical	Difficult, important
Signal quality	Average	Moderate	Superior
Interference/noise	High	Low/medium	None/low
Distance	Within building	Within building	Building-to-building and within building
Typical applications	LAN, WAN, ISDN	LAN, WAN	LAN, WAN, ISDN

Exhibit 5.17: Comparison of transmission/communication media

(D) ***Infrared and radio.*** Infrared and radio provide over-the-air signals. Considering the fact that 40 to 45% of the workforce does not work in an office, true wireless LAN is emerging because of radio-frequency spread-spectrum technology. This technology, which was developed years ago as a secure military radio transmission technique, is approved now for civilian use. It is a viable alternative to cabled LANs. In fact, portable wireless LANs can offer a cost alternative to cabled LANs for disaster recovery or network relocation situations. Cables are unwieldy, unsightly, and obstructive, and difficult to maintain due to lack of cabling diagrams (see Exhibit 5.18).

Advantages of infrared and radio signals	*Disadvantages of infrared and radio signals*
• Enhance mobility • Do not require wire conduits	• Relatively unsecure • Require allocation of the frequency spectrum, a finite resource • Are susceptible to electronic interference

Exhibit 5.18: Advantages and disadvantages of infrared and radio signals

Wireless LANs provide a hand-held spread-spectrum workstation for temporary situations or out-of-the office environments. These LANs transfer files, provide electronic mail, and offer other data services. Each wireless LAN unit contains a radio transceiver, processor, and memory. Interference is possible even with wireless LANs. Transmission is affected by thick concrete walls and metal fixtures and not affected by office partitions and normal wooden walls. A risk in wireless LAN is that anyone with the appropriate receiver device can capture the signal transmitted from one unit to another. Exhibit 5.19 shows the relationships between the topology and transmission medium.

		Topology		
Transmission medium	*Star*	*Bus*	*Tree*	*Ring*
Twisted-pair wire	X	X		X
Baseband coaxial cable		X		X
Broadband coaxial cable		X	X	
Optical fiber				X

Exhibit 5.19: Relationships between LAN topology and transmission medium

(iv) **LAN cable management.** PC/LAN equipment and office personnel often move from one location to another. Cabling, connectors, connectivity boxes, and network interface cards, which are part of a LAN setup, are the most frequently cited causes of LAN failures. LAN downtime is expensive due to lost productivity of end users and even lost revenues. **Cabling,** unlike other computer equipment, is not protected from heat, electrical charges, physical abuse, and damage.

Failures are caused when electrical conductors either break open, short together, or are exposed to electromagnetic forces. Failures are also caused when cables are poorly routed. A common routing problem is placing cables on or near fluorescent light fixtures. Other things to avoid are installing LAN cables parallel to power cables or near switched electrical gear such as motors, relays, or heaters.

If cheap **connectors** are purchased, they may fail from frequent connecting and disconnecting to the LAN. The connector shell may also wear quickly or deform, and retention tabs may weaken or break.

(v) **System backup and environmental considerations for LANs.** Daily **backup procedures** are important so that if the network goes down, only a limited amount of work will be lost. The backup work can be performed either at a local or central site with LAN-based backup hardware or software. It is also a good practice to keep spare, backup PCs and file servers ready to be used at a moment's notice.

Other backup considerations include: (1) placing LAN servers in out-of-the-way areas and in a protected place, (2) designing the network backbone so that if one link goes down, the network can reroute over another link, and (3) installing disk mirroring (the server contains duplicate disks), disk duplexing (the disk controller is duplicated), or server mirroring (the system contains duplicate servers). The server mirroring technique offers greater protection since the potential for failure is not concentrated in a single box. However, server mirroring is expensive and not efficient. Disk mirroring performance has been less than satisfactory due to the fact that when a disk fails, mirroring could not help since it mirrored the failure into the other disk.

Poor **environmental conditions** are another cause of LAN reliability problems. File servers are often located under someone's desk or in a dark, hot closet. File servers are subject to failures caused by electrostatic discharges on dry days, humidity on rainy days, and constant exposure to dirt. File servers should be placed in secure rooms with environmental controls and clean electrical supplies.

(vi) **LAN architecture.** Choosing a LAN software or hardware configuration that will support the desired security features requires an understanding of LAN architectures and the security features provided by the **network operating system (NOS)**. Whereas there are many types of cabling and network interface hardware, there are only two basic logical architectures that are supported on PC-LANs today: (1) peer-to-peer and (2) client-server architectures.

(A) ***Peer-to-peer architectures.*** Peer-to-peer architectures require no dedicated file server because any node on the network may selectively "share" its local hard disk with other nodes on the network. Other peripherals such as printers may also be shared across the LAN. This is a good choice for smaller LAN installations as it has a lower cost-per-node ratio. However, significant security problems exist because of the lack of centralized data storage across the network. Typically, the architecture also has lower performance and requires greater administrative effort to configure and maintain security definitions.

(B) ***Client-server architecture.*** The client-server architecture depends on services provided by dedicated file and print servers. These servers do not provide any direct user application support but provide an optimized design for file level I/O requests and spooled print services. It provides high performance and better security features and is costly. The centralized disk storage architecture provides a more straightforward platform for control of user access and of backup operation than a peer-to-peer architecture. Client-server computing can be bandwidth-intensive due to high performance requirements of workstations, servers, and end users.

Exhibit 5.20 provides an overview of the client-server functions. Most client-server systems are designed for PCs and LAN-based operating systems. The processing of an application is split between a front-end portion executing on a PC or workstation (**client**) and a back-end portion running on a **server**.

The front end typically handles local data manipulation and maintains the user interface, and the back end handles database and other number-crunching processing. Front-end programs, located in the client, are invoked by a user or according to a predefined schedule.

Access to the server is through the database engine, set up by the LAN administrator. The client has no access to the data. Servers provide connections to the data in the database. An interface programming language is needed to connect the client to the server. A typical scenario is as follows: The client issues a command and passes it to the server through interface language mechanism. The server receives the command, verifies the syntax, checks the existence and availability of the referenced objects (data files, libraries), verifies the security rights, and finally executes the command. The resulting data is formatted and sent to the application in the client, along with the return codes, in a format that the client is expecting.

Even though the client-server architecture increases the complexity of the network due to split application development approach, network management tools are available to the network (LAN) administrator to monitor the network. *These tools, in addition to providing reports and sending electronic alarms, help the network administrator to monitor and control traffic capacity, bandwidth, modems, node performance, threshold capacities, and remote systems.*

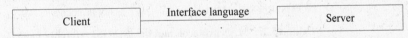

Client	Interface language	Server

Exhibit 5.20: Client-server functions

Client	Server
• Contains front-end programs	• Contains back-end programs (database engine)
• Provides data entry & decision-support screens	• Facilitates access to the data
• Handles ad hoc queries	• Accepts/process requests for data
• Invoked by a user	
• Provides management reporting	• Provides locking mechanism
• Runs batch jobs	• Places data in the database
• No access to the data	• Returns data and status codes to the client
• Heavy user interface	• No user interface
• Provides user-friendly interaction	• Provides system backups, database synchronization, and database protection
• Diskless PC or workstation (more secure)	

(vii) **LAN security.** Evaluation of the work group's security requirements is important. Generally, LANs with low security requirements are less expensive and allow more choices while high security requirements are expensive and allow few options. High-level access controls are needed for classified and sensitive data.

A **high-security LAN** might include the following features:

- Dedicated file server using client-server architecture
- Diskless PCs or workstations remotely booted
- Logical access security control down to lowest level possible (i.e., byte)
- Encryption of passwords
- Password format control
- Security monitoring, accounting, and reporting
- Network encryption devices
- Non-DOS disk format command
- Image backup utility programs
- Fault-tolerant design with the use of disk mirroring, disk duplexing, or server mirroring
- Reduced system privileges to directories, files, records
- No remote log-in
- Automatic logout after dormant periods
- Printers attached to secured file server

A **low-security LAN** might include the following features:

- Peer-to-peer architecture
- Allows DOS disk format command
- Shareable printers across the network
- Bootable workstations with local storage facilities
- No directory, file, record, or byte-level access controls
- Basic password protection

(e) **More on Metropolitan Area Networks.** A metropolitan area network (MAN) is configured for a larger geographical area than a LAN, ranging from several blocks of buildings to entire cities. MANs can be owned and operated either as public utilities or individual organizations. MANs interconnect two or more LANs. Although MANs depend on moderate-to-high data rates as required for LANs, the error rates and delays would be higher than might be obtained on a LAN. MAN is based on the IEEE 802.6 standard—distributed-queue dual-bus (DQDB) standard.

(i) **MAN protocol architecture.** *The MAN protocol architecture can be described in terms of the ISO/OSI reference model), topologies, and internetworking devices (see Exhibit 5.21).*

ISO/OSI Reference Model	MAN Protocols
Data-link layer (upper layer)	DQDB upper layer
Data-link layer (lower layer)	DQDB middle layer
Physical layer	Physical layer

Exhibit 5.21: MAN protocols and the ISO/OSI reference model

Physically, a MAN consists of a transmission medium and nodes that provide user access to the medium. The DQDB standard is divided into three layers: upper, middle, and lower, as shown in Exhibit 5.21. The DQDB provides three types of services that a network must support: (1) connectionless data service, (2) connection-oriented data service, and (3) isochronous service (see Exhibit 5.22).

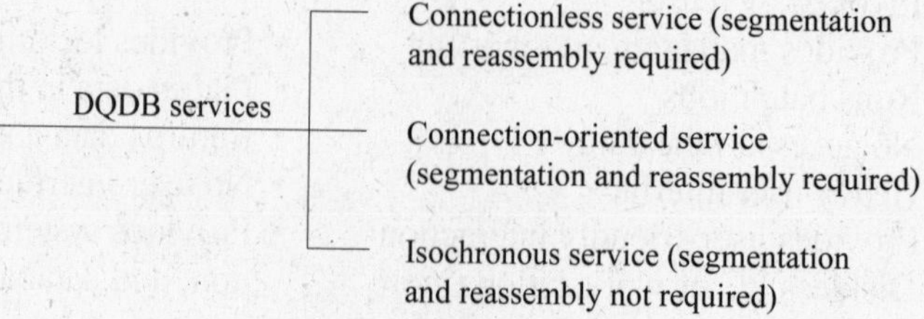

Exhibit 5.22: DQDB services

The connectionless data service supports connectionless communication via the logical link control protocol. Transmission is in the form of fixed-length segments. Both segmentation and reassembly are required. The connection-oriented data service supports the transport segments between nodes sharing a virtual channel connection. Both segmentation and reassembly are required. The isochronous service provides support for users that require constant inter-arrival time. It requires a logical connection but segmentation and reassembly are not required.

(ii) **MAN topologies.** Two categories of MAN topologies exist: (1) DQDB and (2) non-DQDB. Three types exist in the non-DQDB category: (1) tree-based MANs, (2) toroid-based MANs, and (3) LAN-based MANs (see Exhibit 5.23).

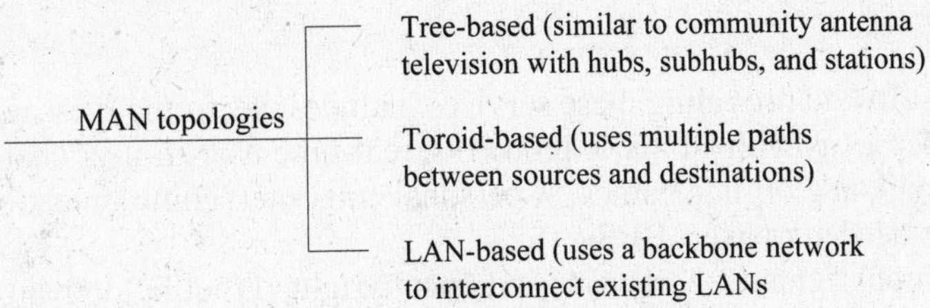

Exhibit 5.23: MAN topologies

Tree-based MANs have the same tree topology as community antenna television (CATV) consisting of hubs, sub-hubs, and stations. These, in turn, are connected to a head-end at the top. **Advantages** include: uses the minimum number of links to interconnect a set of points, can use an existing CATV network, and optimizes the performance of a particular application. **Disadvantages** include: poor reliability of the head, which brings the network down, hub failures, and subhub disconnections.

Toroid-based MANs have multiple paths between sources and destinations that increase the reliability of the network. This, in turn, is helpful in network load balancing. This structure is more complex than linear networks, due in part to complex routines and longer processing time. **Advantages** include: fault tolerance mechanisms, redundant paths, low maximal number of hops, which makes routing easy, and increased throughput. **Disadvantages** include: requirement of complex store-and-forward nodes, recovery of packet with error, and resequence of packets at the destination.

LAN-based MANs use a backbone network to interconnect existing LANs through a broadcast network or a switched network. Bridges or gateways are used for a direct interconnection. A bridge connects two homogeneous LANs and a gateway connects two heterogenous LANs. **Advantages** include: ease of administration to expand the network, easier to regulate traffic efficiently, and better security. A major **disadvantage** is low reliability, in that if the backbone fails, the inter-LAN communication is disrupted.

(iii) **Internetworking devices for MAN.** Interconnecting devices such as bridges, repeaters, routers, and gateways are needed to share resources and information among the networks. This would enable a network user to establish a communication link with a user from another network, and vice versa. In this regard, a MAN can be viewed as an extension of a LAN to cover a metropolitan area. Interconnecting devices may operate at any of the seven layers of the ISO/OSI reference model.

- A bridge operates in data-link layer 2.
- A repeater operates in physical layer 1.
- A router operates in network layer 3.
- A gateway operates in any layer from 4 to 7.

(f) **More on Value-Added Networks.** Value-added carriers lease channels from other common carriers and then provide additional services to customers, using these leased channels. They operate a public data network, where the equipment breaks up the user's data into packets, routes the packets over its network between one location and another, and reassembles them into their original form on the other end. Value-added networks take advantage of the economies of scale. Usually, they share a wider bandwidth, which gives faster response time. Some examples of services provided by VANs include bulletin board services, Internet, electronic data interchange, and dial-in services.

(i) **Bulletin board services.** The range of bulletin board services (BBS) includes sharing tips on a favorite hobby, obtaining business contacts, or starting up a new business. Some computer vendors are using the BBS to provide customer support, whereas others are providing an avenue for their user groups to communicate with each other.

Risks in Bulletin Board Services

A risk in BBS is that employees downloading software from bulletin boards increase a computer virus exposure. A control is to use only shrink-wrapped software or certified shareware.

The software providing these services includes electronic messaging with a full-screen editor, file transfer areas with all major protocols, real-time user-to-user chat facilities, fax support, networked mail, and on-line games. A personal computer, communications software, modem, and telephone are needed to use a BBS.

Both copyrighted (shareware) and uncopyrighted (public-domain) software are available to anyone who calls the BBS. Some questions that must be answered before connecting with the BBS include: How many phone lines are needed? How big a hard disk is required? and What should be the charges for accessing the BBS? The major issue is the cost of running a BBS, including tangible and intangible costs.

(ii) **Internet.** Internet means **internetwork**. It is a worldwide collection of networks that support commercial, educational, research, governmental, and individual user communities. It is called a "network of networks" that use the transmission control protocol/internet protocol (TCP/IP) suite for communications. The Internet is being used as the basis for the National Information Infrastructure in the United States, leading to the information superhighway concept.

Organizations are now using the Internet or considering Internet access for a variety of purposes, including exchanging electronic mail, distributing company information to the public, conducting research, and doing electronic commerce on the information superhighway. Many organizations are connecting their existing internal LANs to the Internet so that LAN workstations can have direct access to Internet services.

The Internet is a set of dissimilar computer networks joined together by means of gateways that handle data transfer and the conversion of messages from the sending network to the protocols used by the receiving network.

The Internet uses a packet-switching network. Digital data are organized into packets and sent through a computer network along the best route available between the source and the destination. A transmitted file, for example, may be broken up into many packets. These packets may take different paths across the network and then be reassembled at their destination.

Two types of gateways exist in the Internet: (1) interior and (2) exterior. The interior gateway is an Internet router that moves information within an autonomous Internet system. Routing information protocol (RIP) is an example of interior gateway protocol, where routers are called gateways. Exterior gateway is an Internet router that moves information from one autonomous Internet system to another.

(iii) **Electronic data interchange.** Electronic data interchange (EDI) is the exchange of routine business transactions in a computer-processable format, covering such traditional applications as inquiries, planning, purchasing, acknowledgements, pricing, order status, scheduling, shipping and receiving, invoices, and payments.

(iv) **Dial-in services.** Many external, commercial electronic databases and on-line systems exist to satisfy a specific customer's need. For example: general services such as electronic mail, real-time conferences, file transfer, game playing, and on-line news are provided, and on-line search systems contain indexes from major magazines and other periodicals on all topics.

(g) **More on Wide-Area Networking.** A WAN is a network that interconnects systems located in a large geographic area, such as a city, a continent, or several continents. A complex network can consist of WANs that span continents or geographic regions within continents and connect smaller, more localized LANs or MANs.

WANs connect intelligent terminals, workstations, personal computers, minicomputers, LANs, and MANs. They use public telecommunication facilities to accomplish this connection. For example, a WAN data-link interconnection can be used to connect two or more physical LANs in different geographical locations. Devices that are available for network interconnection include bridges, repeaters, routers, switches, and protocol converters.

(i) **Synchronous/asynchronous.** Data transmission is of two general types—synchronous and asynchronous—and uses several coding schemes.

Synchronous transmission is the faster rate and requires the receiving terminal to be synchronized bit-for-bit with the sending terminal. This eliminates the need for start-and-stop bits, thereby improving the efficiency (speed) of data transmission.

Asynchronous transmission is the slower rate, such as in telegraph communications with a start and stop of each character. Asynchronous codes are further classified as baudot code and binary coded decimal (BCD) code. Baudot is a 5-level code with 32 possible combinations that is used with some teletype machines. The term baud in baudot means one pulse or code element per second. Baudot uses five bits for the character plus a start and a stop bit. BCD is similar to baudot but has a 6-level code. The extended binary-coded decimal interchange code (EBCDIC) uses an 8-bit data code on IBM mainframe computers. American standard code for information interchange (ASCII) uses seven or eight character bits plus two or three bits for starting and stopping. ASCII is used in personal computers.

(ii) **X.25 standard.** X.25 is an international standard that defines the interface between a computing device and a packet-switched data network. X.25 implements point-to-point connections between two or more user computers. It is a single point of connection for one user computer and a logical point-to-point connection for a number of user computers. This is accomplished through a concept called **virtual circuits** operating in either a permanent mode or a switched mode. The virtual circuits functions in the network layer of the ISO/OSI reference model.

Advantages of X.25 virtual circuits include flexibility in providing a range of functions for implementing multiple-protocol enterprise internetworks, when compared with the conventional telecommunication data links. **Disadvantages** include additional overhead due to handling of multiple protocols and lower throughput due to complex routing decisions.

(iii) **Switched multimegabit data service.** Switched multimegabit data service (SMDS) is provided by several North American public carriers, where it can be viewed as the precursor or the first implementation of Broadband-ISDN (B-ISDN). SMDS is only marginally a competitor of FDDI, where the latter operates in a metropolitan area network (MAN). Rather, SMDS will provide an effective vehicle for connecting LANs in a metropolitan or larger area. SMDS competes more directly with frame relay-based service as another means of connecting LANs together. If SMDS becomes widely installed, then it may offer an advantage for providing wide-area access to those FDDI LANs whose external communications needs include connectivity to many different remote locations.

(iv) **Frame relay.** Frame relay is a new, standardized packet-switching service now being offered by communication carriers for a WAN. In many ways it is a streamlined X.25 packet service. Error recovery with frame relay is end to end, which fits well with the transport layer of the OSI reference model. The reduced processing in switches allows frame relay switches to be faster than their X.25 predecessors. The major market for frame relay is in connecting LANs together. In many cases it will be less expensive to use a frame relay virtual circuit to connect two LANs than to lease a dedicated circuit for that purpose. The major competitor of frame relay for interconnecting LANs is likely to be the SMDS service. Some carriers have both SMDS and frame relay service offerings and choice of the most advantageous service may simply depend on the tariffs.

SMDS VS. FRAME RELAY

- SMDS offers a connectionless service.
- Frame relay is connection-oriented service.

X. 25 VS. FRAME RELAY

- X.25 provides hop-by-hop flow control and recovery from transmission errors.
- Frame relay has simplified flow control and does not recover from transmission errors.

(v) **Virtual private network.** A virtual private network (VPN) can allow employees to connect to the intranet securely, so there are no fears of sensitive information leaving the network unprotected. The Internet alone cannot remove this fear.

A VPN is a private network composed of computers owned by a single organization that share information with each other in that organization (e.g., LAN or WAN). However, a public network is a large collection of organizations or computers who exchange information with each other (e.g., a public telephone system and the Internet).

A VPN blurs the line between a private and public network. With a VPN, a secure, private network can be created over a public network such as the Internet. A VPN can be created using software, hardware, or a combination of the two that provides a secure link between peers over a public network. Control techniques, such as encryption, packet tunneling, and firewalls, are used in a VPN. Tunneling encapsulates a packet within a packet to accommodate incompatible protocols. The packet within the packet could either be of the same protocol or of a completely different one.

The private network is called "virtual" because it uses temporary connections that have no real physical presence, but consist of packets routed over various computers on the Internet on an ad hoc basis. Secure virtual connections are created between two computers, a computer and a network, or two networks. A VPN does not exist physically.

(vi) **Synchronous optical network.** Synchronous optical network (SONET) defines a hierarchy of standardized digital data rates. SONET is intended to provide a specification for high-speed digital transmission over optical fiber. SONET technology can be used for access both to the public network and within the public network. It is installed in a ring topology for a fault-tolerant network.

(vii) **Digital leased lines.** Digital leased lines (T1 and T3 lines) can be used to build a company's leased line private network or it can be used in combination with a public network. When leased lines are used to access a public network the traffic between several sites must be multiplexed over the single access line. Therefore, it is important to be sure that the leased line is fast enough to support this traffic. Higher transmission capacities are available using SONET and the synchronous digital hierarchy technologies.

(viii) **Passive optical networks.** The access network (also called the "last mile"), which exists between the backbone and the business local area network, is still the bottleneck. One solution for this bottleneck problem is to run a separate fiber optical cable from the central office (CO) to every business and home, but the expense of multiple point-to-point links is too great. Another possible solution is for multiple users to share a fiber optical cable as in passive optical network (PON). A PON uses a point-to-multipoint architecture. Because packets destined for a single user are broadcast to multiple users, encryption should be used to provide privacy.

(ix) **Point-to-point protocol.** Point-to-point protocol (PPP) is a full-duplex layer protocol that is very popular for carrying TCP/IP traffic from a user PC to an Internet service provider and for connections between routers and connections between bridges. Features of PPP include address notification, authentication, and link monitoring.

PPP provides a standard way for routers and computers connected over a synchronous, asynchronous, frame relay, SONET, or ISDN WAN link to establish, monitor, and terminate a session and exchange data in between.

PPP has largely replaced serial line Internet protocol (SLIP) as the encapsulation method to carry IP over a dial-up connection. Some advantages of PPP over SLIP include: IP header compression, data compression, error correction, packet sequencing, authentication, and multiprotocol.

The PPP standard specifies that password authentication protocol (PAP) and challenge handshake authentication protocol (CHAP) may be negotiated as authentication methods, but other methods can be added to the negotiation and used as well. New methods of data compression can also be used in the negotiation, which uses the compression control protocol. Handling compression at the end stations ensures that intermediate equipment does not waste time and computing resources compressing the data. Interoperability problems can occur with PPP's implementation, but good PPP software comes with diagnostics to facilitate troubleshooting.

(x) **Digital subscriber line.** A digital subscriber line (DSL) is a faster service than a voice-grade modem. Asymmetric DSL (ADSL) offers a high-speed downstream access to the customer site and a low-speed upstream access from the customer. Examples of downstream services include display of Web pages or large amounts of data. Examples of upstream services include e-mail messages or keystrokes. An advantage of ADSL is that a customer can talk on the telephone at the same time that data are being transferred. One factor that determines the availability of ADSL is the distance to the central office (CO).

5.3 Electronic Funds Transfer

Basically, an electronic funds transfer (EFT) system transfers money and other information electronically from one institution to another. A by-product of this service is the reduction of mountains of paper and time delays, thereby gaining cost efficiencies. For example, banks can transfer money from an account in one bank to another account in another bank, and the federal government can deposit benefits directly into recipients' bank accounts.

A new trend in EFT system is the transmittal of tax information electronically to tax authorities at a central processor. Information such as the amount, tax due, and employer identification number would be provided to the central processor. Some advantages of this approach include fewer errors, lower costs, more timely deposits, and increased elimination of float associated with delays in moving funds.

Some state governments distribute public aid benefits electronically. Benefit recipients who use this system are given magnetic cards with their photographs, which they insert in special electronic devices at the participating check-cashing centers or banks. The cards access computer records to tell the agents the amounts of benefits due.

Other applications include payment of unemployment insurance benefits. Claimants can call the government agency and enter their social security number and personal identification number (PIN). After successfully answering certification questions, claimants are informed that they are to receive their benefits. Participants then gain access to their weekly payments with a plastic card and a PIN through automated teller machines (ATMs) or POS terminals. Those who already have a bank account are given the option to directly deposit their benefits, and those who prefer to receive state-issued checks may continue to do so. This is a clear example of integration of such diverse technologies such as POS, EFT, and ATMs.

5.4 Electronic Commerce

(a) **Overview.** Electronic commerce (e-commerce) is defined as a place where buyers and sellers are connected using computers and networks (the Internet) to buy and sell goods and services. The term electronic business (e-business) is much broader than e-commerce because the former includes distribution of information and customer support, which are lacking in the latter. In other words, e-commerce is a subset of e-business.

E-Commerce and Value Chain

E-commerce is a Web-enabled value chain since the Internet is the enabling technology. Business applications are located on Web servers for wide access to employees and selective access to customers and suppliers.

E-commerce can be grouped into three models: business to consumer (B2C), business to business (B2B), and government to citizen (G2C). On-line stores selling goods directly to consumers is an example of the B2C model. EDI is a critical component of the sales process for many online retailers. B2B e-commerce involves "Internet-enabling" of existing relationships between two companies in exchanging goods and services. EDI is the underlying technology enabling online catalogs and continuous stock replenishment programs. In the G2C model, the federal government is using the Internet to reach its citizens for a variety of information-dissemination purposes and transactions (e.g., Internal Revenue Service, US Postal Service, Social Security Administration). A value chain is created in e-commerce between demand planning, supply planning, and demand fulfillment. The demand planning consists of analyzing buying patterns and developing customer demand forecasts. The supply planning consists of supply allocation, inventory planning, distribution planning, procurement planning, and transportation planning. The demand fulfillment consists of order capturing, customer verification, order promising, backlog management, and order fulfillment.

For the purposes of exploring the relevant security issues, one can divide the e-commerce into four basic classes: (1) electronic mail (e-mail), (2) electronic data interchange (EDI), (3) information transactions, and (4) financial transactions.

E-commerce security issues = E-mail security issues + EDI security issues
+ Information transaction security issues + Financial transaction security issues

(i) **E-mail security issues.** The use of Internet e-mail to carry business-critical communications is growing exponentially. While e-mail provides a low-cost means of communication with customers, suppliers, and partners, a number of security issues are related to the use of e-mail. The security issues include: Internet e-mail addresses are easily spoofed. It is nearly impossible to be certain who created and sent an e-mail message based on the address alone, Internet e-mail messages can be easily modified. Standard SMTP mail provides no integrity checking, there are a number of points where the contents of an e-mail message can be read by unintended recipients, and there is usually no guarantee of delivery with Internet e-mail. While some mail systems support return receipts, when such receipts work at all they often only signify that the user's server (not necessarily the user) has received the message. These weaknesses make it important for organizations to issue policies defining acceptable use of e-mail for business purposes.

(ii) **Electronic data interchange security issues.** Traditional EDI systems allow preestablished trading partners to electronically exchange business data through value-added networks (VANs). The Internet can provide the connectivity needed to support EDI at a substantial cost savings over VAN. However, the Internet does not provide the security services (integrity, confidentiality, and nonrepudiation) required for business EDI. Similar to e-mail over the Internet, EDI transactions are vulnerable to modification, disclosure, or interruption when sent over the Internet. The use of cryptography to provide the required security services has changed this; consequently many companies and government agencies are moving to Internet-based EDI.

Scope of E-Commerce

E-commerce encompasses a broader commerce environment than EDI. Because of this, EDI is a subset of E-commerce. Similarly, E-commerce is a subset of E-business.

(iii) **Information transactions security issues.** Providing information (e.g., stock quotes, news) is a major and costly element of commerce. Using the Internet to provide these services is substantially less expensive than fax, telephone, or postal mail services. Integrity and availability of the information provided are key security concerns that require security controls and policy.

(iv) **Financial transactions security issues.** Computer networks have been used to process financial transactions such as checks, debit cards, credit cards, and electronic funds transfer (EFT). Similar to EDI over VANs, the connectivity options have been limited, and the leased lines are expensive. The Internet provides an opportunity for cost savings in electronic financial transactions. The use of the Internet to carry these types of transactions replaces the physical presentation or exchange of cash, checks, or debit/credit cards with the electronic equivalent. Each of these forms of transactions involves the use of cryptography to provide for integrity, confidentiality, authentication, and nonrepudiation. For example, a standard known as secure electronic transactions (SET) is used for processing credit card transactions over public networks. Use of SET involves three-way transactions between the buyer, the seller, and a financial institution (a bank).

(b) **E-Commerce Software.** E-commerce software should support the following tasks: catalog management, product configuration, shopping cart facilities, e-commerce transaction processing, and Web traffic data analysis.

1. **Catalog management.** Catalog management software combines different product data formats into a standard format for uniform viewing, aggregating, and integrating catalog data into a central repository for easy access, retrieval, and updating of pricing and availability changes.

2. **Product configuration.** Customers need help when an item they are purchasing has many components and options. Buyers use the new Web-based product configuration software to build the product they need online with little or no help from salespeople.
3. **Shopping cart facilities.** Today many e-commerce sites use an electronic shopping cart to track the items selected for purchase, allowing shoppers to view what is in their cart, add new items to it, or remove items from it.
4. **E-commerce transaction processing.** E-commerce transaction processing software takes data from the shopping cart and calculates volume discounts, sales tax, and shipping costs to arrive at the total cost.
5. **Web site traffic data analysis.** Web site traffic data analysis software captures visitor information, including who is visiting the Web site, what search engine and key words they used to find the site, how long their Web browser viewed the site, the date and time of each visit, and which pages were displayed. These data are placed into a Web log file for future analysis to improve the Web site's performance.

(c) **E-Commerce Infrastructure.** Key technology infrastructure for e-commerce applications include Web server hardware, server operating system, server software, e-commerce software, virtual private network (VPN), value-added network (VAN), and the Internet, intranet, or extranet. Strategies for successful e-commerce include: developing an effective Web site that creates an attractive presence and that meets the needs of its visitors (customers), contracting out with Web site hosting service providers or storefront brokers, building traffic into the Web site through meta tag, which is a special HTML tag that contains keywords about the Web site, and analyzing Web site traffic to identify which search engines are effective for your business.

EXAMPLES OF BEST PRACTICES IN ELECTRONIC COMMERCE

- There should be a set of security mechanisms and procedures which, taken together, constitute a security architecture for e-commerce (deals with architecture).
- There should be measures in place to ensure the choice of the correct protocols for the application and the environment, as well as the proper use and exploitation of their features and compensation for their limitations (deals with infrastructure/protocol).
- There should be a mechanism in place to mediate between the public network (the Internet) and an organization's private network (deals with infrastructure/firewall).
- There should be a means to communicate across the Internet in a secure manner (deals with infrastructure/virtual private network).
- There should be a process whereby participants in an e-commerce transaction can be uniquely and positively identified (deals with authentication/digital certificates).
- There should be a mechanism by which the initiator of an e-commerce transaction can be uniquely associated with it (deals with authentication/digital signatures).
- There should be an infrastructure to manage and control public key pairs and their corresponding certificates (deals with authentication/public key infrastructure PKI).
- There should be procedures in place to control changes to an e-commerce presence (deals with applications/change control).
- E-commerce applications should maintain logs of their use, which should be monitored by responsible personnel (deals with applications/logs and monitoring).
- There should be methods and procedures to recognize security breaches when they occur (deals with applications/intrusion detection).
- There should be features in e-commerce applications to reconstruct the activity performed by the applications (deals with applications/auditability).
- There should be a means to maintain a provable association between an e-commerce transaction and the person who entered it (deals with applications/nonrepudiation).
- There should be protections in place to ensure that data collected about individuals are not disclosed without their consent nor used for purposes other than that for which they were collected (deals with applications/privacy).
- There should be a means to ensure the confidentiality of data communicated between customers and vendors (deals with data protection/encryption).

- There should be mechanisms to protect e-commerce presences and their supporting private networks from computer viruses and to prevent them from propagating viruses to customers and vendors (deals with data protection/virus scanning).
- There should be protection over the devices used to access the Internet (deals with availability/protecting the user environment).
- There should be features within e-commerce architecture to keep all components from failing and to repair themselves if they should fail (deals with availability/fault tolerance).
- There should be a plan and procedures to continue e-commerce activities in the event of an extended outage of required resources for normal processing (deals with availability/business continuity planning).
- There should be a commonly understood set of practices and procedures to define management's intentions for the security of e-commerce (deals with policy and governance/policy).
- There should be measures in place to prevent information about customers from being disclosed and not used for purposes other than that for which it was obtained, without the customer's permission (deals with policy and governance/privacy).
- There should be shared responsibility within an organization for e-commerce security (deals with policy and governance/oversight).
- There should be communication from vendors to customers about the level of security in an e-commerce presence (deals with policy and governance/notification).
- There should be a regular program of audit and assessment of the security of e-commerce environments and applications to provide assurance that controls are present and effective (deals with policy and governance/auditing and assurance).

SOURCE: *E-Commerce Security, Enterprise Best Practices*, Information Systems Audit and Control Research Foundation (ISACRF), now known as the IT Governance Institute, 2000, Rolling Meadows, Illinois, USA.

5.5 Electronic Data Interchange

Electronic data interchange (EDI) systems provide computer-to-computer communication. EDI systems are becoming a normal way of exchanging or transmitting documents, transactions, records, quantitative and financial information, and computer-related messages from one computer to another. Some examples of transactions and documents involved are as follows: purchase orders, invoices, shipping notices, receiving advice, acknowledgements, and payments. When payment is involved, the EDI system can be referred to as electronic funds transfer (EFT) system.

EDI is replacing manual data entry with electronic data entry. The objective of EDI is to eliminate manual data entry work and to eliminate or reduce paper mailing and processing delays between two trading parties, for example, buyer and seller, manufacturer and supplier.

Traditional paper-driven systems such as order entry, purchase order, billing, and accounts payable systems are changing significantly with the introduction of EDI-based systems. Some problems with traditional paper-driven application systems are low accuracy, increased mailing and processing times, and high labor and processing costs.

Basically, the transmission of information between two parties can take place in three ways. The first is direct, the second is via a third party service provider, and the third is in the form of computer tapes, disks, and diskettes.

(a) **EDI System.** *Essentially, the EDI system works as follows:*

- The buyer identifies the item to be purchased. Data are entered into the purchasing application system. Translation software creates an EDI purchase order, which is sent electronically to the supplier. The same order is sent to the buyer's accounts payable and goods receiving system.
- A functional acknowledgment, indicating receipt of the order, is automatically generated and electronically transmitted to the buyer.
- The supplier's computer sends the order information to his shipping and invoicing systems.
- Upon receipt by the buyer of the ship notice, the data are electronically entered into the receiving system file.

- The receipt notice is electronically transmitted to the accounts payable application system.
- The ship notice is electronically transmitted to the invoicing application system.
- An invoice is electronically generated by the supplier and transmitted to the buyer. The same information is sent to the supplier's accounts receivable system.
- The invoice is received by the buyer's computer and is translated into the buyer's format. The invoice, receiving notice, and purchase order are electronically matched and reconciled.
- The buyer electronically transmits payment to the supplier's bank through their bank. An electronic remittance advice is transmitted to the supplier.
- Upon receipt of the remittance and notice of payment, the data are transmitted into accounts receivable system, and the buyer account is updated. The buyer is given credit for payment.

(b) **Components of an EDI System.** *The components of an EDI system are standards, software, and networks.* The EDI **standards** consist of formatting standards and communication standards. Formatting standards deal with the type, sequence, and content of an electronic document. Communication standards cover baud rate, protocols, electronic envelopes, and message transmission times. Standards provide a set of common rules, in terms of syntax and formatting, for the development of electronic communications.

In terms of **software,** a translation program is needed to translate company-specific data to EDI standard format for transmission. A reverse translation is performed when data arrive at the organization from external sources.

In terms of **networks,** there are two approaches in common use. In a direct network the computers of the trading partners are linked directly, usually through dial-up modems. A direct network is effective for a limited number of trading partners. As the number of trading partners increases, it is difficult to maintain open lines for all trading partners. The second choice is to use a third-party network, also known as a value-added network (VAN), that acts as an intermediary between trading partners. A VAN maintains a mailbox for both the sender and the receiver.

The VAN receives purchase orders from the sender (buyer), sorts them by seller, and places each seller's purchase orders in his mailbox. At a later time, the seller can dial in to the VAN and retrieve its mail in the form of electronic purchase orders. This approach allows each trading partner to create only one electronic transmission to the VAN rather than having to create a separate electronic transmission for each trading partner.

(c) **Benefits of EDI.** A major benefit is being able to load data, without rekeying, from various formats and placing it where it is needed in a different format for further processing. Besides savings due to reductions in document mailing and processing costs, decreases in data entry personnel costs, and reductions in inventory stock levels, organizations are realizing other significant benefits.

These added benefits include improved operational efficiency in warehousing, shipping, purchasing, and receiving areas; increased sales; increased customer responsiveness; increased ability to compete; and quick access to better information in a timely manner. The users of EDI include organizations in the trucking, retail, shipping, grocery, health care, pharmaceutical, and automotive industries, government, and others.

5.6 Functional Areas of Information Technology Operations

(a) Operating Environment.

(i) **Data input and output procedures.** The data control or production control function is the first line of defense in the computer center against possible delays, errors, omissions, and irregularities. This is due to the fact that many front-end activities such as data entry, job set-up, and job scheduling are performed prior to executing production jobs for application systems. The things that data/production control staff do and how well they do them will have a great impact on subsequent activities such as computer operations, backup and recovery, storage media management, help desk, and report delivery. Consequently, there are many potential risks and exposures in the data/production control work area.

The **goal** of a data control management should be to encourage remote printing where a printer is attached to a local terminal, personal computer, or workstation for timely printing, discourage central printing at the computer center to minimize delays, and labor and print costs, and encourage electronic report viewing facilitated by an automated report distribution software. Electronic report viewing is not a substitute for the hard-copy report printing; rather, report printing can be done in a discretionary manner.

(ii) **Production program execution procedures.** Production control activities include scheduling of jobs and controlling production job turnover procedures, among other things. Some typical activities of a computer operator include execution of production jobs and programs; monitoring of system resources including the computer consoles, hardware preventive maintenance, and operational changes; backing up of program and data files; mounting/unmounting of tapes, cartridges, and disks; recording of operational problems; monitoring of physical security and environmental controls; and housekeeping activities and logging of system activities.

(iii) **Job scheduling practices.** The operations manager has a difficult task in balancing between a certain amount of scheduling work to do and a certain amount of resources with which to do it. Consequently, work must be prioritized based on user business needs. In this regard, most important considerations are peripheral devices (e.g., tape or disk drives) required, job execution time, and memory required. The least important consideration is how the operator interacts with the user. Most production jobs will have a predecessor and successor job to be run.

Job scheduling can be done either manually on paper or automatically using a computer system. Manual scheduling is slow and prone to errors if the computer center environment is complex. The decision whether computer job scheduling is done manually or not depends on various factors such as

- Single CPU or multiple CPUs. Multiple CPUs require an automated job scheduling system.
- Number of total jobs to be run in a time period. The greater the total number of jobs, the greater the need for automation.
- Number of operating shifts. The more work shifts in operation, the greater the need for automation.
- Number of concurrent priority-one jobs to be run. Paper schedules will become complex to manage as the number of concurrent priority-one jobs increases.

Usually, when a new application system is being developed, run-times and other resource requirements (e.g., disk and tape space) are estimated for each job by the system development group. Operations management then determines how best to accommodate these requirements in light of other job needs.

(iv) **Production job turnover procedures.** Production problems stem from hardware failures (10%), systems software failures (20%), and applications software failures (70%). Applications software failures are usually the result of problems originating in or unaddressed by the applications software development and maintenance work area. The most prevalent causes of those failures are

- Incomplete software testing by programmers and functional end users for new application systems development work
- Inappropriate software **regression testing** by programmers for existing application systems maintenance work
- Inappropriate changes made in common program modules such as copy members, macros
- Unreliable paper records and manual procedures in the user and IS departments
- Lack of production/operation acceptance testing by computer operations staff
- Lack of or inadequate quality assurance review by production scheduling and control staff
- Overall poor-quality job turnover procedures
- Inexperienced programmers, production control analysts, and computer operators

Some ways to reduce or eliminate the business risk are to automate the production turnover process and to focus on software configuration management. On-line approvals and automatic transfer of programs from test to production via quality assurance (QA) libraries or from test to production directly will dominate the automation process. A QA library (as shown in Exhibit 5.24) is a staging library where final quality reviews and production set-up procedures take place. Software configuration management helps in identifying the locations and the number of computer machines and in determining the networks that need to be propagated with new or changed software.

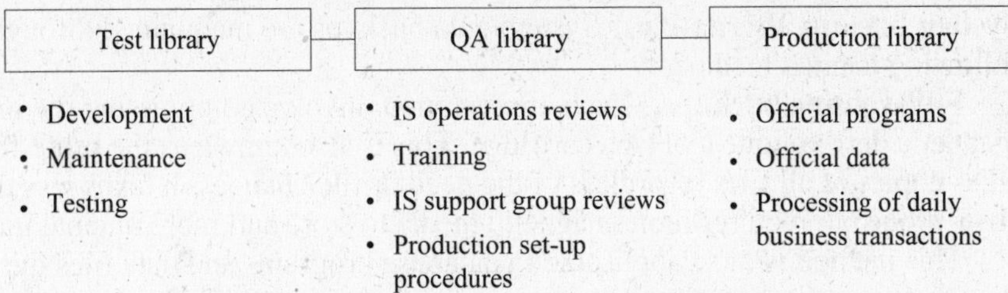

Exhibit 5.24: Libraries involved in a job turnover process

(b) **Computer Operations.** Console operations, system backups, and preventive maintenance work constitute a major responsibility of a computer operator. Other activities include tape/disk handling, system logs, and help-desk function.

(i) **Console operations.** An important task for the computer operator is operating the system console. The operating system sends questions and messages to the operator for a response. It is estimated that 90% or more of these messages are trivial in nature and do not require the operator's attention. Yet, they consume valuable operator's time and cause frustration to the operator due to their speed in presentation. Software is available to automate the console operations and to suppress trivial messages so that the operator responds only to important questions and messages.

Computer operators should have access to system console and operator manuals, not program documentation. They should not perform run-to-run balancing procedures. The console log should contain operator commands, operator messages, and system abends, not data entry errors.

(ii) **System backups.** Hardware failures, disk crashes, power outages, software failures, and other disruptions are normal in computer center operation. Periodic system backups would provide the ability to recover and restart from a failure or disaster and prevent the destruction of information. *System backups include backing up of operational application programs, data files, databases, systems software products, system development programs, utility programs, and others.*

Timely system backups help in reconstructing any damaged files (recovery) and resuming computer program execution (restart). For example, online and real-time systems and database systems require duplicate backup arrangements and extensive backup and recovery and restart procedures.

For online systems, restart procedures identify transactions that were lost when the online process failed. Another related backup mechanism is "checkpoints" which allow program restarts. Checkpoints would be most effective for batch (sequential processing), online data entry and batch update processing and multiprogramming and least effective for online real-time systems due to their instant access and updates. Checkpoints are needed to recover from hardware failures and are usually applicable to sequential files, and direct (random) access files, and tape or disk files. Exhibit 5.25 compares the backup requirements between online and batch systems.

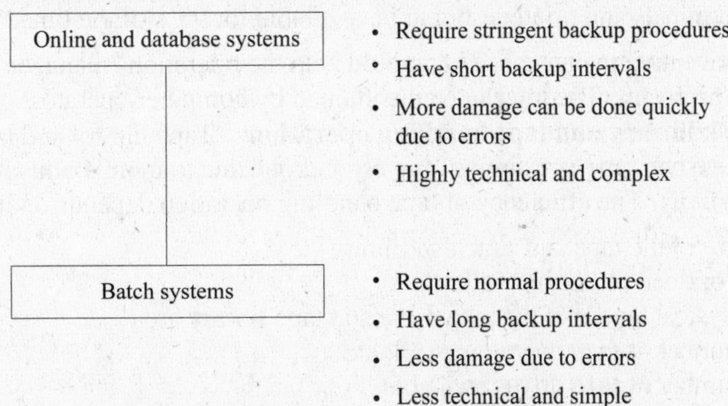

Exhibit 5.25: Backup requirements for online and batch systems

A prerequisite to the performance of timely system backups is the availability of accurate and up-to-date operations documentation (run books), which includes run-time instructions, backup schedules, and recovery/restart procedures for each application system in the production environment. The decision on how often to back up a file is dependent on cost of backup versus expected cost of failure, capability of recreating the file without a backup, and time needed to create a copy.

(iii) **System backup alternatives.** System/data backups are maintained through a combination of the following manual methods:

Full-volume backups, which are common, involve compressing the image copy of an entire magnetic disk volume to a tape/cartridge. This is also known as the brute-force approach since it takes copies of all files regardless of the need or file changes. It takes less time to back up and is less error-prone but requires more magnetic media to store and more manual intervention.

This method is most applicable to database programs and data files due to the logical relationships between data. System recovery is achieved by restoring the database and reapplying transactions from the journal or log. Journals and logs are records of all the transactions that have been processed against a database. The log contains before and after images of transactions for all changes. In the event of a failure, the database is restored and all the changes that have occurred up to the point of failure are reapplied to the database. Some databases are so large that record-level backup is performed whenever a change to the logical database record occurs.

Incremental backups, a new approach, focus only on backing up datasets that have changed since the last full backup. The need for continuous, uninterrupted online system availability leaves a reduced time-window for full backups, which, in turn, justifies the use of incremental backups.

(iv) **Data file backup concepts.** Usually, tape files are backed up using a three-generation (son, father, and grandfather) concept, where each generation represents a time period (e.g., seven or five operating days). Disk files are saved for five or seven generations. Each generation can have multiple copies and be rotated between on-site and off-site. Tape files are a major obstacle to unattended computer center operation due to their labor-intensive nature.

(v) **Preventive maintenance.** The regular practice of preventive maintenance of computer equipment and other system components will provide the assurance of continuity of computing services to end users. Here, computer equipment includes CPU, printers, terminals, and disk/tape drives; other system components include physical channels, control units, cables, air conditioning units, uninterrupted power supply machines, and other mechanical/electrical devices.

The operations manager first needs to analyze the failure rates for each of the computer equipment and system component parts. After knowing the failure rates, the manager should determine the impact of failing equipment or a component on the completion of application system production job schedule. Component failure rates and impact analysis will allow the manager to shift the processing schedules either manually or automatically to balance the workload. Mean-time between failures should be determined for each piece of computer equipment and the system components.

The output of component failure rates and impact analysis can be used to establish system availability objectives and service levels between hardware vendors and computer operations management. Some examples of system availability objectives include

- The CPU should be available for 99% of all scheduled production time.
- Disk/tape drives should be available for 98% of scheduled time
- Terminals and printers should be available for 95% of the time.

A preventive maintenance log would help the operations manager and the hardware vendor in tracking problems. The log can be maintained by computer operators or supervisors.

(vi) **Tape/disk library and tape handling operations.** Tape library and tape handling operations are labor-intensive, time-consuming, and error-prone due to monotonous work and sheer volume of tape mount activity. The efficiency of tape handling operation depends on many factors such as

- Size of the tape and cartridge library
- Workload peaks and valleys
- Physical layout of the tape drive and tape library area
- Number of tape operators available
- Number of tape drives available
- Number of operating shifts per day
- Number of tape mounts that must be made per operating shift
- Technical sophistication of available hardware and software

The decision whether to use tape/cartridge or disk storage media for a data or program file (dataset) should be based on a cost-benefit analysis. Some factors that should be considered include

- Size and complexity of the file (number of records and record types)
- Frequency of file usage (daily, weekly, period-end)

- Volatility of the file (number of records added, changed, and deleted)
- File access method (direct/random, sequential)
- File structure (fixed length, variable length)
- Transportability of the file (off-site storage, third-party processing, remote processing)

The following guidelines, although not absolute, could be useful when deciding between tape/cartridge or disk media:

- Disk storage media is advised when small size, infrequently used, and random access datasets need to be processed.
- Tape/cartridge storage media is advised when large-size, frequently used, and sequentially processed datasets need to be processed. Tape/cartridge files are easy to transport.
- If tape/cartridge is chosen, it is a choice between manual (human) or automated (robotics) handling.
- If disk media is chosen, it is a choice between fixed or removable disk. Fixed disk is faster and cheaper than removable disk. Removable disks can be physically secured by removing and locking them separately if such a need arises.

(vii) **Tape cleaning and degaussing.** In addition to performing recordkeeping of tape and cartridge activity and taking periodic inventory of tapes/cartridges, the tape librarian will be cleaning and recertifying the reel tapes and cartridges to prolong their life. The cleaning equipment should clean both sides of the tape/cartridge, measure the length, test for damaged tape, isolate errors, and retension the tape to industry standards. Cartridges are more reliable and hold more data than reel tapes.

The process of demagnetizing (erasing) the contents of tapes and cartridges is called **degaussing**. It is suggested that when tapes/cartridges are disposed of or no longer in use, they should be subjected to degaussing procedures especially for sensitive data. Disk files are demagnetized by overwriting three times with 0, 1, and a special character, in that order, so that sensitive information is completely deleted.

(viii) **Logging of system activities.** Another important task performed by the computer operations staff is logging and monitoring various systems activities. Transaction log is a processing control, provides an audit trail, and is good for online systems. It is useful for file reconstruction and error tracing if errors occur in updating online files. Ten logs are presented with their contents.

1. Contents of an application transaction log include: transaction code; record type; date and time stamp; user ID or department; terminal ID; transaction amount; transaction activity (add, inquire, delete); and application-specific information.

System Logging Facilities

System logging facilities collect vast amounts of data by design. The key is to determine what types of data to collect and how much.

2. Contents of a database log include: Before images (helps in database roll-back); after images (helps in database roll-forward); input and output file information; access errors; date and time stamp; transaction type and ID; terminal ID; user ID or department; programs used or called; access authorizations; input messages; output messages (transaction was complete or not); and list of data blocks read.
3. Contents of an operating system (console) log include: job ID; date and time stamp; job run times (start and finish times); input and output files used; programs used; disk and tape/cartridge devices used; job completion codes (including abends and successful); computer operator interventions; system diagnostic messages; and file backup times and recovery/restore times.
4. Contents of a telecommunications log include: originating terminal ID; transmission line ID; job ID; communication port ID; date and time stamp; type of application (e.g., CICS, IMS); session type (e.g., bound or not bound); session start and finish times; transmission error messages; user authorization code; transaction ID; message ID; control totals; port/node ID; dial back telephone number; and messages awaiting transmission.

5. Contents of an access control security log include: user ID; terminal ID; date and time stamp; transaction ID; data sets used; job ID; sign-on ID modifications; access rule modifications; type of security violations (**read** when not authorized); unauthorized access attempts and messages; invalid attempts of password; and last activity date. The security system can be found to operate on warning, log, or abort mode.
6. Contents of job accounting log include: job name and ID; job run time with start and finish times; date and time stamps; input and output files used; programs used; user type information (user ID, accounting code, division ID); job completion codes; control totals based on number of records or dollars; input and output devices used; CPU time consumed for the job; and other resource usage data.
7. Contents of problem (help-desk) management log include: a problem number; problem type and description; problem reported time/date; problem source (i.e., failing software, hardware device, network component); name, department, phone number of person reporting the problem; problem resolution status code (i.e., open, closed, transferred) with action dates; name of the (help-desk) person who took the call; name of the person who worked on the problem; and description of final response/resolution of the problem and feedback to the person who reported the problem.
8. Contents of a change management log include: a change number; change type and description; change requestor name and time/date; change source (i.e., failing software or hardware device problem); change status code (i.e., open, closed, deferred) with action dates; name of the person who worked on the change; and description of final outcome of the change and sign-off by the person affected by the change.
9. Contents of a hardware preventive maintenance log include: date/time that a hardware device failed; serial number and location of the hardware device failed; time when service request was made; time when service arrived; time when problem was fixed; description of cause of problem; nature of repair and cost; and warranty period.
10. Contents of system management log include: date and time stamps; datasets accessed; datasets renamed; datasets scratched; system paging activity; job CPU times; job/step termination record; data lost record; jobs using tape bypass label processing; and remote user access.

(ix) **Help-desk function.** In order to provide quality and timely support and service to end users, many computer centers are establishing an end-user support function. This includes an information center, help desk, 24-hour hot-line services, telephone voice response system, and automated problem and change management systems.

A help desk function can implement telephone hot-line services so that end users can call in with their problems and ask pertinent questions. These problems could be related to problems as diverse as printer/terminal operations, operating system malfunctions, telecommunications software incompatibilities, or applications software glitches. The help-desk person will try to solve a problem; if he cannot, he will hopefully route the problem to the right person. Problem logging, routing, and escalation procedures are needed to resolve problems in a timely and proper manner.

Recent innovations such as voice response systems could supplement the help desk function in terms of directing the end user to the appropriate person. Other developments include the implementation of expert systems that aid the help-desk staff in terms of problem diagnosis and resolution.

(c) **Change and Problem Management.** Installation of a change/problem management system or service is another end-user service and support tool where problems and changes are logged, tracked, reported, resolved, and implemented.

Changes can arise from

- Changes in applications and systems software
- Changes in procedures (automated or manual)
- Installation of new software products and equipment
- Introduction of new work tools and techniques
- Changes in equipment and people
- Changes in organizational structure
- Changes in business requirements

Problems can result from

- Operating system failures
- Application program failures
- Processor (CPU or front-end) failures
- Computer terminal failures
- Telecommunication line and equipment failures
- Printer failures
- Personal computer or workstation failures
- Change control failures
- Simply from a failed change

The goals of the computer center operations management should be to

- Stabilize the production environment and limit negative impact (system outages, errors, backouts, and downtime) due to changes or problems.
- Maintain the integrity and security of all program modules, hardware devices, and network components within the production environment.
- Prioritize those changes that are critical to business function versus those changes that can be deferred.
- Coordinate all problems and changes in a controlled and coordinated manner.
- Promote a proactive mode of computer operations instead of a reactive one.

Often, incorrectly implemented changes cause problems. There should be a cross-reference between a change and a problem caused by a change. To some extent, integrity, liability, and availability of computer systems depend on the way the problems and changes are managed, controlled, and secured. Problem management is critical to online processing due to high visibility of problems to end users. Changes can be classified into standard change request, mandatory change requests, and emergency change requests, so that priorities can be established and resources can be allocated accordingly.

(d) **Service-Level Management.** Service-level management is a better way for the computer center management to improve quality of computing services to system users. The computer center management must define a set of user service levels or service objectives that describe application systems, volume of transactions, processing windows, online system response times, and batch job turnaround times. Without defined service levels to monitor against actual performance determined in the resource utilization function, a computer system's capacity limit is difficult to identify. Without service levels, the computer center management will consider that the capacity of a computer is near its limits when the users begin to complain about computer performance.

By monitoring performance against service levels, the computer center management can identify approaching problems in meeting service objectives. In order to achieve these goals, computer center management needs to develop service level objectives for internal use. Some examples of areas requiring service level objectives are

- System capacity during peak hours in terms of average CPU busy, average demand paging rate, and maximum channel busy
- Number of online users, number of online transactions per minute, and number of batch jobs per hour
- Online system average response time in seconds by application
- Percentage of time the online system is available
- Turnaround time for test and production batch jobs processed under each job class by application
- Number of job reruns and time lost due to job reruns
- Number of abnormal terminations (abends) by application program per operating shift

Where applicable, maximum and minimum numbers should be identified for each of these objectives. The rationale behind developing service level objectives internally first is that they provide a basis for negotiating service level agreements with the user community.

After developing service level objectives internally, the computer center management is ready to negotiate with each business user to develop formal service level agreements. Some examples of service level agreements are

- Average response times for each online application system

- Turnaround times for each batch job by application system
- System availability time (system up-time) by each application system
- Accuracy limits in terms of number of errors by cause for each application system
- Number of job reruns by each application system
- Number of transactions to be processed during peak hours in each application system
- Number of production problems by application system per week
- Computer report delivery times by application system
- A plan for reporting service level problems
- Action priorities if services cannot be delivered
- Scheduled meetings to discuss service levels between end users and computer center management

It is important to remember that these service level agreements are not static. They require adjustments and refinements periodically, such as at least once a year or preferably at the time of renegotiation of the agreement with customers (users).

(e) **Separation of Duties in IT Operations.** The objective is to ensure that no one person has complete control over a transaction throughout its initiation, authorization, recording, processing, and reporting. A similar concept applies equally to any operation performed by IT or user department employees. The rationale is to minimize the incompatible functions, which are not conducive to good internal control structure.

It is important to understand that the degree of separation of duties depends on the job level. This means that there is more separation of duties practiced at the lower levels of the organization than at higher levels. The rationale is that somebody at higher levels needs to be in charge of many functions, activities, and operations.

(f) **Separation of Duties in IT Departments.** At a minimum, the following functions in the IT environment should be separated from each other at lower levels.

Incompatible IT functions are

- Data entry and production job scheduling
- Computer operations and applications programming
- Computer operations and systems programming
- Application programming and systems programming
- Systems programming and data security administration
- Data security administration and data administration (includes database administration)
- Data administration and quality assurance
- Database administration and applications programming
- Telecommunication network and computer operations
- Quality assurance and applications development/maintenance
- Quality assurance and systems programming

Compatible IT functions are

- Quality assurance and data security administration
- Help desk and telecommunication networks
- Job control analysis and job scheduling
- Tape librarian and documentation librarian
- Systems analysis and application programming

5.7 Encryption

(a) **Encryption Process.** Encryption is the process of **encoding** information in a predetermined way so that it is unintelligible to anyone who does not know how to **decode** it. The use of encryption techniques for dial-up communications represents the highest form of security. First, it protects the confidentiality of information passing over the communications link by making it unintelligible to snoopers. This is the primary rationale for using encryption. Second, certain modes of encryption operation, for example, cipher block chaining, when combined with an authentication technique, can be used to protect the integrity of messages so that tampering or transmission errors can be identified.

Third, the uniqueness of the encryption key that must be shared by sender and receiver enforces an extremely high degree of user identification. There is one common problem with communications encryption. If the key used by sender and receiver is the only real security, then the security surrounding the procedure used to exchange the key between them becomes extremely important.

- Most present encryption systems rely on the users to transfer keys manually in some way, which may or may not be secure. The intruder may have an opportunity to intercept the key while it is in transit. The level of security afforded by encryption is dependent upon the security of managing the encryption keys. One promising device makes encryption more practical because it manages keys automatically. This unit uses drop-in circuit boards for PCs to create a secure dial-up network. If one user wants to connect with another to exchange sensitive information, the user calls up a special program and requests connection. The board then determines whether the user may make the connection. If so, the board places a telephone call to the other system's board, exchanges session keys encrypted in a higher-level encryption key the two boards share, and enters into the communications session with the session keys operative.

In the newer form of encryption hardware designed for PCs, all circuitry is contained on a single circuit board that is plugged into one of the standard slots on the motherboard, which is located inside the computer housing. Encryption can be implemented in both hardware and software.

(b) **Basic Cryptographic Techniques.** Cryptography is a branch of mathematics based on the transformation of data. It provides an important tool for protecting information and is used in many aspects of computer security. For example, cryptography can help provide data confidentiality, integrity, electronic signatures, and advanced user authentication.

Cryptography relies on two basic components: (1) an algorithm and (2) a key. Algorithms are complex mathematical formulae and keys are strings of bits. For two parties to communicate, they must use the same algorithm(s). In some cases, they must also use the same key. Most cryptographic keys must be kept secret; sometimes algorithms are also kept secret.

There are two basic types of cryptography: (1) secret key systems (also called symmetric systems) and (2) public key systems (also called asymmetric systems) (see Exhibit 5.26). Often, the two are combined to form a hybrid system to exploit the strengths of each type. Which type of key is needed depends on security requirements and the operating environment of the organization.

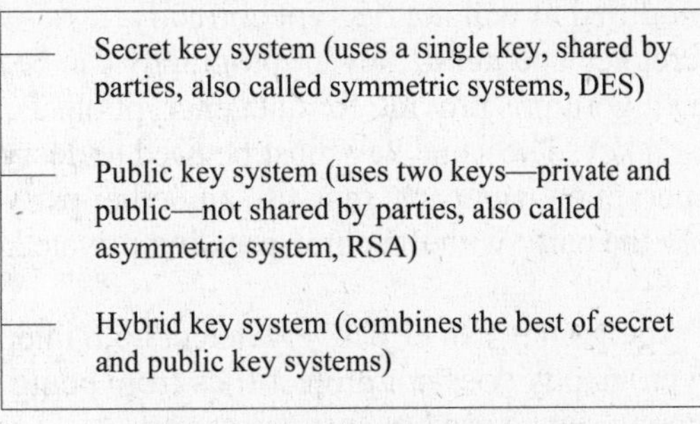

Secret key system (uses a single key, shared by parties, also called symmetric systems, DES)
Public key system (uses two keys—private and public—not shared by parties, also called asymmetric system, RSA)
Hybrid key system (combines the best of secret and public key systems)

Exhibit 5.26: Types of cryptography

(i) **Secret key cryptography.** In secret key cryptography, two (or more) parties share the same key, and that key is used to encrypt and decrypt data. If the key is compromised, the security offered by cryptography is severely reduced or eliminated. Secret key cryptography assumes that the parties who share a key rely on each other to not disclose the key and protect it against modification. The best known secret key system is the data encryption standard (DES) and it is a strong, widely accepted, publicly available cryptographic system. It has been accepted by the American National Standards Institute (ANSI) as the basis for encryption, integrity, access control, and key management standards.

(ii) **Public key cryptography.** Whereas secret key cryptography uses a single key shared by two (or more) parties, public key cryptography uses a pair of keys for each party. One of the keys of the pair is "public" and the other is "private." The public key can be made known to other parties; the private key must be kept confidential and must be known only to its owner. Both keys, however, need to be protected against modification.

Public key cryptography is particularly useful when the parties wishing to communicate cannot rely upon each other or do not share a common key. Examples of public key systems include Rivest, Shamir, and Adleman (RSA) and the digital signature standard (DSS).

(iii) **Hybrid cryptographic systems.** Public and secret key cryptography have relative advantages and disadvantages. Although public key cryptography does not require users to share a common key, secret key cryptography is much faster. Typically, the speed advantage of secret key cryptography means that it is used for encrypting bulk data.

Public key cryptography is used for applications that are less demanding to a computer system's resources, such as encrypting the keys used by secret key cryptography for distribution or to sign messages.

(iv) **Uses of cryptography.** Cryptography is used to protect data both inside and outside the boundaries of a computer system. Outside the computer system, cryptography is sometimes the only way to protect data. While in a computer system, data is normally protected with logical and physical access controls perhaps supplemented by cryptography. However, when in transit across communication lines or resident on someone else's computer, data cannot be protected by the originator's logical or physical access controls. Cryptography provides a solution by protecting data even when the data is no longer in the control of the originator. Four types of uses of cryptography include: (1) data encryption, (2) integrity, (3) electronic signatures, and (4) user authentication (see Exhibit 5.27).

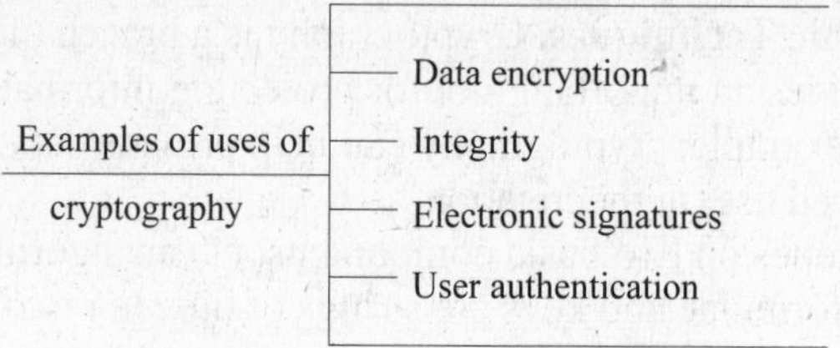

Exhibit 5.27: Uses of cryptography

(A) ***Data encryption.*** One of the best ways to obtain cost-effective data confidentiality is through the use of encryption. Encryption transforms intelligible data, called plaintext, into an unintelligible form, called ciphertext. This process is reversed through the process of decryption. Once data is encrypted, the ciphertext does not have to be protected against disclosure. However, if ciphertext is modified, it will not decrypt correctly.

Both secret key and public key cryptography can be used for data encryption, although not all public key algorithms provide for data encryption. To use a secret key algorithm, data is encrypted using a key. The same key must be used to decrypt the data. When public cryptography is used for encryption, any party may use any other party's public key to encrypt a message; however, only the party with the corresponding private key can decrypt, and thus read, the message.

(B) ***Integrity.*** Cryptography can effectively detect both intentional and unintentional modification; however, cryptography does not protect files from being modified. Both secret key and public key cryptography can be used to ensure integrity.

When secret key cryptography is used, a message authentication code (MAC) is calculated from and appended to the data. To verify that the data has not been modified at a later time, any party with access to the correct secret key can recalculate the MAC. The new MAC is compared with the original MAC, and if they are identical, the verifier has confidence that the data has not been modified by an unauthorized party.

Public key cryptography verifies integrity by using public key signatures and secure hashes. A secure hash algorithm is used to create a message digest. The message digest, called a hash, is a short form of the message that changes if the message is modified. The hash is then signed with a private key. Anyone can recalculate the hash and use the corresponding public key to verify the integrity of the message.

(C) ***Electronic signatures.*** An electronic signature is a cryptographic mechanism that performs a similar function to a written signature. It is used to verify the origin and contents of a message. For example, a recipient of data (e.g., an e-mail message) can verify who signed the data and that the data was not modified after being signed. This also means that the originator (e.g., sender of an e-mail message) cannot falsely deny having signed the data. Cryptography can provide a means of linking a document with a particular person, as is done with a written signature. An electronic signature can use either secret key or public key cryptography; however, public key methods are generally easier to use. **Social engineering** in terms of trickery and coercion are problems with electronic signatures, similar to written signatures.

Simply taking a digital picture of a written signature does not provide adequate security. Such a digitized written signature can easily be copied from one electronic document to another with no way to determine whether it is legitimate. Electronic signatures, on the other hand, are unique to the message being signed and will not verify if they are copied to another document. Cryptographic signatures provide extremely strong proof that a message has not been altered and was signed by a specific key.

Two types of electronic signatures exist: (1) secret key electronic signatures and (2) public key electronic signatures (see Exhibit 5.28).

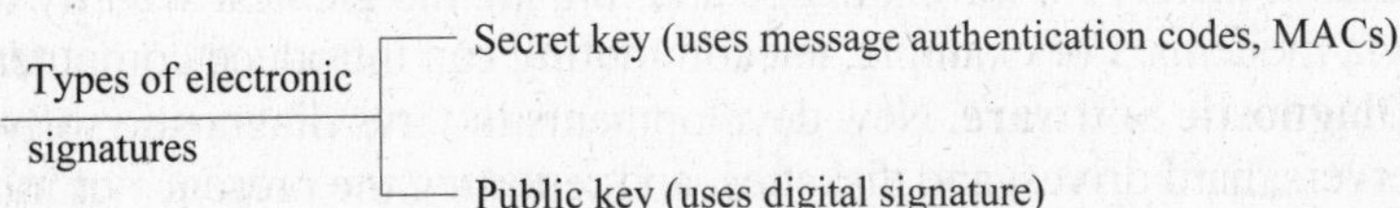

Exhibit 5.28: Types of electronic signatures

Secret key electronic signatures. An electronic signature can be implemented using secret key message authentication codes (MACs). For example, if two parties share a secret key, and one party receives data with a MAC that is correctly verified using the shared key, that party may assume that the other party signed the data. This assumes, however, that the two parties trust each other. Thus, through the use of a MAC, in addition to data integrity, a form of electronic signature is obtained. Using additional controls, such as key notarization and key attributes, it is possible to provide an electronic signature even if the two parties do not trust each other.

Public key electronic signatures. Another type of electronic signature called a digital signature is implemented using public key cryptography. Data is electronically signed by applying the originator's private key to the data. To increase the speed of the process, the private key is applied to a shorter form of the data, called a "hash" or "message digest," rather than to the entire set of data. The resulting digital signature can be stored or transmitted along with the data. The signature can be verified by any party using the public key of the signer. This feature is very useful, for example, when distributing signed copies of virus-free software. Any recipient can verify that the program remains virus-free. If the signature verifies properly, then the verifier has confidence that the data was not modified after being signed and that the owner of the public key was the signer.

(D) ***User authentication.*** Cryptography can increase security in user authentication techniques. Instead of communicating passwords over an open network, authentication can be performed by demonstrating knowledge of a cryptographic key. Using these methods, a onetime password, which is not susceptible to eavesdropping, can be used. User authentication can use either secret or public key cryptography.

SUMMARY OF USES OF CRYPTOGRAPHY

In general, cryptography is used to meet the following four security objectives:

1. **Confidentiality** services restrict access to the content of sensitive data to only those individuals who are authorized to view the data. Confidentiality measures prevent the unauthorized disclosure of information to unauthorized individuals or processes.
2. **Data integrity** services address the unauthorized or accidental modification of data. This includes data insertion, deletion, and modification. To ensure data integrity, a system must be able to detect unauthorized data modification. The goal is for the receiver of the data to verify that the data has not been altered.
3. **Authentication** services establish the validity of a transmission, message, or an originator. (Authentication services also verify an individual's authorization to receive specific categories of information. These services are not specific to cryptography). Therefore, this service applies to both individuals and the information itself. The goal is for the receiver of the data to determine its origin.

4. **Nonrepudiation** services prevent an individual from denying that previous actions had been performed. The goal is to ensure that the recipient of the data is assured of the sender's identity.

5.8 Information Protection

(a) **Computer Viruses.** There is no such thing as a secure computer or network. All computing environments are vulnerable to computer viruses. New and more sophisticated viruses are showing up almost daily and these viruses are unpredictable and grow in an uncontrolled manner. Viruses spread very rapidly from one computing environment to another as well as within an environment. Hackers and intruders, who do it merely for the challenge and fun, are the greatest security threat in networks with dial-in access via modems. For example, telecommuting can introduce computer viruses.

(b) **Virus Diagnostic Software.** New developments in virus diagnostic software include scanning of all network servers, hard drives, and diskettes, and reporting the presence of most commonly known viruses. If a virus is found, the program will identify the virus by name and the name of the file infected and will then allow the user to optionally erase the infected file thereby removing the virus from the computer system. Some virus diagnostic programs even "wipe the file" by writing over the entire program with zeros before erasing it, thus ensuring that the infection cannot be brought back by an unerase program.

Some virus detection programs use encryption-based authenticators that are used to calculate unforgeable digital signatures for whichever data files and/or programs are selected. Any modification of these programs, by a virus or any other means, triggers a change in the signature that is then detectable by the virus detection program.

(c) **Types of Malicious Code.** Malicious code, such as viruses and worms, attacks a system in one of many ways, either internally or externally. Traditionally, the virus is an internal threat, while the worm, to a large extent, is a threat from an external source.

Viruses and worms are related classes of malicious code. Both share the primary objective of replication. However, they are distinctly different with respect to the techniques they use and their host system requirements. This distinction is due to the disjoint sets of host systems they attack. In the past, viruses have been almost exclusively restricted to single-user, single-task personal computers (PCs), while worms have attacked only multiuser systems. This will reverse in the future as the functionality of PCs continues to grow to multiuser and multitask systems.

Hostile software is software that lies hidden from view until it begins reproducing and wreaking havoc with the software and data. Hostile software can damage, erase, hide, or copy applications software or data files, disrupt processing by consuming computing time and disk space, and take over a computer or screen display unexpectedly and display messages that delay the user or cause needless worry.

Hostile software can be grouped into the following categories: virus, worm, bomb, and trap door. Generally, the term virus refers to all hostile software (see Exhibit 5.29 for risks in and controls over hostile software). Symptoms of a virus can include file size increase, change in update timestamp, sudden decrease of free space, or unusual screen activity. A particular hostile software program can fall into more than one category. The following is list of malicious code:

- **Virus.** A virus infects programs already in existence by inserting new code. The primary function of a virus is to reproduce. It may also have a secondary function such as destroying data. When the target program is executed, the virus infects another program. The secondary viral function is then performed at some later time, perhaps using a bomb as a trigger. Characteristics of a virus include replication, requires a host program as a carrier, activated by external action, and replication limited to (virtual) system.
- **Trojan horse.** A Trojan horse is a program that performs a useful function, but also performs an unexpected action—a form of virus. A rental PC or a vendor's product demonstration (demo) diskette could be a potential source of a computer virus.
- **Worm.** A worm differs from a virus in that it reproduces on its own, rather than requiring a program host. Characteristics of a worm include replication, does not require a host (self-contained), activated by creating process (needs a multitasking system), and replication occurs across communication links for network worms.

- **Bomb.** A logic bomb goes off when a program being used normally arrives at a prespecified event (e.g., a financial calculation exceeds a certain dollar amount). A time bomb goes off at a prespecified time.
- **Trap door.** A trap door allows a user to gain more access to more system functions than are normally available. These access privileges can be obtained through a keyboard sequence or system condition (e.g., an aborted system start-up). Once the access is obtained, the user can then manipulate, change, or destroy data.

(i) **How a virus infects a system.** A virus typically infects a system through a floppy disk or network, copying itself undetected onto the user's hard disk under the cover of another legitimate system operation. The virus may then lie dormant until a predetermined date or action occurs. Then, it begins reproducing and carrying out any other actions programmed into it.

Viruses can be introduced through internal or external sabotage or even unintentionally by inexperienced programmers. With the rapid growth in computer networks and the emphasis on ease-of-use over security, the potential for viruses to disrupt and potentially damage hundreds of systems in multiple locations before detection and eradication continues to increase.

(ii) **Detecting a virus.** To detect viruses and prevent them from infecting a computer, several vendors offer antiviral software packages. These packages operate one of three ways.

1. **Execute monitors.** These regulate all potentially damaging system operations, such as writing to a hard or floppy disk. Only the programs that the user specifies are allowed to perform these operations.
2. **File monitors.** These record the state of files in the system using checksums, file size, data encryption, or date/time stamping. The user can compare the records at intervals to detect unexpected changes.
3. **Virus detectors.** These scan files for blocks of code used in known viruses. Because virus developers will change their viruses or develop new ones to work around detection schemes, it is good to update the virus protection software frequently.

PRECAUTIONARY MEASURES TO PREVENT VIRUS INFECTION

- Use only trustworthy sources for new software by dealing directly with vendors and distributors.
- Limit the copying of software by acquiring shrink-wrapped software for each user.
- Protect hardware and software by using write-protect tabs and backing up data frequently.

(iii) **Preventing infection.** A key factor in preventing infection is knowing where viruses come from. The three most common entry points are

1. **Electronic bulletin boards.** Bulletin boards often offer free, downloadable software macros, routines, or games. These can serve as hiding places or Trojan horses for software viruses. Often, computer games are used as a cover for viruses.
2. **Floppy disks.** Viruses often copy themselves onto every floppy disk inserted into a microcomputer, then copy themselves onto the hard disk of each new system in which the floppy is inserted.
3. **Network access.** Many computers are logged onto LANs and WANs through which the virus can spread. Most times, a computer containing the virus logs on (unauthorized) to another computer on the network and transfers the virus.

(iv) **Eliminating a virus after infection.** The following steps should be carried out when a user organization's computer becomes infected with a virus:

1. **Isolate the system.** Disconnect the system from any network, and do not copy files from the infected computer to any other computer.
2. **Back up all data.** Copy the data (but not the applications software) onto diskettes, tapes or disk.

3. **Reinitialize the system.** If the infection is serious, reformat the hard disk, using a low-level format program that destroys all data and file allocation tables.
4. **Reboot the system.** Start up the system again from the master operating system diskette delivered with the hardware with a write-protect tab in place.
5. **Copy viral protection software onto the system.** Install execution monitoring, file monitoring, and virus detection software onto the system.
6. **Reinstall applications software.** Reinstall each packaged application, using the original master diskettes that came with the package, with write-protect tabs in place.
7. **Reinstall data.** Reinstall the data from the backup diskettes or tape, ensuring that the virus detection software is operating.

Potential or actual risks and exposures	Suggested controls or control procedures
• Hostile software (e.g., computer virus, worm, bomb)	• Practice safe computing rules; establish policies regarding shared or external software usage; use diskless PCs and workstations; install antivirus software (detection, identification, and removal tools); use simple checksums, cyclical redundancy checks, or cryptographic checksums on sensitive data; install intrusion detection tools; implement security labels (tags) to sensitive files; use network filter programs and firewall systems; install program change controls (change detection tools); be discrete about granting write permissions to access programs and data.

Exhibit 5.29: Risks in and controls over hostile software

(d) **Privacy.** With information systems, privacy deals with the collection and use or misuse of personal data. The issue of privacy deals with the right to be left alone or to be withdrawn from public view. Privacy at work creates conflict between employers wanting to monitor their employees' work activities and the employees who resent such monitoring. For example, computer workstation software can track employee keystrokes made at the PC keyboard. Another privacy issue is e-mail at work. Courts have ruled that a privileged communication does not lose its privileged character if it is communicated or transmitted electronically. E-mail is a controversial topic where many state and federal laws have been passed in this area.

Another area of privacy concern is the Internet, where a Web site collects personal information when potential or actual customers are buying or selling goods or services or simply inquiring. Individuals should protect their personal information by finding out what data is stored and how it is used, not using a work e-mail system to send personal e-mails, and not sharing personal information without written consent.

(e) **Electronic Mail.** Electronic mail (e-mail) is one of the most popular uses of the Internet. With access to Internet e-mail, one can potentially correspond with any one of millions of people worldwide. Proprietary e-mail systems can be gatewayed to Internet e-mail, which expands the connectivity of e-mail manyfold.

(i) **E-mail policy.** Organizations need policies for e-mail to help employees use electronic mail properly, to reduce the risk of intentional or inadvertent misuse, and to assure that official records transferred via electronic mail are properly handled. Organizational policies are needed to establish general guidance in such areas as

- The use of e-mail to conduct official business
- The use of e-mail for personal business
- Access control and confidential protection of messages, and
- The management and retention of e-mail messages

(ii) **Uses of e-mail lists.** In addition to one-to-one communication, e-mail can support e-mail address lists, so that a single individual or organization can send e-mail to a list of addresses of individual or organizations. E-mail-based discussion groups are another use of e-mail lists. Participants send e-mail to a central mailing list server, and the messages are broadcast to the other participants. This allows subscribers, who may be in different time zones or different continents, to have useful discussions. USENET newsgroups are an elaboration of the e-mail discussion group.

(iii) **E-mail protocols.** The principal Internet e-mail protocols (not including proprietary protocols which are tunneled or gatewayed to the Internet) are: simple mail transport protocol (SMTP), post office protocol (POP), and Interent mail access protocol (IMAP).

An SMTP server accepts e-mail messages from other systems and stores them for the addressees. A POP server allows a POP client to download e-mail that has been received via another e-mail server. IMAP is more convenient for reading e-mail while traveling than POP, since the messages can be left on the server, without having to keep the local list and server list of read e-mail messages in synchronization.

(iv) **E-mail threats.** Several threats exist, including dangerous attachments, impersonation, eavesdropping, mailbombing, and junk and harassing e-mail.

- **Dangerous attachments.** An attacker can attach files to e-mail messages that contain Trojan executables, virus-infected files, or documents that contain dangerous macros. Multipurpose Internet mail extensions (MIME) redefines the format of e-mail messages. It can be used to support security features like digital signatures and encrypted messages. But MIME also has been used to mail virus-infected executables and dangerous messages and attachments.
- **Impersonation.** The sender address on Internet e-mail cannot be trusted, since the sender can create a false return address, or the header could have been modified in transit, or the sender could have connected directly to the SMTP port on the target computer to enter the e-mail.
- **Eavesdropping.** E-mail headers and contents are transmitted in the clear. Consequently, the contents of a message can be read or altered in transit. The header can be modified to hide or change the sender, or to redirect the message.
- **Mailbombing.** Mailbombing is an e-mail-based attack. The attacked system is flooded with e-mail until it fails. Some Internet service providers (ISPs) give temporary accounts to anyone who signs up for a trial subscription, and those accounts can be used to launch e-mail attacks.
- **Junk and harassing e-mail.** Since anyone in the world can send e-mail to anyone, it can be difficult to stop someone from sending it. Most mail systems have some provision for filtering e-mail, that is, searching the e-mail header or body for particular words or patterns, and then filing or deleting the e-mail.

(v) **E-mail safeguards.** The protection provided for e-mail messages, systems, and software should be consistent with the value of the information that will be transmitted over networks. In general, there should be centralized control of e-mail services. Policies should be defined to specify the level of protection to be implemented. The following are some examples of specific controls:

- **Preventing dangerous content.** Attachments to e-mail messages or the messages themselves can be scanned for executables, viruses, macros, and so forth. However, not all dangerous content can be detected or prevented. Users should be warned to treat unusual e-mail messages the same way they treat unusual parcels, with all due caution.
- **Preventing modification and impersonation.** E-mail messages can easily be forged. Digital signatures can be used to authenticate the sender of a message and to protect the integrity of its contents. Digital signature methods generally use a one-way hash or message digest algorithm to detect changes in the contents of a message, and a cryptographic algorithm to protect the hash.
- **Preventing eavesdropping.** Eavesdropping can be prevented by encrypting the contents of the message or the channel over which it is transmitted.

5.9 Evaluate Investment in Information Technology

(a) **Integrated Approach for IT Investment Management.** An IT investment management process is an integrated approach to managing IT investments that provides for the continuous identification, selection, control, life-cycle management, and evaluation of IT investments. This structured process provides a systematic method for organizations to minimize risks while maximizing the return on IT investments.[1]

To be most successful, an IT investment management process should have elements of three essential phases: (1) control, (2) select, and (3) evaluate. However, each phase should not be viewed as a

---

[1] *"Assessing Risks and Returns: A Guide for Evaluating Federal Agencies' IT Investment Decision-Making," US General Accounting Office (GAO), Washington, D.C. February 1997, Version 1.*

separate step. Rather, each is conducted as part of a continual, interdependent management effort. Information from one phase is used to support activities in the other two phases.

CONTROL VS. SELECT VS. EVALUATE

- **Control:** What are you doing to ensure that the projects will deliver the benefits projected?
- **Select:** How do you know you have selected the best projects?
- **Evaluate:** Based on your evaluation, did the system deliver what you expected?

(i) **Critical success factors in IT investment management.** To be successful, an organization's IT investment management processes should generally include the following elements or factors:

- Key organizational decision makers are committed to the process and are involved throughout each project's life cycle.
  - Projects are assessed jointly by operational, financial, and IT managers.
- The investment management process is repeatable, efficient, and conducted uniformly and completely across the organization.
- The process includes provisions for continually selecting, managing, and evaluating projects in the investment portfolio.
- Decisions are made consistently throughout the organization.
  - Decisions at any level of the organization are made using uniform decision criteria.
  - Decisions are driven by accurate and up-to-date cost, risk, and benefit information.
- Decisions are made from an overall mission focus (there is an explicit link with the goals and objectives established in the organization's strategic plan or annual performance plans and with the organization's IT architecture).
- Accountability and learning from previous projects are reinforced.
- The emphasis is on optimizing the portfolio mix in order to manage the risk and maximize the rate of return.
- The process incorporates all IT investments but recognizes and allows for differences between various project types (mission-critical, administrative, infrastructure) and phases (proposed, under development, operational, etc.).

(ii) **Dimensions of the IT investment evaluation approach.** Investment evaluators can assess the control, selection, and evaluation phases from three review levels: (1) process, (2) data, and (3) decisions. In addition to these three phases, there are three critical attributes: (1) repeatability, (2) efficiency, and (3) completeness—that cut across each phase and that should be assessed at each review level.

(A) ***Process.*** This is an assessment of the investment management processes that the organization is following to select IT investments, control, and monitor progress of these investments and to evaluate final results. The central question to be answered is "Does the organization have defined, documented processes for selecting, controlling, and evaluating its IT investments?" The goal in assessing an organization's processes is to identify to what extent the organization has a structure in place for managing and evaluating IT investments.

(B) ***Data.*** An IT investment process cannot operate without accurate, reliable, and up-to-date data on project costs, benefits, and risks. It is the basis for informed decision making. In addition, documentation of management decisions is essential to begin to assemble a track record of results. Evaluating the data involved in the IT investment management process requires evaluating two different types of data.

1. **Ex ante.** The information that is being used as inputs to the IT investment process (e.g., the cost, benefit, and risk analysis that are used to justify the selection and continued funding of projects, the performance measures that are used to monitor a project's progress, etc.)

2. **Ex post.** Information that is produced based on decisions that are made (e.g., project review schedules and risk mitigation plans should be developed once a decision is made to fund a project)

All projects (proposed, under development, operational, etc.) should have complete and accurate project information—cost and benefit data, risk assessments, links to business goals and objectives, and performance measures, as well as up-to-date project-specific data, including current costs, implementation plans, staffing plans, and performance levels. In addition, the organization should have qualitative and quantitative project requirements and decision criteria in place to help screen IT projects, assess and rank projects, and control and evaluate the projects as they move through the various phases of their life cycle

All management actions and decisions that are made should be documented and maintained. Moreover, some decisions require that additional information be produced. For instance, after a project is selected, project-specific review schedules and risk mitigation plans should be developed.

(C) ***Decisions.*** After evaluating the processes that the organization uses to select, control, and evaluate IT investments and the data that are used to make decisions, evaluators will be in a much better position to reach conclusions about the specific decisions that the organization is making. The central focus of analysis is on whether management decisions and actions are being taken using the investment control processes and requisite project data.

The IT investment portfolio should represent a mixture of those projects that best meet the mission needs of the organization. Projects in the portfolio should be consistently monitored, and decisions should be made at key milestones to ensure that the project is continuing to have its expected business or impact with a focus on minimizing risk and maximizing return. Completed projects are evaluated to compare actual performance levels to estimated levels and to feed lessons learned back in to the selection and control phases.

(D) ***Repeatability.*** Repeatability focuses on the extent to which the processes, data, or decisions being reviewed are conducted consistently over time and across different organizational units (recognizing that processes should naturally evolve as lessons are learned and improvements are made).

The following list presents specific guidelines about the repeatability dimension during evaluation of IT investments:

- Projects are selected uniformly across more than one budget cycle; project reviews are conducted for all projects at established intervals; an evaluation methodology is in place and is used to assess all fully implemented projects.
- The organization has identified all necessary information (cost/benefit/risk analyses, proposed schedule, user and business requirements, etc.) for making decisions, and this information is maintained, updated, and used to drive all project decisions. Specific, quantifiable decision criteria have been established and are used at all decision levels.
- Projects are selected and managed based on established criteria or documented justifications.

Two essential aspects of repeatability are whether (1) roles, responsibilities, and authority have been defined and documented and (2) uniform decision criteria are in place.

(E) ***Efficiency.*** Efficiency focuses on how well management processes, the generation of project data, and the function of decision making are working together. The focus is on the overall quality (the accuracy, reliability, and timeliness) of the investment approach. In addition, the same data generated to support IT investment selection, control, and evaluation should be used to manage IT projects through their life cycle.

The following list presents specific guidelines about the efficiency dimension during evaluation of IT investments:

- All projects are subjected to a similar investment management process (consisting of select, control, and evaluate phases), and this process is documented so that everyone knows the steps that are conducted and the analyses that are required.
- Cost, risk, and benefit data, both qualitative and quantitative, are accurate and are updated as information is gained. Project information is readily available, and an organization

track record is maintained. Project results and lessons learned are tracked and aggregated in order to further refine and improve decision making.

- Decisions are being made at the right level. Senior managers' limited time is being utilized to the best extent possible. Actions are quickly taken to address deficiencies.

(F) ***Completeness.*** Completeness focuses on the extent to which all phases of the process (select, control, and evaluate) are being followed and whether use of the IT investment process is institutionalized across the organization. As the evaluation is conducted and questions are asked, a concerted effort should be made to keep these three critical factors in mind. Evaluators should continually ask themselves whether the processes, data, or decisions that they are assessing are repeatable, efficient, and complete.

KEY ELEMENTS IN IT INVESTMENT MANAGEMENT

Select–process: Selection processes include: screening projects, analyzing and ranking all projects based on benefit, cost, and risk criteria, selecting a portfolio of projects, and establishing project-review schedules

Select–data: Selection data include: evidence that each project has met project submission requirements, analyses of each project's costs, benefits, and risks, data on the existing portfolio, and scoring and prioritization outcomes, and project-review schedules

Select–decisions: Selection decisions include: determining whether projects met process-stipulated requirements and deciding on the mixture of projects in the overall IT investment portfolio

Control–process: Control processes include: consistently monitoring projects, involving the right people, documenting all major actions and decisions, and feeding lessons learned back in to the selection phase

Control–data: Control data include: measures of interim results and updated analyses of each project's costs, benefits, schedule, and risks

Control–decisions: Control decisions include: deciding whether to cancel, modify, continue, or accelerate a project and aggregating data and reviewing collective actions taken to date

Evaluate–process: Evaluation processes include: conducting post-implementation reviews using a standard methodology and feeding lessons learned back in to the selection and control phases

Evaluate–data: Evaluation data include: measurements of actual versus projected performance and documented "track record" (project and process)

Evaluate–decisions: Evaluation decisions include: assessing the project's impact on mission performance and determining future prospects for the period and revising the selection and control phases based on lessons learned

---

(b) **IT Acquisition Practices.** The objectives of purchasing, whether it is IT-related or not, are to buy products or services: at the right time and the right price, from the right source, for the right place, and the right service, the right quantity, and the right quality.

Selection and training of competent people to acquire IT products and services are important to maximize purchasing's contribution to total cost reduction and increased competitiveness. The ability to negotiate and sell ideas will be paramount for long-term contracting agreements such as computer hardware and software leases. The relation between the purchasing staff and suppliers/vendors is based on mutual trust and a partnering approach (see Exhibit 5.30).

(i) **Independence.** A clear job description that describes the content and thrust of a job is needed for exacting accountability and definition of duties and responsibilities. The IT purchasing staff should be independent of the IS functional areas such as systems development, computer operations, and telecommunication. The IS purchasing staff should be part of the IT administrative organization that should be reporting directly to the CIO or the director of IT.

Potential or actual risks and exposures	Suggested controls or control procedures
• Fraud or irregularities by purchasing staff and management	• Policies and procedures manual, staff training, job rotation for staff, mandatory staff vacations, signed "conflict of interest" statements for staff

Exhibit 5.30: Risks and controls in purchasing function

(ii) **Budgeting.** Budgeting is a management tool to make individuals responsible and accountable for their actions. Senior management's goals are translated into specific plans and budgets. While goals flow from the top of the organization, budgets should flow up the organization from the lower levels of management such as department managers and line supervisors. The reason is that a budget that has been developed and agreed to at the lower level will have ownership of that individual, and the likelihood of adhering to the budget is higher than otherwise.

Variance analysis, similar to budgets, is a management tool to analyze the differences between what was budgeted for an item and what was actually spent. Corrective actions can be taken by adjusting the budget or reducing future expenditures.

(iii) **Training.** Purchasing staff, similar to other staff, requires professional training and development on a continuing basis. The level of training and the type of training method used depends on the job requirements and the skills, education, and experience of the individual employee.

An effective training program prepares an employee not only for the current job but also for future needs. Attending vendor conferences and exhibitions would be one way of training. Obtaining vendor product demonstrations of new software is another training avenue. An ideal training program fits the employee desires and needs that will motivate him now and benefit him in the long run.

Some of the training and development methods include: on-the-job training programs, manuals, trial-and-error approach, "buddy" system—learning from a colleague, staff meetings, supplier/vendor visits, (7) in-house training programs, professional conferences and seminars, and self-study or college courses.

(iv) **Job rotation.** A buyer rotation is a process in which the employee is rotated from one job to another within or outside the department. The objectives are to provide an expanded base of knowledge, better understanding of interrelationships, and increased decision-making capabilities. The extent to which rotation should be used depends on the individuals involved and their potential to grow and take on more responsibilities.

From a control viewpoint, job rotation minimizes the potential for fraudulent activities such as favoring one supplier over another, getting lower price discounts than normal, and buying more quantity than is needed.

5.10 Enterprise-Wide Resource Planning Software

(a) **Overview of ERP System.** Enterprise-wide resource planning (ERP) software can help organizations in optimizing their value chain, which requires integrating business processes across organizational boundaries through IT.

Value chain = Business process reengineering + Change management + ERP

ERP systems allow employees to access a full database of information that will allow them to complete their tasks. The information can also be shared with customers and suppliers as needed. The ERP system can track business transactions from their origin (at the customer) to order entry through operations and accounting until the transaction is completed. The objective of ERP systems is to integrate all functions within an organization and to become customer-oriented (customer-centric). Companies are using the ERP system for increased business competitiveness.

SAP R/3 system is an example of ERP, where its objective is to standardize business processes across business units, functional departments, and product lines. R/3 is the broadest and most feature-rich ERP system. SAP provides collaborative e-business solutions between companies and their customers and suppliers. More specifically, SAP integrates front office and back office systems, internal and external systems, and unstructured and structured information. The IT department will play a major role in implementing the ERP systems.

SAP and other vendors use push technology to deliver critical software or information over the Internet to their customers. Push technology is an automatic transmission of information over the Internet rather than making users search for it with their browsers. Advantages of push technology are speed and convenience while information overload and clogging up the Internet communications links with data traffic are its disadvantages.

(b) **Advantages and Disadvantages of ERP Systems.** Advantages of ERP systems include: elimination of costly, inflexible legacy systems, improvement of work processes, increase in access to data for operational decision making, and standardization of IT infrastructure (hardware, software, operating systems, and databases). Disadvantages of ERP systems include: expense and time in implementation, difficulty in implementing change in the organization, risks in using one vendor, and difficulty in integrating with other computer systems.

5.11 Operating Systems

(a) **Mainframes and Workstations.** Many control operations are concentrated in systems software, which is defined as a collection of programs or systems that help interconnect and/or control the elements of input devices, computer processing operations, output devices, data files, application programs, and hardware. Typically, systems software is provided by outside vendors. In this section, the operating systems software will be discussed in detail while other systems software products will be highlighted.

(i) **Operating systems software.** The operating system, which is the "brain" of a computer system and a major player in the systems software products group, runs the hardware (e.g., CPU, control units, channels, tape and disk drives, printers, terminals). It is computer software that directs and assists the execution of application programs and provides multiprogramming capability. The part of CPU controlling data manipulation is called the arithmetic-logic unit. It is the data path part of the CPU that has the most influence on its cost versus performance when compared to the other components of the CPU. An application program should be compatible with the hardware, the database management system, and the operating system to run properly.

Major functions of the operating systems software include

- Job initiation and scheduling of input/output (I/O) operation
- Peripheral device operation
- Program loading into memory
- Interrupt handling
- Routing data between a computer's CPU and multiple external storage devices
- Allocating channels to I/O devices
- Dates, stores, and retrieves files to/from primary and secondary storage media

Regardless of vendor, all operating systems software has four components: (1) process management, (2) I/O device management, (3) memory management, and (4) system file management. Each component is discussed briefly.

(A) ***Process management.*** The major focus of process management is executing computer programs. The source code written by a programmer is translated completely to object code either by an assembler or a compiler. One option is to use an interpreter, which works with one source statement at a time, reading it, translating it to machine level, executing the resulting binary instructions, and then moving on to the next source statement. It is important to note that both compilers and interpreters generate machine-level program instructions, but the process is different. Combining object modules to form a load module is done by a linkage editor or loader.

In a **multiprogramming system,** the central processing unit (CPU) processes multiple programs, reads from a disk or tape, and prints on a terminal or printer. The CPU switches from program to program, hence the name multiprogramming. Multiprogramming was made possible due to interrupt and the ability to overlap I/O with internal processing. When there are multiple CPUs operating simultaneously under the direction of one control program, it is called a **multiprocessing system**. One operating system controls the operation and work of two or more processors. Under these conditions, memory, variables, and data files are shared by multiple programs and processes.

A **buffer** is temporary storage in main memory that is used to compensate for the different speeds of storage devices. Buffering makes no difference when internal processing time takes longer than I/O time. If I/O time is longer than processing time, buffering will increase the total job running time. Buffering saves a relatively small percentage of total processing time in a non-multiprogramming environment when internal processing time takes considerably longer than I/O time.

You might ask how the operating system decides which process to run first when more than one process is ready to be run. The scheduling algorithm in the operating system handles this situation and interfaces with an automated job scheduling system to schedule a specific job. The purpose of the operating system-based scheduler is to

- Maximize the number of jobs processed in a given time (a measure of throughput).
- Minimize the response time for online system requests (a measure of effectiveness—the elapsed time between entering a transaction of any kind and seeing the first character of the system's response appear on the screen).
- Keep the CPU busy at all times (a measure of efficiency and productivity).
- Ensure that each process gets an equitable share of CPU resources (a measure of balance and allocation).
- Minimize the time batch job users must wait for the output (a measure of turnaround time—the time between job submission and job completion).

(B) ***Input and output device management.*** The input/output (I/O) devices include both mechanical and electrical parts. The operating system issues commands to the I/O devices, catches interrupts, and handles errors. I/O devices are connected to the computer system through channels and control units.

The operating system deals with **device controllers** assigned to disk drives and tape drives. I/O channels interface with the CPU and the device controller, thus reducing the load of the CPU. Skipping blocks to give the controller time to transfer data to memory is called **interleaving**. Data channels, buffer storage, and released cycle time are used in I/O handling to reduce CPU idle time. A program is said to be "compute-bound" when the time required for computation is greater than the time required for reading and writing.

Operational errors should be handled as close to the hardware as possible. An example of errors is **read errors** caused by specks of dust on the read head. Another error includes **block damage**. If the controller discovers a read error, it should try to correct the error itself. If it cannot, the problem is sent to the device driver for correction, which usually eliminates the problem by reading the entire block again.

Spooling is a way of dealing with dedicated I/O devices in a multiprogramming system. Usually, a spooling library is created for line printers, file transfers over a network, and other tasks. For example, a file ready to be printed is put in a spooled directory and waits its turn for printing. Allowing exclusive access to a dedicated I/O device (e.g., printer, plotter, tape drive) in responding to a user request can lead to a **deadlock** situation in the absence of spooling. Exhibit 5.31 explains a typical deadlock situation.

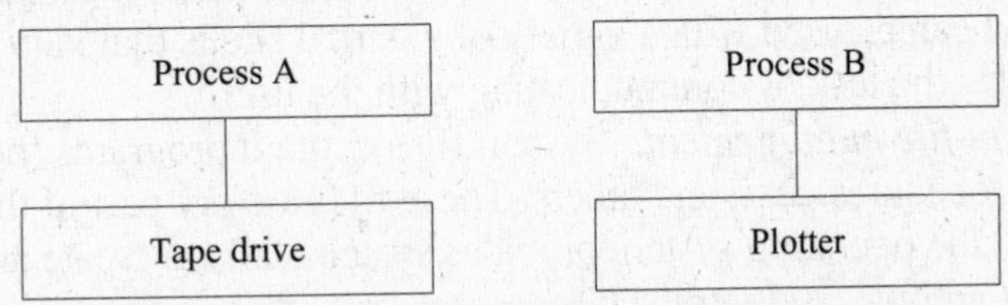

Exhibit 5.31: Deadlock situation in operating systems

Assume that a computer has one tape drive and a plotter, neither of them spooled. Process A requests the tape drive, and Process B requests the plotter. Both requests are granted. After a while, Process A requests the plotter, without giving up the tape drive, and Process B requests the tape drive, without giving up the plotter. Since both resources are being used by their respective processes, neither request can be granted, and they wait forever. This leads to a deadlock situation.

It is important to remember that deadlock can occur in any situation, whether it involves I/O devices, data files, or database programs. In the case of database programs, a program may have to lock several records it is using. For example, Process A locks record R1, Process B locks record R2, and then each process tries to lock the other one's record. However, this is not successful. The reason the deadlock situation occurs is that the system resources can only be used by one process at a time.

Each vendor of the operating system has a different approach to solving the deadlock problem. In general, deadlocks can be prevented by structuring the system so that a process will hold only one resource at a time. It can also be avoided by examining each resource request to see if it leads to a deadlock situation. If it does, the request is simply denied or delayed. In database systems, deadlocks can be avoided by having the database management system automatically intervene and break the deadlock situation. In other cases, deadlocks can be prevented by requiring the database designer to consider avoiding many-to-many and nested program structures.

(C) ***Memory management.*** The memory manager's job is to keep track of which parts of memory are in use or not in use, to allocate memory to required processes, to de-allocate the memory when a process is completed, and to manage swapping between main memory and storage devices (e.g., disk, tape, cartridges) when main memory cannot hold all the processes and programs. **Swapping** moves programs from main memory to disk and back. Boundary protection is needed to prevent mixing of several and different data and program files in the primary storage area.

In the past, programmers had to break down a large program into pieces to fit in the available main memory. Splitting the program into pieces is called **overlays**. This task is time-consuming and tedious. Each program produces a set of memory addresses using indexing, base registers, and segment registers. **Registers** are temporary storage devices that hold control information, key data, and intermediate results. With the invention of virtual memory, the operating system keeps those parts of the program currently in use in main memory and the rest on the disk. **Virtual memory** permits the possibility of program and data size to exceed the amount of main memory available for it.

Virtual memory uses a technique called **paging**. The virtual address space is divided into units called pages. Transfers between memory and disk are always in units of pages. There is a tradeoff between program segmentation and paging. The more the programs are segmented, the greater the number of I/O operations. The greater the number of I/O operations, the greater the paging rate. The greater the paging rate, the longer the system response time. Swapping and paging occur due to lack of sufficient main memory to hold all the programs at once.

Thrashing is a situation that occurs when paging on a virtual memory system is so frequent that little time is left for useful and productive work. The set of pages that a process is currently using is called its working-set. A program causing page faults (run very slowly) every few instructions is said to be thrashing. Another way of looking at thrashing is that it occurs when the number of frames of physical storage allocated to a job falls below the size of its working-set.

Kernel is the core portion of the program that performs the most essential PC-based operating system tasks, such as handling disk I/O operations and managing the internal memory. The kernel can be used with a variety of external shells that vary in their user-friendliness. The shell handles the task of communicating with the user.

(D) ***System file management.*** System files contain programs (both source and object code), data, job procedures, text, and others. These files are not part of the address space of any process. Instead, the operating system provides system calls to create and destroy files; read and write files; store, archive, and retrieve files; copy, sort and merge files; and other tasks. System files are kept in directories, where a directory contains one or more files with pertinent information such as file name, size, type, time created, time last accessed, time last modified, list of disk blocks used, owner's ID, and security level. Sectors, tracks, and cylinders are the unit of allocation for files. A set of tracks is called a cylinder.

Generally, two techniques are used to increase system file performance by reducing disk access time. First, a block cache or buffer cache is used to hide some file blocks in main memory instead of disk. The second technique is the placement of file blocks that are likely to be accessed in sequence close to each other in the same cylinder in order to reduce the amount of disk arm movement.

(ii) **Other types of operating systems.** Other types of operating systems software include network operating systems and distributed operating systems. In a **network operating system,** the users will be aware of the presence of multiple computers, and can log in to remote CPUs and copy files from one

CPU to another. Each CPU runs its own local operating system and has its own users. Network controllers and network management software are needed to operate the system.

The **distributed operating system** consists of multiple CPUs whose locations are transparent to users of the system. It is typical for programs to run on several CPUs at the same time. Because of this, it is possible to switch programs from one CPU to another in the event of hardware malfunction and/or software failures at one location.

(b) **Servers.** Today, servers are very powerful and fast, and perform diverse functions such as transferring files, storing data, communicating outside the network, and processing databases. Because a LAN server is charged with moving large quantities of data from disk and memory onto the network, it is by nature I/O-bound rather than computer-bound, resulting in degraded performance. One way to curb memory operations is with **caching,** a performance-enhancing technique that establishes a small, very-high-speed static RAM cache (or buffer) between main memory and the processor. This approach frees the LAN server from repeated calls to memory. The next time the processor goes looking for data, it will first try to retrieve it from cache memory.

Types of Servers

- File servers
- Database servers
- Print servers
- Communication servers
- Terminal servers
- Facsimile servers
- Image servers
- Network servers
- Mail servers

One of the most common motivations for using a server is resource sharing. The goal is to provide transparent access to organization-wide data distributed across PCs, minis, and mainframe computers while protecting the security and integrity of that data. Next, let us review some of the major servers.

File servers send and receive data between a workstation and the server. A file server is the heart of a LAN. The file server would have to transfer the entire file across the network in order to process it. In a file server approach, each workstation has to provide the services of both a front end and a back end. The bandwidth is limited, too. For these reasons, database servers are better.

Database (e.g., structured query language, SQL) **servers** can access data from mainframes, minicomputers, and other servers, providing a critical link in distributed database systems. It employs client-server architecture for application systems in a distributed computing environment. Distributed computing enables a standard set of resources and services (i.e., directories, files, print queues, named pipes, communications queues, data, programs) residing on different machines in different locations to be available to any workstation connected to the network. Simply stated, the client part of the client-server issues a request to the server, and the server part processes the request and returns the requested information to the client.

Client-server architecture makes it possible for a wide range of front-end client applications such as databases, spreadsheets, and word processors to simultaneously share the same data. A database server supports a high-performance, multiuser, relational database management system. Client-server architecture provides a high level of data integrity, concurrency control, and improved performance.

The database server's distributed update capability allows databases on multiple database servers located in different places to be updated by a single transaction. This ability to scale a system in response to data server requirements provides greater flexibility in accessing geographically dispersed data. Some database servers provide transaction buffering, automatic disk repair, and a real-time tape backup option to guard against hardware problems. More is said about this later.

Print servers allow multiple users and multiple PCs to share an expensive printer such as a high-speed and high-quality laser printer and a plotter. The spooling software may come with the printer software to queue jobs ready to be printed.

Communication servers allow LANS to be connected to WANs as well as enabling a stand-alone PC running under OS/2 to connect directly to a WAN. Communications servers provide 3270 terminal emulation, printer emulation, and file transfer facilities. A communications server uses client-server architecture to provide a gateway between DOS and OS/2-based workstations on a LAN and a host (i.e., mainframe, midrange, mini, or micro) computer. Communications servers share LAN user and password files.

The **terminal server** is a dedicated computer with an asynchronous communications controller and a network interface. Its job is to take keystrokes entered by a user and deliver them to one or more host computers on a network. Terminal servers tie together character-based terminals, printers, and their host computers.

Facsimile (FAX) servers allow a single or many users to transmit high-quality and high-volume documents straight from the PC or workstation disk without passing the document through the scanner of a stand-alone FAX machine. Documents can be sent and received to and from any FAX machine. With FAX modules integrated into the system, both background (FAX application) and foreground (other application) processing can take place simultaneously, which increases productivity.

FAX servers save money by using regular paper instead of the thermal paper needed for a stand-alone FAX machine. By disabling the print feature, confidential documents can be stored and viewed only if access is allowed. FAX application is integrated with electronic mail application and supports multiple scanners. It comes with store and forward features and a detailed activity journal. Most common applications of FAX servers are fast distribution of newsletters, banking and brokerage information, and other time-critical messages to customers or suppliers with FAX machines.

Image servers store and process documents such as loan, credit, employment applications, invoices, and purchase orders. Stored documents can be retrieved later and/or further transmitted to the host computer, or downloaded to a personal computer.

Network servers also called super servers connect LAN users to host (e.g., mainframe) computer sessions and public data networks. These interconnections become fully transparent to users. Super servers are hardware-based unlike others that are software-based (e.g., disk mirroring). Fault tolerance is a major feature of these servers and uses techniques such as disk duplexing. Network servers can handle heavy traffic generated by hundreds or thousands of users with faster I/O rates, and usually come with more disk space.

Mail servers are a part of a network, acting as the central electronic-mail drop for a set of users. All mail messages are routed to this server, which delivers them to the addressees. The recipients run their mail program to read the message. Mail servers can store and forward messages across all computing resources of an organization.

Future server-based applications include directory services providing organization-wide distributed directories and document-management services implementing a lending library concept that lets users "check out" documents for review and revision.

5.12 Application Development and Maintenance

(a) **System Development and Maintenance.** Application systems are developed and maintained to serve system users by providing them with various data processing and information reporting capabilities. Each application system has six major **work areas** during system development or maintenance life cycle (SDLC/SMLC) process (see Exhibit 5.32).

1. Systems planning
2. Systems analysis
3. Systems design
4. Systems development (or construction)
5. Systems implementation
6. Systems operation and maintenance

Some organizations would combine the systems development activity into systems implementation activity. Each work area is divided into phases containing various activities, participants, responsibilities, and end products (deliverables). The process where systems planning, analysis, design, development, and implementation work is done in sequence is the hallmark of the traditional development approach.

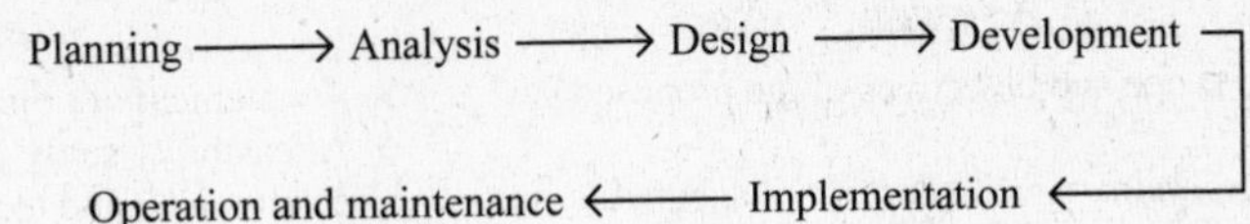

Exhibit 5.32: Sequence of phases in the system development life cycle

A combination of top-down and bottom-up approach is needed to develop a viable system. The top-down approach takes senior management input, long-term goals, and needs whereas the bottom-up approach considers functional user needs and objectives and the existing system strengths and weaknesses.

(i) **System development life cycle phases.** Exhibit 5.33 shows 6 work areas and 14 phases and illustrates the interrelationships between the phases and work areas of the *traditional system development methodology.* It is assumed that in most part the phases follow the sequence outlined. Some of the phases may proceed simultaneously and some independently, while others cannot proceed until the previous phase has been completed. For example, the manuals development phase can proceed at the same time as programs are developed and unit tests are being conducted, whereas the conversion phase cannot proceed until acceptance testing is completed.

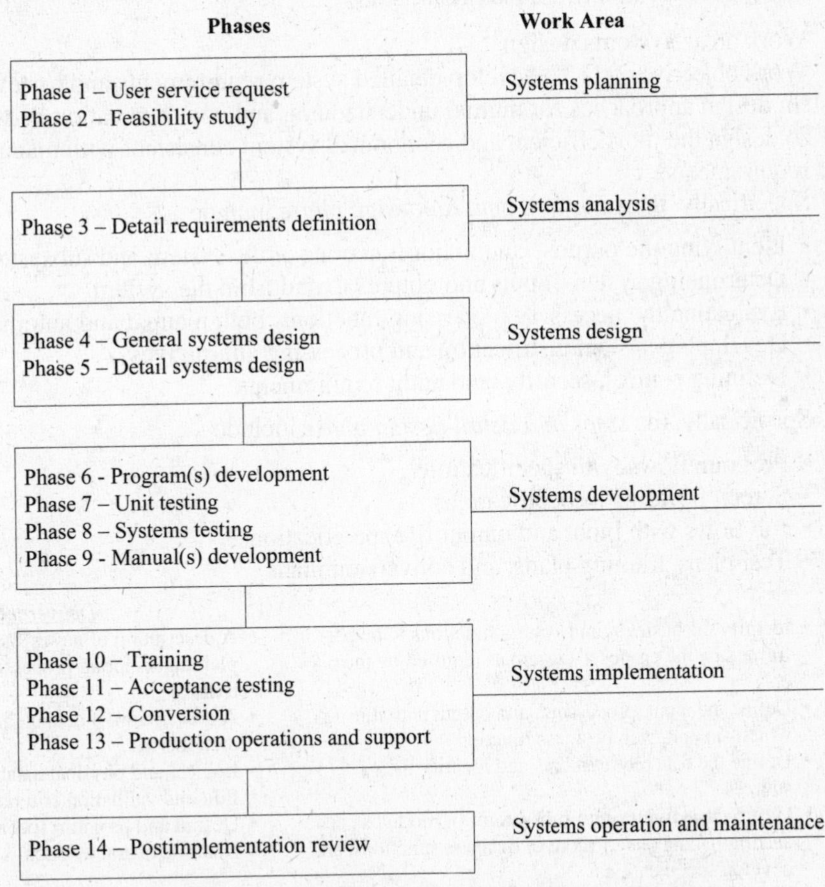

Exhibit 5.33: Traditional system development methodology

(ii) **System development life-cycle activities.** Next, we will present work objectives for each work area, including describing its activities and deliverables.

Work area: **Systems planning (systems investigation)**

Work objectives: To gather adequate information to define the problem to be solved. To provide sufficient economical, operational, and technical information to determine project feasibility.

Activities	*Deliverables*
• Define the scope and objectives of the proposed system • Develop preliminary estimates of costs, benefits, savings and project completion dates • Perform fact-finding analysis • Identify and evaluate the alternative systems solution approaches • Prepare cost-benefit analysis for each alternative • Identify the best possible solution	• A statement of objectives to be accomplished • A feasibility study report describing operational, economical, and technical constraints for each alternative systems solution • Recommendations to management whether to proceed with the system or not • A preliminary system implementation plan

Work area: **Systems analysis**

Work objectives: To conduct analysis of the new system environment and to define business and system requirements.

Activities	*Deliverables*
• Perform data analysis • Perform process analysis • Understand how the current system works • Understand the system user requirements • Define system and business requirements • Define control, security, and audit requirements	• Data and process analysis documents • System and business requirements document

Work area: **Systems design**

Work objectives: (1) To develop detailed system requirements and to develop general and detail system design approaches for mutual understanding and communication between user and IS staff. (2) To design the most efficient and economical system consistent with management's objectives and requirements.

Specifically, the *steps in a general design phase* include

- Identifying the purpose and major functions of the system and subsystems
- Determining system inputs and outputs to and from the system
- Evaluating the necessary processing functions, both manual and automated
- Developing system justification and processing alternatives
- Defining control, security, and audit requirements

Specifically, the *steps in a detail design phase* include

- Program flows with specifications
- Screen flows with specifications
- Job flows with input and output file specifications
- Test plans, training plans, and conversion plans

Activities	*Deliverables*
• Identify the business and system functions to be performed by the proposed system as required by the users • Define the input, processing, and output activities which support each business function • Define the data requirements and identify their sources • Group the activities into subsystems or modules each accomplishing one or more of business functions, and develop specifications • Finalize the control, security, and audit requirements	• A description of new system requirements explaining its input, processing, and output activities • A description of data elements and data dictionaries • Logical and physical databases • Edit and validation criteria • Design and program specifications • Data file characteristics

Work area: **Systems development or construction**

Work objectives: To develop computer programs and to conduct program testing and system testing.

Activities	*Deliverables*
• Develop computer program instructions • Conduct program walkthroughs • Conduct program/unit testing • Conduct system testing of all programs including all interfaces	• Computer program source code • Program/unit test plan and test results • Systems test plan and test results • File conversion plan and approach

Work Area: **Systems implementation**

Work Objectives: To develop user reference and training manuals and train users and IS staff in the use and operation of the system. To conduct user acceptance test of the system and to convert data files.

Activities

- Develop operations and user manuals
- Develop training materials
- Conduct user and IS training
- Conduct acceptance testing of the entire system by users to test all functions, errors, reports, screens, interfaces.
- Identify and document the discrepancies between expected test results and actual test results
- Convert and validate data files and programs
- Conduct pilot conversions or parallel operations

Deliverables

- Operations manual
- User manual
- Training manual
- User acceptance test plan and test results
- Data file conversion results

Three methods exist to implement a new computer system or convert an old system to a new system: (1) direct (complete) cut-over, (2) pilot conversion, and (3) parallel operation. It is important to note that a complete or direct cut-over to a new system is a high-risk approach while phased implementation (pilot or parallel) is a low-risk approach. The reason is that when a new system is implemented at all locations and at all business units as one big step, there are greater chances of failure due to communication and coordination problems among and between all affected people. If the new system is phased in slowly (i.e., one or few locations at a time) any problems discovered can be fixed quickly before going to other locations (see Exhibit 5.34).

Pilot conversion takes place first at one location (division) and then extended later to other locations. Pilot conversion can be an alternative to parallel operation. The purpose is to see if the new system operates satisfactorily in one place before implementing at other locations. In the parallel operation, both the old and the new systems are run for a specific period of time (e.g., two or three months) to study operational problems. A comparison is made between the old and the new system outputs.

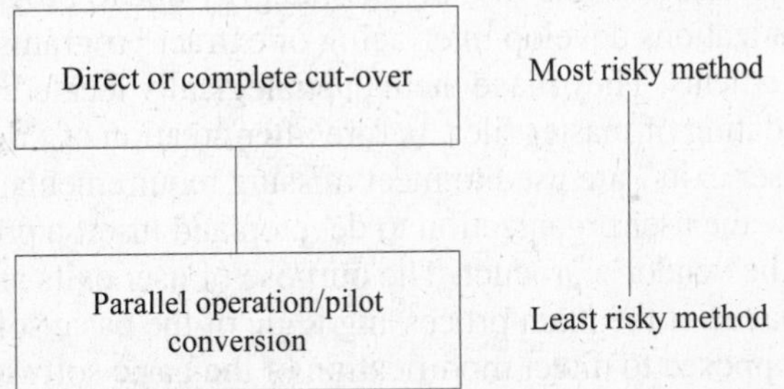

Exhibit 5.34: Risks in system conversion methods

Work Area: **Systems operation and maintenance**

Work Objectives: To run production jobs and to provide production support. To conduct a postimplementation review of the system to ensure that all objectives have been met.

Activities

- Move computer programs to production and run jobs
- Provide production support
- Conduct postimplementation review

Deliverables

- Production problem report
- A list of system enhancements/changes required

(b) **Software Acquisition Methodology.** Some organizations develop all application systems in-house while others develop only unique, one-of-a-kind systems in-house. These are often supplemented by acquiring software packages for normal, standard, or common systems from software vendors.

The system design and programming phases do not exist for software packages while other phases (e.g., planning, requirements analysis, testing, training, and conversion) of traditional system development methodology are still required.

Some of the deciding factors in acquiring and using purchased software packages, compared to in-house development are

- Lower cost to acquire and implement

- Less time to install the package
- Limited IS staff to develop and maintain systems in-house
- Lack of advanced computer skills among the IS staff

(i) **Software package acquisition.** A systematic approach to purchased software package evaluation, selection, and acquisition would include the following steps:

1. Develop software requirements.
2. Establish software selection criteria.
3. Identify several suitable software packages.
4. Develop request for proposal document.
5. Assess software packages for user functions.
6. Assess software vendors and conduct outside user survey.
7. Assess software packages for system/technical functions to assure testability, maintainability, and portability.
8. Assess vendor-supplied documentation.
9. Assess software packages for security, audit, and control features.
10. Perform a cost-benefit analysis.
11. Select a software package.
12. Develop a software contract.

(ii) **Software package modification.** User organizations have three alternatives regarding software adaptation or modification.

1. Modify/change the vendor-supplied basic software.
2. Adapt/change user and IS organization's manual and/or automated operating methods and procedures.
3. A combination of the above.

Adapting the user's and IS's procedures to fit the software is the best approach. Direct modifications to the vendor's software is strongly discouraged by the author and by the vendors because of loss of vendor support and possible loss of data integrity due to program/system modifications.

Some user organizations develop interfacing or extract programs outside the basic software to meet missing requirements. They place them at strategically located points such as front-end, back-end, before/after updating of master files, before/after creation of print files, or some other points. Also, sometimes "user exits" are used to meet missing requirements. User exits are program-calling statements that allow the user organization to develop and insert a processing alternative or capability not available in the vendor's product. The purpose of user exits and interfacing/ extract programs is to prevent disturbance of the main processing logic of the basic software package. This is a preferred approach as opposed to direct modification of the basic software package supplied by the vendor.

(c) **Prototyping.** Definition of software requirements is the biggest and most troublesome area to handle and control for functional users, IS staff, and auditors. Yet, it is the foundation upon which the entire applications software system is built. It is a very simple concept to grasp. If software requirements are incompletely defined and documented, the final product will be incomplete.

A major problem with software requirements is that the software development staff is working against a "moving target" where software requirements are constantly changing because of functional users' inability to define their requirements clearly and completely, communication problems between functional users and IS staff, and natural changes in business functional requirements over the timeframe of the software development project from internal and external sources.

Definition of software requirements is often taken very lightly and most of the time it is skipped or skimped on. Consequently, excessive maintenance of software is needed after the system becomes operational to meet the missing requirements, which should have been addressed earlier.

Prototyping vs. Communications

Prototyping increases communication between people, which is often the major problem in the traditional definition and documentation of software requirements.

An approach that rapidly brings a working version of the system into the hands of the user seems to be a better strategy. This is because users sometimes cannot actually define the system requirements correctly the first time until they have used some or all parts of the system. Prototyping is one way of dealing with the uncertainty, impreciseness, inconsistency, difficulty, and ambiguity involved in defining software requirements and design work. User requirements are not frozen; in fact, changing of user mind is welcomed. Prototyping assures that system requirements are adequately defined and correct through actual user experience in using the model. Prototyping also addresses the question of timely delivery of completed systems. It is especially useful to develop unstructured application systems.

(i) **How prototyping is done.** In practice, software prototyping is done in many ways. Some approaches are: a prototyped system is developed for a single user or multiple users, a prototyped system is programmed in one language for model development and later programmed in or combined with other language(s) to suit the operational (production) environment, a prototyped system is developed for both accounting/financial and nonfinancial systems, a prototyped system is developed to address partial or full system functions, or a prototyped system is developed to build the final (real) system to operate in a production environment.

Different approaches are used to achieve the prototype variations mentioned. This is accomplished either by shortening or replacing the traditional system development life cycle phases. Prototyping can be viewed as the development of a **working model** with test or real (preferred) data using an iterative approach supported by user and developer interaction. Here the user is a functional user and the developer is a data processing staff member whether it is a programmer or systems analyst. Prototyping is done with the use of a **workbench or workstation concept** where the functional user(s) and systems analyst(s) interact with the prototyping software in trying to develop a working model. In some organizations, the Information Center staff can assist the functional users in developing prototyping models. Prototyping is meant to be a learning process in developing usable systems.

Functional users working with the system analyst or programmer/analyst use the model to experiment and understand the system/business requirements. With this approach, system fallacies can be eliminated or minimized quickly before they can get bigger. Usually models include online terminal screens with editing functions for both data input and output, flow logic between screens, error handling rules, and batch reports. System users can define system input, process, and output functions; indicate the sequence of screens and functions; and specify data editing and validation rules to the system analyst. This leads to an accurate data collection and processing which improves the reliability and integrity of the system.

The system model with its inputs, processes, and outputs can be mocked-up either on paper or on computer (preferred) with real data. The model is tested, changed, and retested until users are satisfied with the model. With this approach, end users will get a **look and feel** sense of a proposed system. All changes are handled during successive iterations of the model. Later, these prototyped models are either expanded in the same programming language or rewritten in another programming language to include all functions and features that are expected in a final system. Typically, the final system may use multiple programming languages such as Assembler (a second-generation language), COBOL (a third-generation language), FOCUS (a fourth-generation language), and/or PROLOG (a fifth-generation language). Data flow diagrams and a data dictionary are some of the important tools used to document the prototype features and functions.

There has been controversy whether prototyped systems can be directly moved into production operations. The answer depends on the size, type, and nature of the system (i.e., whether it is a heavy-duty, large and complex, and transaction-based business application system; a decision-support system; a small system; a onetime system; or an ad hoc inquiry system).

Generally, heavy-duty, large and complex, and transaction-based prototyped systems should not be moved as is (directly) into production operations until full-scale design, programming, and testing activities are completed. However, for small and simple systems, onetime systems, decision-support systems, and ad hoc systems, the prototyped system and the production system could be the same.

(ii) **Using software prototyping results.** An organization has at least three choices after a prototype is completed: (1) discard the prototype, (2) move the prototype into production operations as is, or (3) use the prototype as a starting point for the full-scale design work.

- **Alternative 1: Throwaway prototype.** The prototype could be discarded because it is not serving the system objectives or may be addressing wrong problems. In some cases, the model is thrown away because the system performance is so bad that it cannot be improved or that the system cannot be used in multiuser environment.
- **Alternative 2: Use as is.** The prototype could become the actual system that can be operated in a production environment. Usually, this choice is good for application systems with low-volume transactions, operated on a regular or an irregular basis. Examples are decision support systems, ad hoc inquiry systems, onetime systems, small and simple systems, and single-user systems.
- **Alternative 3: Input to full-scale design.** The prototype could become the basis for a full-scale system design, programming, and testing work using the PDLC approach. Usually, this choice is good for application systems with large-volume transactions, with a need for quick response time, and with a need to operate on a scheduled basis. This is where a programming language other than the one used in developing the prototyping model may be implemented for the production environment. Under these conditions, the original prototype model could be "thrown away."

Examples are heavy-duty, large and complex, and transaction-based business application systems whether accounting/financial systems or not.

Exhibit 5.35 presents the major characteristics of the traditional life-cycle methodologies and the prototyping approaches.

<u>Characteristics of life-cycle methodologies</u>

- Suitable to certain requirements and highly structured tasks where requirements can be reasonably defined.
- Uses bottom-up and/or top-down design approach for system analysis and data requirements.
- Applicable to large projects and high user understanding of tasks.
- Provides enhanced management and controls of the development process.
- Cannot give users a functioning system quickly as it requires a lengthy application development time to achieve a functioning system.
- The major phases include defining requirements, designing system, developing code, testing the system, installing the system, and operating the system.
- Anticipates and plans for resource acquisition and use.
- All data files are converted once.

<u>Characteristics of prototype methodologies</u>

- Suitable to uncertain requirements and highly unstructured tasks where requirements are difficult to describe in advance.
- Uses iterative and trial and error approach to define and refine requirements.
- User responsibilities include specifying requirements, evaluating iterations, refining requirements, and communicating changes.
- Management and control of the project could be difficult if not impossible due to a feeling of lax environment.
- Allows experiments with new design approaches without incurring large development costs, thus giving a working model to users quickly.
- The major phases include defining requirements, creating an initial system, refining the requirements, designing the system, developing the system, testing the system, installing the systems, and operating the system.
- Acquires resources on short notice when compared to the traditional approach.
- Data files are continuously reformatted with new system iterations.

Exhibit 5.35: Characteristics of traditional life-cycle and prototyping methods

5.13 Voice Communications

(a) **VoIP Risks and Opportunities.** Voice over Internet protocol (VoIP)—the transmission of voice over packet-switched IP networks—is one of the most important emerging trends in telecommunications. As with many new technologies, VoIP introduces both security risks and opportunities. Lower cost and greater flexibility are among the promises of VoIP for the enterprise, but the technology presents security administrators with significant security challenges. Administrators may mistakenly assume that some digitized voice travels in packets; they can simply plug VoIP components into their already-secure networks and remain secure. Unfortunately, the process is not that simple.

VoIP systems take a wide variety of forms, including traditional telephone handsets, conferencing units, and mobile units. In addition to end-user equipment, VoIP systems include a variety of other components, including call processors/call managers, gateways, routers, firewalls, and protocols. Most of these components have counterparts used in data networks, but the performance demands of VoIP mean that ordinary network software and hardware must be supplemented with special VoIP components. Not only does VoIP require higher performance than most data systems, critical services, such as Emergency 911 (E-911) must be accommodated. One of the main sources of confusion for those new to VoIP is the (natural) assumption that because digitized voice travels in packets just like other data, existing network architectures and tools can be used without change. Unfortunately, VoIP adds a number of complications to existing network technology, and these problems are magnified by security considerations.

Quality of Service (QoS) is fundamental to the operation of a VoIP network that meets users' quality expectations. Unfortunately, the implementation of various security measures can cause a marked deterioration in QoS. These complications range from firewalls delaying or blocking call setups to encryption-produced latency and delay variation (jitter). Because of the time-critical nature of VoIP, and its low tolerance for disruption and packet loss, many security measures implemented in traditional data networks are simply not applicable to VoIP in their current form. Current VoIP systems use either a proprietary protocol, or one of two standards, H.323 and the session initiation protocol (SIP). Although SIP seems to be gaining in popularity, neither of these protocols has become dominant in the market yet, so it often makes sense to incorporate components that can support both. An extension of SIP, the SIP for instant messaging and presence leverage extensions (SIMPLE) standards, is being incorporated into products that support instant messaging. In addition to H.323 and SIP there are two other standards, MGCP and Megaco/H.248, which may be used in large deployments for gateway decomposition. These standards may be used to ensure message handling with media gateways, or however they can easily be used to implement terminals without any intelligence, similar to today's phones connected to a private branch exchange (PBX) system utilizing a stimulus protocol. Until a truly dominant standard emerges, organizations moving to VoIP should consider gateways and other network elements that support both H.323 and SIP. Such a strategy helps to ensure a stable and robust VoIP network in the years to come, no matter which protocol prevails.

Firewalls are a staple of security in today's IP networks. Whether protecting a LAN or WAN, encapsulating a DMZ, or just protecting a single computer, a firewall is usually the first line of defense against would-be attackers. Firewalls work by blocking traffic deemed to be invasive, intrusive, or just plain malicious from flowing through them. Acceptable traffic is determined by a set of rules programmed into the firewall by the network administrator. The introduction of firewalls to the VoIP network complicates several aspects of VoIP, most notably dynamic port trafficking and calls setup procedures.

Network address translation (NAT) is a powerful tool that can be used to provide security and enable several endpoints within a LAN to share the same IP address. The benefits of NATs come at a price. For one thing, an attempt to make a call into the network becomes very complex when a NAT is introduced. The situation is analogous to a phone network where several phones have the same phone number (e.g., a house with multiple phones on one line). There are also several issues associated with the transmission of voice data across the NAT, including an incompatibility with IPsec protocol.

Firewalls, gateways, and other such devices can also help keep intruders from compromising a network. However, firewalls are no defense against an internal hacker. Another layer of defense is necessary at the protocol level to protect the data itself. In VoIP, as in data networks, this can be accomplished by encrypting the packets at the IP level using IPsec, or at the transport level with secure RTP. However, several factors, including the expansion of packet size, ciphering latency, and a lack of QoS urgency in the cryptographic engine itself can cause an excessive amount of latency in the VoIP packet delivery. This leads to degraded voice quality, again highlighting the tradeoff between security and voice quality, and emphasizing a need for speed.

Designing, deploying, and securely operating a VoIP network is a complex effort that requires careful preparation. The integration of a VoIP system into an already congested or overburdened data network could be problematic for an organization's technology infrastructure. An organization must investigate carefully how its network is laid out and which solution fits its needs best.

(b) **VoIP General Guidelines.** The following list provides guidelines for general voice over Internet protocol (VoIP):

- Separate voice and data on logically different networks. Different subnets with separate RFC 1918 address blocks should be used for voice and data traffic, with separate DHCP servers for each.
- At the voice gateway, which interfaces with the PSTN, disallow H.323, SIP, or MGCP, or Megaco/H.248 connections from the data network. Use strong authentication and access control on the voice gateway system, as with any other critical network management components. Strong

authentication of clients towards a gateway is often very difficult. Here, access control mechanisms and policy enforcement may help.

- Use firewalls designed for VoIP traffic, through ALGs or firewall control proxies. Stateful packet filters can track the state of connections, denying packets that are not part of a properly originated call.
- Use IPsec or secure shell (SSH) protocol for all remote management and auditing access. If practical, avoid using remote management at all and do IP PBX access from a physically secure system.
- If performance is a problem, use encryption at the router or other gateway, not the individual endpoints, to provide for IPsec tunneling. Since some VoIP endpoints are not computationally powerful enough to perform encryption, placing this burden at a central point ensures that all VoIP traffic emanating from the enterprise network has been encrypted.

VoIP can provide more flexible service at lower cost, but there are significant tradeoffs that must be considered. VoIP systems can be expected to be more vulnerable than conventional telephone systems, in part, because they are tied into the data network, resulting in additional security weaknesses and avenues of attack. Confidentiality and privacy may be at greater risk in VoIP systems unless strong controls are implemented and maintained. An additional concern is the relative instability of VoIP compared with established telephony systems. Today, VoIP systems are still maturing and dominant standards have not emerged. This instability is compounded by VoIP's reliance on packet networks as a transport medium. The public switched telephone network is ultrareliable. Internet service is generally much less reliable, and VoIP cannot function without Internet connections. Essential telephone services, unless carefully planned, deployed, and maintained, will be at greater risk if based on VoIP. For example, special considerations should be given to E-911 emergency services communications, because E-911 automatic location service is not available with VoIP in some cases.

(c) **VoIP Physical Controls.** Unless the VoIP network is encrypted, anyone with physical access to the office LAN could potentially connect network monitoring tools and tap into telephone conversations. Even if encryption is used, physical access to VoIP servers and gateways may allow an attacker to monitor network traffic. Organizations therefore should ensure that adequate physical security is in place to restrict access to VoIP network components. Physical security measures, including barriers, locks, access control systems, and guards, are the first line of defense. Organizations must make sure that the proper physical countermeasures are in place to mitigate some of the biggest risks such as insertion of sniffers or other network monitoring devices. For example, installation of a sniffer could result in not just data but all voice communications being intercepted.

(d) **VoIP-Ready Firewalls.** Because of the inherent vulnerabilities (e.g., susceptibility to packet sniffing) of operating telephony across a packet network, VoIP systems incorporate an array of security features and protocols. Organization security policy should ensure that these features are used. In particular, firewalls designed for VoIP protocols are an essential component of a secure VoIP system.

(e) **VoIP Training.** Emerging technologies when coupled with network administrators not yet trained on the technology, lax security practices, insufficient controls, and poor understanding of the risks form an especially challenging security environment. Therefore, organizations should carefully consider such issues as administrators' level of knowledge and training in the technology, the maturity and quality of their security practices, controls, policies, and architectures, and their understanding of the associated security risks.

(f) **VoIP Quality of Service Issues.** Quality of service (QoS) is fundamental to the operation of a VoIP network. Unfortunately, the implementation of various security measures can degrade QoS. These complications range from delaying or blocking of call setups by firewalls to encryption-produced latency and delay variation (jitter), QoS issues are central to VoIP security. If QoS were assured, then most of the same security measures currently implemented in today's data networks could be used in VoIP networks. But because of the time-critical nature of VoIP, and its low tolerance for disruption and packet loss, many security measures implemented in traditional data networks just are not applicable to VoIP in their current form. The main QoS issues associated with VoIP that security affects include latency, jitter, packet loss, bandwidth congestion, and speed.

Latency in VoIP refers to the time it takes for a voice transmission to go from its source to its destination. Ideally, we would like to keep latency as low as possible but there are practical lower bounds on the delay of VoIP. Delay is not confined to the endpoints of the system. Each hop along the network introduces a new queuing delay and possibly a processing delay if it is a security checkpoint (i.e., firewall or encryption/decryption point). Also, larger packets tend to cause bandwidth congestion and increased latency. This requires small packets to keep latency at a minimum.

Jitter refers to nonuniform packet delays. It is often caused by low bandwidth situations in VoIP and can be exceptionally detrimental to the overall QoS. Jitter can cause packets to arrive and be processed out of sequence. Applications can be reordered using the sequence number and timestamp field at a cost, increased overhead. When jitter is high, packets arrive at their destination in spurts. A general method to control jitter at VoIP endpoints is the use of a buffer. Jitter can also be controlled at the nexuses of the VoIP network by using routers, firewalls, and other network elements that support QoS. Another method for reducing delay variation is to pattern network traffic to diminish jitter by making as efficient use of the bandwidth as possible. Unfortunately, this constraint is at odds with some security measures in VoIP. Chief among these is IPsec, whose processing requirements may increase latency, thus limiting effective bandwidth and contributing to jitter. Effective bandwidth is compromised when packets are expanded with new headers. Implementing devices that support QoS and improving the efficiency of bandwidth with header compression allows for more uniform packet delay in a secured VoIP network.

VoIP is exceptionally intolerant of **packet loss**. Packet loss can result from excess latency, where a group of packets arrives late and must be discarded in favor of newer ones. It can be the result of jitter, that is, when a packet arrives after its surrounding packets have been flushed from the buffer, it is useless. Sometimes, a packet is not delivered at all. Bandwidth congestion and other such causes of packet loss tend to affect the packets being delivered around the same time. The implementation of forward error correction and packet loss concealment schemes can produce a VoIP network that is less sensitive to packet loss.

As in data networks, **bandwidth congestion** can cause packet loss and a host of other QoS problems. Thus, proper bandwidth reservation and allocation is essential to VoIP quality. Unfortunately, one of the great attractions of VoIP, data and voice sharing the same wires, is also a potential problem for implementers who must allocate the necessary bandwidth for both networks in a system normally designed for one. Congestion of the network causes packets to be queued, which in turn contributes to the latency of the VoIP system. Low bandwidth can also contribute to nonuniform delays (jitter), since packets will be delivered in spurts when a window of opportunity opens up in the traffic. Because of these issues, VoIP network infrastructures must provide the highest amount of bandwidth possible. Header compression is a method for reducing the bandwidth usage of VoIP network.

The key to conquering QoS issues like latency and bandwidth congestion is **speed**. By definition, faster throughput means reduced latency and probabilistically reduces the chances of server bandwidth congestion. Thus every facet of network traversal must be completed quickly in VoIP. The latency often associated with task in data networks will not be tolerated. Chief among these latency producers that must improve performance are firewall/NAT traversal and traffic encryption/decryption routines. Traditionally, these are two of the most effective ways for administrators to secure their networks. Unfortunately, they are also two of the greatest contributors to network congestion and throughput delay.

(g) **Voice Mail.** Voice mail (V-mail) or voice messaging systems are computer-based systems with their own input, editing, storage, retrieval, and transmission of information in the form of natural (human) or synthetic speech. V-mail systems can be PC-based or private branch exchange (PBX). A PBX is a telephone switch located at an end-user site. The PBX is used to connect two end users or an end user and the telephone company network. Each user is given a voice "mailbox" for his own use. Outgoing and incoming messages can be of any length, or they can be fixed. All messages are date- and time-stamped. See Exhibit 5.36 for risks and controls in toll fraud.

Voice-mail system interfaces with the following: private branch exchange system, voice-response system to place purchase orders or inquire status of an account balance in a financial/retail institution, and electronic-mail system to remind that a V-mail message is waiting while the user is on the e-mail session.

Potential or actual risks and exposures	*Suggested controls or control procedures*
• Toll fraud through voice-mail	• Ensure that PINs are truly random; periodically change all PINs; remove all unassigned or unused mailboxes; unpublish the remote access number; block access to long-distance trunks and local lines; deactivate any mailboxes used by intruders; restrict collect calls; and review telephone bills.

Exhibit 5.36: Risks and controls in toll fraud

5.14 Contingency Planning

Computer backup facilities, disaster recovery, business resumption, or contingency planning problems and issues pose major challenges and concerns to IS management, senior management, functional user management, and audit management. *The key issues are how to develop disaster recovery plans, how to test them, how to maintain them, and how to keep the continuity of operations. The major key issue for IS management is to know why we need to plan for disasters and what the objectives are.*

The disaster recovery plan, if it is to be of any value, should cover both IS and functional user departments of the organization. Not only should the recovery plans be available for all departments but they should also be integrated. This "total" plan should address not only mainframe (central) computers, but also minicomputers, midrange computers, microcomputers, and networks of all types (e.g., wide area, local area, metropolitan, value-added, third-party) regardless of their location either inside or outside the organization. The "total" plan also covers manual, automated, and semiautomated functions of the organization.

(a) **Contingency Plan Compared with System Development Life Cycle.** Incorporating disaster recovery requirements into system design would be the best approach and proactive thinking. For example, a facility for restarting at an intermediate stage of processing an application program can be built in to provide continuity of program operation.

A top-down approach is recommended for developing organization-wide disaster recovery and contingency plans especially for the first time. For ongoing maintenance, a combination of top-down and bottom-up approach is advised. This will permit input not only from top management (top-down) but also output from test exercises conducted regularly (bottom-up). A top-down contingency plan approach includes the following steps and involves senior management, line management, IS management, information systems auditors, and functional (end) users: (1) conduct impact analysis, (2) plan design, (3) plan development, (4) plan testing, (5) plan implementation, and (6) plan maintenance.

The above approach can be compared to the traditional development of computer systems using a life cycle approach as shown in Exhibit 5.37.

Systems development life cycle approach	Contingency plan approach
• Conduct systems analysis	• Conduct impact analysis
• System design	• Plan design
• System development	• Plan development
• System testing	• Plan testing
• System implementation	• Plan implementation
• System maintenance	• Plan maintenance

Exhibit 5.37: Comparison of traditional system development with contingency plan approach

The disaster recovery plan can be thought of as various stages in a disaster model building exercise. The stages are progressive, representing higher levels of readiness (planning to implementation). It can also be thought of as reflecting the stages of organizational maturity attained in addressing disaster recovery issues.

(b) **Risk Analysis and Assessment for Contingency Planning.** Risk analysis is a prerequisite to a complete and meaningful disaster recovery planning program. **Risk analysis** is the assessment of threats to resources (assets) and the determination of the amount of protection necessary to adequately safeguard the resources (assets) so that vital systems, operations, and services can be quickly resumed to a normal status in case of a disaster. Essentially, risk analysis and assessment processes addresses the following actions:

- Identify assets (e.g., hardware, software, data, facilities, documentation, supplies).
- Develop a list of potential threats (e.g., fire, flood, tornado) with frequency of their occurrences.
- Correlate threats to assets.
- Rank the threats based on their impact and risk.
- Recommend cost-effective controls to reduce potential threats.

Some basic questions that can be asked about the threat are: How likely is it to occur? What will be the consequence to the organization if it does occur? How predictable are the cycles for occurrence of the threat? The probability of risk must be weighed against the criticality of each asset to be protected. Some questions to ask about the asset are: What would the impact be if the asset were to be suddenly removed? How would loss of the asset impact the organization politically or otherwise?

Once the threat has been identified and its impact defined, the list should be reviewed and threats classified as either acceptable or as risks which must be controlled. To determine the risk imposed by each threat, rank each threat, rank the criticality of the asset, and then evaluate them together. The decision about whether a risk should be tolerated or controlled solely rests with the senior management—not the auditors. There are several actions that can be taken in response to a threat.

- Do nothing. This may be a situation where the threat is remote or the cost of response is excessive and management simply accepts the risk.
- Improve controls.
- Purchase redundant equipment and facilities.
- Remove or spread the vulnerable condition. This is a situation where alternate sources and support for backup are sought. Providing insurance coverage is another form of spreading the risk.

To be meaningful and useful, disaster event scenarios need to be developed. Since there are many scenario levels that can be developed theoretically, it will be effective to limit them to as few levels as possible. The following describes one approach to accomplish this objective:

- **Minor disaster.** It is the lowest level of a disaster where business operations are abnormally interrupted and recovery to normal situation can be accomplished with current resources within a short period of time (e.g., 24 hours).
- **Major disaster.** It is the condition where business operations are seriously interrupted and recovery to a normal situation cannot be effected for an extended period of time (e.g., 48 to 72 hours) and without additional resources.
- **Catastrophic disaster.** It is the condition beyond the previous two situations where severe damage has occurred to building, equipment, software, telecommunications, and network, which renders the organization inoperable for a long time. Extensive additional resources are needed to bring operations to normal conditions.

(c) **Contingency Planning Assumptions.** In developing a disaster recovery plan, many people and many business units and functions participate throughout its development and maintenance phases. Naturally, many assumptions go into the plan development and maintenance activities. Therefore, it is important that all members of the project are informed about all the assumptions so that there is no misunderstanding and misinterpretation of assumptions. Some typical assumptions would include

- All priority level 1 applications will be run first.
- All resources and materials required to restore the processing capability at the recovery site must be obtainable from off-site.
- All data centers will have their own recovery plans to accommodate their uniqueness.
- All the less critical jobs not run during the initial recovery period must be recovered eventually.
- No administrative support (e.g., public relations, security, and risk management) will be immediately available unless it is prearranged and documented.
- Testing and maintenance of the contingency plan must be continual.
- Each application should have its own recovery goal stated in terms of hours or days to recover. Recovery period is the time between the occurrence of a disaster and when the backup computer facility is ready to start processing critical application systems. Note that the recovery goals are not static; they need to be changed as more information is available after testing the plan or during plan development.

(d) **Contingency Planning Requirements.** Senior management personnel of public corporations have a legal responsibility to their stockholders, customers, suppliers, and employees to provide backup computer services so that business functions will continue despite a disaster. Some organizations could not survive more than two or three business days without a computer.

If the disaster recovery plan is not in place and tested regularly, senior management might be subjected to class action suits from stockholders and employees for gross negligence in protecting corporate assets, which include data and information residing in the computer.

The major impetus for disaster recovery or contingency planning is coming from public accountants (external auditors) when they audit data (computer) centers as part of a financial audit, and from internal auditors when they review data centers as a part of the EIS audit program. Both auditors are making recommendations to IS management and senior management to have a fully prepared and tested backup and recovery plan, so that the organization will continue as a going-concern entity.

To be effective, each organization should develop a backup and recovery contingency plan which should be updated as needed, and be tested periodically to ensure its effectiveness. This contingency plan is needed to provide timely computer services to functional users, business customers, and suppliers.

The Planning Committee should be charged with the responsibility for developing a comprehensive Disaster Recovery Plan for the organization. In so doing, a Project Plan should be developed with specific assignments for each member together with milestones, target dates, and deliverables. Periodic management briefings should be scheduled for reporting the progress of the Planning Committee and ensuring continued management guidance, commitment, and support for the planning effort.

(e) **Contingency Plan Development.** A user organization has at least four choices in developing and maintaining the disaster recovery or contingency planning document.

1. **Develop in-house.** Even though this option is inexpensive, it may take a long time to develop the plan due to lack of expertise and the need to develop the plan from scratch. The advantage is that the plan can be tailored to the organization's specific needs, and computer hardware and software configurations.
2. **Buy a software package.** Many commercial vendor organizations are offering a PC-based software package with menu driven features to guide the user through the development of a plan. It is easy to use and more expensive than the in-house choice. However, time can be saved with this approach.
3. **Hire consultants.** Even though this choice is more expensive than the others, time can be saved because of a consultant's expertise with other clients/customers in the same industry, as well as in all industries.
4. **Combination of the above.** The plan can be developed from scratch or with the use of a software package, and then be reviewed by a consultant, who can also provide backup and recovery facilities. The advantage is that the consultant will assess the adequacy of the plan and determine whether it will work on his backup and recovery facilities; the consultant could be completely independent of the backup and recovery facilities.

(f) **Application Systems Prioritization for Contingency Planning.** System prioritization is essential since not every application system can be processed during a disaster. This is because the time window is usually small. Critical application systems need to be determined by ranking each application in terms of potential impact from that application being unavailable. Critical data should be collected for each application system to include the following items:

- Application system name and identifier
- Primary users and data processors and purpose of the system
- Computer processing period with elapsed times and maximum acceptable delay
- Input data sources and their medium
- Output reports and medium with their purpose
- Applications software and supporting systems software requirements
- Backup location for equipment, documentation, special forms, supplies, network, and software

An impact analysis is suggested, which requires two steps: developing an impact matrix (Exhibit 5.38) and prioritizing the criticality levels for each application system. It is the responsibility of computer operations management to ensure that a contingency processing priority code is assigned to each new application system moved into production.

After each application system is weighed in terms of its impact on the organization due to various disruption types, the total score can be converted to priority levels 1 through 3, or other

- Level 1—The system must be processed on schedule (e.g., accounts receivable).
- Level 2—The system can be processed when resources become available (e.g., general ledger).
- Level 3—The system processing can be delayed (e.g., payroll).

Application system name	A	B	C	D	E	F	G	Total
Payroll	1	1	1	1	1	3	3	11
General ledger	1	2	2	2	2	1	3	13
Accounts receivable	3	2	2	3	3	1	3	17

<u>Matrix key</u>

Impact of disruption to:
A = revenues, B = customers, C = operational efficiency, D = ability to achieve profit goals, E = service-levels, F = employees, G = manual recovery effort as an alteranative

Impact weighting factors:
1 = low, 2 = medium, 3 = high

Exhibit 5.38: Application system impact matrix

Instead of levels, each application system can be ranked as critical (with few hours of recovery requirement), important (with few days of recovery requirement), desirable (with several days of recovery requirement).

Those systems that are identified as absolutely critical for conduct of the business should be labeled as critical systems. All of the Level 1 production systems should be prioritized from most critical to least critical. The disaster recovery plan should be developed so that recovery operations are directed toward immediately processing the Level 1 critical application systems. This is followed by Level 2 and Level 3 systems, which will be processed as full recovery operation is reached. The resulting information regarding the status of each application should be conveyed to functional users and an agreement reached concerning the status.

The prioritized list of Level 1 application systems is used to develop an emergency production schedule for use during a recovery operation following a disaster event. The prioritization of the production systems and the production schedule then form the basis for resource identification for the organization disaster recovery plan.

This disaster recovery production schedule should be sufficiently flexible to be adjusted to the timing of the disaster occurrence during the production cycle.

Since there is the potential for extended central (primary) site downtime, it is important that all functional users understand that there is a need for alternate procedures (manual and/or automated) which would provide for continued operation in the event of a disaster, resulting in the nonavailability of central site support for an indefinite period of time. The degree of loss caused by a disaster or disruption is directly related to the length of time the disruption affects business operations.

(g) **Backup Computer Processing Choices.** Many choices are available to a user organization in preparing for a disaster. The following are some major choices available for alternative backup computer facilities:

- **Dedicated contingency facilities.** Also known as "hot sites," where an organization provides fully equipped computer facilities for use in the event one of its subscribers/ customers suffers a computer disaster. Periodic computer testing time is made available to customers. It is the most expensive choice. Large and complex online and database systems use hot-site services. Hot-site is called shared facilities (see Exhibit 5.39).
- **Empty shell facilities.** A fully prepared computer room ("cold site") is maintained by an organization and includes data communication systems, security systems, air conditioning, humidity controls, raised floors, storage and office space, and electrical power. In the event of a disaster, the computer vendor delivers the required hardware and peripheral equipment to the empty shell facility. Usually, empty shell facilities also provide off-site storage of computer files (programs and data), documentation, supplies, source documents, and input forms. Cold site is also called shared facilities.
- **Warm sites.** The configuration lies in between "hot site" and "cold site." It has telecommunications ready to be utilized, and is recommended for users of sophisticated telecommunications and network needs.

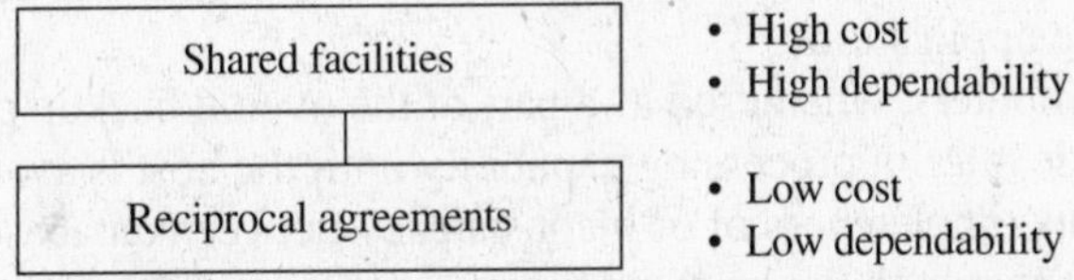

Exhibit 5.39: Shared facilities and reciprocal agreements

- **Rolling recovery sites.** This uses the concept of "computer rooms on wheels" or portable sites, where relocatable, self-contained recovery sites with environmentally conditioned (including raised floors, air conditioning, fire protection, diesel power generators, and security) space is provided by an organization for a fee for emergency computing and telecommunications purposes. The idea is to set up a computer (data) center in a parking lot near the damaged building. Some of the advantages of a rolling cold site are: (a) telecommunications can be reconnected from a point where the communications lines terminated at a manhole, and (b) it saves travel time and money to the nearby hot site location.

- **Vendor backup facilities.** Most major hardware vendors offer their facilities to selected customers in the event of a major computer disaster.
- **Company multiple sites.** Based on the redundancy concept, each site is configured to support the combined computer-processing load of the company.
- **Commercial service providers.** This provides backup and recovery services for their users or customers.
- **Mutual aid (reciprocal processing) agreements.** One organization agrees to provide backup and recovery facilities for another organization with a compatible hardware and software configuration and vice versa. Mutual aid agreements may not prove workable when needed. It is the least expensive choice. Simple and large batch systems are suitable to use a reciprocal processing agreement (see Exhibits 5.39 and 5.40).

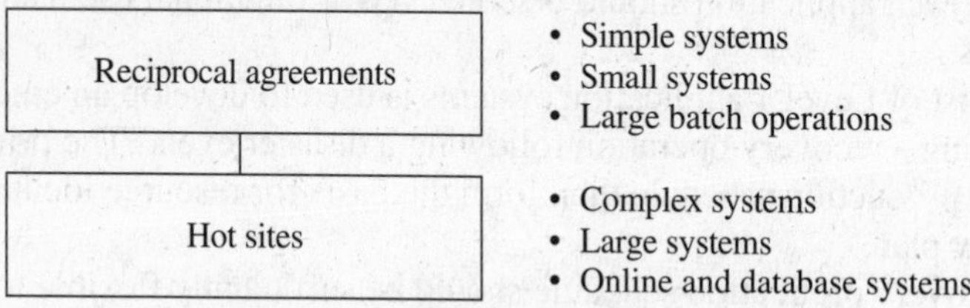

Exhibit 5.40: Reciprocal agreements and hot sites

- **Consortium.** Several organizations pool their resources and build their own backup computer facility for common use.
- **Time brokers.** Time brokers serve as a resource for obtaining backup support. Time brokers find, for a fee, available processing time on other systems. Processing arrangements are made entirely through this third-party service. Time brokers, however, do not guarantee that hardware and software configurations will fully satisfy critical requirements.
- **Empty buildings.** These are warehouses or other buildings, which can be wired, equipped, furnished, and environmentally prepared. In addition, an empty building can provide office space when there is not sufficient space at the backup computer site. When empty buildings are the property of the organization losing the primary computer facility, a more successful recovery may be accomplished than when the buildings are being rented. This may be a viable option in the face of a long outage.
- **Use of microcomputers.** This approach to backup processing integrates operations that can be supported by microcomputers or intelligent terminals. The microcomputer, for example, can be used to perform local processing, storage, data entry and query, and word processing. It may be used as a personal computer or double as a terminal to the mainframe.

  Hence, integration of microcomputers into the organization may ensure less dependence on the central host for computing power. To use this alternative, contingency planners should

  - Determine which operations can be accomplished by a microcomputer.
  - Select commercial data management and other software that can support critical application systems' processing.
  - Select hardware that will not only support current applications but that is flexible enough to support future applications.

    Microcomputers, when used as a part of the overall backup processing strategy, may be able to provide interim processing capability until the host is available. There is a danger, however, of incompleteness of or inconsistency between databases. Database owners should ensure that both the host and microcomputer versions remain compatible.
  - **Reversion to manual processing.** This approach reverts back to a manual operation. It may be a workable choice if manual procedures that duplicate the automated process are documented. If, however, manual procedures are outdated, or simply not available, it may be impractical to rewrite them.

Generally, this option is seldom used with the expectation that critical processing needs can be fully satisfied. It may, however, be a suitable option if used in conjunction with another alternative. For example, planners may find that subsistence functions of a computer system can be supported by a manual process, for a short period, until critical operations are restarted at the alternate location.

- A **combination** of the above options.

(h) **Off-Site Storage Controls.** Off-site storage locations should be identified to store magnetic media, paper documentation, and forms that are needed to run the backup computer in the event of a disaster. Care should be taken to select an off-site storage location whether it is a part of the organization or an outside commercial storage center situated locally or remotely to the primary computer center. Regardless of the choice, the off-site storage location should be well-controlled in terms of recordkeeping of media movement and documentation between on-site and off-site, adequate physical security over the facilities, and environmental controls within the facility.

(i) **Contingency Recovery and Reconstruction Methodologies.** This section discusses the disaster recovery process, teams and compositions, and responsibilities and procedures for conducting disaster recovery operation for any level of disaster.

Experiencing a disaster without preplanned processes, technical personnel skilled in the recovery process and disaster recovery procedures will significantly increase the cost and time necessary to effect a full recovery and return to normal operation. An effective series of disaster recovery procedures that are based upon a well-defined recovery process which has been tested and exercised frequently by skilled personnel will stabilize a crisis situation, and provide managers with a mechanism for directing recovery actions and prevent a disaster from escalating.

(j) **Disaster Recovery Process.** At this point in the planning process, most of the major pieces of the disaster recovery plan have been determined, coordinated and approved, such as the identification of critical application systems, and the identification of equipment and facilities, hardware, systems software, and others. The disaster recovery process should now be defined and described to the extent that the other elements of the disaster recovery plan can be developed.

By stepping through and describing the recovery process for the multitude of possible variations, many of the details that must be addressed will surface and can be reviewed as a part of the planning process. The thought process involved in developing this disaster recovery operations process will aid in identifying the necessary team, responsibilities, team composition, recovery organization, command center, and the procedures necessary to effect a recovery following a disaster.

(k) **Disaster Recovery Teams.** Several teams will be required for a disaster recovery. The exact number of teams should be determined by the management responsible for developing the plan. Each team will have specific responsibilities to perform and will work with other teams to effect full recovery. A team leader should be designated for each team to provide guidance, coordination, and direction to the team effort.

(l) **Disaster Recovery Procedures.** Definitive procedures for use by the disaster recovery organization and each of the teams should provide overall authority for action, guidance, and responsibilities in conducting the recovery operation. Under normal circumstances, several individuals will be developing the procedures.

The procedures should be thoroughly reviewed to insure that all aspects of the recovery process are covered in sufficient detail to preclude confusion during an actual recovery process. The review should also ascertain that the planned recovery process is followed by the appropriate procedures and that the procedures complement one another without conflict.

(m) **Disaster Recovery Training.** The objective is to ensure that disaster recovery plan execution is effective when a disaster occurs. The purpose is to identify the types of training to be provided, the personnel to perform the training, and those to be trained.

Much of the success in executing a disaster recovery plan will be dependent upon how well participants accept the importance of the plan, the credibility of the plan, and the degree and quality of the training provided.

In addition, it is also important that an effective cross training program be in operation to insure that vital functions can effectively be performed in the event key personnel are unavailable at the time of a disaster.

Regular and frequent training in the security policies and procedures should be conducted for all personnel. Strict enforcement of the policies and procedures should be the norm, and all personnel should subscribe to the organization's security policies and procedures. Training in the disaster recovery planned processes should be provided to all personnel of the IS organization to ensure awareness of the process and each individual responsibility in the event of a disaster.

Primary personnel and alternates who are expected to take on specific roles during a disaster should be provided training regarding the overall disaster recovery plan and detailed training in their specific responsibilities. As changes in the plan and the procedures occur, refresher training should be conducted.

(n) **Disaster Recovery Plan Testing Procedures.** The disaster recovery plan should be tested periodically using a fully developed test scenario, a simulated disaster, planned monitoring of results and appraisal of the entire process with revisions and updates to the plan. An untested plan is nearly as bad as having no plan at all. Testing reveals plan shortfalls, weaknesses, and problems—all would help in improving the plan's contents and effectiveness.

Testing of the disaster recovery plan should be carefully planned so that normal operations are minimally disrupted. It is recommended that portions of the plan be tested every six months so that all parts of the plan are tested annually. Each test operation should be monitored by management to enable understanding of the disaster recovery planned operation and to provide effective monitoring of the test, thereby detecting shortcoming and/or problems in the plan and aiding in correcting or updating the plan.

The sequence of first-time testing of the plan at hot-site backup computer facility should include the following subsystems, as not all of them can be tested at once:

- Recovery of operating systems software and other supporting systems software
- Recovery and restoration of production data files
- Recovery of network and telecommunications
- Recovery of specific and individual application systems

After the first-time testing is successful, periodic testing includes prioritized application systems.

A scenario for each test exercise should be developed and approved by executive management. The test exercise should not be announced in advance. Each test scenario should be carefully developed so that all facets of the plan are fully tested on an annual basis.

The test plan should describe the detailed tasks to be performed with timeframes for each task. The test coordinator should log each task's beginning and ending times and record problems and actions taken during the test. These test minutes provide a valuable source of information to identify bottlenecks or gaps in the plan. The chronological description of time-based events will determine the time elapsed for the total test and for each individual task.

In addition to the scheduled testing exercise, the auditor, with the cooperation of senior management, should announce a surprise emergency simulation of a disaster to make sure that people are prepared to handle a real disaster, should it occur.

All test results including the operating system activity, database load and unload activity, telecommunications activity, online system activity, and the review of application system processing results should be documented and published to all affected functional users and IS management.

(o) **Contingency Plan Maintenance Procedures.** Many of the changes and updates to the plan will result from ongoing changes in people, hardware, systems software, applications software, telecommunications and networks, computer operations, changes in business conditions such as mergers and divestures, changes in application system priorities, and other relevant factors. Two methods available for ensuring that the plan is current are: (1) scheduled review of sections of the plan and (2) identification of changes during the plan testing.

Changes that are identified as needed in the plan and the procedures during a test exercise should be carefully noted, and the changes should be made immediately following the test exercise.

To facilitate effective and timely plan maintenance work, it is a good practice to keep a copy of the plan stored on a personal computer or other computer for editing the plan document for additions and changes. If this approach is used, it is important to keep both hard copy and magnetic media as backup at the off-site storage facility. Often the person responsible for maintaining and updating the plan is forgotten after the plan is developed.

(p) **Electronic Vaulting for Contingency Planning.** Manual mode of performing system backups is time-consuming, labor-intensive, and costly. *Electronic vaulting is the ability to store and retrieve backups electronically in a site remote from the primary computer center.* The backup information can be transmitted to off-site from on-site and vice versa. Storage media such as optical disk, magnetic disk, mass storage device, and the automated tape library are some examples of devices used on the receiving end of the electronic vault. Electronic vaulting exploits the significant cost/performance improvements made in telecommunications technologies. Higher bandwidth and lower costs associated with fiber optics and satellite links have made it possible to send complete backup image copies electronically. It is also possible to vault current transaction recovery information (log or journal data) to the remote site in a timely manner.

The **benefits** of electronic vaulting are improved system availability, system performance and reliability, quality of the backup and recovery process, and increased customer (user) service. It makes backup information more accessible by reducing the retrieval time from hours or days to minutes during an interruption or a disaster when time is most valuable. Depending on the application, less information can be maintained online in the computer center that in turn reduces the amount of on-site backup storage needed. It supports automated or unattended computer center operations due to minimal or no human intervention required.

An electronic vault can be located at a recovery site, at a reciprocal site (recovery at the development site and production on the other site), in a third-party location close to the recovery site, or at a commercial hot/cold site.

(q) **Insurance Requirements for Contingency Planning.** A complete inventory of property is not only important for **insurance** purposes but equally useful for disaster recovery planning. The steps involved in this process include

- Determine the cost to replace each inventoried item.
- Inquire where the item could be replaced.
- Know the items that are irreplaceable.
- Determine consequences if the items were lost.

There are at least three methods of property valuation: (1) actual cash value, (2) replacement value, and (3) functional replacement value.

1. **Actual cash value** accounts for the replacement value of an item minus the actual depreciation and obsolescence that have lessened its value. The amount will likely not be enough to adequately replace what was lost.
2. **Replacement value** is the amount it costs to buy the exact piece of property, new, without deducting for depreciation. This is the most commonly used method of all.
3. **Functional replacement value** is the amount paid to replace obsolete machinery with up-to-date models. In rare cases, this cost may actually be less than the original value of the item being replaced.

Replacement value, a far more equitable settlement, is the amount it costs to buy the exact type of computer without deducting for depreciation. Actual cash value accounts for the replacement value of an item minus the actual physical depreciation and obsolescence that have lessened its value. The amount will likely not be enough to adequately replace what was lost. Placing an accurate value on computer equipment is the first step of disaster planning involving insurance. Replacement value, not the actual cash value, should be used for insurance coverage purpose.

Coinsurance represents the percentage of recovery entitled in the event of a total loss. If less than 80% coinsurance requirement is purchased, which is the standard, the cost of any loss sustained will be shared with the insurance company, according to the percentage of coverage purchased.

5.15 Systems Security

(a) **Firewalls.**

(i) **Overview of firewall.** A firewall is a combination of hardware and software placed between two networks that all traffic, regardless of the direction, must pass through. When employed properly, it is a primary security measure in governing access control and protecting the internal system from compromise.

Limitations of Firewalls

Firewalls may provide good control to prevent computer crime from the outside, but they may not prevent computer crime from within an organization.

The key to a firewall's ability to protect the network is its configuration and its location within the system. Firewall products do not afford adequate security protection as purchased. They must be set up, or configured, to permit or deny the appropriate traffic. To provide the most security, the underlying rule should be to deny all traffic unless expressly permitted. This requires system administrators to review and evaluate the need for all permitted activities, as well as who may need to use them. For example, to protect against Internet Protocol (IP) spoofing, data arriving from an outside network that claims to be originating from an internal computer should be denied access. Alternatively, systems could be denied access based on their IP address, regardless of the origination point. Such requests could then be evaluated based on what information was requested and from where in the internal system it was requested. For instance, incoming file transfer protocol (FTP) requests may be permitted, but outgoing FTP requests denied.

Ideally, if an Internet connection is to be provided from within an organization, or a Web site established, the connection should be entirely separate from the core processing system. If the Web site is placed on its own server, there is no direct connection to the internal computer system. However, appropriate firewall technology may be necessary to protect Web servers and/or internal systems.

Placing a "screening router" between the firewall and other servers provides an added measure of protection, because requests could be segregated and routed to a particular server. However, some systems may be considered so critical, they should be completely isolated from all other systems or networks. Security can also be enhanced by sending electronic transmissions from external sources to a computer that is not connected to the main computer.

(ii) **Data transmission and types of firewalls.**

(A) ***Data transmission.*** Data traverses the Internet in units referred to as packets. Each packet has headers that contain information for delivery, such as where the packet is coming from, where it is going, and what application it contains. The firewall techniques examine the headers and either permit or deny access to the system based on the firewall's rule configuration.

All information into and out of an organization should pass through the firewall. The firewall should also be able to change IP addresses to the firewall IP address, so no inside addresses are passed to the outside. Careful consideration should also be given to any data that is stored or placed on the server, especially sensitive or critically important data.

(B) ***Types of firewalls.*** There are at least four types of firewalls that provide various levels of security: (1) screening routers, (2) circuit-level gateways, (3) application gateways, and (4) inspection gateways. For instance, packet filters, sometimes implemented as screening routers, permit or deny access based solely on the stated source and/or destination IP addresses and the application (e.g., FTP). However, addresses and applications can be easily falsified, allowing attackers to enter systems.

Security Ranking of Firewalls

Firewalls listed in the order of security from weak to strong include screening routers, circuit-level gateways and application gateways, and inspection gateways.

Other types of firewalls, such as circuit-level gateways and application gateways, actually have separate interfaces with the internal (Intranet) and external (Internet) networks, meaning no direct connection is established between the two networks. A relay program copies all data from one interface to another, in each direction.

An even stronger firewall, a stateful inspection gateway, not only examines data packets for IP addresses, applications, and specific commands, but also provides security logging and alarm capabilities. This is in addition to historical comparisons with previous transmissions for deviations from normal context.

(C) ***Advantages and disadvantages of firewalls.*** A firewall can greatly improve network security and reduce risks to hosts on the subnet by filtering inherently insecure services and by providing the capability to restrict the types of access to subnet hosts. Consequently, the subnet network environment poses fewer risks to hosts, since only selected protocols will be able to pass through the firewall and only selected systems will be able to be accessed from the rest of the network. Eventual errors and configuration problems that reduce host security are better tolerated. A firewall system offers the following specific **advantages:**

- Concentration of security, where all modified software and logging is located on the firewall system as opposed to being distributed on many hosts
- Protocol filtering, where the firewall filters protocols and services that are either not necessary or that cannot be adequately secured from exploitation
- Hides information, in which a firewall can "hide" names of internal systems or electronic mail addresses, thereby revealing less information to outside hosts
- Application gateways, where the firewall requires inside or outside users to connect first to the firewall before connecting further, thereby filtering the protocol
- Extended logging, in which a firewall can concentrate extended logging of network traffic on one system
- Centralized and simplified network services management, in which services such as FTP, electronic mail, gopher, and other similar services are located on the firewall system(s) as opposed to being maintained on many systems

A firewall not only filters easily exploited services from entering a subnet, it also permits those services to be used on the inside subnet without fear of exploitation from outside systems. A firewall's protection is bidirectional; it can also protect hosts on the outside of the firewall from attacks originating from hosts on the inside by restricting outbound access.

Given these advantages, there are some **disadvantages** to using firewalls, the most obvious being that certain types of network access may be hampered or even blocked for some hosts, including Telnet, FTP, X Windows, and so forth. However, these disadvantages are not unique to firewalls; network access could be restricted at the host level as well, depending on a site's security policy.

A second disadvantage with a firewall system is that is concentrates security in one spot as opposed to distributing it among systems, thus a compromise of the firewall could be disastrous to other less-protected systems on the subnet. This weakness can be countered, however, with the argument that lapses and weaknesses in security are more likely to be found as the number of systems in a subnet increase, thereby multiplying the ways in which subnets can be exploited.

Another disadvantage of firewall is that relatively few vendors have offered real firewall systems; and that most have been hand-built by site administrators. The time and effort that could go into constructing a firewall may outweigh the cost of a vendor solution. There is also no firm definition of what constitutes a firewall; the term "firewall" can mean many things to many people (See Exhibit 5.41).

<u>Advantages of firewalls</u>

- Protection from vulnerable services
- Controlled access to site systems
- Concentrated security
- Enhanced privacy
- Logging and statistics on network use, misuse
- Policy enforcement

<u>Disadvantages of firewalls</u>

- Restricted access to desirable services such as Telnet, FTP, X Windows, NFS.
- Large potential for back doors due to unrestricted modem access.
- Little protection from insider attacks such as copying the data onto a tape and taking it out of the facility.
- World Wide Web (www), gopher, and WAIS do not work well with firewalls.
- Firewalls do not protect against user downloading virus-infected PC programs from Internet archives or transferring such programs in attachments to e-mail. Antiviral controls are needed.
- Firewalls represent a potential bottleneck in throughput since all connections must pass through the firewall.
- Security is concentrated in one spot as opposed to distributing it among systems (all eggs in one basket).

Exhibit 5.41: Advantages and disadvantages of firewalls

(b) **Control Objectives for Information Systems Security.**

(i) **Develop security policies and procedures.** Adequate security policies and procedures, supported by senior management, should be issued to all employees of the organization with a clear security and access control philosophy. This should be followed by formal security awareness and training programs to train employees in protecting both physical and logical assets of the organization. Security is not the responsibility of one group, department, or section of the organization. Instead, it is a shared responsibility between and among all employees and all departments of the organization. Security is no longer limited to the IS department. With widespread use of midrange, mini, and microcomputers throughout the organization, security is pervasive. To prevent legal actions by insiders and outsiders, all security policies and procedures need to be reviewed and approved by legal staff. These procedures should not be so detailed that they would work against the organization when not followed by employees. A mechanism is needed to keep security policies and procedures updated due to changing information technology, regulatory, management, or business requirements.

(ii) **Establish data and system ownership.** Prior to assigning responsibilities and exacting accountabilities from employees, there are three basic organizational responsibilities that should be established by management. These are data/system owners, data/system custodians, and data/system users.

A **data/system owner** is a person or group of persons who pays for the system development, maintenance, and operation or is responsible for the integrity of the data and system. Data ownership may be shared by managers of two or more departments. It is the system sponsor/owner who classifies data, recommends security-related controls, establishes and approves access rules, and assigns custodian(s). Data/system ownership does not imply true ownership rights in a legal sense; hence, owners or employees cannot sell or copy the data or software.

OWNERSHIP RULES—VARIOUS SYSTEMS

- In a traditional system, users can own data files, information groups, or the entire application system.
- In a nonrelational database system, users can own datasets, data fields, information groups, or the entire database.
- In a relational database system, users can own "tables" or "table-spaces"; one user does not necessarily own the entire database.

A **data/system custodian** provides physical and logical access procedures, and implement security controls and access safeguards. Both data owners and data custodians evaluate cost effectiveness of security-related controls.

Data/system users are the actual users of the information on a day-to-day basis. These users are authorized by data owners to read and/or update the information and are monitored by data custodians. Data users, in a way, agree they will follow all the security-related controls established by data owners and data custodians, use the system and its data for its intended purposes, and will not disclose sensitive or confidential information to anyone without explicit permission of the data owner(s). Data users can be classified as primary and secondary users, depending on the degree of usage of system outputs. Access rules must be compatible with employee job description.

Usually, **application system owners** are the functional department managers or division/senior management; **system users** are the functional department employees; and **system custodians** are the data processing (IS) department staff and management.

(iii) **Establish data classification schemes.** Adequate policies and procedures are needed to identify sensitive and critical data and their protection from beginning to end. A data item/file or a document may go through the following life cycle phases. **Life cycle phases for a document or file** can include: origination/creation, transmission/receiving, storage/retrieval, access/use, and retention/disposal.

One way to classify data or a document is to label or mark it as confidential, secret, top secret, sensitive, etc. Those data files are internally or externally marked as such, and access restrictions to those files are closely controlled. *Greater security controls are needed for highly sensitive data and lesser security controls are needed for less sensitive data.*

The key concern is whether a consistent approach was used in evaluating the sensitivity of the information handled and the classification categories used. Usually, financial, personal/personnel, product, and marketing information should be classified and protected.

(iv) **Develop full-scope security program.** To be effective, each organization should develop an overall security plan or program that includes areas such as

- Personnel security and administration
- Software security
- Data security
- Physical security and environmental security

Personnel security and administration refers to the issuing of policies, procedures, and standards; the monitoring of passwords and their violations; and the general administration of security function. Some organizations employ a group of people known as "tiger teams" or "penetration teams" to determine if they can break into a computer system. The focus is on identifying system weaknesses or flaws from a security viewpoint.

Software security and data security can be collectively called logical access security but are treated separately for better clarification of the subject matter. **Software security** refers to access controls over computer program files and terminals. **Data security** refers to access controls over data files, job files, and system libraries. Security rules define who can do what on the system.

Physical security involves a plan dealing with exposures and catastrophes such as fire, water leakage, power failure, power spikes and outages, tornadoes/hurricanes, earthquakes, flood, or explosion; human intervention such as unauthorized entrance, strikes, sabotage, vandalism, civil disorder, theft, and intrusion; and physical damage to computer hardware and peripheral equipment. **Environmental security** refers to measuring and monitoring of heat, humidity, and air conditioning levels.

(v) **Develop security administration goals.** The goal of a security administrator should be to maintain all security rules in one place in order to avoid conflicting, redundant, and uncoordinated security rules and to increase the "trustworthiness" of the security system. A "single rule base" concept, where one rule exists for one user, for the entire computing environment, should be encouraged.

Where possible, security rule verification should be performed at program "run time," instead of "compile time," so that changes to security rules take effect immediately and do not require recompiling of the application program being affected. Recompilation of an application program can take excessive time and could consume heavy system resources.

The security administrator must satisfy the least privilege principle where each user or device is granted the most restrictive set of access rights needed for the specific task.

(vi) **Monitor security program.** Continuous monitoring is required to obtain full benefits from the program. The scope of activities includes reviewing system actions, following up on security violations, and taking corrective actions to improve security weaknesses.

(c) **Different Levels of Control for Information Systems Security.**

(i) **Security levels.** A potential user can be required to go through a series of security levels and layers where the user's identification is verified, validated, and authenticated prior to accessing the desired system resources or functions. A drawback of multiple levels and layers of a security mechanism is that security verification procedures can take more time and can add to system overhead as the number of security levels increases. *The greater the number of security layers, the greater the delay in validating the potential user.* However, this may provide a higher security protection. A balance of security levels is needed considering cost, time, and convenience factors. Several areas or levels where security controls can be placed include

- Sign-on times and session initiation times
- Workstations/terminals/printers
- Utility programs and system commands
- System libraries
- Application programs, menus, functions

- Data files (datasets, databases)

Sign-on time security controls prevent a system user who is not identified on the system from logging on. When the correct combination of user profile name, which is usually the user ID, and when password is entered, the person is allowed on the system. **Session initiation security controls** determine what sessions a user can initiate or be authorized to access.

Workstation or terminal security controls determine who can sign on to a workstation or terminal or who can use a printer. **Security controls over utility programs** prevent unauthorized users from erasing database areas, deleting data files, making backups, or performing other functions, which can affect the integrity of a system. Similarly, **security controls over system commands** prevent unauthorized use of powerful commands such as the override, save, and restore commands. Security controls over system libraries, application programs, and data files are discussed next.

(A) ***Library-level security.*** Computer programs and data files are kept in libraries residing on disks, tapes/cartridges, and other magnetic storage media. These libraries should be protected from unauthorized access, use, and modification. One way to classify system libraries is by their nature such as test, production, and quality assurance. Another way is by function such as data library, and program library. In reality, libraries can be classified as one of the following:

- Data file library by application
- Optical disk library
- Spool library
- Emergency library
- Security library
- General-purpose library
- Documentation library
- Job control library
- Database library by vendor product
- System performance library
- User private library by user
- Backup library
- Vendor library by vendor
- Procedure library
- Job scheduling library
- Recovery library
- Object program library by application
- Executable program library by application, copybook library
- Programmer private library by programmer
- Systems software library for operating systems, utility programs
- System service tools library (e.g., print error log, diagnose/analyze problems, copy screen image)
- Source program library by application, program listing library
- System development and productivity tools library

Library-level security controls determine whether a user can log-on to a particular library. Separate libraries could be set up for source, object, and executable programs in test, production, and quality assurance environments. System libraries can be designated as private (e.g., Joneslib), restricted (e.g., payroll), or public (e.g., syslib). Password security controls should be given a high priority when accessing a library to assure proper security. Similarly, program change controls should be considered when adding, changing, and deleting the contents of a program or data file to assure program/data integrity. For example, application programmers should only be allowed access to the test library, not production code or data libraries. The purpose of separating test and production libraries is to ensure that only authorized program statements are executed on production data. Physical library controls such as a log are required to prevent access to off-line programs.

(B) ***Application-level security.*** Application program-level security controls determine whether a user can access all, some, or none of the programs in a particular library and what the user can do once the access is given (i.e., EXECUTE, EDIT, COPY, COMPILE). Application security can have many levels such as security at volume levels, security at application system level, and so on. Security controls are required at each level to protect the integrity of the application program and its functions from unauthorized execution, use, and modification.

Application level security is depicted in Exhibit 5.42 using an accounts receivable system example. Note that system overhead will increase as the security rule checking progresses from level 1 to level 4. *In general, the deeper (i.e., more levels) the security rule checking, the greater the system overhead.*

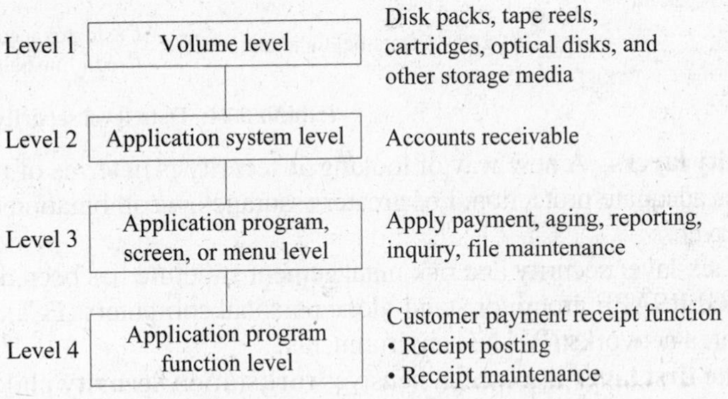

Exhibit 5.42: Application-level security

Application systems can be primarily accessed from two sources: local (on-site) and remote (dial-up). It is the remote access that is riskier than local due to difficulty in identifying the potential caller/user. Security control is enhanced when access restrictions are governed by external security systems software product as well as internal security features built into an application system.

For example, a remote dial-up or dial-in user can be subjected to three levels of security verification procedure. First, dial-in security software or hardware mechanisms verify that the remote user is an authorized one and that he is calling from an authorized location. Second, the user obtains a security clearance from an external or network log-on security software residing on the host computer. Third, an individual application program gives permission to access its menus and functions.

All three levels have to authorize a person to access the desired resource or function as indicated in Exhibit 5.43.

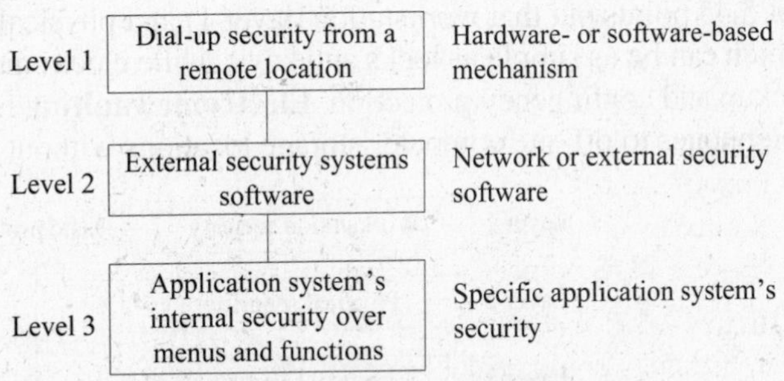

Exhibit 5.43: Dial-up security levels

(C) ***Data-level security.*** Similar to application-level security, data-level security can have many levels such as security at volume level, security at data file level, data record level, and data field level. Security controls are required at each level to protect the integrity of an application data file and its contents from unauthorized access, use, and modification. Data-field-level security controls provide greater assurance of protection than data-file-level security. Data-level security is depicted in Exhibit 5.44 using an accounts receivable system as an example.

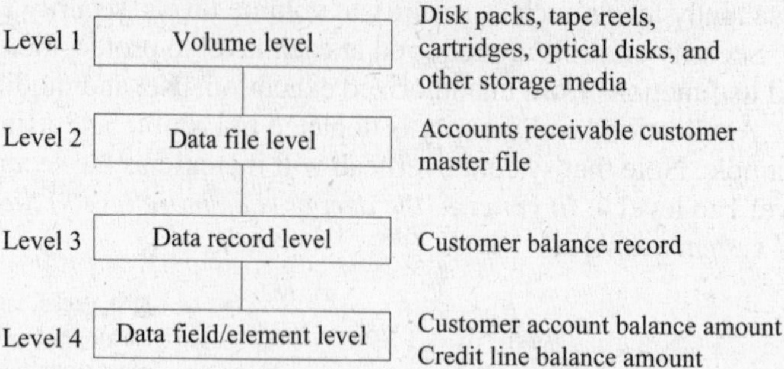

Exhibit 5.44: Data level security

(ii) **Security layers.** A new way of looking at security is in terms of multiple layers since no one layer assures adequate protection. For greater assurance, a combination of security controls is suggested at each layer.

A six-layer security and risk management structure has been defined by Robert Wainwright and the TIGERSAFE group for stand-alone personal computers (PCs), local area networks (LANs), and wide area networks (WANs) environments.[2]

The **first layer** is a comprehensive **workstation security** philosophy and access control directed by hardware, firmware, and software. The **second layer** of security is **physical locks** or tie-downs for a system chassis to prevent theft. The locks ensure control over board removal, and tie-downs provide security for workstations, printers, and monitors.

The **third layer** of security is a **logical access,** menu control system which should allow the security manager or user manager to perform the following functions: set up user access rights; assign project ID codes; establish six-digit user ID codes for host computer processing connection; and log an audit trail of application program and data file usage.

Data file encryption is the basis of the **fourth layer** of security. Sensitive programs, reference files, and changing data files should be encrypted, have cyclic redundancy check (CRC) performed, and be password controlled.

The **fifth layer** of security involves **encryption for network** transmission. Each data file, sensitive program, and personal electronic-mail type information should be encrypted.

Finally, a corporate **contingency/backup** philosophy should be developed for the **sixth layer** of security. By using encryption and key management packages, all backed-up files can be stored in an encrypted mode for privacy and security control. Exhibit 5.45 depicts six security layers.

Exhibit 5.45 points out that workstation (layer 1) and physical security (layer 2) are basic protections which can be as simple as locks and keys, while electronic vaulting (layer 6) provides advanced backup and contingency protection. **Electronic vaulting** is where backup files are transmitted over telephones to off-site computer storage locations without human intervention.

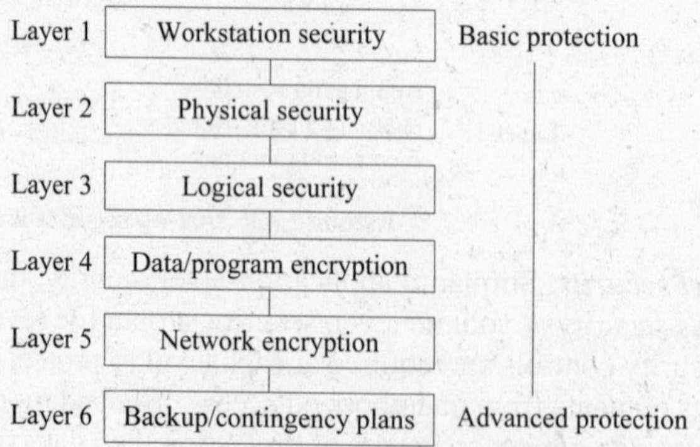

Exhibit 5.45: Six security layers

(iii) **Hardware-based security.** Essentially, there are two major components of a computer-processing environment from a security viewpoint: (1) hardware and (2) software.

---

[2] *ISPNews, INFO Security Product News, Vol.1, No.1, MIS Training Institute Press, Inc., Framingham, MA, March/April 1990.*

Basically, the hardware and computer environment may include

- A centralized computer center where local and/or remote terminals are connected to a host computer
- Distributed data processing networks with many nodes
- Remote job entry (RJE) terminals connected to the central computer
- Microcomputers linking to host computers
- Micros connected to each other through a local area network (LAN)
- LANs connected to wide area networks (WANs)
- Value-added networks (VANs), third-party networks, connected to WANs
- Metropolitan networks (MANs) connected to WANs
- LANs connected to MANs

All of these are used with communications equipment such as terminal controllers, communications controllers, multiplexers, bridges, routers, repeaters, gateways, and modems. Routers, bridges, and gateways are used to connect LANs with WANs. The host computer could be a mainframe, midrange, mini, or microcomputer. The location of these computers could be local or remote, domestic or international, home or away from home.

Some major hardware-related security devices focus on dial-up communication ports and lines including (1) one-end security devices such as port protection devices and security modems, and (2) two-end security devices such as user authentication tokens, smart cards, terminal device authentication methods, line encryption devices, and message authentication methods. Other hardware-related security devices include access control cards (smart cards, magnetic stripe cards), modems, onetime password, and biometrics-based access control mechanisms. Each item is discussed below.

(iv) **Security for dial-up lines.** It is now common knowledge that computer enthusiasts (hackers, hobbyists, pranksters) have broken into a number of government and business computer systems (NBS Special Publication 500-137.)[3] They have gained illegal access via the common dial-up telephone and the communications ports which are connected to almost every computer system. They then exploit weaknesses in software access controls to enter the system itself.

CONTROL GUIDELINES FOR DIAL-UP LINES

Dial-up lines pose risk to the organization. There are a number of ways that better dial-up communications protection can be achieved. This may include a combination of presently available operating system features, simple modifications to the operating system, improved administrative security procedures, and hardware protection devices.

Dial-up communications may not be protected properly. Manual procedures are highly recommended if the system is generally kept in a high-security posture, and during periods when no dial-up traffic is expected, such as evenings and weekends.

The typical dial-up communication differs from direct connection in that the major portion of the linkage consists of the public telephone network. The very nature of dial-up communication implies that the user may be anywhere in the world where the telephone network reaches. Anyone who comes into possession of the telephone number for a computer's dial-up port may attempt to gain access. The computer, then, must assume the job of screening incoming calls to verify the terminal connection itself is valid. Modems and telephone sets are present at both ends, with a port at the host computer end. A **port** is a socket into which a dedicated terminal or modem is plugged so that it may communicate with the host.

Computer system intruders, whether they are hackers or more serious criminals, could not be successful if there were not one or more serious weaknesses in the systems they attack. This leads to computer-related fraud and abuse.

(v) **Software approaches to dial-up security.** There is a set of control measures that are already either available in the typical host computer operating system or can be added to the operating system. In

[3] *"Security for Dial-Up Lines," National Bureau of Standards (NBS) Special Publication 500-137, US Department of Commerce, Gaithersburg, Maryland, May 1986.*

addition, procedures for administering these controls can often be improved to make them significantly more effective. A discussion of software-based controls follows.

(A) ***User identification and passwords.*** A good password system should include: large enough number of passwords, based on minimum length (at least six characters) and composition (at least ten different characters to select from), to permit a minimum of 1,000,000 passwords for the lowest level of security; secure, storage, entry, and transmission of the passwords so they are protected from disclosure to unauthorized individuals, that retries after invalid entry are limited, and authentication such that the password is required each time the individual logs on; ownership and distribution of passwords should be controlled in such a way that the password is known only to the individual owning it; source of the password such that it is selected at random or selected by users (not related to their personal identity, history, or environment); and maximum lifetime of say 60 or 90 days or one year for the lowest level of security, with speedy replacement after compromise is suspected or when the owner no longer has authorized access. Passwords should protect both local and remote accesses to the computer system.

(B) ***Effective password management procedures.*** If users select the passwords, there should be a mechanism to ensure those selected are not short in length, trivial, or otherwise easily guessed. In addition, adequate password change criteria should be set up so the passwords will not stay active on the system after they are no longer needed or it is suspected unauthorized persons have gained access to them. System management procedures should ensure the system protects the passwords from unauthorized disclosure. Minimum password protection should be provided during data file editing and maintenance procedures. Problems associated with password management and administration usually require people-based solutions, not technical.

(C) ***System event logging as protection.*** Automatic logging of important system events has many uses. In terms of system security, logging represents a warning device to help make system administrators aware of improper user practices or attempts at intrusion. With this knowledge, they can take any number of corrective actions to reduce the problem. Without adequate system logging, there is usually no clear way to determine a system is being attacked. Audit files or journals can be used as backup for recovering lost data and to provide a historical record of file accesses to detect security violations.

(D) ***Access rules.*** A set of access rules should be developed for all users describing their privileges in the system. These rules can then be checked each time users attempt to perform functions on the system. A number of minicomputers and mainframes have this capability inherent in their operating systems, or commercial software packages can be obtained to perform the same functions.

(vi) **Three approaches to communications link protection.** In protecting any set of communications ports, there are three basic approaches. These are manual procedures, one-end security devices, and two-end security devices.

(A) ***Manual procedures.*** The most direct way to protect any communications link is simply to keep it disabled except when needed. Manual procedures may then be used by computer operators to activate ports when actually needed, typically in direct response to a request by a potential user at the time of need. These manual procedures may involve turning on a modem, physically connecting a plug, or throwing a switch. This approach may be the cheapest and most practical solution if the dial-up communications mode is used only on demand or for emergency work (e.g., a programmer doing a "fix" on a production system from home).

(B) ***One-end security devices.*** The solution involves direct hardware protection of only one end of the communications link, either on the host computer or on the user's terminal. In effect, this provides a separate password on the communications link itself.

Port protection devices (PPD) are placed on the host end of the circuit. A PPD may be placed between modem and the port or between modem and telephone set. All PPDs require the user to enter a separate authenticator (e.g., password) in order to access the computer's dial-up ports. This set of password tables, external to and independent of the computer's operating system, is characteristic of PPDs. All have mechanisms to limit the number of sign-on attempts per telephone connection.

Call-back or dial-back to the call originator is a second level of user authentication beyond the standard PPD password tables. If call-back is used, a typical sequence of user connection is as follows: the user dials the computer access number and is connected to the PPD. The PPD requires the user to enter a PPD table password and then hangs up the line. The PPD searches its table and, if the password is found, identifies the user's telephone number that matches the password. The PPD then makes a return call to the user. Once connection takes place, the PPD becomes passive in the circuit.

Many models of PPD provide some form of logging or other warning signal of dial-up attack. Systems which use the call-back approach may need to record enough information to generate telephone usage bills to system users, since the host incurs all telephone toll charges with this approach.

Security-modems are intended for installation on user terminals. They incorporate a set of outbound call-screening security functions into a standard single-user modem, in effect controlling access to the host from the user end. Usually, they will not operate as normal modems for dial-out purposes until the user enters a specified password. Inside the modem, these passwords are matched in a secured table with dial-out telephone number sequences necessary to connect the user to specified host computers. The table also can be used to transmit a complete log-on sequence to the host once connection is made. This is a **weak control** since it relies upon secrecy of the phone number, which can be obtained by listening to the output of the modem.

(C) ***Two-end security devices.*** More security is gained by using a matched set of hardware protective devices for both ends of the dial-up circuit (computer and terminal) to **prevent snooping or tampering** with communications traffic. In this approach, there is a security device attached to or used with each user terminal plus a matching device or comparable application software used by the host computer.

There are four types of devices that belong to the two-end solution: (1) user authentication with or without "tokens," (2) terminal device authentication methods, (3) line encryption devices, and (4) message authentication methods.

User authentication. User authentication can be thought of simply as making sure people are who they say they are before allowing access to any element of a computer system. User authentication is not as easy as having a security guard check photographs on ID badges. Some computer system users may never actually enter the computer facility but instead access the system from a remote workstation. A potential intruder may be able to pose as a legitimate remote user and thus may never have to physically break into a computer room in order to abuse the system. Electronic authentication of all users attempting to log on to the system is necessary to address such threats.

User authentication typically involves verification of information which the user can be required to supply during a log-on procedure. The information to be verified is drawn from at least one of the following categories: something the user **knows** (e.g., passwords or biographic information), something the user **has** (e.g., a magnetic stripe card or a smart card), and some physical characteristic of the user indicating **who** the user is (e.g., fingerprints, retina scans, or other biometrics information).

In general, the more information each user must submit, the more time consuming and costly the user authentication process. At the same time, system overhead will increase which could degrade performance. However, requiring all users to submit information from each of the three categories provides the best defense against intruders attempting to masquerade as legitimate users.

From an intruder's point of view, attempting to pose as an authorized computer user might seem a fairly straightforward attack. It might involve guessing passwords or forging magnetic stripe cards in order to elude the system's user authentication scheme. A more devious approach would be to masquerade not as a human user but as a host computer or some other equipment in the system. An intruder could conceivably intercept communication lines between an unsuspecting user and a host computer and capture data which the user attempts to send to the host. The intruder could mimic messages which would have ordinarily been sent from the host to the user, and the user would have no reason to suspect an invasion of the system. The intruder could use such a technique to appropriate not only a few files which the user happens to transmit, but the user's password as well, especially for future masquerading endeavors.

A user authentication token is a small item, such as a plastic "smart-card," given to each authorized system user, that must be used to gain access to the system. Each token has a special algorithm or some other unique and noncopyable identifier embedded in it. The host computer can challenge the user in some way that can only be responded to correctly by means of the token. There are two varieties of user authentication tokens. The simpler and cheaper variety is hand-held and requires no terminal attachments. The user must read the authentication information from a liquid crystal display on the token and then enter it as a response via the terminal when challenged. In some cases, the user must first read a challenge string on the terminal and enter it into the token via keys. The host reads the authentication information and compares it to the "right" answer it has generated before deciding to approve access.

The second variety of user authentication is simpler to use but may be more costly. It requires the user to place his token into a device connected to the terminal. This attachment can accept the challenge from the host, use the algorithm in the token to perform the required calculations, and then transmit the response to the host for verification. The token can take the form of a small plastic device with embedded microcircuitry, or in a somewhat less secure approach it can be a plastic card with a magnetic stripe.

Terminal device authentication methods. Some terminal authentication devices are very similar in operation to user authenticators. There are three basic methods for positively identifying the user terminal by "two-end" challenge-response techniques. The **first method** is an assignment of unique terminal identifiers, called answer-back memory. The host system can use this feature by sending a standard character (ASCII) code as a challenge to the terminal that will cause it to respond with the "answer-back memory" contents for authentication. Some telecommunications packages and modems have these features. A **second method** of terminal identification uses matching pairs of devices inserted in the communications circuit. One device is placed between the terminal and modem, and the other is attached to the host computer's port.

In the **third method,** hybrid versions of terminal authenticators are available, including the capability to authenticate each user at the same time. Some allow insertion of a magnetic striped card. Another product uses a similar method, in which each user must insert a thick plastic card with embedded identification circuitry into the unique terminal unit.

New approaches to prevent **spoofing attacks** includes altering a cryptographic unit to a user's terminal to authenticate the terminal to the host computer.

Line encryption devices. Encryption is the process of **encoding** information in a predetermined way so that it is unintelligible to anyone who does not know how to **decode** it. The use of encryption techniques for dial-up communications represents the highest form of security. First, it protects the confidentiality of information passing over the communications link by making it unintelligible to snoopers. This is the primary rationale for using encryption. Second, certain modes of encryption operation, for example, cipher block chaining, when combined with an authentication technique, can be used to protect the integrity of messages so that tampering or transmission errors can be identified.

Third, the uniqueness of the encryption key, which must be shared by sender and receiver, enforces an extremely high degree of user identification. There is one common problem with communications encryption. If the key used by sender and receiver is the only real security, then the security surrounding the procedure used to exchange the key between them becomes extremely important.

Most present encryption systems rely on the users to transfer keys manually in some way, which may or may not be secure. The intruder may have an opportunity to intercept the key while it is in transit. The level of security afforded by encryption is dependent upon the security of managing the encryption keys. One promising device makes encryption more practical because it manages keys automatically. This unit uses drop-in circuit boards for PCs to create a secure dial-up network. If one user wants to connect with another to exchange sensitive information, the user calls up a special program and requests connection. The board then determines whether the user may make the connection. If so, the board places a telephone call to the other system's board, exchanges session keys encrypted in a higher-level encryption key the two boards share, and enters into the communications session with the session keys operative.

In the newer form of encryption hardware designed for PCs, all circuitry is contained on a single circuit board that is plugged into one of the standard slots on the motherboard, which is located inside the computer housing. Encryption can be implemented in both hardware and software.

Message Authentication Methods

According to NIST Special Publication 500-157, **cryptography** is the art or science of secret communications. It involves methods for converting information which is sensitive or secret from an intelligent plain text form to an unintelligible cipher text form.

The process of converting plain text to cipher text is called **encryption;** the reverse process (converting cipher text to plain text) is called **decryption**. Most cryptographic algorithms make use of a secret value called a key. Encryption and decryption are easy when the key is known, but decryption is intended to be virtually impossible without the key used for encryption. This is true except for public schemes, where they don't require both parties knowing (sharing) the same key. Furthermore, one of the keys is public—it needs no security.

Disguising and concealing secret messages via encryption has been the traditional purpose of cryptography. More recently, however, the use of cryptography for message (or data) authentication has become widespread. **Message authentication** is a process for detecting unauthorized changes made to data that has been transmitted between users or machines or to data that has been retrieved from storage.

Message encryption techniques can be used for plain text messages, which do not necessarily have to be kept secret, as well as for encrypted messages. By using cryptography in message authentication, a special tamper-proof checksum, often referred to as **message authentication codes (MAC)**, can be generated.

A cryptographic MAC is calculated using an encryption algorithm and a secret key. If the key is unknown, even a very small change to a message will cause an unpredictable alteration of the MAC. Therefore, any intruder who intercepts authenticated messages and attempts to modify them will not know what the corresponding MAC for the altered message should be. Thus, cryptography can be used to ensure the safety of information by making it unreadable or unalterable without detection through encryption and message authentication. The MAC may then be checked by the recipient by duplicating the original MAC generation process. Usually, MAC is used in electronic funds transfer systems where it is important to verify that the contents of a message have not been changed, since these messages are in effect electronic checks subject to fraud or embezzlement.

(vii) **Software-based security.** This section includes a discussion of security features available in operating systems software, access control security software, cryptographic keys and digital signatures, and network security systems.

(A) ***Operating systems software.*** A large number of operating systems software products permit the use of **exits** or **hooks** to locally-developed procedures as part of the user sign-on function or at other processing points to meet unique user/system requirements. At the same time, some exits could be used as a means to bypass control options of the operating systems software. It is the operating systems feature that permits no more than a few invalid sign-on tries per session. Once the limit has been reached, the computer can be forced to break the connection. Many operating systems already have the capability to do this, but this capability often must be turned on. A somewhat risky follow-on action is to time-out the line for some period so that it may not be used. The potential problem with the time-out tactic is that it could possibly be turned against the organization by an intruder whose intent was to harass, by attacking each port in turn until all the lines were tied up.

The operating system could send an alarm and message to the system security administrator while the attack is still under way. To be most effective, this should be done without terminating the connection or warning the intruder. Then it is possible to trace the call or take other actions as appropriate.

Operating systems software can be used to log certain events such as

- All system-level user entry/exit activity, such as log-on and log-off
- All starts and stops of sensitive processes or applications, especially if it can be determined they are done by unauthorized individuals
- All accesses to sensitive data and program files, especially if it can be determined that they are done by unauthorized individuals
- All other forms of access violations, such as improper time of day, directory, terminal, communications entry mode, or failed access attempts

(B) ***Cryptographic keys and digital signatures for computer networks.***

Cryptographic keys. A key notarization system may be used in conjunction with a cryptographic device to provide increased data security. Key management involves the secure generation, distribution, and storage of cryptographic keys. If the key management is weak, then the most secure cryptoalgorithm will be of little value. In fact, a very strong cryptoalgorithm used in a weak key management system can give a false sense of security. Online communications, file encryption, off-line mail, and digital signatures all are to be protected. Key notarization is presented to help provide security while maintaining the required flexibility.

Secure Communication Guidelines

Secure communication involves preventing the disclosure of plain text, detecting fraudulent message modification, detecting fraudulent message insertion or deletion, and detecting fraudulent replay of a previously valid message.

The **key notarization system** may be used in computer networks along with key notarization facilities to

- Securely communicate between any two users
- Securely communicate via encrypted mail (off-line)
- Protect personal (non-shared) files
- Provide a digital signature capability

Digital signatures. A digital signature is a form of authentication and was developed in conjunction with public key systems. In such systems the decryption key is not equal to, and cannot be computed from, the encryption key. Encryption keys may be made public while decryption keys are kept secret. A digital signature is decrypted using the secret decryption key and sent to the receiver. The receiver may encrypt, using the public key, and may verify the signature, but the signature cannot be forged since only the transmitter knows the secret decryption key. The cryptoalgorithm must have the property that decryption of the signature followed by encryption equals the original signature. Nonpublic keys' algorithms can also be used for digital signatures. The point here is that the decrypt key is not shared.

(C) ***Network security systems.*** Some security products provide network-level security by granting application and functional level access to users of an online transaction processing system. Security is further ensured through a unique process of encrypting information during network transport and storage and through an enhanced authentication process used to verify the identity of the online system user. Some desirable features of this kind of systems are

- The ability to complement the host-based access control security system
- The ability to operate seamlessly (no boundary limits) within multiple-host computer environments

A network security policy generally specifies

- How data transmissions between two systems will be protected from unauthorized reception or corruption
- How access to resources in one system will be granted to entities on another system
- How security breaches, deviations, and exceptions between two systems will be reported

- How audit trail information will be collected, and how and to whom that information will be reported

(d) **Logical Security.** Logical security is software based and usually involves entering a user ID or a password, using a card or biometrics device, or a combination. There are at least five ways the logical security can be implemented as shown in Exhibit 5.46.

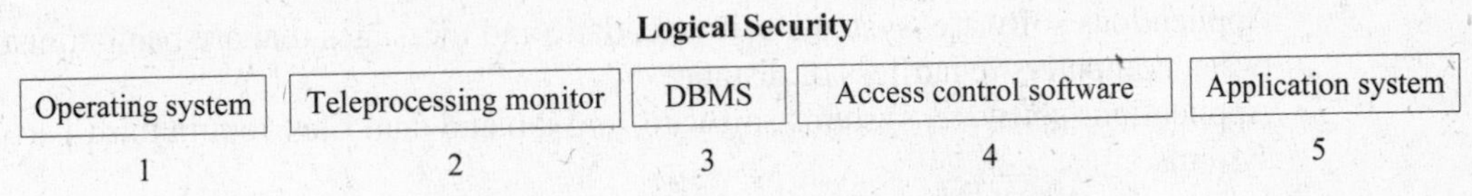

Exhibit 5.46: Ways to implement logical security

Notes

1. & 2. The security features provided by the operating systems software and teleprocessing monitor are not complete.

3. The security features provided by the database management system (DBMS) are not complete but they can be supplemented with the access control security software.

4. The security features provided by the access control security software are reasonably complete in terms of protecting data and program files, system libraries, and computer terminals.

5. The security features built into the applications system can be supplemented with the access control security software in terms of allowing access to specific functions.

The access control security software determines the access level allowed to the application system and/or the database system. For example, each data element in the database is assigned a security level similar to a function in the application system. The access control security software works in conjunction with the DBMS and the application system to provide a comprehensive security protection and it is external to them. It acts like an umbrella in protecting access to computer resources (data and program files, etc.)

Regardless of the security software used, all system users should be identified to and authenticated by the system. To accomplish this, a two-step process is suggested. In step 1, a public information known to others such as user name is used to first validate a user. This is followed by a more secret validation (step (2) using private information such as passwords. The type of second-level validation depends on the criticality of the information to be protected (see Exhibit 5.47).

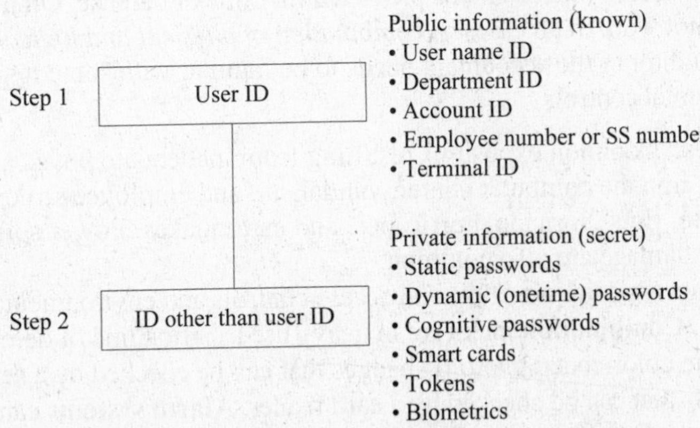

Exhibit 5.47: Steps in user identification and authentication

Static passwords are normal passwords with or without expiration time and they are reusable. Dynamic passwords change every time the password-generating device is used. Cognitive passwords use fact-based and opinion-based cognitive data as a basis for user authentication. An example of cognitive questions and answers that are known only to the user is: What is your favorite vegetable or flower?

As information systems become more complex, there is no simple solution to the problem of providing complete or even adequate computer security. Logical security is located in the access control software and usually involves entering a user ID and a password into the system for identification and authentication. All logical access paths need to be identified and analyzed for possible unauthorized access and security breach. Specific plans may, for example, need to be designed for the protection of

- Applications software, systems software, and job and data files maintained within the organization's host computer(s)
- Applications software, systems software, and job and data files maintained in personal computers or workstations, either stand-alone or connected
- Applications software, systems software, data, and messages that are being transmitted between computers regardless of distance
- Applications software, systems software, and job and data files kept in third-party computer systems
- Information kept in identification cards used to access the system (e.g., smart cards)

Usually, logical access paths or entry points to a computer system may include one or more of the following avenues connected to one or more networks of dissimilar architectures and vendor platforms:

- Connected micro or personal computers using LANs, MANs, VANs, and WANs located inside or outside the organization
- VDU/CRT terminals connected to host computers either inside or outside the organization.
- Direct computer-to-computer connections between two hosts
- Satellite and microwave relay links
- Directly wired terminals via coaxial cables, twisted pairs, or optical fibers to the host computer
- Terminals linked up through multiplexers and accessed through local or remote communications controllers
- Terminals hooked up through dial-up ports and multidrop leased lines
- System/operator consoles
- Employee dialing up a PC at work from a PC at home or other location. This, in turn, is connected to the host computer

(e) **Physical and Environmental Computer Security.** Although logical access controls are effective, they alone are not enough. Usually, logical access controls are expensive and time-consuming. They add overhead or delay to the system processing and cause performance problems. Sometimes, simple and inexpensive physical security mechanisms should be considered to provide cost-effective security solutions. Physical security mechanisms provide a first line of defense. On the other hand, physical security controls may not work in all cases. *A combination of physical and logical security controls might be needed.* The auditor or the accountant needs to be familiar with some major physical security devices and environmental controls.

(i) **Exposures.** Common exposures resulting from inadequate physical access controls are unauthorized entry into the computer center, vandalism, and employee strikes. Environmental exposures include fire, flood, tornado, hurricanes, and earthquakes. Power spikes, brownouts, and outages, and water damage are also common.

(ii) **Physical access controls.** Physical access controls and environmental controls are needed to reduce exposures. **Combination locks** are in heavy use as a first line of defense for computer center facilities. So are color-coded photo ID badges that can be checked by a **security guard** and magnetic stripe cards that can be checked by a card reader. **Alarm systems** can be installed to alert people for possible detection of problems such as fire, burglary, water under raised floors, or power supply line. Audible alarms can alert the operator at the console for any hardware-related problems such as computer circuitry malfunctions, parity bits in the memory, and horizontal and vertical parity in tape and disk storage.

Automated teller machines used in banking often have a **video camera** to take pictures of customer transaction activities (transaction cameras) or to monitor the area (surveillance cameras) to detect holdups or robberies. The cameras employed may be film cameras or closed-circuit television (**CCTV**) cameras. Many banks use both types of systems based on specific applications and considerations. In CCTV, there is no distinction between transaction cameras and surveillance cameras. The same cameras are used for both applications. A major distinction between systems lies in the fact that a CCTV system requires a video cassette recorder. Each camera is connected to a recorder.

The recorders provide the photographic evidence of all activity monitored by the cameras, which can be used for fraud investigations.

(iii) **Environmental controls.** Smoke, heat, and fire detection equipment and **fire extinguishers** are commonly found in the data center. Auxiliary electric power generators and uninterruptible power supply (**UPS**) equipment are needed to provide continuous clean power to the computer and its facilities and to prevent data loss. Heat and humidity control devices are also needed to regulate the environment. An air-conditioning system can minimize the CPU downtime due to overheating. Humidifiers should be used to reduce static voltages that could damage equipment, data, and programs. A gauss meter should be used periodically to test for the presence of magnetic fields originating from disk and tape drives. Magnetic fields, if not tested, can **degauss** or erase information on tapes and disks.

The manual monitoring of environmental controls for proper functioning of motor generators, water chillers, air conditioning units, and humidifiers is time-consuming, error-prone, and unreliable as it requires constant attention.

The recovery process from damage can be slow. The automation of monitoring and controlling the environmental system can help minimize the damage and speed up the recovery process. The major objective is to reduce the effect of a disaster resulting from malfunctioning of the environmental system. The **benefits** of automation are

- Environmental system probes connected to personal computer (PC) software can perform automatic diagnosis and analysis.
- When an environmental system threshold has been exceeded, the PC software can begin the telephone voice system and/or beeper notification of key personnel.
- Database integrity can be maintained due to orderly shutdown of the host system through the help of the PC software before a disaster hits. Noncritical systems should be shut down first so that critical applications stay up.
- The host computer can be directed to open problem management records when a problem is detected.

(f) **Logical Access Controls.** Logical access controls include passwords, personal identification numbers (PINs), and user identification codes (IDs); tokens; smart cards; and biometrics. Each is discussed next.

(i) **Passwords.** If passwords are used for access control or authentication measures, users should be properly educated in password selection. Strong passwords consist of at least six to eight alpha numeric characters, with no resemblance to any personal data. PINs should also be unique, with no resemblance to personal data. Neither passwords nor PINs should ever be reduced to writing or shared with others.

Other security measures should include the adoption of onetime passwords, or password aging measures that require periodic changes. Encryption technology can also be employed in the entry and transmission of passwords, PINs, user IDs, and so on. Any password directories or databases should be properly protected, as well.

Password guessing programs can be run against a system. Some can run through tens of thousands of password variations based on personal information, such as a user's name or address, or words in the dictionary. It is preferable to test for such vulnerabilities by running this type of program as a preventive measure, before an unauthorized party has the opportunity to do so. Incorporating a brief delay requirement after each incorrect login attempt can be very effective against these types of programs. In cases where a potential attacker is monitoring a network to collect passwords, a system utilizing onetime passwords would render any data collected useless.

When additional measures are necessary to confirm that passwords or PINs are entered by the user, technologies such as token, smart cards, and biometrics can be useful. Utilizing these technologies adds another dimension to the security structure by requiring the user to possess something physical.

(ii) **Tokens.** Token technology relies on a separate physical device, which is retained by an individual, to verify the user's identity. The token resembles a small hand-held card or calculator and is used to generate passwords. The device is usually synchronized with security software in the host computer such as an internal clock or an identical time-based mathematical algorithm. Tokens are well suited for onetime password generation and access control. A separate PIN is typically required to activate the token.

(iii) **Smart cards.** Smart cards resemble credit cards or other traditional magnetic stripe cards, but contain an embedded computer chip. The chip includes a processor, operating system, and both read only memory (ROM) and random access memory (RAM). They can be used to generate onetime passwords when prompted by a host computer, or to carry cryptographic keys. A smart card reader is required for their use.

(iv) **Onetime password.** This is also called **see-through security device** where a new password code is generated each time an access is requested to a host computer. The user carries a handheld device and uses it to generate a password code. One approach is that both the host and the handheld device are synchronized in internal timing. The correct number for a user is linked through the entry of the user's PIN. The handheld device displays a code that changes, say, every one minute. Different devices display unique codes. The host, on successful comparison, grants access to the user.

MORE ON CARDS

Card Access Control Systems

The basic card reader is a stand-alone unit for single door control that is programmed through a built-in digital panel. For extra security, both an authorized card and a personal identification number can be required to gain access. More sophisticated systems increase card capacity and include features such as automatic door locking and unlocking to a programmed schedule and visual indication in plain English of all programming commands.

Other access control systems with card reader technologies include: a badge, key-tag, or card, waved at a reader mounted on a wall, specially treated wires embedded in plastic cards that can be sensed by a reader, and a readable magnetic stripe.

Smart Card

A smart card is a credit-card-sized device, containing one or more integrated circuit chips, which performs the functions of a microprocessor, memory, and input/output. Smart cards, and other related devices may be used to provide an increased level of security in applications requiring controlled access to sensitive information.

On a superficial level, a smart card system resembles conventional data storage card systems, such as automated teller machine (ATM) systems, which employ magnetic stripe cards. However, because smart cards have computing powers and greater capacity for protected data storage, smart card systems can provide increased flexibility and security in many applications.

Magnetic Stripe Card

The magnetic stripe card, currently one of the most widely used storage cards, consists of a plastic card with a thin strip, or stripe, of magnetic material affixed to its surface. Small spots along the stripe are magnetized in varying degrees to form a code representing the stored data. The card is inexpensive to make. The widespread use and ease of production of the magnetic stripe card has made it a target for counterfeiting and fraud. Some counterfeit cases included collecting discarded receipts and recording PINs by observing customers making transactions at ATMs. The receipts were then used to produce counterfeit magnetic stripe cards.

Recently magnetic stripe manufacturers have developed techniques to increase the security of the magnetic stripe card. Some methods involve recording special markings or numbers in the magnetic stripe that cannot be duplicated by standard magnetic stripe production methods. A would-be counterfeiter, hopefully, will not be able to determine where the special markings are, nor how to reproduce them, thereby being unable to reproduce a functional copy of a stolen card. Another technique is to store the information in the card in secret code so anyone trying to illegally read the card will obtain only scrambled data. In addition to possible forgery and illegal reading of stored data, the magnetic stripe card may be susceptible to erasure if placed near other magnetic materials.

Difference between the Smart Card and the Magnetic Stripe Card

The magnetic stripe card is a passive data storage device. In this sense, the word passive indicates the card itself cannot control the writing of information into the storage area nor the subsequent retrieval of the information by an authorized, or an unauthorized, user. The smart card, on the other hand, is an active device, capable of independently performing calculations and controlling access to its own memory.

(v) **Modems.** If computers are to be connected over longer distances, modems are utilized. Modems are devices that convert computer output to an analog signal for transmission over telephone lines. They also convert the analog signal to a digital signal at the receiving end. The range of options available on modems is quite large. Simple units do little more than perform the digital-to-analog signal conversion. More intelligent units, **smart modems,** can automatically dial numbers, store messages for delayed transmission, and perform a number of the other functions.

(vi) **Biometrics.** Biometrics involves identification and verification of an individual based on some physical characteristics, such as fingerprint analysis, hand geometry, or retina scanning. This technology is advancing rapidly, and offers an alternative means to authenticate a user. Various biometrics are discussed either to complement or substitute the normal password mechanism.

(A) ***Eye retina recognition control systems.*** Imposter-proof access control biometrics security systems are available today using retinal identification technology. The user's eyes are scanned to authenticate the user. These systems are used in high-security organizations such as defense and research. Card-based access systems can interface with biometrics system.

(B) ***Fingerprint match systems.*** In some systems, fingerprints are compared against the database of authorized users. Usually, a personal identification number is needed to retrieve the central fingerprint file. Other systems employ a high-speed matching technique, which compares fingerprint data against an entire database of authorized users. This eliminates the need for entering a personal identification number to retrieve the central fingerprint file. The system is particularly suitable for high-volume situations such as banking and retail applications. The system tolerates fingerprint stretch and compression and is not sensitive to print rotation. Similarly, palm-print and hand-geometry can be recognized.

(C) ***Voice verification systems.*** Voice verification systems control access to data or facilities from remote locations with a telephone call. Voice "prints" are one of several biometrics technologies that measure the physical human traits that make people unique. The system links into a conventional private branch exchange (PBX) and controls access via voice verification to extensions that could connect to a computer through a modem, facsimile machines, or to anyone requiring caller identification before answering the call. Authorized callers enroll by recording a personal identification number and a brief phrase of their own choice, guided by vocal prompts. The system compares voiceprints and allows permission to authorized persons only. Voice identification/verification system is least likely to be compromised when compared to use of passwords, ID badges, and combination keys.

(D) ***Typing rhythm recognition system.*** People exhibit certain keying styles when they are working at a keyboard. Systems are available to detect any deviations from established keying patterns.

(E) ***Signatures.*** Similarly, human signatures can be verified by comparing them to an established signature style based on length of time, hand pressure, speed, or direction of writing.

5.16 Databases

(a) **Database Management Systems Software.** A database contains facts and figures on various types of information such as sales, costs, and personnel. These files are collectively called the firm's database. A database is a collection of related data about an organization, intended for sharing of this data by multiple users. A database management system (DBMS) is comprised of software, hardware, and procedures. The DBMS acts as a software controller enabling different application systems to access large number of distinct data records stored on direct access storage devices (e.g., disk).

The DBMS should be compatible with the operating system environment and it handles complex data structures. Unauthorized access to data elements is a major concern in a database system due to concentration of data. The DBMS helps in providing user interface with the application system through increased accessibility and flexibility by means of "data views."

Advantages (objectives) of a DBMS are

- Provide minimum data redundancy resulting in data consistency.
- Provide data independence from application programs except during computer processing.
- Provide consistent and quality information for decision-making purpose.
- Provide adequate security and integrity controls.
- Facilitate uniform development and maintenance of application systems.
- Ensure that all applicable standards (e.g., documentation, data naming, data formats) are observed in the representation of the data.
- Provide shared access to data.
- Improve program maintenance due to separation of data from programs.
- Provide a single storage location for each data item.
- Separate file management tasks from application programs.
- Programs access data according to predefined subschema.
- Provides built-in backup and recovery procedures.

Disadvantages of a DBMS are

- Can be expensive to acquire, operate, and maintain
- Requires additional main memory
- Requires additional disk storage
- Requires knowledgeable and technically skilled staff (e.g., DBA, DA)
- Results in additional system overhead thereby slowing down the system response time
- Needs additional CPU processing time
- Requires sophisticated and efficient security mechanisms
- Difficult to enforce security protection policies

Redundancy of data is sometimes necessary when high system performance and high data availability are required. The tradeoff here is the cost of collecting and maintaining the redundant data and the system overhead it requires to process the data. Another concern is synchronization of data updates in terms of timing and sequence. Ideally, the synchronization should be done at the system level, rather than the application level.

A DBMS understands the structure of the data, and provides a language for defining and manipulating stored data. The primary functions of the DBMS are to store data and to provide operations on the database. The operations usually include create, delete, update, and search of data. It is generally known that most DBMS products require extensive file backup and recovery procedures and require more processing time. Some essential features supported by most DBMSs are

- **Persistence.** Persistence is the property wherein the state of the database survives the execution of a process in order to be reused later in another process.
- **Data sharing.** Data sharing is the property that permits simultaneous use of the database by multiple users. A DBMS that permits sharing must provide some **concurrency control** (locking) mechanism that prevents users from executing inconsistent actions on the database.
- **Recovery.** Recovery refers to the capability of the DBMS to return its data to a consistent and coherent state after a hardware or software failure.
- **Database language.** The database language permits external access to the DBMS. The database language may include the Data Definition Language (DDL), the Data Manipulation Language (DML), the Data Control Language (DCL), and an ad hoc query language. The DDL is used to define the database schema and subschema. The DML is used to examine and manipulate contents of the database. The DCL is used to specify parameters needed to define the internal organization of the database, such as indexes, buffer size. Ad hoc query language is provided for interactive specification of queries.
- **Security and integrity.** Security and authorization control, integrity checking, utility programs, backup/archiving, versioning, and view definition are other features of most DBMS. Integrity checking involves two types: semantic and referential. **Semantic integrity** refers to the declaration of semantic and structural integrity rules (e.g., typing constraints, values of domain constraints, uniqueness constraints) and the enforcement of these rules. Semantic integrity rules may be auto-

matically enforced at program run time, at compile time, or may be performed only when a message is sent. **Referential integrity** means that no record may contain a reference to the primary key of a nonexisting record. Cascading of deletes, one of the features of referential integrity checking, occurs when a record is deleted and all other referenced records are automatically deleted.

(b) **Database Design Approaches.** First, user requirements are specified to the conceptual model, which represents "user views" of the database. When the conceptual model is presented to the DBMS, it becomes a logical model, external model, or schema/subschema. The type of DBMS is not a factor in designing a conceptual model, but the design of a logical model is dependent on the type of DBMS to be used. This means that the conceptual model is, or should be, independent of a DBMS.

Second, the logical model is converted to a physical model in terms of physical storage media such as magnetic disk, tape, cartridge, or drum. The physical model, which is also called an internal model, considers the type of access methods needed, the type of indexing techniques required, and the data distribution methods available.

Schemas/Subschemas

- A logical view of an entire database is called schema. Schemas may be external, conceptual, or internal. A synonym for schema is a "view."
- A subschema is a part of schema. In other words, a schema is made up of one or more subschemas.
- A logical data model presents a view of data.

Logical database design is the process of determining an information system structure that is independent of software or hardware considerations. It produces logical data structures consisting of a number of entities connected by one-to-one or one-to-many relationships, subject to appropriate integrity checking. The objective is to improve the effectiveness of an information system by maximizing the accuracy, consistency, integrity, security, and completeness of the database.

Physical database design is the implementation of a logical design in a particular computer system environment. It deals with retrieval and update workloads for the system and the parameters required (i.e., average time required for random/sequential access to a track, length of a track, and disk cylinder sizes) for the hardware environment. The objective is to improve the performance of the information system by minimizing the data entry time, data retrieval time, data update time, data query time, and storage space and costs.

For large, logically complex databases, physical design is an extremely difficult task. Typically, an enormous number of alternatives must be explored in searching for a good physical design. Often, optimal or near-optimal designs cannot be discovered, resulting in the creation of inefficient and costly databases. Following are the suggested action steps required in a physical database design:

- Analyze workload complexity and characteristics.
- Translate the relationships specified in the logical data structures into physical records and hardware devices, and determine their relationships. This includes consideration of symbolic and direct pointers. **Symbolic pointers** contain the logical identifier of the other. **Direct pointers** contain the physical address of the other. Both pointers can coexist.
- Fine-tune the design by determining the initial record loading factors, record segmentations, record and file indexes, primary and secondary access methods, file block sizes, and secondary memory management for overflow handling.

Exhibit 5.48 depicts the relationships between conceptual, logical, and physical models.

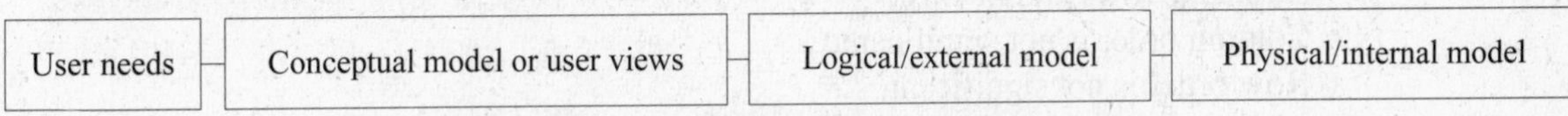

Exhibit 5.48: Relationships between database models

Prior to developing a full-scale database, a prototype may be undertaken to finalize user/technical requirements of the application system. Later, the prototype can be merged into normal system design phase for security, controls, recovery, and performance considerations.

Another way of looking at the database models is from the design focus and features of the database itself. Exhibit 5.49 presents a list of features with their focus between a physical data model and a logical data model.

Physical data model	Logical data model
• Concerned with physical storage of data (internal schema) • Concerned with the entities for which data are collected • Describes how the data are arranged in the defined storage media (e.g., disk) from a program and programmer viewpoints • Physical in nature in the sense that it describes the way data are physically located in the database	• Concerned with user-oriented data views (external schema) • Concerned with entities for which data are collected • Describes how the data can be viewed by the designated end user • Conceptual in nature (conceptual schema) in the sense that it describes the overall logical view of the database

Exhibit 5.49: Features of physical and logical data models

A data model describes relationships between the data elements and is used as a tool to represent the conceptual organization of data. A relationship within a data model can be one-to-one (e.g., between patient and bed in a hospital environment—at any given time, one bed is assigned to one patient), one-to-many (e.g., between hospital room and patients—one hospital room accommodates more than one patient), and many-to-many (e.g., between patient and surgeon—one surgeon may attend to many patients and a patient may be attended by more than one surgeon). A data model can be considered as consisting of three components.

1. **Data structure**—The basic building blocks describing the way data is organized
2. **Operators**—The set of functions that can be used to act on the data structures
3. **Integrity rules**—The valid states in which the data stored in the database may exist

The primary purpose of any data model is to provide a formal means of representing information and a formal means of manipulating the representation. A good data model can help describe and model the application effectively. A DBMS uses one or more data models as described below.

Data Model Types

- Relational
- Hierarchical
- Network
- File inversion
- Object
- Distributed

(i) **Relational data model.** The relational data model (e.g., DB2) consists of **columns,** equal to data fields in a conventional file, and **rows,** equal to data records in a conventional file, represented in a **table**. Data is stored in tables with keys or indexes outside the program. For example, in a hospital environment, a patient table may consist of columns (patient number, name, and address) and the values in the column (patient number, 1234; patient name, John Jones; patient address, 100 Main Street, Any Town, USA.) are represented in rows.

The columns of the table are called "attributes" while the rows are called "tuples." A set of actual values an attribute may take are drawn from a "domain." The primary key to the patient table is patient number. The following is a description of properties of a relational data model:

- All "key" values are defined.
- Duplicate rows do not exist.
- Column order is not significant.
- Row order is not significant.

Some major **advantages** of a relational model are its simplicity in use and true data independence from data storage structures and access methods. Some major **disadvantages** are low system performance and operational efficiency compared to other data models.

(ii) **Hierarchical data model.** From a comparison point of view, the hierarchical data model (e.g., IMS) can be related to a family **tree concept,** where the parents can have no children, one child, or more than one child. Similarly, a tree is composed of a number of branches or nodes. A number of trees or data records form a database. Every branch has a number of leaves or data fields. Hence, a hierarchical tree structure consists of nodes and branches. The highest node is called a "root" (parent—level 1) and its every occurrence begins a logical database record. The dependent nodes are at the lower levels (children—level 2, 3 ...).

The following is a description of the properties of a hierarchical data model:

- A model always starts with a "root node."
- A parent node must have at least one dependent node.
- Every node except the root must be accessed through its parent node.
- Except at level 1, the root node, the dependent node can be added horizontally as well as vertically with no limitation.
- There can be a number of occurrences of each node at each level.
- Every node occurring at level 2 must be connected with one and only one node occurring at level 1, and is repeated down.

Some major **advantages** of a hierarchical data model are its proven performance, simplicity, ease of use, and reduction of data dependency. Some major **disadvantages** are that addition and deletion of parent/children nodes can become complex and that deletion of the parent results in the deletion of the children.

(iii) **Network data model.** The network data model (e.g., IDMS/R) is depicted using blocks and arrows. A block represents a record type or an entity. Each record type, in turn, is composed of zero, one, or more data elements/fields or attributes. An arrow linking two blocks shows the relationship between two records types. A network database consists of a number of areas. An area contains records, which in turn contain data elements or fields. A set, which is a grouping of records, may reside in an area or span a number of areas. Each area can have its own unique physical attributes. Areas can be operated independently of, or in conjunction with, other areas.

Exhibit 5.50 depicts the network data model, where a patient is described as an owner record type and surgery is denoted as member record type in the set type patient-has-surgery.

The following is a description of the properties of a network data model:

- A set is composed of related records.
- There is only a single "owner" in a set.
- There may be zero, one, or many members in a set.

Some major **advantages** of a network data model are its proven performance and the accommodation of many-to-many relationships that occur quite frequently in real life. Some major **disadvantages** are its complexity in programming and loss of data independence during database reorganization and when sets are removed.

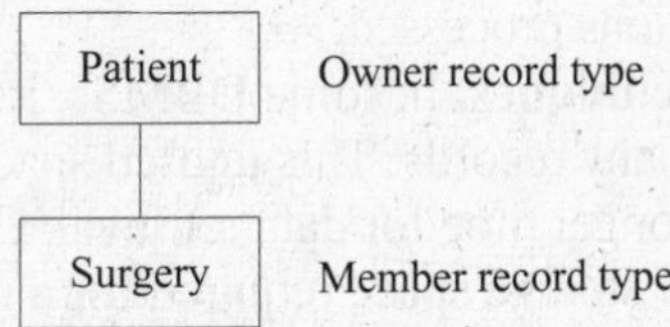

Exhibit 5.50: Network model

(iv) **Inverted file data model.** In the inverted file data model (e.g., ADABAS), each entity is represented by a file. Each record in the file represents an occurrence of the entity. Each attribute becomes data field or element in the file. Data fields are inverted to allow efficient access to individual files. To accomplish this, an index file is created containing all the values taken by the inverted field and pointers to all records in the file.

Some major **advantages** of the inverted file data model are its simplicity, data independence, and ease of adding new files and fields. Some major **disadvantages** are difficulty in synchronizing changes between database records/fields and index file.

(v) **Object data model.** The object data model is developed by combining the special nature of object-oriented programming languages (e.g., Lisp, C++) with DBMS. Objects, classes, and inheritance form the basis for the structural aspects of the object data model. Objects are basic entities, which have data structures and operations. Every object has an object ID that is a unique, system provided, identifier. Classes describe generic object types. All objects are members of a class. Classes are related through inheritance. Classes can be related to each other by superclass or subclass relationships, similar to entity-relationship-attribute model, to form class hierarchies. Class definitions is the mechanism for specifying the database schema for an application. For example, the class PERSON has an attribute SPOUSE whose data type is also PERSON.

Object DBMS also supports data sharing, provides concurrency controls and system recovery, and handles cooperative transaction processing and data versioning. Engineering applications such as computer-aided design systems, office information systems, and artificial intelligence (knowledge-based) systems require the use of cooperative transaction processing and data versioning techniques.

Version management is a facility for tracking and recording changes made to data over time through the history of design changes. The version management system tracks version successors and predecessors. When objects constituting a portion of the design are retrieved, the system must ensure that versions of these objects are consistent and compatible. System development efficiency and handling of complex data structures are some **advantages** of the object data model. Some **disadvantages** include new technology and new risks, which requires training and learning curves.

(vi) **Distributed data model.** The distributed database model can be thought of as having many network nodes and access paths between the central and local computers and within the local computer sites. Database security becomes a major issue in a truly distributed environment, where data itself is distributed and there are many access paths to the data from far-flung locations.

Data in a distributed database resides in more than one physical database in the network. **Location transparency,** in which the user does not need to know where data is stored, is one of the major goals of a distributed database data model. Similarly, programmers do not have to rewrite applications and can move data from one location to another, depending on need.

(c) **Database Checkpoints.** A technique used to start at certain points in the execution of a program after the system fails or detects an error is called "checkpoints." In the case of a backout, it is possible to go back to the last checkpoint instead of starting at the beginning of a program. Checkpoints are relatively easy to implement in batch programs and cumbersome for online programs due to concurrent processing.

A drawback of checkpoints is that they degrade system performance. The database designer needs to balance between the number of checkpoints and the time interval between two checkpoints. Usually, the higher the number of checkpoints, the greater is the degradation of performance, even though the easier the recovery process. On the other hand, if the time interval between two checkpoints is long, the degradation of performance is less at the cost of more difficult recovery. A trade-off exists between the number of checkpoints and the time interval between two checkpoints.

Some of the *criteria for designing and implementing checkpoints* may include the following items: time interval, operator action, number of changes to the database, number of records written to the log tape, and number of transactions processed.

(d) **Database Compression Techniques.** In some DBMSs, it is common to find unused space in the database due to the deletion of many records. This unused space widens the distance between the active database records, resulting in longer time for data retrieval. Compression or compaction techniques can be used to reduce the amount of storage space required for a given collection of data records. In addition to saving storage space, compression saves disk input and output (I/O) operations. However, CPU activity will increase to decompress the data after it has been retrieved. A tradeoff exists between the I/O savings and additional CPU activity. Indexes always gain from the use of compression technique. Both pointers and data values can be compressed too.

(e) **Database Reorganization.** A fragmentation of space or unused space occurs as a result of a deletion of some records in the database. This could happen during initial loading or after the reloading of the database. A normal practice is to reorganize the database by

- Copying the old database onto another device such as tape (which can act as a backup copy of the database)
- Reblocking the valid records
- Reloading the valid records

- Excluding the records marked "deleted" during this process

Besides reclaiming unused space, reorganization can arrange the records in such a way that their physical sequence is the same or nearly the same as their logical sequence. It is also possible to arrange the records so that the more frequently accessed ones are stored on a disk, whereas the rarely accessed or less frequently accessed records are stored on tape. Other reorganization efforts could result from changing block sizes, buffer pool sizes, prime areas, and overflow areas.

(f) **Database Restructuring.** Databases go through changes after their creation, usually because of usage patterns, priorities of the application systems, or performance requirements. New record types and new data elements may be added to the database. Access controls and database procedures may need to be changed. Implementing all of these changes is called "restructuring" the database at the logical and physical level.

Relatively speaking, database reorganization is a minor activity, and restructuring is a major activity. Usually, reorganization does not affect the existing application systems and procedures, whereas restructuring does affect them. Normally, there are three types of changes in restructuring.

- **Logical changes** in terms of adding or deleting data elements, combining a number of records, changing the relationship between records
- **Physical changes** in terms of channels and disk configuration to minimize contention, adding or removing some pointers
- **Procedural changes** in terms of backup and recovery procedures and access control security rules

(g) **Database Performance Monitoring.** An important responsibility of a DBA is to monitor the performance of the database. The DBMS can consume large amounts of computer resources (i.e., memory, disk space) and can take long processing times due to design complexity. Often, a performance-monitoring tool and/or utility programs are utilized to take internal readings of the database and its components. The objective is to identify performance-related problems and take corrective action as quickly as possible.

(h) **Database Utility Programs.** The DBA needs the following utility programs to make his work more effective and efficient:

- Load and restore routines can be used to create the initial version of the database.
- Dump and reload routines can be used to dump (unload) the database to backup storage for recovery purposes and to reload the database from such a backup copy.
- Statistical routines can be used to compute and analyze various performance statistics such as file sizes and database values.
- Reorganization routines can be used to rearrange the data in the database to improve performance.
- Programs can be used to analyze database pointers and broken chains.
- Reconfiguring routines can be used to reconfigure the pointers in the database.
- Programs can be used to archive journal files.
- Programs can be used to initialize database files.
- Routines can be used to fix journal problems.
- Programs can be used to roll-back or roll-forward database updates.
- Routines can be used to expand database page size.
- Programs can be used to restructure database contents.
- Routines can be used to print and clear the log area of the data dictionary.

(i) **Data Dictionary Systems Software.** A data dictionary is an alphabetical listing that describes all the data elements (fields) in an application system and tells how and where they are used. It defines each data element's characteristics, properties, and processes, including the size of the data field and record, the volume of records, the data field editing and validation rules with maximum and minimum values, the security levels or ratings, and the frequency of use and of changes of data elements.

Used properly, a data dictionary presents a top-down structure or definition of a complex data element. The data editing and validation rules available in the data dictionary can be used to prevent the entry of inaccurate data into the system. The data dictionary can be used as a corrective control because of its "where-used" information, which can be used to trace data backward and forward through the transaction as an audit trail.

A data dictionary or directory (DD) system is a central repository of an organization's data elements and their relationships. The DD stores critical information such as data sources, data formats, data us-ages, and data relationships. In this regard, a DD can be a database itself—storing data about data. A DD provides cross-references between groups of data elements and databases, and indicates which computer programs use which databases. A DD is a tool to develop and maintain database as well as nondatabase application systems. Usually, automated software is used to manage and control the data dictionary. A manual DD can become inconsistent quickly with what is actually in the system. An automated DD supports the objectives of minimum data redundancy, maximum data consistency, and adequate data integrity and security.

The data dictionary can be dependent on a DBMS or it can be stand-alone. A dependent DD uses the underlying DBMS to manage and control its data, and it is a part of the DBMS. A stand-alone DD is a separate package from the DBMS package. *A DD may be active or passive with the DBMS software.* An active DD requires all data descriptions for a database defined or available at one time. On the other hand, a passive DD may or may not require a check for currency of data descriptions before a program is executed. Some major advantages of each approach are described below.

Advantage of an active data dictionary system

- Provides quick access to the data in the database
- Tracks database accesses and actions
- Provides valuable statistics for improving system performance
- Minimizes redundancy in storage of data descriptions
- Facilitates system documentation
- Improves data editing and validation controls
- Works well with database files

Advantages of a passive data dictionary system

- Less risk of commitment to a DBMS
- Ease of implementation
- Data descriptions can be done on a piecemeal basis
- Works well with conventional data files
- Serves as a documentation and communication tool

Some of the major reports that can be obtained from a DD and its interface systems are

- Access control reports
- Audit trail reports
- Cross-reference reports
- Data elements and their relationships with their usage frequencies
- Summary, change, error, and ad hoc reports

In summary, a data dictionary provides the following benefits:

- It provides a consistent description of data as well as consistent data names for programming and data retrieval. This in turn provides consistent descriptive names and meanings.
- It shows where-used information such as (1) what programs used the data items, (2) which files contain the data items, and (3) which printed reports display the data items.
- It provides data integrity through data editing and validation routines.
- It supports elimination of data redundancy.
- It supports tracing of data item's path through several application programs.
- It describes the relationships among the entities.

(j) **Data Warehouse.** The purpose of a data warehouse is information retrieval and data analysis. It stores precomputed, historical, descriptive, and numerical data. It is the process of extracting and transferring operational data into informational data and loading it into a central data store or "warehouse." Once loaded, users can access the warehouse through query and analysis tools. The data warehouse can be housed on a computer different from production computer.

A data warehouse is a storage facility where data from heterogeneous databases are brought together so that users can make queries against the warehouse instead of against several databases. The warehouse is like a big database. Redundant and inconsistent data are removed from the databases and subsets of data are selected from the databases prior to placing them in a data warehouse. Usually, summary data, correlated data, or otherwise massaged data is contained in the data warehouse.

Data integrity and security issues are equally applicable to warehouses as they are to databases. An issue is: what happens to the warehouse when the individual databases are updated?

Data modeling is an essential task for building a data warehouse along with access methods, index strategies, and query language. For example, if the data model is relational, then an SQL-based language is used. If the data model is object-oriented, an object-based language may be appropriate.

Metadata management is another critical technology for data warehousing. Metadata will include the mapping between the data sources (databases) and the warehouse. Another issue is whether the warehouse can be centralized or distributed.

DATABASE VS. DATA WAREHOUSE

- A database contains raw data.
- A data warehouse contains massaged (cleaned up) data.
- Users query many points with heterogeneous databases.
- Users query only a single point with data warehouse.

(k) **Data Marts.** A data mart is a subset of a data warehouse. It brings the data from transaction processing systems (TPSs) to functional departments (i.e., finance, manufacturing, and human resources) or business units or divisions. Data marts are scaled-down data warehouses, where targeted business information is placed into the hands of more decision makers.

DATA MART VS. DATA WAREHOUSE

- Data mart provides a detailed data for a specific function of a business.
- Data warehouse provides a summary data for the entire business.

(l) **Data Mining.** Data mining can be applied to databases as well as to data warehouses. A warehouse structures the data in such a way so as to facilitate query processing. Data mining is a set of automated tools that convert the data in the warehouse into some useful information. It selects and reports information deemed significant from a data warehouse or database.

Data mining is the process of posing a series of queries to extract information from the databases. A data warehouse itself does not attempt to extract information from the data contained in the warehouse. One needs a data mining tool to do this.

There are several types of data mining applications, including data classifications, data sequencing, data dependencies, and deviation analysis. Data records can be grouped into clusters or classes so that patterns in the data can be found. Data sequencing can be determined from the data. Data dependencies such as relationships or associations between the data items can be detected. Deviation analysis can be performed on data. Fuzzy logic, neural networks, and set theory are some techniques used in data mining tools.

Data mining techniques can also be used as intrusion detection, fraud detection, and auditing the databases. One may apply data mining tools to detect abnormal patterns in data, which can provide clues to fraud. A security problem can be created when a user poses queries and infers sensitive hypotheses. That is, the inference problem occurs via data mining tool. A data mining tool can be applied to see if sensitive information can be deduced from the unclassified information legitimately obtained. If so, then there is an inference problem. An inference controller can be built to detect the motives of the users and prevent the inference problem from occurring. The inference controller can be placed between the data mining tool and the database. Since data mining tools are computationally intensive, parallel processing computers are used to carry out the data mining activities.

Examples of application of data mining include: market segmentation, where it identifies the common characteristics of customers who buy the same products, customer defection, where it predicts which customers are likely to leave the company, fraud detection, where it identifies which transactions are most likely to be fraudulent, direct marketing, where it identifies which prospects are the target for mailing, market basket analysis, where it identifies what products or services are commonly purchased together, and trend analysis, where it reveals the difference between a typical customer this month versus last month.

DATA MINING AND DATA AUDITING

- Data mining is a user tool to select information from a data warehouse.
- Data mining is an auditing tool to detect fraud, intrusions, and security problems in a data warehouse.

(m) **Virtual Databases.** A virtual database is created when data from multiple database sources is integrated to provide a total perspective on a specific topic. It is virtual in that such database does not exist physically, but is created on demand. For example, an auditor comparing performance of a multiplant organization can use virtual database technology to view key operating and financial ratios of each plant side-by-side.

(n) **Online Analytical Processing.** Online analytical processing (OLAP) programs are available to store and deliver data warehouse information from multidimensional databases. It allows users to explore corporate data from a number of different perspectives, such as product, geography, time, and salesperson.

OLAP servers and desktop tools support high-speed analysis of data involving complex relationships, such as combinations of a company's products, regions, channels of distribution, reporting units, and time periods. Access to data in multidimensional databases can be very quick because they store the data in structures optimized for speed, and they avoid using structured query language (SQL) and index processing techniques. In other words, multidimensional databases have greater retrieval speed and longer update times.

Consumer goods companies (e.g., retail) use OLAP to analyze the millions of consumer purchase records and transactions captured by electronic scanners at the checkout stand. This data is used to spot trends in purchases and to relate sales volume to store promotions (coupons) and store conditions (displays). The data in OLAP is generally aggregated giving information such as total or average sales in dollars or units. Users can examine the OLAP's hierarchical data in the time dimension such as sales by year, by quarter, by month, by week, or by day.

5.17 Software Licensing

Copyright laws protect the software. The act of illegally (not paying for) copying, duplicating, or using the software is called software piracy. Internet privacy involves illegally gaining access to and using the Internet. Many companies on the Internet receive customer fees for their research, services, information (sports, market analysis), and even products. When unauthorized people use such services illegally, Internet firms lose revenues. Both software piracy and the Internet piracy are growing steadily.

(a) **Software Licensing Practices.** There are many variations of software licensing practices available that the internal auditor needs to be familiar with. The following information is to be known along with its **criteria**.

(i) **PCs, LANs, and workstations.** The following list indicates how software is licensed for PCs, LANs, and workstations:

- Major characteristics of the application whether it is a single-user or multiple-user application
- Major classification of software agreements such as single user program or multiple user software
- The multiuser software is further subdivided into
  - A site license
  - A perserver license
  - A per personal computer license
  - A number-of-users license
- Maximum number of concurrent users—regardless of the machine in use, a LAN software license can be bought only for the number of employees who would use the software simultaneously. Either LAN operating system or a utility program can monitor concurrent access to the software on a network.
- Floating licenses—in a client-server environment, it is a practice to buy a single copy of a software program and obtain a client license for each workstation. In this arrangement, the specified number of licenses are bought and that only required workstations can use it. It does

not matter who uses them as long as the number of users does not exceed the number contracted for. Floating licenses are distributed by the server when a license request is received from a client.

(ii) **Mainframe, mini, and midrange computers.** The auditor should be aware of the following requirements for a successful and complete software contract negotiation:

- The basis for the license per CPU machine
- Specifying most "favored customer" status generally through price concessions
- Arbitration clauses where disputes are submitted for binding arbitration
- Cancellation clauses with time periods and charges required
- Software fixes, upgrades, and future options
- Responsibility for the independent or subcontractors provided by the vendor
- Responsibility for inherent defects in the software or hardware
- Insurance requirements on the software product or the hardware device
- Software and hardware maintenance requirements
- Notification of unauthorized use or possession of vendor software
- Document and software reproduction rights and limitations
- Computer virus damage, detection and prevention requirements
- Access to source code and its modifications
- Global use of software and hardware

(b) **Software Piracy.** The vast majority of the software involved in software piracy legal cases is off-the-shelf, PC software, such as word processing, spreadsheets, graphics, and databases. The issue is illegal use, copying, and distribution of software both inside and outside the organization. Here, illegal means a user has not paid for the software.

Software piracy policies are needed to protect the organization from legal suits by owners. The policy should include

- Prohibiting illegal copy and use of software.
- Developing a software inventory management system that includes a list of popular application programs. This list can be compared to the organization's purchase orders, original software diskettes, or original documentation manual.
- Checking the hard disks for illegally copied software periodically.
- Making illegal copying of software grounds for employee dismissal.
- Requiring all employees to sign a statement of not using illegal software at their work and not using the illegal software taken from work to home.
- Prohibiting copying of internally-developed software.
- Prohibiting pirated externally-developed software from being brought into the organization.
- Monitoring of all sensitive programs from illegal copying.

(c) **Copyright Laws.** Copyright laws give protection to the author for almost anything he created that can be expressed in a tangible form. Under the law, only the author or copyright owner may make copies unless they grant permission to others. When the author sells the copyright, the new owner takes over all the rights and privileges of the author.

Computer programs are copyrightable. Source code, microcode, and object code can be copyrighted. Blank forms can be copyrighted if they convey some information by their organization and have considerable originality. Similarly, computer terminal screens can be copyrighted if they are part of a computer program and vice versa. However, procedures, concepts, and principles cannot be copyrighted.

One computer program is said to be an **infringement** on the other when the alleged infringing product and the copyrighted product contain many similar design features and functions. Although the structure, sequence, and organization of a computer program is protected by copyright, the physical order of the subroutines and their calling sequences are not protected.

Input formats are copyrightable in some courts while in others it is not. Statistical formulas are not copyrightable when they are used in an input format. Even innocent or unintentional infringers may be liable for using a copyrighted material without the written permission of the owner.

Legal penalties for copyright infringement may include injunction, punitive damages, and possible criminal prosecution. However, it does not include payment of actual damages as well as any profits. Attorneys' fees and costs may be awarded.

Fair use is a defense against a charge of copyright infringement. Fair use depends on

- The amount of the material and the economic impact of the material that was "taken"
- The nature of the copyrighted work
- The nature and purpose of the use, that is, whether it is commercial or not

When a teacher copies substantial portions of a text for his students, it is not a fair use. If what is copied is a small portion of the text it would come under fair use. *Selling illegal copies of software for profit would not be fair use, whereas making one backup copy for archival purposes would be fair use.*

When consultants, software developers, and employees are doing work for an organization, the organization becomes the owner of the work products. In order for an organization to claim product ownership, the work should be a part of an employee's job description.

(d) **Information Systems Contracts.**

(i) **Penalties.** If the customer/client refuses to pay due to nonperformance by vendor/contractor, can the contractor "electronically repossess" the software that he developed/maintained for the customer or supplied to the customer? The question is, who is right?

Even where it is clear that the client had wrongfully refused to pay for the contractor work, **electronic repossession of software** is not always justified. The contractor/developer's claim for payments due does not automatically include a right to repossess or disable the software, especially without going to the court. One exception is when the contractor is the owner or has a personal property interest in the software product. Disabling of computer software could interrupt business operations and customer services.

Even where the vendor has an arguable right to "repossess" or disable the software, the manner in which the repossession is executed may itself be wrongful. If a contractor/developer must access the customer/client's computer in order to remove or disable the software, this may constitute a violation of federal and/or state computer crime statutes.

If a contractor disables the client's software, the client can sue the contractor for trespass, intentional interference with contractual relations, and breach of contract.

Automatic disabling mechanisms such as "time/logic bombs," "drop-dead devices," "trojan horses," "access keys," are the insertion of illegal and unauthorized program code into the computer system, to be activated by the system date on the computer, by turning up a counter, or by occurrence of some specific event or condition. Are these mechanisms legal?

Software disabling mechanisms by vendor/contractor require advance notice to the client, that is, prior to entering into the software agreement.

Courts do not appreciate the idea that business operations are at the mercy of, or slave to, a computer. The courts would prohibit the vendor from activating the drop-dead device if prior notice is not given to the customer. However, courts would allow a vendor to activate a drop-dead device where notice of the device was included in the contract. In either case, such contractual protection will not protect the vendor/contractor if the vendor itself is in default, that is, nonperformance.

(ii) **Acceptance testing for contracts.** The following list provides guidelines for acceptance testing of contracts:

- A well-drafted contract will not guarantee the quality of software development and maintenance work, but it can provide the developer a strong incentive to do the job right, and it can give the client some legal protection in the event there is a problem.
- Every software acquisition or development contract should include one element—the right to conduct an acceptance test. Successful completion of an acceptance test should be a condition that must be met before final payment is made to the contractor or vendor. If the software does not perform properly, the final payment should be withheld until the contractor/vendor corrects the problem, refunds the amounts previously paid, fixes the software without pay, or provides some other remedy.
- Defining what constitutes acceptance testing is a major question and concern. Here, the buyer or the client needs to evaluate both the performance and the reliability of the software. It is important that the specifications contained in the contract be clear, thorough, and complete since the test results are measured against these specifications.

The contract should define the obligations of each party during the acceptance test. Examples are

- Is the test done by the client, vendor, third party, or in combination?
- Who should supply or prepare the test data?
- Who should correct the software problems during the test?
- How long is the postinstallation support provided?
- What happens if the software fails, is defective, or inoperable? What is the fallback plan?
- How is the software acceptance communicated?
- When does the warranty begin?

Some of choices the customer can exercise when the software does not work as expected are

- Return the software
- Cancel the contract
- Obtain a refund of all or partial sums paid
- Accept the defective software at a reduced price

5.18 Web Infrastructure

Web infrastructure consists of hardware, software, services, networks, protocols, policies, and procedures. It is discussed in terms of the Internet, intranet, and extranet. Web management issues in terms of security, privacy, and service bottlenecks are presented.

(a) **The Internet.**

(i) **Connection to the Internet.** Connection to the Internet is accomplished in three different ways. A user may obtain an account on a host connected to the Internet and access Internet services by means of that host. Through a commercial online service provider, a user may connect a PC or workstation directly to the Internet with that PC or workstation becoming an Internet host with its own Internet address. Finally, an organization may connect its own network to the Internet and become a network on the Internet referred to as an Internet subnet. Routers and modems are used in the connection to the Internet.

(ii) **Internet hosts.** Internet hosts are one of two types: (1) client hosts, generally a DOS/Windows PC, which only access services on the Internet provided by other hosts; or (2) server hosts, generally Unix PCs or workstations, which provide services on the Internet to other hosts but may also access services from other hosts.

(iii) **Internet common services.** The Internet is a worldwide "network of networks" that use the TCP/IP (transmission control protocol/ Internet protocol) protocol suite for communications. The Internet is being used as the basis for the National Information Infrastructure in the U.S.A. There are a number of services associated with TCP/IP and the Internet. The most commonly used service is electronic mail, implemented by the simple mail transfer protocol (SMTP), terminal emulation for remote terminal access (Telnet), and file transfer protocol (FTP). Beyond that, there are a number of services and protocols used for remote printing, remote login, remote file and disk sharing, management of distributed databases, and information-based services.

Specifically, the Internet common services include

- **SMTP** provides a facility for users to send messages to other users on the Internet. It specifies how two mail messages interact and the format of control messages they exchange to transfer mail. Examples of commercial services consist of electronic mail, journals, and newspapers.
- **Telnet** allows a user to sign on to another computer or host. Examples of services provided by Telnet include electronic mail and commercial services such as accessing journals, databases, and news.
- **FTP** allows a user to either send or retrieve files to or from another host. It is a high-level protocol for transferring files from one computer to another.
- **DNS** (Domain name service) used by Telnet, FTP, and other services for translating host names to IP addresses.
- **Information-based services** such as: gopher (a menu-oriented information browser and server that can provide a user-friendly interface to other information-based services), wide area information service (WAIS) which is used for indexing and searching with databases of files, and World Wide Web (WWW), and a superset of FTP. Mosaic is a popular WWW client using the hypertext transfer protocol (http). WWW servers on the Internet are providing knowledge bases in various organizations.

- **RPC-based services**—Remote procedure call (RPC) services, such as: network file system (NFS), which allows systems to share directories and disks and causes a remote directory or disk to appear to be local, and network information services (NIS), which allow multiple systems to share databases, (e.g., the password file), and permit centralized management.
- **X Window System**—A graphical windowing system and set of application libraries for use on workstations.
- **rlogin, rsh, and other "r" services**—Employs a concept of mutually trusting hosts, for executing commands on other systems without requiring a password.

Although TCP/IP can be used equally well in a LAN or WAN environment, a common use is for file and printer sharing at the LAN level and for electronic mail and remote terminal access at both the LAN and WAN levels. Gopher and Mosaic are increasingly popular; both present problems to firewall designers.

WHICH INTERNET SERVICE IS PROVIDING WHAT?

- SMTP is used for sending and receiving electronic mail.
- TELNET is used for connecting to remote systems connected via the network, uses basic terminal emulation features.
- FTP is used to retrieve or store files on networked systems.
- Domain name service (DNS) is used by Telnet, FTP, and other services for translating host names to IP addresses.
- Network file system (NFS) allows systems to share directories and disks, causes a remote directory or disk to appear to be local.
- Network information services (NIS) allows multiple systems to share databases, e.g., the password file, to permit centralized management. Both NFS and NIS are part of remote procedure call (RPC) services.

(iv) **Internet protocols.** TCP/IP is more correctly a suite of protocols including TCP and IP, UDP (user datagram protocol), ICMP (Internet control message protocols), and several others. The TCP/IP protocol suite, which is a four-layer model, does not conform exactly to the open systems interconnection's seven-layer model.

(A) ***IP.*** The IP layer receives packets delivered by lower-level layers, (e.g., an Ethernet device driver) and passes the packets "up" to the higher-level TCP or UDP layers. Conversely, IP transmits packets that have been received from the TCP or UDP layers to the lower-level layer. IP packets are unreliable datagrams in that IP does nothing to ensure that IP packets are delivered in sequential order or are not damaged by errors. IP does contain an option known as IP Source Routing, which can be used to specify a direct route to a destination and return path back to the origination. However, this option can be used by intruders to trick systems into permitting connections from systems that otherwise would not be permitted to connect. Thus, since a number of services trust and rely on the authenticity of the IP source address, this is problematic and can lead to break-ins and intruder activity.

Internet and the Security

A number of TCP and UDP services provide poor levels of security in today's Internet environment. It is difficult to know or assess the true risks of using the Internet.

(B) ***TCP.*** If the IP packets contain encapsulated TCP packets, the IP software will pass them "up" to the TCP software layer. TCP sequentially orders the packets and performs error correction, and implements **virtual circuits,** or connections between hosts. The TCP packets contain sequence numbers and acknowledgements of received packets so that a packet received out of order can be reordered, and damaged packets can be retransmitted.

(C) ***UDP.*** It is used for services that are query-response oriented, such as NFS. There is no error correction or retransmission of misordered or lost packets. UDP is therefore not used for connection-oriented services that need a virtual circuit. It is easier to spoof UDP packets than TCP packets, since there is no initial connection setup (handshake) involved (since there is no virtual circuit between the two systems). Thus, there is a higher risk associated with UDP-based services.

(D) ***ICMP.*** Its purpose is to transmit information needed to control IP traffic. It is used mainly to provide information about routes to destination addresses. ICMP can cause TCP connections to terminate "gracefully" if the route becomes unavailable. ICMP redirect messages can be used to trick routers and hosts acting as routers into using "false" routes; these false routes would aid in directing traffic to an attacker's system instead of a legitimate trusted system. This could in turn lead to an attacker gaining access to systems that normally would not permit connections to the attacker's system or network.

(v) **Internet security-related problems.** Some of the problems with Internet security are a result of inherent vulnerabilities in the services (and the protocols that the services implement), while others are a result of host configuration and access controls that are poorly implemented or overly complex to administer.

Security problems include installation of sniffer programs to monitor network traffic for usernames and static passwords typed in by users, use of weak, static or reusable passwords, ease of spying and spoofing, where an attacker's host can masquerade as a trusted host or client, and poor configuration of host systems which can result in intruders gaining access. A solution is to install an Internet firewall, which is a device that sits between the user organization network and the outside Internet. It limits access into and out of user network based on the user organization's access policy. A firewall can be set up to allow access only from specific hosts and networks or to prevent access from specific hosts. In addition, one can give different levels of access to various hosts; a preferred host may have full access, whereas a secondary host may have access to only certain portions of the user host's directory structure.

MORE ABOUT INTERNETS

- The Internet applications include electronic mail, voice mail, instant messaging, telecommuting, videoconferencing, Internet phone service, EDI, distance learning, file transfer, and news groups.
- The server is the source of Web documents and applications and the protocols used to deliver them. The server also interacts via gateway interfaces with databases and other information sources.
- Information push is a situation where employees are inundated with requests for information, orders, and dates to remember. This is referred to as push technology where information is automatically transmitted to users over the Internet (webcasting). Most push systems rely on HTTP or Java technology to collect content from Web sites and deliver it to users' desktops.
- Java is an object-oriented programming language based on C++ that allows small programs (applets) to be embedded within a hypertext markup language (HTML) document.
- Information pull is where employees are empowered to seek out relevant information. This is referred to as pull technology where users search for information with their browsers.
- The Web browser is the user interface of an intranet. The most standard form of a Web client is a stand-alone desktop computer connected to the LAN running a Web browser such as Netscape Navigator or Microsoft Internet Explorer. Thus a Web browser is closely related to a Web client.
- A Web page is a document on the World Wide Web containing links to other Web pages. It consists of an HTML file, a graphics file, and a script file.
- HTML tags let the Web browser know how to format text (i.e., heading, list, body text, images, and sound).
- Extensible markup language (XML) is markup language for Web documents containing structured information, including words, pictures, sounds, and other elements.

- Backbone is one of the Internet's high-speed, long-distance communications links.
- Uniform resource locator (URL) is an assigned address on the Internet for each computer. Hypertext links are maintained using URLs.
- Hypermedia are tools that connect the data on Web pages, allowing users to access topics in whatever order they wish.
- Content streaming is a method for transferring multimedia files over the Internet so that the data stream of voice and pictures plays more or less continously. It allows users to browse large files in real time.
- A chat room is a facility that enables two or more users to engage in interactive conversations over the Internet.
- An Internet service provider (ISP) is any company that provides access to the Internet.
- Serial line Internet protocol (SLIP) or point-to-point protocol (PPP) is a communications protocol that transmits packets over telephone lines, allowing dial-up access to the Internet.
- A Web server provides documents and files requested by client such as a Web browser.
- A Web document is synonymous with a Web page.
- The Web browser is the user interface of an intranet and provides navigating information. At the heart of an intranet is the Web server. Since an intranet is based on a system of requests and responses, the server controls and administers that flow of information through the TCP/IP protocol.
- Web servers handle requests and return the information in the form of either Web pages or other media types, such as pictures, sound, and video. In addition to supplying documents, the Web server is also responsible for ensuring the security of requests from outside the organization or within.

(b) **Intranet.** An intranet is simply Internet technology put to use on a private network. Intranet is an internal network within an organization to facilitate employee communications and information sharing. Organizations are posting information to their internal Web sites and using Web browsers as a common collaborative tool. An example of an intranet application is a customer database accessible via the Web. Sales staff could use this database to contact customers about new product offerings and send them quotes. Other applications include internal phone books, procedures manual, training manual, and purchase requisition forms.

A virtual private network (VPN) can allow employees to connect to the intranet securely, so there are no fears of sensitive information leaving the network unprotected. The Internet alone cannot remove this fear.

A VPN is a private network composed of computers owned by a single organization that share information with each other in that organization (e.g., LAN or WAN). However, a public network is a large collection of organizations or computers who exchange information with each other (e.g., a public telephone system and the Internet).

A VPN blurs the line between a private and public network. With a VPN, a secure, private network can be created over a public network such as the Internet. A VPN can be created using software, hardware, or a combination of the two that provides a secure link between peers over a public network. Control techniques, such as encryption, packet tunneling, and firewalls, are used in a VPN. Tunneling encapsulates a packet within a packet to accommodate incompatible protocols. The packet within the packet could either be of the same protocol or of a completely different one.

The private network is called "virtual" because it uses temporary connections that have no real physical presence, but consist of packets routed over various computers on the Internet on an ad hoc basis. Secure virtual connections are created between two computers, a computer and a network, or two networks. A VPN does not exist physically.

MORE ABOUT INTRANETS

- Using an intranet, an organization can link up its current operating systems using a common network protocol, thus eliminating the problem of sharing information between different computer systems. In addition, for older legacy systems that do not fit into the network protocol framework, intranets offer the capability to seamlessly integrate database entry and query through a system of gateways.

- Intranets encourage and allow collaboration among workers regardless of their location. Intranets also facilitate telecommuting between work and employees on the road because remote access is built in.
- Intranet is a kind of local area network (LAN) based on Internet technology. Just like on the Web, intranet users get to most information via a Web browser. Intranets increase employee productivity through simplified workflow systems. Intranet is an add-on to a LAN, not a replacement. Intranets are cheaper to maintain than LANs. They are easy to set up and customize. Intranets can be installed on LANs, MANs, and WANs to allow employees to collaborate at the departmental, corporate, and even global level.
- An intranet is a private network that relies on the same protocols used by computers on the Internet to talk to each other. This includes TCP/IP, the World Wide Web, and electronic-mail protocols. Java programming language is the de facto standard of the intranet and the Internet. Java is an object-oriented language based in part on the popular C++. Since intranets are connected between customers, suppliers, and the organization, access to information is a vital concern. Firewalls and routers will keep intruders out of the intranets.
- Groupware is an alternative to intranets, where the former is good for document sharing, mail exchange, and group discussion. On the other hand, intranets facilitate external and internal communications more efficiently.
- One major advantage of the intranet over groupware is the Internet's inherent platform independence (e.g., Web pages written on a Macintosh computer would look the same when viewed from a Sun workstation regardless of the distance between them). In addition to being easy to set up, intranets use the concept of layered communication protocols. There are seven layers between the physical network media and the applications running on the host machines.
- Intranets are modeled after the Internet, where the former is a collection of Web pages. The publisher is the means by which information is published, Web pages created, and applications developed. intranets will become a quick and efficient method for accessing and publishing information, allowing existing information sources, such as databases or company documents, to be leveraged.
- The clients of an intranet are machines enabled with Web browsers that allow them to view documents written in hypertext markup language (HTML).
- The basic elements of intranet security tools are encryption, authentication, and filtering. In addition to the use of these tools, vigilant monitoring of all network connections is required on a regular basis. Each time a new feature is added to a network, the security implications should be reviewed.
- Intranets facilitate virtual corporation concept through dial-in facilities or leased lines.
- Intranets promote business process reengineering through organized and fluid flow of information.

(c) **Extranet.** While the scope of an intranet is limited to a customer organization, the scope of extranet includes vendor or customer organizations that do business with the suppler organization. Extranets are intranet-based networks restricted to select audiences such as vendors, clients, and other interested parties outside the organization. In other words, intranets talk to extranets through the Internet-based technology.

Security and performance concerns are different for an extranet than for a Web site or network-based intranet. Authentication and privacy are critical on an extranet so that information is protected from unauthorized users. Performance in terms of response time must be good for customers and suppliers. Secured intranet and extranet access applications require the use of a VPN.

(d) **Web Management Issues.** Managing the Web is not easy since no on one owns it on a global basis in terms of access, security, hardware, software, privacy, and control. The Web is managed at the local level as there is no centralized governing body. Service bottlenecks occur due to overloaded routers, slow modems, and the use of twisted-pairs of copper wires. Suggested solutions include: upgrading the backbone links by installing bigger, faster "pipes," improving routers with increased hardware capacity and efficient software to provide quick access to addresses, prioritizing traffic going through the backbone, and installing digital subscriber line (DSL) and cable modems to speed Internet access.

Regarding privacy, many Internet sites use cookies to gather information about users who visit their Web sites. A cookie is a text file that an Internet company places on the hard disk of a computer system. These text files keep track of visits to the site and the actions users take. This tracking can be disabled with special software.

Regarding security, cryptography, firewalls, encryption, and digital signatures can be used to protect Web resources from unauthorized access.

(e) **More on Security Risks Associated with the Internet.** Utilization of the Internet presents numerous issues and risks that must be addressed. The risks will not remain static. As computer technologies evolve, security controls will improve; however, so will the tools and methods used by others to compromise data and systems. Comprehensive security controls must not only be implemented, but also updated to guard against current and emerging threats.[4]

Uses of the Internet may include information-only, information transfer, or fully transactional sites on the World Wide Web (Web), or the capability to access the Internet may exist from within the organization.

The Internet is inherently insecure. By design, it is an open network, which facilitates the flow of information between computers. Five areas of concern relating to both transactional and system security risks include: data privacy and confidentiality, data integrity, authentication, nonrepudiation, and access control and system security. Next, these security risks and security measures (controls) to mitigate the security risks are presented.

(i) **Security risk: data privacy and confidentiality.** Unless otherwise protected, all data transfers, including electronic mail, travel openly over the Internet and can be monitored or read by others. Given the volume of transactions and the numerous paths available for data travel, it is unlikely that a particular transmission would be monitored at random. However, programs such as sniffer programs can be set up at opportune locations on a network, like Web servers (i.e., computers that provide services to other computers on the Internet), to simply look for and collect certain types of data. Data collected from such programs can include account numbers (e.g., credit cards, deposits, or loans) or passwords.

Due to the design of the Internet, data privacy and confidentiality issues extend beyond data transfer and include any connected data storage systems, including network drives. Any data stored on a Web server may be susceptible to compromise if proper security precautions are not taken.

(ii) **Security risk: data integrity.** Potentially, the open architecture of the Internet can allow those with specific knowledge and tools to alter or modify data during a transmission. Data integrity could also be compromised within the data storage system itself, both intentionally and unintentionally, if proper access controls are not maintained. Steps must be taken to ensure that all data is maintained in its original or intended form.

(iii) **Security risk: authentication.** Essential in electronic commerce is the need to verify that a particular communication, transaction, or access request is legitimate. To illustrate, computer systems on the Internet are identified by an Internet Protocol (IP) address, much like a telephone is identified by a phone number. Through a variety of techniques, generally known as "IP spoofing" (i.e., impersonating), one computer can actually claim to be another. Likewise, user identity can be misrepresented as well. In fact, it is relatively simple to send e-mail which appears to have come from someone else, or even send it anonymously. Therefore, authentication controls are necessary to establish the identities of all parties to a communication.

(iv) **Security risk: nonrepudiation.** Nonrepudiation involves creating proof of the origin or delivery of data to protect the sender against false denial by the recipient that the data has been received or to protect the recipient against false denial by the sender that the data has been sent. To ensure that a transaction is enforceable, steps must be taken to prohibit parties from disputing the validity of, or refusing to acknowledge, legitimate communications or transactions.

(v) **Security risk: access control and system security.** Establishing a link between an organization's internal network and the Internet can create a number of additional access points into the internal operating system. Furthermore, because the Internet is global, unauthorized access attempts might be

---

[4] *"Security Risks Associated with the Internet," Federal Deposit Insurance Corporation (FDIC), Washington, D.C. 1997.*

initiated from anywhere in the world. These factors present heightened risk to systems and data, necessitating strong security measures to control access. Because the security of any network is only as strong as its weakest link, the functionality of all related systems must be protected from attack and unauthorized access.

Specific risks include the destruction, altering, or theft of data or funds; compromised data confidentiality; denial of service (system failures); a damaged public image; and resulting legal implications. Perpetrators may include hackers, unscrupulous vendors, former or disgruntled employees, or even agents of espionage.

The following sections represent potential areas of vulnerability related to access control and system security risks. They include system architecture and design, security scanning products, logical access controls, security flaws and bugs/active content languages, and viruses/malicious programs.

(A) ***System architecture and design.*** The Internet can facilitate unchecked and/or undesired access to internal systems, unless systems are appropriately designed and controlled. Unwelcome system access could be achieved through IP spoofing techniques, where an intruder may impersonate a local or internal system and be granted access without a password. If access to the system is based only on an IP address, any user could gain access by masquerading as a legitimate, authorized user by "spoofing" the user's address. Not only could any user of that system gain access to the targeted system, but so could any system that it trusts.

Improper access can also result from other technically permissible activities that have not been properly restricted or secured. For example, application layer protocols are the standard sets of rules that determine how computers communicate across the Internet. Numerous application layer protocols, each with different functions and a wide variety of data exchange capabilities, are utilized on the Internet. The most familiar, hyper text transfer protocol (HTTP), facilitates the movement of text and images. But other types of protocols, such as file transfer protocol (FTP), permit the transfer, copying, and deleting of files between computers.

Telnet protocol actually enables one computer to log in to another. Protocols such as FTP and Telnet exemplify activities which may be improper for a given system, even though the activities are within the scope of the protocol architecture.

The open architecture of the Internet also makes it easy for system attacks to be launched against systems from anywhere in the world. Systems can even be accessed and then used to launch attacks against other systems. A typical attack would be a denial of service attack, which is intended to bring down a server, system, or application. This might be done by overwhelming a system with so many requests that it shuts down. Or, an attack could be as simple as accessing and altering a Web site, such as changing advertised rates on certificates of deposit.

(B) ***Security scanning products.*** A number of software programs exist which run automated security scans against Web servers, firewalls, and internal networks. These programs are generally very effective at identifying weaknesses that may allow unauthorized system access or other attacks against the system. Although these products are marketed as security tools to system administrators and information systems security personnel, they are valuable to anyone and may be used with malicious intent. In some cases, the products are freely available on the Internet.

(C) ***Logical access controls.*** A primary concern in controlling systems access is the safeguarding of user IDs and passwords. The Internet presents numerous issues to consider in this regard. Passwords can be obtained through deceptive "spoofing" techniques such as redirecting users to false Web sites where passwords or user names are entered, or creating shadow copies of Web sites where attackers can monitor all activities of a user. Many "spoofing" techniques are hard to identify and guard against, especially for an average user, making authentication processes an important defense mechanism.

The unauthorized or unsuspected acquisition of data such as passwords, user IDs, e-mail addresses, phone numbers, names, and addresses, can facilitate an attempt at unauthorized access to a system or application. If passwords and user IDs are a derivative of someone's personal information, malicious parties could use the information in software programs specifically designed to generate possible passwords. Default files on a computer, sometimes called "cache" files, can automatically retain images of such data received or sent over the Internet, making them a potential target for a system intruder.

(D) ***Security flaws and bugs/active content languages.*** Vulnerabilities in software and hardware design also represent an area of concern. Security problems are often identified after the release of a new product, and solutions to correct security flaws commonly contain flaws themselves. Such vulnerabilities are usually widely publicized, and the identification of new bugs is constant. These bugs and flaws are often serious enough to compromise system integrity. Security flaws and exploitation guidelines are also frequently available on hacker Web sites. Furthermore, software marketed to the general public may not contain sufficient security controls for business organizations.

Newly developed languages and technologies present similar security concerns, especially when dealing with network software or active content languages which allow computer programs to be attached to Web pages (e.g., Java, ActiveX). Security flaws identified in Web browsers (i.e., application software used to navigate the Internet) have included bugs that, theoretically, may allow the installation of programs on a Web server, which could then be used to back into an organization's system. Even if new technologies are regarded as secure, they must be managed properly. For example, if controls over active content languages are inadequate, potentially hostile and malicious programs could be automatically downloaded from the Internet and executed on a system.

(E) ***Viruses/malicious programs.*** Viruses and other malicious programs pose a threat to systems or networks that are connected to the Internet, because they may be downloaded directly. Aside from causing destruction or damage to data, these programs could open a communication link with an external network, allowing unauthorized system access, or even initiating the transmission of data.

(vi) **Security measures for the Internet.** Security measures (controls or safeguards) such as encryption, digital signatures, certificate authorities and digital certificates, firewalls and security scanning tools, and logical access controls will be discussed next.

(vii) **Security measures: encryption.**

(A) ***Encryption method.*** Encryption, or cryptography, is a method of converting information to an unintelligible code. The process can then be reversed, returning the information to an understandable form. The information is encrypted (encoded) and decrypted (decoded) by what are commonly referred to as "cryptographic keys." These "keys" are actually values, used by a mathematical algorithm to transform the data. The effectiveness of encryption technology is determined by the strength of the algorithm, the length of the key, and the appropriateness of the encryption system selected.[5]

Because encryption renders information unreadable to any party without the ability to decrypt it, the information remains private and confidential, whether being transmitted or stored on a computer system. Unauthorized parties will see nothing but an unorganized assembly of characters. Furthermore, encryption technology can provide assurance of data integrity as some algorithms offer protection against forgery and tampering. The ability of the technology to protect the information requires that the encryption and decryption keys be properly managed by authorized parties.

(B) ***Cryptographic key systems.*** There are two types of cryptographic key systems: (1) symmetric and (2) asymmetric. With a symmetric key system (also known as secret key or private key system), all parties have the same key. The keys can be used to encrypt and decrypt messages, and must be kept secret or the security is compromised. For the parties to get the same key, there has to be a way to securely distribute the key to each party. While this can be done, the security controls necessary make this system impractical for widespread and commercial use on an open network like the Internet. Asymmetric key systems can solve this problem.

In an asymmetric key system (also known as a public key system), two keys are used. One key is kept secret, and therefore is referred to as the "private key." The other key is made widely available to anyone who wants it, and is referred to as the "public key." The private and public keys are mathematically related so that information encrypted with the private key can only be decrpyted by the corresponding public key. Similarly, information encrypted with the public key

[5] *Ibid.*

can only be decrypted by the corresponding private key. The private key, regardless of the key system utilized, is typically specific to a party or computer system. Therefore, the sender of a message can be authenticated as the private key holder by anyone decrypting the message with a public key. Importantly, it is mathematically impossible for the holder of any public key to use it to figure out what the private key is. The keys can be stored either on a computer or on a physically separate medium such as a smart card.

Regardless of the key system utilized, physical controls must exist to protect the confidentiality and access to the key(s). In addition, the key itself must be strong enough for the intended application. The appropriate encryption key may vary depending on how sensitive the transmitted or stored data is, with stronger keys utilized for highly confidential or sensitive data. Stronger encryption may also be necessary to protect data that is in an open environment, such as on a Web server, for long time periods. Because the strength of the key is determined by its length, the longer the key, the harder it is for high-speed computers to break the key code.

SYMMETRIC KEY SYSTEM VS. ASYMMETRIC KEY SYSTEM

- In a symmetric key system, only one key is used to encrypt and decrypt a message. All parties have the same key, which must be used to encrypt and decrypt a message. Security can be compromised. Data Encryption Standard (DES) uses one key.
- In an asymmetric key system, two keys are used to encrypt and decrypt a message. Information encrypted with the **private key** can only be decrypted by the corresponding **public key**. Information encrypted with the **public key** can only be decrypted by the corresponding **private key**. Security cannot be compromised. Rivest, Shamir, and Adelman (RSA) encryption technique uses two keys.

(viii) **Security measures: digital signatures.** Digital signatures authenticate the identity of a sender, through the private, cryptographic key. In addition, every digital signature is different because it is derived from the content of the message itself. The combination of identity authentication and singularly unique digital signatures results in a transmission that cannot be repudiated.

Digital signatures can be applied to any data transmission, including electronic mail. To generate a digital signature, the original, unencrypted message is run through a mathematical algorithm that generates what is known as a message digest (a unique, character representation of the data). This process is known as the "hash." The message digest is then encrypted with a private key, and sent along with the message. The recipient receives both the message and the encrypted message digest. The recipient decrypts the message digest, and then runs the message through the hash function again. If the resulting message digest matches the one sent with the message, the message has not been altered and data integrity is verified. Because the message digest was encrypted with a private key, the sender can be identified and bound to the specific message. The digital signature cannot be reused, because it is unique to the message. In the above example, data privacy and confidentiality could also be achieved by encrypting the message itself. The strength and security of a digital signature system is determined by its implementation, and the management of the cryptographic keys.

(ix) **Security measures: certificate authorities and digital certificates.** Certification authorities and digital certificates are emerging to further address the issues of authentication, nonrepudiation, data privacy, and cryptographic key management. A *certificate* authority is a trusted third party that verifies the identity of a party to a transaction. To do this, the certification authority vouches for the identity of a party by attaching the authority's digital signature to any messages, public keys, etc., which are transmitted.

Obviously, the certificate authority must be trusted by the parties involved, and identities must have been proven to the certificate authority beforehand. *Digital certificates* are messages that are signed with the certificate authority's private key. Digital certificates identify the certificate authority, the represented party, and could even include the represented party's public key.

The responsibilities of certificate authorities and their position among emerging technologies continue to develop. They are likely to play an important role in key management by issuing, retaining, or distributing public and private key pairs.

(x) **Security measures: firewalls and security scanning tools.**

(A) ***Firewalls.*** A firewall is a combination of hardware and software placed between two networks that all traffic, regardless of the direction, must pass through. When employed properly, it is a primary security measure in governing access control and protecting the internal system from compromise.

(B) ***Security scanning tools.*** Security scanning tools should be run frequently by system administrators to identify any new vulnerabilities or changes in the system. Ideally, the scan should be run both with and without the firewall in place so the firewall's protective capabilities can be fully evaluated. Identifying the susceptibility of the system without the firewall is useful for determining contingency procedures should the firewall ever go down. Some scanning tools have different versions with varying degrees of intrusion/attack attempts.

(xi) **Security measures: logical access controls.** Logical access controls include passwords, personal identification numbers (PINs), and user identification codes (IDs); tokens; smart cards; and biometrics (see Exhibit 5.51).

Security risks	Security measures
• Data privacy and confidentiality	• Implement encryption.
• Data integrity	• Implement encryption.
• Authentication	• Implement encryption, digital signatures, certificate authorities, and digital certificates.
• Nonrepudiation	• Implement encryption, digital signatures, certificate authorities, and digital certificates.
• Access control and system security	• Implement firewall technologies with alerts and detection mechanisms; install logical access controls (passwords, tokens, smart cards, biometrics); install antivirus products; communicate with computer emergency response team coordination center and Internet newsgroups to identify software bugs and flaws; keep up with software releases and security patches provided by vendors; accept or reject the downloading of active content languages (e.g., Java, ActiveX); protect the Web servers and browsers by running security scanning tools periodically; and install packet tunneling techniques to manage packets properly.

Exhibit 5.51: Security risks and security measures (controls) associated with the Internet

5.19 Operational Application Systems

(a) **Operational Application Systems Defined.** Application-oriented information systems encompass all areas of business and nonbusiness computerized systems. Each application system is designed to perform specific functions, similar to a manual system, with clearly defined input, processing, and output activities.

Example of Application Systems

- General ledger
- Insurance claims processing
- Accounts payable
- Demand deposits
- Payroll
- Welfare payments
- Order entry
- Tax administration
- Sales forecasting
- License administration
- Manufacturing scheduling
- Accounts receivable

Most application systems are not fully developed all at one time. Rather, they evolve during the course of time. If controls are built into the application systems during software development, it does not guarantee that they will function properly once the system is operational. Therefore, to ensure a sustained and effective functioning of controls, each application system that is operational requires periodic review, testing, and evaluation of automated and manual internal controls.

Application systems attain operational status after they are either developed in-house or acquired from vendors and then installed into the production area. Application system controls are primarily concerned with data being originated, prepared, entered, processed, stored, accessed, transmitted, secured, controlled, and used. Application systems are usually classified as specific to each industry such as banking and manufacturing or across industry such as general ledger, payroll.

To be effective, one of the major purposes of application systems should be to provide accurate, timely, and relevant data and information to support management decision making at all levels. This will lead to accomplishment of the organization's goals and objectives.

(b) **Data Origination, Preparation, and Input.** There are several approaches to data preparation and data entry into the application system. In some cases, the data are captured on a paper (source) document like a sales order or purchase order. The source documents are batched into small groups and entered into the system either by functional users or central data entry operators through the use of terminals. In other cases, there is no externally generated source document since the customer calls in and places an order with the organization.

Data Processing Rules

- If an error occurs when processing a transaction, processing should be continued with that transaction and all errors and rejected transactions should be listed in a report or displayed on a computer terminal.
- When updating a batched file, and if end-of-file condition is reached on the master file before end-of-file on the transaction file, then the application program should post the remaining transactions to the master file.

Regardless of the method used to capture the data, the entered data are edited and validated for preventing or detecting errors and omissions. Therefore, access controls and data editing and validation controls are important to ensure that quality data are entering into the application system.

Program-based controls are embedded in online data entry programs in the form of data editing and validation routines. These routines will ensure data integrity. The sequence of events followed by the computer center in a typical batch data entry and batch updating or online data entry and batch updating environment would include

- Batching records of transactions or source documents
- Converting (keying) transactions or documents to machine-readable form
- Validating input transactions
- Updating the master file with new transactions
- Generating hard-copy reports

(c) **Data Processing.** Processing controls should satisfy the following objectives: all transactions are authorized prior to processing, all approved transactions are entered quickly in their entirety and accepted by the system, and all transactions are accurately and quickly processed. Understanding the nature of computer processing is critical. Although there are some common controls, controls will be different between batch and online processing. Similar to data input, data editing and validation controls are important during computer processing. Therefore, more use of program-based processing controls is needed to ensure data integrity and security.

The process of carrying forward control totals from one run to another is known as **run-to-run balancing**. Run-to-run control totals are program processing-based controls. Examples could be the number of records in a file and amount totals for certain data fields. The objective is to maintain the accuracy and completeness of data as it passes through computer programs and processing operations (i.e., processing control). It is good to automate the batch report balancing and reconciliation procedures and return this function to the functional user departments. Functional user control of report balancing activity increases the chances of correcting the source of out-of-balance conditions. This is due to intimate knowledge the users have about the nature of transactions and their interrelationships. Computer operators should not perform run-to-run balancing procedures.

(d) **Data Output.** There are many output devices in use. Some examples are terminals, printers, plotters, microfilm, microfiche, and voice response units. System output documents are photographed onto a roll of film and stored on microfilm, microfiche, and optical disk. Audio response systems will help people to inquire about a customer's bank balance, get the time and temperature readings, and obtain a telephone number from a directory. Usually, system outputs are in the form of hard-copy reports. Trends indicate that paper will be replaced by online viewing of reports on a terminal.

Balancing, distribution, and retention of system outputs are of major concerns to management and the auditor alike since they affect the quality and timeliness of data and usefulness of the system.

(e) **Documentation.** System documentation is a key element of system operations. Without correct and complete documentation, new users cannot be trained properly, programmers cannot maintain the system correctly, users of the system cannot make any meaningful references to the system functions and features, management or anyone else cannot understand the system functions and features, and reviewers of the systems (e.g., auditors) cannot make objective evaluation of the system functions and controls.

Application system documentation is classified into six categories: system, program, computer operations, help desk, network control, and user. This classification is based on the major user of the documentation. For example, help desk documentation is used by help desk staff.

(f) **Data Integrity.** Data and information are not synonymous. **Data** are a collection of facts and figures, and it is **raw. Information** is derived from data in response to a particular need, and it is **processed**. Integrity is binary in nature: it exists or it does not. **Information quality** has a parallel meaning to data integrity. Information quality means meeting system user requirements. Quality is a matter of characteristics.

The perception of quality depends upon the purpose for which information is to be used. For information to be useful, it should be available where, when, and in the form it is required with costs equal to or less than benefits to be derived from it.

The data has a certain degree of quality, and the user has some expectations of quality. If the data quality equals or exceeds the expectations of quality, the data has integrity; otherwise, it does not. Other factors of data quality, in addition to completeness, accuracy, and timeliness, are relevance and validity. Relevance is a measure of the appropriateness of the data item in relation to the user's problem or need. Validity is a notion of external reference or correspondence. Data may be valid but not relevant, or may have low validity but still be relevant.

Data integrity is the heart of any application system. Data integrity controls ensure the reliability and usability of data and information in making management decisions. The higher the integrity of controls, the greater the credibility and reliability of the application system. Here, data integrity refers to **five control attributes:** (1) completeness, (2) accuracy, (3) authorization, (4) consistency, and (5) timeliness.

DATA INTEGRITY RULES AND CONTROLS

- A directive control will ensure that people follow data integrity rules consistently.
- A preventive control will stop a data integrity violation from happening.
- A detective control will recognize a data integrity violation.
- A corrective control will fix or repair the damage done by a data integrity violation.
- A recovery control will help in recovering or restoring from a disaster caused by a data integrity violation.

MULTIPLE-CHOICE QUESTIONS (1-469)

Control Frameworks

1. The "A" in the IIA's SAC model refers to which of the following?

a. Authorization.
b. Auditability.
c. Assurance.
d. Assessment.

2. Providing assurance to management on the availability capability, functionality, protectability, and accountability of computer systems and automated information is the heart of which of the following?

a. COSO model.
b. SysTrust model.
c. SAC model.
d. COBIT model.

3. The building blocks to achieving assurance objectives in the SAC model do **not** include which of the following?

a. People.
b. Processes.
c. Technology.
d. Customers.

4. Privacy concerns and issues are discussed under which of the following components of the SAC model?

I. Availability.
II. Capability.
III. Protectability.
IV. Accountability.

a. I and II.
b. I and III.
c. III only.
d. III and IV.

5. The ability to receive, accept, process, and support business transactions is part of which of the SAC model's assurance objectives?

a. Availability.
b. Capability.
c. Functionality.
d. Accountability.

6. Efficiency of computer systems and effective use of computing resources are part of which of the following SAC model's assurance objectives?

a. Availability.
b. Capability.
c. Functionality.
d. Accountability.

7. System hang-ups are part of which of the following SAC model's assurance objectives?

a. Availability.
b. Capability.
c. Functionality.
d. Accountability.

8. The concept of nonrepudiation is discussed in which of the following SAC model's assurance objectives?

a. Availability.
b. Capability.
c. Functionality.
d. Accountability.

9. Which of the following components of the SAC model appear to be in conflict with others?

a. Availability and recovery.
b. Accountability and privacy.
c. Capability and reliability.
d. Functionality and facilities.

10. The **main** theme of ISACA's Control Objectives for Information and Related Technology (COBIT) is

a. Control orientation.
b. Audit orientation.
c. Technical orientation.
d. Business orientation.

11. According to the ISACA's COBIT, control includes all of the following **except:**

a. Policies.
b. Procedures.
c. Programs.
d. Practices.

12. According to the ISACA's COBIT, control objectives follow the principles of

a. Reengineering.
b. Simultaneous engineering.
c. Concurrent engineering.
d. Information engineering.

13. The ISACA's COBIT model focuses on which of the following?

a. IT planning.
b. IT governance.
c. IT standards.
d. IT infrastructure.

14. According to the ISACA's COBIT, business requirements for information do **not** specifically refer to which of the following?

a. Quality requirements.
b. Fiduciary requirements.
c. Security requirements.
d. Audit requirements.

15. According to the ISACA's COBIT, IT resources do **not** specifically refer to which of the following?

a. Capital.
b. Data.
c. Technology.
d. Facilities.

16. According to the ISACA's COBIT, control objectives are defined in a

a. Product-oriented manner.
b. Policy-oriented manner.
c. Process-oriented manner.
d. Control-oriented manner.

Data and Network Communications and Connections

17. What type of network consists of nodes connected to one central site that controls the network and has all communications flowing through the central site?

a. Star.
b. Ring.
c. Bus.
d. Synchronous.

Items 18 through 22 are based on the following:

An old, established insurance company with 4,500 employees and 150 sales offices has been using the same mainframe system for 10 years to support regional offices and company analysts with low-speed terminal links. The company sells individual and group life and health insurance policies and investment products. Because data transfer charges are high and the transmissions are slow, not everyone who needs it has had access to the mainframe system.

Management views the lack of a responsive system as especially troublesome given its desire to increase the company's market share by 15 percent over the next three years. Management believes its growth goal is realistic if the company could respond more quickly to the needs of policy owners and new customers.

Everyone agrees that users need faster access to policy information, but hardly anyone agrees on how to achieve it. The two most popular approaches to improving access and supporting new applications are (1) to integrate existing separate databases on an upgraded mainframe and (2) to install local area network (LAN)-based PCs with communications software for formatting data base queries and sending them to headquarters. Even the company's 250 information systems professionals are evenly divided in their support for the two alternatives.

18. In the existing system, data transfer charges are high because

a. All users communicate in a star network with the host.
b. All users communicate via LANs with the host.
c. For host communication, users communicate in a star network and via LANs.
d. System development costs prohibit reconfiguring the network.

19. Maintaining policy information only in a single computer has the advantage of

a. Increasing the speed of regional office access to policy data.
b. Permitting evolutionary growth in capabilities.
c. Avoiding loss of control due to data fragmentation.
d. Increasing system availability for all users.

20. Maintaining policy information only on LANs at regional offices has the advantage of

a. Increasing the speed of regional office access to policy data.
b. Avoiding loss of control due to data fragmentation.
c. Increasing headquarters staff's access to policy data.
d. Reducing the need to replicate data at multiple sites.

21. Maintaining all policy information only on a single computer has the disadvantage of

a. Permitting local autonomy over local data.
b. Increasing communication costs and access time.
c. Underutilizing a star communications network.
d. Requiring update propagation across sites.

22. Maintaining all policy information only on LANs at regional offices has the disadvantage of

a. Increasing communication costs and access time.
b. Decreasing the availability of local data.
c. Restraining incremental growth at regional offices.
d. Increasing the difficulty of compiling aggregate policy statistics.

23. Payroll master file updates are sent from a remote terminal to a mainframe program on a real-time system. A control which works to ensure accuracy of the transmission is a(n)

a. Echo check.
b. Protection ring.
c. Hash total.
d. Integrated test facility.

24. A medical clinic has eight personal computers, four printers and one plotter, all networked together in one building. This type of network is called

a. Ring.
b. Star.
c. Local area.
d. Wide area.

25. As the number of computers in an organization increases, many organizations find it useful to interconnect them by a communications network. A type of network that is used to support interconnections within a building is known as a(n)

a. Local area network.
b. Wide area network.
c. End user network.
d. Baseband network.

26. When two devices in a data communications system are communicating, there must be agreement as to how both data and control information is to be packaged and interpreted. Which of the following terms is commonly used to describe this type of agreement?

a. Asynchronous communication.
b. Synchronous communication.
c. Communication channel.
d. Communication protocol.

27. Which of the following is a device used in a data communications system to interleave the slow data transmissions of many different terminal devices in order to fully utilize the capacity of a medium- or high-speed data communication line?

a. Multiplexer.
b. Modem.
c. Coaxial cable.
d. Bus.

28. Which of the following terms applies to a telecommunications network used to connect computers with other computers, peripherals, and workstations that are in fairly close proximity?

a. Distributed system.
b. Local area network.
c. Protocol.
d. Wide area network.

29. Distributed computing provides several advantages over a centralized computer. Which of the following is **not** an advantage?

a. Communications costs are generally lower.
b. Alternate processing locations are available in case one site's computer is not functioning.
c. Security measures are easier to provide.
d. Investment in hardware is smaller for each site than for a central site.

30. A company does business in seven states. Its offices maintain regional databases on their own minicomputers, which are linked to the mainframe computer at headquarters.

These minicomputers periodically relay summarized data to the home-office mainframe computer, where they are used to update a corporate database. This company uses a system known as

a. Distributed data processing.
b. Parallel-systems method.
c. Inventory method.
d. Strategic-planning system.

31. Audit team members can use the same database and programs when their microcomputers share a hard disk and printer on a local area network (LAN). Which communication device enables a microcomputer to connect to a LAN?

a. A network interface card that plugs into the motherboard.
b. An internal modem that plugs into the motherboard.
c. An external modem with a cable connection to a serial port.
d. A fax modem that sends signals through telephone lines.

32. What type of information system utilizes communications capabilities to make needed data and computing capability available to end users at separate locations?

a. Distributed processing system.
b. Time-sharing system.
c. Online processing system.
d. Personal computing system.

33. An auditor is planning an audit of a customer information system, which uses a local area network (LAN) with personal computers (PCs). Increased risks associated with the company's use of a LAN and PCs, as opposed to use of a mainframe, could include all of the following **except:**

a. Lack of documentation of procedures to ensure the complete capture of data.
b. Poor security of data residing on the PCs.
c. Problems with failures of the hardware used for processing data.
d. Incomplete data communications.

34. Which of the following networks provides the **least** secure means of data transmission?

a. Value-added.
b. Public-switched.
c. Local area.
d. Private.

35. Response time on a local area network (LAN) was so slow that programmers working on applications kept their code on their own workstations rather than on the server. As a result, daily backups of the server did not contain the current source code. The best approach to detect deteriorating response time is

a. Parallel testing.
b. Integrated test facility.
c. Performance monitoring.
d. Program code comparison software.

36. There are several kinds of hardware and software for connecting devices within a network and for connecting different networks to each other. The kind of connection often used to connect dissimilar networks is a

a. Gateway.
b. Bridge.
c. Router.
d. Wiring concentrator.

37. Many companies and government organizations would like to convert to open systems in order to

a. Get volume discounts from equipment vendors.
b. Achieve more economies of scale for equipment.
c. Use less expensive computing equipment.
d. Facilitate the integration of proprietary components.

38. Securing client/server systems is a complex task because of all of the following factors **except:**

a. The use of relational databases.
b. The number of access points.
c. Concurrent operation of multiple user sessions.
d. Widespread data access and update capabilities.

39. The International Standards Organization (ISO) has developed standards for ring networks, which include fault management, configuration management, accounting management, security management, and performance monitoring. Which of the following controls would be included in the performance monitoring standards?

a. Reporting the failure of network fiber-optic lines.
b. Recording unauthorized access violations.
c. Compiling statistics on the number of times that application software is used.
d. Allocating network costs to system users of the network.

40. Terminal emulation software allows the microcomputers in a local area network (LAN) to act as mainframe terminals. Departmental LAN users also request information from the company's central database on the mainframe and process this information using end-user computing (EUC) applications developed by the departmental users. In this environment, all of the following are major control risks **except:**

a. Employees may use their individual microcomputers for personal gain.
b. Microcomputers may have inadequate computing power for screen displays when performing terminal emulation.
c. Departmental users may follow inadequate backup procedures for EUC applications.
d. Employees may make unauthorized copies of office automation software for their personal use.

Items 41 and 42 are based on the following:

A national retailer required more detailed data to help stock its stores with the right products and to increase its turnover. Such data amounted to several gigabytes per day from each store. A new high-speed company-wide network was needed to transmit and analyze the data.

41. The company wanted the features, functionality, and control of a sophisticated voice and data network without the cost of the components or the staff to maintain it. Which of the following options would be most suitable?

a. Private wide area network.
b. Integrated services digital network.
c. Value-added network.
d. Virtual private network.

42. All of the options in the previous question involve using the services of a telecommunications provider and impact the company's in-house networks. Management recognized the need to prepare the company for changes resulting from the enhanced external network services. For this purpose, what management action would be appropriate?

a. Optimize in-house networks to avoid bottlenecks that would limit the benefits offered by the telecommunications provider.
b. Plan for rapid implementation of new capabilities in anticipation of ready acceptance of the new technology.
c. Downsize the company's disaster recovery plan to recognize the increasing role of the telecommunications provider.
d. Enhance the in-house network management to minimize dependence on the telecommunications provider for network management.

43. Compared to closed systems, open systems are characterized by

a. Less expensive components.
b. Decreased interoperability.
c. More dependence on particular vendors.
d. More restricted portability.

44. A growing company is opening ophthalmic diagnostic centers in major population areas. In each area there are several centers, usually no more than twenty miles apart. In order to share inventory and special diagnostic skills, the company intends to network all the centers together. In each major population area, the company will most likely install a configuration known as a metro area network (MAN) which

a. Provides protocol conversion, message sorting, and message forwarding.
b. Connects multiple sites with multiple workstations for shared use of common resources.
c. Defines protocols and formats for the transfer of business information between application systems on different computers.
d. Implements the open systems interconnection (OSI) transport layer for managing end-to-end network transmissions.

45. Of the following, the most likely factor relating to poor response time in a telecommunications network is

a. The absence of network monitoring software.
b. Allocation of network costs across applications.
c. Incorrect software initialization options.
d. Multiple vendors providing the network components.

Items 46 through 50 are based on the following:

A department store company with stores in 11 cities is planning to install a network so that stores can transmit daily sales by item to headquarters and store salespeople can fill customer orders from merchandise held at the nearest store. Management believes that having daily sales statistics will permit better inventory management than is the case now with weekly deliveries of sales reports on paper. Salespeople have been asking about online inventory availability as a way to retain the customers that now go to another company's stores when merchandise is not available. The planning committee anticipates many more applications so that in a short time the network would be used at or near its capacity.

46. As the planning committee identified the many applications that the proposed network could support, the committee realized that a significant risk could be

a. Incomplete, inadequately tested, or unauthorized application software.
b. Lack of enthusiasm for installing and using the new network in the stores.
c. Patent and trademark violations when using new application software.
d. Inability to obtain needed network components from vendors as usage increases.

47. The planning committee identified several applications that would make the company's stores more competitive. One was an online gift registry system for customers such as those about to be married. The system would then allow other customers in any of the company's stores to view the information listed in the registry. Once purchased, an item would be deleted from the list. In order to maintain adequate security, the system should have the following restrictions on access:

a. Customers and salespeople have read privileges only.
b. Customers and salespeople have update privileges.
c. Customers have update privileges; salespeople have read privileges.
d. Customers have read privileges; salespeople have update privileges.

48. Management charged the planning committee with the responsibility of identifying the significant risks associated with a network and evaluating their potential impact. A significant risk is that

a. Salespeople may be reluctant to use the system.
b. The network will require expensive nonstandard components.
c. Customers may feel threatened by the use of the network.
d. The network operating costs may not be fully projected.

49. The best kind of network for this application is a

a. Local area network.
b. Wide area network.
c. Value-added network.
d. Private branch exchange.

50. The planning committee was concerned that unauthorized people might attempt to gain access to the network. If the company installs a network using leased lines, then it should ensure that

a. Phone numbers for the network are kept confidential.
b. Tone suppression devices are installed on all ports.
c. Transmission facilities on its premises are secure.
d. Network availability is limited to certain times of the day.

51. Securing client/server systems is a complex task because of all of the following factors **except:**

a. The use of relational databases.
b. The number of access points.
c. Concurrent operation of multiple user sessions.
d. Widespread data access and update capabilities.

52. Which of the following is a benefit of a successful client/server architecture implementation?

a. Reduced time required to develop and maintain new business applications.
b. Reduced data network traffic.
c. Reduced complexity when troubleshooting user problems.
d. Centralization of data and processing.

53. To identify those components of a telecommunication system which present the greatest risk, the internal auditor should first

a. Review the open systems interconnect (OSI) network model.
b. Identify the network operating costs.
c. Determine the business purpose of the network.
d. Map the network software and hardware products into their respective layers.

54. Response time on a local area network (LAN) was so slow that programmers working on applications kept their code on their own workstations rather than on the server. As a result, daily backups of the server did not contain the current source code. The best approach to detect deteriorating response time is

a. Parallel testing.
b. Integrated test facility.
c. Performance monitoring.
d. Program code comparison software.

55. Having an accurate inventory of hardware, software, and communication components of a wide area network (WAN) system and an accurate account of enhancements in the system

a. Minimizes reliance on external parties.
b. Ensures timely installation of new components.
c. Helps to isolate faults in the network.
d. Maximizes system availability to users.

56. Which of the following is considered to be a server in a local area network (LAN)?

a. The cabling that physically interconnects the nodes of the LAN.
b. A device that stores program and data files for users of the LAN.
c. A device that connects the LAN to other networks.
d. A workstation that is dedicated to a single user on the LAN.

57. Large organizations often have their own telecommunications networks for transmitting and receiving voice, data, and images. Very small organizations, however, are unlikely to be able to make the investment required for their own networks and are more likely to use

a. Public switched lines.
b. Fast-packet switches.
c. Standard electronic mail systems.
d. The Internet.

58. A real estate brokerage firm is moving into a building that was already equipped with extensive telephone wiring. The firm is considering the installation of a digital private branch exchange (PBX) to connect computers and other office devices such as copying machines, printers, and facsimile machines. A limitation of using a PBX-based system for this network is that

a. The firm would be dependent on others for system maintenance.
b. The system cannot easily handle large volumes of data.
c. Coaxial cabling would have to be installed throughout the building.
d. Relocating devices in the office would be difficult and expensive.

Electronic Funds Transfer

59. Which of the following represents the greatest exposure to the integrity of electronic funds transfer data transmitted from a remote terminal?

a. Poor physical access controls over the data center.
b. Network viruses.
c. Poor system documentation.
d. Leased telephone circuits.

60. Which of the following **most** significantly encouraged the development of electronic funds transfer systems?

I. Response to competition.
II. Cost containment.
III. Advances in information technology.
IV. Improvements in automated control techniques.
V. The development of data encryption standards.

a. I, II, and IV.
b. II, III, and IV.
c. II, IV, and V.
d. I, II, and III.

61. Which of the following is a risk that is higher when an electronic funds transfer (EFT) system is used?

a. Improper change control procedures.
b. Unauthorized access and activity.
c. Insufficient online edit checks.
d. Inadequate backups and disaster recovery procedures.

62. Which of the following risks is **not** greater in an electronic funds transfer (EFT) environment than in a manual system using paper transactions?

a. Unauthorized access and activity.
b. Duplicate transaction processing.
c. Higher cost per transaction.
d. Inadequate back-up and recovery capabilities.

Electronic Commerce

63. Which of the following is **not** an application in business-to-business (B2B) commerce model?

a. Electronic data interchange.
b. Electronic retailing.
c. Data exchanges.
d. Application service providers.

64. Which of the following is **not** an application in business-to-consumer (B2C) commerce model?

a. Auctions and reverse auctions.
b. Software sales.
c. Exchanges and auctions.
d. Stock trading.

65. When organizations that produce the same or similar products or services share information, this is called what information interchange?

a. Horizontal.
b. Lateral.
c. Vertical.
d. Serial.

66. When a manufacturer uses electronic data interchange (EDI) to monitor the stock level of its products at retailers for the purpose of automatically replacement merchandise, this is an example of

a. Horizontal integration.

b. Lateral integration.
c. Vertical integration.
d. Serial integration.

67. Settlement of electronic-commerce transactions using credit cards is most common in

a. North America.
b. Europe.
c. Asia.
d. South America.

Electronic Data Interchange

68. Companies now can use electronic transfers to conduct regular business transactions. Which of the following terms **best** describes a system where an agreement is made between two or more parties to electronically transfer purchase orders, sales orders, invoices, and/or other financial documents?

a. Electronic mail.
b. Electronic funds transfer.
c. Electronic data interchange.
d. Electronic data processing.

69. Which of the following is an accepted example of electronic data interchange?

a. Request for an airline reservation by a travel agent.
b. Withdrawal of cash from an automated teller by a bank's customer.
c. Transfer of summary data from a local area network to a centralized mainframe.
d. Placement of order entry transactions from a customer to its supplier.

70. Consider the following computer applications:

1. At a catalog sales firm, as phone orders are entered into their computer, both inventory and credit are immediately checked.
2. A manufacturer's computer sends the coming week's production schedule and parts orders to a supplier's computer.

Which statement below is true for these applications?

a. Both applications are examples of electronic data interchange (EDI).
b. Both applications are examples of online real-time processing (OLRT).
c. The first application is an example of EDI and the second is an example of OLRT.
d. The first application is an example of OLRT and the second is an example of EDI.

71. The emergence of electronic data interchange (EDI) as standard operating practice increases the risk of

a. Unauthorized third-party access to systems.
b. Systematic programming errors.
c. Inadequate knowledge bases.
d. Unsuccessful system use.

Items 72 through 88 are based on the following:

A pillow manufacturer tracks its production manually. That process results in continuing inaccuracies in inventory and production records on monthly production of about one million pillows in three plants. Not knowing how much raw materials inventory is needed, the company maintains surplus inventory of about 25 days' production usage at each plant so it can meet its delivery commitments.

The company makes pillows to order for large-volume customers that have given it one year to (1) implement electronic data interchange (EDI) for sending and receiving business data for orders, shipping instructions, confirmations, and payments and (2) affix bar codes to each carton and pillow. The company believes it would also be advantageous to implement EDI with its suppliers as a means to facilitate just-in-time inventory. The company is fully aware that its automation plan is ambitious, but management senses that the company really has no choice if it is to remain in business.

Production begins with the receipt of an order, when a blank production sheet is prepared. As the order progresses through production, each worker writes in the quantity of raw materials and production hours added at each stage. Packers load finished pillows into cartons and update the order sheet to show that the order is complete. When an order is shipped, its production sheet goes to data entry where clerks key the data to update inventory records. Often there are errors, but even when there are none, there is a significant delay between shipping an order and updating inventory records. Consequently, the company never really knows how much inventory it has or the quality of individual shipments still in inventory.

The quality of raw materials matters because customers expect their shipments to be of uniform quality. The quality of the final product varies in direct proportion to the quality of its raw materials. Consequently, when the quality of raw materials varies, production workers requisition more materials from inventory to maintain consistent quality. The unused materials go back into inventory.

72. The company could maintain more current records of raw materials inventory by installing bar codes on inventory and scanning them when inventory is

a. Counted.
b. Replenished and relieved.
c. Removed from production due to defects.
d. Adjusted for financial statement purposes.

73. To automate production tracking, the functions should be performed in the following order:

a. Analysis, design, construction, and implementation.
b. Design, analysis, construction, and implementation.
c. Analysis, design, implementation, and construction.
d. Design, analysis, implementation, and construction.

74. The business reason for automating production tracking is to

a. Reduce the payroll by reducing the number of production workers.
b. Facilitate more effective management of production.
c. Identify production workers who are working slowly.
d. Determine which vendors habitually ship defective materials.

75. Suppose the company reduced average inventory levels to three days. The **best** control for the potential exposure that the lower inventory level creates is to

a. Plan to take physical inventory when raw material inventory is depleted.
b. Hire security guards to protect inventory to avoid loss of any raw materials.
c. Ensure that suppliers are qualified initially and remain qualified.
d. Negotiate with other suppliers that could ship raw materials in two months.

76. After the company implements electronic data interchange (EDI) to communicate with its customers, an appropriate control for ensuring authenticity of the electronic orders it receives is to

a. Encrypt sensitive messages such as electronic payments for raw materials received.
b. Perform reasonableness checks on quantities ordered before filling orders.
c. Verify the identity of senders and determine whether orders correspond to contract terms.
d. Acknowledge receipt of electronic payments with a confirming message.

77. A control the company could use to detect forged electronic data interchange (EDI) messages is to

a. Acknowledge all messages initiated externally with confirming messages.
b. Permit only authorized employees to have access to transmission facilities.
c. Delay action on orders until a second order is received for the same goods.
d. Write all incoming messages to a write-once/read-many device for archiving.

78. Although the company and its largest customers will invest in the trading relationships, there is still the potential for disputes over the contents of messages. The **best** practice for ensuring that the company will be able to substantiate its version of events in the case of a disagreement over the contents of a customer's order is to

a. Write all incoming messages to a tape file.
b. Mail the customer a confirmation for large orders.
c. Write all messages to a write-once/read-many devices.
d. Agree to submit all disagreements to arbitration.

79. Before sending or receiving electronic data interchange (EDI) messages, the company should

a. Execute a trading partner agreement with each of its customers and suppliers.
b. Reduce inventory levels in anticipation of receiving shipments.
c. Demand that all its suppliers implement (EDI) capabilities.
d. Evaluate the effectiveness of its use of (EDI) transmissions.

80. The **best** approach for minimizing the likelihood of software incompatibilities leading to unintelligible messages is for the company and its customers to

a. Acquire their software from the same software vendor.
b. Agree to synchronize their updating of electronic data interchange (EDI)-related software.
c. Agree to use the same software in the same ways indefinitely.
d. Agree to write their version of the electronic data interchange (EDI)-related software.

81. Regardless of whether the company develops, buys, leases, or pays for the use of the software for electronic data interchange (EDI) transmissions, internal audit should be responsible for evaluating whether the software

a. Was developed in a controlled environment.
b. Is backed up adequately to permit recovery.
c. Was acquired with adequate review by legal counsel.
d. Meets business objectives.

82. One of the company's objectives is to reduce the variation in the quality of raw materials. The **most** efficient approach for reducing the handling of unsuitable materials is to

a. Inspect raw materials before making them available for production.
b. Inspect raw materials before accepting them from suppliers.
c. Require suppliers to include a quality assessment with each shipment.
d. Work with suppliers to help them deliver more uniform materials.

83. After implementing electronic data interchange (EDI) with suppliers, the company discovered a dramatic increase in the prices it paid the single supplier of some special materials for its primary product line. After consulting with the supplier, the company determined that the supplier had assumed the risk of not having inventory and raised its prices accordingly since the company was the only buyer for the special materials. The best approach for managing inventory in this situation is for the company to

a. Give the supplier more information about expected use of the materials.
b. Demand that the supplier reduce the prices of the materials.
c. Find another supplier to replace the one charging higher prices.
d. Change its product line so the special materials are no longer needed.

84. If the cycle time for manual purchase orders is 25 days, composed of 4 days preparation, 3 days in the mail, 14 days in process at the supplier, and 4 days for delivery of raw materials, the shortest possible cycle time if the company fully implemented electronic data interchange (EDI) with suppliers would be

a. 21 days.
b. 18 days.
c. 4 days.
d. 1 day.

85. If implementing electronic data interchange (EDI) with suppliers permitted more frequent orders and more frequent communication about them, the company could be more effective by using electronic data interchange (EDI) to

a. Reduce costs by reducing raw materials inventory.
b. Ensure that it always maintained a 25-day buffer stock.
c. Track materials through production to completed orders.
d. Schedule production to reduce the number of setups required.

86. To be even more effective, the company was considering investing in automated equipment to decrease setup times. The payback period was not considered quick enough to justify the investment. The company could refine the analysis of the investment by considering

a. No other factors since the only benefit from the equipment is to decrease setup times.
b. Reductions in inventory permitted by reducing average batch sizes.

c. Efficiencies gained by getting suppliers to deliver better quality raw materials.
d. Economies achieved by bar coding batches of raw materials before production.

87. Suppose a major supplier responded to the company's request to implement electronic data interchange (EDI) by asking the company to share raw materials usage data so it could smooth its production. The most effective response to this request would be for the company to send the supplier

a. The requested data daily via electronic data interchange (EDI).
b. Usage data via weekly reports.
c. Monthly production reports.
d. No data at all because it is confidential.

88. Suppose the company begins bar coding raw materials and production, implements electronic data interchange (EDI) with suppliers and customers, and invests in new automated equipment for production. A risk associated with these changes is that

a. The company will be less able to respond to customers' inquiries about their orders.
b. Having less raw materials inventory will increase the likelihood of stockouts.
c. The company will be less responsive to customers because it has less finished goods inventory.
d. Employees may fail to modify their efforts consistent with the new approaches.

89. Electronic data interchange (EDI) offers significant benefits to organizations but it is not without certain major obstacles. Successful EDI implementation begins with which of the following?

a. Mapping the work processes and flows that support the organization's goals.
b. Purchasing new hardware for the EDI system.
c. Selecting reliable vendors for translation and communication software.
d. Standardizing transaction formats and data.

90. A company using EDI made it a practice to track the functional acknowledgments from trading partners and to issue warning messages if acknowledgments did not occur within a reasonable length of time. What risk was the company attempting to address by this practice?

a. Transactions that have not originated from a legitimate trading partner may be inserted into the EDI network.
b. Transmission of EDI transactions to trading partners may sometimes fail.
c. There may be disagreement between the parties as to whether the EDI transactions form a legal contract.
d. EDI data may not be accurately and completely processed by the EDI software.

91. Which of the following is likely to be a benefit of electronic data interchange (EDI)?

a. Increased transmission speed of actual documents.
b. Improved business relationships with trading partners.
c. Decreased liability related to protection of proprietary business data.
d. Decreased requirements for backup and contingency planning.

92. In a review of an electronic data interchange (EDI) application using a third-party service provider, the auditor should

I. Ensure encryption keys meet ISO standards.
II. Determine whether an independent review of the service provider's operation has been conducted.
III. Verify that only public-switched data networks are used by the service provider.
IV. Verify that the service provider's contracts include necessary clauses, such as the right to audit.

a. I and II.
b. I and IV.
c. II and III.
d. II and IV.

93. As organizations move to implement electronic data interchange (EDI), more of them are turning to the use of value added networks (VANs). Which of the following **would not** normally be performed by a VAN?

a. Store electronic purchase orders of one organization to be accessed by another organization.
b. Provide common interfaces across organizations thereby eliminating the need for one organization to establish direct computer communication with a trading partner.
c. Maintain a log of all transactions of an organization with its trading partner.
d. Provide translations from clients' computer applications to a standard protocol used for EDI communication.

Functional Areas of IT Operations

94. An organization's computer help-desk function is usually a responsibility of the

a. Applications development unit.
b. Systems programming unit.
c. Computer operations unit.
d. User departments.

95. Good planning will help an organization restore computer operations after a processing outage. Good recovery planning should ensure that

a. Backup/restart procedures have been built into job streams and programs.
b. Change control procedures cannot be bypassed by operating personnel.
c. Planned changes in equipment capacities are compatible with projected workloads.
d. Service level agreements with owners of applications are documented.

96. In traditional information systems, computer operators are generally responsible for backing up software and data files on a regular basis. In distributed or cooperative systems, ensuring that adequate backups are taken is the responsibility of

a. User management.
b. Systems programmers.
c. Data entry clerks.
d. Tape librarians.

97. One control feature in tape management systems is the ability to

a. Limit the accessibility of production libraries.
b. Prohibit access to unauthorized data views.
c. Restrict jobs from bypassing label processing.
d. Control access to privileged utility programs.

98. An online teller application goes down while transactions are in process. The best control to ensure that each in-progress transaction is completed successfully when the system resumes operation is

a. Manual reconstruction of in-process transactions by tellers.
b. Automatic restart that prompts tellers to complete in-process transactions.
c. Computer reconciliation of accepted-item totals.
d. Manual reconciliation of accepted-item totals.

99. In a large organization, the biggest risk in **not** having an adequately staffed information centers help-desk is

a. Increased difficulty in performing application audits.
b. Inadequate documentation for application systems.
c. Increased likelihood of use of unauthorized program code.
d. Persistent errors in user interaction with systems.

100. Which of the following would **not** be appropriate to consider in the physical design of a data center?

a. Evaluation of potential risks from railroad lines and highways.
b. Use of biometric access systems.
c. Design of authorization tables for operating system access.
d. Inclusion of an uninterruptible power supply system and surge protection.

101. Which of the following is **not** a typical output control in IT operations?

a. Reviewing the computer processing logs to determine that all of the correct computer jobs executed properly.
b. Matching input data with information on master files and placing unmatched items in a suspense file.
c. Periodically reconciling output reports to make sure that totals, formats, and critical details are correct and agree with input.
d. Maintaining formal procedures and documentation specifying authorized recipients of output reports, checks, or other critical documents.

102. Minimizing the likelihood of unauthorized editing of production programs, job control language, and operating system software can best be accomplished by

a. Database access reviews.
b. Compliance reviews.
c. Good change control procedures.
d. Effective network security software.

103. Which control, when implemented, would best assist in meeting the control objective that a system has the capability to hold users accountable for functions performed?

a. Programmed cutoff.
b. Redundant hardware.
c. Activity logging.
d. Transaction error logging.

104. Query facilities for a database system would most likely include all of the following **except:**

a. Graphical output capability.
b. Data dictionary access.
c. A data validity checker.
d. A query-by-example interface.

105. Inefficient usage of excess computer equipment can be controlled by

a. Contingency planning.
b. System feasibility studies.
c. Capacity planning.
d. Exception reporting.

Encryption

106. An organization could incur material losses if a competitor gains access to sensitive operating information contained in computer files. The controls most likely to prevent such losses are

a. Controlled disposal of documents and encryption of data files.
b. Encryption of data files and frequently changed passwords.
c. Primary and secondary key integrity checks and encryption of data files.
d. Primary and secondary key integrity checks and frequently changed passwords.

107. To reduce security exposure when transmitting proprietary data over communication lines, a company should select

a. Asynchronous modems.
b. Authentication techniques.
c. Call-back techniques.
d. Cryptographic devices.

108. Encryption protection is **least** likely to be used in which of the following situations?

a. When transactions are transmitted over local area networks.
b. When wire transfers are made between banks.
c. When confidential data are sent by satellite transmission.
d. When financial data are sent over dedicated, leased lines.

109. A controller became aware that a competitor appeared to have access to the company's pricing information. The internal auditor determined that the leak of information was occurring during the electronic transmission of data from branch offices to the head office. Which of the following controls would be most effective in preventing the leak of information?

a. Asynchronous transmission.
b. Encryption.
c. Use of fiber-optic transmission lines.
d. Use of passwords.

110. An insurance firm uses a wide area network (WAN) to allow agents away from the home office to obtain current rates and client information and to submit approved claims using notebook computers and dial-in modems. In this situation, which of the following methods would provide the best data security?

a. Dedicated phone lines.
b. Call-back features.
c. Frequent changes of user IDs and passwords.
d. End-to-end data encryption.

111. The encryption technique that requires two keys, a public key that is available to anyone for encrypting messages and a private key that is known only to the recipient for decrypting messages, is

a. Rivest, Shamir, and Adelman (RSA).

b. Data encryption standard (DES).
c. Modulator-demodulator.
d. A cypher lock.

112. The use of message encryption software
a. Guarantees the secrecy of data.
b. Requires manual distribution of keys.
c. Increases system overhead.
d. Reduces the need for periodic password changes.

113. The information systems and audit directors agreed on the need to maintain security and integrity of transmissions and the data they represent. The best means of ensuring the confidentiality of satellite transmissions would be
a. Encryption.
b. Access control.
c. Monitoring software.
d. Cyclic redundancy checks.

Information Protection

114. What is the **best** thing a microcomputer user should do if a program takes longer than usual to load or execute?
a. Test the system by running a different application program.
b. Reboot the system.
c. Run antivirus software.
d. Back up the hard disk files to floppies or diskettes.

115. Which of the following is the best program for the protection of a company's vital information resources from computer viruses?
a. Stringent corporate hiring policies for staff working with computerized functions.
b. Existence of a software program for virus prevention.
c. Prudent management policies and procedures instituted in conjunction with technological safeguards.
d. Physical protection devices in use for hardware, software, and library facilities.

116. The best preventative measure against a computer virus is to
a. Compare software in use with authorized versions of the software.
b. Execute virus exterminator programs periodically on the system.
c. Allow only authorized software from known sources to be used on the system.
d. Prepare and test a plan for recovering from the incidence of a virus.

Items 117 and 118 are based on the following:

One major category of computer viruses is programs that attach themselves to other programs, thus infecting the other programs. While many of these viruses are relatively harmless, some have the potential to cause significant damage.

117. Which of the following is an indication that a computer virus is present?
a. Frequent power surges that harm computer equipment.
b. Unexplainable losses of or changes to data.
c. Inadequate backup, recovery, and contingency plans.
d. Numerous copyright violations due to unauthorized use of purchased software.

118. Which of the following operating procedures increases an organization's exposure to computer viruses?
a. Encryption of data files.
b. Frequent backup of files.
c. Downloading public-domain software from electronic bulletin boards.
d. Installing original copies of purchased software on hard disk drives.

119. A company makes snapshot copies of some often-used data and makes them available in files on the mainframes. Authorized users can then download data subsets into spreadsheet programs. A risk associated with this means of providing data access is that
a. Data replicas may not be synchronized.
b. Data fragments may lack integrity.
c. Data transactions may be committed prematurely.
d. Data currency may not be maintained.

120. Managers at a consumer products company purchased microcomputer software only from recognized vendors and prohibited employees from installing nonauthorized software on their microcomputers. To minimize the likelihood of computer viruses infecting any of its systems, the company should also
a. Restore infected systems with authorized versions.
b. Recompile infected programs from source code backups.
c. Institute program change control procedures.
d. Test all new software on a stand-alone microcomputer.

121. An organization installed antivirus software on all its microcomputers. The software was designed to prevent initial infections, stop replication attempts, detect infections after their occurrence, mark affected system components, and remove viruses from infected components. The major risk in relying on antivirus software is that antivirus software may
a. Not detect certain viruses.
b. Make software installation overly complex.
c. Interfere with system operations.
d. Consume too many system resources.

122. Because of competitive pressures to be more responsive to their customers, some organizations have connected their internal personal computer networks through a host computer to outside networks. A risk of this practice is that
a. Viruses may gain entry to one or more company systems.
b. Uploaded files may not be properly edited and validated.
c. Data downloaded to the personal computers may not be sufficiently timely.
d. Software maintenance on the personal computers may become more costly.

123. Six months after a disgruntled systems programmer was fired and passwords disabled, the company's mainframe computer was brought to a halt when it suddenly took over control of itself and erased all of its own files and software. The most likely way the programmer accomplished this was by
a. Returning to the computer center after six months.
b. Planting a computer virus through the use of telephone access.
c. Having an accomplice in the computer center.
d. Implanting a virus in the operating system.

124. The major risk in relying on antivirus software is that antivirus software may
   a. Not detect certain viruses.
   b. Make software installation overly complex.
   c. Interfere with system operations.
   d. Consume too many system resources.

125. The duties properly assigned to an information security officer could include all of the following **except:**
   a. Developing an information security policy for the organization.
   b. Maintaining and updating the list of user passwords.
   c. Commenting on security controls in new applications.
   d. Monitoring and investigating unsuccessful access attempts.

126. Which of the following is an advantage of electronic mail systems?
   a. They are more cost-effective than other methods of delivering information.
   b. They are easier to use than manual systems.
   c. They are inexpensive to implement.
   d. The system is available to all those want to use it.

127. Who is responsible for securing an electronic mail message?
   a. The receiving ISP.
   b. The message sender.
   c. The sending ISP.
   d. The message receiver.

128. Which of the following is used to prevent electronic mail spoofing?
   a. Pretty good privacy.
   b. Point-to-point protocol.
   c. Microcom networking protocol.
   d. Password authentication protocol.

129. Regarding electronic mail security, which one of the following items is **most** important and drives the other items?
   a. A procedure.
   b. A policy.
   c. A standard.
   d. A guideline.

130. The internal auditor is reviewing a new policy on electronic mail. Appropriate elements of such a policy would include all of the following **except:**
   a. Erasing all employees' electronic mail immediately upon employment termination.
   b. Encrypting electronic mail messages when transmitted over phone lines.
   c. Limiting the number of electronic mail packages adopted by the organization.
   d. Directing that personnel do not send highly sensitive or confidential messages using electronic mail.

131. The list of modern communication systems extends well beyond the telephone and postal service. These new systems can be distinguished by the features or capabilities they provide. Thus, features such as: answer, edit, forward, send, read, and print would indicate a system called
   a. Electronic mail.
   b. Voice store-and-forward.
   c. Desktop publishing.
   d. Digital communications.

132. Which of the following statements are correct regarding electronic mail security?
   I. Electronic mail can be no more secure than the computer system on which it operates.
   II. Confidential electronic mail messages should be stored on the mail server as electronic mail for the same length of time as similar paper-based documents.
   III. In larger organizations, there may be several electronic mail administrators and locations with varying levels of security.

   a. I only.
   b. I and II only.
   c. I and III only.
   d. II and III only.

133. Which of the following statements regarding security of electronic mail is correct?
   a. All messages on the Internet are encrypted thereby providing enhanced security.
   b. Passwords are effective in preventing casual access to another's electronic mail.
   c. Supervisory-level access to the file server containing electronic messages would not give access to the file containing electronic mail messages without first decrypting the security control log.
   d. Passwords are not needed with discretionary access control.

134. A corporation receives the majority of its revenue from top-secret military contracts with the government. Which of the following would be of greatest concern to an auditor reviewing a policy about selling the company's used microcomputers to outside parties?
   a. Whether deleted files on the hard disk drive have been completely erased.
   b. Whether the computer has viruses.
   c. Whether all software on the computer is properly licensed.
   d. Whether the computer has terminal emulation software on it.

135. Within an integrated financial system, which of the following is **not** a major risk consideration associated with the accounts receivable component of the system?
   a. Credits may be applied to improper accounts.
   b. Updates of credit ratings may be untimely.
   c. Financial or management reporting may be inaccurate.
   d. Transactions may occur with unauthorized vendors.

Items 136 through 140 are based on the following:

The computer center of a company processes its prior week's sales invoices, as well as its returns and allowances, at the end of the week. Cash receipts, however, are processed and deposited daily. Each morning the mail receipts clerk prepares the cash receipts prelist in duplicate. The original prelist goes to the head cashier together with the checks and an adding machine tape. The duplicate copy goes to the accounts receivable supervisor. The separate remittance advices are sent to the data input clerk. At midday, the head cashier prepares the bank deposit slip, which is taken to the bank. After returning from the bank, the head cashier compares the original prelist to the validated bank deposit slip, initials the documents, and files them in chronological order.

The following morning the accounts receivable supervisor receives a summarized processing list from the computer center with various control totals from the nightly accounts receivable update. The total on the prior day's duplicate cash receipts prelist is then compared with the total showing the difference between the prior days beginning and ending accounts receivable subsidiary ledger totals. The amount shown on yesterday's duplicate cash receipts prelist was $35,532.32. This morning the difference between the beginning and ending subsidiary ledger totals was $35,541.32.

136. What is the **most** likely reason for the difference between the two amounts?

a. A remittance advice was recorded twice.
b. An irregularity occurred during data output.
c. A transposition error occurred.
d. The total on the cash receipts prelist was miscalculated.

137. What is the first thing that the accounts receivable supervisor should do to try to resolve the discrepancy in the two amounts?

a. Call the head cashier to determine the amount deposited.
b. Manually recalculate the total on the cash receipts prelist.
c. Compare the accounts receivable subsidiary ledger total with the total in the accounts receivable general ledger account.
d. Send a copy of the prelist and the summary processing list to the internal audit department.

138. The company probably uses which of the following processing systems?

a. Batch processing for cash receipts and sales invoices.
b. Real-time processing for cash receipts, batch processing for sales invoices.
c. Online credit check inquiries.
d. Remote batch processing for cash receipts.

139. Assume the difference occurred because the input clerk keyed in the wrong amount during data input. Which of the following would **most** likely detect such an error?

a. Check-digit verification.
b. A sequence check.
c. A field check.
d. Batch total controls.

140. Which of the following is **most** likely **not** a true statement about the company?

a. If the two control totals agree, the amount posted to each subsidiary ledger account is correct.
b. If a customer is required to prepay for a custom order, the subsidiary ledger account will have a credit balance.
c. On the last day of the month, sales are understated.
d. The grandfather-father-son technique can be used as a file protection procedure in this system.

141. A mail-order retailer of low-cost novelty items is receiving an increasing number of complaints from customers about the wrong merchandise being shipped. The order code for items has the format *wwxxyyzz*, where *ww* is the major category, *xx* is the minor category, *yy* identifies the item, and *zz* identifies the catalog. In many cases, the wrong merchandise was sent because adjacent characters in the order code had been transposed. The best control for decreasing the number of orders with the wrong merchandise is to

a. Require customers to specify the name for each item they order.
b. Add check-digits to the order codes and verify them for each order.
c. Separate the parts of the order code with hyphens to make the characters easier to read.
d. Use a master file reference for all order codes to verify the existence of items.

142. A mail-order retailer has just modified its processing programs to charge each customer the appropriate sales tax. The best approach for detecting whether sales taxes are applied correctly is to

a. Move the program code that computes sales taxes to a single program and make this program part of the processing sequence.
b. Change the operator input screens to show the computation of sales taxes so the operator can verify the computation.
c. Modify the program code to prompt the operator to ask customers whether their areas have sales taxes and enter the appropriate rates.
d. Add the program code to sort orders by area, compute taxes in aggregate, and compare the amount with the sum of individual taxes charged for each area.

143. One class of data processing error is the failure to enter all the data that should be presented to the system. Which one of the following would you expect management to install in their effort to detect this class of error?

a. Existence check.
b. Control totals.
c. Limit check.
d. Reasonableness check.

144. To ensure the completeness of update in an online system, separate totals are accumulated for all transactions processed throughout the day. The computer then agrees these totals to the total of items accepted for processing. This is an example of

a. Run-to-run controls.
b. Computer matching.
c. Computer sequence check.
d. One-for-one checking.

145. A mail-order retailer in the United States has had difficulty getting the customer's ZIP (mail) code and two-letter state abbreviation to correspond. Telephone order-takers could verify the ZIP (mail) code and state with the customer if they had an indication that they did not match. The **best** approach in the online environment for ensuring that the ZIP (mail) code and the state abbreviation match is

a. Implementing a master file lookup of the ZIP (mail) code to verify the state abbreviation.
b. Implementing a master file lookup of the state abbreviation to verify the ZIP (mail) code.
c. Requiring operators to enter the ZIP (mail) code only and generating the state abbreviation from a master file lookup.
d. Requiring operators to enter the state abbreviation only and generating the ZIP (mail) code from a master file lookup.

146. A central computer system has the ability to produce output on laser printers in departments. Users specify where their output is to be printed, but some users give the wrong destination code and tie up others' printers needlessly. The **best** approach for ensuring that printing occurs on the right device is to

a. Permit departments to cancel printing that does not belong to one of its employees.
b. Create destination defaults for printing based on each employee's departmental affiliation.
c. Put all the printers in one location so that it is irrelevant which device does the printing.
d. Train current users in how to specify the right designation codes for their printing.

147. A company's labor distribution report requires extensive corrections each month because of labor hours charged to inactive jobs. Which of the following data processing input controls appears to be missing?

a. Completeness test.
b. Validity test.
c. Limit test.
d. Control total.

148. An update program for bank account balances calculates check digits for account numbers. This is an example of

a. An input control.
b. A file management control.
c. Access control.
d. An output control.

149. An online bank teller system permitted withdrawals from inactive accounts. The best control for denying such withdrawals is a

a. Proof calculation.
b. Check-digit verification.
c. Master file lookup.
d. Duplicate record check.

150. The purpose of a cycle processing control, based on the preparation and comparison of control totals before and after processing, is to mitigate the risk of

a. Missing or improper transactions.
b. Transmission errors.
c. Lost transactions after a restart.
d. Recording transactions in the wrong period.

151. You have a message waiting for you when you sign-on to your terminal. It states, "Your purchase request #5796 for $15,000 could not be processed because of lack of certifiable funds in your budget. Please contact your budget analyst, ext. 4932." This is an example of error

a. Prevention.
b. Detection.
c. Correction.
d. Recovery.

152. Insurance company clerks enter customers' claims into an online editing program that maintains a direct access file of open claims. In many cases, data from different sources about the same claim are not available for entry at the same time. The fact that data entry for a single claim can occur in more than one data entry session increases the risk that

a. Backups of customer claim data might be incomplete or untimely.
b. The audit trail for claim data might not exist in machine-readable form.
c. Data are unreliable.
d. Data entry clerks might enter fraudulent claim data.

153. The best control in an edit program for loan applications to ensure that a logical relationship exists between the amount advanced, the number of repayments to be made, and the repayment installments is

a. A dependency check.
b. A reasonableness check.
c. A format check.
d. An existence check.

154. The purpose of check digit verification of an account number on an update transaction is to

a. Verify that the account number corresponds to an existing account in the master file.
b. Prevent an incorrect, but valid, match of the update transaction to the master file.
c. Ensure that supporting documentation exists for the update transaction.
d. Require the account number to have the correct logical relationship with other fields.

155. A firm has a computer-based inventory control system. The organization's internal auditor wishes to have reasonable assurance that inventory data received at the terminals are accurately entered into the system. Which of the following application controls would best achieve such assurances?

a. Sequence checking.
b. Batch totals.
c. Limit checking.
d. Check-digit.

156. Before each employee pay raise was effective, a data entry operator entered new wage rates for salaried and hourly employees. The operator mistakenly entered $100 instead of $10 for an hourly rate. The best control for preventing this error from resulting in an over-payment of wages to the employee is use of

a. A reasonableness check.
b. Self-checking digit.
c. Prior data matching.
d. A mathematical accuracy check.

157. In testing controls over online processing, which of the following demonstrates the characteristics of restart procedures?

a. Searching memory locations in online files for particular stored values.
b. Relaying input data back to originating terminals to verify submitted transactions.
c. Identifying transactions which were lost when the online operating system failed.
d. Changing the contents of memory locations within particular online data files.

158. A data-entry clerk typed the account number 36798 into the computer for a customer's payment on account when the account number that should have been typed was 37698 resulting in the wrong customer's account being updated. What input control would have prevented this error?

a. Check-digit.
b. Control totals.
c. Limit check.
d. Value test.

159. Which of the following are sources of data for computer processing?

a. Protocols.
b. Multiplexors.
c. Machine-readable documents.
d. Fiber optic lines.

160. Output controls ensure that the results of computer processing are accurate, complete, and properly distributed. Which of the following is **not** a typical output control?

a. Reviewing the computer processing logs to determine that all of the correct computer jobs executed properly.
b. Matching input data with information on master files and placing unmatched items in a suspense file.
c. Periodically reconciling output reports to make sure totals, formats, and critical details are correct and agree with input.
d. Maintaining formal procedures and documentation specifying authorized recipients of output reports, checks, or other critical documents.

Items 161 and 162 are based on the following:

A mortgage broker prepared sample mortgage payment schedules on a personal computer to illustrate different payment plans to prospective loan customers. The schedules were especially helpful for loans with variable rates because the schedules illustrated how loan balances would fluctuate over multiyear horizons with different interest rate trends. The mortgage company's literature was not nearly as helpful, and the broker was convinced the schedules helped customers understand and appreciate the sophisticated loan types, which led to more loans.

161. To the extent the schedules incorporate erroneous logic, it is most likely that the schedules would

a. Understate the potential volatility of loan balances over time.
b. Overstate the potential volatility of loan balances over time.
c. Exhibit a conservative bias in the portrayal of loan balances.
d. Fail to illustrate the potential range of loan balances over time.

162. The potential risk of erroneous logic in the schedules could best be minimized by

a. Adequate independent testing of the application.
b. Ensuring adequate backup procedures for the application.
c. Designing control procedures for sharing the schedules.
d. Requiring adequate documentation for the schedules.

163. A validation check used to determine if a quantity-ordered field contains only numbers is an example of a(n)

a. Input control.
b. Audit trail control.
c. Processing control.
d. Data security control.

164. A computer program will not generate month-end balances if transactions are missing. This is an example of a

a. Preventive control.
b. Detective control.
c. Corrective control.
d. Discretionary control.

165. Which of the following controls would assist in detecting an error when the data input clerk records a sales invoice as $12.99 when the actual amount is $122.99?

a. Batch control totals.
b. Echo check.
c. Limit check.
d. Sign check.

166. Which of the following would be the **most** important control objective in the audit of an online order entry system that maintains information critical to management decisions?

a. Data integrity.
b. User documentation.
c. System efficiency.
d. Rejected and suspense item controls.

167. Input to a payroll program included a data field with a code specifying either weekly or monthly payments to the employee. A third payment period type, biweekly, was added, but no changes were made to the payroll program. Subsequently, when the program encountered a transaction for a biweekly employee, the amount was calculated as if the employee were paid on a weekly basis. The error was discovered when biweekly employees complained that they had been underpaid. The control that would most likely have prevented this error is

a. Internal redundant calculation.
b. Validity checking.
c. Explicit checking by value.
d. Checkpoint/restart processing.

168. A hash total of employee numbers is part of the input to a payroll master file update program. The program compares the hash total to the total computed for transactions applied to the master file. The purpose of this procedure is to

a. Verify that employee numbers are valid.
b. Verify that only authorized employees are paid.
c. Detect errors in payroll calculations.
d. Detect the omission of transaction processing.

169. A control to verify that the dollar amounts for all debits and credits for incoming transactions are posted to a receivables master file is the

a. Generation number check.
b. Master reference check.
c. Hash total.
d. Control total.

170. The best control for identifying missing and duplicate transactions over long time periods is

a. Manual agreement of a batch register.
b. Computer agreement of batch totals.
c. A batch sequence check.
d. A cumulative sequence check.

171. In an online inventory system, an update program flags the sequence number file as the last step prior to actually updating the inventory. Occasionally, the inventory update never occurs. A control for detecting these update omissions is to

a. Perform proper data matching of transactions and master file records.
b. Require use of the self-checking digits.
c. Reconcile counts of sequence flags set and records updated.
d. Make memo updates to the database with subsequent processing.

172. One concern of a user of a computer service center is that one firm's transactions may accidentally be used in the process of updating a second firm's master files. The control procedure that would best provide assurance of the integrity of the master files during updating processes is a check for

a. Completeness of input such as a computer sequence check.
b. Correct master files such as a header label.
c. Input accuracy such as a check of detail reports.
d. Accuracy of file maintenance such as review of exception reports.

173. The last few records on a payroll master file on tape were omitted in an update run because the processing program failed to read to end-of-file. A control for detecting the incomplete processing in this situation is

a. A computer sequence check for transactions.
b. Reconciliation of record counts.
c. Computer matching of update transactions.
d. One-for-one checking of detail reports.

174. The best method for determining the effectiveness of an application system is to perform a check of

a. The redundancy controls to ensure that a data item is processed only once.
b. Computer performance using hardware and software monitors.
c. The edit routines that ensure the correctness and completeness of data and processes.
d. Product use and degree of user satisfaction.

175. An online stores requisition system requires users to input the stock number of the item, the number of units they are requesting, and the job order to which the units will be applied. A new clerk confused the requisitions and returns procedures and preceded the numbers of units with minus signs. A control for preventing this error is a

a. Size test.
b. Sequence check.
c. Type check.
d. Sign test.

176. A computer operator has been removing the last page from one copy of a printed report before it is distributed to authorized users. The operator has been giving the page, which contains inventory turnover summary information, to a competitor. The best corrective action is to employ

a. Retention control.
b. Spooler control.
c. Distribution logs.
d. End-of-job markers.

177. What specific audit test would be used to ensure that an update of a master file is performed accurately?

a. Reconcile computer-generated totals with totals on the update reports.
b. Perform cutoff testing.
c. Reconcile time cards with job cost sheets.
d. Review update reports for proper authorization for processing.

178. In an order-entry system, in which manually prepared source documents are input online for immediate processing, which of the following is an example of an appropriate input/output control?

a. Password authorization procedure.
b. Check-digit validation procedure.
c. Hash total verification.
d. Backup/recovery procedure.

179. Many online computer systems maintain a log of all incoming transactions. The transactions log is useful for file reconstruction and error tracing if errors occur in updating online files. Which of the following terms best describes a transactions log?

a. Input control.
b. General control.
c. Processing control.
d. Application development control.

180. When readying data to update a payroll file, the clerk enters the number of employees having record changes and the sum total of their ID numbers. The purpose of these added data items is to provide

a. Backup.
b. Feedback.
c. An audit trail.
d. Processing control.

181. The greatest risk associated with end users modifying standard procedures to get subsets of financial and operating data that were not originally accessible is that

a. The data obtained might be incomplete or lack currency.
b. The data definition might become outdated.
c. The mainframe data might be corrupted by end users' updates.
d. Repeated downloading might fill up end users' microcomputers.

182. Prevention of unauthorized modifications to computer applications can be accomplished through the use of

a. Programmed checks.
b. Batch controls.
c. Implementation controls.
d. One-for-one checking.

183. To avoid invalid data input, a bank added an extra number at the end of each account number and subjected the new number to an algorithm. This technique is known as

a. Optical character recognition.
b. A check-digit.
c. A dependency check.
d. A format check.

184. What technique could be used to prevent the input of alphabetic characters into an all numeric identification number?

a. An existence check
b. A check-digit.
c. A dependency check.
d. A format check.

185. Preventing someone with sufficient technical skill from circumventing security procedures and making changes to production programs is best accomplished by

a. Reviewing reports of jobs completed.
b. Comparing production programs with independently controlled copies.
c. Running test data periodically.
d. Providing suitable segregation of duties.

186. Which of the following actions would best address a concern that data uploaded from a microcomputer may be erroneous?

a. The mainframe computer should be backed up on a regular basis.
b. Two persons should be present at the microcomputer when it is uploading data.
c. The mainframe computer should subject the data to the same edits and validation routines that online data entry would require.
d. Users should be required to review a random sample of processed data.

187. Which of the following application controls would offer reasonable assurance that inventory data were completely and accurately entered?
a. Sequence checking.
b. Batch totals.
c. Limit checking.
d. Check-digits.

188. Image processing systems have the potential to reduce the volume of paper circulated throughout an organization. To reduce the likelihood of users relying on the wrong images, management should ensure that appropriate controls exist to maintain the
a. Legibility of image data.
b. Accessibility of image data.
c. Integrity of index data.
d. Initial sequence of index data.

189. Data from receiving and inspection activities are keyed into the new manufacturing system and compared to recorded purchase order and scheduled receipt data. Accounting management has requested, and has been using, special copies of all purchase orders and receiving reports generated at time of receipt to verify supplier invoice data. Accounting has resisted installing computer software that integrates the manufacturing system with accounting operations because the conversion would be additional work for accounting and would reduce the level of documentation available to be filed with supplier invoices. The auditor finds no errors during tests of accounts payable transactions. The auditor should
a. Recommend that an interface should be installed between manufacturing and accounting to eliminate paper copies.
b. Expand the scope of the audit to verify the entry of receiving and inspection data in manufacturing.
c. Recommend copies of purchase orders be generated at the time the purchase order is sent to the supplier.
d. Expand the scope of the audit to test whether purchasing and receiving information is accurate as recorded in the manufacturing system.

Evaluate Investment in IT

190. Management information systems represent a significant investment by most businesses. A primary concern of management is that the system
a. Must meet the business needs of the organization.
b. Must employ the latest technology.
c. Might consume too much time and money during testing.
d. Was designed using CASE (computer-aided software engineering) tools rather than traditional methods.

191. Acquisition of information technology (IT) products and services should be
a. Selection-driven.
b. Control-driven.
c. Evaluation-driven.
d. Investment-driven.

192. Organizations should view information technology (IT) function as a
a. Business center.
b. Risk center.
c. Business enabler.
d. Business inhibitor.

193. Information technology (IT) in an organization should be treated as a(n)
a. Profit center.
b. Cash flow.
c. Asset.
d. Expense.

194. The best plan for responding to quickly changing information requirements is to foster
a. Greater online access to information systems.
b. Competitive pressures for enhanced functions in systems.
c. Closer linkage between organizational strategy and information.
d. More widespread use of automated controls.

195. There are significant differences in the characteristics of information required for strategic planning decisions and operational control. Which of the following statements concerning characteristics of information is correct?
a. Operational control information is not primarily historical in nature.
b. The required accuracy for operational control information is usually low.
c. The scope of strategic planning information is well defined and narrow.
d. Strategic planning information is normally company-oriented rather than department- or process-oriented.

Enterprise-Wide Resource Planning (ERP) Software

196. Which of the following promises to integrate information used in all functions of an organization into a unified computing system?
a. Supply-chain management.
b. Enterprise-wide resource planning.
c. Customer relationship management.
d. Capacity requirement planning.

197. The main reason manufacturing companies are implementing an enterprise-wide resource planning (ERP) system is to
a. Increase productivity.
b. Reduce inventory.
c. Share information.
d. Reduce investment.

198. Manufacturing companies should justify implementation of an enterprise-wide resource planning (ERP) system from a
a. Cost perspective.
b. Business perspective.
c. Technology perspective.
d. Marketing perspective.

199. Which of the following is a controversial issue when implementing an enterprise-wide resource planning (ERP) system in an organization?

a. Reduced costs.
b. Improved efficiency.
c. Access to information.
d. Fewer errors.

200. Electronic-business application of enterprise-wide resource planning (ERP) system includes which of the following?

I. Customer relationship management.
II. Supply chain management.
III. Capacity requirement planning.
IV. Material requirement planning.

a. I only.
b. II only.
c. I and II.
d. III and IV.

201. An enterprise-wide resource planning (ERP) system uses which of the following as its major strategic theme?

I. Create switching costs.
II. Lower production costs.
III. Raise barriers to entry.
IV. Lock in buyers.

a. I and II.
b. II and III.
c. III and IV.
d. I and IV.

Operating Systems

202. Which new issues, associated with rapidly advancing computer technology, create new risk exposures for organizations?

a. Changes in organizational reporting requirements and controls over computer abuse.
b. Controls over library tape procedures.
c. Complexity of operating systems and controls over privacy of data.
d. Changes in organizational behavior.

203. A veterinary hospital uses a computer application program to provide client-billing statements after each animal visit. Which of the following functions requires the assistance of the operating system?

a. Retrieve each animal's file.
b. Extract the animal owner's name from record.
c. Sum fees due for visit.
d. Update remaining balance.

204. Which of the following is a specialized program that performs routine and repetitive functions such as sorting data?

a. Compiler programs.
b. Application software.
c. Utility programs.
d. Operating system.

205. An example of microcomputer software which can perform diagnostic tests, control input and output, and manage disk operations is a(n)

a. Spreadsheet.
b. Database manager.
c. Graphics package.
d. Operating system.

206. The part of a computer system controlling data manipulation is the

a. Operating system.
b. Arithmetic-logic unit.
c. Primary storage.
d. Job control program.

207. Users in one department of a company developed a batch mainframe program to obtain financial information for their cost center. The program extracts data from the general ledger system's master file backup tape. The program calls for the current generation of the tape backup. Which of the following error conditions are the users most likely to become aware of?

a. A preliminary monthly closing file was used.
b. The job did not complete successfully.
c. The wrong program version was used.
d. The program contained errors in its processing logic.

208. The primary purpose of a data buffer is to

a. Compensate for the differences in the rates of flow of data from input/output devices to the central processing unit (CPU).
b. Compensate for the differences in the lengths of records in a file.
c. Compensate for the differences in the execution time in various program instructions.
d. Compensate for the differences in the volume of data that can be transmitted between communication devices.

209. A program that edits a group of source language statements for syntax errors and translates the statements into an object program is a(n)

a. Interpreter.
b. Compiler.
c. Debugger.
d. Encrypter.

210. A program that allocates memory and responds to interrupts will also

a. Translate source code to object code.
b. Initiate input/output operations.
c. Create load module libraries.
d. Map virtual views onto base tables.

211. Detecting errors in real memory is a function of

a. Memory protection.
b. Parity checking.
c. Validity checking.
d. Range checking.

212. A review of the system activity log kept by the operating system would reveal which of the following problems in the processing of the inventory

a. In recording the transaction, an inventory purchase was inadvertently recorded as an inventory usage.
b. The dollar amount of an inventory purchase transaction had two of the digits transposed.
c. The inventory master file, which is scheduled to be updated every Friday, was updated on Sunday.
d. An inventory purchase was recorded twice on the transaction file to be used in updating the master file.

213. A computer program produces periodic payrolls and reports. The program is a(n)

a. Operating system.
b. Application program.
c. Report generator.
d. Utility program.

214. Which of the following translates a program written in a high-level language into a machine language for execution?
a. Assembler.
b. Asynchronous translators.
c. Compiler.
d. Artificial intelligence.

215. A computer program that provides for inventory control is an example of a(n)
a. System program.
b. Application program.
c. Utility program.
d. Operating program.

216. Routing data between a computer's central processing unit and multiple external storage devices is a function of the
a. Application program.
b. Utility program.
c. Operating system.
d. Communication system.

Application Development and Maintenance

217. What is a control concern when a department independently installs part of an accounting system on a microcomputer and uploads the output to the company mainframe?
a. Traditional controls used in the development, testing, and documentation of systems may not have been used.
b. The capabilities of the application may reflect only the needs of that department.
c. The department using the system may not fully understand the mainframe architecture.
d. The microcomputer system application may not allow the use of computer assisted auditing techniques (CAAT).

218. With the help of analysts and programmers from the central information technology (IT) group, the commercial lending department of a bank developed an expert system for analyzing risks in new loan applications. The prototype pleased the loan officers, but an internal auditor was concerned about the lack of a backup and recovery procedure. The **best** choice for assigning the responsibility of backup/recovery of data files is
a. A commercial lending department manager.
b. A central information systems group analyst.
c. A central information systems group programmer.
d. An internal auditor.

219 The accountant who prepared a spreadsheet model for workload forecasting left the company and the person's successor was unable to understand how to use the spreadsheet. The best control for preventing such situations from occurring is to ensure that
a. Use of end-user computing resources is monitored.
b. End-user computing efforts are consistent with strategic plans.
c. Documentation standards exist and are followed.
d. Adequate backups are made for spreadsheet models.

220. The best control for the potential risk of lack of necessary security and recovery controls in end-user developed systems is
a. Ensuring compatibility of information systems with organizational objectives.
b. Management oversight to ensure adequate procedures.
c. Validation of the knowledge base.
d. Testing of controls in development and production.

221. In assessing risk for an application in an end-user computing (EUC) environment, which of the following types of risk should be given the **least** weight?
a. Application risks.
b. Environmental control risks.
c. Risks inherent in the application's software and hardware combination.
d. Technological obsolescence risk.

Items 222 and 223 are based on the following:

A cost analyst for a manufacturer used a spreadsheet program to forecast monthly sales. Special promotions were common practice in the industry, and the spreadsheet was used to forecast the effect of discounts on complementary product lines. The spreadsheet model underestimated sales on some product lines, which led to production bottlenecks and the delay of deliveries beyond contract terms. Upon investigation, it was learned that the analyst failed to apply the discount to all complementary product lines.

222. This failure is an example of a
a. Logic error.
b. Hardware error.
c. Typing error.
d. Crossfooting error.

223. The best approach for minimizing the occurrence of similar kinds of errors in other spreadsheets is
a. Permitting only trained systems professionals to develop spreadsheets.
b. Requiring independent review and testing of spreadsheet models.
c. Ensuring that all spreadsheet models contain appropriate crossfooting.
d. Enforcing documentation standards for multiuse spreadsheet models.

224. One trend was that end users with minimal computer literacy will be able to develop and use their own computer programs to solve complex problems such as investment decisions. Which of the following is a likely outcome associated with a widespread increase in end-user programming?
a. Improved documentation of end-user programs.
b. Unintentional errors due to inexperienced programmers.
c. Increased demand on centralized MIS departments to design end-user applications.
d. A decrease in the risk of fraud and irregularities.

Items 225 through 227 are based on the following:

A company has been working on the development of a new payroll package. The company has hourly workers, and overtime pay is a common occurrence in the busy season. During the slow season, employees are allowed to take leave without pay without losing employee benefits. The company has a payroll deposit plan, and employees may withhold contributions to various charitable organizations.

225. Program testing of this new payroll package should occur within which phase of the systems development life cycle?
a. Design stage.
b. Construction stage.
c. Analysis stage.
d. Implementation stage.

226. Which of the following types of test transaction techniques is **most** likely to be used during the development of this payroll package?
a. Test data.
b. Integrated test facility (ITF).
c. Embedded audit modules.
d. System control audit review files (SCARF).

227. Which of the following is the **least** risky method of converting from the existing payroll system to the new system?
a. Direct cutover method.
b. Parallel method.
c. Prototyping method.
d. Modular/phased method.

228. The risk of hastily developed, ineffective systems is heightened by
a. Growing organizational reliance on information systems.
b. Competitive pressures for enhanced functions in systems.
c. Greater emphasis on internal control.
d. Use of knowledge-based systems.

229. Systematic and rigorous testing of programmed controls reduces the risk of misplaced reliance on
a. Management oversight to ensure adequate procedures.
b. Proliferation of knowledge-based systems.
c. Closer linkage between organizational strategy and information.
d. Automated controls.

230. A control for ensuring that the source code and the executable code for a program match each other is
a. Verifying that the program move request is authorized.
b. Requiring program, system, and parallel testing of the code.
c. Authorizing programmer access to test libraries only.
d. Recompiling source code into the production load library.

231. While the system development life cycle (SDLC) approach to information system development has proven helpful, a major disadvantage of SDLC is
a. That there is no necessary link between organizational strategy and system requirements.
b. The tendency to accept a prototype as the final product.
c. Difficulty in managing the development process.
d. Inability to involve users in the process.

232. A computer programmer fraudulently altered the accounts payable program to have certain valid vendor checks mailed to a personal address. At that point, they were deposited to a fraudulent account. The control to prevent this misappropriation would be to
a. Compare all payees on checks to the names in the check register.
b. Compare all dollar totals on the check run to the accounts payable postings.
c. Ensure that only documented, independently tested, and approved changes are made to application programs.
d. Require all system access passwords to be changed on a regular basis.

233. Computer program change control procedures ensure that
a. Only authorized programmers make changes to programs.
b. Backup copies of data files are maintained online.
c. There are no inappropriate executions of production programs.
d. There are no unauthorized changes to data files.

234. Documentation of decision rules is important for both information system analysts and users. Which of the following methods of documenting decision logic would be appropriate when presenting pairs of conditions and a resulting decision?
a. Pseudo code.
b. Matrix.
c. Flow chart.
d. Payoff table.

235. An insurance firm which follows the systems development life cycle (SDLC) concept for all major information system projects is preparing to start a feasibility study for a proposed underwriting system. Some of the primary factors the feasibility study should include are
a. Possible vendors for the system and their reputation for quality.
b. Exposure to computer viruses and other intrusions.
c. Methods of implementation such as parallel or cutover.
d. Technology and related costs.

Items 236 through 245 are based on the following:

A large bank has 24 major application systems supporting more than 200 different kinds of customer accounts ranging from standard checking and savings accounts to sophisticated trust accounts. The systems have been developed over two decades in several languages and database systems. Individually, the systems work as intended with minimal errors. However, different systems have different user interfaces, and that increases both the training time for new account representatives and the likelihood of misuse of the systems.

Ten years ago, account representatives were generally familiar with all the account types and could make good recommendations to customers regarding which accounts to select. Now, however, only a few account representatives are familiar with most of the account types, and even they have trouble helping customers select the best portfolio of accounts for their individual financial situations. Management became concerned that the quality of customer service was dependent upon which account representative was contacted by the customer. The customer received good service if the account representative was familiar with the account types most suitable for the customer.

After many discussions, management is convinced the bank will fall behind its competitors if it does not do better at managing its relationships with customers. It is also clear that the bank cannot implement all new systems at once. After many meetings, management and the account representatives could not agree, however, on how the new system should work or what the user interfaces should include.

236. The new account management system is characterized by

a. Uncertain requirements and unstructured tasks.
b. Certain requirements and unstructured tasks.
c. Uncertain requirements and high user understanding of tasks.
d. Certain requirements and low user understanding of tasks.

237. The best development approach for the new account management system is

a. Life cycle.
b. Bottom-up design.
c. Prototyping.
d. Top-down design.

238. Compared to prototyping, life cycle methodologies are appropriate for problems involving

a. High user understanding of tasks and large project size.
b. Low user understanding of tasks and small project size.
c. Low user understanding of tasks and uncertainty of requirements.
d. Uncertainty of requirements and large project size.

239. The major phases in a life cycle methodology are

a. Define requirements, design system, refine requirements, and revise/enhance system.
b. Define requirements, design system, develop code, test system, install system, and operate system.
c. Define requirements, create initial system, develop code, install system, and operate system.
d. Define requirements, create initial system, refine requirements, and revise/enhance system.

240. In addition to specifying requirements, user responsibilities in prototyping are to

a. Modify programs, refine requirements, and evaluate iterations.
b. Modify programs, develop code, and operate systems.
c. Create initial systems, communicate requirements, and operate systems.
d. Evaluate iterations, refine requirements, and communicate refined requirements.

241. Advantages of life cycle methodologies are

a. Lower overall development costs when requirements change frequently.
b. Ability to give users a functioning system quickly.
c. Reduced application development time to achieve a functioning system.
d. Enhanced management and control of the development process.

242. Advantages of prototyping are

a. Ability to try out implementations without incurring large development costs.
b. Early definition of complete requirements and conceptual design.
c. Easy specification of control points and associated control procedures.
d. Enhanced management and control of the development process.

243. Assume that after some time, the bank developed its account management system and trained its account representatives who were then able to use it successfully, much to the delight of customers. Further, suppose that after a period of use, the bank intends to add another type of account. Implementing the new account type would require revising system menus, adding data fields, and expanding the update cycle to another master file. The best development approach for the new account type is

a. Prototyping.
b. Hierarchy-input-process-output.
c. Life cycle.
d. Simulation.

244. A contingency approach to choosing an application development strategy means that an organization adopts

a. A single requirements development assurance method.
b. Multiple methods as appropriate for individual projects.
c. Any one of several common life cycle methodologies.
d. Prototyping for all projects with uncertain requirements.

245. The principal rationale for prototyping is that it is easier to

a. Divide a project into manageable segments at the beginning rather than to impose control after development is underway.
b. React to an existing application system rather than to specify desired features for a future system.
c. Anticipate and plan for resource use rather than to acquire resources on short notice.
d. Convert data files once rather than to reformat data continually with new project iterations.

246. Which of the following should be emphasized before designing any system elements in a top-down approach to new systems development?

a. Types of processing systems being used by competitors.
b. Computer equipment to be used by the system.
c. Information needs of managers for planning and control.
d. Controls in place over the current system.

247. With sufficient technical skill and detailed program knowledge users can circumvent security procedures and make changes in production programs. Prevention of this possibility is enhanced by

a. Review of a report of jobs processed.
b. Comparison of production programs with independently controlled copies.
c. Periodic running of test data.
d. Suitable segregation of duties.

248. One stage of development associated with a proposed system application is the feasibility study. An assessment of the user and managerial environment in which the system will be implemented is associated with which aspect of feasibility?

a. Operational.
b. Motivational.
c. Technical.
d. Economic.

249. A controlled approach to systems development that consists of initially designing a relatively basic system and then refining the design during continued use of the system is described as

a. Top-down.
b. Modular.
c. Prototyping.
d. Prompting.

250. For internal control over computer program changes, a policy should be established requiring that

a. The programmer designing the change should be responsible for ensuring that the revised program is adequately tested.
b. All program changes be supervised by the IT control group.
c. To facilitate operational performance, superseded portions of programs should not be deleted from the program run manual.
d. All proposed changes be approved by a responsible individual and logged.

251. The plant controller intends to expand the chart of accounts to permit the designation of department numbers for cost accounting. An important control associated with the implementation of this change to the accounting system software is

a. Review of use of restricted utilities.
b. Inspection of attempted accesses.
c. Appropriate written authorization.
d. Maintenance of backup master files.

252. In order to be more responsive to its customers, a bank wants a system that would permit account representatives to consolidate information about all the accounts belonging to individual customers. Bank management is willing to experiment with different approaches because the requirements are evolving rapidly. The best development approach for this system is

a. Prototyping.
b. System development life cycle model.
c. Structured analysis and design technique.
d. Hierarchy-input-process-output.

253. A major disadvantage of the life cycle approach to system development is that it is **not** well suited for projects that are

a. Structured.
b. Large.
c. Complex.
d. Unstructured.

Items 254 through 263 are based on the following:

A manufacturer intends to develop a new system to implement activity-based cost accounting for its three plants, which produce earth-moving equipment to order. Two of the plants make parts which are shipped to the third plant for assembly and distribution to customers. The largest equipment is shipped in pieces and assembled at the customer's location. Parts and raw materials from suppliers go directly to the plants. The manufacturer provides maintenance service on its equipment anywhere in the world. There are eleven regional sales offices worldwide.

The existing chart of accounts contains 4-digit account numbers, which are inadequate for coding the departmental and activity-related information required for activity-based cost accounting. The existing cost accounting system is based on allocation of plant-wide overhead rates. Sales expenses are currently treated as administrative expense, but are to be treated as an activity in the new system. In the absence of compelling reasons not to do so, the manufacturer wants to relate all costs to the activities that drive them.

254. The **conceptual design report** for the system should include

a. Initial drafts of operator and user documentation of account number coding.
b. Initial draft of security and backup plans and procedures.
c. Outlines of operator and user documentation of account number coding.
d. Outlines of equipment assembly instructions for assemblers.

255. The **conceptual design report** for the system should include

a. Justification for implementing a system to generate activity-based costs.
b. A schedule for converting from the existing chart of accounts to the new one.
c. A plan for assuring that account numbers are translated correctly.
d. Sample output formats for reporting components of activity costs.

256. The **conceptual design report** for the system should include

a. Description of input requirements for job cost posting from activities.
b. Documentation of the operational feasibility of revised job cost transactions.
c. Hierarchy-input-processing-output documentation of requirements for job cost posting from activities.
d. Plan for gaining user acceptance of new job cost posting procedures.

257. The **conceptual design report** for the system should include

a. An explanation of procedures for ensuring integrity of job costs.
b. A plan for quality assurance for the development of the system.
c. A description of controls and their place in the processing flow.
d. A plan for postimplementation review of the activity-based costing system.

258. The **conceptual design report** for the system should include

a. An explanation of the flow of job cost transactions through programs.
b. A specification of the overall structure of programs for processing job cost transactions.

c. A description of the communications requirements to and from plants.
d. An explanation of the general flow of job cost transactions.

259. The **detailed system design specification** for the system should include

a. An explanation of the general flow of job cost transactions through the system.
b. A system design showing the flow of job cost transactions through programs.
c. A description of the relationships of input, processing, and output for job costing.
d. A statement of the flow of job cost transactions through organizational units.

260. The **detailed system design specification** for the system should include

a. Testing plans for the communications network linking the plants and sales offices.
b. A plan for postimplementation review of the data communications network.
c. Specifications for data communications to and from the plants and sales offices.
d. Explanation of functions to be performed via the communications network.

261. The **detailed system design specification** for the system should include

a. An explanation of procedures for ensuring integrity of job costs during operation of the system.
b. A plan for ensuring integrity of converted job cost files.
c. A control design showing controls to be implemented at various points in the flow of job cost posting.
d. An analysis of procedures for converting account numbers.

262. The **detailed system design specification** for the system should include

a. An estimate of hardware requirements to support increased processing for job costing.
b. Schedule of expected cost and benefits from having activity-based job costing.
c. Hardware specifications for new hardware to support increased data storage requirements for job cost data.
d. A testing plan for new hardware acquired to support the new job costing system.

263. The **detailed system design specification** for the system should include

a. An explanation of procedures for ensuring integrity in the use and operation of the job costing system.
b. A description of user responsibilities in the correct operation of the system.
c. An application test or quality assurance plan for the remainder of the development.
d. Outlines for operating manuals needed for correct operation of the system.

264. Prototyping and structured development are two different general approaches to the process of developing and implementing computer-based application systems. Which of the following is a **distinguishing feature** of the prototyping approach to systems development?

a. User statements of system requirements are accepted as being complete and firm and to be developed as defined.
b. At the completion of each development stage, there are formal procedures to verify compliance with system requirements.
c. Whenever requirements are found to be incorrect or inadequate during development, the specifications are revised by returning to the requirement determination process with users.
d. Assurance that systems development requirements are adequate and correct is obtained through actual user experience during the system development.

265. A large government agency with a multivendor computer center had difficulties in the past making different database management systems work with existing operating systems. To prevent continuing compatibility problems associated with the acquisition of new database management software and to achieve cost-effective operating results, the agency should specify in the bid request

a. The required operating system environment.
b. The identity of the preferred database management software.
c. The kinds of data manipulation required of the database management software.
d. Required transaction throughput rates and data storage volumes.

266. The development stage of the systems development life cycle (SDLC) approach to application system development includes all of the following activities except:

a. Coding of computer programs.
b. Testing of computer programs.
c. User-oriented design of the application.
d. Detailed design of flows and processes in the application processing systems.

267. Using systems concepts to decompose information system requirements and define the boundaries and interfaces of subsystems is known as

a. Top-down design.
b. Subsystem prototyping.
c. Hierarchy-input-process-output.
d. Structured design.

Items 268 through 276 are based on the following:

A mail-order company offering only natural fiber clothing has been phenomenally successful. In fact, its success threatens its existence unless it can automate its order entry, shipping, and billing system. The company wants a system that will automate at least the following functions:

1. Online entry of orders from mail and telephone
2. Validation of order detail and credit authorization.
3. Invoice, mailing label, and back-order notice printing
4. Order fulfillment and stock record maintenance
5. Computation of shipping charges for private carrier shipping
6. Analysis of stock levels and preparation of purchase orders
7. Tracking of customer sources (e.g., from catalogs or advertisements on television and in magazines)
8. Demand forecasting based on early orders for items

9. Analysis of buying patterns based on customer order history

268. The best sequence of order entry tasks in the new system would be

a. Customer master file lookup, customer credit validation, order detail entry, order detail validation.
b. Order detail entry, order detail validation, customer master file lookup, customer credit validation.
c. Customer master file lookup, order detail entry, order detail validation, customer credit validation.
d. Order detail entry, customer master file lookup, customer credit validation, order detail validation.

269. If clerks will be pulling merchandise from the warehouse shelves, invoices and mailing labels should be printed in the order of

a. Customer postal codes.
b. Customer numbers.
c. Stock number sequence.
d. Stock numbers in the warehouse.

270. If all requirements could not be incorporated in the system due to lack of development personnel, the phase most likely to be deferred is

a. Validation of order detail and credit authorization.
b. Invoice, mailing label, and back-order notice printing.
c. Analysis of stock levels and preparation of purchase orders.
d. Analysis of buying patterns based on customer order history.

271. The best time to capture data about customer sources is at

a. Order entry.
b. Stock ordering.
c. Credit rejection.
d. Order filling.

272. For repeat customers, the best control for ensuring that the company ships an order to the right customer is

a. Customer master file lookup at data entry.
b. Key verification of customer name and address.
c. Reconciliation of rejected orders with valid orders.
d. Maintenance of a suspense file for incomplete orders.

273. A detective control for ensuring that stock shrinkage is minimal is

a. Screening new warehouse clerks to hire only individuals likely to be trustworthy.
b. Reconciling stock positions with stock receipts, valid orders, and orders shipped, with supervisor follow-up of discrepancies.
c. Restricting use of terminals authorized for read-only access to information about stock levels to warehouse supervisors.
d. Adjusting stock levels so that only merchandise needed for sale is kept in the warehouse.

274. Which of the following is not a control for ensuring that customers **receive** the merchandise they ordered and paid for?

a. Ask customers to return a post-paid card indicating their receipt of goods.
b. Reconcile records of customer orders, stock positions, and completed orders with orders shipped.
c. Review customers' inquiries about undelivered goods.
d. Have the customer service department periodically ask customers to verify receipt of goods.

275. The best means to ensure that duplicate goods were not shipped is to

a. Require that all parts of an order be shipped together in the same package.
b. Screen new warehouse clerks to hire only individuals likely to be trustworthy.
c. Match records of goods shipped with records of valid orders.
d. Allow shipping clerks to access online information to correct errors.

276. The best approach to developing the system is the

a. Life cycle approach.
b. Contingency approach.
c. Prototyping approach.
d. Iterative approach.

277. The process of converting a high-level computer language to a machine language for operation and storage is performed using

a. Translation by a compiler.
b. Transformation by a kernel program.
c. Transmittal by an encoder.
d. Conversion by an object code.

278. Using standard procedures developed by information center personnel, staff members download specific subsets of financial and operating data as they need it. The staff members analyze the data on their own microcomputers and share results with each other. Over time, the staff members learn to modify the standard procedures to get subsets of financial and operating data that were not accessible through the original procedures. The greatest risk associated with this situation is that

a. The data obtained might be incomplete or lack currency.
b. The data definition might become outdated.
c. The mainframe data might be corrupted by staff members' updates.
d. Repeated downloading might fill up staff members' microcomputers.

279. Criteria to determine how much control to build into an application system should include all of the following **except** the:

a. Importance of the data in the system.
b. Feasibility of using network monitoring software.
c. Level of risk if a specific activity or process is not properly controlled.
d. Efficiency, complexity, and expense of each control technique.

280. An electronics firm has decided to implement a new system through the use of rapid application development techniques. Which of the following would be included in the development of the new system?

a. Deferring the need for system documentation until the final modules are completed.
b. Removing project management responsibilities from the development teams.
c. Creating the system module by module until completed.

d. Using object development techniques to minimize the use of previous code.

281. Minimizing the likelihood of unauthorized editing of production programs, job control language, and operating system software can best be accomplished by

a. Database access reviews.
b. Compliance reviews.
c. Good change-control procedures.
d. Effective network security software.

282. Both users and management approve the initial proposal, design specifications, conversion plan, and testing plan of an information system. This is an example of

a. Implementation controls.
b. Hardware controls.
c. Computer operations controls.
d. Data security controls.

283. Traditional information systems development procedures that ensure proper consideration of controls may not be followed by users developing end-user computing (EUC) applications. Which of the following is a prevalent risk in the development of EUC applications?

a. Management decision making may be impaired due to diminished responsiveness to management's requests for computerized information.
b. Management may be less capable of reacting quickly to competitive pressures due to increased application development time.
c. Management may place the same degree of reliance on reports produced by EUC applications as it does on reports produced under traditional systems development procedures.
d. Management may incur increased application development and maintenance costs for EUC systems, compared to traditional (mainframe) systems.

284. Traditional information systems development and operational procedures typically involve four functional areas. The systems analysis function focuses on identifying and designing systems to satisfy organizational requirements. The programming function is responsible for the design, coding, testing, and debugging of computer programs necessary to implement the systems designed by the analysis function. The computer operations function is responsible for data preparation, program/job execution, and system maintenance. The user function provides the input and receives the output of the system. Which of these four functions is often poorly implemented or improperly omitted in the development of a new end-user computing (EUC) application?

a. Systems analysis function.
b. Programming function.
c. Computer operations function.
d. User function.

285. For traditional systems, change control ensures that the production system was created from the correct version of the authorized programs. Operating in client/server environments has the potential to increase the complexity of change control. One change-control function that is required in client/server environments, but is **not** required in mainframe environments, is to ensure that

a. Program versions are synchronized across the network.
b. Emergency move procedures are documented and followed.
c. Appropriate users are involved in program change testing.
d. Movement from the test library to the production library is controlled.

286. A company often revises its production processes. The changes may entail revisions to processing programs. Ensuring that changes have a minimal impact on processing and result in minimal risk to the system is a function of

a. Security administration.
b. Change control.
c. Problem tracking.
d. Problem-escalation procedures.

287. In spite of management's insistence on following procedures, there have been occasions, usually associated with emergencies, in which a program in the test library was used for the company's operations. A risk of using test library programs in emergency situations is that

a. The personnel preparing the programs may not be authorized to write or modify them.
b. The programs may not be further tested before being placed into production permanently.
c. The integrity of the production library is threatened under such circumstances.
d. Operational personnel may not be fully satisfied with the output of the programs.

288. Object technology provides a new and better way of enabling developers and users to build and tailor applications. In light of this technology, what action should management take with respect to its older (legacy) systems?

a. Plan for rapid migration of legacy systems to object-based applications.
b. Consider the more stable legacy systems as initial candidates for conversion.
c. Investigate the integration of object-based capabilities with legacy systems.
d. Defer the use of object technology until the legacy systems need replacement.

289. Prudent managers will recognize the limits within which expert systems can be effectively applied. An expert system would be most appropriate to

a. Compensate for the lack of certain technical knowledge within the organization.
b. Help make customer-service jobs easier to perform.
c. Automate daily managerial problem solving.
d. Emulate human expertise for strategic planning.

290. For which of the following applications would the use of a fuzzy logic system be the most appropriate artificial intelligence (AI) choice?

a. Assigning airport gates to arriving airline flights.
b. Forecasting demand for spare auto parts.
c. Ventilating expressway tunnels.
d. Diagnosing computer hardware problems.

291. When a new application is being created for widespread use in a large organization, the principal liaison between the information technology (IT) department and the rest of the organization is normally a(n)

a. End user.
b. Application programmer.
c. Maintenance programmer.
d. Systems analyst.

292. Graphical notations that show the flow and transformation of data within a system or business area are called
a. Action diagrams.
b. Program structure charts.
c. Conceptual data models.
d. Data flow diagrams.

293. A systems development approach used to quickly produce a model of user interfaces, user interactions with the system, and process logic is called
a. Neural networking.
b. Prototyping.
c. Reengineering.
d. Focus groups.

294. Methods to minimize the installation of unlicensed microcomputer software include all of the following **except:**
a. Employee awareness programs.
b. Regular audits for unlicensed software.
c. Regular monitoring of network access and start-up scripts.
d. An organizational policy that includes software licensing requirements.

295. Which of the following risks is more likely to be encountered in an end-user computing (EUC) environment as compared to a mainframe computer system?
a. Inability to afford adequate uninterruptible power supply systems.
b. User input screens without a graphical user interface (GUI).
c. Applications that are difficult to integrate with other information systems.
d. Lack of adequate utility programs.

296. Which of the following is **not** a method for implementing a new application system?
a. Direct cutover.
b. Parallel.
c. Pilot.
d. Test.

297. The review process for auditing end-user computing (EUC) controls at the application level involves which of the following?
a. Evaluating EUC administration, policies and procedures, and end-user support.
b. Identifying EUC applications, performing application risk ranking, and documenting and testing controls.
c. Reviewing training, user satisfaction, and data ownership.
d. Evaluating physical security, logical security, backup, and recovery.

298. Change control typically includes procedures for separate libraries for production programs and for test versions of programs. The reason for this practice is to
a. Promote efficiency of system development.
b. Segregate incompatible duties.
c. Facilitate user input on proposed change.
d. Permit unrestricted access to programs.

299. In traditional information systems, computer operators are generally responsible for backing up software and data files on a regular basis. In distributed or cooperative systems, the responsibility for ensuring that adequate backups are taken is the responsibility of
a. User management.
b. Systems programmers.
c. Data entry clerks.
d. Tape librarians.

Items 300 and 301 are based on the following:

Anticipating increasing trading volume, a stock brokerage firm approved the modification of existing programs to permit higher transaction volumes. After the firm used the revised programs, it learned about some unrecorded trades when customers complained about missing confirmations.

300. When program test results were approved, the revised programs were authorized and copied to the production library. This practice is an example of
a. Prototyping.
b. Program integration.
c. System development life cycle.
d. Change control.

301. The most likely failure in the implementation of the revised programs was lack of adequate
a. Desk checking.
b. Change authorization.
c. Volume testing.
d. Feature documentation.

302. With the growth of microcomputers, some organizations are allowing end users to develop their own applications. One of the organizational risks of this policy is
a. That user requirements will not be well met.
b. Reduced control of data.
c. Increased applications backlog.
d. Increased development time.

303. Select the pair of components that would be included in a system's planning and development project for a company's planned decision support system for resource allocations.
a. Physical system design and variance analysis.
b. Procedure development and multiplexing constraints.
c. Feasibility assessment and telematics design.
d. Information requirement analysis and database design.

Items 304 through 306 are based on the following:

Because the backlog for the corporate information technology (IT) development group at a large telephone company was longer than two years, the marketing department proposed to undertake its own development of queries and reporting programs that would access the company's mainframe relational databases. For over a year, the marketing department had been making progressively less accurate predictions about sales demand in its primary markets. The department attributed this to the inability to access current data about customers, sales, service levels, and equipment maintenance histories. Because their predictions were so inaccurate, there were frequent backlogs in production when sales demand was underestimated, which resulted in customers buying service and equipment from other companies. When sales demand was overestimated, there was excess inventory that became obsolete before it could be sold.

304. The marketing analysts became very comfortable using the query language and report writer. It became common for individual analysts to design, write, and finish a report in an hour or less. The marketing manager was generally pleased with this but found that the most complex reports never seemed to be correct. The most likely cause for the errors is inadequate

a. Testing.
b. Change control.
c. Documentation.
d. Access control.

305. After using the mainframe report writer for several months, the marketing analysts gained confidence in using it, but the marketing department manager became concerned. Whenever analysts revised reports they had written earlier, the coding errors kept reappearing in their command sequences. The manager was sure that all the analysts knew what the errors were and how to avoid them. The most likely cause of the reappearance of the same coding errors is inadequate

a. Backups.
b. Change control.
c. Access control.
d. Testing.

306. The director of IT development initially refused the marketing department's request, saying "allowing marketing people to write their own programs could affect our mission-critical applications to the point of crippling the company." This statement reflects the IT director's belief that marketing employees would

a. Be unable to learn to write queries and programs that accessed the mainframe databases.
b. Spend time on programming to the detriment of other aspects of their job performance.
c. Write inefficient programs that would degrade overall system performance.
d. Get access to sensitive information, which might be compromised or misused.

307. The marketing department's proposal was finally accepted, and the marketing employees attended a class in using the mainframe report writer. Soon, the marketing analysts found that it was easier to download the data and manipulate it on their own microcomputers than to perform all the data manipulation with the mainframe report writer directly. One analyst became highly skilled at downloading and wrote downloading command sequences for the other employees. When the analyst left the company for a better job, the department had problems making modifications to these command sequences. The department's problems are most likely due to inadequate

a. Documentation.
b. Data backup.
c. Program testing.
d. Antivirus software.

Items 308 and 309 are based on the following:

A large bank developed a new integrated customer information system to replace formerly separate systems for deposits, credit reporting, and account management. Customer service representatives liked the new system until they discovered that its account management system did not cover all types of accounts. As a result of this flaw, several customers were initially denied loans for which they were actually qualified and threatened to move their business to another bank.

308. The audit involvement that would most likely help the bank to avoid this kind of flaw in future systems is

a. A design review.
b. An application control review.
c. A source code review.
d. An access control review.

309. After the system was changed so the account management functions included all the account types, the customer service representatives noticed that occasionally the consolidated customer profiles had inflated balances. This flaw in the system could have most likely been prevented by better

a. User specifications.
b. Application control reviews.
c. Testing procedures.
d. Software mapping analyses.

310. A computer programmer has altered the payroll program so that, during each payroll processing cycle, the dollar value of the operator's payroll check will be doubled. A control that would detect or prevent this fraud is

a. Control total comparison of the number of time cards submitted and the number of checks generated.
b. Implementation of an authorization and testing procedure for payroll program changes.
c. Distribution of paychecks by the treasurer's office.
d. Computation of a hash total on the field containing the employee's social security number.

311. In reviewing a feasibility study for a major office automation project, an internal auditor should determine if the study

a. Provided a preliminary plan for converting existing manual operations and clerical functions.
b. Considered the cost/benefit of the conversion.
c. Provided management with assurances from independent consultants that the automation was justified.
d. Included an evaluation of internal controls for each planned application.

312. An appropriate internal auditing role in a feasibility study is to

a. Serve on the task force for the preliminary survey.
b. Ascertain if the feasibility study addresses cost-benefit relationships.
c. Determine the requirements for preparing a manual of specifications.
d. Participate in the drafting of recommendations for the computer acquisition and implementation.

313. In an accounts receivable system, the internal auditor discovered that source code and executable modules did not correspond. A control that would decrease the likelihood of this situation is to

a. Require updating of executable modules from compilation of authorized source code.
b. Enforce the use of separate development and production libraries.
c. Require management authorization for source code changes.
d. Install access control procedures for source code libraries.

314. In the context of a traditional system development life cycle, database design occurs during
a. Detailed analysis and design.
b. Conversion and implementation.
c. Information requirements analysis.
d. Program and procedure development.

315. The practice of maintaining a test program library separate from the production program library is an example of a(n)
a. Organizational control.
b. Physical security.
c. Input control.
d. Concurrency control.

316. It is not uncommon to find newly designed information systems that fail to meet user requirements. A control over system design to prevent this problem is
a. Project planning.
b. User involvement.
c. Structured programming.
d. System development life cycle.

317. An internal auditor is a member of a study group, which is evaluating the potential purchase of an optical disk storage unit. Which of the following is a key consideration in evaluating the proper use of peripheral devices such as an optical disk storage unit?
a. Use of hardware performance monitors.
b. Use of software performance monitors.
c. Direct observation of operating performance.
d. Vendor-supplied performance standards.

318. An internal auditor is reviewing a feasibility study for a new demand deposit application. One of the auditor's objectives will be to evaluate
a. Internal schema.
b. Program correctness.
c. Operational feasibility.
d. Detailed process design.

319. A convenience store chain is developing a new integrated sales and inventory system for its stores. Which of the following implementation techniques would involve the most risk?
a. A complete cutover.
b. Phased implementation.
c. Parallel running.
d. A pilot test.

320. A large savings and loan association plans to develop a computer system to allow depositors to pay regular bills (such as phone, utility and credit cards) by phone. The best approach to guide the development of this system would be
a. PERT.
b. Prototyping.
c. Feasibility study.
d. System development life cycle.

Voice Communications

321. Attacks against wireless technologies include which of the following?
a. Spamming and loss of availability.
b. Spoofing and loss of integrity.
c. Eavesdropping and loss of confidentiality.
d. Cracking and loss of authenticity.

322. Which of the following merit protection in the use of wireless technologies?

I. Privacy of location.
II. Privacy of equipment.
III. Privacy of transmission contents.
IV. Privacy of third parties.

a. I and II.
b. I and III.
c. III and IV.
d. II and III.

323. Which of the following is inherently less secured in the use of wireless technologies?
a. Digital formats.
b. Analog formats.
c. Error detecting protocols.
d. Error correcting protocols.

324. Which of the following are more efficient and secure for use in wireless technologies?
a. Spread spectrum.
b. Radio spectrum.
c. Radio signals.
d. Radio carriers.

325. Which of the following is inherently efficient and difficult to intercept in the use of wireless technologies?
a. Code division multiple access, CDMA.
b. Time division multiple access, TDMA.
c. Public switched telephone network, PSTN.
d. Very small aperture terminal, VSAT.

326. Voice encryption uses which of the following algorithms?
a. RSA.
b. 3DES.
c. IDEA.
d. DES.

327. Which of the following is illegal in the US regarding wireless technologies?
a. When a scanner is purchased regardless of its use.
b. When the electronic serial number altering software is purchased.
c. When the electronic serial number altering software is sold.
d. When a scanner is used with intent to defraud.

328. Which of the following is illegal in the US regarding wireless technologies?

I. Phone cloning.
II. Fraudulent billing.
III. Fraudulent roaming.
IV. Call selling.

a. I and II.
b. I and IV.
c. II and III.
d. III and IV.

329. Which of the following is **not** an effective control against telephone cloning?
a. Digital encoding.
b. Electronic signatures.
c. Call screening system.
d. Digital technologies.

330. Which of the following is the true purpose of "ping" in wireless technologies?

a. The pinging tells the filters on the network.
b. The pinging tells the frequencies of the network.
c. The pinging tells the location of a phone user.
d. The pinging tells the troubles on the network.

331. Which of the following can prevent telephone tumbling attacks?

a. Call screening system.
b. Call pattern recognition software.
c. Precall validation system.
d. Postcall validation system.

332. Analog cellular phone systems are prone to which of the following attacks?

a. Tumbling attacks.
b. Cloning attacks.
c. Pinging attacks.
d. Pirating attacks.

333. A technique used to perpetrate wireless fraud is which of the following?

a. Scaling.
b. Roaming.
c. Cloning.
d. Browsing.

Contingency Planning

334. Contingency planning alternatives can vary by computer processing environment. A company is **least** likely to use a reciprocal processing agreement for

a. Small systems.
b. Large batch operations.
c. Online teleprocessing facilities.
d. Small batch operations.

335. Contingency plans for IT operations should include appropriate backup agreements. Which of the following arrangements would be considered too vendor-dependent when vital operations require almost immediate availability of computer resources?

a. A "hot site" arrangement.
b. A "cold site" arrangement.
c. A "cold and hot site" combination arrangement.
d. Using excess capacity at another data center within the organization.

336. Which of the following best describes the **primary** reason that organizations develop contingency plans for their IT operations?

a. To ensure that they will be able to process vital transactions in the event of any type of disaster.
b. To ensure the safety of important records.
c. To help hold down the cost of insurance.
d. To plan for sources of capital for recovery from any type of disaster.

337. Greater reliance of management on information systems increases the exposure to

a. Unauthorized third-party access to systems.
b. Systematic programming errors.
c. Inadequate knowledge bases.
d. Business interruption.

338. An essential element of a disaster-recovery plan is a statement of the

a. System development standards for the organization.
b. History of modifications to the operating system.
c. Applications planned for new development.
d. Responsibilities of each organizational unit.

339. Because of a power surge, a read/write head damaged the surface of the disk volume containing the savings account master file used by an online savings account update and inquiry program. At the time of the failure, there were 20 active teller terminals connected to the program. The disk damage was the only physical damage resulting from the power fluctuation. Possible recovery steps are

1. Restart the online update and inquiry program.
2. Restore the savings account master file from the good records on the original disk.
3. Restore the savings account master file from the most recent file backup.
4. Display each teller's last transaction and prompt each teller to reenter any subsequent transactions.
5. Apply transactions occurring since the last complete file backup to the master file.
6. Prompt tellers to reenter their last transaction.

The best recovery procedure comprises which of the following sequence of steps?

a. 2,5,1,6
b. 2,5,1,4
c. 3,5,1,4
d. 3,5,1,6

340. In one company, the application systems must be in service 24 hours a day. The company's senior management and information systems management have worked hard to ensure that the information systems recovery plan supports the business disaster recovery plan. A crucial aspect of recovery planning for the company is ensuring that

a. Organizational and operational changes are reflected in the recovery plans.
b. Changes to systems are tested thoroughly before being placed into production.
c. Management personnel can fill in for operations staff should the need arise.
d. Capacity planning procedures accurately predict workload changes.

341. Which of the following is necessary to determine what would constitute a disaster for an organization?

a. Risk analysis.
b. File and equipment backup requirements analysis.
c. Vendor supply agreement analysis.
d. Contingent facility contract analysis.

342. Some companies have been the target of terrorist attacks in recent years. The **best** approach to avoid having a data center be selected as a terrorist's target is to

a. Ensure that the disaster recovery plans are fully tested.
b. Harden the electrical and communications systems against attack.
c. Maintain as low a profile as possible for the data center.
d. Monitor the locations and activities of known terrorists.

343. A company's management is aware that it cannot foresee every contingency even with the best planning. Management believes, however, that a more thorough recovery plan increases the ability to resume operations quickly after an interruption and thus to

a. Maintain the same level of employment.
b. Minimize the cost of facility repair.
c. Fulfill its obligations to customers.
d. Receive the maximum benefit from planning.

Items 344 and 345 are based on the following:

In the annual review of the data center of a nationwide mortgage servicing company, the internal audit manager was concerned about the data center not having an adequate contingency plan. The audit manager was especially concerned because the data center was located close to a river that occasionally flooded and in the vicinity of a major railroad and a major highway.

344. Even though floodwaters might not reach the data center, being located adjacent to a river is associated with the risk that in the event of a significant flood

a. Customers might refuse to do business with the company.
b. Expensive equipment might need to be replaced.
c. Employees might be unable to report for work.
d. Many customers might fail to make timely payments.

345. Management acted on the internal auditor's recommendation to prepare a contingency plan. The most critical aspect of the plan would be to provide for

a. Monitoring for fraud or abuse during recovery.
b. Continuation of mortgage servicing.
c. Security and control over information assets.
d. Minimizing expenses during recovery periods.

346. A number of disasters have occurred around the globe in recent years. In response to the potential for a devastating impact on their organizations, internal auditors should encourage management to develop a crisis management program. Identify the first stage in the development of a crisis management program.

a. Formulate contingency plans.
b. Conduct a risk analysis.
c. Create a crisis management team.
d. Practice the response to a crisis.

Items 347 through 349 are based on the following:

An automobile and personal property insurer has decentralized its information processing to the extent that headquarters has less processing capacity than any of its regional processing centers. These centers are responsible for initiating policies, communicating with policyholders, and adjusting claims. The company uses leased lines from a national telecommunications company. Initially, the company thought there would be little need for interregion communication, but that has not been the case. The company underestimated the number of customers that would move between regions and the number of customers with claims arising from accidents outside their regions. The company has a regional center in an earthquake-prone area and is planning how to continue processing if that center, or any other single center, were unable to perform its processing.

347. The company has considered several alternatives for replacing the hardware required for a regional center's processing. An advantage of using a third-party cold site is that

a. Personnel employed at the site would be familiar with company operations.
b. Travel expenses would be minimized for company personnel.
c. No additional equipment would be required at the regional centers.
d. The replacement site could be up and running in a few hours.

348. Unfortunately, the company has not revised its contingency plan since the time when its data processing was mostly centralized at headquarters. The existing plan is likely to be out of date because of

a. Changes in equipment, data, and software.
b. Inadequate processing capability at headquarters.
c. Lack of arrangements for a backup site for headquarters.
d. Personnel turnover at regional centers.

349. The company considered mirroring the data stored at each regional center at another center. A disadvantage of such an arrangement would be

a. Lack of awareness at headquarters of the state of processing.
b. Increased cost and complexity of network traffic.
c. Interference of the mirrored data with original source data.
d. Confusion on the part of insurance agents about where customer data are stored.

Items 350 and 351 are based on the following:

Many organizations are critically dependent on information systems to support daily business operations. Consequently, an organization may incur significant loss of revenues or incur significant expenses if a disaster such as a hurricane or power outage causes information systems processing to be delayed or interrupted. A bank, for example, may incur significant penalties as a result of missed payments.

350. Which of the following management activities is essential to ensure continuity of operations in the event a disaster or catastrophe impairs information systems processing?

a. Review of insurance coverage.
b. Electronic vaulting.
c. Change control procedures.
d. Contingency planning.

351. Which of the following activities is necessary to determine what would constitute a disaster for an organization?

a. Risk analysis.
b. File and equipment backup requirements analysis.
c. Vendor supply agreement analysis.
d. Contingent facility contract analysis.

352. A large property insurance company has regional centers that customers call to report claims. Although the regional centers are not located in areas known to be prone to natural disasters, the company needs a disaster recovery plan that would restore call answering capacity in the event of a disaster or other extended loss of service. The best plan for restoring capacity in the event of a disaster would be to reroute call traffic to

a. A cold site that duplicates regional facilities.
b. A hot site that duplicates regional facilities.
c. A third-party service center.
d. Nonaffected regional centers.

353. The system requiring the most extensive backup and recovery procedures is

a. A batch system for payroll processing.
b. A database management system for online order entry.
c. A file-oriented system for billing clients.
d. An index sequential access method file system for inventory and materials request planning.

354. A firm was running the payroll program when a temporary power outage occurred. When power resumed, it was discovered that the computer had terminated the payroll program's processing. Which of the following would best ensure continuity of operations?

a. A system to copy the master files and associated transaction files.
b. A facility for restarting at an intermediate stage of processing.
c. A review of the console log.
d. A formal procedure to transfer processing to another location.

355. The best evidence that contingency planning is effective is to have

a. No processing interruptions during the past year.
b. Comprehensive documentation of the plan.
c. Signoff on the plan by the internal audit activity.
d. Successful testing of the plan.

356. A company's management has expressed concern over the varied system architectures that the organization uses. Potential security and control concerns would include all of the following **except:**

a. Users may have different user ID codes and passwords to remember for the several systems that they use.
b. There are difficulties in developing uniform security standards for the various platforms.
c. Backup file storage administration is often decentralized.
d. Having data distributed across many computers throughout the organization increases the risk that a single disaster would destroy large portions of the organization's data.

357. A review of the system activity log kept by the operating system would reveal which of the following problems in the processing of the inventory?

a. In recording the transaction, an inventory purchase was inadvertently recorded as an inventory usage.
b. The dollar amount of an inventory purchase transaction had two of the digits transposed.
c. The inventory master file, which is scheduled to be updated every Friday, was updated on Sunday.
d. An inventory purchase was recorded twice on the transaction file to be used in updating the master file.

358. A total interruption of processing throughout a distributed information technology system can be minimized through the use of

a. Exception reporting.
b. Fail-soft protection.
c. Backup and recovery.
d. Data file security.

Systems Security

359. Which of the following are examples of security boundary controls?

a. Patches and probes.
b. Fences and firewalls.
c. Tags and labels.
d. Encryption and smart cards.

360. Which of the following **cannot** defend login spoofing?

a. Providing a secure channel between the user and the system.
b. Installing hardware reset button.
c. Implementing cryptographic authentication techniques.
d. Installing input overflow checks.

361. Both session hijacking and eavesdropping attacks can be prevented by which of the following?

a. SET.
b. PPP.
c. MIM.
d. SSL.

362. Many of the vulnerabilities in firewalls are due to which of the following reasons?

a. Incomplete firewall rules or network traffic rules.
b. Misconfigured firewalls or a lack of administrative monitoring.
c. Incorrect source IP addresses or destination IP addresses.
d. Misconfigured target ports or target addresses.

363. Which one of the following firewalls is simple, inexpensive, and quick to implement?

a. Static packet filter firewall.
b. Dynamic packet filter firewall.
c. Application gateway firewall.
d. Stateful inspection gateway firewall.

364. Which of the following firewalls is **most** secure?

a. Packet filtering firewall.
b. Screened subnet firewall.
c. Screened host firewall.
d. Dual-homed gateway firewall.

365. Who should **not** be given access to firewalls?

a. Primary firewall administrator.
b. Functional users.
c. Backup firewall administrator.
d. Network service manager.

366. The screened subnet firewall acts as which of the following?

a. A fast packet network.
b. A digital network.
c. A perimeter network.
d. A broadband network.

367. Which of the following provides a security service in authenticating a remote network access?

a. Remote access server.
b. Windows NT server.
c. An exchange server.
d. A DNS server.

368. Market research personnel for a manufacturer frequently access computer data on customer and product sales. Password protection for these users would be

a. Inappropriate.
b. Use of a market research department password.
c. Use of individual passwords.
d. Use of individual user passwords plus separate access passwords for customer data and product data.

369. The capability for computers to communicate with physically remote terminals is an important feature in the design of modern business information systems. Which of the following risks associated with the use of telecommunications systems is minimized through the use of a password control system?

a. Unauthorized access to system program and data files.
b. Unauthorized physical availability of remote terminals.
c. Physical destruction of system program and data files.
d. Physical destruction of remote terminals.

370. A company has recently installed new accounts payable system, which is personal computer (PC)-based. Six PCs are networked and have access to the mainframe accounts payable database system. After signing on to the system, a portion of the database can be downloaded to the network user. The data entry and edit programs are resident on the network and can be downloaded to individual PCs for execution. Which of the following controls would be appropriate to ensure that accounts payable information is not removed from the system without approval?

a. Password validation at sign-on to the system.
b. Data encryption should be utilized at the PC level.
c. Data file access control software installed on both the network and the mainframe.
d. Key locks be utilized on the PCs.

371. Which of the following security controls would best prevent unauthorized access to sensitive data through an unattended data terminal directly connected to a mainframe?

a. Use of a screen saver with a password.
b. Use of workstation scripts.
c. Encryption of data files.
d. Automatic log-off of inactive users.

372. The information systems director is concerned that someone might be able to enter fictitious orders from store terminals. Of the following, the best control for minimizing the likelihood of such an occurrence is to

a. Encrypt outward bound transmissions from the stores.
b. Require change control procedures for programs.
c. Enforce password control procedures for users.
d. Encourage employees to report suspicious activity.

373. The information systems and audit directors also agreed that maintaining the integrity of the system that kept inventory data was crucial for distributing correct product quantities to stores. The best way to ensure the integrity of this application software is through

a. Access controls for terminals in the receiving department.
b. Audit trails for items sold and received.
c. Change controls for inventory software.
d. Monitoring software for the network.

374. To increase the security of application software, the internal audit director recommended that programmers be given diskless workstations. Using diskless workstations would increase security by

a. Making theft of programs more difficult.
b. Reducing workstation maintenance expense.
c. Imposing a stricter level of access control.
d. Prompting programmers to work more closely together.

375. Which of the following is an objective of logical security controls for information systems?

a. To ensure complete and accurate recording of data.
b. To ensure complete and accurate processing of data.
c. To restrict access to specific data and resources.
d. To provide an audit trail of the results of processing.

376. Which of the following audit tests should be performed by an internal auditor who is reviewing controls over user authentication procedures?

a. Verify password masking at data terminals.
b. Review how proper separation of duties is established using access control software.
c. Review procedures concerning revocation of inactive users.
d. All of the above.

377. Identify a control that could cost-effectively minimize unauthorized use of a home banking system.

a. Automatic dial-back.
b. Message sequencing.
c. Encryption.
d. Dedicated lines.

378. Although dial-in lines with a callback feature are less vulnerable than dial-in lines without a callback feature, a weakness of callbacks on dial-in lines is the

a. Absence of logging of attempted sign-ons.
b. Inability to disconnect after invalid access attempts.
c. Existence of call-forwarding devices.
d. Required display of user codes and passwords.

379. A dial-up order entry system is used by salespeople to enter customer orders from the customers' locations via portable computers assigned to each salesperson. Unauthorized persons, using their own equipment, have entered fraudulent transactions into the order entry system. A control that would permit only authorized persons using portable computers to access the system is

a. A callback procedure.
b. An error-correcting code.
c. Frequent access code revalidation.
d. Modem equalization.

380. Biometric authentication systems are automated methods of verifying or recognizing the identity of a person based on physiological or behavioral characteristics. Which of the following might be used in a biometric system to authenticate a user?

a. PIN code.
b. Password.
c. Employee badge.
d. Voice.

381. Which of the following is an important senior management responsibility with regard to information systems security?

a. Assessment of exposures.
b. Assignment of access privileges.
c. Determining ownership of data.
d. Training employees in security matters.

382. Which of the following would normally be the functions of security software?
a. Authenticates user identification and controls access to information resources.
b. Logs the activity of the computer system including the time each program is started and when each file is accessed.
c. Displays the data typed into a terminal keyboard.
d. Records and monitors changes to program source code and object code files.

383. The primary objective of security software is to
a. Control access to information system resources.
b. Restrict access to prevent installation of unauthorized utility software.
c. Detect the presence of viruses.
d. Monitor the separation of duties within applications.

384. Because log-on procedures may be cumbersome and tedious, users often store log-on sequences on their personal computers and invoke them when they want to use mainframe facilities. A risk of this practice is that
a. Sensitive data on the personal computers would be more vulnerable to exposure.
b. Anyone with access to the personal computers could log-on to the mainframe.
c. Backup procedures for data files would not be as effective.
d. Users with inadequate training would make more mistakes.

385. To gain access to a bank's online customer systems, users must validate themselves with a user identification code and password. The purpose of this procedure is to provide
a. Data security.
b. Physical security.
c. Context-dependent security.
d. Write-protection security.

386. The data security administrator is responsible for
a. Planning and managing overall needs for data resources.
b. Ensuring the integrity of data in a shared data environment.
c. Determining and monitoring controls over access to data.
d. Making data available to users when and where it is needed.

387. A company has a dial-up facility allowing the employees to gain access to the computer when they are not on the premises. The most effective way to prevent unauthorized access to the computer is to use
a. Callback.
b. Modem.
c. Echo check.
d. Console log.

388. The increased presence of the microcomputer in the workplace has resulted in an increasing number of persons having access to the computer. A control that is often used to prevent unauthorized access to sensitive programs is
a. Backup copies of the diskettes.
b. Passwords for each of the users.
c. Disaster recovery procedures.
d. Record counts of the number of input transactions in a batch being processed.

389. A five-member personnel department shares one computer terminal. To maintain computerized employee records, the list of employees has been divided alphabetically among the five members of the department. Minimum password protection for computer access should be provided at the level of
a. Terminal access.
b. File retrieval.
c. File editing.
d. System access.

390. All administrative and professional staff in a corporate legal department prepares documents on terminals connected to a host LAN file server. The best control over unauthorized access to sensitive documents in the system is
a. Required entry of passwords for access to the system.
b. Physical security for all disks containing document files.
c. Periodic server backup and storage in a secure area.
d. Required entry of passwords for access to individual documents.

391. Securing client/server systems is a complex task because of all of the following factors **except:**
a. The use of relational databases.
b. The number of access points.
c. Concurrent operation of multiple user sessions.
d. Widespread data access and update capabilities.

392. Unauthorized alteration of online records can be prevented by employing
a. Key verification.
b. Computer sequence checks.
c. Computer matching.
d. Database access controls.

393. A password is an example of
a. A physical control.
b. An edit control.
c. A digital control.
d. An access control.

394. Computer program libraries can best be kept secure by
a. Installing a logging system for program access.
b. Monitoring physical access to program library media.
c. Restricting physical and logical access.
d. Denying access from remote terminals.

395. Which of the following database controls would be **most** effective in maintaining a segregation of duties appropriate to the users' reporting structure within an organization?
a. Access security features.
b. Software change control procedures.
c. Dependency checks.
d. Backup and recovery procedures.

396. After a security review, a company determined that all employees in the bid preparation department should have access to common data such as current costs but that access to data pertaining to specific bids should be restricted to employees working only on that bid. The company keeps all bid-related data together in an integrated database. To enable selective access to bid data, the company needs data security software that restricts access to records based on

a. The type of resource.
b. Statistical summaries.
c. The age of the records.
d. Data item contents.

397. When a sign-maker's business was small, there were only three employees in information systems (IS), and all of them had access to the development and production libraries, which facilitated getting systems implemented quickly. IS has 10 employees now but is still operating as before. The IS manager senses that the unrestricted access creates the risk of untested programs being installed in the production library. Which one of the following password controls would protect the libraries, yet still permit some of the efficiencies of open access?

a. Restrict updating to one position but permit read access to source code for everyone in IS.
b. Permit updating for everyone in IS but restrict read access to source code to one position.
c. Restrict updating and read access to one position.
d. Permit updating and read access for everyone in IS.

398. A clerk in a retailer's buying department watched a merchandise buyer use the online purchasing system and subsequently accessed the same system with the clerk's user number to read confidential sales forecasts. The clerk sold the information to a competitor, who preempted the retailer's sales. The best control for preventing such occurrences is

a. Ensuring that the database design is relational.
b. Restricting access to authorized individuals.
c. Requiring before and after images of transactions.
d. Reconciling monetary totals for input sessions.

399. Data access security related to applications may be enforced through all the following **except:**

a. User identification and authentication functions incorporated in the application.
b. Utility software functions.
c. User identification and authentication functions in access control software.
d. Security functions provided by a database management system.

400. Microcomputers with software to access corporate databases were installed for all production supervisors, one of whom sold sensitive pricing information to a competitor. The best preventive control for such situations is to ensure that

a. Program change procedures are established and enforced.
b. Passwords are required to validate user identification numbers.
c. Data ownership resides with the most appropriate users.
d. Access privileges are established on a need-to-know basis.

401. Which of the following is most likely to increase the risk of unauthorized user access?

a. Growth in end-user development.
b. Competitive pressures for enhanced functions in systems.
c. Greater online access to information systems.
d. Growing organizational reliance on information systems.

402. A new accounts receivable clerk, working for a wholesaler, noticed that a customer had apparently changed addresses. The clerk accessed the customer's computer file and revised all addresses. One week later the customer complained that goods were being sent to the wrong address. The primary control to prevent this occurrence is

a. Policy dissemination.
b. Training on data entry.
c. Communication from the customer.
d. Database security.

403. Passwords are often components of control systems over IT facilities. A password is an example of

a. Physical control.
b. Edit control.
c. Digital control.
d. Access control.

Items 404 and 405 are based on the following:

A company distributes revenues from various theatrical productions to the different investors after deduction of certain management and development expenses. The company also retains its interest in production profits. Income is distributed according to a master agreement signed by all parties and maintained for each production. A unique number is assigned to each agreement. After the investment clerk enters master agreement information into the master file, the clerk verifies a report of the update. Ownership percentages must total 100 percent in order to pass the input edit. Owners not already active in the customer/vendor master file will be rejected. Updates to the ownership master file are reported to all affected owners. Master file passwords are permanently assigned. Income distribution checks are produced automatically each month by the system. When the customer/vendor clerk is on vacation, the general accounting clerk fills in.

404. Which of the following procedures associated with the distribution of income requires improvement?

a. Master agreement identification.
b. Input proofing.
c. Ownership percentage edits.
d. Customer/vendor edit.

405. Which of the following is most likely to result in unauthorized transactions?

a. General accounting clerk filling in for customer/vendor clerk.
b. Updates to the ownership master reported to all affected owners.
c. Master file passwords permanently assigned.
d. Income checks produced automatically by the system.

406. An equipment manufacturer maintains dial-up ports into its order entry system for the convenience of its customers worldwide so they may order parts, as they need them. The manufacturer promises 48-hour delivery anywhere in the world for 95% of these parts orders. Due to the cost and sensitive nature of certain electronic parts, the manufacturer needs to maintain secure access to its order entry system. The best technique for monitoring the security of access is

a. Integrated test facility for the order entry system.
b. Tracing of transactions through the order entry system.
c. Transaction selection of order entry transactions.
d. Logging of unsuccessful access attempts.

407. A bank employee had access to automated teller machines (ATMs) account codes and obtained personal identification number (PINs) by looking over the shoulders of the bank's ATM customers. With this information, the employee created fraudulent ATM cards with a machine that wrote the cards' magnetic strips. The bank's ATMs detected the fraudulent cards, and the bank was able to catch the person in the act of using a fraudulent card. The control strength in the bank's system that was most responsible for stopping this unauthorized access was

a. Strict control over bank customers' account codes and PINs.
b. Transaction validation of cards to detect fraudulent ATM cards.
c. Restriction of bank employee exposure to knowledge of ATM operation.
d. Control over access to machines that write magnetic strips on cards.

408. Bank tellers and their supervisors sign on to an online deposit system with their employee numbers, which are readily available to all tellers. The bank wants to prevent teller access to certain approval functions, such as withdrawals over a specified dollar limit. The best control for implementing this restriction would be

a. Tagging.
b. Callback.
c. Passwords.
d. Logs.

409. An audit of the electronic data interchange (EDI) area of a banking group revealed the facts listed below. Which one indicates the need for improved internal control?

a. Employees may only access the computer system via an ID and an encrypted password.
b. The system employs message sequencing as a way to monitor data transmissions.
c. Certain types of transactions may only be made at specific terminals.
d. Branch office employees may access the mainframe with a single call via modem.

410. Which of the following statements is most accurate regarding the data security of an online computer system protected by an internal user-to-data access control program?

a. Access to data is controlled by restricting specific applications to specific files.
b. Access to data is controlled by restricting specific terminals to specific applications.
c. Security will be dependent upon the controls over the issuance of user IDs and user authentication.
d. The use of this type of access control software will eliminate any significant control weaknesses.

411. Which of the following database controls would be most effective in maintaining a segregation of duties appropriate to the users' reporting structure within an organization?

a. Access security features.
b. Software change control procedures.
c. Dependency checks.
d. Backup and recovery procedures.

412. Because much of the data involved in daily operations would be helpful to competitors if they had access to it, a company authorizes access for employees to only the data required for accomplishing their jobs. This approach is known as access on a(n)

a. Need-to-know basis.
b. Individual accountability basis.
c. Just-in-time basis.
d. Management-by-exception basis.

413. A company is very conscious of the sensitive nature of company information. Because company data are valuable, the most important thing that the security administrator should monitor is

a. Multiple access to data by data owners.
b. Management authorization of modified access.
c. Access to operational data by privileged users.
d. Data owner specification of access privileges.

Databases

414. Which of the following is **not** true? Relational databases

a. Are flexible and useful for unplanned, ad hoc queries.
b. Store data in table form.
c. Use trees to store data in a hierarchical structure.
d. Are maintained on direct access devices.

415. The ability to add or update documentation items in data dictionaries should be restricted to

a. Database administrators.
b. System programmers.
c. System librarians.
d. Application programmers.

416. Database management systems are categorized by the data structures they support. Which of the following data structures treats data like a series of tables?

a. Network.
b. Hierarchical.
c. Relational.
d. Indexed sequential.

417. Enabling users to have different views of the same data is a function of

a. The operating system.
b. A program library management system.
c. The database management system.
d. A utility program.

418. The function of a data dictionary is to

a. Mark the boundary between two consecutive transactions.
b. Organize and share information about objects and resources.
c. Specify system users.
d. Specify privileges and security rules for objects and resources.

419. Planning for and controlling the data used throughout the enterprise and throughout the data resource life cycle is

a. Enterprise modeling.
b. Data administration.
c. Conceptual modeling.
d. Database administration.

Items 420 and 421 are based on the following:

An online database management system for sales and receivables was recently expanded to include credit approval transactions. An evaluation of controls was not performed prior to implementation.

420. If certain data elements were not defined in the expansion, the following problem could result:
a. Unlimited access to data and transactions.
b. Incomplete transaction processing.
c. Unauthorized program execution.
d. Manipulation of the database contents by an application program.

421. To prevent unauthorized access to specific data elements, the database management system should contain which of the following controls?
a. Sign-on verification security at the physical terminals.
b. Password specifications for each data file or element.
c. Periodic tests of the system using production databases.
d. Terminal security used in lieu of passwords for each data element or file.

422. A work in process data model for a manufacturer shows that quantities of raw materials and labor hours are related to job order numbers and that raw materials and labor hours are related to their costs. This data model is a
a. Decision model.
b. Database model.
c. Logical model.
d. Physical model.

423. The update response time for the Accounts Payable System has recently increased from three seconds to twenty seconds. The system utilizes a relational database (RDBMS) and has interactive update and reporting. Which of the following is the most likely cause of the degradation in response time?
a. Excess tablespace for the RDBMS.
b. Large input/output buffers for the RDBMS.
c. Interactive queries that read the entire RDBMS.
d. Large decrease in the number of interactive users.

424. In a database, there are often conditions that constrain database records. For example, a sales order cannot exist unless the corresponding customer exists. This kind of constraint is an example of
a. Normalization.
b. Entity integrity.
c. Internal schema.
d. Referential integrity.

425. A database has three record types: (1) for suppliers, which contains a unique supplier number, a supplier name, and a supplier address; (2) for parts, which contains a unique part number, a part name, a description, and a location; and (3) for purchases, which contains a unique supplier number, which references the supplier number in the supplier record, a part number, which references the part number in the part record, and a quantity. This database has a
a. Single flat file structure.
b. Hierarchical structure.
c. Relational structure.
d. Network structure.

426. An important function of a database administrator is
a. Reviewing database output for errors and omissions.
b. Scheduling daily database operations.
c. Redefining and restructuring the database.
d. Evaluating internal controls for hardware.

427. Of the following, the greatest advantage of database architecture is
a. Data redundancy can be reduced.
b. Conversion to a database management system is inexpensive and can be accomplished quickly.
c. Multiple occurrences of data items are useful for consistency checking.
d. Backup and recovery procedures are minimized.

428. The term schema is used in the literature on database systems to denote a view or model of data. Three major schemas are the external schema, the conceptual schema, and the internal schema. Which of the following is a unique feature of the internal schema?
a. It describes the user's view of a part of the database.
b. It describes the user's model of data, which is needed.
c. It describes the way data is physically stored in the database.
d. It describes the overall logical view of the database.

429. In preparing to audit an electronics wholesaler, the auditor learns that all ordering, purchasing and inventory records are contained in and administered by a single, integrated software package which is also used to generate regular management reports as well as ad hoc reports. This software package is best characterized as a(n)
a. Management information system.
b. Decision support system.
c. Artificial intelligence system.
d. Database management system.

430. A data model is an abstract representation of data, which is used to describe the way data items are organized and related. Which of the following is the distinction between logical and physical models of data?
a. Logical models of data are concerned with the physical storage of data.
b. Logical models of data are concerned with the entities for which data is collected.
c. Logical models of data are practical rather than conceptual in nature.
d. Logical models of data are user-oriented ways of describing data.

431. Occasionally, a database user may send an incorrect update to the database. "Undoing" the update is difficult because the old data has been replaced by the new, incorrect data. The feature of a system that would allow the user to "undo" the mistake is classified as error
a. Prevention.
b. Detection.
c. Correction.
d. Recovery.

432. An advantage of a data dictionary is that its use
a. Facilitates complete identification of instances of use of data items.
b. Ensures that all descriptive names and meanings are consistent.
c. Encourages the appropriate level of normalization of data models.
d. Eliminates the need for conceptual modeling in database design.

433. A logical view of an entire database is a
a. Hierarchy.

b. Network.
c. Schema.
d. Subschema.

434. A professor needs to monitor students in each class. Information needed includes the student's major, address, telephone number, and grades on various assignments. A view of how all this data relates and how it can be used is called a
a. Physical data model.
b. Rational data model.
c. Logical data model.
d. Sequential data model.

435. In a database system, locking of data helps preserve data integrity by permitting transactions to have control of all the data needed to complete the transactions. However, implementing a locking procedure could lead to
a. Inconsistent processing.
b. Rollback failures.
c. Unrecoverable transactions.
d. Deadly embraces (retrieval contention).

436. All of the following are methods for distributing a relational database across multiple servers **except:**
a. Snapshot (making a copy of the database for distribution).
b. Replication (creating and maintaining replica copies at multiple locations).
c. Normalization (separating the database into logical tables for easier user processing).
d. Fragmentation (separating the database into parts and distributing where they are needed).

437. To properly control access to accounting database files, the database administrator should ensure that database system features are in place to permit
a. Read-only access to the database files.
b. Updating from privileged utilities.
c. Access only to authorized logical views.
d. User updates to his/her access profiles.

438. Users making database queries often need to combine several tables to get the information they want. One approach to combining tables is known as
a. Mail merge.
b. Joining.
c. Projecting.
d. Pointing.

439. One of the benefits of a single integrated information system is
a. Closer program-data linkage.
b. Increased data redundancy.
c. Reduced security.
d. Increased data accessibility.

440. Which of the following best describes what is contained in a data dictionary?
a. An organized description of the data items stored in a database and their meaning.
b. A description of record layouts used by application programs.
c. A description of the privileges and security rules governing database users.
d. Before and after images of updated records in a database.

441. An overall description of a database, including the names of data elements, their characteristics, and their relationship to each other would be defined by using a
a. Data definition language.
b. Data control language.
c. Data manipulation language.
d. Data command interpreter language.

442. The data security administrator is responsible for
a. Planning and managing overall needs for data resources.
b. Ensuring the integrity of data in a shared data environment.
c. Determining and monitoring controls over access to data.
d. Making data available to users when and where it is needed.

Items 443 through 450 are based on the following:

Five brand managers in a consumer food products company met regularly to figure out what price points were being lowered by their competitors and how well coupon promotions did. The data they needed to analyze consisted of about 50 gigabytes of daily point-of-sale (POS) data from major grocery chains for each month. The brand managers are competent users of spreadsheet and database software on microcomputers. They considered several alternative software options to access and manipulate data to answer their questions.

443. The selected option is unlikely to use a hierarchical database system because
a. A hierarchical database system requires multiple joins.
b. Programming queries for it are too costly and time consuming.
c. Point-of-sale data are too sensitive for routine access.
d. Summarization of point-of-sale data would not answer the questions.

444. The limiting factor in the brand managers' use of a relational database system to answer their ad hoc questions would be
a. Understanding what individual data records represent.
b. Obtaining computer resources for complicated queries.
c. Distinguishing primary and foreign keys in the data.
d. Lack of management interest in using the results.

445. The brand managers tried to import the point-of-sale (POS) data into microcomputer spreadsheets for analysis. Their efforts were unsuccessful, most likely because of
a. The complexity of the mainframe data structure and the large volume of data.
b. The difficulty of establishing access privileges for each subset of the mainframe data.
c. Inconsistencies in the mainframe data due to lack of integrity constraints on the data files.
d. Error-prone transmission links for downloading the data from the mainframe data files.

446. The organization's senior management was pleased that its brand managers were taking the initiative to use sales data creatively. The information systems director, however, was concerned that the brand managers might be creating standard queries that would provide erroneous results for decision making. The best approach for ensuring the correctness of the brand managers' queries is

a. A source code review of the queries.
b. A code comparison audit.
c. A transaction retrieval and analysis.
d. An input/output analysis.

447. After abandoning spreadsheets as their analysis tool, the brand managers were successful in downloading limited subsets of the point-of-sale (POS) and using the data to populate relational database files on their microcomputers. They could then access the data using a relational query language. One of the downloaded files contained actual sales by product by store, and another contained projected sales by product by store. In order to compare actual and projected sales by product by store, a query would have to include

a. Projecting the two tables on product and store identification codes.
b. Projecting the two tables on product identification codes.
c. Joining the two tables on product and store identification codes.
d. Joining the two tables on product identification codes.

448. Eventually, the brand managers chose a data analysis tool and report writer that permitted multidimensional views of the data. The tool could support different views, such as actual versus projected sales by region, actual versus projected sales by product, and projected sales by product and by region. In order to see the data in such views, the brand managers would need to specify

a. A protocol for data transmission.
b. Access privileges by user number.
c. Integrity constraints for the data.
d. Criteria for retrieving the data.

449. One of the brand managers suspected that the point-of-sale (POS) data for some of the stores were inaccurate because sales fluctuated widely for products that had steady sales in other stores. The best approach for determining whether the POS data for these products are accurate is to compare

a. Sales for similar size stores.
b. Sales to the quantities shipped.
c. Sales for consecutive years.
d. Sales of similar products in the same period.

450. Another brand manager suspected that several days of the point-of-sale (POS) data from one grocery chain were missing. The best approach for detecting missing rows in the data would be to

a. Sort on product identification code and identify missing product identification codes.
b. Sort on store identification code and identify missing product identification codes.
c. Compare product identification codes for consecutive periods.
d. Compare product identification codes by store for consecutive periods.

451. A function of a data dictionary is to

a. Document processing steps.
b. Ensure design consistency.
c. Maintain data integrity.
d. Coordinate program interfaces.

452. A physical database is an integral component of which of the following systems?

a. The operating system.
b. The database system.
c. The user system.
d. The system management facility.

453. Which of the following database models is considered to be the most versatile?

a. The hierarchical model.
b. The tree model.
c. The network model.
d. The relational model.

454. The primary purpose of a database system is to have a single storage location for each

a. File.
b. Record.
c. Database.
d. Data item.

455. Providing a consistent official description of data as well as consistent data names for programming and retrieval is the function of the

a. Database management system.
b. Data administrator.
c. Data dictionary.
d. Schema.

Software Licensing

456. A department purchased one copy of a word processing software program for internal use. The manager of the department installed the program on the manager's office computer and then made two complete copies of the original diskettes. Copy number 1 was solely for backup purposes. Copy number 2 was for use by another member of the department. In terms of software licenses and copyright law, which of the following is correct?

a. Both copies are legal.
b. Only copy number 1 is legal.
c. Only copy number 2 is legal.
d. Neither copy is legal.

457. Pirated software obtained through the Internet may lead to civil lawsuits or criminal prosecution. Of the following, which would reduce an organization's risk in this area?

I. Maintain a log of all software purchases.
II. Audit individual computers to identify software on the computers.
III. Establish a corporate software policy.
IV. Provide original software diskettes to each user.

a. I and IV only.
b. I, II, and III only.
c. II and IV only.
d. II and III only.

458. Use of unlicensed software in an organization

I. Increases the risk of introducing viruses into the organization.
II. Is not a serious exposure if only low-cost software is involved.
III. Can be detected by software checking routines that run from a network server.

a. I only.
b. I and II only.

c. I, II, and III.
d. I and III only.

459. Which of the following approaches is the most effective way to detect an illegal copy of application software in a microcomputing environment?
a. Carefully examine the external labels of software diskettes.
b. Determine if end-user passwords are properly employed.
c. Compare the serial number loaded onto the software to the software vendor's serial number.
d. Obtain a proof of purchase from software vendor.

Web Infrastructure

460. Which of the following statements is correct regarding the Internet as a commercially viable network?
a. Organizations must use firewalls if they wish to maintain security over internal data.
b. Companies must apply to the Internet to gain permission to create a home page to engage in electronic commerce.
c. Companies that wish to engage in electronic commerce on the Internet must meet required security standards established by the coalition of Internet providers.
d. All of the above.

461. The most difficult aspect of using Internet resources is
a. Making a physical connection.
b. Locating the best information source.
c. Obtaining the equipment required.
d. Getting authorization for access.

462. An information systems administrator had a very specific question about the functioning of an integrity feature in a proprietary database management system. The administrator knew of no other organization that had installed those databases but did know how to post the question where other knowledgeable persons would see it and respond to it. Such a place would be
a. A file search program, such as Archie.
b. The wide area information servers (WAIS).
c. An Internet group, such as a Usenet group.
d. The open systems interconnection (OSI) organization.

463. The Internet is made up of a series of networks, which include
a. Gateways to allow mainframe computers to connect to personal computers.
b. Bridges to direct messages through the optimum data path.
c. Repeaters to physically connect separate local area networks (LANs).
d. Routers to strengthen data signals between distant computers.

464. The process of sending unsolicited electronic-mail messages to a large number of recipients in a marketing campaign is called
a. Surfing.
b. Spamming.
c. Priming.
d. Pumping.

465. A network that uses computer technologies such as Web servers, HTML, and XML to serve the internal needs of an organization is called a(n)
a. Internet.
b. Intranet.
c. Extranet.
d. Thinnet.

466. A network that uses computer technologies such as Web servers, HTML, and XML to link an organization to its suppliers is called a(n)
a. Internet.
b. Intranet.
c. Extranet.
d. Thinnet.

467. Which of the following is **not** an impediment to global information systems?
a. Differences in payment mechanisms.
b. Cultural differences.
c. Legal barriers.
d. Internet protocols.

468. With reference to using the Web infrastructure for international commerce, the process of "glocalization" means
a. Think globally, act locally.
b. Think locally, act globally.
c. Think about local need and preferences.
d. Think about global needs and preferences.

469. A company has a very large, widely dispersed internal audit department. Management wants to implement a computerized system to facilitate communications between auditors. The specifications require that auditors have the ability to place messages in a central electronic repository where all auditors can access them. The system should facilitate finding information on a particular topic. Which type of system would best meet these specifications?
a. Electronic data interchange.
b. Electronic bulletin board system.
c. Fax/modem software.
d. Private branch exchange.

MULTIPLE-CHOICE ANSWERS AND EXPLANATIONS

1. c	63. b	125. b	187. b	249. c	311. b
2. c	64. c	126. a	188. c	250. d	312. b
3. d	65. a	127. b	189. a	251. c	313. a
4. d	66. c	128. a	190. a	252. a	314. a
5. a	67. a	129. b	191. d	253. d	315. a
6. b	68. c	130. a	192. c	254. c	316. b
7. c	69. d	131. a	193. c	255. d	317. d
8. d	70. d	132. c	194. c	256. a	318. c
9. b	71. a	133. b	195. d	257. a	319. a
10. d	72. b	134. a	196. b	258. d	320. d
11. c	73. a	135. d	197. c	259. b	321. c
12. a	74. b	136. c	198. b	260. c	322. b
13. b	75. c	137. a	199. a	261. c	323. b
14. d	76. c	138. a	200. c	262. c	324. a
15. a	77. a	139. d	201. d	263. c	325. a
16. c	78. c	140. a	202. c	264. d	326. a
17. a	79. a	141. b	203. a	265. a	327. d
18. a	80. b	142. d	204. c	266. c	328. b
19. c	81. d	143. b	205. d	267. d	329. a
20. a	82. d	144. a	206. b	268. c	330. c
21. b	83. a	145. a	207. b	269. d	331. c
22. d	84. c	146. b	208. a	270. d	332. a
23. a	85. a	147. b	209. b	271. a	333. c
24. c	86. b	148. a	210. b	272. a	334. c
25. a	87. a	149. c	211. b	273. b	335. b
26. d	88. d	150. a	212. c	274. b	336. a
27. a	89. a	151. a	213. b	275. c	337. d
28. b	90. b	152. c	214. c	276. a	338. d
29. c	91. b	153. a	215. b	277. a	339. c
30. a	92. d	154. b	216. c	278. a	340. a
31. a	93. d	155. b	217. a	279. b	341. a
32. a	94. c	156. a	218. a	280. c	342. c
33. c	95. a	157. c	219. c	281. c	343. c
34. b	96. a	158. a	220. b	282. a	344. c
35. c	97. c	159. c	221. d	283. c	345. b
36. a	98. b	160. b	222. a	284. a	346. b
37. c	99. d	161. d	223. b	285. a	347. c
38. a	100. c	162. a	224. b	286. b	348. a
39. c	101. b	163. a	225. b	287. b	349. b
40. b	102. c	164. a	226. a	288. c	350. d
41. d	103. c	165. a	227. b	289. b	351. a
42. a	104. c	166. a	228. b	290. c	352. d
43. a	105. c	167. c	229. d	291. d	353. b
44. b	106. b	168. d	230. d	292. d	354. b
45. c	107. d	169. d	231. a	293. b	355. d
46. a	108. a	170. d	232. c	294. c	356. d
47. d	109. b	171. c	233. a	295. c	357. c
48. d	110. d	172. b	234. b	296. d	358. b
49. b	111. a	173. b	235. d	297. b	359. b
50. c	112. c	174. d	236. a	298. b	360. d
51. a	113. a	175. d	237. c	299. a	361. d
52. a	114. c	176. d	238. a	300. d	362. b
53. c	115. c	177. a	239. b	301. c	363. a
54. c	116. c	178. b	240. d	302. b	364. b
55. c	117. b	179. c	241. d	303. d	365. b
56. b	118. c	180. d	242. a	304. a	366. c
57. a	119. d	181. a	243. c	305. b	367. a
58. b	120. d	182. c	244. b	306. c	368. c
59. d	121. a	183. b	245. b	307. a	369. a
60. d	122. a	184. d	246. c	308. a	370. c
61. b	123. d	185. d	247. d	309. c	371. d
62. c	124. a	186. c	248. a	310. b	372. c

373. c __ __	390. d __ __	407. b __ __	424. d __ __	441. a __ __	458. a __ __
374. a __ __	391. a __ __	408. c __ __	425. c __ __	442. c __ __	459. c __ __
375. c __ __	392. d __ __	409. d __ __	426. c __ __	443. b __ __	460. a __ __
376. a __ __	393. d __ __	410. c __ __	427. a __ __	444. b __ __	461. b __ __
377. a __ __	394. c __ __	411. a __ __	428. c __ __	445. a __ __	462. c __ __
378. c __ __	395. a __ __	412. a __ __	429. d __ __	446. a __ __	463. a __ __
379. c __ __	396. d __ __	413. c __ __	430. d __ __	447. c __ __	464. b __ __
380. d __ __	397. a __ __	414. c __ __	431. d __ __	448. d __ __	465. b __ __
381. a __ __	398. b __ __	415. a __ __	432. a __ __	449. b __ __	466. c __ __
382. a __ __	399. b __ __	416. c __ __	433. c __ __	450. d __ __	467. d __ __
383. a __ __	400. d __ __	417. c __ __	434. c __ __	451. c __ __	468. c __ __
384. b __ __	401. c __ __	418. b __ __	435. d __ __	452. b __ __	469. b __ __
385. a __ __	402. d __ __	419. b __ __	436. c __ __	453. d __ __	
386. c __ __	403. d __ __	420. b __ __	437. c __ __	454. d __ __	
387. a __ __	404. b __ __	421. b __ __	438. b __ __	455. c __ __	
388. b __ __	405. c __ __	422. c __ __	439. d __ __	456. b __ __	1st: __/469 = __%
389. c __ __	406. d __ __	423. c __ __	440. a __ __	457. b __ __	2nd: __/469 = __%

Control Frameworks

1. (c) In 1994, the IIA's SAC model was enhanced by changing the "auditability" to "assurance" to recognize the important perspectives of governance and the alliances—both within an organization and between business partners—needed to assure effective security, auditability, and control of information.

Subject Area: information technology—control frameworks. Source: Author.

2. (c) Components (assurance objectives) of the IIA's SAC model include availability, capability, functionality, protectability, and accountability. The SAC model sets the stage for effective technology risk management by providing a framework for evaluating the electronic-business control environment. These assurance objectives provide the "framework" for the SAC model. SysTrust is AICPA's information technology and control model.

Subject Area: information technology—control frameworks. Source: Author.

3. (d) The building blocks to achieving assurance objectives include people, processes, technology, investment, and communication. Customers are part of external market forces along with competitors, regulators, citizens, and owners. The building blocks are internal to an organization.

Subject Area: information technology—control frameworks. Source: Author.

4. (d) Privacy concerns and issues are discussed under protectability and accountability components of the SAC model. The protectability objective focuses on logical and physical security controls to ensure that authorized access and to deny unauthorized access to servers, application systems, and information assets. The accountability objective focuses on ensuring that transaction processing is accurate and complete.

Subject Area: information technology—control frameworks. Source: Author.

5. (a) "Availability" means the ability to receive, accept, process, and support business transactions at all times in a manner acceptable to an organization's customers (e.g., 7/24/365).

Subject Area: information technology—control frameworks. Source: Author.

6. (b) Efficiency of computer systems is an aspect of capability that leads to effective use of computing resources. Management's goal is to achieve and maintain an efficient and effective balance across the organization. The capability objective focuses on end-to-end reliable, timely completion and fulfillment of all business transactions.

Subject Area: information technology—control frameworks. Source: Author.

7. (c) Functionality means computer systems provide necessary facilities, responsiveness, and ease-of-use to meet user needs and expectations. To help ensure functionality, the auditor evaluates controls that monitor and provide feedback. Some of these might include the display of progress indicators following input, positive confirmation of transactions, or monitoring user abandonment of transactions, or system "hang-ups."

Subject Area: information technology—control frameworks. Source: Author.

8. (d) The accountability objective includes the concept of nonrepudiation. This means that once authenticated, a user cannot disclaim a transaction, as might happen when an online brokerage user seeks to break a trade that turned out to be a bad idea that they nonetheless actually caused.

Subject Area: information technology—control frameworks. Source: Author.

9. (b) Accountability and privacy appear to be in conflict. Accountability means identifying the source of a transaction, while privacy might deny meaningful identification of the transaction. Accountability and privacy issues must be reconciled with care.

Subject Area: information technology—control frameworks. Source: Author.

10. (d) The focus of COBIT is business orientation, not audit, control, or technology. The control objectives are linked to business objectives.

Subject Area: information technology—control frameworks. Source: Author.

11. (c) COBIT defines control as "the policies, procedures, practices, and organizational structures designed to provide reasonable assurance that business objectives will be achieved . . . ."

Subject Area: information technology—control frameworks. Source: Author.

12. (a) Control objectives are defined using the principles of business reengineering.

Subject Area: information technology—control frameworks. Source: Author.

13. (b) COBIT has been developed as a generally applicable and accepted standard for good IT security and control practices. COBIT is the breakthrough IT governance tool that helps management understanding and manages the risks associated with IT.

Subject Area: information technology—control frameworks. Source: Author.

14. (d) In the business requirements for information, COBIT combines the quality, fiduciary, and security requirements, but not audit requirements.

Subject Area: information technology—control frameworks. Source: Author.

15. (a) The IT resources identified in the COBIT include data, application systems, technology, facilities, and people. Money, or capital, was not retained as an IT resource for classification of control objectives because it can be considered as an investment in any of the above resources.

Subject Area: information technology—control frameworks. Source: Author.

16. (c) Control objectives are defined in a process-oriented manner following the principles of business reengineering. The scope of the COBIT contains four domains, seven information criteria, 34 high-level control objectives, and 318 detailed control objectives.

Subject Area: information technology—control frameworks. Source: Author.

Data and Network Communications and Connections

17. (a) In a star network, nodes are connected to a central location that controls the network and all nodes communicate through the central site. Choice (b) is incorrect because in a ring network, each node receives messages from one node and sends messages to the next node. Choice (c) is incorrect because in a bus network, each node shares a common communication path so that all nodes receive simultaneous messages sent by a node. Choice (d) is incorrect because synchronous is a communications protocol where characters are sent at a fixed rate by synchronizing the transmitting and receiving devices.

Subject Area: Information technology—data and network communications and connections. Source: CIA 1193, III-23.

18. (a) In the existing system, data transfer charges are high because all users communicate in a star network with the host for data that could be maintained locally. Choice (b) is incorrect because in the existing system, all users communicate in a star network since there are no LANs. Choice (c) is incorrect because in the existing system, all users communicate in a star network since there are no LANs. Choice (d) is incorrect because the company will have system development costs no matter which alternative it chooses.

Subject Area: Information technology—data and network communications and connections. Source: CIA 593, III-87.

19. (c) If all policy information is kept in a single computer, there is no overhead for consolidating data fragmented across multiple databases. Choice (a) is incorrect because maintaining policy information only in a single computer decreases the speed of regional office access to policy data. Choice (b) is incorrect because maintaining policy information only in a single computer restrains evolutionary growth in capabilities because the single computer must be upgraded. Choice (d) is incorrect because maintaining policy information only in a single computer decreases system availability because all users are subject to interruptions of the single computer.

Subject Area: Information technology—data and network communications and connections. Source: CIA 593, III-88.

20. (a) Maintaining policy information only on LANs at regional offices has the advantage of increasing the speed of regional office access to policy data because long-distance communications are avoided for routine, repetitive transactions and inquiries. Choice (b) is incorrect because maintaining policy information only on LANs at regional offices means that there may be some loss of control due to data fragmentation. Choice (c) is incorrect because maintaining policy information only on LANs at regional offices may decrease headquarters staff's access to policy data because communications are required to access the policies stored at the regional offices. Choice (d) is incorrect because even though policy data are stored at regional offices, some data need to be replicated at headquarters.

Subject Area: Information technology—data and network communications and connections. Source: CIA 593, III-89.

21. (b) Maintaining all policy information only on a single computer has the disadvantage of increasing communication costs and access time because each user must communicate with the single computer. Choice (a) is incorrect because permitting local autonomy over local data is an advantage of distributed, not centralized, arrangements. Choice (c) is incorrect because maintaining all policy information only on a single computer has the disadvantage of over-using a star communications network. Choice (d) is incorrect because maintaining all policy information only on a single computer does not have the disadvantage of requiring update propagation across sites because there is only one site.

Subject Area: Information technology—data and network communications and connections. Source: CIA 593, III-90.

22. (d) Maintaining all policy information only on LANs at regional offices has the disadvantage of increasing the difficulty of compiling aggregate policy statistics because the relevant source data are maintained on multiple LANs. Choice (a) is incorrect because maintaining all policy information only on LANs at regional offices has the advantage of decreasing communication costs and access time at the regional offices. Choice (b) is incorrect because maintaining all policy information only on LANs at regional offices has the advantage of increasing the availability of local data. Choice (c) is incorrect because maintaining all policy information only on LANs at regional offices has the advantage of facilitating incremental growth at regional offices.

Subject Area: Information technology—data and network communications and connections. Source: CIA 593, III-91.

23. (a) An echo check provides a feedback loop by transmitting data received back to the source unit for validation with the original data. It is a hardware control. Choice (b) is incorrect because a protection ring prevents accidental writing on a tape file for mostly batch systems. A real-time system would not utilize tape files. Choice (c) is incorrect because hash totals are utilized to control data sent to a batch system not a real-time system. It is a software control. Choice (d) is incorrect because integrated test facilities are useful in testing real-time systems but cannot be utilized to ensure completeness of data transmissions. It is a software control.

Subject Area: Information technology—data and network communications and connections. Source: CIA 1192, II-31.

24. (c) Local area networks (LANs) connect computers with other computers, peripherals (e.g., printers, plotters) and workstations that are fairly close in proximity such as in a building or multiple buildings within a campus. Choice (a) is incorrect because of insufficient information to classify in this manner. A ring is a type of LAN topology where each member of the network gets access to the communication channel for a set time at predefined intervals. Topology refers to the manner in which a network is physically connected. Choice (b) is incorrect because of insufficient information to classify in this manner. A star is a type of LAN topology where it facilitates the sharing of resources such as hard disks, which are located at the central node. Choice (d) is incorrect because wide area networks (WANs) deal with long distances greater than 30 miles or 50 km. WANs connect system users who are geographically dispersed through public telecommunication facilities.

Subject Area: Information technology—data and network communications and connections. Source: CIA 1192, III-38.

25. (a) A local area network is the appropriate type of network. Choice (b) is incorrect because wide area networks provide communication over long distance. Choice (c) is incorrect. This is a distractor because of the term "end user," but this is not a type of network. Choice (d) is incorrect because baseband network is a term used to describe networks that are used **only** for data communications.

Subject Area: Information technology—data and network communications and connections. Source: CIA 592, III-26.

26. (d) A protocol is the agreement as to how both data and control information shall be packaged and interpreted in a data communications system. Choice (a) is incorrect because asynchronous communication is a type of data transmission where each character is transmitted separately with corresponding "start" and "stop" signals. Choice (b) is incorrect because synchronous communication is a type of data transmission where a number of characters are sent as a unit with start and stop signals for the entire unit. Choice (c) is incorrect because a communication channel is the medium used to connect components in a data communications system.

Subject Area: Information technology—data and network communications and connections. Source: CIA 592, III-37.

27. (a) A multiplexer is used to interleave the slow data transmissions of many different terminal devices in order to fully utilize the capacity of a medium- or high-speed data communication line. Choice (b) is incorrect because a modem is a device which is used to convert analog data transmissions into digital form or vice versa. Choice (c) is incorrect because a coaxial cable is a data communication line, not a device. Choice (d) is incorrect because a bus is part of the internal structure of a microprocessor.

Subject Area: Information technology—data and network communications and connections. Source: CIA 1191, III-24.

28. (b) A local area network (LAN) is a telecommunications network used to connect computers and other devices in close proximity. Choice (a) is incorrect because a distributed system is an arrangement of computers in an organization involving several separate computer complexes in which each one performs local processing operations. Choice (c) is incorrect because protocol refers to the rules governing communications between two pieces of equipment. Choice (d) is incorrect because a wide area network (WAN) is a telecommunications network used to connect computers over a broad geographic area.

Subject Area: Information technology—data and network communications and connections. Source: CIA 591, III-37.

29. (c) This is not an advantage because security becomes more difficult when there are more sites to secure. Choices (a) and (b) are incorrect because they are advantages of distributed computing. Choice (d) is incorrect because the cost of hardware for each site would be much less than for a central site.

Subject Area: Information technology—data and network communications and connections. Source: CIA 591, III-38.

30. (a) A distributed data processing system maximizes the advantages of both centralized and decentralized systems. Each facility has its own computer, which is linked to a central mainframe. Choice (b) is incorrect because in centralized data processing one computer serves the entire organization. Choice (c) is incorrect because in decentralized data processing separate computer systems are provided to each facility, but the individual systems are not integrated. Choice (d) is incorrect because in time-sharing, several customer firms share time on a computer operated by an outside company.

Subject Area: Information technology—data and network communications and connections. Source: CIA 591, III-88.

31. (a) A network interface card links microcomputers and printers together in a local area network that is connected by coaxial cable, twisted pair, or optical fiber. The card creates an address for the microcomputer, transmits data, and monitors incoming messages. Choices (b,) (c), and (d) are incorrect because modems are used to connect microcomputers to regular telephone lines.

Subject Area: Information technology—data and network communications and connections. Source: CIA 594, III-23.

32. (a) Decentralization of computerized data processing functions through the interconnection of computer hardware. Choice (b) is incorrect because time-sharing systems are terminal-oriented systems that are connected to a central processing site. Choice (c) is incorrect because an online processing system operates under direct control of the CPU. Choice (d) is incorrect because a personal computing system is a microcomputer resource dedicated to a single user usually in a stand-alone configuration.

Subject Area: Information technology—data and network communications and connections. Source: CIA 1193, III-20.

33. (c) This is not considered a major risk as PCs have similar hardware components to mainframe computers. The integrity of the hardware is quite high. Choice (a) is incorrect because a major concern with LANs is that users are responsible for building and maintaining procedures for capturing and processing data. One of the major problems associated with this form of end-user computing is that users often do not do a good job of documenting procedures. Choice (b) is incorrect because security is a major concern for sensitive data residing on a PC and/or a LAN. Choice (d) is incorrect because data communications are always a high risk factor on LANs because they do not happen automatically. The auditor will need to gain assurance that the company has mechanisms, including reconciliations, to ensure complete data communications.

Subject Area: Information technology—data and network communications and connections. Source: CIA 597, I-20.

34. (b) Public-switched networks are open to the general public and offer the least level of security. Choice (a) is incorrect because value-added carriers would provide data security and error procedures. Choice (c) is incorrect because local area networks would inherently limit data transmission exposures. Choice (d) is incorrect because private networks provide security through limited access and dedicated facilities.

Subject Area: Information technology—data and network communications and connections. Source: CIA 597, III-45.

35. (c) Performance monitoring is the systematic measurement and evaluation of operating results such as transaction rates, response times, and incidence of error conditions. Performance monitoring will reveal trends in capacity usage so that capacity can be upgraded before response deteriorates to the point that users behave in unintended or undesirable ways. Choices (a), (b), and (d) are incorrect because they deal with applications software, not response times.

Subject Area: Information technology—data and network communications and connections. Source: CIA 597, III-67.

36. (a) A gateway, often implemented via software, translates between two or more different protocol families and makes connections between dissimilar networks possible. Choice (b) is incorrect because a bridge joins network segments so they appear to be one physical segment. Choice (c) is incorrect because a router connects two or more network segments, such that the segments maintain their separate logical identities. Choice (d) is incorrect because a wiring concentrator accepts twisted-pair cabling from each of several PCs in the same LAN.

Subject Area: Information technology—data and network communications and connections. Source: CIA 597, III-68.

37. (c) Converting to open systems increases the number of vendors from which substitutable components could be acquired, which increases price competition for equipment. Choice (a) is incorrect. In general, running open systems tends to increase the number of vendors, which decreases the amount of the average purchase from any one vendor, thereby decreasing the opportunities for volume discounts from vendors. Choice (b) is incorrect. In general, running open systems allows organizations to scale their computing facilities to a precise size, which may be inconsistent with attempting to achieve economies of scale due to larger volumes concentrated in fewer sites. Choice (d) is incorrect. In general, running open systems reduces an organization's reliance on proprietary components, which reduces the need for their integration into existing systems.

Subject Area: Information technology—data and network communications and connections. Source: CIA 597, III-70.

38. (a) Client/server implementation does not necessarily use relational databases. Choices (b) and (c) are incorrect because these factors make security complex in client/server environments. Choice (d) is incorrect because this is also a factor that makes client/server security complex.

Subject Area: Information technology—data and network communications and connections. Source: CIA 597, III-77.

39. (c) Recording software usage is a performance management control. Choice (a) is incorrect because failure reporting is a fault management function. Choice (b) is incorrect because access violations are a security management function. Choice (d) is incorrect because cost allocation is an accounting management function.

Subject Area: Information technology—data and network communications and connections. Source: CIA 1196, III-60.

40. (b) PCs have sufficient computing power for screen displays during terminal emulation (PCs have more computing power than terminals). Choice (a) is incorrect because having employees use PCs for personal gain is a control risk. Choice (c) is incorrect because inadequate backup procedures are a control risk. Choice (d) is incorrect because unauthorized copying of software is a control risk.

Subject Area: Information technology—data and network communications and connections. Source: CIA 1196, III-38.

41. (d) A Virtual Private Network is a carrier-provided service in which the public switched network provides capabilities similar to those of private lines but at a lower cost. Choice (a) is incorrect because a Private Wide Area Network is one that an individual business firm maintains for its own use. Choice (b) is incorrect because Integrated Services Digital Network (ISDN) is an international standard for transmitting voice, video, and data over phone lines. Choice (c) is incorrect because a value-added network (VAN) is a data-only, multipath, and third-party-managed network.

Subject Area: Information technology—data and network communications and connections. Source: CIA 1196, III-71.

42. (a) A number of bottlenecks (e.g., in-house analog technology) may limit the benefits that can be derived from the external network. Choice (b) is incorrect because resistance to change, inflexible organization structures, and skepticism of the technology should be expected and must be successfully managed if the company is to reap the benefits of the technology. Choice (c) is incorrect because as individuals rely on communications to perform their daily tasks, it becomes imperative for a network to be essentially 100% available. The company should enhance its disaster recovery plan to recognize this fact. Choice (d) is incorrect because network management is a function within the company; it will become more of a partnership arrangement with the communications carrier or provider.

Subject Area: Information technology—data and network communications and connections. Source: CIA 1196, III-72.

43. (a) Open systems are characterized by less expensive components because there are more sellers of open as opposed to closed system components, which makes open components more like commodity products. Choice (b) is incorrect because open systems are characterized by more, not less, interoperability because more of the open components work with each other than is the case in closed systems. Choice (c) is incorrect because open systems are characterized by less dependence on particular vendors because users have choices of vendors as sources for components. Choice (d) is incorrect because open systems are characterized by more, not less, portability because open components are designed to industry-wide standards rather than proprietary standards.

Subject Area: Information technology—data and network communications and connections. Source: CIA 1196, III-73.

44. (b) A MAN (metro-area network) connects multiple sites with multiple workstations for shared use of common resources. Choice (a) is incorrect because value-added networks (VANs) provide protocol conversion, message storing, and message forwarding for specific transactions such as EDI. Choice (c) is incorrect because electronic data interchange (EDI) supports the transfer of business information in formatted form between application systems on different computers. Choice (d) is incorrect because TCP/IP is a network protocol that implements the OSI transport layer for managing end-to-end network transmissions.

Subject Area: Information technology—data and network communications and connections. Source: CIA 1196, III-71.

45. (c) Incorrect software initialization options could be the source of poor response time. Choice (a) is incorrect because monitoring would give evidence for the source of poor response time but lack of monitoring would not cause poor response. In fact, monitoring itself incurs overhead, which would degrade response time. Choice (b) is incorrect because network cost allocations are typically executed on a single computer and generally do not place any significant demand on the network. Choice (d) is incorrect because multiple-vendor sourcing for network components is often a means of improving response time in that an organization can acquire just the hardware and software components it needs.

Subject Area: Information technology—data and network communications and connections. Source: CIA 596, III-46.

46. (a) The pressure for the department store to be competitive is so great that there may be a significant risk that applications software could be incomplete, inadequately tested, or unauthorized. Choice (b) is incorrect. On the contrary, management has stated its intention to install the network, salespeople have been asking for features that the network could provide, and the planning committee has identified many potential applications. Choice (c) is incorrect because these types of violations do not occur with in-house development. Choice (d) is incorrect because given the standard nature of the network, it is unlikely that the company would not be able to obtain needed components from vendors as usage increases.

Subject Area: Information technology—data and network communications and connections. Source: CIA 596, III-52.

47. (d) Customers with read privileges can examine the gift registry lists to make their selections, and salespeople can update the gift registry with actual purchases. Choice (a) is incorrect because reserving all system functions for salespeople would restrict access more than is required for adequate security and would hinder use of the system for maximum benefit. Choices (b) and (c) are incorrect because customers should not have update privileges to prevent them from corrupting data files, intentionally or accidentally.

Subject Area: Information technology—data and network communications and connections. Source: CIA 596, III-53.

48. (d) Given the company's lack of experience with networks, a significant risk is that the network operating costs may not be fully projected with the result that the company would incur unanticipated costs after the network is installed. Choice (a) is incorrect because salespeople are already asking for network features to help them do their jobs so they are unlikely to be reluctant to use the system. Choice (b) is incorrect. The required features are typical of networks and its overall size makes it a midrange system, hence, the network should not require expensive nonstandard components. Choice (c) is incorrect because customers are so used to companies managing inventory with computer systems that they expect such systems and take their business to the companies with the best supply practices.

Subject Area: Information technology—data and network communications and connections. Source: CIA 596, III-54.

49. (b) A wide area network (WAN) is the best kind of network because it can connect many sites located across a broad geographical distance. Choice (a) is incorrect because a local area network (LAN) is generally limited to short distances (e.g., 2,000 feet radius of the servers). Choice (c) is incorrect because a value-added network (VAN) is, in general, more expensive than a private network such as a WAN for high-volume communications. Choice (d) is incorrect because a private branch exchange (PBX) is an electronic switch that transfers telephone calls, which does not have the network capabilities needed by the company.

Subject Area: Information technology—data and network communications and connections. Source: CIA 596, III-55.

50. (c) If the company installs a leased-line network, it should ensure that transmission facilities on its premises are secure. Choice (a) is incorrect because in a leased-line network, there are no phone numbers. Choice (b) is incorrect because in a leased-line network, there are no phone numbers and hence no ports with tone devices for incoming calls. Choice (d) is incorrect because limiting network availability to certain times of the day is often associated with public switched lines, not leased lines, to reduce the time during which unauthorized people could potentially gain access to the system.

Subject Area: Information technology—data and network communications and connections. Source: CIA 596, III-56.

51. (a) Client server implementation does not necessarily use relational database. Choices (b) and (c) are incorrect because these factors make security complex in client/server environments. Choice (d) is incorrect because this is also a factor that makes client/server security complex.

Subject Area: Information technology—data and network communications and connections. Source: CIA 596, III-66.

52. (a) This is a benefit of a successful implementation. Choice (b) is incorrect because data transmission costs usually go up. Choice (c) is incorrect because systems may not benefit from replacement of mainframes. Choice (d) is incorrect because client/server usually results in decentralization of data and/or processing.

Subject Area: Information technology—data and network communications and connections. Source: CIA 596, III-67.

53. (c) This will be the best first step. Choice (a) is incorrect because this may be done as part of audit preparation. Choice (b) is incorrect because this may be an audit step. Choice (d) is incorrect because this may be a subsequent audit step.

Subject Area: Information technology—data and network communications and connections. Source: CIA 596, III-72.

54. (c) Performance monitoring is the systematic measurement and evaluation of operating results such as transaction rates, response times, and incidence of error conditions. Performance monitoring will reveal trends in capacity usage so that capacity can be upgraded before response deteriorates to the point that users behave in unintended or undesirable ways. Choice (a) is incorrect because parallel testing involves testing both old and new programs. Choice (b) is incorrect because integrated test facility involves testing data through real and simulated programs. Choice (d) is incorrect because program code comparison software focuses on comparing old and new versions.

Subject Area: Information technology—data and network communications and connections. Source: CIA 595, III-76.

55. (c) Lack of adequate inventories of network, hardware, and software components and lack of records of changes in components increase the difficulty of isolating faults in any part of the system. There may be subtle differences in components or successive versions of the same components, which lead to incompatibilities that cause failures. Choice (a) is incorrect. To the extent the system incorporates components from external parties, the company is dependent on them. Choice (b) is incorrect. Having an accurate inventory of hardware, software, and communications components and an accurate account of changes in the components would make timely installation of new components easier but would not guarantee timely installation of new components. Choice (d) is incorrect. Having an accurate inventory of hardware, software, and communications components and an accurate account of changes in the components may be helpful in maintaining system availability but availability depends on the appropriateness of the configuration and the ability of service personnel to keep the system running.

Subject Area: Information technology—data and network communications and connections. Source: CIA 595, III-78.

56. (b) A file server, providing files for users of the LAN, is one type of server. Choice (a) is incorrect because the cabling is the telecommunications link. Choice (c) is incorrect because a network gateway connects the LAN to other networks. Choice (d) is incorrect because a workstation that is dedicated to a single user is a client.

Subject Area: Information technology—data and network communications and connections. Source: CIA 1194, III-21.

57. (a) Companies can use public switched lines on a per transmission basis, which would be the most cost-effective way for low-volume users to conduct telecommunications. Choice (b) is incorrect because fast-packet switches receive transmissions from various devices, break the data into packets, and route them over a network to their destination. Public switched lines are installed by telecommunication utility companies and other large companies that have their own networks. Choice (c) is incorrect because electronic mail systems have no capability for voice and data transmissions. Choice (d) is incorrect because the Internet does not provide telephone connections.

Subject Area: Information technology—data and network communications and connections. Source: CIA 1195, III-40.

58. (b) Since PBX-based systems use telephone wiring (most often copper wire), they cannot easily handle very large volumes of data. Choice (a) is incorrect because the company would be responsible for all maintenance of the equipment although it could contract for service. Choice (c) is incorrect because PBX-based systems use telephone wiring. LANs require their own coaxial cabling. Choice (d) is incorrect because PBX-based systems are under the firm's control; the firm can reconfigure devices and rearrange facilities as it sees fit.

Subject Area: Information technology—data and network communications and connections. Source: CIA 1195, III-58.

Electronic Funds Transfer

59. (d) Represents a direct exposure to breaching data integrity since it represents the use of public lines that can be easily identified and tapped and thus requires that adequate security measures be adopted. Choice (a) is incorrect because it represents a secondary exposure for compromise of remote data communications lines. That is, it is a secondary rather than a primary exposure to compromise of the communications circuit. Choice (b) is incorrect because exposures from network viruses can be minimized through the implementation of "safe computing practices" such as where to buy software or who can access what on the system. Choice (c) is incorrect because poor system documentation is a secondary exposure thus causing inconvenience to system users and maintainers.

Subject Area: Information technology—electronic funds transfer. Source: CIA 593, III-31.

60. (d) Item 1 is correct because competition has been a strong motivator in the financial services industry in the development of EFT systems. Item 2 is correct because maintaining costs in a highly competitive industry can be aided by leveraging information technology. Item 3 is correct because advances in information technology, especially telecommunications technology, have made EFT systems possible. Item 4 is incorrect because improvements in automated control techniques have been the result of industry taking advantage of the trends that have influenced the development of information technology. Item 5 is incorrect because data encryption standards have been in response to the increase in the use of telecommunications technology.

Subject Area: Information technology—electronic funds transfer. Source: CIA 1193, III-17.

61. (b) Unauthorized access is a risk, which is higher in an EFT environment. Choices (a), (c), and (d) are incorrect because these are risks common to all information technology environments.

Subject Area: Information technology—electronic funds transfer. Source: CIA 1196, III-63.

62. (c) Per transaction costs are lower with electronic funds transfer. Choice (a) is incorrect because it is a major risk factor, inherent to electronic funds transfer (EFT). Choice (b) is incorrect because it is another inherent risk factor. Choice (d) is incorrect because it is a critical risk factor.

Subject Area: Information technology—electronic funds transfer. Source: CIA 596, III-64.

Electronic Commerce

63. (b) Examples of applications in business-to-business (B2B) include electronic data interchange (EDI), exchanges and auctions, online business alliances, and application service providers (ASP). Electronic retailing is an example of business-to-consumer (B2C) commerce model.

Subject Area: Information technology—electronic commerce. Source: CBM, Volume 4.

64. (c) Exchanges and auctions are examples of business-to-business (B2B) commerce model. Others are examples of business-to-consumer (B2C) commerce model.

Subject Area: Information technology—electronic commerce. Source: CBM, Volume 4.

65. (a) Horizontal interchange means information is shared between organizations producing the same or similar products or services. Airline companies and financial institutions are examples of this category.

Subject Area: Information technology—electronic commerce. Source: CBM, Volume 4.

66. (c) Vertical integration means the output of an organization is used as input of another organization.

Subject Area: Information technology—electronic commerce. Source: CBM, Volume 4.

67. (a) Use of credit cards for electronic commerce is most common in North America followed by Asia. Debit cards are popular in Europe.

Subject Area: Information technology—electronic commerce. Source: CBM, Volume 4.

Electronic Data Interchange

68. (c) Electronic data interchange (EDI) refers to the electronic transfer of documents between businesses and between customers and suppliers. Choice (a) is incorrect. E-mail can send text or document files, but the term encompasses a wide range of transfers. Electronic data interchange specifically applies to the system described in the question. Choice (b) is incorrect. Electronic funds transfer (EFT) refers to the transfer of money. Choice (d) is incorrect. Electronic data processing (EDP) is a generic term, which refers to computerized processing of transaction data within organizations.

Subject Area: Information technology—electronic data interchange. Source: CIA 594, III-26.

69. (d) Placement of order entry transactions from a customer to its supplier is an accepted use of electronic data interchange between trading partners. Choice (a) is incorrect. A request for an airline reservation requires an online real-time reservations system. Choice (b) is incorrect. Withdrawal of cash from an automated teller is accomplished via online transactions to copies of master files. Choice (c) is incorrect. The transfer of summary data to headquarters may be accomplished with point-to-point communications, known as distributed computing.

Subject Area: Information technology—electronic data interchange. Source: CIA 1192, III-30.

70. (d) Choice (d) is the correct answer. Online real-time processing (OLRT) systems are used when time is of the essence. Inventory availability and good credit status are important to process a customer's order. The scope of EDI can include computer-to-computer communication as well as communication between a manufacturer and his supplier. Choice (a) is incorrect. The first is not EDI since it is not computer to computer. Choice (b) is incorrect. The second is not OLRT since processing does not take place, only communication. Choice (c) is incorrect. The first is OLRT and the second is EDI.

Subject Area: Information technology—electronic data interchange. Source: CIA 593, III-59.

71. (a) Electronic data interchange (EDI) for business documents between unrelated parties has the potential to increase the risk of unauthorized third-party access to systems because more outsiders will have access to internal systems. Choice (b) is incorrect. Systematic programming errors are the result of misspecification of requirements or lack of correspondence between specifications and programs. Choice (c) is incorrect. Inadequate knowledge bases are a function of lack of care in building them. Choice (d) is incorrect. One of the benefits of EDI is to improve the efficiency and effectiveness of system use.

Subject Area: Information Technology—electronic data interchange. Source: CIA 593, III-38.

72. (b) The company could maintain more current records of inventory by installing bar codes and scanning them when inventory is replenished and relieved. Choice (a) is incorrect. Scanning bar codes only when inventory is counted will not keep inventory records accurate because it does not take into account almost daily changes. Choice (c) is incorrect. Inventory records need not be updated when inventory is removed from production due to material defects because inventory was decreased when the raw materials first entered production. Choice (d) is incorrect. There is no physical movement of goods when inventory value is adjusted for financial statement purposes.

Subject Area: Information technology—electronic data interchange. Source: CIA 1193, III-37.

73. (a) In order, the functions to be performed are analysis of user requirements, design of processes and data structures, construction of programs and files, and implementation of the system. Choice (b) is incorrect. Determining user requirements through analysis must precede design of the system. Choice (c) is incorrect. Construction of a system must precede its implementation. Choice (d) is incorrect. Determining user requirements through analysis must precede design of the system. Construction of a system must precede its implementation.

Subject Area: Information technology—electronic data interchange. Source: CIA 1193, III-38.

74. (b) The main objective of automating production tracking is to facilitate more effective management of production (e.g., by increasing product quality and improving response to customers). Choice (a) is incorrect. Automating production tracking may or may not reduce the number of production workers. Choice (c) is incorrect. Automating production tracking may, as a byproduct, help identify production workers who work slowly, but that is not the business objective. Choice (d) is incorrect. Automating production tracking may, as a byproduct, determine which vendors ship defective materials often, but that is not the business objective.

Subject Area: Information technology—electronic data interchange. Source: CIA 1193, III-39.

75. (c) The best control for the potential exposure that the lower inventory level creates, namely, the risk that the company will run short of raw materials, is to ensure that suppliers are qualified initially and remain qualified. Choice (a) is incorrect. Taking physical inventory when raw material inventory is low is a good idea for reducing the cost of taking physical inventory, but this would not address the potential exposure of being short of raw materials for production. Choice (b) is incorrect. If the company reduces inventory, the need to hire security guards to protect inventory should decrease. Choice (d) is incorrect. Negotiating with other suppliers that could ship raw materials in two months would not be useful for a company whose inventory level is only three production days.

Subject Area: Information technology—electronic data interchange. Source: CIA 1193, III-41.

76. (c) A control for ensuring the authenticity of electronic orders received is to verify (1) the identity of senders by matching them with an authorized list of senders and (2) the correspondence of orders with contract terms. Choice (a) is incorrect. Encrypting sensitive messages such as electronic payments for raw materials received is an appropriate step for messages the company sends but does not apply to messages it receives. Choice (b) is incorrect. Performing reasonableness checks on quantities ordered before placing orders is a control for ensuring the correctness of the company's own orders, not the authenticity of its customers' orders. Choice (d) is incorrect. Acknowledging receipt of electronic payments with a confirming message is good practice but will not authenticate orders from customers.

Subject Area: Information technology—electronic data interchange. Source: CIA 1193, III-42.

77. (a) If the company acknowledges messages initiated externally, then the alleged sender would have the opportunity to recognize that it had not sent the message and could notify the company of the potential forgery. Choice (b) is incorrect. Permitting only authorized employees to have access to transmission facilities controls for unauthorized access to the facilities but would not detect forged EDI messages. Choice (c) is incorrect. Delaying action on orders until a second order is received for the same goods defeats the purpose of using EDI, namely, rapid communication followed by rapid response. Choice (d) is incorrect. Writing all incoming messages to a write-once/read-many device is a good practice, but it will not detect forgeries.

Subject Area: Information technology—electronic data interchange. Source: CIA 1193, III-43.

78. (c) Writing all messages to a write-once/read-many device ensures that in the event of a dispute, the company can reproduce the messages exactly as it received and produced them. Choice (a) is incorrect. Writing all incoming messages to a tape file does not yield a completely defensible copy of the messages because tape files can be rewritten. Choice (b) is incorrect. Mailing confirmations to customers defeats the purpose of using EDI for business data exchange. Choice (d) is incorrect. Agreeing in advance to submit all disagreements to arbitration is a good policy even though it would not ensure the company would not be liable.

Subject Area: Information technology—electronic data interchange. Source: CIA 1193, III-44.

79. (a) Before sending or receiving electronic data interchange (EDI) messages with its customers and suppliers, the company should execute a trading partner agreement with its customers and suppliers so that all parties understand their responsibilities, the messages each will initiate, and how they will interpret the messages. Choice (b) is incorrect. The company may intend to reduce inventory levels, but that is unrelated to the timing of first sending and receiving electronic data interchange (EDI) messages. Choice (c) is incorrect. The company may want to demand or encourage all its customers and suppliers to implement electronic data interchange (EDI) capabilities, but that is independent to sending and receiving messages to customers and suppliers. Choice (d) is incorrect. It is not possible to evaluate the effectiveness of electronic data interchange (EDI) transmissions until after they occur.

Subject Area: Information technology—electronic data interchange. Source: CIA 1193, III-45.

80. (b) If the company and its customers will agree to synchronize their updating of electronic data interchange (EDI)-related software, then they will minimize the likelihood of unrecognizable or unintelligible messages due to software incompatibilities. Choice (a) is incorrect. The company and its customers may get their electronic data interchange (EDI)-related software from the same vendor but still have software incompatibility problems if they do not synchronize their installation of updated versions. Choice (c) is incorrect. As business requirements change, it may not be possible to use the same software in the same ways indefinitely. Choice (d) is incorrect. Even if the company and its customers each write their own version of the electronic data interchange (EDI)-related software, there will be synchronization problems with updates.

Subject Area: Information technology—electronic data interchange. Source: CIA 1193, III-46.

81. (d) Regardless of whether the company develops, buys, leases, or pays for the use of the software for electronic data interchange (EDI), internal audit should be responsible for evaluating that the applications meet business objectives. Choice (a) is incorrect. If the company developed its own software, internal audit would be responsible for evaluating that the software was developed in a controlled environment. Choice (b) is incorrect. If the company developed and maintained its own software, internal audit would be responsible for evaluating that the software is backed up adequately to permit recovery in the event of a system failure. Choice (c) is incorrect. If the company purchased, leased or paid for the use of the software, internal audit would be responsible for evaluating that the software was acquired with legal counsel review of contract terms.

Subject Area: Information technology—electronic data interchange. Source: CIA 1193, III-47.

82. (d) The most efficient approach for reducing the variation is to work with suppliers to help them deliver more uniform materials and thus avoid the costs of inspecting and handling any materials not immediately suitable for production. Choice (a) is incorrect. Inspecting raw materials before making them available for production would ensure higher quality materials for production but would not decrease the volume of materials that were unsuitable. Choice (b) is incorrect. Inspecting raw materials before accepting them from suppliers would ensure higher quality materials for production but would not decrease the volume of materials that had to be handled. Choice (c) is incorrect. Requiring suppliers to include a quality assessment with each shipment would make the quality known in advance but would not decrease the volume of materials that had to be handled.

Subject Area: Information technology—electronic data interchange. Source: CIA 1193, III-48.

83. (a) If the company gave the supplier more information about use of the materials, the supplier could plan its production better so that it could reduce its inventory of the materials and then reduce the price of the materials. Choice (b) is incorrect. The company could demand that the supplier reduce the prices of the materials, but the supplier could then decline to supply them. Choice (c) is incorrect. The company could attempt to find another supplier to replace the one charging higher prices, but since the materials are special, other suppliers would probably charge higher prices for the same reasons the original supplier did. Choice (d) is incorrect. If the special materials are needed in the primary product line, it is unlikely that the company would discontinue it before investigating other alternative (e.g., working with the supplier to help the supplier manage its inventory).

Subject Area: Information technology—electronic data interchange. Source: CIA 1193, III-49.

84. (c) Four days is the minimum cycle time because physical delivery requires four days. Choice (a) is incorrect. This cycle time does not include reductions possible by using electronic data interchange (EDI) to eliminate mail time and supplier process time. Choice (b) is incorrect. This cycle time does not include reductions possible by using EDI to eliminate supplier process time. Choice (d) is incorrect. The cycle time cannot be reduced below the delivery time of four days with implementation of EDI alone—more efficient transportation would be required.

Subject Area: Information technology—electronic data interchange. Source: CIA 1193, III-50.

85. (a) If implementing electronic data interchange (EDI) with suppliers permitted more frequent orders and more frequent communication about them, the company could reduce costs (e.g., inventory carrying costs) by reducing raw materials inventory. Choice (b) is incorrect. The company could ensure that it always maintained the 25-day buffer stock, but there would be no reason to do so if it could ensure more reliable deliveries by ordering more frequently. Choice (c) is incorrect. Tracking materials through production is not an example of EDI, which is intercompany exchange of business information. Choice (d) is incorrect. Scheduling production is not an example of EDI, which is intercompany exchange of business information.

Subject Area: Information technology—electronic data interchange. Source: CIA 1193, III-51.

86. (b) Shortening setup times permit smaller average batch sizes which permits reductions in inventory leading to decreased inventory holding costs. Choice (a) is incorrect. There are other factors and not considering them is shortsighted. Choice (c) is incorrect. Getting suppliers to deliver better quality raw materials is independent of an investment to decrease setup times. Choice (d) is incorrect. Coding batches of raw materials is independent of an investment to decrease setup times.

Subject Area: Information technology—electronic data interchange. Source: CIA 1193, III-52.

87. (a) Sending the supplier the requested data daily via electronic data interchange (EDI) would permit the supplier to smooth its production and thus let it hold down its costs. Choice (b) is incorrect. Sending the supplier usage data via weekly reports is better than none at all, but daily data are better. Choice (c) is incorrect. Sending the supplier usage data via monthly production reports is better than none at all, but daily data are better. Choice (d) is incorrect. Sending the supplier no data at all because it is confidential will probably lead to the supplier increasing its prices to the company in order for it to assume the increased risk entailed by having to be more responsive to the company's orders (i.e., the supplier assumes the cost of the inventory the company no longer maintains).

Subject Area: Information technology—electronic data interchange. Source: CIA 1193, III-53.

88. (d) Beginning bar coding for raw materials and production, implementing electronic data interchange (EDI) with suppliers and customers, and investing in new automated equipment for production creates the risk that employees may fail to modify their efforts consistent with the approaches, resulting in dysfunctional behavior (e.g., machine operators persisting in maximizing throughput rather than producing high-quality products to order). Choice (a) is incorrect. Instead of being less able to respond to customers' inquiries about their orders, the company should be better able to respond to customers' inquiries about their orders. Choice (b) is incorrect. Instead of being more likely to have stockouts, having less raw materials inventory because of the shift to better controlled ordering via EDI will decrease the likelihood of stockouts. Choice (c) is incorrect. The company produces only to order so there is no finished goods inventory before or after the changes.

Subject Area: Information technology—electronic data interchange. Source: CIA 1193, III-54.

89. (a) Marked benefits come about when EDI is tied to strategic efforts that alter, not mirror, previous practices. Applying EDI to an inefficient process results in the ability to continue doing things wrong, only faster. Choice (b) is incorrect. The prerequisite for EDI success is an understanding of the mission of the business and the processes and flows that support its goals, followed by cooperation with external partners. Hardware concerns are after. Choice (c) is incorrect. Before applying EDI technology to the business, EDI must be viewed as part of an overall integrated solution to organizational requirements. Choice (d) is incorrect. EDI is not a solution by itself. Instead of thinking about how to send transactions back and forth, a company has to first think about the entire process from both ends.

Subject Area: Information technology—electronic data interchange. Source: CIA 597, III-51.

90. (b) Tracking of customers' functional acknowledgments, when required, will help to ensure successful transmission of electronic data interchange (EDI) transactions. Choice (a) is incorrect. To address this issue, unauthorized access to the EDI system should be prevented, procedures should be in place to ensure the effective use of passwords, and data integrity and privacy should be maintained through the use of encryption and authentication measures. Choice (c) is incorrect. Contractual agreements should exist between the company and the EDI trading partners. Choice (d) is incorrect. The risk that EDI data may not be completely and accurately processed is primarily controlled by the system.

Subject Area: Information technology—electronic data interchange. Source: CIA 597, III-52.

91. (b) Improved business relationships with trading partners is a benefit of electronic data interchange (EDI). Choice (a) is incorrect. EDI transmits document data, not the actual document. Choice (c) is incorrect. Liability issues related to protection of proprietary business data is a major legal implication of EDI. Choice (d) is incorrect. EDI backup and contingency planning requirements are not diminished.

Subject Area: Information technology—electronic data interchange. Source: CIA 596, III-57.

92. (d) Items II and IV are correct. Determination whether an independent review of the third-party service provider has been performed (and appropriate follow-up) is required (Item II). Reviewing the third-party provider's contract is an appropriate audit step (Item IV). Item I is incorrect because using a third-party service provider does not mean encryption is utilized. Item III is incorrect because public switched data networks are not directly related to EDI applications.

Subject Area: Information technology—electronic data interchange. Source: CIA 596, III-59.

93. (d) Companies must purchase their own software to translate to a national standard protocol (either ANSI X.12 in the US or EDIFACT in Europe and most of the rest of the world). Once the data are in the standard format, the VAN handles all the communication. Choice (a) is incorrect because VANs normally act as a clearinghouse and storage house for communications between different organizations. Choice (b) is incorrect because VANs provide a common communication interface, thus eliminating the need for each company to establish independent communication with each of its trading partners. Choice (c) is incorrect because VANs establish logs of transactions as a basis for recordkeeping and audit trail.

Subject Area: Information technology—electronic data interchange. Source: CIA 1195, III-62.

Functional Areas of IT Operations

94. (c) Help desks are usually a responsibility of computer operations because of the operational nature of their functions (e.g., assisting users with systems problems involving prioritization and obtaining technical support/vendor assistance). Choice (a) is incorrect because applications development is responsible for developing systems. After formal acceptance by users, developers typically cease having day-to-day contact with system users. Choice (b) is incorrect because the responsibility of systems programming is to implement and maintain system-level software such as operating systems, access control software, and database systems software. Choice (d) is incorrect because the responsibility of user departments is to interact with application systems as planned. User departments typically do not have the expertise necessary to solve their own systems problems.

Subject Area: Information technology—functional areas of IT operations. Source: CIA 1196, III-55.

95. (a) An essential component of a disaster recovery plan is that the need for backup/restart has been anticipated and provided for in the application systems. Choice (b) is incorrect because change control procedures should not be bypassed by operating personnel, but that is not generally a consideration in disaster recovery planning. Choice (c) is incorrect because planned changes in equipment capacities should be compatible with projected workloads, but that is not generally a consideration in disaster recovery planning. Choice (d) is incorrect because service level agreements with owners of critical applications should be adequate, but that is not generally a consideration in disaster recovery planning.

Subject Area: Information technology—functional areas of IT operations. Source: CIA 596, III-39.

96. (a) In distributed or cooperative systems, the responsibility for ensuring that adequate backups are taken is the responsibility of user management because the systems are under the control of users. Choice (b) is incorrect because in distributed environments, there will be no systems programmers comparable to those at central sites for traditional systems. Choice (c) is incorrect because in distributed environments, there may be no data entry clerks because users are typically performing their own data entry. Choice (d) is incorrect because in distributed environments, there are no tape librarians.

Subject Area: Information technology—functional areas of IT operations. Source: CIA 596, III-75.

97. (c) A security control feature in tape management systems is the ability to restrict jobs from omitting label processing, which would make tapes vulnerable to unauthorized access. Choice (a) is incorrect because tape management systems are for managing tape libraries, not production program libraries on disk. Choice (b) is incorrect because prohibiting access to unauthorized data views is a security feature of database management systems. Choice (d) is incorrect because tape management systems are for managing tape libraries, not for controlling access to utility program libraries on disk.

Subject Area: Information technology—functional areas of IT operations. Source: CIA 595, III-70.

98. (b) The best control is automatic restart that prompts tellers to complete partial transactions. Choice (a) is incorrect because manual reconstruction of in-process transactions by tellers is more subject to error than an automated restart that prompts tellers to complete in-process transactions. Choice (c) is incorrect because computer reconciliation of accepted-item totals should indicate the dollar magnitude of unfinished transactions but would not help individual tellers complete their most recent transactions. This kind of reconciliation is typically applied in batch rather than to online systems. Choice (d) is incorrect because manual reconciliation of accepted-item totals should indicate the dollar magnitude of unfinished transactions but would not help individual tellers complete their most recent transactions. This kind of reconciliation is typically applied in batch rather than to online systems.

Subject Area: Information technology—functional areas of IT operations. Source: CIA 1190, II-33.

99. (d) The biggest risk in not having an adequately staffed help desk is that users will unknowingly persist in making errors in their interaction with the information systems. Choice (a) is incorrect because application audits should be about the same difficulty with or without an adequately staffed help desk. Choice (b) is incorrect because preparation of documentation is a development function, not a help desk function. Choice (c) is incorrect because the likelihood of use of unauthorized program code is a function of change control, not of a help desk.

Subject Area: Information technology—functional areas of IT operations. Source: CIA Model Exam 2002, III-43.

100. (c) Authorization tables for operating system access address logical controls, not physical controls. Choice (a) is incorrect because external risks should be evaluated to determine the center's location. Choice (b) is incorrect because biometric access systems control physical access to the data center. Choice (d) is incorrect because power supply systems and surge protection are included in data center design.

Subject Area: Information technology—functional areas of IT operations. Source: CIA Model Exam 2002, III-46.

101. (b) Matching the input data with information held on master or suspense files is a processing control, not an output control, to ensure that data are complete and accurate during updating. Choice (a) is incorrect because review of the computer processing logs is an output control to ensure that data are accurate and complete. Choice (c) is incorrect because periodic reconciliation of output reports are an output control to ensure that data are accurate and complete. Choice (d) is incorrect because maintaining formal procedures and documentation specifying authorized recipients is an output control to ensure proper distribution.

Subject Area: Information technology—functional areas of IT operations. Source: CIA Model Exam 2002, III-47.

102. (c) Program change control comprises: (1) maintaining records of change authorizations, code changes, and test results; (2) adhering to a systems development methodology (including documentation); (3) authorizing changeovers of subsidiary and headquarters' interfaces; and (4) restricting access to authorized source and executable codes. Choice (a) is incorrect because frequently, the purpose of database reviews is to determine if: (1) users have gained access to database areas for which they have no authorization and (2) authorized users can access the database using programs that provide them with unauthorized privileges to view and/or change information. Choice (b) is incorrect because the purpose of compliance reviews is to determine whether an organization has complied with applicable internal and external procedures and regulations. Choice (d) is incorrect because the purpose of network security software is to provide logical controls over the network.

Subject Area: Information technology—functional areas of IT operations. Source: CIA Model Exam 2002, III-49.

103. (c) Activity logging provides an audit trail of user activity. Choice (a) is incorrect because programmed cutoff controls mitigate the risk of recording transactions in the wrong period. Choice (b) is incorrect because redundant hardware is a control over hardware malfunction. Choice (d) is incorrect because transaction error logging controls transactions rather than user terminal activity.

Subject Area: Information technology—functional areas of IT operations. Source: CIA Model Exam 2002, III-50.

104. (c) The least likely feature of a query tool would be a data validity checker because the database system has already enforced any validity constraints at the time the data were inserted in the database. Any further data validity checking would be a function of a user application program rather than a query. Choice (a) is incorrect because most query tools include the capability of presenting the results of queries graphically. Choice (b) is incorrect because query tools include data dictionary access because that is how they know what table attributes to present to users. Choice (d) is incorrect because query tools typically have a query-by-example interface.

Subject Area: Information technology—functional areas of IT operations. Source: CIA Model Exam 2002, III-55.

105. (c) The plan should include goals and objectives, an inventory of current capacity, and a forecast of future needs. Choice (a) is incorrect because contingency planning refers to the arrangements for alternative processing facilities in the event of equipment failure. Choice (b) is incorrect because the feasibility study is one of the phases in the systems development life cycle. Choice (d) is incorrect because exception reports are meant to highlight problems and bring them to the attention of management.

Subject Area: Information technology—functional areas of IT operations. Source: CIA Model Exam 1998, III-80.

Encryption

106. (b) Encryption limits an intruder's ability to understand and use the data; frequently changed passwords limit unauthorized access to the files. Choice (a) is incorrect because controlled disposal of documents is not limited to computer files; choice (b) is more complete. Manually maintained files must be protected too. Choices (c) and (d) are incorrect. Key integrity checks are not access-related controls. Key integrity checks prevent the updating process from creating inaccuracies in keys. Each of these choices is partially complete from the encryption and password point of view.

Subject Area: Information technology—encryption. Source: CIA 593, I-30.

107. (d) Cryptographic devices protect data in transmission over communication lines. A key notarization can be used in conjunction with a cryptographic device to provide increased data security. Key management involves the secure generation, distribution, and storage of cryptographic keys. Choice (a) is incorrect because asynchronous modems handle data streams from peripheral devices to a central processor. Choice (b) is incorrect because authentication techniques confirm that valid users have access to the system. Choice (c) is incorrect because callback techniques are used to ensure incoming calls are from authorized locations.

Subject Area: Information technology—encryption. Source: CIA 592, I-32.

108. (a) Various factors need to be considered. Encoding is important when confidential data are transmitted between geographically separated locations that can be electronically monitored. Although LANs may need encryption protection, the type of data and the described communication media make the other options appear more vulnerable. Choices (b), (c), and (d) are incorrect because encryption is often used in these situations.

Subject Area: Information technology—encryption. Source: CIA 594, III-13.

109. (b) Encryption is the conversion of data into a code. While data may be accessed by tapping into the transmission line, an encryption "key" is necessary in order to understand the data being sent. Choice (a) is incorrect because asynchronous transmission does not prevent theft of data; it speeds up the transmission process. Choice (c) is incorrect because fiber-optic transmission lines will improve the quality of the transmission, but will not prevent theft of data. Choice (d) is incorrect because use of passwords will control access at the sending location, and will limit access to the head-office computer. Passwords, however, will not prevent someone from tapping into the transmission line.

Subject Area: Information technology—encryption. Source: CIA 597, I-5.

110. (d) Encryption of data from entry to the network and its return would provide the best security. Choice (a) is incorrect because dedicated phone lines would not be cost effective or available to field agents. Choice (b) is incorrect because field agents would not always be located at the same phone line to permit dial-up call back usage. Choice (c) is incorrect because passwords may be compromised by computer software.

Subject Area: Information technology—encryption. Source: CIA 1196, III-59.

111. (a) RSA requires two keys: the public key for encrypting messages is widely known but the private key for decrypting messages is kept secret by the recipient. Choice (b) is incorrect because DES requires only a single key for each pair of communicants that want to send each other encrypted messages. Choice (c) is incorrect because a modem is used for telecommunications. Choice (d) is incorrect because a cypher lock is a physical device.

Subject Area: Information technology—encryption. Source: CIA 1196, III-77.

112. (c) The machine instructions necessary to encrypt and decrypt data constitute system overhead, which means that processing may be slowed down. Choice (a) is incorrect because no encryption approach absolutely guarantees the secrecy of data in transmission although encryption approaches are considered to be less amenable to being broken than others. Choice (b) is incorrect because keys may be distributed manually, but they may also be distributed electronically via secure key transporters. Choice (d) is incorrect because using encryption software does not reduce the need for periodic password changes because passwords are the typical means of validating users' access to unencrypted data.

Subject Area: Information technology—encryption. Source: CIA 1196, III-78.

113. (a) Encryption is the best means of ensuring the confidentiality of satellite transmissions because even if an unauthorized individual recorded the transmissions, they would not be intelligible. Choice (b) is incorrect because access control applies to gaining entrance to the application systems, not to the format of transmissions. Choice (c) is incorrect because monitoring software is designed to monitor performance (human or machine) for specified functions such as number of tasks performed or capacity utilized. Choice (d) is incorrect because cyclic redundancy checks are complex computations performed with the data bits and the check bits in data transmissions to ensure the integrity, but not the confidentiality, of the data.

Subject Area: Information technology—encryption. Source: CIA 596, III-47.

Information Protection

114. (c) The described condition is a symptom of a virus. Many viruses will spread and cause additional damage by performing choices (a), (b), and (d). Use of an appropriate antivirus program may identify and even eliminate a virus infection. Choice (a) is incorrect because the application program could be infected with the computer virus. Choice (b) is incorrect because the entire operating system could be infected with the computer virus. Choice (d) is incorrect because the data files on floppies or diskettes could be infected with the computer virus.

Subject Area: Information technology—information protection. Source: CIA 594, III-29.

115. (c) Acceptably safe computing can be achieved by carefully crafted policies and procedures used in conjunction with antivirus and access control software. Choice (a) is incorrect. Hiring policies can provide assurance of qualified personnel for operation of the system, but cannot prevent introduction of viruses from bulletin boards or from outside sources. Choice (b) is incorrect. Software programs can identify and neutralize known viruses but may not recognize and properly neutralize new strains of a computer virus. Choice (d) is incorrect. Physical protection devices can reduce access but cannot prevent introduction of viruses by errant employees or from outside sources.

Subject Area: Information technology—information protection. Source: CIA 593, II-20.

116. (c) Allowing only authorized software from known sources to be used on the system reduces the likelihood of introducing a computer virus onto the system via software. Choice (a) is incorrect because comparing software in use with authorized versions of the software is a detective measure, not a preventative measure. Choice (b) is incorrect because executing virus exterminator programs periodically on the system is a detective/corrective measure, not a preventative measure. Choice (d) is incorrect because preparing and testing a plan for recovering from the incidence of a virus is a corrective measure, not a preventative measure.

Subject Area: Information technology—information protection. Source: CIA 591, III-24.

117. (b) Unexplainable loss of or changes to data files are symptomatic of a virus attack. Choice (a) is incorrect because power surges are symptomatic of hardware or environmental (power supply) problems. Choice (c) is incorrect because inadequate backup, recovery, and contingency plans are symptomatic of operating policy and/or compliance problems. Choice (d) is incorrect because copyright violations are symptomatic of operating policy and/or compliance problems.

Subject Area: Information technology—information protection. Source: CIA 1196, III-40.

118. (c) There is a risk that downloaded public domain software may be contaminated with a virus. Choices (a) and (b) are incorrect because viruses are spread through the distribution of computer programs. Choice (d) is incorrect because original purchased software should be virus-free and cannot legally be shared.

Subject Area: Information technology—information protection. Source: CIA 1196, III-41.

119. (d) Snapshot files are recreated at intervals (e.g., daily, weekly, or monthly). Therefore, the data will not be as current as the file from which they were extracted. If the data are so old that they are no longer useful, then they lack currency. Choice (a) is incorrect. Data replication is the approach of wholly replicating data on multiple devices to improve accessibility. No replicas are involved in this use of snapshots. Choice (b) is incorrect. Data fragmentation is the approach of distributing data across different locations such that the fragments from the different locations must be put together to give the complete file. No data fragmentation is involved in this use of snapshots. Choice (c) is incorrect. Premature committing of transactions occurs when some but not all the required data for a business transaction are written. The snapshot approach does not involve any writing of transactions to files, which means that committing transactions is not associated with the snapshot approach.

Subject Area: Information technology—information protection. Source: CIA 1196, III-47.

120. (d) Software from recognized sources should be tested in isolation because even vendor-supplied software may be infected with viruses. Choice (a) is incorrect. If viruses infect a system, the company should restore the system with authorized software, but this procedure would not minimize the likelihood of the system being infected initially. Choice (b) is incorrect. If viruses infect programs that the company wrote, it should recompile the programs from source code backups, but this procedure would not minimize the likelihood of the system being infected initially. Choice (c) is incorrect. Instituting program change control procedures is good practice, but this would not minimize the likelihood of the system being infected initially.

Subject Area: Information technology—information protection. Source: CIA 595, III-67.

121. (a) A risk in relying on antivirus software is that antivirus software only works for known viruses and may not be completely effective for variants of known ones. In other words, there is no guarantee that the software identifies all viruses. Choice (b) is incorrect because antivirus software is unlikely to make software installation overly complex. Choice (c) is incorrect because antivirus software need not interfere with system operations because its execution scheduling can be set in advance not to interfere with running programs. Choice (d) is incorrect because antivirus software can be set to execute at times when it would not consume too many system resources (for example, at startup).

Subject Area: Information technology—information protection. Source: CIA 1195, III-37.

122. (a) Connecting all networked personal computers through a host computer to outside networks increases the exposure of all company computers to viruses coming from the outside. Choice (b) is incorrect. Whether uploaded files are properly edited and validated is independent of whether external links to other networks exist. Choice (c) is incorrect. Whether data downloaded to the personal computers is sufficiently timely is independent of whether external links to other networks exist. Choice (d) is incorrect. Whether software maintenance on the personal computers becomes more costly is independent of whether external links to other networks exist.

Subject Area: Information technology—information protection. Source: CIA 1195, III-61.

123. (d) In this way the code is hidden and the mainframe's clock can be monitored to assure a safe time delay. Choice (a) is incorrect because it assumes that access is restricted. Choice (b) is incorrect because it assumes password protection. Choice (c) is incorrect because most computer crime is by individuals.

Subject Area: Information technology—information protection. Source: CIA 1190, III-19.

124. (a) A risk in relying on antivirus software is that antivirus software only works for known viruses and may not be completely effective for variants of known ones. In other words, there is no guarantee that the software identifies all viruses. Choice (b) is incorrect because antivirus software is unlikely to make software installation overly complex. Choice (c) is incorrect because antivirus software need not interfere with system operations because its execution scheduling can be set in advance not to interfere with running programs. Choice (d) is incorrect because antivirus software can be set to execute at times when it would not consume too many system resources (for example, at startup).

Subject Area: Information technology—information protection. Source: CIA Model Exam 2002, III-71.

125. (b) The information security officer should not even know the user passwords. These are normally stored by a computer in encrypted format, and users change them directly. Choices (a), (c), and (d) are incorrect because each one of them is an appropriate duty of the information security officer.

Subject Area: Information technology—information protection. Source: CIA 596, III-44.

126. (a) Once in place, electronic mail can deliver information faster and more cost effectively. Choice (b) is incorrect. They require that users have access to appropriate hardware and have been trained in how to log on and use the various features of the system. Choice (c) is incorrect. All senders and receivers must be wired into the network and acquire the necessary hardware to utilize the system. Choice (d) is incorrect. Only individuals who have been given appropriate access passwords and identification codes recognized by the system can use it.

Subject Area: Information technology—information protection. Source: CIA 1193, III-24.

127. (b) The person or the organization sending an e-mail message has the utmost responsibility for the message's security. This is because the sender is initiating the message.

Subject Area: Information technology—information protection. Source: Author.

128. (a) Pretty good privacy (PGP) is a cryptographic software application for the protection of computer files and electronic mail. PGP provides a very good authentication mechanism and reasonable confidentiality protection. Point-to-point protocol (PPP) connects two TCP/IP devices over a standard serial line, such as a common telephone link. Microcom networking protocol (MNP) defines various levels of error correction and compression for modems. Password authentication protocol (PAP) is a handshaking protocol.

Subject Area: Information technology—information protection. Source: Author.

129. (b) A policy is management directive that sets the tone for the electronic mail (e-mail) security. Policy is the most important one and drives the other items, such as a procedure, standard, or guideline. Choice (a) is incorrect because procedures are derived from policies. Procedures are detailed instructions to comply with the e-mail security. Choice (c) is incorrect because standards are derived from policies. Choice (d) is incorrect because guidelines are derived from policies. Standards are mandatory whereas guidelines are suggestive in nature.

Subject Area: Information technology—information protection. Source: Author.

130. (a) The company should have access to the business-related e-mail that is left behind. Access to e-mail can also be critical in business or possible criminal investigations. The privacy concerns of the individual case must be mitigated by compelling business interests: the need to follow-up on business e-mail and to assist in investigations. Choice (b) is incorrect. Encryption helps prevent eavesdropping of unauthorized persons trying to compromise e-mail messages. Choice (c) is incorrect. Such standards simplify the job of managing technology and reduce the possibility that the system will remove encryption when it passes messages from one system to another. Choice (d) is incorrect. This is an appropriate privacy control technique because of the inherent weaknesses in e-mail security.

Subject Area: Information technology—information protection. Source: CIA 596, III-60.

131. (a) Electronic mail system has those features that the other systems do not have. Choice (b) is incorrect because it lacks Read and Print capability. Choice (c) is incorrect because only Edit and Print are listed. Choice (d) is incorrect because it refers to method of transmission, not features.

Subject Area: Information technology—information protection. Source: CIA 1190, III-20.

132. (c) Items I and III are correct. Item II is incorrect because a confidential mail message should not be retained on the server once the user has downloaded it to a personal computer (PC).

Subject Area: Information technology—information protection. Source: CIA Model Exam 1998, III-41.

133. (b) Passwords are effective against the casual intruder. Choice (a) is incorrect because messages on the Internet are not encrypted. It is the sender and receiver's responsibility to encrypt confidential information. Choice (c) is incorrect because if someone gains access to the server, they can download the file of messages and gain access to the messages without working with any security log. Choice (d) is incorrect because discretionary access does not completely eliminate the need for passwords.

Subject Area: Information technology—information protection. Source: CIA Model Exam 1998, III-54.

134. (a) While most delete programs erase file pointers, they do not remove the underlying data. The company must use special utilities that fully erase the data. This is especially important because of the potential for top-secret data on the microcomputers. This risk is the largest because it could cause them to lose military contract business. Choice (b) is incorrect because this could create a liability for the company if a virus destroyed the purchasing party's data or programs. However, the purchasing party should use anti-viral software to detect and eliminate any viruses. This concern, while important, is not as serious as the one in choice (a). Choice (c) is incorrect because the purchasing party has a responsibility to insure that all their software is properly licensed. If the company represented that all the software was properly licensed, this could create a liability. However, this liability is not as serious as the implication from choice (a). Choice (d) is incorrect because terminal emulation software is widely available.

Subject Area: Information technology—information protection. CIA 597, III-63.

135. (d) Transactions with unauthorized vendors are risks associated with the accounts payable component of an integrated system. Choices (a), (b), and (c) are incorrect because each choice is a risk associated with the accounts receivable component.

Subject Area: Information technology—information protection. Source: CIA 594, III-28.

136. (c) The amount of a discrepancy between two batch totals often provides a clue about the error. When a difference can be divided evenly by 9, a transposition error may have occurred during data input where the column amounts in two adjacent columns are exchanged. Other possibilities to consider include looking for transactions exactly equal to the amount of the discrepancy or transactions equal to half of the discrepancy. In the later case, a transaction may have been incorrectly debited or credited. Choice (a) is incorrect. The nature of the discrepancy, a small number in an even dollar amount evenly divisible by 9, suggests that double recording is less likely than a transposition error. Choice (b) is incorrect. If an error or irregularity had occurred, it would have been likely during data input, not output. Choice (d) is incorrect. If the prior day's cash receipts prelist were wrong, the Head Cashier is likely to have discovered and reported this either when preparing the bank deposit or after agreeing the prelist to the validated bank deposit.

Subject Area: Information technology—information protection. Source: CIA 594, III-35.

137. (a) This takes a short period of time and includes external verification of the amount on the cash receipts prelist. This would prove that an error was made during data input suggesting that further investigative effort should be concentrated there. Choice (b) is incorrect. The external validation in choice (a) is better, as well as more efficient. Choice (c) is incorrect. The narrative implies that the accounts receivable General Ledger Account is updated when the accounts receivable subsidiary ledgers are updated. Thus, there would be no difference between these amounts. Choice (d) is incorrect. Minor errors should be investigated and corrected by operating personnel.

Subject Area: Information technology—information protection. Source: CIA 594, III-36.

138. (a) Batch processing is probably used. Choice (b) is incorrect. Cash receipts are not updated immediately as they occur. Choice (c) is incorrect. This is not discussed, nor is it likely considering the technological state of the described systems. Choice (d) is incorrect. It is not a remote location.

Subject Area: Information technology—information protection. Source: CIA 594, III-37.

139. (d) Computerized batch processing environments need batch total controls to detect errors that cannot be discovered through other input edit checks. The other listed controls would not detect an input error in a dollar amount; they are designed to detect other errors. Choice (a) is incorrect because check-digit verification is used when a self-checking digit is included in an identification number. It can detect errors in fields, such as account or inventory numbers. Choice (b) is incorrect because a sequence check looks for numerical or alphabetical sequence discrepancies. Choice (c) is incorrect because a field check detects if the input characters are of the expected type (i.e., alpha, numeric, or alpha/numeric).

Subject Area: Information technology—information protection. Source: CIA 594, III-38.

140. (a) The totals could agree, but individual payments could be posted to wrong accounts. This would not be caught by the above procedures. Choices (b) and (c) are incorrect because these derive from the logic of the narrative. Choice

(d) is incorrect because this is typically used for batch processing.

Subject Area: Information technology—information protection. Source: CIA 594, III-39.

141. (b) Having check digits in the order codes and verifying them for each order would detect transposed digits. Choice (a) is incorrect. Having customers specify the name for each item they order would let the company correct erroneous order codes once they had been detected, but would not, in general, detect erroneous codes. Choice (c) is incorrect. Separating the parts of the order code with hyphens would make the characters easier to read, but would not cure the problem of transposed characters. Choice (d) is incorrect. Using a master file reference for all order codes would verify the existence of items, but would not detect erroneous order codes in which transposed characters in an order code match other items.

Subject Area: Information technology—information protection. Source: CIA 1193, I-29.

142. (d) Sorting orders by area, computing taxes in aggregate, and comparing the amount with the sum of individual taxes charged for each area verifies that the individual computations were performed correctly. Choice (a) is incorrect. Moving the program code that computes sales taxes to a single program and making this program part of the processing sequence is a good system design approach, but it does not guarantee that sales tax processing is complete. Choice (b) is incorrect. Changing the operator input screens to show the computation of the sales tax so the operator can verify the computation would not ensure correct application of sales taxes because the operator will generally not know what the appropriate computation is. Choice (c) is incorrect. Modifying the program code to prompt the operator to ask customers if their areas have sales taxes and enter the appropriate rates is unlikely to ensure correct application of sales taxes because customers may not know the right rates or may deny that their areas impose the taxes.

Subject Area: Information technology—information protection. Source: CIA 1193, I-30.

143. (b) A control total is a test of completeness. Choice (a) is incorrect because an existence check is a test of accuracy. Choice (c) is incorrect because a limit check is a test of accuracy. Choice (d) is incorrect because a reasonableness check is a test of accuracy.

Subject Area: Information technology—information protection. Source: CIA 1193, I-27.

144. (a) Run-to-run controls for an online system are as described. Choice (b) is incorrect because computer matching compares transaction data to referenced fields or records. Choice (c) is incorrect because computer sequence checks identify changes or breaks in a numerical sequence. Choice (d) is incorrect because one-for-one checking generally requires manual comparisons of input data elements to processing results.

Subject Area: Information technology—information protection. Source: CIA 1193, II-25.

145. (a) Looking up the ZIP (mail) code in a master file of ZIP (mail) codes would permit the operator to verify the state abbreviation while talking to the customer. Choice (b) is incorrect. Looking up the state abbreviation is insufficient to permit the operator to verify the ZIP (mail) code. Choice (c) is incorrect. This is a less reliable control, since it requires verbal verification of the states rather than computer matching. Choice (d) is incorrect. In general, it is not feasible to determine ZIP (mail) codes from street, city, and state addresses that can be entered in multiple ways.

Subject Area: Information technology—information protection. Source: CIA 1193, II-29.

146. (b) Creating destination defaults for printing based on each employee's departmental affiliation removes the requirement of employees specifying the destination code and the opportunities for misspecification that send printing to the wrong device. Choice (a) is incorrect. Permitting departments to cancel printing that does not belong to one of their employees might free up printers faster but would antagonize other departments' employees. Choice (c) is incorrect. Putting all the printers in one location might result in efficient printer use, but the constraints of centralized facilities are exactly why users want decentralized facilities for printing in their departments. Choice (d) is incorrect. Training users in how to specify the right designation codes for their printing will help current users, but will not ensure that they use the right codes or those subsequent employees will understand the codes.

Subject Area: Information technology—information protection. Source: CIA 1193, II-31.

147. (b) Validity tests are used to ensure that transactions contain valid transaction codes, valid characters, and valid field size. Choice (a) is incorrect because completeness tests are used to ensure that the input has the prescribed amount of data in all data fields. Choice (c) is incorrect because limit tests are used to determine whether the data exceeds certain predetermined limits. Choice (d) is incorrect because control totals are used to reconcile system input to the source document totals.

Subject Area: Information technology—information protection. Source: CIA 593, I-9.

148. (a) Check-digit verification is an example of an input control. Choice (b) is incorrect because check-digit verification is not a file management control. Internal label check is an example of a file management control. Choice (c) is incorrect because check-digit verification is not an access control. Password is an example of access control. Choice (d) is incorrect because check-digit verification is not an output control. Report balancing is an example of an output control.

Subject Area: Information technology—information protection. Source: CIA 593, I-23.

149. (c) A master file lookup is the best control for denying withdrawals on inactive accounts. Choice (a) is incorrect. A proof calculation is the use of a predefined algorithm to be performed on the information in a telecommunications transmission to verify that no transmission errors occurred. Choice (b) is incorrect. A check-digit verification is used to control the accuracy of input of reference numbers but would not deny access to an inactive but valid account. Choice (d) is incorrect. A duplicate record check ensures that duplicate records are not processed.

Subject Area: Information technology—information protection. Source: CIA 593, I-24.

150. (a) Cycle processing controls mitigate the risk of missing or improper transactions. Batch control or hash total control is an example of cycle processing control. Choice (b) is incorrect because proof calculations mitigate the risk of transmission errors. Choice (c) is incorrect because restart and recovery controls mitigate the risk of lost transactions when processing is interrupted. Choice (d) is incorrect because programmed cutoff controls prevent improper cutoff and mitigate the risk of transactions being recorded in the wrong period.

Subject Area: Information technology—information protection. Source: CIA 593, II-24.

151. (a) The error in this case is overspending the budget. The control prevented this from occurring. Choice (b) is incorrect because detection occurs after the fact. It is untimely. Choice (c) is incorrect because correction fixes the error, comes after the fact. Choice (d) is incorrect because recovery relates to automated detection of error conditions and attempts by the software (usually vendor software such as a database) to recover from an error condition.

Subject Area: Information technology—information protection. Source: CIA 593, III-43.

152. (c) If claim data for a claim is entered in multiple sessions, then there must be a programmed control to verify that the claim data are complete before payment is authorized. Choice (a) is incorrect because backups might be incomplete or untimely, but not because there are multiple data entry sessions for the same claim. Choice (b) is incorrect because the audit trail is independent of whether multiple clerks enter data about the same claim. Choice (d) is incorrect because data entry clerks might enter fraudulent claim data whether data entry is accomplished in one session or in several sessions.

Subject Area: Information technology—information protection. Source: CIA 593, III-48.

153. (a) A dependency check would test whether the data elements for a loan application are logically consistent. Choice (b) is incorrect because a reasonableness check tests whether the data contents entered fall within predetermined limits. Choice (c) is incorrect because a format check ensures that all required data are present in the prescribed form. Choice (d) is incorrect because an existence check tests whether the entered data codes are valid codes held on the file or in the program.

Subject Area: Information technology—information protection. Source: CIA 593, III-49.

154. (b) Check-digit verification of account numbers prevents incorrect, but valid, matches of an update transaction to the master file. Check-digit verification prevents single digit errors from leading to erroneous updates. Choice (a) is incorrect because verifying that the account number corresponds to an existing account in the master file is a master file reference check. Choice (c) is incorrect because ensuring that supporting documentation exists for update transactions is a document reconciliation control. Choice (d) is incorrect because requiring a field to have the correct logical relationship with other fields is a dependency check.

Subject Area: Information technology—information protection. Source: CIA 1192, I-31.

155. (b) Batch total checks provide a reasonably good test for completeness to accuracy input. Choice (a) is incorrect because sequence checking provides a reasonably good test for completeness of input but does not test accuracy. Choice (c) is incorrect because limit checks are useful to determine whether an entry is within acceptable limits, only. Such limitation makes the limit check unusable to test the accuracy of input. Choice (d) is incorrect because a check digit allows the computer to automatically reject incorrect entries. The cumbersome computation required to establish the check digit, however, tends to limit its use to a few key entries. They are never used to test accuracy of input for an entire working document.

Subject Area: Information technology—information protection. Source: CIA 1192, I-34.

156. (a) A reasonableness check of wage rates based on job classification would have detected this error before an overpayment occurred. Choice (b) is incorrect because self-checking digit detects account number transposition. Choice (c) is incorrect because in this example, there is no prior data for matching. Choice (d) is incorrect because a mathematical accuracy check verifies the results of computation but would not have detected this error.

Subject Area: Information technology—information protection. Source: CIA 1192, II-33.

157. (c) Restart procedures tell computer users which transactions were lost when the operating system failed. Choice (a) is incorrect because online debugging tests of programs involve searching memory for particular values. Choice (b) is incorrect because feedback to originating terminals identifies transactions that were lost or never submitted for processing. Choice (d) is incorrect because online debugging tests of programs permit changing the contents of memory locations.

Subject Area: Information technology—information protection. Source: CIA 1191, I-32.

158. (a) The check-digit control is designed to catch transposition errors. Choice (b) is incorrect because control totals are intended to ensure completeness of processing. Choice (c) is incorrect because limit checks are intended to determine whether a data value falls within certain limits. Choice (d) is incorrect because a value test is used to check a data field for a certain value.

Subject Area: Information technology—information protection. Source: CIA 1191, II-29.

159. (c) Machine-readable documents are sources of data for computer processing. Choice (a) is incorrect because protocols are specified forms of agreements as to how data and control data are packaged for transmission. Choice (b) is incorrect because multiplexors are types of equipment to divide communication lines into segments to facilitate data transmission. Choice (d) is incorrect because fiber-optic lines are types of channels for rapid transmission of data.

Subject Area: Information technology—information protection. Source: CIA 591, III-32.

160. (b) Matching the input data with information held on master or suspense files is a processing control, not an output control, to ensure that data are complete and accurate during updating. Choice (a) is incorrect because review of the computer processing logs is an output control to ensure that data are accurate and complete. Choice (c) is incorrect because periodic reconciliation of output reports is an output control to ensure that data are accurate and complete. Choice (d) is incorrect because maintaining formal procedures and documentation specifying authorized recipients is an output control to ensure proper distribution.

Subject Area: Information technology—information protection. Source: CIA 597, III-37.

161. (d) To the extent the schedules incorporate erroneous logic, there is the potential for the schedules to fail to illustrate the potential range (understate or overstate the potential volatility) of the loan balances over time. Choice (a) is incorrect because the schedules could understate the potential volatility of loan balances over time but could also overstate it. Choice (b) is incorrect because the schedules could overstate the potential volatility of loan balances over time but could also understate it. Choice (c) is incorrect because the schedules could exhibit a conservative bias in the portrayal of loan balances but could just as easily exhibit an aggressive bias.

Subject Area: Information technology—information protection. Source: CIA 596, III-41.

162. (a) Any potential risk of erroneous logic in the schedules could be minimized by adequate independent testing of the application to detect any errors that the broker could not recognize. Choice (b) is incorrect. The application should have adequate backup procedures, but that would not detect or correct logic errors in the schedules. Choice (c) is incorrect. To the extent the schedules are shared with other brokers, there should be adequate control procedures, but that would not detect or correct logic errors in the schedules. Choice (d) is incorrect. There should be adequate documentation for the schedules, but that would not detect or correct logic errors in the schedules.

Subject Area: Information technology—information protection. Source: CIA 596, III-42.

163. (a) A validation check at data entry that verifies that a quantity field contains only numbers is an example of a programmatic means of ensuring the accuracy of the value in that no nonnumeric characters are permitted; this is an input control. Choice (b) is incorrect because the purpose of an audit trail control is to ensure that a chronological record of all relevant events in a system has been recorded. Choice (c) is incorrect because a processing control ensures that data are complete and accurate during updating. Choice (d) is incorrect because a data security control ensures that only authorized individuals are permitted to access and use a system.

Subject Area: Information technology—information protection. Source: CIA 1195, III-63.

164. (a) A preventive control is designed to prevent errors from occurring. In this case, the missing transactions are noted by the computer program. Choice (b) is incorrect. Usually, detective controls are needed when preventive controls are not in place. When there is a choice, preventive controls are much preferred since they cost less to correct. Choice (c) is incorrect. Corrective controls fix both detected and reported errors. It is too late by the time the corrective controls are needed. Choice (d) is incorrect. Discretionary control is a distracter here since there is no such term in computer controls.

Subject Area: Information technology—information protection. Source: CIA 594, III-31.

165. (a) The other controls would not find this error. Only batch control does. Choice (b) is incorrect because this is a hardware control that checks for accuracy in data transmission; it is not an input control. Choice (c) is incorrect because this would only work if the two amounts were reversed, and there was a dollar limit on invoices. Choice (d) is incorrect because this control checks for positive or negative field restrictions.

Subject Area: Information technology—information protection. Source: CIA 594, III-14.

166. (a) Management relies on the integrity of the system data and programs in making critical business decisions. Choice (b) is incorrect because user documentation, while an important technique in teaching controls, is not a specific overall control objective. Choice (c) is incorrect because efficiency would not affect the basis of critical management decisions using information provided by the system. Choice (d) is incorrect because rejected and suspense item controls represent only a portion of the techniques used to insure information integrity.

Subject Area: Information technology—information protection. Source: CIA 1193, III-18.

167. (c) Explicit checking for data values with error messages for unknown values would have detected the biweekly employee pay requests and generated error messages rather than erroneous checks. Choice (a) is incorrect because redundant calculations check the results of calculations performed in another manner (e.g., to verify that machine idiosyncrasies do not affect results). Choice (b) is incorrect because the input itself was valid, so validity checking would not have detected the error. Choice (d) is incorrect because checkpoint/restart processing permits the operator to restart a failed program without rerunning the entire process.

Subject Area: Information technology—information protection. Source: CIA 590, I-21.

168. (d) Comparing the hash totals gives assurance that transactions were processed once and only once. Choice (a) is incorrect because check-digit processing and master file look-ups verify that employee numbers are valid. Choice (b) is incorrect because completeness tests verify that all authorized employees are paid. Choice (c) is incorrect because hash totals are independent of authorized payroll payments.

Subject Area: Information technology—information protection. Source: CIA 590, I-22.

169. (d) At the end of the run, the processing program can compare control totals of debits and credits entered on a control record with totals determined by summing the debit and credit entries posted to the file. Choice (a) is incorrect because a generation number check verifies that the right version (generation) of a data file is used in processing. Choice (b) is incorrect because a master reference check verifies that an input data field matches a corresponding field in a file to be updated. Choice (c) is incorrect because a hash total gives assurance that all records were processed by comparing totals of sums of data fields (e.g., account numbers, that normally would not be added in actual processing).

Subject Area: Information technology—information protection. Source: CIA 590, I-23.

170. (d) In a cumulative sequence check, sequence numbers flag transaction table entries so there is a record of which transactions were processed. This record permits detection of attempted duplicate transactions and missing transactions. This question pertains to input controls. Choice (a) is incorrect because manual agreement of a batch register gives assurance that the batch totals agree but does not identify the specific missing or duplicate transactions. Choice (b) is incorrect because computer agreement of batch totals gives assurance that the batch totals agree but does not identify the specific missing or duplicate transactions. Choice (c) is incorrect because batch sequence checks perform sequence checks within single batches only.

Subject Area: Information technology—information protection. Source: CIA 1190, I-33.

171. (c) Reconciling record counts of sequence flags set and records updated would detect situations in which records were not updated. This question pertains to lack of controls associated with processing systems. Choice (a) is incorrect. Performing prior data matching of transactions and master file records ensures that the right master file record is updated but does not ensure that the record is updated. Choice (b) is incorrect. The control account technique ensures that the correct master file generation is used. Choice (d) is incorrect. Making memo updates to the database with subsequent processing permits detection of duplicate updates but does not ensure that the update occurred.

Subject Area: Information technology—information protection. Source: CIA 1190, I-36.

172. (b) A header label would alert the computer operator as to what the contents of the file being loaded were and would require an acknowledgement before the processing was to begin. Choice (a) is incorrect because this would check to make sure that given a preassigned numbering sequence there were no missing items in the input group. Choice (c) is incorrect because this would check the detail of the input items. It would not verify that the update transactions belonged with the firm whose master file was being updated. Choice (d) is incorrect because this report would provide information on exceptions in the update transactions that were encountered that require further action before the processing will be complete.

Subject Area: Information technology—information protection. Source: CIA 590, I-25.

173. (b) Reconciliation of record counts would detect the missing records on the updated master file. This question pertains to lack of controls associated with files. Choice (a) is incorrect because a computer sequence check for update transactions would detect missing update transactions but not omitted master file records. Choice (c) is incorrect because computer matching of update transactions would detect missing update transactions but not omitted master file records. Choice (d) is incorrect because one-for-one checking of detail reports would detect erroneous updates for individual transactions but not detect omitted master file records.

Subject Area: Information technology—information protection. Source: CIA 1190, II-35.

174. (d) Only by determining user satisfaction of a system can its effectiveness be determined. Choice (a) is incorrect because redundancy controls are application controls for computer processing and are not intended to determine system effectiveness. Choice (b) is incorrect because computer performance evaluation using monitors is a technique to determine computer efficiency. Choice (c) is incorrect because edit routines are application controls for data input and are not intended to determine system effectiveness.

Subject Area: Information technology—information protection. Source: CIA 1190, II-38.

175. (d) A sign test would have prevented the error because data input with the wrong sign would have been detected. Choice (a) is incorrect because a size test verifies that fields and records have permissible lengths. Choice (b) is incorrect because a sequence check verifies that sequence numbers of logical records are valid. Choice (c) is incorrect because a type check verifies that a data field contains data of the right data type (e.g., numeric alphanumeric, or logical).

Subject Area: Information technology—information protection. Source: CIA 590, II-22.

176. (d) Using end-of-job markers to mark the last page of the printed output would permit control section staff and users to verify that they have received the entire report and take appropriate action if they have not received the entire report. Choice (a) is incorrect because retention control is the practice of collecting and destroying output after its useful life has expired. Choice (b) is incorrect because spooler controls prevent access to disk copies of printed output as it waits to be printed. Choice (c) is incorrect because distribution controls govern the manner of delivering whole reports to authorized users.

Subject Area: Information technology—information protection. Source: CIA 590, II-23.

177. (a) This would verify that the changes to the various fields that the totals were calculated on were the same as those submitted. Choice (b) is incorrect because this would check to make sure that changes were recorded in the proper period, not that the changes were properly recorded. Choice (c) is incorrect because this would merely check that the hours workers reported as being worked were the same as the number of hours assigned to the various jobs. Choice (d) is incorrect because this would merely check to make sure that all changes submitted to be processed were properly authorized.

Subject Area: Information technology—information protection. Source: CIA 590, II-24.

178. (b) Check-digit validation of input records is an input/output control. Choice (a) is incorrect because password authorization is a general control over access to terminals. Choice (c) is incorrect because hash totals are appropriate for batch processing. Choice (d) is incorrect because backup and recovery procedures are a processing control.

Subject Area: Information technology—information protection. Source: CIA 1190, III-23.

179. (c) Processing controls ensure that processing is accurate. Choice (a) is incorrect because input controls are designed to detect errors in the conversion of data to machine-readable format. Choice (b) is incorrect because general controls function internal to information system operations to ensure that applications run correctly and that the facilities are operational. Choice (d) is incorrect because application development controls relate to the development of application systems, not their operation.

Subject Area: Information technology—information protection. Source: CIA 1190, III-24.

180. (d) This is a record count and a hash total. Choice (a) is incorrect because this is not a duplication. Choice (b) is incorrect because this is not an echo check. Choice (c) is incorrect because this is not for individual transactions.

Subject Area: Information technology—information protection. Source: CIA 590, III-31.

181. (a) Staff members may not be aware of how often they need to download data to keep it current, or whether their queries, especially the ones they modified, get all the information. Choice (b) is incorrect because downloading data does not affect the data definitions. Choice (c) is incorrect because the end users are downloading data only, not uploading, so the end users are unlikely to corrupt the mainframe data. Choice (d) is incorrect because the downloading procedures could replace previously downloaded files on the end users' microcomputers.

Subject Area: Information technology—information protection. Source: CIA Model Exam 1998, III-45.

182. (c) Implementation controls are designed to ensure that only authorized program procedures are introduced into the system. Choice (a) is incorrect because programmed checks are used to check the potential accuracy of input data (for example, a range check). Choice (b) is incorrect because batch controls are used to ensure the completeness and accuracy of input and update. Choice (d) is incorrect because one-for-one checking is a technique used to check individual documents for accuracy and completeness of data input or update.

Subject Area: Information technology—information protection. Source: CIA Model Exam 1998, III-56.

183. (b) A check digit is an extra reference number that follows an identification code and bears a mathematical relationship to the other digits. This extra digit is input with the data. The identification code can be subjected to an algorithm and compared to the check digit.

Subject Area: Information technology—information protection. Source: CIA Model Exam 1998, III-57.

184. (d) With a format check, the computer checks the characteristics of the character content, length, or sign of the individual data fields.

Subject Area: Information technology—information protection. Source: CIA Model Exam 1998, III-58.

185. (d) When duties are separated, users cannot obtain a detailed knowledge of programs and computer operators cannot gain unsupervised access to production programs. Choice (a) is incorrect because the reviews of jobs processed will disclose access, but will not prevent it. Choice (b) is incorrect because comparison of production programs and controlled copies will disclose changes, but will not prevent them. Choice (c) is incorrect because periodic running of test data will detect changes, but will not prevent them.

Subject Area: Information technology—information protection. Source: CIA Model Exam 1998, III-59.

186. (c) This could help prevent data errors. Choice (a) is incorrect because this practice is a wise control, but it does not address the issue of the integrity of uploaded data. Backups cannot prevent or detect data-upload problems, but can only help correct data errors that poor upload caused. Choice (b) is incorrect because this control may be somewhat helpful in preventing fraud in data uploads, but it is of little use in preventing errors. Choice (d) is incorrect because this control is detective in nature, but the error could have already caused erroneous reports and management decisions. Having users try to find errors in uploaded data would be costly.

Subject Area: Information technology—information protection. Source: CIA Model Exam 1998, III-64.

187. (b) Batch total checks provide a reasonably good test for completeness and accuracy of input. Choice (a) is incorrect because sequence checking provides a reasonably good test for completeness of input but does not test accuracy. Choice (c) is incorrect because limit checks are useful to determine whether an entry is within acceptable limits only. Such limitation makes the limit check unusable to test the accuracy of input. Choice (d) is incorrect because a check digit allows the computer to automatically reject incorrect entries. The cumbersome computation required for establishing the check digit, however, tends to limit its use to a few key entries. Check digits are never used to test accuracy of input for an entire grouping of input.

Subject Area: Information technology—information protection. Source: CIA Model Exam 1998, III-72.

188. (c) If index data for image processing systems are corrupted, users will likely be relying on the wrong images. Choice (a) is incorrect because legibility of image data is important to its use, but is independent of using the wrong image. Choice (b) is incorrect because accuracy of image data is important to its use, but is independent of using the wrong image. Choice (d) is incorrect because maintaining the initial sequence of index data may not be possible as the image data is modified and images are added/dropped.

Subject Area: Information technology—information protection. Source: CIA Model Exam 1998, III-74.

189. (a) The additional resources and energy to produce copies of selected transactions, and compare data on the copies to data on the supplier invoices, are not efficient and do not add value or control. Choice (b) is incorrect because there is no indication that receiving or inspection data contain errors. Choice (c) is incorrect because generating copies of the initial purchase orders would not add value; initial purchase order data might have been changed. Choice (d) is incorrect because this procedure is not necessarily based on the results of the testing.

Subject Area: Information technology—information protection. Source: CIA 595, III-18.

Evaluate Investment in IT

190. (a) According to the IIA's SAC report, it is one of the highest rated risks by 40% of the respondents. Choice (b) is incorrect because all organizations desire to utilize the latest technology that can be economically justified but this was not listed as a concern of management related to management information systems success. Choice (c) is incorrect because testing is time-consuming and expensive but it was not listed as a concern of management related to management information system success. Choice (d) is incorrect because use of CASE tools generally enhances the chances of success rather than increases risk.

Subject Area: Information technology—evaluate investment in IT. Source: CIA 593, III-32.

191. (d) Buying IT products and services can be a high-risk, high-return undertaking that requires strong management commitment and a systematic process to ensure successful outcomes. By using an investment-driven management approach, many organizations have significantly increased the realized return on IT investments, reduced the risk of cost overruns, and schedule delays, and made better decisions about how their limited IT dollar should be spent.

Subject Area: Information technology—evaluate investment in IT. Source: CBM, Volume 4.

192. (c) IT function is business enabler—a necessary step in mitigating risks, increasing revenues, increasing competitive advantage, and developing new products and services.

Subject Area: Information technology—evaluate investment in IT. Source: CBM, Volume 4.

193. (c) It is becoming increasingly important that organizations think of their IT projects as investments. With the emphasis on outcome-oriented performance measures, the contribution of IT to achieving business goals and objectives is being recognized.

Subject Area: Information technology—evaluate investment in IT. Source: CBM, Volume 4.

194. (c) An important management challenge is to integrate the planning, design, and implementation of complex application systems with the strategy of the organization, which will permit the best possible response to quickly changing information requirements. Choice (a) is incorrect. Independent of a strategy-IS linkage, greater online access may or may not be helpful. Choice (b) is incorrect. The marketplace creates competitive pressures for enhanced functions in systems. Choice (d) is incorrect. More pervasive use of automated controls may be independent of responding quickly to changing information requirements.

Subject Area: Information technology—evaluate investment in IT. Source: CIA 593, III-42.

195. (d) Strategic planning information is a highly summarized (aggregate) data rather than detailed data. Choice (a) is incorrect because operational control information does primarily use historical data. Choice (b) is incorrect because the required accuracy for operational control information is high. Choice (c) is incorrect because the scope for strategic planning information is very wide.

Subject Area: Information technology—evaluate investment in IT. Source: CIA 1192, III-25.

Enterprise-wide Resource Planning (ERP) Software

196. (b) Enterprise-wide resource planning (ERP) software integrates the information used by an organization's functions and departments into a unified and consistent computing system so that information is shared quickly and effectively.

Subject Area: Information technology—enterprise-wide resource planning (ERP) software. Source: Author.

197. (c) To compete globally, organizations must have the ability to share information quickly and effectively across the entire organization. "Information islands" would not achieve this goal. Management wants to integrate common business practices across the company and multiple business units.

Subject Area: Information technology—enterprise-wide resource planning (ERP) software. Source: Author.

198. (b) ERP system should be justified based on return on investment (ROI) criterion and from business perspective. Sometimes, the ERP system may not provide an immediate or extremely large ROI; it still may be necessary just to stay in business.

Subject Area: Information technology—enterprise-wide resource planning (ERP) software. Source: Author.

199. (a) Implementation of an ERP system can lead to significant benefits, including reduced costs, improved efficiency, more complete access to information, and fewer errors. However, critics of ERP system reported that ERP system can increase the IT costs and staff head counts. This is because multiple, additional computer systems to link with ERP system are needed to smooth functioning of ERP system thus increasing the overall costs.

Subject Area: Information technology—enterprise-wide resource planning (ERP) software. Source: Author.

200. (c) Electronic-business application of ERP system include customer relationship management (CRM) and supply chain management (SCM). Companies that invest in SCM systems report reduction in cycle time, inventory levels, and production costs. Capacity requirement planning (CRP) and material requirement planning (MRP) system can be part of SCM.

Subject Area: Information technology—enterprise-wide resource planning (ERP) software. Source: Author.

201. (d) Switching costs are expenses incurred when a customer stops buying a product or service from one business and starts buying it from another. One way to lock in buyers in a free market is to create the impression that an organization's product is significantly better than the competitor's, or to enjoy a situation in which customers fear high switching costs. ERP application is a good example of this strategy.

Subject Area: Information technology—enterprise-wide resource planning (ERP) software. Source: Author.

Operating Systems

202. (c) Advancing computer technology presents more complex audit environments and data privacy is an integral part of the complexity. Choice (a) is incorrect because changes in organizational reporting requirements are not new issues related to advancing computer technology. Choice (b) is incorrect because controls over library tape procedures have not been materially changed by advancing computer technology. Choice (d) is incorrect because changes in organizational behavior are not directly associated with auditor responsibilities in advancing technology.

Subject Area: Information technology—operating systems. Source: CIA 591, II-33.

203. (a) It requires input from secondary storage. Choice (b) is incorrect. Within the file, no input/output required. Choices (c) and (d) are incorrect because they are self-contained within the program.

Subject Area: Information technology—operating systems. Source: CIA 592, III-34.

204. (c) Utility programs are specialized programs that perform common routine and repetitive functions. Choice (a) is incorrect because compiler programs translate programs coded by programmers into machine-level instructions. Choice (b) is incorrect because application software consists of programs that perform specific information processing for users. Choice (d) is incorrect because the operating system directs and assists the execution of application programs.

Subject Area: Information technology—operating systems. Source: CIA 1191, III-22.

205. (d) Operating systems perform the functions described. Choice (a) is incorrect because spreadsheets make calculations, define output, etc. Choice (b) is incorrect because database manager is an organizational function exercising control over who may access the database. Choice (c) is incorrect because graphics describes a software package used to produce graphs, charts, etc.

Subject Area: Information technology—operating systems. Source: CIA 1191, III-26.

206. (b) The arithmetic-logic unit of a central processing unit (CPU) controls all data manipulation. Choice (a) is incorrect because the operating system is a set of programs, which manage access to and use of system resources. Choice (c) is incorrect because primary storage accepts the results of processing but does not control processing. Choice (d) is incorrect because the job control program communicates between user programs and the operating system.

Subject Area: Information technology—operating systems. Source: CIA 591, III-81.

207. (b) The system output can be reviewed to ensure that the job completed successfully, that is, producing the user report. Choice (a) is incorrect. The tape backup file may reflect a preliminary close or an intermediate point in the final close. The users may not be aware of this from the system output. Choice (c) is incorrect. Users may submit different program versions from their personal libraries rather than out of production libraries, without being aware of the differences. Choice (d) is incorrect. An assumption may be made that the program works correctly but the integrity of the processing logic may not have been verified.

Subject Area: Information technology—operating systems. Source: CIA 597, III-53.

208. (a) Data buffers are used to hold large blocks of logical records, thereby compensating for relatively slow transfer rate of data from/to input/output devices. Choice (b) is incorrect. Differences in lengths of records in a file are accommodated by setting aside space in the file control block for the longest record that will be encountered. Choice (c) is incorrect. There is no compensation for the differences in the execution time in various program instructions. Choice (d) is incorrect. Multiplexers and concentrators compensate for the differences in the volume of data that can be transmitted between communication devices.

Subject Area: Information technology—operating systems. Source: CIA 1194, III-32.

209. (b) A program that edits a group of source language statements for syntax errors and translates the statements into an object program is a compiler. Choice (a) is incorrect because an interpreter edits source language statements for syntax errors and translates them into executable code, but it interprets source statements one statement at a time, not as a group as a compiler does. Choice (c) is incorrect because a debugger is a program that traces program execution or captures variable values for the purpose of helping the developer find program errors. Choice (d) is incorrect because an encrypter is a program that converts ordinary text to encoded text that cannot be deciphered without access to the encryption key and procedure.

Subject Area: Information technology—operating systems. Source: CIA 1194, III-24 and 1196, III-53.

210. (b) Initiating input/output operations is a function of the operating system, which allocates memory and responds to interrupts. Choice (a) is incorrect because translating source code to object code is a function of compilers and interpreters. Choice (c) is incorrect because creating load module libraries is a function of the linkage editor. Choice (d) is incorrect because mapping virtual views onto base tables is a function of a database management system.

Subject Area: Information technology—operating systems. Source: CIA 1194, III-30.

211. (b) Parity checking, a hardware control, detects single bit errors in memory locations. Choice (a) is incorrect because memory protection prohibits programs from accessing memory outside their designated ranges. Choice (c) is incorrect. For hardware, validity checking verifies that a machine-level instruction is a valid instruction; for applications, validity checking verifies that transaction data is complete, authorized, and reasonable. Choice (d) is incorrect because range checking verifies that input data values are within predetermined ranges.

Subject Area: Information technology—operating systems. Source: CIA 590, II-20.

212. (c) Since the activity log records the time each job is started and finished, as well as the resources consumed by the job, this problem would be detected by a review of the log. Choice (a) is incorrect. This would not result in a software failure hence would not appear on the activity log. A data recording control would be needed to catch this error, such as a read after write check. Choice (b) is incorrect. This would not result in a software failure hence would not appear on the activity log. A batch total of the dollar amount of the purchases to be posted would be needed to catch this error. Choice (d) is incorrect. This would not result in a software failure hence would not appear on the activity log. A record count of the number of transactions to be submitted would be needed to catch this error.

Subject Area: Information technology—operating systems. Source: CIA 1190, III-29.

213. (b) An application program, such as a payroll program, performs useful work for an organizational function. Choice (a) is incorrect because operating systems direct and manage use of computer resources such as the CPU and peripheral devices. Choice (c) is incorrect because a report generator is a program that accepts high-level coding statements and creates program code to execute them. Choice (d) is incorrect because a utility program accepts commands, such as copying and sorting, from users and manipulates the designated files accordingly.

Subject Area: Information technology—operating systems. Source: CIA 1190, III-37.

214. (c) A compiler is a translator that translates higher-level languages into machine language. Choice (a) is incorrect because an assembler is a translator that translates assembly (lower-level) language into a machine language. Choice (b) is incorrect because an asynchronous translator is a distracter. There is an asynchronous transmission. Choice (d) is incorrect because artificial intelligence (AI) is a field of research that uses computers to solve problems that appear to require human-like intelligence.

Subject Area: Information technology—operating systems. Source: CIA 590, III-29.

215. (b) Application programs are user programs for specific tasks. Choice (a) is incorrect because system programs are those that provide the interface with the computer for the execution of application programs. Choice (c) is incorrect because utility programs are part of system programs, which perform common tasks such as sorting, merging, listing, etc. Choice (d) is incorrect because an operating program is not a recognized type of program.

Subject Area: Information technology—operating systems. Source: CIA 590, III-30.

216. (c) This is one of many functions of the operating system, which is the brain for the computer. The major functions are input/output control, memory management, and process management. Choice (a) is incorrect because application programs can route data but it is most often done by the operating system. Choice (b) is incorrect because utility programs seldom handle data. Choice (d) is incorrect because communication systems are too general.

Subject Area: Information technology—operating systems. Source: CIA 590, III-33.

Application Development and Maintenance

217. (a) System development procedures and controls that are well established in the centralized IT environment do not exist in user departments. Choice (b) is incorrect because this is a principle motivation for developing end-user systems. Choice (c) is incorrect because end-user systems can be developed to serve departmental needs without understanding mainframe architecture. Choice (d) is incorrect because the inability to accommodate computer assisted auditing techniques is not a control weakness.

Subject Area: Information technology—application development and maintenance. Source: CIA 1193, I-37.

218. (a) Management of the commercial lending department has the ultimate responsibility for data integrity and availability of its applications. Choice (b) is incorrect because the function of a central IT group analyst is to help develop applications for users. Choice (c) is incorrect because the function of a central IT group programmer is to help develop applications for users. Choice (d) is incorrect because the function of an internal auditor is to assess the appropriateness of controls.

Subject Area: Information technology—application development and maintenance. Source: CIA 1193, III-31.

219. (c) The reason the accountant's successor could not use the forecasting model was because there was inadequate documentation. Choice (a) is incorrect because end-user computing resources should be monitored, but the lack of monitoring is not the reason the accountant's successor could not use the forecasting model. Choice (b) is incorrect because end-user computing efforts should be consistent with strategic plans, but lack of consistency is not the reason the accountant's successor could not use the forecasting model. Choice (d) is incorrect because maintaining adequate backups for spreadsheet models is necessary, but lack of adequate backup is not the reason the accountant's successor could not use the forecasting model.

Subject Area: Information technology—application development and maintenance. Source: CIA 593, II-27.

220. (b) The technology trend of increasing end-user development of systems has the risk of lack of necessary security and recovery controls, which can be mitigated by management oversight to ensure adequate procedures. Choice (a) is incorrect because ensuring compatibility of IT with organizational objectives will not ensure adequate security and recovery controls in end-user developed systems. Choice (c) is incorrect because validation of the knowledge base will not ensure adequate security and recovery controls in end-user developed systems. Choice (d) is incorrect because testing of controls in development and production will not ensure adequate security and recovery controls in end-user developed systems.

Subject Area: Information technology—application development and maintenance. Source: CIA 593, III-35.

221. (d) A single firm cannot control the technological obsolescence risks resulting from advancements in computer hardware and software. It is a subset of the risk of high or unnecessary costs. Choice (a) is incorrect because a firm can control the application risks resulting from bad system design and implementation. It is a class of risk and is very pertinent to an EUC application. Choice (b) is incorrect because a firm can control environmental risks such as interfaces of an EUC system with people. It is a class of risk and is very pertinent to an EUC application. Choice (c) is incorrect because a firm can control the risks inherent in the application's software and hardware combination. Problems resulting from these risks can be resolved by the company's technical support staff and/or computer vendor support staff. It is a class of risk and is very pertinent to an EUC application.

Subject Area: Information technology—application development and maintenance. Source: CIA 593, III-62.

222. (a) The spreadsheet logic was flawed in that it failed to apply discounts to all complementary product lines. The logic error was due to human error. Choice (b) is incorrect because the error is independent of the operation of hardware. Choice (c) is incorrect because there was no misentry of keystrokes in spreadsheet cells. Choice (d) is incorrect because crossfooting is the independent summing of rows and columns and comparison of results. There was no crossfooting error in the spreadsheet model.

Subject Area: Information technology—application development and maintenance. Source: CIA 592, I-38.

223. (b) Independent audit and testing of spreadsheet models by knowledgeable persons is the best approach for validating model logic and thus the integrity of a spreadsheet. Choice (a) is incorrect. Although trained systems professionals are less likely to make logic errors, all significant spreadsheet models should be independently reviewed. Spreadsheet models are useful precisely because users that are not trained systems professionals can prepare them. Trained systems professionals are not available to develop all the spreadsheet models that organizations need. Choice (c) is incorrect. Specifying crossfooting for all spreadsheet models would detect some spreadsheet logic errors, but not all of them. Crossfooting would not have detected this error. Choice (d) is incorrect. Enforcing documentation standards for multiuse spreadsheet models is a good practice for promoting correct use of spreadsheet models used repetitively but is unlikely to detect logic errors like this one.

Subject Area: Information technology—application development and maintenance. Source: CIA 592, I-39.

224. (b) Unintentional errors due to inexperienced programmers are one of the dangers associated with a widespread increase in end-user programming. Choice (a) is incorrect because improved documentation of end-user programs is not a likely outcome associated with a widespread increase in end-user programming. Choice (c) is incorrect. While there will be an increased demand on centralized MIS departments to support end-user applications, design is undertaken by end-users. Choice (d) is incorrect because a potential increase (not decrease) in the risk of fraud and irregularities is one of the dangers associated with a widespread increase in end-user programming.

Subject Area: Information technology—application development and maintenance. Source: CIA 592, III-36.

225. (b) Major testing of the developed system occurs before implementation. In the construction (development) stage, program testing is performed after programmers write programs. Choice (a) is incorrect because in the design stage, system inputs and outputs are defined; program and screen flows are specified. Choice (c) is incorrect because in the analysis stage, system analysts perform both data and process analysis. Choice (d) is incorrect because in the implementation stage, user manuals are developed; all affected parties are trained; and user acceptance testing is conducted.

Subject Area: Information technology—application development and maintenance. Source: CIA 594, III-32.

226. (a) Integrated test facility (ITF), embedded audit modules, and system control audit review files (SCARF) are normally used to audit transactions during normal operations, not during the development stage. Choices (b), (c), and (d) are incorrect because these techniques are used after the system is developed.

Subject Area: Information technology—application development and maintenance. Source: CIA 594, III-33.

227. (b) The parallel method allows a comparison between the old and new system outputs. Discrepancies between the two systems can be identified and corrected. Choice (a) is incorrect because the direct cutover method is a high-risk approach due to communication and coordination problems that can occur between and among all affected parties. Choice (c) is incorrect because prototyping method is not used in converting the existing system to a new system. It is an alternative to the traditional method of developing computer systems. Choice (d) is incorrect because modular or phased method is a vague term here as it applies to anything.

Subject Area: Information technology—application development and maintenance. Source: CIA 594, III-34.

228. (b) As competitive pressures for enhanced functions in systems increase, development groups will be under more pressure to implement systems quickly, which increases the risk of hastily developed, ineffective systems. Choice (a) is incorrect because growing organizational reliance on information systems increases the risk of business interruption. Choice (c) is incorrect because greater online access to information systems increases the risk of unauthorized access. Choice (d) is incorrect because use of knowledge-based systems increases the risk of inadequate knowledge bases.

Subject Area: Information technology—application development and maintenance. Source: CIA 593, III-39.

229. (d) More pervasive use of automated controls increases the need for more systematic and rigorous testing in development and production of programmed controls since there are fewer compensating manual controls. Choice (a) is incorrect because management oversight controls for end-user development risks, not reliance on automated controls. Choice (b) is incorrect because proliferation of knowledge-based systems increases the risk of inadequate knowledge bases. Choice (c) is incorrect because closer linkage between organizational strategy and information is a strength not a weakness.

Subject Area: Information technology—application development and maintenance. Source: CIA 593, III-41.

230. (d) Recompiling source code into the production load library ensures that the source and executable codes match because the executable code was created from the source code. Choice (a) is incorrect. Verifying that the program move request is authorized ensures that a change was authorized, not that the source and executable code match each other. Choice (b) is incorrect. Requiring program, system, and parallel testing of the code ensures that the code meets test specifications, not that the source and executable code match each other. Choice (c) is incorrect. Authorizing programmer access to test libraries only ensures that programmers do not have access to production libraries, not that the source and executable code match each other.

Subject Area: Information technology—application development and maintenance. Source: CIA 593, III-46.

231. (a) This is a major reason for project failure. Choice (b) is incorrect because it is true for prototyping, not SDLC. Choice (c) is incorrect because SDLC is designed to enhance process management. Choice (d) is incorrect because users can and often do play important roles.

Subject Area: Information technology—application development and maintenance. Source: CIA 593, III-60.

232. (c) All application changes must be documented and subject to testing and approval. Choice (a) is incorrect because vendor payees were not changed; check register would show that the checks were issued to authorized vendors. Choice (b) is incorrect because total dollars were not altered; there is no out-of-balance condition. Choice (d) is incorrect because password usage would typically include the programmer.

Subject Area: Information technology—application development and maintenance. Source: CIA 1192, I-37.

233. (a) Program change control procedures help ensure that only authorized programmers make changes to programs by restricting access to programs in production libraries to only authorized programmers. Choice (b) is incorrect because program change control procedures are independent of backup procedures for data files. Choice (c) is incorrect because inappropriate executions of production programs can be detected by reviews of job logs of jobs executed. Choice (d) is incorrect because ensuring against unauthorized changes to data files is a function of access control software.

Subject Area: Information technology—application development and maintenance. Source: CIA 1192, II-32.

234. (b) A matrix permits showing a pair of conditions and one resulting action or decision. Choice (a) is incorrect because pseudocode shows the decision logic in the if-then format. Choice (c) is incorrect because a flow chart represents a decision with each of its paths. Choice (d) is incorrect because a payoff table represents two or more states of nature, two or more decision alternatives, and the appropriate outcomes (payoffs).

Subject Area: Information technology—application development and maintenance. Source: CIA 1192, III-23.

235. (d) This is needed to establish technical feasibility and cost. Choice (a) is incorrect because this would come after the feasibility study. Choice (b) is incorrect because this is part of the information requirements phase. Choice (c) is incorrect because this would be part of the implementation and operations stage.

Subject Area: Information technology—application development and maintenance. Source: CIA 1192, III-39.

236. (a) The new account management system is characterized by uncertain requirements (e.g., lack of unanimity about requirements) and unstructured tasks (e.g., the varying nature of analyzing customers' financial situations). Choice (b) is incorrect because the new account management system is not characterized by certain requirements. Choice (c) is incorrect because the new account management system is not characterized by high user understanding of tasks. Choice (d) is incorrect because the new account management system is not characterized by certain requirements.

Subject Area: Information technology—application development and maintenance. Source: CIA 1192, III-85.

237. (c) Prototyping is the best development approach because it permits evolutionary design/development that lets user responses to a developing system guide future development. Choice (a) is incorrect because the system development life cycle (SDLC) approach requires certain requirements and structured tasks, neither of which is present in this system. Choice (b) is incorrect because bottom-up design is an SDLC approach for data analysis requiring certain requirements and structured tasks, neither of which is present in this system. Choice (d) is incorrect because top-down design is an SDLC approach for decision analysis requiring certain requirements and structured tasks, neither of which is present in this system.

Subject Area: Information technology—application development and maintenance. Source: CIA 1192, III-86.

238. (a) The higher user understanding of tasks and the larger project size, the more appropriate life cycle methodologies are for the problem. Choice (b) is incorrect because the lower user understanding of tasks and the smaller project size, the less appropriate life cycle methodologies are for the problem. Choice (c) is incorrect because the lower user understanding of tasks and the more uncertain requirements, the less appropriate life cycle methodologies are for the problem. Choice (d) is incorrect because the more uncertain requirements and the larger project size, the less appropriate life cycle methodologies are for the problem.

Subject Area: Information technology—application development and maintenance. Source: CIA 1192, III-87.

239. (b) Define requirements, design system, develop code, test system, install system, and operate system are the major life cycle phases. Choice (a) is incorrect because define requirements, design system, refine requirements, and revise/enhance are some phases from both life cycle and prototyping. Choice (c) is incorrect because define requirements, create initial system, develop code, install system, and operate system are some phases from both life cycle and prototyping. Choice (d) is incorrect because define requirements, create initial system, refine requirements, and revise/enhance system are the phases in prototyping.

Subject Area: Information technology—application development and maintenance. Source: CIA 1192, III-88.

240. (d) Specifying requirements, evaluating iterations, refining requirements, and communicating refined requirements are user responsibilities in prototyping. Choice (a) is incorrect because modifying programs is a developer responsibility. Choice (b) is incorrect because modifying programs is a developer responsibility. Choice (c) is incorrect because creating the initial system is a developer responsibility. Operating the system is an operator responsibility.

Subject Area: Information technology—application development and maintenance. Source: CIA 1192, III-89.

241. (d) Life cycle methodologies provide enhanced management and control of the development process because they divide the process in manageable steps. Choice (a) is incorrect because overall development costs are higher when requirements change frequently in a life cycle methodology. Choice (b) is incorrect because life cycle methodologies are unable to give users a functioning system quickly. Choice (c) is incorrect because life cycle methodologies require lengthy application development time to achieve a functioning system.

Subject Area: Information technology—application development and maintenance. Source: CIA 1192, III-90.

242. (a) Because of planned successive refinement to the system, prototyping has the ability to try out implementations without incurring large development costs. Choice (b) is incorrect because in prototyping, requirements and conceptual design may not be complete, even in the last prototype version. Choice (c) is incorrect because in prototyping, control points and associated control procedures are often omitted in order to obtain a functioning system sooner. Choice (d) is incorrect because life cycle methodologies, not prototyping, provide enhanced management and control of the development process because they divide the process in manageable steps.

Subject Area: Information technology—application development and maintenance. Source: CIA 1192, III-91.

243. (c) Requirements are certain and users agree on task structure so life cycle is the best approach. Choice (a) is incorrect because prototyping is not needed because requirements are certain and users agree on task structure. Choice (b) is incorrect because hierarchy-input-process-output (HIPO) is a documentation technique. Choice (d) is incorrect because simulation, a technique for emulating the process, is not needed because requirements are certain.

Subject Area: Information technology—application development and maintenance. Source: CIA 1192, III-92.

244. (b) A contingency approach to choosing an application development strategy means that an organization adopts multiple methods as appropriate for individual projects. Choice (a) is incorrect because using a single requirement development assurance method for all projects increases the likelihood of a mismatch between the project and project characteristics. Choice (c) is incorrect because adopting one life cycle methodology is the same as adopting a single requirement development assurance method. Choice (d) is incorrect because uncertain requirements are consistent with a prototyping approach, but the organization should also consider other factors such as the degree of task structure, user comprehension of the tasks, and the developer's proficiency with the technique.

Subject Area: Information technology—application development and maintenance. Source: CIA 1192, III-93.

245. (b) The principal rationale for prototyping is that it is easier to react to an existing application system than to specify desired features for a future system, especially in cases in which requirements are uncertain. Choice (a) is incorrect because dividing a project into manageable segments at the beginning instead of imposing control after development is underway is a rationale for life cycle. Choice (c) is incorrect because anticipating and planning for resource use rather than acquiring resources on short notice is a rationale for life cycle. Choice (d) is incorrect because converting data files once rather than reformatting data continually with new project iterations is a rationale for life cycle.

Subject Area: Information technology—application development and maintenance. Source: CIA 1192, III-94.

246. (c) Users' information needs and objectives should be primary. Choice (a) is incorrect because competitors' processing may be irrelevant or totally unknown. Choice (b) is incorrect because emphasis should first be on the purposes and needs of the new system—not on equipment. Choice (d) is incorrect because controls related to the old (current) system could be irrelevant or unimportant to the new system.

Subject Area: Information technology—application development and maintenance. Source: CIA 592, I-29.

247. (d) When duties are separated, users cannot obtain a detailed knowledge of programs and those developing and/or maintaining programs cannot gain unsupervised access to production programs. Choice (a) is incorrect because the reviews of jobs processed will disclose access, but will not prevent it. Choice (b) is incorrect because comparison of production programs and controlled copies will disclose changes, but will not prevent them. Choice (c) is incorrect because periodic running of test data will detect changes, but will not prevent them.

Subject Area: Information technology—application development and maintenance. Source: CIA 592, I-31.

248. (a) Operational feasibility addresses whether the system will work within the constraints of the user and managerial environment. Choice (b) is incorrect because motivational feasibility refers to the probability that the organization is motivated to support the development and implementation of the system. Choice (c) is incorrect because technical feasibility is associated with the prospects that existing technology exists to allow the system development. Choice (d) is incorrect because economic feasibility is related to an assessment of expected benefits versus costs.

Subject Area: Information technology—application development and maintenance. Source: CIA 592, II-28.

249. (c) Prototyping involves fine-tuning the design over continued use. Choice (a) is incorrect because top-down design is represented from the beginning as a hierarchy with general control modules at the top and detailed modules further down. Choice (b) is incorrect because modular approach is the controlled design with small sets of processing instructions called modules. Some are used only once and others more than once. Choice (d) is incorrect because prompting is a type of feedback provided in user systems dialog to guide users through a task or decision sequence.

Subject Area: Information technology—application development and maintenance. Source: CIA 592, II-29.

250. (d) This control prevents unauthorized program changes by a single individual. Choice (a) is incorrect because someone should test program changes other than the programmer. Choice (b) is incorrect because program changes are not the responsibility of the control group. Choice (c) is incorrect because a complete history of the program does not facilitate operating performance.

Subject Area: Information technology—application development and maintenance. Source: CIA 592, II-36.

251. (c) Appropriate written authorization of the change, including an explanation of the need, what the change requires, and the authorization itself, is an important control associated with the implementation of this change. Choice (a) is incorrect because review of use of restricted utilities is an important control over the activities of systems programmers, who have access to utility programs that others are not authorized to access. Choice (b) is incorrect because reviewing attempted accesses is an important step in ensuring that access control is effective. Choice (d) is incorrect because maintenance of backup master files is important in any system to ensure data integrity.

Subject Area: Information technology—application development and maintenance. Source: CIA 1191, I-28

252. (a) Prototyping is the best approach because the requirements are difficult to specify in advance and requirements are likely to change significantly during development. Choice (b) is incorrect because the system development life cycle (SDLC) model is appropriate for highly structured operational applications whose requirements can be defined in advance. Thus, it is not suitable for the bank's application. Choice (c) is incorrect because structured analysis and design technique, which is a specific type of the SDLC model. Choice (d) is incorrect because hierarchy-input-process-output (HIPO) is a specific type of the system development life cycle model.

Subject Area: Information technology—application development and maintenance. Source: CIA 1191, III-29.

253. (d) Prototyping would be better since system requirements are not well defined. Experimentation of new design approaches by few participants is encouraged. The system goes through many iterations of trial-and-error until the design and outputs are satisfied. Choice (a) is incorrect because it is well suited for structured projects since they require exact specifications of the system requirements. Choice (b) is incorrect because it is well suited for large projects where project management controls can be implemented to complete the project on schedule and within budget. Choice (c) is incorrect because it works well for complex projects where many participants need to be coordinated and communicated with.

Subject Area: Information technology—application development and maintenance. Source: CIA 1191, III-31.

254. (c) The overall conceptual design report should include outlines of operator and user documentation of account number coding. Choice (a) is incorrect because the initial drafts of operator and user documentation of account number coding are prepared after management has accepted the conceptual design report. Choice (b) is incorrect because the initial draft of security and backup plans and procedures should be part of the detailed design phase, not the conceptual design phase. Choice (d) is incorrect because equipment assembly instructions are unaffected by the new system and hence would not be part of the conceptual design report.

Subject Area: Information technology—application development and maintenance. Source: CIA 1191, III-40.

255. (d) Sample output formats for reporting components of activity costs are a component of the overall conceptual design report. Choice (a) is incorrect because justification for implementing a system to generate activity-based costs is a component of the feasibility assessment, not the overall conceptual design report. Choice (b) is incorrect because the schedule for converting from the existing chart of accounts to the new one will be a product of the conversion phase. Choice (c) is incorrect because the plan for assuring that account numbers are translated correctly will be a product of detailed system design, not the overall conceptual design.

Subject Area: Information technology—application development and maintenance. Source: CIA 1191, III-41.

256. (a) Description of input requirements for job cost posting from activities is part of the overall conceptual design report. Choice (b) is incorrect because documentation of the operational feasibility of revised job cost transactions is a part of the feasibility assessment, not the overall conceptual design. Choice (c) is incorrect because hierarchy-input-processing-output (HIPO) documentation of requirements for job cost posting from activities would be a product of detailed system design. Choice (d) is incorrect because a plan for gaining user acceptance of new job cost posting procedures would be a product of the conversion phase.

Subject Area: Information technology—application development and maintenance. Source: CIA 1191, III-42.

257. (a) Explanation of procedures for ensuring integrity of job costs is part of overall conceptual design. Choice (b) is incorrect because the plan for quality assurance for the development of the system is a component of detailed systems design, not conceptual design. Choice (c) is incorrect because a description of controls and their place in the processing flow is a component of detailed systems design, not conceptual design. Choice (d) is incorrect because a plan for post-implementation review of the activity-based costing system would be prepared after the system has been installed, not during the conceptual design.

Subject Area: Information technology—application development and maintenance. Source: CIA 1191, III-43.

258. (d) An explanation of the general flow of job cost transactions is a component of the conceptual design. Choice (a) is incorrect because an explanation of the flow of job cost transactions through programs is a component of detailed system design, not conceptual design. Choice (b) is incorrect because a specification of the overall structure of programs for processing job cost transactions is a component of detailed system design, not conceptual design. Choice (c) is incorrect because a description of the communications requirements to and from plants is a component of detailed system design, not conceptual design.

Subject Area: Information technology—application development and maintenance. Source: CIA 1191, III-44.

259. (b) A system design showing the flow of job cost transactions through programs is a component of the detailed system design specification. Choice (a) is incorrect because an explanation of the general flow of job cost transactions through the system is a component of conceptual design, not detailed system design. Choice (c) is incorrect because a description of the relationships of input, processing, and output for job costing is a component of conceptual design, not detailed system design. Choice (d) is incorrect because a statement of the flow of job cost transactions through organizational units is a component of conceptual design, not detailed system design.

Subject Area: Information technology—application development and maintenance. Source: CIA 1191, III-45.

260. (c) Specifications for data communications to and from the plants, sales offices, and headquarters are part of the detailed system design specification. Choice (a) is incorrect because a plan for testing the communications network linking the plants and sales offices is a component of conversion, not detailed system design. Choice (b) is incorrect because a plan for postimplementation review of the data communications network is a component of conversion, not detailed system design. Choice (d) is incorrect because explanation of functions to be performed via the communications network is a component of conceptual design, not detailed system design.

Subject Area: Information technology—application development and maintenance. Source: CIA 1191, III-46.

261. (c) A control design showing controls to be implemented at various points in the flow of job cost posting is a component of detailed system design. Choice (a) is incorrect because an explanation of procedures for ensuring integrity of job costs during operation of the system is a component of conceptual design, not detailed system design. Choice (b) is incorrect because a plan for ensuring integrity of converted job cost files is a component of conversion, not detailed system design. Choice (d) is incorrect because an analysis of approaches for converting account numbers is a component of information requirement analysis, not detailed system design.

Subject Area: Information technology—application development and maintenance. Source: CIA 1191, III-47.

262. (c) Hardware specifications for new hardware to support increased data storage requirements for job cost data is a component of detailed system design. Choice (a) is incorrect because an estimate of hardware requirements to support increased processing for job costing is a component of feasibility assessment, not detailed system design. Choice (b) is incorrect because a schedule of expected cost and benefits from having activity-based job costing is a component of feasibility assessment, not detailed system design. Choice (d) is incorrect because a testing plan for new hardware acquired to support the new job costing system is a component of conversion, not detailed system design.

Subject Area: Information technology—application development and maintenance. Source: CIA 1191, III-48.

263. (c) An application test or quality assurance plan for the remainder of the development is a component of detailed system design. Choice (a) is incorrect because an explanation of procedures for ensuring integrity in the use and operation of the job costing system is a component of conceptual design, not detailed system design. Choice (b) is incorrect because a description of user responsibilities in the correct operation of the system is a component of conceptual design, not detailed system design. Choice (d) is incorrect because a set of outlines for operating manuals needed for correct operation of the system is a component of conceptual design, not detailed system design.

Subject Area: Information technology—application development and maintenance. Source: CIA 1191, III-49.

264. (d) This is a distinguishing feature of the prototyping approach to systems development. Choice (a) is incorrect because this describes an acceptance assurance strategy, which is appropriate to structured development. Choice (b) is incorrect because this describes a linear assurance process, which is appropriate to structured development. Choice (c) is incorrect because this describes an iterative assurance process, which is appropriate to structured development.

Subject Area: Information technology—application development and maintenance. Source: CIA 591, III-21.

265. (a) Since working with the installed operating systems is a requirement, the agency should put that fact in the request for bids to vendors. In the absence of a specific stated requirement, vendors may ignore the compatibility issue. Choice (b) is incorrect because specifying the identity of the preferred database management software would preclude bids for other products that might be better and may be prohibited by governmental contract regulations. Choice (c) is incorrect because specifying the kinds of data manipulation required of the database management software is necessary for a successful acquisition, but data manipulation alone would not address operating system compatibility issues. Choice (d) is incorrect because specifying required transaction throughput rates and data storage volumes is necessary for successful acquisitions, but transaction rates and data volumes do not address operating system compatibility issues.

Subject Area: Information technology—application development and maintenance. Source: CIA 591, III-25.

266. (c) This is a part of the definition stage, not the development stage. Choices (a), (b), and (d) are incorrect because each one is a part of the development stage.

Subject Area: Information technology—application development and maintenance. Source: CIA 591, III-39.

267. (d) Structured design is the process of using systems concepts to decompose information system requirements and define the boundaries and interfaces of subsystems. Choice (a) is incorrect because top-down design is the practice of defining a system by its general purpose and progressively refining the level of detail in the form of a hierarchy. Choice (b) is incorrect because it is not a meaningful term. Choice (c) is incorrect because hierarchy-input-process-output (HIPO), is a documentation technique relying on stylized charts depicting different levels of detail of a system.

Subject Area: Information technology—application development and maintenance. Source: CIA 591, III-40.

268. (c) The most efficient sequence is customer master file lookup, order detail entry, order detail validation, customer credit validation. Choice (a) is incorrect because customer credit validation cannot be performed before the order amount is known, which is determined through order detail entry and order detail validation. Choice (b) is incorrect because if orders were entered before customers are identified, orders from nonpaying customers would then be cancelled. Choice (d) is incorrect because customer credit validation cannot be performed before the order amount is known, which is determined through order detail entry and order detail validation.

Subject Area: Information technology—application development and maintenance. Source: CIA 591, III-90.

269. (d) The best sequence for invoices and mailing labels corresponds to the most efficient sequence for the clerks to pull the merchandise, which is the stock number sequence in the warehouse. Choice (a) is incorrect because it is easier to resort sealed packages in groups than it is for clerks to pull merchandise from warehouse shelves at random. Choice (b) is incorrect because customer number sequence for invoices and mailing labels means clerks must pull merchandise at random and packages will have to be sorted in ZIP code order. Choice (c) is incorrect because stock number sequence may not coincide with warehouse stock number sequence, which would mean clerks must pull merchandise at random.

Subject Area: Information technology—application development and maintenance. Source: CIA 591, III-91.

270. (d) Analysis of buying patterns based on customer order history would be helpful for fine-tuning merchandise selection and stock replenishment, but they could be deferred in the short run. Choice (a) is incorrect because validation of order detail and credit authorization is an integral part of an order entry/shipping/billing system. Choice (b) is incorrect because invoice, mailing label, and back-order notice printing are integral parts of an order entry/shipping/billing system. Choice (c) is incorrect because analysis of stock levels and preparation of purchase orders are integral parts of an order entry/shipping/billing system.

Subject Area: Information technology—application development and maintenance. Source: CIA 591, III-93.

271. (a) Order entry is the best time to capture data about customer sources because that is where the data are available, on the paper order sent through the mail or as customers place orders over the telephone. Choice (b) is incorrect because customer source information is unrelated to stock ordering. Choice (c) is incorrect because credit rejection does not affect all customers and occurs after the company needs customer source information. Choice (d) is incorrect because order filling is independent of customer source information.

Subject Area: Information technology—application development and maintenance. Source: CIA 591, III-94.

272. (a) Customer master file lookup at data entry is the best control for ensuring that the company ships an order to the right customer. For each order, the system will perform a customer master file lookup, which the data entry clerk will confirm if the right customer name/address has been retrieved. Choice (b) is incorrect because key verification is often used on batch input but is rarely used on online input. Choice (c) is incorrect because reconciliation of rejected orders with valid orders does not ensure that the company only ships orders to the right customers. This reconciliation ensures that orders are eventually shipped. Choice (d) is incorrect because maintenance of a suspense file for incomplete orders ensures that incomplete orders are eventually shipped or otherwise accounted for. It does not ensure that the company ships orders only to the right customers.

Subject Area: Information technology—application development and maintenance. Source: CIA 591, III-95.

273. (b) The best control for ensuring that stock shrinkage is minimal is reconciling stock positions with stock receipts, valid orders, and orders shipped. Discrepancies between any two of these would be discovered by periodic reconciliation. Choice (a) is incorrect because screening new warehouse clerks for trustworthiness is a good management practice, but it is not guaranteed to control stock shrinkage. Choice (c) is incorrect because restricting use of terminals authorized for read-only access to information about stock levels to warehouse supervisors is not likely to control stock shrinkage because read-only access would not permit someone to manipulate stock records to conceal a discrepancy. Choice (d) is incorrect because adjusting stock levels so that only merchandise needed for sale is kept in the warehouse is good practice because it minimizes stock levels, but it is not likely to control shrinkage of the stock in the warehouse.

Subject Area: Information technology—application development and maintenance. Source: CIA 591, III-96.

274. (b) Reconciling records of completed orders with orders shipped will determine orders not shipped but will not detect orders shipped but not received. Choice (a) is incorrect because asking customers to return a post-paid card indicating their receipt of goods is often used with shipment of high-value items, but not with low-value items. Customers are unlikely to return the cards (which would be a significant expense) routinely, so the company would still be unaware of undelivered goods. Choice (c) is incorrect because auditing the company's responses to customers' inquiries about undelivered goods will detect instances where merchandise was not shipped, not shipped timely, or shipped but not received. Choice (d) is incorrect because reconciling stock positions with valid orders and orders shipped would not identify individual orders shipped but not received.

Subject Area: Information technology—application development and maintenance. Source: CIA 591, III-97.

275. (c) Matching records of goods shipped with records of valid orders would detect duplicate shipments for the same order. Choice (a) is incorrect because requiring that all parts of an order be shipped together in the same package is an unworkable practice since mail-order companies typically ship partial orders. Choice (b) is incorrect because screening new warehouse clerks to hire only individuals likely to be trustworthy is good practice, but it is unlikely to ensure no duplicate shipments. Choice (d) is incorrect because allowing shipping clerks to access online information to correct errors is more likely to facilitate duplicate shipments than it is to reduce them. The accuracy and integrity of customer and order information is the responsibility of data entry clerks.

Subject Area: Information technology—application development and maintenance. Source: CIA 591, III-98.

276. (a) The life cycle approach is appropriate for this system because requirements are well defined, tasks are highly structured, and requirements are unlikely to change for the duration of development. Choice (b) is incorrect because the contingency approach is appropriate for situations in which requirements are uncertain, users are unlikely to be able to articulate requirements, and tasks are highly unstructured. Choice (c) is incorrect because the prototyping approach is appropriate for situations in which requirements are difficult to specify in advance or when requirements may change significantly during development. Choice (d) is incorrect because the iterative approach is the prototyping approach.

Subject Area: Information technology—application development and maintenance. Source: CIA 591, III-100.

277. (a) A compiler translates a high-level language into machine code. Choice (b) is incorrect because a kernel program is a sample program of small size executed on alternative computer configurations to provide information useful in making computer acquisition decisions. Choice (c) is incorrect because an encoder is used in transmitting coded messages through a communication system. Choice (d) is incorrect because object code is machine-readable code, and therefore it has no conversion application itself.

Subject Area: Information technology—application development and maintenance. Source: CIA 1192, III-28.

278. (a) Staff members may not be aware of how often they need to download data to keep it current, or whether their queries, especially the ones they modified, get all the information. Choice (b) is incorrect because downloading data does not affect the data definitions. Choice (c) is incorrect because the staff members are downloading data only, not uploading, so the staff is unlikely to corrupt the mainframe data. Choice (d) is incorrect because the downloading procedures could replace previously downloaded files on the staff members' microcomputers.

Subject Area: Information technology—application development and maintenance. Source: CIA 597, III-36.

279. (b) Network monitoring software does not involve controls within an application system. Choice (a) is incorrect. For example, major financial and accounting systems, such as a system that tracks purchases and sales on the stock exchange, must have higher standards of controls than a system to inventory employee training and skills. Choice (c) is incorrect. The likely frequency of a problem and its potential damage should determine how much control is built into a system. Choice (d) is incorrect. For example, complete one-for-one checking may be time-consuming and operationally impossible for a system that processes hundreds of thousands of utilities payments daily. But it might be possible to use this technique to verify only critical data such as dollar amounts and account numbers, while ignoring names and addresses.

Subject Area: Information technology—application development and maintenance. Source: CIA 597, III-38.

280. (c) The new system would be developed module by module. Choice (a) is incorrect because system documentation is not eliminated or deferred by using rapid application development. Choice (b) is incorrect because project management involves development teams. Choice (d) is incorrect because object development might not be of use; if it were, it would increase usage of previous code.

Subject Area: Information technology—application development and maintenance. Source: CIA 597, III-48.

281. (c) Program change control comprises: (1) maintaining records of change authorizations, code changes, and test results; (2) adhering to a systems development methodology (including documentation); (3) authorizing changeovers of subsidiary and headquarters' interfaces; and (4) restricting access to authorized source and executable codes. Choice (a) is incorrect. Frequently, the purpose of database reviews is to determine if: (1) users have gained access to database areas for which they have no authorization, and (2) authorized users can access the database using programs that provide them with unauthorized privileges to view and/or change information. Choice (b) is incorrect. The purpose of compliance reviews is to determine whether an organization has complied with applicable internal and external procedures and regulations. Choice (d) is incorrect. The purpose of network security software is to provide logical controls over the network.

Subject Area: Information technology—application development and maintenance. Source: CIA 597, III-49 and 595, III-77.

282. (a) Implementation controls occur in the system development process at various points to ensure that implementation is properly controlled and managed. Choice (b) is incorrect because hardware controls ensure that computer hardware is physically secure and check for equipment malfunction. Choice (c) is incorrect because computer operations controls apply to the work of the computer department and help ensure that programmed procedures are consistently and correctly applied to the storage and processing of data. Choice (d) is incorrect because data security controls ensure that data files on either disk or tape are not subject to unauthorized access, change, or destruction.

Subject Area: Information technology—application development and maintenance. Source: CIA 597, III-62.

283. (c) There is a prevalent risk that management may rely on EUC reports to the same degree as reports produced under traditional systems development procedures. Choice (a) is incorrect because EUC systems typically increase flexibility and responsiveness to management's information requests. Choice (b) is incorrect because EUC systems typically reduce application development cycle time. Choice (d) is incorrect because EUC systems typically result in reduced application development, and maintenance, costs.

Subject Area: Information technology—application development and maintenance. Source: CIA 1196, III-36.

284. (a) The systems analysis is often incomplete or improperly omitted. Choice (b) is incorrect because the programming function cannot be omitted. Choice (c) is incorrect because the computer operations function cannot be omitted. Choice (d) is incorrect because the user function cannot be omitted.

Subject Area: Information technology—application development and maintenance. Source: CIA 1196, III-37.

285. (a) In client/server environments, change control must also ensure synchronization of programs across the network so that each client and each server are running from the same versions of the programs; in mainframe environments, there may be only one copy of the production system that is executed so that synchronization of programs is not required. Choice (b) is incorrect because emergency move procedures should be documented and followed in both mainframe and client/server environments. Choice (c) is incorrect because appropriate users should be involved in program change testing in mainframe and in client/server environments. Choice (d) is incorrect because movement from the test library to the production library should be controlled in both mainframe and client/server environments.

Subject Area: Information technology—application development and maintenance. Source: CIA 597, III-73.

286. (b) Change control is the process of authorizing, developing, testing, and installing coded changes so as to minimize the impact on processing and the risk to the system. Choice (a) is incorrect because security administration deals with adding or deleting user to/from the system. Choice (c) is incorrect because problem tracking is the process of collecting operational data about processes so that it can be analyzed for corrective action. Choice (d) is incorrect because problem escalation procedures are a means of categorizing problems or unusual circumstances so that the least skilled person can address them.

Subject Area: Information technology—application development and maintenance. Source: CIA 1196, III-49.

287. (b) A risk associated with such programs is that the programs may not be tested further before being placed into production permanently. The temptation is to place the test library program into production if it appeared to run satisfactorily. Choice (a) is incorrect because such programs can be assumed to have been prepared by authorized personnel. Choice (c) is incorrect because the integrity of the production library is not threatened because no changes were made to the production library. Choice (d) is incorrect because test library programs are run in such circumstances because the personnel involved believe that using them is better than using the prior programs or no programs at all.

Subject Area: Information technology—application development and maintenance. Source: CIA 1196, III-50.

288. (c) Legacy systems represent a significant investment and may still provide adequate service. Moving forward, IT departments will find opportunities to add object-oriented capabilities to existing systems. Choice (a) is incorrect because the costs of migrating legacy systems to an open environment and retraining the personnel who would develop and maintain them preclude any rapid transition. Choice (b) is incorrect because legacy systems that are difficult to modify and maintain are better candidates for conversion to object technology. Choice (d) is incorrect because object technology is an important part of the way forward for developers and users and should be explored as a better approach for implementing business applications.

Subject Area: Information technology—application development and maintenance. Source: CIA 1196, III-65.

289. (b) The use of expert systems has helped to improve the quality of customer service in applications such as maintenance and scheduling. Choice (a) is incorrect because expert systems codify and apply existing knowledge, but they do not create knowledge that is lacking. Choice (c) is incorrect because expert systems do best in automating lower-level clerical functions. Choice (d) is incorrect because virtually all successful expert systems deal with problems in which there are relatively few alternative outcomes and in which these possible outcomes are all known in advance.

Subject Area: Information technology—application development and maintenance. Source: CIA 1196, III-68.

290. (c) Fuzzy logic systems are suitable for dealing with imprecise data and problems that have many solutions. These systems have been applied successfully to applications such as ventilating expressway tunnels. Choice (a) is incorrect because the requirement in this instance is to make the process of gate assignment quick and consistently correct. This requirement calls for an expert system rather than a fuzzy logic system. Choice (b) is incorrect because neural networks rather than fuzzy logic systems provide the technology to undertake sophisticated forecasting and analysis. Choice (d) is incorrect because diagnosing problems with equipment such as computer hardware requires a knowledge base and extensive rule-based programs. These are characteristics of an expert system.

Subject Area: Information technology—application development and maintenance. Source: CIA 1196, III-69

291. (d) The systems analysts are the principal liaison between the IT group and the rest of an organization because the analyst's job is to translate business problems and requirements into information requirements and systems. Choice (a) is incorrect because the end user's job is to conduct the business of the organization, not to be the interface between the IT group and the rest of the organization. Choice (b) is incorrect because the application programmer's job is to convert information requirement specifications into new application systems. Choice (c) is incorrect because the maintenance programmer's job is to modify existing programs in response to authorized changes in program function.

Subject Area: Information technology—application development and maintenance. Source: CIA 1196, III-70.

292. (d) That is the definition of a data flow diagram. Choice (a) is incorrect because action diagrams are process logic notations that combine graphics and text to support the definition of technical rules. Choice (b) is incorrect because program structure charts are graphical depictions of the hierarchy of modules or instructions in a program. Choice (c) is incorrect because conceptual data modules are independent definitions of the data requirements that are explained in terms of entities and relationships.

Subject Area: Information technology—application development and maintenance. Source: CIA 596, III-69.

293. (b) Usually prototyping is accomplished with a software tool. Choice (a) is incorrect because it may include prototyping tool, but is much more. Choice (c) is incorrect because reengineering is a much broader concept than prototyping— prototyping could be used in this reengineering, however. Choice (d) is incorrect because a more traditional approach could include use of a prototyping tool.

Subject Area: Information technology—application development and maintenance. Source: CIA 596, III-70.

294. (c) This technique will not affect introduction of unlicensed software. Choice (a) is incorrect because this technique works. Choice (b) is incorrect because it is a must to test the "other" controls that should be in place. Choice (d) is incorrect because it is the basis for all good controls in a written policy.

Subject Area: Information technology—application development and maintenance. Source: CIA 596, III-71.

295. (c) This risk is considered unique to end-user computer (EUC) system development. Choices (a) and (b) are incorrect because these risks relate to traditional information systems and EUC environments. Choice (d) is incorrect because this risk relates to all computing environments.

Subject Area: Information technology—application development and maintenance. Source: CIA 596, III-61.

296. (d) While all systems should be tested before implementation, "test" is not an approach to implementation. Choice (a) is incorrect because a complete cutover is done after thorough testing. Choice (b) is incorrect because new and existing systems run in tandem for a period. Choice (c) is incorrect because pilot locations implemented, then others cutover.

Subject Area: Information technology—application development and maintenance. Source: CIA 596, III-62.

297. (b) Applications must be found, risk-ranked, and "traditionally" reviewed. Choice (a) is incorrect because this process is used to review organizational level EUC controls. Choices (c) and (d) are incorrect because these are only parts of a review, not a phase, or process.

Subject Area: Information technology—application development and maintenance. Source: CIA 596, III-63.

298. (b) Separating production and test versions of programs facilitates restricting access to production programs to only the individuals, such as computer operators, who need access, thus separating the incompatible functions of operators and programmers. Choice (a) is incorrect because production and test programs can only be separated if there is a specific procedure for installing programs in production libraries. Thus maintaining the separation requires its own procedure, which may decrease development efficiency. Choice (c) is incorrect because separating production and test versions of programs is independent of facilitating user input on proposed changes. Choice (d) is incorrect because separating production and test versions of programs restricts access to programs.

Subject Area: Information technology—application development and maintenance. Source: CIA 596, III-36.

299. (a) In distributed or cooperative systems, the responsibility for ensuring that adequate backups are taken is the responsibility of user management because the systems are under the control of users. Choice (b) is incorrect because in distributed environments, there will be no systems programmers comparable to those at central sites for traditional systems. Choice (c) is incorrect because in distributed environments, there may be no data entry clerks because users are typically performing their own data entry. Choice (d) is incorrect because in distributed environments, there are no tape librarians.

Subject Area: Information technology—application development and maintenance. Source: CIA 595, III-80.

300. (d) The practice of authorizing changes, approving test results, and copying developmental programs to a production library is program change control. Choice (a) is incorrect because prototyping is the practice of rapid development of a system containing essential features for the purpose of eliciting user comments, which drive successive iterations of the prototype system. Choice (b) is incorrect because program integration does not have a standard meaning. Choice (c) is incorrect because system development life cycle (SDLC) practice described is often assumed to be incorporated in well-controlled SDLC but is not thought of as SDLC.

Subject Area: Information technology—application development and maintenance. Source: CIA 1194, III-25.

301. (c) The most likely implementation failure was lack of adequate volume testing. If the programs had been tested with sufficient volumes of transactions, the deficiency would have been detected before actual trades went unrecorded. Choice (a) is incorrect because desk checking, a programmer's review of program code, verifies program logic for individual transactions and would be unlikely to detect the program's inability to process continuing transactions. Choice (b) is incorrect because the changes were authorized and planned, and the changeover was anticipated. Choice (d) is incorrect because the enlarged trading volume may or may not have been documented, but that was not the reason for the failure.

Subject Area: Information technology—application development and maintenance. Source: CIA 1194, III-26.

302. (b) Private files can proliferate. Choice (a) is incorrect because this will improve with less chance of user-analyst distortion. Choice (c) is incorrect because this will reduce applications backlog. Choice (d) is incorrect because this will reduce development time.

Subject Area: Information technology—application development and maintenance. Source: CIA 1194, III-35.

303. (d) Two important systems plan components are information requirement analysis and database design. Choice (a) is incorrect because variance analysis refers to the comparison of standards with actual performance results. Choice (b) is incorrect because multiplexors are physical devices to interleave transmissions of hardware such as modems. Choice (c) is incorrect because telematics describes the integration of computer and communications technologies.

Subject Area: Information technology—application development and maintenance. Source: CIA 1194, III-40.

304. (a) Inadequate testing is the most likely cause for the coding errors in the most complex reports. It is difficult to design a test which will satisfy all data criteria in a complex environment. Choice (b) is incorrect because there may be inadequate change control, but that is not the reason for errors in the most complex reports. Choice (c) is incorrect because there may be inadequate documentation, but that is not the reason for errors in the most complex reports. Choice (d) is incorrect because there may be inadequate access control, but that is not the reason for errors in the most complex reports.

Subject Area: Information technology—application development and maintenance. Source: CIA 1195, III-33.

305. (b) Inadequate change control is apt to lead to previously corrected errors recurring because the analysts were reusing erroneous code rather than corrected code. The solution to the problem is better program change control procedures. Choice (a) is incorrect because there may be inadequate backups, but that is not the cause of analysts reusing erroneous code. Choice (c) is incorrect because there may be inadequate access control, but that is not the cause of analysts reusing erroneous code. Choice (d) is incorrect because there may be inadequate testing, but that is not the cause of analysts reusing erroneous code.

Subject Area: Information technology—application development and maintenance. Source: CIA 1195, III-34.

306. (c) The IT director's statement reflects the belief that non-IT professionals are apt to write inefficient queries and programs because they do not understand the data structure well enough to avoid relational operations such as multitable joins that require more processing capacity than may be available. Choice (a) is incorrect because with adequate training, marketing and other professional employees would be capable of writing their own queries and programs with query and report-writing software. Choice (b) is incorrect because programming does take time, but the marketing department has ascertained that it can only do its job better with access to more current production data. Choice (d) is incorrect. If it is to do its job, the marketing department must have access to the data required for it to make useful predictions.

Subject Area: Information technology—application development and maintenance. Source: CIA 1195, III-35.

307. (a) The command sequences should have been documented so that other analysts could use and modify them readily. Choice (b) is incorrect. There may have been inadequate data backup procedures, but the inability of other analysts to understand the command sequences is not a function of inadequate data backup procedures. Choice (c) is incorrect. There may have been inadequate testing, but the inability of other analysts to understand the command sequences is not a function of inadequate testing. Choice (d) is incorrect. There may have been inadequate use of antivirus software, but the inability of other analysts to understand the command sequences is not a function of inadequate use of antivirus software.

Subject Area: Information technology—application development and maintenance. Source: CIA 1195, III-36.

308. (a) Because this flaw was a design error, a design review, an audit of the design of the system before it is programmed, is the audit involvement most likely to help avoid this kind of flaw in future systems. Choice (b) is incorrect because an application control review is a review of the effectiveness and appropriateness of controls in an existing application. Choice (c) is incorrect because a source code review is the selective examination of source code to verify or test controls in an application. Choice (d) is incorrect because an access control review is an evaluation of the effectiveness and appropriateness of access controls.

Subject Area: Information technology—application development and maintenance. Source: CIA 1195, III-59.

309. (c) The flaw should have been detected by the examination of test data. Choice (a) is incorrect because data errors are not generally addressed by user specifications. Choice (b) is incorrect because application control review is the identification, analysis, testing, and evaluation of controls in application systems, usually performed on systems already in use. Choice (d) is incorrect because software-mapping analysis is used to detect nonexecuted code in software.

Subject Area: Information technology—application development and maintenance. Source: CIA 1195, III-60.

310. (b) This would have prevented the programmer from being able to alter the working copy of the payroll program without having received proper authorization. The program would have been thoroughly tested and the results checked before the new program was implemented. Hence this control would have prevented the current situation from occurring. Choice (a) is incorrect because this would merely verify that for each input (timecard) there is one output (a check) was generated. The problem of generating a check with an incorrect dollar value would not be assisted by this control. Choice (c) is incorrect because distribution of the checks by the treasurer's office provides control in the possibility of a check going to the wrong person but would not aid in detecting a check generated for the wrong dollar value. Choice (d) is incorrect because hash total on the field social security number would not have assisted in any way in detecting the illegal change in the program or the generation of a check for an improper dollar value. A hash total would only verify that all records were processed.

Subject Area: Information technology—application development and maintenance. Source: CIA 590, II-26.

311. (b) The study at this point should consider the activity that takes place, the needs of the user, the type of equipment needed, the cost, and the potential benefit to the specific area and the company in general. Choice (a) is incorrect because the feasibility study will not deal with this amount of detail. Conversion plans will most likely be included in the system design. Choice (c) is incorrect because such assurances should come from those who will be affected by the conversion and are implied in the study of the larger issue of cost/benefit. Choice (d) is incorrect because the feasibility study will not deal with the controls needed in the new system; such issues are addressed during design and specification.

Subject Area: Information technology—application development and maintenance. Source: CIA 590, II-9.

312. (b) This is a proper role for the internal auditor in a feasibility study. Choices (a) and (c) are incorrect because these are the roles for users and functional management. Choice (d) is incorrect because this is a role for computer experts.

Subject Area: Information technology—application development and maintenance. Source: CIA 1190, I-38.

313. (a) Requiring updating of executable modules from compilation of authorized source code would ensure that executable modules corresponded to the source code. Choice (b) is incorrect because enforcing the use of separate development and production libraries are good practice, but it does not ensure that source code and executable modules correspond. Choice (c) is incorrect because requiring management authorization for source code change ensures that source code changes are authorized but does not ensure correspondence between source versions and executable forms. Choice (d) is incorrect because installing access control procedures for source code libraries ensures control of source code libraries but does not ensure control over access to executable libraries.

Subject Area: Information technology—application development and maintenance. Source: CIA 1190, I-35.

314. (a) Detailed analysis and design is the portion of the system development life cycle in which physical database design occurs. Choice (b) is incorrect because detailed analysis and design occurs prior to conversion and implementation. Choice (c) is incorrect because detailed analysis and design occurs after information requirement analysis. Choice (d) is incorrect because detailed analysis and design occurs before program and procedure development.

Subject Area: Information technology—application development and maintenance. Source: CIA 1190, I-31.

315. (a) Maintaining separate test program and production program libraries is an organizational control. Choice (b) is incorrect because physical security prevents unauthorized personnel from coming and going at will. Choice (c) is incorrect because input controls validate the completeness, accuracy, and appropriateness of input data. Choice (d) is incorrect because concurrency controls prohibit conflicting requests for database access from interfering with each other.

Subject Area: Information technology—application development and maintenance. Source: CIA 590, I-20.

316. (b) It is the most likely to provide assurance. Choice (a) is incorrect because it is not related to requirements. Choice (c) is incorrect because it is a computer programming technique. Choice (d) is incorrect because it is too broad.

Subject Area: Information technology—application development and maintenance. Source: CIA 1190, III-16.

317. (d) Vendor-supplied performance standards provide a means for evaluating the proper use of peripheral devices. Choice (a) is incorrect because a hardware monitor is a tool used to collect performance data, but it does not provide a standard for evaluating the proper use of a device. Choice (b) is incorrect because a software monitor is a tool used to collect performance data, but it does not provide a standard for evaluating the proper use of a device. Choice (c) is incorrect because direct observation of operating performance is a method of collecting data, but it does not provide a standard for evaluating the proper use of a device.

Subject Area: Information technology—application development and maintenance. Source: CIA 1190, III-27.

318. (c) Operational feasibility is a component of a feasibility study. Choice (a) is incorrect because the design of internal schema is a component of detailed analysis and design. Choice (b) is incorrect because evaluating program correctness is a function of the testing phase. Choice (d) is incorrect because detailed process design is a component of detailed analysis and design.

Subject Area: Information technology—application development and maintenance. Source: CIA 1190, III-35.

319. (a) A complete cutover means that all stores would implement the new system simultaneously, which would preclude comparing the results of the old and new systems. The company is also unlikely to have the personnel required to implement the new system in all stores at once. Choice (b) is incorrect because phased implementation means the new system would be implemented in phases. Given the integrated nature of the new system, phasing it in is not feasible. Choice (c) is incorrect because parallel running means that both old and new systems run simultaneously for a time. Store personnel are unlikely to have the time to run both systems at once. Choice (d) is incorrect because a pilot test at one or a small number of stores would allow the company to evaluate the new system, modify the system based on pilot results, and then implement the refined system in all stores.

Subject Area: Information technology—application development and maintenance. Source: CIA 1190, III-36.

320. (d) System development life cycle (SDLC) is best for large integrated systems. Choice (a) is incorrect because PERT is a means of tracking a project, not a guide. Choice (b) is incorrect because prototyping is used for small or narrow systems. Choice (c) is incorrect because feasibility study is only one step in the process.

Subject Area: Information technology—application development and maintenance. Source: CIA 590, III-40.

Voice Communications

321. (c) Wireless technologies invite privacy and fraud violations more easily than wireline (wired) technologies due to their broadcast nature. The privacy implications of widespread use of mobile wireless technologies are potentially serious for both individuals and businesses. There will be a continuing need to guard against eavesdropping and breaches of confidentiality, as hackers and scanners develop ways to listen in and track wireless communications devices.

Subject Area: Information technology—voice communications. Source: Author.

322. (b) There are two main types of information that merit protection in the wireless context: the contents of a call or transmission and the location of the sender or recipient. Items 2 and 4 are distracters.

Subject Area: Information technology—voice communications. Source: Author.

323. (b) Wireless data network providers claim that their digital systems are inherently more secure than analog cellular telephony because of their digital formats and error-checking and correction protocols.

Subject Area: Information technology—voice communications. Source: Author.

324. (a) New digital communications systems such as time division multiple access (TDMA) or code division multiple access (CDMA) use spread spectrum much more efficiently than analog cellular and other traditional radio systems. The spread spectrum technology uses a wide band of frequencies to send radio signals. The other choices are distracters.

Subject Area: Information technology—voice communications. Source: Author.

325. (a) CDMA is more efficient and secure than TDMA because it uses spread spectrum technology more efficiently. Instead of assigning a time slot on a single channel, CDMA uses many different channels simultaneously. CDMA is also inherently more difficult to crack because the coding scheme changes with each conversation and is given only once at the beginning of the transmission.

Subject Area: Information technology—voice communications. Source: Author.

326. (a) Voice encryption schemes are based on RSA algorithm to provide privacy protection over mobile or cellular phones. The main constraints with encryption are the slow speed of processing and the lag that occurs if signals take too long to pass through the system.

Subject Area: Information technology—voice communications. Source: Author.

327. (d) Under current law, a scanner is only illegal if it is used with intent to defraud. Possession of or sale of electronic serial number (ESN)-altering software is currently legal. These scanners are intended for bench testing only, but cloners use them for illegal purpose to listen in on cellular phones. These scanning devices typically monitor cellular signaling channels and display broadcasted electronic serial numbers (ESN) and mobile identification numbers (MIN) pairs.

Subject Area: Information technology—voice communications. Source: Author.

328. (b) Phone cloning and call selling are two major illegal activities in the US. In phone cloning, cloners pick up electronic serial numbers (ESN) and mobile identification numbers (MIN) pairs on busy streets or highways with scanning equipment that is legally available, although their use for this purpose is illegal. Call selling is an illegal activity conducted with cloned cellular telephones.

Subject Area: Information technology—voice communications. Source: Author.

329. (a) Telephone cloning is the practice of reprogramming a phone with stolen electronic serial numbers (ESN) and mobile identification numbers (MIN) pairs from another phone. Digital encoding schemes are known and can be broken, given enough time and computing power, even though the equipment to pick out numbers is more costly. Other techniques are effective against telephone cloning.

Subject Area: Information technology—voice communications. Source: Author.

330. (c) To monitor the state of the network and be able to respond quickly when calls are made, the main cellular controlling switch periodically "pings" all cellular telephones. This pinging lets the switch know which users are in the area and where in the network the telephone is located. This information can be used to give a rough idea of location of the phone user to help catch the fraud perpetrator. Vehicle location service is an application of the ping technology. The other choices are distracters.

Subject Area: Information technology—voice communications. Source: Author.

331. (c) A telephone tumbling attack is where a fraud perpetrator randomly or sequentially changes the electronic serial numbers (ESN) and/or mobile identification numbers (MIN) after each call. Because the cellular switch takes some time to verify each number, some proportion of calls may get through the system before the system denies access. Wireless telephone providers can install precall validation systems to detect this type of fraud.

Subject Area: Information technology—voice communications. Source: Author.

332. (a) With traditional analog cellular systems, "tumbling" attacks are quite simple. Tumbling is the practice of programming a phone with electronic serial numbers (ESN)/mobile identification numbers (MIN) pairs until a valid combination is found.

Subject Area: Information technology—voice communications. Source: Author.

333. (c) Cloning is the practice of reprogramming a phone with an electronic serial numbers (ESN)/mobile identification numbers (MIN) pairs from another phone. Cloners pick up the ESN/MIN pairs on busy streets or highways with scanning equipment. Cloners record these number pairs and send them to other cities, where carriers may be unable or unlikely to verify that the number is in use elsewhere. In the remote city, participants in the fraud scam use a standard PC to reprogram the ESN/MIN pairs in a cellular telephone. Scaling is the ability to change in size or configuration to suit changing conditions. Roaming is the practice of using a cellular phone in cellular networks outside the user's home system. Browsing is searching for information to attack.

Subject Area: Information technology—voice communications. Source: Author.

Contingency Planning

334. (c) Online teleprocessing would generally not involve a reciprocal processing agreement. They use shared facilities such as hot-site services. Choices (a), (b), and (d) are incorrect because reciprocal processing agreements are often used for small systems and for large/small batch operations.

Subject Area: Information technology—contingency planning. Source: CIA 594, III-30.

335. (b) A "cold site" has all needed assets in place except the needed computer equipment and is vendor dependent for timely delivery of equipment. Choice (a) is incorrect because a "hot site" has all needed assets in place and is not vendor dependent. Choice (c) is incorrect because a "cold and hot site" combination allows the "hot site" to be used until the "cold site" is prepared and is thus not too vendor dependent. Choice (d) is incorrect because excess capacity would ensure that needed assets are available and would not be vendor dependent.

Subject Area: Information technology—contingency planning. Source: CIA 593, I-42.

336. (a) This is the primary reason because continuity of operations is dependent upon the ability to properly process vital transactions. Choices (b) and (c) are incorrect because they are not the best choices. These are secondary reasons. Choice (d) is incorrect because it is not the best choice; sources of capital are seldom included.

Subject Area: Information technology—contingency planning. Source: CIA 593, II-41.

337. (d) As management relies more on information systems for crucial functions, system failures have the potential to interrupt business. Choice (a) is incorrect because the exposure of unauthorized third-party access to systems is increased by the absence of adequate access controls to systems. Choice (b) is incorrect because systematic programming errors are the result of misspecification of requirements or lack of correspondence between specifications and programs. Choice (c) is incorrect because inadequate knowledge bases are a function of lack of care in building them.

Subject Area: Information technology—contingency planning. Source: CIA 593, III-37.

338. (d) An essential element of a disaster recovery plan is a statement of the responsibilities of each organizational unit. Choice (a) is incorrect because system development standards for the organization are an element of management control; they are not part of a disaster recovery plan. Choice (b) is incorrect because the history of modifications to the operating system is an element of management control through documentation; it is not part of the disaster recovery plan. Choice (c) is incorrect because the applications planned for new development are part of management planning and control; they are not part of a disaster recovery plan.

Subject Area: Information technology—contingency planning. Source: CIA 593, III-54.

339. (c) The use of restart and recovery procedures eliminates the need to reprocess all data in the event of a processing failure. Choice (a) is incorrect. The original disk was damaged, thus preventing a full update from that source. Also, each teller should begin with the transaction following the last one logged before the power surge. Choice (b) is incorrect. The original disk was damaged, thus preventing a full update from that source. Choice (d) is incorrect. Each teller should begin with the transaction following the last one logged before the power surge.

Subject Area: Information technology—contingency planning. Source: CIA 591, III-80.

340. (a) A crucial aspect of recovery planning for the company is ensuring that organizational and operational changes are incorporated in the plans because such changes have the potential to make the recovery plans inapplicable. Choice (b) is incorrect because it is vital that changes to systems be tested thoroughly before being placed into production, but that is not a part of recovery planning. Choice (c) is incorrect because a good recovery plan would specify how operational staff might be replaced should the need arise, but their replacements might not be management personnel. Choice (d) is incorrect because being able to predict workload changes accurately permits a company to minimize its information systems facility costs, but that is not a part of recovery planning.

Subject Area: Information technology—contingency planning. Source: CIA 1196, III-39.

341. (a) Risk analysis is necessary to determine an organization's definition of a disaster. Choice (b) is incorrect because system backup analysis is a contingency planning strategy to react to a disaster. Choice (c) is incorrect because vendor supply agreement analysis is a contingency planning strategy to react to a disaster. Choice (d) is incorrect because contingent facility contract analysis is a contingency planning strategy to react to a disaster.

Subject Area: Information technology—contingency planning. Source: CIA 1196, III-42.

342. (c) The best approach to avoid having the data center identified as a terrorist's target is to establish as low a profile as possible for the data center. This is done by refraining from (1) identifying the building on the outside as a data center, (2) showcasing the data center through glass windows, of (3) advertising the important role the data center plays in operations. Choice (a) is incorrect because ensuring that the disaster recovery plans are fully tested would not contribute to avoiding being selected as a terrorist target. Choice (b) is incorrect because hardening the electrical and communications systems so that they could withstand some kinds of attacks would not contribute to avoiding being selected as a terrorist's target. Choice (d) is incorrect because monitoring the locations and activities of known terrorists, even if permitted by law, would not by itself help the company avoid having the data center selected as a terrorist's target.

Subject Area: Information technology—contingency planning. Source: CIA 1196, III-43.

343. (c) The better the recovery plans, then the more likely the company would be to resume operations quickly and fulfill its obligations to customers. Choice (a) is incorrect because the company may or may not maintain the same level of employment after a disaster (e.g., a disaster that destroys productive capacity in one plant may lead to layoffs). Choice (b) is incorrect because thorough planning may or may not minimize the cost of facility repair (i.e., the best approach may be to undergo more expensive repair sooner in order to resume operations sooner). Choice (d) is incorrect because the maximum benefit from planning is that it prompts action to avoid the most likely or most devastating events with the potential to interrupt business. Management would be delighted if planning ensured that business was never interrupted and thus that the recovery plan was never invoked.

Subject Area: Information technology—contingency planning. Source: CIA 1196, III-48.

344. (c) If the area floods, some employees may be unable to report for work due to flooded roads or to the demands on them to care for injured loved ones or their own damaged property. Choice (a) is incorrect because customers are unlikely to refuse to do business with the company because mortgagee customers generally do not have control over how mortgaging servicing rights are assigned. Choice (b) is incorrect because as long as floodwaters do not reach the data center, there should be no special threat to the equipment. Choice (d) is incorrect because the company is a nationwide mortgaging servicing company, and most payments will be coming from places other than the immediate vicinity, which would most likely not be affected by a flood in the local area. Mail containing payments might be delayed, but large groups of customers are unlikely to fail to make payments.

Subject Area: Information technology—contingency planning. Source: CIA 596, III-37.

345. (b) The most critical aspect of the planning would be to provide for continuation of mortgage servicing because without mortgage servicing, the company would be out of business. Choice (a) is incorrect because deterring and detecting fraud or abuse while processing in recovery mode is important, but that is not the most critical aspect to consider. Choice (c) is incorrect because there should be control over information assets at all times but that is not the most critical aspect. Choice (d) is incorrect. Of course, the company would want to minimize expenses during recovery periods but not at the expense of continuing to service mortgages.

Subject Area: Information technology—contingency planning. Source: CIA 596, III-38.

346. (b) The risk analysis is performed to seek out potential vulnerabilities. Choice (a) is incorrect because contingency plans are put into place when something goes wrong. However, first the possibility of that particular crisis should have been analyzed. Choice (c) is incorrect because the crisis management team is formed after the risk analysis has been conducted and contingency plans have been developed. The team is composed of specialists in different fields to best insure appropriate response to emergencies. Choice (d) is incorrect because practice is the last phase of the program and is periodically conducted using differing scenarios to promote teamwork and effectiveness.

Subject Area: Information technology—contingency planning. Source: CIA 595, III-14.

347. (c) If the company arranged for a third-party cold site to replace a nonfunctioning regional center, the company would not have to install additional equipment at the regional centers. Choice (a) is incorrect because personnel employed at the site would not be familiar with company operations because they work for the third party, not the company. Choice (b) is incorrect because using a cold site may actually increase travel expenses because company personnel would have to travel to the site. Choice (d) is incorrect because typically, cold sites require a minimum of 24 hours before being operational in order to permit software and data installation and testing.

Subject Area: Information technology—contingency planning. Source: CIA 595, III-71.

348. (a) The company has decentralized its information processing since the last revision to the plan. Choice (b) is incorrect. For its functions, headquarters has adequate processing capability. Choice (c) is incorrect. If the company were depending on a cold site for the times when facilities were unavailable, lack of arrangements for cold site backups would be crucial. Having a cold site, however, may or may not be required, depending on the best plan. Choice (d) is incorrect. Personnel turnover by itself is not a reason for a contingency plan to be outdated because new personnel would be trained for their jobs, which would include recovery procedures for processing.

Subject Area: Information technology—contingency planning. Source: CIA 595, III-72.

349. (b) Mirroring the data an another regional center would cause the company to incur the cost and complexity of greater network traffic that would be required to send and synchronize the replicated data. Choice (a) is incorrect because headquarters would be no more unaware of processing than is now the case. Choice (c) is incorrect because the mirrored data would most likely be kept in segregated files; there would be no interference with the data originally kept at each regional center. Choice (d) is incorrect because agents would not have to change their procedures because they would continue using the system as before.

Subject Area: Information technology—contingency planning. Source: CIA 595, III-73.

350. (d) Contingency planning is a management activity, which is essential to ensure continuity of operations in the event a disaster impairs information systems processing. Choice (a) is incorrect because review of insurance coverage is an aspect of risk analysis, and a much narrower concept than contingency planning. Choice (b) is incorrect because electronic vaulting is a technology which may be used to address contingency planning issues. Choice (c) is incorrect because change control procedures do not ensure continuity of operations.

Subject Area: Information technology—contingency planning. Source: CIA 1194, III-22.

351. (a) Risk analysis is necessary to determine an organization's definition of a disaster. Choice (b) is incorrect because system backup analysis is a contingency planning strategy to react to a disaster. Choice (c) is incorrect because vendor supply agreement analysis is a contingency planning strategy to react to a disaster. Choice (d) is incorrect because contingent facility contract analysis is a contingency planning strategy to react to a disaster.

Subject Area: Information technology—contingency planning. Source: CIA 1194, III-23.

352. (d) Rerouting call traffic to nonaffected regional centers is the best approach because it minimizes cost, maximizes the company's control over the reconfiguration, and permits calls to be answered by the company's skilled personnel. Choice (a) is incorrect because duplicating regional facilities in a cold site would be overly expensive and would still not provide equipment, software, or personnel. Choice (b) is incorrect because duplicating regional facilities in a hot site would provide space, equipment, and some software but would be overly expensive and would still not provide personnel. Choice (c) is incorrect because rerouting call traffic to a third-party service center would be overly expensive because of personnel cost, and service center personnel would not be trained for the company's calls.

Subject Area: Information technology—contingency planning. Source: CIA 1195, III-38.

353. (b) A database management system (DBMS) for online order entry requires the most extensive backup and recover procedures. This is due to complexity of processing, quick propagation of errors, and the difficulty of determining database status after failures. Choices (a), (c), and (d) are incorrect because batch and file-oriented systems do not require the most extensive backup and recovery procedures since error propagation can be controlled between successive runs.

Subject Area: Information technology—contingency planning. Source: CIA 1190, III-17.

354. (b) A formal procedure for restarting at an intermediate stage of processing would ensure continuity of operations for the situation. This would solve the problem of a program being terminated before the normal ending and avoid the need to reprocess the whole run. Choice (a) is incorrect. The problem that occurred was a discontinuation in the processing. There was no problem in either the master program file or the transaction files that were being processed. While backup copies are a necessary part of a contingency plan, they will not solve the situation that was presented. Choice (c) is incorrect. A review of the console log provides information on all operating system activity, maintains an equipment utilization record, and identifies operator-initiated actions. This does not provide a feasible solution for the situation. Choice (d) is incorrect. Since power has been restored and the computer is working there is no need to transfer processing to another location in this situation. This is an advisable procedure that should be in a contingency plan but there is no need to implement it now.

Subject Area: Information technology—contingency planning. Source: CIA 1190, III-28.

355. (d) The only way to know whether contingency planning has been effective is to test the plan, by simulating an interruption or by conducting a paper test with a walk-through of recovery procedures. Choice (a) is incorrect because the absence of processing interruptions indicates nothing about the interruptions that might occur in the future, especially those that are not under the organization's control. Choice (b) is incorrect because contingency plan may have comprehensive documentation, but until the plan is tested, an organization has no indication of its effectiveness. Choice (c) is incorrect because audit signoff is one indicator of plan quality, but until the plan is tested, an organization has no indication of its effectiveness.

Subject Area: Information technology—contingency planning. Source: CIA Model Exam 2002, III-77.

356. (d) This would not cause a control concern; it is a potential advantage to distributed systems of various architectures versus centralized data in a single mainframe computer. Choice (a) is incorrect because password proliferation is a considerable security concern because users will be tempted to write their password down or make them overly simplistic. Choice (b) is incorrect because consistent security across varied platforms is often challenging because of the different security features of the various systems and the decentralized nature of those controlling security administration. Choice (c) is incorrect because under centralized control, management can feel more confident that backup file storage is being uniformly controlled. Decentralization of this function leads to lack of consistency and difficulty in monitoring compliance.

Subject Area: Information technology—contingency planning. Source: CIA 1196, III-66.

357. (c) Since the activity log records the time each job is started and finished, as well as the resources consumed by the job, this problem would be detected by a review of the log. Choice (a) is incorrect because this would not result in a software failure hence would not appear on the activity log. A data recording control would be needed to catch this error, such as a read after write check. Choice (b) is incorrect because this would not result in a software failure hence would not appear on the activity log. A batch total of the dollar amount of the purchases to be posted would be needed to catch this error. Choice (d) is incorrect because this would not result in a software failure hence would not appear on the activity log. A record count of the number of transactions to be submitted would be needed to catch this error.

Subject Area: Information technology—contingency planning. Source: CIA 1190, III-29.

358. (b) The capability to continue processing at all sites except a nonfunctioning one is called fail-soft protection, an advantage of distributed systems. Choice (a) is incorrect because exception reporting can be used to control correctness and timeliness of updates but cannot minimize the impact of an interruption. Choice (c) is incorrect because backup procedures are intended to prevent the recovery process from introducing any erroneous changes into the system after computer failure. Choice (d) is incorrect because data file security is intended to prevent unauthorized changes to data files.

Subject Area: Information technology—contingency planning. Source: CIA Model Exam 1998, III-75.

Systems Security

359. (b) A firewall is an example of logical access control while fences provide a physical security and perimeter access control. When these two controls are combined they provide a total boundary control. By limiting access to host systems and services, firewalls provide a necessary line of perimeter defense against attacks thus providing logical security boundary control. Similarly, perimeter fences provide a physical security boundary control for a facility or building. A probe is a device programmed to gather information about a system or its users. A patch is a modification to software that fixes an error in an operational application system on a computer. The patch is generally supplied by the software vendor. Tags and labels are used in access controls. Encryption and smart cards are used in user identification and authentication mechanisms.

Subject Area: Information technology—systems security. Source: Author.

360. (d) Input overflow checks ensure that input is not lost during data entry or processing and are good against input overflow attacks. These attacks can be avoided by proper program design. Log-in spoofing can be defended against by providing a secure channel between the user and the system. A hardware-reset button on a personal computer can be very effective in removing some kinds of spoofing attacks. Cryptographic authentication techniques can increase security but only for complex systems.

Subject Area: Information technology—systems security. Source: Author.

361. (d) The secure sockets layer (SSL) protocol is the technology used in most Web-based applications. When both the Web client and the Web server are authenticated with SSL, the entire session is encrypted providing protection against session hijacking and eavesdropping attacks. SET is security electronic transaction protocol. PPP is a point-to-point protocol, and MIM is a man-in-the-middle attack. Choices (a), (b), and (c) are distracters here.

Subject Area: Information technology—systems security. Source: Author.

362. (b) A well-configured firewall is very difficult to bypass. And there is no substitute for monitoring by diligent and vigilant system/security administrators.

Subject Area: Information technology—systems security. Source: Author.

363. (a) A static packet filtering firewall is the simplest and least expensive way to stop messages with inappropriate network addresses. It does not take much time to implement when compared to other types of firewalls.

Subject Area: Information technology—systems security. Source: Author.

364. (b) The screened subnet firewall adds an extra layer of security by creating a network where the bastion host resides. Often called a perimeter network, the screened subnet firewall separates the internal network from the external. This leads to stronger security.

Subject Area: Information technology—systems security. Source: Author.

365. (b) Firewalls should not be used as general-purpose servers. The only access accounts on the firewalls should be those of the primary and backup firewall administrators and the network service manager, where the latter manages both administrators. Functional users should not be given access to firewalls since they do not contain business-related application systems.

Subject Area: Information technology—systems security. Source: Author.

366. (c) The screened subnet firewall acts as a perimeter network. If there is an attack on the firewall, the attacker is restricted to the perimeter (external) network and therefore is not attacking the internal network.

Subject Area: information technology—systems security. Source: Author.

367. (a) The remote access server (RAS) provides the following services: when a remote user dials in through a modem connection, the server hangs up and calls the remote user back at the known phone number. The other servers mentioned do not have this kind of dial-in and callback dual control mechanism.

Subject Area: information technology—systems security. Source: Author.

368. (c) Access limited to users with valid passwords. Choice (a) is incorrect. Both types of data are sensitive and need protection. Choice (b) is incorrect. Would not identify the user. Choice (d) is incorrect because it is excessive and burdensome.

Subject Area: Information technology—systems security. Source: CIA 593, III-61.

369. (a) Password control systems are used to prevent unauthorized access to system program and data files. Choice (b) is incorrect. Physical locks and other such devices are used to prevent unauthorized physical availability of remote terminals. Choice (c) is incorrect. Organizational controls for security and protection are necessary to prevent physical destruction of system program and data files. Choice (d) is incorrect. Organizational controls for security and protection are necessary to prevent physical destruction of remote terminals.

Subject Area: Information technology—systems security. Source: CIA 593, III-56.

370. (c) Data access control software on the network and mainframe will limit access to the data to authorized users only. Choice (a) is incorrect. While validation at sign-on to the system will limit access, it will not effectively prevent data being removed without permission. Choice (b) is incorrect. Data could be taken electronically from the network file server or the mainframe. Choice (d) is incorrect. While key locks will limit access to the PC and thus to the data, it will not effectively prevent data being removed without permission.

Subject Area: Information technology—systems security. Source: CIA 1192, I-32.

371. (d) Automatic log-off of inactive data terminals may prevent the viewing of sensitive data on an unattended data terminal. Choice (a) is incorrect because screen savers do not prevent the viewing of data on an unattended data terminal. Choice (b) is incorrect because scripting is the use of a program to automate a process such as startup. Choice (c) is incorrect because encryption of data files will not prevent the viewing of data on an unattended data terminal.

Subject Area: Information technology—systems security. Source: CIA 597, III-76.

372. (c) Enforcing password control procedures would make it more difficult for an unauthorized person, such as a competitor intending to disrupt the distribution patterns, to gain prolonged entry. Choice (a) is incorrect. Encrypting transmissions from the stores would increase the difficulty of eavesdropping on the transmissions but would not deter someone from entering bogus transactions. Choice (b) is incorrect. Requiring change control for programs ensures that program changes are authorized, tested, and documented. Choice (d) is incorrect. Encouraging store employees to report suspicious activity is a good practice, but such activity might go undetected.

Subject Area: Information technology—systems security. Source: CIA 596, III-48.

373. (c) Change control is the set of procedures that ensure that only authorized, tested programs are run in production. Choice (a) is incorrect. Access control ensures that only authorized persons have access to specific or categories of information resources, but is not enough by itself to ensure integrity of application software. Choice (b) is incorrect. Audit trails permit audits of transaction updates to data files, not programs. Choice (d) is incorrect. Monitoring software is designed to monitor performance (human or machine) for specified functions such as number of tasks performed or capacity utilized.

Subject Area: Information technology—systems security. Source: CIA 596, III-49.

374. (a) Using diskless workstations would increase security by making it impossible to copy software to a floppy disk from a programmer's diskless workstation. Choice (b) is incorrect because using diskless workstations might decrease maintenance expense, but this would not affect security of programs. Choice (c) is incorrect because access control is programmatic and would not be affected, in general, by switching to diskless workstations. Choice (d) is incorrect because switching to diskless workstations might or might not prompt programmers to work more closely together.

Subject Area: Information technology—systems security. Source: CIA 596, III-50.

375. (c) Logical security controls restrict access to specific data and resources. Choice (a) is incorrect because this is the objective of input controls. Choice (b) is incorrect because this is the objective of processing controls. Choice (d) is incorrect because this is an objective of output controls.

Subject Area: Information technology—systems security. Source: CIA 595, III-37.

376. (a) Password masking procedures are directed at user authentication (i.e., guaranteeing that a valid password is known only by the intended person). Choice (b) is incorrect because methods used to establish user privileges within the access control software are concerned with user access to applications. Choice (c) is incorrect because procedures concerning revocation of inactive users are directed at identification. Inactive users should no longer be accepted.

Subject Area: Information technology—systems security. Source: CIA 595, III-38.

377. (a) Automatic dial back requires reconnection of authorized contact before processing. Choice (b) is incorrect because message sequencing detects gaps or duplicate messages. Choice (c) is incorrect because encryption scrambles messages for security transmissions. Choice (d) is incorrect because dedicated lines are impractical for a home banking system because of their cost.

Subject Area: Information technology—systems security. Source: CIA 1194, III-39.

378. (c) The existence of call-forwarding devices makes callback/dial-in lines vulnerable because the devices may transfer access from an authorized telephone number to an unauthorized one. Choice (a) is incorrect because attempted sign-ons can be logged whether a callback feature is present.

Choice (b) is incorrect because the ability to disconnect after invalid access attempts is a function of access control software, not the callback feature. Choice (d) is incorrect because displaying user codes and passwords is not a function of the callback feature.

Subject Area: Information technology—system security. Source: CIA 1190, II-32.

379. (c) Required access code revalidation on a recurring basis would prevent unauthorized persons from being able to continue to enter unauthorized transactions. Choice (a) is incorrect. In callback procedures, the communications system terminates the inbound call and initiates an outbound call to the designated telephone number for that user. Since the salespeople have no fixed telephone number, callback procedures would not control this access. Choice (b) is incorrect. Error correcting codes repair damaged transmissions but cannot detect or prevent unauthorized access. Choice (d) is incorrect. Modem equalization controls for line errors but cannot detect or prevent unauthorized access.

Subject Area: Information technology—systems security. Source: CIA 590, II-21.

380. (d) A person's voice is a personal characteristic. Choice (a) is incorrect because PIN code is personal knowledge. Choice (b) is incorrect because a password is personal knowledge. Choice (c) is incorrect because an employee badge is a possession.

Subject Area: Information technology—systems security. Source: CIA 595, III-39.

381. (a) Assessment of exposures is a senior management responsibility related to the establishment of organizational policy with regard to information systems security. Choice (b) is incorrect because assignment of access privileges is a task of security management. Choice (c) is incorrect because determining ownership of data is a task of security management. Choice (d) is incorrect because training employees in security matters is a task of security management.

Subject Area: Information technology — systems security. Source: CIA 1194, III-28.

382. (a) Authentication and subsequent access to computer resources are the primary functions of security software. Choice (b) is incorrect because activities of the computer are recorded on the operating system log and include when each program is started, the files it accesses, and when the programs terminate execution. Choice (c) is incorrect because hardware monitors display the data typed onto terminal keyboards. Choice (d) is incorrect because monitoring and recording changes to program source and object code are the functions of source code library maintenance software.

Subject Area: Information technology —systems security. Source: CIA 1194, III-31.

383. (a) The objective of security software is to control access to information systems resources such as program libraries, data files, and proprietary software. Choice (b) is incorrect because security software will control the use of utilities, but not the installation. Choice (c) is incorrect because antivirus software detects the presence of viruses. Choice (d) is incorrect because security software may be a tool to establish separation of duties, but does not monitor it.

Subject Area: Information technology—systems security. Source: CIA 1195, III-32.

384. (b) Since storing the log on sequences makes logging on easier, anyone with access to the personal computer could potentially log on to the mainframe. Choice (a) is incorrect because keeping the log-on sequences on the personal computers would not make sensitive data on the personal computers more vulnerable to exposure. Choice (c) is incorrect because keeping the log-on sequences on the personal computers would not affect the effectiveness of backup procedures for data files. Choice (d) is incorrect because keeping the log-on sequences on the personal computers would tend to reduce the number of user mistakes because using automated log-ons would reduce the knowledge required for users to log on to the mainframe.

Subject Area: Information technology—systems security. Source: CIA 1195, III-64.

385. (a) Validating access to data security software with user codes and passwords provides logical security over the systems and the data they can access. Choice (b) is incorrect because sign-on sequences do not provide physical security. Choice (c) is incorrect because context-dependent security refers to access control based on the content of a sequence of database inquiries. Choice (d) is incorrect because write-protection security is provided by the absence of a write-enable ring on tapes and the presence of a write-protect tab on floppy disks.

Subject Area: Information technology—systems security. Source: CIA 1190, I-32.

386. (c) The data security administrator is responsible for determining and monitoring controls over access to data. Choice (a) is incorrect because the database administrator is responsible for planning and managing overall needs for data resources. Choice (b) is incorrect because the database administrator is responsible for ensuring the integrity of data in a shared data environment. Choice (d) is incorrect because making data available to users when and where it is needed is a responsibility of the database administrator.

Subject Area: Information technology—systems security. Source: CIA 1190, II-30.

387. (a) The callback technique would prevent unauthorized access to the computer when using a dial-up facility. The callback technique is a two-step control. First the connection is broken after the caller has identified himself and given the call number allowing reconnection. The system checks for authorization by the caller; if the authorization is verified the computer is reconnected. If there is no authorization the computer is not reconnected. Choice (b) is incorrect. The modem (modulator/demodulator) is a device that allows a connection between a computer and a terminal to be made from a remote location through the use of telephone lines. Choice (c) is incorrect. The echo check is a control used to verify that information sent by a sender is identical to the information received by the recipient. The information sent is echoed back by the recipient to the sender; if the message received by the sender is not identical to what was sent the transmission is tried again. Choice (d) is incorrect. The console log has nothing to do with controlling access to the computer. The log lists all operating system activity, maintains an equipment utilization record, and identifies operator-initiated actions.

Subject Area: Information technology—systems security. Source: CIA 1190, III-33.

388. (b) Passwords would restrict access to the files, thereby preventing authorized users from being able to gain access to the sensitive programs. Choice (a) is incorrect. Backup copies would allow the firm to rebuild its data files using the transaction files that were made since the most recent backup. This would not prevent the unauthorized person from gaining access to the sensitive program. Choice (c) is incorrect. Echo check is commonly associated with transmission of information between computers over telephone lines. An echo check would not prevent unauthorized access to the sensitive programs. It merely checks to verify the correctness of the transmitted information. Choice (d) is incorrect. Record counts verify the number of transactions being submitted in the batch that is being processed. They do not prevent unauthorized access to sensitive programs.

Subject Area: Information technology—systems security. Source: CIA 590, II-25.

389. (c) Editing is limited to assigned records. Choices (a) and (b) are incorrect because all employees could edit every record, which is not good. Choice (d) is incorrect because system access is too general to be of any use.

Subject Area: Information technology—systems security. Source: CIA 590, III-41.

390. (d) Required entry of passwords for access to individual documents is the best single control over unauthorized access to sensitive documents in the system. This question pertains to output controls. Choice (a) is incorrect. Password security for access to the system permits all departmental employees access to all documents in the system. Choice (b) is incorrect. There are no floppy disks in this system. Choice (c) is incorrect. Periodic server backup and storage in a secure area is a good security/backup procedure, but it would not prevent access to sensitive documents online.

Subject Area: Information technology—systems security. Source: CIA 1190, I-34.

391. (a) Client/server implementation does not necessarily use relational databases. Choices (b), (c), and (d) are incorrect because these are factors that make security a complex matter in client/server environments.

Subject Area: Information technology—systems security. Source: CIA Model Exam 1998, III-77.

392. (d) Users can gain access to databases from terminals only through established recognition and authorization procedures; thus, unauthorized access is prevented. Choice (a) is incorrect because key verification ensures the accuracy of selected fields by requiring a different individual to rekey them. Choice (b) is incorrect because sequence checks are used to ensure the completeness of input or update data by checking the use of preassigned document serial numbers. Choice (c) is incorrect because computer matching entails checking selected fields of input data with information held in a suspense or master file.

Subject Area: Information technology—systems security. Source: CIA Model Exam 1998, III-73.

393. (d) Passwords are a form of access controls since they limit access to computer systems and the information stored in them. Choice (a) is incorrect because physical controls limit access to an area and do not include passwords. Choice (b) is incorrect because edit controls test the validity of data. Choice (c) is incorrect because digital controls are examples of physical controls.

Subject Area: Information technology—systems security. Source: CIA Model Exam 1998, III-66.

394. (c) Restricting physical and logical access secures program libraries from unauthorized use, in person and remotely via terminals. Choice (a) is incorrect because installing a logging system for program access would permit detection of unauthorized access but would not prevent it. Choice (b) is incorrect because monitoring physical access to program library media would control only unauthorized physical access. Choice (d) is incorrect because denying all remote access via terminals would likely be inefficient and would not secure program libraries against physical access.

Subject Area: Information technology—systems security. Source: CIA Model Exam 1998, III-70.

395. (a) Restrict users to functions and data compatible with organizational structure. Choice (b) is incorrect because it provides controls over software changes for application development functions. Choice (c) is incorrect because it provides controls over form and type of data entered by users. Choice (d) is incorrect because it provides controls over continued availability of data resources to users.

Subject Area: Information technology—systems security. Source: CIA 1193, II-35.

396. (d) Restricting access on the basis of data values within a record (e.g., bid identity) would enable the selective access the company wants. Choice (a) is incorrect because restricting access on the basis of the type of resource would not permit selective access based on values in a record. Choice (b) is incorrect because restricting access on the basis of statistical summaries would not be helpful in preparing bids. Choice (c) is incorrect because restricting access on the basis of the age of the stored records would not enable the selective access the company wants because some needed data would be new and some would be old.

Subject Area: Information technology—systems security. Source: CIA 1193, III-30.

397. (a) Restricting updating to one position would protect the libraries from unauthorized updating, and permitting all IS employees read access to source code would let them continue to obtain the efficiencies of being able to read others' code. Choice (b) is incorrect because permitting updating for everyone is the current situation, which is risky; restricting read access to source code to one position creates more inefficiency than existed before. Choice (c) is incorrect because restricting updating and read access to one position protects the libraries but creates the inefficiency of no others being able to read the source code. Choice (d) is incorrect because permitting updating and read access for everyone in the information systems department is the current situation, which created the risk.

Subject Area: Information technology—systems security. Source: CIA 1193, III-55.

398. (b) Restricting access to authorized individuals would prevent the use of unauthorized user numbers for unauthorized access. Choice (a) is incorrect. Ensuring that the database design is relational facilitates the use of views, but would not by itself prevent clerks from having read access to confidential information. Choice (c) is incorrect. Requiring before and after images of transactions are a good backup/recovery practice but would not prevent unauthorized read access. Choice (d) is incorrect. Reconciling monetary totals for input sessions helps maintain data integrity but would not prevent unauthorized read access.

Subject Area: Information technology—system security. Source: CIA 593, I-25.

399. (b) Utility programs are one of the more serious "holes" in data access security since some of them can actually bypass normal access controls. Choice (a) is incorrect. Although there is a migration of control of this type away from applications to other software, the large bulk of these controls still reside in application software. Choice (c) is incorrect. Access control software has as one of its primary objectives improving data access security for all data on the system. Choice (d) is incorrect. Most database management systems provide for improved data access security while they are running.

Subject Area: Information technology —systems security. Source: CIA 593, II-23.

400. (d) Individuals should have only the access privileges required for their job functions. Production employees typically do not need access to pricing information. Choice (a) is incorrect. Program change procedures should be established and enforced to ensure the validity of processing, but lack of enforcement of program change procedures was not the reason the supervisor was able to access the pricing information. Choice (b) is incorrect. Requiring users to have and use passwords to validate their identification numbers is essential to good control, but the lack of a password was not the reason the supervisor was able to access the pricing information. Choice (c) is incorrect. Data ownership should reside with the most appropriate users, but the lack of appropriate ownership was not the reason the supervisor was able to access the pricing information.

Subject Area: Information technology—systems security. Source: CIA 593, II-28.

401. (c) Greater online access to information systems creates the risk of increased unauthorized access to systems, which can be mitigated by authenticating transactions for authorized users. Choice (a) is incorrect. Management oversight controls are needed for the growth in end-user development. Choice (b) is incorrect. Integration of all phases of system development controls is needed for competitive pressures for enhanced functions in systems. Choice (d) is incorrect. Increased attention should be given to validating development phase controls for growing organizational reliance on information systems.

Subject Area: Information technology—systems security. Source: CIA 593, III-40.

402. (d) Proper security would prevent changes by an accounts receivable clerk. Choice (a) is incorrect because it is too vague a response in this case. Choice (b) is incorrect because training cannot cover all contingencies. Choice (c) is incorrect because the customer did not wish to effect a change.

Subject Area: Information technology—systems security. Source: CIA 593, III-58.

403. (d) Passwords are a form of access controls since they limit access to computer systems and the information stored in them. Choice (a) is incorrect because physical controls limit access to an area and do not include passwords. Choice (b) is incorrect because edit controls test the validity of data. Choice (c) is incorrect because digital controls are examples of physical controls. They focus primarily on switches, gears, and instrumentation.

Subject Area: Information technology—systems security. Source: CIA 592, II-31.

404. (b) Proofing of input data by the individual responsible for data entry is generally not recommended. Choice (a) is incorrect because assigning a unique number to the signed agreement will provide adequate identification control for the master agreement. Choice (c) is incorrect because ensuring that ownership percentages total to exactly 100% is a reasonable edit control. Choice (d) is incorrect because ensuring that only owners who exist in the customer/vendor file may receive payments makes unauthorized payments to fictitious owners more difficult.

Subject Area: Information technology—systems security. Source: CIA 592, II-33.

405. (c) Making passwords permanent negates the controlling power of passwords. Choice (a) is incorrect because this represents no particular risk to the revenue distribution system. Choice (b) is incorrect because reporting all updates to affected owners should help identify any improper changes. Choice (d) is incorrect because having all income checks produced by the system is a control, not a weakness.

Subject Area: Information technology—systems security. Source: CIA 592, II-34.

406. (d) The system should monitor unsuccessful attempts to use the order entry system since repeated attempts could suggest someone is trying random or patterned character sequences in order to identify a password. Choice (a) is incorrect. Integrated test facility (ITF) is a technique by which an auditor selects transactions and processing functions and applies the transactions to a fictitious entity during a normal processing cycle, along with regular transactions. ITF has no ability to determine whether the data themselves are legitimate. Choice (b) is incorrect. Tracing follows the path of a transaction during processing but is inadequate to determine whether a transaction is legitimate. Choice (c) is incorrect. Transaction selection uses an independent computer program to monitor and select transactions for internal audit review. Like tracing, it fails to determine whether a transaction is legitimate. It would be an appropriate technique to apply to transactions suspected to be illegitimate.

Subject Area: Information technology—systems security. Source: CIA 592, III-27.

407. (b) Detecting the fraudulent cards allowed the bank to monitor ATM use and catch the individual. Choice (a) is incorrect because the former employee obtained account codes or PINs by observing customers at the ATMs. The bank should encourage its customers to keep their account information secret but must take independent steps to detect and prevent use of fraudulent cards. Choice (c) is incorrect because this individual has, at one time, been authorized to know about ATM operation. Choice (d) is incorrect. The bank should restrict access to machines capable of writing magnetic stripes on cards to only those employees who need them for their job. Individuals skilled in electronics can, however, obtain parts they assemble themselves so banks are unable to restrict access to stripe-writing machines.

Subject Area: Information technology—systems security. Source: CIA 591, III-26.

408. (c) Using passwords would permit supervisors to authenticate themselves to the system as supervisors. Tellers, not knowing the supervisors' passwords, could not invoke supervisor-only functions. Choice (a) is incorrect because tagging is the practice of marking specific transactions for subsequent investigation. Choice (b) is incorrect because call-back is a procedure in which the system disconnects the caller and calls the external entity's telephone number of record before letting the terminal session proceed. Choice (d) is incorrect because logs of access and attempted functions by employee would detect teller use of unauthorized functions but would not prevent tellers from using them.

Subject Area: Information technology—systems security. Source: CIA 591, III-42.

409. (d) The system should employ automatic dial-back to prevent intrusion by unauthorized parties. Such a system accepts an incoming modem call, disconnects, and automatically dials back a prearranged number to establish a permanent connection for data transfer or inquiry. Choice (a) is incorrect. The procedure described is considered acceptable. Encrypted passwords further decrease the likelihood of unauthorized access. Choice (b) is incorrect. Message sequencing detects unauthorized access by numbering each message and incrementing each message by one more than the last one sent. Such a system detects when a gap or duplicate has occurred. Choice (c) is incorrect. Allowing certain types of transactions (such as payroll transactions) to be made only at specific terminals minimizes the likelihood of unauthorized access.

Subject Area: Information technology—systems security. Source: CIA 591, III-50.

410. (c) This effective administration of user IDs and authentication procedures is the key to enforcing personal accountability, the basis for the user-to-data authorization technique. Choice (a) is incorrect because this is a job-to-data authorization technique. Choice (b) is incorrect because this is a terminal-to-data authorization technique. Choice (d) is incorrect because the use of access software alone does not address all access security risks.

Subject Area: Information technology—systems security. Source: CIA 597, I-51.

411. (a) Access security features restrict users to functions and data compatible with organizational structure. Choice (b) is incorrect because software change control procedures provide controls over software changes for application development functions. Choice (c) is incorrect because dependency checks provide controls over form and type of data entered by users. Choice (d) is incorrect because backup and recovery procedures provide controls over continued availability of data resources to users.

Subject Area: Information technology—systems security. Source: CIA 597, I-56.

412. (a) Access on a need-to-know basis means that access is authorized only as is required for employees to perform authorized job functions. Choice (b) is incorrect because individual accountability means that individuals with access to data are responsible for the use and security of data obtained via their access privileges. Choice (c) is incorrect because just-in-time means arranging delivery of inventory or materials as close to the time they would be incorporated into products as is possible rather than maintaining large quantities of inventory or materials. Choice (d) is incorrect because management-by-exception means spending managerial time on exceptional conditions on the grounds that attending to exceptions is a better approach to management than spending time on the transactions or processes that are operating in their normal ranges.

Subject Area: Information technology—systems security. Source: CIA 1196, III-46.

413. (c) The security administrator should report access to data or resources by privileged users so that the access can be monitored for appropriate and authorized usage. Choice (a) is incorrect. Multiple access to data by data owners, the individuals responsible for creating and maintaining specific data, is a normal occurrence. Choice (b) is incorrect. Management authorization of modified access is expected as needs or conditions change. These events are not typically reported. Choice (d) is incorrect. Data owner specification of access privileges is normal and is typically maintained by the system and need not be reported by the security administrator.

Subject Area: Information technology—systems security. Source: CIA 1196, III-54.

Databases

414. (c) Hierarchical databases use tree structures to organize data; relational databases use tables. Choices (a), (b), and (d) are incorrect because these are true statements about relational databases.

Subject Area: Information technology—databases. Source: CIA 594, III-25.

415. (a) Access must be controlled to ensure integrity of documentation although "read" access should be provided to other parties, as it is important for applications development and maintenance. Database administrators (DBAs) are responsible for adding and updating data elements into the data dictionary. Choices (b), (c), and (d) are incorrect because each choice is an improper function. Each of these parties has no need to add or update documentation items into data dictionaries.

Subject Area: Information technology—databases. Source: CIA 594, III-27.

416. (c) A relational database is a structure where data records are maintained as tables. Choice (a) is incorrect because network structures are where data records are arranged in parent-child or owner-member configurations. Choice (b) is incorrect because it is a special form of network structure where data records are arranged in hierarchical segments of ordered sets of related records. Choice (d) is incorrect because it is a method that stores records sequentially but allows them to be located directly through indexes.

Subject Area: Information technology—databases. Source: CIA 1193, III-25.

417. (c) One of the functions of the database management system (DBMS) is to enable users to have different views of the same data. Choice (a) is incorrect because the operating system regulates the use of the components of the computer system. Choice (b) is incorrect because a program library management system controls the movement of programs and job control statements into and out of the production program libraries. Choice (d) is incorrect because utility programs have special purpose functions (e.g., sorting, printing, or copying).

Subject Area: Information technology—databases. Source: CIA 1193, III-32.

418. (b) The function of a data dictionary is to organize and share information about objects and resources. Choice (a) is incorrect because the database management system (DBMS) log contains checkpoint records that mark the boundary between two consecutive transactions. Choice (c) is incorrect because the data dictionary is software that specifies data elements, not system users. Choice (d) is incorrect because the data control language specifies privileges and security rules for objects and resources.

Subject Area: Information technology—databases. Source: CIA 1193, III-33.

419. (b) Data administration is planning for and controlling the data used throughout the enterprise and throughout the data resource life cycle. Choice (a) is incorrect because enterprise modeling is creating an organization-wide model of activities for supporting overall goals. Choice (c) is incorrect because conceptual modeling is depicting in broad terms the perceived needs of system owners/users. Choice (d) is incorrect because database administration is the management of physical design, database design implementation, database-monitoring specifications, database availability, and database security.

Subject Area: Information technology—databases. Source: CIA 1193, III-34.

420. (b) Failure to completely define the program specification blocks (PSB) prevents the application program from accessing or changing data, resulting in incomplete processing. Choice (a) is incorrect because data element definition allows application programs to access or change data; therefore, if they are not defined, no access takes place. Choice (c) is incorrect. Without the program specification blocks, the application program cannot access data and cannot execute. Choice (d) is incorrect. The desired manipulation of the database contents by an application program cannot take place if program specification blocks are not defined.

Subject Area: Information technology—databases. Source: CIA 593, I-27.

421. (b) Passwords should be specified before the user may access a file or data element. Choice (a) is incorrect because sign-on verification identifies a particular user as being present at the physical terminal, but does not prevent access. Choice (c) is incorrect because test databases, not production databases, should be used to test the system. Choice (d) is incorrect. If no passwords are required, then control is nonexistent.

Subject Area: Information technology—databases. Source: CIA 593, I-28.

422. (c) A logical data model shows relationships among entities. Choice (a) is incorrect because a decision model shows what data are needed to make particular decisions. No decision is implied in this example. Choice (b) is incorrect because database model does not necessarily describe a data model. Choice (d) is incorrect because a physical data model shows actual storage conventions on the storage media.

Subject Area: Information technology—databases. Source: CIA 593, III-50.

423. (c) The reading of the entire RDBMS would place serious I/O demands on the system; exactly the thing that would cause serious degradation of response time. The response time is defined as the elapsed time between the start of an inquiry and the beginning of the response. Choice (a) is incorrect. For the most part, excess table space improves response time for an RDBMS. A tablespace is a page set used to store the records of one or more tables in the RDBMS program. Choice (b) is incorrect. Large-size buffers would increase the storage space for system files thus improving the system response time. Choice (d) is incorrect. The number of interactive users affects the system response time—the greater the number of users, the slower the response time would be. Here, a large decrease in the number of interactive users would improve the system response time.

Subject Area: Information technology—databases. Source: CIA 593, III-44.

424. (d) In a database, referential integrity means that an entity such as a sales order can only reference an entity such as a customer that exists. Choice (a) is incorrect because normalization is the practice of decomposing database relations to remove data field redundancies and thus reduce the likelihood of update anomalies. Choice (b) is incorrect because in a database, entity integrity means that each thing or relationship in the database is uniquely identified by a single key value. Choice (c) is incorrect because in a database, internal schema means the ways the data are physically organized on the disk.

Subject Area: Information technology—databases. Source: CIA 1192, III-35.

425. (c) This database has a relational structure since there are no links, which are not contained in the data records themselves. Choice (a) is incorrect because each record type corresponds to a flat file, but there are multiple structures rather than a single flat file structure. Choice (b) is incorrect because a hierarchical structure would have a tree structure with embedded links instead of explicit data values. Choice (d) is incorrect because a network structure would have bidirectional pointers instead of explicit data values.

Subject Area: Information technology—databases. Source: CIA 1192, III-36.

426. (c) Restructuring and redefining the database is the function associated with a database administrator. Choice (a) is incorrect because reviewing output is a control group and user function. Choice (b) is incorrect because scheduling daily operations is not a database administrator function. Choice (d) is incorrect because evaluating hardware is not a function associated with a database administrator.

Subject Area: Information technology—databases. Source: CIA 592, I-30.

427. (a) The database contains all related files thus eliminating the duplication of data in several independent files. Choice (b) is incorrect because conversion to a database is often costly and time consuming. Choice (c) is incorrect because a flat file system, not a database, has multiple occurrences of data items. Choice (d) is incorrect because using a database does not reduce the need for appropriate backup and recovery procedures. Due to the absence of data redundancy and to quick propagation of data errors through applications, backup and recovery procedures are just as critical in a database as they are in a flat file system.

Subject Area: Information technology—databases. Source: CIA 592, III-28.

428. (c) The internal schema describes the way data is physically stored in the database. Choice (a) is incorrect because the external schema describes the user's view of a part of the database. Choice (b) is incorrect. Neither of the three schemas does this; the external schema is a formalized and probably simplified view of the user's mental view of data. Choice (d) is incorrect because the conceptual schema describes the overall logical view of the database.

Subject Area: Information technology—databases. Source: CIA 592, III-35.

429. (d) A database management system can be viewed as the only "door" to the physical storage of data in a database. Choice (a) is incorrect because management information systems (MIS) seldom contain data. Choice (b) is incorrect because a decision support system (DSS) would also contain models. Choice (c) is incorrect because an artificial intelligence system (AIS) would have an inference engine.

Subject Area: Information technology—databases. Source: CIA 1191, III-19.

430. (d) Logical models of data are user-oriented ways of describing data. Choice (a) is incorrect because physical models of data are concerned with the physical storage of data. Choice (b) is incorrect because both physical and logical models of data are concerned with the entities for which data is collected. Choice (c) is incorrect because logical models of data are conceptual in nature.

Subject Area: Information technology—databases. Source: CIA 1191, III-21.

431. (d) Error recovery procedures allow the user to reconstruct the prior state of the database by logging the before and after images of the record therefore "undoing" the error. Choice (a) is incorrect because error prevention involves providing the user with specific instructions so that the user knows what to do and avoids making errors. Choice (b) is incorrect because error detection involves providing immediate notification that an error has been detected by way of an error message. Choice (c) is incorrect because error correction techniques usually are in the form of a question and ask the user to respond and verify the request before the transaction is processed.

Subject Area: Information technology—databases. Source: CIA 1191, III-27.

432. (a) Using a data dictionary ensures complete identification of instances of use of data items. Choice (b) is incorrect because using a data dictionary does not ensure that descriptive names and meanings are consistent because development personnel must decide the correspondence between descriptions and meanings. Choice (c) is incorrect because using a data dictionary is independent of selecting the appropriate level of normalization of data models. Choice (d) is incorrect because using a data dictionary does not eliminate the need for conceptual modeling in database design.

Subject Area: Information technology—databases. Source: CIA 1191, III-28.

433. (c) A schema is a logical view of an entire database. Choice (a) is incorrect because a hierarchy is a way of organizing a database. Choice (b) is incorrect because a network is a way of organizing a database. Choice (d) is incorrect because a subschema is a logical view of a portion of a database.

Subject Area: Information technology—databases. Source: CIA 591, III-23.

434. (c) Logical data models allow users to describe, think about, and use data without worrying about its physical storage. Choice (a) is incorrect because a physical data model is concerned with how the data is physically stored in the various storage media and devices. Choice (b) is incorrect because this answer is a distracter because the logical models attempt to describe reality. This answer may sound reasonable to some candidates. Choice (d) is incorrect because a sequential data model is not a recognized model type.

Subject Area: Information technology—databases. Source: CIA 591, III-33.

435. (d) A deadly embrace occurs when two transactions each have a lock on a data resource that the other transaction needs to run to completion. When deadly embraces occur, the database system must have an algorithm for undoing the effects of one of the transactions and releasing the data resources it controls so that the other transaction can run to completion. Then, the other transaction is restarted and permitted to run to completion. If deadly embraces are not resolved, response time worsens or the system eventually fails. Choice (a) is incorrect because inconsistent processing is the phenomenon of a database transaction having different effects depending on when it is processed. Data locking ensures consistent processing. Choice (b) is incorrect because a rollback failure is the inability of the database software to undo the effects of a transaction that could not be run to completion. Data locking does not cause rollback failures although data locking may lead to situations in which rollback is required. Choice (c) is incorrect because transactions are said to be unrecoverable when the database software cannot reconstruct in sufficient detail a transaction so that it can be run to completion.

Subject Area: Information technology—databases. Source: CIA 1196, III-75.

436. (c) It deals with the process of database design, not distribution. Choice (a) is incorrect because it involves making a copy of the database for distribution. Choice (b) is incorrect because it involves creating and maintaining replica copies at multiple locations. Choice (d) is incorrect because it deals with separating the database into parts and distributing where they are needed.

Subject Area: Information technology—databases. Source: CIA 596, III-65.

437. (c) One security feature in database systems is their ability to let the database administrator (DBA) restrict access on a logical view basis for each user. Choice (a) is incorrect because if the only access permitted is read-only, then there could be no updating of database files. Choice (b) is incorrect because permitting catalog updating from privileged software would be a breach of security, which might permit unauthorized access. Choice (d) is incorrect because updating of users' access profiles should be a function of a security officer, not the user's supervisor.

Subject Area: Information technology—databases. Source: CIA 596, III-51.

438. (b) Joining is the combining of one or more tables based on matching criteria. For example, if a supplier table contains information about suppliers and a parts table contains information about parts, the two tables could be joined on supplier number (assuming both tables contained this attribute) to give information about the supplier of particular parts. Choice (a) is incorrect because mail-merge feature combines letter writing and label printing functions. Choice (c) is incorrect because projecting involves estimating future values based on past values. Choice (d) is incorrect because pointing refers to showing the desired function.

Subject Area: Information technology—databases. Source: CIA 595, III-75.

439. (d) Increased data accessibility is a benefit of a single integrated information system. Choice (a) is incorrect because closer program data linkage or independence is not a benefit. Choice (b) is incorrect because redundancy is reduced which is a benefit. Choice (c) is incorrect because the need for security measures is not reduced.

Subject Area: Information technology—databases. Source: CIA 1194, III-36.

440. (a) A data dictionary is a repository of definitions of data contained in a database. Choice (b) is incorrect because a source code application file definition describes the record layouts used by an application program. Choice (c) is incorrect because the data control language describes the privileges and security rules governing database users. Choice (d) is incorrect because a database recovery log file records the before and after images of updated records in a database.

Subject Area: Information technology—databases. Source: CIA 1194, III-37.

441. (a) The data definition language (DDL) defines the database structure and content, especially the schema and subschema descriptions, including the names of the data elements contained in the database and their relationship to each other. DDL is used to define (that is, determine) the database. Choice (b) is incorrect because the data control language (DCL) is a type of database language used to specify the privileges and security rules governing database users. DCL is used to specify privileges and security rules. Choice (c) is incorrect because data manipulation language (DML) provides application programs with a facility to interact with the database to facilitate adding, changing and deleting either data or data relationships. DML provides programmers with a facility to update the database. Choice (d) is incorrect because data command interpreter languages are symbolic character strings used to control the current state of database management system operations. Also, database query language (DQL) is used for ad hoc queries.

Subject Area: Information technology—databases. Source: CIA 1194, III-38, 1196, III-57, and 597, III-42.

442. (c) The data security administrator is responsible for determining and monitoring controls over access to data. Choice (a) is incorrect because the database administrator is responsible for planning and managing overall needs for data resources. Choice (b) is incorrect because the database administrator is responsible for ensuring the integrity of data in a shared data environment. Choice (d) is incorrect because making data available to users when and where it is needed is a responsibility of the database administrator.

Subject Area: Information technology—databases. Source: CIA 1190, II-30.

443. (b) Programming queries for a hierarchical database are costly and time consuming, and even if the programs could be written, there likely would be inadequate machine resources to execute them in a production environment. Choice (a) is incorrect because hierarchical database systems do not have commands for joins, which are standard features in relational systems. Choice (c) is incorrect because the point-of-sale data are clearly proprietary, but the reason for having the data is that brand managers can use it to manage the business. Choice (d) is incorrect because point-of-sale (POS) data contain precisely the information that, if summarized appropriately, would answer questions about product sales and coupon use.

Subject Area: Information technology—databases. Source: CIA 1195, III-44.

444. (b) The limiting factor in the brand managers' use of a relational database system for ad hoc queries would be obtaining computer resources for complicated queries for the large volume (50 gigabytes) of data. Choice (a) is incorrect because the brand managers already know what the data represent because they understand the data that point-of-sale terminals capture in grocery stores. Choice (c) is incorrect because distinguishing primary and foreign keys in the data will be relatively straightforward since the brand managers are already familiar with the data. Choice (d) is incorrect because management would be highly interested in the results of performing queries to answer the ad hoc questions.

Subject Area: Information technology—databases. Source: CIA 1195, III-45.

445. (a) Their efforts were unsuccessful because of the high complexity of the mainframe data structure and the large volume of data. Since spreadsheets lack Structured Query Language (SQL) query capabilities, there is no way to manipulate the huge volume of data into two-dimensional views that can be readily imported into spreadsheets. Choice (b) is incorrect because access privileges for the point-of-sale (POS) data would have to be established, but this is a routine operation. Choice (c) is incorrect because inconsistencies in the mainframe data due to lack of integrity constraints on the data files might make spreadsheet analysis not as correct as desirable, but they would not make the downloading and subsequent analysis unsuccessful. Choice (d) is incorrect because transmission links for downloading the data from the mainframe data files can be made sufficiently error free to accomplish the downloading.

Subject Area: Information technology—databases. Source: CIA 1195, III-46.

446. (a) A source code review of the brand managers' queries would detect erroneous queries, which would be corrected. Choice (b) is incorrect because a code comparison audit is used to compare two versions of the same program to verify that only authorized code is executed. Choice (c) is incorrect because a transaction retrieval and analysis is a sampling approach to collecting data about transactions to verify correct processing. Choice (d) is incorrect because an input/output analysis traces transactions from input to output.

Subject Area: Information technology—databases. Source: CIA 1195, III-47.

447. (c) Joining the two tables on product and store identification codes matches up the two files on product and store identification codes, which enables comparisons of actual and projected sales by product by store. Choice (a) is incorrect because projecting is the relational operator that creates column subsets from a file. Projecting would still leave actual and projected sales in different files. Choice (b) is incorrect because projecting is the relational operator that creates column subsets from a file. Projecting would still leave actual and projected sales in different files. Choice (d) is incorrect because joining the two tables on product identification codes matches up the two files on product identification code but not on store identification code.

Subject Area: Information technology—databases. Source: CIA 1195, III-48.

448. (d) In the mainframe database, the data exist in files or tables, not in the formats interesting to brand managers. Therefore, before users can see views of the data, the data must be retrieved and represented as views. Choice (a) is incorrect because protocols for data transmission will be determined by IT telecommunications personnel, not by users. Choice (b) is incorrect because there may be different access privileges for different users, but specifying access privileges by user number does not cause data to be retrieved in any format. Choice (c) is incorrect because there will be integrity constraints for data entering the original database on the mainframe, but they are independent of specifying how data views will be presented to users.

Subject Area: Information technology—databases. Source: CIA 1195, III-49.

449. (b) Actual sales cannot be greater than the quantities available for sale so a comparison would reveal whether actual sales are inaccurate to the point of exceeding quantities available for sale. Choice (a) is incorrect because actual sales may vary across stores so the comparison would not isolate data inaccuracies. Choice (c) is incorrect. Since actual sales may fluctuate across years, comparing sales across years may not isolate data inaccuracies. Choice (d) is incorrect. Since actual sales for similar products may vary significantly, comparing sales for similar products in the same period may not isolate data inaccuracies.

Subject Area: Information technology—databases. Source: CIA 1195, III-50.

450. (d) Comparing product identification codes by store for consecutive periods would detect instances where, in consecutive periods, specific products had no sales, which might indicate missing data. Choice (a) is incorrect because product identification codes are unlikely to be consecutive, which means that many of the apparently missing numbers would not correspond to products. Choice (b) is incorrect because sorting on store identification code will likely give a sequence that includes all the product identification codes. Choice (c) is incorrect because comparing product identification codes for consecutive periods would not detect missing rows in the data because each product appears in the sales for some store.

Subject Area: Information technology—databases. Source: CIA 1195, III-51.

451. (c) Maintaining data integrity is a function of a data dictionary. Choice (a) is incorrect because documenting processing steps is a function of programs and their documentation. Choice (b) is incorrect because ensuring design consistency is a function of design review. Choice (d) is incorrect because coordinating program interfaces is a function of "requirements definition and design" phases.

Subject Area: Information technology—databases. Source: CIA 1190, III-31.

452. (b) The main components of the database system are the database, the database administrator, and the database management system. Choice (a) is incorrect because the operating system consists of a series of programs whose main purpose is to control and coordinate the running of the computer and its many functions. Choice (c) is incorrect because the database management system is an integral component of the database system. It consists of two software programs, one for data manipulation and one for data definition. It is the coordinator between the database and the application programs. Choice (d) is incorrect because the system management facility (SMF) collects and stores data that reflects the activity that takes place within the computer.

Subject Area: Information technology—databases. Source: CIA 1190, III-32.

453. (d) Since data is organized in two-dimensional tables, developers find the relational database models easier to construct than the complex cobwebs that result when using the hierarchical and network models. Choice (a) is incorrect because the hierarchical model organizes data through the development of relationships that are strictly one-to-many. The construction is difficult for when adding data elements to the database since the data is hard-coded the index must be completely redefined. Choice (b) is incorrect because the hierarchical model is another name for the tree model. For the above reasons this response is incorrect. Choice (c) is incorrect because the network model organizes data through the development of relationships that are many-to-many. The construction is difficult for when adding data elements to the database since the data is hard-coded the index must be completely redefined.

Subject Area: Information technology—databases. Source: CIA 1190, III-34.

454. (d) The purpose is to eliminate redundant data storage. Choice (a) is incorrect because databases are not organized by file. Choice (b) is incorrect because records do not organize databases. Choice (c) is incorrect because databases are an end result but not the purpose.

Subject Area: Information technology—databases. Source: CIA 590, III-36.

455. (c) This is a function of the data dictionary. Choice (a) is incorrect because database management system (DBMS) is too general. Choice (b) is incorrect because data administrator is too general. Choice (d) is incorrect because schema relates, not describes, data.

Subject Area: Information technology—databases. Source: CIA 590, III-38.

Software Licensing

456. (b) A backup copy is legal under the copyright law. Choice (a) is incorrect because only copy number 1 is legal. Choice (c) is incorrect because any copy other than a backup copy is illegal and is a license violation. Choice (d) is incorrect because only copy number 1 is legal.

Subject Area: Information technology—software licensing. Source: CIA 597, III-40.

457. (b) These steps will discourage illegal software usage. Choices (a) and (c) are incorrect because allowing users to keep original diskettes increases both the likelihood of illegal copies being made and the loss of diskettes. Choice (d) is incorrect because maintaining a log also protects an organization since a log documents software purchases.

Subject Area: Information technology—software licensing. Source: CIA 1196, III-64.

458. (a) Unlicensed software is more likely to have a virus. Choice (b) is incorrect because option II is not true: the cost of the software is not a consideration. Choice (c) is incorrect because software checking routines are detective/

corrective and not preventative. Choice (d) is incorrect because option I is correct.

Subject Area: Information technology—software licensing. Source: CIA 596, III-73.

459. (c) This is the most effective approach to detect an illegal copy of application software. The serial number usually appears on the screen immediately after the loading of the software. Choice (a) is incorrect because this is an approach, but not the most effective one. Choice (b) is incorrect because this approach is related to access control. Choice (d) is incorrect because this is an approach, but not the most effective one.

Subject Area: Information technology—software licensing. Source: CIA 1194, III-34.

Web Infrastructure

460. (a) Companies who wish to maintain adequate security must use firewalls to protect data from being accessed by unauthorized users. Choice (b) is incorrect because anyone can establish a home page on the Internet. Choice (c) is incorrect because there are no security standards for connecting to the Internet, nor is there a coalition of Internet providers, which dictate such standards. The lack of such standards is a major problem with the Internet.

Subject Area: Information technology—Web infrastructure. Source: CIA Model Exam 1998, III-43.

461. (b) The most difficult aspect of using Internet resources is locating the best information given the large number of information sources. Choice (a) is incorrect because there is no limitation on the number of access ports. Choice (c) is incorrect because the only equipment required for accessing Internet resources is a computer, a modem, a telephone line, and basic communication software. Choice (d) is incorrect because organizations routinely provide Internet access to their employees, and individuals can obtain access through individual subscriptions to commercial information service providers.

Subject Area: Information technology—Web infrastructure. Source: CIA Model Exam 1998, III-69.

462. (c) Usenet groups on the Internet were established so those users could post questions to which other users could reply. Choice (a) is incorrect because Archie is a directory of files available on the Internet. Choice (b) is incorrect because wide area information servers (WAIS) help users find specific files on the Internet. Choice (d) is incorrect. OSI is open systems interconnection, a protocol suite for multivendor networking.

Subject Area: Information technology—Web infrastructure. Source: CIA 597, III-78.

463. (a) Gateways connect Internet computers of dissimilar networks. Choice (b) is incorrect because bridges connect physically separate LAN's. Choice (c) is incorrect because repeaters strengthen signal strength. Choice (d) is incorrect because routers determine the best path for data.

Subject Area: Information technology—Web infrastructure. Source: CIA 1196, III-56.

464. (b) Spamming is the practice of sending unsolicited electronic-mail messages in a marketing campaign.

Subject Area: Information technology—Web infrastructure. Source: CBM, Volume 4.

465. (b) An intranet is a computer network within an organization that uses Internet technologies such as hypertext markup language (HTML) and extensible markup language (XML) to communicate. Thinnet is related to transmission media.

Subject Area: Information technology—Web infrastructure. Source: CBM, Volume 4.

466. (c) An extranet is similar to an intranet, but its purpose is to facilitate communications and trade between an organization and its business partners, such as suppliers. It is not meant to serve customers. Unlike an intranet, an extranet is not limited to employee use. It may be thought of as the part of an intranet that is extended to business partners. Thinnet is related to transmission media.

Subject Area: Information technology—Web infrastructure. Source: CBM, Volume 4.

467. (d) Internet protocols are the standard for the entire Internet regardless of geographical location of computers. The other three choices are true impediments to global information systems.

Subject Area: Information technology—Web infrastructure. Source: CBM, Volume 4.

468. (c) Organizations must plan and design their global Web sites so that they also cater to local needs and preferences.

Subject Area: Information technology—Web infrastructure. Source: CBM, Volume 4.

469. (b) The definition of bulletin boards includes, "A computer system that functions as a centralized information source and message switching system for a particular interest group. Users dial up the bulletin board, review and leave messages for other users, as well as communicate to other users on the system at the same time." Choice (a) is incorrect. EDI is for the electronic transmission of business information (purchase orders, invoices, etc.) from one computer to another. EDI may feature electronic mail between trading partners, but it does not offer central repositories where it can store messages for many parties to read. Choice (c) is incorrect. Fax/modem software facilitates communications by sending messages. It converts paper documents or software files into electronic images for transmission to other parties. Through fax/modem software can store images of faxes received, it does not meet the criteria of ease of finding information a particular topic. Choice (d) is incorrect. The PBX is a telecommunication system that routes calls to particular extensions within an organization. The PBX may facilitate a bulletin board, but does not feature electronic messaging itself.

Subject Area: Information technology—Web infrastructure. Source: CIA 1196, III-61.

C

J

K

L

Q

T

U

V